Praise for *Reel Bad Arabs*

"A long overdue look at the portrayal and perception of Arabs and Muslims in contemporary culture."

—The Washington Report on Middle East Affairs

"Every college and public library should own this important book."

—Choice

"A sharp and acerbic look at negative movie stereotypes of an entire ethnicity. Starkly relevant, soberly honest, and highly recommended."

—Bookwatch

"In light of the tragedy of September 11th, it is even more important to read and digest Shaheen's book. Only when the world stops demonizing people, will this be a safer place to live."

—John L. Peterson, The Anglican Communion

"The stereotyping of Arabs in American movies is an old story, yet it is a story that, until now, no one has told. Shaheen has broken the silence with a book that will be the indispensable starting point for all future research on this neglected topic. The impact, even in summary, of scores of plots, one more vulgar and ignorant than the next, is numbing in its sheer ugliness. Shaheen attacks the stereotype not by denouncing it but, far more devastatingly, by documenting it."

—Jack Miles, Pulitzer Prize winning author and columnist at Beliefnet.com

"This world-class presentation sets the facts straight about Hollywood's Arabs. Jack Shaheen, an articulate arbiter of fair play, has written a sterling book. It is a major contribution to the literature of film, and will change the way you think about movies and slanderous screen images."

—Casey Kasem, radio and TV personality

"If you can cut us, we do not bleed? I ask all my Jewish friends to come to the defense of their Semitic cousins."

—F. Murray Abraham, Academy Award-winning actor

"A must-read!...[Shaheen's] book should be in all libraries nationwide, especially those of government officials and filmmakers."

—Camelia Anwar Sadat

"If you think overt racism in America is dead, think again. Jack Shaheen has shown in depressing detail in his book, Reel Bad Arabs, that anti-Semitism in motion pictures is more virulent than ever provided the Semites being portrayed are Arabs. Films from Exodus (1960) to Rules of Engagement (2000) have relentlessly stereotyped Arabs and Muslims in ways that would fit seamlessly into Der Stürmer and the films of Nazi Germany."

—James E. Akins, Middle East specialist and former US diplomat

"*[A] rousing wake-up call. Anybody concerned about education, racial justice, democracy, and critical literacy should buy and read this book, and then pass it on to a friend.*"
—Henry A. Giroux, author of *The Mouse That Roared: Disney and the End of Innocence*

"*For years, with rare passion and eloquence, Jack Shaheen has raised a constant, resonating voice on behalf of the Arab in America. An undaunted warrior devoted to righting the wrongs of distortion that have too long persisted, Shaheen has displayed unwavering dedication to the cause of fair play for ethnic groups who have suffered from misrepresentation by our film industry—Arabs most of all. For his courage in protecting the integrity of an entire people against the tides of prejudice in American mass culture, we are all deeply in his debt.*"

—Asaad Kelada, television and stage director

"*When presented with this vast compendium about movie Arabs, I was at first delighted. But all too soon my emotions turned to sadness, then to anger. Were this book about movie Africans, Asians, Jews, Italians, Latinos, or Native American Indians, the American public would be outraged. Yet, for some perverted reason, we passively accept the film industry's immoral stereotyping of Arabs that* Reel Bad Arabs *documents with such convincing power. In bringing together upwards of 1,000 motion pictures, Shaheen moves from professor to prophet. The reader is moved to exclaim, 'Enough!'*"

—Fred Strickert, professor of religion, Wartburg College

"*Jack Shaheen is a one-man anti-defamation league who has exposed Hollywood's denigration of Arabs in most, if not all, of its films. His book casts light on the stereotyping Arabs have suffered at the hands of movie makers. But as they learn tolerance, this too shall pass.*"
—Helen Thomas, distinguished journalist, White House correspondent and author

"*This important book delivers a frank and incisive look at how, for more than 100 years, American motion pictures have narrowly portrayed an entire people. Shaheen deserves plaudits for giving us this detailed, painstaking, and insightful study. His book is a must for all who care about the often abused teaching power of film images.*"
—Carlos E. Cortés, author of *The Children Are Watching: How the Media Teach about Diversity*

"*...Some day, as a society, we will look back in horror at the routine media vilification of Arabs, especially in motion pictures, and wonder how the American public could have put up with it for so long...When we can come to terms with the evidence and analysis that Shaheen provides, we will rid ourselves of the delusion that mass media outlets have informed us about Arab people.*"
—Norman Solomon, nationally syndicated columnist, author of *The Habits of Highly Deceptive Media*

"*This is a valuable contribution to both the casual film goer and the film scholar.*"
—James M. Wall, senior contributing editor, *The Christian Century*

REEL
BAD
ARABS

How Hollywood
Vilifies a People

JACK G. SHAHEEN

FOREWORD BY WILLIAM GREIDER

OLIVE
BRANCH
PRESS

An imprint of Interlink Publishing Group, Inc.
NEW YORK • NORTHAMPTON
www.interlinkbooks.com

With Love to Bernice, Michael, and Michele

First published in 2001 by

OLIVE BRANCH PRESS
An imprint of Interlink Publishing Group, Inc.
99 Seventh Avenue • Brooklyn, New York 11215 and
46 Crosby Street • Northampton, Massachusetts 01060
www.interlinkbooks.com

Library of Congress Cataloging-in-Publication Data

Shaheen, Jack G., 1935-
  Reel bad Arabs : how Hollywood vilifies a people / Jack G. Shaheen ;
foreword by William Greider.
    p. cm.
  ISBN 1-56656-388-7
  1. Arabs in motion pictures. I. Title.
  PN1995.9.A68 S54 2001
  791.43'65203927--dc21
                                        2001003040
Printed and bound in Canada

To request our complete 48-page full-color catalog,
please call us toll free at **1-800-238-LINK**, visit our
web site at **www.interlinkbooks.com**, or write to
Interlink Publishing
46 Crosby Street, Northampton, MA 01060
E-mail: sales@interlinkbooks.com

CONTENTS

ABBREVIATIONS

AA	Allied Artists	AFIC	*American Film Institute Catalog*
ACI	Action International	D	director
AI	American International	EP	executive producer
BV	Buena Vista	IMDb	internet movie database
CAN	Cannon	MAG	*Magill's Survey of Cinema*
COL	Columbia	MPH	*Motion Picture Herald*
DW	DreamWorks	MPW	*Motion Picture World*
EMB	Embassy	NYT	*The New York Times*
FOX	Fox Studios	OS	original screenplay
INT	International	P	producer
HOL	Hollywood	Rel.	released by
LIP	Lippert	S	story by
MGM	Metro-Goldwyn-Mayer	SP	screenplay
MIR	Miramax	VAR	*Variety*
MON	Monogram	W	writer
NL	New Line	*NS	film not screened by author
NLC	New Line Cinema		
NWP	New World Pictures		
OR	Orion		
PAR	Paramount		
REP	Republic		
RKO	RKO Radio		
SA	Seven Arts		
TOU	Touchstone		
TWE	Trans World Entertainment		
TCF	Twentieth Century-Fox		
TRI	Tristar		
UNI	Universal		
UA	United Artists		
UI	Universal-International		
WAR	Warner		
WB	Warner Bros.		
WP	Warner-Pathe		

Note: Studios, production, and releasing companies not listed are spelled out in the synopses.

ACKNOWLEDGEMENTS

I am deeply grateful to my lovely and remarkable wife, Bernice. Her keen attention to detail and her tireless and enthusiastic assistance guided me during this book's long development. Always Bernice stood by me, with complete faith in my writings. And in me. She is the wind beneath my wings, and it is impossible to thank her enough.

My gratitude goes as well to my wise and true literary agent, James C. G. Conniff. I thank him for his loyalty and for his innumerable wise decisions about content. His expertise and generous encouragement were indispensable.

Special thanks to Greg Montjoy-Bass. His proofing, editing, and considerable computer skills helped prepare the manuscript for publication.

I am especially appreciative of the support and love given me by my children, Michael and Michele.

Heartfelt thanks to my publisher, Michel Moushabeck, and his creative staff, notably Juliana Spear, Katrina Yeager, Moira Megargee, and Pam Thompson.

And, I acknowledge departed family members of 1118 Worthington Avenue, Clairton, PA: My mother, Nazara, grandparents Jacob and Naffa, Aunt Ann, Uncle Bo, and Uncle Mike. Their unselfish love instilled in me the faith that tolerance can triumph over intolerance.

FOREWORD

Hollywood is our great national entertainer and also the most effective teacher of our young. It is the authoritative creator of commonly shared attitudes and feelings and even the shared experiences of Americans. Hollywood is also, as this book documents in troubling detail, the leading source of propagandistic images that damage and isolate some citizens and can destroy the possibility of ever achieving genuine democratic relationships among us. The power to depict certain "others" as innately strange and dangerous—as foul creatures not like the rest of us—is surely as devastating as the physical force of weaponry. The malign images segregate some Americans from the whole experience of citizenship, impeding their capacity to speak and act for themselves in political life or intimidating any public leaders who dare to speak for them.

This is the cloud that shadows Arab-Americans still and induces a kind of blindness among other Americans, who have unwittingly consumed the propaganda for generations in the process of being entertained. Folk prejudice is ancient among different peoples, of course, and not likely ever to disappear entirely. But Jack G. Shaheen's inquiry is about manufactured prejudice—a product that stokes feelings of distrust and loathing. We can argue at length about how much of this process is accidental and unintentional, how much is purposeful and politically motivated. But the larger point that Shaheen documents is the perpetuation of this malignancy among us at the center of American's popular culture. Indeed, he argues that, as other groups have protested and won redress against prejudicial stereotypes, as the Cold War ended and the familiar bogeyman of Soviet Communists was retired, the stereotypical confinement of Arabs has actually grown worse in films.

This book poses important challenges to the film industry, but it also asks questions of the rest of us. Why does our desire to experience a good story induce us to swallow the defamation so passively? Do we always need some one or other as villain to dread and despise? Or are we perhaps capable—as Americans, as human beings—of rising above the ugly stereotypes, escaping from their deleterious effects and joining Arab-Americans in protest? One might start the process of escape by reading Shaheen's account as if you and your children are Arabs too. As he describes your image as it is portrayed in American film, ask yourself how it feels.

—William Greider

William Greider is national correspondent for *The Nation* and author of *One World, Ready or Not: The Manic Logic of Global Capitalism.*

viii

INTRODUCTION

The culture for which Hollywood has shown its greatest contempt has been the [Arab or] Middle East culture.[1]

—Max Alvarez, editor of *Cinecism*

The popular caricature of the average Arab is as mythical as the old portrait of the Jew. He is robed and turbaned, sinister and dangerous, engaged mainly in hijacking airplanes and blowing up public buildings. It seems that the human race cannot discriminate between a tiny minority of persons who may be objectionable and the ethnic strain from which they spring. If the Italians have the Mafia, all Italians are suspect; if the Jews have financiers, all Jews are part of an international conspiracy; if the Arabs have fanatics, all Arabs are violent. In the world today, more than ever, barriers of this kind must be broken, for we are all more alike than we are different.[2]

—Sydney Harris

For the great enemy of truth is very often not the lie—deliberate, continued and dishonest—but the myth—persistent, persuasive and unrealistic. Too often we hold fast to the clichés of our forebears.[3]

—President John F. Kennedy

Al tikrar biallem il hmar. By repetition even the donkey learns.

This Arab proverb encapsulates how effective repetition can be when it comes to education: how we learn by repeating an exercise over and over again until we can respond almost reflexively. A small child uses repetition to master numbers and letters of the alphabet. Older students use repetition to memorize historical dates and algebraic formulas.

For more than a century Hollywood, too, has used repetition as a teaching tool, tutoring movie audiences by repeating over and over, in film after film, insidious images of the Arab people. I ask the reader to study in these pages the persistence of this defamation, from earlier times to the present day, and to consider how these slanderous stereotypes have affected honest discourse and public policy.

Genesis

In this first comprehensive review of Arab screen images ever published, I document and discuss virtually every feature that Hollywood has ever made— more than 900 films, the vast majority of which portray Arabs by distorting at every turn what most Arab men, women, and children are really like. In gathering the evidence for this book, I was driven by the need to expose an injustice: cinema's systematic, pervasive, and unapologetic degradation and dehumanization of a people.

1

When colleagues ask whether today's reel Arabs are more stereotypical than yesteryear's, I can't say the celluloid Arab has changed. That is the problem. He is what he has always been—the cultural "other." Seen through Hollywood's distorted lenses, Arabs look different and threatening. Projected along racial and religious lines, the stereotypes are deeply ingrained in American cinema. From 1896 until today, filmmakers have collectively indicted all Arabs as Public Enemy #1—brutal, heartless, uncivilized religious fanatics and money-mad cultural "others" bent on terrorizing civilized Westerners, especially Christians and Jews. Much has happened since 1896—women's suffrage, the Great Depression, the civil rights movement, two world wars, the Korean, Vietnam, and Gulf wars, and the collapse of the Soviet Union. Throughout it all, Hollywood's caricature of the Arab has prowled the silver screen. He is there to this day—repulsive and unrepresentative as ever.

What is an Arab? In countless films, Hollywood alleges the answer: Arabs are brute murderers, sleazy rapists, religious fanatics, oil-rich dimwits, and abusers of women. "They [the Arabs] all look alike to me," quips the American heroine in the movie *The Sheik Steps Out* (1937). "All Arabs look alike to me," admits the protagonist in *Commando* (1968). Decades later, nothing had changed. Quips the US Ambassador in *Hostage* (1986), "I can't tell one [Arab] from another. Wrapped in those bed sheets they all look the same to me." In Hollywood's films, they certainly do.

Pause and visualize the reel Arab. What do you see? Black beard, headdress, dark sunglasses. In the background—a limousine, harem maidens, oil wells, camels. Or perhaps he is brandishing an automatic weapon, crazy hate in his eyes and Allah on his lips. Can you see him?

Think about it. When was the last time you saw a movie depicting an Arab or an American of Arab heritage as a regular guy? Perhaps a man who works ten hours a day, comes home to a loving wife and family, plays soccer with his kids, and prays with family members at his respective mosque or church. He's the kind of guy you'd like to have as your next door neighbor, because—well, maybe because he's a bit like you.

But would you want to share your country, much less your street, with any of Hollywood's Arabs? Would you want your kids playing with him and his family, your teenagers dating them? Would you enjoy sharing your neighborhood with fabulously wealthy and vile oil sheikhs with an eye for Western blondes and arms deals and intent on world domination, or with crazed terrorists, airplane hijackers, or camel-riding bedouins?

Real Arabs

Who exactly are the Arabs of the Middle East? When I use the term "Arab," I refer to the 265 million people who reside in, and the many more millions around the world who are from, the 22 Arab states.[4] The Arabs have made many contributions to our civilization. To name a few, Arab and Persian physicians and scientists inspired European thinkers like Leonardo da Vinci. The Arabs invented algebra and the concept of zero. Numerous English words—algebra, chemistry, coffee, and others—have Arab roots. Arab intellectuals made it feasible for Western scholars to develop and practice advanced educational systems.

In astronomy Arabs used astrolabes for navigation, star maps, celestial globes, and the concept of the center of gravity. In geography, they pioneered the use of latitude and longitude. They invented the water clock; their architecture inspired the Gothic style in Europe. In agriculture, they introduced oranges, dates, sugar, and cotton, and pioneered water works and irrigation. And, they developed a tradition of legal learning, of secular literature and scientific and philosophical thought, in which the Jews also played an important part.

There exists a mixed ethnicity in the Arab world—from 5000 BC to the present. The Scots, Greeks, British, French, Romans, English, and others have occupied the area. Not surprisingly, some Arabs have dark hair, dark eyes, and olive complexions. Others boast freckles, red hair, and blue eyes.

Geographically, the Arab world is one-and-a-half times as large as the United States, stretching from the Strait of Hormuz to the Rock of Gibraltar. It's the point where Asia, Europe, and Africa come together. The region gave the world three major religions, a language, and an alphabet.

In most Arab countries today, 70 percent of the population is under age 30. Most share a common language, cultural heritage, history, and religion (Islam). Though the vast majority of them are Muslims, about 15 million Arab Christians (including Chaldean, Coptic, Eastern Orthodox, Episcopalian, Roman Catholic, Melkite, Maronite, and Protestant), reside there as well.

Two Fulbright-Hayes lectureship grants and numerous lecture tours sponsored by the United States Information Service (USIS) enabled me to travel extensively throughout the region. While lecturing and living in fifteen Arab countries, I came to discover that like the United States, the Arab world accommodated diverse, talented, and hospitable citizens: lawyers, bankers, doctors, engineers, bricklayers, farmers, computer programmers, homemakers, mechanics, businesspeople, store managers, waiters, construction workers, writers, musicians, chefs, architects, hairdressers, psychologists, plastic surgeons, pilots, and environmentalists.

Their dress is traditional and Western. The majority are peaceful, not violent; poor, not rich; most do not dwell in desert tents; none are surrounded by harem maidens; most have never seen an oil well or mounted a camel. Not one travels via "magic carpets." Their lifestyles defy stereotyping.

As for Americans of Arab heritage, prior to World War I, nearly all the Arabs immigrating to America were Christians: Lebanese, Palestinians, and Syrians. Today, the majority of the United States' Arab-American population is also Christian; about 40 percent are Muslim.

Through immigration, conversion, and birth, however, Muslims are America's fastest growing religious group; about 500,000 reside in the greater Los Angeles area. America's six to eight million Muslims frequent more than 2,000 mosques, Islamic centers, and schools. They include immigrants from more than 60 nations, as well as African-Americans. In fact, most of the world's 1.1 billion Muslims are Indonesian, Indian, or Malaysian. Only 12 percent of the world's Muslims are Arab. Yet, moviemakers ignore this reality, depicting Arabs and Muslims as one and the same people. Repeatedly, they falsely project all Arabs as Muslims and all Muslims as Arabs. As a result, viewers, too, tend to link the same attributes to both peoples.

In reality, of course, Mideast Arabs—and Arab-Americans—are more than a bit like you and me. Consider, for example, two typical Arab-American families—the Jacobs and the Rafeedies. Jacob Mike Jacob, my grandfather, worked in the mills outside of Pittsburgh for nearly twenty years. Albert Rafeedie, my father-in-law, served in the United States Army during World War I; following the war he ran dry goods stores in Minneapolis and Los Angeles.

Both Jacob and Albert emigrated to America in the early 1900s. Their wives and children served their country during World War II and the Korean War, working in aircraft factories in the 1940s, enlisting in the US Army, Air Force, and Navy. Yet, I have never seen their likes in a Hollywood movie—Arab immigrants and their children making good in America, just like the Irish, Italian, and Polish immigrants.

Hollywood's past omission of "everyday" African-Americans, American Indians, and Latinos unduly affected the lives of these minorities. The same holds true with the industry's near total absence of regular Arab-Americans. Regular Mideast Arabs, too, are invisible on silver screens. Asks Jay Stone, "Where are the movie Arabs and Muslims who are just ordinary people?"[5]

Why is it important for the average American to know and care about the Arab stereotype? It is critical because dislike of "the stranger," which the Greeks knew as xenophobia, forewarns that when one ethnic, racial, or religious group is vilified, innocent people suffer. History reminds us that the cinema's hateful Arab stereotypes are reminiscent of abuses in earlier times. Not so long ago—and sometimes still—Asians, American Indians, blacks, and Jews were vilified.

Ponder the consequences. In February 1942, more than 100,000 Americans of Japanese descent were displaced from their homes and interred in camps; for decades blacks were denied basic civil rights, robbed of their property, and lynched; American Indians, too, were displaced and slaughtered; and in Europe, six million Jews perished in the Holocaust.

This is what happens when people are dehumanized.

Mythology in any society is significant. And, Hollywood's celluloid mythology dominates the culture. No doubt about it, Hollywood's renditions of Arabs frame stereotypes in viewer's minds. The problem is peculiarly American.

Because of the vast American cultural reach via television and film—we are the world's leading exporter of screen images—the all-pervasive Arab stereotype has much more of a negative impact on viewers today than it did thirty or forty years ago.

Nowadays, Hollywood's motion pictures reach nearly everyone. Cinematic illusions are created, nurtured, and distributed world-wide, reaching viewers in more than 100 countries, from Iceland to Thailand. Arab images have an effect not only on international audiences, but on international movie makers as well. No sooner do contemporary features leave the movie theaters than they are available in video stores and transmitted onto TV screens. Thanks to technological advances, old silent and sound movies impugning Arabs, some of which were produced before I was born, are repeatedly broadcast on cable television and beamed directly into the home.

Check your local guides and you will see that since the mid-1980s, appearing each week on TV screens, are fifteen to twenty recycled movies projecting Arabs as dehumanized caricatures: *The Sheik* (1921), *The Mummy* (1932), *Cairo* (1942), *The Steel Lady* (1953), *Exodus* (1960), *The Black Stallion* (1979), *Protocol* (1984), *The Delta Force* (1986), *Ernest In the Army* (1997), and *Rules of Engagement* (2000). Watching yesteryear's stereotypical Arabs on TV screens is an unnerving experience, especially when pondering the influence celluloid images have on adults and our youth.

Early on, Plato recognized the power of fictional narratives, asserting in his *Republic*: "Those who tell the stories also rule society." Functioning as visual lesson plans, motion pictures, like composed stories, last forever. They help to shape our thoughts and beliefs. "It is time to recognize that the true tutors of our children are not schoolteachers or university professors but filmmakers...," writes Benjamin R. Barber in *The Nation*. "Disney does more than Duke; Spielberg outweighs Stanford."

Actor Richard Dreyfuss made this comment, "There are film artists who affected me more than any textbook, civics teacher, or even a lot of what my parents taught me. And, that's big."[6] If Barber and Dreyfuss are right—and I believe they are— what can we expect our children to know and feel about Arabs? After all, teenagers not only watch a lot of television, they are avid moviegoers and nowadays purchase "four out of ten movie tickets."[7]

Arabs, like Jews, are Semites, so it is perhaps not too surprising that Hollywood's image of hook-nosed, robed Arabs parallels the image of Jews in Nazi-inspired movies such as *Robert and Bertram* (1939), *Die Rothschilds Aktien von Waterloo* (1940), *Der Ewige Jude* (1940), and *Jud Süss* (1940). Once upon a cinematic time, screen Jews boasted exaggerated nostrils and dressed differently—in yarmulkes and dark robes—than the films' protagonists. In the past, Jews were projected as the "other"—depraved and predatory money-grubbers who seek world domination, worship a different God, and kill innocents. Nazi propaganda also presented the lecherous Jew slinking in the shadows, scheming to snare the blonde Aryan virgin.

Yesterday's Shylocks resemble today's hook-nosed sheikhs, arousing fear of the "other." Reflects William Greider, "Jews were despised as exemplars of modernism," while today's "Arabs are depicted as carriers of primitivism—[both] threatening to upset our cozy modern world with their strange habits and desires."[8]

Though Arabs have been lambasted on silver screens since cameras started cranking, the fact remains that it is acceptable to advance anti-Semitism in film—provided the Semites are Arabs. I call this habit of racial and cultural generalization "The New Anti-Semitism." I call it "new" not because stereotypical screen Arabs are new (they aren't) or because anti-Semitism against Jews is dead (it isn't). I use the word "new" because many of the anti-Semitic films directed against Arabs were released in the last third of the twentieth century, at a time when Hollywood was steadily and increasingly eliminating stereotypical portraits of other groups.

Few would argue that today's Jew is subjected to the type of stereotyping in film that existed in the first half of the century. I hope and believe those days are gone forever. But this earlier incarnation of anti-Semitism, where Jews were portrayed as representing everything evil and depraved in the world, has in many ways found a new life in modern film—only this time, the target is Arabs.

Flashback. In the 1930s, the star director of Hitler's cinema was Viet Harlan, whose *Jud Süss* (1940) encouraged Germans to despise Jews.

Fast forward to two producers with a political agenda: Menachem Golan and Yoram Globus. In 1982 Yoram Globus was appointed Israel's director of the Film Industry Department, a unit that monitors all movies made in Israel. Meanwhile, back in the United States, Globus and co-producer Golan formed the American film company Cannon. Under the Cannon label, the producers functioned as cinematic storm troopers, churning out upward of 26 hate-and-terminate-the-Arab movies. In Cannon's *Hell Squad* (1985), *The Delta Force* (1986), and *Killing Streets* (1991), Las Vegas showgirls, US Marines, and US special forces in turn kill off Palestinians.

Writing about Edward Zwick's *The Siege* (1998), Roger Ebert picks up on this theme: "The prejudicial attitudes embodied in the film are insidious, like the anti-Semitism that infected fiction and journalism in the 1930s—not just in Germany but in Britain and America."[9]

Though there are several major reasons why the stereotype has endured for a century-plus—politics, profitable box offices, apathy, and the absence of Arab-Americans in the industry—the fact remains: "You can hit an Arab free; they're free enemies, free villains—where you couldn't do it to a Jew or you can't do it to a black anymore," affirms Sam Keen.[10]

Because of Hollywood's heightened cultural awareness, producers try not to demean most racial and ethnic groups. They know it is morally irresponsible to repeatedly bombard viewers with a regular stream of lurid, unyielding, and unrepentant portraits of a people. The relation is one of cause and effect. Powerful collages of hurtful images serve to deepen suspicions and hatreds. Jerry Mander observes, screen images "can cause people to do what they might otherwise never [have] thought to do..."[11]

One can certainly make the case that movie land's pernicious Arab images are sometimes reflected in the attitudes and actions of journalists and government officials. Consider the aftermath of the 19 April 1995 bombing of the federal building in Oklahoma City. Though no American of Arab descent was involved, they were instantly targeted as suspects. Speculative reporting, combined with decades of harmful stereotyping, resulted in more than 300 hate crimes against them.[12]

Months following the tragedy, even Henry Kissinger cautioned, "In an age when far more people gain their understanding from movies... than from the written word, the truth is not a responsibility filmmakers can shrug off as an incidental byproduct of creative license."[13] Frequent moviegoers may even postulate that illusionary Arabs are real Arabs.

Our young people are learning from the cinema's negative and repetitive stereotypes. Subliminally, the onslaught of the reel Arab conditions how young Arabs and Arab-Americans perceive themselves and how others perceive them, as well. Explains Magdoline Asfahani, an Arab-American college student: "The most common questions I was asked [by classmates] were if I had ever ridden a camel or if my family lived in tents." Even worse, "I learned at a very young age [that] every other movie seemed to feature Arab terrorists."[14]

It must be trying for young Arab-Americans to openly express pride in their heritage when they realize that their peers know only Hollywood's *reel* Arabs—billionaires, bombers, and bellydancers—which is to stay, they don't know *real* Arabs at all.

The stereotype impacts even well established Arab-Americans. When Academy Award winner [*Amadeus* (1984)] F. Murray Abraham was asked what the "F" in F. Murray Abraham stood for, he said: "F stands for Farid. When I first began in the business I realized I couldn't use Farid because that would typecast me as a sour Arab out to kill everyone. As Farid Murray Abraham I was doomed to minor roles."[15]

The Stereotype's Entry

How did it all start? Obviously, filmmakers did not create the stereotype but inherited and embellished Europe's pre-existing Arab caricatures. In the eighteenth and nineteenth centuries, European artists and writers helped reduce the region to colony. They presented images of desolate deserts, corrupt palaces and slimy souks inhabited by the cultural "other"—the lazy, bearded heathen

Arab Muslim. The writers' stereotypical tales were inhabited with cheating vendors and exotic concubines held hostage in slave markets. These fictional renditions of wild foreigners subjugating harem maidens were accepted as valid; they became an indelible part of European popular culture. The *Arabian Nights* stories especially impacted Western perceptions. Until 1979, the *Arabian Nights'* 200-plus tales had been printed in more languages than any other text except the Bible.

During the early 1900s, imagemakers such as the Frenchman Georges Méliès served up dancing harem maidens and ugly Arabs. In Méliès' mythic Arabia, Arabs ride camels, brandish scimitars, kill one another, and drool over the Western heroine, ignoring their own women. In Méliès' *The Palace of Arabian Nights* (1905), submissive maidens attend a bored, greedy, black-bearded potentate; a stocky palace guard cools the ruler, fluttering a huge feather fan.

From the beginning, Méliès and other moviemakers conjured up a mythical, uniform "seen one, seen 'em all" setting, which I call "Arab-land." The illusory setting functions as a make-believe theme park complete with shadowy, topsy-turvy sites, patronized by us all. Arab-land is populated with cafes and clubs like the "Shish-Ka-Bob Cafe" and "The Pink Camel Club," located in made-up places with names such as "Lugash," "Othar," "Tarjan," "Jotse," "Bondaria," and "Hagreeb."

The desert locale consists of an oasis, oil wells, palm trees, tents, fantastically ornate palaces, sleek limousines, and, of course, camels.[16] To complement Arab-land's desert landscapes producers provide performers with "Instant Ali Baba Kits." Property masters stock the kits with curved daggers, scimitars, magic lamps, giant feather fans, and nargelihs. Costumers provide actresses with chadors, hijabs, bellydancers' see-through pantaloons, veils, and jewels for their navels. Robed actors are presented with dark glasses, fake black beards, exaggerated noses, worry beads, and checkered burnooses. Contemporary film-makers embellished these early stereotypical settings and characters, trashing Arabs as junk dealers who smash automobiles. As ever, both autos and Arabs are recast as refuse.

In *The Desert Song* (1929), producers display devout and daring Arabs riding across swift-swept sands, helping the French protagonists defeat evil French colonialists. Flash forward to *The Desert Song* remakes of 1943 and 1953. Both films are decidedly different from the 1929 version. Here, the producers opt to frame Arabs as an unruly, unkempt, feuding lot—one of them is even pro-Nazi.

King Solomon's Mines (1950) contains no Arabs. Yet, Cannon's *Allan Quatermain and the Lost City of Gold* (1987), a remake of *King Solomon's Mines*, presents sleazy Arabs trying to rape the blonde heroine (Sharon Stone).

Only one villain, a lumbering mummy, appears in Universal's classic film, *The Mummy* (1932). Attempting to duplicate the original's success, Universal released in 1999 an $80 million movie displaying the reawakened mummy as a superhuman terminator intent on killing Western protagonists. Assisting him are hordes of Egyptian baddies: a fat and lecherous prison warden, saber-wielding mummies, desert bandits, and zombie look-a-likes carrying torches.

Observes film critic Anthony Lane,

> Finally there is the Arab question. The Arab people have always had the roughest and most uncomprehending deal from Hollywood, but with the death of the Cold War the stereotype has been granted even more wretched prominence. In *The Mummy* (1999), I could scarcely believe what I was watching... So, here's a party game for any producers with a Middle Eastern setting in mind; try replacing one Semitic group with another—Jews instead of Arabs —and THEN listen for the laugh.[17]

Unfortunately Lane's poignant comments had no effect on Universal. They still populate their 2001 sequel, *The Mummy Returns*, with repugnant caricatures.

Islam, particularly, comes in for unjust treatment. Today's imagemakers regularly link the Islamic faith with male supremacy, holy war, and acts of terror, depicting Arab Muslims as hostile alien intruders, and as lecherous, oily sheikhs intent on using nuclear weapons. When mosques are displayed onscreen, the camera inevitably cuts to Arabs praying, and then gunning down civilians. Such scenarios are common fare.

Film criticism is an integral part of the cultural landscape. Allegations of moviemakers' discriminatory practices are hardly new. Documentary filmmakers as well as scholars have commented upon Hollywood's stereotypes of other groups. Especially informative are insightful and incisive texts: *The Hollywood Indian, From Sambo to Superspade, The Jew in American Cinema, The Latin Image in American Film, Hollywood's Wartime Woman*, and *The Kaleidoscopic Lens: How Hollywood Views Ethnic Groups*. What I find startling is that although sordid-looking reel Arabs regularly imperil the very heartland of civilized societies, so little attention has been given to the plethora of Arab screen portraits in cinema texts until now.

Andrew Dowdy's text *The Films of the Fifties: The American State of Mind*,[18] for example, offers a detailed examination of the "movie culture of the fifties." More than 100 films released during the fifties featured Arab caricatures. Yet, Dowdy does not mention a single Arab scenario.

From 1930–34 Hollywood released more than 40 fiction films featuring Arabs. Thomas Doherty writes about this period in his 1999 *Pre-Code Hollywood: Sex, Immorality and Insurrection in American Cinema 1930–34*. He points out that "racism [propelled] a hefty percentage of the escapist fantasies of pre-code Hollywood." To support his thesis, Doherty cites stereotypical portraits of American Indians, Africans and African-Americans, Asians and Asian-Americans, Jews and Jewish-Americans, Irish and Irish-Americans and Italians and Italian-Americans. But Doherty does not mention Arabs or Arab-Americans at all.

From 1929 through 1956, Hollywood produced a total of 231 movie sound serials, averaging 8.5 serials a year.

> The racial attitudes of the period [were] none too enlightened. For the most part... Orientals were portrayed as sinister cultists bent upon the destruction of the white race; blacks were merely ignorant natives who followed the leader who most successfully played upon their primitive superstitions.

write Ken Weiss and Ed Goodgold in *To Be Continued...*, their book on the period.[19] The authors make no mention, however, of the Arab caricatures that appeared in thirteen movie serials from 1930–1950.

These early serials are important because they present several firsts. *The Black Coin* (1936) was the first film to portray an Arab skyjacker threatening to blow up a plane. Another, *Radio Patrol* (1937), introduced Arab immigrants as shoddy criminals threatening America, while *Federal Agents vs. Underworld, Inc.* (1948) displayed federal agents contesting "evil" Nila, the cinema's first Arab woman terrorist. During an invasion of the United States Nila, a reel Egyptian assassin, convinces her comrades to "rise up against the [Western] infidels." After Nila sets off a bomb, she tries to gun down a federal agent.

Surprisingly, all sorts of hokey Arab caricatures pop up in movie serials, beginning with the cliffhanger *Son of Tarzan* (1920) up to and including *Adventures of Captain Africa* (1955). Negative stereotyping of the Arab thrives profusely in eighteen cliffhangers, notably in the *Captain Africa* serial. This thrill-a-minute drama presents heroic Westerners and Africans crushing Arab slavers and terrorists, as well as pro-Nazi Arabs.

Some decent Arabs appear, albeit briefly, in three serials. In *The Vigilante* (1947), an Arab arrives in time to save the American protagonist. In *Queen of the Jungle* (1935), Arabs befriend Americans. And an intelligent and attractive Egyptian heroine appears in *The Return of Chandu* (1934).

As most serials are low-budget ventures, the performances suffer. At times, serial actors portraying Arabs speak gibberish; other robed characters speak with Southern drawls and thick Italian accents.

Determined to maximize profits, as soon as the serials exited movie theaters, producers rushed back to the editing tables. They selected key scenes, then spliced and edited the serial footage, transforming the most interesting frames into ten feature-length motion pictures. By successfully managing to extend the staying power of yesteryear's Arab serials, the producers' serial stereotypes reached new audiences.

A Basis for Understanding

In this book, I list and discuss, in alphabetical order, more than 900 feature films displaying Arab characters. Regrettably, in all these I uncovered only a handful of heroic Arabs; they surface in a few 1980s and 1990s scenarios. In *Lion of the*

Desert (1981), righteous Arabs bring down invading fascists. Humane Palestinians surface in *Hanna K* (1983) and *The Seventh Coin* (1992). In *Robin Hood, Prince of Thieves* (1991), a devout Muslim who "fights better than twenty English knights," helps Robin Hood get the better of the evil Sheriff of Nottingham. In *The 13ᵗʰ Warrior* (1999), an Arab Muslim scholar befriends Nordic warriors, helping them defeat primitive cavemen. And in *Three Kings* (1999), a movie celebrating our commonalities and differences, we view Arabs as regular folks, with affections and aspirations. This anti-war movie humanizes the Iraqis, a people who for too long have been projected as evil caricatures.

Most of the time I found moviemakers saturating the marketplace with all sorts of Arab villains. Producers collectively impugned Arabs in every type of movie you can imagine, targeting adults in well-known and high-budgeted movies such as *Exodus* (1960), *Black Sunday* (1977), *Ishtar* (1987), and *The Siege* (1998); and reaching out to teenagers with financially successful schlock movies such as *Five Weeks in a Balloon* (1962), *Things Are Tough All Over* (1982), *Sahara* (1983), and *Operation Condor* (1997). One constant factor dominates all the films: Derogatory stereotypes are omnipresent, reaching youngsters, baby boomers, and older folk.

I am not saying an Arab should never be portrayed as the villain. What I am saying is that almost *all* Hollywood depictions of Arabs are *bad* ones. This is a grave injustice. Repetitious and negative images of the reel Arab literally sustain adverse portraits across generations. The fact is that for more than a century producers have tarred an entire group of people with the same sinister brush.

Hundreds of movies reveal Western protagonists spewing out unrelenting barrages of uncontested slurs, calling Arabs: "assholes," "bastards," "camel-dicks," "pigs," "devil-worshipers," "jackals," "rats," "rag-heads," "towel-heads," "scum-buckets," "sons-of-dogs," "buzzards of the jungle," "sons-of-whores," "sons-of-unnamed goats," and "sons-of-she-camels."

Producers fail to recognize that "Allah" is Arabic for God, that when they pray, Arab Christians and Muslims, use the word "Allah." When producers show Jewish and Christian protagonists contesting Arab Muslims, the Western hero will say to his Arab enemy in a scornful and jeering manner, "Allah." The character's disrespectful "Allah's" mislead viewers, wrongly implying that devout Arab Muslims do not worship the "true God" of the Christians and Jews, but some tribal deity.

Still other movies contain the word "Ayrab," a vulgar Hollywood epithet for Arab that is comparable to dago, greaser, kike, nigger, and gook.

All groups contain some Attila-the-Hun types; some Israelis and Latinos are militant zealots; some Irishmen and Arabs are terrorists; some Italians and Indonesians are gangsters; some Asians and Africans are rapists; and some Americans and Englishmen are child-abusers. Every group has among its members a minority of a minority committing heinous acts. Yet, the overwhelming majority of all people are regular, peace-loving individuals who vigorously object to violent crimes.

These pages represent the foundation for making sense of Hollywood's Arab narratives. The vast majority of the 900-plus features that I scrutinize here are English-language feature films and movie serials made by Hollywood. I use "Hollywood" in the generic sense, as some movies theatrically released in the United States were produced by independent American filmmakers, as well as by producers from Australia, Canada, England, France, Sweden, Spain, Germany, Italy, and Israel. Documentaries and movies made for television are not included.

Given time constraints and the vast numbers of Arab scenarios, my discussions of some non-viewed films are brief, usually one or two paragraphs. Many silent movies were destroyed, and some sound features are not yet available on video. I was unable to see about 140 features, including silent classics with stereotypical Arabs such as *Beau Sabreur* (1928), and *A Daughter of the Gods* (1916). When I refer to these non-viewed movies, I rely solely on my only available source: film reviews.

Research and Methodology
I began the research process that forms the content of this book in 1980. For two decades I searched for, collected, and studied motion pictures related to Arab portraits and themes. Assisting me was my research partner—my wife Bernice. Initially, to identify the films, we launched extensive computer searches. We put into play dozens of keywords such as bedouin, Egypt, Algiers, desert, and sheikh. Using keywords as a guide, we examined thousands of movie reviews, searching for "Arab" story lines, settings, and character casts.

I proceeded to uncover and write about more than 900 features, released between 1896 and 2001. During the research, I sometimes came across movie titles and reviews that misdirected me. For example, critics and promotions for Universal's horror film, *The Mad Ghoul* (1943), refer to Egyptians using "ancient Egyptian gases" to stun one's victims. In fact, the movie displays generic "natives," and makes no mention of Egyptians or their gases. Fully expecting to see Egyptians and harem maidens in *The Sphinx* (1933) and *Lost in a Turkish Bath* (1952), I purchased the films. But *The Sphinx*, a murder mystery, has no Arabs; and *Lost in a Turkish Bath* is about an American canary salesman, not dancing maidens.

In the late 1980s, I began visiting various research centers to screen and study those motion pictures not available on video, television, or in movie theaters. I screened scores of feature films, about a quarter of those I discuss here, at various institutions: the Library of Congress (Motion Picture, Broadcasting, and Recorded Sound Division), Washington, DC; the Film and Television Archive, University of California, Los Angeles; the Wisconsin Center for Film and Theater Research, University of Wisconsin, Madison; and the Museum of Modern Art, New York City.

At these centers, I also examined primary reference works, and thousands of motion picture reviews dating from when cameras started cranking to the present. I relied on sources such as *Motion Picture Daily*, *Motion Picture Guide*, *Motion Picture Herald*, *Motion Picture News*, *Motion Picture World*, *International Motion Picture Almanac*, *Moving Picture World*, *American Film Institute Catalog*, *Film Daily Yearbook of Motion Pictures*, *Halliwell's Film Guide*, *The New York Times*, *Variety*, *Hollywood Reporter*, *Photoplay*, *Magill's Survey of Cinema*, *Landers Film Reviews*, and *Showman's Reviews*. In the mid-1990s, I began using the Internet Movie Database, an invaluable resource.

Additionally, I appraised every film listed in movie/video guidebooks and catalogs, including those published by individual collectors. I shopped at obscure video rental stores and garage sales, rummaging through videos, checking out cassette covers and plot descriptions. Weekly, I scrutinized TV/film guide magazines and texts.

For those especially hard-to-find movies-on-video, I placed advertisements in film magazines. Surprisingly, channel surfing led me to discover dozens of unknown films. Without warning ugly Arabs would suddenly surface on our TV screens. And friends, colleagues, relatives, video rental clerks, and film buffs directed me to fresh films.

From the research, I came to discover that Hollywood has projected Arabs as villains in more than 900 feature films. The vast majority of villains are notorious sheikhs, maidens, Egyptians, and Palestinians. The rest are devious dark-complexioned baddies from other Arab countries, such as Algerians, Iraqis, Jordanians, Lebanese, Libyans, Moroccans, Syrians, Tunisians, and Yemeni.

Locked into a cycle of predictable plots, these five basic Arab types—Villains, Sheikhs, Maidens, Egyptians, and Palestinians—pop up in a hodgepodge of melodrama and mayhem. Repeatedly, Arab evil-doers are seen in every sort of film imaginable: sword-and-sandal soaps, Foreign Legion and terrorist shoot 'em-ups, camel-operas, musical comedies, magic-carpet fantasies, historical tales, movie serials, and even contemporary dramas and farces that have absolutely nothing to do with Arabs.

When you come across rigid and repetitive movies brandishing stereotypical slurs and images, keep in mind not all negative images are alike; there are distinctions and nuances. Some Arab portraits are dangerous and detestable and should be taken seriously; others are less offensive. And pay special attention to those Arabs you *do not see* on movie screens. Missing from the vast majority of scenarios are images of ordinary Arab men, women and children, living ordinary lives. Movies fail to project exchanges between friends, social and family events.

Nor should you expect to encounter friendly children, those real Arab youths who participate in sporting events, or who are Boy Scouts and Girl Scouts. Absent also are frames showing gracious and devout Arab mothers and fathers, grandmothers and grandfathers, caring for each other and their neighbors.

Such scenes are as sparse as geysers in the Sahara.

Do not expect to see movie characters patterned after Arab scholars, those innovative individuals who provided us with the fundamentals of science, mathematics, medicine, astronomy, and botany. Arab seamen pioneered navigational techniques, enabling them to traverse oceans. The Arabs brought to Indonesia and Spain a fresh and vigorous religion, new technology, and new knowledge that helped transform the civilizations.

To guide the reader, I present more than 900 films in alphabetical order. In each of my silent and sound entries, I highlight specific scenes and dialogue pertaining to on-screen Arabs. I also include summaries of scenarios, cast listings, and production credits. Throughout, I pay particular attention to the five Arab character types—Villains, Sheikhs, Maidens, Egyptians, and Palestinians—many of which overlap.

In addition, I offer several appendices:

1) A.K.A.—Alternate Titles. Many of these films have different titles in video release, or in distribution worldwide.

2) Best List.

3) Recommended Films. These scenarios offer balanced and humane portraits; young people may view them without being ashamed of their heritage.

4) Worst List.

5) Cannon (Golan-Globus) Films.

6) Epithets Directed at the Film Arab.

7) Reel Arabia: Hollywood's Arab-Land.

8) Silent Shorts, Travelogues, and Documentaries.

9) Films for Future Review.

10) Glossary: Arabic words and phrases.

Villains

Beginning with *Imar the Servitor* (1914), up to and including *The Mummy Returns* (2001), a synergy of images equates Arabs from Syria to the Sudan with quintessential evil. In hundreds of movies "evil" Arabs stalk the screen. We see them assaulting just about every imaginable foe—Americans, Europeans, Israelis, legionnaires, Africans, fellow Arabs, even—for heaven's sake—Hercules and Samson.

Scores of comedies present Arabs as buffoons, stumbling all over themselves. Some of our best known and most popular stars mock Arabs: Will Rogers in *Business and Pleasure* (1931); Laurel and Hardy in *Beau Hunks* (1931); Bob Hope and Bing Crosby in *Road to Morocco* (1942); the Marx Brothers in *A Night in Casablanca* (1946); Abbott and Costello in *Abbott and Costello in the Foreign Legion* (1950); the Bowery Boys in *Bowery to Bagdad* (1955); Jerry Lewis in *The Sad Sack* (1957); Phil Silvers in *Follow that Camel* (1967); Marty Feldman in *The*

Last Remake of Beau Geste (1977); Harvey Korman in *Americathon* (1979); Bugs Bunny in *1001 Rabbit Tales* (1982); Dustin Hoffman and Warren Beatty in *Ishtar* (1987); Pauly Shore in *In the Army Now* (1994); and Jim Varney in *Ernest In the Army* (1997).

Some protagonists even refer to Arabs as "dogs" and "monkeys." As a result, those viewers laughing at bumbling reel Arabs leave movie theaters with a sense of solidarity, united by their shared distance from these peoples of ridicule.

In dramas, especially, Hollywood's stars contest and vanquish reel Arabs. See Emory Johnson in *The Gift Girl* (1917); Gary Cooper in *Beau Sabreur* (1928); John Wayne in *I Cover the War* (1937); Burt Lancaster in *Ten Tall Men* (1951); Dean Martin in *The Ambushers* (1967); Michael Caine in *Ashanti* (1979); Sean Connery in *Never Say Never Again* (1983); Harrison Ford in *Frantic* (1988); Kurt Russell in *Executive Decision* (1996); and Brendan Frasier in *The Mummy* (1999).

Perhaps in an attempt to further legitimize the stereotype, as well as to attract more viewers, in the mid-1980s studios presented notable African-American actors facing off against, and ultimately destroying, reel Arabs. Among them, Eddie Murphy, Louis Gossett, Jr., Robert Guillaume, Samuel Jackson, Denzel Washington, and Shaquille O'Neal.[20]

In the Disney movie *Kazaam* (1996), O'Neal pummels three Arab Muslims who covet "all the money in the world." Four years later, director William Friedkin has actor Samuel Jackson exploiting jingoistic prejudice and religious bigotry in *Rules of Engagement* (2000). The effects of ethnic exploitation are especially obvious in scenes revealing egregious, false images of Yemeni children as assassins and enemies of the United States.

To my knowledge, no Hollywood WWI, WWII, or Korean War movie has ever shown America's fighting forces slaughtering children. Yet, near the conclusion of *Rules of Engagement*, US marines open fire on the Yemenis, shooting 83 men, women, and children. During the scene, viewers rose to their feet, clapped and cheered. Boasts director Friedkin, "I've seen audiences stand up and applaud the film throughout the United States."[21] Some viewers applaud Marines gunning down Arabs in war dramas not necessarily because of cultural insensitivity, but because for more than 100 years Hollywood has singled out the Arab as our enemy. Over a period of time, a steady stream of bigoted images does, in fact, tarnish our judgment of a people and their culture.

Rules of Engagement not only reinforces historically damaging stereotypes, but promotes a dangerously generalized portrayal of Arabs as rabidly anti-American. Equally troubling to this honorably discharged US Army veteran is that *Rules of Engagement*'s credits thank for their assistance the Department of Defense (DOD) and the US Marine Corps. More than fourteen feature films, all of which show Americans killing Arabs, credit the DOD for providing needed equipment, personnel, and technical assistance. Sadly, the Pentagon seems to condone these Arab-bashing ventures, as evidenced in *True Lies* (1994), *Executive*

Decision (1996), and *Freedom Strike* (1998).

On November 30, 2000, Hollywood luminaries attended a star-studded dinner hosted by Defense Secretary William Cohen in honor of Motion Picture Association President, Jack Valenti, for which the Pentagon paid the bill—$295,000. Called on to explain why the DOD personnel were fraternizing with imagemakers at an elaborate Beverly Hills gathering, spokesman Kenneth Bacon said: "If we can have television shows and movies that show the excitement and importance of military life, they can help generate a favorable atmosphere for recruiting."

The DOD has sometimes shown concern when other peoples have been tarnished on film. For example, in the late 1950s, DOD officials were reluctant to cooperate with moviemakers attempting to advance Japanese stereotypes. When *The Bridge Over the River Kwai* (1957) was being filmed, Donald Baruch, head of the DOD's Motion Picture Production Office, cautioned producers not to over-emphasize Japanese terror and torture, advising:

> In our ever-increasing responsibility for maintaining a mutual friendship and respect among the people of foreign lands, the use of disparaging terms to identify ethnic, national or religious groups is inimical to our national interest, particularly in motion pictures sanctioned by Government cooperation.[22]

Arabs are almost always easy targets in war movies. From as early as 1912, decades prior to the 1991 Gulf War, dozens of films presented allied agents and military forces—American, British, French, and more recently Israeli—obliterating Arabs. In the World War I drama *The Lost Patrol* (1934), a brave British sergeant (Victor McLaughlin) guns down "sneaky Arabs, those dirty, filthy swine." An American newsreel cameraman (John Wayne) helps wipe out a "horde of [Arab] tribesmen" in *I Cover the War* (1937).

In *Sirocco* (1951), the first Hollywood feature film projecting Arabs as terrorists, Syrian "fanatics" assail French soldiers and American arms dealer Harry Smith (Humphrey Bogart). *The Lost Command* (1966) shows French Colonel Raspeguy's (Anthony Quinn) soldiers killing Algerians. And, Israelis gun down sneaky bedouins in two made-in-Israel films, *Sinai Guerrillas* (1960) and *Sinai Commandos* (1968).

Arabs trying to rape, kill, or abduct fair-complexioned Western heroines is a common theme, dominating scenarios from *Captured by Bedouins* (1912), to *The Pelican Brief* (1993). In *Brief,* an Arab hitman tries to assasinate the protagonist, played by Julia Roberts. In *Captured,* desert bandits kidnap a fair American maiden, but she is eventually rescued by a British officer. As for her bedouin abductors, they are gunned down by rescuing US Cavalry troops.

Arabs enslave and abuse Africans in about ten films, including *A Daughter of the Congo* (1930), *Drums of Africa* (1963), and *Ashanti* (1979). Noted African-American filmmaker Oscar Micheaux, who made "race movies" from 1919 to

1948, also advanced the Arab-as-abductor theme in his *Daughter of the Congo*. Though Micheaux's movies contested Hollywood's Jim Crow stereotypes of blacks, *A Daughter of the Congo* depicts lecherous Arab slavers abducting and holding hostage a lovely Mulatto woman and her maid. The maiden is eventually rescued by the heroic African-American officers of the 10th US Cavalry.

Anti-Christian Arabs appear in dozens of films. When the US military officer in *Another Dawn* (1937) is asked why Arabs despise Westerners, he barks: "It's a good Moslem hatred of Christians." Islam is also portrayed as a violent faith in *Legion of the Doomed* (1959). Here, an Arab is told, "Kill him before he kills you." Affirms the Arab as he plunges a knife into his foe's gut, "You speak the words of Allah." And, in *The Castilian* (1963), Spanish Christians triumph over Arab Muslim zealots. How? By releasing scores of squealing pigs! Terrified of the pigs, the reel Arabs retreat.

Arabs invade the United States and terrorize innocents in *Golden Hands of Kurigal* (1949), *Terror Squad* (1988), *True Lies* (1994), and *The Siege* (1998). *The Siege* is especially alarming. In it, Arab immigrants methodically lay waste to Manhattan. Assisted by Arab-American auto mechanics, university students, and a college teacher, they blow up the city's FBI building, kill scores of government agents, blast theatergoers, and detonate a bomb in a crowded bus.

I discussed the movie's violent images with director Edward Zwick in New York on April 2, 1998. Zwick told me that because some scenes show innocent Arab-Americans being tossed indiscriminately into detention centers, the film would "provoke thought." Provoke violence, more likely, I thought.

I pointed out that his scenario may be fiction, but the terrorists' on-screen killings take place in a real city—the Arabs are rounded up in Brooklyn, where many peace-loving Arab-Americans reside. After watching reel Arab terrorists murder more than 700 New Yorkers, I said, some viewers may think that Arab-Americans belong in those camps.

Zwick argued that he had created balance in the film, pointing out that actor Tony Shalhoub plays a decent Arab-American FBI agent. Zwick's token good guy reminded me how yesteryear's producers tried to justify their hostile depictions of American Indians. In movies showing savage Indians massacring settlers, they would point to Tonto, claiming balance. *The Siege's* virulent and prejudicial images continue to trouble me, profoundly.

Oily Arabs and robed thugs intent on acquiring nuclear weapons surface in roughly ten films. See *Fort Algiers* (1958) and *Frantic* (1988).

At least a dozen made-in-Israel and Golan-Globus movies, such as *Eagles Attack at Dawn* (1970), *Iron Eagle* (1986), and *Chain of Command* (1993), show Americans and/or Israelis crushing evil-minded Arabs, many of whom are portrayed by Israeli actors.

More than 30 French Foreign Legion movies, virtually a sub-genre of boy's-own-adventure films, show civilized legionnaires obliterating backward desert bedouin. These legion formula films cover a span of more than 80 years, from *The Unknown* (1915) to *Legionnaire* (1998). Scenarios display courageous, outnumbered legionnaires battling against, and ultimately overcoming, unruly Arabs. Even Porky Pig as a legionnaire and his camel join in the melee, beating up bedouins in the animated cartoon, *Little Beau Porky* (1936).

Movies imply savage imagery by applying indiscriminately to Arabs and Native Americans both the colonialist's expression "tribes." Prototypes of cowboy shoot-'em-ups, screen legionnaires bring down Arabs much the same way as US Cavalrymen terminate Indians. Three *Beau Geste* movies, faithful adaptations of P.C. Wren's 1926 book, portray British legionnaires as American cowboys; they shoot Arabs as if they were Indians.

Though screen Arabs and Indians share commonalities, there are some differences. Celluloid Indians are projected as war-like and cruel, but unlike reel Arabs, they are seldom depicted as venal, greedy, or hypocritical. And, some films, notably *Broken Arrow* (1950), *Dances with Wolves* (1990), and *Last of the Mohicans* (1992), portray Native Americans as "noble" savages.

I never expected to encounter movies pitting Cowboys against Arabs, but I came across eight shoot-'em-ups, released from 1922 through 1952. Galloping from the Wild West to the Arabian desert in search of adventure and romance are cowboy favorites Tom Mix, Hopalong Cassidy, and Hoot Gibson. Six-shooters drawn, the men in white hats gun down "foul" Arabs. To paraphrase General Philip Henry Sheridan, the images imply that the only good Arab is a dead Arab.

Observes William Greider of the *Washington Post*, "Much of what Westerners 'learned' about Arabs sounds similar to what nineteenth-century Americans 'discovered' about Indians on this continent... acceptable villains make our troubles so manageable." In the past, imagemakers punctuated "anti-human qualities in these strange people," American Indians. They projected them as savages, not thinking like us, "not sharing our aspirations." Once one has concluded that Indians thrive on violence, disorder, and stealth, it becomes easier to accept rather than challenge "irrational" portraits. Today, says Greider, "The Arab stereotypes created by British and French colonialism are still very much with us."[23]

Film producers, broadcast journalists, and military leaders echo Greider's Arab-as-Indian analogy. Seeing marauding desert Arabs approach, the American protagonist in the war movie *The Steel Lady* (1953) quips, "This is bandit area, worse than Arizona Apache." In talking up his film *Iron Eagle* (1986), producer Ron Samuels gushed: Showing an American teen hijacking a jet and wiping out scores of Arabs "was just the kind of story I'd been looking for... *It reminded me of the old John Wayne westerns*" [my emphasis].

Seeing Arabs about to attack, an American soldier in *Hot Shots! Part Deux* (1993) warns his buddies: "Indians on the warpath." After Demi Moore terminates Arabs in her role as a Navy SEAL recruit in *G.I. Jane* (1996), she tells her SEAL pals: "Let's get out of Dodge."

Declares *Scholastic* magazine, American Indians are our "new energy sheikhs!" To boost this absurd declaration, the editors placed on their March 5, 1980 "Senior Weekly Reader" cover a stereotypical American Indian sitting "astride a camel [not a horse] laden with containers labeled Gas, Oil, and Coal. Explains Carlos Cortés in his insightful book, *The Children Are Watching: How the Media Teach about Diversity*, the editors' disrespectful Indian-as-sheikh image reinforces "the negative image of Arabs as manipulative moguls while simultaneously using 'Arabness' to frame—better yet—taint Native Americans."

In the mid-1980s, as CNN reporter Mike Greenspan[24] was filing a report from the Israeli-Lebanese border, the camera cut to Israelis on horseback. Greenspan tagged the Israelis "Cowboys" defending against Lebanese "Indians." And days prior to the 1991 Gulf War, a US Army Colonel appeared on CNN News to tell the viewers he was dispatching "scouts" to "Indian country."

I discuss a few scenarios that focus on Iranians/Persians, such as *The Invincible Six* (1970) and *Into the Night* (1985). Though Iranians are not Arabs, I've added the films because some filmmakers and viewers mistakenly perceive them as Arabs, and for a personal reason. The heavies in *Into the Night* are tagged "Shaheen's boys." Since I'm a Shaheen myself, it grates.

Sheikhs

The word "sheikh" means, literally, a wise elderly person, the head of the family, but you would not know that from watching any of Hollywood's "sheikh" features, more than 160 scenarios, including the Kinetoscope short *Sheik Hadj Tahar Hadj Cherif* (1894) and the Selig Company's *The Power of the Sultan* (1907)—the first movie to be filmed in Los Angeles. Throughout the Arab world, to show respect, people address Muslim religious leaders as sheikhs.

Moviemakers, however, attach a completely different meaning to the word. As Matthew Sweet points out, "The cinematic Arab has never been an attractive figure... in the 1920s he was a swarthy Sheik, wiggling his eyebrows and chasing the [Western] heroine around a tiled courtyard. After the 1973 oil crisis..." producers revitalized the image of the fabulously wealthy and slothful sheikh, only this time he was getting rich at the expense of red-blooded Americans; "he became an inscrutable bully—a Ray-Ban-ed variation of the stereotypes of the Jewish money lender."[25]

Instead of presenting sheikhs as elderly men of wisdom, screenwriters offer romantic melodramas portraying them as stooges-in-sheets, slovenly, hook-nosed potentates intent on capturing pale-faced blondes for their harems. Imitating the stereotypical behavior of their lecherous predecessors—the "bestial" Asian, the black "buck," and the "lascivious" Latino—slovenly Arabs move to swiftly and violently deflower Western maidens. Explains Edward Said, "The perverted sheikh can often be seen snarling at the captured Western hero and blonde girl... [and saying] 'My men are going to kill you, but they like to amuse themselves before.'"[26]

Early silent films, such as *The Unfaithful Odalisque* (1903), *The Arab* (1915), and *The Sheik* (1921), all present bearded, robed Arab rulers as one collective stereotypical lecherous cur. In *The Unfaithful Odalisque*, the sheikh not only admonishes his harem maiden, he directs a Nubian slave to lash her with a cat-o'-nine-tails. In *The Sheik* (1921), Sheikh Ahmed (Valentino) glares at Diana, the kidnapped British lovely and boasts: "When an Arab sees a woman he wants, he takes her!"

Flash forward 33 years. Affirms the sheikh in *The Adventures of Hajji Baba* (1954): "Give her to me or I'll take her!"

Moving to kidnap and/or seduce the Western heroine, clumsy moneyed sheikhs fall all over themselves in more than 60 silent and sound movies, ranging from *The Fire and the Sword* (1914) to *Protocol* (1984). Sheikhs disregard Arab women, preferring instead to ravish just one Western woman.

But Hollywood's silent movies did not dare show Western women bedding sheikhs. Why? Because America's movie censors objected to love scenes between Westerners and Arabs. Even producers experiencing desert mirages dared not imagine such unions.

Some viewers perceived Valentino's *The Sheik* (1921) to be an exception to the rule. Not true. Valentino's Sheikh Ahmed, who vanquishes Diana, the Western heroine in the movie, is actually a European, not an Arab. This helps explain why the European lover-boy dressed in Arab garb was viewed so positively by his essentially female audience. Note the dialogue, revealing Ahmed to be a European:

Diana, the heroine: "His [Ahmed's] hand is so large for an Arab."
Ahmed's French friend: "He is not an Arab. His father was an Englishman, his mother a Spaniard."

Other desert scenarios followed suit, allowing the hero and heroine to make love, but only after revealing they were actually Western Christians!

In Europe, it was otherwise. As early as 1922, a few European movies such as *The Sheikh's Wife* (1922) countered fixed themes, showing Western heroines embracing dashing Arab sheikhs.

Both good and evil sheikhs battle each other in about 60 Arabian Nights fantasies, animated and non-animated. A plethora of unsavory characters, wicked viziers, slimy slavers, irreverent magicians, and shady merchants contest courageous princes, princesses, lamp genies, and folk heroes such as Ali Baba, Sinbad, Aladdin and, on occasion, the benevolent caliph. You can see some of them in the four *Kismet* fantasies (1920, 1930, 1944, 1955), *Prisoners of the Casbah* (1955), and *Aladdin* (1992).

Even animated cartoon characters thump Arabs. My childhood hero, Bugs Bunny, clobbers nasty Arabs in *1001 Rabbit Tales* (1982). Bugs trounces an ugly genie, a dense sheikh, and the ruler's spoiled son. My other cartoon hero, Popeye, also trounces Arabs. In the early 1930s, Fleischer Studios' lengthy Popeye cartoons presented Arab folk heroes as rogues, not as champions. Popeye clobbers, not befriends, Ali Baba and Sinbad in *Popeye the Sailor Meets Ali Baba's Forty Thieves*, and *Popeye the Sailor Meets Sinbad the Sailor.*

Beginning in the mid-1970s, fresh directors also projected Arab leaders through warped prisms. Emulating their predecessors' stereotypes they, too, displayed Western heroines fending off over-sexed desert sheikhs.

Yet, there are dramatic differences in sheikh images. Once-upon-a-time Arabian Nights movies, such as *Ali Baba Goes to Town* (1937) and *Aladdin and His Lamp* (1952), show indolent sheikhs lounging on thrones. But, contemporary films present oily, militant, ostentatious sheikhs reclining in Rolls Royces, aspiring to buy up chunks of America.

Today's films present anti-Christian, anti-Jewish Arab potentates perched atop missile bases, armed with nuclear weapons, plenty of oil, and oodles of cash. Using Islam to justify violence, today's reel mega-rich hedonists pose a much greater threat to the West, to Israel, and to fellow Arabs than did their predecessors. You can catch a few of their kind in *Rollover* (1981), *Wrong Is Right* (1982), *The Jewel of the Nile* (1985), and *American Ninja 4: The Annihilation* (1991).

Scantily clad harem maidens attend sheikhs in more than 30 scenarios. The rulers shrug off some, torture others, and enslave the rest. Enslaving international beauties in the X-rated movie, *Ilsa: Harem Keeper of the Oil Sheikhs* (1976), is a depraved Arab ruler and his cohort—Ilsa, the "She-Wolf of the S.S." Depraved sheikhs also subjugate dwarfs and Africans; see *Utz* (1992) and *Slavers* (1977).

Often, producers falsify geopolitical realities. During WWII many Arab nations actively supported the Allies. Moroccan, Tunisian, and Algerian soldiers, for example, fought alongside French troops in North Africa, Italy, and France. Also, Jordanian and Libyan troops assisted members of the British armed services. And, late in the conflict, Egypt, Saudi Arabia, and Iraq declared war on Germany.[27]

Yet, most movies fail to show Arabs fighting alongside the *good* guys. Instead, burnoosed pro-Nazi potentates, some belonging to the "Arabian Gestapo," appear in more than ten sheikh movies; see, for example, *A Yank in Libya* (1942), *Action in Arabia* (1944), and *The Steel Lady* (1953). As early as 1943, about fifty years before the Gulf War, *Adventure in Iraq* (1943) depicts the US Air Force bombing the pro-German Iraqi ruler's "devil-worshiper" minions into oblivion.

From the start, protagonists ranging from Samson to 007 have battled burnoosed chieftains. Flashback to the 1900s. Two 1918 films, *Tarzan of the Apes* and *Bound in Morocco*, show Tarzan and Douglas Fairbanks, respectively, trouncing shifty sheikhs.

Cut to the 1940s. Abbott and Costello, Bing Crosby and Bob Hope, follow suit by belittling Arabs in *Lost in a Harem* (1944) and *Road to Morocco* (1942).

Advance to the 1950s. The Bowery Boys and Tab Hunter thrash robed rulers in *Looking for Danger* (1957) and *The Steel Lady* (1953), respectively.

Flash forward to the 1960s and the 1970s. Elvis Presley, Pat Boone, and Jerry Lewis deride Arabs in: *Harum Scarum* (1965), *The Perils of Pauline* (1967), and *Don't Raise the Bridge, Lower the River* (1968). Other stars bashing sheikhs were Ron Ely in *Slavers* (1977), Michael Douglas in *The Jewel of the Nile* (1985), Cheech and Chong in *Things Are Tough All Over* (1982), and Eddie Murphy in *Best Defense* (1984). And I almost forgot—Burt Braverman drubs two of movie land's ugliest sheikhs in *Hollywood Hot Tubs 2: Educating Crystal* (1990).

The movies of the 1980s are especially offensive. They display insolent desert sheikhs with thick accents threatening to rape and/or enslave starlets: Brooke Shields in *Sahara* (1983), Goldie Hawn in *Protocol* (1984), Bo Derek in *Bolero* (1984), and Kim Basinger in *Never Say Never Again* (1986).

Finally, five made-in-Israel films lambast sheikhs. Particularly degrading is Golan and Globus' *Paradise* (1981). A combination of Western teenagers and chimpanzees finish off the "jackal," a Christian-hating bedouin chieftain, and his cohorts.

Maidens

Arab women, meanwhile, are humiliated, demonized, and eroticized in more than 50 feature films.

Half-Arab heroines as well as mute enslaved Arab women appear in about sixteen features, ranging from foreign legion films to Arabian Nights fantasies. "The Arabian Nights never end...," writes William Zinsser.

> It is a place where young slave girls lie about on soft couches, stretching their slender legs, ready to do a good turn for any handsome stranger who stumbles into the room. Amid all this décolletage sits the jolly old Caliph, miraculously cool to the wondrous sights around him, puffing his water pipe... This is history at its best.[28]

Stereotypical idiosyncrasies abound, linking the Arab woman to several regularly repeated "B" images:

1. They appear as bosomy bellydancers leering out from diaphanous veils, or as disposable "knick-knacks," scantily-clad harem maidens with bare midriffs, closeted in the palace's women's quarters.

2. Background shots show them as Beasts of Burden, carrying jugs on their heads. Some are "so fat, no one would touch them."

3. In films such as *The Sheltering Sky* (1990) they appear as shapeless Bundles of Black, a homogeneous sea of covered women trekking silently behind their unshaven mates.

4. Beginning in 1917 with Fox's silent *Cleopatra*, starring Theda Bara, studios labeled Arab women "serpents" and "vampires." Subsequently, the word "vamp," a derivation of that word, was added to English dictionaries. Advancing the vampire image are movies such as *Saadia* (1953) and *Beast of Morocco* (1966). Both display Arab women as Black magic vamps, or

enchantresses "possessed of devils."

5. In *The Leopard Woman* (1920) and *Nighthawks* (1981) they are Bombers intent on killing Westerners.

When those dark-complexioned femmes fatales move to woo the American/British hero, they are often disappointed. The majority of movies, such as *Outpost in Morocco* (1949), posit that an Arab woman in love with a Western hero must die.

A few films allow Arab maidens to embrace Western males. In *A Café in Cairo* (1925) and *Arabesque* (1966), actresses Priscilla Dean and Sophia Loren appear as bright and lovely Arab women. Only after the women ridicule and reject Arab suitors, does the scenario allow them to fall into the arms of Western protagonists.

Regrettably, just a handful of movies—*Anna Ascends* (1922), *Princess Tam Tam* (1935), *Bagdad* (1949), *Flame of Araby* (1951), and *Flight from Ashiya* (1964), present brave and compassionate Arab women, genuine heroines. There are also admirable queens and princesses in several Cleopatra films and Arabian fantasy tales.

The costume is one way imagemakers make personal and political statements. By covering the reel Arab woman in black and relegating her to silence, the costumer links her with oppression. But throughout the Arab world, from Bahrain to Lebanon, women wear a wide variety of apparel. Some don the traditional black cloaks and veils; others dress in the latest Western fashions, whether it be jeans, designer dresses, or bikinis.

Taken together, her mute on-screen non-behavior and black-cloaked costume serve to alienate the Arab woman from her international sisters, and vice versa. Not only do the reel Arab women never speak, but they are never in the work place, functioning as doctors, computer specialists, school teachers, print and broadcast journalists, or as successful, well-rounded electric or domestic engineers. Movies don't show charitable Arab women such as those who belong to the Mosaic Foundation, which donates millions to American hospitals. Points out Camelia Anwar Sadat, Syria and Egypt gave women the right to vote as early as Europe did—and much earlier than Switzerland. Today, women make-up nearly one-third of the Egyptian parliament. You would never guess from Hollywood's portrayal of Arab women that they are as diverse and talented as any others. Hollywood has not yet imagined a woman as interesting as Ivonne Abdel-Baki, the daughter of Lebanese immigrants and Ecuador's ambassador to Washington. Abdel-Baki, a specialist in conflict resolution, graduated from Harvard University's Kennedy School of Government and is fluent in five languages. Or De' Al-Mohammed, the University of Missouri's blind fencing star.[29] And many, many more.

Addressing movie land's "B" stereotypes is my friend, a Palestinian film industry lawyer with two children. She, like Ms. Al-Mohammed and other bright, highly-educated Arab women, defy the stereotype. Concerned about stale screen portraits of women, she questions whether future films will present more honest images. "Many Arab women like myself work outside the home," she said. "Some wear hijabs, others do not. What we wear, what kind of clothes other women choose to wear, should not matter. What matters most is how we live our lives, especially that we manage quite well to care for our little ones. Why doesn't Hollywood make movies showing us bonding with and assisting other women, those like myself who are finding the proper balance between family and professional life?" Why not, indeed?

Egyptians

Egyptian caricatures appear in more than 100 films, from mummy tales to legends of pharaohs and queens to contemporary scenarios. Reel Egyptians routinely descend upon Westerners, Israelis, and fellow Egyptians. Interspersed throughout the movies are souk swindlers as well as begging children scratching for baksheesh. An ever-constant theme shows devious Egyptians moving to defile Western women; see Cecil B. DeMille's *Made for Love* (1926) and *Sphinx* (1981).

Stephen Spielberg's films *Raiders of the Lost Ark* (1981), *Young Sherlock Holmes* (1986), and *Indiana Jones and the Last Crusade* (1989) merit special attention, as do Golan-Globus' 1960s scenarios, made-in-Israel: *Cairo Operation* (1965) and *Trunk to Cairo* (1965). The producers paint Egyptians as nuclear-crazed and pro-Nazi. Their scenarios are particularly objectionable given the real-life heroics of the Arab Brotherhood of Freedom, a group of brave Egyptians who sided with the Allies during World War II.

Imagemakers are not so harsh with Queen Cleopatra. Beginning with Helen Gardner's *Cleopatra* (1912), Hollywood enlisted stars such as Ava Gardner, Theda Bara, Vivian Leigh, Sophia Loren, Claudette Colbert, and Elizabeth Taylor to portray Egypt's seductive queen. Approximately fifteen movies show Egypt's queen, encircled by stereotypical maidens, pining over Roman leaders. Only four movies display Egyptian queens romancing Egyptians. The majority display Egyptian royals feuding with fellow Egyptians as well as Rome's soldiers.

A few movies, such as Cecil B. DeMille's *The Ten Commandments* (1923) and DreamWorks' Jeffrey Katzenberg's *The Prince of Egypt* (1998), feature Egyptian rogues trying to crush heroic Israelites. I found the animated *Prince of Egypt* to be less offensive than DeMille's scenarios. Though Katzenberg's movie displays plenty of Egyptian villains, *Prince of Egypt* offers more humane, balanced portraits than do DeMille's 1923 and 1956 versions of *The Ten Commandments*. DeMille's 1923 film shows Egyptian guards beating "the dogs of Israel" and Pharaoh's ten-year-old son whipping Moses.

From the start, moviemakers linked Egypt with the un-dead. In Georges Méliès' film *The Monster* (1903), the camera reveals a bearded Egyptian magician removing a skeleton from its casket. Presto! He transforms the bony thing into a lovely maiden. But, not for long. The cunning magician changes the woman back into a skeleton.

Say "Egypt" and producers think "Mummies" and "Money." Beginning with Vitagraph's *The Egyptian Mummy* (1914) and *Dust of Egypt* (1915), Hollywood presented about 26 mummy films. In order to spook viewers, cinematographers placed gauze over the camera's lens, creating chilling, dreamlike, and exotic moods. Topping the list is Universal's *The Mummy* (1932). Due to a fine screenplay and Boris Karloff's performance as the mummy Imhotep, this classic stands the test of time as *the* mummy film. Other popular mummy movies are *The Mummy's Hand* (1940), *The Mummy's Tomb* (1942), and *The Mummy's Revenge* (1973).

Mummy plots are relatively simple: Revived mummies and their caretaker "priests" contest Western archaeologists. In most scenarios, the ambitious gravediggers ignore tomb curses. So of course they suffer the consequences for daring to reawaken Egypt's sleeping royals. Meanwhile, the Westerners dupe ignorant, superstitious, and two-timing Egyptians.

Once fully revived, the bandages-with-eyes mummy lusts after the archaeologist's fair-skinned daughter. And, the mummy crushes panicked Egyptian workers and all crypt violators—"infidels," "unbelievers," and "heretics." Occasionally, movies like *The Awakening* (1980) pump up the action by offering decomposed horrors; also in this one, a queen's evil spirit so contaminates the Western heroine, she kills her father.

Obviously, there's more to the state of Egypt, the most heavily populated of all Arab countries, than pyramids and curses. Egypt is comprised of a people who take pride in their culture and their long and honorable history. Moving to modernize its economy and to improve the living standards of its population, Egypt now boasts more than fourteen state universities. The likes of scholarly students or noted Egyptian archeologists, men like the celebrated Kamal El Malakh, are absent from movie screens.

Nor do screenwriters present scenarios patterned after Egypt's renowned journalists and authors, like Rose El-Yousef and Nobel Laureate Naguib Mahfouz. Egyptians, like most other Arabs, are deeply religious and are noted for their warm hospitality. In villages and throughout cosmopolitan cities like Cairo and Alexandria, *Ahlan wa Sahlan* (Welcome, this is your home) is spoken as often as "good morning."

Though I do not analyze Mexican "Aztec" mummy and mayhem features, it's important to point out that Aztec scenarios correspond with Egyptian curse movies. See *Curse of the Aztec Mummy* (1959), *Attack of the Mayan Mummy* (1963), and *Wrestling Women Versus The Aztec Mummy* (1964). Even *Robot Versus the Aztec Mummy* (1959) emulates Hollywood's Egyptian formula films, with a tomb inscription that warns archaeologists: "He who defiles the tomb runs the risk of death. Those disregarding the warning perish."

Palestinians

Observed Mark Twain, "We are all ignorant, just about different things." When it comes to the Middle East, many Americans are ignorant about the history and plight of the Palestinian people. One reason is that moviegoers may mistakenly believe *reel* Palestinians, those ugly make-believe film "terrorists," are *real* Palestinians. Should this be true, then what must viewers think of Palestinians after exiting movie theaters?

To assume viewers acquire some true knowledge of Palestinians after watching the 45 Palestinian fiction films that I discuss here is both dangerous and misleading. It's the same as thinking that you could acquire accurate knowledge of Africans by watching Tarzan movies, or that you would know all about Americans after watching movies about serial killers.

More than half of the Palestinian movies were released in the 1980s and 1990s; nineteen from 1983–1989; nine from 1990–1998. Absent from Hollywood's Israeli-Palestinian movies are human dramas revealing Palestinians as normal folk—computer specialists, domestic engineers, farmers, teachers, and artists. Never do movies present Palestinians as innocent victims and Israelis as brutal oppressors. No movie shows Israeli soldiers and settlers uprooting olive orchards, gunning down Palestinian civilians in Palestinian cities. No movie shows Palestinian families struggling to survive under occupation, living in refugee camps, striving to have their own country and passports stating "Palestine." Disturbingly, only two scenarios present Palestinian families.

Watching these, I questioned the defamation of Palestinians. Is there an unwritten cinematic code stating Hollywood will present all Palestinians as irrational and *bad,* all Israelis as rational and *good?*

One year after the state of Israel was born, the film, *Sword of the Desert* (1949), presented Palestine according to the popular Zionist slogan, as a land without a people—even though the vast majority of people living in Palestine at the time were, in fact, Palestinians. This myth—no-Palestinians-reside-in-Palestine—is also served up in *Cast a Giant Shadow* (1966) and *Judith* (1966).

A decade after *Sword of the Desert* Paul Newman declared war on the Palestinians in *Exodus* (1960). Hollywood's heroes followed suit. In *Prisoner in the Middle* (1974), David Janssen links up with Israeli forces; together they gun down Palestinian nuclear terrorists. Films from the 1980s such as *The Delta Force* (1986) and *Wanted: Dead or Alive* (1987) present Lee Marvin, Chuck Norris, and Rutger Hauer blasting Palestinians in the Mideast and in Los Angeles. In the 1990s, Charlie Sheen and Kurt Russell obliterate Palestinians in Lebanon and aboard a passenger jet, in *Navy SEALs* (1990) and *Executive Decision* (1996).

In *Ministry of Vengeance* (1989) filmmakers dishonor Palestinians and American military chaplains as well. In lieu of presenting the chaplain, a Vietnam veteran, as a devout, non-violent man, the minister exterminates Palestinians. The minister's parishioners approve of the killings, applauding him.

Seven films, including *True Lies* (1994) and *Wanted Dead or Alive* (1987), project the Palestinian as a nerve-gassing nuclear terrorist. In more than eleven movies, including *Half-Moon Street* (1986) *Terror in Beverly Hills* (1988), and *Appointment with Death* (1988), Palestinian evildoers injure and physically threaten Western women and children.

The reader should pay special attention to *Black Sunday* (1977), Hollywood's first major movie showing Palestinians terrorizing and killing Americans on US soil. Telecast annually the week of Super Bowl Sunday, the movie presents Dahlia, a Palestinian terrorist, and her cohort Fasil. They aim to massacre 80,000 Super Bowl spectators, including the American President, a Jimmy Carter look-alike.

Dictating numerous Palestinian-as-terrorist scenarios is the Israeli connection. More than half (28) of the Palestinian movies were filmed in Israel. Nearly all of the made-in-Israel films, especially the seven Cannon movies, display violent, sex-crazed Palestinian "bastards [and] animals" contesting Westerners, Israelis, and fellow Arabs.

I believe Cannon's poisonous scenarios are not accidental, but rather propaganda disguised as entertainment. Even in the early 1900s studio moguls knew that motion pictures could serve propagandists. Following WW I, Adolph Zukor, the head of Paramount Pictures affirmed this film-as-propaganda fact, saying fiction films should no longer be viewed as simply "entertainment and amusement." The war years, he said, "register[ed] indisputably the fact that as an avenue of propaganda, as a channel for conveying thought and opinion, the movies are unequaled by any form of communication."[30]

Gratuitous Scenes and Slurs

Shockingly, producers insert egregious, amoral Villains, Maidens, Sheikhs, Egyptians, and Palestinians in more than 250 movies that have absolutely nothing to do with Arabs or the Middle East. I refer to these films as cameos. Appearing like unexpected jumbo potholes on paved streets, nasty Arabs clutter hundreds of non-Arab scenarios—and even noted filmmakers such as Steven Spielberg, Francis Ford Coppola, and Ridley Scott participate in this. See *The Black Stallion* (1979), *Back to the Future* (1985), *Young Sherlock Holmes* (1985), and *G.I. Jane* (1997).

Renowned writers such as Neil Simon, Tom Wolfe, and Paddy Chayefsky also tarnished Arabs. About 40 films, including *Network* (1976), *Chapter Two* (1979), and *The Bonfire of the Vanities* (1990), contain discriminatory dialogue.

Between 1980–2001, Hollywood released more than 120 of these cameo features. Apparently, studio executives looked the other way, approving the insidious anti-Arab insertions. How would reasonable moviegoers react had the villains not been Arab? What if these hundreds of cameo movies had saturated audiences not with visions of "primitive" Arabs, but rather with cruel celluloid caricatures of other groups? Would you walk away in anger, thinking

Hollywood's slanderous insertions were intentional and discriminatory? Or would you leave the theater in an apathetic state, believing the corruptive insertions to be harmless and accidental?

Why the Stereotype?

Ask a film industry executive, director, or writer whether it is ethical to perpetuate ethnic or racial stereotypes and you can expect a quick negative response. How then, to explain that since 1970, these very same individuals produced, directed, and scripted more than 350 films portraying Arabs as insidious cultural "others?"

Either filmmakers are perpetuating the stereotype unknowingly, and would immediately disassociate themselves from such activities were they to realize the implications of their actions, or they are doing so knowingly and will only stop when sufficient pressure is brought to bear on them.

It is difficult to imagine that screenwriters who draft scenes of fat, lecherous sheikhs ogling Western blondes, or crazed Arab terrorists threatening to blow up America with nuclear weapons, are not precisely aware of what they are doing. But we sometimes forget that one of the elements that makes stereotyping so powerful, and so hard to eliminate, is that it is self-perpetuating. Filmmakers grew up watching Western heroes crush hundreds of reel "bad" Arabs. Some naturally repeat the stereotype without realizing that, in so doing, they are innocently joining the ranks of the stereotypes' creators.

Huge inroads have been made toward the elimination of many racial and ethnic stereotypes from the movie screen, but Hollywood's stereotype of Arabs remains unabated. Over the last three decades stereotypical portraits have actually increased in number and virulence.

The Arab stereotype's extraordinary longevity is the result, I believe, of a collection of factors. For starters, consider print and broadcast "if it bleeds it leads" news reports. Like most Americans, creators of popular culture (including novelists, cartoonists, and filmmakers), form their opinions of a people, in part, based on what they read in print, hear on the radio, and see on television. Like the rest of us, they are inundated and influenced by a continuous flow of "seen one, seen 'em all" headlines and sound bites.

New reports *selectively* and relentlessly focus on a minority of a minority of Arabs, the radical fringe. The seemingly indelible Arab-as-villain image wrongly conveys the message that the vast majority of the 265 million peace-loving Arabs are "bad guys."

The image began to intensify in the late 1940s when the state of Israel was founded on Palestinian land. From that preemptive point on—through the Arab-Israeli wars of 1948, 1967, and 1973, the hijacking of planes, the disruptive 1973 Arab oil embargo, along with the rise of Libya's Muammar Qaddafi and Iran's Ayatollah Khomeini—shot after shot delivered the relentless drum beat that all Arabs were and are Public Enemy #1.

Right through the 1980s, the 1990s, and into the twenty-first century, this "bad people" image prevailed, especially during the Palestinian intifada and the Israeli invasion of Lebanon. In 1980, the rabid followers of Iran's Ayatollah Khomeini held 52 Americans hostage at the US Embassy in Teheran for 444 days. Nightly, TV cameras blazoned across the planet Khomeini's supporters chanting "Death to America!" and calling our country "the Great Satan" as they burned our flag and, in effigy, Uncle Sam himself.

At the height of the Iranian hostage crisis anti-Arab feelings intensified, as 70 percent of Americans wrongly identified Iran as an Arab country. Even today, most Americans think of Iranians as Arabs. In fact, Iranians are Persians, another people altogether.

Mindlessly adopted and casually adapted, the Arab-as-enemy stereotype narrows our vision and blurs reality. Juicy and marketable news headlines are picked up and repeated by the global news services, triggering further misunderstandings.

It got worse in the 1990s. Two major events, the Iraqi invasion of Kuwait that led to the Gulf War, and the bombing of New York City's World Trade Center, combined to create misguided mindset, leading some Americans to believe all Arabs are terrorists and that Arabs do not value human life as much as we do. As a result, some of us began even perceiving our fellow Americans of Arab descent as clones of Iraq's Saddam Hussein and the terrorist Osama bin Laden. Well, I think you get the picture.

Damaging portraits, notably those presenting Arabs as America's enemy, affect all people, influencing world public opinion and policy. Given the pervasive stereotype, it comes as no surprise that some of us—and the US State Department—find it difficult to accept Egyptians, Moroccans, Palestinians, and other Arabs as friends.

Not only do these violent news images of extremists reinforce and exacerbate already prevalent stereotypes, but they serve as both a source and excuse for continued Arab-bashing by those filmmakers eager to exploit the issue. In particular, the news programs are used by some producers and directors to deny they are actually engaged in stereotyping. "We're not stereotyping," they object. "Just look at your television set. Those are real Arabs."

Such responses are disingenuous and dishonest. As we know, news reports by their very nature cover extraordinary events. We should not expect reporters to inundate the airwaves with the lives of ordinary Arabs. But filmmakers have a moral obligation not to advance the news media's sins of omission and commission, not to tar an entire group of people on the basis of the crimes and the alleged crimes of a few.

Taken together, news and movie images wrench the truth out of shape to influence billions of people. Regrettably, gross misperceptions abound and continue to plaster on movie screens, those distorted "pictures in our heads" that Walter Lippmann bemoaned some 70 years ago.

Why would anyone take part in the denigration of a people knowingly? I think one answer is the Arab-Israeli conflict. Though the majority of moviemakers are fair-minded professionals, there are some who, in the interests of pursuing their own political or personal agenda, are willing to perpetuate hate. These individuals may be expected to continue to indict Arabs on movie screens for as long as unjust images are tolerated.

New York Times columnist Maureen Dowd offers another answer: "[S]tereotypes are not only offensive [but] they are also comforting. They... exempt people from any further mental or emotional effort. They wrap life in the arch toastiness of fairy tale and myth. They make complicated understandings unnecessary."[31] Convenient stereotypes make everyone's job easier. Rather than having to pen a good joke, the writer inserts a stumbling, bumbling sheikh. Looking for a villain? Toss in an Arab terrorist—We all know what they look like from watching movies and TV. No thought required. As for the audience? Well, it also makes some of us feel better to see ourselves as superior to someone else. If one is no longer allowed to feel superior to Asians, Jews, Latinos, or blacks, at least we can feel superior to those wretched Arabs.

For some producers, Arabs are convenient scapegoats. Asked to explain why his *Iron Eagle* (1996) displayed heinous Arabs, writer-director Sidney J. Furie had this to say to NBC producer Arthur Lord:

> Look, [in movies] there always has to be a bad guy. And, so you make one up... an acceptable bad guy. I mean, it has to be something. It has to be somebody, cause there's good and evil. Something has to represent evil. And in our picture, as an example, we didn't give the country a name and we didn't say it was Arab. I mean you have to be an idiot not to think it was [Arab]. But, so what![32]

And, don't forget about peer pressure. I recall asking one producer why he and his co-workers never projected in comedies and dramas Arabs and Arab-Americans as "regular" folk. To my astonishment, he confided, "Jack, some of us are reluctant to present good Arabs, even good Arab-Americans in our movies, because we'll be labeled pro-Arab."

Certainly, the Department of Defense's rubber-stamping of motion pictures that lambast Arabs plays a role. The fact is, the government has a history of playing a role in what movies do and don't get made. As early as 1917, the federal government not only acknowledged the power of film to influence political thought, it took on the wrongful role of censor. As soon as the United States declared war on Germany, the government declared that no Hollywood movie could arouse prejudice against friendly nations. The 1917 film *The Spirit of '76* reveals heroic American revolutionaries such as Patrick Henry and Paul Revere. But, some frames show British soldiers committing acts of atrocities. As England was our World War I ally, the government protested; a judge declared producer Robert Goldstein's movie advanced anti-British sentiments. Calling the film "potent German propaganda,"[33] the judge sentenced Goldstein to prison.

Greed, too, is an incentive. Bash-the-Arab movies make money. Thus, some producers exploit the stereotype for profit.

Other moviemakers fail to offer a corrective because they may be indolent, inflexible, and/or indifferent. Certainly, in the past, ignorance, the handmaiden of bigotry, was a contributing factor.

The absence of vibrant film criticism is another cause. A much-needed recourse against harmful Arab images would be more vigorous criticism emanating from industry executives and movie critics. I recall, still, Bosley Crowther's *New York Times* review of *Adventure in Sahara* (1938). Instead of criticizing stereotypes, Crowther advanced them, writing: "We know the desert is no picnic and you can't trust an Arab very far."

Another factor is silence. No significant element of public opinion has yet to oppose the stereotype; even scholars and government officials are mum. New York's Andrew Cuomo, for example, is running for governor of New York, a state where many Americans of Arab heritage reside. Cuomo is "very interested in the topic of discrimination" and stereotyping; he is alert to the fact that there is "a robust hunger for vulgar stereotypes in popular culture." Imagemakers, he says, are "still stereotyping Italian-Americans, Irish-Americans, African-Americans, Indian-Americans and American Jews."[34] Yet, Cuomo fails to mention coarse stereotypes of Arab-Americans. If we are ever to illuminate our common humanity, our nation's leaders must challenge *all* hateful stereotypes. Teachers need to move forward and incorporate, at long last, discussions of Arab caricatures in schools, colleges, military, and government classrooms.

Ethnic stereotypes do not die off on their own, but are hunted down and terminated by those whom the stereotypes victimize. Other groups, African-Americans, Asian-Americans and Jewish-Americans, have acted aggressively against discriminatory portraits. Arab-Americans as a group, however, have been slow to mobilize and, as a result, their protests are rarely heard in Hollywood and even when heard, are heard too faintly to get the offenders to back off.

Another reason is lack of presence. With the exception of a few movies, *Party Girl* (1995) and *A Perfect Murder* (1998), Arab-Americans are invisible on movie screens. One reason, simply put, is that there are not many Arab-Americans involved in the film industry; not one is a famous Hollywood celebrity.

What does their absence have to do with contesting stereotypes? Well, one answer is that movie stars have clout. Consider how Brad Pitt altered the scenario, *The Devil's Own* (1996). After reading the initial script, Pitt protested, telling the studio the screenplay made him "uneasy" because it was loaded with stereotypes—"full of leprechaun jokes and green beer." The dialogue, he argued, unfairly painted his character as a stereotypical Irish "bad" guy. Explains Pitt, "I had the responsibility to represent somewhat these [Irish] people whose lives have been shattered. It would have been an injustice to Hollywood-ize it." Unless changes were made to humanize the Irish people, especially his character, Pitt "threatened to walk." The studio acquiesced, bringing in another writer to make the necessary changes.

Also, when it comes to studio moguls, not one Arab American belongs to the media elite. The community boasts no communication giants comparable to Disney's Michael Eisner, DreamWorks' Jeffrey Katzenberg, Fox's Rupert Murdoch, or Time-Warner's Ted Turner.

The lack of an Arab-American presence impacts the stereotype in another way. The industry has a dearth of those men and women who would be the most naturally inclined to strive for accurate and balanced portrayals of Arabs. But a number of high-level Arab Americans in the industry over the course of time would rectify the situation. It's difficult to demean people and their heritage when they're standing in front of you, especially if those persons are your bosses.

Not so long ago, women and minorities were excluded from studios' executive offices. Not anymore. Explains director Spike Lee, "Look at the number of women in the film industry now—Amy Pascal is running Sony, you have Sherry Lansing at Paramount, and Stacey Snider at Universal—and twenty years ago there were no women heads of studios... This is a gradual process."[35]

Contesting cinema's defamatory images is as American as apple pie. From the beginning, America's blacks, Jews, and Irish moved to break down walls of mistrust and suspicion. What did these diverse peoples have in common? Well, they formed pressure groups, lobbying the industry for more balanced images.

In the early 1900s, "Cinema's new presence as a form of mass entertainment made ethnic groups more sensitive to the way they were portrayed on the screen," explains Charles Musser. Though "film stereotypes faded only slowly," says Musser, "egregious representations were often followed by protest."

It began with the Irish. The year, 1907. The manager of the Lyric Theater in Providence, Rhode Island, screened a comedy about Murphy, a drunken Irishman. Abruptly,

> Irish film-goers in nearby Pawtucket [became] so outraged when they saw the picture that they threatened to destroy the Lyric [unless the film] was banned. [Enter] Mayor McCarthy of Providence. [He] saw the show, and banned the film.

Declared McCarthy: This movie is "a deliberate insult to a respectable race."[36]

Another "respectable race" was tarred in D.W. Griffith's *The Birth of a Nation* (1915), in which all blacks are portrayed as brutes. As a result, the film stirred up race hatred against blacks, prompting the Ku Klux Klan to use it for Klan recruiting. The Mayor of Boston, James Curley, refused to ban or censor the film. He shrugged off protests from the NAACP's Boston branch, arguing, "the objections to *The Birth of a Nation* as racist propaganda would be no more valid than protests against

Shakespeare's *Henry VIII* for maligning the Roman Catholic church."

One year later, members of the B'nai Brith protested the portrayal of Jews as Christ-killers in D.W. Griffith's biblical epic *Intolerance* (1916). Argued the B'nai Brith, too many Jewish extras surrounded the cross where Christ was to be crucified. Griffith responded by burning the protested footage. And, he re-shot the controversial crucifixion scene, adding Roman extras, deleting some Jewish ones. A decade later, Jewish groups objected to Jewish images in Cecil B. DeMille's spectacle, *The King of Kings* (1927). DeMille, too, deleted the offending scenes. Later, Will Hayes, the chairman of the film censorship board, said that in the future, he and his committee would consult the B'nai Brith on films with subjects of Jewish interest.

Regrettably, America's Arabs do not yet have an organized and active lobby in Los Angeles. To bring about fundamental changes in how motion pictures project Arabs, a systematic lobbying effort is needed. Though the Arab-American and Muslim-American presence is steadily growing in number and visibility in the United States, only a few Arab-Americans meet with and discuss the stereotype with filmmakers. When dialogue does occur, some discriminatory portraits are altered. Declares a February 3, 2001 Council on American-Islamic Relations (CAIR) fax: "The villains in Paramount's upcoming film, *The Sum of All Fears*, were changed to "European neo-Nazis." CAIR officials acknowledged Paramount for this important change, as Tom Clancy's book, on which the movie is based, presents Arab Muslims detonating a nuclear device at the Super Bowl in Denver. In a letter to CAIR, the film's director, Phil Alden Robinson, wrote: "I hope you will be reassured that I have no intention of portraying negative images of Arabs or Muslims."

Ongoing informal and formal meetings with movie executives are essential. Such sessions enable community members to more readily explain to producers the negative effects misperceptions of Arabs have on their children as well as on American public opinion and policy. Also, Arab-Americans need to reach out and expand their concerns with well-established ethnic and minority lobbying groups—with Asians, blacks, Jews, Latinos, gays and lesbians, and others.

Positives

To see is to make possible new ways of seeing. In this book, I have tried to be uncompromisingly truthful, and to expose the Hollywood stereotype of Arabs for all to see.

While it is true that most filmmakers have vilified the Arab, others have not. Some contested harmful stereotypes, displaying positive images—that is, casting an Arab as a regular person.

In memorable well-written movies, ranging from the Arabian nights fantasy *The Thief of Bagdad* (1924), to the World War II drama *Sahara* (1943), producers present Arabs not as a threateningly different people but as "regular" folks, even as heroes. In *Sahara*, to save his American friends, a courageous Arab soldier sacrifices his life.

Note this father and son exchange from the film *Earthbound* (1980):

Son: "Why do they [the police] hate us, so?"
Father: "I guess because we're different."
Son: "Just because somebody's different doesn't mean they have to hate 'em. It's stupid."
Father: "It's been stupid for a long time."

At first, I had difficulty uncovering "regular" and admirable Arab characters— it was like trying to find an oasis in the desert. Yet, I discovered more than 50 motion pictures sans Arab villains, five percent of the total number reviewed here. Refreshingly, the movies debunk stale images, humanizing Arabs.

As for those Arabian Nights fantasies of yesteryear, only a few viziers, magicians, or other scalawags lie in ambush. Mostly fabulous Arabs appear in *The Desert Song* (1929), *Ali Baba and the Forty Thieves* (1944), *Son of Sinbad* (1955), and *Aladdin and His Magic Lamp* (1969). The movies present viewers with brave and moral protagonists: Aladdin, Ali Baba, and Sinbad. Emulating the deeds of Robin Hood and his men of Sherwood Forest, Arabs liberate the poor from the rich, and free the oppressed from corrupt rulers.

Worth noting is the presence of glittering Arabs in non-fantasy movies. A heroic Egyptian princess appears in the movie serial, *Chandu the Magician* (1932). A courageous Egyptian innkeeper assists British troops in *Five Graves to Cairo* (1943). *Gambit* (1966) displays a compassionate Arab entrepreneur. In *King Richard and the Crusaders* (1954), Saladin surfaces as a dignified, more humane leader than his counterpart, Richard.

Some independent Israeli filmmakers, notably those whose movies were financed by the Fund for the Promotion of Israeli Quality Films, allow viewers to empathize with Palestinians, presenting three-dimensional portraits. To their credit, producers of *Beyond the Walls* (1984) and *Cup Final* (1992) contest the self-promotional history and Palestinian stereotypes spun out by most other filmmakers. Both movies show the Palestinian and the Israeli protagonist bonding; the two men are projected as soul-mates, innocent victims of the Arab-Israeli conflict.

I recommend several top-notch movies, produced in Australia, France, Germany, and Italy. Three of the films offer telling illustrations of how prejudice impacts Arabs, blacks, Jews, and Germans. See *Ali: Fear Eats the Soul* (1974), *The Camel Boy* (1984), and *Hate* (1995).

Solutions

The time is long overdue for Hollywood to end its undeclared war on Arabs, and to cease misrepresenting and maligning them.

All I ask of filmmakers is to be even-handed, to project Arabs as they do other people—no better, no worse. They should enjoy at the very least relative immunity from prejudicial portrayal.

Established professionals and young, energetic moviemakers should step forward and create movies that change the way viewers perceive reel Arabs. They should incorporate this axiom: The denigration of one people, one religion, is the denigration of all people, all religions. As Holocaust survivor and Nobel Prize winner Elie Wiesel reminds us, no human race is superior, no religious faith is inferior; every nation has its share of bad people and good people.

I challenge Hollywood's producers to acknowledge unjust portraits of the past century and embrace Wiesel's wisdom, taking the high ground and projecting Arabs as ordinary and decent world citizens.

Affirms Thoreau, "It is never too late to give up our prejudices... Men [and women] hit only what they aim at." Filmmakers should remember to aim high and heed the advice of DreamWorks' chairman Jeffrey Katzenberg, who told me: "Each of us in Hollywood has the opportunity to assume individual responsibility for creating films that elevate rather than denigrate, that shed light rather than dwell in darkness, that aim for the highest common denominator rather than the lowest."

A few producers did aim high, creating fresh scenarios humanizing Arabs. *The Lion of the Desert* (1981) and *The 13th Warrior* (1999), not only explored the various facets of the human heart, but also the films made money at the box office.

Imagemakers could illuminate the human condition and enhance tolerance by revising classics such as *Crossfire* (1947) and the Academy Award-winning film *Gentleman's Agreement* (1947). The producers combined truth with cinematic sensitivity and skill, resulting in two memorable films. *Crossfire* details the tragic consequences of an ex-soldier's (Robert Ryan) anti-Semitic actions. To better understand the nature of prejudice, *Gentleman's Agreement's* protagonist, a crusading reporter portrayed by Gregory Peck, feigns being a Jew, and writes about anti-Semitism. The journalist's son questions his father's assignment:

Son: "What's anti-Semitism?"
Father: "Some people don't like other people just because they're Jews."
Son: "Why? Are some bad?"
Father: "Some are. Some aren't. Just like everybody else."

As both Arabs and Jews are Semites, revised versions of the two excellent 1947 movies would serve to sensitize viewers as well as imagemakers. An altered *Crossfire* could show an Arab American as a victim of prejudice. A fresh *Gentleman's Agreement* could reveal a reporter feigning to be Arab, writing about the new anti-Semitism.

Another way to curtail insidious portraits is to provide imagemakers with the long-awaited evidence—as found in this book—revealing that for more than a century Hollywood has targeted the Arab as the "other." The evidence documented here is intended to fill the empty desert between Hollywood and the Arabs that until now has seemed untraversable. Writing it has convinced me that the discussion of screen Arabs is not only historically relevant, but a legitimate and important undertaking.

I am confident this book will find its place in college classrooms. When young people, especially students of the cinema, are aware how moviemakers' tainted brushes have discolored Arabs, up-and-coming filmmakers will alter stereotypical portraits.

Openness to change is an American tradition. Not so many years ago, imagemakers repeatedly projected American Indians, Asians, Italians, and Latinos as cultural "others." No longer.

Ultimately, it is a matter of conscience and morality. Filmmakers opting to shed light would join a select and distinguished group—innovative, spirited men and women who not only contested stale stereotypes, but created more honest and humane portraits.

Overlooked in nearly all the films is this telling fact: The Arabs are an exceptionally hospitable people. Most Arabs I know are warm, outgoing, and friendly, abiding by the proverb, "Even this small room is space enough for 1,000 friends." I still recall my visit to Manama, Bahrain, in the summer of 1981. Seeking to escape the noonday heat and traffic snarls, I meditated at the entrance of a cool and peaceful mosque. After some time, Mohammed, a smiling cab driver who had just finished saying his ritual prayers, approached me. It was obvious to him that I was an exhausted visitor. Mohammed offered me some bottled water, insisting he take me to my host's home, gratis. His soft-spoken words and kindness ruled the moment; all I could say was "Thank you." Throughout the region, such helpful gestures are common.

When I think about how cinema's injurious stereotypes stand in stark contrast to the warm and hospitable Arabs I know, my thoughts turn to my late friend Alex Odeh, a poet, and a champion of human rights. In his poem, Alex equates stereotypes with lies:

> Lies are like the dead ashes;
> when the wind of truth blows,
> the lies are dispersed like dust...
> and disappear.

As for the future, I believe my children Michael and Michele will witness the demise of reel bad Arabs, and see the stereotypes slowly fade away like the smile on the Cheshire cat, into an overdue oblivion.

This book, the result of two decades of research, has been a daunting enterprise. To be sure, there are movies I have missed. Though I am appending a list of about 120 feature films that call for analysis, there are still plenty of films out there with hostile Arabs. Thus, I invite you, good reader, to rally round the cause, to join me in wiping the shadows of unjust portraits off the silver screen. Contest slanderous portraits whenever you see them— now and in the morrow.

Assist me in identifying stereotypes, beyond those cited here. I look forward to hearing from you and reading your evaluations of undiscovered and upcoming motion pictures with negative and positive Arab themes, characters, dialogue, and settings. Your role as a non-commissioned observer is especially important because it will help you bring to the cause a continuing reminder for producers and writers that they have an obligation—but also an opportunity to live up to their humanitarian responsibilities. Your input will add to my interpretation of new films I am already researching. Cumulatively, our joint efforts may lead to another edition. When and if it does, I will gratefully acknowledge the source of every contribution I can use. My e-mail address is info@interlinkbooks.com.

To paraphrase an Arab proverb, *Eed wahdeh ma fiha tza'if,* one hand alone does not clap. Believe me, by working together we will shatter the stereotype.

Abbott and Costello in the Foreign Legion (1950), UI. *Bud Abbott, Lou Costello, Patricia Medina, Walter Slezak, Douglass Dumbrille, Wee Willie Davis. See* Beau Hunks (1931). VILLAINS, SHEIKHS

Arabs vs. Abbott and Costello, Arabs vs. legionnaires. While rescuing legionnaires, the duo mock and topple Algerian "bandits." Abbott and Costello's 25th film reveals scantily-clad slave girls and dancing harem maidens. The Breen Office, concerned about the costuming of the harem girls, issued this statement to the producers: "We wish to emphasize... with all the force at our command, the necessity of guarding most carefully the problem of costumes in this picture. As we review the material, it seems to us that there are many occasions for difficulties with inadequate costumes for the women in the harems and the like to crop up during the course of the filming of the picture. We recommend this problem to your most careful supervision..."[37]

Scene: Brooklyn. A popular wrestler, "Abdullah the Assassin" (Davis), gets homesick and skips off to Algeria. His US promoters dispatch Jonesy and Max (Bud and Lou) to bring Abdullah back to the US.

• Algeria. Duped into joining the Foreign Legion, Bud and Lou dodge desert cutthroats and pursue slave maidens. Abdullah's evil cousin, Sheikh Hamud El Khalid (Dumbrille), raids the railroad. Intent on extorting monies from the rail company, Hamud moves to kill Bud and Lou.

• Auction block. Lou ponders whether he can purchase slave girls for "$1.25 down and $1.00 a month." He outbids Hamud, receiving six "knick-knacks." Furious, Hamud plans "an extremely painful death"; his men attack Bud and Lou in a back alley. Enter Nicole (Medina), a French undercover agent posing as an Arab; she saves them.

• Abdullah is told that unless he returns home, he will be obliged to marry Sheikh Hamud's daughter. He asks, "Is she a dog?"

• The desert. An alligator displays an old Arab's false teeth. Arabs on horseback try to catch up with Bud and Lou's jeep. The action is similar to a scene in *Ride 'Em Cowboy* (1942) in which American Indians chase the protagonists. Acting as stereotypical Indians, Arabs function as fodder for cheap laughs.

• Hamud's sneaky men slay a legion patrol.

• Hamud's camp. Bud and Lou dupe Arabs into fighting Arabs. Employing "Arabian onions" they floor Arabs with a single breath. A press release for the movie stated that during the shoot Lou Costello ate "two Arab apples." But the Arab apples were really raw onions. Costello swears they gave him strength for his wrestling bouts with Abdullah.[38]

• Hamud plans to dynamite Fort Apar, but Bud and Lou turn the tables on him. They convince Hamud's men to enter the Legion Fort. Then, they blow up the fort, killing gobs of Arabs. See the cartoon "Little Beau Porky." In it, "Ali Mode," a fat, black-bearded desert bandit and his "Riff Raffs" also charge the Legion fort. But Porky and a camel extinguish them.

Dialogue: Wearing bedouin garb, Bud and Lou protest: "Hey, we're not Arabs!"

Notes: TV viewers still see legionnaires tumbling desert Arabs. For example, reruns of Buster Crabbe's TV series Captain Gallant of the Foreign Legion (1955),[39] surface on the Nostalgia channel. Thirty-nine of the 65 half-hour episodes were actually filmed in Morocco, in cooperation with French authorities. In 1957, Merle Oberon hosted on CBS-TV the half-hour British adventure series *Assignment Foreign Legion.* In each episode Oberon appears as a foreign correspondent assigned to North Africa. The TV series was filmed on location in Algiers, Morocco, and Spain.

• See Hal Roach's short *Arabian Tights* (1933), starring Charlie Chase. Here, too, Americans with the foreign legion contest desert "Algerian hillbillies." Bearded Arabs toting sabers disguise themselves as harem maidens. When the legionnaires remove their veils—surprise! A legionnaire removes a hair from the wealthy sheikh's beard, then attaches it to an out-of-tune violin. Desert Arabs speaking gibberish hold the blonde heroine hostage. In the end, the sheikh with "plenty of money" and the legionnaires unite, opening a business. The camera cuts to a US amusement park banner stating: "Sheik Ali Chase's Oriental dancers, Admission 10 cents."

• Also see *The World of Abbott and Costello* (1964). Comedian Jack E. Leonard narrates this film compilation of stock footage taken from films such as *Abbott and Costello in the Foreign Legion* (1950) and *Abbott and Costello Meet the Mummy* (1955).

Abbott and Costello Meet the Mummy (1955), UNI. *Bud Abbott, Lou Costello, Marie Windsor, Michael Ansara.* EGYPTIANS, MAIDENS

Bud and Lou confront Klaris, a 4,000 year-old mummy. And, they deride feuding Egyptians. Egyptians vs. Egyptians. P.T. Barnum began marketing sarcophagi and mummies in 1823.

Scene: Stock footage of Egypt displays camels and pyramids. Cut to two Egyptian sects; one coveting Princess Ara's treasures, the other wanting to keep her riches intact. Both cults worship Klaris, keeping the mummy alive with secret "nourishment."

• Cultists move to pilfer a sacred medallion, killing the noted Egyptologist, Dr. Gustav Zoomer. Though "it means death to whoever holds it," the medallion may pinpoint Ara's fortune.

• The cult leader, Madame Rontru (Windsor), a femme fatale with killer hirelings, threatens Bud and Lou, the "infidels."

• Egyptian policemen acting as buffoons collide with Egyptian curs.

• The desert. A trap door leads to a secret passageway beneath a pyramid. Inside, the pyramid, Klaris guards Princess Ara's Tomb. Lou spots the mummy, screaming, "Bandages with eyes!" How can Bud and Lou dispatch this mummy? Dynamite does the job!

• Lou dons Arab garb; Bud poses as a mummy. Together, they bring down the cultists, and then secure Princess Ara's long-lost treasures.

• Bud and Lou also preserve the memory of Klaris. Using Ara's treasures, they transform the mummy's temple into "Café Klaris," a modern nightclub. Musicians dressed as mummies play swing music, bellydancers perform. Properties include a water pipe, skeletons, bats, snakes, and poison darts.

Notes: Recommended viewing is "Mummy Daddy," the first tale in Stephen Spielberg's film *Amazing Stories: The Movie III* (1987). Spoofing mummy films, this fine yarn begins on a shooting set of a Hollywood mummy movie. The director tells the actor portraying the screen mummy, "Legend has it years ago around the turn of the century, there was a traveling Gypsy carnival and they had this mummy, an evil Egyptian king named Ra. They used to charge a nickel a look—big box office in those days. [One night] the thing comes to life, the few who made it out alive swore... that it still roams the bogs, these very bogs we're working in." The actor-mummy laughs. Later, however, the real mummy Ra does surface from the swamp. Mistakenly thinking the actor-mummy is the real mummy, angry villagers with guns and torches track the actor-clad-in-mummy garb. Surprisingly, both mummies are preserved.

Comedians contesting mummies is a familiar theme. For example, Monarch's 1998 not-so-humorous TV movie, *The All-New Adventures of Laurel and Hardy: For Love or Mummy*, features a reincarnated mummy surfacing in the United States. Promptly, Stan and Ollie begin contesting Ferouk, an Egyptian villain. Ferouk is intent on nabbing the archeologist's daughter and linking the woman up with the mummy permanently. In time, Stan and Ollie, bring down Ferouk, rescue the heroine, and seal the mummy back into its tomb.

Abdulla the Great (1956), a.k.a. Abdullah's Harem, UNI. *Kay Kendall, Sydney Chaplin, Gregory Ratoff, Alex D'Arcy, Marina Berti. P, D: Gregory Ratoff. Filmed in Egypt. Some scenes reveal an authentic Egyptian palace.*
SHEIKHS, EGYPTIANS, MAIDENS, WORST LIST

A European model brings down an Arab monarch. Supposedly, the melodrama parallels the life of Egypt's King Farouk.

Scene: Bondaria, a mythical Arab country. Ruthless King Abdulla (Ratoff) surrounds himself with electric trains, "bought" women, and bellydancers. Though he knows the military weapons he purchases will misfire and likely kill his own men, he approves the arms sale, then feeds pigeons.

• Abdulla repeatedly moves to sleep with Ronnie (Kendall), a European model. Though he offers treasures, Ronnie repels the potentate's advances, preferring the company of Captain Farid (Chaplin), a young Army officer. Yet, Ronnie never embraces the Egyptian Captain. Critical of Abdulla's reign, Farid tells Ronnie, "I don't want you to think we're all like that (Abdulla)," and, "The Army is the last hope of our people. We hope to drive him out and become free."

• Farid shows Ronnie "common folk." Boarding a felucca, they observe locals dancing and singing. Says Ronnie, "It's a beautiful song. I like your people." This scene is atypical, as almost the entire film shows Ronnie running from Abdulla.

• Arabs take women. Abdulla's assistant Marco (D'Arcy) warns women reluctant to sleep with Abdulla, "His Majesty's will is the law here, and we intend to enforce our laws." Sighs Marco, "Women are like flowers. Enjoy them. Admire them. But change them often and always keep a fresh supply on hand."

• The rotund, gluttonous degenerate is obsessed with seducing the European. Thus, he dispatches henchmen to drug Ronnie, "that foreign lady," and take her to his yacht. Here, clumsy Abdulla tries to rape her, but fails. Counters Ronnie, "I don't like you. I don't respect you." Moans Abdulla, "You are a beautiful devil sent to destroy me. If only Allah would give me strength."

• In the end, Abdulla loses both his sanity and the throne. His city is aflame, and the Army moves to invade the palace. Still, the ruler frolics with bellydancers. One maiden, Aziza (Berta), stands by his side.

Note: In most films, Western women do not bed Arabs, or Iranians. Consider Universal's *Caravans* (1978), a film about Iranians shooting Iranians. The movie, shot entirely in Iran at the height of favorable US-Iranian relations, displays a stiff Iranian colonel and his unhappy bride (Jennifer O'Neill), the daughter of a noted US politician. No between the sheets scenes. In fact, when the US heroine runs off and joins a mountain chieftain (Anthony Quinn), she never even smooches, let alone sleeps with him.

The Abominable Dr. Phibes (1971), AIP. *Vincent Price.* EGYPTIANS

In need of an eternal life formula? Visit a pharaoh's tomb! In this silly yarn Egyptians function as props.

Scene: Dr. Phibes (Price) attempts to reanimate his dead wife, Victoria. Boarding a ship, he departs for Egypt in search of the "secret river of life." Supposedly, here, under "a mountain range where pharaohs once resided, rests the key to resurrection, eternal life."

• A puzzled British police inspector questions why Phibes stores his organ below deck. Quips the inspector, "Organ music is bound to go down well with the Arabs."

• The desert, inside the "Temple of Hibiscus." The Temple boasts an underwater cave filled with scorpions, skeletons, a pharaoh's tomb, and secret passageways. Intent on reviving Victoria, Phibes employs some "elixir of life" drops.

• Believing several doctors caused Victoria's death, Phibes opts to punish them. Utilizing bats, locusts, and frogs, he prepares to launch "the ten plagues of the Pharaoh" curse. As frightened Egyptian workers run off, Phibes sighs, "The Arabs are gone."

• Inexplicably, Arab music underscores the final scenes, showing the mad Phibes wearing an Egyptian robe and headdress.

Action in Arabia (1944), RKO. *George Sanders, Virginia Bruce, H.B. Warner, Jamiel Hasson, and Michael Ansara* (as Hamid, a pro-Nazi Arab). Originally to be billed *The Fanatic of the Fez*, RKO changed the title because of US involvement in the Mideast during WWII. SHEIKHS, VILLAINS

1941 Damascus. Arabs vs. Americans. A US journalist, a French spy, and "good" Arabs upset pro-Nazi Arabs. An American reporter functions as Arabia's savior. See also *A Yank in Libya* (1942), *I Cover the War* (1937).

Scene: As camels trek through the desert, the narrator says, "Damascus, a breeding place for espionage and intrigue." Cut to Gordon (Sanders), an American journalist. Yvonne (Bruce), the Western heroine, tells him, "I'd give anything to be out of the Middle East, anything." Sighs Gordon, "Damascus is certainly mysterious and intriguing." Fearing Germany has placed undercover agents in Syria, he quips: "The new saviors of Islam—the Nazis." Gordon says, "The Arabs could play devil with the Allied armies." He tags an Arab, "You murderous little snake."

• Arab vs. Arab. Pro-Axis Sheikh Hareem (Hasson), intends "to lead the tribes against the Allies." Sheikh Rashid (Warner), the Arabs' "spiritual leader" who favors the Allies, refuses to participate.

• In the souk, as Arabs dicker over pricing camels and carpets, rumpled hagglers and panhandlers harass Gordon as he walks along the "street of beggars."

• Pro-Nazi Arabs, including one who speaks perfect German, attack Rashid's desert castle, killing scores. One Arab warns Gordon, "I shall kill you."

• Hareem's face is superimposed over his "wandering savages." "Somewhere in the desert," Hareem's rifle-toting Arabs link up with the Nazis. But Sheikh Rashid arrives in time to convince the pro-Nazi "tribes" to join the Allies and reject Hareem's war proposals. Mounting their camels, Rashid's pro-Western followers attack, terminating Hareem, his bandits, and the Nazis.

• A "bond of true friendship"; Rashid presents Gordon with a gift.

Dialogue: Chalmers, a US reporter, arrives in Damascus; he tries to speak with Sheikh Rashid's daughter. At once, her two mute bodyguards corner him. Says Chalmers, "What is this, the Middle Ages?" "No," says Gordon, "it's the Middle East. But it sometimes comes to the same thing."

• The US Embassy official in Damascus does not care about Syrians, telling Gordon, "Suppose somebody did talk the Arabs into going in on the wrong side. So what? What could a lot of camels and rifles do against artillery and tanks and planes?"

Note: The film's caricatures did not faze NYT critic Bosley Crowther, who wrote that the movie "is good fun" (19 February 1944).

• Similar themes, different settings are found in two films, *Jungle Siren* (1942) and *Law of the Jungle* (1942). Here, in equatorial Africa, Nazis gain the assistance of Africans, corrupting local chiefs and stirring up "the natives" against the Allies.

• Back in 1937, cinematographers Merian C. Cooper and Ernest B. Schoedsack shot desert footage for RKO, complete with wandering camels and nomads. The footage, originally intended to be used for a *Lawrence of Arabia* epic, was stored in studio vaults for seven years. As the Lawrence film never materialized, RKO inserted Cooper and Schoedsack's 1937 desert footage into *Action in Arabia*.

Adventure in Iraq (1943), WB. *John Loder, Ruth Ford, Warren Douglas, Paul Cavanagh, Manuel Lopez, Bill Crago.* Based on William Archer's stage play, *The Green Goddess.* SHEIKHS

1943 Iraq. Sheikh Ahmid's "devil worshipers" vs. the Allies. Iraqis capture and hold hostage an English pilot and an American couple.

Scene: An allied plane encounters engine problems. George Torrence (Loder), an American, warns British pilot Doug Everett (Douglas) not to land "in the wastelands of Iraq. Try to find a place with some civilization."

• Mechanical problems force a landing. The trio spot "a castle in this godforsaken wilderness." Alerts George, "This part of the desert is filled with devil worshipers. There are tough Arab tribes that lie in the foothills and only come out to rob and kill. They mistrust all Europeans; they can be pretty nasty customers."

• Arabs surface, whisking off Doug, George, and his wife, Tess (Ford). Quips George, "Weird-looking ducks, aren't they!"

• Arabs as devil worshipers. On entering the mythical kingdom of Jotse, the protagonists see Arabs bowing before a serpent, "the image of Satan." Clasping a staff with a bronze peacock at its tip, the "High Priest (Lopez) archbishop, so to speak" arrives, tagging the hostages, "unclean creatures." Then, he points to the peacock, explaining that the bird made possible the devil's entrance into the Garden of Eden.

• The camera focuses on two "native girls" in a trace. "How long will they stay that way?" asks Doug. "For years," he is told. "Part of their religion. No white man's ever been able to approach them." The implication here is that Arab women are not Caucasians.

• Appearing on a white horse and greeting the hostages is Sheikh Ahmid (Cavanagh); the ruler speaks several languages. "The religion of my people has always been primitive," he says, "idolatry and superstition. We know very well we are barbarians." Yet, "many nations covet my oil." Ahmid favors an alliance with Germany, saying he is negotiating oil rights with Hitler; the German "offer is most attractive." Note: See *Harem Girl* (1952).

• Not only does the British Army control Iraq, says Ahmid, the British also sentenced his three brothers to death; they spied for the Nazis. Surprisingly, Ahmid approves of the executions, saying, "my brothers are fanatics." He regrets the British did not "have them strangled; [this is] a traditional method of ending disagreements in my family. Family affection is seldom a strong point. Uncles seldom love cousins."

• Ahmid's castle. "Quite a place here, palace and fortress all in one," says George. His description applies to other screen potentate's castles; see *Jewel of the Nile* (1985) and *Protocol* (1984).

• Feigning remorse, Ahmid tells the hostages they will soon perish at the "sacrificial altar. It is a promise to the evil one... The priests demand the death of foreigners." And if I deny "these devil worshipers their prejudices, I lose the throne," he says.

• Doug, the British pilot, tries to escape; Ahmid's Arabs kill him.

• Maidservants bathe and dress Tess; she exclaims, "I've read about rooms like this— the Arabian Nights." One maiden tells her, though "Highness has many ladies, many wives, highness fall head, line, and sinker for you."

• Ahmid woos Tess, saying, "Of all the fair ladies to grace this room, you are the most exquisite. You will be my first and only queen." Our son will "rule the world." Not if Tess can help it.

• As George and Tess trod through the souk, ugly screeching Arabs torment them. Speaking Arabic, the High Priest curses the couple. Says Ahmid, "I apologize for the manner of my people. Their fanaticism is beyond my control." He regrets "this medieval punishment; death alone will not appease my people."

• In time, US fighter planes commanded by US Capt. Bill Carson (Crago) arrive, hovering over the city. Capt. Carson demands Ahmid release the hostages. Ahmid hesitates; Carson's planes drop bombs.

• Carson insists Ahmid release Tess and George. Ahmid asks about terms; barks Capt. Carson, "It's the policy of the American government never to bargain with gangsters!" As Ahmid hesitates, Carson's planes "proceed with the attack." A bomb drops near Ahmid's castle; he purrs, "I bow to your superior forces."

Adventure in Sahara (1938), COL. *Paul Kelly, C. Henry Gordon.* *NS.
Notes from "With the Foreign Legion," NYT (19 December 1938: 19). VILLAINS
Legionnaires bring down desert Arabs.

Scene: Two legionnaires, Jim Wilson (Kelly), and Capt. Savatt (Gordon), surface at Fort Agadez, "the last outpost in the Sahara."

• Savatt's heroics save the fort from "an Arab attack."

• The desert. Wilson's mutinous behavior enables "Arab ambushers" to pick off, "one at a time," Savatt and his starving troops.

• Legionnaire mutineers move to fight fellow legionnaires. Again, the Arabs attack. Suddenly, all legionnaires unite in a common purpose, defeating the Arab horde.

Note: This is the NYT review in which Bosley R. Crowther writes: "We know the desert is no picnic and that you can't trust an Arab very far."

Adventures of Captain Africa (1955), COL. 15 episodes. *John Hart, Bern Welden, Paul Marion, Lee Roberts, June Howard, Rick Vallin.* Stock footage is employed from the serial *The Desert Hawk* (1944). CLIFFHANGERS, SHEIKHS, VILLAINS, MAIDENS

Arabs vs. Africans, vs. Arabs, vs. Americans.

Scene: Credits, displayed at the start of all fifteen episodes show Arabs killing Arabs. In a mythical Arab nation, complete with palace, souk, underground cave, and tents, Arabs wield sabers and duel.

• The European, "Borid" (Roberts), and his evil Arabs go up against Captain Africa (Hart), a few good Arabs, and some natives.

• Numerous scenes show Arabs enslaving Africans, Arabs fighting Arabs, and Captain Africa punching out Arabs.

• The "sinister liar of the [Arab] tyrant dictator houses a gorilla." Captain Africa, clad in Arab garb, tumbles the huge gorilla, saves Caliph Hamid's life, and "frees the slaves."

• Captain Africa's friend Ted (Vallin) romances Arab Princess Rhonda (Howard).

• The final episode. Captain Africa returns Hamid, the deposed caliph, to "his rightful throne." Says the Princess, "We must give thanks to the great Captain Africa who makes all things possible"; he has prevented Germany, "a great Northern power," from ruling Arabia.

Adventures of Hajji Baba (1954), TCF. *John Derek, Elaine Stewart, Don Randolph, Paul Picerni, Rosemarie Bowie. SP: Richard Collins.* MAIDENS

This entertaining Arabian Nights adventure displays fleshy harem maidens and an evil sheikh. A lovely Arab Princess embraces a poor Persian barber. Heroic "Turkamen" women help the protagonists tumble the sheikh. See *The Thief of Baghdad* (1924).

Scene: A hodgepodge of desert settings. Imprisoned maidens are sold as slaves.

• The weak Caliph (Randolph) warns his daughters, Princess Fawzia (Stewart), "Think of all the wives Sheikh Nur el-Din (Picerni) has had and how he's treated them." The "heartless" sheikh tells the Caliph, "Give her [the Princess] to me or I"ll take her!" The sheikh demands Fawzia wed him. He intends to make the Caliph's kingdom his own. Should Fawzia balk, he vows to poison her.

• Introducing Ayesha (Bowe), the leader of the Turkamen women. Previously enslaved by the sheikh, this red-haired, blue-eyed beauty declares, "I am not meant to be any man's slave." Brandishing sabers, Ayesha and her valiant, scantily-clad women move to crush the sheikh and his cohorts.

• Hajji (Derek) the barber endures palace tortures and he prevents his beloved Princess from being seduced by the sheikh. Hajji duels and tumbles the potentate.

• A palace guard says, "By the beard of Allah." Echos Hajji, "I swear by Allah's beard."

• The commoner Hajji and Princess Fawzia are united. The Caliph notes the prophet Mohammed said "the greatest power in the world is love."

Note: Nat King Cole sings the "Hajji Baba Song," written by Dimitri Tromkin.

The Adventures of Marco Polo (1938), UA. *Gary Cooper, Basil Rathbone.* CAMEOS

Mute Arabs as rescuers.

Scene: Marco Polo (Cooper) goes off to meet Khan, the Chinese ruler. En route, a raging storm destroys Polo's ship. Several Arabs appear and deliver the twelfth-century traveler and his companion safely to shore.

Note: The Khan's cunning prime minister Ahmed (Rathbone), who maintains secret torture chambers, could be viewed as an Arab or Chinese cur. Ahmed, who opposes Polo, moves to nab the throne and the princess.

The Adventures of Prince Achmed (1925), a.k.a. The African Sorcerer, Silhouette Films, Potsdam, Germany. Silent. *D: Lotte Reiniger.* Cinema's first full-length animated motion picture (over 300,000 frames of silhouetted figures). MAIDENS, RECOMMENDED

Prince Achmed and other Arab heroes and heroines vs. the sorcerer. Islam is respected.

Scene: Baghdad, the birthday of the Caliph, jugglers entertain the "commander of the faithful." A hook-nosed sorcerer demands the Caliph allow him, not Aladdin, to wed the Caliph's lovely daughter, Princess Dinarzade. With her brother, the "young and brave" Prince Achmed, the Princess escapes by flying off on Peacock, a magic horse, to magical islands.

• Though nude dancers entertain the Prince, he falls in love with Princess Peribanu, whisking her off to "the sacred city of the celestial empire," in China. The Chinese emperor insists Peribanu marry him, but the Prince prevents the wedding.

• In Baghdad, the sorcerer guides Aladdin to the magic lamp. As Aladdin refuses to turn over the lamp, the sorcerer leaves him to die in the cave. Aladdin lights the lamp, and white doves appear. The sorcerer perishes.

• The enchanted palace. Prince Peribanu and Prince Achmed live here happily ever after. Aladdin and Dinarzade, too, are united.

• Final frames reveal the towers and palaces of Baghdad. The subtitles acknowledge Islam: "The voice of the *muezzin,* calling the faithful to prayer rose from the minarets... There is no God but Allah, no safety and no refuge save in Allah, the Glorious and the Great."

Note: The Caliph takes an oath, swearing "by the beard of the prophet."

The Adventures of Sinbad (1962), a.k.a. Adventures of Sinbad the Sailor, a.k.a. Arabian naito: Shindobaddo no boken, Toei Films, Japan. Animated. S, D: *Masao Kuroda.* RECOMMENDED

Japanese animators present Arab heroes, a few villains. No offensive songs; Islam is revered. Props and special effects include a boiling lava pit, flying electric eels, carnivorous plants, a giant roc, and an "evil hell bat."

Scene: In this animated children's adventure film, Sinbad plays the lute and marries the brave princess.

• Arabs move to dethrone an evil vizier, whose cohorts boast beaklike noses. As the villains move to attack Sinbad and his crew, the vizier barks, "Kill them. Go find them and kill them."

• Though the benevolent princess drugs her prison guards, she muses, "They're all good-hearted men."

• Sinbad's men kneel and pray, "Allah is the one and only God. Praise be to Allah the merciful. Allah protect us. We trust you to show us the straight path of peace and safety."

• Sinbad squashes the vizier and his saber-wielding accomplices. Earlier, Sinbad uncovered valuable diamonds. He opts not to keep the treasure, telling the princess, "I have the most wonderful jewel in the world. It's you, princess. It's you."

Note: U.B. Iwerks' animated "Cinecolor" cartoon *Sinbad the Sailor* (1935, Celebrity Pictures), does not feature Sinbad as an Arab hero. Featured instead is a short Anglo-looking Sinbad, resembling Popeye the Sailor. He boasts long, white sideburns and puffs a pipe. Briefly, Sinbad's crewmen surface, several wearing white headdresses.

• No Arab characters are featured in the non-animated Russian film *The Magic of Voyage of Sinbad* (1962), which before being dubbed into English, was released in Russia in 1952 under the title, *SADKO*.

• See Toho's non-animated Japanese film *The Adventures of Sinbad* (1963), a.k.a. *The Lost World of Sinbad* (1965), featuring actor Toshiro Mifune as the mythic hero. Scenes show Sinbad defeating a land-grabbing ruler and crushing a witch who turns folks into stone.

The Adventures of Sinbad (1979), MGM/UA. Animated. *Voice of Telly Savalas.* RECOMMENDED

Benevolent Arabs.

Scene: Sinbad (Savalas) weaves a story, telling it to his son Alibar about his past adventures. Flashback. Baghdad's citizens gather around their kind Caliph. Brandishing the magic lamp, the Caliph says, "I wish clothing and food for my friends." Suddenly, the wicked old man of the sea pops up, stealing the lamp.

• Sinbad moves to retrieve the lamp, contesting sea pirates, two giant rocs, and a giant cyclops tagged Baba Moustafa.

• Good triumphs over evil. Sinbad returns the magic lamp to the compassionate Caliph. Keeping his promise, Baghdad's potentate shares the treasures.

Note: Sinbad functions as a scoundrel in the Fleischers' lengthy two-reel cartoon, *Popeye the Sailor Meets Sinbad the Sailor* (1936). Here, the animated Sinbad is tagged Abu Hassan, the scourge of the Middle East. He and his Arab cohorts try to terminate Popeye. Moving to enslave Olive and Wimpy, Abu Hassan barks to a giant roc, "Wreck that ship [Popeye's] and bring me the woman [Olive]." But, Popeye rescues his pals, defeating Abu Hassan and his dastardly quacks. Though this cartoon displays an irreverent Sinbad, it was so successful that theater owners often billed *Popeye the Sailor Meets Sinbad the Sailor* over the accompanying feature.

The Adventures of Tarzan (1921), Numa. Silent. 15 episodes. *Elmo Lincoln.* Footage in this serial is from two Tarzan features, *Tarzan of the Apes* (1918) and *The Adventures of Tarzan* (1921). CLIFFHANGERS, SHEIKHS, VILLAINS

In Africa, Tarzan, Jane, Africans, and jungle animals struggle against Arab slavers and their Russian cohort Rohoff. All 15 episodes display "Arab slave traders." Arabs are tagged "bandits," "buzzards of the jungle," and "devils." Affirms Tarzan: "We shall fight these devils with fire." In the end, Tarzan prevents the Arabs from overpowering the Africans of Opar and taking their gold and women.

Scene: The camera reveals Sheikh Ben Ali and his henchmen, notably, Hagar. States the title card, "Hagar is begging for money he does not need, while his eyes and ears gather what information may be useful to the desert underworld."

• Sheikh Ben Ali's horde kidnaps Jane; they trap and torture Tarzan and murder Waziri tribe members.

• In episode five, "Flames of Hate," an elephant rescues the kidnapped Jane, trouncing an Arab guard.

• Final frames reveal lions gobbling Ben Ali, who "dies as he lives—violently."

Note: Stated on *The Adventures of Tarzan* video cover, this blurb: Viewers will see "Tarzan battling lions, a crocodile, a giant ape, [and] *Arabs* [emphasis mine]."

The African Magician (year unknown), a.k.a. Amina and the Forty Thieves. *NS. Notes from Jeff Rovin's *The Encyclopedia of Super Villains* (New York: Facts on File, 1987). VILLAINS

En route to China, an African magician asks his nephew, Aladdin, to collect the magic lamp from a cave. Aladdin refuses; his uncle "shuts him up in the cave." Inside, the boy uncovers a "magic ring" and escapes. Returning home, Aladdin conjures up from the magic lamp, "a powerful genie." And, he weds the princess. But, the evil uncle reappears; he grabs the lamp and whisks Aladdin's princess off to Africa. Aladdin follows the culprit, rescues the princess, and poisons the magician. Finally, Aladdin goes to China where he terminates the magician's brother, who is even "more wicked, more cunning."

Against All Flags (1952), UNI. *Errol Flynn, Maureen O'Hara, Anthony Quinn.* CAMEOS, MAIDENS

Arab women as mute chattel.

Scene: In about 1700 pirates invade the ship of "the grand mogul, the emperor of India." A crescent moon with star is embossed on the ship's main sail. The pirates move to kidnap the female passengers. The Arabic-speaking Hassan, a fat, bald-headed eunuch, lowers his head, flooring a few. Next, dense Hassan runs smack into the flag pole, knocking himself out.

• The mogul's men (clad in baggy white pants, red turban-like caps, and vests) are easily crushed. Seeking protection, the "daughter of the emperor of India hides in the prayer closet." Yet, the pirates nab the princess, along with her clad-in-harem-garb "Moorish females."

• Seeking protection, the veiled maidens gather around the princess' governess, Mrs. McGregor. The governess tags them, "these lambs."

• The pirate base, a Republic on the Island of Madagascar. After an auctioneer parades the ten Moorish maidens in front of boisterous pirates, he sells them to the highest bidders as "lawful wedded wives." The maidens trod off with their unkempt pirates; no one contests their bondage; they are never again seen.

Note: Stereotypical images also surface in *The King's Pirate* (1967), the remake.

Air Force One (1997), COL. *Harrison Ford, Glenn Close.* CAMEOS

Dialogue links terrorists with Arab countries.

Scene: This post Cold War drama reveals radicals from Kazakhstan holding the US President (Ford) and his family hostage aboard Air Force One. When discussing where the villains might land the plan, a White House aide remarks, "Iraq, Libya, Algeria"—three Arab nations. Also, several times aides say rescue forces should be dispatched to "Iraq."

Airplane II: The Sequel (1982), PAR. *Robert Hays, Stephen Stucker.* CAMEOS, VILLAINS

Iranians as Arab hostage-takers.

Scene: Credits roll. On screen, this blurb: "Houston, the Future." Cut to a blue "Iran Air Courtesy Bus" arriving at an airport. Two rifle-wielding thugs, wearing fatigues and checkered kuffiyehs, steer four blindfolded US hostages into the terminal.

• Passengers, including a mute Arab wearing a kuffiyeh, board a lunar shuttle. Blink twice and you miss him.

• Closing credits. An airline employee, Jacobs (Stucker), reiterates the history of the world. Explains Jacobs, "First, the earth cooled. And then the dinosaurs came but they got big and fat and they all died and turned into oil. And then the Arabs came and they bought Mercedes-Benzes."

Aladdin (1986), CAN. *Bud Spencer, Janet Agren.*

Amazingly, there is nothing "Arabian" about this feature; no Arabs and no Arabian Nights settings.

Scene: Miami, Florida. An American genie (Spencer) appears; he wear slacks and a casual shirt. The genie and a teenage boy proceed to nab local hoodlums.

Notes: Attentive viewers may spot a magic carpet and lamp.

• The British TV movie *Bernard and the Genie* (1991), telecast on A&E, offers a much different perspective, as the film displays a devout, spirited jinn from "Palestine." Throughout, the jinn assists an unlucky London art dealer, granting him Christmas wishes.

• The delightful children's film *The Incredible Genie* (1997, from Kushner-Locke) also offers refreshing portraits. Here, an American explorer and his guide Ali are trapped beneath an Egyptian pyramid. Suddenly, a rampaging desert mummy attacks. The explorer grabs a loose bandage, unraveling the creature. Escaping, the explorer returns to the US with a magic lamp. When a teen named Simon (Matt Koruba) comes across the lamp he rubs it and out pops a 2,001-year-old jinn (Tom Fahn). Throughout the film, the benevolent genie wears Arab garb. Initially the genie doesn't do "anything right"; i.e., he turns Simon's typical home into a crusader castle, complete with villainous knights. Yet, he and Simon become inseparable friends. An evil American scientist nabs the genie, ordering the wish-grantor to conjure up destructive armaments. The genie refuses and is tortured. Says Simon, "Stop, you're hurting him... he doesn't like making weapons." Simon knows the only way to save the genie is "to send him back into his own time," which the boy does, saying, "You gave me a special friend. It's you, it's you, genie." After dispatching the genie safely home, Simon returns to school. Here, he presents a history report on Arab culture, telling classmates a "little known fact... ancient Arabians invented the first numeral system."

Aladdin (1992), Bevanfield. Animated. *Voices of Derek Jacobi, Edward Woodward.*

Though the film opens in "a town in Morocco," 99 percent of the action occurs "someplace in China." No threatening Chinese caricatures—not one! Aladdin appears as the "chosen one." All townspeople are benevolent folk. No offensive lyrics.

Scene: This version differs dramatically from other Aladdin films. All the characters are Chinese—including Aladdin, his mother, the princess, and the sultan.

• Two genies are featured. An elderly man resembling a leprechaun appears as the lamp genie; the lamp is hidden at the bottom of a fig tree. And a black ring genie by the name of "Jorda" pops up, saying to Aladdin, "Hey, dude!" And, "Gimme five!" Aladdin and the princess speak with crisp English accents; the Vizier and his cohorts possess thick, foreign accents. Unlike Disney's threatening Jafar, this film's Vizier is appealing.

Aladdin (1992), Disney. Animated. *Voice of Robin Williams.* D: John Musker, Ron Clements. Music and lyrics by Alan Menken, Howard Ashman, and Tim Rice.
VILLAINS, MAIDENS

This film, Disney's 31st animated feature, received two Academy Awards. Also, it was the studio's second most financially successful film ever. Costing $35 million to produce, in 1992 this film ranked number five in [US] rental earnings, taking in $60 million. Hit movies such as *Aladdin* often earn more money from international rights, video sales, and rentals than they do from domestic motion picture theaters. See my essay "*Aladdin:* Animated Racism" (*Cineaste* XX:1).

Background: Various forms of the Aladdin story go back as far as AD 800. Explains Jeff Rovin, the Aladdin tale is not limited to the Mideast: "It has a long oral tradition and appears in the lore of other lands. In the "Bohemian tale of Jenik," for example, the magic prop is not a lamp, rather "an enchanted watch." Though "the princess is evil, the events in the story are largely the same." Also, in "an Albanian folk tale, the 'lamp' is a magic stone, the villain, an evil Jew."[40]

Around the turn of the century, pioneer filmmakers presented brief versions of *Aladdin.* And, beginning with *Aladdin's Lamp* (1907), moviemakers began lengthening and dramatizing the Aladdin fantasy. A dozen-plus fantasies appeared, complete with an unusual array of genies ranging from a nearly naked female genie to an animated jolly green giant jinn.

U.B. Iwerks' black-and-white cartoon *Aladdin and the Wonderful Lamp* (1934), also presents the protagonists, Aladdin and the princess, as Westerners. As for the other Arabs, the animator offers stereotypical characters, displaying them with long beards and bulbous noses. Also appearing are a "Slave of the Lamp," a rotund Sultan, and dancing girls.

In the Fleischer Popeye cartoon, *Aladdin and His Wonderful Lamp* (1939), the "Arab" genie appears as an effeminate simpleton. And, in the Bugs Bunny cartoon, *A-Lad-In His Lamp* (1948), the genie sides with Bugs, quashing the fat caliph.

In this version, Disney animators anglicize the film's heroes, Aladdin, Princess Jasmine, and the Sultan. Conversely, they paint all the other Arabs as ruthless, uncivilized caricatures. The animators attribute large bulbous noses and sinister eyes to palace guards and merchants. Throughout, the action and dialogue imply that Arabs are abhorrent types, that Islam is a brutal religion. Aladdin's mother does not appear in the film, rather on the cutting room floor. Producers set the film not in fifteenth-century Baghdad, a center of Arab culture, but in Agrabah, a backward mythical kingdom. Occupying Agrabah's foreboding desert castle, complete with Arabesque cupolas, are thieves, harem maidens, and ugly vendors. Out "to slice a few throats," and speaking with idiotic accents, are hiss-able villains: Jafar and his bizarre cohorts.

Scene: Opening frames reveal a shady *al-rawi* (storyteller). Sitting atop a camel, he travels through the desert singing "Arabian Nights." The slanderous lyrics are reminiscent of a song from *Peter Pan* (1953) vilifying American Indians. In part, *Aladdin's* opening lyrics go thus:

> Oh I come from a land,
> From a faraway place,
> Where the caravan camels roam.
> Where they cut off your ear,
> If they don't like your face,
> It's barbaric, but hey, it's home.

Why begin a children's film with lyrics such as "barbaric," and "cut off your ear?" Why declare a culture "barbaric?" In June 1993, in response to public pressure, Disney executives deleted two lines from these opening lyrics for its video version. They cut "Where they cut off your ear," and "If they don't like your face," but retained, "It's barbaric, but hey, it's home"—not quite enough to change the message. As a 14 July 1993 NYT editorial stated, "To characterize an entire region with this sort of tongue-in-cheek bigotry, especially in a movie aimed at children, borders on the barbaric."

• Scabbards raised, hook-nosed Arab guards chase Aladdin. Why? Because the boy took a loaf of bread. Shouts a guard, "I'll have your head for a trophy, you street rat." In reality, those visiting the Arab world's souks encounter mostly friendly merchants offering them coffee or tea, usually gratis. But this film presents a grotesque Arab street vendor, scabbard poised, threatening to remove Princess Jasmine's hand. Why? Because she took an apple to feed a starving child. In reality, punitive laws apply only to repeat offenders, those refusing to repent for crimes that are far more serious than apple-lifting. And hand-chopping is not implemented anywhere in the Arab world, except for major criminal cases in one country, Saudi Arabia. Taking provisions is not a crime, provided one needs food. Islam teaches that any person who steals out of poverty or hunger should never to be punished. Instead, Muslims are advised to give generously to such a person, to provide food and shelter.

• Throughout *Aladdin*, producers disregard Arab culture, even the language. Not only are Arabic names mispronounced, but Agrabah's storefront signs, ostensibly written in Arabic, are actually nonsensical scribbles!

• Professor Joanne Brown of Drake University is especially critical of the film's Arab portraits. The villains display "dark-hooded eyes and large hooked noses," wrote Brown in an editorial in the *Des Moines Register* (22 December 1992). "Perhaps I am sensitive to this business of noses because I am Jewish." Brown goes on to say how she distressed she would be had Disney created a feature length cartoon based on a Jewish folktale, displaying all Jews as Shylocks.

• Though Disney denigrates *Aladdin*'s Arabs, the studio humanizes its animated creatures in *The Little Mermaid* (1989), as well as Native Americans in *Pocahontas* (1996). To test my thesis, review the three features, comparing Agrabah's Arabs with *The Little Mermaid*'s undersea creatures and *Pocahontas*' villagers. Explains Yousef Salem, former spokesman for California's South Bay Islamic Association, "All the bad guys have beards and large bulbous noses, sinister eyes and heavy accents, and they're wielding swords constantly. Aladdin doesn't have a big nose; he has a small nose. He doesn't have a beard or a turban. He doesn't have an accent. What makes him nice is they've given him this American character... I have a daughter who says she's ashamed to call herself an Arab, and it's because of things like this."[41]

• On a positive note, Disney's sensitivity sessions with concerned Arab Americans helped the studio avoid the same kind of stereotyping in *Pocahontas*. Mike Gabriel, the film's director, affirms that from the beginning, the image of the Native American "was a clear concern since we had been blasted by Arab [American] groups for defamatory song lyrics in 1992's *Aladdin*."[42]

• In June 1993, six months after Arab Americans and others contested the movie's anti-Arab images, Disney management under Jeffrey Katzenberg offered at a meeting to submit future projects involving anything Arabic to the American-Arab Anti-Discrimination Committee (ADC) for review—prior to production. Explains my friend, ADC member, Don Bustany, who attended the meeting:

> This became known as the policy of prior consultation. Disney employed the practice with the American-Indian community in its production of *Pocahontas* (1995) but, in its feature films *In the Army Now* (1994), *Father of the Bride, Part II* (1995), and *Kazaam* (1996), the studio reneged on its promise to the Arab-American community. By that time, Katzenberg had departed Disney, with some highly publicized acrimony between him and Disney CEO Michael Eisner, to form DreamWorks with Stephen Spielberg and David Geffen... In his first DreamWorks animated production, *The Prince of Egypt* (1998), Katzenberg employed his policy of prior consultation by meeting with literally scores of representatives of the three Abrahamic faiths—Christianity, Islam, and Judaism, and dozens of members of secular human rights organizations. Sometime later, in a private conversation, I praised Katzenberg for instituting such an enlightened policy as prior consultation. Katzenberg replied, "Thanks, but that wasn't my idea. It was Michael's [Eisner's]."

• Two years following *Aladdin*, Disney again presented young viewers with insulting lyrics, this time in their video sequel, *The Return of Jafar* (1994). Ten million copies sold, making it one of the 20 top-selling videos of all time.[43] In part, the offending lyrics:

> Arabian Nights like Arabian Days... they shock and amaze.
> Pack your shield, pack your sword,
> You won't ever get bored,
> Though beaten and gored, you might.

The Return of Jafar's grotesque Arabs are carbon copies of *Aladdin*'s caricatures. Palace goons and buck-toothed thieves try to kill Aladdin. One villain tries to knife Iago,

Aladdin's parrot. The lead Arab thief, Abismal, refers to his cohorts as "jerks," and as "my surly band of desert skunks." Protesting Abismal's greedy actions, his jerks move to slice him in half.

Disney received scores of letters and calls criticizing *The Return of Jafar* and questioning why the filmmakers featured so many negative stereotypes. Tad Stones, the film's co-producer responded, saying, "In storytelling you have to concentrate on the hero, not add a bunch of characters who are also good guys. The hero should be standing alone against impossible odds." Stones contradicts himself. Aladdin does not "stand alone." In fact, he is surrounded and aided by plenty of good non-Arab characters: Abu, the monkey; Iago, the parrot; Raja, the tiger; the flying carpet; and the blue Genie.[44]

• Two years following the release of *The Return of Jafar*, Walt Disney Television Animation released the second *Aladdin* sequel for home video, *Aladdin and the King of Thieves* (1996), produced and directed by Stones. For ... *Thieves*, Disney's TV animation team consulted with Arab-American specialists. Subsequently, the opening song announcing Aladdin and Jasmine's "royal wedding" differs dramatically from the earlier scores: "There's a party here in Agrabah...What could possibly go wrong?"

This time around, the animators present a dark-complexioned Aladdin and Jasmine. Yet, the blue genie still tags them "Jas," and "Al." Refreshingly, Agrabah's citizens appear as decent folk, not as caricatures, and the sultan functions as a compassionate, wise potentate. Also, Aladdin discovers the "father he never knew," Kassim, leader of the infamous forty thieves. Still, Disney fails to project good-natured thieves robbing the rich, assisting the poor. Instead, the film's "fight-like-demons" thieves are "worse than demons." The thieves and Kassim's enemy Saluk break into the palace, wrecking Aladdin and Jasmine's wedding. And the palace guards, the dense Captain Rasoul and his chubby buck-toothed men, are still goons. But Stones deserves some credit for offering several telling segments, such as Aladdin bonding with his father, who tells him, "We never hurt the innocent." Also, Kassim saves Aladdin's life, and vice versa. Final frames show Kassim and Aladdin uniting, bringing down Saluk and the forty thieves. Now a reformed man, Kassim refuses to steal the "ultimate treasure, the Hand of Midas," telling Aladdin, "It's you. You, son, are my ultimate treasure."

• Disney's TV Animation team also produced "Master of the Djinni" (1987), an animated half-hour *Duck Tales* segment. Here, Uncle Scrooge and nephews Huey, Dewey, and Louie search for "the lost gold of Aladdin." Emerging from Aladdin's "magic lamp" is a dense, turbaned, 2,000-year-old genie. Promptly, he dispatches Uncle Scrooge back to the desert, to the time of Scheherazade. Trekking through the desert, Scrooge and the boys encounter an evil sultan, complete with harem maidens. The ruler's ugly "desert bandits"—one is sketched as a hippo—move to feed them "to the crocodiles." Though Scrooge, the boys, and Scheherazade are surrounded by palace guards, a "good" emir's "camel troops" arrive, just in time to rescue them. Interestingly, a Bullwinkle cartoon shows Aladdin's wicked uncle-magician trying to shoot off his nephew's head with a cannonball!

Note: Viewers interested in Aladdin tales should view the animated 26-minute special *Aladdin and the Wonderful Lamp* (1993, Rabbit Ears Production), telecast on Showtime, 3 April 1995. Here, the action occurs not in Arabia, but in "Isfahan, Persia." Traditional Mideast music underscores this illustrated tale. Refreshingly, only one cur appears—a dark, bearded, hook-nosed Arab. The special contains no fat stupid guards, and no cheating merchants. Both a lamp and ring genie are featured, the lamp genie resembles a huge green Buddha. Aladdin's lovely white-robed princess and her handmaidens are dark-complexioned. Briefly, Aladdin's father and mother appear. This ... *Wonderful Lamp* brought back fond memories of reading the tales of Aladdin's heroics to my children, from a 1950s edition of *The Arabian Nights*.

• A good-natured, tiny, dark-complexioned female genie wearing Arab garb appears in "Madeline and the Magic Carpet," a segment (broadcast on ABC-TV, September 16, 1995) from the popular TV series *The New Adventures of Madeline*. Here, the "littlest genie" employs magic while feeding pigeons. Singing, "You find magic when you find a friend," the lovely genie delivers flowers and ice cream to children. Also featured is a kind "Persian storyteller"; appearing at Madeline's school, the Persian relates a moving narrative, all the girls applaud.

• To its credit, Disney deleted a sombrero-wearing character from a video game related to the hit movie *Toy Story 2* (1999). The Latino caricature never appeared in the movie itself, but the video's mustachioed villain drew fire from activist Latinos.[45]

• U.B. Iwerks' charming animated color cartoon *Aladdin and the Wonderful Lamp* (1934) also displays an Anglo Aladdin and princess, plus a rotund sultan and Arab dancing maidens residing in an arabesque palace. But unlike Disney's *Aladdin*, Iwerks' likeable tale does not boast slanderous songs, nor does the cartoon display an evil vizier or dense guards and a blue genie. Instead, a generic cur sells "new lamps for old," and the helpful slave of the lamp appears as an American-Indian wrestler.

Aladdin: The Story of the Wonderful Lamp (1923), Federated.

Silent. *Joe Rock*. D: Rock and Norman Taurog. SHEIKHS

Though this satirical reworking of the Aladdin fable is set in "a town in far-off China," Arab morons surface.

Scene: In China, Chinese townsfolk gather around Aladdin (Rock), who appears and behaves as an anxious American youth.

• Abruptly, near-naked blacks hoist a rig holding a fat Arab potentate. When Aladdin tries to prevent the ruler from stepping into a puddle and wetting his feet, the dense Arab steps on the coat Aladdin placed over the puddle, sinking deep into the mud hole.

• Appearing also, is "The Moorish magician, a treacherous scamp." And, "the slave of the lamp" appears; wearing a lengthy white nightgown, this genie resembles a clown.

• As a dog bites the potentate's butt, the Arab vows to "behead" its owner, Aladdin.

• Introducing Aladdin's counterpart, an Anglo princess wearing Chinese garb. The Arab ruler's guards, who wear Chinese garb as well, brandish their swords, surrounding Aladdin. The genie intervenes and grants the Arab his special wish. Poof! Fair-complexioned maidens pop up, fondling the potentate.

Note: A *New York Herald* newspaper strip also linked the heroic deeds of Western youths with Aladdin's lamp. From 1904–1907, "The Wish Twins and Aladdin's Lamp" focused on 10-year-old twins who, after acquiring the magic lamp, satisfy childhood wishes, such as running a candy store, soaring in the air, and playing pranks on adults.

Aladdin from Broadway (1917), Vitagraph. Silent. *Laura Winston.* Based on the novel *Aladdin from Broadway*, by Frederic Stewart Isham (1913). MAIDENS

Scene: After the heroine, Faimeh, is sold into slavery, she is forced to wed Amad, an ugly merchant. Rescuing Faimeh from the Arab's clasp is the American, Jack Stanton. Posing as an Arab beggar, Jack secures Faimeh; they run off into the desert. Though Amad and his henchmen pursue the duo, they fail to nab them.

• Faimeh discovers that Stanton is not really a beggar, but a New York millionaire. And, Stanton discovers that Faimeh is not Arab, but English; "She had been captured by the Turks when she was a child." Abruptly, amour! Stanton, the American, whisks the fair British maiden off to the US; they are wed in a "Christian ceremony." In short, a Westerner in Arab garb is the hero; the "Arab" heroine is English; Arabs slavers take Western women.

Aladdin and His Lamp (1952), MON. *Patricia Medina, Johnny Sands, Charles Horvath, John Dehner.* P: Walter Wanger. MAIDENS

This children's fantasy shows Arabs fighting Arab slavers. The commoner, Aladdin, weds the royal princess.

Scene: Baghdad. Introducing the courageous "Princess of all Arabia," Jasmine (Medina). The film's two-toned Cinecolor process presents lovely Jasmine joining forces with the pickpocket, Aladdin (Sands), and the Caliph, her father. Opposing them are two knaves, Prince Borka (Dehner), who wants to bed Jasmine and rule Baghdad, and the evil magician, Mahmoud.

• Borka kidnaps the benevolent Caliph. After binding him to "the wheel of torture," he kills the ruler.

• In the souk slave market, Arabic music underscores Arab slavers auctioning off "The Damascus Dancers." The camera closes in on ugly old Arabs leering, prodding, even poking the enslaved dancers.

• Aladdin uncovers the magic lamp. The emerging genie (Horvath) cautions him about employing the three wishes. To be free from this "curse," warns the genie, "I'm obliged to murder the master of the lamp." Later, when Borka takes possession of the lamp, the genie crushes him.

On treatment of Islam: The auctioneer displaying scantily-clad women tells lecherous Arab onlookers, "Allah welcomes you!" When receiving a high bid, he shouts, "Allah be praised."

• Some movie theaters promoted ticket sales for this film by posting large lobby cards displaying seductive, smiling harem maidens sprawling on sofa cushions, with this caption: "The World's Most Gorgeous Harem Beauties."

• The genie-crushing-Arab motif is also prevalent in two animated cartoons, *A Lad and His Lamp* (1929) and *A-Lad-In His Lamp* (1948). In Pathe's 1929 cartoon, the genie helps a heroic mouse rescue the enslaved heroine and crush nasty Arab cats. In Looney Tunes' 1948 cartoon, the genie assists Bugs Bunny; they bring down Baghdad's wicked caliph.

Aladdin and His Magic Lamp (1968), a.k.a. Aladdin's Magic Lamp, Gorky Films, Russia. Animated. Dubbed in English. *Voices of Boris Bystrov, Dodo Chogovadze.* VILLAINS, MAIDENS

Mostly, Arab heroics.

Scene: This animated feature from Russia offers an ethical genie and an evil magician. Swinging his sword, the magician attempts to slice "handsome" Aladdin in half.

• The nasty magician orders the lamp genie to crush Aladdin; the genie refuses, sparing Aladdin's life. This unique genie is no slave-of-the-lamp. He takes sides; befriending Aladdin, the genie helps bring down the foul magician.

• Appearing throughout are pleasant folk such as Aladdin's mother and other citizens of Baghdad. They all respect their beloved princess. But, "whoever is caught looking at the princess will lose his head."

• Participating at the princess's joyous wedding ceremony is a "time-honored chess master," carrying a giant chess board.

On treatment of Islam: Arabs say, "Allah gives us the morning"; "Allah gives us this lovely day."

Aladdin and His Magic Lamp (1969), Jean Image Production, France. Animated. *Voices of Gordon Heath, Steve Eckardt.* MAIDENS, SHEIKHS

No menacing Arabs appear in this light-hearted adventure by French animator, Jean Image. The knavish magician's antics are humorous, not threatening. Heroics are exhibited by Aladdin, the princess, and the sultan. Scene: Why does the rich, black-bearded "Great Magician of Egypt" want to secure the magic lamp? So that he may nab the princess and become the earth's "most powerful man." This "Master of the Underworld," who boasts a huge proboscis, resides in the Sphinx's eye. Here, his cohort, an owl, gives him bubble baths. Also, another villain, the "Grand Vizier," tries to secure the princess for his wealthy son.

• Aladdin's kingdom appears as a bright, benevolent place. Cheerful music underscores children at play.

• In the souk, a shady merchant gives Aladdin a gold coin in exchange for several gold plates.

• The sultan declares Aladdin shall wed the princess. Fireworks, "festivity and merriment" fill the screen. Aladdin's mother, an attractive woman wearing a veil, joins the festivities.

• When Aladdin learns the princess is missing, he tells the sultan, "I swear by Allah, I will find her." Aiding Aladdin is "Moustafa, the servant of the ring."

• A "servant of the lamp" genie also appears; he obeys whoever controls the lamp.

• Aladdin exchanges blows with the evil magician, knocking him flat. As soon as Aladdin rescues the princess, the ring genie assists, dispatching the Master of the Underworld and his owl inside "a crystal ball, forever."

Aladdin and the Magic Lamp (1982), a.k.a. Aladdin and His Wonderful Lamp, Toei Films, Japan. Animated. *Voices of Kristy McNichol, John Carradine.* SHEIKHS, VILLAINS

Reliable Arabs surface in this rags-to-riches animated tale. No offensive songs; the townsfolk are likeable people. The protagonists—Aladdin, his benevolent mother, the wise sultan, the lovely princess, a chipmunk, and "The Servant of the Ring"—contest the corrupt vizier, the wicked wizard, and his black crow.

Scene: Dependable Aladdin woos the Princess; he secures her, then loses her. In the end, they wed.

• The evil wizard dispatches several huge statues to crush Aladdin. Next, he tries to saw the youth in half. After snatching the princess, the wizard purrs, "When are we getting married?" She retorts, "Never."

• During a flying carpet duel, the wizard sends gliding through the air, a huge pair of scissors; the giant scissors snip away at Aladdin's carpet.

• The finale. After toppling the vizier, Aladdin links up with his beloved princess. Then, he assists needy villagers, giving them newly discovered treasures. Deciding it's best to create their own magic, the couple toss the magic lamp onto a truck, and pitch the key.

Note: The wizard tags Aladdin "jackal" and "you son of a camel."

Aladdin and the Wonderful Lamp (1917), a.k.a. Aladdin and His Wonderful Lamp, FOX. Silent. *Francis Carpenter, Violet Radcliffe, Virginia Lee Corbin.* D: C.M. Franklin, S.A. Franklin. See FOX's *Ali Baba and the 40 Thieves* (1918). RECOMMENDED

William Fox's child-stars appear as likeable Arabs in this charming kiddie fantasy. The sultan, his palace guards, and Baghdad's townspeople are all likeable folk.

• Aladdin, portrayed by a bushy-haired blonde boy (Carpenter), woos the film's princess (Corbin), calling her, "my white-petaled rose."

• Treatment of Islam: Unlike scenes in Disney's *Aladdin* (1991), souk scenes show devout Arabs praying in "Baghdad, City of the Faithful."

• The Princess calls the evil alchemist, el-Talib (Radcliffe), a "little pig with a moustache."

• El-Talib nabs Aladdin and seals him inside a huge cave. Next, the magician acquires the magic lamp and threatens the sultan. To save her father and Baghdad, the princess reluctantly agrees to wed the alchemist. In time, Aladdin recovers the lamp and calls on the genie, who promptly turns the magician into a "fish peddler."

• Actor Elmo Lincoln stars as the genie.

Aladdin's Lamp (1907), Pathe. Silent. RECOMMENDED

This seven-minute film displays a not-so-nice court magician. Aladdin falls for the sultan's daughter. Romance flourishes, thanks to a lamp genie's playful antics.

Scene: The camera displays the "Underground Kingdom of Gold"; here, the evil "Court Magician" moves to trap Aladdin. Assisting the youth are the genie, the princess, the sultan, and palace guards.

• Initially, the genie appears as a pixie; his bushy hair and horns mesh with his Court Jester's outfit. Later, the genie appears as a giant, complete with huge horns and a humped back.

• Aladdin assists an elderly woman. Poof, she turns into a fairy princess. Next, she and others help bring about the magician's demise.

Aladdin's Other Lamp (1917), Rolfe Photoplays. Silent. *Viola Dana, Robert Walker.*

This 100-percent-Anglicized version of the Aladdin tale is set in a Western boarding house for seafarers. The genie, tagged "Jehaunarana," pops out of an "Oriental lamp." Not only does this helpful genie move to restore Patsy Smith's foster-father's leg, he decorates her room.

Alf's Button (1930), Gaumont. *Tubby Edlin, Will Kellino.* *NS. Notes from VAR (16 April 1930). MAIDENS

A helpful genie emanates from Aladdin's lamp. Thanks to the genie, Alf acquires an Arabian Nights abode. Subsequently, attractive females appear, entertaining Alf at his posh palace.

Note: See two comedy features, *Alf's Carpet* (1929) and *Alf's Button Afloat* (1938). *NS. Notes from MPG.

In *Alf's Carpet*, a London bus driver discovers a magic carpet, enabling him to rescue his friend "from the clutches of an evil sheikh." *Alf's Button Afloat* reveals "the magic lamp of Aladdin." The lamp grants Alf "improbable wishes which turn his fate comedic."

Algiers (1938), RKO. *Charles Boyer, Hedy Lamarr, Gene Lockhart, Joseph Calleia, Leonid Kinskey.* Remake of the French film *Pepe le Moko* (1937), starring Jean Gabin. See *Casbah* (1948). VILLAINS, CAMEOS

Arabs as tattered props. A dismal Algerian casbah serves as the setting for a tragic European romance. Pepe (Boyer), a likable French criminal tagged "King of the Thieves," eludes French police by abiding in the casbah. But when Pepe falls for a beautiful Parisian (Lamarr), he rushes out of the casbah and is killed.

Scene: A clash of cultures. Before credits roll, the soundtrack echoes the muezzin's call to prayer, followed by an upbeat French tune, then haunting Arabic music. Intones the narrator: Algeria is a place "where blazing desert meets the blue Mediterranean, and modern Europe jostles ancient Africa."

• "There is not one casbah," says the narrator, "but hundreds; there are thousands. It is easy to go in—not so easy to come out!" Cut to a maze of winding narrow alleyways and corridors. The casbah's population, intones the narrator, "includes many drifters and outcasts... from all parts of the world [even] criminals. Supreme on these heights rules one man, Pepe le Moko, wanted by the French police." In *Pepe le Moko* (1937) the narrator is more explicit, stating: The casbah contains "smelly pits and doorways full of vermin" and Algerian women "so fat no one would touch them."

• Algeria's French police tell the newly arrived inspector from Paris, "The reality of the casbah is something stranger than anything you could've dreamed." It's like "entering another world, a melting pot for all the sins of the earth... the filth of centuries." Arabic music underscores souk scenes: haggling merchants, beggars, idle women, men playing cards and smoking nargelihs.

• Regis (Lockhart), an obese, unshaven police informer who wears Arab clothing, "sells his friend" (Pepe) to the police "at bargain prices." Pepe's comrades, notably those who shoot Regis, wear Western clothing.

• A blind Algerian beggar moves to enter Pepe's room. He pounds his cane on the floor; screeching music materializes. To Pepe, the casbah is "like being in a grave." I can't stand much more of it," he says (in the original, Pepe shouts, "I hate the casbah!").

• When Pepe meets the "wonderful" Gaby (Lamarr), he expresses a longing for Paris, "where they speak French." He yearns to ride "the subway, eat 'potatoes,' [and sip] coffee on the boulevard."

• Seeing an Algerian lady wearing a white abaya, Gaby says, "The women look so mysterious." Counters Inspector Silmane (Calleia), "No doubt they'd say the same about you."

• Another police informer trying to nab Pepe is L'Arbi (Kinskey); he wears a fez.

• Jealous that Pepe loves Gaby, Pepe's Spanish sweetheart Inez goes to the police, telling them that Pepe plans to leave the casbah. Cut to the shipping dock. When Pepe tries to board the ship, to be with Gaby, a policeman shoots him. Sighs Inspector Silmane, "I'm sorry, Pepe. He thought you were trying to escape." Responds Pepe, "And so I have my friend"; to him, death is better than living in the casbah. (In *Pepe Le Moko*, Pepe also feels imprisoned within the casbah's "native" quarters. But the film concludes with Pepe being captured. Rather than face prison, Pepe shoots himself.)

Note: Supposedly, the often-imitated "Come with me to the casbah" expression is derived from *Algiers*. Yet, Pepe, who hates the casbah, never speaks this line. Given the film's theme, perhaps Pepe should say, "Help get me out of the casbah!"

As the two informers, Regis and L'Arbi, wear Arab garb, they could be Algerians.

Ali: Fear Eats the Soul (1974), Tango Films, Germany. *Brigitte Mira, El Heidi ben Salem.* D: Rainer W. Fassbinder. BEST LIST

The film deals with discrimination against Arabs and against Germans daring to love them. A handsome Moroccan mechanic and his German mate experience prejudice in post-war Munich. Mocking the couple are shopkeepers, apartment dwellers, cleaning ladies, and restaurant waiters.

Scene: Soothing Arab music underscores credits. Ali (Ben Salem) rejects an attractive German bar girl's advances. His Arab co-workers and his German pals call him Ali, but his real name is "El Hedi ben Salem MuBarek Mohammed Mustapha." Entering the bar to escape the rain is Frau "Emmy" Kurowski (Mira), a homely German widow in her late 50s. After she orders a "cola," Ali asks her to dance. The tall, dark, bearded Ali enjoys dancing with Emmy.

• Emmy invites Ali to her flat. He stays the night and they make love. In the morning, Ali insists on paying Emmy room and board. He does not want to be perceived as a kept man. Later, he confides in Emmy, telling her how he feels about his life in Germany. "German master—Arab dog," says Ali. Adding, "Arab nichts [not] human in Germany." Sighs Ali, "Maybe German right. Arab not person."

• Seeing Emmy with Ali, several German ladies whisper they would "die of shame" if anyone saw them with a "foreigner."

• Back at the bar, an attractive German woman watches Ali and Emmy dance. She points out that Ali is twenty years younger than Emmy. "It's plain unnatural," she says. "Of course it won't work. How can it?"

• Throughout, scenes show the couple being harassed. When Emmy's children arrive at the flat and discover she has married Ali they are furious. Her son Bruno smashes the TV set, telling her, "You can forget you have children," then exits. A German merchant refuses to serve Ali. When Emmy enters the shop demanding service, she is insulted. Seeing his wife cry, Ali says, "I love you." Restaurant waiters isolate the couple, placing them in far-off corner tables, away from other patrons. After Emmy's cleaning lady sees Ali, she confesses, "He's good looking, you know and so clean." Asks Emmy, "What do you mean?" "Well, I always thought they never washed," says the cleaning woman.

• Ali's stomach ulcers force him to go to the hospital. The doctor says he cannot return to work for six months. Too much "stress." Explains the doctor, this happens to all foreign workers.

• Final frames show that prejudices may be unlearned. Some Germans accept the couple. We see a smiling Ali with Emmy at his side.

Note: See Fassbinder's film *Fox and His Friends* (1975). Here, one telling set-in-Morocco scene shows class prejudice against Arabs; the scene comments on the residues of colonialism. Two vacationing Western protagonists invite a local Moroccan to their room. But, the colonized Arab hotel clerk refuses to admit the local, explaining it's hotel policy not to admit Arab guests. For a fee, however, the clerk offers to dispatch to the room some of the hotel's own Arab workers.

Ali Baba and the 40 Thieves (1918), FOX. Silent. *George E. Stone.* D: Sidney Franklin. *NS. Notes from VAR (17 November 1919).

This "kiddy" film features William Fox's child actors, Gertrude Messinger and Raymond Nye, who portray the Arab protagonists.

Around 1900, Charles Pathe released a color-tinted film, *Ali Baba and the Forty Thieves*.

Ali Baba and the Forty Thieves (1944), UNI. *Jon Hall, Maria Montez, Kurt Katch, Andy Devine, Moroni Olsen, Fortunio Bonanova.* D: Arthur Lubin, SP: Edmund L. Hartmann. RECOMMENDED

Arab heroics. The story of Ali Baba "was told orally for at least nine centuries before scholar Antoine Galland, a Frenchman, transcribed it in 1704." The story may "be older than that since a similar tale exists in the writings of Greek historian Herodotus, circa 450 BC." In the Greek version, "the hero robs a treasure house then undergoes trials similar to those of Ali Baba."[46]

Scene: This set-in-the-Mideast Robin Hood tale displays good Arabs stealing from rich Mongol tyrants. The revered thieves turn over needed money to poor Iraqis.

• Flashback, the palace garden. The Caliph of Baghdad's son, young Prince Ali and the red-haired girl, Princess Amara, vow to remain united.

• Flash forward. Amara (Montez) rebuffs the advances of Hulagu Khan (Katch), the Mongol ruler.

• Several scenes show the heroic Prince Ali (Hall), Abdullah, (Devine), and Old Baba

(Bonanova), chief of the forty thieves, contesting the Mongol villains—notably Khan and Cassim (Puglia), an Iraqi traitor.

• The thieves encourage Baghdad's citizens to challenge Khan's Mongol horde. Declares the caliph (Olsen), though Baghdad's brave are armed with only stones and sticks, they are willing to "die for freedom."

• Approaching a solid wall of rock, the thieves cry out, "Open Sesame." The rock parts, allowing them to enter.

• Old Baba advises Ali, "Allah be with you"; and "Avenge your father (the Mongols killed his father, the caliph) and free your people."

• Khan's Mongols spot forty large crocks being delivered to the palace. Believing Ali's men are hiding in the crocks, Khan's minions plunge their swords through the skin covers. Surprisingly, Ali's men are already inside the palace. They rout the Mongols. Afterwards, Prince Ali and Princess Amara wed.

Notes: U. B. Iwerks' animated color cartoon *Ali Baba* (1936) offers an altogether different perspective of the 40 thieves. Here, the Arab robbers and their fat bearded leader appear not as heroic liberators, but as rampaging dark-complexioned camel-riding bandits toting shotguns, robbing the poor. Not to fret; an Anglo-looking Ali Baba and his father thwart the villains, smashing jugs over their heads. When the dense leader and his sidekick try gunning down Ali Baba, they shoot one another instead. Final frames show the captured thieves wearing white underwear, trekking across the desert to return the stolen gold.

• Sinful Arabs also appear in an animated Japanese cartoon, *Ali Baba's Revenge* (1982). Here, "King Ali Baba the 33rd" functions as a ruthless, effeminate ruler, ordering citizens to be "removed from the land." Declares the non-Arab protagonist, Huick, "Ali Baba must be stopped; he's only brought sorrow and pain. We want our happiness back."

• In the Heckle and Jeckle animated cartoon "Arabian Nights and Days" (1937), the crows declare "Open Sesame." Entering the treasure cave, they contest a despondent "Allah Baba Bear," who warns them about a fez-wearing "evil genie [that] stole the princess." The crows fly off on Allah Baba's "magic rug," rescue the blonde princess, then transform the wicked genie into a benevolent jinn.

Ali Baba Goes to Town (1937), TCF. *Eddie Cantor, Tony Martin, Douglas Dumbrille, Roland Young, Louise Hovick, June Lang.* MAIDENS

Arabs vs. Arabs, vs. Americans. Eddie Cantor liberates feuding "Bag-daddies and Bag-mammies."

Scene: Movie aficionado Al Babson (Cantor) bursts onto a shooting set, interrupting the filming of an Ali Baba film. Suddenly, Al swallows an overdose of painkillers and passes out; Al dreams he is Ali Baba's son. Flashback to ancient Baghdad, where Al appears as young Ali Baba. When evil Prince Musah (Dumbrille) and his sinister sister, Sultana (Hovick), move to murder the good-hearted sultan, Abduallah (Young), Al intervenes. Furious, Prince Musah tries to dump Al into a pot of boiling oil.

• Mistakenly thinking his "trick knife" terminated Al, Musah quips, "Killing Baba made me a heel." Affirms Sultana, "He made me a sourpuss."

• Though townspeople starve, Prince Musah's royal cohorts digest gobs of food. Lovely Princess Miriam (Lang), who loves the peasant leader, Yusuf (Martin), assists the "hungry people of the streets."

• Inside multicolored tents, luscious dancing maidens perform. The sultan boasts "365 wives." A screen record?

• Perceiving Al (he wears harem garb) as an Arab woman, the love-struck Musah coos, "Would you like to join my harem?" To distract Musah, Al does the "dance of the seven veils."

• As Baghdad's citizens think Al is a sorcerer, they bow before him.

• Aiding Al is "Omar, the carpet man." Omar creates a flying carpet; Al mounts the magic carpet and, in-flight, vanquishes Prince Musah. Al also rescues the sultan from Musah's soldiers.

• Thanks to Al, the commoner Yusuf unites with Princess Miriam. And, democracy comes to Baghdad. The sultan's wives cast their ballots in favor of Al, who is elected president.

• Treatment of Islam: As Al delivers an election speech, the camera cuts to the muezzin atop a mosque, calling Arabs to prayer. When Al sees the Muslims pray, he ridicules this solemn moment by rolling his eyes and acting flabbergasted.

• Al adopts the principles of President Franklin D. Roosevelt's New Deal. Baghdad's wealthy citizens, including their camels and wives, are taxed. Quips Al, "They take of those who have too much and give to those who have too little."

Note: Inside a tent, two Arabs dance to swing music. Al joins in, making the spectacle look even more ridiculous.

• Dressed in Arab garb, Cantor sings and tap dances in blackface to the song, "Swing is Here to Stay." Talented African-Americans perform for about 14 minutes.

Ali Baba and the Seven Saracens (1964), a.k.a. Hawk of Baghdad, AI. *Gordon Mitchell, Don Harrison.* SHEIKHS

This good guy vs. bad guy Italian-made swashbuckler features Ali Baba (Harrison) and his rebel band, along with lovely Fatima and the "people," defeating the wicked potentate Omar and his merciless oppressors.

Scene: Omar's desert palace contains harem quarters, secret passageways, a huge gong, and "the great stone door." Says a persecuted Arab, "You're the scum of the earth, Omar."

• As the "country has been cursed, cursed by that devil, Omar," Ali Baba challenges the potentate. Riding horse-drawn chariots, à la Ben Hur, Omar and Ali duel.

• Omar dons a black, armored vest; he looks like a tyrant plucked from a Robin Hood film. Ali Baba's hat exhibits a huge white feather.

• After Ali Baba and his men free enslaved maidens, they slug Omar's cohorts. Says Ali Baba, "The tyranny is over, liberty! This is the greatest joy in my life."

• The finale. Ali Baba reigns as Baghdad's new king; lovely Fatima's at his side.

Ali Barboyou et Ali Bouf a l'huile (1907), a.k.a. Delirium in a Studio, Georges Méliès. Silent short. SHEIKHS

In an "oriental" setting, French filmmaker Georges Méliès illustrates violence and trick photography.

An executioner converses with several dancing maidens. Concurrently, four men wearing turbans and pantaloons appear before a chopping block. Wielding a huge saber, the executioner cuts off their heads, then tosses them into a barrel. Suddenly, all four heads pop up and flip back to their bodies. Now fully restored, the men even the score by cutting the executioner in half. All ends well when the executioner's lower half joins his upper body.

Ali and the Talking Camel (1960), MIR. *Henry Geddes, Haj Mohammed.* Filmed in Libya. RECOMMENDED

The action focuses on Ali, a poor, courageous boy, and his devout father.

Scene: Ali and his talking camel, Mehair, encounter two jewel thieves. One thief is an Arab professor; the other, a Westerner. Curiously, the chatting dromedary does much of Ali's thinking for him.

• Libyan policemen and members of the Arab Camel Corp appear as competent officials.

• At the hospital, Ali attends his ill father.

• In the Libyan desert, Ali's jeep breaks down. To the rescue, an American helicopter pilot. Emblazoned on the pilot's chopper: US Air Force. Ali asks the pilot, "We are broken down; can you give us a lift?" Nods the American, "Okay boy, hop aboard."

• Ali, Mehair, and the police inspector rein in the two thieves. After Ali receives the reward money, he rushes to the hospital, paying his "father's hospital bills."

Note: Six of this movie's eight lead characters are portrayed by Arabs, or by actors possessing Arab roots.

All Aboard (1926), First National. Silent. *Johnny Hines, Edna Murray.*
*NS. Notes from VAR. EGYPTIANS, SHEIKHS

An Egyptian lecher kidnaps the US heroine, who is rescued by the American protagonist.

When Hines, an American shoe clerk, declares he knows a short route to the pyramids, an Egyptian travel agency employs him. When Hines discovers a sheikh has abducted an American woman, he swats the Arab kidnapper, freeing her.

Allan Quatermain and the Lost City of Gold (1987), CAN. *Richard Chamberlain, Sharon Stone, James Earl Jones.* SP: Gene Quintano. CAMEOS, VILLAINS

This African-based adventure, a sequel to *King Solomon's Mines* (1950), shows sloppy Arabs intent on raping the Western heroine.

Scene: A sleazy Arab dupes Quatermain (Chamberlain) into buying a phony vest, one that supposedly protects the wearer from knives and bullets.

• An Arab moves to rape Quatermain's blonde fiancée, Jesse (Stone). Jesse eludes his grasp, but four more Arabs corner her. Enter Quatermain's right-hand man, the African protagonist, Umslopogaas (Jones). Single-handedly, Umslopogaas runs off the lecherous Arabs. See *Never Say Never Again* (1983).

• Credits include "Toothless Arab." No Arabs appear in *King Solomon's Mines* (1950).

Amarcord (1974), Italian. SP, D: Federico Fellini. Academy Award: Best Foreign Film. CAMEOS, MAIDENS, SHEIKHS

Fellini recalls his younger days, circa 1930s. Supposedly, Fellini's nostalgic reminiscences of family life in Fascist Italy are fact-based. But his 1930s Arabs are, in all likelihood, fictitious. Featured in Fellini's home town of Rimini are priests, prostitutes, teachers, children, and loveable mothers and fathers. Then, midway through the film, Fellini injects a stereotypical rich Emir and his mute wives. The Arab women function as mute exotics and as subservient objects.

Scene: "His majesty's harem." Maidens covered head-to-toe in white file out of a bus; only their eyes are visible. Lugging white bundles, the mute women march into the "Grand Hotel's" ornate lobby. Observes the narrator, "A sheikh came to the hotel with his 30 concubines." Two fez-wearing black guards waving sabers lash the maidens' backsides, and bark "*yallah*" [move it] in Arabic. Though a huge black-bearded guard stands motionless, his two fez-wearing cohorts bow before the Emir, then guide him toward the elevator. Before entering the lift, the short, fat Emir flirts with the hotel's maids.

• Evening, outside the hotel. The camera reveals an unkempt Italian named Bisceni peddling "beans, olives, and toasted melon seeds." Abruptly, thirty white veiled maidens appear, beckoning Bisceni. From their balconies they toss down white-sheeted ropes.

• The smiling Bisceni climbs up the hotel balcony, where the emir's harem maidens reside. Bisceni appraises the Arabian Nights setting: Lounging about and anxious to please him, are near-naked maidens. These women are the world's fastest change artists; it took only seconds for them to exchange their white draped garments for exotic garb. Exclaims Bisceni, "Sweet Jesus, the pussy!" The maidens wiggle seductively around the pool, tempting the Italian. Quips the narrator, "He [Bisceni] claims that making no distinction between the beautiful and the ugly, he polished off twenty-eight that night."

The Ambassador (1984), a.k.a. The Peacemaker, CAN. *Robert Mitchum, Ellen Burstyn, Rock Hudson, Fabio Testi, Donald Pleasance.* P: Menachem Golan, Yoram Globus. Based on Elmore Leonard's novel *52 Pick-Up*. Filmed in Israel. PALESTINIANS

Ruthless Palestinians murder Israeli and Palestinian peacemakers. Palestinian extremists prevent Americans and Israelis from bringing peace to the region.

Scene: Superimposed on screen before the credits roll, a message summarizes the scenario: "A group known as the PLO (Palestine Liberation Organization) has vowed never to recognize Israel's right to exist. [In the film, Israeli Defense Minister Eretz (Pleasance) repeats this line three times, embellishing the statement with declarations such as: "They also massacre children."]... A PLO splinter group, SAIKA, spreads terror on both the Israelis and the Arabs to prevent peace."

• In the desert, US Ambassador Peter Hacker (Mitchum) and his security advisor Frank Stevenson (Hudson) discuss peace with four Palestinians from Bir Zeit University. Suddenly, Israeli soldiers and SAIKA radicals wearing red-and-white kuffiyehs appear. The Israelis and Palestinians open fire, killing three students. The camera displays close-ups of Palestinian assassins, not of Israeli assassins.

• Mustapha Hashimi's (Testi) antique store. Hashimi speaks "five different languages, [is] a graduate from Rome University [and is] an astute businessman." Mustapha is also "one of the most powerful people in the PLO, a rich aristocratic Arab." He gives a lovely necklace to the US ambassador's attractive wife, Alex (Burstyn). "Take it, as a gift from one who admires you very, very much," he says. Alex goes to Mustapha's flat where they make love. Later, when Mustapha finds out that Alex is the ambassador's wife, he acts responsibly, saying, "You must go. For your own protection. For your husband's protection."

• Palestinian radicals set off an explosion by the Jaffa Gate; eleven are killed, Alex is injured. The ambassador is advised not to speak with any PLO members.

• Both Mustapha and the ambassador are determined to pursue peace. Says the ambassador, "I believe that peace can come to this land when all people of good will can, as I said, sit and reason together." The ambassador meets with students at Hebrew University. Mustapha engages students at Bir Zeit University.

• Roman ruins, the desert. Palestinian and Israeli students gather to exchange ideas about peace. Mustapha tells them, "I was a refugee when I was thirteen... I want more than anything for all of us to live in peace." He and the ambassador shake hands. After the students light candles, a much-needed dialogue commences. Had *The Ambassador* ended here, one could say this was a telling film. But, no. The next scenes serve to enhance the Palestinian-as-terrorist stereotype.

• A Palestinian who survived an earlier Palestinian-Israeli surprise attack, informs SAIKA about the Israeli-Palestinian gathering. SAIKA members rush off to the ruins, shattering the peace movement. One Palestinian moves to stab the ambassador in the back; Mustapha intervenes, saving the diplomat's life. Cut to SAIKA radicals gunning down the students. Abruptly, Israeli soldiers arrive, mowing down the Palestinians. A bloodbath.

• The final scene. Israelis and Palestinians gather in front of the ambassador's residence. Holding candles they chant: "Peace. Peace." The ambassador says that peace is not impossible. "There is hope. Maybe the next generation will make it better."

Note: Only Palestinians, not Israelis, appear as murdering villains disrupting peace.

• In *The Ambassador* and in other movies, the kuffiyeh is linked with the stereotypical Palestinian Muslim terrorists attacking innocents. "But the cotton headdress has a colorful history that transcends the stereotype, crossing political, social, and cultural boundaries of the region," notes US anthropologist, Ted Swedenburg. The red-and-white headgear of kings and camel drivers is worn for various reasons. It can be seen throughout the Arab world, from the palaces of Saudi Arabia to the outback of Yemen. To shield their heads from the sun, Arab men don checkered kuffiyehs. Yasser Arafat uses the kuffiyeh as a symbol of the Palestinian quest for statehood. Palestinian youths, to hide their identities when contesting Israeli soldiers, wrap kuffiyehs around their faces. The headgear also protects them from tear gas rounds. Non-Arabs also brandish headdresses. Early Zionists who settled in Palestine—including David Ben-Gurion, Israel's first prime minister, wore kuffiyehs. As a *Baltimore Sun* headline put it, the "Kuffiyeh is above Fashion, Faction."[47]

The Ambushers (1967), COL. *Dean Martin, David Mauro, Beverly Adams.*
VILLAINS

In Mexico, agent Matt Helm (Martin) prevents an unrighteous Arab's "organization" from procuring a US flying-saucer.

Scene: Sporting dark glasses and a red tarboosh, rich Hassim (Mauro) seizes one of Helms' partners. Later, when Hassim meets with a power-mad rogue, the Arab boasts,

"I am empowered to offer you a large sum for the aircraft [flying saucer] in your possession."

• Hassim tells Helm, "May good fortune smile upon you." Retorts Helm, "May a thousand tigers break every bone in your body." Tigers!?

• Hassim moves to secure the aircraft, passing the guard a fifth of "excellent scotch," saying, "Have a drink, my friend." The watchman drinks; Hassim takes a rope from under his fez and chokes him. The moral here? Beware Arabs bearing gifts!

• The myth: Arabs are mechanically inept. Hassim double-crosses the spy, Lucy (Adams), a curvaceous redhead. Though Lucy's technical adeptness, not his, gives him access to the saucer, the Arab strangles her, saying, "I knew you knew how to open it."

• Moving to escape with this prized possession, Hassim jumps into the saucer, closing the hatch. Abruptly, plenty of smoke appears! The burnt-to-a-crisp Hassim pops up, screaming.

American Ninja 3: Blood Hunt (1989), CAN. *David Bradley.*
CAMEOS, SHEIKHS

Terrorist sheikhs surface in this martial arts drama.

Scene: Credits roll. Cut to a mad terrorist in "Port San Luco, Triana," moving to auction off a deadly virus. All the bidders are generic types, with one exception—two mute Arabs wearing white burnooses appear. The terrorist refers to the Arabs, saying, "There will be no more inefficient highjackings, no bungled kidnaping, no mistimed bombings." The two Arabs depart in a limousine.

• Later, the Arabs resurface at another gathering of virus bidders.

American Ninja 4: The Annihilation (1991), CAN. *Michael Dudikoff, Ron Smerczak, Robin Stille, James Booth, Ken Gampu.* Filmed in the Kingdom of Lesotho. Based on characters created by the EPs, Avi Kleinberger and Gideon Amir. See *Chain of Command* (1993). SHEIKHS, WORST LIST

A US school teacher, Delta Force commandos, and African villagers defeat a nuclear-mad Islamic sheikh, his Ninja guards, and his Arab cohorts. Slurs target Islam.

Scene: In the US, a CIA official explains that Sheikh Ali Maksoud's (Smerczak) "assassins" are killing African civilians. Maksoud's men hide out "in an old British fort up in the mountains, [and] have taken hostage three commandos, and Sarah (Stille), a Peace Corps worker." An aide chimes in, "Those [Arab] bastards are on the verge of creating a nuclear device small enough to fit into a suitcase to carry into New York."

• Africa. Maksoud's men call themselves "God's Freedom Fighters"; his "assassins" torture their four US captives, demanding $50 million for their release.

• The bearded Maksoud sits at a reviewing stand and observes Ninjas employing their fierce skills. Watching, nearby, are immobile, mute Arabs brandishing weapons. Their passivity implies they are not robust athletes. A Ninja dies. Exclaims Maksoud, "It's as if they are almost proud to die at my command. I always try to impress upon my people that to die in holy battle is a passport to heaven." Retorts Maksoud's cohort, Mulgrew (Booth), a bright Britisher, "You always were full of shit!" Maksoud says nothing.

• Maksoud enjoys watching Mulgrew whip the hostages, saying "Do not kill them... They shall give far more pleasure to Allah and myself, alive."

• Speaking mumbo jumbo, not Arabic, Maksoud falls to his knees and prays. Quips Mulgrew, "Mecca is that way, chap."

• In Beirut, Maksoud and Mulgrew acquire the bomb to nuke New York. Maksoud attends a reception for "Third World Finance Ministers"; says the US Ambassador, "Who invited that scum?" The American tags Maksoud a "pig" and a "bastard."

• Returning to Africa, Maksoud stares at the bomb, saying, "There she is, made by the hand of Allah to bring the Great Satan to his knees." He sets the detonation timer. When Mulgrew enters, clicking off the switch, he berates the dense Arab for his foolish act. Sighs Maksoud, "It fills me with ecstasy to think that I was one second from meeting Allah!"

• The bomb is placed onto a helicopter; Maksoud tells the pilot, "It has enough power to blow New York off the face of the earth. Allah go with you."

• The four abused American captives are delivered to Maksoud. Ninja villains and nasty Arabs wearing kuffiyehs and robes, scream: "Kill! Kill! Kill the infidels! Kill the unbelievers!" Shouts Maksoud, "Allahu Akbar!" (God is great!). Adding, "True believers, last night I heard a jackal scream in the mountain. It was an omen sent to me by Allah to tell me that I have been too merciful to my children, because the Great Satan has not fulfilled the just demands." He screams, "Let the execution begin." The villains bind the Americans to wooden crosses; woodpiles are placed at their feet and set ablaze.

• Enter a Delta Force rescue team. Joining the squad are local villagers, Dr. Tomba (Gampu), an African-American, and an American schoolteacher, Joe Armstrong (Dudikoff). They charge Maksoud's stronghold, free the prisoners, and terminate the villains.

• Maksoud rushes off to board the chopper. "Where to?" asks the pilot. "Mecca," says Maksoud. Mulgrew spots the fleeing Maksoud, shouting: "You Arab prick. You bloody wogs are all the same, a bunch of incompetents, the whole bloody lot of you," he says. Suddenly, the chopper explodes, killing Maksoud.

• Coincidence? The sadistic Islamic sheikh shares the last name of Dr. Clovis Maksoud who, for more than a decade, served as the Arab League's Ambassador to the United Nations.

• Arab villains appear in other Ninja films, e.g. Paramount's TV movie *The Last Ninja* (1983) written by Ed Spielman and starring Michael Beck. Though this set-in-Dallas TV movie focuses on generic US terrorists, two Arab heavies are inserted. After the terrorists wire their "hostages (research scientists) to explosives," one heavy appears; speaking with an Arab accent he shouts: "We are wasting time. Shoot them!" Enter the Ninja protagonist, Ken (Beck), who is the adopted son of an American-Japanese family. Promptly, Ken confronts the Arab, "Haj," who wears a reversible burnoose, white on one side, black-and-white checks on the other. Ken kills Haj and all the other terrorists. Next, he frees the hostages.

The American President (1995), COL. *Michael Douglas, Annette Bening.*
SP: Aaron Sorkin. CAMEOS, LIBYANS

In this romantic comedy about a widower President courting a lovely environmental lobbyist, Arabs bomb a US weapons system. See *Broadcast News* (1987).

Scene: The US president (Douglas) kisses his date (Bening). An aide arrives, stating, The "Libyans have just bombed C-Stan" [a new weapons system]. Presidential advisors prepare to retaliate, "to hit" those responsible for the attack, specifically "Libyan Intelligence headquarters located in a downtown building." Aware that it is "a tough decision to bomb" as many innocents may die, the president orders the attack during "the night shift, [when only a few] people are working in the building." Says the President, "Somewhere in Libya right now, a janitor is working the night shift at Libyan intelligence headquarters. And he's going about doing his job because he has no idea that in about an hour he's going to die in a massive explosion."

• A fine line exists between fiction and reality. Journalist Christopher Hitchens refers to the above scene, pointing out that President Clinton used similar words to help justify an American bombing attack in Sudan. Explains Hitchens:

> Speaking to an audience on Martha's Vineyard, a few days after ordering the destruction, by a volley of cruise missiles, of the Al-Shifa plant in Khartoum, President Bill Clinton repeats, basically, what the fictitious president in *The American President* says: "I was here on this island up till 2:30 in the morning, trying to make absolutely sure that at that chemical plant there was no *night shift* [emphasis mine]. I believed I had to take the action I did, but I didn't want some person who was a nobody to me—but who may have a family to feed and a life to live and probably had no earthly idea what else was going on there—to die needlessly."[48]

• On hearing President Reagan say he learned how to deal with terrorists from the Rambo movies [*First Blood* (1982), *Rambo: First Blood Part II* (1985), and *Rambo III* (1988)], Dr. Thomas Radecki, chairperson of the National Coalition on Television Violence, said, "It is a dangerous thing that the president is learning something from movies that are distortions rather than reality."

American Samurai (1992), CAN/Global. *David Bradley, Mark Dacascos.*
Filmed at GG Studios in Israel. CAMEOS, SHEIKHS

Arabs as callous zealots.

Scene: Istanbul, Turkey. Arena fighters duel to the death. Prominently displayed during fight scenes are mute Arabs wearing dark glasses and white kuffiyehs. More than twenty-four times, the camera cuts to the Arabs, usually a group of four, betting, drinking, wringing their hands, clenching their teeth, and applauding when the fighter's blood flows, or when a grappler's head is chopped off. Only Arabs are singled out. No other arena audience members are depicted as Mexicans wearing sombreros, Africans wearing traditional costumes, Scots donning kilts, Asians wearing straw hats, or Jews wearing yarmulkes.

• Istanbul's "number one nightspot, especially for the Saudis." Here, a bellydancer links up with a white-robed Arab wearing a kuffiyeh.

• The film's protagonist (Bradley) shows his date for the evening photographs of a "sliced up Saudi Prince." Her only comment: "Not exactly dinner material."

Americathon (1979), UA. *Harvey Korman, John Ritter.* S, SP, D: Neil Israel.
SHEIKHS

This film mocks most people and introduces a first: Hebrabs—a blend of Israelis and Arabs. The "Hebrabs," a robed group of silly radicals, nab and hold hostage the US President. Only one Hebrab wears a yarmulke, but scores don Arab garb, advancing the Arab-as-terrorist stereotype.

Scene: 1998 USA. To save the nation from bankruptcy, President Chet Roosevelt (Ritter), stages a 30-day telethon, hosted by Monty Rushmore (Korman). Why a telethon? The US needs $400 billion to pay back an American Indian loan. Appearing are power-hungry Hebrabs. "They are the united people of Israel and Arabia under the banner of United Hebrab Republic, a country conceived by aggression, world domination, and having a good time on a Saturday night."

• Hebrabs tease a maiden; they lust "for anything blonde."

• Wearing sunglasses and robes, two unsightly Hebrabs move to sabotage the telethon. One says, "We've got to knock this off, put our commandos on the air." Suddenly, Hebrabs take over the telethon. Cut to a newspaper headline, stating: "Terrorists Sabotage Telethon—They Kidnap the President."

• A Hebrab party. "Praise the Jews," says a robed man. "Praise the Arabs," yells his yarmulke-wearing cohort.

Note: Actor Harvey Korman also appears in *First Family* (1980), a film where he gives Arab diplomats the boot and the finger.

Anna Ascends (1922), PAR. Silent. *Alice Brady, Robert Ellis, Howard Fisk.*
*NS. Notes from VAR (17 November 1922). Adapted from Harry C. Ford's 1920 Broadway play. Notes on the play from Kathy Baum's program. MAIDENS

Hollywood's first and only feature film displaying a noble Arab immigrant. This rags-to-riches story focuses on Anna, a Syrian immigrant, who writes a bestselling novel.

Film summary: New York's "Little Syria" during World War I. Anna Ayyoub (Brady), a recently arrived immigrant, works as a waitress in Said Coury's coffee house. Enter Howard Fisk (Ellis), a wealthy New Yorker. He and Anna fall in love. Their courtship ends abruptly, however, when a gem smuggler tries to force Anna into prostitution. During a struggle, Anna stabs the pimp. Fearing the hustler is dead, Anna flees, taking up residence elsewhere. Three years pass. Anna learns English at night school, and goes on to write a novel. In the end, love comes full circle as she is reunited with Howard Fisk and they live happily ever after.

Stage play summary: Explains author Harry Ford, "The idea of writing *Anna Ascends* came first into my mind during the winter of 1912, when I met and finally knew very intimately a Syrian family living in Washington, DC. Their family life, their clean way of living impressed me." Arab culture also impressed Ford. "I figured here is a people who could read and write probably six thousand years before the northern 'blue eyes'... who had a fine culture along with the great Egyptian dynasties... Hence I figured why not write a Syrian drama...?"

• The Players of Utica (NY) rendered a successful stage production of *Anna Ascends* (1–4 August 1991).

• Filmmakers generally ignore the Arab immigrant experience. Of early films, only *Anna Ascends* and the documentary *The Syrian Immigrant* (1920) focused on Arab immigrants.

Another Dawn (1937), a.k.a. Caesar's Wife, WB. *Errol Flynn, Kay Francis, Ian Hunter, Clyde Cook, George Regas.* SHEIKHS, VILLAINS

Arabs vs. Arabs, vs. British. Two Western military officers crumble a sheikh's anti-Christian "heathens."

Scene: A Sahara outpost. US Capt. Denny Roark (Flynn) and British Col. Wister (Hunter) love Julia Ashton (Francis), an American. Their wooing is placed on hold— warring Arabs threaten the peace.

• Superimposed over sand dunes, this message: "A remote outpost where a handful of the King's best preserve a precarious peace amongst the warring natives, at the cost of much British blood spilt in the desert sand."

• Arabs-as-buffoons. Three bedouin ride into the legion fort. One greets the British guard by bowing, and saying "Assalamu Aleikum" [Peace be with you.] The guard mocks the Arab, repeating three times, "Salamulakum."

• The treacherous Arab, Achaben (Regas), appears as "a powerful warring sheikh who controls the river water that is the life and livelihood of the peaceful tribes in the valley below." Explains Capt. Roark, "Of course it's not greed that prompts his raiding. It's a good Moslem hatred of Christians." The camera shows Achaben's men "raiding and burning peaceful Arabs."

• As the British patrol scans the desert, Roark says, "The Arabs have pretty nasty ideas for entertaining prisoners." Suddenly, Acaben's bandits appear atop sand dunes; the music swells; the Arabs attack.

• Roark's men describe the conflict:

Soldier #1: How many you got?
His pal: Chalk up two.
Another: You dirty yellow-heathen, you!
Sgt. Murphy: [after being wounded] Around my neck, a medal. Take it off and throw it
    away. I don't want these heathens finding me dead with a Saint Christopher on me.

At other times, Arabs are referred to simply as "heathens."

• Roark bumps off scores of Arabs. He transmits a radio message, "Outnumbered six to one, five dead, ammunition running low, can hold out to sunset." He has only "one chance in a hundred" of surviving.

• Roark triumphs; the Arabs retreat. Shouts fellow soldier, "We done 'em in, sir. We done 'em all in. Pity there weren't more of them."

• Achaben's cohorts build a makeshift dam, "cutting off a much-needed water supply to peaceful Arabs." Thus, "about 500 men, women and children will only have enough water to last for 24 hours. Death and drought are imminent," says an officer. Adding, Achaben cannot "be bribed," unless, of course, it is "a terrific amount."

• To foil Achaben's scheme, Col. Wister sacrifices his life. He flies off in a plane low on fuel and drops several bombs over the dam. The water is released, the villagers saved. But, the plane crashes.

Anthony Adverse (1936), WB. *Frederic March.* CAMEOS, VILLAINS

Message: Anti-Christian Arabs enslave, torture, and kill Africans.

Scene: To pay his debts, Adverse (March), retreats to Africa and becomes a dealer "in slaves." A monk, Brother Francois, accompanies him.

• For 2½ minutes Arabs function as heartless slave traders. Drum beats and chants announce the arrival of shackled Africans. Arab "Chiefs" are told, "By the blessing of Allah, trading will begin this day at the firing of the gun." Cut to bearded, white-robed Arabs whipping the slaves.

• The auction block. Arabs insist Adverse's aide give them more money for their slaves. Barks one, "Only seven pounds?"

• The monk tends an ailing black slave; consider the dialogue:

Arab: "I see Father Francois is still helping the cripples."

Adverse: "The [Arab] Chiefs hate him. They call him the white devil doctor."

Brother Francois [*To the Arab throng*]: "Have you no pity?"

Adverse: [*The Arabs threaten the monk; Adverse intervenes*] "I've said that Brother Francois may have the rejected slaves and I say it again. He protects only those slaves you kill because they've been rejected."

Note: Credits do not state the Arab slavers' names.

Antony and Cleopatra (1913). Imported by George Kleine. Italian, with English subtitles. Silent. *Antonio Novelli*. Photographed in Egypt. EGYPTIANS, MAIDENS

Note: In 1908 Vitagraph released its version of *Anthony and Cleopatra*. And, in 1910 Pathé produced a French silent, *Antony and Cleopatra*. In this Italian version of the epic love story, complete with impressive crowd scenes and settings, offers a not-so-likeable queen. Pursuing the Roman warrior are Cleopatra, the abandoned Octavia (Antony's wife), and a lovely slave girl.

Scene: Concerned about her future, Cleopatra visits an oracle; an elderly woman conjures up "a sacred flame."

• After Antony arrives in Egypt, he "falls easily under the spell of the Egyptian [Queen]." Octavia tries to bring Antony back to Rome. Failing, she turns on Cleopatra, calling her "a serpent." And, she begs the queen to release her husband.

• Cleopatra discovers the slave girl is out to woo Antony, so, "the Pagan Queen" directs guards to whip the slave. She also considers tossing her to awaiting crocodiles. "Thus did the queen defend her love."

• Declare Egyptian conspirators: Let us "rid our people of this Roman [Antony's] presence." They administer to Antony "a sleeping potion."

• After Antony's death the "half-savage" queen tries to win Octavius' love. The conquering Roman not only rejects her, he threatens to whisk Cleopatra off to Rome "in chains." The queen grasps the asp to her bosom and dies.

Antony and Cleopatra (1972), RANK. *Charlton Heston, Hildegard Neil*. Adapted by Heston. Filmed in Spain. EGYPTIANS, MAIDENS, RECOMMENDED

Handmaidens and eunuchs attend Cleopatra (Neil); her sexual attributes bring down Rome's greatest warriors.

Scene: As soon as Antony's (Heston) battle with Caesar commences, the Egyptian commander signals his troops to disperse. Shouts Antony (in a line straight out of Shakespeare), "This fool Egyptian hath betrayed me."

• Final scenes show a devoted Cleopatra. As Antony perishes, the queen commits suicide rather than submit to the conquering Octavius Caesar.

Note: See Renée Goscinny's animated French comedy, *Astérix and Cléopatre* (1992), featuring Astérix, not Antony, as the champion who captures Cleopatra's attention. Here, too, dancing harem maidens perform for the queen. Injected into the scenario, however, is a talking camel and pet tiger. In the end, Astérix vanquishes Roman soldiers and a jealous, inept Egyptian architect.

Appointment with Death (1988), CAN. *Peter Ustinov, Lauren Bacall, Hayley Mills, Jenny Seagrove, Carrie Fisher, Piper Laurie.* SP: Anthony Shaffer, Peter Buckman. D: Michael Winner. Filmed in Israel. PALESTINIANS

Propaganda? Mute Palestinians as beggars, cheats, and rapists.

Scene: 1937 Palestine, the docks. As Palestinians appear in the background, a Western tourist reads from a guidebook: "Jerusalem was the capital of Judea and Samaria. The Jewish people had a state in biblical times." Nodding approval is Agatha Christie's Belgian sleuth, Hercule Poirot (Ustinov). Cut to devout Jews praying at the Wailing Wall. The camera does not show Palestinians praying in churches or mosques.

• At an outdoor cafe an elderly, unattractive Arab bellydancer performs. Cut to an attractive blue-eyed tourist, Dr. Sarah King (Seagrove), anxiously awaiting her friend's arrival. Suddenly, ominous Mideast music underscores the appearance of two ugly Palestinians, frightening Sarah.

• At an archaeological site, some Palestinians ride camels, others wield picks and shovels. Unkempt, aggressive Palestinian boys surround British tourists, asking for baksheesh (tips). Quips the American matriarch (Bacall), "The Arabs have a nose for who tips the most." Next, a wealthy English woman gives money to a fat bearded Arab, complaining: "Are you sure this is the normal fee for the work?"

• In the souk, Sarah moves to purchase from a bearded Arab a butterfly pin. "I give a special price, twenty dinars," says the merchant. Quips Poirot, "Offer him five." The Arab shakes his head. Poirot and Sarah walk away; the Arab shouts: "Five dinars; I give in." Unlike this film's stereotypical merchant, most Arab vendors are honest and courteous. Bargaining is expected; most exchanges between buyers and sellers are pleasant experiences. Almost always, hospitable vendors offer customers complimentary soft drinks or coffee.

• In an alley, Sarah spots the body of a dead Palestinian. Frightened, she picks up the gun that killed him. Suddenly, a dozen-plus swarthy Palestinians wearing kuffiyehs and fezzes threaten Sarah, encircling her. As the scruffy mute men close in on Sarah, the music swells. Next, the Palestinians pull daggers. In time, British officers arrive, shooting. The Palestinians run off.

Note: Though this film is set in 1937 Palestine, the word "Palestinians" is never mentioned. All Palestinians are mute and devious, except Hassan, who utters about six words.

• Agatha Christie's book, on which the film is based, also advances Arab stereotypes. For example, in the book an English woman complains: "The sheikh wanted to kidnap me." Plus, one Arab mocks other Arabs, saying, "They are all very stupid bedouin, understanding nothing."

• In *Summertime* (1955), Rossano Brazzi portrays a Venice shopkeeper who behaves honestly, like most Arab shopkeepers. He captures the heart of the visiting US heroine (Katherine Hepburn). As Hepburn spots a lovely red goblet in Brazzi's window, she enters the merchant's store, asking the price. Brazzi says, "10 thousand lire." Hepburn moves to pay, but the Italian refuses to take the money. Smiling, he explains that one should never accept the initial asking price, adding that it is customary for customers, especially tourists, to "bargain." Promptly, the honest Brazzi reduces to goblet's price to 8,700 lire.

Appointment with Fear (1985), Galaxy Int. *Michele Little*. CAMEOS, EGYPTIANS

Egyptian rituals and murder.

Scene: In Los Angeles, a hospital patient takes leave of his body. Materializing into solid form, he commits murder. Why such violent behavior? Police Sergeant Kowalski cites evil spirits and Egyptian customs. "The Egyptians," explains Kowalski, "believe that when a person sleeps, his other self goes out and does things."

• Closing credits reveal Egyptian tomb paintings.

The Arab (1915), a.k.a. A Night in Cairo, Lasky. Silent. *Edgar Selwyn* (Jamil), *Gertrude Robinson* (Mary). *NS. Notes from AFIC. SHEIKHS

The Arab (1924), MGM. Silent. *Roman Novarro* (Jamil), *Alice Terry* (Mary). *NS. Notes from AFIC and NYT (14 July 1924). This Rex Ingram production was filmed in Tunisia, complete with 800 camels and 400 horses. SHEIKHS

Both silent films are based on Edgar Selwyn's play, *The Arab*. MGM's *The Barbarian* (1933), with Roman Novarro, is also adapted from Selwyn's play. A copy of Ingram's *The Arab* (1924) is available at the Czech Film Archive in Prague.

Both feature Anti-Christian Arab Muslims vs. the Turks. Even before Valentino's *The Sheik* (1921), "the beguiling beauty of Anglo-Saxon [Christian] maidens wrought havoc with the hearts of [Muslim] Arabian chieftains."

Summary: El Kirouan, Syria. An "unscrupulous Turkish governor's Mohammedans" prepare to slaughter a "group of Christian children." Joining them are Syrian "fanatics [who] sharpen their sticks to use as weapons on the 'infidels.'" Saving "the foreigners from being massacred" is Jamil, the "best dragoman in the world." Jamil's knows little English; for example, believing a written-in English letter flatters him (it does the opposite), he proudly reads the missive, which states: "Jamil is the finest little liar in this country of liars, and as a dragoman he is a bunco artist."

Jamil, the courageous son of a respected sheikh, successfully leads an army of "white-clad" bedouin against the Turkish troops. Next, he enters the harem, rescuing Mary, a missionary's daughter, from an evil potentate's clutches. Later, the Muslim, Jamil, declares his love to Mary, vowing to become a Christian. Obliged to leave for England, Mary promises to "return to him." Why does the film fail to show Mary and Jamil at the altar? Explains the VAR critic, the "happy ending is wisely left open" in spite of the fact "the handsome noble Moslem has saved her and her whole white family and flock [and has] given up his indigenous rascalities for her and fallen in love with her; yet he is tan, by birth and tradition, and she is white—oh, so white" (16 July 1924).

Note: According to Liam O'Leary's *Rex Ingram: Master of the Silent Cinema*, Ingram felt a strong affinity for the Arab people, approving of "their... attitude toward life."[49] In 1927, Ingram wrote "In the desert all men are free and equal. Their code is the unwritten law of hospitality." In Tunis, while shooting scenes for *The Arab*, he found the "relaxed atmosphere agreeable." He and his wife Alice even adopted an Arab youth, Abd-el-Kader, "who played in several of their films." And, Ingram befriended the Bey who presented him with "his personal court jester, Shorty Ben Mairech. [Shorty] remained with Rex for many years," appearing in many of his movies. Ingram became profoundly steeped in Arab traditions and customs: He studied Arabic, wrote a novel about Arab life entitled *The Legion Advances*, decorated his villa with "Moorish *objets d'art*," and donated his collection of Arab art to the Cairo Museum. During WWII, Ingram offered to assist Washington's policymakers with his knowledge of the Arab peoples. ·

• Filmmakers did not allow Anglo-Saxon heroines to kiss Arabs. Yet, in Jesse L. Lasky's brilliant anti-war film *The Captive* (1915), which was released the same year as *The Arab*, the Balkan heroine embraces the Turkish protagonist. Throughout, action scenes reveal warring Montenegrans and Turks. In spite of the war, Sonya (Blance Sweet), a Montenegran peasant girl, falls in love with Mahmud (House Peters), an imprisoned Turkish nobleman. After the conflict ceases, Mahmud declares his love, telling Sonya, "I want you to come with me as my wife." Sonya balks, "You are a great nobleman. I am a peasant." All ends well. Final scenes show Mahmud, Sonya, and her young son, linked together as a family. They managed to contest ethnic hatreds.

Arabesque (1966) UNI. *Sophia Loren, Gregory Peck, Alan Badel, Kiernon Moore, Carl Duering, George Coulouris.* MAIDENS

Arabs vs. Arabs, Arabs vs. Americans. Scenarios occasionally show a movie star, such as Sophia Loren, portraying an Arab—an Arab who detests other Arabs and opts to love a Westerner. In *Arabesque*, the clad-in-Western-garb Yasmin Azier (Loren), battles Arabs and romances an American professor.

Scene: Arab assassins kill Ragheeb (Coulouris), an Arab professor. Cut to Ragheeb's conspiring wife, an ugly woman wearing a black abaya.

• London. David Pollock (Peck), an American professor of languages on exchange, falls for Yasmin, a seductive agent. As soon as Yasmin meets Pollock, they make love. Yasmin tells him, "You must believe me. I hate them [Yussef and Beshravvi, two Arabs]."

• Yasmin feigns being the devoted mistress of Beshravvi (Badel), an effete shipping magnate who collects things. How does Beshravvi react when Yasmin flaunts her shapely body while modeling latest fashions? The "degenerate" Arab could care less. Beshravvi's unseemly behavior parallels that of the villain Karim Hatimi in *Half Moon Street* (1986); he too is painted as an "Arab-not-digging-sex." See also Malouf, a collector of women, in *24 Hours to Kill* (1966).

• Beshravvi's London mansion. Surfacing are "nasty [Arab] characters,"and a falcon that "eats only flesh." Beshravvi's men want to assassinate Prime Minister Hassan. Only Pollock stands in their way.

• To assist Pollock, Yasmin feigns befriending the scheming Yussef (Moore). When her cover is blown, both Beshravvi and Yussef try to kill her and Pollock. The protagonists rush off to a zoo. The Arabs pursue them; one riddles the zoo's aquarium with bullets.

• Yussef nabs Pollock. "The Marines can't save you now," he says. Yasmin, however, rescues her lover.

• Pollock tells the respected Arab leader, Prime Minister Hassan (Duering), "The fact is, there are very few men on this earth whom I admire more than you." Replies Hassan, "No man is greater than the people he serves, Mr. Pollock. Your respect should be for them."

• Seeing Beshravvi's assassins closing in, Pollock asks Hassan: "Can you ride, Mr. Prime Minister?" Astonished, Hassan retorts, "You ask that of an Arab?" They mount their steeds and gallop off.

• From the beginning, the "good" espionage agent, Yasmin, works to prevent fellow

Arabs from murdering Prime Minister Hassan. With Pollock's help, she saves Hassan's life. All the Arab villains die; some are so inept they accidentally shoot themselves. Yasmin and Pollock resume amour.

Note: Loren portrays an intelligent, attractive Arab woman; why not present her in Arab garb? Only once does she wear a Middle Eastern dress.

• Why show so many Arab curs killing Arabs? Why never Arab good guys beating up generic villains?

• Why not present Gregory Peck as an Arab-American professor? Viewers could have seen, for the first time, a brave Arab-American scholar loving an Arab woman.

Arabia (1922), a.k.a. Tom Mix in Arabia, FOX. *Tom Mix, Barbara Bedford, Edward Piel, Hector Sarno.* *NS. Notes from AFIC. See *King Cowboy* (1928). The SP is from Mix's unpublished story "An Arabian Knight." VILLAINS, SHEIKHS

Cowboy and Arabs vs. Arabs. "Overpowering the outlaw band," Mix preserves "the throne of a desert prince." And, he frees the US heroine from the Arab villain's clutches.

Summary: An Arab prince visiting the US moves to wed a Follies beauty. But the ruling sultan and his cohorts disapprove. To elude them, the prince induces Mix to double for him. The two swap clothes. Thinking Mix is the prince, the sultan's men whisk him off to Arabia. Here, Mix meets two endangered Americans, Janice Terhune (Bedford) and her father, a specialist in "dead languages." Forthwith, Mix, the "dashing horseman," restores order to a kingdom in peril. The cowboy crushes a "powerful pretender to the throne." And, he rescues the kidnaped Janice from an "evil counterfeit" sheikh. After restoring the rightful sultan to the palace, Mix and Janice prepare "to leave for America."

Note: Robert S. Birchard, author of *King Cowboy Tom Mix and the Movies*, told me that *Arabia* is considered a lost film. Explains Birchard, Twentieth Century-Fox had a devastating vault fire in 1937, "and virtually all of the Fox Film corporation original negatives were lost." Mix's other Arabian movie, *King Cowboy* (1928), is also a lost film. See Birchard's analysis of *King Cowboy* in his *King Cowboy...* (p 176).

Arabian Adventure (1979), EMI. *Christopher Lee, Peter Cushing, Milo O'Shea, Capucine, Emma Samms, Puncet Sira, Oliver Tobias, Milton Reid.*

This camel-opera features "good" Arabs, a magic sapphire, a pet monkey and an enchanted rose. A few curs appear, including a malevolent genie.

Scene: Once a place "fit for honest men," mythical Jadoor is now ruled by a usurper, the magician Alquazar (Lee). Backstabbing spies and evil Khasim (O'Shea) assist the magician; they imprison the kind caliph.

• Before Prince Hasan (Tobias) may wed Princess Zuleria (Samms) he must "achieve the impossible"—secure a magic rose. "Allah be with you," says Zuleria; "Only the bravest of princes could attempt such a task." Hasan tells Jadoor's denizens, "This is our freedom we are fighting for."

• The adroit beggar boy, Majeed (Sira), joins Hasan. Flying off on a magic carpet, they search for the rose. The camera reveals the desert and snow-capped mountains.

• Intent on preventing Hasan from acquiring the rose, the magician intervenes, turning the prince into a toad.

• The wicked released-from-the-bottle Jinnee (Reid) does not offer Hasan three wishes. Instead, the Jinnee grants himself a wish—to murder his liberator, Hasan.

• Hasan recovers from the Jinnee's threats and the magician's spell. He brings down Jadoor's tyrants. Then, he and the boy, Majeed, free the imprisoned caliph and other prisoners.

Finis: Hasan links up with Princess Zuleira. Sighs the caliph, "The days of evil are over."

Note: A mean Arab buys some water for the dehydrated Majeed, then deliberately spills it. Also, street thugs nearly kill Majeed. On flying carpets, Majeed and Khasim duel.

• Guards don black medieval outfits, resembling attire worn by King Arthur's foes.

Arabian Dagger (1908), Pathe. Silent, one reel. *NS.

Listed in Library of Congress files. I could neither locate reviews nor find the print.

Arabian Fantasy (1904). Silent. *NS.

Listed in Library of Congress files. I could neither locate reviews nor find the print.

An Arabian Knight (1920), Haworth. Silent. *Sessue Hayakawa, Lillian Hall, Elaine Inescourt, Fred Jones.* *NS. Notes from AFIC. See *The Barbarian* (1933). EGYPTIANS

Egyptians fight Egyptians. In this movie, released one year prior to *The Sheik* (1921), the Western heroine falls for an Egyptian. A screen first?

Summary: In Luxor, Abdul Pasha (Jones) and his "hashish-maddened horde" threaten Elinor (Hall), the ward of a noted US archeologist. But Ahmed (Hayakawa), a dissolute Egyptian donkey tender, saves Elinor. Later, Ahmed secures her love.

Note the reincarnation theme. Elinor's sister Cordelia (Inescourt) believes that she is an Egyptian princess and that Ahmed is the reincarnation "of the prince she lost and loved 2,000 years earlier."

• In 1922, Ernest Lubitsch's German film *Loves of Pharaoh* (1922) starring Emil Jannings, was released in the US. In it, the Pharaoh (Jannings) opts to place on his throne an Ethiopian slave girl instead of the Ethiopian ruler's daughter. So, war breaks out. Egyptians defend themselves against invading Ethiopians.

Arabian Knight (1995), a.k.a. The Thief and the Cobbler.

A Richard Williams film. Animated. *Voice of Vincent Price.* MAIDENS

Arabs vs. Arabs. Animator Richard Williams presents a non-Arab hero—Tack, an Anglo cobbler. Yet, Baghdad's King Nod, Princess Yum-Yum, and Baghdad's denizens appear as animated Arabs. They contest a wizard's evil Arabs, a fez-wearing black parrot and General One-Eye's army of darkness.

Scene: Resembling a straw doll, the blue-eyed hero Tack moves to prevent "Baghdad, the golden city," from being occupied by generic villains—General One-Eye and his cohorts. Plus, the cobbler thwarts a sorcerer's attempt to nab the heroine.

• Intent on ruling Baghdad, the wizard, Zig-Zag (Price), schemes to wed Yum-Yum. The princess refuses, declaring, "There's a mind in the body of this pretty miss." Affirms

King Nod, "She can only marry a man pure of heart."

• Zig-Zag's black-cloaked Arabs wield whips. And, "desert outlaws" threaten Tack Inc. Eventually, Yum-Yum and a heroic witch who employs her power "for the forces of good" save Baghdad. They, along with Tack, bring down both the sorcerer and General One-Eye.

• After Tack, the first "Arabian Knight," weds the princess, the narrator intones this message: "So, next time you see a shooting star, be proud of who you really are. Do in your heart what you know is right and you, too, shall become an Arabian Knight." (Can *anyone* become an "Arabian Knight"? In this blue-eyed movie world, could an Arab?)

Arabian Love (1922), FOX. Silent. *John Gilbert, Barbara Bedford*. SP: Jules Furthman. *NS. Notes from VAR (19 May 1922). SHEIKHS, RECOMMENDED

Bedouin assist American lovers.

Summary: The American protagonist, Norman Stone (Gilbert), kills "a French officer who has abused "his sister." Fleeing into the desert, Norman links up with "an Arab band." Later, he meets the Frenchman's widow, Nadine (Bedford); they fall in love. But when Nadine finds out that Norman murdered her husband, she "lays a trap for her lover." Too late, she "learns the true story behind the crime and forgives him." Abruptly, French soldiers surface, preparing to attack. But the soldiers fail to apprehend Norman. "*His Arab friends arrive in time to rescue him* [emphasis mine] from the troops intent on his capture." Final scene reveal the reunited lovers, Nadine and Norman, passing over a hill into the sunset.

Note: This film shows what viewers seldom see. As the writer Emma Freud says in a PBS four-hour travelogue, *Legendary Tales* (1994), "The hospitality of the bedouin is legendary and overwhelming... it makes one feel embarrassed of how we in the West often treat outsiders." Moved by a bedouin's charity toward "unexpected" guests, she says, "He has almost nothing, yet he gave us half. The generosity to strangers is part of a religious duty."

Arabian Nights (1942), UNI. *Jon Hall, Turhan Bey, Leif Erikson, Maria Montez, Thomas Gomez, Shemp Howard, John Qualen, Billy Gilbert, Sabu.* P: *Walter Wanger*. MAIDENS, VILLAINS

In Baghdad, white-robed Arabs fight black-robed Arabs. Two brothers move to secure Scheherazade's hand, and the throne. Haroun al Rashid (Hall) "has too many enemies," including his cruel brother, Kamar (Erickson).

Scene: Shots reveal the palace, a desert fortress, a dungeon, and desert tents. Filling the screen are Arab acrobats, jugglers, beggars, and gobs of harem maidens wearing peek-a-boo pants and displaying bare midriffs. Among the "vultures" poised for prey are the Grand Vizier, a slaver, palace guards, and Kamar. Torture ploys include the "punishment of the slow death" via the stretching wheel and the poison-in-the-ring trick.

• Schehrazade (Montez) refuses to marry a man she does not love. When she rejects the Grand Vizier's advances, he sells her. Whip in hand, Hakim the Slave Trader (Gomez) barks, "Where we're sending you, not even Allah himself can find you." Schehrazade will not allow Hakim to remove her veil.

• The slave market. Enslaved women are imprisoned behind wooden bars. Disheveled

Arabs bid; the camera cuts to a dirty old man, barely able to walk. At times, the dialogue mocks Islam. A beggar and others say: "By the beard of the Prophet." And, "By the beard of Allah."

• Providing comic relief are Schehrazade's not-so-bright sidekicks, Aladdin (Qualen) and Sinbad (Howard).

• Baghdad's denizens, especially Haroun, love and respect Schehrazade; she is referred to as "a woman whose beauty shames the beauty of the desert sunset." Affirms a storyteller, "Her skill and beauty made her an idol of the people."

• Thinking Haroun is a commoner, Schehrazade tends his wounds, saving his life.

• Haroun and his followers, especially Ali ben Ali (Sabu), crush the villains. Blending with Haroun is Schehrazade, "a woman to make men dream." The couple intend to live "in peace and happiness all their days."

Note: It was said to be in Harun al Rashid's tenth-century Baghdad that Scheherazade kept her husband at bay. She spun her "Thousand and One Nights" stories of Ali Baba and Aladdin and of beguiling women and lascivious men, telling of golden palaces and silver ponds, eunuchs and slaves.

• As early as 1905, French filmmaker Georges Méliès produced fantasy Arabian tales such as *The Arabian Night's Palace.* In 1794, a century before motion picture cameras began cranking, *The Arabian Nights Entertainment* was one of four "best sellers" published in the United States.[50] Arabian Nights stories are not exclusively Arab; the sources of many tales are Persian, Hindu, and Chinese.

• During the 1940s and 50s, Latino and Latina performers such as Maria Montez, Patricia Medina, Ramon Navarro, Cesar Romero, and Gilbert Roland were called on to portray Arabs. Producers believed their skin color and accents made them ideal types for exotic adventures and desert soap operas.

• The 30-minute Rankin/Bass animated cartoon *The Arabian Nights* (1972), displays a light-complexioned hero and heroine. Conversely, villains such as the "Cruel Caliph of the Blue City" are dark. The heavies boast huge noses, only a few teeth. See *Aladdin* (1992). In one scene, the Cruel Caliph places the hero inside a coffin, telling saber-wielding guards to chop him in half. "No one who enters my kingdom leaves it alive," he chuckles. One sign states: "Honest Old Omar's Fast Deals in Flying Carpets."

• Following the release of Phil Tucker's burlesque bump-and-grind show on film, *Bagdad after Midnight* (1952), Arab characters and settings became part of the X-rated film genre. In *Bagdad after Midnight*, the comical protagonist winds up in the mythical "Kingdom of Pomonia." He coos as the "Passionate Pasha's" shapely, semi-nude women in harem garb strip down to their panties. Twenty-two years after *Bagdad after Midnight*, and three-plus decades after Universal's *Arabian Nights*, United Artists released Pier Paolo Pasolini's X-rated film, *The Arabian Nights* (1974). In Pasolini's racy feature, Schehrazade spins tales about Arabia's genies, maidens, and licentious sheikhs. Appearing are erotic princesses, as well as enslaved boys and girls. For some viewers, the nude scenes may overshadow flimsy Arab vs. Arab sequences. Also, surfacing in the XXX-rated feature, *A Taste of Genie* (1986), are a genie, several debauched sheikhs, and nude harem maidens. Credits reveal names like: "Khamir U Bitch."

Around the World (1943), RKO. *Kay Kyser.*

This musical comedy displays, briefly, well-groomed Egyptians.

Scene: Bandleader Kay Kyser and his entourage head for the Middle East. Superimposed over their aircraft, the words, "Iran, Palestine, Cairo, Algiers, Casablanca."

• Cairo. Kyser prepares to entertain US servicemen. Surfacing are two neat Egyptians, a guide and a merchant wearing a suit, tie, and fez.

Around the World in 80 Days (1956), WB. *David Niven, Gilbert Roland.*
CAMEOS

Arabs as backdrops.

Scene: Spain. Four mute, bearded Arab bodyguards protect a potentate (Roland).

• The port at Suez. Arab music introduces an elderly beggar. Surfacing also is a woman carrying a fruit tray on her head. Well-dressed Egyptians wear red fezzes.

Ashanti (1979), a.k.a. Ashanti: Land of No Mercy, WB. Israeli co-production. *Michael Caine, Peter Ustinov, Kabir Bedi, Beverly Johnson, Omar Sharif, Rex Harrison, William Holden, Zia Mohyeddin, Marne Maitland, Eric Pohlman.* SP: Stephen Geller, from Alberto Vasquez Figueroa's novel, *Ebano.* This multi-million dollar film was shot in Israel. Roll Films provided production facilities. VILLAINS, SHEIKHS, WORST LIST

Ashanti encourages blacks to hate Arabs. Sleazy Arab slavers abuse Africans, selling them to Saudi Arabian potentates. Arabs vs. Westerners, Arabs vs. Arabs. Deranged Arabs attempt to rape a missionary-doctor. An Arab father kills his son.

Scene: Present-day Africa. Arabs on camels force chained blacks to march across the desert. Credits state: "This story is based on fact." Counters scholar Douglas Porch, "By 1900 the days of Moroccan slavery were over...Slave markets in coastal towns ceased to exist in the nineteenth century.[51]

• A rural village, two World Health Organization (WHO) doctors, David Linderby (Caine) and his beautiful black wife Anassa (Johnson), assist ill Africans. Anassa, who speaks four languages, goes for a swim. Abruptly, Djamil (Mohyeddin), an ugly Arab slaver, rushes from behind bushes and nabs her. Anassa and African boys are placed in chains and tossed into the back of a truck. The key slavers are Suleiman (Ustinov) and Djamil, his unstable son.

• Suleiman's battered truck pulls into a gas station. The African attendant wants to sell a black boy, demanding "two hundred dollars." Suleiman offers "twenty dollars." Argues the man, "But look, you paid more for your petrol." Referring to the imprisoned "fourteen" slaves in his truck," Suleiman says, "People have not gone up in price like petrol... thirty dollars." The African takes "thirty-five dollars" and screams, "Oh, you filthy Arabs are spoiling everything!"

• David examines a map of the "slave route... littered with corpses." Englishman Brian Walker (Harrison) tells David that unless the Arab slavers are stopped "before they reach the Red Sea," Anassa will "disappear forever." Walker's friend, US chopper pilot Capt. Jim Sandell (Holden), offers to assist.

• Lounging on pillows, Suleiman sips Turkish coffee. Anassa is brought to him. As Anassa works with the UN, Suleiman muses, we must find a "special buyer for you," we must "find some special market."

• When Suleiman discovers that Djamil has stashed away unaccounted-for monies, he beats his son with a cane, declaring, "I am a good father."

• Suleiman shoots down Sandell's chopper. Cut to Suleiman's camel-riding Arabs leading the chained Africans across the desert. Why use camels? Why not Land Rovers?

• David and Malik (Bedi), an Arab "vulture," mount camels and pursue Suleiman. Why is Malik chasing Suleiman? Because Suleiman took Malik's family; Malik's wife was "raped, sodomized, had her throat cut." Still, "no trace" of his children.

• Suleiman sniffs the air. Abruptly, several scruffy bedouin approach. Seeing Anassa, the bedouin leader (Maitland) demands: "I want her." Suleiman gives the bedouin a rifle, and "the other woman," a young black "virgin." Leering, the bedouin grabs the girl.

• David and Malik spot some Arab slavers. Malik attacks. After killing several, he tells David these dead Arabs are "not [with] the caravan of Suleiman." He and David free the young Africans. But, explains Malik, they will still be slaves. Only if other Arab slavers take them, says Malik, can the young Africans survive. At the very least, their owners will "give them food, give them work."

• Anassa feigns being interested in Djamil; he releases her. Then he moves to seduce her. Anassa slugs the Arab, and runs off. After Djamil knifes a fellow "stupid bastard" slaver, he nabs the fleeing Anassa and goes to rape her. Suleiman appears and shoots his son, twice, in the legs. He leaves the crippled, bleeding Djamil in the desert to die.

• Near the Red Sea. Malik kills a rich slaver, El-Kabir (Pohlman), "a filthy, groveling pig," who, ironically, boasts several times, "I'm honorable man." El-Kabir manages a "fattening" house, where slaves are fed before being sold into slavery. Hidden under El-Kabir's floor rugs is a trap door that leads to a pit with scores of slaves inside, flies buzzing around them.

• At a seaport, a slave auction commences. A German bargains with an Arab over "three girls." ONE OF THE MOST OFFENSIVE SCENES EVER FILMED. As young African children are paraded, close-ups reveal Arabs as lecherous, effeminate slobs.

• An oil-rich sheikh as slaver. Wealthy Prince Hassan (Sharif), a "Harvard graduate," appears with Suleiman. Seeing the "drugged" Anassa, he says, "very good, and you say that no man has touched her?" Suleiman nods, asking for "two hundred thousand dollars." Quips Hassan, "That's a high price, even for a virgin." When Hassan learns the "beautiful" Anassa is a UN doctor, with a husband," he gives Suleiman "twenty-thousand dollars."

• The "Palace Hotel." Malik and David corner Suleiman. Malik vows "not to kill" Suleiman, but David shoots the slaver.

• Hassan's yacht. The prince assures Anassa that after "a year, perhaps sooner," he will release her. She is "precisely" what he has been "looking for." My father is "very old, [with] a bad heart." It is his "dearest wish that he dies, blissfully, in your arms," says Hassan. Exclaims Anassa, "You want me to be an old man's whore for my freedom?" I am "a dutiful son," says Hassan; you will be paid "very handsomely. You see, in these days a lady's honor is much less important than the price of oil, and my country practically floats on the stuff."

• Malik and David board Hassan's yacht and kill several Arabs. When Malik moves to save David's life, he is shot. At long last, Anassa and David are reunited. Yet, Hassan manages to safely cruise off.

Note: For additional information, see my essay, "Ashanti: The Arab as Black Slaver" (*Middle East Perspective*, December 1979).

• Responding to my letter regarding *Ashanti*'s Arabs, Ted Ashley, chairman of Warner Bros., wrote on 31 May 1979: "Warner Bros. never read the original script of *Ashanti*. It was acquired by us as an appendage to another more significant production arrangement for a two part film to be produced by a major motion picture star." Adds Ashley, "Your letter causes me to appreciate your concern (about stereotypes) and to remain alert in terms of the future... I obviously regret any negative impact the film may have."

• Michael Caine told *People* magazine that the only film "he did for money, knowing beforehand that it would be dreadfully awful, was *Ashanti*." On hearing that "it was a film hardly anybody saw," Caine said, "Good. Let's hope it stays that way" (4 May 1987).

• Peter Ustinov also portrays a debauched Arab in *John Goldfarb Please Come Home* (1964).

Assignment in Brittany (1943), MGM. *Pierre Aumont.* CAMEOS, VILLAINS

Arabs as France's enemies. This WWII melodrama about the French Resistance reveals heroic Frenchmen contesting a Gestapo agent. But, opening frames show a Free French officer stabbing an Arab.

Attack of the Killer Tomatoes! (1977), Four Square Productions. *David Miller.* This low-budget spoof of disaster thrillers is a staple at "Worst" Film Festivals. CAMEOS, VILLAINS

Arab money; Arab heroics.

Scene: Muses the US president, "[Remember how] I used the Statue of Liberty as collateral on that Arab loan?" And, "How does the old girl look in the Dead Sea?"

• A man wearing a khaki uniform and sunglasses enters a restaurant and asks the owner, "Have you any falafel?" Promptly, the owner attacks him. After recognizing the khaki-clad man is his friend, the owner quips, "My God! It's Muamar Khadafi."

• A football stadium. America's "crack" citizens prepare to attack the treacherous tomatoes. Among the Americans intent on crushing the tomatoes is one "foreigner": a bearded white-robed, sword-wielding Arab wearing sunglasses and a burnoose.

Austin Powers: International Man of Mystery (1997), NL. *Mike Myers, Will Ferrell.* SP, Co-P: Mike Myers CAMEOS

This spoof of 1960s James Bond movies displays an inept Arab cad.

Scene: Opening frames show Dr. Evil (Myers) and his cohorts moving to terminate British super-agent, Austin Powers (Myers). One of Dr. Evil's underlings, Mustafa (Ferrell), a prototypical Arab villain wearing a large red fez, bungles his assignment. Displeased, Evil pushes a red button, dumping Mustafa into an incinerator.

The Awakening (1980), OR. *Charlton Heston, Susannah York, Stephanie Zimbalist.* See *Blood from the Mummy's Tomb* (1972). Filmed in Egypt. Both movies are based on Bram Stoker's novel, *The Jewel of the Seven Stars.* EGYPTIANS, MAIDENS

Egyptians as sexual deviants. Beware desert tranquility, swaying palm trees, and crystalline Nile waters. Lurking in Egyptian tombs are restless spirits waiting to unleash curses on Westerners.

Scene: The "Valley of the Sorcerer." Archaeologists tamper with the tomb of Queen Kara, a cruel and murderous ruler. Her 3,800-year-old tomb bears this inscription: "Do Not Approach the Nameless One Lest Your Soul Be Withered." Yet, archaeologists dig away, hastening her timeless curse.

• Believing ancient spells are harmless, British Egyptologist Matthew Corbeck (Heston) uncovers Kara's tomb.

• Egyptians sing a few songs. Briefly, two Egyptian archeologists surface. One, especially, detests Corbeck. He berates Corbeck for stealing Egypt's valuable relics and placing them in British and American museums.

• Corbeck tries to stop Kara's vengeful spirit from possessing his daughter, Margaret (Zimbalist).

• Flashback. Queen Kara's unpleasant past is revealed. Her father, a really weird dandy, murders young Kara's lover and then forces his daughter to bed and wed him. Later, Kara kills her father and takes "hideous revenge." Egyptians had good reason to be "terrified of her" because she "slaughtered everyone who had ever spoken to her father. She must have killed thousands."

• Back to the present. Kara's evil spirit enters Margaret's body. Corbeck is doomed, as are Egyptian workers who stand in Margaret's way. Abruptly, "evil spirits" induce Corbeck to sleep with Margaret. Later, instead of blaming himself for the seduction, Corbeck tells his daughter, "You're a bad girl."

• Kara's hateful spirit guides Margaret to kill her father; she lets loose a huge boulder, crushing Corbeck "instantly."

Note: See Joe Pollack's comments on *The Awakening* under *Sphinx* (1981).

Babes in Bagdad (1952), UA. *Paulette Goddard, Gypsy Rose Lee.* *NS.
Notes from NYT (5 April 1954) and VAR (10 December 1952). MAIDENS

Baghdad's harem maidens revolt! Outsmarting dense sultans, they achieve "equality."

Summary: This filmed-in-"Exotic Color" Arabian Nights tale displays Arab women upending ancient Baghdad's clinging caliph. A retinue of scantily-clad maidens, chaperoned by Kyra (Goddard) and Zohara (Lee), also contest wicked viziers, and oust polygamous sheikhs. In the end, the women triumph, acquiring men of their choosing. Writes the NYT critic, "This is definitely one harem to avoid."

Baby Boom (1987), UA. *Diane Keaton.* SP: Charles Shyer, Nancy Meyers.
D: Shyer. CAMEOS, MAIDENS

A submissive Muslim Arab.

Scene: Manhattan. Diane Keaton, who portrays a liberal business executive, acquires custody of a 13-month-old girl. In need of a nanny, she interviews several applicants. Among the aspirants is a Muslim Arab woman wearing a black abaya that covers her from head to toe. Only the woman's hands and a small portion of her face are visible. The applicant promises, "I will teach your daughter to properly respect a man" and "I speak only when spoken to. I do not need a bed. I prefer to sleep on the floor."

Note: See also *Father of the Bride Part II* (1995).

Baby, It's You (1983), PAR. A John Sayles film. *Rosanna Arquette, Vincent Spano.* CAMEOS, SHEIKHS

In this romantic comedy about a rich high school girl in 1960s New Jersey, a "white" girl may date an Italian or a Jew, but not an "Arab."

Scene: Actor Vincent Spano, who is referred to in this film as "the sheikh," runs into difficulties when he tries to date Jill Rosen (Arquette), the daughter of a Jewish doctor:

> Spano: "What's your name?"
> Jill: "Jill. What's yours?"
> Spano: "They call me the sheikh."
> Jill: [*Shocked, she withdraws*] "Are you an Arab?"
> Spano: [*Surprised*] "No. I'm Italian."

• Later, the excited Jill boasts to her friend, "He asked me out. His name is the sheikh." Jill's pal gasps: "He's an Arab?" The underlying assumption, of course: It's not okay to date a guy with Arab roots.

Note: What a difference three-plus decades make. In MGM's roaring musical *Good News* (1947) students tagged "sheikh," sans disclaimers, were considered cool. Throughout the film, coeds tag the handsome and sought-after males, "sheikhs." Swoons one, "The sheikhs will be here any minute." Another says of the football team captain, "And what a sheikh!"[52]

Back to the Future (1985), UNI. A Steven Spielberg film. *Michael J. Fox, Christopher Lloyd.* Co-W, D: Robert Zemeckis. CAMEOS, VILLAINS, WORST LIST

This time-travel comedy shows a young teen, Marty McFly (Fox), and a crazed scientist, Dr. Brown (Lloyd), duping and decimating nuclear Arab terrorist "bastards."

Scene: Opening credits roll. States a TV anchorman: A "Libyan terrorist group" has stolen some plutonium.

• Dr. Brown brags about hoodwinking the Arabs, chuckling, "A group of Libyan nationalists wanted me to build them a bomb, so I took their plutonium and in return gave them a shoddy bomb casing full of used pinball machine parts."

• A three-minute shoot-em-up scene begins when two inept Libyans in a van try to gun down the protagonists. One Libyan wears a red-and-white kuffiyeh. As soon as their van enters the Twin Pines Mall parking lot, Libyans shoot at Brown and Marty. Screams Brown, "Oh, my God, they found me." One crazed Libyan machine-guns Brown; he drops to the pavement. Screams Marty, "Nooooo! Bastard." Next, the Libyan, who spouts garbled mishmash, goes to shoot Marty. But, the Arab's gun jams. Meanwhile, his dense cohort cannot start the van's engine. Marty jumps into Brown's DeLorean, a plutonium powered time-machine auto. The two Libyans pursue Marty, firing away. Their van closes in; one goes to fire a rocket. Too late. Flooring the pedal, Marty shouts, "Let's see if you bastards can do ninety." He and the car disappear into the past.

Note: In May 1987, I was in Washington, DC, having dinner with several Arab-American friends. In the adjoining room, my host's daughter was watching *Back to the Future.* After watching Arab terrorists shoot at the protagonists, the anxious girl rushed into the dining room. "I can't watch anymore," she said, "I don't want to see those bad Libyans."

• The year's biggest box office draw, seen by more than 53 million people, *Back to the Future* grossed $190 million.

• At the time the movie was made in 1985, the only Mideast nation with nuclear weapons, perhaps as many as 100, was Israel.

• Richard O. Duran and Jeff O'Haco appear in the credits as "Terrorist," "Terrorist Van Driver."

Background to Danger (1943), WB. *George Raft, Frank Puglia.* SP: W.R. Burnett. D: Raoul Walsh. Based on Eric Ambler's novel. CAMEOS

This set-in-Turkey WWII thriller pits US agents against Nazi spies. Appearing are wily Syrians trying cheat an American FBI man.

Scene: As the narrator intones, "There remain only a few uneasy neutrals," a Mideast map appears on screen, displaying Iraq, Turkey, Iran, and Syria.

• Aleppo, Syria. A sign at the crowded train station reads: "Baghdad Istanbul Express." Cut to FBI agent Joe Barton (Raft) asking a Syrian vendor (Puglia) for some chewing gum. The Syrian inflates the price; Barton protests. "Forty cents for a pack of gum? Not me brother! Here's a franc; call it a deal," he says. Another Syrian butts in; he tries to hawk some linens. Then, the two hustlers begin arguing. Barton tosses a coin. As they move to retrieve it, one Syrian's goods fall to the ground. Other Syrians drop to their knees, scrambling for the coin. Barton boards the train; the screeching Syrian pursues him. Barton laughs.

Bagdad (1949), UI. *Maureen O'Hara, Paul Christian, Vincent Price, Frank Puglia, John Sutton.* SP: Robert Hardy Andrews. MAIDENS

Revolt, revenge, romance, and derring-do in old Baghdad. An Arab princess and prince topple Turkish and Arab renegades. Bedouin surface as courageous, "grateful people."

The "Coming Attractions" preview of *Bagdad* outlines the plot. Declares the narrator: "Baghdad, ageless city of intrigue and treachery... What is your pleasure? Dancing girls, perhaps, or desert raiders? It's all yours, all the fighting fury, all the glamour you ever thrilled to! BAGDAD." On screen, scenes of action and romance. Intones the narrator: "Against this exotic background the screen brings you the story of Princess Marjan, a woman of a hundred moods, tempting and beguiling, charming and desirable, imperious and vengeful, pitting her beauty and courage against the desert's savage warriors."

Scene: From atop a mosque, the call to prayer. Desert bedouin pray. Cut to Princess Marjan (O'Hara) and Baghdad's military ruler, the Turkish Pasha, Ali Nadim (Price). Wearing a blue military outfit and red fez, the Pasha says, "Baghdad, the Arabs abode of peace, where for seven centuries there has been no peace."

• The Black Robes appear from behind dunes, attacking the caravan. Sighs the Pasha, "I must bargain with thieves and murderers. It is written in the Koran, what is to be, will be."

• A hotel room. A tubby and unscrupulous merchant tries to con the princess into paying too much for some dresses. Twice, he says, "I am a poor man with many hungry children." Quips the princess, "Be silent, brother to a barrel."

• The princess, who was brought up in England, soon learns that her "people are homeless," that her father was "slain by treachery" by the villainous Black Robes. She vows revenge "on a blood enemy." A bedouin mocks her, saying: "Who will avenge? Thou? A woman?" Retorts the princess, "You will obey me as you would my father."

• Intent on avenging her father's killer, the princess asks the Turkish Pasha for assistance. She does not know that the Pasha and Raizul (Sutton), the leader of the Black Robes, are as amicable as serpents, that it was Raizul, with the Pasha's help, who killed her father.

• The princess and Pasha dine at the "Cafe IFrangi," Baghdad's only European restaurant. Arab dancers and musicians perform, waiters serve flaming kebabs.

• The souk. The Pasha's guards fail to kill the heroic Hassan (Christian), Raizul's "good" cousin. Hassan woos the princess. She sings, in part, "Where the moon can bring desire, Oh, beware of Baghdad."

• Islam is respected. A beggar treads through the souk, exclaiming: "Alms for the love of Allah." As Hassan goes to ride off for help, a friend advises, "Allah be with thee." Falsely accused of murder, Hassan says, "In the name of Allah, I ask only for time to prove the truth."

• At an oasis, bedouin chiefs discuss whether Hassan committed murder. The Pasha dispatches his robed renegades to kill them.

• The bedouins defend themselves from the attack. Employing "an old bedouin trick," they dump disgusting gourds into the villains' steaming food kettles. After the robed assassins partake of this horrible stew, they clutch their stomachs and fall to the ground, violently ill.

• The Pasha ascertains the Princess leads the bedouins. He tells Raizul, "You have a method prescribed by desert law for the punishment of prisoners. You bury them in the sand up to their necks. Then your lances inflict a slow death. A thrust for each eye and one for each ear. It might be amusing." Cut to three bedouin, buried in sand up to their heads. The villains' spears pierce their faces. Another torture method is described, not shown. An Arab tells his prisoner: After you are "buried in the sand and honey placed upon thy head," the ants will feed upon the honey.

• The Pasha's men are about to maim the princess. In time, Hassan and the bedouins appear, eliminating the Pasha and routing Raizul's Black Robes. Final frames display the princess, united with Hassan.

Bagdad after Midnight (1954). *George Weiss, Dick Kimball, Genii Young, Mae Blondell, Dimples Morgan.* D: Phil Tucker. SHEIKHS, MAIDENS

Message: This X-rated burlesque-on-celluloid shows a dense American tourist (Kimball) in pre-Saddam Baghdad ogling stripteasers clad in Arab garb. The Sheikh of Pomonia (Wood) also exploits harem maidens.

Scene: The "Passionate Pasha of Pomonia's" palace; six harem maidens lounge at the potentate's feet. Boasts the ruler, "I won this one in a horse race." And, "I picked this lovely little dancer up last week in a slave market." My vizier, he says, "is very unhappy; he married three wives last week."

• Arab-clad dancers perform burlesque routines; some dances are exotic. Other numbers are out-and-out stripteases. For example, some women appear from behind the curtains, face the camera, and strip down to their pasties.

Note: Nude scenes notwithstanding, humiliating portraits of Arab men and women in this X-rated film parallel outlandish images prevalent in other mainstream feature films. For example, in AI's *Goliath and the Sins of Babylon* (1963), Babylonian potentates function as depraved, lecherous caricatures. Babylon's king demands "thirty of the loveliest young virgins of the land"—to put them "to death." Fortunately, Goliath deposes the evil ruler, freeing the "virgins."

The Barbarian (1933), MGM. Working title: *Man on the Nile. Ramon Novarro, Myrna Loy, Reginald Denny, Edward Arnold.* Note ballad, "Love Song of the Nile" (Nacio Herb Brown and Arthur Freed). SP: Edgar Selwyn, who also wrote *The Arab* (1915). In 1924, MGM released a remake of *The Arab.* EGYPTIANS

A sincere Egyptian weds the half-Egyptian heroine and vanquishes Egyptian villains.

Scene: Cairo. After Jamil El Shehab (Novarro), a learned prince fluent in several languages, poses as a dragoman, he and Pasha Achmed (Arnold), an unscrupulous Egyptian, decide to woo a visiting English socialite Diana Standing (Loy). Diana is "the fiance of Achmed's very dear friend," Gerald (Denny).

• On purpose, Jamil behaves as "a nasty fellow." After Diana employs him, he keeps "popping up" in unique places. Cut to Diana's bedroom; Jamil watches her undress. Diana is advised to be careful, as "All these natives need is a little encouragement."

• Hoping to separate herself from Jamil, Diana fires him and employs another caravan guide, Ben Ali. Unexpectedly, Jamil appears at her desert camp, startling her.

> Diana: "Where's Ben Ali?"
> Jamil: "I persuaded him to give his place to me."
> Diana: "How?"
> Jamil: "Egyptian fashion."
> Diana: "Egyptian fashion?"
> Jamil: [*Tongue in cheek*] "You get them from behind, put a knife at their throat, and if they are not persuaded, you cut!"
> Diana: Furious, she draws a whip and lashes Jamil.

• Diana leaves the caravan, rushing off to Achmed's retreat house. Here, Egyptian maidens bathe and dress her. As Diana came to Achmed's abode, the smitten Arab truly believes she wants him to love her. Misreading Diana's intentions,, he moves to bed her. Jamil arrives, saving Diana.

• Egyptian vs. Egyptian. The angry Pasha dispatches three men to abduct Diana. At an oasis Jamil protects Diana, killing the Pasha's men.

• Jamil and Diana make love.

• The couple enter Jamil's village. Egyptians, including Jamil's father, welcome Diana. Confesses Jamil, They "are noble people and I am their prince. I offer you all the love of an Arab for one woman. I ask you to be my wife."

• Prior to the marriage ceremony, maidens again bathe Diana, then clothe her in Arab garb. Abruptly, she becomes upset, tossing a cup of water into Jamil's face, humiliating him in front of his people. Jamil grabs a whip and strikes her. Diana asks that the ceremony be canceled. Jamil concurs; Diana departs.

• Diana tells Egyptian troops to find Jamil and to punish him. "Every grain of sand is being sifted," says the Colonel.

• Just as Diana is about to wed the Englishman, Gerald, Jamil arrives, declaring: "Either I live for you or die for you. It is for you to choose." Diana abandons Gerald at the altar, running off with Jamil. See *The Graduate* (1967).

• A 1933 scenario that permits an Egyptian to marry an English socialite?! Not exactly. Final frames show Diana and Jamil cruising down the Nile. Diana alludes to "a call of the blood," telling Jamil, "Did you know my mother was an Egyptian?" Sighs Jamil: "I wouldn't care if she was Chinese." See *The Sheik* (1921). Still, the half-English socialite chooses an Egyptian over her English fiancé.

Barbary Sheep (1917), PAR. Silent. *Elsie Ferguson, Lumsden Hare, Macy Harlan, Alex Shannon, Pedro de Cordoba.* *NS. Notes from MAG review by Anne Louise Lynch. All of Ferguson's films, including this one, writes Lynch, "were destroyed in a studio fire." Based on Robert Hitchens' novel, *Barbary Sheep.* SHEIKHS

This conventional yarn shows a shady Arab intent on seducing the Western heroine. Also, Arab vs. Arab.

Scene: Bored living in England with Claude (Hare), her "prosaic [English] husband," Lady Katherine "Kitty" Wyverne (Ferguson) fantasizes "an adventurous interlude," convincing Claude to travel to Algeria, and "the gateway to the desert."

• Kantara, Algeria. A moonlit desert camp. Benchaalal (de Cordoba), a singer of songs, sweet-talks Kitty. Unknown to Kitty, this Arab chieftain is treacherous.

• As Claude's been away for some time hunting sheep, Kitty's "primitive passions grow." Meanwhile, the lecherous Benchaalal "brags" to an innkeeper "about his conquests of French officers' wives."

• Evening, the desert. Unable to check her "desire for the mysterious Arab," Kitty dons her expensive necklace and rushes off to Benchaalal. Instead of embracing her, he tears the diamonds from her neck, then tries to rape her. To the rescue comes Marabout, an older Arab. He "leaps onto Benchaalal's back" and pulls out a knife, fatally stabbing the evil Benchaalal. Explains Marabout, this man killed my only daughter, "for the diamond necklace she always wore."

The Baron's African War (1943), REP. *Rod Cameron.* SHEIKHS

In this re-edited feature, taken from the movie serial *Secret Service in Darkest Africa* (1943), Rod Cameron brings down pro-Nazi Arabs and their German cohorts.

Beast of Morocco (1966), a.k.a. Hand of Night, British Pathe. *William Sylvester, William Dexter, Alizia Gur.* Filmed in Morocco. MAIDENS

Arab as vampire princess. See Theda Bara's *Cleopatra* (1917).

Scene: "There's no such thing as a vampire," declares the Western archeologist. Abruptly, Marisa (Gur), a fourteenth-century Moroccan vampire princess surfaces, along with "Omar" and her "servants of the night." Marisa moves to ravage the young British protagonist, Paul Carver (Sylvester), and his French girlfriend. She sends Omar to attack Carver, the "infidel."

• Carver begins experiencing nightmares, visualizing Marisa and Omar residing inside some caskets. Marisa beckons him, purring, "The darkness isn't strange to those who dwell in it."

• Carver becomes obsessed with these "secrets of the dark." Before long, his unrealistic nightmares become all-too-real. Marisa, "a being of darkness," actually emerges from her underground tomb and embraces him. "You must choose between light [purity] and darkness [sin]," she purrs. Though Carver has allowed himself to move "down the road into the dark," he balks. "There was never love between us, Marisa," he says. "For a time I was captivated by the darkness in you."

• Finally, Carver sees the light, opting to romance his French girlfriend.

• The rejected Marisa swears "revenge upon the whole race of men." Ages ago, she was an "unfaithful" wife and was "entombed alive by her jealous husband." Cut to an ancient inscription: "Here lives one who does not sleep, but who walks the night of death to make all mankind her slave."

Beat the Devil (1954), UA. *Humphrey Bogart, Jennifer Jones, Robert Morley, Manuel Serano.* SP: Truman Capote, John Huston. D: Huston. CAMEOS, SHEIKHS

Odd-ball Arabs and Western con artists surface in this offbeat comedy. An eight-minute scene, complete with abrasive Arab music, relates several messages: Do not get stranded in Arabia; Arab women submit to men; "haggle" if you wish to seem Arab; to dupe an Arab, slip him a few bucks and promise him a Hollywood starlet.

Scene: Forced to abandon ship, Western uranium hunters, including Billy (Bogart), came ashore in an Arab country. One asks, "Where are we?" A shot is heard, several Arabs on horseback appear atop sand dunes. Speaking gibberish, they encircle the group.

• After the Arabs rough up the Westerners, they deliver them to Ahmed (Serano), the ruling despot. A youth fans the nargelih-smoking Ahmed. My country, sighs Ahmed, "is in a state of unrest." Filling the soundtrack, wailing voices of Arabs being tortured by Ahmed's men. Petersen (Morley) calls Ahmed a "swine,"adding, "I spit on you." His remarks are not rebuffed.

• Gwendolen (Jones) starts to speak, Ahmed interrupts. "In my country a female may speak," he says, "but her words are not heard."

• Imprisoned by Ahmed, Billy boasts he is a "friend of Rita Hayworth." Sighs Ahmed, "Tell me more." Billy offers to "write a letter of introduction" to the actress, saying, "She'll fall immediate victim to your charms." Believing Billy, Ahmed releases the group.

• Admiring Billy's ability to dicker, Ahmed says, "I believe you must have Arab blood." See *Appointment with Death* (1988), in which Lauren Bacall says, Arabs "have a nose for bargaining."

Beau Geste (1926), PAR. Silent. *Ronald Coleman, William Powell, Neil Hamilton, Ralph Forbes, Norman Trevor, Noah Berry, Alice Joyce.* The first of three films adapted from P.C. Wren's novel. See *Beau Geste* (1939), *Beau Geste* (1966), and *The Last Remake of Beau Geste* (1977). VILLAINS

Legionnaires exterminate desert Arabs. Barbaric bedouin bandits pop up from behind desert dunes, circle, and charge the Legion fort. In Cowboys-and-Indians films, scalping Indian primitives emerge from behind hilltops, circle, then attack the cavalry fort.

Scene: The Sahara. Major de Beaujolais (Trevor) and his legionnaires enter Fort Zinderneuf. Cut to dead legionnaires propped at their firing stations, victims of an "Arab attack."

• Evening, the fort ablaze. Needing reinforcements, the Major dispatches volunteers. On screen: "What mysterious power moves here? Dead men stand to arms... Then—a fortress disappears in Fire. These happenings, strange and terrible."

• Flashback to Lady Brandon's (Joyce) British estate, 15 years earlier. Lady Brandon's wards, the Geste boys—Beau (Coleman), Digby (Hamilton), and John (Forbes)—ask a visiting Captain "about the Legion and fighting the Arabs." Explains the Captain, "[The] Legion... is the exile of the self-condemned. And the fiercest of all the Arabs are the Tuaregs." The boys play-act, pretending to be Arabs. They place white sheets over their clothes, don burnooses, and feign dueling with sabers.

• Now grown, the Geste youths learn that Lady Brandon's priceless diamond, the "Blue Water," is missing. Each claims to be responsible. For honor's sake, all three join the Legion.

• Cut to Fort Zinderneuf, "the last outpost in the Sahara... often under fire from Arab outlaws." The Gestes terminate mute, robed Arabs.

• Final frames show a swarm of Arabs charging the fort, withdrawing, then re-attacking. Brave legionnaires prop their dead comrades onto the parapets. Declares the Sergeant (Berry), "[We've] got the Arabs completely fooled—those dead men on the walls will save us."

• Treatment of Islam: On screen, this message: "The Arabs at prayer." Quips the Sergeant, "They believe in God. We believe in France." As legionnaires sing the French anthem, Arabs fire away, picking the legionnaires off one by one. Though Beau and Digby perish, John Geste survives.

• In time, Legion reinforcements arrive, saving the fort. Defeated, the screaming, faceless Arabs ride off.

Note: Rightly so, this film and the other Geste films portray no anti-Jewish views. But the novel slurs a "representative of the Chosen People." Wren describes a young Hebrew merchant as a man with "a curved nostril, pendulous nose, [and] large ripe lips" who works in a "dark, mysterious shop." He characterizes Jews as unprincipled hagglers and as a "chatty race."

• This movie was filmed in Arizona, at a cost of nearly $1 million.

Beau Geste (1939), PAR. *Gary Cooper, Ray Milland, Robert Preston, Brian Donlevy.* VILLAINS

Bedouins liquidate scores of Fort Zinderneuf's legionnaires. In the end, reinforcements arrive; the Arabs "are beaten."

Scene: Fort Zinderneuf, littered with lifeless legionnaires.

• Bedouin bring two near-dead legionnaire deserters to Sgt. Markoff (Donlevy), the fort's brutal commander. The Sergeant tells the Arabs to "drive the men back into the desert." They do.

• Unlike the 1926 and 1966 films, this 1939 version presents a desert Arab as a two-faced snitch. The Arab tells legionnaires that fellow bedouins plan to attack.

• In all Geste films, distant camera long shots display bedouins as ants, crouching on giant mole hills.

• Duping Arabs. Dead legionnaires are elevated at their posts. Bedouins fall for the ruse, believing the fort is "fully manned" with "a thousand men."

• Four legionnaires observe bedouin bandits at an oasis. Asks one, "How many would you say?" Quips his pal, "Forty or fifty." One legionnaire blows his bugle; his three comrades fire some shots. Abruptly, the dense bedouins run off. The bugle sound precipitated fear, the bedouins thought they were "being attacked by the whole legion."

Note: French government officials complained to producers, saying this Geste remake did not depict legionnaires fairly.

• Leon Schlesinger's animated cartoon *Little Beau Porky* (1936) displays Porky Pig as a heroic legionnaire. Defending the legion fort, Porky and his two-humped camel machine-gun "Ali Mode" and his desert bandits.

• For a very different account of a Westerner's encounter with bedouins, see John Dos Passos's *Orient Express* (1927), *Journeys between the Wars* (1938), and *The Best Times: An Informal Memoir* (1966). In 1921 Dos Passos arrived in Iraq and immediately befriended Jassem al-Rawwaf, a bedouin caravan master. He spent 39 days with al-Rawwaf's caravan as they traveled across the Syrian desert to Damascus. To Dos Passos, al-Rawwaf and his bedouin were "the finest people I had ever met. These desert people, more than any people I had ever known, seemed to take a man for what he was. Each man stood up by himself, in the fearful wind, under the enormous sky. What did I care how long it took to get to Damascus?" He wrote to one friend, "There was never a more pleasant method of traveling." To another, "This caravan across the desert is the finest thing in my life." After the caravan arrived in Damascus, Dos Passos wrote, "I felt like kissing their feet I was so fussy and gawky beside them. I've never known people so intense, so well balanced, so gentle. I actually found myself crying after I said good-bye to them."[53]

Beau Geste (1966), UNI. *Guy Stockwell, Doug McClure, Leslie Nielsen, Joe De Santis.* VILLAINS

This Geste displays "scum of the earth" Westerners as legionnaires. Though some may be "liars" and "thieves," all are expert Arab killers.

Scene: A nightclub. Arab women sit on the legionnaires' laps. An attractive bellydancer performs, backed by Arab musicians.

• The Sahara desert. Clad-in-blue Tuaregs launch fire balls at the Legion fort. Abruptly, they wield sabers and charge. The Arab horde enters the fort. Though outnumbered, legionnaires shoot them dead.

• The Arabs retreat. Stunned, a legionnaire asks, "It was all over [for us] and then they fell back. Why?" Explains Major Beaujolais (De Santis), "It's not just us; relief is on the way." Boasts the Major, "My gallery of heroes."

Note: Hollywood's irresistible desert legion sagas *never* project humane, heroic Arabs.

Beau Hunks (1931), MGM. *Stan Laurel, Oliver Hardy.* D: James W. Horne. VILLAINS

This Geste jest shows legionnaires using thumb-tacks to rout the "Chief of the Riff-Raff" and his dense "Riffians." Islam is ridiculed. Opening credits state that director Horne plays the chief of the Riff-Raff, "Abul Kasim K'Horne."

Scene: The desert. Stan and Ollie arrive at the legion fort. An Arab warns the Colonel that bedouin "are preparing to make an attack." When asked how many, the Arab informer slurs Islam, saying: "They number more than the hairs in the head of Mohammed."

• A legion rescue squad moves to aid trapped legionnaires. They head out for Fort Arid, "plague spot of the desert, sweltering for 20 days under a Riffian attack."

• Though outnumbered and "ammunition nearly done," Arid's commander will not surrender. Cackles the Arab leader, "Then the bones of your beloved legionnaires will lie bleaching on the desert sand." Quips the officer, "Go back to your scavengers."

• Treatment of Islam: The Arabs storm Fort Arid, shouting "Allah be with thee [and] Allah be praised."

• Ollie and Stan arrive and toss a few grenades, blowing up the bedouins. Next, they beat back the knife-wielding bedouins. How? By placing those thumb-tacks, point-side-up on the ground. When bare-footed Arabs enter the fort, the tacks injure their feet. Grasping their damaged soles, the "Chief of the Riff-Raff" and his screaming "1,921 Riffians" cease firing, surrendering to the legionnaires.

• Credits include: "3,897 Arabs" and "1,400 Riffians."

Note: In RKO's winsome desert farce *The Flying Deuces* (1939), Laurel and Hardy poke fun of legionnaires, not Arabs. Only one strolling bedouin appears in that film.

Beau Ideal (1931), RKO. *Ralph Forbes, Lester Vail, Loretta Young, Leni Stengel, George Rigas, Irene Rich.* Based on P.C. Wren's 1928 novel, sequel to the silent *Beau Geste* (1926). MAIDENS, VILLAINS, WORST LIST

Willing to do anything to bed the Western protagonist, the half-Arab, half-French dancer betrays Arabs. Plus, double-crossing Arabs massacre legionnaires. Islam equals violence; Muslim bedouin hate Christians. As for the legionnaires, one affirms "We are hard, but we are just."

Scene: A desert fort. The camera displays dead legionnaires, murdered by Arabs. Two survivors, Otis Madison (Vail) and John Geste (Forbes), are about to collapse into an abandoned grain pit. In time, the Emir (Rigas) and dancer Zuleika (Stengel), his half-French mistress, rescue them.

• When the Emir entertains legion officers, he seems friendly and supportive of France. An officer says the Emir has "generous and powerful influence among the tribes." Cut to Zuleika, "the angel of death," conspiring with the Emir.

> Zuleika: There has been another religious outbreak.
> Emir: The Muhammadans against the Christians.
> Zuleika: Every guard and convict in the [Legion] camp has been massacred.
> Emir: Allah is good to help us in our holy mission.

• The Emir's palace. "Half-caste" Zuleika dances seductively for Otis. She drops into the legionnaire's lap and puckers up. Otis recoils. Zuleika spits in his face, shouting "You Christian dog!" Still, she betrays her Arab comrades:

> Zuleika: Today is the day of the big Arab uprising. There will be an attack on them, before
>   they can prepare. They [legionnaires] will be butchered like pigs. The Emir has planned
>   it for a long time.
> Otis: But the Emir is a friend of the French.
> Zuleika: The Emir hates the French. When the call to prayer is heard, thousands of the
>   faithful will answer. But under their cloaks, they carry guns and swords.
> Otis: The treacherous swine. A massacre?
> Zuleika: Yes, a massacre, my friend. Not a Christian will be left alive.

• Zuleika requests "a small favor." I want to get out of this country," she tells Otis. "I want to live in Paris. I hate these brown-skinned!"

• When Otis vows to whisk her off to Paris, she dresses him as an Arab. Advises Zuleika, "When you go out, cry and pray as they do, to Mohammed." In reality, Muslims pray always to God, never to Mohammed.

• After Arabs pray, they gather around the Emir, flaunting rifles and swords. Screams the Emir, "Kill! In the name of Allah, kill!" Shouting, they run off. I have never seen a movie showing militant Jews in synagogues, or radical Christians in churches, who flaunt weapons, and scream "Kill! In the name of God, kill!" as the "Muslims" in this film do. Such declarations would be abhorrent.

• The Emir's faceless, white-robed Arabs charge the Legion fort. Otis, his fellow legionnaires, and the French Cavalry troops machine-gun all of them.

• Otis spots Zuleika in the arms of a Major. The officer offers Zuleika a "house, two cars, and alimony." Otis rejoices... he need not take Zuleika to Paris.

Beau Sabreur (1928), PAR. *Gary Cooper, Evelyn Brent, Noah Berry, Mitchell Lewis*. *NS. Notes from VAR (25 January 1928) and NYT (24 January 1928). Adapted from P.C. Wren's novel. VILLAINS, SHEIKHS

Legionnaires vs. Arabs, Americans in Arab garb vs. Arabs.

Summary: "An Algerian desert." In this "billed sequel" to Beau Geste movies, Legion Major Henri de Beaujolais (Cooper) moves to deliver a treaty to Sheikh El Hammel (Berry). Supposedly, the treaty could suppress the "native uprising" instigated by "the disciples of Allah." And, the treaty could lock in French control of Algerian "territory." The ruler, El Hammel, appears as an indolent, obese potentate "who has his vassals help him to stand up after a heavy meal, or a period of cross-legged sitting on downy cushions."

El-Hammel spots American writer Mary Vanbrugh (Brent) and is smitten. The sheikh refuses to sign the French treaty unless Mary joins his harem. Though Mary rejects the sheikh's proposal, he does sign the treaty. And, he blows up fellow Arabs. El Hammel makes good use of "desert mines which he explodes in a secret chamber by means of an electric switch." Mary also joins the melee, fatally shooting the "natives' evil leader," "Sulieman the Strong" (Lewis).

Note: As *Beau Sabreur's* legionnaires' began dropping desert Arabs, audiences in New York's Paramount theater applauded. See *Iron Eagle* (1986), *True Lies* (1994), *Executive Decision* (1996), and *Rules of Engagement* (2000).

• In the end, Sheikh El Hammel and his vizier reveal their real identities: they are Bud and Hank, two adventurous Americans. Thus, the American heroines pair off with the men.

Beauties of the Night (1952), a.k.a. Les belles de nuit, Franco-London Films. *Gerard Philipe, Gina Lollobrigida*. D: Rene Clair. Winner of the International Critics Award, Vienna Film Festival. CAMEOS, MAIDENS

An exotic and elegant Arab woman.

Scene: A French composer (Philipe) dreams he is a soldier stationed in 1830s Algeria. The dream shows French soldiers fighting Arabs. The composer-as-soldier enters a desert tent. Welcoming him is a scantily clad Algerian, beautiful Leila (Lollobrigida). She asks, "Who are you?" He says, "The composer of an opera." Exclaims Leila, "An opera!" Instantly, she prepares herself for amour, purring, "Fair enemy, your victory is complete." Suddenly, the composer's dream ends.

Behind that Curtain (1929), FOX. *Boris Karloff, E.L. Park, Warner Baxter.* CAMEOS

Hollywood's first Charlie Chan talkie. The scenario has India, Persia, and Arabia as the same country. Arabs are props.

Scene: Colonel Beacon's boasts that he is off to "Persia": "goin' to India, into the Persian desert." Arab music underscores desert scenes; souk vendors speak Arabic. Camels and elephants appear.

• As soon as a plane lands in the desert, denizens clad in Arab garb begin shouting in Arabic. They rush to the aircraft, anxious to greet Sahib Hanna, the "Persian" government's envoy. Sahib tells Colonel Bacon, "You are on the sand of my country. I order obeyment."

• Near Teheran's "Palace Hotel." The muezzin chants in Arabic, calling the faithful to prayer.

Bella Donna (1915), Lasky. Silent. *Pauline Frederick, Thomas Holding, Julian L'Estrange.* *NS. Notes from AFIC. Adapted from the book by Robert Hichens. EGYPTIANS

Bella Donna (1934), Twickenham. *Conrad Veidt.* *NS. EGYPTIANS

To love an Egyptian is fatal. In this miscegenation tale, a prosperous Egyptian appears as an immoral gigolo.

Summary: As soon as she arrives in Egypt, London's Bella Donna (Frederick) meets up with Baroudi (L'Estrange), a wealthy Egyptian. [His] "brutal manner attracts her." Promising Bella Donna amour, Baroudi convinces the alluring English lady that he's smitten with her. After a time, the Egyptian convinces her to poison her husband, the Honorable Nigel Armine. When her murder attempt fails, Bella Donna rushes to Baroudi hoping he will provide needed comfort and affection. But, she sees that Baroudi prefers "another woman." Abruptly, the Egyptian dismisses her. The despondent Bella Donna wanders into the desert, perishing in a sandstorm.

Note: See *Barbary Sheep* (1917). Here, too, tragedy occurs when a Western woman and an Arab fall in love.

The Belles of St. Trinian's (1954), AA. *Alastair Sim, Hermoine Baddeley.* Based on Ronald Searle's cartoons. CAMEOS, MAIDENS, SHEIKHS.

A dense, opulent, polygamous sheikh and his near-mute daughter appear in this comedy, set in a British girl's school.

Scene: Arabia, the ruler's castle. The Sheikh of "Makyad's" maidens flirt with American soldiers. The GIs are in Makyad building "air bases," with the sheikh's blessings.

• The sheikh, who dons a headdress the size of a tablecloth, insists that Fatima, his daughter, be educated at St. Trinian's. Why? Because his racehorses train near the school.

• The sheikh has more Arab wives than he can count, yet he lusts after a beautiful Western woman. When he tells his secretary to make the arrangements, she gives him a no-can-do sign. This woman, she says, is off-limits; she's a "Western journalist."

• The sheikh not only has too many wives, he has "at least seventeen other daughters"—so he cannot remember who Fatima's mother is. He tells the secretary to check the files.

• St. Trinian's. Here, the dark-complexioned Fatima functions as a mere "foreign" observer; she speaks only four sentences.

• St. Trinian's lacks funds. Yet, the school can survive, provided the sheikh's horse, "Arab Boy," wins a major race.

• British gamblers try to prevent Arab Boy from winning. But, due to the imaginative actions of St. Trinian's school girls, Arab Boy wins the race.

Ben Hur (1907), Kalem. Silent. *NS. SHEIKHS

Thanks to the cooperation of the Brooklyn Fire Department, the studio filmed five chariot races. Kalem promoted the film as: "Positively the Most Superb Moving Picture Spectacle Ever Produced in America." What few frames remain of the 1907 *Ben Hur* are used in *The Chariot Race* (1907).

Ben Hur (1926), MGM. Silent. *Ramon Novarro, Francis X. Bushman, Carmel Myers.* SHEIKHS, MAIDENS

A stereotypical Egyptian temptress.

Summary: This biblical epic focuses on an enslaved Judean prince and Messala, his Roman betrayer. Years in production, *Ben Hur* was released at a then-record cost of $4 million. Messala's (Bushman) mistress Iras (Myers), a sly Egyptian siren, attempts to ravish Judah (Novarro), but fails.

Ben Hur (1959), MGM. *Charlton Heston, Stephen Boyd, Hugh Griffith.* SHEIKHS, RECOMMENDED

Screenwriter Karl Tunberg pens Arab and Jew as friends. Unlike the 1926 movie, no Egyptian femme fatale surfaces here.

Scene: Wealthy Sheikh Ilderim (Griffith) travels to Jerusalem to see the chariot races. Accompanying the sheikh are his "eight wives" and four white horses. En route, this wise and tolerant Arab, befriends Judah (Heston). The sheikh respects some of Judah's beliefs, questioning others. "One God I can understand," he says, "but one wife—that's not generous."

• The sheikh serves Judah a scrumptious meal, then offers Judah his finest horses. Why? He wants Judah to ride against Messala and others in the upcoming great chariot race.

• Several scenes present Arabs and Jews as oppressed peoples under Roman rule. Working together, fellow Semites contest the ruling Romans.

• Before the race, the sheikh pins on Judah's garb, a Star of David. "The Star of David will shine out for your people and my people," he says, "and blind the eyes of Rome."

• The great race commences; the sheikh and his Arab companions cheer Judah on to victory.

Note: *Ben Hur* received eleven Academy Awards. Heston won the Oscar for best actor; Griffith, for best supporting actor. Box office receipts for the first year—$40 million.

Bengazi (1955), RKO. *Richard Carlson, Richard Conte, Mala Powers, Victor McLaglen.* VILLAINS

Arabs appear as threatening curs. At an ancient Libyan shrine, marauding desert "natives" entrap Westerners. Nasty Arab boys.

Scene: Bengazi, a nightclub owned by an Irishman, Donavan (McLaglen). Dickering Arabs fill the club; a female vocalist sings in Arabic.

• When a lovely Irishwoman (Powers) enters the club, assertive Libyan youths nab her luggage. Before being run off, they hassle her for money.

• Evening, a desert sanctuary. After Westerners uncover buried riches, Arabs surround them. The protagonists cannot see the Arabs, yet the Arabs can see them. (Do Arabs see better in the dark?)

• Finally, the Westerner protagonist (Conte) offers to return the discovered gold. The Arabs withdraw, allowing the protagonists to leave.

Dialogue: Arabs are labeled "tribes" and "natives."

Best Defense (1984), PAR. *Eddie Murphy, Dudley Moore.* SP: Gloria Katz, Willard Huyck. Made in Israel. Israeli actors portray Kuwaiti soldiers. SHEIKHS, MAIDENS, VILLAINS, WORST LIST

Best Defense is based on Robert Grossbach's 1975 novel, *Easy and Hard Ways Out.* Grossbach's novel is set is Saigon, Vietnam, circa 1966. He writes about the US Air Force trying to curtail "North Vietnamese aggression." No Arabs are mentioned. Not once. But for the movie, the screenwriters switched the location to 1984 Kuwait. Arabs bomb Arabs; a US officer mocks Kuwaiti soldiers, women and children. And the soldier slanders Islam. Why did they mock Islam? Why did they falsify Kuwait as a backward camel burg? And, why did they project the Kuwaiti as anti-American goons? Did shooting the film in Israel prompt the writers to change the locale from Vietnam to Kuwait?

In switching their location, it seems they also mixed up some facts. Writers Katz and Huyck present Iraqis as the villains, but in the early 1980s, when the duo adapted *Best Defense* for the screen, the US government considered Iran, not Iraq, to be Enemy Number One. In the 1980s, America and its Arab allies, especially Kuwait, aided Iraq. They feared Iran would invade and occupy Kuwait and other Gulf states. For example, during the Iran-Iraq conflict (1980–1988), Iranian airplanes directed missiles at Kuwaiti and Saudi oil tankers. During the Iran-Iraq war, Europe, the US, Kuwait, and other Arab nations provided unyielding military and financial support to Iraq. Many Americans still believe Iranians are Arabs. All-too-few know that Iran is a Persian country, that its inhabitants speak Farsi. This is one reason why some people thought the Iran-Iraq war was a war between two Arab nations.

Scene: Sunrise; a mosque. The call to prayer is heard. Cut to US Army officer Landry (Murphy) in bed with a mute Kuwaiti woman. Ridiculing the prayer call, Landry quips, "Somebody ask for a wake-up call?" Landry tells the Kuwaiti he bedded, "Thanks for the belly dance."

• The camera consistently displays camels everywhere—even on boulevards! When Landry spots a few, he screams, "What's this camel shit!?" These camel scenes are absurd. During the 1980s and 90s, this writer spent months lecturing and traveling throughout Kuwait. The streets are congested, but not with camels—with scores of pick-up trucks and sleek autos, ranging from Toyotas to Mercedes-Benz. A visitors wanting to see camels must travel far out into the Kuwaiti desert, where only a few camel markets exist.

• A US Army locker room. Introducing two horny, stupid Kuwaiti, who speak with Israeli accents. The soldiers unzip their pants and play with themselves. One even toys with a fire extinguisher. Landry laughs. Had two African American soldiers behaved as perverts, would Landry laugh?

• A reviewing stand. Preparing to inspect a new American super tank, US Army officers link up with robed Kuwaiti. One officer stutters; he tries but cannot explain what the US and Kuwait have in common. "Kuwait and America share a common heritage," he says. Stuttering and stammering to come up with a commonality, he blurts out: "Like, ah, ah, ah, ah, ah—your desert. We, too, have deserts." Abruptly, Landry's inept Kuwaiti soldiers steer the tank into the stand, demolishing it, a Mercedes-Benz, and a house.

• Some confused Kuwaiti gather around the tank, muttering mumbo jumbo. Translates a soldier: "They say they're very scared and they surrender." Barks Landry, "I'm sick and tired of this Lawrence of Arabia shit, I'm going home." (When I saw this in the theater, at this point, he wasn't the only one who wanted to go home!)

• Iraqi planes bomb Kuwait, killing some Kuwaiti and Americans. During the Iraqi attack, Landry tells his Kuwaiti soldiers, "Pull out your prayer rugs."

• The film's Kuwaiti detest Americans. Veiled women in black, even children, toss stones and firebombs at Landry. When Landry's tank gets stuck, he roars at stone-throwing kids, "Okay, you desert rats—now you die!"

• An Iraqi helicopter appears. Landry's tank dispatches a missile, blowing up the chopper. The previously hostile Kuwaiti cheer. Quips Landry, "So many talented people in the desert."

Best Revenge (1983), Lorimar. *John Heard, John Rhys-Davies, Levon Helm, Tim McCauley, Lorenzo Campos.* Filmed in Spain and Canada. VILLAINS

Moroccans coveting drugs kill family members, imprison and beat Americans.

Scene: In Tangier, Charlie (Heard) and Bo (Helm) move to smuggle drugs valued at $4 million into the US "This guy from Morocco, can we trust him?" asks Charlie. Chuckles Bo, "Trust him? Hell yeah. Moustafa's a good Ayrab. He's never killed nobody he didn't have to." And, Bo asks, "You ever wrestle an Ayrab?" Throughout, Bo calls Arabs "Ayrabs."

• A shack surrounded by goats, chicken, and sheep. Cut to mute Moroccan hagglers threatening Moroccan officials and policemen. Says the uneasy Charlie, "I just want to get home in one piece." The hagglers torment Charlie; he screams: "Leave me alone." In the souk, a whore grabs Charlie; he shakes her off.

• Charlie spits out some water, complaining, "What's all this weirdness here, I hate weirdness...This place stinks. The food's going right through me." Retorts Bo, "You like goat meat, huh?" Quips Charlie, "Ugh."

• Moroccan police yank Charlie and Bo from their hotel room, tossing them in jail. Next, they badly beat Bo.

• A Moroccan drug producer, Moustafa (Rhys-Davies), bribes a policeman; Bo and Charlie are free. "If there is money," boasts Moustafa, "anything can be arranged."

• Moustafa's cousin, a police inspector (Campos), demands more of a cut from an impending drug sale. He argues, "My cousin is in charge of the operation. He refuses to pay me for the drug deal. Since he refuses to pay me, you will." Protests Moustafa, "I did pay my cousin, but he wanted more."

• Absalom (McCauley), Moustafa's son, assists the Americans. But, when Absalom tries to pass a police roadblock, the inspector kills the youth. The enraged Moustafa shoots dead the inspector. Moustafa loses his son and a cousin.

• Final frames. Profiting $1 million from the drug deal, Bo and Charlie appear in "safe" Spain, enjoying retirement.

Dialogue: Moustafa tags his police inspector cousin, "the Devil." The inspector calls his relative, Absalom, "son-of-a-whore... son-of-a-thief." When Absalom runs a Moroccan cyclist called "Screaming Eagle" off the road, Bo quips, "He's gone, like a hog in a restaurant."

Beyond Justice (1992), Titanus. *Rutger Hauer, Omar Sharif, Carol Alt, Kabir Bedi.* Filmed in Morocco, with government cooperation. SHEIKHS, WORST LIST

Contemporary Morocco—camel-riding villains abide in the desert. Moroccans vs. Moroccans, vs. Americans. A desert sheikh kidnaps his American-Arab grandson. To the rescue, an ex-CIA agent and his three hirelings. They terminate 100-plus Moroccans and free the boy, returning him to his American mother.

Scene: Before credits roll, producers set up the film's theme—"Kill lots of Arabs." In an Arabesque room, several "Party of God" heavies and a fat Arab sheikh wearing a red fez abuse their American prisoner, Professor Kurson. The sheikh tries to force Kurson into making a false statement, wanting him to say: "A democracy always gives in." Abruptly, Western mercenaries arrive. They free Kurson and blow up the Arabs.

• In the US, Christine Sanders (Alt) learns that Robert, her 12-year old son, has "been kidnaped." She asks James Burton (Hauer), an ex-CIA agent, to find and rescue the boy.

• Though Christine has been separated from her Moroccan husband (Bedi) for ten years, she knows he's the culprit who whisked Robert off to Morocco. Why? Because, "Thus, it is written [in the Holy Koran]."

• Tafout's desert castle, Morocco. The Emir (Sharif) welcomes his grandson Robert and his divorced son, saying: "If you had not done it [kidnapped Robert], you would have died along with that foreign woman you so stupidly married." Warns the Emir, "No foreigner shall be able to take him [Robert] from this land; [it is his] destiny to lead his people." Sighs a Moroccan, "The Emir's got his own little world out there."

• Moroccans tag Westerners "infidels." And, Moroccans contend kidnaping is not "an unforgivable sin."

• En route to Tafout's castle, Burton and his pals gun down "about twenty" blue-robed Arabs. Next, his cohorts kill twenty more "predators on the ridge."

• The castle. After young Robert uncovers a secret passageway, he stares into the desert sighing, "Allah's furnace... it's just like in [Hollywood's] adventure stories."

• Burton's men enter the castle and shoot down 50-plus Moroccans. And rescue Robert.

• Arab vs. Arab. The Emir's men kill Robert's father. Next, the "son-of-a-dog" Selim, the Emir's arch-enemy, appears. Selim's "predators" kill scores of the Emir's guards. And, they take Robert hostage.

• Burton's men to the rescue. They attack Selim's camp, liquidating more Moroccans. Next, the Emir and his men appear, shooting scores of Selim's cohorts.

• Selim and the Emir fight; the Emir liquidates Selim; Burton and group return Robert to his mother. Where opening frames show the kidnapped Robert being whisked off to Morocco on an "Air Maroc" plane, now closing frames show the liberated Robert and his mother departing Morocco for the United States on an "Air France" jet.

Note: Why did Moroccan officials endorse this film? Why did Omar Sharif agree to portray a backward Emir? See *Ashanti* (1979).

Beyond Obsession (1982), a.k.a. Beyond the Door. *Tom Berenger, Marcello Mastroianni.* Filmed in Morocco. CAMEOS, VILLAINS

Debauched Moroccans.

Scene: In Marrakech, "passions run high." Surfacing are a Moroccan female impersonator, a prostitute, and a terrorist. At a club, live sex acts are performed. Quips a Westerner, Moroccan women "are all dark."

• A vulgar Moroccan boy assaults a Western woman. Taking a knife, he slits open her jeans.

Beyond the Walls (1984), April. *Arnon Zadok, Muhammad Bakri, Assi Dayan, Rami Danon, Boaz Sharambi.* Israeli film in Hebrew, with English subtitles. SP: Benny Barbash. D: Uri Barbash. PALESTINIANS, BEST LIST

A triumph of human relationships. Inside an Israeli maximum security prison, guards use wooden truncheons on prisoners. Yet, Israelis and Palestinians defy their captors, preventing officials from exploiting prejudices.

Scene: Appearing in the prison dining area, Uri (Zadok), leader of the Israeli prisoners, and Issam (Bakri), the Palestinian chief. Issam warns Uri, If you "hurt Assaf [an Israeli prisoner called "Arab-lover" because he had contacted the PLO] ...you deal with us." Counters Uri, "This ain't Fatah-land, we make the rules here."

• Scenes reveal the Israeli warden and his security chief conspiring to advance hatreds. An Israeli prisoner threatens Doron, an Israeli homosexual. Issam and the Palestinians intervene, protecting Doron.

• Uri and Issam share deep commitment to their families. Uri begs his young daughter Sigi to return to school. And, though Palestinians are looking after Issam's wife, Maha, and their son, he, too, worries. Appraising a family photograph, Issam recalls when he first met Maha.

• The recreation room. An Israeli prisoner, the "Nightingale," wins a talent contest and appears on Israeli television, singing, in part, "Just your hand can set me free... just your hand waits for me... I need your hand." The song, a metaphor for amity, implies that friendship may set Palestinians and Israelis free. Cut-a-ways show the prisoners' embracing the lyrics.

• The short-lived feelings of unity are shattered when the TV announcer interrupts the talent show, declaring that Arab "terrorists" have killed "six people, including two children." Abruptly, violence erupts. The security chief's stooge kills an Israeli prisoner, Hoffmann, then frames the Palestinians. More violence. Inside the cell block, the camera reveals bloodied Israelis and Palestinians.

• Issam tries explaining to his Palestinian cellmates that the Jews are not "our enemies. That's how they [the prison authorities] control the prison," says Issam.

• The warden summons Issam. He orders him to lie, to say that the Palestinians "killed Hoffmann." Counters Issam, I "can't admit to what I didn't do." Guards beat him, then dispatch Issam to the prison's "hole."

Eight: Uri ends up in solitary in an adjoining cell, and he and Issam bond. Note the dialogue:

> Issam: These games [of violence] are too costly for you and for us. If we had done it [killed Hoffmann], we'd have been proud to admit it. We must do something.
> Uri: Issam, we ain't the same. We don't do nothin' together. [*He gives Issam a cigarette*]
> With you it's a method, to throw a bomb and run, like into a fish pond, as long as you kill one fish. Blowing up a bus is war?
> Issam: Strafing a refugee camp is war? It's like a thousand buses.

• The dining area. Released from their cells, Uri and Issam convince the prisoners to go on a hunger strike. On cue, most men toss food trays. Not everyone is pleased. "I don't strike with no Arabs," says one.

• During the hunger strike, the warden unsuccessfully tries to force Doron to lie, to say the Palestinians killed Hoffmann. As Doron cannot withstand the pressure, he hangs himself. Later, Uri finds and shares with Issam. Doron's missive reveals an Israeli guard killed Hoffman, that the Israeli warden wanted him to falsely implicate Issam. Uri acts, telling fellow Israelis the warden is "responsible for deaths on our blocks." Strike with the Arabs, he tells them; "You can be free. To be free you get to choose. Choose to be true to yourself. Or else you play into their hands; you become their stooge."

• Seven days pass; the strike continues. Aware that Issam's absence will terminate the strike, the warden plays on Issam's emotions, delivering to the prison his wife Maha and his son; Issam is free to leave. Standing behind bars, they wait for Issam, to take him home.

• Guards open Issam's cell door. Israeli and Palestinian prisoners focus on Issam. The Palestinian steps out of his cell, assesses his family, then steps back into the cell. Uri claps, then shouts, "Issam." All the prisoners clap; they want Issam to walk away and to be with his loved ones. Urges Uri, "You have a pretty woman. Go. Go." Decisively, Issam does approach his wife, saying, "Maha. Go back home." He cries, as does Uri. Issam's willingness to remain ensures solidarity, trust, unity, mutual respect, and hope.

• Had Issam left the prison, the authorities would have triumphed. Without Issam, hostilities would have resumed.

• The Palestinians and Israelis bond. The prisoners join together singing a refrain of the Nightingale's song, "Just your hand can set me free."

Note: Israelis and Palestinians were involved in the making of Barbash's film. Also, actual prison wardens and ex-prisoners participated. Rashed Mashrawi from Gaza designed the sets; a Palestinian and an Israeli, Muhammad Bakri and Arnon Zadok, served as co-directors.

• *Beyond the Walls*, the first film ever screened in Israel's Knesset, attracted large numbers of Israeli-Palestinian viewers. During the first year, about 70 percent of the potential cinema audience attended showings. Also screening the film were selected Israeli and Palestinian neighborhoods, schools, and universities. Yet, several times, the late Rabbi Kahane and his group tried to blow up theaters screening the film.

• Academy Award nomination for "Best Foreign Film." Recipient of the International Critics Award, 1984 Venice Film Festival. Made in Israel for $550,000, 20 percent of which was provided by the Fund for the Promotion of Israeli Quality Films.

• See also *Peace of Mind* (2000), the first documentary film shot jointly by Israeli and Palestinian youths. The documentary focuses on a year of their lives, beginning after they return home from a Maine summer camp run by Seeds of Peace. Annually, this organization brings together Israeli and Palestinian teens, guiding them to nurture friendships so they may in turn help resolve conflicts between fellow Semites.

The Big Fisherman (1959), Centurion. *Howard Keel, Herbert Lom, John Saxon, Susan Kohner, Marion Seldes, Martha Hyer, Ray Stricklyn, Alexander Scourby, Mark Dana.* SP: Howard Estabrook, Rowland V. Lee. Based on Lloyd C. Douglas' novel. SHEIKHS

The Big Fisherman should focus on the life of Simon Peter, one of Christ's first apostles. But, the Arabs vs. Arabs motif dominates. Appearing are an evil Arab potentate, a lovely Arabian-Judean princess, and a brave Arabian prince. Some Arabians and Judeans unite, contesting Roman rule.

Scene: "Arabia During the Memorable Years of the First Century." Benevolent King Zendi (Dana) compliments Princess Fara (Kohner), the "child of that vile Judean, Herod, for learning Greek so quickly." Zendi also cares for Fara's seriously ill mother, Arnon (Seldes), an Arabian princess. Arnon's wicked husband, Herod Antipas (Lom), Tetarch of Galilee, abused and deserted her.

• Royal Prince Voldi (Saxon) loves Princess Fara. So does King Zendi's unrighteous son, Prince Deran (Stricklyn); his "thoughts are dark and bitter." Deran moves to woo Fara; she rejects him." Furious, Deran objects, then plays the race card, saying, "It's against the law. She is not a true Arabian; she is half-Judean."

• Deran threatens to *take* Fara, "I can still have you as my queen, much closer than a wife," he says. She resists; he tries to force himself on her.

• After Princess Arnon dies, Fara decides to leave her Arabian sanctuary. Says King Zendi, "May all the Gods guide you." Voldi joins Fara. They vow to find and kill Rome's puppet ruler, Fara's father, Herod Antipas. Earlier scenes show a brave Arabian trying to bring down Herod; he fails.

• At an inn, three Judean bandits try to assassinate a Roman Magistrate (Scourby). Prince Voldi intervenes, killing the thugs and saving the Magistrate's life.

• Arriving in Galilee, Fara meets Simon Peter (Keel). He shelters her and Voldi. Soon, they learn King Zendi has died, most likely assassinated by his son, Zendi. They rush back to Arabia. The now-crippled tyrant, Zendi, rules. His guards lash Voldi.

• Arabs and Simon Peter convince King Zendi to take "a sacred vow." Zendi promises to allow Voldi and Fara to depart Arabia in peace, provided Simon Peter's God creates a miracle, enabling him to once again, walk. The miracle occurs. Zendi walks, then breaks his promise and tries to brutalize the couple. The Arabian Chiefs, however, step forward. They dispense with Zendi; a man not keeping his word is unworthy to rule Arabia. Abruptly, Zendi collapses, and dies.

Finis: Voldi is declared Arabia's new ruler. Fara appears at his side; "We must both try to bring a new day of peace," she says. "You to Arabia, and I to the hearts of the Judeans."

The Big Red One (1980), Lorimar. *Lee Marvin, Mark Hamill.* W, D: Samuel Fuller. Filmed in Israel. CAMEOS

Scene: North Africa, November 1942. Surfacing on a "miserable Algerian beach," a US WWII Infantry squadron. In the background, camels, donkeys, and some Arabs.

• A Tunis hospital, run by the Germans. A wounded US sergeant (Marvin), moves to escape. Lying on the bed next to his, a critically wounded Arab. Insensitive to the Arab's suffering, the sergeant reaches out, grabbing the Arab's white thobe. The American puts on the dying Arab's thobe and heads for the exit. A liberating US soldier sees the clad-in-Arab-garb sergeant, barking, "What are you doing wrapped up in an Ayrab bed sheet?"

Bitter Victory (1958), Transcontinental. *Richard Burton, Curt Jurgens, Ruth Roman, Robert Pellegrin.* Shot in Libya "with the kind cooperation of the British war office and of Her Majesty's forces in Libya."

WWII Libya. British officers feud; a brave Arab acts as desert guide.

Scene: British soldiers clad in white thobes attack a German complex, returning to base with Axis documents.

• A knowledgeable Arab desert guide, Mokrane (Pellegrin), joins the patrol. Mokrane, a friend of British Captain Jimmy Leith's (Burton), has assisted the British for five years. "It will be very good to work with you, again," says the Captain. "Without him," Jimmy tells a soldier, "I'd probably be dead."

• Needing water, patrol members rush to a well. Shouts Mokrane, "Wait. It may be poisoned." Though the water is drinkable, Mokrane's warning is valued.

• Earlier, Jimmy's arch enemy, Major Brand (Jurdens), left the Captain and two soldiers to die in the desert. Now, the Major allows a scorpion to sting the Captain. When the scorpion strikes, the soldiers panic; they have no medical supplies. Mokrane acts: taking a knife, he cuts Jimmy's leg, then sucks and spits out the poison. Next, he kills a camel, giving Jimmy needed fluids. A soldier observing Mokrane's skills exclaims, "Blimey, a gent with guts!"

• As Mokrane knows Major Brand wants to kill the afflicted Jimmy, he reasons the only way to save the Captain is to kill the Major. But when Mokrane moves to kill Brand, the Major shoots him dead. Though the soldiers are shocked to see Mokrane's body, they shed no tears. Nor is there a eulogy or funeral service.

Note: Opening frames briefly display mute Arabs on horseback. A British soldier shoots them. Quips Major Brand, "Nice work."

The Black Coin (1936), Weiss-Mintz. 15 episodes. *Dave O'Brien, Pete de Grasse.* SP: George M. Merrick, the producer of *Yank in Libya* (1942), a feature that uses footage from this serial. CLIFFHANGERS, VILLAINS, CAMEOS

Anti-Christian Arabs vs. the US Secret Service and the British government. The villains, Ali Ben Aba (de Grasse) and his robed cohorts, only appear in the first episode.

Episode one: Tangier, the desert. Arabs chase two Justice Dept. officials. Agent Walter Prescott (Graves) fires four shots; four Arabs die.

• Ali Ben Aba's Arabs are kidnappers and smugglers; they ship contraband to Mexico. They are superstitious and anti-Christian. Why? Because "Various Christian symbols," such as the saint Santa Clara, are embedded on "pieces of [Arab] silver." The Arabs believe the silver coins "carry a curse," and turn black. "The coins are devil-cursed," says an American, "and according to the Arabs, so are all of those who hold the black coins."

• Surfacing is a bellydancer and some musicians. Cut to a dreadful beggar shouting, "Allah, Allah, deliver me from the curse of the black coin."

• Declares the "shrewd rascal" Ali: "The people who ride in that plane must never take off." BOOM! Ali and his anti-Christian Arabs blow up the plane carrying Secret Service agents. Afterwards, agent Prescott says: "The Arab [Ali] was at the bottom of it."

• A jailed American dupes his Arab guard. How? By shouting, "Hey." See John Wayne dupe his Arab captors in *I Cover the War* (1937).

Slurs: Muslims are tagged "Musselmen." A Westerner asks why conflict exists between "the Musselmen and the Christian Crusaders." Explains Ali, "[It is] Mohammedan law."

The Black Rose (1950), TCF. *Tyrone Power, Jack Hawkins, Herbert Lom.*
SP: Talbot Jennings. Based on Thomas B. Costain's novel. Filmed in Morocco. CAMEOS, SHEIKHS

An avaricious Arab merchant and beggar children detest Christians. Most of the action focuses on the two heroic Englishmen trying to rescue a lovely "girl of English blood, the 'Black Rose,'" from the heathen Kubla Khan's clutches.

Scene: Norman-Saxon rivalry prompts the Saxon leader, Walter (Power), and his friend Tristram (Hawkins) to flee England. Off they go to the Orient, to "search for knowledge." En route, they pause in an Arab country. Arabic music underscores shots of camels, tents, and mumbling folk. Several unkempt children steal tomatoes and toss them at the duo. Tristram expresses anger. Explains Walter, "The Crusades have given these people enough reason not to love Christians."

• Seeking to link up with an Arab caravan, the men search for the "biggest merchant," a man "likely to be the biggest pirate, too." After they tip an Oriental wearing a white headdress, he introduces them to his Arab "master."

• The master, Anthemus (Lom), resides in an ornate palace and lounges on a oriental rug. Seeing the Englishmen approach he sighs, "[You] do not look important to me. I warn you that every minute of my day must show me a profit." The Arab tells them that he is presenting the Khan with a "caravan of gifts, eighty-one of the most beautiful women of this land." Soon, says Anthemus, "I will be the richest merchant in the world."

• As Walter and Tristram are not "prepared to pay well" to travel in the master's caravan, the Arab dismisses them. Content to earn a "smaller profit," the Arab's servant opts to take them along. But he warns the Englishmen, do not approach the Muslim general's men; they "would enjoy cutting a Christian's throat."

• The Englishmen join the Arab's caravan. Cut to "a camel driver who came too close to the women's tent" being brutally whipped.

The Black Stallion (1979), UA. *Kelly Reno, Mickey Rooney, Doghmi Larbi.*
EP: Francis Ford Coppola. CAMEOS, VILLAINS, WORST LIST

This film is adapted from William Farley's book about a young boy's adventures with an Arabian horse. More than 12 million copies of the *Stallion* text have been sold worldwide. Farley's book does not reveal an ugly, uncouth Arab. In the book, a benevolent Arab sheikh befriends an American boy, giving the youth the Arabian's first foal. In Coppola's movie, however, a nasty Arab abuses an Arabian horse and violates an American boy.

Scene: During a sea voyage the boy, Alec. Ramsey (Reno) sees an Arabic-speaking tough (Larbi) whip a beautiful Arabian horse.

• Seeking to befriend the horse, Alec leaves several sugar cubes near the Arabian. Before the horse can consume the cubes, the Arab appears. Seeing Alec with the horse, the angry Arab grabs him, scaring Alec off. The Arab spots one remaining cube and promptly pops the sugar into his own mouth. In Farley's book, no Arab whips the horse, no Arab threatens the boy, and no Arab steals and gulps a sugar cube.

• A horrific storm. As the ship is sinking, Alec's father attaches a life vest to his son. Trying to maintain his footing, Alec clasps the deck railing, but slips and falls. Looking up, he sees the Arab. Abruptly, the Arab seizes Alec. Pulling a knife, the Arab tries to remove the boy's life vest. In time, Alec's father appears. He knocks the Arab onto the deck. The ship sinks.

• Alec and the horse survive. Credits tag the villain simply "Arab."

The Black Stallion Returns (1983), MGM, UA. *Kelly Reno, Vincent Spano, Woody Strode, Jodi Thelen, Allen Goorwitz, Ferdinand Mayne.* EP: Francis Ford Coppola. Based on Walter Farley's novel. Filmed in Morocco. VILLAINS, SHEIKHS, MAIDENS, WORST LIST

Quarrelsome Arabs vs. thieving, brutal Arabs. An Arab youth indulges the American hero as Tonto indulged the Lone Ranger. This absurd scenario claims Arabs are unable and unworthy of owning and riding their own horses. Only Alec Ramsey (Reno) is deemed worthy to ride an Arabian stallion. The Americans tag the horse "the Black." In Arabic, *aswad* means black. But here Arabs tag the horse "Shetan"—Satan in Arabic.

Scene: Intones the narrator—Every five years "the tribes of the Sahara race their horses... this is the land of the Sahara, where the finest horses are bred. To the victor go the best horses from the losing tribes, bringing prestige, wealth, and powers." Farley's text is similar: "For the law of the desert is that blood calls for blood, and death for death. A blood feud between desert tribes might easily last fifty years or more."

• 1947. The Ramsey farm outside New York City, evening. Abruptly, two Arab curs from the Urak appear. Kurr (Goorwitz), a Yasser Arafat look-alike, sets the horse's stable on fire. Young Alec manages to free the Black from the flames; the Arabs seize the stallion. Note: Arabs do not set a farm ablaze in Farley's text.

• Seeing an Arab leaving the city with the stallion, a New York immigration officer quips, "I doubt that this horse is for sale."

• Alec pursues the two kidnappers, stowing away on a plane en route to Casablanca. Morocco looks like a desert junkyard, complete with wrecked cars, shabby buses, and camels.

• Kurr and his cohort rob Alec, then abandon him.

• An Arab youth, Raj (Spano), assists Alec. The boys hop onto a broken-down bus. Atop the moving-at-a-snail's-pace bus are unkempt Arabs and their shoddy baggage.

• Sheikh Abu Ben Ishak (Mayne) and Tabari (Thelen), his attractive daughter, display grace, providing Alec with nourishment and hospitality. After Ben Ishak places a blanket over the exhausted boy, he tells him that his tribe needs the stallion to win the intertribal race. In the novel, Farley also paints Ben Ishak as a gentleman who agreeably settles with 15-year-old Alec and the others before taking the horse to Arabia.

• Scenes show that no Arab can mount the Black; the horse tosses all Arabs—even Tabari. The horse allows only Alec to ride.

• At the intertribal horse race, Arabs race their horses. Alec rides the Black to victory, defeating Raj and all the Arab riders. As a result of Alec's grit and valor, feuding tribal leaders cease feuding and embrace each other.

• Final frames show the Black pining to stay in Morocco. Not because the stallion favors his Arab owners, but because the horse wants to roam around with other Arabians. Should Arabs dare try mounting the Black, they will fall.

Black Sunday (1977), PAR. *Robert Shaw, Bruce Dern, Marthe Keller, Fritz Weaver, Victor Campos, Bekim Fehmiu.* Based on Thomas Harris' novel.

PALESTINIANS, MAIDENS

The first feature film to display Palestinian terrorists on American soil; they invade Los Angeles, Washington, DC and Miami, killing 15 Americans. At the Super Bowl they try to massacre 80,000 spectators, including the US president.

Scene: Beirut, a Black September base. Palestinians Dahlia (Keller) and her lover Nageeb (Campos) make love. Israel's Major Kabakov's (Shaw) soldiers attack, killing scores, including Nageeb. On screen, Palestinian bodies are tossed about like disposable clay pigeons.

• Dahlia and her cohorts decide to strike American civilians "where it hurts, where they feel most safe." Dahlia seduces and enlists the aid of a former Vietnam prisoner of war, Mike Lander (Dern). Aware of the Palestinians' terror plan, Major Kabakov and his Israelis cooperate with an FBI official, Corley (Weaver).

• The United States. Robert, Kabakov's Israeli colleague, is injured and taken to a hospital. Robert has a daughter in "Jerusalem, Israel"; his mother, father, and two sons are dead. Posing as a nun, Dahlia enters Robert's room and kills him.

• Kabakov warns an Egyptian diplomat that unless he helps them track the Palestinian assassins he will be responsible for the deaths of innocent Americans. Reluctantly, the Egyptian confesses: "Dahlia Iyad, of Arab-German extraction. Born on a farm near Haifa, Palestine, 1948. Her father, brother, killed by Israeli commandos in war of same year. She, sister, mother, expelled '49, lived in a tent, in desert refugee camp, Gaza. Sister raped in war of '56. Refugee camp, Jordan, joined Black September... Here is her face," he tells Kabakov. "Look at it. After all, in a way she is your creation."

• Dahlia meets with Fasil (Fehmiu), a Palestinian who helped "organize the attack [on Israeli athletes] at the Olympic Village." They opt to proceed with their plan to blow up the Super Bowl. Attempting to elude the FBI's trap, Fasil take a young woman hostage, then kills some civilians.

• Miami, the Super Bowl. During the film's climax, stock footage of an actual football game appears on the screen, showing the Pittsburgh Steelers playing the Dallas Cowboys. The camera cuts to coaches Chuck Noll and Tom Landry, and the American president, a Jimmy Carter look-alike.

• Steering the blimp over the stadium, Dahlia and Mike try to detonate a cluster bomb. In time, thanks to Major Kabakov's heroics, they are terminated.

Note: Some critics embrace fixed Palestinian stereotypes. In his NYT review, critic Vincent Canby writes, "Miss Keller has some difficulty portraying a Palestinian terrorist, looking, as she does, as beautiful and healthy and as uncomplicated as a California surfer" (1 April 1977).

• Decades prior to *Black Sunday*, movie land presented Nila, the first Arab woman terrorist. In the 1948 movie serial, *Federal Agents vs. the Underworld, Inc.* Nila bombs civilians. Two years later, United Artists released a thriller [*Conspiracy in Teheran* (1950), a.k.a. *The Plot to Kill Roosevelt*] featuring a wealthy Persian trying to kill Franklin D. Roosevelt. The Persian cur, who conspires with international arms dealers and Nazis, believes the President's assassination will prompt US forces and Russian troops to fight each other, thus prolonging WWII. In the end, reports the NYT critic, a British journalist and Russian ballerina foil the plot (11 March 1950).

The Black Tent (1956), Rank. *Anthony Steel, Donald Sinden, Andre Morell, Donald Pleasence, Anna Maria Sandri.* Filmed in Libya. The producers received "the cooperation of the Libyan government and army." SHEIKHS, BEST LIST

Bedouin and Englishmen oppose the Germans. The Western protagonist weds an Arab.

Scene: Libya, WWII. David (Steel), a British officer, is wounded. Attending the officer is Sheikh Salem (Morell), his daughter, Mabrouka (Sandri), and bedouins. Salem's men protect David from the Germans.

• Several scenes reveal David and Sheikh Salem as chums. In contrast to other WWII desert dramas, e.g. *Tank Force* (1958), this film shows an Allied soldier and bedouins fighting against the Axis.

• Sheikh Salem tells the injured David, "Sleep, now. You are among friends." And, "My home is yours. Do as you wish."

• Inside a black tent, bedouins kneel and pray. David tells Salem he is ready to resume fighting. Affirms the sheikh again, "My house is your house—also my sword."

• Islam is revered. When David asks Salem for Mabrouka's hand in marriage, the Arab says, "We in our faith recognize the brotherhood of man under the solvent rule of Allah." Affirms Mabrouka, "With faith you can make anything happen."

• The wedding ceremony, complete with traditional Arab music and dancing. One year later, Mabrouka gives birth to a son, Daoud (Sharkey).

• Sir Charles, David's wealthy brother, wants Daoud to live in England. The 12-year-old hesitates. Advises Salem, his grandfather, "You must serve your own heart." Cut to Daoud viewing children at play in the Libyan desert. The youth opts to remain with fellow bedouin. He burns the deed granting him monies and property in England.

• One of Salem's men, Faris, envies Mabrouka's happiness with David. So, he conspires with the Germans, hoping to trap and kill David.

• Behind German lines. Salem and David engage in guerrilla warfare. David sacrifices his life so the sheikh may live.

Note: Even recommended movies may contain clichéd moments. An Arab guide (Pleasence), tells Sir Charles, "I have pictures of girls in Tripoli. Perhaps you find nice girls in Bedouin tents? I will arrange scenes of great delight for you. I am noted for it." Retorts Sir Charles: "I'm sure you are, but I have more important things to think about." Quips the guide, "What can be more important than girls?"

Blazing Saddles (1974), WB. *Harvey Korman, Cleavon Little, Gene Wilder, Mel Brooks.* CAMEOS, VILLAINS

This spoof of westerns presents Nazis and their Arab cohorts preparing to attack pioneers. One scene shows the villains assisting "Ridge Rock's" evil land speculators.

Scene: After the main villain (Korman) tells his gun hands, "You're about to embark on a great crusade to stamp out runaway decency in the West," the camera reveals six Nazis, their arms raised in the "Heil Hitler" position. Cut to two robed Arabs, brandishing rifles.

Blazing Sand (1960), a.k.a. Brennender Sand, a.k.a. Burning Sands, a.k.a. Sinai Guerrillas, Ran Film. *Daliah Lavi, Gurt Guenter Hoffman.* W, P, D: Raphael Nussbaum. Dubbed in English. Filmed in Israel, Jordan. VILLAINS

Israelis vs. bedouins.

Scene: Beer Sheba's souk; a donkey pulls a cart. Arab music accents a backward place. An Arabic-speaking Israeli sips coffee with bedouin; his friends buy bedouin garb and camels.

• Six Israelis move to secure King Solomon's "valuable scrolls." They dress as bedouin and "cross the border," entering Sinai, "enemy territory."

• The disguised Israelis encounter five armed bedouins on camels. Easily, they dupe the Arabs. An Israeli tells the bedouins that his "wife and baby have the cholera," that he is "taking them to the witch doctor." After the Arabs let them pass, the Israelis laugh.

• Later, one bedouin fires at Dina (Lawrie). He misses, killing her donkey.

• The Israelis arrive at Citra. Says Mike, "The whole place belonged to us, now we have to come here illegally."

• Inside Citra's "temple" they uncover portions of "King Solomon's scrolls." They also locate their seriously injured friend, Marco, who soon dies.

• A bedouin advances. Dina shoots him dead.

• More bedouins appear; they kill all but one of the six Israelis. As for the Solomon's scrolls, the wind scatters them.

Note: At the time the movie was being filmed, Jordan and Israel were not at peace. Yet, for this Israeli co-production, German filmmaker Nussbaum gained permission to film in Jordan. The Citra scenes were shot in Petra, Jordan.

• Credits state that two real Arabs portray the film's two bedouin: "Sheikh Ode Abu Mamar" and "Salegh Ibn Abdulla."

• Nussbaum wrote and directed another anti-Arab desert drama, *Sinai Commandos* (1968), featuring actor Robert Fuller.

Blink of an Eye (1991), Capitol. *Michael Pare, Janis Lee, Uri Gavriel, Amos Lavi, Sasson Gabai.* P: Jacob Kotzky. Filmed at "United Studios of Israel." VILLAINS, WORST LIST

Two Americans and a Kurd eradicate Iraqi "terrorists." The Iraqis move to seize plutonium. Israeli actors portray Iraqis.

Scene: The CIA's director's wife dreams her daughter Kathryn (Lee), who works at a Kurdish refugee camp, is taken prisoner by an Iraqi "terrorist organization." Fearing his wife's nightmare may become a reality, the director sends Sam (Pare), a "spiritual warrior" with "ESP training," to the camp to protect Kathryn.

• The Kurdish camp. Mozaffar (Lavi) and his Iraqi "terrorists" attack, murdering scores of civilians, including a boy. Also, the Iraqi "terrorists" blow up a "plane over Cyprus," killing "over 200 people." Unexpectedly, Mozaffar kills his own brother.

• Moans the CIA director, "[Mozaffar is] bargaining my daughter like some fucking camel."

• Sam arrives at the camp. He, Kathryn, and Izmir (Gavriel), a Kurd whose villagers suffered from an Iraqi "poison gas" attack, terminate scores of Iraqis. Khalil (Gabai), a "terrorist" linked with Mozaffar, complains that Sam's group has terminated too many of his troops. Barks Kahlil: "What takes so long to take one American woman? Three people against all your men!"

• Iraqis capture Sam, toss him in jail and torture him. See *Iron Eagle* (1986), *Death Before Dishonor* (1987).

• Posing as an Arab, Kathryn enters the Iraqi jail. She pours gasoline over several Iraqi guards, then vows to ignite her lighter onto their gas-drenched uniforms unless they free Sam. She and Sam escape. Cut to a dense Iraqi. He fires his weapon, setting himself and his prison comrades ablaze.

• Sam terminates Mozaffar; the protagonists are rescued. And, Izmir recites a Kurdish proverb: "When the end is good (meaning the killing of Arabs), everything is good."

Dialogue: Iraqis are tagged "terrorists" and "assholes." Khalil and his cohorts speak with thick accents, fracturing the English language.

Blood Feast (1963), Box Office Spectaculars. *Thomas Wood, Mal Arnold*. CAMEOS, EGYPTIANS

Beware Americans clad in Egyptian garb and ancient Egyptians.

Scene: A modern metropolis. Several scenes present the lunatic (Ramses) trying to create a live Egyptian Love Goddess. In order to obtain needed body parts, Ramses kills American women, adding specimens from their anatomies to his Egyptian Goddess.

Blood from the Mummy's Tomb (1971), AI. Remade as *The Awakening* (1980). *Andrew Keir, Valerie Leon*. EGYPTIANS, MAIDENS

Intending to make his "mark on the world of Egyptology," a British archaeologist tampers with evil mummies. He ignores the reel fact: Those who violate tombs perish.

Scene: Professor Fuchs removes Princess Tera's mummy from her tomb, transporting Tera's body to England. Soon, the spirit of Tera, the "Queen of Darkness," emerges in Fuchs' lovely daughter, Margaret.

• Scenes reveal Princess Tera's severed hand bringing "evil and destruction." As in *Blood from the Mummy's Tomb* (1972) and *The Awakening* (1980), a dead Egyptian maiden is reincarnated as a vengeful murderess.

Bloodsport (1988), CAN. *Jean Claude Van Damme, Leah Ayres*. CAMEOS, VILLAINS

This martial-arts drama presents Van Damme as Frank Dux, an American special forces officer. When Arab rogues manhandle an attractive American journalist, Janice (Ayres), Dux floors them.

Scene: A Hong Kong bar. An ugly "Syrian fighter" wearing a red burnoose grabs Janice's wrist and demands: "You come upstairs with me for an interview." Barks Janice, "Like hell I will." Insists the Syrian, "You want [to sleep with] Hossein, no?" Quips Janice, "No! Hossein is an asshole. Leave me alone." Angry, Hossein goes to slug Janice. Dux arrives. He employs a swift coin trick, easily duping the dense Syrian. And, he saves Janice from the nasty Arabs.

• The arena of the international martial-arts competition. Dux fights Hossein. Arabic writing is embossed on the Syrian's trunks. Hossein fights dirty; he sneaks behind Dux, boasting, "Now I show you some trick or two." Presto! Dux flattens Hossein.

Bolero (1984), CAN. *Bo Derek, Greg Bensen, Andrea Occhipinti, Mickey Knox.* W, D: John Derek. SHEIKHS, CAMEOS

This sexual romp perpetuates the myth that sheikhs "are all counterfeit." When the blonde Western heroine goes to bed a sleepy-eyed Moroccan, her sexual fantasies shatter.

Scene: The 1920s. College graduate Arye McGilvary (Bo Derek) watches the silent classic movie *The Sheik* (1921) and decides sex with an Arab would be a marvelous experience. Off she goes to Morocco, intent on awarding her virginity to a Valentino substitute.

• A Moroccan hawker (Knox) guides Ayre to a nightclub. Inside, some bellydancers and baby camels. "What do you do with camels?" she asks. Quips the Moroccan, "They are for sale." The Arabs spots a young sheikh (Bensen) smoking a nargelih. He ushers Ayre toward him, whispering, "Allah is kind."

• Ayre tenders her virginity; the Oxford-educated Arab accepts. She requests a romantic horseback jaunt through the desert. But the clumsy Arab cannot mount a horse; nor can he lift Ayre off her feet. He proposes a plane ride.

• The desert. Greeting the couple are screaming bedouins, firing guns. Shrugs the sheikh, "I've only been to this place three times."

• Inside a tent, a Moroccan woman dances. "They do incredible things with their stomachs," sighs the sheikh. Stimulated, Ayre moves to bed the Arab; he opts to puff a nargelih. Finally, he slowly creeps toward the naked Ayre. Rendering a "traditional Arab custom," he pours milk and honey over her body, then collapses. The dejected Ayre sighs, "Why are they all counterfeit?"

• Following her disillusioning encounter with the wimpish Arab, Ayre flies off to Spain. Here, she finds "ecstasy" with a genuine lover—a Spanish bullfighter (Occhipinti).

• Three Arab hirelings charge into Ayre's bedroom, carrying her off. The kidnappers deliver Ayre to the wimpish Moroccan. He barks, "I'm taking you like my father took my mother... What I do is correct."

• All ends well. Easily, Ayre rebuffs the clumsy Arab, returning safely to embrace her Spanish lover.

Bomba and the Hidden City (1950), MON. *Johnny Sheffield, Sue England, Paul Guilfoyle, Leon Belasco, Charles La Torre.* SP: Carrol Young. SHEIKHS, MAIDENS, VILLAINS

Bomba vs. Sheikh Hassan, a rich and repugnant bandit who takes women and kills fellow Arabs.

Scene: Hidden City. Surrounding the "tyrant" Hassan (Guilfoyle) are harem maidens and a black slave toting a huge feather fan. Hassan gained the throne by killing the parents of Zita (England), a lovely Arab maiden. Zita does not know she is the throne's rightful heir.

• Bomba (Sheffield), however, sees Hassan murder Zita's parents. Hassan acts, directing assassins to "deal with him (Bomba) as you would any other animal." Says Abduallah (La Torre), "Have no fear your highness, he [Bomba] won't be captured alive. I'll see to it."

• Gun-toting Arabs capture Bomba. After Abduallah binds and whips him, he pulls a knife, stabbing the jungle boy in the back.

• Zita arrives in time to assist the injured Bomba. Tending his wounds, she says, I "like" Bomba "very much.[I am] afraid of Hassan." Sighs Bomba, "Bad thing, make girl slave!"

• Hidden City's procurer, Raschid (Belasco), arrives at Hassan's camp. "What brings you here? Surely, no village would trust you to bring its taxes," says Hassan. Acknowledges Raschid, "No, your excellency, that they wouldn't."

• Raschid drugs several "new maidens [that he] selected for Hassan's household." Hassan lifts their veils, choosing Zita, the one who "dances and sings and makes wonderful spice cakes."

• As a "reward" for delivering Zita, Hassan appoints the slaver, Raschid, as his new gatekeeper. Raschid expresses anger; he expected money! "May the fleas of a thousand camels nest in your beard," he grunts.

• Now revived, Bomba crushes Hassan's cohorts. Grabbing a rifle, Hassan fires at Bomba. He misses; the bullet kills another Arab.

• Hassan runs out of ammunition. He runs off, stumbling over a cliff and dropping into the water. Abruptly, crocodiles devour the Arab.

• After Bomba secures all the "bad" Arabs, the camera cuts to Queen Zita. She reigns in Hidden City.

The Bonfire of the Vanities (1990), WB. A Brian De Palma film. *Bruce Willis, Melanie Griffith, Alan King.* SP: Michael Christopher. Based on Tom Wolfe's bestselling novel. CAMEOS, SHEIKHS, WORST LIST

In this film about Wall Street opportunists and black-white controversies, the dialogue slanders Arab Muslims and the holy city of Mecca.

Scene: Lovely Maria (Griffith) explains to Peter (Willis) why her husband, Arthur (King), "is pleased with himself. He just closed a new deal," she says, "a charter business going to take Arabs to Mecca on airplanes. The airplanes are all from Israel." Cut to a posh New York restaurant. Gloating, Arthur recounts his "Mecca" trip, telling Peter, "The best one happened a couple of weeks ago. The plane goes off the runway... We were going to Mecca, see. And the plane is full of Arabs with these animals. Goats, sheep, chickens. I mean they don't go anywhere without those goddam animals. We had to put plastic in the cabins. You know they urinate, defecate. The plane goes off the runway. I was scared shitless. I look in the cabin. Calm. Quiet. They're picking up their luggage, their animals, and they're looking out the little window, fire on the wings. They're waiting for the doors to open like nothing happened. Then it dawns on me. They think it's normal. They think that's how to stop a plane. The wing's in the sand, and you let it spin around before it stops. They've never been on a plane before; they think this is how you do it." Peter smiles; the slurs stand.

The Boost (1988), Hemdale. *James Woods, Sean Young.* SP: Darryl Ponicsan. Based on Benjamin Stein's *Ludes*. CAMEOS, SHEIKHS

The scenario concerns a California real estate hustler, Mr. Brown (Woods) and his drug-addicted wife (Young). Saudis buying up the USA are tagged "Ayrabs."

Scene: Boasts Mr. Brown, "I do some research on these big guys [from New York]. It turns out they're in bed with the Saudis." Their biggest problem, says Brown, is that "they're buying up office buildings and shopping centers." So, I have "to structure their deal so that it doesn't look like the Ayrabs are buying up the country."

• Quips Brown, "You know what these [New York] guys are gonna be doing'? Carrying around some Arab's dick!"

Bound in Morocco (1918), PAR. Silent. *Douglas Fairbanks, Pauline Curley, Edythe Chapman.* W, D: Allan Dawn. *NS. Notes from the NYT (29 July 1918) and MPW (10 August 1918: 888). SHEIKHS, VILLAINS

A Moroccan desert sheikh's "wild tribes" hold an American mother and her daughter hostage. To the rescue, the American protagonist. Writes the NYT's critic, *Bound In Morocco* offers "a plentiful supply of people who look like Arabs." The MPW reviewer said, "Hopping through Morocco while the wild tribes battle, Fairbanks acrobatics from the harem to the hot sands."

Summary: A young American (Fairbank) travels by car "near the desert of Sahara." He discovers that "a couple of American women—a mother and a daughter" (Chapman and Curley) were kidnaped by a potentate intent on expanding his harem. And, that "the daughter has been selected by a native ruler to 'augment' his extensive harem." At the sheikh's abode, the American watches Arab maidens "bathing au naturel, doing 'cooch' dances." The sheikh's men nab the American, and tie him to a prison wall. The protagonist escapes, "scattering Arabs all over the sandy soil." And, he frees the US heroines from the ruler's harem. They escape "by means of automobile, motorcycle and horse."

Bowery to Bagdad (1955), AA. *Leo Gorcey, Huntz Hall, Eric Blore, Joan Shawlee, Rick Vallin, Paul Marion.* SP: Elwood Ullman. D: Edward Bernds. See *Aladdin* jinni films. VILLAINS, SHEIKHS, MAIDENS

This Aladdin's lamp scenario reveals bumbling Arabs vs. Arabs; Arabs vs. US criminals; Arabs vs. the Bowery Boys.

Scene: Stock footage presents Baghdad, circa 1700; camels trek through the desert. Cut to "Aladdin's magic lamp" being pilfered from the sultan. Explains the narrator, "The weary quest for the lamp leads to the new world, to a city called by some, 'Baghdad on the Hudson.'" Superimposed over New York's skyscrapers are two bearded Arabs (Vallin, Marion) scouring shops in search of their sultan's treasured lamp.

• Louie's Sweet Shop. Satch (Hall) has a "broken-down teapot" (Aladdin's lamp) worth "two-bits"; some gangsters, the "Boys," and the two Arabs try to snatch the lamp.

• Satch rubs the lamp. Popping out is a British-accented jinni wearing a wide sash and a turban (Blore); he gulps booze and flirts with damsels. Though he is called "monkey," "stupid," "crazy-looking character," and an "animated Turkish towel," the jinni boasts, "I am the slave of the lamp; your wish is my command."

• Louie's back room. Baghdad's turbaned Arabs snatch the lamp. "It's mine," says one. "Yours? It's mine," says the other. They fight each other, then pull knives on the Bowery Boys. But, the "Boys" are formidable foes. The Arabs run off.

• Sighs Louie, "They [the Arabs] almost cut me up like a hot pastrami." An Arab puts a knife to Satch's throat, warning,. "Where's the lamp? We will "cut your heart out."

• Seeing the lamp on a desk an Arab exclaims: "Heaven be praised. Together, we shall rule the world." Abruptly, New York thugs arrive and beat up the Arabs. The jinni tells the duo, "You're a disgrace to dear old Baghdad. Go home!" The Arabs vanish.

• Abruptly, the two Arabs, the jinni, plus the now-clad-in-Arab-garb Satch and Jones (Gorcey), are whisked off to the sultan's harem quarters in ancient Baghdad. The astonished Jones asks, "Where are we?" Says Satch, "Baghdad." Jones: "I wanna go home."

• The sultan's giggling maidens attend the "Boys." The women fan the Americans with an ostrich feather fan, feed them grapes and give them manicures. Says Jones, "I may be persuaded to dilly-dally with these dillies for a bit." Enter the sultan, barking, "Don't you know it's death to anyone who sets foot into the harem? I'll cut you into small pieces and feed you to the vultures."

• In the end, the sultan regains his magic lamp. Satch and Jones are wished safely back to the Bowery.

A Boy Ten Feet Tall (1965), TCF. Originally released in the UK as *Sammy Going South* (1963), SA. *Edward G. Robinson, Zia Mohyeddin, Constance Cummings, Fergus McClelland.* SP: Denis Cannan. D: Alexander Mackendrick. EGYPTIANS

A British boy travels from Egypt to South Africa. En route, he encounters inhospitable and uncaring Egyptians and a deceptive Syrian.

Scene: Port Said, November 1956. Speaking Arabic into a loudspeaker, an Egyptian warns fellow Egyptians about the British invaders. This message appears on the screen: "For seven days the British attacked this city..." Cut to Sammy (McClelland), a 10-year-old British youth at play inside his parents' flat. Seeing Mahmoud, an Egyptian youth he knows, Sammy follows Mahmoud, running off to the docks. Suddenly, British planes attack; the boy ducks for shelter.

• Sammy rushes home; the plane's bombs have destroyed the flat; his parents have perished. In what seems to be a warm and friendly gesture, Mahmoud extends his hand, leading Sammy away from the rubble. Unexpectedly, Mahmoud hits Sammy, then runs off with other Egyptian boys, leaving the boy alone.

• A deserted road. An Egyptian driver halts his bus, forcing Sammy off. Why? The boy lacks money. So much for Egyptian hospitality.

• Evening, an Arab peddler (Mohyeddin) with three donkeys offers to help, telling Sammy: "Don't be frightened. I'm not Egyptian. I'm Syrian—I'm pro-British." Later, "the Syrian" makes a fire, baking and sharing bread with Sammy. When the peddler goes to make another fire, he asks Sammy to gather some stones. Regrettably, Sammy puts "the wrong stones in the fire." An explosion blows out the Syrian's eyes." In pain, and fearing Sammy will leave him alone to die, the Syrian grabs some handcuffs, attaching his arm to Sammy's.

• Morning; vultures appear. The Syrian has died. After finding the key, Sammy removes the cuffs, takes the peddler's money and departs with his donkeys. Sammy shows no remorse; he leaves the uncovered peddler's body for the vultures. Near the conclusion, Sammy feels guilty, telling the wise Western protagonist, Mr. Wainwright (Robinson), about his behavior with the Syrian. Wainwright assures Sammy he did nothing wrong, saying: This peddler didn't care about you; "he was after your [aunt's reward] money!"

The Brass Bottle (1963), UNI. *Tony Randall, Burl Ives, Barbara Eden, Ann Doran, Kamala Devi.* Sequel to *The Brass Bottle* (1923). Both based on F. Ansley's novel. MAIDENS

The benevolent genie Fakrash (Ives) pops out of an antique magic bottle and attends a needy architect, Harold Ventimore (Randall).

Scene: Bearded Fakrash, who sings in Arabic, wears a turban, white shirt, vest and baggy pants. After Harold releases him from the bottle, Fakrash expresses gratitude, offering to help the architect develop several new subdivisions. No other architect dare intervene, cautions Fakrash. He also vows to arrange a marriage for Harold, fix some horse races, provide him with harem maidens, and bricks of gold.

• Fakrash spots the police, exclaiming, "The Philistines; they shall be destroyed." He conjures up a row of elephants, placing them in front of the cops.

• Fakrash transforms Harold's domicile into an Arabian Nights boudoir, complete with camels, waiters, slaves and dancing girls. Protests Harold, "This is not Baghdad; it's Pasadena."

• Harold's romantic overtures always flop. When Fakrash tries to replace Harold's sweetheart, Sylvia (Eden), with "100 wives, or 50," the architect balks, "Not even two; it's against the law."

• Determined to please Harold, Fakrash summons "Terza" (Devi), a beautiful Arab dancing girl. Surprise! Terza woos and wins the genie; Fakrash opts to wed her.

• Thanks to Fakrash, Harold's confidence soars. The architect secures a contract to build a new, fashionable subdivision, and he marries Sylvia.

Dialogue on Arab cuisine: Quips a character, "The eyes of lamb dipped in honey is a rare Phoenician delicacy."

Note: Fakrash reminds me of another charitable genie, "Lenny" of "Palestine," who appears in the 1991 British TV film *Bernard and the Genie.* Lenny, too, befriends his Western master, saying, Think of me as your "close friend," especially now, during Christmas, "when the multitudes gather in Jerusalem." Underscoring the genie's advice, the song "God Rest Ye Merry Gentlemen."

Brewster's Millions (1914), Lasky. *NS. Notes from AFIC. CAMEOS, SHEIKHS

Brewster's Millions (1921), PAR. No Arabs appear.

Brewster's Millions (1945), PAR. No Arabs appear.

Brewster's Millions (1985), UNI. *Richard Pryor, John Candy.* CAMEOS, SHEIKHS

In the 1914 film, Monty Brewster (Edward Abeles) "rents and repairs a yacht to sail around the world." No sooner does Brewster dock at a Middle Eastern port, then an Arab sheikh moves to secure for his harem the protagonist's darling, Peggy Grey (Winifred Kingston). In time, Brewster "saves his childhood sweetheart from abduction."

In the 1985 film, after Monty Brewster (Pryor) acquires 30 million dollars a hustler advises him, "Arabs live in the desert. No water. No Arab farmers. It's all desert... [let's transport] an iceberg to supply water to Arab desert dwellers." We can charge them "five dollars for a glass."

The Brides of Fu Manchu (1966), SA. *Christopher Lee.* CAMEOS

An Arab helps drop Fu Manchu and he rescues enslaved women.

Scene: The megalomaniac Fu Manchu holds beauties hostage. To the rescue, Abdul, who dons a red fez and a white thobe. After freeing the women, he hands them weapons, saying, "All the ladies, they are my friends." Abdul and the ladies battle Fu Manchu and his cohorts.

The Brigand (1952), COL. *Anthony Dexter, Anthony Quinn, Donald Randolph, Mari Blanchard, Walter Kingsford.* SP: Jesse Lasky Jr. D: Phil Karlson. CAMEOS, VILLAINS

Arabs contest Arabs. This revamped version of the *Prisoner of Zenda* centers upon intrigues at an eighteenth-century Spanish court. Throughout, Spaniards vs. Spaniards. But opening scenes show dueling Arabs killing other Arabs.

Scene: Initial frames reveal this message: "Early in the nineteenth century... the Moroccan desert... a small caravan is moving slowly on its way." Cut to the Arab sultan's guards escorting Spain's ambassador to Mandorra (Randolph) and his blonde wife, Doña Dolores (Blanchard). Suddenly, Arab brigands attack. Arabic music underscores the action. Cut to the sultan's champion, Captain Carlos (Dexter). Carlos and his men crush the Arabs.

• Inside the sultan's tent, coffee is served to the ambassador. Carlos enters, telling the ruler (Kingsford), "Abdul bin Mustafa and his brigands are dead. They refused capture, choosing to fight to the end." Sighs the sultan, "Praise Allah." The sultan tells the ambassador that although Carlos is Spanish, he is a "skillful and courageous" officer.

Bright Lights, Big City (1988), MGM/UA. *Michael J. Fox, Phoebe Cates.* SP: Jay McInerney. CAMEOS, PALESTINIANS

A joke contends Palestinians killed an American model.

Scene: Soon after Jamie Conway's (Fox) attractive wife Amanda (Cates) jilts him, Jamie's friend tries to cheer him up in a Big Apple bar. Jamie meets a lovely model, who inquires about Amanda. Jamie's friend intervenes, offing this face-saving story: "Didn't you hear?" he says. "She was in Paris showing the fall collection. Got hit by a burst of terrorist crossfire, Palestinians and French police. Senseless death. She was an innocent..."

Broadcast News (1987), TCF. *William Hurt, Holly Hunter.* CAMEOS, VILLAINS

Libyans bomb Americans. Injected into this romantic comedy, a 3½-minute scene targeting Arabs. See *The American President* (1995).

Scene: A TV network's newsroom. A photogenic anchorman (Hurt) goes on the air with a special Middle East report. Prompted by his girlfriend (Hunter), he announces that the "Joint Chiefs are meeting, there's a massive movement of US military might." Adding, "at 10:07 AM, a Libyan fighter plane attacked a United States military installation" in Italy. "The Libyan MIG-21 dropped all four of its bombs on the Air Station," says the anchor. "There are some 500 men and women stationed there... Naturally, we shot down the plane. Libya has always been an outlaw nation." As he speaks, stock footage of Muamar Khadafi appears on the TV screen.

The Bugs Bunny/Road Runner Movie, (1979), a.k.a. The Great American Bugs Bunny Road Runner Chase, WB. A Chuck Jones film, displaying some of WB's best cartoon shorts. CAMEOS, VILLAINS

Included in the film, this excerpt from the cartoon short *Ali Baba Bunny* with Daffy Duck and Bugs, the insouciant bunny. The camera reveals a desert cave filled with treasures and the magic lamp. Cut to an ugly green genie with pointed teeth; he pursues Bugs and Daffy. The green genie reduces Daffy to the size of a pearl, shouting, "Dog! You have desecrated the spirit of the lamp."

Bugs Bunny's Third Movie: 1001 Rabbit Tales (1982), WB. Animated compilation. VILLAINS, SHEIKHS

Cartoon heroes mock an Arab father and his son.

Scene: Clasping a book, "1001 Tales for Toddlers," Bugs Bunny mistakenly pops up at Sultan Sam's (Yosemite Sam) desert palace. An Arab guard's scabbard beckons Bugs.

• The sultan, tagged the "pinhead potentate," continually tries pleasing his son, "crabby Prince Abadaba." The ruler hires Bugs to tell Abadaba stories. The departing storyteller warns Bugs, "That rotten kid in there doesn't need a storyteller, he needs an exorcist!"

• The sultan thrusts his saber into Bugs' tail, giving notice that unless he reads "Little Red Riding Hood," "Jack and the Beanstalk," and other tales to his "spoiled, rotten, loud-mouthed cry-baby son," he will be "boiled in oil." Bugs resists; the guards dump him in the dungeon. Awaiting Bugs, a pot of boiling oil.

• "Crabby" Abadaba might be more amused, suggests the sultan, if "some storytellers from Hollywood" could be adducted and sent to the palace "as hostages."

• Inside a cave, Bugs and his pal, Daffy Duck, search for hidden treasures. Hassan, a huge, dense Arab guard wielding a huge saber attacks. Hassan chases Daffy, shouting several times, "Hassan chop!" The "Hassan chop" scenes are identical to the "Hassan chop" scenes that appear in a 1979 Road Runner film.

• Daffy finds the magic lamp and rubs it. Out pops an ugly green genie. Instead of serving Daffy, the genie afflicts him.

• Riding atop flying carpets, Bugs and the sultan duel.

• Final scenes show the beleaguered Daffy as "Crabby" Abadaba's new storyteller. Bugs flees the palace, returning to the U.S. of A.

Dialogue: The sultan calls his aide, "Son of an unnamed goat."

Bulldog Drummond in Africa (1938), Congress. *John Howard, Reginald Denny.* CAMEOS

Scene: Stock footage introduces "Arbi, Morocco." Mulling about are veiled Arab women, men wearing fezes, and some donkeys.

• At the Hotel du Maroc, Drummond's American girlfriend asks, "Do you think we could be married in Morocco? Or would they make us use a Mohammedan priest?" Quips Drummond, "Well, then we'd be Muhammadans. And I could have a harem."

Bulletproof (1988), Cinetel. *Gary Busey, Darlanne Fluegel, Henry Silva.* SP: T.L. Langford Carver. S: Steve Carver. VILLAINS, WORST LIST

Exit the Red Menace—enter the Arab Menace! One Los Angeles policeman wipes out 80 Arab "terrorists." Arabs who despise Christians move to invade America. Attended by Russians, Cubans, and Nicaraguans, the Arabs steal "Thunderblast," a US super tank, then hide out at a Mexican border town. Here, the villains, who don red-and-white-checkered kuffiyehs, rape a Marine Captain, imprison priests and nuns, and slay American soldiers.

Scene: An American military officer briefs the policeman, McBain (Busey), about "communist inspired guerilla terrorists" in Mexico. "We recently confirmed the presence of enemy forces just 300 miles [from] our border... Cubans, Nicaraguans, Ayrabs." Cut to a TV set displaying evil Arabs.

• The Arabs hold Capt. Devon Shepard (Gluegel), McBain's former sweetheart, hostage. He leads a rescue mission, pledging to rescue the hostages and to bring back the bulletproof tank. McBain is told "an enemy force of about 80" awaits him. "80 to 1, no problem," he quips.

• Capt. Devon mocks her Arab captors, "You clowns are a little far from the shores of Tripoli." Barks the "Ayrab" leader Kartiff (Silva), "In my country, a woman shows respect... I despise women like you," and, "By Allah, you will die for this."

• Arabs chain the hostages, including Father Riley, Sister Mary, and another nun, to a makeshift mission cell. Pleads Father Riley, the prisoners are sick and hungry, "God have mercy." Snaps Kartiff, "Your God, not mine."

• Note the dialogue and interaction between Kartiff and Devon:

Devon: I'll never sell out to you, scum.
Kartiff: You still have not learned respect. In my country women...
Devon: Respect for you? Don't make me laugh. In your country you treat women like camels and send young boys to their death in the name of your excuse for God. Believe me, nobody is impressed!
Kartiff: Blasphemy. [*He slaps her; Devon slaps him back*] I love it when a woman fights, makes the prize that much more enjoyable. [*Pulling out a knife*] You will obey me. Take off your clothes. Obey me, woman. [*Brings the blade to her throat*]
Devon: Go fuck your camel. [*Kartiff rapes her*]
Sister Riley: [*Hearing Devon's screams*] "God help her."

• McBain is captured; he escapes. A Latino rebel officer berates Kartiff, saying that as the Arab is technically inept, the American got away. "Fool, if it were not for me, you would have blown us all to your precious Allah... You and your weakness for women." Says Kartiff, McBain "cannot live long in the desert." Quips the officer, "Your people do, don't they?"

• Acting as a one-man killing machine, McBain nabs the tank and slays the "terrorists." Kartiff begs a Russian officer, "You must stop him." Too late. Capt. Devon crushes Kartiff with the super tank.

Note: Writes *Washington Times* critic Tom Breen, "Mr. Silva is so loathsome in this role [Kartiff] that it's hard to refrain from yelling at him in the theater something like, 'You miserable rat, Silva, I hope you finally get yours. You're disgusting'" (19 May 1988).

Bulworth (1998), TCF. *Warren Beatty.* W, P, D: Beatty. CAMEOS

Included in this stinging criticism of American politics and corporate moguls is a rap song with some lyrics that satirize the US relationship to the Arab world.

Scene: At his political rally, California Senator Bulworth (Beatty) sings "Big Money," a rap tune. Midway through his song Bulworth belts out, "Exxon, Mobil, the Saudis and Kuwait; If we still got the Middle East, the atmosphere can wait. The Arabs got the oil; we buy everything they sell. But if the brothers raise the price, we blow 'em all to hell." Drum cymbals clash as Bulworth prompts others to chime in: "Now let me hear you say it. Saddam, Saddam!"

Bunker Bean (1936), a.k.a. His Majesty, Bunker Bean, RKO.

Owen Davis Jr. Based on the play by Lee Wilson Dodd. EGYPTIANS

This sound version of *His Majesty, Bunker Bean* (1918) also employs a dead Egyptian pharaoh as a role model. The heroic mummy, Ram Tah, boosts Bunker Bean's (Davis Jr.) confidence. Viewing the sawdust reproduction of Ram Tah, Bean convinces himself that he is the reincarnated pharaoh. Courage suddenly replaces Bean's anxieties; he thwarts swindlers and moves to wed the heroine.

Burning Sands (1922), Lasky. Silent. *Wanda Hawley, Milton Sills, Jacqueline Logan.* *NS. Notes from NYT (8 September 1922). EGYPTIANS

Paramount billed *Burning Sands* as "the answer to *The Sheik.*" English heroics and Egyptian villainy.

Summary: An unwelcome Egyptian pursues Lizette (Logan), a French dancing girl. To the rescue, the Western protagonist, Daniel Lane (Mills). Expressing gratitude, Lizette tells Lane about an Arab uprising. Promptly, Lane and the "British cavalry" bring down rebellious desert Egyptian "tribes." Lane also overpowers a British traitor. This turncoat not only sides with the Egyptian rebels, he tries to seduce the Western heroine, Murial Blair (Hawley).

Business and Pleasure (1931), FOX. *Will Rogers, Jetta Goudal.* Based on Booth Tarkington's novel. *NS. Notes from AFIC (Record 2459). VILLAINS, CAMEOS

Desert Syrians and a fortune-teller vs. Will Rogers.

Summary: A business cruise. When fortune-teller Madame Momora (Goudal) learns that an American, Earl Tinker (Rogers), plans "to corner the Damascus steel market," she decides to put Tinker out of business, permanently. Momora travels to the Syrian desert and, "to impress the Arabs," she operates a radio. Hearing voices and music over this radio, of all things, "persuade(s) them to abduct Tinker." Momora tells the bedouins to kill Tinker. But, Tinker escapes from them. Not only does he expose the deceitful Momora, he convinces his bedouin captors to arrest her.

Dialogue: Tinker's wife is relieved when learning that couscous is food, and not "a code word" for Tinker's "presumed affair with Momora."

Cabaret (1972), AA. *Liza Minnelli, Joel Grey.* SP: Jay Presson Adler, D: Bob Fosse. CAMEOS, SHEIKHS, MAIDENS

Winner of eight Academy Awards, this dramatic musical focuses on the horrors of Nazism. Briefly, the film offers an exotic view of an "Arabische Nacht."

Scene: Berlin, the early 1930s; the Kit Kat Club. Behind the stage curtain, silhouettes of performers wearing Arab garb. Three scantily-clad harem maidens attend a sheikh. As he puffs a water pipe, one maiden places a bunch of grapes between her toes. Then, she seductively extends her leg, offering grapes to the sheikh. The second woman offers him wine. Throughout the scene, another maiden cools the ruler with a feather fan.

Caesar and Cleopatra (1946), UA. *Claude Rains, Vivien Leigh, Stewart Granger, Anthony Harvey.* SP: George Bernard Shaw. In 1946, this was England's most costly film. EGYPTIANS, MAIDENS, RECOMMENDED

Shaw's screenplay reveals compelling, three-dimensional characters. Vivien Leigh's Cleopatra is neither wicked nor tragic. Yet, she nearly brings down the Roman empire. Egypt's Queen appears as a young, alluring woman intent on helping her people. And Ptolemy (Harvey), her younger brother, functions as an astute official, not as an inept, arrogant, effeminate brat as in *Cleopatra* (1963). Claude Rains' Caesar is a benevolent ruler, wooing the spirited Cleopatra with rhetoric. Caesar helps her to become "a real, real queen."

Scene: Caesar not only loves Cleopatra, he admires Egypt and the Egyptians. At the Sphinx he says, "Rome is a madman's dream. This Egypt is my reality." Also, he praises Egypt's soldiers, "Only a handful have held the palace against my army."

• Cleopatra tries to convince Caesar that her ambitious brother, Ptolemy, should be driven out of Egypt. In return for his help, she promises to guide his soldiers to India's riches. Believing Cleopatra is not strong enough to rule, Caesar hesitates. Only after Caesar learns that Cleopatra killed a palace intruder does he support her.

• To settle this dispute, Caesar's Roman soldiers and Cleopatra's loyal Egyptians battle Ptolemy's Roman and Egyptian followers. When Caesar leaves for Rome, Cleopatra takes Ptolemy's place on the throne.

Note: Excellent performances, brilliant sets, and lovely costumes. Regrettably though, at times the film operates as a recorded stage play, moving at a snail's pace.

A Café in Cairo (1925), Hunt Stomberg Prod. Silent. *Priscilla Dean, Robert Ellis.* *NS. Notes from NYT (18 March 1925). MAIDENS, EGYPTIANS

An Egyptian woman rescues her US paramour from desert bandits. Egyptians vs. Americans. This "silent" film was shown with an onstage "spoken" drama.

Summary: The movie screen shows dagger-wielding Egyptian heavies "binding and gagging" the American hero, Barry (Ellis), and tossing him "over the castle wall," into "the Nile's wintry depths." The submerged Barry wears a "white shirt, dress waistcoat, pressed trousers and patent leather shoes." Nadia (Dean), the Egyptian heroine, "being an Oriental, is dressed less extensively." She plunges into the Nile, rescuing her "American sweetheart." As *A Café in Cairo* is a combination screen and stage drama, after the Nile rescue scene, "the screen artistically dissolves into a stage set, and the principals in the flesh appear," briefly.

A Café in Cairo was considered to be "quite reminiscent of the 'thrilling' serials" and the screen and stage mix a "novel approach." Yet, the NYT critic said it was not "particularly effective."

Cairo (1942), MGM. *Jeanette MacDonald, Robert Young, Ethel Waters, Dooley Wilson, Eduardo Ciannelli.* SP: John McClain. Waters sings, "Buds Won't Bud." EGYPTIANS

In this WWII musical satirizing spy films, Egyptians and their Nazi cohorts oppose Americans. African-Americans demean Arabs. Displayed are the heroics of two Americans, movie star Marcia Warren (MacDonald) and war reporter Homer (Young). They prevent Egyptians and Nazi agents from bombing 5,000 American soldiers. The Egyptian heavies are Hassan, a technical genius tagged an "Arabian Wizard of Oz," and a shady Arab tagged the "Mongol Oriental."

Scene: Hassan (Ciannelli) places explosives inside a radio-controlled plane, boasting, "If any part of the plane hits any part of the American transport ship, it will blow it to bits."

• Operating a model airplane, Hassan demonstrates how he plans to release the bombs, via radio control. The camera closes in on the sinister, bearded, fez-wearing Hassan, then abruptly cuts to American servicemen aboard a troop ship, singing.

• In time, Homer the journalist wrecks Hassan's radio controlled plane. British agents shoot Hassan, then nab Nazi agents.

Note: Why not display a Nazi scientist as the antagonist instead of Hassan, the Egyptian? Why not show Hassan working with the Allies, against the Nazis?

• Dialogue. African-American actors ridicule Islam, everything "Ayrab." For example, distressed about not being back in the States, Warren's maid Cleona (Waters) tells the actress, "I miss everything you miss—plus." Cleona wants to woo "a nice colored boy." She complains that in Egypt she can only meet a man "who goes around in a nightgown, in which case he turns out to be an Ayrab." Hector (Wilson) appears from the pyramid's shadows wearing a thobe. When the robed Hector approaches Cleona, she balks, fearing he is an Egyptian. Note the dialogue:

Cleona: Don't look at me. I ain't Mecca.
Hector: [*He smiles*]
Cleona: Go on, just bow three times and go. Don't think that outfit you got on scares me 'cause I've handled 'em bigger and better with pants on.

Hector: Don't let this nightgown fool you, honey.
Cleona: What kinda Ayrab talks like that?
Hector: [*Explaining why he is in Cairo*] I wasn't doin' so good back there [in Hollywood], except in the movies. There wasn't an Ayrab picture shootin' that I didn't play an Ayrab."
Cleona: Oh, now you eatin' regular?
Hector: No, not all the time. Must be their religion or somethin.' Fastin' goin' on night and day. And when they do eat, I can't eat it.
Cleona: Bein' an Ayrab ain't much fun. You been missing' more than you know. [*They sing a song*]

• No Egyptian heavies surface in Columbia's 1943 thriller, *Passport to Suez.* Set in Alexandria, *Passport to Suez* displays the Lone Wolf [Warren William] and British agents nabbing German spies intent on seizing the Suez canal. A few Egyptians appear in the background. They function as waiters, attending patrons at the club, "Yankee Inn."
• When the Lone Wolf's valet, Jamison, opens an umbrella, a tall dark-complexioned Egyptian becomes frightened; he runs off, screaming.

Cairo (1963), MGM. *George Sanders, Richard Johnson, Faten Hamama, John Meillon.* Filmed at "Arabian Studios," Egypt. Arab actors perform a variety of roles, ranging from shop owners to doctors. EGYPTIANS

Balanced portraits, but with a warning: Do not tamper with a pharaoh's treasures.
Scene: A criminal tagged the Major (Sanders) enlists shady British and Egyptian accomplices. Determined to heist "Tut-ankh-amen's" jewels, the men break into the Cairo Museum. They intend to execute a foolproof robbery; they fail.
• The hashish-smoking Ali (Johnson), "a little crook, crazy about roulette, crazy about drugs," assists the Major. And, he cautions the Major not to tamper with treasures.

Ali: Are you superstitious?
Major: No, why?
Ali: They say to touch anything of the pharaoh's is unlucky.

• Ali's comments are on target. During the attempted heist some of the Major's criminals are shot, others are imprisoned. Perhaps to illustrate that some Arabs are Christians, an Egyptian priest appears at the criminal Willy's (Meillon) funeral.
• Efficient Egyptian police officers collaring the Major are men of integrity, refusing to take bribes.
• Final frames. Superimposed over the Egyptian countryside, a bust of the pharaoh.
Note: Egyptian women sing and bellydance at "The Cleopatra Club."

Cairo Operation (1965), A Menachem Golan Prod. Filmed in Israel. *NS. EGYPTIANS

This is the first Arabs-out-to-nuke-Israel film. Producer Menachem Golan punches anti-Arab rhetoric into overdrive. German specialists, assisted by primitive Egyptians, move to launch atomic missiles against Israel.
Professor Ella Shohat writes that Golan's film displays "a narrative contrast between the scientifically advanced Germans and the backward Arabs... here united in their evil acts." Adding, "German scientists... work for the Egyptians in the effort to develop atomic missiles against Israel."[54]

Cairo Road (1950), Free Lance. *Eric Portman, Lawrence Harvey, Maria Mauban and "introducing the Egyptian Artiste CAMELIA."* Original music by Na'im al-Basri. Filmed in Egypt. See *The Camels are Coming* (1934). EGYPTIANS

1945 Cairo. Brilliant British sleuths crush Egyptian hashish-peddlers.

Scene: Opening credits acknowledge the assistance of the "Egyptian government, the administrative achievements of the Cairo City Police, the Egyptian Coast Guards Administration and the Egyptian Frontiers Force in their relentless efforts to pursue and suppress the evil traffic in obnoxious drugs." Conversely, final frames display on screen, this message: "Distributed throughout the world except the Middle East."

"The Cleopatra Club"; Two British protagonists, police chief Colonel Youssef Bey (Portman), and his colleague, Lt. Mourad (Harvey), seek to terminate a world-wide narcotics smuggling ring based in Cairo. They're determined to nab scores of Egyptian smugglers, and the main "dealers in narcotics in the Middle East, three non-Egyptian brothers—Lombardi, Rico, and Pavlis."

• In order to ascertain whether Egyptians use camels to haul narcotics, British soldiers direct the animals to walk through a "radar-type" detector device. Should hashish be hidden on a camel, the detector's needle swings to the right.

• Do not trust a camel boy: A British Police Captain suspects an Egyptian boy of toting hashish. Unless the youth confesses, the officer threatens to kill his baby camel. Seeming sincere, the boy begs the officer to spare the camel. Then the Captain sees tucked into the lying boy's shirt, several drug packets.

• Thanks to British ingenuity, members of the Egyptian Camel Corps riding white camels apprehend the smugglers.

California Suite (1978), COL. *A Ray Stark Prod. Alan Alda, Jane Fonda.* SP: Neil Simon. CAMEOS

A swank Beverly Hills Hotel. The protagonist (Alda) boasts to his ex-wife (Fonda) that New York is "an exciting, vibrant, stimulating, fabulous city. But it's not Mecca. It just smells like it."

The Camel Boy (1984), Yoram Gross Studio. Animated and live action. Voices: *Barbara Frawley, Ron Haddrick.* P, D: Yoram Gross. The SP is based on Gross's book documenting the journeys of 20th century explorers. Filmed in Australia. RECOMMENDED

This children's story focuses on Ali, a courageous youth who treks across Australia's great Victoria desert.

Scene: The early 1920s. Ali, his grandfather, Moussa, and two other Arabs from the Gulf village, Bhustan, arrive in Australia, along with five camels.

• Before returning to Bhustan, the helpful Arabs tell Moussa, "May your desert bloom with flowers."

• As the Australian government "is offering a reward to those who find the shortest way across the desert," Ali, Moussa, the camels, and two Aussies, Barnaby and Morgan, prepare to compete. They hope to complete their 2,000-mile journey in two months.

• Islam is respected. Moussa is offered a beer; he shakes his head, saying, "My beliefs forbid me to drink alcohol." Evening, inside Moussa's tent, the elderly man prays.

• In Arabic, Ali means " exceptional bravery." Twice, Ali rescues his companions. Wild dogs attack the caravan; Ali routs the animals. Next, Ali and Moussa rescue Morgan from drowning. "He's a good kid," says Barnaby. The grateful Barnaby carves the name, "Ali," on a coin, placing it around the boy's neck.

• A horrific sandstorm. Ali and his trusted camel, Aziza, ride off during the storm. They find an oasis, returning with ample water. But they are not able to save the faltering Moussa.

• Mourning the death of his beloved grandfather, Ali sheds tears.

• After successfully completing their journey, Ali returns to Bhustan. Here, the animation ceases, live action begins.

• Years pass. An Australian boy travels to Bhustan, presenting the now grown-up Ali with a baby camel, Aziza's daughter. The young camel becomes a mascot in Bhustan's army.

The Camels are Coming (1934), Gainsborough. *Jack Hulbert, Anna Lee.* *NS. Notes from MPH. EGYPTIANS

Posing as an Arab ruler, a British officer (Hubert) assigned to Egypt's Camel Corps entraps Egyptian drug smugglers. This hashish scenario resembles *Cairo Road* (1950).

Cannonball Run (1981), TCF. *Burt Reynolds, Jamie Farr.* W: Brock Yates. CAMEOS, SHEIKHS

This farce centers around a cross-country auto race. Participating is a ludicrous Arab sheikh (Farr); he tries to buy women as well as "southern California." Boasts the wealthy Arab, who has already run down three camels, "The Cannonball will fall to the forces of Islam." Abruptly, the sound of a lightning bolt.

Scene: The desert. Two Arabs riding camels mock the not-so-bright sheikh who will race the "infidel Americans."

• The United States. The sheikh, attended by two mute bodyguards, parks his Rolls at the hotel, telling the clerk, "Twelve suites. Better yet, the entire floor."

• Prior to the Cannonball race, two American women warn the Arab, "Time for you to punch out."

• During the race, the sheikh pulls up at a drive-thru and orders some fast-food. The waitress asks for six dollars. The Arab gives her a gold ring, then hands her a wad of bills. "Keep the change," he says. Vowing to return, he quips, "Have you ever considered joining a harem?"

• A policeman tags the sheikh a "damn camel jockey." When the cop gives him a ticket, the Arab whines, "And my mother was considering buying southern California."

• Concluding scenes. All the "good racers" but not the sheikh, beat up the villains, members of the Hell's Angels.

Note: On real Arab auto racers: In 1996, Bobby Rahall won the Indy 500. Ray Harroun, nicknamed "The Bedouin," came out of retirement to win the Indy 500 in 1911. For this race Harroun installed a rear-view mirror. Born in Spartansburg, PA, "The Bedouin" served in the Navy during the Spanish-American War. An innovative designer and builder of race cars, this engineer invented the automobile bumper and fender. In 1914, he designed a Maxwell passenger car that ran on kerosene. The second Maxwell car in the 1914 "Indy" displayed another Harroun innovation—"a two-way radio so the driver could communicate with the pits!" Harroun owned an automobile factory, built and designed a monoplane, and designed the M5 bomb carrier for the Army, which was employed during the Vietnam conflict. Harroun is considered one of "the most talented engineers" of "all pre-WWI American drivers."[55]

Cannonball Run II (1984), WB. *Burt Reynolds, Ricardo Montalban, Jamie Farr.* W: Hal Needham. CAMEOS, SHEIKHS

The moronic Arab, Abdul bin Falafel (Farr), competes in a cross-country race. Actor Doug McClure appears as Abdul's blonde slave. Throughout, Abdul is called "the Arab."

Scene: A mosque in an Arab city. The ruling sheikh (Montalban) tells Abdul, "Son of my ugliest wife, you must win the Cannonball race." To assist Abdul, the potentate gives him more than a million dollars.

• The US. A half-naked woman appears, enticing Abdul not to enter the race. Mobsters monitor Abdul's erratic driving habits. "Only a moron would race like that," says one. They move to kidnap Abdul, saying, "We're gonna rip off the Arab."

• Abdul hands the thugs a chunk of bills. "Here, buy yourself a clothing store." And, "Allah came to me one night... and said spread the wealth before Khomeini gets it."

• The gangsters hold Abdul hostage. As they shave him, Abdul sings, "Look sharp, feel sharp." And, "I like the song so much I bought the company."

• The gangsters dump Abdul into a room straight out of the Arabian Nights. Three nearly-nude women fan and massage Abdul. He purrs, "I have a weakness for blondes and women without moustaches." One mobster declares Abdul's father will fork over ransom money. Affirms his pal, "The sheikh's father hates him."

• The camera reveals Sammy Davis, Jr., Dom De Luise, and Burt Reynolds posing as harem maidens. De Luise belly dances.

• A fight breaks out. Shouts the cowardly Abdul, "Get me somebody to hide behind."

• Abdul offers to buy the mobsters' joint for "$9 million, a drop in the well." When the gang hesitates, Abdul ups the ante: "$48 million!"

Slurs: Abdul employs a chimpanzee as his driver. The chimp, who wears a burnoose, kisses Abdul's father. The potentate stares at Abdul, smiles, then exclaims with delight: "Now, if your mother could kiss like that!" This ape kiss is reminiscent of a similar smooch in a Heckle and Jeckle cartoon, *The Desert Rat.* Here, a camel kisses an Arab who looks like a "rat."

Note: As early as 1925, producers injected chimpanzees into Arab scenarios. Hal Roach's 12-minute silent short, *Grief in Bagdad,* for example, presents a chimp in Arab garb ridiculing and besting nasty Arabs. The short begins with a starving Arab woman asking a robed Arab for assistance; he refuses. The chimp intervenes; he snitches a loaf of bread, giving it to the needy woman. Seeing a sleeping Arab, the chimp grabs some rope, ties the Arab's legs, then attaches the bound Arab to a donkey. Two more chimps wearing Arab garb appear: a sheikh and a princess. The chimp-as-sheikh moves to woo the chimp-as-princess; she rejects him. One scene mocks Islam. Cut to live actors portraying Arabs; they bow, kneeling to pray. Cut to a chimp clad in Arab garb happily bouncing atop their backs.

Captain Blood (1952), COL. *Louis Hayward, Ted de Corsia, Jay Novello.*
SP: Robert Libott, D: Ralph Murphy. EGYPTIANS, CAMEOS

From Jamaica to Martinique, the heroic swashbuckler and "great slave-liberator," Captain Blood (Hayward), crushes blackguards, including "the Egyptian" (Novello).

Scene: At a Spanish tavern, an attractive maiden vows to assist the captain. But when Blood arrives at her flat, he finds the woman dead — "an Egyptian dagger" in her back. Abruptly, the captain's foes appear — the Egyptian, who dons a red shirt, a red vest, and a red fez, and Easterling (de Corsia). The Egyptian holds a dagger to Blood's throat, boasting: "I am a man of experience. Raise your hands." Before collecting the reward of "10,000 pieces of eight" for Blood's capture, Easterling dispatches the Egyptian to bring back a jug of wine. "Hop to it, ya little squirt," he blurts.

• When the Egyptian returns, the clever captain provokes Easterling, saying, "You [and the Egyptian] are partners, I presume." Protests Easterling, "Partners, me eye. He works for me." The angry Egyptian pulls a dagger, "You are wrong my friend," he says, "From now on we divide everything in two parts... the same." Knowing the Egyptian cannot be trusted—after knifing the Spanish woman "he was going to pocket her gold necklace for himself"—Easterling pulls a pistol and shoots the Egyptian dead. "Well, that's one way of dissolving a partnership," he says. Then, Easterling stares at the corpse, muttering, "Look at 'em, bad little Arab." Wham! Blood floors Easterling and escapes.

Captain Sinbad (1963), MGM. *Guy Williams, Heidi Bruhl, Pedro Armendariz, Abraham Sofaer.* RECOMMENDED

This light-hearted adventure features plenty of romance and comedy. Arabs contest some Arab heavies.

Scene: From his impenetrable castle, the wicked ruler, El Karim, (Armendariz) dispatches cohorts to whip innocents, tagged "dogs."

• Opposing El-Karim are Sinbad (Williams), Calgo, the magician (Sofaer), Princess Jana (Bruhl), her father and townsfolk.

• Why is El-Karim immune from death? Because the potentate's living heart remains outside his body, safely tucked away in the "White Tower." As long as magical power protects his heart, El-Karim will remain invulnerable.

• El-Karim kidnaps the princess. Sinbad and his men, along with brave citizens, move to rescue Jana, and to destroy El-Karim's throbbing ticker. Princess Jana would rather be beheaded than wed the tyrant.

• Scheherazade-type music underscores Sinbad's bravery. En route to the White Tower, he crushes crocodiles and a 12-headed ogre.

• An elephant goes to crush Jana; Sinbad arrives, saving her. As for El-Karim's living heart, finally, it expires.

Note: Russia's enchanting *Magic Voyage of Sinbad* (1952) was released in the US and dubbed into English. The movie, in which the Russian Sinbad wears Viking garb, contains no Arab characters or settings. In search of a peaceful place, Sinbad and his men encounter colorful characters; e.g., the magical bird of happiness, a bird with a woman's head, plus Viking warriors, dancing Indian maidens, even Neptune.

• Japan's Toshiro Mufune stars as Sinbad in AI's release, *The Lost World of Sinbad* (1964). No Arab characters or settings appear in this dubbed-in-English film.

Yet, familiar personalities appear; e.g., a wicked vizier and an evil witch; they turn honorable men into stone. The vizier "takes the girls as mistresses. When through with them, they're all killed." Other curs bind innocent women to chains. Barks one, "He who has no money must give up his daughter."

The Captain's Paradise (1953), UA. *Alec Guinness, Yvonne De Carlo.* See *Song of Scheherazade* (1947). CAMEOS

The film is set in Ceuta, an enclave of Morocco, a municipality belonging to metropolitan Spain. Yvonne De Carlo does not portray a Moroccan beauty. Instead, De Carlo surfaces as Nita, the British protagonist's (Guinness) Spanish sweetheart. Nita, the "solution to man's happiness on earth," dances the flamenco, not the dubke.

Scene: In the initial frames, Arabs trod alongside donkeys and camels. Also, Arabs wearing fezzes, robes, and veils appear in the background.

Captured by Bedouins (1912), Kalem Company. Silent. *Gene Gauntier.* SP: Gauntier. Shot in Egypt. VILLAINS

Western heroes wearing Arab garb crush bedouins. In 1912, the motif of Arabia vs. the West surfaced. The desert becomes as a hostile place; crude bedouins take Western heroines hostage, attempt seduction, and demand monies.

Scene: In Cairo, British Lt. Grieg proposes to Doris Barnett, an American. After Doris agrees to wed the lieutenant she "slips away secretly to ask the Sphinx if she has acted wisely." Eight gruff "prowling bedouins" appear, nab Doris and whisk her off to their "native village."

• The bedouins demand "ransom" money. Lt. Grieg blackens his face and dons Arab garb. Grieg, "A Strange Arab," enters the bedouin camp, rescuing Doris from her straw prison.

• Bedouins pursue the couple; Grieg and Doris take cover. Using their camel as a shield, they fire at charging bedouins. Next, fez-wearing soldiers appear, running off the bedouins. This scene could easily be transformed into a Cowboys-and-Indians scenario. Replace camels with horses; replace the bedouins with Indians; and replace Egyptian rescue squad with US Cavalry troops.

Note: About the time *Captured by Bedouins* was being filmed, Victorian author Gertrude Bell, adviser to kings and diplomats, journeyed alone throughout the Arab world. Never was she robbed, raped, or injured. Commoners, as well as Arab leaders, loved and respected Bell. During her travels, Bell was surrounded by bedouin men who spoke almost no English. Yet, she bonded with the bedouins, sleeping in tents, riding camels and horses.[56]

Carpet from Baghdad (1915), Selig. Silent. *NS. Notes from AFIC (1911–1920: 127). VILLAINS

Americans nab Arab treasures; Arabs mishandle an antiquity. See *Maroc 7* (1967).

Summary: The Pasha tells Mohammad, his servant, to guard "the sacred Carpet of Baghdad." But a New York entrepreneur-turned-crook steals the carpet. He runs off to Baghdad and sells the carpet to Mr. Jones, an antique dealer. Mohammed catches up with the two Americans and employs desert torture. During a sandstorm, the two men escape. Jones arrives safely in New York, stolen carpet in hand. The frustrated "Mohammed bows in resignation to Allah's will."

Carry on Cleo (1965), Governor Films. *Sidney James, Kenneth Williams, Amanda Barrie.* SP: Talbot Rothwell. EGYPTIANS, MAIDENS

A harmless and entertaining spoof of Elizabeth Taylor's *Cleopatra* (1963). Gags are evenly directed at Romans and Egyptians.

Scene: Throughout, viewers witness a mute bodyguard, a white-bearded soothsayer, harem maidens, and bungling Romans. Props include a giant feather fan and a poison asp.

• Examples of burlesque humor. Vestal virgins lounge about in Cleopatra's (Barrie) bed chamber, where "the siren of the Nile takes ass's-milk baths."

• Cleopatra appears before Caesar (Williams) rolled up in a carpet. When guards release the carpet's cords, out rolls the "ambitious battle-ax."

Casablanca (1942), WAR. *Humphrey Bogart, Ingrid Bergman, Frank Puglia, Dan Seymour, Paul Henreid.* SP: Julius J. Epstein, Phil G. Epstein, Howard Koch. VILLAINS

This patriotic romantic classic made largely by European immigrants (the director hailed from Hungary, an Austrian penned the music, the art director came from Germany and the cast includes Russians and Hungarians) shows the American protagonist helping a freedom fighter flee the Nazis. Moroccans appear as backdrops: unprincipled vendors, waiters, rug dealers, a doorman, and a juggler.

Scene: WW II, Casablanca, French Morocco. The souk reveals Moroccan merchants and French-speaking police.

• Rick's Cafe. A bearded Arab barterer appraises a lovely European woman's diamond bracelet. She pleads, "Can't you make it a little more, please?" Sighs the Arab, "Sorry Madame, but diamonds are a drug on the market. There are diamonds everywhere. Everybody sells diamonds." He offers her "two thousand four hundred." Though distressed, she accedes. The Arab hands her some bills, leaving with the bracelet.

• In the souk, an Arab vendor (Puglia) tries to induce Ilsa Lund (Bergman) to buy some linen, telling Ilsa, "You will not find a treasure like this in all Morocco, Mademoiselle. Only 700 Francs." Rick (Bogart) enters the frame. "You're being cheated," he says. The startled Moroccan lowers the price; "Ah, the lady's a friend of Rick's. For friends of Rick's we have a small discount. Did I say 700 Francs? You can have it for 200." Abruptly, he withdraws the "200" price tag, purring, "For special friends of Rick's we have a special discount, 100 Francs." Though the Arab exhibits a new "100" price tag, Ilsa and Rick depart.

Note: Though set in Casablanca, the film short-changes Moroccans. No scenes reveal freedom-loving Moroccans befriending Rick, helping him and brave Europeans to crush the Nazis. But apparently the absence of heroic Moroccan characters did not concern Morocco's King Hassan, for on 7 April 1992, Hassan hosted a party in New York's Museum of Modern Art, celebrating the film's 50th anniversary.

• In the shortlived 1950s TV series, *Casablanca*, Arab caricatures also surface. The series featured actor Charles McGraw as Rick Jason. The program was telecast every third week on ABC-TV, September 1955–April 1956. A one-hour 1956 episode,

"The Siren Song," displays a fat mute Arab wearing dark glasses "still thinking he's a big shot." The fez-wearing Arab stuffs food into his mouth, then stalks Elsa (Mari Blanchard), the blonde protagonist. Elsa is asked, "Why does he always follow you? He's repulsive. Why doesn't he go back to Arabia where he belongs?" Quips Elsa, "Just ignore him, like I always do."

Casablanca Express (1990), Trylon. *Jason Connery.* Filmed in Morocco. VILLAINS

Moroccans in cahoots with Nazis vs. Western commandos. Islam is respected. When critic Joe Bob Briggs introduced this film set in Morocco on the Movie Channel (24 August 1991), he inexplicably slurred the Kuwaiti. Said Briggs, During the Gulf War, those people, "the Kuwaiti, turned out to be scum. They were scum."

Scene: 1942. A commando (Connery) is assigned to protect Winston Churchill from being kidnaped. Cut to unkempt Arab hawkers lurking in a Moroccan souk. They force the commando to halt. The Arabs and their Nazi cohort move to knife the commando; he kills two.

• Arabs on a train carry chickens.

Treatment of Islam: An imam wearing a fez moves to befriend a Catholic priest and three nuns. When the imam says, "Allah," the Christians snub him, implying their God and his "Allah" are different. Later, the nun and the dying priest respectfully acknowledge the imam, asking him to administer last rites. The imam tells the priest, "May Allah be with you, brother."

Casbah (1948), UI. *Tony Martin, Peter Lorre, Yvonne DeCarlo, Marta Toren, Hugo Haas, Katherine Dunham* and dancers. *Casbah* and *Algiers* (1938), starring Charles Boyer, are both remakes of the French film *Pepe Le Moko* (1937), with Jean Gabin. VILLAINS

This tragic European "romance musical" about a French criminal who hates life in the casbah displays Arabs as ragged props. One Arab character appears, the shady Omar. Tony Martin sings seven songs.

Scene: The casbah. European tourists step down from their bus. Cut to a veiled Arab woman tossing dirty water onto some steps. Cautions Omar (Haas), the fez-wearing guide. "Not wise to be alone in the streets of the casbah." Omar flirts with the women tourists; they ignore him.

• A Paris official orders the local inspector, Silmane (Lorre), to arrest the French fugitive, Pepe (Martin). Explains Silmane, such an arrest is impossible; the casbah contains too "many thieves." Pepe can only be nabbed if he is lured out of the casbah. Inside, he has "50 thousand friends."

• One of Silmane's men poses as a scruffy Algerian, but fails to nab Pepe. Then police invade the casbah. Residents toss melons and vegetables in alleyways; the police stumble and Pepe escapes.

• Pepe meets Gaby (Toren), a sophisticated and beautiful European, and falls in love. A montage of unsightly images reveals: flute players, beggars, and Abdullah eating fire. Suddenly, Pepe, who desperately wants to be back in France, screams, "Gotta get out of here. The dirt and the noise, day in and day out. I'm getting fed up."

• Pepe exits the casbah. As he rushes to meet Gaby, he is fatally shot.

Treatment of Islam: Silmane explains to Gaby the holy time of Ramadan. During the fasting period, he says, one "can't eat [before sundown] or have sex. Of course, there are exceptions. Invalids, tourists, they don't have to fast." Quips Gaby, "Mohammed must have been in favor of the tourist business."

Cast a Giant Shadow (1966), UA. *Kirk Douglas, Frank Sinatra, John Wayne, Yul Brynner, Senta Berger, Haym Topol, James Donald.* SP, D: Melville Shavelson. Filmed in Israel. PALESTINIANS, VILLAINS, WORST LIST

Palestinians are defined as a people without a land. Performers Frank Sinatra, Yul Brynner, John Wayne, and Kirk Douglas bring down Arab aggressors. Surly Syrians and Egyptians vs. appealing Israelis and an American Colonel.

Scene: 1947 New York City. Credits state: "The major events in this film actually happened. Some of them are still happening." When Israeli Major Safir (Donald) is told, "Six nations promise to drive you into the sea," Safir moves to convince Colonel David Mickey Marcus (Douglas), an American Jew and an advisor to President Roosevelt, to go to Israel. The Major refers to a statement made by Ibn Saud, "There are 50 million Arabs. What does it matter if we lose 10 million and kill all the Jews?" Major Safir counters by citing Jerusalem's Grand Mufti, "I declare a Holy War. Murder them. Murder them all," he said. The harsh citation prompts Marcus to leave for Israel, where he intends to train Israeli soldiers to kill Arabs.

• American General Randolph (Wayne) tells David, "Your friends may have the Bible in their favor but the Arabs have the oil. You think the State Department is going to hesitate choosing up sides? Five Arab nations [want to] shove Israel into the Mediterranean," says the general. Next, Randolph vows to compel State Department officials to side with Israel.

• Palestine, the airport. Mute Palestinians appear as props; they walk alongside camels and donkeys. A disagreeable Palestinian youth munching a sandwich shoots at a truck, then resumes eating.

• Israelis as victims of Palestinian terror. Jews die "standing up." The camera reveals a Jewish woman's hands tied to a burning bus, a knife-carved Star of David etched into her bloodied back. Says an Israeli, "The Arabs [not Palestinians] in the country have never learned to love us." "I know the Arab leaders hate each other worse than they hate you. So, they don't have anything to die for and they don't trust each other," explains Marcus.

• David visits the bedouin, Abou ibn Kader (Topol). Inside the Arab's tent some musicians accompany an attractive bellydancer. Abou grabs handfuls of foodstuffs, forcing the reluctant David to digest edibles. Abou slaps the dancer, hard, then dispatches her and the musicians. Next, he spits on his sleeve and places a record, "The Sheik of Araby," on a gramophone. Abou asks Marcus, "Why do you want to take... our desert? [rather than land] By what right?" Counters Marcus, "The Jews aren't destroying your land. For the first time the desert is blooming." Abou, the "friendly" bedouin, decides to side with the Israelis; he thinks they will triumph. Not only does Abou betray the Syrian position, he directs the Israelis to "a path through the hills to Jerusalem," enabling them to defeat the Arab Legion.

• A mountain path. Syrian troops pin down Israeli soldiers, including lovely Magda (Berger). Three repulsive-looking Syrians advance, screaming, "Come on, Magda." After

Marcus rescues her, he says, "All my life I've been looking for where I belong. It turns out to be here [Israel]." Marcus and Magda embrace "between a rose bush and the moonlight."

• Egyptian tanks fire on innocents, killing an Israeli woman soldier. Declares an Israeli, Arab Legion forces wearing red-and-white kuffiyehs "slaughtered" defenseless Israeli families; "wheat fields are irrigated with their blood."

• The Israelis triumph. Assisting in the victory are Vince (Sinatra), an American soldier of fortune, a Scotsman, and other Westerners. When the State of Israel is officially announced, Israelis stand and sing the anthem. Cut to Jewish immigrants arriving in Palestine, singing, "Hava Nagila."

Note: Not one frame reveals Palestinian sufferings. Viewers do not see Israelis killing lovely brave Palestinian women soldiers; Palestinians do not sing their anthem; nor does the camera show heroic bedouins, Egyptians, or Syrians.

• Excluded from films focusing on Israel-Palestinian strife are some needed facts. In 1948, although Palestinians residing in Palestine outnumbered the Jews by more than a two-to-one majority, the United Nations gave the minority [the Jews] 55 percent of the land. The remaining 45 percent of land was not allocated to the Palestinians, but rather to the Kingdom of Jordan. This is why it is called the West Bank. Only one movie shows Israelis destroying the homes of Palestinian families. Yet, since 1948 the Israelis have razed to the ground about 500 Palestinian villages that existed within its own borders, not to mention the West Bank, creating thousand of refugees and refugee camps. Still, thousands of Palestinians reside in these camps. For decades, the Israeli forces have been implementing an old British policy, destroying an entire family's home, and/or its olive orchards, whenever a single member was even *suspected* of wrong doing. Though not aware of what crime they are accused of, Israeli armed forces round up and imprison thousands of Palestinians. Yet, the prisoners who await trial are never told why they are jailed. At times, soldiers terrorize families, they barge into Palestinian homes late at night, threaten the occupants, destroy furniture, and whisk away young people.

The Castillan (1963), WB. *Cesar Romero, Broderick Crawford.* See *El Cid* (1961). VILLAINS

Spain, 350 years prior to the Crusades. Opening and final frames show Arab Muslims persecuting and raping Christians. Pigs defeat Arabs!

Scene: On screen, a tenth-century map of Spain. Explains the narrator: "The Moors swept over Spain and by rape and slaughter struck fear into all Europe."

• As Abdelraman's Arabs kill Spaniards, destroy Christian religious relics and torch villages, Spanish women weep.

• Clad-in-white Christian women as "tribute." Before the Spanish women are given to the Arab leaders, the heroic Spanish nobleman, Fernan Gonzales (Romero), intercedes. He overpowers debauched Arabs.

• Gonzales considers whether the Arabs could win an upcoming battle. Not to worry, says a Spanish soldier, "Arabs are afraid of certain animals [pigs]!"

• Duping Arabs. Though "outnumbered 100 to 1," Gonzales' Spanish Christians triumph over the Arabs. Why? Because when the pigs appear, the frightened Arabs run off. Dozens of "squealing pigs" pursue them.

Dialogue: An Arab is tagged "half-man, half-horse."

The Ceremony (1964), UA. *Laurence Harvey, Sarah Miles, John Ireland, Robert Walker Jr.* P & D: Laurence Harvey. *NS. Notes from NYT (14 May 1964: 34). VILLAINS

"Obviously gloom and foreboding lurk in the corridors and cells" of the dingy old prison in Tangier, where much of the action occurs. In prison, Sean McKenna (Harvey), an innocent man, awaits execution for a murder he tried to prevent.

Chain of Command (1993), CAN. *Michael Dudikoff, Keren Tishman, Todd Curtis, R. Lee Ermey, Eli Danker* (often portrays evil Arabs), *David Menachem, Steve Greenstein, Yaron Levi Sabag, Michael Greenspan.* P: Yoram Globus. Filmed in Israel (G.G. Studios). Israeli actors portray Arabs. VILLAINS, WORST LIST

An anti-Arab film from Israeli producer Yoram Globus. One American kills 60-plus Arab "terrorists"—Arabs are "barbecue."

Scene: Ominous music underscores credits. The camera reveals the "Western Oil Co. Station No. 7 Republic of Qumir." Seated at a table playing cards are Al Ross (Dudikoff), an ex-Green Beret, and Moustafa (Sabag). Noting Al's bottle of Jack Daniel's, Moustafa says, "The prophet teaches us to abstain from alcohol. Perhaps you would play better if you drank less."

• Rawlings (Curtis), the American heavy, smuggles into the station scores of clad-in-blue Arab "terrorists." After American workers are taken hostage, Rawlings and his Arabs blow up the station. He and his cohorts terminate scores of "dispensable" Arabs, including Moustafa.

• Qumiri Secret Headquarters. Unknown to Al, Colonel Hakkim (Danker) is in cahoots with Rawlings. The Colonel and Rawlings are responsible for the station tragedy. Yet, the Colonel frames Al, the "infidel," for the killings. The Colonel also blames the CIA and an underground group, the Qumiri Liberation Initiative (QLI), for the attack.

• Appearing at the Hotel Paradise, sans air conditioning, is lovely Maya (Tishman). She kills two of Hakkim's men, then runs off with Al to the QLI's hideout.

• Intending to free American hostages, Maya, Al and the QLI leader (Menachem), invade the "terrorist's camp." Al suggests some strategies. As the QLI leader does not listen, the "bad" Qumiris entrap and kill scores of "good" QLIs. Abruptly, Al takes charge. He bombs and machine-guns scores of "terrorists," boasting, "time for a little barbecue." Next, Al frees the hostages. The inept QLI leader tells Al, "You fought well, almost as an Arab." Al smiles.

• US Embassy, Qumir. Ambassador Dwayne Mosby (Greenstein) tells his aide, "Qumir is one of the few governments in this part of the world that is even remotely friendly to the United States." Mosby, however, does not trust Hakkim. He refuses to hand over to the "son-of-a-bitch classified information."

• Ahmed, a cabby who likes jazz, takes Al to his home. Maya greets Al. Surprise! She is not a Qumiri, after all! Neither is Ahmed. Maya explains they are "with Mossad, Israeli foreign intelligence." She and Al make love. (In Globus films, always an attractive Israeli, never a lovely Arab, romances the American hero.)

• Al discovers that "somebody wants to rush in and take over the country for themselves." That "somebody" is Western Oil CEO Ben Brewster (Ermey). Employed by Brewster are Rawlings, Colonel Hakkim, and Rawlings' "trained Arabs."

• Al and Maya are delivered to Brewster. Boasts Brewster, my "corporate takeover" of Qumir will net "trillions." I'll have my "own little private Arab country; I'll keep the "natives happy."

• Abruptly, Al crushes Brewster and Rawlings. Next, he wipes out plenty of "Arab mercenaries." In the end, Al and Maya embrace.

Note: Actors speak Arabic with Israeli accents.

Treatment of Islam: In two scenes, the Muslim call to prayer is heard just before Arabs kill Arabs.

• Ex-CNN reporter Michael Greenspan appears in this film, portraying a TV "journalist."

• Globus' images are even more heinous than those surfacing in the X-rated film *Up the Gulf* (1991). *Up the Gulf* displays "Arab terrorists in Beirut... in need of a shower." The Arabs hold hostage the American protagonist. And, they rape a female prisoner. All ends happily. The American's girlfriend flies off to Lebanon; she frees her sweetheart and brings down the Arab "terrorists."

Chandu the Magician (1932), FOX. *Edmund Lowe, Bela Lugosi, Irene Ware, June Vlasek, Virginia Hammond, Henry B. Walthall, Weldon Heyburn.* Based on a radio serial. CLIFFHANGERS, EGYPTIANS, MAIDENS

In this movie serial, an Egyptian Princess Nadji and her American sweetheart oppose evil Egyptians. The movie's theme—Arabs-seek-to-destroy-the-world—precedes nuclear destruction plots that appear in films such as *Cairo Operation* (1965), *Operation Thunderbolt* (1977), *Wrong is Right* (1982), and *True Lies* (1994).

Scene: Egypt. The Arab villain Roxor (Lugosi) wants to become "king" of the world. Roxor, "a human monster hailing from the last of an ancient family that lived in Alexandria," kidnaps the inventor of a death-ray, Robert Regent (Walthall). Boasts Roxor, "This death-ray means an end to goodness. London, New York—all the cities will perish."

• After a sneaky Egyptian peers through a window and frightens the American lovely, Betty Lou (Vlasek), the Egyptian peeping tom howls. Asks Chandu (Lowe), "What's that?" Quips Mrs. Regent (Hammond), "Only a dog down by the river."

• Roxor's cohort, Abdullah (Heyburn), goes to rape Princess Nadji (Ware). Quips Roxor, "A new slave for your harem?"

• Unless Nadji helps the "heartless [Roxor] become a modern pharaoh," he threatens to annihilate innocents. "They shall bow before me," he says. Declares Nadji, "My life belongs to my people."

• Roxor kidnaps Betty Lou (she wears only a slip). He whisks her off to the slave market, intending to sell her. Disguised as an Arab, Chandu rescues Betty Lou. Numerous films offer similar scenes, showing Western protagonists donning Arab garb, rescuing Western heroines from nasty Arabs. See especially the James Bond film *Never Say Never Again* (1983). Here, a disguised 007 (Sean Connery) saves the Western heroine (Kim Bassinger) from Arab perverts.

• Regent's death-ray explodes; Roxor dies. Rubble crushes Abdullah and his cohorts.

• The magician, Chandu, is locked in a coffin and tossed into the river. Yet, he emerges unscathed. "I have come out of a coffin from the depths of the Nile," he says.

• Finale. Moonlight. The lovebirds, Egyptian Princess Nadji and Chandu, the American hero, kiss—a multi-cultural smooch that escaped the scrutiny of Code members.

Note: In 1934, the Fox Film Corporation released two feature films, *The Return of Chandu* and *Chandu on the Magic Isle*. Both films were edited from the 12-part serial *The Return of Chandu*, which is listed separately.

Chapter Two (1979), COL, Ray Stark Prod. *James Caan, Joseph Bologna*. SP: Neil Simon. CAMEOS

Writer Neil Simon slurs Arabs.

Dialogue: Seconds into the film, Leo Schneider (Bologna) greets his despondent brother George (Caan) at the airport, asking "How was London?" Barks George, "Full of Arabs." (Would it be permissible for Simon to write, "Full of Jews?")

Chariots of Fire (1981), TCF. *Ben Cross, John Gielgud, Ian Holm*. EP: Dodi Fayed. P: David Putnam. Academy Award: Best Picture. CAMEOS

An Arab-Italian trainer befriends a Jewish student at Cambridge; based on a true story.

Scene: Jewish student Harold Abrahams (Cross) is part of Britain's 1924 Olympic track team. The Master of Trinity College (Gielgud) expresses concern, asking Abrahams whether he really does work with a foreign coach:

Abrahams [*proudly*]: Mr. Mussabini. Yes.
Trinity Don: Is he Italian?
Abrahams: Of Italian extraction, yes.
Don [*upset*]: Oh, I see.
Abrahams: But not all Italian.
Don [*pleased*]: I'm relieved to hear that.
Abrahams [*boasting*]: He's half-Arab.

• Abrahams calls his Arab-Italian trainer Mussabini (Holm) "the finest, most balanced clearest-thinking athletic coach in the country. I am honored that he considers me worthy of his complete attention... He's the best."

Charlie Chan and the Curse of the Dragon Queen (1981), American Cinema. *Peter Ustinov, Brian Keith*. SP, P: Jerry Sherlock. CAMEOS

In this spoof of Chan films, a dead "Ayrab."

Scene: A San Francisco police inspector (Keith) examines the bodies of several victims, recently drowned inside an elevator. One victim wears a white thobe. Grunts the inspector, "I don't know why in the hell he's wearing that dress...Put him down as an Ayrab, an unidentified Ayrab."

• Prior to its release, Asian-American groups picketed this film. They protested because "of the film's stereotypical portrayal by an Occidental (Ustinov) of a major Asian character (Chan)."

Charlie Chan in Egypt (1935), FOX. *Walter Oland, Thomas Beck, Rita Cansino, Nigel De Bruller, Stepin Fetchit.* EGYPTIANS

No Egyptian heavies; blacks appear as buffoons.

Scene: The treasures of Egyptian high priest, Ameti, unexpectedly appear in Europe. To find out why, Charlie Chan (Oland) travels to the land of the pharaohs. Naturally, Chan solves the mystery. Fez-wearing Egyptian police are not as perceptive as Chan, but then, who is?

• Chan's driver, Snowshoes (Stepin Fetchit), appears as an inferior and superstitious black, afraid of a secret Egyptian tomb. Snowshoes not only rolls his eyes and smokes a water pipe, he carries a razor blade in his pocket. When characters bark orders, Snowshoes obliges. NYT Critic Andre Sennwald praised Fetchit's portrayal of Snowshoes: "Stepin Fetchit, the master of slow motion... manages as usual to be both hilarious and unintelligible" (24 June 1935).

• The film's costumers seem to view the Near East and the Middle East as one and the same: Rita Hayworth's Egyptian maiden is clad in Indian garb, including a sari.

Charlie Chan in Panama (1940), TCF. *Sidney Toler, Frank Puglia.* CAMEOS, EGYPTIANS

A fez-wearing Egyptian salesman surfaces in Panama City.

Scene: A German agent moves to destroy the US Fleet and the Panama Canal. Cut to a suspected collaborator—an Egyptian businessman, Achmed Halide (Puglia). He owns the "Achmed Halide Tobacco" shop, and beckons patrons, saying, "Come to me for the best cigarettes."

• A cemetery. Chan's son Jimmy thinks Achmed may be a German spy. Pointing to the Egyptian's tomb, he declares, "What would a guy (Achmed) that's alive want with a tomb?" Explains Miss Finch, "Consider his nationality and possible religion." Affirms Chan, "Miss Finch is right. Not exceptional for Egyptian to prepare final resting place before death."

Chasing Danger (1939), TCF. *Preston Foster, Lynn Bari, Wally Vernon, Henry Wilcoxon, Joan Woodbury, Harold Huber, Jody Gilbert.* SP: Leonardo Bercovici, Robert Ellis, Helen Logan. D: Ricardo Cortez. VILLAINS, MAIDENS

All too familiar hokum. French legionnaires vs. Arab desert tribes in revolt.

Scene: Fort El-Hamed, Algeria. Opening frames display French troops battling desert Arabs. Cut to the American office of "Graphic Newsreel," where its wire service receives this bulletin: "Fifth company foreign legion... entire garrison reported to have been massacred." Promptly, Graphic Newsreel's chief dispatches newsmen Steve Mitchell (Foster) and Waldo (Vernon) to Algeria. See *I Cover the War* (1937), which also shows newsmen tangling with Arab rebels.

• Arab-land. Quips a French officer: "Algeria is a strange place. There are avenues of escape which make even the Apache slums of Paris look simple in comparison... A European found there [in a souk after dark] is inviting an early funeral."

• When Steve moves to woo Renee (Bari), an Arab woman delivering weapons to the uprising nomads, she rebuffs him, advising, "My father was Arabian. It was his dream to someday lead a revolt against the French in North Africa. He fought for it and died for it."

• Arab vs. Arab. In the souk, Arab rebels capture Steve and Waldo. Believing Renee betrayed her Arab comrades to the Americans, Hazila (Woodbury) orders the Arab rebels to shoot Steve and Waldo. Renee protests, "This is no time to listen to a woman's jealous tongue." Abruptly, Andre Duvac (Wilcoxon), a French Intelligence officer arrives, rescuing the trio and killing the Arab guards.

• Arabs on horseback appear atop sand dunes; they charge the Graphic Newsreel van. Quips Waldo, "Here come a bunch of those guys in their nightshirts..." Waldo and Steve also tag Arab garb "bathrobe" and "kimono."

• Karashar, a walled Arab city. Arab rebels imprison Waldo and Steve. Cut to Teeda (Gilbert), a dense, rotund, mostly mute Arab damsel; she swoons over Waldo. Mistakenly, Waldo removes Teeda's veil. Cut to shouting Arabs; one warns: "No one removes a Karashar woman's veil unless it's her future husband."

• The giggling Teeda vows to help Waldo and Steve escape, provided Waldo kisses her. Waldo resists, shouting: "Keep away from me." When Steve reminds Waldo they've got to get out of prison before they get their "throats cut," he retorts, "That's better than having her kill me her way."

• Out of jail, Steve disguises himself as an Arab woman. A rebel mistakes Steve for an Arab woman. Steve floors the Arab, then transmits a message to French intelligence, revealing the rebel's hideout. Meanwhile, the rebels capture several legionnaires; among their prisoners, Andre. Abruptly, the Arabs practice "an old Arabian custom," tying Andre to a wild horse. Arabs cheer as the horse drags "him around till it knocks his brains out. Just an old Arabian lawn party."

• Some French military planes appear, dropping bombs on the rebels. Steve and Waldo free Andre, then they machine-gun fleeing Arabs.

• Renee finds out that Carlos (Huber), the non-Arab leader of the revolt, deceived her. He never intended to liberate the Arabs. Instead, Carlos bargained "with a certain European country (most likely, Germany), promising to "turn over Northern Africa to them when the French were driven out." Though Andre is taking Renee back to France to face trial, he tries to console her, saying she may be pardoned for her crime. "France has always been generous," says Andre, "and you'll be able to do a lot to promote her friendship with your countrymen."

Finis: The flighty Teeda still pursues Waldo, trying desperately to embrace him. Waldo refuses; angry Arabs enter the frame. Insists Teeda's father, "You will marry my daughter whose veil you removed." Waldo runs off, pursued by Teeda and the Arabs.

Cheech & Chong's Next Movie (1980), UNI. *Cheech Marin, Tommy Chong.* SP: Chong, Marin. D: Chong. See *Things are Tough All Over* (1982). CAMEOS

Cheech and Chong mock Arabs and link an Arab-American businessman with oil-rich Arabs.

Scene: As credits roll, the camera reveals a "Texaco" gas station. The drug-dazed duo Cheech and Chong, appear toting a garbage can. They pilfer gas from the station, filling the huge can. As gasoline flows into the can, the camera cuts to the mustachioed attendant, "a dude too busy watching his money." Parked directly behind Cheech and Chong is the station tow truck. Several times, the camera displays the station owners' names, emblazoned on the truck's door: "SAYDIS & SAYDAT." After Cheech and Chong fill their can with gasoline, they move toward their car. Smiling, Cheech sings: "Ahab the Ayrab, sheikh of the burning sands."

Children of Rage (1975), Emmessee Production, British-Israeli.

Simon Ward, Helmut Griem, Olga Georges-Picot, Richard Alfieri, Robert Salvio. SP, D: Arthur Allan Seidelman. Filmed in Israel. PALESTINIANS, MAIDENS

Palestinian radicals initiate terror. Two Palestinians are peacemakers—a bright nurse and an intelligent commando leader. Though they befriend an Israeli doctor, the film's message remains: Israelis intending to make peace with Palestinians die.

Scene: Palestinians blow up an Israeli bus. Israeli soldiers surface, killing most of the Palestinians. At an Israeli hospital, Dr. David Shalom (Griem) attends a seriously wounded Palestinian, Ahmed Saleh. David recognizes the Palestinian as his former classmate, but he cannot save Ahmed's life. Some Israelis, including David's father, tag Palestinians "savages," "terrorists," and "murderers." Counters David, peace will come only after "Israelis start to deal with their grievances." Says David, "This was their land, their homes." Returns his father, "It's our land; we earned it. They can find a place."

• Jerusalem. Sighs Mr. Saleh, Ahmed's father, "I am an old man. My oldest son is killed and I look around here [this house], and there is no reason. My friends did not run away in 1948, and I will not run away now. I was born here and I will die here." Ahmed's 19-year-old brother, Omar (Alfieri), declares, "I want to avenge my brother's death." Cut to a Palestinian military camp. The leader barks to recruits, "Realize every one of you, you came here to die. But you will die in the earth of your homeland."

• Posing as an Israeli, Omar goes to a dance hall. When an Israeli girl moves to befriend him, he rejects her. Suddenly, Omar places a bomb inside a book. Igniting the explosive, the bomb kills scores of Israeli teens.

• Wounded by the explosion, Omar runs off to an enclave near the Israeli-controlled border. The camera reveals Omar's sister, Leyla (Georges-Picot), a Palestinian nurse working with the Israeli doctor, David. Both attend Palestinian fighters. As David dresses Omar's wounds, the youth barks, "You'll never have my friendship." Says David, "Well, at least take mine." Omar departs, warning Leyla to "be careful."

• Ibrahim (Andreu), the Palestinian commander, and David become friends. Explains Ibrahim, "In 1948 all my family [they were farmers], went to Lebanon. Nine years later we came back. Where are you from?" Replies David, "Austria." Says Ibrahim, I want to "live in Palestine as you live in Palestine, with all the rights that you have." Affirms David, "To have a safe home... Yes, I think that's what we all want."

• As there is no camp hospital to treat Palestinian soldiers, David and Leyla decide to build a makeshift infirmary. Yet, Palestinian radicals toss stones at the facility. Protests Ibrahim, "Save your rocks for Israel!"

• Ibrahim's prejudiced assistant, Abdullah (Salvio), who hates all Israelis, even David, warns Ibrahim, "They rule you, those arrogant Israeli pigs and their American friends... It's our turn [to use terror]. No Israeli should feel safe in their beds."

• Abdullah fatally shoots David. Israelis bomb Ibrahim's camp, killing nearly all the Palestinians, including Omar. Only Leyla survives.

The Chipmunk Adventure (1987), Samuel Goldwyn. Animated.

SP, P: Janice Karman, Ross Bagdasarian. SHEIKHS, EGYPTIANS

The Chipmunks and the Chipettes participate in an around-the-world balloon race, traveling to Mexico, Italy, Greece, and Holland. Along the way, they encounter, briefly, two generic villains. Midway through the scenario they are nabbed by nasty Arabs.

Scene: The desert. The camera shows evil Jamal's camel-riding bedouins stumbling over themselves. After much struggling, they bring down the Chipettes' balloon and drag them off to the palace. Inside the throne room, a young prince cackles, "I will rule the world." And, "I want the girls... I keep the girls." The prince tells his Arab guards, "Prepare [Brittany] for the engagement ceremony. In ten years I will make her one of my wives. The ceremony will take place promptly at dawn." The guards haul the girls, Jeanette, Eleanor, and Brittany, off to the harem quarters.

• The girls now wear harem garb; Arab maidens attend Brittany. "If you think I'm marrying that pint-sized twerp," says Brittany, "you're nuts. I don't care how important he is, how rich he is."

• Evening. The girls move to escape; poisonous green rattlesnakes appear, surrounding them. But the girls "charm" the rattlers, escaping in their balloon.

Chu Chin Chow (1934), Gaumont. *George Robey, Francis K. Sullivan, Anna May Wong.* *NS. Notes from NYT (21 September 1934). VILLAINS

This comic operetta adapted from the tale of "Ali Baba and the 40 Thieves" shows Ali Baba bringing down nasty Arabs. Featured is Zahrat (Wong) an unfaithful and vengeful slave girl. The musical features colorful costumes, the familiar "Open, Sesame" password, and scimitar battles. Opposing Ali Baba are greedy Kassim and Abu Hassan, villains who prey upon Baghdad's merchants.

• In 1923, a silent film version of *Chu Chin Chow* was released in England. The movie was so successful, it "ran for more than 2,000 performances in London." See *Ali Baba and the Forty Thieves* (1918).

The City of Lost Men (1935), COL. This full-length film is one of two features compiled from the 12-episode movie serial, *The Lost City* (1935). VILLAINS

Cleopatra (1912), State Rights. A Helen Gardner Prod. Silent. *Helen Gardner.* D: Charles L. Gaskill. *NS. Notes from MPW, James Reeves Harrison, "Helen Gardner's Idealization of Cleopatra," (859–60). EGYPTIANS

Harrison praises Gardner's Cleopatra, saying she displays "keen intelligence" as Antony's "steadfast, devoted and determined" lover. "She is not to be turned from him by the armies of the world, by the fleets of the world, nor by the [Roman] diplomats of the world." In the end, "she could stand the loss of a battle, the loss of a throne, but not the loss of the man [Antony]." Adds Harrison, "I think her (Gardner's) performance will rank as one of the greatest ever shown on the screen up to the present time... Cleopatra... Helen Gardner—they are one and indivisible in this rare [five-reel] production."

Note: In 1899, the Egyptian enchantress made her debut in Frenchman Georges Méliès' short film, *Cleopatra*. The Egyptian queen then appeared in three more high-budget Hollywood films after this Helen Gardner production. (See next three entries.)

Cleopatra (1917), FOX. Silent. *Theda Bara, Fritz Leiber, Thurston Hall.* *NS. Notes from Ronald Bower in *MAG* (322–5). One of AFI's "Ten Most Wanted Lost Movies." EGYPTIANS

Fox studios spent "approximately $500,000" on this *Cleopatra* film, which featured a "cast of about thirty thousand men and women" and branded the queen a "serpent" and a "vampire." The promotions department went all out to promote Theda Bara as the stunning queen; the dark-haired actress became Hollywood's first femme fatale. Studio releases claimed Bara was of "exotic Arabian ancestry." In reality, Bara was born "Theodosia Goodman," in Cincinnati, Ohio, the daughter of a local tailor (see IMDb). Studio moguls invented the name Theda Bara, using it as an acronym for "Arab Death." Bara embellished the myth, boasting she was born in the shadow of the pyramids. The actress personified what came to be known as the vamp, luring helpless men to their death.

Fox Film's publicity unit churned out releases and posters tantalizing viewers with this question: "What will be your verdict after you see Theda Bara's portrayal of the passions and pageants of Egypt's vampire queen?" Notes critic Ronald Bowers, "Due to Bara's international success, the word 'vamp,' an accepted derivation of the word 'vampire' which describes a woman who uses her attractions to win passionate love and brings her lover to a debased, humiliated, or impoverished condition," was added into "the English language [and later] dictionaries." Critics applauded Bara's performance, saying she made a convincing "Serpent of the Nile."

After *Cleopatra* was completed, writes Bowers, Fox's colorful press releases swayed even Bara, prompting her to proclaim: 'I know I am a re-incarnation of Cleopatra. I live Cleopatra, I breathe Cleopatra, I am Cleopatra!'" Fox's $1.00 reserved seat souvenir program contained an essay entitled, "In all seriousness, 'Is Theda Bara a reincarnation of Cleopatra?'"

Bara's 1917 film is "believed to have been lost," and is included on the AFI's 'Ten Most Wanted' list." See *Serpent of the Nile* (1953).

Cleopatra (1934), PAR. A Cecil B. DeMille Prod. *Claudette Colbert, Warren William, Henry Wilcoxon, Ian Keith*. EGYPTIANS, MAIDENS, RECOMMENDED

Cleopatra (Colbert) appears as a powerful, respected, and dignified Queen. Intent on preserving Egypt, she seduces Rome's mightiest leaders, Caesar and Antony. This brilliant ploy leads her to the threshold of world domination. Though Cleopatra's brother, Ptolemy, seeks to rule, he never appears on screen. No scenes depict brother-sister hatred.

Scene: 48 BC. Egypt's prime minister kidnaps Cleopatra, mockingly referring to the bound and gagged ruler as "Queen of the Desert." With you "out of the way," he says, "the Romans can deal with your brother" (Ptolemy). The warrior queen escapes, killing the prime minister. She returns home in time to prevent Caesar (William) from signing an ill-advised treaty with Ptolemy, an agreement that would rob "Egypt's treasury."

• After Caesar sees Cleopatra stab an assassin, he vows to divorce his wife and to wed her. Recognizing her political ambitions, he takes Cleopatra to Rome.

• "I am Egypt," says sultry Cleopatra to Caesar. The Queen's presence in Rome causes criticism. As slaves carry her on a decorative litter, Romans quip, "Caesar is tamed by a woman." Antony (Wilcoxon) berates his friend, "That woman is making an Egyptian out of you. [You may] change the character of Rome to Egypt. But you cannot bring an Egyptian Queen as ruler over Rome."

• When Caesar is assassinated, Antony visits Cleopatra. Thinking Roman senators dispatched Antony to set her "in chains," she gets him drunk, cooing, "I'm dressed to lure you, Antony." And she does. At first, she intends to use the warrior, not fall in love with him.

• Cleopatra's barge. En route from Tarsus to Egypt, she seduces Antony. The camera reveals hundreds of dipped oars moving in flawless rhythm; decorative Egyptian women place pearls and jewels at the lovers' feet. Encompassing the couple, "birds from the Nile." Cleopatra coddles Antony with wine and "clams from the sea."

• Resting in Antony's arms, the serene Cleopatra concedes, "I am no longer a Queen; I am a woman." Though passionately in love, she becomes angry with Antony when learning he plans not "conquest, but union." In Rome, Octavian (Keith) protests Cleopatra's influence, shouting, "Who is this poisonous snake that wrecks our men?"

• Antony could return home a hero, provided he kills Cleopatra. He refuses. Fearing for her lover's safety, Cleopatra goes to Rome with an olive branch. She offers Egypt to Octavian, provided he spares Antony.

• Actium. Antony's Egyptians battle Octavian's Romans. Wrongly assuming Cleopatra has betrayed him, the defeated Antony kills himself. Seeing Antony die, Cleopatra, too, takes her own life.

Note: The movie contains eye-filling shots of licentious Egyptians; writhing dancing girls, scantily-clad maidens bearing jewels, and virgins riding bulls.

• Consider the accomplishments of another Egyptian queen, Hatshepsut. She ruled Egypt from 1503 to 1482 BC. Under Hatshepsut's jurisdiction, the arts flourished and Egyptians prospered, initiating fresh trade routes to the East.

Cleopatra (1963), TCF. *Elizabeth Taylor, Richard Burton, Rex Harrison, Roddy McDowall.* Filmed in Egypt. EGYPTIANS, RECOMMENDED

In the early 1960s, this $40 million movie was the most expensive one ever made. Running 4 hours, 3 minutes, it was also the longest American-made commercial film. It opened at New York's Rivoli Theater, 12 June 1963, sans intermission.

Featured here are Cleopatra's (Taylor) courtships and fatal love affairs with Caesar (Harrison) and Antony (Burton), complete with a poison asp slithering from a basket to Cleopatra's breast. Especially impressive are the spectacular barge and battle displays, dazzling dance routines, Cleopatra's suicide, and the Queen's arrival in Rome; she appears on a grand, portable sphinx. Creative cinematography, realistic costumes, and authentic ancient Roman and Egyptian settings provide spectacular sights. The scenario also refers to Roman politics and Egypt's contributions to societies, noting that Rome's greatness came about, in part, because of Egypt's richness of corn, wheat, gold, and jewels.

Scene: Declares a Roman, "Cleopatra speaks seven languages." To gain power she "was known to employ torture, imprison [innocents] and even [use] her own sexual talents, which are said to be considerable." Later, Caesar tells Cleopatra "You have a way of mixing politics and passion."

• The movie's primary Egyptian villain is Cleopatra's brother, King Ptolemy. The screeching, effeminate Ptolemy and his inept sidekick try to poison Cleopatra.

• Cleopatra discovers that Caesar's soldiers accidentally destroyed Alexandria's "Great Library"; mourning the loss of never-to-be replaced classics, she berates the ruler.

• Elizabeth Taylor's Cleopatra, like Claudette Colbert's, lives for Egypt. The women do not appear as serpents or vampires, but rather as splendid, stunning Queens, devoted to their beaus, steadfast and attentive to the welfare of their people. Cleopatra's love of Antony takes precedence over political ambitions. Before Richard Burton's Antony confronts Octavian's Roman forces at the Battle of Actium, Taylor's Cleopatra embraces him, declaring, "Without you, this isn't a world I want to live in, much less conquer."

Note: To the producer's credit, Cleopatra's attendants are not projected as mute caricatures, rather as loyal, lovely, and intelligent women.

• Both the 1963 and 1934 *Cleopatra* movies are available on videocassette.

• The X-rated film, *The Notorious Cleopatra* (1970), displays Cleopatra, Antony, and Caesar making a different kind of history; they advance kinky bedroom maneuvers.

• See *Serpent of the Nile* (1953) and *Legions of the Nile* (1960).

• A 1998 *Highlander* TV segment entitled "The Pharaoh's Daughter" focuses on Cleopatra's reawakened handmaiden, Nefertiti. The 2,000-year-old Nefertiti appears as a vindictive and unforgiving Egyptian. This lovely moves to kill villains and innocents, including the Highlander's friend, as well as the protagonist himself. Defending himself, he beheads her, albeit reluctantly.

Cleopatra Jones (1973), WB. *Tamara Dobson.* CAMEOS

The heroine, Ms. Jones (Dobson), stamps out a narcotics ring. Aiding her are a karate-chopping agent, Arabs, Turks, and Frenchmen.

Scene: Turkey. As credits roll, bedouins and camels approach some tents. Ms. Jones emerges from a helicopter. Greeting her are three Arabs wearing white burnooses, plus French and Turkish military officers. Says Jones, "This is the largest poppy field I've ever seen, worth $30 million on the street. Burn it!" Jones' pilot, "Hisham," ignites the field.

Cleopatra's Daughter (1961), a.k.a. Daughter of Cleopatra, Explorer. Italian, dubbed in English. *Debra Paget, Robert Alda, Erno Crisa, Corrado Pani.* EGYPTIANS, MAIDENS

This sword-and-sandal scenario shows corrupt Egyptian guards killing Egyptian villagers.

Scene: Egypt, twenty years following Queen Cleopatra's death. Palace guards hold Shila (Paget), the daughter of Cleopatra, hostage. If Shila does not agree to marry evil King Nemorat (Pani), she'll "be thrown to the crocodiles."

• Palace conspiracies. After Nemorat's Uncle, Kefren (Ceisa), poisons the pharaoh, he frames Shila for King Nemorat's death. Kefren's guards dispatch and seal Shila beneath the pyramids, inside the pharaoh's tomb. Arriving in time to save Shila is Resi (Manni), a warm and compassionate physician who loves her. Resi's heroics prevent Cleopatra's daughter from being buried alive inside the crumbling tomb. Several not-so-nice Egyptians, however, perish. The liberated Shila now moves to bring "happiness to tortured souls."

• Romance triumphs; Shila and Resi ride off together.

Cloak and Dagger (1984), UNI. *Dabney Coleman, Henry Thomas.* SP: Tom Holland. CAMEOS, VILLAINS

This espionage thriller concerns a young computer expert's friendship with an imaginary international spy. The opening displays America's enemies—Russians and Arabs.

Scene: The Russian Embassy. Jack Flack (Coleman) the swashbuckling super-spy, brings down some Russian agents. Suddenly, a bearded Arab wearing a white thobe appears. Drawing a dagger, he charges Flack. The agent twists the dagger into the Arab's stomach. Finis.

Club Paradise (1986), WB. *Robin Williams, Jimmy Cliff, Bobby Ghisays, Louis Zorich.* SP: Harold Ramis, Brian Doyle-Murray. See *Earthbound* (1980). CAMEOS, SHEIKHS

A dense Arab sheikh (Ghisays) surfaces in two scenes, each about a minute. The Arab and a Swiss businessman (Zorich) want to buy an unspoiled island resort. If successful, they intend to build commercial eye-sores, ruining the island's natural surroundings. Saving the day, a retired Chicago fireman.

Scene: An unspoiled resort in the Caribbean. Visiting fireman Jack Moniker (Williams) and the island's Reggae performer, Ernest Reed (Cliff), worry that outsiders will purchase the resort and then erect high-rise condominiums, factories, even a nuclear power plant.

• The sheikh's yacht, "Moolah." The sheikh's cohort hands him a model of an Arabian Nights domicile, boasting, "I have a surprise, a new residence for you." The sheikh examines the model. Expressing excitement, the Arab considers turning the island into his private Arabian fantasy land. Quips a henchman, "Incredible. This guy's got a heart like Dumbo." Hearing the word, "Dumbo," the Arab frowns. Explains an aide, "Dumbo the elephant, with the big ears." As he does not understand English, the Arab emits a perplexed look.

• Fireman Jack cautions the main player behind the deal, Mr. Big, "I know how these guys operate. A year from now your little Swiss and Arab friend will turn on you, and give you a hosing for a lifetime." Mr. Big nods.

• In the end, the Swiss and the sheikh are advised, "Forget this place. You guys are going to love the Caymans." Cut to the sheikh's yacht, the "Moolah," traveling on.

The Cobra (1968), ACI. *Dana Andrews, Peter Martell, Anita Ekberg, Omar Zolficar, Giovanni Petrucci.* *NS. Notes from VAR (10 April 1968). VILLAINS

International actors appear in this thriller focusing on US Treasury agents trying to nab smugglers who transport opium via desert oil pipelines. Most of the action occurs in Lebanon; other locales are Turkey and Jordan. In this one, the only good Arab is a dead Arab.

Summary: Arab heroin traffic is controlled by Peking's "Red Chinese" and their cohorts. The villains intend "to destroy the moral fiber of our [American] nation." Enter the protagonist, Martell (Rand). After firing bullets into an unarmed Arab, he eradicates an oil-rich trafficker and boasts: "I'm your judge, jury, executioner."

Code Name Vengeance (1989), AI. A David Winters film. *Robert Ginty, Cameron Mitchell, Shannon Tweed, James Ryan.* P, D: David Winters. VILLAINS, WORST LIST

Arabs vs. Arabs, vs. Americans. An ex-CIA agent crushes brutal Arabs.

Scene: Contemporary Arabia. The rebel leader Tabrak (Ryan) and his black-robed men liquidate Arabs. Invading a pro-Western ruler's home, they kidnap Crown Prince

Tala, his mother, and Ms. Cooper, the prince's US tutor. Quips a US agent, "Well, I guess that's the end of [our] missiles being installed over there."

• The "hawk-nosed" Tabrak delivers Ms. Cooper's head on a platter; stuffed inside the victim's mouth, a note demanding he rule the country. "This Tabrak," says an American, "is like a jackal." See *Paradise* (1981).

• Tabrak's Arabs tie their Arab prisoners to a tree and shoot them.

• At a hospital, Western doctors and nurses attend Tabrak's wounded. Abruptly, Tabrak's troops enter. Do they express thanks? No! They shoot everyone, even bedridden patients. One of Tabrak's men rapes an Arab woman. Another pours gas over a fellow Arab, burning him alive.

• Tabrak declares: "Victory is at hand. We will throw off the diseased Western puppet (the current ruler) who claims to be of our blood." His cohorts raise clenched fists.

• Says Prince Talal, "I'm not scared, mother, but who is going to help us?" To the rescue, ex-CIA agent Monroe Beiler (Ginty). Monroe brings order out of chaos. He obliterates Tabrak and his Arabs.

Commando (1964), AI. *Stewart Granger, Carlos Casaravilla.* See *Lost Command* (1966). VILLAINS

Outnumbered legionnaires vs. Algerian brutes.

Scene: The 1961 French-Algerian war. Captain LeBlanc (Granger) and his legionnaires move to nab and bring back alive Ben Balad (Casaravilla), an Algerian rebel leader. LeBlanc is told, "Without him, the whole rebellion has to collapse. [If anything goes wrong] you'll have three million Arabs chasing you."

• At a bar, a lovely Arab dancer performs. One legionnaire places a key into a slingshot and fires, striking the dancer's navel and injuring her. No one cares.

• A legionnaire who prefers to see only "dead Arabs" tells Balad, "All Arabs look alike to me." He calls Balad a "pig," then spits in his face. No one contests his actions.

• In the desert, legionnaires pick off Arabs. Dozens of dead Algerians fill the frame.

• Outside a church, the bodies of an Arab man and woman; Ben Balad's men killed the couple. Only their son survives. On a wall, this inscription: "Death to traitors. Algeria for the Algerians." Grunts a legionnaire, "Nice way to give Algeria to the Algerians."

• Algerians are compared to Nazis. Ben Balad moves to comfort the dead couple's son, placing his hand on the boy. Quips a legionnaire, "Very moving. When I was a little boy, a Nazi officer put his hand on my head, just like that. But, before he shot my parents, not after!" Ben Balad asks Capt. LeBlanc why this one legionnaire hates Arabs. Says the Captain, "He had a wife, young and pretty. One day he came home and he found her on the floor, with her throat cut. And that's not all that happened."

• Algerians vs. Christians. A cross appears in the foreground—dead legionnaires in the background.

• Ben Balad's men capture LaBlanc's friend, Garcia. They tie Garcia to a post and ignite a fire. To prevent Garcia from suffering, LaBlanc shoots him. He denounces the Arabs' ruthless act. Says Ben Balad, "And the French, Captain? Have you never tortured or murdered? Are you so pure? There are no rules in this war and that's what makes it so frightening. There is only one tragedy for all of us." (But the movie doesn't portray LaBlanc's legionnaires as barbarians.)

• Captain LaBlanc returns his prisoner to the fort. He expects to see Ben Balad hang. But the war has ceased. Ben Balad is whisked off to Paris, protected by the same Frenchmen who earlier sought his demise. Before he departs, Balad extends his hand to LaBlanc, who takes it.

Commandos (1968), Star Classics. *Lee Van Cleef, Jack Kelly.* CAMEOS, VILLAINS

The North African desert. An Arab appears as a shady hotel keeper.

Scene: October 1942. Italian and US forces confront a fat, unshaven Arab in his "Hotel Du Paris." The Arab, who dons a bright red fez, confesses he housed the "enemy." Later, the grubby Arab pleads, "Save the well, sir, [and] may Allah protect you."

Company Business (1991), MGM. *Gene Hackman, Mikhail Baryshnikov, Nadim Sawalha.* SP, D: Nicholas Meyer. See Meyer's *The Seven-Per-Cent Solution* (1976). CAMEOS, SHEIKHS

An unscrupulous Saudi as an arms merchant.

Scene: CIA and KGB agents pursue rogue CIA agent Sam Boyd (Hackman) and ex-KGB agent Pyiotr Grushenko (Baryshnikov). The duo seek sanctuary in Berlin. Sam decides to hide out with Faisal (Sawalha), a Saudi arms dealer "so rich he could ski uphill." Faisal used to sell Stinger Missiles with defective parts to the Contras, says Sam. He became really "rich. He's got toilet seats that are 14-karat gold, more beautiful women than you've ever seen outside of Las Vegas."

• Surprisingly, Faisal's Berlin mansion has no electricity; the place is vacant. Why? Because Faisal's destitute. The Arab complains to Sam that he can no longer hawk weapons to anyone, "Contras, Cubans, Lithuanians, not even the PLO." Thus, Sam and Pyiotr depart. Abruptly, CIA agents enter the mansion, killing Faisal.

Note: NYT critic Vincent Canby writes the "movie has a *funny scene* [emphasis mine] involving a Saudi Arabian arms merchant" (24 April 1992).

• Screenwriter Meyer mocks Japanese and Columbians. A fat Columbian surfaces as a drug dealer. One character quips, the Japanese "own the whole fuckin' country."

Condorman (1981), Disney. *Michael Crawford, Oliver Reed.* CAMEOS, SHEIKHS

ABSCAM revisited.

Scene: The hero, Condorman, dupes the Russian villain. How? By posing as a bearded sheikh. Perpetuating the ludicrous Arab stereotype, Condorman dons a thobe and sunglasses, wears gaudy rings, and drives a Rolls-Royce. Condorman even speaks with a phoney Mideast accent. An onlooker falls for the ruse, saying, "He was nothing more than a bedouin. Then, several months ago he struck oil, and now he's the richest man in the world."

• A businessman asks Condorman-as-Arab, "Do you think our North Sea will produce oil?" Grunts Condorman before exiting, "Ugh! A caesar salad's worth." And, "Ugh! I have to close a deal for Rhode Island."

Coney Island (1943), TCF. *Betty Grable, George Montgomery, Cesar Romero, Phil Silvers.* CAMEOS, SHEIKHS, MAIDENS

This film features "In My Harem," a 1913 tune by Irving Berlin. At the time Berlin wrote it, Arabia was under the Ottoman Empire and many Americans, even US immigration officials, confused Arabs and Turks. When my Lebanese grandparents arrived at Ellis Island in the early 1920s, US immigration officers wrote "Turk" on their documents.

Scene: Surfacing at an American fairground, two con artists (Montgomery, Silvers). To make a buck, they set up a "cooch show." Feigning to be Arabs, Sultan Ben Asha and Abou, the men don Oriental garb. Determined to "pack 'em in," they promise onlookers "a night in a Turkish harem." They tell onlookers, "Watch a young Turkish maiden sold to the sultan for 20 pieces of silver." And, you'll see "ten genuine Turkish harem girls."

• Cut to Abou, surrounded by coddling, dancing maidens. The women sing Berlin's *In My Harem*. The lyrics adulate American women, not Turkish maidens. Bellows the American looking after a Turkish soldier's harem:

> In my Harem, there's Rosie, Josie, Posie...
> Wives for breakfast, wives for dinner, wives for supper time;
> Lots of fancy dancing and it doesn't cost a dime...
> I've got a thousand wives...
> And ev'ry one of them has got a perfect figure...
> How can a man get lonesome with a thousand wives?
> In my Ha-rem, there's Fannie, Annie, and Jenny,
> And the dance they do would make you wish you were in a harem with Pat Ma-lone.

Note: Also Betty Grable sings "Miss Lulu From Louisville" in black face with a curly black wig.

The Corsair (1914), Eclectic. Silent. *Crane Wilbur, Anna Rose, M.O. Penn.* *NS. Notes from AFIC. SHEIKHS

Sheikhs abduct and imprison women. Pirates vs. Arabs. See *The Long Ships* (1964).

A lecherous Arab sultan (Penn) and a dashing Barbary pirate (Wilbur) fall for Medora (Rose), a lovely Arab slave girl. The lecherous sultan nabs the "captive maiden," placing Medora in his harem. The pirate moves to rescue Medora. The Arab guards grab and imprison him. But, thanks to Medora's inventiveness, she and the corsair escape. As for the debauched sultan, he is "slain in the harem bath."

Courage under Fire (1996), TCF. *Denzel Washington, Meg Ryan.* SP: Patrick Sheane Duncan. D: Edward Zwick. See *G.I. Jane* (1997) and Zwick's *The Siege* (1998). VILLAINS

This first major studio release about the Gulf War displays the telling effects of "friendly fire." Americans kill Iraqis.

Scene: January 1991. As credits roll, CNN stock footage of the Gulf War appears—scenes display Saddam Hussein, President George Bush, Muslims praying, bombs dropping and desert camels.

• The desert. After Lt. Colonel Nathaniel Serling (Washington) prays alongside his troops, he and his colleague say, "Let's kill 'em all; let's eat 'em up!"

• The colonel's tank battalion pursues Iraqis. The Americans destroy an Iraqi tank, and machine-gun faceless Iraqis. Cut to some Iraqi soldiers; their arms raised, surrendering.

• The United States. To ascertain whether Captain Karen Walden (Ryan), a female officer who was killed during the war, merits the Medal of Honor, the colonel interviews three surviving soldiers. Each one relates his version of what happened after their helicopter, flown by Walden, was downed. Four flashbacks reveal US-Iraqi desert battle scenes, showing "ragheads up on the ridge" shooting at American soldiers. Repeatedly, Walden's men kill scores of Iraqis, then blow up an enemy tank. Though Iraqis down Walden's chopper, her men fire away at Iraqi "fuckers" and "ragheads," terminating scores. Walden and her pinned-down soldiers continue killing Iraqis until some rescue choppers arrive, enabling the men to escape. Though the seriously injured Walden is left alone, she grabs a pistol and machine gun, mowing down charging Iraqis. And, the rescue choppers shoot and napalm Iraqis.

Note: Only one actor is crediting with portraying an Iraqi: Bob Aspia as the "Iraqi tank commander." Probably, stunt men portrayed the Iraqis being shot.

Cover-Up (1991). A Manny Coto Film. *Dolph Lundgren, Lou Gossett Jr.* SP: William Tannen. Made in Israel. VILLAINS, MAIDENS

Israel. The scenario focuses on a vengeful marine officer. Two lines label Arab Muslims as extremists and mute Arabs appear as whores, but this film shows that not all movies made in Israel are alike.

Scene: A naval base in Tel Aviv. As two Arab drive a truck full of cabbages and munch sandwiches, the truck suddenly explodes, killing the Arabs and eight marines. Says the TV announcer, "A religious extremist group out of Baghdad has claimed responsibility... A group claiming to be Black October says they are responsible."

• *Los Angeles Times* reporter, Mike (Lundgren), examines photos of Palestinians, saying,: "Black October is the biggest terrorist group we've ever seen. It's based in Iraq. It has links with Shiite Moslems [and the] PLO [and is] "funded by Libya, Iran, as well as Syria." Warns Mike, Black October's "maniacs" acquired a sample of an "odorless nerve gas that kills instantly." They can "kill 50 thousand people, minimum."

• An Arab arms dealer, Adnan Zahadi, kidnaps Mike, telling him him that a US colonel, not Arabs, exploded the truck. The colonel wants America to declare war, explains Zahadi, so he blames the deaths of the marines on Black October.

Note: After the camera reveals a beautiful outdoor Israeli restaurant, cut to the seedy Oasis Hotel, belonging to Arabs. Arab music accents the presence of two whores perched on the hotel's balcony.

The Crusades (1935), PAR. *Loretta Young, Henry Wilcoxon, Ian Keith, Katherine DeMille, C. Aubrey Smit.* P: Cecil B. DeMille, S. Howard Lamb. See *King Richard and the Crusaders* (1954). VILLAINS

The Third Crusade. Richard the Lionhearted and Christian monarchs, whose armies hail from Germany, Hungary, Russia, and Sicily, battle Saladin's coarse Muslims. DeMille's film implies that it is morally right for "religious" Europeans to pursue and murder "unbelieving" Arab Muslims. The footage reveals Muslims as slavers and non-believing savages raping Christian women. Briefly, Saladin appears as a compassionate Muslim leader.

The theme, Muslim Arab vs. Christian Crusader, surfaced in the cinema during the early 1900s. See *A Tale of the Crusades* (1908) and *The Crusaders* (1911).

Scene: Jerusalem, "a city sacred to men." The muezzin calls the faithful to prayer. Intones the narrator, "The Saracens [a medieval word for Muslim Arabs of the Levant] ...are crushing the Christians to death."

• For three-plus minutes, Muslim Arabs lay waste to Jerusalem. Muslims toss Bibles, crosses and icons, including those of the Virgin Mary, into a raging fire. Similar images appear in *El Cid* (1961).

• Inside city walls, Arab slavers auction off chained Christian women. [Actor J. Carrol Naish portrays one of the slave sellers; actress Ann Sheridan appears as one of the Christian slave girls]. One Arab grabs a blonde, asking, "How much am I bid?" When the poor woman asks permission to pray, Arabs mock her. As slavers drag her off, she kisses a cross.

• A Christian hermit (Smith) clutches a cross, warning "the King of the Infidels" Saladin (Keith), "Woe to you, unbeliever." Says Saladin, "My life is in the hands of Allah."

• The hermit returns to England, advising King Richard (Wilcoxon), Let us "go forth to war for the cross. Come to the army of the cross. Fight for the Lord our God."

• In the Levant, Richard meets Saladin, barking, "Bring wine for the infidel." Says Saladin, "We of the true faith drink no wine." Captivated by Richard's wife, Queen Berengaria (Young), Saladin says, "I offer peace to you, foes of Islam." Richard responds to Saladin's peace offer by drawing his huge sword, "We're going to slaughter you," he says. Undaunted, Saladin tosses a silk handkerchief in the air, slicing it with his blade. Richard's men tag his skill "black magic."

• An arrow wounds Queen Berengaria; Saladin rushes her off to his tent, vowing, "I will not let her die." Later, he confesses, "And here is the love of Saladin." Says Berengaria, "It would not bring me happiness; I am your captive. I do not love you."

• Evening. Seeing Crusaders and the hermit approaching the walled city of Acre, a Muslim guard warns, "Halt Christian dog, or we'll kill your Holy Man." Undaunted, the hermit declares, "I command you, in the name of God, attack!" To illustrate that this film's Muslim Arabs, with the exception of Saladin, are barbarians, Muslims brutally slay the hermit.

• God favors European Christians. Singing religious hymns, Richard's men attack and triumph. Later, the victorious Crusaders flaunt "the cross of our Lord, the cross on which He died."

• Though "outnumbered ten to one" the Crusaders move to attack Jerusalem, to rescue their Queen. Sighs Saladin to the Berengaria, "You shall see the foes of Islam swept like dust before the might of Allah." Gasps the Queen, "God forbid."

• A traitor from Richard's camp visits Saladin, offering to kill Richard. "I have no traffic with assassins," says Saladin. "Away with this dog."

• Saladin's soldiers save Richard from doublecrossing European assassins. The grateful King tells Saladin, "By Allah, I wish you had been my brother, not my foe." Explains the Queen, "He (Saladin) saved my life." Saladin proposes a pact, "I offer you peace; all will be free. I offer you terms you could never win." Saladin also asks Richard for Berengaria's hand. Reluctantly, she agrees. Soon, Saladin realizes the Queen loves Richard "deeply"; he returns her. Clutching a cross, she credits not Saladin for her release, but the Christian God.

• Religious hymns underscore shots of enslaved Christian women in chains emerging from Jerusalem's Muslim dungeons. The released prisoners raise crosses. Cut to Christians entering Jerusalem and attending church services. As Saladin initiated the peace accords, why doesn't the camera show devout Arab Muslims and Arab Christians praying in Jerusalem's mosques and churches?

Note: Reel Christian soldiers are not as vicious as reel Muslim Arabs. No scenes show the Christian Crusaders enslaving and abusing Muslim women, or torching mosques.

• Some Italian filmmakers emulated DeMille's scenario. *The Mighty Crusaders* (1961), an Italian "Superscope" film produced by Octavio Poggi and starring Sylva Koscina, displays heroic Christian "crusaders" slashing inferior Muslim "infidels." Those interested in discussing similarities between Arab and black stereotypes should screen this film and DeMille's *The Crusades*, along with D.W. Griffith's *The Birth of a Nation* (1915).

• In the AI release, *The Attack of the Moors* (1964), an Italian movie dubbed in English, the camera reveals Arab Muslims "raiding all of [France's] provinces."[57] The Muslims intend to kidnap and hold hostage the King's two children. This film's Muslims fight Christians, and battle fellow Muslims. Again, reel Muslims "show no mercy"; they bind and whip Christian women and children. Conversely, the heroic French knight, Roland, tells Salina, the Muslim heroine tending his wounds, "A Christian knight does not fight women." Though Salina loves Roland, she balks. "Your faith divides us; I'm a Muhammadan," she says. Sighs Roland, "Our God is the same if you love me." (The fact is, Muslims, Christians, and Jews *do* believe in the same God.)

Salina learns that the Muslim leader wooing her, Ibn Saleh, has killed her father. She shouts, "You murdering swine! Marry you? Never!" In time, the King of France arrives, assisting Roland's forces; they rout Ibn Saleh's Muslims. "This is a great victory for Christianity," boasts the king. Surprisingly, Salina decides to marry Roland. Why? Because final frames reveal that she is part-Christian. Her Muslim handmaiden explains, "Your mother was not of the same God and faith as we are. She was a noble Spanish lady." See *The Sheik* (1921).

• An historical footnote on the crusades. Western religious and political leaders garnered support for their conflict against the Saracens, a people with whom most Europeans had no contact by launching propaganda campaigns depecting the Muslims as violent, backward, and inhuman infidels. In 1095, Pope Urban II advanced the demonization process, calling Muslims "the wicked race... wholly separated from God." And, in 1095, the Pope also ordered Europe's Christians to seize the Holy Sepulcher in Jerusalem.[58]

Cup Final (1992), Local Production. Hebrew and Arabic, with English subtitles, some English. *Moshe Igve, Muhammad Bakri, Sharon Alexander.* SP: Eyal Halfon. Filmed in Israel. PALESTINIANS, BEST LIST

Humane Palestinians.

Scene: June 1982. As the Israeli Army invades Lebanon, the camera reveals bound and blindfolded Palestinian captives.

• Though PLO fighters blow up an Israeli vehicle, two Israeli soldiers survive, Galilli (Alexander) and Cohen (Igve). As the Palestinian squad heads for Beirut, a Palestinian orator-doctor, Dottore, tends Galilli's wounds.

• The Palestinians serve coffee and freshly picked lemons to their Israeli prisoners. Yet, Cohen says, "These guys are bastards."

• One Palestinian mentions the "Mejiddo jail"; Galilli corrects him, saying, "Kibbutz Mejiddo, Kibbutz!" Counters Dottore, "My family had a lot of land in Mejiddo, now we live in Geneva." Affirms Abu Eyash, you Israelis confiscated our land; my home was "Beit Sachur, near Jerusalem."

• An Israeli squad fires on the Palestinians. The prisoner, Galilli, runs off and is fatally shot. One Palestinian comforts the other prisoner, Cohen, saying, "Do not be afraid." Cohen, who runs a boutique, has a wife and two children.

• When Ziad (Bakri), an ex-pharmacy student whose family resides in Italy, searches Cohen's wallet, he uncovers two tickets to Barcelona's World Cup soccer matches. "You like football?" Ziad asks Cohen. The Israeli nods, saying he supports Italy, "a very good team." Later, Ziad tells his men to give Cohen the good news, "Italy won, two-nil."

• Abu Eyash's Lebanese friends welcome the Palestinians into their home. The men switch on the TV and watch soccer. Suddenly, a young Palestinian squad member, Fatchi, a diabetic, passes out. As he has no more insulin, he could soon die.

• Cohen and a Palestinian clad in a blue tuxedo bounce a ball. Soon, Palestinian soldiers join in, playing soccer. Afterwards, Cohen shows the squad his wife's photograph.

• The men come across an Arab wedding ceremony, complete with Arab food, music, and dancing. Cohen dances with a young Palestinian woman.

• Told that needed insulin for Fatchi may be acquired from a Christian village, George dons a crucifix; he and Dottore go there.

• George and Dottore return to the camp with a large box of insulin. When Fatchi moves to thank them, he steps on a booby trap and is killed.

• Near Beirut, the squad takes cover in a damaged facility, the "Paradise Club." Cohen and Ziad play pool. Each time Ziad sinks a ball, he shouts the names of Palestinian cities—"Nablus, Hebron."

• The men are in need of food. Yet, Ziad concentrates on locating a TV set so they can watch Brazil play Italy. Eventually, the squad comes across a posh, deserted home. Here, they watch the soccer match. Upstairs, Cohen takes a bath. The squad's only extremist, Shukri, grabs the naked Cohen, dumping his head into the toilet, humiliating the Israeli. Ziad appears, forcing Shukri to stop.

• The Palestinians approach Beirut; a sniper shoots Dottore dead. Cohen goes berserk, fearing the Palestinians will now shoot him. Comforts George, "Relax, nobody wants to kill you."

• Cohen sees Beirut's night lights, sighing, "Haifa." Muses Abu Eyash, "Who knows what's waiting for us in Beirut?"

• Cohen knows the Israelis are near Beirut. He tries to convince the Palestinians to surrender, promising he will help them with the Israelis.

• Cohen asks Ziad whether Italy or Germany will win the match? "Italy, of course," affirms Ziad. Cohen says, "Of course, we must win." "We must win," nods Ziad. Hoping Ziad will not be killed, Cohen gives the Palestinian his soccer ticket.

• Beirut, evening. At a road block, Israeli guards, too, watch the final soccer match on television. Abruptly, the soldiers spot the squad. They fire, seriously injuring Abu Eyash. Ziad rushes to aid his friend. The Israelis shoot him. George and Mussa are also killed.

• Stock footage shows the Italians winning the world cup. Cut to an Israeli ambulance attending injured Palestinians. Cut to Cohen wearing a Palestinian kuffiyeh. Alone, he grieves.

Note: See Eyal Halfon's telling feature, *Circus Palestina* (1998). The film focuses on European circus performers in the West Bank, their encounters with Israelis and Palestinians. Scenes display Palestinians under occupation raising their flag, Israelis destroying it. Confesses the Israeli protagonist, "Too many promises have been given to too many people on one land." The film was financed by the Fund for the Promotion of Israeli Quality films.

Cupid versus Women's Rights (1912). Silent. *NS.

I could locate no reviews, only this: Romance "in the shadows of the pyramids."

The Curse of the Mummy's Tomb (1964), COL. *Terence Morgan, Fred Clark, Ronald Howard, Jeanne Roland, George Pastell, Bernard Rebel, Dickie Owen.*
EGYPTIANS

Beware Ramses' two murdering sons, Omar and Adam. Omar, a reawakened tomb mummy, kills intruders. Adam, Omar's "immortal" brother, kills him.

Scene: "Egypt, in the year 1900"; the desert. The camera reveals a tortured Westerner, Professor Dubois (Rebel), his arms bound to two poles. Three clad-in-black Egyptians approach Dubois; one pulls a knife. Smiling, he plunges the blade into Dubois' stomach. Next, he cuts off the professor's hand, tossing it to a leering cohort. Vultures fill the screen.

• In the desert, the heroine, Annette Dubois (Roland), echoes anxieties, "These old tombs give me the creeps."

• An Egyptian official, Hashmi Bey (Pastell), believes in tomb curses; he warns visiting Western archaeologists, "All persons present at the opening of the coffin shall die. You cannot run away from the curse of the mummy's tomb. We're all doomed to die for this act of desecration." And they do die.

• Bey's advice is ignored; "the finest mummified specimen ever known" is unearthed and whisked off on a world tour.

• Victorian London, brother vs. brother. Surfacing is the revived mummy, Omar. He is the brother of an immortal, Adam Beauchamp. Stealing through the fog, Omar stalks brother Adam. When Adam moves to kill the lovely Annette, Omar stops him.

• London's underground sewers. Adam and Omar battle; tons of debris crash down, killing Ramses' two sons.

Note: A monkey eats a tasty "Turkish Delight."

The Dancer of the Nile (1923), William P.S. Earle Production. Silent. *Carmel Myers, Malcolm McGregor, June Eldridge.* *NS. Notes from AFIC.
EGYPTIANS, MAIDENS

An Egyptian princess and an Egyptian dancing girl vie for Prince Tut's affections. Tut weds the dancer. As for the princess, she "finds another prince and marries him."

Dangerous When Wet (1953), MGM. *Esther Williams, William Demarest, Donna Corcoran, Richard Alexander.* D: Charles Walters. EGYPTIANS

In this aquatic tale, all the swimmers are in great shape, except for one—a sour, blubbery Egyptian.

When Katy (Williams), a gifted American, decides to swim the English channel an elderly seaman offers some advice, "I've seen 'em come and I've seen 'em go. And there's many [of swimmers] I've helped drag out, more dead than alive." Abruptly, waddling duck music underscores the appearance of one aspirant, "The Egyptian" (Alexander). Katy's amazed mother (Corcoran) watches the dour-looking, grossly overweight swimmer walk towards the coast. She shakes her head and frowns, as if to say: This man belongs in a Fat Farm! Next, competitors from other nations appear: Germany, Denmark, Canada, Argentina, Brazil, England, Norway, Finland, and France. Unlike the clumsy and chubby Egyptian, these muscular swimmers are physically fit.

Dark Streets of Cairo (1940), a.k.a. Streets of Cairo, UNI. *Sigrid Gurie, Katherine DeMille, George Zucco, Rod LaRocque, Ralph Byrd, Eddie Quillan, Sigfried Arno, Yollande Mollot.* SP: Alex Gottlieb. EGYPTIANS

Observed the NYT critic, this film's Egyptians are "knife throwers and assorted evil-doers who plot killings, gem thefts and sundry forms of torture for their victims in the murky taverns of Cairo" (2 December 1940).

Scene: In Cairo, an American archaeologist is murdered. Introducing Abadi (Zucco), a wily merchant. He and his "secret defenders" steal the "seven jewels of the seventh Pharaoh." A gem cutter makes copies of the jewels, but Abadi's thugs kill the artisan, and two other Arabs.

• A US photographer, Jerry Jones (Quillan), hands an Arab a flash bulb; it explodes, covering the man's face with a dark substance. The frightened Egyptian runs off.

• Jerry is told, when Egyptians "want to get rid of someone" they take him for "a trip down the Nile." The villain Hessien (Brandon) calls Jerry "one of the infidels from the American expedition."

• Another sleazy, pathetic merchant: The Egyptian Khattab (Arno) informs the US protagonists, Ellen (Gurie) and Dennis (Byrd), that nine dollars is a fair price to pay for a showy trinket. "I'm a poor man," he purrs; "my wife and children haven't eaten all day." They bargain; Khattab accepts seventy-five cents. So much for reel Egyptian candor.

• The action shifts to Brooklyn; Hessien intends to kill Jerry and his ex-sweetheart, Margo (Mollot). Hessien tosses knives at the couple; Jerry tags Hussien, "fink-face."

• Back in Cairo, Ellen enters Abadi's shop. Seeing her, Dennis exclaims, "A white woman under forty! Is this a mirage?" The implication here?—that Egyptian women are not "white"? Abadi holds Ellen hostage, promising Dennis he will not harm her. Dennis socks the Arab, declaring, "I never trusted a snake before."

• Abadi's attractive Western wife, Shari (deMille), also loves a Westerner—Inspector Joachim (LaRocque). Shari helps Joachim trap the "snake." Passing through a secret revolving door, they move to recover the stolen "jewels of the pharaoh."

• Thanks to Shari and Joachim, the police nab the "secret defenders." Abadi is liquidated and the stolen jewels are returned.

• Now rid of their oppressive Arab mates, the Western heroines embrace Western men. Brooklyn's Margo embraces Jerry; Shari unites with Inspector Joachim.

Note: Other Egyptians appearing in this film are a blind beggar, deceitful waiters, and a jazz band—"Stuff Abdullah and the Cairo Hot Cats."

A Daughter of the Congo (1930), Micheaux Pictures. *Loretta Tucker, Clarence Reed.* *NS. Notes from Alan Gevinson's *Within Our Gates: Ethnicity in American Feature Films, 1911–1960* (p 262). VILLAINS

In this, the first talking picture produced by an African-American film company, Arab slavers kidnap a mulatto girl.

Africa. En route to marry the powerful Chief Lodango, Lupelta, a young mulatto woman raised by Africans, pauses to bathe. Abruptly, Arab slavers capture Lupelta and her maid. Cut to heroic African-American officers serving with the 10th US Cavalry. "They encounter the [Arab] slave hunters, rescue Lupelta, and imprison the men responsible for her capture."

A Daughter of the Gods (1916), FOX. Silent. *Annette Kellerman, William Shay, Hal De Forest, Rica Allen, Edward Boring.* *NS. Notes from AFIC (p 194). MAIDENS, SHEIKHS

Gnomes defeat Arabs. An Arab prince opts to romance a mermaid, rather than an Arab. A sultan and two Arab women, "treacherous Zarrah," and "The Witch of Evil," vs. fellow Arabs. See *Beast of Morocco* (1966).

The Witch of Evil (Allen) vows to employ her powers and bring back to life Prince Omar (Shay), the sultan's son. On one condition. The ruler (De Forest) must help her "destroy" Anita (Kellerman), a beautiful mermaid. He agrees. Thus, Omar is restored. The Sultan imprisons Anita, but her dancing arouses him. Before he moves to take Anita, Prince Omar arrives, whisking her safely off to "Gnome-land."

Scheming to grab the sultan's lands, "a nearby sheikh" places his evil daughter, Zarrah (Horner), into the ruler's harem. Zarrah promptly murders the sheikh, then "instigates a revolt." Anita and the gnomes charge the sultan's palace, routing Zarrah's Arab cohorts. Zarrah, who survives the attack, moves to secure Prince Omar. As Omar is repulsed by her "advances," Zarrah "stabs him to death." In the end, Omar's soul is being "reunited to the spirit of Anita."

Kellerman, an international star, appears nude and nearly nude. Fox re-released the film in 1920, using this blurb: "The screen marvel that will never know a yesteryear."

David and Bathsheba (1951), TCF. *Gregory Peck.* CAMEOS, EGYPTIANS

A one-liner. Egyptians vs. Hebrews.

When David (Peck) receives an ornate dagger from Egypt's ruler, he quips, "The pharaoh probably hopes I'll cut my throat with this."

Dawn of the Mummy (1981), Harmony Gold. *Brenda King, Barry Sattels, John Salvo.* Filmed in Egypt. *NS. Notes from VAR (6 January 1982). EGYPTIANS

Contemporary Egypt. Western photographers search for exotic backdrops. When they come across a mummy's burial ground, they begin setting up their equipment for a shoot.

Promptly, four beautiful American models pose for some "glamour magazines." At the same time, three gold-diggers desecrate the sealed mummy's tomb. Abruptly, the revived mummy and his guards appear—it seems the intense heat from the photographers' lights rekindles a 3,000-year-old royal mummy and his guards. Employing "cannibalism, they bite chunks out of the grave robbers as well as bystanders."

The VAR reviewer writes: "This picture should be entombed permanently."

Days of Wine and Roses (1962), WB. *Jack Lemmon, Lee Remick.* Based on a story by J.P. Miller. CAMEOS, MAIDENS

Two American alcoholics fall in love. Perhaps intending to instill a sexual atmosphere, the producer inserts a bellydancer.

Scene: A public relations specialist (Lemmon) delivers to a yacht, several blonde hookers to entertain his clients. Evening. The men drink and cuddle the blondes; also, an alluring bellydancer, accompanied by Arab musicians, performs.

The original *Days of Wine and Roses*, presented on "Playhouse 90" (2 October 1958) starred Cliff Robertson and Piper Laurie. The teleplay, also penned by J.P. Miller, mocks Arabs. In that production, women-for-hire pamper oil-rich Arabs, not US businessmen. Opening scenes reveal a party in progress. The camera cuts to a scale model of an oil well; photographs of oil wells cover the walls. The American host, Mr. Trayner, declares, "Here's to my pal, Prince Hamid. Long may his association with the Trayner Drilling Corporation be fruitful and glorious." Cut to several on-the-make women encircling the smiling "oil-rich highness." The mute Arab wears a suit and tie; covering his head is a large, striped scarf. As Hamid's robed and burnoosed Arabs mingle, the prince makes a move on the heroine (Laurie). She walks away. The protagonist (Robertson) links up with her, saying that Eddie, a mutual friend, quit his P.R. job. "Why did he quit?" she asks. "A little item called personal integrity," he quips. "Eddie doesn't agree that getting dates for potentates is part of public relations." This four-minute Arab scene concludes with the camera focusing on several women about to cuddle his "oil-rich highness."

Dead of Night (1987), a.k.a. Mirror of Death, Vista. *Julie Merrill.* SP: Gerry Daly. EGYPTIANS, MAIDENS

An Egyptian empress' wicked spirit overpowers the young American heroine, causing her to brutally slay several men.

Scene: After Sara's (Merrill) boyfriend David abuses her, she seeks guidance from an occult book. Suddenly, Sara conjures up the evil spirit of an Egyptian empress, Queen Sura (Merrill).

• Presto! Queen Sura's spirit takes possession of Sara's mind and body. When Sara whispers, "Sura, Sura, Sura," the Egyptian Queen's supernatural fury takes hold. As a result, Sara decapitates David, with her bare hands.

• The Egyptian's evil spirit also directs Sara to rip out Bobby's heart, which she does.

• The Queen even wants Sara to kill April, her sister, and Richard, April's friend. But April knows something is amiss; she cautions Sara, "You are becoming possessed by an ugly demon."

• In time, the police arrive, preventing Sara from killing April. The cops shoot Sura; the Egyptian Queen's body vanishes. As Sura's demonic spirit evaporates, Sara returns to her true, normal self.

Deadline (1986), Virgin Vision. *Christopher Walken, Hywel Bennett, Ette Ankri, Marita Marschall, Amos Lavie.* SP: Hanan Peled. D: Nathaniel Gutman. Filmed in Israel. Israeli actors portray Arabs. PALESTINIANS, VILLAINS

Palestinian extremists vs. Palestinian peacemakers vs. radical Lebanese Christian militiamen, the Phalange. All-too-few scenes show massacred Palestinians. Their bodies are selectively framed to prevent viewers from empathizing with them. Numerous historical inaccuracies advance gross distortions.

Scene: 1982 Lebanon. As bombs explode [viewers are not told that Israeli planes are dropping the bombs], American news reporter Don Stevens (Walken), scans a road map. Cut to three Arab boys, blindfolded; they are shot dead.

• In Beirut, Habib, a Lebanese cab driver tries to pawn whiskey, dirty pictures, and hashish. He tells Stevens, "Out of Women? Out of gas? Call Habib." As Stevens edits his video report for ABS-TV, he hears bombs exploding. "Beirut is the closest thing to hell on earth," he grumbles.

• Stevens interviews a PLO leader, Yessin Abu-Riadd. The Palestinian advocates not war, but "diplomacy." He tells Stevens, "We cannot rely on our Arab brothers." Soon, Stevens learns that he has been duped, that his earlier interviewee was an imposter, a man posing as Yessin. Soon, the imposter is murdered. Cut to a PLO camp resembling a slum. Here, a Palestinian tells Stevens, "It's still time for a gun, not for diplomacy or talk."

• Christian Phalangists kidnap Stevens; they rough him up, cautioning, "This is Lebanon, not Disneyland. [The Palestinians] stole our homes and raped our sisters." Inside the Phalange stronghold, militia members gleefully use live Palestinians as target-practice, shooting Palestinian boys in the back.

• A Palestinian camp. Young men with rifles train to kill. Boasts the leader, "For every PLO fighter we have a brother to take his place."

• The apartment of the gentle Yessin (Lavie) and his five-year old son, Daoud. "If I say to the world I recognize the state of Israel it will not change anything," he tells Stevens. Explains Yessin, the Palestinians are "the world's new wandering Jews." Stevens begins taping the interview. Two Palestinians enter, shooting Yessin.

• Stevens registers anger. Quips Hywel Bennett (Jessop), a British journalist, "It's only a bloody Palestinian. Here, no one needs a reason to kill, just kill as you can." A young Palestinian woman, Samira (Ankri), put Stevens in touch with Yessin. As a result, some Palestinians want to kill her, including her ex-boyfriend, a man interested only in cars and gifts. Samira, who is constantly being maligned by fellow Palestinians, is taken in by Stevens.

• At a refugee camp, Palestinians kick and slug Stevens, then shoot at his car. After a blonde nurse, Linda Larson (Marschall), tends Stevens' bruises, the duo visit a morgue; bodies fill the screen. Among the dead, an ABS journalist. Stevens, too, is marked for death.

• PLO members shoot a Palestinian physician. Believing Linda works for Mossad, the PLO demands Stevens deliver her to them. Linda admits the Mossad did offer her a job. But, she fell in love with Yessin. Now, she aids the Palestinians.

• Linda rushes to Stevens with a warning; the Palestinians intend to "blow up everyone in it [the Phalange office], including the President." If this happens, she says, the Phalange will retaliate, eradicating all the Palestinians in the Chatila compound. Stevens drives off to warn the Israelis. The Israeli soldiers express concern, saying they want everyone to be "alive, alive." The camera shows the Israelis moving toward the Chatila compound, giving viewers the false impression Israeli forces intend to stop the impending calamity.

• Stevens rushes to the Chatila camp, warning a Palestinian leader about the upcoming Phalange attack. "Go where?" sighs the Palestinian. Is just like 1948, 1956, and 1967. Go where? We will not run. We will stay and fight." This scene and others show Palestinians as irrational fanatics, not as butchered innocents. The camera shows camp residents chanting in Arabic, "With our soul and blood." Cut to the battered Samira; Palestinians have beaten her. Christian Phalangists enter the Chatila camp; they massacre innocent women and children, including Samira.

• Final frames show a Palestinian exodus. Among the displaced persons, the wounded five-year-old Daoud, being attended to by Linda.

Note: In reality, an Israeli tribunal looking into the 1982 Israeli invasion of Lebanon found that Israeli General Ariel Sharon was indirectly responsible for the Sabra-Chatila massacre of Palestinian civilians. The bloodbath, carried out by Israel's allies, Lebanese Christian militias, cost Sharon his job; he was forced to resign as defense minister. The Israelis were responsible for the safety of Palestinian families inside the camps; yet "General Sharon, as the Israeli Kahane Commission later substantiated, opened the way for the Phalange [Christian militiamen] to enter the camps and massacre more than a thousand Palestinians," many of whom were killed in their beds, writes Ann Zwicker Kerr. An American Embassy staff member surveying the massacre of Palestinians told Ann's husband Malcomb Kerr, who was serving as president of the American University of Beirut at the time, that the Israelis supervised the whole thing. "I don't know what reports you are getting [in the States] about the massacre," said Professor Kerr, "but here there is no one who doesn't hold Israel responsible, as they let the Haddad people [Phalange] into the area in the first place and sat by and watched through binoculars as the massacre took place."[59]

• For a more compelling and accurate perspective of Lebanon's civil strife, see *West Beirut* (1998).

• BBC Films' made-for-television movie *Deadline* [(1988), John Hurt. SP: Tom Stacey. P: Innes Lloyd. D: Richard Stroud. Released on video in US by City Lights Entertainment] also focuses on feuding Arabs, albeit not so many nor so violent. The action occurs in "oil-rich Awad," where anti-Western "Islamic revolutionaries ignite a coup." Khaki-clad troops invade the palace, seriously wounding the pro-West potentate. Leading the revolt is the arrogant Hatim, the deposed ruler's son. Hatim boasts to a British journalist, "We Arabs are a people of God or we are nothing." Due primarily to the Western journalist's courage, Hatim's takeover ends. The benevolent ruler returns to the throne. The West no longer need fear that Awad's oil flow will cease.

Deal of the Century (1983), WB. *Chevy Chase, Gregory Hines, Richard Libertini.* CAMEOS, SHEIKHS.

Ridicules Latinos, showing them as preening colonels, menacing soldiers, and ragged rebels. And, sheikhs are disdained.

Scene: At an "Arms For Peace" exhibit mute, robed Arabs check out US military weapons. "They [the mute Arabs] don't seem like the kind of people I'd like to associate with," says one American. Barks another, "We're gonna bomb you [Arab] guys. Go home. Go home!"

• The American weapons salesman (Chase) seeks advice on how to negotiate with the Central American despot. The salesman meets with Sheikh Magossi (Libertini), "the richest arms dealer in the world." Near Magossi's jet, the camera reveals the Arab's white Rolls Royce. The plane's interior reveals a posh Arabian nights room. Smiling, the crafty Magossi offers the American negotiating tips.

Death before Dishonor (1987), NWP. *Fred Dryer, Brian Keith, Paul Winfield, Joanna Pacula, Kasey Walker, Rockne Tarkington, Muhammad Bakri.* SP: John Gatliff, Lawrence Kubik. P: Kubik. D: Terry J. Leonard. Filmed in Israel; Israeli actors portray Arab "terrorists." See *Wanted: Dead or Alive* (1987). PALESTINIANS, WORST LIST

Writes NYT critic Janet Maslin, *Death before Dishonor's* Palestinian "terrorists [are] depicted as worthless, lying scum" (20 February 1987). Israelis, the marines, and US Marine Sergeant Jack Burns (Dryer)—a marine with a mission—crush baby-killing Palestinians and a German terrorist.

Scene: Nicosia, the Israeli ambassador's residence. The Palestinian terrorist Gavrill (Bakri) and Sonia, his German cohort (Walker), place a pillow over a guard's head, then shoot him and the maid. Blood and flesh splatter the screen. Next, using an Uzi automatic, the terrorists machine-gun the Israeli ambassador's young son, the ambassador, his wife, and their little girl. Cut to splattered blood on white linen drapes. Cut to spilt red wine slowly trickling from the ivory table cloth. (See opening frames of *The Little Drummer Girl* (1984), here, too, Palestinians kill an Israeli ambassador.)

• A terrorist fortress in the desert. Presenting Ellie (Pacula), an Israeli spy feigning to side with Palestinian radicals. Boasts the bearded terrorist Abu Jihad (Tarkington), "Her photographs of the victims [massacred in refugee camps] brought us much public support."

• Jemal, the US Embassy. Mulling about are camels, sheep, and donkeys, as well as fruit vendors and women wearing black abayas. As soon as Sgt. Jack Burns arrives, unkempt Jemalis attack. Some Jemalis pound their fists onto Burns' car windows; others parade signs stating "DEATH TO AMERICANS," "YANKEE OUT." Still others burn the American flag. An outraged marine barks, "Look at those bastards burning our flag. I'd like to kick their asses." Cut to Sgt. Burns telling a shady Jemali official, "For a one-camel country... you've had a lot of wars over the past twenty years. And you never seem to win any." Cut to Jemali soldiers contesting Palestinian terrorists wearing checked red-and-white kuffiyehs.

• The Palestinians hijack a truck carrying weapons. They grab the guns and kill scores of Jemalis. Barks Burns, "Son-of-a-bitch, those people killed civilians." Sighs an apathetic Jemali, "In the Middle East people die every day. Some from poverty, some from war." Retorts Burns, "Bullshit. Tell your terrorist [Palestinian] friends this, don't get us mad." Affirms the American ambassador, Virgil Morgan (Winfield), "We will not negotiate with terrorists."

• Abu Jihad's hideout. A sly Jemali houseboy makes it possible for the terrorists to kidnap, then torture, Marine Colonel Holloran (Keith) and another marine. When told to talk, the Colonel refuses, saying, "Go fuck yourself." The German, Sonia, grabs a "made-in-America" power tool, drilling a hole in the Colonel's hand. Next, a Palestinian grabs the drill and goes to penetrate a bloodied marine's leg. But, the marine snatches the drill. He thrusts it into the Palestinian's heart, shouting, "Now, you die!" The terrorists shoot the marine, dumping his body in front of the US Embassy.

• The Palestinians capture the Mossad photographer, Ellie. They dump her into the Colonel's cell. "We're in this together," she tells him. Cut to an Israeli Mossad officer telling Sgt. Burns he knows where the terrorists are hiding. Here come the marines. They kill scores of Arabs but fail to rescue the Colonel.

Treatment of Islam: One Palestinian tells the spying houseboy, "Would you like to get back at these marines. Allah will praise you." The boy nods, then blows up the US Embassy and himself. Cut to rubble everywhere, a damaged US flag and a child's doll. [See the doll scene in *Wanted: Dead or Alive* (1987).] Sighs the ambassador, "What kind of savages would do this? Blood everywhere." Observing a dead marine he says, "His mother wouldn't recognize him." Marines are told to "go home," that "this isn't your war." Rebuffs a marine, "It is now!"

• An Israeli agent poses as a Jemali food peddler. He tells his Mossad colleagues, There are "only eight of us" to attack the terrorist stronghold; "that makes it about even—twelve to one." The agent recruits Burns' marines, explaining, "Two international terrorists committed crimes against our people [in Nicosia] and yours. We thought you and your men would like to join us." Asks Burns, "What about [enlisting help from] the Jemalis?" Quips the Israeli, "You can't trust them." The marines link up with the Israelis; off they go to terminate Palestinians.

• At the Palestinian desert fortress, an Abu Jihad cohort quips, "How weak these Americans are." We will "give back the Colonel in little pieces." To the tune of "From the Halls of Montezuma," Israelis and marines enter the fortress, killing 60-plus Palestinians. Sonia and Abu Jihad try to escape; Sgt. Burns drops them. In the end, a marine hoists the American flag.

• A film such as this always makes me ask: What if Hollywood made such extreme anti-Israeli movies in Arab countries, using Arab actors to portray Israeli terrorists? How would such films be perceived?

• An ad for this film in the *St. Louis Post-Dispatch* contained this promotional blurb from Chris Chase's *New York Daily News* review: "John Wayne would have loved *Death before Dishonor*. An old-fashioned adventure movie, fast, slick, bloody and the good guys win."

• On the Today show (17 February 1987), Dryer, whose TV series *Hunter* also vilified Arabs, told NBC-TV's Bryant Gumbel:

Dryer: [The film] is about patriotism and terrorism.
Gumbel: This is another film shot in Israel; some say some of these films involve Arab-
    bashing.
Dryer: Arabs certainly are doing it [committing acts of terrorism]... Arabs have been found
    to take part in it. Those are the ones singled out by the news media.

Note: Credits thank "Lt. Colonel Fred Peck and the United States Marine Corps for Their Cooperation in the Making of this Motion Picture." See *Rules of Engagement* (2000).

The Death Merchants (1973), Liberty. *Jason Robards, Hardy Kruger.* D: Reza S. Badiyi, Uri Massad. Filmed in Germany and Israel. PALESTINIANS, MAIDENS

Israeli agents vs. Palestinian radicals. The film contends that coexistence is not feasible, not between Palestinians and Israelis, nor even between Palestinians and Palestinians.

Scene: Israel. Islam equals violence: After an imam's call to prayer, Palestinians toss a bomb in front of a Palestinian physician's home. The explosion seriously injures Dr. Amir's six-year-old daughter, Munera.

• The movie's primary terrorists are Samir, who operates in Europe, and Amina, Dr. Amir's sister; they reside in Jerusalem. Aware Amina's group is responsible for his son's injury, Dr. Amir slaps her face, saying, "My baby's leg blown off, I spit on you."

• Hamburg, Germany. Palestinian heavies kill a photographer. His body has "eleven stab wounds."

• Berlin. Amina poses as a French journalist. She befriends Arthur (Kruger), a German-Jewish lawyer who lost his father in the Holocaust. Amina and her Palestinian cohorts wrongly believe Arthur is a spy called Herzog.

• Purring "my little Arab girl," Arthur makes love to Amina. The smitten Arthur follows Amina to Israel.

• An Israeli official explains to Arthur that when the Six Day War ended the Israelis never took Palestinian homes. Arthur believes him. No one counters the Israeli's lie about real history.

• Israel's intelligence chief (Robards) informs the naive Arthur, "By the way, she's (Amina) a terrorist." Angry Arthur rebukes all Palestinians, especially Amina. To say "millions of my people are homeless," he says to Amina, is a lame excuse for fighting. People like you "dredge up the past and send the youth to die for he future. I am sick of it." Sighs Amina, "All I have left is hate; please don't take it from me."

• Too late, Amina realizes Arthur is actually not the spy, Herzog. Still, she betrays her lover. In an alley, Amina and her Palestinian cohorts shoot Arthur dead. Afterwards, the Palestinian leader censures Amina. Why? Because she slept with Arthur, a Jew.

Death on the Nile (1978), PAR. *Peter Ustinov, Bette Davis, Angela Lansbury.* Filmed in Egypt. EGYPTIANS

In this Agatha Christie whodunit, Belgian sleuth Hercule Poirot (Ustinov) cruises up the Nile with a boatload of Westerners. Most Egyptians function as backdrops; occasionally, the dialogue demeans Egyptians. The camera reveals, briefly, some local scenes; miniature mosques, sundry souks, and swaying palms. Camels, goats, and donkeys roam about cosmopolitan Luxor, Cairo, and Alexandria.

Scene: A European woman aboard a Nile steamer spots several playful Egyptian youths at the riverbank. The boys wave to her; she smiles. For a brief moment viewers may think cultures connect. But this impression is short-lived. Abruptly, the boys turn around, drop their shorts, and bare their buttocks. The shocked woman scowls.

• Egyptian husbands are devious money-grubbers. When a European governess learns that her French maid may wed an Arab, she protests, saying, "She wants to get married to an Egyptian, no less... I had him checked out. He had a wife already [and] he wouldn't touch her without a dowry." Another Westerner mentions an oppressive Egyptian who "sent his woman back to her people," and still demanded her "dowry."

• The steamer arrives in Luxor; Egyptian children hustle tourists for loose change.

• Egyptian ship captains regularly command the Nile cruises. Yet strangely, *Death on the Nile* shows a stereotypical Indian, not a competent Egyptian, piloting the steamboat.

Deception (1992), MIR. *Andie MacDowell, Liam Neeson, Viggo Mortensen, Lydia Lenossi.* Filmed in Egypt, with a $24 million budget. Original title, *Ruby Cairo.*
EGYPTIANS, MAIDENS

One-third of the action occurs in Egypt. The American heroine, Bessie Faro (MacDowell), encounters foreboding Muslims and a money-grubbing Egyptian woman. Cairo is portrayed as a bed of thieves.

Scene: Alexandria. Arab music underscores Bessie's arrival. She makes a phone call from a tacky pay booth, complete with broken windows and Arab graffiti.

• At Cairo's crowded hall of "Foreign Residents," Bessie pleads earnestly with a selfish clerk, Miss Abou Seif (Lenossi), "You've got to help me." The Egyptian agrees to "assist," provided Bessie pays. "You need to find someone who has a reason to help you," purrs the clerk. Bessie nods, and pulls out a handful of 20- and 50-dollar bills. She is about to give the Egyptian two 20-dollar bills. Suddenly, Abou Seif grabs those, as well as a wad of bills from Bessie's other hand.

• Abou Seif enters Bessie's hotel room. Seeing a candy bowl, she remarks that Egyptian children like sweets, especially during the holy month of Ramadan. "May I?" she asks. Bessie nods. The Egyptian sucks a sweet. Suddenly, she grabs handfuls of "Turkish Delights" and stuffs them inside her purse.

• A Western aid worker, Fergus Lamb (Neeson), finds out that fifty sacks of food are missing from his "Feed the World" shipment. Fergus confronts his distributor, Ed. "Fifty? That's nothing," barks Ed. "In a town like this [Cairo], there's a thief born every minute." Fergus remains mum.

• Briefly, Egypt's Coptic Christians appear. Bessie and Fergus observe a Coptic church service. Says Fergus, "There's real charity here. These people know good things the rest of the world has forgotten. They know how to pray and they know how to look after each other."

• Compare Bessie's visit to a mosque: Harsh Arab music fills the soundtrack, and in stark contrast to the serenity of the Coptic church, the mosque's praying Muslims seem menacing. Frightened, Bessie rushes off.

• Finally, Bessie links up with her presumed dead husband, Johnny (Mortensen). She soon learns that Johnny's a cur; he smuggles poison gas inside bags of food grain; the gas will be used for chemical weapons. Explains Johnny, "You gotta understand. Life is different, here. This ain't a city. It's an ant heap. Ants got it better than these people."

• Johnny decides to kill Bessie. Suddenly, two Mexicans appear on a Cairo street. They shoot Johnny dead.

Note: Compare the portaits of Greeks vs. those of Egyptians. When a troubled Bessie appears at an Athens bank, a lovely Greek bank clerk comforts her, becoming Bessie's helpmate. The benevolent Greek woman's only concern is to assist Bessie. On the other hand, Cairo's clerk, Abou Seif, a cold, stiff opportunist, uses and abuses Bessie.

• *Deception* fails to display attractive Egyptian women wearing stylish hijabs. In many Arab countries, especially Egypt, high-fashion hijab stores are very successful. Women from all over the Mideast visit Cairo's two-floor shopping mall, purchasing a variety of brightly colored hijabs from stores such as the "Salaam Center for Veiled Women," "High Couture," and "Proper Guidance for Women." And, at Wafeya Sadek's Islamic designer studio women buy custom-made "veils of velour, chiffon, satin, or lace." Some are "decorated with beads and other trinkets"; others feature "intricate purple, green or blue paisley patterns."[60]

The Delta Force (1986), CAN. A Golan-Globus film. *Chuck Norris, Lee Marvin, Martin Balsam, Joey Bishop, Lanie Kazan, Robert Vaughn, Robert Forster, David Menachem (Mustafa) Assaf Dayan, Hanna Schygulla, Shelly Winters, George Kennedy.* SP: James Bruner, D: Menachem Golan. P: Golan and Yoram Globus. Filmed in Israel. PALESTINIANS, WORST LIST

Arabs vs. the US military and American civilians, notably Jews and Christians. Unkempt Palestinian and Lebanese skyjackers, members of the "New World Revolution," reroute a passenger jet to Beirut. Wham! An elite US military unit obliterates them. Points out Detroit Free Press critic Tom Hundley, "much of the film was shot in Israel": the Beirut airport scenes at Ben Gurion airport, street scenes in a Jewish suburb near Tel Aviv. Adds Hundley, "the F-16s used in an aerial dogfight were provided by the Israeli military, [but] Israel is not mentioned in the film's credits" (7 February 1986).

Most Golan-Globus films, especially those of the 1980s and 1990s, are filmed in Israel and feature Israeli performers as Palestinian terrorists.

Functioning as bogus-history, this fiction film is loosely based on the June 1985 hijacking of TWA 847. No US commando team terminated the TWA hijackers. After 17 days, diplomats, not miliary men, brought about the release of all 39 hostages, with one major exception: the murdered US sailor. Tragically, real Arab terrorists killed him.

Scene: In Iran, American military forces fail to evacuate Americans hostages.

• Athens, Greece. The camera shows the interior of an ATW [not TWA] airplane. An Arab hijacker bursts from the lavatory, gun in hand, shouting, "God be praised." He and his cohort direct the pilot to "fly to Beirut." As they hit passengers, the Arabs boast, "We are prepared to die... Do not provoke me."

• One hijacker checks Mrs. Goldman's (Kazan) purse, finding a ring. Emblazoned on her ring, a Hebrew inscription. "There are Israelis aboard this plane," he says. Abruptly, male passengers are relegated to one side of the plane, women to the other.

• The hijackers demand the flight attendant, Ingrid (Schygulla), identify passengers with Jewish names. "No," says Ingrid, "remember the Nazis? The death camps? You don't want to be like them." Counters an angry Arab, "The Jews stole Palestine." He slugs Ingrid, then he and his aide savagely beat a US Navy diver. Says a Jewish passenger, "We survived once. We can do it again." Cut to a tattoo on his arm; the man survived a Nazi concentration camp.

• At the Pentagon, the US Command activates the Delta Force, dispatching the unit to Israel. General Woodbridge (Vaughn) tells the commandos, "Israel is America's best friend in the Middle East." Major McCoy (Norris) and Colonel Alexander (Marvin) concur with the general. The elated Colonel Alexander tells the Israelis, "You guys have done it before. Now it's our turn."

• On the plane, the terrorists nab an American with Russian roots. The man protests, "I'm not Jewish; I'm not a Jew." Abruptly, Father O'Malley (Kennedy) steps forward saying, "I'm Jewish, just like Jesus Christ"; the Arabs slug him. These Muslim Arab skyjackers hate Christians. Shouting "Allah be praised" and "May Allah grant us this victory," they torture innocent passengers. One Arab even snatches a nun's cross. See *Hostage* (1986).

• Abdul (Forster), a Palestinian who acts as a Nazi, announces, "We have declared war against the US Zionists and Israel. It's your government we fight, your White House... One day I will go there. I will drive a truck, and the truck, it will blow... Don't think we don't have friends in America. Don't be surprised. One day, one day..." Abdul vows to kill all the hostages, one "every five minutes."

• After beating the US Navy diver, the terrorists shoot and toss the young man's body onto the runway.

• The plane lands in Beirut. Cut to several huge posters of a grim Ayatollah Khomeini. Terrorists wearing black hoods greet their "brothers." Intending to "manipulate the press," they free women and children. Whispers a youngster, "They don't like Jews, Mama." She nods, "No, they don't like Jews." the terrorists haul off the Jewish hostages, covering their heads with hoods.

• A Greek Orthodox priest appears; quips a terrorist, "I don't trust the priest." Cut to the priest informing Israelis where the hostages are hidden; the terrorists kill him.

• US Major McCoy receives attack orders. "It's a go; take 'em down," he says. Posing as tourists the Delta Force team arrives in Beirut; they crush the Arabs and free the Jewish hostages. The Major fires a rocket, blasting Abdul. Growls McCoy, "Sleep tight, sucker." After exterminating 50-plus Arabs, the commandos go to Israel, and receive a hero's welcome.

Note: Actor Lee Marvin was asked his opinion of the film; "I like what the picture says... Audiences love to see the bad guy get it. Well, go see *Delta Force*," said Marvin. Adding, "we start blowing up everybody. That's the good old American revenge."[61]

• The "biggest party of the entire [1986] American Film Market was Cannon Group's black-tie gathering for 3,500 to 4,000 to celebrate the opening of its new building." Among the attendees were "15 or so protestors from the American-Arab Anti-Discrimination Committee holding a candlelight vigil to protest *The Delta Force*." The protest "turned out to be something of a non-event, though police were everywhere."[62]

• Writes Vincent Canby in the NYT, *The Delta Force* "will be the 1986 film to beat for sheer, unashamed, hilariously vulgar vain-gloriness" (14 February 1986). Though some action films appeal to "a sense of nationalism... force as a solution as depicted in *Delta Force* and other similar works is a very dangerous message," says critic Michael Elkin. Affirms Israel's award-winning filmmaker, Rafi Bukaee, "I hate films like *Delta Force*... [They] don't show [Arabs as] human beings."[63]

• Critic Michael Medved argues that viewers' concerns about Arab-bashing films are not necessarily justified. "There is a disproportionate representation of Arab people in terrorism. It would be absurd to have a terrorist threatening to blow up a plane and have his name be Smith," writes Medved. The critic does not say that regardless of culture, creed, or color, every group boasts some individuals who commit violence— as the Oklahoma City bombing showed. Or, the example of Menachem Rubinowits, a 22-year-old Israeli man who was arrested in the public gallery of the US House of

Representatives, for trying to detonate a bomb he had carried into the building. Reports *US News & World Report*, the bomb "could have destroyed most of the gallery and crowded chamber."[64]

• At no point does *The Delta Force* point out the fact that in 1983, the indiscriminate bombing of Shiite Muslim and other Lebanese homes by the US battleship New Jersey caused countless casualties. One of the Lebanese Shiites who hijacked a June 1985 TWA Flight ran up the aircraft's aisle shouting "New Jersey." Later, he told a passenger that shells emanating from the New Jersey had killed his wife and daughter.

• A St. Martin's paperback of the same name was released with *The Delta Force*, which came out about the same time as the Arab-bashing film *Iron Eagle* (1986).

• In *Operation Delta Force II*, a 1997 Nu Image TV movie telecast on HBO, producer-director Yossi Wein embellishes *The Delta Force*'s kill-Arab scenario. Wein gives his 1997 Delta Force unit even more lethal ways of killing more Arabs than Golan and Globus's 1986 Delta unit displayed. The movie opens with several Delta Force commandos invading an Arab military base in "Amadiya, Nothern Iraq." The Delta leader, Captain Long, explains the mission's purpose: "Basically, we poke their [Iraqi] eyes out and secure our guys." Wein's reel Iraqis really take it on the chin. Before rescuing their imprisoned friends, the US commandos liquidate more than 100 Iraqis, machine-gunning them and igniting them with rockets. These US-Iraqi shoot-em-up and spit-em-out scenes last about 15 minutes, non-stop. To ensure the viewer knows for certain the Delta team is extinguishing khaki-clad Iraqis, Wein makes sure that every "enemy" soldier dons a red-and-white checkered kuffiyeh.

Amazingly, the movie is not even about Arabs: after the opening Iraqi scenes, remaining frames focus on an American radical and his generic terrorists. They take over a Russian nuclear submarine, a Russian missile base and the "Northern Star" cruise ship, carrying "2,842 passengers." The Delta team saves the day.

Delta Force Commando II (1990), a.k.a. Priority Red One, SURF.

Fred Williamson, Van Johnson, Richard Hatch. CAMEOS, VILLAINS

Americans vs. Americans. The US hero feigns being an Arab arms dealer [see *Condorman* (1981)].

Scene: Intent on inciting a clandestine nuclear missile operation, US General John McCailand (Johnson) and his cohorts steal missiles from a government base. In order to distract investigators, the general blames others. "Terrorism seems to be on the rise recently. A few hours ago in a Belgrade hotel, *they* [emphasis mine] shot the CIA official who is responsible for the Mideast Department."

• American drivers carrying "warhead missiles" are killed. Cut to the American protagonist (Hatch); he dons a black-and-white kuffiyeh. An ugly man with a beard approaches him, offering to buy weapons. The men agree on the price; the bearded man hands the American some money. Assassins sneak up on him; the American floors them, saying, "There's guys out here that will slit their mother's throat for a crust of bread."

• In the end, the US commandos bring down the US conspirators.

Delta Force 3: The Killing Game (1991), CAN. A Golan-Globus film.

Nick Cassavetes, Eric Douglas, John Ryan, Candace Brecker, Dan Turgeman, Jonathan Cherchi, Yacov Banai. SP: Andy Deutsch, Greg Latter, Boaz Davidson. P: Davidson. Filmed in Israel. Israeli actors portray Palestinian terrorists. PALESTINIANS, SHEIKHS, MAIDENS

Palestinians appear as slimy seducers of innocents, and as nuclear terrorists about to blow up Miami. Assisting them is a crazed sheikh. Opposing them, American and Russian commandos.

Scene: Arab music underscores the action. As credits roll, two clad-in-black Arab women affix a bomb to their near-naked colleague. Cut to Moscow. Inside an auditorium, an Arab receives an "international prize for peace." The camera pans to the woman in black, carrying the bomb. Abruptly, she grabs the Arab, shouting, "Allahu Akbar." The bomb explodes, killing her and the man. Superimposed on screen, this message: "In the name of Allah!" [Also see suicidal Arabs in *Wrong Is Right* (1982)].

• The Pentagon. A military officer sees on TV, the Palestinian terrorist Kahlil Kedal (Cherchi) demanding "complete withdrawal of all forms of Western interference in the Arab world." Kedal threatens to "dispatch the American people to the Hell they deserve," declaring, "I will continue to send messengers of death into the Western world." Quips a general: "One of his crazy followers [Hussein] is ready to take out half of New York City."

• Chatila, Lebanon. Instead of mute Palestinians showing empathy for the woman who martyred herself in Moscow, they toss bills into a basket. Declares Kedal to Hussein (Turgeman): "Go. Deliver our gift [a nuclear bomb] to the world."

• Quantico, Virginia's Urban Attack Training Center. Charlie (Cassavetes) and Sergei (Ryan) teach American and Russian soldiers how to best kill Palestinians.

• Miami, Florida. An underground parking garage. Using a baseball bat, Kedal's cohorts smash the legs of Wendy Jackson (Brecker), a JCBS-TV producer. Abruptly, Hussein arrives, chasing them off. Feigning friendship, Hussein visits Wendy in the hospital. After he brings her flowers, Wendy says, "I feel safe with you." Cut to Hussein planting a nuclear device in her wheelchair.

• The Mideast. Standing amidst piles of used tires, Kedal and his Palestinians puff hashish on a nargelih. One of his Palestinian cohorts sees an American-Russian patrol. He tells Kedal, "Let's go; we'll kill them all"— but instead the Americans and Russians kill most of Kedal's men.

• When Kedal arrives at Sheikh Mahmud's Mideast fortress, Arabs cheer. The rotund sheikh (Banai) embraces Kedal. Cut to the American-Russian squad. Posing as Palestinians, they attack the fortress. One Palestinian tries to rape Irenia, the Russian Captain. Irenia knifes him in the gut. Eventually, she is captured; a Palestinian cuffs her to a post, then hits her; Irenia spits in his face. Kedal arrives, attaching a bomb to her waist.

• The souk, the desert, and a fortress: In all three locales, the American-Russian team bring down masses of Palestinians wearing black-and-white kuffiyehs, as well as robed Arabs. Fifty-plus bodies litter the screen. Also, the unit nabs Kedal.

• Scenes show Arabic-speaking Palestinians sacrificing their lives for Kedal and "the cause."

• Miami's JCBS-TV's studio is telecasting the show "Current Events." Cut to Hussein; he machine-guns the program's host. Next, he holds the lame Wendy hostage. Hussein yanks her hair and slaps her face. American soldiers and Kedal enter the studio. Kedal pleads with Hussein not to detonate the nuclear device.

• Shouting "Allahu Akbar," Hussein kills Kedal, then tries to explode the nuclear bomb. The protagonists kill him.

Note: Characters refer a mythical country, El Qutar. Note the similarity to Qatar, a real Arab nation. In 1997, Showtime followed its telecast of *Delta Force 3: The Killing Game* with another hate-the-Arab scenario, *American Ninja 4: The Annihilation* (1991).

• Interestingly, the same year these movies were released, the following editorial statement, referring to the outcome of Madrid's Arab-Israeli peace talks, appeared in the NYT: "Madrid now denotes the end of the stereotype of 'the Arabs' as a hostile unreasoning monolith. That change may not be sufficient, but is a necessary condition, for peace" (5 November 1991).

The Demon (1918), METRO. Silent. *Edith Storey, Lewis Cody.* Based on a novel by Alice Muriel Williamson and Charles Norris Williamson. *NS. Notes from AFIC (p 204). MAIDENS

Algeria. After Jim Lassells inherits his cousin Harold's fortune, he ascertains who murdered Harold—the Arab sultan.

When Arabs auction off Perdita at a slave market, Lassells buys her. Then, he whisks Perdita off, not to his bedroom, but "to a convent in Corsica to be educated."

Years later, Lassells meets up with Perdita. On discovering she is really half-American—"the long-lost daughter of his cousin Harold"—he falls in love and they marry!

Desert Attack (1961), a.k.a Ice Cold in Alex (1958), TCF. *John Mills, Anthony Quayle.* Filmed in Libya. CAMEOS, EGYPTIANS

The action occurs in "Tobruk, 1942," yet not one Libyan surfaces. No Arabs fight alongside the British. Libya is portrayed as a desert without people. Opening credits state, "The producers wish to express their sincere thanks to the Government of the United Kingdom of Libya for their friendly cooperation."

Just before the film ends, an Egyptian bartender serves British soldiers "four cold beers."

Desert Bride (1928), COL. *Betty Compson, Allan Forrest, Otto Matiesen.* P: Harry Cohn. D: Max Cohn. *NS. Notes from AFIC (p 178). VILLAINS

Kassim Ben Ali's (Mateisen) nationalists capture French intelligence officer Maurice (Forrest), and his "sweetheart," Diane (Compson). Though Kassim tortures the couple, they refuse to "divulge information." French troops to the rescue; they storm Kassim's "fortress," killing the Arab. Next, they rout his rebels and rescue the couple.

Desert Command (1948), Mascot. This feature film is an edited version of *The Three Musketeers* (1933), a 12-episode foreign legion serial with John Wayne. VILLAINS

The Desert Hawk (1944), COL. 15 episodes. *Gilbert Roland, Mona Maris, Frank Lackteen, Ben Welden, Egan Brecher.* See *Tarzan the Fearless* (1933). CLIFFHANGERS, SHEIKHS, MAIDENS

In mythical Ahad, brother vs. brother. This palace/desert movie serial poses a question: Will Kasim, the "good" Arab, or Hassan, the "bad" Arab, secure the throne? Actor Gilbert Roland portrays both brothers. Hassan tries to seduce Princess Azela. All 15 episodes display Arabs. Some Arab slavers surface.

Scene: The camera displays a souk, cave, mosque, and coffee shop. Inside Ahad's palace, bellydancers perform. The palace contains an execution chamber and a treacherous floor panel; when the panel opens, innocents plunge below onto daggers.

• In episode one, an Arab guard spots "the ruthless tyrant" Hassan knife the vizier in the back. "You shouldn't have killed him right here in the throne room," says the guard. Retorts Hassan, "It saves putting him in the dungeon and having to feed him." Aiding Hassan are the chief chamberlain, Fuad (Lackteen), and the evil "Brothers of the Sword."

• Hassan makes a move on Princess Azela (Maris). She threatens to kill herself rather than submit to a false caliph.

• Kasim moves to resume his rightful place on the throne. He assumes the role of the Desert Hawk and throughout this cliffhanger, scenes show Kasim thwarting brother Hassan's sinister plots. Kasim, who robs the rich and feeds the poor, functions as the "symbol of hope for the poor and oppressed." Among his supporters are Princess Azela, the beggar Omar (Welden), Omar's daughter, and the "Grey Wizard" (Brecher). When the wizard shakes his carpet, out pop attractive dancers.

• Hassan's dog "Satan" nearly gobbles Kasim.

• Asks one of Hassan's dense Arabs, "What if the townspeople resist our taking their belongings?" Grunts Hassan, "That's why you and your men wear scimitars."

• The camera reveals black slaves en route to the auction block trekking across the desert; Hassan's Arab whip them. See *Ashanti* (1979).

• Hassan and his cohorts are defeated; Kasim secures the throne.

Note: In episode two, the vicious "Brothers of the Sword" intend to break Kasim in half; they tie him to two horses. In episode four, the Brothers move to burn Kasim alive. Then they toss knife after knife at the bound Kasim, missing every time.

Dialogue: An Arab is tagged, "You treacherous dog." And, an Arab knife thrower speaks with a southern accent.

Treatment of Islam: Throughout, Kasim says, "Allah be with you." And, seeing Kasim's men gather at the mosque, Hassan's men are advised, "This is holy ground. You don't dare harm or arrest anyone inside a mosque." They do not.

The Desert Hawk (1950), UI. *Yvonne De Carlo, Rock Hudson, Jackie Gleason, Richard Greene.* MAIDENS, RECOMMENDED

In this sand-and-sandal movie, the Arab princess is a beautiful, courageous, intelligent and independent woman, devoted to family. Desert duels display Arabs and Persians. Omar, the Desert Hawk and the Iraqi Princess Schehrazade oppose Arab bandits, "the Assassins," and Prince Murad's evil Persians.

Scene: Teheran's Prince Murad (Greene) tells the slave master Abdul to drag some chained "young maidens to the slave markets." The mute ladies will be sold to the highest bidders.

• Assisting Murad is Kibar, the Assassins' leader; Kibar's cohorts wear steel-pointed helmets. The Assassins' secluded hide out, the "Palace of a Thousand Delights," boasts an ornate pool and pleasure chamber. In the chamber, some maidens lounge on pillows, other dance. Still others attend the Arabs. Located beneath the sexual pleasure room is a torture chamber, headed by the "master of the lash."

• Determined to bring down Murad is a Persian blacksmith, Omar, the Desert Hawk (Hudson). Daily, Omar, "a champion of his people, risks his life to free innocents from bondage."

• Omar rescues imprisoned bedouins. He asks the freed bedouins to join him, declaring, "What are you, men or jackals?" As they fear Murad's forces, the bedouins run off.

• The souk. Women are sold into slavery; cunning men engage in hoaxes. The sly Sinbad (Gleason) sells bogus treasure maps; crafty Aladdin dupes customers with the stale ploy, "Which of the three cups contains the pea?"

• Omar spots the Iraqi lovely, Schehrazade (DeCarlo), and sighs, "Such priceless beauty. I have no harem," he tells her. "It is written in the Koran that a man who knows too many loves may never cherish one. There is no precedent for beauty such as yours."

• Schehrazade, a woman who could never "marry a man she could not love," falls for Omar. A "holy man" presides over the Iraqi princess's wedding to the blacksmith.

• Iraqi maidens protect Schehrazade from Murad's grip. When Murad demands that Schehrazade reveal herself, her attendants step forward. One at a time they tell Murad: "I am Schehrazade." The assassins try to force one maiden into identifying the real Schehrazade. Though they lash her, she refuses to talk.

Finis: "Allah is with us," says Omar as he storms Murad's palace. Assisting Omar are Aladdin, Sinbad, Princess Schehrazade, and her father, Baghdad's caliph. Harem maidens, too, join in the melee. Omar defeats Murad and his assassins. The caliph honors him, declaring, "I salute a valiant warrior."

Desert Hell (1958), TCF. *Brian Keith, Barbara Hale.* S, P, D: Charles Marquis Warren. VILLAINS

Legionnaires kill the "unseeable ones."

Scene: Arab music accents the trudging of three legionnaires across the desert. One drops, two reach the fort. Explains Captain Edward (Keith), "They're all dead." Our patrol was "hit from nowhere." By whom? asks the General. "I didn't see them. They couldn't be seen," says the Captain, "we never saw a thing."

• The black dots spotted across the white desert sands turn out to be black-robed Tauregs.

• Edward's patrol goes to warn the fort's legionnaires that the Tauregs will attack. An unsettled legionnaire says, "You can't fight an enemy you can't see. Ever see the work un-see-ables do to a man's body?... When he [the mute "native" who acts as the legionnaires' guide] was a child, they cut out his tongue, killed all his family."

• Tauregs abuse a legionnaire; they place him in the spread eagle position, then bind his hands and feet to four posts.

• A dressed-in-white "Holy Man" prays, offering a wounded legionnaire last rites. The Tauregs intend to kill the "Holy Man" and frame the legionnaires.

• In time, fresh legionnaires arrive, saving the Holy Man. And, the legionnaires crush unruly Tuaregs, preventing an uprising. Boasts a Legion officer, "The Tuaregs threatened to end 25 years of peace and plunge the desert tribes into a holy war. [But a] patrol of the legion dealt with the situation."

Note: Often scenarios depict robed Tauregs as Arabs, and vice versa.

Desert Legion (1955), UI. *Alan Ladd, Richard Conte, Arlene Dahl, Akim Tamiroff.* VILLAINS, MAIDENS

Arabs vs. legionnaires, vs. Arabs.

Scene: As credits roll, the camera reveals two menacing Arabs lurking behind a sand dune; they check out Paul Lartal's (Ladd) legion squad. An officer cautions Lartal, "Don't expect any fun around here. This territory breeds the fanatical murderer. Every year it's a new one. [Beware Omar Ben Khalif]; All he does is kill and disappear." Abruptly, the Arabs attack. Lartal's men are "shot from behind by Omar's men"; Lartal collapses.

• Lartal awakens in Madera, the "Lost City of Peace." Lovely Marjana (Dahl) and her French father, Si Khalil (Bergei), tend his wounds.

• "Evil can flourish, even in a paradise," explains Si Khalil, the founder of Madera. Suddenly, from behind the curtains comes an Arab wielding a scabbard. He charges Lartal. But, the clumsy Arab stumbles, knifing himself.

• Later, Si Khalil tells Lartal, "I leave Madera in your hands, my son." Cut to the main villain, the clad-in-black Crito (Conte). He also appears as the bandit, Omar Ben Khalif. Crito not only wants to bed Marjana, he intends to rule Madera. He threatens Lartal, "You were tried by my followers this morning. A fair trail. Death by stoning."

• Failing to kill Lartal, Crito moves to attack his legionnaires, boasting: "I will convince them that many lives will be spared." And, I will tell them that "if they lay down their arms we will be merciful, as usual." He and his rebels laugh.

• Lartal recovers from his wounds. In time, the legionnaire helps Madera's "good" Arabs, as well as his legion friends, crush the deceptive Crito and his cohorts.

Finis: Lartal and Marjana marry; together they rule Madera.

Note: Oriental dances are performed by two Indians, Sujath and Asoka.

Desert Mice (1960), Rank. *Sidney James.* *NS. Notes from VAR (13 January 1960). CAMEOS

The scenario concerns British troops. Appearing briefly, the "keeper of an Algerian brothel."

Desert of Fire (1971), Nuova. Italian, dubbed in English. *Giuseppe Abbobbati, George Wang, Zohra Faiza.* D: *Renzo Merusi.* SP: Landro Lucchetti, Renzo Merusi. Filmed in Tunisia. VILLAINS, MAIDENS

Arabs vs. Westerners; Arabs vs. Africans; Arabs vs. fellow Arabs. The half-Arab heroine rides off with the blonde Western hero.

Scene: The desert. The bare-chested clad-in-black El-Marish and his bandits attack, robbing four Westerners. El-Marish tells his cohorts he'll split the money "four ways." Instead, he shoots his men.

• A nearby village. El-Marish lies again, telling villagers that some bandits "attacked the jeep that carried the payroll. The filthy beasts, they murdered my friends."

• Cut to Abdullah and Ali, his son, visiting with Sir John, an Englishman. Abdullah wants his son Ali to marry Sir John's half-Arab, half-English daughter, the "infidel" Joanna. Retorts Sir John, "She's the daughter of an Englishman and must marry one." Sighs Joanna, "No, I am not white. I'm a Berber." Cut to Sir John's wife, a rotund, militant Arab.

• El-Marish's camp. The Arab strips his hostage, Joanna, then goes to rape her. She runs off shouting, "You filthy animal; you pig; you disgusting swine."

• Joanna's mother links up with El-Marish and his Arab bandits. They gun down Tunisian soldiers as well as scores of Africans. Afterwards, El-Marish complains that Joanna prefers being with Bill, a blonde Westerner: "Your daughter! That bitch would make love to a camel for a glass of wine."

• Bill and El-Marish fight. Joanna's mother saves Bill's life; she shoots El-Marish dead. Why? Because she finds out that El-Marish had assassinated her father.

Finis: Bill and Joanna ride off into the sunset.

Desert Pursuit (1952), MON. *Wayne Morris, Virginia Grey, George Tobias, Anthony Caruso, Emmett Lynn, John Doucette.* SP: W. Scott Darling. Based on Kenneth Perkins' short story "Horse Thieves' Hosana." The film's working title: *Starlight Canyon.* VILLAINS

Cowboys and Indians gun down Arabs. This thin-as-the-veil-of-a-houri scenario mocks Arab Muslims.

Scene: 1870s California, "more than a decade" after Arabs were brought to America to assist "the American Camel Corps of the US Army." The camels once carried "supplies and mail across Death Valley." Arab music is infused when the words "Camel Corps" are spoken.

• In Nevada, cowboy Ford Smith (Morris) discovers gold. His elderly friend, Leatherface (Lynn), explains to Ford that camels are no longer necessary—because the US Army "couldn't find the right cuss words to get 'em to move." Also, he tells Ford to watch out for some Arabs, notably "Hassan, the Arab" (Caruso).

> Leatherface: [Hassan] was selling that there Mormon-whiskey to the sheep herders and to
>   some of the prospectors. They're after you!
> Ford: Who, the camels?
> Leatherface: No. The Ayrabs... they're after your gold.

• No sooner does an attractive ex-blackjack dealer named Mary Smith (Grey) arrive, she befriends Ford and Leatherface. Intending to elude the Arabs, Ford and Mary take the gold, mount their horses, and ride off for San Bernardino via Death Valley.

• As Leatherface is now alone, Hassan's cohort, Kafan (Doucette), who dons a mini-fez, sneaks behind the elderly man. The Arab crushes Leatherface's head with a rifle butt. When Hassan asks his cohort whether he has the ammunition, Kafan sighs, "Stupid fool that I am... I forgot to buy ammunition." Exclaims Hassan, "By the beard of the Prophet!" Mumbling gibberish, the camel-riding Arabs pursue Ford and Mary.

• Hassan and his men catch up with Ford. Hassan tries to deceive Ford, offering the cowboy "a little Mormon whiskey... In the name of the compassionate one, listen. I am from Arabia," says Hassan, and I am "a friend of all America. We have decided to be brothers of the road." Counters Ford, "You're Hassan, the Arab!" Abruptly, Hassan's other cohort, Ghazili (Tobias), grabs Mary. Ford trounces the Arab.

• The anxious Mary tells Ford: "They're gonna get us, sooner or later." If they get me, says Ford, "Divvy up the gold. Give it to the widows or the orphans."

• Ford and Mary enter an Indian village; "Mission Indians" are holding a Christmas Eve ceremony. Commemorating the birth of the Christ child, the praying Indians welcome them. Touched by the Indian worship service and their hospitality, Ford gives them some gold, enough to "take care of the old and sick for many years."

• During their Catholic mass, the Indians spot Hassan and his Arabs approaching. Regrettably, the Indians wrongly perceive them to be the Three Wise Men. Abruptly, they bow. Ford tells Hassan, "The Indians think you're saints." The Arabs play along; one "blesses" a child.

• Christmas morning. As two Indians guide Ford and Mary out of the village, Hassan's men attack. A shoot-out! The Indians and Ford shoot two Arabs dead. Ford and Mary ride off, smiling.

Desert Sands (1955), UA. *Ralph Meeker, Marla English, John Carradine, Keith Larsen*. P: Howard W. Koch. See *Outpost in Morocco* (1949). VILLAINS, SHEIKHS, MAIDENS

Legionnaires vs. a Christian-hating sheikh and bedouins. As a Moroccan woman is infatuated with a legionnaire, Arabs are terminated. See *Outpost in Morocco* (1949).

Scene: Captain Malcomb's (Meeker) legion relief column enters a besieged fort. One survivor approaches them explaining that desert Arabs attacked the fort, slaughtering most of the legionnaires. We were "cut to pieces, butchered like animals." Legionnaires with the relief column are shocked. Says one, Look, "a burning cross with a man on it... it looks like a legionnaire." Says another, "I've never seen such mutations, slow death like this. [The Arabs'] knives are sharp and they use them expertly."

• Introducing Sheikh El-Zanal (Larsen) and his Arab cohorts. They demand Malcomb (Meeker) surrender his relief squad. Malcomb refuses. The Arabs charge the fort several times; finally, El-Zanal's rebels triumph. Boasts the sheikh, "In time, we shall lead every tribe in North Africa."

• El-Zanal tells his legionnaire prisoners, "You will know pain like few men have endured... Par-Islam will no longer be a dream but a reality."

• El-Zanal finds out that legionnaires did not murder his father. His Uncle Jata (Carradine) hired assassins to do the deed. Promptly, El-Zanal confronts his uncle, saying, "You have my thanks." Later, a furious woman attendant fatally knifes Jata. As a rule, reel legionnaires sacrifice themselves to save friends and family; reel Arabs kill family members.

Note the dialogue between El-Zanal and Zara (English), his sister.

El-Zanal: Once they [the legionnaires] have served their purpose, they will be killed.
Zara: But you gave your word.
El-Zanal: This is a crusade. Anything is justified.
Zara: Suppose we make him [Capt. Malcomb] think as we do?
El-Zanal: I have yet to meet a foreigner who can think as we do.
Zara: He must not die. He's the man I want.

• Feigning interest in Zara so he may escape, the bound prisoner Malcomb kisses her. Presto! The smitten Zara frees him. For the love of Malcomb, she also betrays her brother and fellow Arabs. In return, Malcomb gags and binds Zara.

• The legionnaires triumph. Quips one, "They're (the Arabs) running like carpet-baggers." Cut to dead Arabs; their bodies are "plastered all over the desert." As for Zara, she and other Arabs are relegated to a legion cell.

Treatment of Islam: Arabs kill legionnaires—in the name of "par-Islam."

Dialogue: Arabs are tagged "Ayrab," "filthy butcher," and "pig."

The Desert Song (1929), WB. Silent. *John Bolen, Carlotta King.* SP: Harvey Gates. RECOMMENDED

The Desert Song (1943), WB. *Dennis Morgan, Irene Manning.* SP: Robert Buckner. VILLAINS

The Desert Song (1953), WB. *Gordon MacRae, Kathryn Grayson.* SP: Roland Kibbee, who also penned *Ten Tall Men* (1951), *A Night in Casablanca* (1946). VILLAINS

All three Warner Brothers versions of Sigmund Romberg's operetta are based on the play by Lawrence Schwab, Otto Harbach, and Oscar Hammerstein. Though all three *Desert Song* movies are discussed here, only the 1929 silent film is recommended viewing. Anti-Arab images are prevalent in both the 1943 and 1953 films.

These movies feature the Westerner as an Arabian Robin Hood. The 1929 movie and the 1926 Broadway stage production feature only courageous Arabs; the 1943 and 1953 sound versions project plenty of Arab villains. Nasty Moroccans contest Westerners and Moroccans. And, an Arab leader appears as a Nazi-sympathizer. All three movies are set in French Morocco, and in all three the Western protagonists fall in love and harem maidens dance, bathe, and lounge about. In none is the heroic Riff leader an Arab, but instead a Westerner tagged the Red Shadow/El Khobar.

Desert Song's Western heroes have dual identities. Yes, they are dashing champions who wear red costumes. But, they also feign being wimps, musicians, or students. In the *Desert Song* of 1943, the hero plays the piano. In the 1953 film, the protagonist is an archeology student. Seeing the film's protagonists don Red Shadow garb is like watching Clark Kent change into Superman.

In the 1929 film, French military men rather than Arabs are the heavies, notably a French officer called "the butcher." Another cur is the Red Shadow's father, a French general who enjoys dispatching soldiers to kill Arab villagers. The Red Shadow's friends are Moroccans, notably Ali Bin Ali. The Red Shadow and Ali lead an uprising against French forces. Boasts the Red Shadow to the Riffs, No "man can prove himself a better fighter than I am. Does any one of you care to try me in single combat? Any man in Morocco?"

Islam is revered in this version: Ali tells his friend, "Go, with the blessings of Allah." Still though, Arab women are represented, albeit briefly, by a Moroccan dancer tagged "Tiger Claws." She boasts, "My mother says if you must hurt [someone], find a hurt that is worse [than anything], then kill. I know a way." The Red Shadow rejects her advances; she moves to hurt the Frenchman.

The 1943 movie features a Moroccan villain, Yousseff; he happens to be a "very rich Arab." Yousseff exploits Moroccans, deceives the French, and sides with the Axis. Yousseff intends to turn over a newly constructed railroad to the Nazis. The Red Shadow foils the scheme. He and French forces attack Yousseff's palace, killing the Arab traitor and some Nazis. Thinking the French will give "all rights and liberties for the Riff tribes," The Red Shadow says, "One wrong guy's death (Yousseff"s) can solve the problems of thousands." Moroccans are tagged "savages." Retorts the Red Shadow, "Savages about their freedom, about thirty thousand have died for it. The only cultural benefit they've had from our civilization is a kick in the face." A Western bartender says of Muslims, "It's a shame these Muhammadans don't drink."

Again, in the 1953 movie, the villainous Yousseff pops up. This time, plenty of scheming Moroccan cutthroats assist him. The Moroccans plan to overthrow the French and starve Moroccan villagers. In the end, the Red Shadow not only crushes Yousseff and his marauders, he rescues the Western heroine from the Arab's clutches.

Note: The Berber tribe, El Riff, resides in the northern Atlas mountains of Morocco and Algeria. Adult males wear a veil (tegelmoust), a long blue cloth covering the face, with a slit left for the eyes. See *The Wind and the Lion* (1975).

The Desert Warrior (1961), Pontiac. Italy-Spain, dubbed in English.
Ricardo Montalban, Carmen Sevilla, Anna Maria Ferrero, Gino Cervi. SHEIKHS, MAIDENS

Arabs vs. Arabs; daughter vs. father.

Scene: The establishing shot reveals Egypt's sphinx and the pyramids. Cut to the tyrant, Ibrahim (Cervi), moving to become the new ruler in Magda, Spain. The Arab orders his accomplice, Selim, to destroy Sultan Omar's men, which Selim does. The camera reveals Selim and his soldiers examining dead Arabs, including the body of the "beloved" sultan, and gloating.

• Ibrahim plans to dispense with several wives, "especially some of the fat ones."

• Waving sabers, Selim's black-robed Arabs ignite a village, massacring innocents.

• The marketplace. Sultan Omar's son, the white-robed Prince Said (Montalban), tells the crowd to help him win back what rightfully belongs to him—the throne. Cut to the desert. Here, Prince Said and his men attack Ibrahim's caravans. Said's men also nab Princess Amina (Ferrego), Ibrahim's daughter. Feigning to be a commoner, she sings "Destiny." In part, the lyrics: "Burning desert, unchain me, let me go; set me free."

• The souk. Disguised, Said mingles with his people. Later, he romances Amina; they kiss near the pyramids. Amina rides off; "May Allah protect you," says Said.

• One of Ibrahim's cohorts dies. Angry, Ibrahim jails and threatens to behead the innocent. Armed with a bow and arrow, Said rescues the imprisoned men.

• The throne room; Ibrahim's Arabs whip fellow Arabs. Ibrahim warns his cohort Selim to measure up, or "I'll feed you to the dogs."

• Prince Said grabs Magda's precious scimitar, "a symbol of power." But Selim tosses a dagger, injuring the prince. Said runs off, collapsing near the maiden Zulieka's (Sevilla) hut; she heals him. Later, Selim tortures, then terminates Zulieka.

• The palace. Bellydancers perform. Ibrahim tells his daughter, Amina, to wed "the traitor and mercenary" Selim. Amina refuses. Says Ibrahim, "I swear by Allah" you will obey me.

• Selim imprisons Prince Said; promptly, Amina frees the prince. Meanwhile, the two villains, Selim and Ibrahim, duel. Selim wins. Cut to Said's men penetrating palace walls, vanquishing the bad guys. Said and Selim cross swords; Said triumphs and rescues Amina from her cell.

Finis: Said becomes the new potentate; at his side, the beaming Princess Amina.

Note: Ibrahim's palace guards don black robes and huge cone-shaped hats, not head dresses. The film's bow-and-arrow/saber battle scenes feature scores of Italian extras.

Devil and the Deep (1932), PAR. *Gary Cooper, Charles, Laughton, Tallulah Bankhead, Paul Porcasi.* SP: Ben Levy, D: Marion Gering. CAMEOS

An Arab country, off the coast of North Africa. British submarine Commander Sturm (Laughton), an obsessively jealous man, falsely accuses his wife, Pauline (Bankhead), of having an affair. Clad in a seductive dress, the distraught Pauline runs into the street at night. Abruptly, she is jostled by a crowd of Arab men; they are rushing to see performing folk dancers. Loud and disturbing Arab music underscores the action. Pauline is about to collapse. In time, Lt. Sempter (Cooper) appears, whisking her away from the cacophonous crowd and into the shop of Hassan (Porcasi), the Arab.

• The assertive Hassan insists on selling something to the couple. Note the dialogue.

Hassan: What can I sell the lady? Surely there is something the gentleman would like to give the lady!
Sempter: Go away, will you!
Hassan: But sir, I have shawls like nobody else.
Sempter: I don't need a shawl.
Hassan: But the lady?
Sempter: Oh, go to the devil!
Hassan: Lady, I am a poor man. What am I to do? Sir, you are in my shop; you must be just.

Sempter relents, giving the bearded Hassan "30 dinars" for a bottle of "rare scent." He and Pauline rush off to a deserted oasis. Here, Pauline accidentally spills the perfume, exclaiming: "Oh heavens, it's an amazing scent; ... you should get your money back."

Diamonds Are Forever (1971), MGM/UA. *Sean Connery, Charles Gray, Frank Olegario.* SP: Richard Maibaum, Tom Mankiewicz, D: Guy Hamilton. CAMEOS, EGYPTIANS

James Bond (Connery) slugs a rotund Egyptian gambler (Olegario).

Scene: A casino in Cairo. Before credits roll, the camera reveals a fat, bearded Egyptian wearing a red fez and dark glasses. The unpleasant-looking Egyptian sits at a gambling table, playing cards. After examining his cards, the Egyptian grumbles to the dealer: "Hit me!" Abruptly, 007 appears and hits the Egyptian's jaw. Next, Bond convinces the Egyptian to help him locate his nemesis, Blofeld (Gray). The scene lasts 17 seconds.

Note: Credits bill actor Frank Olegario as "Man in Fez."

The Dishonored Medal (1914), Reliance. Silent. *Miriam Cooper, George Gebhard.* *NS. Notes from AFIC. MAIDENS

French legionnaire Lt. Dubois deceives and seduces an innocent Algerian woman, Zora. Soon, the Frenchman deserts Zora and their baby boy. When Zora is killed, the benevolent Sheikh Ahmed raises El Rabb, Zora's son, as his own. Befriending El Rabb is the sheikh's son, Bel Kahn. Flash forward. Both El Rabb and Bel Kahn declare their love for Anitra, a lovely woman who is half-Arab. Unexpectedly, Lt. Dubois reappears. He forces Anitra into his tent and moves to seduce her. Meanwhile, El Rabb and Bel Kahn lead a revolt of independence. Though "the Algerians are almost entirely wiped out," El Rabb penetrates the French officer's quarters, fatally stabbing Dubois and saving Anitra.

Dr. Phibes Rises Again (1972), AI. *Vincent Price.* CAMEOS, EGYPTIANS

Uncultivated folk, such as peculiar bellydancers, dwell in Egypt.

Scene: A Western voyeur watches a gyrating bellydancer kiss a huge snake.

• Dr. Phibes (Price) kills the voyeur, then affixes a label to the victim's amulet. This mark represents one of the ten "solemn curses wished upon the Pharaohs for keeping the Israelites in bondage."

• Phibes and his cohort move to acquire a special reincarnation drug, hidden in a Pharaoh's chamber. Confesses Phibes' accomplice, "I am obsessed with life. Somewhere in Egypt the obsession will be answered."

Note: A passenger ship en route to Egypt. On ascertaining Phibes' organ is stored below deck, the British inspector comments, "Organ music? Bound to go down well with all those Arabs."

Don Juan DeMarco (1995), New Line, American Zoetrope. *Marlon Brando, Johnny Depp, Bill Capizzi, Geraldine Pailhas.* P: Francis Ford Coppola. SP, D: Jeremy Levin. SHEIKHS, MAIDENS

Injected into Coppola's bizarre comedy are stereotypical scenes of Arabs and Arabia. The camera reveals a palace and slave market. Appearing are a sultan, a sultana, a eunuch, and several harem maidens. The Arab sequence lasts about seven minutes.

Scene: A psychologist's office. Here, Dr. Jack Mickler (Brando) questions the delusional Don Juan (Depp), a youth with a romantic vision of the universe. As Juan tells Mickler about his past, the camera reveals his memories: Scenes display Juan's wonderful Mexican family and his sweetheart, Dona Ana (Pailhas).

• Unexpectedly, Juan switches from good memories of Mexico to Arabia. He tells Dr. Mickler that his ship docked in "some obscure Arabian sultan's [kingdom] where all the passengers were immediately sold into slavery." The camera reveals ugly Arabs in a slave market, bidding to buy the captured men, including the bound Juan. Amazingly, a sultan's wife buys Juan; he is "led off [to the palace] by her eunuch."

• The sultan's palace. Disguised as an Arab maiden, Juan is about to be "presented to the sultana." Guarding her bedroom are two clad-in-Arab-garb midgets. Muses Juan, "The sultan had a harem of 1,500 young women so the demands he placed on his wives were relatively minor." The sultana goes to seduce Juan; he backs off. She pulls out, then withdraws, a knife. Juan succumbs, making love to "the magnificent sultana." Sighs Juan, "For the next two years my days were spent with the sultana; my nights were spent with the 1,500 young women from the sultan's harem."

• The harem quarters. Juan fears "being discovered by the sultan." Cut to the rotund sultan (Capizzi) encountering the clad-in-harem-garb Juan. Frightened, Juan bows. The sultan winks, then whispers to the eunuch that he wants to fool around with Juan, purring: "You may rise my little dove." Sighs Juan, "All good things must end."

• Juan boards a departing ship; hundreds of Arab women wave good-bye. In the background, the desert, palm trees, a tent, and camels. Says Juan, "I had learned to love in a thousand ways."

Don't Drink the Water (1969), Avco Embassy. *Jackie Gleason, Estelle Parsons, Avery Schreiber, Joan Delaney.* SP: R.S. Allen, Harvey Bullock, and Woody Allen (based on his play). EP: Joseph E. Levine. CAMEOS, SHEIKHS

This comedy concerns a New Jersey couple trapped inside Vulgaria, a mythical Iron Curtain country. Yet, the movie displays a tubby, rich, lecherous sheikh with a harem.

Scene: Vulgaria. Inside the US Embassy, two American tourists, Mr. and Mrs. Hollander (Gleason, Parsons) and their attractive daughter (Delaney). Abruptly, the Sultan of Bashir (Schreiber) wearing a lengthy white burnoose, barges in. Trailing the sheikh are his four colorfully-garbed wives. The bearded sheikh raises his arms; the mute women sit. The sheikh struts along at an embassy party; the wives trail behind.

• Leering at the Hollander's daughter, Susan, "this [Arab] clown" purrs, "You know I am thinking of adding an American girl to my harem." Barks Susan's father, "Drop dead...you sand clam...Who do you think you are, some big shot because you own some oil wells?" Pointing to the Arab's wives, Mr. Hollander says, "I don't like my government doing business with sex maniacs."

• The sheikh rushes out of the embassy. Quips Hollander, "Goodbye fatso!" Later, at a posh hotel, Hollander and the ambassador's son dupe the sheikh. The two men bind and gag the potentate, then clad themselves in Arab garb and drive off.

Don't Raise the Bridge, Lower the River (1968), COL. *Jerry Lewis, Terry Thomas, Jacqueline Pearce.* SP: Max Wilk, based on his novel. See Arab caricatures in Lewis' *The Sad Sack* (1957) and *Money from Home* (1953). SHEIKHS

Arabs as buffoons. Western protagonists dupe an Arab sheikh into buying bogus plans for "some kind of a high-speed electric [oil] drill."

Scene: A mute fez-wearing man pulling a zebra approaches an American, George Lester (Lewis). Barks Lester, "Not now." Minutes later, the fez man pops up in Lester's hotel room; again, Lester shoos him away. Final frames. Again, the zebra man pesters Lester. The fez man boasts he can "breed zebras with white stripes."

• Lester's British pal, con-artist H. William Homer (Terry-Thomas), says he's been appointed the "new purchasing agent for the [Arab] government of Sumalia." Homer points to a smuggled dentist's chair and drill, exclaiming, "All those for the rotten teeth of Sumalia."

• Homer and Lester intend to bilk an "old sheikh of 50 thousand pounds." How? By selling the dense Arab some spurious plans for a new electric oil drill. Says Homer, I can imagine "tears of gratitude coming to the old sheikh's bad eyes if you were to turn over the [bogus] blueprints."

• In Portugal, Sumalia's emir and his aide examine Homer's mock plans. Sensing the Arabs are bewildered, Homer says, "Patience, gentlemen—the pyramids weren't built in a day." Finally, the grunting aide yanks wads of "dollars" from a briefcase, handing the loot to Homer.

• The chase! The Arabs realize they've been hoodwinked. The sheikh places a dagger to Homer's throat; Lester covers the Arab with some drapes. The Arabs chase after Homer and Lester, cornering them. Lester and Homer dump flowers over the Arabs' heads, pouring water. Next, Islam is mocked. Lester wails mumbo-jumbo; the two Arabs halt, bow, and pray.

• Conclusion. Trying to dupe his wife Pamela (Pearce), Lester dons Arab garb. Pamela tells Homer, "You should be ashamed of yourself, coming in here with this fake sheikh!"

Note: Credits state: "Arab," "Bearded Arab," and "Zebra Man."

Double Edge (1992), Castle Hill. *Faye Dunaway, Amos Kollek, Shmuel Shiloh, Muhammad Bakri, Makram Khouri, Michael Shneider.* P: Kollek and Rafi Reibenbach. W, D: Amos Kollek. Filmed in Israel. PALESTINIANS, WORST LIST

Israelis vs. Palestinians. Palestinians vs. Palestinians, vs. Americans. Israelis are humane folk; Palestinians are not. In Israel, an American journalist (Dunaway) interviews four Israelis and two Palestinians. In the film, they appear as themselves: Teddy Kollek, Abba Eban, Rabbi Meir Kahane, Naomi Altaratz, Ziad Abu Za'yad, and Hanan Ashrawi.

Scene: *New York Herald* reporter Faye Milano (Dunaway), who empathizes with the Palestinians, arrives in Israel for a three-week stay. Faye spots David (Kollek), an Israeli novelist, hitchhiking to Jerusalem. She picks him up, then tells David about a shooting in the West Bank town of Nablus—three Arab [not Palestinian] boys were shot. Next, she asks David why Israel has different-colored license plates. "The blue ones belong to the Arabs of the West Bank"; says David, "they're not Israeli citizens." Says Faye, "Sure makes them easy to spot." Counters David, "There are a lot of Arab terrorists in this country; this is a dangerous place... I'm the good guy."

• "East Jerusalem, Arab Part of the City." Israeli soldiers surround Palestinian school girls; one soldier clubs a youth. Faye brandishes her press ID, the soldier stops. Next, she tries to comfort the injured girl. The Palestinian spits in Faye's face and runs off.

• Surfacing is Faye's newspaper colleague, Moshe (Shiloh); his son was killed during Israel's 1982 invasion of Lebanon. The two journalists go off to Nablus to meet with the intifada leader Shafik (Khouri). Shafik's son, Omar, was killed by Israelis.

• An Israeli Army press censor berates Faye. Why? She publishes articles sympathetic to Palestinians. Insists Faye, "I am fair." Later, Israeli censors take away her press card. One of Faye's stories identified an Israeli guard who was deporting Palestinians. Later, Palestinians kill the guard.

• Israelis deport Palestinians, including Shafik, to Lebanon. Moshe justifies the deportation process, saying: "If he wasn't doing anything they wouldn't deport him."

• Faye dines at the home of Shafik's nephew, Mustafa (Bakri). To Faye, Mustafa is "not a terrorist"; Israelis say he is. Abruptly, soldiers enter, arresting Mustafa.

• In Nablus, Faye and her friend Max (Shneider) chat with Israelis. Cut to a rooftop; Palestinian boys pee on the troops. Earlier, Palestinians dropped a cement block from the window, killing an Israeli soldier. Israeli soldiers and reservists, including David, haul off the youths. Next, the Israelis dynamite a Palestinian house. When Faye mentions a "brain-dead" Palestinian boy, David protests, "Palestinians send their children to do their fighting; we can't surrender to them because they're children."

• In Ramallah, two "friendly" Palestinian youths burn tires; "they're doing it for your benefit," says David. "They love reporters." Suddenly appearing with a machine gun is an Israeli extremist, Joey Greenberg, "a new immigrant from New York." Greenberg fires at some Palestinian kids; David floors him.

• Masked Palestinians chanting "PLO" flaunt large photographs of Yasir Arafat and Saddam Hussein. Palestinians rejoice when the photograph of a dead 22-year-old Israeli policeman is revealed, the young man was stabbed five times in the chest.

• Faye tells David, "What I feel most is confusion—who's right and who's wrong? Who are the good guys?" Suddenly, they kiss and make love. Later, David says, "If I were a Palestinian Arab, I'd throw stones... but I'm an Israeli." Cut to Moshe. "A bus was attacked on the way to Jerusalem"; he says, "thirty are wounded; an Israeli mother and her three children were killed." Comments Max, "You should see the Arabs who were beaten up by the Israelis today over that bus incident."

• At a hospital, Faye sees a Palestinian mother grieving over her "brain-dead" son. Earlier, Faye wrote a story stating an Israeli blast injured the boy. Now, she learns, too late, that the youth seriously burned himself cooking in the kitchen.

• In Nablus, Faye and David meet with Mustafa and several masked Palestinians. Mustafa shows her some photographs of his Uncle Shafik. Apparently when Shafik tried to return to the West Bank, a Palestinian betrayed him. Sighs Mustafa, he "was ambushed and killed by his own people."

• Mustafa requests a favor; Faye obliges. She delivers Mustafa's note to a Palestinian's home. As the Palestinian reaches for the note, Mustafa and his men shoot him, then hang his bloodied body in the square. Screams Faye, "You bastard, you used me." Affirms Mustafa, "Yes, I had to use you. He's a traitor, a collaborator."

Finis: Faye, David, and Sarah, his daughter, drive off to have a picnic lunch. Boom! David's car has a flat. While David fixes the tire, a Palestinian boy, Salim, appears. He feigns friendship. Suddenly, Salim tries to snatch Sarah's doll; failing, he goes away. David takes Sarah to the bathroom. As Faye is alone, a dozen-plus grim-faced Palestinian youths surround the vehicle, gawking at her. The boys steal her camera, then close in. Realizing the Palestinians want to hurt her, Faye locks herself inside the car. First, the youths violently shake the auto. Next, they clasp stones and clubs and start smashing the vehicle. In self-defense, Faye grabs a pistol. She exits the car and confronts the Palestinians. Standing on the car's roof is Salim; he moves to crush Faye's head with a boulder. In time, she spots Salim. Faye points the gun at the youth. Seeing the weapon, Salim hesitates. Freeze frame.

• In short: When an Israeli dies, Palestinians rejoice; deceitful Palestinians kill fellow Palestinians; Israelis are not responsible for the "brain-dead" Palestinian boy; ugly Palestinians youths intend to kill a US journalist.

Down and Out in Beverly Hills (1986), TOU. *Nick Nolte, Little Richard, Reza Bashar, Joseph Makkar.* CAMEOS, MAIDENS

Dark-complexioned rich men with harems are not welcome in Beverly Hills. Some viewers may perceive the film's wealthy Iranians to be Arabs, especially as so many films show black-clad maidens attending wealthy Arabs.

Scene: Beverly Hills homeowner Chris Goodnight (Little Richard) watches a tanned Iranian, followed by several mute women wearing black, moving into the area.

"There goes the neighborhood," he quips. Noticing a party-in-progress, the newcomer (Bashar) asks, "Why were we not invited?"

• The protagonist, Jerry Baskin (Nolte), approaches the new resident's black limousine. Seated inside the car, five black-clad women. Abruptly, the man takes a wad of bills and gives Jerry "five hundred." Why is he so generous? Because Jerry spoke with his son and gave the boy (Makkar) "an apple."

Dragnet (1987), UNI. *Dan Aykroyd, Tom Hanks.* CAMEOS

This parody of Jack Webb's famous TV show mocks Islam.

Scene: The narrator introduces Los Angeles. On screen, people of "every race, color, creed, and persuasion." As the narrator discusses religion, the camera reveals religious symbols representing several faiths, as well as houses of workshop. When the narrator says, "but God," the viewer sees a church and a statue of the Virgin Mary. When he says, "No matter how…" the viewer sees a synagogue and Star of David; as he continues, "he is worshiped," the viewer sees a mission and a sign stating, "There is hope for all who enter here." And, when the narrator intones, "chose in his wisdom to deposit here," the viewer sees a gold dome. As a variety of religious symbols have just appeared, one expects to see the gold dome resting atop a mosque. But, no. The camera tilts down, revealing the dome to be atop the "Ali Baba Motel."

Dream Wife (1953), MGM. *Cary Grant, Deborah Kerr, Betta St. John, Eduard Franz, Buddy Baer.* St. John sings "Tarji's Song" and "Ghi-ll, Ghi-ll, Ghi-ll," by Charles Wolcott and Jamshid Sheibani. MAIDENS

Arab women are obedient, like dogs. This battle-of-the-sexes comedy also belittles Arab cuisine, customs, language, and behavior. The liberated US heroine prevails, vanquishing Cary Grant.

Scene: Mythical Arabia, Bakistan's palace. Princess Tarji (St. John) dances for Clemson Reade (Grant), an American. The ruler (Franz) informs Reade that Bakistani maidens are brought up "to make men happy. Women are wives and mothers, as Allah intended them to be. They are not taxi-cab drivers and wrestlers."

• In the US. Reade fears Effie (Kerr), his fiancée, cares more about the US government's oil deal with Bukistan, than him. So, Reade proposes marriage to Princess Tarji. A state department official points to the globe, saying, "Here's Bakistan [on one side] and here's the United States [the other side]. We have just one thing in common— oil." [See *Best Defense* (1984), where Americans and Arabs have in common "the desert."]

• Reade tells his pals, "There must be a girl somewhere who thinks it's a wonderful career just to have a home and babies, whose only thought is to make her husband happy." Boasts Reade, I prefer to wed an Arab woman, one who was "trained from the day she was born to be a dream wife." Women like Effie, he says, think of careers first, husbands, second.

• Reade proposes. Presto! Tarji's dowry, consisting of a goat herd and one camel, is delivered to his New York office.

• Tarji, accompanied by a retinue of harem maidens and a bodyguard (Baer), appears at an American airport. Wearing a thobe over his suit, Reade greets her. Since Tarji does not speak English and Reade does not speak Arabic, they play charades, confusing onlookers.

Boy: Look Mommy, look at the funny man [Reade].
Man: I'll bet he's some kind of nut.
Woman: Maybe he's making a movie.
Man: Or advertising some kind of cigarette.
Other Man: I wonder how many wives he has.
Woman: I'll bet he's from India.
Man: Arabia.
Other Man: Afghanistan.

• At the hotel, the manager protests the Bakistanis' strange behavior. Reade tries to calm him, "They're not different than any of us. They live just like you and me." Yet, these reel Bakistanis are different; they are 100 percent *not* like you and me. The hotel room resembles a 1920s Arabian Nights chamber. As some Arabs sleep on the floor, several harem maidens prance about the room. "One of the dancing girls discovered the telephone, and won't get off it."

• After Reade marries Tarji she will become his wife, his "property." Says Effie, Tarji must "walk three paces behind her husband... "Her only concern is to please you."

• At Bakistan's Consulate, "goat meat is served." Men, only, are served "drinks." The women sit at separate tables.

• Reade tells his pals that Tarji behaves like his dog, Brutus. Complains Reade, when Brutus walks, Tarji follows, when the dog stops, she stops.

• Declares Bakistan's ruler: America "is foolish to allow women in government." When he meets talented Effie, however, the potentate changes his mind. He offers her arak, a Lebanese anise drink. Impressed with Effie, he agrees to the Bakistani-US oil deal.

• Finally, Reade realizes that liberated Effie, not obedient Tarji, is the right woman for him. From Effie, her new mentor, the now-liberated Tarji learns "a new word, freedom." Boasts Tarji, "Woman not have to obey man she not love."

Dreamboat (1952), TCF. *Clifton Webb, Ginger Rogers.* SP, D: Claude Binyon.
VILLAINS

A four-minute scene from a silent movie shows a heroic legionnaire shooting desert bedouins, slugging robed Arabs, and ogling bellydancers.

Scene: Much to the chagrin of a now-respected college professor, Thornton Sayre (Webb), his past life as an actor is revealed. Two decades earlier Sayre was a Hollywood movie celebrity, starring in silent films as a dashing musketeer, a World War I flying ace, an expert Latino swordsman, and a fighting legionnaire. Now, television stations are airing the professor's old movies, causing embarrassment at the college.

• A fashionable bar. Sayre sits on a stool, orders a drink, and stares at the TV set. The TV screen displays Sayre portraying a dashing legionnaire in an old silent movie. On the TV screen, desert bedouins emerge from behind dunes, firing at pinned-down legionnaires. Sayre-as-legionnaire machine-guns masses of Arabs. The title card reads: "That was no easy battle. Tonight we sleep like the dead." Sayre does not sleep; he moves to nab his foe. The camera displays a seedy Arab club, complete with an attractive wiggling Arab bellydancer (Rogers). When she dances, robed Arab patrons open their mouths wide, panting. Sayre enters the club, as does a nasty Arab. Note the dialogue, displayed on title cards. The dancer warns Sayre, "Flee—before he kills you!" Retorts Sayre, "This lout? He will trip over his own hulk!" And he does. A fight occurs; Sayre triumphs, punching out all the Arabs. Fade out.

Drums of Africa (1963), MGM. *Mariette Hartley, Lloyd Bochner, Torin Thatcher, George Sawaya.* See *Allan Quatermain and the Lost City of Gold* (1987) and *Ashanti* (1979). Producers insert footage from *King Solomon's Mines* (1950). VILLAINS, SHEIKHS

In East Africa, Arabs vs. Africans, vs. Westerners. Arab slavers kidnap the American heroine.

Scene: Western and African slavers enslave blacks and murder missionaries, including a nun. The slavers "live by selling their fellow human beings. Killing means nothing to them." An Arab wearing an orange kuffiyeh collaborates with the slavers. He kidnaps Ruth (Hartley), the Western heroine.

• Jack Cuortemayn (Thatcher) frets about Ruth. "They'll probably sell her," he says; "Arab caravans come up from the valley of the white Nile and buy the slaves from them."

• Ruth is considered "a valuable piece of merchandise." Boasts her captor, "The fact that you are ignorant of the male sex will double your price." The implication here? Arabs pine for virgins. "Cleaned and properly dressed," says a slaver, "you are going to be quite an attraction in Alexandria, Damascus."

• Inside a cave. A laughing, lecherous Arab "sheikh" manhandles Ruth. To the rescue, Cuortemayn and Moore (Bochner). They free Ruth, killing the Arabs as well as other slavers. A "good" African assists; he spears an Arab villain in the belly, then plunges a knife into another Arab.

Finis: Cuortemayn stumbles, falling to the ground. An armed Arab fails to shoot Cuortemayn. Instead, the Arab stares at him. Abruptly, Moore grabs his rifle butt, flooring the dense Arab.

Drums of the Desert (1940), MON. *Ralph Lord, Peter George Lynn, Lorna Gray, Neyle Marx, Jean del Val, Mantan Moreland, Boyd Irwin, William Costello, Alberto Morin.* SP: Dorothy Reid, Joseph West. S: John T. Neville. VILLAINS

In Algeria, Arabs vs. legionnaires, vs. blacks. Stereotypical blacks and Arabs.

Scene: Legionnaire Lt. Paul Dumont (Byrd) woos the heroine, Helene Larouche (Gray). Next, en route to join his regiment Dumont meets up with Sheikh Abdullah (Costello). Abdullah has returned to Algeria to share with "tribesmen," the "benefit of the culture" he has absorbed while living in Paris.

• Legion headquarters, Fort Haroun. Introducing Sgt. Blue Williams (Moreland), who hails from Harlem, and his Senegalese regiment. Functioning as paratroopers, Williams and his squad are stereotypical blacks. The men cannot count to ten. Plus, they speak broken English, saying: "ain't that somethin'," "get that boy," and "we is." One man is tagged "Meatball," another, "Satchel."

• Unexpectedly, Abdullah's robed cohorts, his brother, Ben Ali (Marx), and Hassan (Morin), "the sand diviner," attack the legion "infidels" and the paratroopers. Ben Ali slinks into Paul's tent, wounding Captain Andre (Irwin). Another Arab fatally stabs Satchel; he "cut him, pretty bad." After the Arabs retreat, Sgt. Williams quips, "They sure come and go fast."

• Fort Haroun's commander, Colonel Fouchet (del Val), sentences the captured Ben Ali to death. Abdullah begs Fouchet to spare his brother's life; he refuses. As the legion firing squad shoots Ben Ali dead, Abdullah plans "reprisals for the execution of his brother."

• A club. Legionnaires applaud lovely Arab dancers. Outside in the souk, an Arab flute player coaxes a "cobra" from a basket. Paul advises Helene, "These dark-complexioned [Arab] gentlemen are vendors. Don't pay any attention to them. They'll sell you lots of apples, turnips, and beets."

• The sand diviner's tent. Hassan warns Paul and Helene, "Death hovers near, to someone close to you." When the couple uncovers some stolen legion rifles, Hassan's men appear, nabbing them. Sgt. Williams appears. He grabs Hassan's "Nubian" henchman," and places a razor [a stereotypical act] to the Nubian's throat. Williams learns that Abdullah's men, who hold Paul and Helene hostage, are hiding out at a nearby oasis.

• Abdullah's camp. The Arab moves to attack the legion fort. Abruptly, Williams' Senegalese troops arrive. Tossing grenades, they rout the Arabs, free the couple and terminate Abdullah.

• The proud Sgt. Williams presents Paul with a photograph of his Senegalese squad, with only one signature, his. Confused, Paul asks why the other men did not sign. But they have, chuckles Williams. Cut to the photograph: Squad members placed X's beneath their pictures.

Ducktales The Movie: Treasure of the Lost Lamp (1990), Walt Disney. *Huey, Duey, Louie, Webby, Scrooge McDuck, Merlock, and Dijon.* VILLAINS

The protagonists search for treasures belonging to Collie Baba and the forty thieves. Not one heroic, fun-loving Arab character appears.

Scene: Uncle Scrooge and his nephews fly off to Arabia; "In the desert, the sun burns like a hot kabob!" While searching for Collie Baba's gold, they demolish Arab ruins and frighten off mute, cowardly Arabs. Only in this scene are Arabs clearly identified. Appearing throughout is the movie's dark "Oriental," clad-in Arab-garb villain, Dijon. He boasts a hooked nose and speaks with a peculiar Indian-Arab accent.

• Dijon aids Merlock, a wicked sorcerer. Feigning friendship, he links up with Scrooge's party.

• Dijon, a cunning third-world blunderer, refuses to enter Baba's treasure cave. "The camels will be lonesome, it's time for my nap," he says. Scrooge sees Dijon and Merlock stealing Baba's gold, "I smell a couple of desert rats...I knew that weasel's [Dijon's] prices were too good to be true," exclaims Scrooge.

• In Duckburg, an all-American genie emerges from Baba's lamp. As the lamp emanates from Arabia, why not display a heroic Arab genie? The genie warns Dijon, don't give Merlock the lamp, or "you'll be the hot falafel."

• Dijon steals the lamp, plus all of Scrooge's treasures. Pleased with himself, Dijon sits atop the stolen loot and orders "goat's milk." Says Dijon, "Everything smells more delicious here, even me!"

• Throughout, Merlock changes shapes. He appears as a cougar, even a cockroach. When he learns Dijon has nabbed the lamp, he calls him a "disloyal swine." Abruptly, Merlock turns Dijon into a jackass.

• In the end, Scrooge brings down Merlock, restoring Dijon to his former self. Dijon thanks Scrooge. How? By stealing Scrooge's gold, again.

Note: As early as the 1930s, animators displayed shady looking Oriental characters— clones of Dijon. For example, a bearded, dark-complexioned "mystic" with a large nose, and few front teeth, appears in Leon Schlesinger's "Hamateur Night," a Warner Brothers cartoon. This inept, white-turbaned Oriental is called "Swami River." Brandishing a huge sword, he performs his "basket trick." An Anglo volunteer from the audience plops into the basket. Cut to the mystic thrusting his sword, repeatedly, into the basket. Arab music underscores the action. Suddenly, the volunteer moans. The mystic lifts the lid, peers inside, sighs, then shakes his head.

The Dust of Egypt (1915), Vitagraph. Silent. *Antonio Moreno, Edith Storey, Charles Brown.* *NS. Notes from MPW (p 233). Based on the play, *The Dust of Egypt.* EGYPTIANS, MAIDENS

Warning: Do not dream about a mummy princess.

An Egyptian mummy, Princess Amenset (Storey), is delivered to the home of Mr. Lascelles (Moreno). Lascelles falls asleep and dreams that the mummy princess has awoken. She fouls up modern inventions, annoys the butler, harasses Mrs. Lascelles, and tries to poison Mr. Lascelles. Suddenly, Lascelles wakes up, relieved the princess nightmare has ended.

Eagles Attack at Dawn (1970), a.k.a. Ha pritza ha gdola, CAN. *Rick Jason, Peter Braun, Yehoram Gaon, Yoseph Shiloah.* SP: Menachem Golan and Joseph Gross. Filmed in Israel. Israeli actors perform as Arabs. VILLAINS, WORST LIST

In this Golan/Globus production a vastly outnumbered Israeli squad terminates dense, vicious Syrian Muslims.

Scene: Inside El Musir, a Syrian prison, 30 miles from the Israeli border, Syrian Major Haikal (Shiloah) tortures Eli (Gaon), a captured Israeli. Scores of Syrians surround Eli, yet he escapes.

• In Israel, Eli asks his friends for assistance. "They are beating them [Israeli prisoners] day and night. They will kill them; they will hang them. They are killing them with torture," he says. Someone suggests they notify the United Nations; Eli angrily injects, "If we wait for the UN, they will rot."

• Eli leads an Israeli squad into Syria. Near the prison, the Israelis nab and hold hostage a burnoosed Syrian who lives with a goat. Eli dons Arab garb, goes to a nearby mosque and prays. Next, Eli asks a Syrian prison guard to help him free the Israeli prisoners. Affirms the guard, "I am Druze. I have children in Israel... Tell my family I helped you."

• Anticipating an Israeli attack, Major Haikal shouts, "We've got to catch them. But let's use our brains, our brains." The Israelis enter the prison compound. Cut to Syrian guards mistakenly killing Syrians. Inept Syrian troops fire away, mistakenly hitting a petrol tanker, prompting an explosion.

• Dense Syrian guards shoot at their major. He screams, "What are you shooting at, you idiots!" Armed with machine guns and grenades, the Israelis kill dozens of Syrians. One spineless Syrian hides under a desk. Even the cowardly major surrenders. He orders his men to drop their weapons and gather in the prison yard. Here, the Israelis belittle the captured Syrians.

• The major tries to escape; Syrian guards mistakenly kill him. The clad-in-Arab-garb Israelis escape. They set up a mine field, just in case the Syrians opt to pursue them.

• The squad enters Israel. The camera reveals green fields and water. This lovely scene stands in stark contrast to Syria's dry, rocky plateau.

Earthbound (1980), Taft Int. *Burl Ives.* SP, P: Michael Fisher. CAMEOS, SHEIKHS

Arabs try to ravage the American countryside. See *Club Paradise* (1986).

Scene: This family film shows Midwest protagonists befriending space aliens. A mute sheikh appears, threatening to destroy the local environment. Warns the protagonist (Ives), "Some people [Arabs] intend to tear down his hotel [so they can] build condominiums. But not on this land." As he speaks, the camera reveals mountains, trees, birds, and deer.

• Appearing is an Arab wearing dark glasses and a white headdress, plus his cohort, Mr. Madden, an unscrupulous US businessman. Bemoans the protagonist, these two are trying to "sell my hotel right from under me... [They want] to buy this place to put up a twenty-story monstrosity."

• In the end, Madden's scheme to "sell [the hotel] to the sheikh" fails. Protests Madden, "I have nothing to gain from this [hotel] sale... except a $200,000 finders fee from the sheikh." The camera reveals the outflanked sheikh, scowling.

East Meets West (1936), Gaumont. *George Arliss, Ballard Berkeley.* SP: Edwin Greenwood, Maude Howell. *NS. Notes from NYT. Based on Greenwood's stage play, *Lake of Life*. SHEIKHS

The action occurs off the Mediterranean shoreline, in the "small and vital [Arab] country, Rungay." The story concerns the "imperialist ambition of the East against the grave concern of the West." Rungay's wise, compassionate sultan (Arliss) matches wits with British and Japanese diplomats. Throughout, the sultan "remains calm while all the others are in one state of hysteria or another, and [in the end, he] comes up with a political coup." The sub-plot focuses on Nazim, the sultan's son (Berkeley), who loves an English official's wife.

East of Sudan (1964), COL. *Anthony Quayle, Sylvia Syms, Jenny Agutter, Joseph Layode, Johnny Sekka, Edward Ellis.* SP: Jud Kinberg. See *Ashanti* (1979), *Yankee Pasha* (1954). VILLAINS, WORST LIST

In the jungle, anti-Christian Sudanese Muslim slavers vs. British Christians and Africans. Viewers are cautioned: "The Arab slaver is only one day away!"

Scene: 1880s Sudan. General Gordon declares that he wants slave trading to cease. Cut to brutal Arabic-speaking Muslims wearing white turbans and thobes attacking Batash, a British outpost near Khartoum. Two British soldiers, Baker (Quayle) and Murchison, appear. They rescue from the clutches of Arab slavers, English governess Margaret Woodville (Syms) and the Emir's daughter, Asua (Agutter).

• Sudanese Muslims view a Christian cross that is posted above an Egyptian officer's grave. They tear down the cross, then spit on the Christian's grave.

• Margaret spots an Arab following them, asking, "What could we have that could be of any value to them?" Barks Baker, "Look, do you know the market price of a white woman in these parts? A woman with fair hair?"

• The Britishers meet an educated African, Prince Kimrasi (Sekka). I "was a slave for the Arabs... for five years," says Kimrasi. Sighs Baker, "You know what the Arabs are like. They took you as a slave!" Affirms the prince, "[The] Arabs are like a great sickness; some it takes, others it leaves. Always it has been so." Cut to a sly African chief, Gondoki (Layode); he wants to sell the heroines to the Arabs. The prince refuses. The two men fight; the prince triumphs.

• Bemoans the prince, "The Arabs have put fear in their [his people's] hearts. They say there is no use fleeing them." As soon as the prince's men and the Britishers escape, a herd of elephants appears; the elephants trample the Arab slavers.

• Arriving in Khartoum, the survivors see Arab hordes controlling the British fort. Baker crawls into the fort, freeing British prisoners. Next, Baker blows up the arms arsenal; dozens of Arabs go up in smoke. The Arab flag is lowered; the Union Jack raised.

Note: Perhaps *East of Sudan* reflects the views of Sir Alfred Lyall and Evelyn Baring, the Earl of Cromer (1841–1917). From 1883 to 1907, Baring was governor of Egypt, including modern Sudan. Explains historian Bruce Fetter: Baring's anti-Egyptian beliefs became "a textbook for colonial administrators"; his ideas might be considered ludicrous had they not been "so pervasive and determinative of colonial policy, especially with regard to education." Sir Alfred Lyall's writings, in part, influenced Baring's perceptions of Arabs. Writes Lyall: "Accuracy is abhorrent to the Oriental mind. Every Anglo-Indian official should always remember that maxim. Want of accuracy, which easily degenerates into untruthfulness, is in fact the main characteristic of the Oriental mind... The mind of the Oriental... is eminently wanting in symmetry. His reasoning is of the most slipshod description." Remember, "the grave and silent Eastern(er) is "devoid of energy and initiative, stagnant in mind, wanting in curiosity about matters which are new to him, careless of waste of time and patient under suffering."[65]

The Egyptian (1954), TCF. *Edmund Purdom, Jean Simmons, Victor Mature, Gene Tierney, Michael Wilding, Bella Darvi, Anitra Stevens, Peter Ustinov.* D: Michael Curtiz. SP: Philip Dunne, Casey Robinson. EGYPTIANS, MAIDENS

Egypt's pharaoh believes in a single, living God; an underlying theme is a bid for monotheistic understanding. Religion, sex, and the quest for power pit Egyptian against Egyptian.

Scene: Egypt, 1358 BC, at the dawn of monotheism; Egypt rules the world. In Thebes, a humane Egyptian physician and his childless wife attend the poor. They adopt an abandoned child, Sinuhe (Purdom).

• After the pharaoh dies, Egypt's priests, who believe in numerous Gods, declare to citizens, "People of Thebes, ask pity of the Gods." Cut to Sinuhe and his muscular classmate Horemheb (Mature) hunting lions. The lion attacks a praying man; Horemheb kills the animal. Soldiers spot Horemheb and Sinuhe attending the man; they haul the duo to the court of the new pharoah, Akhanton (Wilding).

• The pharaoh rewards the duo. Born of a cheese-maker, Horemheb becomes the pharaoh's officer of the guard; Sinuhe becomes the court physician.

• Sinuhe and Horemheb attend a raucous party at Nefer's bawdy house. Sinuhe falls for Nefer (Darvi), a gold-digging, heartless Babylonian vamp. Nefer warns him to find another woman, saying she uses men: "If you wish to give me a present, do so. But ask nothing in return. I'm an evil woman... go!" Amazingly, Sinuhe presents Nefer with the gift given to him by the pharaoh—a valuable necklace.

• Sinuhe's half-sister, Baketamon (Tierney), moves to save the smitten doctor from Nefer's charms. She dispatches Horemheb to Nefer's abode, along with a valuable bracelet, and a note requesting that she dump Sinuhe. When Sinuhe spots Nefer with his comrade he loses control, saying to Horemheb, "Never call me your friend again."

• Nefer convinces Sinuhe to present her with the deeds of his foster parent's homes. Abruptly, her servants toss him into the street. The lovesick Sinuhe retreats to his childhood home, only to learn his parents are dead. He reads their note, stating they love and forgive him. As he has no money for a respectful burial, Sinuhe does hard labor for three months, working side-by-side with condemned criminals at an embalmment center. Finally, he earns sufficient funds to place his parents' bodies in the Valley of the Kings.

• A local bar maid, Merit (Simmons), confesses she loves Sinuhe, telling him that all women are not like Nefer: "Can't you believe in a love that asks for nothing?" Merit, Sinuhe, and his servant Kaptah (Ustinov) escape the embalmment arena.

• Sinuhe resumes practicing medicine. As he treats only wealthy patients he soon becomes rich and famous. In exchange for saving a foreign leader's life, Sinuhe receives an invincible iron sword. Sinuhe opts to use his mighty sword to bring down Egypt's pharaoh, a devout ruler who worships one God. Yet, the pharaoh moves to repay Sinuhe's treachery with kindness, saying to the priests, "Right or wrong, I will not order death."

• Sinuhe attends the dying Nefer; instead of gloating he empathizes with her plight, telling Kaptah, "Revenge leaves you as empty as fame and fortune." Confused, Kaptah asks, "Master, what is it you want?"

• Merit attends an orphan child who wants to be a doctor. Finally, Sinuhe realizes that he loves Merit; he also agrees to become the boy's father.

• Sinuhe's half-sister Baketamon and Horemheb convince him to drug the pharaoh. Why? So that he, Sinuhe, will become the new ruler. Aware that Sinuhe has poisoned him, the pharaoh offers forgiveness, saying: "The house of God is all creation... He is the creator of all things, the loving spirit that lives in all our hearts... God forgives everything. He forgives you."

• Horemheb and the high priests kill the pharaoh's followers, those Egyptians believing in one God. Among their victims, Merit.

• Sinuhe, who now believes in one God, is exiled. No matter. He tells Horemheb, the new pharaoh, that he will go among the people as a slave and attend the ill. "A man cannot be judged by the color of his skin, by his clothes, his jewels or his triumphs, but only by his heart," he says. Adding, "He who uses mercy is superior" to those unwilling to forgive; "we have but one master, a God who made us all. Only his truth is immortal and in his truth all men are equal."

The Egyptian Mummy (1914), Vitagraph. Silent. *Bill Quirk*.
EGYPTIANS

This harmless comedy links "elixir of life" recipes with mummies.

As Professor Hicks wants to test his "elixir of life" formula, he places a newspaper ad requesting the company of an Egyptian mummy. The protagonist, Dick Graham (Quirk), reads the ad, which promises a "wonderful fluid restoring to life." Graham comes across a vagrant, whom he dresses in mummy garb and whisks off to the professor's lab, duping Hicks into thinking the disguised bum is a real mummy. Finally, after some elixir shenanigans, the professor realizes his patient, the bandaged bum, is not a real mummy after all; he and Graham share some laughs.

El Cid (1961), AA. *Charlton Heston, Sophia Loren, Herbert Lom.* See *The Crusades* (1935). VILLAINS

Eleventh century Spain. Spanish Christians vs. Spanish Christians, vs. Muslim Moors. Muslims vs. Muslims. Christians and Muslims are heroes and bigots. The dialogue misleads viewers into thinking the Muslim god is different from the Christian god.

Scene: The clad-in-black Moorish leader, Ben Yusef (Lom), orders Moorish rulers to help him conquer Spain's "infidels." Says Yusef, "The Prophet has commanded us to rule the world... Let your doctors invent new poisons for arrows. Let your scientists invent new war machines and then, kill, burn... I will sweep up from Africa and let the empire of the one God, the true God, Allah, first spread across Spain, then across Europe, then the whole world."

• Islam equals violence. The call to prayer heard; cut to a plundered Spanish village, aflame. Asking God for a savior, a priest prays before a wooden crucifix of Jesus, pierced with arrows. Says the priest, Muslims "destroy our towns, our people [are] in bondage." His prayer is answered; appearing is Rodrigo Diaz de Bivar, better known as El Cid (Heston).

• El Cid captures several Moorish kings. One prisoner, the emir, warns Heston about Yusef's quest for "wars, death and destruction. Blood and fire more terrible than has ever been seen by a living man." Surprisingly, El Cid decides to release his prisoners. Thus, the emir pledges "eternal friendship in the name of Allah," telling El Cid, "I pledge never to attack King Ferdinand's country." Another Moor also vows not to attack. But, he breaks his vow.

• King Ferdinand dies; his sons fight each other. Trying to save the "good" son's life, El Cid crushes thirteen Spaniards. Too late. The "bad" son triumphs. And, he refuses to meet with the "good" Moorish Kings. "We're a Christian kingdom," he says. "We speak only with Christians." Most of his Spanish-Christian followers support the king's show-no-mercy-to-the-Moors policy. Lovely Chimene (Loren) berates El Cid: "Moors? You let Moors live! Why?" Not only is El Cid banished from the palace, he is forced to duel and kill Chimene's father.

• Seeking vengeance, Chimene hires a Spanish assassin (Vallone). The assassin and some Moors ambush El-Cid. In time, the emir his white-robed Moors rout the villains. Says the emir, "You were betrayed by one of your own." Sighs El Cid, "Betrayed by a Christian. Saved by a Moor."

• Evening, the steady pounding of Moorish drums. After Yusef's black-robed troops invade Valencia's castle, Yusef reveals his scheme, prompting Ferdinand's sons to duel. "The word will spread, Christian brother kills Christian brother," he shouts. "Allah" made it so.

• The emir and "good" Moors join with El Cid's Spanish troops. Before the battle at Valencia, El Cid tells the emir, "You'll make a Moslem of me yet, my lord. How can anyone say this (the sight of Spaniards and Moors united against Ben Yusef) is wrong?" Notes the emir, "They will, though. On both sides."

• Aware that people trapped inside Valencia's castle are starving, the emir says:

"May Allah make our siege a short one." El Cid's troops enter the castle. The Moorish king who broke his vow of peace to El Cid, is killed.

• Yusef nabs and tortures the Spaniard hired by Chimene to kill El Cid. Declares the Spaniard, "El Cid will never die." Exclaims Yusef, "Then this will be more than a battle. It will be our God against yours." Yusef pulls a knife, thrusting it into the Spaniard's gut.

• Evening. Observing Yusef's dark-robed soldiers, El Cid says, "The enemy has no face."

• On the first day of fighting, El Cid is wounded. Though the emir personally tends his wounds, El Cid dies. Hearing the Spanish champion has perished, Yusef declares victory, shouting, "Allah be praised, El Cid is dead." Not really.

• Morning, the next day. The Moors are duped into believing that El Cid is immortal. Spanish soldiers strap El Cid's body onto his white stallion; off they go into the Muslim camp. Seeing the "renewed" El Cid riding toward them, the Moors panic and retreat. Horses trample Yusef. The scene is not real history, rather the legend built around El Cid.

Note: Yusef and his black-robed Muslim troops appear as religious fanatics. They surface primarily at night, accompanied by a steady beat of war drums. At some point in the scenario, someone should say: All peoples—Jews, Christians, and Muslims—use and abuse religion for political gain. But this film only shows devout Christians, not Muslims, praying. And only Muslims are shown desecrating Christian churches.

Emanuelle around the World (1977), Embassy. French, dubbed in
English. *Laura Gemser*. Sexual situations. SHEIKHS

Oily Arab slavers take Western women; Arab vs. Arab.

Scene: Emanuelle (Gemser) and her journalist friend, Cora, move to stop a "Mideast white slavery ring." Warns Cora, "Tourists from America" are being held hostage "in the harem of a sheikh."

• Though "the sheikh's harem" is located in Iran, the emir speaks Arabic and all his cohorts wear Arab garb, burnooses and white thobes. The emir, a graduate of the Harvard Business School, goes to bed Cora and Emanuelle. Quips Cora, "You Arabs have energy resources."

• Sighs a lovely enslaved woman, "Many of the girls are never seen again; [they're taken to] a brothel on the Ivory Coast." Cora and Emanuelle discover the slaver's identity; telling the emir that his aide, Kassim, is "a slave trader [operating] a white slavery ring." Kassim refuses to release his Western prisoners unless "lucrative oil contracts are arranged." Abruptly, the emir catches up with Kassim, terminating the Arab's slavery trade.

Emanuelle in Bangkok (1976), City Lights. *Laura Gemser*. Filmed in
Morocco. CAMEOS

Final frames in this un-rated film display Moroccans romping around with Emanuelle and Janet, her blonde companion.

Scene: In the desert, Emanuelle's car breaks down. Surfacing are a band of black-burnoosed, white-robed, saber-wielding, gun-toting Arabs. Emanuelle and Janet check out the bedouins, nod approvingly and ride off with them.

• Inside an Arabian Nights tent, nearly nude bellydancers, backed by Arab musicians, flex their torsos. Janet and Emanuelle opt to participate. Smiling, they remove their blouses and also dance. Cut to several burnoosed Arabs. They encircle the women, covering them with their dark, lengthy burnooses. Fade to black.

Emanuelle in Egypt (1977), Dimenson. Italian, dubbed in English.

Laura Gemser, Annie Belle, Tarik Ali. W, D: Brunello Rondi. EGYPTIANS

This R-rated scenario, filmed in Egypt, passed Egypt's censors.

Scene: Egypt. A Western cameraman takes photographs of the nearly nude Emanuelle. Cut to scores of young, dead Egyptians; their bodies fill the screen. Next, the camera reveals the naked Emanuelle; she and the photographer make love.

Note: Nubian songs are performed by the Aswan Folklore Group. Also, the villagers of So'Hel, Aswan sing.

Embassy (1972), a.k.a. Target Embassy, Hemdale. *Richard Roundtree, Max von Sydow, Chuck Connors, Ray Milland, Marie-Jose Nat.* P: Mel Ferrer. SP: William Fairchild. Based on Stephen Coulter's novel. Filmed in Lebanon. MAIDENS

A Lebanese woman appears as a bright and courageous doctor in love with an African-American diplomat.

Scene: US Embassy, Beirut. A Soviet official, Gorenko (von Sydow), seeks political asylum. An American diplomat, Shannon (Roundtree), and his colleagues move to protect the Russian from assassins.

• Outside the Embassy. Lebanese students flaunt signs: "Yankee-Go-Home," "American Imperialism Out." Lebanese policemen arrive; Lebanese tussle with Lebanese.

• Shannon sleeps with the Lebanese doctor he loves, lovely Laure (Nat).

• "To try and keep the Russian alive," Laure performs a difficult "abdominal operation." She saves Gorenko's life; aiding Laure is an American nurse.

• A "gun-wielding wild man," Kesten (Connors), enters the hospital and holds Laure hostage. Unless she tells him where Gorenko is lodged, he will shoot her. Laure refuses to reveal the Soviet official's whereabouts. Later, Shannon tells her, "You were great."

• The airport. Shannon and a state department official argue about what to do with Gorenko. Meanwhile, Laure tells the duo, "Stop squabbling over him as though he was a piece of paper or something, and get him into this ambulance... I can at least try and keep him alive. Now!" They place Gorenko into the ambulance; Laure attends him.

The English Patient (1996), MIR. *Ralph Fiennes, Kristin Scott Thomas, Juliet Binoche, Naveen Andrews.* SP, D: Anthony Minghella. Based on Michael Ondaatje's novel. Filmed in Tunisia. MAIDENS

In the pre-WWII desert of North Africa, Arabs assist Westerners and vice versa. The story concerns Hungarian Count Almasy (Fiennes) and his tragic affair with Katherine (Scott Thomas), a British cartographer's wife.

Scene: Though bedouins are relegated to minor roles, opening frames show them rescuing Almasy from his broken plane, which the Germans shot down. To ease his pain, bedouins carefully apply indigenous medicines to Almasy's badly burned body.

• During desert expeditions Almasy and his international team of Western cartographers speak Arabic. The Arabs and the English participate in sing-a-longs, belting out tunes such as "Yes, we have no bananas," and the "Jellyroll Blues."

• Islam is revered. Praying Arabs say, "Allahu Akbar."

• The desert. A bedouin accidentally falls from a moving truck. Swiftly, his British supervisors assist.

• A sandstorm completely covers the incapacitated truck. Trapped inside are three bedouins. Digging fanatically, Almasy and Katherine locate the buried vehicle, rescuing the Arabs.

• In Tobruk, a German officer demands a Libyan Muslim nurse slice off an American prisoner's thumbs. Cut to the shocked faces of two German soldiers; they oppose this order. The Arab nurse, however, obeys the Nazi officer, and removes the American's thumbs.

Note: Enhancing religious tolerance. Inside a darkened church, the camera reveals Kip, a Sikh demolitions expert (Andrews). With him is his companion Hana (Binoche), an Allied nurse. Kip hands Hana a lighted torch, then hoists her to the church ceiling. The light reveals the cathedral's colorful biblical motifs; Hana rejoices.

Ernest in the Army (1997), Monarch. *Jim Varney, David Muller, Christo Davids, Hayley Tyson, Ivan Lucas, Farouk Valley Omar.* SP: Jeffrey Pillars, Joseph Dattorre. S, D: John Cherry. VILLAINS

An army reservist crushes an Arab tyrant and his cohorts. See *In the Army Now* (1994).

Scene: The desert. Arab soldiers haul off bloodied Arab prisoners, blindfolded. Destroyed army vehicles, barbed wire, and wasted weapons appear in the background.

• "ARIZIA," a Gulf nation. The potentate, Omar Habib Tufute (Lucas) plays golf. He informs his cohorts they will soon invade neighboring "Karifistan." Should US forces intervene, Omar vows to crush the "infidels." A golf ball hits a pole flying the US flag; the flag falls.

• One of Omar's prisoners says, "There will be one man... from the West to humble the [Arizia] tyrants of the earth." Cut to Valdosta, Georgia. Ernest Worrell (Varney) is gathering golf balls.

• Ernest joins the army's 97th reserve unit. Abruptly, the reservists are told that Arizia possesses "a large pluton missile," and that an invasion of Karifistan is imminent. Cut to Omar's soldiers "devouring" Karifistan's "oppressed, crushing everything in their path." A starving Arab boy, Ben-Ali (Davids), grabs an apple. One of Omar's soldiers chases him.

• Unveiling his new pluton missile, Omar shouts, "Allah be praised... I will bring the infidels to their knees!" Omar's screaming soldiers fire their weapons.

• Ernest befriends Ben-Ali; he prevents three Arab youths from beating the boy.

• Omar's "goons" kidnap a blonde US TV reporter, Cindy (Tyson). Cindy will not allow Omar to kiss her hand.

• Omar straps a UN colonel to a missile; his men chant "Tufute, Tufute!"

• Thanks to Ernest, Cindy escapes. Cut to the ruler's dense soldiers mistakenly beating up each other. Omar's freed prisoners join in, bringing down the culprits.

• "Operation Sand Trap." Ernest thwarts Omar's missile launch. When asked, "Who do you think you are, Rambo?" Ernest says, "Almost." Omar and his troops chase after Cindy and Ernest. Cindy grabs a gun and mows down the pursuers. [See *G.I. Jane* (1997).] Concurrently, Ernest tosses a few bombs, blasting even more Arabs. Finally, using one of his rock-hard pancakes, he floors the bearded, bald Omar.

Note: This direct-to-video movie also mocks a US Army general.

Escape from L.A. (1996), a.k.a. John Carpenter's Escape from LA, PAR. A John Carpenter film. *Kurt Russell, Valerie Golina.* SP, P: Russell, Carpenter, Debra Hill. D: Carpenter. CAMEOS, MAIDENS

US government profiling damages an Arab Muslim woman. The film's primary villains are the American president and a Peruvian.

Scene: The year 2013, "Los Angeles Island." (The city was separated from the mainland by earthquake.) After the president signs "Directive 17," all "undesirable and unfit" people are dispatched to the island. Declares the president, these folks are not suitable "to live in moral America... we're throwing out the trash, they'll never come back."

• Tucked away somewhere on the island is a weapon capable of eradicating the world's power supplies. The protagonist, Snake (Russell), is coerced into retrieving it. When Snake arrives on the island, he befriends an attractive Arab Muslim woman, Tasmila (Golina). Flaunting a rose tattoo above her bosom, Tasmila offers to read Snake's future. Later, they make love. Concerned for Snake's safety, Tasmila guides him to a safe place.

• Impressed by Tasmila's wisdom, Snake asks: "Why are you here?" Sighs Tasmila, "I was a Muslim in South Dakota. All of a sudden, they made it a crime." Suddenly, she is shot dead.

Escape from Zahrain (1962), PAR. *Yul Brynner, Sal Mineo, Marilyn Rhue, Jack Warden.* MAIDENS, RECOMMENDED

Arabs seeking freedom befriend an American. Briefly, Arab villains surface.

• Barks the ruler of a mythical Arab nation, "May (Sheikh) Sharif (Brynner) burn in hell... There will be no trial. Kill him." Why eradicate Sharif? Because if Sharif "were to live he'd remind the people that the ruler failed to keep his promises to build schools and hospitals."

• Courageous Arab students encircle a military van. Inside the van, the ruler's hostages: Sharif, Ahmed (Mineo), a young militant, and Huston (Warden), an American who embezzled $200 thousand from Zahrain Oil. Abruptly, the prisoners escape. Huston calls one escapee "raghead," and "Frankenstein, a perfectly appalling fellow."

• The escapees head for the frontier. A European-educated Arab nurse, Laila (Rhue), drives the truck. Impressed, the young Ahmed tells her, "I think women should be as free as men." Huston spouts some colonial propaganda: "If someone didn't step in to help you [Arabs], you'd still be rubbing sticks together to make a fire." Sighs Sharif, "You're just as stuck with us, as we are with you." At times, the ruler's soldiers try to stop the escapees; they fail.

• Sharif lectures Laila, "You're still trying to be European, but you're not. And if you keep trying you"ll become nothing and belong nowhere. You are Arab. Your roots are strong... deep and strong." Sharif was also educated in Europe, but he "didn't adopt their view." Bemoans Sharif, the Europeans control Zahrain; half the wealth goes to outsiders, the remaining half to corrupt Zahrani bureaucrats. This is why "independence is something that has to be fought for."

• A military plane attacks, destroying their truck. When Ahmed moves to save Laila's life, he is fatally shot. Clasping the student's hand, Sharif says, "When a boy of eighteen dies in your arms, it isn't glorious."

• Desert villagers assist the escapees, giving them a vehicle. Huston advises Laila not to try and liberate her country, quipping, "Aren't you a little tired of sand in your food?" Retorts Laila, "I am Arab, Mr. Huston, I am used to it."

• Mutual respect and cooperation. Huston, the American, and the Arabs, Sharif and Laila, work together. They monitor the dictator's communications, read maps, repair the vehicle, and fix flat tires. Finally, they arrive at the frontier.

Finis: Sharif and Houston shake hands. Acknowledges Huston, "Ahmed was a nice boy." Affirms Sharif: "They all are."

Treatment of Islam: A man dies; Sharif pauses to say prayers.

Espionage in Tangiers (1965), Douica. Italian-Spanish, dubbed in English. *Luis Davila.* D: Gregg Tallas. Filmed in Morocco. VILLAINS

Stolen, an atomic gun, "the most terrible weapon that mankind has ever dreamed of." The American protagonist (Murphy) flies off to Tangiers to nab the thieves. Moroccans as disposable properties.

Scene: Tangiers. A pleasant souk. The first Moroccan to appear is a corpse. The second is a man "mixed up with narcotics [and] spying; [he'll] do anything for 100 francs." Abruptly, he is shot. And the third Moroccan: a dense vendor.

Eve of Destruction (1991), OR. *Gregory Hines.* CAMEOS, VILLAINS

A one-liner. When a destructive computer called "Eve" murders several people, the protagonist (Hines) quips: "Looks like a bad night in West Beirut." As Eve's nuclear capabilities are getting "out of hand," military personnel consider blaming the unexpected deaths on the "Iraqis or Libyans. Whoever's on top of your shit list."

Executive Decision (1996), WB. *Kurt Russell, Halle Berry, David Suchet.* SP: Jim Thomas, John Thomas. P: Joel Silver. PALESTINIANS

Eight dark-complexioned Palestinian Muslims vs. an elite US anti-terrorist unit. Palestinian terrorists hijack a Boeing 747 en route to Washington, DC; 406 passengers are aboard. The Palestinians beat and kill innocents, including a US senator. Chanting Allahu Akbar, the maniacal Muslims intend to unload enough DZ-5 nerve gas to kill nearly everyone on the Eastern seaboard—40 million people. Actor David Suchet, who portrays the lead terrorist, is best known for his portrayal of Hercule Poirot on the PBS series *Mystery*.

Scene: London. Holding the Holy Koran in one hand and a bomb in another, a Palestinian fanatic enters the Marriott Hotel, blowing up himself and scores of diners.

• Nagi Hassan (Suchet) and his Muslim cohorts hijack an Oceanic Air passenger jet. They rough up passengers and murder a blonde stewardess. As Nagi demands "50 million in gold bullion," cut to a map displaying the terrorists' target—Washington, DC

• To the rescue, US Major David Grant's (Russell) multicultural (Asian, black, and Latino soldiers) anti-terrorist crew. A Stealth superjet takes off, piggybacking underneath the hijacked Oceanic plane, enabling Grant's squad to board the jet.

• Throughout, devout Islamic practices are equated with terror. Implying the Holy Koran encourages the killing of innocents, the camera reveals a Muslim terrorist's ring displaying the word, "Allah." When asked whether mistreating people has anything to do with his "cause," Nagi says, "It says here in the Koran." Before and after killing passengers, Nagi prays. And when he spots several F-14's approaching, Nagi shouts: "It's the sword of Islam... sent to deliver a blow to the belly of the infidel." Exclaiming "Allahu Akbar" (God is Most Great), Nagi boasts to a cohort, "We are the true soldiers of Islam."

• Nagi, whom the Israeli agents tag the "Jaffa bastard," refuses to allow the African-American flight attendant (Berry) to serve food to non-Muslim passengers. Only Muslims may dine, he says. Why? Because "Allah has blessed all the people of Islam."

• Nagi kills an American senator. Then he prays, warning, "Any further threats will result in a passenger being killed every minute."

• In the end, Major Grant's squad wipes out the terrorists. Before Nagi dies, he screams, "Allahu Akbar."

Note: Though the credits state that Nagi Hassan is portrayed by David Suchet, the credits do not offer names for Nagi's cohorts; they are simply billed as "Terrorists." Two American Muslim actors, Sayed Badreya and Majed Ibrahim, portray two of these terrorists. Distressed because far too many scenes presented Islam in "a disgraceful manner," they persuaded director Stuart Baird to remove several objectionable anti-Muslim scenes. Not only did the original script contain a rape scene, said Ibrahim, but Jews were targeted as the primary hijacking victims. Baird, however, was "sympathetic to the [some of the] concerns raised by Muslims." Said Ibrahim, "[All I] tried to do was damage control... My dream is to some day make a movie that shows Arabs and Muslims as hard-working people, unlike what most Americans know about them."[66]

• Excerpts from some reviews: "*Executive Decision* is an edge-of-the-seat, thinking person's thriller," according to Larry King in *USA Today* (13 April 1996). The Toronto *Globe and Mail*'s Christopher Harris: [Villains are] "the same generic, Allah-praising Muslims who pop up in thriller after thriller. Enough already!... It would be nice to have a change of bad guys in the movies... to prevent this ethnic group from being demonized" (15 March). *Hilton Head News*' Jim Littlejohn: "I have a problem these days with our new stage villains turning out to be Palestinians at every turn." When it comes to "ethnic and national bogeymen, our Arabic friends get it in the neck every time" (3 April). Ray Rinaldi of the *St. Louis Post-Dispatch*: "Once again the bad guys are Middle East terrorists... it's enough to make you consider taking Amtrak" (15 March). *Entertainment Weekly*'s Owen Gleiberman: "[A]nother go-around on a ride that never ends... [The Palestinians] are portrayed as if they were the staff of the world's meanest falafel establishment." He reported that during the preview screening "some audience members whistled and clapped when the good guys kicked ass, terminating gun-toting Muslims" (22 March). Strangely, a few weeks after Gleiberman's EW review criticized the stereotypes, a capsule review stated, "Will kids want to watch it? Yes—and you might just let them. The movie is successful and smart" (19 April).

In her *LA Times* essay "The Villainous Depiction of Muslims," Grace Song pointed out that the Muslim villain's reading of the Koran "associated mainstream Islamic practices with terrorism." Imagine a movie featuring a clone of Yitzhak Rabin's assassin, Yigal Amir, reading from the Torah, and then killing bystanders. Filmmakers, argued Song, "would think twice before drawing that hideous connection." *Executive Decision*, *True Lies*, and other Hollywood movies "fuel the fire of racism against Muslims... [T]he security and comfort of our Islamic faith [has] become the symbolic embodiment of terror" (1 April).

In her NYT review, Janet Maslin complained of "unexplained Arab fanatics who draw on every ethnic cliché. The [American] Arab groups that protested unflattering stereotypes in *True Lies* have a stronger complaint about this [film]" (15 March).

• Just before *Executive Decision*'s debut, Steven Emerson claimed in the *Wall Street Journal* that America's Muslims were supporting Middle East terror, and that President and Mrs. Clinton were consorting with "the American Muslim Council," a group that "champions... Islamic terrorist groups in the US" (12 March). On 16 March, four days after Emerson's column and two days following the film's release, two Denver DJs burst into a Denver mosque and harassed worshipers. One announcer wore a mock turban; the other played the national anthem on a trumpet. The radio station broadcast the mosque incident, live.

• From 17–26 March, *Executive Decision* was the highest grossing film in the country. Warner Brothers' spokesperson defended the film's stereotypes, saying the movie was "portraying a make-believe situation." Said Diane Gursky, "We did not and do not intend to hurt anyone's feelings by this movie." Another executive chimed in, "These are unfortunately the headlines of the moment." (Since when are newspaper headlines used as an excuse to vilify a people? The "headlines of the moment" regularly display heinous acts committed by non-Muslims, Christians, Jews, Hindus, Buddhists and so forth.)

• Days before *Executive Decision* appeared in movie theaters, Warner Brothers executives invited Muslim and Arab leaders to a special screening. Afterwards, Nihad Awad, executive director of Council On American-Islamic Relations (CAIR), posed this question, "Why is it the norm in movies for a Muslim to be a terrorist?" CAIR asked the studio to edit offensive scenes; studio executives balked, saying it was too late for such modifications. Two weeks later, however, following another CAIR meeting, Warner Brothers agreed to make "eight changes" for *Executive Decision*'s video and television release. Later, CAIR issued a press release stating that the studio promised "to seek our assistance in advance of production of future projects involving Arabs and Islam."

• In 1997, Royal Oaks Entertainment distributed its direct-to-video feature, *Strategic Command*. The scenario is similar to this one, with one major exception: No Arab terrorists appear. In *Strategic Command*, generic terrorists hijack a plane, taking the US vice president and others hostage. Unless the terrorists receive $100 million, they threaten to unleash "the most destructive element ever created—the highly lethal chemical weapon, Bromex 365." Here, too, US commandos board the in-flight jet, crushing the terrorists.

Exodus (1960), UA, Otto Preminger Productions. *Paul Newman, Eva Marie Saint, Ralph Richardson, Jill Hayworth, John Derek, Lee J. Cobb, Sal Mineo.* SP: Dalton Trumbo. D: Preminger. Based on Leon Uris's novel. PALESTINIANS, WORST LIST

In the 1950s, when Americans were largely apathetic about Israel, the eminent public relations consultant Edward Gottlieb was called on "to create a more sympathetic attitude" toward the newly established state. And so, he sent Leon Uris to Israel to write a novel, which became the bestseller *Exodus*. "Uris' novel solidified America's impressions of Israelis as heroes, of Arabs as villains; it did more to popularize Israel with the American public than any other single presentation through the media."[67]

Exodus introduced filmgoers to the Arab-Israel conflict, and peopled it with heroic Israelis and sleazy, brutal Arabs, some of whom link up with ex-Nazis. Set in Palestine in 1947, Arabs aligned with ex-Nazis commit atrocities against fellow Arabs and non-Arabs. Jews wearing Arab garb terminate Arabs. Westerners and others, such as Hank, a Greek businessman, supply needed weapons, and fight and die for Israel. The movie's only "good Arab" becomes a dead Arab.

Scene: An American woman's bad feelings about Jews dissipate. Kitty Fremont (Saint), a widowed nurse from Indiana, is asked to tend Jewish refugees. Kitty balks, saying, "I don't know anything about them, I feel strange about them." "In what way?" asks a British officer. Admits Kitty, "Now that you mention it, I can't think. It's just a feeling I get." Soon, Kitty befriends Israeli nationalist Ari Ben Canaan (Newman). She warns him, "The Arabs won't let you keep it [Palestine]. 500,000 Jews against 50 million Arabs! You can't win." When she learns the Arabs will attack, Kitty tells Ari, "I'm with you!"

• A British solider tells an Israeli youth, Dov (Mineo), "Don't wander into the Arab section. Run into one of the Grand Mufti's gangsters [and] they'll kill you, son. They'll slice your throat."

• Declares British General Sutherland (Richardson), "The Arabs simply won't keep the peace... The Arabs are fanatic on the subject of Jewish immigration."

• The camera reveals Jewish refugees aboard the ship, *Exodus*. They are warned, "The Grand Mufti of Jerusalem, who sat out the war as Hitler's guest in Berlin, has met with representatives of the Arab nations to coordinate action against Palestinian Jews in the event partition is granted."

• The camera reveals Jewish refugees in British detention camps, a "barbed wire jungle."

• Aboard the *Exodus*, the Star of David flag flutters in the wind. The ship's 611 refugees go on a hunger strike. Mothers are willing to sacrifice themselves and their children for freedom in a Jewish state. Cut to a young couple, elderly men playing chess, and violin players.

• Irgun members bomb the King David Hotel. Declares a radio announcer, "91 bodies have been discovered so far." Throughout, the Irgun terrorists are tagged "freedom fighters." Ari Ben Canaan plans to release "93 Jewish prisoners," including those Irgun bombers who ignited the King David Hotel. When an Irgun member asks Ari, "What about the 400 Arabs in that prison?" Ari quips, "If you turn 400 Arabs loose they are going to run in 400 different directions."

• Believing Arabs will attack a Jewish youth camp, 300 children depart. A Jewish solider is asked about reinforcements, "How many men did you bring?" Only a few truckloads, he says, but "from the Arab side it looks like an army."

• Ari's men enter a Turkish bath; mute Palestinians promptly surrender.

• Ari's father, Barak (Cobb), and a Hagana community leader, cite the Bible, telling General Sutherland what God said to Moses, "Go unto Pharaoh and say unto him, thus sayeth the Lord: Let my people go, that they may serve me." Exodus. Chapter 7, verse 26."

• Barak addresses Jews, saying, "[We] changed these mosquito-infested swamps into such [fertile] fields. On a quiet night you can hear the corn grow... The Grand Mufti of Jerusalem has asked you [Palestinians] to either annihilate the Jewish population or abandon your homes, and your land, and seek the weary path of exile. We [Jews] implore you, remain in your homes and we shall work together as equals in the state of Israel."

Ari echo's his father's advice, telling the crowd: "Now, we'll be equal citizens in the free state of Israel. Why should they [the Palestinians] go anywhere. This is their home as well as ours. Don't you see, we have to prove to the world that we can get along together."

• As Barak dedicates a new kibbutz, he thanks a charitable Arab village leader who donated the land. Next, Taha, the film's token Arab, utters a few words, "We dwell together as friends. It is natural that we should live in peace." Cut to Barak. He condemns Arab brutes, explaining that the kibbutz is named after Daphne, a Jewish girl. Daphne "was a young soldier [only seventeen]. And the Arabs captured her and they tortured her to find out things from her. But she wouldn't tell. So they sent her back in a sack, tied to the back of a mule. They cut off her hands and feet and they gouged out her eyes."

• A German wearing a white suit asks Taha to join an attack on a Jewish youth camp. I have "eighty Arab storm troopers" under my command, he says. Taha refuses, saying, "Why must we slaughter defenseless children?"

• Sighs Taha, "When the Syrian Arabs murdered my father in his mosque, Ari's father saved my life, and my heritage." Ari warns Taha not to return to his village. Says Taha, "I am a Moslem; I cannot kill another Arab." Cut to Taha's body, hanging from a rope, in his deserted Arab village. Painted on a nearby wall, the Star of David.

• At the Jewish camp Dov tells the refugee Karen, "Stay down, girl, there are Arabs out there." Later, the Arabs kill young Karen.

• Ari buries in one grave, the Arab, Taha (Derek), and the 15-year-old European refugee, Karen [Hayworth]. Says Ari, "The day will come when Arab and Jew will share a peaceful life in this land they have always shared in death."

• Prior to the Jewish victory, Ari's men say "Arabs... have been infiltrating the valley... There have been two ambushes... uprising in progress... We're heavily outnumbered." Jewish children in the kibbutz are told, "Arabs have been leaving [their] villages." At no time does a character say Jewish troops are terrorizing the Palestinians, forcing them from their homes.

Note: In 1937, two-plus decades prior to *Exodus*, the Ray Film Company's, *The Holy Oath*, a Yiddish language film with English subtitles advanced a similar "good" Jews and "bad" Arabs theme. Screened in New York City, *The Holy Oath*'s objective was not so much to entertain audiences, rather to muster viewers' support for a worldwide Jewish movement to gain and rebuild Palestine. To engage viewers, *The Holy Oath* shows Arabs, not Jews, at Jerusalem's wailing wall. Throughout *The Holy Oath*, the Jewish protagonist declares that God gave this land [Palestine], flowing with milk and honey, to the people of Israel. To illustrate, footage selectively displays bedouins roaming the sterile cities of Hebron and Jerusalem. The film concludes with the Jewish people enjoying life in the booming nation of Israel. Featured in the film, the song, "In the Arabian 'doine.'" Interestingly, as President Franklin D. Roosevelt's wife, Eleanor, thought the Palestinians were nomads, she believed there would be no problems evicting Palestinians from their homes.[68]

• Never spoken in this movie are these words: "Palestinian," "Palestinian Arab," "Palestinian village," "Palestinian state." Instead, *Exodus*' Jews, Arabs, and Westerners say: "Arab," "Arab village," and "independent Arab state." On two occasions, the phrase, "Palestinian Jews," is mentioned.

The Exorcist (1973), WB. *Ellen Burstyn, Linda Blair, Max von Sydow.* W, P: William Peter Blatty. CAMEOS

A priest befriends Iraqi archaeologists.

Scene: An excavation site in northern Iraq. As Arabs dig, sheep roam. An Iraqi boy informs the priest (von Sydow) that workers have "found something, small pieces." Speaking Arabic, Von Sydow chats with Arab archaeologists. Next, the priest hugs his Arab colleague.

• One of the uncovered artifacts foretells danger, "evil against evil." The priest sees two dogs fighting, and glances up at a statue, "The Demon." From Iraq, the film shifts to the Georgetown area of Washington, DC. Here, "evil" possesses a young girl.

Eye For Eye (1918), Nazimova Prod. Silent. *Nazimova, Charles Bryant.* *NS. Notes from AFIC (p 254). MAIDENS

The Arab heroine romances a French officer, double-crossing fellow bedouins.

The sheikh's daughter, Hassouna (Nazimova), rescues French Captain de Cadiere (Bryant) from hostile bedouins. As she was disloyal, bedouins abandon Hassouna, leaving her "to die in the desert." But Hassouna is rescued and goes on to become a dancer. No sooner does Captain de Cadiere adopt her, Hassouna's ex-Arab suitor surfaces. The Arab deceives her, saying that the Frenchman "was responsible for the death of her family." For a moment, her affection for the officer "turns to hatred." Not for long. Her love "is too great" to do de Cadiere "harm." In the end, she discovers the truth. The jealous bedouin's charges against her French Captain are "false."

Eyes of the Mummy (1918), a.k.a. Die Augen der Mummie Ma.

Ernst Lubitsch's silent film with German subtitles. *Pola Negri, Emil Jannings.* MAIDENS

Scene: Cairo's souk. As a magician performs, children steal food and vendors hawk wares to Western tourists.

• Inside a tomb. Introducing a Western tourist in love with the maiden, Ma (Negri). He moves to save her from the clutches of the insanely jealous Radu (Jannings). The Westerner and Radu fight; Radu's defeated. Ma and the tourist ride off together. Later, they wed.

• Ma's husband's home. Various tutors teach Ma manners. Finally, her husband decides to present Ma to some guests. He hosts a swank party for fellow Westerners. As Ma cannot waltz, she dons Egyptian garb and dances, seductively, for the guests. Gaping, the men approve; the women do not.

• Radu sneaks into the home. Seeing Ma's portrait on the wall, the enraged Egyptian plunges a dagger into the painting. Next, Radu searches the home, uncovering Ma's whereabouts. The Egyptian fatally knifes Ma, then himself.

The Fall of Babylon (1910), Gaumont. Silent. *NS. MAIDENS

The Fall of Babylon (1919), D.W. Griffith. Silent. An expanded version of his film *Intolerance* (1916). My summary is of the 1919 film. MAIDENS

539 BC. Scantily-clad Arab maidens are sold at the "marriage market. Money [is] paid for beautiful women." Barks the auctioneer, "What am I bid for this gentle dove?" One Arab woman performs "the dance of undulation." Babylonians [today's Iraqis] fight Persians [today's Iranians]. Final frames show Cyrus's Persians defeating Belshazzar's Babylonians.

Father of the Bride Part II (1995), TOU. *Steve Martin, Diane Keaton, Eugene Levy, Kimberly Williams.* SP: Nancy Meyers, Charles Shyer. P: Meyers, Shyer. D: Shyer. CAMEOS

Into this classic feel-good family movie, Disney-owned Touchstone injects three scenes (totaling about five minutes) of ugly Mideast Americans. Before this one, all the 'Bride' movies going back to the Spencer Tracy, Elizabeth Taylor film *Father of the Bride* (1950) focused on love and marriage; not one vilified a people.

Scene: In Los Angeles, George Banks (Martin) opts to sell his and Nina's (Keaton) "Brady Bunch" home on 24 Maple Drive. Abruptly, coarse buyers surface—the rich, unkempt Mr. Habib (Levy) and his wife. Even the movie's ferocious Dobermans behave better than this uncaring duo. Habib smokes, needs a shave, and speaks with a heavy accent. When Mrs. Habib tries to speak, Habib shouts gibberish at her, a mix of Farsi and Arabic. Mrs. Habib heels, reinforcing the stereotype of the Arab woman as a mute, submissive nonentity. Sleazy Habib tells George, "We like house, very much. You sell, we pay top dollar!" And, "We need house, especially the dishes." As a down payment, he hands George, one at a time, 15 1,000-dollar bills. Then, he insists the Banks' "be out in 10 days... or no deal."

• 24 Maple Drive. George and his soon-to-be-wed daughter Annie (Williams), recall past sentiments, the time when they carved their initials on the tree, and when they played basketball. Habib arrives. Shattering their memories, he commands, "You got a key, George. The key!" Slowly, George hands him the key. Habib tosses his cigarette onto the neat walkway. The message? There goes the neighborhood.

• Morning, the next day. Habib and his uniformed wrecking crew move to tear down George's home. Steering a huge yellow wrecking ball, Habib boasts to George, "See, I demolish house, put two in its place." Pleads George, "I built this fence. I planted this grass. Don't bulldoze my memories, man. I'm begging you." Though Habib has owned the house for only a day, he preys on George's emotions and rips him off. Trying to save his residence, George is more than generous, offering Habib $50,000 more than what Habib paid for the home. Yet, Habib refuses to take the money. He wants more. Only after he extorts $100,000 from George does Habib decide to return the house.

Note: *Entertainment Weekly* critic Ken Tucker writes, "The caricature of a cold, rich... [Habib] amounts to a glaring ethnic slur" (15 December 1995).[69]

Fatima (1897), International. Silent. MAIDENS

Fatima (1912), Cines Films. Silent. *NS. Notes from Adbelmajid Hajji's dissertation, "The Arab in Silent Cinema" (University of Kansas, 1993). RECOMMENDED

Two brothers, the magistrate Malik and young Omar, love the same woman. Malik dispatches brother Omar to a distant land to fetch his intended, the beautiful Fatima. On the return journey home Omar falls hopelessly in love with Fatima, and vice versa. Yet, Omar remains faithful to his [brother's] trust." Malik attempts to gain Fatima's love; he woos her and offers her presents. But, he soon realizes she loves Omar, his brother. Intent on making her happy, Malik permits Fatima to wed the man of her choice, Omar.

This refreshing film does not reveal Malik as a stereotypical Arab "who is polygamous, sensual, and cruel." Rather, Malik appears as "a respectful individual," a man of honor. Omar, too, shares such integrity. After confessing to his mother that he loves Fatima, Omar acts honorably, refusing to injure Fatima or his brother. Fatima's actions, too, counter the stale stereotype. She is not as a cheating harem maiden, but a devout, honest, and faithful woman.

Fatima's Dance (1907), International. Silent. MAIDENS

Silent movies debuted in 1892 in Thomas Edison's West Orange, New Jersey New Theater. At his "movie studio," Edison managed to project moving pictures onto a screen large enough to be viewed by more than one or two persons. Four years later, on April 23, 1896, the first program of silent motion pictures in the United States was screened in New York, at the Koster and Bial's Music Hall. A year later, Edison presented *Fatima*, with the Egyptian sensation of the 1896 Chicago World's Fair. Fatima's famous *danse du ventren* shocked audiences.

I first saw the three-minute *Fatima* in the summer of 1965 at the University of California, Los Angeles. The film history instructor screened both the 1897 and 1907 films, the censored and uncensored versions, both of which featured the well-endowed houchie-couchie dancer: Fatima.

The uncensored cut of *Fatima* reveals an obese, dark-haired, and olive-eyed woman in Arab garb, her navel exposed. She performs a belly dance. As the dance commences, the swaying of her hips becomes more pronounced.

The censored version offers identical images, with one major exception. Some exhibitors objected to the dancer's pronounced movements. Thus, they blotted out the offending portions of Fatima's sensuous shimmy, placing bar grids that look like a wooden fence over her midriff and hips.

A decade later, *Fatima's Dance* surfaced, containing identical footage. *Fatima's Dance* was part of Showtime's November 1, 1996 TV special, *Sex and the Silver Screen*, hosted by Raquel Welch.

The fact that bellydancers appeared in early films is not surprising. At the turn of the century, in vaudeville and burlesque circles, Arab bellydancers were familiar fare. In a paper presented at the Southeastern Middle East and Islamic Studies Seminar in 1993, Virgina Polytechnic Professor Charles Kennedy said that the dancer's "costume was always strictly oriental, a short bolero with coin decorations, a white chemise, harem pantaloons and a wide sash." As early as 1895 barkers tagged the bellydancer "Little Egypt," and "one hundred and fifty Oriental beauties" accompanied her. Barkers would shout, "This way for the streets of Cairo... Pre-sen-ting Little Egypt! For ten cents, see her prance, see her wiggle... When she dances every fiber and every tissue of her anatomy shakes like a jar of jelly from our grandmother's Thanksgiving dinner." And, "Now, gentlemen, I don't say she's hot. But I do say she's as hot as a red hot stove on the fourth of July in the hottest county in the state."

At the Chicago (1893) and St. Louis (1904) World Fairs, barkers would ramble the "Street of Cairo," hyping dancers such as "Belle Fatima," and "Little Egypt." As a result, crowds flocked to Chicago's most popular village, the "Street of Cairo." In a little less than one decade, "Little Egypt" became the generic name for the belly and oriental dancer, capturing the popular imagination with a stereotype that has endured ever since. The dancer Fahreda Mahzar, who came from Damascus, Syria, not Cairo, Egypt, was called "Little Egypt" and the "Darling of the Nile." Fahreda's success at the Chicago Fair prompted the Egyptian Theater to feature dancing girls performing continuously, from 10 AM to 10 PM. Not everyone, however, was pleased. Kennedy cites one critic's impressions: "It was a suggestively lascivious contorting of the abdominal muscles, which is extremely ungraceful and shockingly disgusting."

A Chicago Fair historical document contains similar criticisms. A photograph of three Egyptian women is displayed, with this caption: Contrary to what writers of Oriental stories say about the beautiful "houris of the East, close contact reveals them as we behold them here, destitute of animation, formless as badly stuffed animals, as homely as owls, and as graceless as stall-fed bovines."

Kennedy contends that "There was no way for audiences to know or appreciate the status of professional dancers in the Middle East or the rigorous training required." The women were packaged and then displayed as things of pleasure, benefitting men. Thus, the performances of dancers such as "Little Egypt," "Belle Fatima," and other "bewitching ballerinas" initiated "negative and ethnic and gender stereotypes about Middle Eastern women. From the American standpoint the negative associations of the undulating movements of the torso were sufficient to denigrate the performers." Americans wrongly assumed "these women represented a lower class," says Kennedy. "No ordinary Western woman looked at one of these performances with anything but horror."[70]

Interestingly, though Chicago's 1893 fair "was supposed to commemorate human rights," blacks were ridiculed. "When fair officials finally decided to hold a special 'Colored People's Day,' they made it into a cruel joke, with free watermelons for all African-American visitors."[71]

• Four decades later, the houchie-couchie dance surfaces in Walt Disney's animated short, "A Good Time for a Dime" (1941); the cartoon displays a duck as an Arab dancer. When Donald Duck frequents an arcade, he spots a mutoscope featuring the "Dance of the Seven Veils." The exotic title arouses Donald. He deposits a penny, then ogles the veiled, clad-in-harem-garb Daisy Duck.

Fazil (1928), FOX. Silent. *Charles Farrell, Greta Nissen.* D: Howard Hawks. *NS. Notes from Rob Edelman's essay in MPW (pp 425–7). SHEIKHS

Caution—Westerners should not wed Arabs. A dashing Arab ruler, Prince Fazil (Farrell) and the attractive Parisian Fabienne (Nissen) marry. For a time, they reside happily in Paris. But Fabienne enjoys socializing with Europeans, prompting the prince to become "overbearingly jealous and protective." This reel Moroccan is "a classic male chauvinist" who thinks "a good Arabian wife cannot have men friends." Disturbed by his wife's behavior, Fazil returns to Arabia and "establishes a harem." To Fabienne, the desert is "a prison." Yet, she leaves Europe, returning to Fazil. She confesses her love and agrees to stay at the Moroccan's desert palace. But she will "not submit to him"; nor will she accept his "traditions"—namely, his "harem."

Fazil demands "obedience," and he insists on keeping his "concubines." Fabienne protests; he imprisons her. As friends move to help Fabienne escape, Fazil is shot. "Though mortally wounded," he poisons Fabienne. Final frames show the two "united in death—where, they hope, they can find happiness." Oddly, the sheet music for "Neopolitan Nights," the movie's theme song, displays on its cover a romantic couple embracing.

This scenario reflects changing perceptions of Arabs. In the early 1920s, some common bywords were "vamp," "flapper," and "it." And, thanks to Valentino, "sheik." By the end of the decade, the "sheik" craze had nearly evaporated. Observes critic Rob Edelman, *Fazil* "was released several years past the height of the 'sheik' craze" and "did poorly at the box office." In "1928 audiences were no longer interested in Arab princes... by the 1930s the idea of 'sheik' was a joke. Arab chieftains could no longer be taken seriously as screen lovers. Sheiks were satirized."

In the 1970s, says Edelman, producer-director Stanley Kramer announced the production of *The Sheiks of Araby*, a comedy about "the oil crisis." The film was never made. Explains Edelman, "Contemporary sheiks are associated more with power and money than with romance."

Note: Fazil's attitudes about European women are similar to those expressed by an African officer in *Guns at Batasti* (1964). Here, a British soldier lectures African troops about equal opportunity, emphasizing that English women serve in government. An African interrupts, "What uses, sir, do English women have in Parliament? To carry water?" His African pals laugh.

Federal Agents vs. Underworld, Inc. (1948), REP. 12 episodes. *Kirk Alyn, Rosemary La Planche, Carol Foreman, Jack O'Shea.* Re-edited and released as the feature: *Golden Hands of Kurigal* (1949). See *Perils Of Nyoka* (1942). CLIFFHANGERS, VILLAINS, MAIDENS, EGYPTIANS

Invading the United States, an Arab woman as terrorist. See *Black Sunday* (1977). Federal agents vs. Nila, the Egyptian "female fanatic," and her Arab cohorts.

Scene: Action occurs in America and in the caves, tunnels, tents, and tombs of mythical Abistahn. US agents Dave (Alyn) and Laura (La Planche) move to secure the famous "Golden Hands of Kurigal." Why? Because when one places the statue's two golden hands together and then translates the hieroglyphic inscriptions, the secret to "unknown treasures and gold" will be revealed. At times, the agents don Arab garb.

• Nila, Ali (O'Shea), and their cohorts plus some underworld gangsters are out to acquire the "Hands." If the Egyptians get the treasures, warns a US agent, "the peoples of Abistahn [will be] under Nila's evil domination." To dull the senses of a foe, Nila uses a "rare oriental herb."

• Nila tells her followers, "Rise up against the infidels." Affirms Ali, "The infidels tried to surprise us." Though Ali and other "tribesmen" wear burnooses and thobes, they speak gibberish, not Arabic.

• In the US, Nila tries to kill Dave. First she shoots at him, then she sets off a bomb.

• The US Immigration Bureau. Dave examines files containing information on immigrants from Abistahn. The files are labeled: "ABISTAHNIAN ALIENS IN THIS COUNTRY." The camera reveals an Abistahnian flag tattooed onto an alien's arm.

• Examining Nila's shoe, Dave says, "Nila's been stepping in a swamp area." Quips Laura, "Too bad she didn't step into quicksand up to her neck."

Finis: The statue, the "Golden Hands of Kurigal," crushes Nila. Says Dave, "Seeking to destroy others, Nila succeeded in destroying herself." And Nila gasps her last, with a southern accent.

The Fifth Element (1997), COL. *Bruce Willis.* EGYPTIANS

The first ten minutes of this $90 million science fiction epic are set in Egypt, the birthplace of civilizations. Appearing are lazy children and a frightened high priest.

1914 Egypt. An Egyptian boy atop a donkey delivers water to loud Egyptian youths. Next, the boy goes inside an ancient tomb, giving some water bags to two Western archaeologists. An Egyptian priest enters the tomb area. He frets that the archaeologists may uncover dangerous truths, so he moves to drug them, permanently. Suddenly, aliens descend from their spaceship. They warn the priest, who is their human contact, "evil is at hand; war is coming!" The aliens depart; the action shifts to New York City, the mid-23rd century.

Fire and the Sword (1914), Kismet. Silent. *Isabel Rea, Tom McEvoy.* *NS. Notes from George Blaisdell's review in MPW (p 815). See *Protocol* (1984). SHEIKHS

A sheikh abducts an American woman. Arabs seeking to secure the heroine kill fellow Arabs. To the rescue, an American reporter.

Summary: In Tangier, the Grand Vizier abducts Helen (Rea), the daughter of a rich American. When the Arab moves to whisk Helen off to Fez, an aroused sultan intervenes, abruptly snatching Helen from the vizier, "which starts trouble and eventually revolt."

Intent on rescuing Helen is a Western journalist (McEvoy), aided by some "good [Arabs] of the dark-skinned type." But the sultan's men nab the journalist, dumping him in the palace torture chamber. Here, "The captured newspaper reporter is suspended by his thumbs... and lifted from the floor with what purports to be a great iron ball tied to his feet."

In the end, the reporter and Helen escape to New York and get engaged.

• Studio press releases called *Fire and the Sword* an "International photo play of love and daring, utilizing 10 acres of flames and 1,000 people," complete with "wall-scalings, hand-to-hand combats, revolution, much shooting and burning."

• Two critics on the film's Arabs. George Blaiswell of MPW: "The backgrounds have a strong resemblance to a certain part of Coney Island where Arabs much do congregate... The mob scenes contain many Arabs—there can be no mistaking that." After visiting Coney Island's Luna Park to see Arabs performing at a "Fire and Sword" stage attraction, the VAR reviewer wrote, "Those Arabic beggared natives [in the film] look suspiciously like a lot of foreigners [that] Ben Hassan Ali brought over for the amusement exhibition in America."

Fire over Africa (1954), COL. *MacDonald Carey, Maureen O'Hara, Binnie Barnes, Ferdy Mayne.* Filmed in Morocco. See *Cairo Road* (1950). VILLAINS, MAIDENS

US agents defeat international curs, including a Moroccan. Arab prostitutes.

Scene: As the narrator intones "Tangier, known as the smuggler's triangle," cut to donkeys and camels parading the casbah's narrow streets. Continues the narrator, criminals "are building the secret fires which burn over North Africa, contraband for all. Although there is no industry, somehow men make fortunes. While Tangier produces nothing, it does create two things: sudden riches, and sudden death." Abruptly, a man in an alley is shot.

• Arriving in Tangier are two American agents, Logan (Carey) and Dane (O'Hara). They move to crush the international smugglers.

• "Frisco's Bar," run by Frisco (Barnes), an American woman. Mute Moroccan prostitutes perch on bar stools. Frisco offers Dane a drink; Dane points to the whores and quips, "No thanks. I'm not a member of the union."

• The Moroccan, Mustapha (Mayne), who owns "Ali Baba's Bazaar" feigns friendship with the Dane and Logan. Later, he moves to kill them. Hidden in the bazaar's back room: the smugglers' communications center.

Finis: Dane and Logan smash the smugglers, taking down the cartel.

Firewalker (1986), CAN. *Chuck Norris, Lou Gossett Jr.* P: Menachem Golan and Yoram Globus. CAMEOS, VILLAINS

This adventure saga takes place in a Central American jungle, where the American protagonists search for lost treasure. Yet, producers Golan and Globus inject Arabs.

Scene: Opening frames reveal repulsive Arabs chasing the protagonists (Norris, Gossett, Jr.) across "200 miles of stinking' desert." Arab music underscores the action. The bearded Arab "bandits" scream as they toss a grenade at the two men. The Arabs close in. "Maybe they're running out of gas," quips a protagonist.

• The Arabs nab the Americans. They bind their hands and feet, then stretch them out, in the spread-eagle position. Right after the Arabs depart, the protagonists escape.

• Moaning about the hazards of treasure hunting in Central America, one protagonist quips: "This whole idea was stupid, stupid." Indeed.

First Family (1980), WB. *Bob Newhart, Harvey Korman, Maurice Sherbanee.* W, D: Buck Henry. CAMEOS, SHEIKHS

The film lampoons White House officials and Arabs. A crude Arab diplomat clashes with US diplomats.

Scene: The UN. A robed Arab delegate (Sherbanee) brandishing a dagger in his belt argues with US delegates. The Arab blows his nose with gusto, prompting the US delegate to quip, "A fascinating display of bodily eruptions." The US delegate tells the Arab to shape up, to "apply his limited powers of concentration to the subject at hand." Retorts the Arab, "You are not fit to suck my hat." Barks the American, "He [the Arab] can meet me in the parking lot wherever he chooses, even if he's wearing a dress. The Arab tosses his dagger at the delegate and walks off. Sighs a US general, he's "a maniac wearing a bed sheet."

First Strike (1984), Tekstar. *Stuart Whitman, Persis Khambatta.* VILLAINS

The Russians move to occupy Syria and other countries and gain control of Arab oil. In Berlin, a Russian spy acquires top-secret US Navy submarine ballistic missile codes. The Russians plan to use the codes to gain control of the American nuclear submarine, the U.S.S. *Cobra.* After taking over the *Cobra,* they intend to launch a "first strike" on Syria's oil regions. The Russians intend to blame the Americans for the attack. Then, they plan to occupy Syria, and wind up with Arab oil. In reality, Syria has no oil fields.

• Boasts a Russian: "We have just delivered five 30-megaton ballistic missiles to Syria. They will be available for launch shortly." A KGB officer complains that "the Syrians are fools. They could jeopardize our entire operation." The Russians warn Syrian officials, "The Americans are probably after your oil fields. Of course the Soviet Union will stand behind you… The American fleet? They are steaming toward your shores. I suggest to you—attack first."

• A Soviet double-agent, Sylvia Kruger (Khambatta) boards the *Cobra.* She guns down the captain (Whitman) and 10-plus crew members. Next, she and her aide launch two nuclear missiles into Syria. Though the Russians are responsible for the Syrian attack, they dupe the Syrians into believing the villainous Americans launched the missile.

• The Syrians retaliate. They launch ICBM's, destroying 90 percent of the US fleet. Exclaim the Russians, "The world will believe the United States initialed the use of nuclear weapons… We will take the Middle East oil fields… the Mediterranean will be ours." Their rejoicing is short-lived; the Americans regain control of the *Cobra* and destroy the Russian fleet. Cut to officials with the state department and Russians agreeing to a cease-fire.

Five Graves to Cairo (1943), PAR. *Franchot Tone, Anne Baxter, Akim Tamiroff, Erich von Stroheim.* Co-W & D: Billy Wilder. Filmed twice before, first in 1927 and then in 1939 as *Hotel Imperial.* EGYPTIANS, RECOMMENDED

This WWII drama displays a heroic Egyptian innkeeper. The Egyptian, a French woman, and a British corporal discover the location of Germany's secret supply depots, enabling the Allies to rout Axis forces at El Alamein.

Scene: The "Hotel Empress of Britain," a desert hotel located near the Libyan-Egyptian border. Victorious Nazis now occupy the hotel; previously the British lived there. Managing the hotel is Farid (Tamiroff), a daring, fidgety Egyptian. Assisting Farid is Mouche (Baxter), a brave French maid. Risking their lives, they aid a wounded British soldier, Corporal John Bramble (Tone).

• On viewing his after-dinner dessert, German Field Marshal Rommel (von Stroheim) quips, "Rice pudding in Egypt. One never knows if it's raisins or flies." [See *Table For Five* (1983).] The soldiers laugh. Farid wants the Germans out of Egypt. "When I think of it," he sighs, "there will be swastikas on the mosques of Cairo."

• In the end, Farid uncovers a vital clue, ascertaining where the Germans store their supplies. Declares Cpl. Bramble, "Farid, you're a great man." Thanks to Farid and Mouche, his French maid, Bramble reaches British forces, pinpointing the supply location. The Allies destroy German supply depots, then go on to defeat Rommel's troops.

Five Weeks in a Balloon (1962), TCF. Irwin Allen Prod. *Red Buttons, Fabian, Barbara Eden, Cedric Hardwicke, Peter Lorre, Barbara Luna, Billy Gilbert, Richard Haydn, Henry Daniell Marshall.* SP: Irwin Allen, Charles Bennett, Albert Gail. Based on a Jules Verne story set in 1862. See *Road to Morocco* (1942). SHEIKHS

An alternate title of this silly Arab-bashing film might well be: *Five Weeks in Arabland.* Opening frames mislead the viewer, contending the scenario will focus on Westerners out to prevent international thugs from exploiting West Africans. Not so. Instead, the film shows ugly Arab slavers kidnaping and selling women. Also, violent sheikhs from three Arab nations try to kill the Western protagonists. Islam is vilified.

Scene: Intent on traveling 4,000 miles to "no man's land," Western explorers board a unicorn-shaped balloon. Joining them is Donald O'Shay (Buttons), a "pleasant inoffensive" newspaper man from New York, and Sir Henry (Haydn), "The Scourge of the Desert."

• The camera reveals Zanzibar, complete with foul Arabs and screeching maidens. Arab music underscores the action. O'Shea prevents an Arab slaver from auctioning off a lovely Arab maiden, Makia (Luna). He hits one Arab over the head with his cane, then runs off with Makia shouting, "Here come the marines." Pursuing Arabs speak gibberish, wield knives and swords—and stumble all over themselves. O'Shea socks some; he tosses live chickens at others. At the same time, goats rush past a bellydancer.

• O'Shea and Makia seek sanctuary at the British consulate. Jacques (Fabian), O'Shea's pal, boasts, "Slave traders whipped her, but he saved her." An Englishman warns O'Shea, in Zanzibar, if you dare "rescue a slave, they'll cut you to pieces and kill the rest of us, too." A rotund Arab guard tries to remove Makia from the consulate; she punches him, yelling, "Fat pig." Previously, she tagged another Arab, "He fat pig."

• Makia and O'Shay rush off to the balloon; O'Shea tosses suitcases to the Arabs below. Some scramble to retrieve the cast-off garments. Others try to destroy the balloon.

• En route to "the Volta river," Makia, who speaks with a Spanish accent, purrs, "Pasha O'Shea, he save me... He own me now." Sighs O'Shea, "I don't want her."

• An unexpected storm whisks the balloonists off to Hazak, a mythical Arab country. As the balloon nears the souk, the "natives" scream, then run off with their camels. "As long as they're afraid of the balloon," says Prof. Ferguson (Hardwicke), "we might be safe."

• Speaking Arabic, an Arab falls to his knees before the balloon. He shouts, twice, "Allahu Akbar," [God is Great]. Other Arabs bow, too. Tall guards brandishing sabers remain mute. Explains Ferguson, "They believe our balloon is the moon," and that O'Shea is "the Moon God because he's redheaded and handsome. And the Moon God is paying [them] a visit."

• The drunken sultan's (Gilbert) palace. Maidens fan the "dead drunk" potentate. "The sultan's a God, here," the balloonists are told.

• The palace's main hall displays a banquet table, a huge gong, some fire blowers, acrobats, dancers, and Arabs chasing maidens.

• Ahmed the slaver (Lorre) presents the sultan with a gift—Susan Gale (Eden), a blonde, blue-eyed Western maiden. The kidnaped Gale, a teacher from Virginia, once taught at a mission. But, Arab slavers raided the place and kidnapped her. Refusing to be enslaved, she runs off with the balloonists.

• In the souk, Makia dances for some Arabs; a goat watches. Abruptly, Arabs wearing headdresses that resemble blue tablecloths, chase after the Westerners. Ahmed tries to stab the professor.

• Ahmed, who stole precious jewels from the sultan,, sighs, "Allah gives, Allah takes away." Explains Ahmed, "I wasn't born to work." "I don't like it... I'm not a slave. I sell them!"

• Arabs leading a camel caravan across the desert glance upward. Seeing the balloon, they become frightened and run off.

• As soon as the balloonists touch down in "the forbidden city of Timbuktu," black-robed Arabs attack, hauling them off.

• Arabic-speaking guards dump four balloonists into the palace dungeon, complete with skeletons. Quips the ruler, Agelba (Daniell), "So, the white demons come to Timbuktu." He tells his prisoners, "You are Christians, infidels. You will all "die at sunset."

• The slaver's block. The dense sultan's cousin auctions off Makia. Disguised as Arabs, Jacques and O'Shea outbid everyone, and "free" her.

• The four prisoners are to be executed right after "the call for evening prayer from the minaret [when] all the faithful bow toward Mecca."

• The prisoners are taken to the mosque's top minaret. The muezzin ["holy man"] chants the call to prayer. Anticipating the beheading ceremony, Arabs bow, and pray.

• From the balloon, the rescue party begins shooting Arab executioners; O'Shea hurls several black-robed Arabs to the ground. The prisoners escape, unscathed.

• Final frames, Africa. The balloonists spot and bring down some generic heavies. And the English flag is firmly planted in West Africa.

Note: Scenes equate Islam with violence. Arabs move to execute Westerners atop a mosque during prayer time. And, a Westerner declares that Arab Muslims worship a "Moon God." Thirty years later, author Robert Morey promoted the same fabrication. He writes, "solid, overwhelming archeological evidence verifies that Islam is nothing more than a revival of the ancient moon god cult," and that the "pagan Arabs worshiped the moon god... the pagan religion of the moon god."[72]

Flame of Araby (1951), UNI. *Jeff Chandler, Maureen O'Hara, Maxwell Reed, Lon Chaney Jr.* MAIDENS, RECOMMENDED

Using "the sling of David," a bedouin leader and his men bring down red-bearded Corsairs.

Scene: Maureen O'Hara portrays Princess Tanya, "the fairest jewel of all Araby." To assist her ailing father, Tanya will ride through Tunis' streets "unveiled, unclothed, if need be."

• When Tanya meets the bedouin Tamerlane (Chandler), she muses, "I find much to be admired in his untamed spirit." Both she and Tamerlane try to reign in a wild black stallion.

• Enslaved "Christian" women are brought before Tanya's wicked cousin, Medina (Reed), the film's only Arab cur. Medina selects a "fair" maiden; his Corsair cohorts approve.

• Medina conspires with the Corsairs; they poison Tanya's father.

• Islam is respected. Princess Tanya tells Tamerlane, "Teach me the joys, the simple blessings of Allah." Says her handmaiden, "May Allah protect you from [Medina's] evil shadows that walk the aisles of this palace."

• Tamerlane crushes the Corsairs and Medina. And, he weds Princess Tanya.

Note: Located in Saudi Arabia, Medina is one of Islam's holiest cities. So, why tag the villain, Medina? The NYT critic ridicules Islam, writing that this "preposterous" film, "is enough to curl the beard of the prophet (20 December 1951).

• The same year it released *Flame of Araby*, UNI also released *The Golden Horde* (1951). Here, Ann Blyth stars as the courageous Persian princess of Samarkand. *Horde's* scenario closely resembles *Araby's*. Both films feature intelligent Arab heroines beset by non-Arab adversaries. In *Araby*, Corsairs are walloped. In *Horde*, Mongols are repelled. Yet, *Horde* offers no Arab heroics. English crusaders, not brave bedouins, help *Horde's* princess defeat the villains.

Flame of Stamboul (1951), COL. *Richard Denning, Lisa Ferraday, George Zucco, Paul Marion, Peter Brocco, Donald Randolph, Norman Lloyd, Daniel B. Ullman.* EGYPTIANS

This espionage drama features American heroes and Egyptian thugs.

Scene: Cairo, stock footage of the pyramids. Cut to the Café Sahara; US agent Larry Wilson (Denning) plays the piano. Wilson's mission? To nab "the Voice" (Zucco), an Egyptian out to secure the Suez Canal secrets. Outside the cafe, beggars mingle. Inside, a French woman performs, Lynette Garay (Ferraday), "the Flame of Stamboul."

• The cafe's owner, a spy tagged "Hassan the goat" (Randolph), orders Lynette to woo Ahmed (Marion), the ugly son "of one of the wealthiest men in Egypt." Lynette tries to acquire from Ahmed "the plans for the defense of the Suez Canal."

• Hassan intends to give the Suez Canal secrets to "the Voice" (Zucco), who, in turn, will sell the documents to the top bidder, probably, the Germans.

• The Sahara desert. Egyptian heavies kill Wilson's sidekick, Joe Baracca (Lloyd), an Armenian-American from Fresno.

• Finally, Wilson collars "the Voice" in his "hideout, a strange room." The Egyptian villain sits "in the dark behind some lights."

Note: American protagonists also contest anti-Western Egyptians in the TV show *Jet Jackson*, a.k.a. *Captain Midnight.* The TV program displays Jackson and his secret squadron "in the land of mystery (Egypt) battling enemies of the free world." In Cairo, near the pyramids, the American hero foils an "enemy plot to take over the Middle East." He crushes a German villain and his Egyptian gun-running cohorts who are trying to "set up a local revolution." Even the American heroine excels. Posing as a 5,000 year-old Egyptian princess, she tells Egyptian villains to watch out or she will initiate "the curse of the pharaohs." The frightened Egyptians run off. Frank Lackteen, who portrays many reel Arab villains, appears as Hassem, the Egyptian heavy.

Flame of the Desert (1919), Goldwyn Pictures. Silent. *Geraldine Farrar, Lou Tellegen.* *NS. Notes from NYT (17 October 1919). See *Burning Sands* (1929). SHEIKHS, EGYPTIANS

An English lord posing as a sheikh prevents Egyptian "natives" from revolting against the British. The movie contains "effective street and fight scenes."

In this precursor to *Lawrence of Arabia*, an Englishman (Tellegen), "properly disguised" in Arab garb, passes himself off as "a sheikh of the desert." He "escapes detection by natives and Englishmen, including Lady Isabelle (Farrar). The disguised lord "represents the natives in London [and] sits in on their innermost councils." He overhears the Arabs "plotting the overthrow of British rule." In the end, after the "sheikh-Englishman" saves Lady Isabelle, he reveals his true identity.

Perhaps this film's screenwriters were influenced, in part, by British novelist John Buchan. In his 1916 book, *Greenmantle*, Buchan writes that Englishmen easily take on other identities, notably Mideast Muslims. "The truth is," writes Buchan, "we are the only race on Earth that can produce men capable of getting inside the skin of remote peoples." To illustrate, Buchan describes the heroics of Sandy, an Englishman, posing as a Muslim "Holy Man." Sandy "was turbaned and rode like one possessed... as he rode it seemed the fleeing Turks were stricken still, and sank by the roadside with eyes strained after his unheeding figure."[73]

Fleetwing (1928), FOX. Silent. *Barry Norton, Dorothy Janis, Ben Bard. S: Elizabeth Pickett.* SP, D: Lambert Hiller. *NS. Notes from VAR (25 July 1928). VILLAINS, SHEIKHS

Arab vs. Arab. A young Arab, Ami (Norton), not only reigns in the white stallion, Fleetwing, he "rescues the maiden, Thurya (Janis) from the slave market."

Unexpectedly, the maiden Thurya is "sold to a cruel sheikh." Ami moves to rescue her, but is captured. The film's villain, Zeki (Bard), acquires a machine gun. Off he goes to wipe out Ami's villagers. In time, Ami escapes, turning "the machine gun on its owners." Ami slays Zeki, then unites with his intended, Thurya.

Flight From Ashiya (1964), UA. *Yul Brynner, Daniele Gaubert.* MAIDENS, RECOMMENDED

An American GI falls in love with a Tunisian woman.

Scene: Yul Brynner appears as Sergeant Mike Takashima, a US serviceman. Mike, who is half-Polish, half-Japanese, reflects on his Army days.

• Flashback to WWII, Tunisia, 1942. Mike meets Leila Gaubert, a Tunisian "from a good family." He is smitten.

• At the beach, an enhancing tolerance scene. Mike proposes marriage. He promises Leila that when the war ends, he will become an "Arab," and live with her in Tunisia, "any time, any day." Leila hesitates, telling Mike, "I love you, but I am a Moslem." So what, says Mike, my mother was "a Buddhist," my father, a "Seventh Day Adventist."

• Germans troops invade the city. To halt the German advance, Mike sets sticks of dynamite under a bridge. At the same time, Leila begins searching for her lover, pausing on the dynamite-rigged bridge. Though Mike moves to warn her, the dynamite detonates, demolishing the bridge and killing Leila.

The Flight of the Phoenix (1966), TCF. *James Stewart, Peter Finch, Alex Montoya Barrie Chase.* SP: Lukas Heller. CAMEOS, VILLAINS

Bedouins as savages.

Scene: An "ARABCO" cargo plane carrying Western oil workers and soldiers crashes in the Libyan desert. The near-dead men are stranded. Suddenly, they spot a "raiding party," a dozen hostile bedouins on camels. Captain Harris (Finch), a British officer, and Frank Towns (Stewart), the American pilot, discuss whether they should seek help from the bedouins.

> Harris: They look friendly enough.
> Towns: I wouldn't count on it.

• Captain Harris and a companion decide to approach the bedouins. As they trek toward the bedouin camp, ominous Arab music swells.

• The following day, Towns finds the two men dead, their throats slit. Enraged, Towns empties his revolver into a lame camel left behind by the bedouins.

• Later, a crew member witnesses a mirage, imagining a sensuous bellydancer, Farida (Chase).

• Compare this portrayal of bedouins with Antoine de Saint-Exupéry's in the wake of his own plane crash in the Libyan desert: "The Arab looked at us without a word… race, language, religion were forgotten. There was only this humble nomad with the hands of an archangel on our shoulders… You, Bedouin of Libya, who saved our lives… You are Humanity… our beloved fellow man. I shall recognize you in the faces of all mankind. You came toward me in an aureole of charity and magnanimity bearing the gift of water."[74]

Flight to Tangier (1953), PAR. *Jack Palance, Joan Fontaine.* W, D: Charles Marquis Warren. CAMEOS, VILLAINS

Mute Moroccan "natives" assist a Russian spy.

Scene: In "exotic" Tangier, US and Soviet agents hunt for a cache of money. As veiled Moroccan women stroll, disheveled Arabs pull donkeys.

• Though Tangier's "international" police force boasts no Moroccans, mute Arabs collaborate with a Soviet agent. Boasts the agent: "These natives work for pay. My pay."

The Flying Deuces (1939), a.k.a. Flying Aces, RKO. *Stan Laurel, Oliver Hardy.* CAMEOS

Some Arabs surface on camels, others appear in the background. Legionnaires, not Arabs, are the butts of pranks.

Encircled by legionnaires, a smiling Arab plays the flute. Legionnaires Stan and Ollie sneak out of the fort, concealed underneath the over-sized robes of two Arabs.

Follow That Camel (1967), Rank. *Phil Silvers, Joan Sims, Bernard Bresslaw, Angela Douglas, Anita Harris, Jim Dale.* VILLAINS, SHEIKHS, MAIDENS, WORST LIST

Dense Arabs vs. legionnaires. Arabs take women. Arabs are tagged "dogs" and "monkeys." Islam is mocked.

Scene: An Englishman, Bertram O. West (Dale), joins the Legion. Cut to Ms. Zig Zig's Cafe. Here, Arab musicians play and an Egyptian bellydancer (Harris) wiggles. The dancer plops onto Sergeant Nocker's (Silvers) lap, cooing, "I have just come from Egypt." Nocker says, "Ah, Egypt. Land of mystery, home of the fairies." Injects a recruit, "You mean pharaohs." Affirms Nocker, "I know what I mean." Later, Nooker calls Arabs, "Ayrabs" and "these monkeys."

• The fort. As legionnaires raise their flag, they spot a pair of white bloomers with the inscription: "Death to all Legion infidels... the flaming sword has spoken." The "flaming sword" is the emblem of Sheikh Abdul (Bresslaw). Cut to Abdul's cohorts checking out the fort.

• Abdul, who needs a shave and a dentist, has no front tooth. Yet, Abdul boasts "12 wives." He calls his comrades, Riff and Raff, "you dogs."

• A cafe. Abdul spots Lady Jane (Douglas) and moves to whisk her off to "El-Nookie," a desert oasis. "I desire her; bring her to me," he pants. As Lady Jane rejects him, Abdul drugs her drink. Abruptly, the drugged Lady Jane dreams of dashing Bertram, not ugly Abdul.

• The Egyptian dancer, a *reel* jezebel, lures Nocker and Bertram off to her pad, located on the "Street of Many Fools." She floors the men, then hauls them off to Abdul's camp.

• Shouts Abdul, "The infidels at the fort will be destroyed. It has been ordained by the prophet, Mustafa Leak." Abdul bows; his men shout: "Mustafa Leak." Next, they kiss the ground. Nooker asks to speak with "Mustafa Leak." Arabs shout: "Mustafa Leak," and again bow. Quips Nooker, "I don't know. [Mustafa Leak] must be number one on the hit parade." Nooker, Jane, and Bertram shout "Mustafa Leak"; the Arabs bow, enabling them to escape.

• Nooker and Bertram encounter near-naked harem maidens inside a tent. Sighs Nooker, "Allah is smiling on me... By their laws, they [the Arabs] can't enter here."

• Abdul's Arabs nab Nooker and Bertram. After placing them spread-eagle on the sand, they tie their arms and legs to wooden stakes. Overhead, buzzards fly. "The desert sun will bake them alive," purrs Abdul. Then, the Arab moves to make Lady Jane his "13th wife."

• The plot thickens. Will Nooker and Bertram survive in time to warn fellow legionnaires about Abdul's attack? Will they save Lady Jane from Abdul's claws?

• Abdul lusts after the clad-in-harem-garb Jane, purring: "Go to my tent. The hour of your fulfillment approaches." Lady Jane refuses to move. The Arabs force her inside the tent.

• Arabs offer gold "to the glory of Abdul." Next, Arab music underscores Arabs thrusting their fingers into food trays, sloppily gobbling foodstuffs.

• Asks a legionnaire wanting to rescue Lady Jane, "That [Arab] mob against six of us?" The outnumbered legionnaires have little ammunition and only a dash of water. So, they dupe the Arabs. [See *I Cover the War* (1937).] The legionnaires place a record on a gramophone. Abruptly, a military march with men's voices blares throughout the camp. On hearing loud military voices, Abdul's Arabs imagine marching legion reinforcements are nearby; they panic. Finally, Abdul discovers the gramophone. Too late. A legion regiment does arrive, routing the Arabs. As for Lady Jane, her "virginity" remains intact.

Dialogue: After an Arab shoots an alarm clock, a legionnaire quips, "[They] can't seem to cope with technology."

For the Boys (1991), TCF. *James Caan, Bette Midler.* SP: Neal Jimenez, Lindy Laub. D: Mark Rydell. CAMEOS, MAIDENS

Dancers wearing harem garb are talented performers.

Scene: Dixie Leonard (Midler) and Eddie Sparks (Caan), are tagged "America's sheikh-est couple." They tour from the Pacific to North Africa, entertaining American troops for three-plus decades. Preparing an Arabian Nights number for their TV show, Eddie dons a sheikh's outfit. Preceding Eddie's appearance are dancers dressed as harem maidens. The attractive women tap-dance, then perform synchronized leg kicks.

The Formula (1980), MGM. *George C. Scott, Marlon Brando, Marthe Keller.* W, P: Steve Shagan, based on his own book. CAMEOS, SHEIKHS

Arabs as oily terrorists.

Scene: When a policeman (Scott) investigates his friend's murder, he comes across a sinister plot involving a secret Nazi formula for synthetic fuel. He learns that the Arabs and the oil companies are trying to prevent the synthetic fuel formula from surfacing.

• The cop spots "a red crescent" marking on the policeman's dead friend, exclaiming, "[Since] 1968, one of the Middle East terrorist groups" has placed this symbol on their victims.

• Scott tells an American oil tycoon (Brando) that: "A bunch of bandits with towels around their heads have got us [Americans] by the nuts." Acknowledges the tycoon, "But they've got the oil. Bribery is a way of life in the Middle East. They call it baksheesh over there."

• The tycoon is told, the "Arabs" will be blamed for high gas prices. He quips, "I think you're missing the point. "We [the oil companies] are the Arabs."

Note: Writer-producer Shagan served as executive producer of the *Tarzan* television series. In some episodes, Shagan shows brutal Arabs enslaving Africans. Shagan's book, *The Formula*, contains more anti-Arab remarks than the film. For example, Shagan writes about "a Saudi grease man, a bloodsucking professional pimp" and his entourage "being entertained by young boys and blonde English prostitutes." And: "I will see those Satanic Muslim robes of his burn in hell."[75]

• Only about half of OPEC's members are Arab nations. Yet, when *The Formula* was being shown in theaters, Shagan blamed all Arabs for America's economic problems. He also implied Iranians are Arabs. He told a National Public Radio reporter: "We don't have 52 hostages in Teheran [Iran], we have 230 million hostages to these sheikhdoms and cartels. We are all hostages. We are paying 9 billion dollars a year in ransom for their oil. You can't stop inflation if you are paying this kind of dough. You can't" (8 January 1981).

Fort Algiers (1958), UA. *Yvonne DeCarlo, Carlos Thompson, Leif Erickson, Raymond Burr.* VILLAINS, SHEIKHS

Legionnaires and a French singer squash Algerians bent on owning and operating their own "oil fields."

Scene: Fanatical Arabs brandishing rifles invade a legion fort; bodies of legionnaires fill the screen. Scream the Arabs: "Victory! The fort is ours." As the French flag is being detached, the villain Amir (Burr) declares, "Make sure no legionnaire is left alive."

• "Araba," Algiers. Amir's cohorts uncover and then beat up a French spy. The French military agent, Yvette (DeCarlo), suspects Amir's men (Burr) murdered her legionnaire brother. Yvette correctly assumes Amir is staging the uprisings, that the Arab intends to take over and control the Arab oil fields.

• Amir wants to bed Yvette; he invites her to his palace. She balks, then accepts his invitation. "Do I have to buy the place to get you? You'll have all the protection of my armed guards," he says. "I don't even have a harem."

• Desert Arabs track marching legionnaires.

• At the palace, Amir tells visiting sheikhs, "Our full forces will take over the oil fields... We will have the sympathy of the entire world...We will crush anyone who stands in our way." Sheikh Haroon, who refuses to take part in the uprising, decides to leave. Amir intercedes, offering him tea and purring, "We must not part in anger." Abruptly, Amir's aide knifes Haroon in the back. See *Goldfinger* (1964).

• Western ingenuity triumphs. Amir's men invade the oil fields. Though vastly outnumbered, Yvette, her legionnaire beau, Jeff (Thompson), plus several oil workers and some legionnaires, fend off the Amir's charging Arabs. The defenders places dynamite sticks beneath the sand. When Arabs run over these sand traps, the dynamite detonates. Arab bodies fill the frame. Next, the protagonists toss bottles, filled with nitroglycerin. BOOM! More Arab rebels drop. Finally, a legion squad arrives, routing the remaining rebels. Jeff punches out Amir.

Note: In most legion films, legionnaires do what Arabs never do—act as civilized folk. Legionnaires sit around the campfire, play musical instruments, and reminisce about family.

40,000 Horsemen (1942), Charles Chauvel Production. *Grant Taylor, Betty Bryant.* Produced "with the cooperation of the [Australian] Department of Defence." The film pays tribute "to the men of the 1st and 2nd Australian Cavalry Divisions." RECOMMENDED

This atypical WWI drama reveals Arabs as valiant men and women. They help British and Australian forces defeat the Germans. An Arab saves the Western heroine.

Scene: 1916 Jerusalem, the "Holy Land." Germans march into the city, terrorizing Arabs. German soldiers destroy Paul Rouget's wine shop, then move to hang him. Rouget tells his friend, Abdul, "They are coming for my daughter [Juliet]. Take her to my friend, Sheikh Abu Bin Rashid." In time, Abdul saves Juliet (Bryant).

• The "Cafe Chantant." After seductive Egyptian women dance, they fraternize with Australian soldiers.

• El Arish. The white-bearded Sheikh Abu Bin Rashid treats Juliet as if she were his own daughter, guarding her from flirtatious German soldiers. Seeing a German officer, the sheikh spits, then tells Juliet: "I work for England and for France. Arab women are [also] willing to battle the Germans."

• Othman, one of the sheikh's men protecting Juliet, says to her: "May Allah be with you." He goes to warn the British of an impending attack; the Germans kill him.

• The Germans capture Juliet's Australian beau, Red Gallagher (Taylor), sentencing him to hard labor at Beersheba. An Arab patriot, Ismet, enters the German prison camp, shoots the guard, and rescues Gallagher.

Finis: "German domination throughout the Holy Land" ends. Arab villagers welcome the victorious Australians. Shaking hands with the British officer, Sheikh Rashid says, "These friendly sheikhs and I hail you with delight. El Arish is yours."

Note: Quips an Aussie soldier: "There's nothing in this damn country but sand and shadows."

• Using a two-headed coin, Aussies dupe two Arabs. First, they strip merchants of their garments. Next, they place the Arabs' pantaloons and fezzes onto donkeys' asses.

The Four Feathers (1915), Metro. Silent. *Edgar L. Davenport, Howard Estabrook, Irene Warfield.* *NS. Notes from AFIC (1911–20: 303). VILLAINS

The Four Feathers (1921), Stoll. Silent. *Harry Ham.* D: Rene Plaissetty. *NS. VILLAINS

The Four Feathers (1929), PAR. Silent. *Richard Arlen, Fay Wray, William Powell.* *NS. VILLAINS

The Four Feathers (1939), London Film Productions. *John Clements, Ralph Richardson, Clive Baxter, Jack Allen, Donald Gray, John Laurie.* D: Zoltan Korda. VILLAINS

Storm over the Nile (1955), a.k.a. The Four Feathers, Big Ben & London Film Productions. *Anthony Steel, Christopher Lee.* D: Zoltan Korda.

The Four Feathers (1977), Norman Rosemont Productions and Trident Films Ltd. (TV). *Beau Bridges, Jane Seymour.* D: Don Sharp. VILLAINS

Six versions of A. E. W. Mason's story (a seventh is in pre-production). All the movies show the British protagonist rescuing comrades and fighting off screaming dervishes. In the 1977 made-for-TV movie, Arabs wielding sabers and rifles sneak up on British troops and scream: Allahu Akbar (God is great)!

Presented here is an analysis of the 1939 movie, which was filmed on the Nile's east bank, the same spot where General Gordon was killed. The producer (Alexander Korda) used thousands of Sudanese extras. A UA (distributor) poster shows screaming villains on horseback wielding rifles. Underneath the poster, this blurb: "8,000 Savage Dervishes Roar Down the Screen in Violent Onslaught!"

Scene: On screen, this message: "In 1895, the rebellious army of cruel dervishes enslaved and killed many thousands of defenseless... [The English General in command] Gordon, appealed for help from England, but no help came." Next, this newspaper headline: "Gordon murdered in Khartoum."

• Waving swords and spears, camel-riding Sudanese dash through desert villages. They take down the British flag, replacing it with their own black flag.

• Ten years after the fall of Khartoum. News of renewed dervish brutalities prompt British officials to avenge Gordon's death. They dispatch the British army to the Sudan. Introducing Harry Faversham's comrades; they serve with General Kitchener's Anglo-Egyptian army. Harry does not. Thus, his friends present Harry (Clements) with white feathers of cowardice.

• Harry moves to shake off the "coward" label. An Egyptian doctor provides Harry with tanned skin, and administers some camouflage surgery. Cut to the desert, where the disguised Harry masquerades as a Sengali tribe member.

• Quips a British officer, "When the dervishes catch a white man they cut his nose off, and hang him by his toes."

• A British patrol slaughters dervishes. Next, some dervishes nab and bind Harry's friends, Lt. Willoughby (Allen) and Lt. Burroughs (Gray). Camels drag the bound duo through scorching desert sands. In Omdurman, the dervishes toss the officers into a cage, fastening chains around their necks.

• Who will free them? Inside the prison dungeon, Harry surfaces. He removes the officers' chains. Next, Harry brings down their dervish captors.

• Just when it looks as though the dervishes will defeat General Kitchner's troops, "brave man" Harry and his friends arrive. They gain control of the arsenal, eradicating the Madhi's (Laurie) dervishes. Harry's heroics enable Kitchner's Anglo-Egyptian army to triumph, and the British take Khartoum. A few Egyptians wearing fezzes appear in the background. Though Egyptians did in fact fight along side the British, the film displays only British soldiers excelling.

Note: In fact, General Kitchner's troops were never in danger of losing this battle. Historian Douglas Porch describes the actual event. On "September 1, 1898, Kitchner arrived at Omdurman, across the Nile from Khartoum, with a force of over 20,000 men, gunboats mounting a hundred guns and a vast supply of camels and horses." The next morning, at "dawn, 50,000 Sudanese tribesmen in a line four miles long attacked the British. They were massacred. Within a short two hours over 10,000 bodies lay in piles over the desert. Surveying the battlefield, Kitchner said the enemy had been "given 'a good dusting.' The Sudan was now British." Interestingly, when Kitchner met with Marchand, the leader of the French expedition in the Sudan, the General wore his Egyptian uniform, complete with "red fez."[76]

• Scholar John Lewis Burckhardt, "one of the first Europeans to assume the identity of an Arab," took the name, Sheikh Ibrahim Ibn Abdullah. According to Sari Naisr, "[Burckhardt's] disguise was successful enough to escape the detection of Arabs and Englishmen alike."[77]

Four Jills in a Jeep (1944), TCF. *Carol Landis, Kay Francis, Martha Raye.* CAMEOS

In this patriotic movie, starlets entertain US soldiers. As soon as the actresses' military plane lands in the Algerian desert, the camera reveals camels and Arabs. Viewers see more of the camels than they do of the Arabs.

Foxhole in Cairo (1960), PAR. *Robertson Justice, Fenella Fielding, Gloria Mestre.* EGYPTIANS, MAIDENS

Cairo, WWII. Egyptians and Nazis vs. Westerners and Israelis. The villain? Ameana (Mestre), an Egyptian bellydancer. The heroine? Yvette (Fielding), an Israeli. All Egyptians in this film are pro-Nazi, anti-British.

Scene: A British officer berates a shady Egyptian bartender, "As long as you're paid [for informing], what do you care? You'd go to them [the Germans] if you're paid better. Give me information on any new faces in Cairo and you'll get a bonus." Affirms the wily bartender, "May Allah bless you and keep you."

• Germans posing as British soldiers secure four British trucks, not five: Quips an Allied soldier, "Perhaps the Arabs pinched it [the other truck] sir."

• Appearing at Cairo's train station, an Axis spy; his mother was German, his father, Egyptian. The spy fidgets; the Egyptian boy carrying his suitcases has vanished. Assures an elderly Egyptian, "Don't worry, it'll be all right. You don't know Egyptian servants when they work for Egyptians." Later, the spy's suitcases are returned, intact.

• Spying for the Germans, a mysterious, seductive, and cruel Egyptian dancer, Ameana. She loathes Westerners, saying, "I dream to see the English driven out of Egypt... and Germany winning the war, and our people free. I'll do anything to help the country."

• Ameana betrays a young British officer. After she drugs him, she gives the officer's secret documents to her colleague, the half-Egyptian spy. Unaware the documents are false, the spy dispatches them to Germany.

• Cut to Evette, an Israeli agent. She and Ameana tussle; Evette kills the Egyptian.

Frantic (1988), WB. *Harrison Ford, Emmanuelle Seigner, Betty Buckley*. Co-W, D: Roman Polanski. VILLAINS

Arab "terrorists" move to acquire nuclear components. Arabs are kidnappers and opulent drunks.

Scene: Paris, the Grand Hotel. The wife (Buckley) of Richard Walker (Ford), an American surgeon, disappears. The hotel clerk tells Walker: Your wife was with a man who "had an accent, not American... like the Middle East." Affirms an official, "I believe they're Arabs."

• Earlier, at the airport, Walker mistakenly picked up an Arab's suitcase. Now, the Arabs want it back. The Arab case contains a "stolen" mechanism that "triggers detonation of nuclear devices." An Arab warns Walker, "You want your wife back, you get my suitcase."

• Inside a parking garage. Three Arabs corner the surgeon. One holds a knife at his wife's throat. Abruptly, Israeli agents pop up. An Arab is killed. Walker grabs the dead Arab, props him against the car's steering wheel and drives off.

• An official with the US Embassy advises Walker not to worry about encountering some Israelis, "They're probably on our side," he says.

• A young and beautiful French woman, Michele (Seigner), aids Walker. She tells him to check out the "Touch of Class" nightclub; it's "full of rich Arabs. It's really square."

• At the club, a Western woman confesses she "can't stand this [Arab] music." Nor can she tolerate the rude behavior of three drunken Arab doctors.

• Walker examines the Arab's suitcase; inside is a nuclear component. The component is hidden inside a souvenir model of the Statue of Liberty.

• A bridge, near the Seine. Walker clashes with treacherous Arabs; he grabs one Arab, pounding his head to the ground. The subjugated Arab pulls a knife; Israelis shoot him. Before he dies, the beaten Arab intentionally kills Michele. Throughout the film, Israelis kill Arabs.

• Intent on nabbing the nuclear component, the villains close in on Walker; he tosses the Liberty nuclear "souvenir" into the Seine.

Note: The Arab-as-nuclear-terrorist motif surfaces in many films, including: *Operation Thunderbolt* (1977), *Wrong Is Right* (1982), *Back to the Future* (1985), *Ground Zero* (1988), *American Ninja 4: The Annihilation* (1991) and *True Lies* (1994).

• Polanski, who as a youth saw "German propaganda newsreels," knows the telling effects of propaganda.[78] So, why does he project *Frantic*'s Arabs as he does? In 1988, Israel was the only country in the Mideast known to have nuclear weapons. As of this writing, Israel has not signed the Nuclear Non-Proliferation Treaty. A spy for Israel, a Jewish-American named Jonathan Pollard, is currently serving time in an American prison for stealing nuclear devices and plans and smuggling them into Israel. Given these facts, why didn't Polanski reverse the roles of protagonists and antagonists, and present Israelis as nuclear smugglers?

Freedom Strike (1998), Royal Oaks. Direct to video. *Michael Dudikoff, Jay Anthony, Nicholas Kadi*. SP: G. E. Mallow, D: Allan A. Goldstein. VILLAINS, WORST LIST

Again, actor Michael Dudikoff liquidates Arabs. A UN strike force crushes Syrian nuclear terrorists. In the credits, the producers thank for their cooperation: "The Department of Defense, the Department of the Navy, and the US Marine Corps"

Scene: The year 2001; the UN approves an "International Special Operation Strike Force Team... code name, Freedom Strike." Cut to a ZNN-TV announcer reporting on the "Gulf Wars." Warns the announcer: "A nuclear weapons system outside Damascus, Syria is days away from becoming fully operational." Cut to Damascus' fatigue-clad Syrians speaking Arabic. Invading the Syrian coast, a UN special ops team.

• Special ops leader Tom Dickson (Dudikoff) and his men attack Syrian headquarters; they kill about 17 Syrians. A US fighter tags a Syrian pilot "bastard," then blasts him.

• Following the successful attack against the Syrians, the ZNN-TV reporter announces a ceasefire: "The two-year Arab wars [between Iran, Iraq, Syria, and Saudi Arabia] came to a close when UN forces took control of downtown Damascus."

• In Damascus, scores of Syrians protest the ceasefire. Quips an American combatant, "[This is a] holy war that's been raging for two thousand years." Cut to a bearded Syrian Colonel, Abdul Rama (Anthony), criticizing the UN treaty. Cut to inept Arab assassins attempting to kill the US president. One assassin injures, instead, the Syrian president. Thus, he kills himself. A Syrian tries to knife Tom; but, he knifes himself. Boasts Tom, "The good news is we got the bad guys."

• Colonel Rama, says the President's advisor, is behind "many of the anti-treaty terrorist groups, as well as bombings in Tel Aviv." Cut to the "son-of-a-bitch" Rama; his inflammatory rhetoric stirs the Syrians.

• Rama's radicals kill UN guards. Next, they take over the Syrian Weapons Center. Rama decides to launch some nuclear missiles. Thus, Tom's team invades Syria, again. Once more, an American pilot tags a Syrian pilot, "bastard," then kills him.

• Rama's Syrians deliver prisoners—unarmed Americans and UN guards—into a courtyard. They tie the prisoners' hands behind their backs, then prepare to shoot them in the back. In time, Tom's men arrive. They free the prisoners, terminate scores of Rama's Syrians, and thwart the nuclear launch.

Note: Arab-American actor Nicholas Kadi, who is often typecast as a kuffiyeh-clad Arab, portrays a Syrian officer. Several years ago, Kadi and I addressed stereotypes on CBS-TV's *48 Hours* (30 January 1991). Kadi expressed disappointment, saying he was typecast and that his Arab screen roles seldom allow him to speak. Instead of talking, directors would tell him to impart "a lot of threatening looks, threatening gestures, threatening actions. Every time we [he and other actors portraying Arab villains] said

'America,' we'd [be directed to] spit," he said. "There are other kinds of Arabs in the world besides terrorists. I'd like to think that some day there will be a positive Arab role out there."

Fun with Dick and Jane (1977), COL. *George Segal, Jane Fonda.* CAMEOS, SHEIKHS

Corrupt Arabs in cahoots with US businessmen.

Dick Harper (Segal) loses his job with "Taft Aerospace." At home, Harper views a live TV report about Taft, his ex-employer. Taft's president is testifying at a Congressional hearing. Asked whether his company accepts bribes, the president lies. Quips Harper, "You know, guys [Arabs] walk into his office and walk out again with 200,000 cash in a briefcase." At a Taft party, the camera reveals a mute, smiling Arab clasping a "briefcase." Other Arabs, the party's only identifiable ethnic group, are in attendance.

The Fury (1978), TCF. *Kirk Douglas, Andrew Stevens.* SP: John Farris, based on his own novel. Produced in cooperation with US-Israel Productions, Herzila Studios (Israel). CAMEOS, PALESTINIANS, SHEIKHS

An American agent tries to protect his son from evil US agents. Arabs appear as hateful, disposable objects.

Scene: "Mideast, 1977." Peter (Douglas), a professional super agent, tries to save his psychic son Robin (Stevens) from being nabbed by a corrupt US Government agent. He and Robin relax on an Israeli beach, mingling with tourists. Suddenly, assassins clad in Palestinian garb attack. From atop a mosque, they shoot Israeli bathers. Next, the assassins single out Peter. Before being shot, Peter kills several men. Though the attacking terrorists might well be US agents posing as Palestinians, Robin believes Arabs murdered his father. "They [the Arabs] killed my dad," he screams; "they killed my dad."

• Not-so-nice US agents nab Robin. Later, they show him a film of Palestinian-clad assassins killing innocents on the Israeli beach.

• "Chicago, 1978," an amusement park. Robin spots a strolling group of mute, robed sheikhs. He views these Arabs as monsters. When two robed Arabs ride a Ferris wheel, Robin's anger mounts. Unleashing his psychic powers, Robin forces the wheel to spin out of control. Abruptly, sparks fly, the wheel bolt is released and the two robed Arabs are thrown from the wheel. The Arabs crash through a large restaurant window, falling onto a table occupied by other Arabs.

G.I. Jane (1997), HOL. *Demi Moore, Viggo Mortensen, Anne Bancroft.* D: Ridley Scott. CAMEOS, VILLAINS

Are women in the US Navy "suited for all jobs?" Will Jordan O'Neil (Moore), the first female Navy SEALs trainee, survive the military's toughest training camp? Will she "measure up," setting an example for other SEALs women? To show that O'Neil has what it takes to be a "world-class warrior," frames present her and fellow SEALs landing off the Libyan coast, blowing up Arabs. Mega-macho O'Neil also rescues her sergeant (Mortensen).

Scene: Florida, a SEALs Training Camp, "one of the most grueling anywhere." O'Neil is asked, "How' d you like to spend time in an Arab prison?" "After spending six months with you, Slovnak," she quips, "I may just volunteer!"

• Training exercises are canceled; the SEALs are dispatched to "hostile waters." "Iran or Iraq?" asks one. He is told, "Libya." Their mission? To help a Ranger recovery squad retrieve a "US nuclear-powered satellite [with] weapons-grade plutonium."

• Arab music introduces the Libyan coast. The drill sergeant, O'Neil, and other trainees occupy a domed ruin. Anticipating an Arab attack, the SEALs plant some grenades, setting an explosive sand trap.

• The SEALs spot "bedouins, two o'clock, twenty-five, thirty, mixed weapons." Concurrently, the camera reveals camels, jeeps, bedouins, and Libyan soldiers.

• A bearded Arab wearing a black-and-white checkered head scarf lights a cigarette, then moves toward O'Neil. Via walkie, the sergeant warns her, "He's a big boy, gonna take him from behind." And he does.

• Hearing the shots, Arabic-speaking soldiers come running. "The Chief's got a shit-load of trouble coming," quips a SEAL. Though isolated from his squad, the drill sergeant begins "picking em off." Tossing a grenade, he kills two. But Arabs shoot him, twice.

• Seeing more Arabs close in, O'Neil runs between bullets, rescuing her sergeant. Boasts O'Neil, "We're sucking them in; we're sucking them in." As soon as the Arabs infiltrate "the kill zone," the SEALs detonate their trap area, killing scores. "Hey O'Neil," says a SEAL, "I'd go alone with you any day!" Barks O'Neil, "Let's get the hell out of Dodge."

• US choppers arrive, hauling the SEALs safely off. "The [satellite] cargo [is] safe in hand."

Note: Reviewing *G.I. Jane*, EW's Owen Gleiberman writes, "At the end, [director] Scott stages a ludicrous (and chaotically edited) military skirmish in Libya, the sole purpose of which is to prove that women can—and should—go into combat. It's sheer propaganda" (Fall Double Issue 1997).

• An African-American SEAL empathizes with O'Neil. During WWII, he says, the Navy would not permit his father or other blacks to fight on battleships. They could serve only as "cooks." When blacks questioned their assignments, they were told, "Negro's can't see at night." Crewmen tagged his father the "new nigger on the block."

• O'Neil tells her C.O., "Just treat me the same, no better, no worse... the more everybody fucks with me, the more I'm gonna gut it out." When Texas Senator Lillian De Haven (Bancroft) tries to oust her from the SEALs, O'Neil barks, "What are you trying to say, that no woman's life is more valuable than a man's?"

• Though some "military consultants" assisted the producers, the US Navy Department did not.

• Hollywood is a subsidiary of Disney.

• Unlike those Arab Muslim caricatures surfacing in *G.I. Jane*, a compassionate, bright Muslim appears as a Navy SEAL trainee in *Silver Strand* (1977), Showtime's TV-Movie written and directed by Douglas Day Stewart. Here, Rahman (Anjul Nigam), a Muslim from Bangladesh, befriends the film's protagonist, Brian Del Piso (Gil Bellows). Scenes show the men bonding. Rahman provides Brian with needed guidance, saying, "You're the captain of your soul." After the clad-in-white Rahman prays, he explains to Brian, "We are required to pray five times a day." Brian kids Rahman about his not-so-manly physique. Quips Rahman, "I am stronger than I appear." As it turns out, Rahman is indeed much stronger. The Master Chief harasses all SEAL recruits, especially Rahman, calling him "raghead" several times. Note the dialogue:

Rahman: What did you call me, Master Chief?

Chief: I called you raghead. That's what I call all you Ayrabs. Now get out of my face.
  Move it! [The Chief tells the SEALs to dive into a pool and hold their breaths for as
  long as feasible.]

Chief: What's the matter, Mr. Raghead, you're not afraid of water, are you?

Rahman: No, sir.

Chief: Liar. You live in a country where floods periodically kill millions of your
  countrymen. You're fuckin' terrified of drowning, aren't you, Mr. Raghead?

Abruptly, Rahman dives into the pool; he remains underwater for longer than anyone,
"four minutes, 8 seconds." Surfacing, Rahman proclaims to the Chief, "I am required by
my religion to pray five times a day. I try to fit it in whenever I can." Angry, the Chief
walks off, saying "fuckin' Raghead." In the end, Brian saves Rahman's life. When Brian
is accused of a crime he did not commit, Rahman steps forward, successfully defending
his friend.

Gallipoli (1981), PAR. *Mel Gibson, Mark Lee, David Argue.* A Peter Weir film. CAMEOS, EGYPTIANS, MAIDENS

WWI, Cairo. Australian soldiers confront disagreeable Egyptian prostitutes and
cheating merchants.

Scene: Cairo, July 1915. Appearing in the background, the pyramids and the Sphinx.
Australian soldiers, including outback runners Frank (Gibson) and Archy (Lee), mill
about their tents, then play football. Abruptly, robed Egyptians mumbling Arabic appear.
They try to hawk artifacts. "Hello Australia," says one. The troops ignore the Egyptians.
Later, some Egyptian youths try to sell the soldiers some eggs.

• Barks the commander: "Men, you are shortly to be set loose on the local inhabitants,
who, you will be surprised to find, don't look at all like you." The soldiers laugh. "Beware
of the local eggs, and the local liquor, which is poisonous." He also warns them not to
sleep with Egyptians. To do so, he says, would result in "a legacy which is horribly painful
and may get you sent home to face embarrassing questions from girlfriend or wife."

• An Egyptian village. A playful youth runs off with a trooper's hat. Children cling to
a soldier's uniform, begging. Soldiers dicker with a merchant selling fresh, warm milk.
He demands five piasters. The Aussie offers two, "the official price." To ride donkeys,
some generous soldiers pay "ten piasters."

• Inside a cafe, an Egyptian hawks dirty postcards. One soldier wearing a red fez,
Snowy (Argue), ponders sleeping with an Egyptian. "What harm can it do? " he asks.
Warns Frank, "Life is cheap here, Snowy, and the women have no respect for
themselves."

• A soldier displays an artifact he purchased, boasting it's "1,000 years old." "How
much did ya pay for it? " asks his friend. "Two quid," he says. His comrade shows him
an identical artifact, boasting, I paid "five bob." Quips Snowy, "See, what did I tell ya?
These Egypt-os are a pack of thieves."

• Upset at being duped, the men confront the merchant at his shop. The bearded,
rotund owner, who dons a robe and red fez, tells the soldiers, "Ahlan wa Sahlan, Ahlan
wa Sahlan [Welcome, Welcome]. What can I do for you gentlemen?" Says a soldier, "We
Australians come to your country as guests."You cheated my friend, charging him "two
pounds" for a relic worth only "five shillings." Injects Snowy, "Tell him to cough up with

the money... They're bloody thieves." A soldier tells the Egyptian to refund Snowy's money. The Egyptian refuses, saying, "No, no, no, no. This [relic] is not mine. This is yours...This is not mine." Frank smiles. Then he destroys the merchant's shop; relics crash to the floor. "OK, OK." shouts the Egyptian, "Take your money and go!" After the men depart a soldier confesses, "It was the wrong shop." No one pays attention.

• One soldier tries to take a photo of a veiled woman in black carrying a jug on her head. She runs off.

• Several Egyptian prostitutes approach the soldiers saying, "We clean. No dirty. We very clean." Snowy watches his friends go off with the women, complaining, "They're common; They're cheap. I'm disgusted, what are ya' gonna say to your wives on your wedding night?"

Gambit (1966), UNI. *Michael Caine, Shirley MacLaine, Herbert Lom.* SP: Jack Davies and Alvin Sargent. SHEIKHS, BEST LIST

This fine spy spoof displays a sophisticated Arab sheikh.

Scene: Planning to dupe a wealthy Arab art collector, Ahmad Shahbandar (Lom), are a suave British cat burglar, Harry Dean (Caine), and a lovely Eurasian dancer, Nicole Chang (MacLaine). They intend to snatch a priceless treasure—the sculpted head of Ahmad's late wife, whom Nicole happens to resemble.

• Hoodwinking Ahmad, "the richest man in the entire world," will not be easy. Wearing a fez and sporting a monocle, Ahmad seems to be a typical screen sheikh. He is not. Possessing humor, intelligence, and compassion, this art connoisseur truly loved his wife. He knows Harry and Nicole intend to rob him. Yet, perhaps to help ease the pain of his wife's loss, Ahmad plays along for the sport of it.

• Arabia. Genteel music underscores the potentate's country, an agreeable place. The call to prayer is heard. Tidy souks reveal helpful merchants assisting Westerners.

• Ahmad's penthouse. Nicole and Harry move to heist the sculpture. Harry gets away; Nicole is caught. Yet, Ahmad releases her. Surprisingly, he offers her and Harry "a second chance."

• Harry confesses to Ahmad that his sculpted head of his late wife is safe and sound, that he tucked the sculpture inside the sheikh's statue of Buddha. Your priceless artifact never left the penthouse, confesses Harry.

• Final frames reveal Harry preparing to market several sculptures—all fake—of Ahmad's late wife.

The Garden of Allah (1936), UA. *Marlene Dietrich, Basil Rathbone, John Carradine, Joseph Schildkraut, Henry Brandon.* P: David O'Selznick. Based on Robert Hichens' novel. Sequel to two silent films: Selig Polyscope's *The Garden of Allah* (1916) and MGM's *Garden of Allah* (1927). MAIDENS, VILLAINS

The Garden of Allah's Arab women are vengeful and greedy. Most of the action takes place at a "Trappist monastery." The camera does not display mosques, nor Muslims at prayer. The Sahara serves as a refuge for Europeans. See *The Sheltering Sky* (1990).

Scene: Algeria, the desert. Some Algerians appear. The men function as mystics and dimwits, the women as illiterate and dangerous caricatures.

• When Domini Enfilden's (Dietrich) invalid father dies, she seeks solace in the Sahara where she hopes to discover "peace and happiness." Instead, Domini encounters a scruffy Algerian "Sand Diviner"(Carradine); his "prophecy" is not encouraging.

• Batouch (Schildkraut), an Arab handyman, ridicules his cousin, Hadj (Brandon), calling him a "swine." Batouch tries to teach Hadj English; the dense Arab stumbles badly, prompting even a camel to laugh. Batouch points to the camel, directing Hadj to "go [and] give your brother some hay."

• Toothless Algerians appear, gaping at a money-grubbing Arab dancer. Clasping two daggers, the dancer nearly murders her lover. Confused by such behavior, Domini says, "She loves him and she tries to kill him?"

• Giggling Arab women begin fondling Domini. Explains Count Amteoni (Rathbone), "They're curious about a European woman. They seldom see one." See *Sahara* (1983).

Note: For *The Garden of Allah*, UA launched an extensive promotional campaign, including essay contests. The essay winners received free trips to Egypt. Newlyweds toured the country in trucks, complete with portable tents for two.

Gas (1981), PAR. *Donald Sutherland, Gershon Resnik, Brian Nasimok.* CAMEOS, SHEIKHS

This comedy about a phony fuel shortage displays a perverted sheikh.

Scene: A Midwest town. An unsightly sheikh wearing dark glasses, Fawsi Ibn Fawsi (Nasimok), sits in a limo embellished with Arabian Nights decor. The Arab holds a phone in one hand and a sex manual in the other. Irritating Arab music underscores Fawsi's phone conversation with a woman. In broken English, the sheikh purrs, "I drive my Cadillac in your love tunnel." The woman hangs up. Undaunted, Fawsi continues: "Foreplay! Ah, I like foreplay. I phone three girls."

• A gas station, a long line of waiting cars. Abruptly, Yassir (Resnik), the sheikh's chauffeur, jumps the limo to the front of the waiting autos. Note the dialogue:

Attendant: You go to the back of the line, Ayatollah.
Sheikh: I am Saleh Ibn Saleh.
Attendant: I don't care if you're the Son of Sam.
Sheikh: Yassir, behead him!
Yassir: [protesting] It's America.
Sheikh: Then run him over, ignorant son of a sheep herder.

• Upset, Yassir walks off. Flashing his green card, he tells the potentate he will "open a falafel stand." Retorts the sheikh, "Come back here so that I may injure you." The attendant warns Fawsi, "You get this pimp-mobile outta here." The inept sheikh grasps the wheel, and smashes into the car behind him.

Gas Pump Girls (1978), David A. Davies Prod. *Kirsten Baker, Huntz Hall, Dave Shelley, Jack Jozefson.* W: Davies, Joel Bender, Issac Blech. P, D: Davies. See *Happy Hooker Goes to Washington* (1977). CAMEOS, SHEIKHS

Scene: Uncle Joe's (Hall) gas station lacks customers. His business is located across the street from Mr. Friendly's (Shelley) "We'll Be Here Forever" Pyramid station. Friendly's station has tons of customers. Joe's niece, June (Baker), to the rescue. She and several "pretty young girls" wearing halter tops and short shorts transform Joe's run-down station into "Joe's Super Duper." Soon, Pyramid's customers are rushing to Joe's.

• The Pyramid Petroleum Products (PPP) building. Scantily clad beauties wearing harem garb attend Mr. Big (Jozefson), "a real oily character." Speaking with an Indian accent, Mr. Big tells Mr. Friendly he no longer need fret about competition from "Joe's."

• A "No Gas Today" sign appears at Joe's pumps. Says June, "There's something fishy goin' on around here." Joe cannot buy gas, but Friendly can. June moves to see Mr. Big, though "nobody gets to see him, not unless he's some goddamn Arab sheikh or something."

• Arab music underscores the action. Feigning to be Arabs, June's pals don white thobes, harem outfits and black veils; they drive off in a black limo to see Big. A phony "sheikh" barks mumbo jumbo at the PPP gate guard, he lets June Inc. enter.

• Inside PPP. Three authentic Arabs spot June's phony group. Quips one [in Arabic], "If those [kids] are real Arabs, I'll eat my camel!"

• June tells Mr. Big, "We're from Joe's Super Duper Service Station. Why can't you ship Joe any gas. You're the meanest man I ever met. You think just because you have all the money and power, you can play with everyone's lives." Moved by June's plea, Mr. Big says, "I need some time to think about it."

• Uncle Joe's station is now linked with PPP; business thrives. As for Mr. Friendly, he works for Joe.

The Ghoul (1933), Gaumont. *Boris Karloff, Cedric Hardwick, Ralph Richardson, Harold Huth, Dorothy Hyson.* Remade as a comedy, *No Place Like Homicide* (1962). Critics consider *The Ghoul* Britain's first true horror feature.
EGYPTIANS

An English mummy murders an Egyptian culprit.

Scene: British Egyptologist Professor Moriant (Karloff) emerges from the grave. The stiff-as-a-hieroglyph Moriant moves to punish the thieves who ran off with his precious "eternal light."

• Emerging from the shadows is Mahmoud, a sneaky Egyptian out to nab the mummy's precious eternal light jewel for himself. Mahmoud sneaks up on an Englishman; placing a knife to the man's throat, he says, "The eternal light goes back to the tomb from which you stole it… I shall be among the trees, watching." Suddenly, the risen-from-the-dead Moriant appears, killing Mahmoud.

• Moriant, a mummy who engraves ancient symbols onto his chest with a knife, desperately wants this jewel. Why? Because its light will bestow eternal life and open "the gates of paradise."

• Appearing is a dapper not-to-be-trusted Egyptian Aga-ben (Huth). Aga-ben, who also seeks the "eternal light," moves to befriend Betty Harlow (Hyson), an English woman.

• A full moon reveals Moriant's tomb. Nearby, a statue of Anubis, some candles and Betty with the special "light." Abruptly, Aga-ben snatches the "eternal light" from Betty. He shuts the tomb door on her, running off. In time, the police rescue Betty and collar Aga-ben.

The Gift (1982), a.k.a. Le cadeau, Rel. Goldwyn. *Claudia Cardinale, Pierre Mondy, Renzo Montagnani, Clio Goldsmith.* CAMEOS, MAIDENS, SHEIKHS

In this French-Italian sex farce a happily married 55-year-old French banker receives a unique retirement gift—a beautiful call girl. Injected into the comedy are perverted sheikhs. The Arabs reject their wives, moving to bed Europeans; the prostitutes dismiss the sheikhs, preferring Frenchmen.

Scene: A French hotel. After an English woman reluctantly spends the evening with Sheikh Faycal (Montagnani) of Katar, she complains to her female friend, "I'd give anything to go back to normal men." Her friend agrees, then gripes about an old prince from "Abu Dhabi who sprinkles camel urine all over himself and wants you to sing to him."

• Introducing Emir Faycal's mute wives; they are covered in cloth from head to toe. Two bodyguards lead the women into their hotel room. Cut to the Emir rushing after a call girl. No European woman wants to sleep with Faycal.

• A woman-for-hire explains how Faycal became so rich. When he was drilling "for water in his yard, [he] found oil, more than 200 million barrels." Now, the Emir's dealing with the French, paying "cash [for] ready-to-plug-in nuclear reactors."

• A French banker accidentally enters the Emir's suite. Immediately, the Arab's giggling wives begin fondling the man.

• The banker's son boasts he's bedding a "sleek bellydancer from Morocco."

The Gift Girl (1917), Bluebird Photoplays. Silent. *Louise Lovely, Emory Johnson, Wadsworth Harris, Winter Hall.* *NS. Notes from AFIC (p 320). VILLAINS, MAIDENS

In Arabia, "Mohammedans" care for "Rokaia (Lovely), an "orphaned English girl." But, when Rokaia grows up she is "ordered to marry a fat [Arab] merchant," Malec (Harris). Distressed, Rokaia "flees to Paris." Here, she falls in love with a college student, Marcel (Johnson). Unexpectedly, Malec arrives, confronting her in the city. The couple's "happiness is threatened." The rejected Malec "forcibly [tries to] take Rokaia" back to Arabia. Western heroes intervene: "Marcel and his fellow students fend the [Arab] merchant off and all ends happily."

Gladiator (2000), DW, UNI. *Russell Crowe, Oliver Reed, Djimon Hounsou, Omar Djalili.* SP: John Logan, William Nicholson, David Franzoni. S: Franzoni. D: Ridley Scott. See *GI Jane* (1997). CAMEOS, VILLAINS

Here, moviemakers inject a band of Arab slavers and a dirty desert Arab village into this splashy Roman sword-and-sandal scenario, set in AD 180.[79]

Scene: Maximus's home, Spain. Following the battle of Germania, Roman soldiers burn the home of Maximus (Crowe), Rome's "greatest General." The soldiers crucify his son and wife. Seriously wounded, Maximus collapses. Suddenly, Arabic-speaking men abduct Maximus.

• A camel caravan, complete with slaves. One slave kidnapped by the Arabs is an African (Hounsou); he tends Maximus' wounds, cautioning, "Don't die, or they [the Arabs] will feed you to the lions." The camera reveals two grotesque Arab slavers.

• The caravan arrives at mythical "Zaccahabar, a Roman province" resembling a backward Arab desert burg. (Note the resemblance to Zanzibar, an island off the coast of Tanzania.) The Zaccahabar scenes last about 25 minutes. Introducing a sly Arab slaver played by Omar Djalili, who is also a slimy Arab in *The Mummy* (1999). The slaver, who needs a bath and shave, attempts to sell Maximus and the African to Proximo (Reed), a Roman who procures gladiators. The Arab slaver barks, "we can negotiate," "bargain," and I give you "a special price." Finally, Proximo acquires Maximus and the African; he gives the slaver much less than his asking price.

• As Proximo's gladiators, the two men fight before Arab crowds in Zaccahabar, a "flea-infested" "shit hole." Finally, they move on to Rome, where they battle in the Coliseum before Romans and the emperor.

Note: When asked about the Arab-as-slaver scene, Harvard Professor Kathleen Coleman, an authority of Roman history who served as a consultant on *Gladiator* said, "I was not present during any of this process, so when I saw the preview I was unpleasantly surprised... I was under the impression that although the plot was fictitious, DW wanted the atmosphere to be authentic. But that is evidently not the case... I'm quite sure Arab slave-traders would not have penetrated Spain (where the scene was set) to kidnap Maximus."[80]

To insert ugly Arabs into *Gladiator* is both ridiculous and false. No band of defeated combatants, yet alone far-off Arab slavers, could ever invade the homes of Roman soldiers. I have found nobody specializing in Roman history who knows of any small band of Arab slavers plundering Rome's soldiers' homes from AD 180 to 1483. [81]

The Glass Sphinx (1967), AI. *Robert Taylor, Anita Ekberg, Angel Del Pozo, Ahmed Kamis.* Filmed in Egypt. EGYPTIANS

Amidst pyramids and palm trees, Egyptian bandits try to kill the American protagonist. Also appearing, a loyal Arab guide, a bellydancer, musicians, and policemen.

Scene: A clumsy Egyptian moves to murder noted archaeologist, Karl Nichols (Taylor), boasting, "Professor Nichols is not leaving this city alive." Instead of killing Nichols, the dense Egyptian kills himself.

• Why is Nichols "obsessed with the legend of the glass sphinx?" Because the underground tomb may contain "mysterious elixir," a magic cure-all that supposedly kept a pharaoh alive for more than "two hundred years." Nichols' superstitious, unruly Egyptian workers are wary about the expedition, declaring, "We will have much bad luck because we have [Western] women with us on this expedition."

• Arabs as Indians. In the desert, scores of "primitive" Egyptians flaunting rifles surface atop sand dunes. Though these "marauders [who] attack caravans" and burn tents outnumber the archaeologist's' expedition party, Nichols ignites some dynamite. The explosions compel the bandits to retreat.

• Nichols cautions lovely Paulette (Ekberg), "Nights on the desert give the illusion of romance." But the European villain, Alex (Del Pozo), threatens Paulette: I'm going to "exchange merchandise. You're going to a tribe," he says. "You're going to them [Arabs]." And, Alex delivers her to the marauders' tent camp. Cut to several ugly Egyptian bandits. They order Paulette to "dance." She refuses, and is told, "If you want to live, obey." Slowly, Paulette sways to the Arab music. Says Nichols, "We've gotta get her out of here." Abruptly, an Arab shoots Paulette dead.

• Alex and cohorts locate the glass sphinx. But when one of his men removes an eye from the sphinx, a curse materializes. Poison gas emerges, killing the Arab bandits and Alex.

Note: Though costumes and settings may vary, many screen images similarly show Arabs and Indians as heathens. In the desert/on the plains, "screeching" Arabs/"screaming" Indians charge legion/cavalry forts that shelter outnumbered legionnaires/pioneers. Hordes also attack caravans/stage coaches, kidnapping and raping blonde heroines.

Treatment of Islam: After Nichol's fatally wounded Egyptian guide saves the archaeologist's life, he asks, "Lift my face toward Mecca, my friend."

Dialogue: Characters speak gibberish, not Arabic.

A Global Affair (1964), MGM, SA. *Bob Hope.* CAMEOS

Scene: Speaking at the United Nations, the American protagonist (Hope) declares, "Each nation of our busy planet has fine cultural aspects... great poetry, fine music, noble ideals." Suddenly, an abandoned baby girl surfaces in the UN building. All the UN representatives volunteer to adopt her, but the American protagonist receives temporary custody of the child. Cut to two smiling Arabs bringing stuffed animals to the infant. Later, an African and an Arab diplomat help the girl ride an elephant.

The Golden Blade (1953), UNI. *Rock Hudson, Piper Laurie, Gene Evans, George Macready, Steven Geray.* S, SP: John Rich. VILLAINS, MAIDENS

Arabs vs. Arabs. "Jafar, the prince of treason," moves to squash the caliph.

Scene: Baghdad's hero, Harun (Hudson), rides across desert sands to link up with his father's caravan. Says the narrator: Harun is "unaware that Allah in His mysterious ways, had chosen to press upon his brow, the thumb of destiny." When Harun nears the camp, he sees tents-on-fire. Arab villains stab his father and his followers. Harun's dying father gives his son, now "the protector of all Islam," a medallion, saying, "Seek out the true maker of these crimes... May Allah keep you."

• Baghdad's souk displays an elderly beggar, animals and numerous shops, including "the House of Barcus the Greek." An Arab pretender incites the crowd; he tries to blame the kind caliph for the caravan tragedy. Princess Khairuzan (Laurie), the caliph's daughter, challenges the man's lies. A fight ensues; palace guards arrive. As the guards whisk the princess off, she tosses tomatoes at the pretender, calling him "son-of-a-flea-bitten-camel."

• Harun moves to aid the princess. He takes from Barcus' shop, the "magic sword of Damascus." As the weapon cuts through iron, Harun boasts, "While I hold this sword no danger can ever harm me."

• The palace throne room and grand hall reveal a large gong, decorative pots, incense burners, and feather fans. Appearing in the harem quarters are maidens, a eunuch, and a dancer. Nearby, the vizier, Jafar (Macready), and his dense son, Hadi (Evans), plot the caliph's demise.

• The caliph orders his daughter to marry Hadi. She scoffs, "Do you want me to marry an accident?" Fighting off palace guards with the "magic sword of Damascus," Harun frees the princess. When Hadi tells Jafar about Harun's "magic sword," his father beams, saying: "At last, your brain competes with your muscle."

• Declares the caliph: The winner of an upcoming joust may wed the princess. Jafar not only produces a "perfect copy" of the "magic sword," but he dupes Harun into using the "copy." Thus, during the joust, Hadi bests Harun. After Jafar drugs Harun, he tags him the "enemy of Basra." Moans Harun, "I was drunk without drinking."

• The princess takes a bubble bath; scantily clad maidens prepare her for Hadi. The drunken Hadi tries to seduce her. Harun arrives; he and the princess escape. The caliph learns of Jafar's treachery. Too late. One of Jafar's men stabs the ruler in the back.

• Jafar tells the crowd: "Long Live Caliph Hadi!" Jafar, Hadi, and some "strongmen" try to remove the real "magic sword" from a stone column. They fail. Harun arrives, easily extracting the sword. Suddenly, columns crumble. Hadi, Jafar and their cronies are crushed.

• The princess tells her people: "Behold, with the sword of Damascus we restore our lives to former peace." Noting Harun, she says, "Upon him who saved us, I bestow the title, El-Rashid, he who follows the righteous cause. Long live Harun." She and Harun kiss.

Note: Why do producers tag Harun's pal, "Barcus, the Greek"? As the action takes place in Baghdad, why not call him, "Barcus, the Iraqi"?

• Baghdad's palace guards wear Crusader-type outfits, pointed steel helmets and armor; they look like medieval soldiers.

Golden Hands of Kurigal (1949), REP. This feature film showing Arab fanatics battling American agents is a re-edited release of a 12-episode serial, *Federal Agents vs. Underworld, Inc.* (1948). VILLAINS

The Golden Idol (1954), AA. *Johnny Sheffield, Anne Kimbell, Paul Guilfoyle, Lane Bradford.* P, W, D: Ford Beebe. VILLAINS, SHEIKHS

Bomba trounces an evil Arab and his cohorts.

Scene: A village. Arab music underscores shots of dogs, chickens, primitive huts and gun-toting Arabs. Inside the palace, black slaves and harem maidens attend Prince Ali Ben Mamoud (Guilfoyle). Beneath the palace, a large pit holding a wild boar and a Bengal tiger.

• A priceless golden idol, considered to be the "last evidence of a lost civilization," belongs to the Watusi, a peaceful African tribe. Yet, Ali not only nabs the idol, the Arab tortures the Watusi chief "with fire." Bomba (Sheffield),"a devil in human form," catches up with Ali's Arabs, and takes the idol from them. Ali hires an expert hunter, Joe Hawkins (Bradford), to track Bomba. Later, Bomba brings down Joe.

• Bomba always outwits Ali. Easily, Bomba punches out the Arab and his palace guards. The inept Ali tries to kill Bomba. Instead, Ali shoots his own guard.

• Abruptly, Arabs cease tracking Bomba. Why? Because the sun has set, and Arabs cannot see at night.

• To prevent Ali from torturing the heroine, Karen Marsh (Kimbell), Bomba vows to return the golden idol to Ali's camp. Ali's Arab guards who follow Bomba cannot "keep up"; they insist he "slow down." Bomba halts, then slugs an Arab. Another Arab swings a rifle at Bomba's head. He misses, flooring his Arab ally. Next, Bomba clubs a knife-toting Arab.

• A river basin. After a shoot-out, Ali's guards surrender. Suddenly, Ali stumbles, falling into the river. A huge snake spots the Arab, crushing him.
• Bomba returns the golden idol to the grateful Watusi.

The Golden Salamander (1951), Pinewood. *Trevor Howard, Anouk Aimee, Herbert Lom, Peter Copley.* Filmed in Tunisia. VILLAINS

Tunisia as a soiled backdrop with panhandling kids. Europeans vs. Europeans.

Scene: A large map displays the cities, Tunis and Kabarta. Cut to David Redford (Howard); the archaeologist enters Kabarta's Café des Amis. A British pianist performs. Anna (Aimee), a Frenchwoman, owns the bar; she tells David that Tunisia is "that kind of country, violent." David wants to employ some Tunisians; he needs their help to repair some damaged cargo crates containing vital relics. The artifacts are to be shipped to the British Museum.

• In the souk, children beg. David gives one child some coins; others scream, then surround him. A French policeman runs the boys off, advising, "Ignore them. But keep your hands in your pockets. [This Arab market's] always the same... my nerves, my indigestion, all ruined."

• Aribi (Copley), a Tunisian, helps David employ some Arabs. The men, says Aribi, want "100 Francs an hour." Anna protests, saying "30" is fair. Aribi suggests "60"; David insists on "50." What matters most is not the money, quips Aribi, rather "the honor of the work." "Aribi is a good workman," says Anna, "but watch him. He'll steal the laces out of your shoes and sell them back to you." (David spends 65 Francs postage to send an express letter from Kabarta to Tunis. Yet, he convinces his Tunisian workers to accept only 50 Francs an hour.)

• Viewing a Tunisian town, David says, "It looks beautiful from here." Counters Anna, "Yes, from here. But... it's not a nice town, dirty and corrupt."

• In a cafe, David and Anna drink coffee; a Tunisian wedding party passes. Men dance, playing traditional instruments. Explains Anna, "They're taking the bridegroom to the hammam (a Turkish bath). He must be washed before they take him to his bride. It's a form of purity. Do you think it's a nice custom?" David nods, "It's wonderful."

• A murder occurs; David tries to call the police but the phone lines are down. "That's what happens," says Anna, "the bedouins cut the wire; they make bracelets out of it." Grunts David, "They would."

Note: Credits state: "The cooperation and help of the French and Arab authorities is gratefully acknowledged."

The Golden Treasure (1982), MIR. *Kenneth Nash, Elizabeth White.* Filmed in Egypt. EGYPTIANS

Present-day Egyptians uncovering hidden treasures are as profane as their predecessors. Egyptians move to bump off the American protagonist.

Scene: A desert dig. A British couple and their two children search for hidden jewels. Cut to Youssef and Ali, two Egyptian rogues lugging baskets filled with rocks.

• Ali and Youssef stumble across the sought-after treasures. They remain mum. The Egyptians intend to keep the loot for themselves. To celebrate, they slop corn-cobs as pigs.

• Youssef and Ali move to sell the jewels off to an American, Jeff. As he refuses to buy them, they kidnap Jeff, dumping him into a desert pit. Next, the thieves slug Ramsey, Jeff's Egyptian friend.

• Eventually, the authorities nab Ali and Joussef. After the rich treasure site is disclosed, the Western protagonists and Ramsey celebrate.

The Golden Voyage of Sinbad (1974), COL. *John Phillip Law, Caroline Munro, Tom Baker.* Special effects: Ray Harryhausen. RECOMMENDED

Heroics are omnipresent; only one Arab cur. This 1970s fantasy resembles action-packed tales of 1950s Saturday matinee films.

Scene: Out to acquire a magical golden tablet, Baghdad's legendary hero, Sinbad the Sailor (Law), and his crew confront a foul wizard, "a great black bat of a man," Prince Koura (Baker).

• On a mysterious island, Sinbad defeats opponents—a ferocious statue with six arms, a flying griffin, and a one-eyed centaur.

• Sinbad falls for a beautiful slave girl, Margiana (Munro), and vice versa.

• Numerous battle scenes; Sinbad Inc. triumph. Finis. "With the help of Allah," Sinbad brings down Koura and his cohorts.

Dialogue: "Trust in Allah, but tie up your camel."

Goodbye, New York (1985), a.k.a. Crazy House, Castle Hill. *Julie Hagerty, Ezra Ahazon.* W, D: Amos Kolleck. An Israeli-U.S. movie, filmed in Israel. CAMEOS, PALESTINIANS

Israeli actors appear as lecherous Palestinians. The film's Palestinians try to seduce a Jewish-American tourist, Nancy Callaghan (Hagerty).

Scene: In Israel, a bearded, unkempt, camel-riding Palestinian (Ahazon) tries to defile Nancy. He fails.

• Nancy enters a Palestinian shop; she tries on an Arab garment. As Nancy removes her Western clothes, the camera shows the Palestinian shopkeeper leering. He suggests a price, Nancy offers less. The bargaining continues. Eventually, Nancy realizes the bargaining is all about sex. The Palestinian wants her, not money. Nancy exits the shop.

Note: Writer-director Kolleck is the son of Jerusalem's former mayor.

Grand Larceny (1987), MGM. *Marilu Henner, Omar Sharif.* CAMEOS

A one-liner; a Libyan as an imaginary villain.

In this comedy crime-caper, a wealthy man (Sharif) and his colleagues test the heroine's skills. The rich man and his cohorts concoct a false tale about a stolen horse. On purpose, they mislead the heroine (Henner), telling her to watch out for "the brother of the defense minister of Libya." The Libyan, they say, "who gambles at Nice's roulette tables, wants to develop a racing stable." Thus, they add, the Arab is about to nab their $5-million race horse. Though the heroine falls for the ruse, in the end she proves her mettle.

The Great Sinner (1949), MGM. *Gregory Peck, Ava Gardner.* CAMEOS, SHEIKHS

A polygamous potentate.

1860s. A private card game is in progress at a European gambling resort. Two bearded men wearing fezzes wait on tables. Cut to a really big game. A man wearing a white turban raises the bet, "fifty thousand." Whispers an elderly gentleman, "He's a mystery to me, a man with a kingdom, and a harem. Why on earth does he gamble?" Quips his companion, "He wants to forget his thirty-second wife." All gamblers except the turbaned man are Europeans and Americans.

Ground Zero (1994), a.k.a. Bloodfist VI: Ground Zero, New Horizons. *Don "The Dragon" Wilson* (a world kick-boxing champion), *Leonard Turner, Steve Garvey, Jonathan Fuller.* SP: Bob Kerchner, Brendan Broderick. A Roger Corman film. See *True Lies* (1994), *Executive Decision* (1996), *The Siege* (1998). VILLAINS, WORST LIST

A "global emergency." Arab nuclear terrorists vs. the US military. Invading America, an Arab Muslim madman and his "Party of Allah" cohorts slay dozens of airmen and special forces troops. They intend to nuke millions: "Projected Death Toll 375 Million People."

Scene: Nebraska, the Strategic Air Command's "Nuclear Missile Base." The terrorists attack, gaining "control of 20 ICBM's, each with a 1.2 megaton nuclear warhead." Among the bad guys, Ali, Ahmed, and Hassad.

• The head terrorist, Fawkes (Fuller), warns an American general: "The brethren of the Party of Allah demand from you 100 million dollars in gold." Quips the general, "They call themselves the Party of Allah?"

• Says Fawkes, the "Prophet Mohammed" has said that "the more people who die for a cause, the stronger that cause shall become." Balderdash! The Prophet Mohammed never made such a statement.

• Note the dialogue between two American officers:

Col. Briggs: We finally came up with something on this Party of Allah. It's a small Islamic fundamentalist organization out of New York. The FBI has an open file on them and one of the members is Joseph Fawkes.
US general: American?
Col. Briggs: No, Arab. His real name is Hassan Al-Hazar!
US general: So, what have we got? A crazy camel-driver! Shit! [The General also tags Al-Hazar's men "rat-bastards," and "sons-of-bitches."]

• Islam equals violence. An African-American electronics specialist tries to foil the Arabs' launch of the ICBM. Al-Hazar kills the man. Next, Al-Hazar extends his arms and prays: "Praise be to God, sustainer of worlds." The Arab checks the launch controls, then resumes praying: "With hopes of martyrdom... Praise be to God."

• US Sgt. Corrigan (Wilson) moves to stop the launch. He slugs Al-Hazar. But Al-Hazar kicks Corrigan in the gut, shouting: "I am the will of Allah... the fist of Mohammed." Then he slams a gun to Corrigan's face, warning, "And the world shall witness my holocaust." Al-Hazar extends his arms in prayer, hits the launch button, and screams: "For my country's two million martyrs and the children of Islam." In time, Corrigan recovers; he terminates Al-Hazar and prevents the ICBM from lifting off.

Note: Not all terrorist scenarios demonize Arab Muslims. For example, in *Live Wire* (1992), a New Line Cinema release, written by Bart Baker and starring Pierce Brosnan, the villains are generic types—not one heavy dons Arab garb; not one speaks Arabic; not one equates "Islam," "Allah," or "the Prophet" with violence. *Live Wire's* scenario focuses on *international* terrorists liquidating corrupt American senators opposing a "Mideast anti-arms bill." Though closing credits refer to the main terrorist as "Mikhail Rashid," his reel cohorts call him Mikhail, not Rashid.

Guns and Guitars (1936), REP. *Gene Autry, Smiley Burnett.* P: Art Levine. MAIDENS, CAMEOS

The scenario shows Gene Autry battling unscrupulous cattlemen.[82] Yet, a five-minute scene presents Smiley Burnett as a stereotypical "Arab harem girl." Blacks, too, are mocked. A stylish African-American tap-dancer wearing Arab garb is tagged "Eight-Ball."

Scene: Texas. An unscrupulous character wanting to become the sheriff offers "free beer" to prospective voters. Quips an opponent, "It's very hard to compete with free beer. [But] there's "an antidote for everything." Unexpectedly, the crowd exits the beer stand—to watch Burnett posing as a harem maid. Clad in flimsy garb and wearing a veil, Burnett performs as Princess Zara, an Arab dancer. With him, on stage, is Eight-Ball, who plays the flute.

• This scene burlesques and ridicules Arabs and blacks. As Eight-Ball plays the flute, onlookers are told: "Step inside and see Egypt's Princess Zaza. Watch her wiggle, watch her shake and don't forget to watch that snake." The clad-in-harem-garb Burnett squirms to and fro, then clasps a false snake. Says the barker, Princess Zaza "is not only an oriental dancer, but a mind reader as well." He asks Zaza, "What's underneath your hat?" Sighs Zaza, "Nothing!"

Gymkata (1985), MGM. *Kurt Thomas.* CAMEOS, VILLAINS

Americans are not welcome in Arab souks.

Scene: The US could secure a much-needed "star wars" missile base in a far off nation, provided gymnast Jonathan Cabot (Thomas) wins a martial arts contest. En route to compete, Cabot stops off in an unnamed Arab country. On screen, a mosque; an imam calls the devout to evening prayer.

• A crowded souk; hawking their wares are men wearing red fezzes. One bearded merchant asks Cabot, "You are American?" "Yeah!" brags Cabot. The man throws a cup of water into gymnast's face, ands runs off shouting, "Yankee, go home." Explains the US agent with Cabot, "There's just a little anti-American sentiment running around." Suddenly, someone shoots the agent dead.

• Several men try to assassinate Cabot, first in the souk, then at an Arabesque abode. Cabot crushes the would-be assassins, declaring, "Well, that cleans things up around here."

Half Moon Street (1986), RKO. *Sigourney Weaver, Michael Caine, Nadim Sawalha, Keith Buckley.* SP: Bob Swain, Edward Behr, based on Paul Theroux's 1984 novel, *Doctor Slaughter.* D: Swain. PALESTINIANS, MAIDENS

Scene: London, cut to a mosque. Cut to a limousine accommodating three mute Arab women; they are covered in black, and wear black and yellow face masks. Cut to the

American heroine, Professor Lauren Slaughter (Weaver), jogging. The editing suggests Arab women yearn to be as liberated as Lauren.

• During a discussion about terrorism, someone points out that a Libyan exile may be the culprit behind a recent car bomb. Next, Hugo Van Arkady, one of 5,000 men who control the world, tells Lauren that among this ruling group are "more Arabs than you'd expect."

• For a time, Lauren works at London's Institute of Middle East Studies. But as she does not receive a grant to conduct research in Kuwait, she opts to become a high-class hooker. Her escort service, the Jasmine Agency, links her up with an irritable Kuwaiti sheikh and a radical Palestinian who masquerades as a respectful businessman, Karim Hatimi (Sawalha). Though Karim, who "put(s) people together," sleeps with Lauren, the camera reveals no passion. Instead, the viewer sees two shuffling bodies hidden under satin sheets. Occasionally, unpleasant grunts are heard. Later, sexless Karim watches the topless Lauren riding an exercise bike. Smiling, Karim takes photographs.

• Lauren meets Lord Samuel Bulbeck (Caine), a British diplomat moving to bring Israelis and Arabs together. When they make love sparks fly; Lauren's nude body is revealed.

• Karim permits Lauren to live rent-free in his flat on Half Moon street—a street "crawling with Arabs and prostitutes." Unknown to Lauren, sinister types bug her apartment.

• Karim also gives Lauren a gold half-moon crescent-shaped pendant studded with diamonds. Lauren is taken aback by the "Arab good will," asking, "Why are you being so nice to me?" Karim lies, saying, "I like you. You're a friend... friendship is everything." Actually, Karim, who opposes Bulbeck's Mideast peace efforts, deceives Lauren. Using Lauren and "Arab money," he and his nasty cohorts intend halt the peace process by bumping off Lord Bulbeck.

• Intending to kill Lord Bulbeck, a hired assassin enters Lauren's flat. He expects to see and kill the Englishman. Only Lauren is present. A struggle takes place; Lauren brings down the assassin Karim arrives; Lauren is relieved to see him. But for the first time, Karim's true nature surfaces, as he wants Lord Bulbeck dead. Karim becomes violent; he yanks the pendant from Lauren's neck, slugs her, and pulls a gun to her head. To the rescue, British agents. They barge into the flat, shooting Karim and rescuing Lauren.

Note: In Theroux's book, several kinky Arabs assist Karim.

The Half-Naked Truth (1932), RKO. *Lee Tracy, Lupe Velez.* MAIDENS, CAMEOS

A Mideast dancer portrayed by a Latina actress weds the Anglo protagonist.

Scene: Appleton, Pennsylvania. During the city's carnival, "La belle Sultana" (Velez), does the "dance of the seven veils [and] the sacred dance of the muscles." Carnival hucksters tag her "Sultana," and "Princess Erotica of Turkey." Plus, they bark she has escaped "from a harem."

• A Broadway theater. The stage set looks like an Arabian Nights chamber. When Sultana dances, the audience hisses. Promptly, Sultana removes her "oriental" garb. She belts out a jazzy song. Enthusiasts cheer.

Hanna K. (1983), UNI. *Jill Clayburgh, Muhamad Bakri, Jean Yanne, Gabriel Byrne. SP: Franco Solinas and Constantin Costa-Gavras. P: Michele Ray. D: Costa-Gavras. Filmed in Israel.* PALESTINIANS, RECOMMENDED

This pre-intifada movie sympathizes with the displaced Palestinian protagonist. He illegally enters Israel to reclaim his Palestinian family's home, confiscated by the Israelis. Initial and final frames present Palestinians as victims. Says director Costa-Gavras, "The film is about a human problem. It tries to explain there is a problem in Israel. The problem is that there are Palestinians living there under certain kinds of pressure. For years we didn't think about that problem." We wanted to show "the human problem," he says, "which could lead to war, a larger war, moral bankruptcy... there must be a land for the Jewish people. And there must also be a land for the Palestinian people. And this right—for both these people—must go through the mutual recognition of this right."[83]

Scene: The front yard of a Palestinian family's home; as a mother cuddles her child the camera reveals Israeli soldiers patrolling the area. Cut to Palestinian captives, their arms tied, inside an Israeli military truck. Abruptly, a soldier discovers Selim (Bakri), hiding in a nearby well. Before the Israelis haul off Selim and their other prisoners, Palestinian women rush into the house, removing furniture. The Israelis explode the house; the family reacts, silently.

• Jerusalem. Selim tries to explain that although he was expelled from Israel, he re-entered the country to reclaim his ancestral home, which Israeli officials seized from his family years before. Defending him is Hanna Kaufman (Clayburgh), an American Jew with a passion for justice. Selim has ample funds to pay Hanna for her services. During the trial, Hanna, not Selim, requests an interpreter.

• Hanna asks an Israeli solider how to reach the village Selim calls home, Koufar Ramaneh, "in existence since the fifth century." Barks the soldier, "Doesn't exist, better get an up-to-date map." He says she must mean the Hebrew town, "Kfar Ramon." When Hanna asks a newly arrived Russian immigrant what happened to the old village, the immigrant replies that the Arabs are "in the countryside, not here."

• Hanna enters Selim's ancestral home, now a museum. Above the doorway, an Arabic inscription and photographs of Selim's family. One photo shows Selim's mother holding him. Outside, a Palestinian tending his flock mumbles repeatedly, "Koufar Ramaneh."

• Selim's second trial. The Palestinian's rights and ownership of the family home are debated. Argues Hanna, that house was his. He wants to it back, fairly, by going through proper channels. Explains Hanna, over a five-year period the Israeli-born Selim "sent one dozen letters" requesting an entry visa. But, "he never received an answer." She poses a telling question. Is there one law for Palestinians, another for Jews? Counters Joshue Herzog (Byrne), the district attorney whose child Hanna carries, "The defendant [Selim] is not a citizen of this country. He is not a citizen of any country... He just wants to go home. His parents were transferred to a refugee camp. They wound up in Lebanon... There are two million more behind him." Retorts Hanna, "Maybe he doesn't exist at all."

• Following Selim's trial, Professor Leventhal convinces Hanna to concur with the harsh verdict. He says Selim will serve only eight months. Afterwards, he could be issued papers and become a citizen of South Africa. "Would you make us a minority surrounded by a sea of Arabs?... Now that we are a country we must defend it," he says. Retorts Hanna, "By refusing the same thing [an identity] to others?" "Yes," says Leventhal, "if necessary, yes."

• The Israeli court labels Selim a terrorist, convicting him of illegal entry. Now imprisoned, Selim goes on a hunger strike. Six months pass; on learning "he is dying" Hanna gets Selim paroled. She takes the Palestinian into her home; Selim and Hanna become lovers.

• Later, Selim tends Hanna's child, calling him "little Omar." The baby's biological father is the Israeli district attorney; he warns Hanna, "I thought my son's name was David... If I were you I wouldn't let my son go around with a terrorist as a babysitter... It wouldn't be the first time they used a baby carriage for bombs." The child exemplifies the conflict. Should both parties share the land? Or does the country belong only to the Israelis? Hanna complains about the district attorney to a friend, "It's Selim he can't accept. We get along well together."

• Hanna follows Selim to an abandoned refugee camp. Years ago, Selim and his parents lived there. Pointing to where shells once landed, he tells Hanna, "Come in and see for yourself." Next, they embrace.

• A terrorist attack occurs near Koufar Ramaneh; several Israelis are injured. Selim is blamed for the incident. Asked whether he had "anything to do with it," the Palestinian sighs, "What can I say? The decision has already been made." Selim goes to little Omar's room; he hugs the boy, then hands him to Hanna. Abruptly, armed Israelis appear. Selim tells Hanna, "I'll be seeing you."

• In spite of the unjust accusations, the soft-spoken, non-violent Selim does not scream, nor shout. Nor does he move to kill little Omar, a common screen terrorist act.

Note: The Hanna Kaufman character may be patterned after Israeli defense attorney, Felicia Langer. Following the 1967 war, Langer began representing Palestinians in Israeli military courts.

• *Hanna K.* was attacked by some conservative critics, who expressed alarm about the movie's "pro-Palestinian" stance and "biased" account of the Israeli-Palestinian conflict. As the movie's debut attracted much controversy, UNI began withdrawing the film from distribution. *Hanna K.* never opened in Boston. Nor was the film commercially shown in Washington, DC.[84]

In 1984, however, *Hanna K.* was screened before those attending the 1984 American-Arab Discrimination Committee's conference, in Washington, DC. Professor Edward Said explained that as the film "deals directly with the rights of the Palestinians," commercial distributors have not made it available to most movie theaters in this country. Affirmed producer Michele Ray, "after the Paris opening, European critics were hostile. Not one wrote about the political theme of the film, about the Palestinian people's rights. This is the first time this has happened to Costa."

• Immediately after the film's release, the New York office of the Anti-Defamation League of B'nai B'rith (ADL) sent out a six-page political analysis condemning *Hanna K.* On 10 October 1983, an ADL Media Watch memorandum was dispatched to regional offices, advising members how to best address *Hanna K.*'s "inaccuracies and prejudicial implications" in the press. Wrote Shimon Samuels, ADL's European office director and Abba Cohen, assistant director of the Middle Eastern Affairs Department, "The film teaches us nothing about present-day realities... Costa-Gavras resorts, at times, to the insidious and hateful. There is the implication of a determined Israeli policy that seeks to erase all traces of Palestinian presence from the West Bank and Gaza." The film "is a shallow and meaningless story, beset with oversimplifications, inaccuracies, and distortions. It lends nothing to thoughtful discussion; it offers nothing for those who wish for peace."

• A few days after the ADL memo (14 October 1983) critic John Simon of *New York Magazine* appeared on ABC-TV's *Nightline* segment, "The Movies." Here, Simon reiterated ADL's argument. Simon blasted *Hanna K.*, telling host Ted Koppel that the movie was "meant to be sympathetic to the P.L.O." Countered Costa-Gavras: "The movie has nothing to do with the P.L.O. We never say P.L.O. in the film. Never. Not once. The film is about a human problem." Next, actor Charlton Heston appeared, explaining to *Nightline* reporter Jeff Greenfield that some movies do in fact impact policies. "Film is far and away the most powerful tool for shaping human opinion, that has ever been devised by the hand of man. They not only can, but always have, made political statements; but [movies] also [make] profound social statements," said Heston. Chimed in actor Gene Hackman, "There are films that are made as political films which are really propaganda films."

• Though *Hanna K.* was filmed mostly in Israel, director Costa-Gavras shot the opening scene—the Israeli soldiers evicting a Palestinian family and dynamiting their home—in Italy.[85]

The Happy Hooker Goes to Washington (1977), CAN. *Joey Heatherton, Jerry Fisher*. W: Robert Kaufman. P, D: William A. Levey. See *Gas Pump Girls* (1978). CAMEOS, SHEIKHS

A perverted, "militant" sheikh speaking with a high-pitched, effeminate voice tries to rule the world's economy. To foil the Arab's ambitions, the CIA enlists the bedroom skills of a noted blonde hooker, Xaviera Hollander (Heatherton).

Scene: Washington, DC. "Looking for a fall guy," some senators accuse Xaviera of promoting "sexual excesses in America." A CIA agent intervenes, recruiting Xaviera as an "undercover" agent. Explains the agent, "Middle East men are meeting in Miami Beach. If "egocentric Sheikh Ali" [Fisher] attends, a war" may result. This would be "disastrous for the economy of the free world."

• Xaviera examines photographs of the tubby Ali; he lounges on pillows, attended by harem maidens. This "oil billionaire is the most militant, most ruthless leader," says the agent. Plus, he is the "absolute ruler of 48 million subjects whose average per capita income is $49.11 cents a year, before taxes. His people hate him."

• To "save America," Xaviera moves to keep Ali "away from the Miami meeting."

• Miami Beach, pool side. Xaviera cuddles the red-robed Ali, then takes him to a diner. States the sign: "MOGEN DAVID Kosher Meat Products." Here, the lisping Ali munches "a pastrami sandwich" that drips down his chin onto the table.

• To gain Ali's confidence, Xaviera tells a fib. "The Israeli soldiers took my village in the Sinai," she purrs. After they "captured me," they did nasty things. It was "horrible." Next, she propositions Ali. "What would my wives say; they would be jealous!" exclaims Ali. "I am the Sheikh of Steel. My mighty member is like an oil derrick... [I am] the potentate of potency." Xavier clasps Ali's "derrick," then pulls her hand back, sighing, "It's not much of a gusher, is it?" Bemoans Ali, "It's a mirage. You can help?"

• Ali's Arabian Nights bedroom, complete with a bare-chested eunuch. Beneath red silken sheets, Xaviera's bedroom skills transform "the pussycat of the oasis [into] the lion of the desert." To show his "appreciation," Ali asks Xaviera to be his "head wife, [his] only wife." Also, he vows "to distribute the wealth of [his] country to all; to place two camels in every garage."

• Ali's hotel suite. Arab music underscores an orgy in progress. Harem maidens and nudes nuzzle. Ali boasts to Xaviera that he and a US senator on his "payroll," are "in the business of white slaving. We go way back," says Ali. The senator "gives me certain votes on legislation and I give him certain favors." As the senator is in cahoots with Ali, Xaviera no longer need fret about him wanting to jail her for "sexual excesses."

• Arab rulers depart Miami Beach, fully aware that Xaviera's bedroom antics saved America, indeed, the world.

Hard Hunted (1992), Malibu. *W, D: Andy Sidaris.* CAMEOS, VILLAINS

Americans stop an Arab country from acquiring a nuclear device.

Scene: Hidden inside a statue of Buddha is a stolen "nuclear trigger." Moving to purchase the device are "three emissaries from the Middle East." Fearing the "trigger" may wind up in "Iraq," American agents retrieve the Buddha. Next, the women crush the villain who was trying to hawk the device to the Arabs.

Harem (1985), Sara Film Prod. *Ben Kingsley, Natassja Kinski, Dennie Goldson.* Filmed in Morocco. Credits thank "The National Center of Moroccan Cinema." SHEIKHS, MAIDENS

Contemporary Arabia. In this $10-million-dollar R-rated film, Prince Selim (Kinglsey), a desert oil sheikh kidnaps Diane (Kinski), a lovely New York stock exchange trainee, and imprisons her in his palace harem. Arab women are vilified. Mingling inside an Arab palace are chickens, camels, and donkeys.

Scene: A New York boat dock. Prince Selim's henchmen drug Diane's sweet tea drink.

• Diane awakes "locked up" at Selim's desert palace. Gawking, semi-nude Arab women and children surround her. Among them, a black eunuch, Massoud (Goldson). Maidens shave their legs; others yodel and clap their hands, still others rub the body of a naked woman.

• Diane tries to ascertain her whereabouts. Peering outside, she sees a desert dotted with black tents, and a Rolls Royce. Nearby, a few trucks; Western men mingle.

• Frightened, Diane runs off into the desert and collapses. When she is returned to the palace, Massoud tells her, "Home, [this is] your home. [You no longer] have to worry about money, taxes, rent."

• Diane asks mute, ogling Arab maidens, "What do you do here to pass the time?" They watch a porno film, laughing as the on-screen couple fornicate atop a horse. Protests Diane, "I can't be sitting around here waiting for some phony sheikh to come and rape me."

• Appearing is a wrinkled Arab matriarch, one of Prince Selim's grandfather's "favorite wives." The covered-in-black woman looks like Darth Vader's wife.

• Cackling old women prepare Diane for seduction. They comb her hair, apply lipstick and make-up, and put henna on her face and hands. Next, they cover Diane in black.

• Diane enters Sheikh Selim's quarters wearing a gold cross, symbolizing perhaps,

Christian protection from a Muslim prince. Cut to Selim playing "Schubert" on an out-of-tune piano. Chickens and donkeys roam about; the camera closes in on a caged monkey, reflecting Diane's captivity.

• Selim admits he had his men watch Diane "for a long time." He reveals some photographs taken of her and her New York relatives. "In my country we often choose a wife from a photograph. The veil," says Selim, "presents unpleasant surprises." Selim's declaration about not being able to see his wife until after a marriage is nonsense, applying to, perhaps, two percent of the Arab population.

• Selim's harem maidens and Diane hop into Mercedes-Benzes and Land Rovers and drive off to the sea. Here, music blares from portable radios. As one youth drinks a Coke, the women sing. Only Diane undresses, and goes for a dip.

• Selim allows his Arab maidens to "have lovers, even children." Yet, he questions whether "the women are content." Cut to Massoud functioning as Selim's "pimp." Evenings, he arranges for the women to depart, to sleep with Westerners.

• Selim and Diane drive off in his black Ferrari. Camels block the road; but they manage to arrive in time to check into a hotel room. Here, they confess they like each other and make love. Later, Selim tells Diane he never beds palace maidens. "Most of them are daughters," he says, "sisters of my cousins, of my fathers."

• Concluding scenes illustrate the film's theme: East and West are incompatible. Though Selim loves a Western woman and vice versa, their cultures prevent a happy union. See *Fazil* (1928), and other miscegenation films. Diane is reluctant to "give up" her lover, saying, "We can't stay here forever." Begs Selim, "There's no reason to go back" [to New York].

• The palace, morning. Western men invade and trash palace rooms as well as violate Selim's maidens. Angry, Selim becomes irrational. He spots a man, poolside, brushing his teeth. Selim, who had "never killed" anyone, shoots him. Selim points to his father's picture, telling Diane, "Him? Many he terrorized."

• Aware that a lasting relationship with Diane is not possible, Selim chooses an Arab woman—reluctantly, like selecting a morsel from a row of crumbs.

• Diane departs for New York. The despondent Selim walks alongside the palace pool. Thinking the prince is an intruder, an Arab guard mistakenly shoots him.

Note: This film humiliates Arab women, showing them simply lounging about, occasionally serving Selim. The mostly mute maidens function as part-time whores. An elderly woman appears not as benevolent mother or grandmother, but as a toothless hag.

Harem Girl (1952), COL. *Joan Davis, Peggy Castle, Arthur Drake, Paul Marion, Donald Randolph.* S, SP, D: Edward Bernds. See *Road to Morocco* (1942), *Harum Scarum* (1965). SHEIKHS, MAIDENS

Move over Lawrence of Arabia. In this slapstick comedy Susie Perkins (Davis), a secretary from Cedar Rapids, Iowa, becomes Arabia's deliverer. Given Susie's heroics, writer Bernds should tag this film: *Susie of Arabia.* Plenty of nonsensical desert palace hullabaloo reveals obese and oily sheikhs exploiting maidens.

Scene: Opening credits. Arab music underscores a series of on-screen sketches showing Arabs beating up Arabs.

• Arriving in the "mysterious Mideast" is Susie Perkins (Davis), a US secretary-companion to the "real-live Princess Shareen" (Castle). Susie expects "a sheikh on a white horse" will woo her. No such luck. She soon learns there's "no romance [in this] strange little country; [it] slumbers like it did 100 years ago." Says Shareen, "Nothing is happening here, nothing."

• An Arab knifes an Arab; quips Shareen, "My life is in constant danger... At any moment an assassin's knife may strike." The princess points to "that crawling little snake of a hotel manager," telling Susie, "I don't know whom to trust but you; there are spies everywhere."

• A knife-wielding Arab lunges at Shareen. Susie's "well-honed judo abilities" stave off the assassin. "Beat it or I'll blow your burnoose off," declares Susie.

• Dressing as an Arab, Susie says, "Is this how they wear 'em in the harem?"

• Sheikh Jamal (Randolph) tries to bump off Shareen. Why? Because he wants to profit from the kingdom's immense, untapped oil resources. Explains Jamal, "Don't you know what we have here? Oil! Oil to last the world 1,000 years." Before Jamal can cash in on the "black gold," he has to uncover an ancient scroll.

• Arabs opposing Jamal will be "herded together like cattle for the slaughter."

• Inside Sheikh Nassib's palace, maidens dance. Jamal threatens Shareen, telling her: Marry the debauched Abdul Nassib (Blake), a "sheep-faced idiot, or die." Susie rushes off and disguises herself as Nassib's concubine, Fatima. After Susie ridicules Arab dancing, Nassib swings into action, trying to seduce her. Susie tosses pillows, flooring the lecherous sheikh. Undaunted, he pursues her.

• Maidens tell Susie their harem mistress is an "old goat." Says Susie: Demand your rights; "organize, you have power." Asks a puzzled maiden, "Power? We have power?" Says Susie, "Collective bargaining, girls; organize." Adding, It's not right, "one wolf owning twenty wives. [Remember], 3,000 years ago one of the ruler's 40 wives cut his head off."

• The now-organized maidens are ordered to dance; they refuse. Next, the women stage a sit-down strike. And, they convince Jamal's soldiers to obey them, not the sheikh. Moans Jamal, "My men are as helpless as kittens." Susie and the maidens slug the sheikh's buffoons.

• Evil Arab "slave traders" attack the camp of Majeed (Marion), a dashing rebel. Shouts Majeed, "We'll teach those jackals a lesson." In time, legionnaires arrive, nabbing Jamal and preventing his cohorts from torturing Shareen and Majeed.

• Arabs wielding swords are no match for Susie. A "good" Arab cites her judo heroics, saying, "Thanks to this brave woman we have a chance to strike a blow for freedom." Majeed tells Susie, "We can never thank you enough." As for Princess Shareen, she regains the throne.

Note: Nassib is tagged "fat and dumb," a "lard bucket," and a "croaking bull frog."

• This silly film contends an Arab can only rule provided he possesses a ridiculous property, such as a "secret scroll." Another example of this theme: 40-plus years after *Harem Girl*, a "Mr. Gadget" cartoon displays "Fast Abdul," the "sneakiest thief" around, endangering an Arab kingdom. Why is the nation threatened? Because Abdul ran off with the country's "sacred scimitar."

• Bernds also worked on *Bowery to Bagdad* (1955), and he penned *Looking for Danger* (1957).

Harem Scarem (1932), Mermaid Comedies. *Al St. John, Aileen Cook, Harriet Hilliard.* S: Andrew Bennison. SHEIKHS, MAIDENS

The message of this film: Trouncing Arabs builds confidence. Appearing in Baghdad are stereotypical Arabs and blacks.

Scene: In Harlem, the protagonist Al visits Prince Yoggi, a phony black prophet wearing Arab garb. Al seeks advice on how to improve his love life.

• Yoggi takes Al into the back room, directing him to stare into a cloudy crystal ball. The entranced Al begins imagining himself as a "brave lover from the old days." Explains Yoggi, "[You] robbed the rich and helped the poor, 3,000 years ago in Bagdad, in the harem of the Pasha."

• Flashback to Baghdad—a palace harem. Al, wearing Robin Hood garb, serenades maidens. When Arab guards arrive, he floors them, then he ignites gunpowder. Poof! The Pasha and his muscular black attendants are floored. Al returns to the harem, embracing an attractive blonde who was held "captive for three months." When two huge eunuchs try to intervene, Al socks them. Dancing maidens vie for Al's affection; black musicians wearing fezzes entertain.

• Ahmed and his saber-wielding Arabs enter the harem and try to behead Al. He takes a club and floors Ahmed and men. The triumphant Al shouts "Ala-Kazaar."

• Flash forward—New York City, the present. Charged with confidence after bringing down the Arabs, Al defies his nasty boss and embraces his true love.

Note: The Walt Disney's cartoon, *Mickey in Arabia* (1932) also displays the sheikh-as-kidnapper. In the cartoon, a frothing-at-the-mouth potentate surfaces. He is a fat, bearded cat. The ruler abducts Minnie Mouse, whisking her off to his desert stronghold. Mickey to the rescue! He invades the desert palace. The dense ruler grabs two pistols, firing away. Though he misses Mickey, he nearly kills scurrying palace guards. Next, the sheikh retrieves a huge saber and several knives. He slings the knives at Mickey, but the daggers bounce back, undressing the Arab lecher. In the end, the pajama-clad sheikh leaps at Mickey; he misses, landing head first in the sand. In the end, palace guards toss spears at Mickey and Minnie. Their blades miss the heroes, piercing instead the sly sheikh's protruding butt. Struck with terror, the sheikh runs off.

Harum Scarum (1965), MGM. *Elvis Presley, Mary Ann Mobley, Michael Ansara, Fran Jeffries, Jay Novello.* P: Sam Katzman. SP: Gerald D. Adams. SHEIKHS, MAIDENS

This musical desert drama should be re-titled *Elvis of Arabia*. Elvis gets the Arabian Princess. And he rescues good Arabs from evil ones.

Scene: Contemporary Arabia. After Arab officials screen Elvis' new film, *Sands of the Desert*, they applaud, enthusiastically. Pleased at the response, the US ambassador tells Elvis, "Your good-will tour in this part of the world will be most helpful to the state department."

• Thanking his hosts, Elvis performs—live. The lyrics go, in part, "A sheikh so rich and grand, with dancing girls at your command... Make love the way I can."

• Elvis agrees to accompany the lovely Aishah (Jeffries) to her kingdom. "When you come to my country," she warns, "you will be stepping back 2,000 years!"

• In the desert, Aishah serves Elvis a beverage. He takes a sip and collapses. Abruptly, black-clad "Assassins" appear from the shadows, whisking Elvis off to the "Palace of Jackals."

• Beautiful harem maidens attend a revived Elvis. Says one, "[You are] in the Garden of Paradise. This kingdom has been isolated from the rest of the world for 2,000 years."

• A would-be Arab deliverer offers to help Elvis escape, provided he forks over "$10,000, US." Asks Elvis, "Where's the airport?" He's told, "We have no airport. [And] There are no cars."

• Elvis links up with a unique group of rebels, including a dwarf, an orphan, and Princess Shalimar (Mobley).

• Elvis' deliverer tells the rebels, "Meet my most valuable client. He is an American, which means nothing. But he is filthy rich, which means something... Allah help my filthy rich client and all that foreign aid." Throughout, Arabs mention "American foreign aid." Unexpectedly, Elvis' liberator suddenly turns him over to the Assassins.

• Aishah and her cohorts vow to murder the orphans, and to inflict Elvis with the "death of 1,000 cuts." They will spare Elvis and the others, provided Elvis assassinates the king, Princess Shalimar's father. Elvis asks the villains whether he can trust them. "In over 1,000 years no leader of the Assassins has violated a promise," she says. But, the Assassin chief intends to slice the orphans' throats—no matter what! Elvis refuses to murder the ruler; he is imprisoned and lashed.

• After Elvis escapes, he finds out the main villain is Prince Dragna (Ansara), the king's brother. Dragna wants to control "The Bakir Oil Company" so that he can earn "millions." Dragna even manages to deceive his niece, Shalimar. Early on, she believed him loyal, saying: "The protection of my father comes first to you, Uncle. I honor you for it."

• The palace. Elvis and the orphans defeat the Assassins. The king and Dragna duel.

• Later, seeing the king and Dragna playing chess, Elvis expresses bewilderment. Explains the king, "I couldn't kill my own brother. But I am sending him into exile with his favorite chess player (Aishah)."

• Elvis tells the king, "I'm in love with your daughter."

• An American nightclub. Elvis and some Arab maidens perform. In the audience, the king and Princess Shalimar. Cut to Elvis kissing Shalimar.

Dialogue: The Chief Assassin shouts at Elvis, "On your feet, unbeliever... infidel pig!"

Note: Writes NYT critic Vincent Canby, *Harum Scarum* is about "a Hollywood star, a mythical Arab kingdom and some oil rights. Every line of dialogue sounds like a song cue, and about every other one actually is" (16 December 1965).

• Arab women appear as orphans, dancing girls, and decorative maidens.

• See Max and Dave Fleischer's silent cartoon, *Harem Scarem* (1928). Here, a live actor portrays a violent sultan. The actor-sultan sketches two cartoon characters, Ko-Ko the Clown and Fritz. What follows next, writes specialist Mark Langer, is "one of the most gruesome moments in animation." The actor-sultan picks up Ko-Ko and Fritz, "pulls out a knife and slices their heads off. The heads fall to the ground, blink once, and lie motionless." Observes Langer, "the violence here is committed by a living character [the actor-sultan] upon cartoon characters." Eventually, "the chopped-off heads of Ko-Ko and Fritz sprout legs and walk back into their bodies." Abruptly, "razor-wielding [Arab] guards" appear, chasing them through the potentate's harem.[86]

• In the Bugs Bunny cartoon, *Hare-abian Nights* (1962), the sheikh is portrayed by

Yosemite Sam. Wearing Arab garb, Sam-as-sheikh dumps American entertainers, including "El-vis," into a "crocodile pit." Bugs tags the sheikh, Ayrab, "the stupidest character of them all."

Hate (1995), a.k.a. La haine, Polygram. *Vincent Cassel, Hubert Kounde', Said Taghmaoui.* D, SP: Mathieu Kassovitz. Best Film, 1995 Cesar Awards. RECOMMENDED

This French film displays three boys of different races as friends: Sayid (Taghmaoui), an Arab; Vinz (Cassel), a Jew; and Hub (Koundé), a black.

Scene: Just outside Paris, a run-down housing project. Police trounce an Arab youth, Abdel Ichaha. Later, Abdel dies from the beatings.

• Police also abuse Hub, Vinz, and Sayid. "An Arab in a police station doesn't last an hour," says Sayid.

• As Vinz trims Sayid's bushy hair, he jokes that the Arab's new cut could frighten most anyone.

• Skinheads threaten the boys. Cautions Hub, "We learned... hate breeds hate."

• Police nab, then bind Hub and Sayid to a chair. Next, they beat them. Barks one policeman, "You Arab son-of-a-bitch."

• Skinheads move to impair Hub and Sayid; armed with a gun, Vinz chases them off. He refuses to shoot one violent skinhead.

• A large TV screen displays a news story about the death of young Abdel Ichaha. Unexpectedly, a policeman arrives, terrorizing Vinz. Accidentally, the policeman's gun goes off, fatally shooting Vinz. Distraught at seeing Vinz die, the non-violent Hub points a gun at the cop.

Hawmps (1976), Mulberry Square Prod. *James Hampton, Gino Conforti, Christopher Connelly, Slim Pickens, Denver Pyle.* D: Joe Camp, SP: William Bickley, Michael Warren.

Based on a true story, the action occurs in the southwest, circa 1856, just before the Civil War. Hadji Ali (Conforti), a likeable Arab, teaches US cavalry troops how to ride camels.   But too little attention is given to the Arab protagonist's actual achievements. Instead, scenes show US cavalry members coping with camels. *Hawmps'* soldiers treat Arabian camels better than most scenarios treat Arabs.

Scene: Texas. Should the US cavalry use camels or horses as pack animals? The military opts to import camels. Chaperoning the camels is Hadji Ali, a trainer and veterinarian of sorts. The soldiers nickname Hadji, "Hi Jolly."

• Hadji, who speaks English with a British accent, introduces himself to the commanding officer: "Origin, Arab. Education, Oxford, class of 1854, camel instructor extraordinaire, at your service, sir."

• Initially, soldiers such as Uriah Tibbs (Connelly) and Naman Tucker (Pickens) balk at working with the Arab. But after Hi Jolly teaches the men to mount and ride camels, the troops accept and befriend him.

• Hi Jolly, who dons a huge orange burnoose, also flaunts a monocle. He also swaggers with a saber at his side.

• Hi Jolly barges into Col. Hawkins' (Pyle) office with the camel Sheba at his side.

As Sheba is ill, Hi Jolly wants permission to contact a doctor. Stunned, the colonel says, "What was that?" Says a fellow officer, "That was a camel, sir." Protests the officer, "No, no, I mean the one with the tablecloth on its head."

• Sharpening his saber, Hi Jolly tells the troops, "Arabian horses are great for the desert, [but] nothing can beat the camel."

• A saloon fight. Hi Jolly tries to assist his pals. But, he's promptly punched out. The next morning, the bruised and bandaged Arab walks with a crutch. Limping off to duty, he advises, "There's an old proverb that goes, 'May Allah guide your way, and may the breath of a thousand camels be always at your back.'"

• A cavalry unit with "great Arabian horses" offers to race Col. Hawkins' camel riders. The camels, not the horses, go on to "win the west."

• A telegram arrives, celebrating the completion of a new railroad system. As camels are no longer needed, Tibbs and Tucker are ordered to turn the animals "loose in the desert."

• Fast forward—10 years later, a farm. The retired Hi Jolly and his camel-corps cohorts tend several friendly camels.

Note: This film is based on fact. In 1857, cameleer Hadj Ali, nicknamed Hi Jolly, plus other Arabs [and Turks] came to the United States at the request of the government, to set up a camel corps that would expedite mail service throughout the southwest.

Known for his love of camels, Hi Jolly remained in the West until the early twentieth century. To acknowledge his contributions to the cavalry, in 1953 the Arizona highway department erected over this Arab-American's grave, a pyramid-shaped tombstone, topped with a metal camel. The monument inscription reads:

THE LAST CAMP OF HI JOLLY
Born somewhere in Syria about 1828.
Died at Quartzsite on December 16, 1902.
Came to this country on February 16, 1856.
Camel Driver Packer Scout
Over thirty years a faithful aid to the U.S. government.[87]

• Prior to the Civil War, Americans experienced a Zouave craze. Men, women and children wore Zouave garb—baggy trousers, ornate skirts, vests, and tasseled red fezzes. Its origins? The French army in North Africa during the 1830s. Red was associated with elite regiments.

Head (1968), COL. *The Monkees, William Bagdad.* SP: Bob Rafelson, Jack Nicholson. SHEIKHS

Nonsensical vignettes poke fun of Arabs, Italians, Native Americans, others.

Scene: The desert. The "black sheik" (Bagdad) rides up to a Coke machine. He whispers "psst," then rides off.

• Clad as an Arab potentate, Mickey enters an arabesque room. As he smokes a nargelih, harem maidens surround him.

• Final scenes, the desert. The Monkees and some Arabs pop up. Suddenly, the black sheik and some Arabs yell, "Lalalalalala." They drink Coke. A tank blows up the Coke machine; and again, they holler.

Heaven Can Wait (1978), PAR. *Warren Beatty, Julie Christie, Vincent Gardenia.* SP: Beatty, Elaine May. See *Ishtar* (1987). The 1978 and 1943 versions of *Heaven Can Wait* are remakes of the movie, *Here Comes Mr. Jordan,* (1941). CAMEOS, SHEIKHS

Another Beatty/May film blemishing Arabs. See Victor Ayoub's comments on *True Confessions* (1981).

Scene: Concluding frames show the police inspector (Gardenia) investigating the death of a millionaire, Mr. Farnsworth (Beatty). The inspector answers a ringing telephone, saying, "Yes, your Majesty." Next, he grimaces and slams down the receiver, disapprovingly shouting, "Just another Arab! That Farnsworth was into everything."

• In TCF's 1943 version of *Heaven Can Wait,* starring Don Ameche, director Ernst Lubitsch has the protagonist (Ameche) attend a "Follies" stage show. One of the show's musical numbers features a bearded Arab ruler surrounded by maidens. Sings the potentate:

> I'm the Sheik of Araby;
> You'll all belong to me.
> At night when you're asleep,
> Into your tent I'll creep.
> The stars that shine above
> Will light our way to love.
> You'll rule this land with me,
> The Sheik of Araby.

Hell Squad (1985), CAN. *Bainbridge Scott, Tina Lederman, Marvin Miller, William Bryant, Glen Hartford.* SP, P, D: Kenneth Hartford. PALESTINIANS, SHEIKHS, WORST LIST

Vegas show girls eliminate Palestinians. The movie's anti-Palestinian theme is evidenced in the credits, which state, "The Producers Wish to Thank... the 47 members of the PLO who played themselves as terrorists." Written on the video cassette cover, this blurb: Nine gorgeous Las Vegas entertainers "trade in their g-stings for military khaki and submachine guns when they're recruited by an elite branch of 'The Agency' as a special covert commando unit." Their mission? "To rescue a United States ambassador's son who is being held hostage by a mid-eastern terrorist organization." The showgirls "free the young man from his demented captors."

Scene: Afer a neutron bomb explodes, stock footage reveals a mythical Arab country. Cut to Jack Steward (Hartford), the US ambassador's son, being chauffeured through a souk. Suddenly, fatigue-clad Palestinians wearing burnooses shoot the driver, taking Jack hostage. Cut to a hilltop fortress, "somewhere near the Syrian border." The prisoner, Jack, is chained to a wall.

• The Palestinians want to manufacture an "ultra-neutron bomb." To do so they need to acquire "the formula for the secret fuel." They tell the US ambassador to deliver the formula "or by Allah, your son will be returned to you, organ by organ."

• The ambassador's aide initiates our "secret weapon." Flying to Vegas, the aide recruits nine showgirls for a rescue mission. At first, only Jan (Scott) displays the necessary fighting skills. But, after ten training days, all the women become "expert commando fighters."

• Stock footage of "Tarjan," an Arab city. The nine commandos dance at a nightclub. Arab bellydancers also perform.

• One commando boasts about her posh suite. Quips her friend, "It's British influence, otherwise we'd be staying in tents." The women do not bathe one at a time. Instead, they plop into a communal tub. Evidently, though Tarajan has "plenty of oil," there's "a water shortage."

• The desert. Wearing red berets, khaki shorts, tight blouses, and black boots, the commandos steer their jeeps inside the Arab fort. Cut to Arabs playing cards and drinking beer. The Vegas squad barges into the room; the women punch out, machine-gun, and knife Jack's kidnappers. The camera pans from the women's pleased faces to Arab bodies.

• Back at the hotel, the showgirls celebrate by taking another bath. At 5AM they depart on another mission. Bam! They explode even more Arabs in their tents.

• Sighs Jan, "We've raided and killed dozens of Arabs, and none of them seem to be terrorists." Next, Jan and her friends dance; Arab men toss money at their feet.

• At the nightclub, the American owner (Bryant) greets his Arab patrons, reluctantly. After shaking hands with one, he wipes his hand. "I guess I better start greeting the little [Arab] bastards. Drink up, you scum bums. I need all the money I can get, so I can get out of your stinking country," he says.

• Evening. Palestinians invade the showgirls' suite. They whisk the women off to their camp, chaining them to a wall. Appearing is an ugly, obese Arab, "the sheikh" (Miller). One showgirl tags him a "slob."

• The Palestinian guards deliver a ferocious animal. Barks the sheikh to the women, I'll "feed each one of you to the tiger." Suddenly, the sheikh stumbles, stepping on the tiger's tail. Abruptly, the angry tiger gobbles up the ungainly sheikh. The women free themselves, punch out the guards and hitch a ride to safety.

• Intent on rescuing Jack, the heroines swim to the Arab fortress. Cut to the battered and bruised hostage, Jack Steward. Using unique arrows, the showgirls exterminate the Palestinian kidnappers. After freeing Jack, they blow up the fortress.

Finis: The US ambassador is reunited with his son. And, thanks to the showgirls, the neutron bomb's "secret fuel" remains a secret.

Note: Israelis portray Arabs. Credits state: "Principal terrorists."

• Twice, Jan admits they "wiped out a group of innocent Arabs." Yet, she and her commandos never show remorse.

• This film was made circa 1983, and released theatrically overseas in 1985. Via an agreement with MGM/UA, CAN placed *Hell Squad* into video stores in 1986.

The Hell with Heroes (1968), UNI. *Rod Taylor, Claudia Cardinale, Harry Guardino. See Tangier (1983).*

Algeria as a seedy backdrop.

Scene: A bar in Oran, Algeria. As a bellydancer performs, an American says, "Basically, it's a fertility dance."

• In the souk, ragged Algerian beggar boys hustle a newly arrived tourist. He throws the youths some coins, grumbling, "Come on, get away, get away!"

• The American villain, Lee Harris (Guardino), deceives his friend, Mackay (Taylor), saying that in the desert "some Algerian terrorists" ambushed his men. The truth is, the "terrorists" responsible for killing his men are Westerners.

• Mackay, not an Algerian, cares for and attends homeless Arab youths. Declares Mackay, "I believe in teenagers."

• The Algerian youths save Mackay's life. Not only do they track Harris, the chief smuggler, they help Mackay nab Harris' Western cohorts.

Note: Credits label Arab youths "urchins."

Hercules and the Tyrants of Babylon (1964), AI. *Rock Stevens* (Peter Lupus on the TV series, *Mission Impossible*), *Helga Line, Mario Petri*. VILLAINS

Hercules vs. Babylonians and Assyrians. From evil potentates, Hercules rescues enslaved innocents, notably a princess "dear" to him.

Scene: "Babylon, 3,000 Years Ago." Hercules (Stevens) brings down black robed tyrants—Babylonians and Assyrians.

• Babylon's "three sovereigns" encourage their guards to torment female slaves. The soldiers whip the enslaved women, then bind them to wooden poles.

• In Babylon's souk, Hercules confronts a fat Arab auctioneer; he floors the slaver.

Finis: Mighty Hercules rescues his princess, then uses his strength to crush the villains, crumbling all of Babylon.

Hercules of the Desert (1964), AI. Italian, dubbed in English. *Kirk Morris.* VILLAINS, MAIDENS

Hercules vs. Arabs; Arabs vs. Arabs; Arab slavers.

Scene: The Arab princess, Farida, and her vizier, attack fellow Arabs of the El-Sikuri region, seizing their "land of the green pastures." Barks Farida, "Show no mercy; a kingdom is at stake."

• After Farida's troops destroy Arab tents, they slaughter bedouins. Next, they haul Arab "girls away as slaves." As they bind the girls' hands to the horses' saddles, a soldier remarks, "They'll bring a good price at the slave market."

• Barks an Arab auctioneer to some Arabs, "Just a few pieces of gold and you can buy these enchanting young girls... Imagine how these beauties would look in your harem."

• Arriving is Hercules (Morris), "the man of a thousand legends who reappeared on earth to help the weary and oppressed." Says a joyous Arab of the El-Sikuri, "Allah sent him."

• Farida captures Hercules. Her soldiers try to crush Hercules, setting into motion a huge, moving wall. The strength of Hercules prevails; he crushes Farida and her cohorts.

• Thanks to Hercules, a decent Arab's "prophesy comes true"; the bedouins of El-Sikuri return to their "green pastures."

Hercules Unchained (1959), WB. *Joseph E. Levine, Steve Reeves, Sylvia Lopez.* EGYPTIANS, CAMEOS

In this sand and sandal scenario, Egyptians obey a malicious queen.

Scene: Located beneath Queen Omphale's (Lopez) palace is a combination torture chamber/wax museum. Here, Egyptian servants pour hot wax over live bodies, then display the victims.

• The queen tells several Egyptians wearing head scarfs and half-skirts, "You Egyptians are so clever; I am almost certain you'll find a way of even preserving life." Rebuts one, "Life is different; we cannot create the soul of man." Retorts the queen, "Still, it must be exciting, your work... to fix for eternity, man's character. Just the man, the way he looks, the way he stands."

Note: In the Embassy release of the Italian film *The Beast of Babylon Against the Son of Hercules* (1963), a.k.a. *Hero of Babylon*, a cunning queen and her evil potentate oppress multitudes, tossing white-clad virgins into raging fires. In the end, Hercules (Gordon Scott) defeats the tyrants.

Here Come the Girls (1951), PAR. *Bob Hope, Rosemary Clooney.* CAMEOS, SHEIKHS

To love an Arab is splendid, suggests the ballad, "On the Desert Sand."

Scene: Appearing in this musical comedy within a musical are a dozen scantily-clad "wives of the sultan," lounging on the stage set. Rosemary Clooney enters. Clad in Arab garb, she croons, "I'm mad about a sheik; I must have his embrace." The maidens gyrate; Clooney warbles on:

Oh, Ali Baba, be my baby
maybe we'll make love, oh baby, on the desert sand
Ali Baba sell your harem, harem scarem
Come into my tent... you belong to me.

• Bob Hope appears as a clumsy tap-dancing sultan with "pierced ears." Asked, "How many wives does a sultan have?" Hope-as-sultan quips, "Fifty."

Hero at Large (1980), MGM. *John Ritter, Andrew Masset, Alan Rich.* SP: A. J. Carothers. CAMEOS

The dialogue tarnishes Arabs.

Scene: An unemployed actor, Steve Nichols (Ritter), lunches with his agent, Marty Fields (Rich). As Steve munches "a corned beef sandwich," Jerry (Masset), another hard-luck actor, rushes to their table. Jerry thanks Steve for helping him get the "Schlitz commercial"; he kneels and lowers his head. Quips Fields, "Who's the Arab?" Steve glosses over the slur.

• When Jerry leaves the restaurant, Fields berates Steve for helping Jerry get the beer commercial. "Did I get ten percent from that Arab?" asks Fields.

The Heroes (1972), UA. *Rod Steiger, Rod Taylor, Claude Brasseur, Rosanna Schiaffino.* CAMEOS, MAIDENS

For a buck, a double-crossing Arab sells his sisters. Arab women as prostitutes.

Scene: The North African country, "Oran," WWII. Two Allied soldiers hawk stolen military supplies to Ali, a "black marketeer." Cut to a mosque; the imam calls the faithful to prayer. Boasts a GI (Brasseur), "We can trust Ali, he's like my brother."

• Screaming Arab kids unload a military truck. The GI's pal (Taylor) sighs, "I hope they give us the truck back."

• Two veiled, clad-in-black women appear. Quips the trustworthy GI, "Those are his

[Ali's] sisters, all included in the price." Inside a bedroom, the soldiers and Ali's mute sisters remove their clothing and have sex.

• Later, the embarrassed soldiers appear on the beach, wearing only shorts and shoes. Moans one, "Oh, we can trust Ali, eh, and his two sisters?... I wonder who took my watch." Affirms his pal, "We've been double-crossed."

• In the desert, Arabs stand guard outside a tent. Inside, veiled women pamper an Italian wearing a white thobe. Soon, several near-naked Arab women appear in bed alongside the Italian and a GI. Brags the Italian, "We got the girls! We got spaghetti!"

Hey Rookie (1944), COL. *Ann Miller.* CAMEOS, SHEIKHS

Scene: Ann Miller sings "Streamlined Sheik."[88] Surrounding her are several clad-in-Arab-garb performers. See *Here Come the Girls* (1951).

Hideous Kinky (1999), BBC Films. *Kate Winslet, Said Taghmaoui, Bella Riza, Carrie Mullan.* SP: Billy Mackinnon. D: Gillies MacKinnon. Shot in Morocco MAIDENS.

A handsome, benevolent Moroccan man romances the British heroine. And, he diligently looks after her two daughters. The British girls love the Moroccan as much as he cares for them. Nasty Moroccan women.

Scene: Marrakech 1972. Introducing Julia (Winslet), a single mother, anxiously awaiting child support checks from her daughters' philandering English father. As the checks never arrive, Julia makes hand-stitched dolls and translates poetry to help support her children, eight-year-old Bea (Riza), and six-year-old Lucy (Mullan). Julia resists going home, saying, "London's cold, cold and sad."

• Interspersed throughout are souk scenes displaying busy merchants, musicians, dancers, even comedians.

• Julia meets Bilal (Taghmaoui), an acrobatic performer and laborer who hauls stones for a living. Soon, Bilal becomes her lover. Bilal, a Moroccan of modest means, loves Julia. After making love, Julia attends Bilal's bruised back. Bilal functions as the girls' surrogate father; he regularly shows them affection, and they return his love. When Bilal rehearses his acrobatic act, the girls try emulating his skills, performing somersaults.

• Seeing Julia pocket money from selling her dolls, two dressed-in-black Moroccan women appear, assaulting her. Returning to her flat, Julia spots three heavy Moroccan women wearing her clothes. The women laugh, refusing to return the garments. Julia charges them; they knock her to the ground.

• Bilal takes Julia and the girls to his village; women greet them, tossing rose petals.

• Bilal's efforts to raise needed money fail; he and Julia separate.

• One girl becomes ill; Julia has no money for the needed medicine. She becomes desperate. Aware of the girl's illness and the need for Julia to return to England, Bilal sells his precious uniform. In fact, he steals the uniform, then sells it to purchases return-home tickets for Julia. Fearing what may happen to Bilal should the authorities find him, Julia initially balks at taking money from him.

Finis: A fast-moving train. Julia, Bea, and Lucy depart for England. Seeing a truck move alongside their train, Julia and the girls rejoice. Driving the truck is Bilal. The smiling Bilal bids them a fond farewell; a lengthy red sash brandishes in the wind.

The Hill (1965), MGM. *Sean Connery, Harry Andrews.* CAMEOS, MAIDENS

A British prison stockade, located in a North African military outpost. Surfacing for 12 seconds in a seedy bar is a mute, grotesque bellydancer. Shaking her fat, the Arab woman closes in on some British soldiers. Abruptly, two dogs appear and chase her off. As the woman scrambles for safety, the soldiers laugh and whistle.

Hill 24 Doesn't Answer (1955), a.k.a. Giv'a 24 eina ona, Israel Motion Picture Studios. *Edward Mulhare, Arich Lavi, Michael Wagner, Haya Haraeet.* SP: *Thorold Dickinson, Peter Frye.* P, D: Dickinson. The first feature made entirely in Israel. *NS. Notes from Ella Shohat's *Israeli Cinema: East/West and the Politics of Representation* (Austin: University of Texas Press, 1989). PALESTINIANS

According to the VAR critic, this film "could be used for [Israeli] fundraising functions" (18 May 1955). The action takes place during the British Mandate over Palestine. Paying homage to heroic Israelis are three episodes from the 1948 war. One segment shows four outgunned and outnumbered Israeli soldiers, including an American Jew born in Palestine, defending a hill outside Jerusalem. Arab hordes kill them.

Episode one: "The portrayal of the British Mandate reflects not only the fact that the film was made by a British filmmaker," writes Shohat, "but also the warm relations between Britain and Israel at the period the film was made. In 1956 Israel, Britain, France fought together against Egypt." As for the Arabs, they "are anonymous both as individual characters and as a collective." Jordanian and Egyptian soldiers surface as "agents of violence." The camera's long shots of Palestinian soldiers wearing kuffiyehs serve to distance the viewer from their humanity (61–62). Also, the producers reinforce the categorization of the Druze as "good natives"; well-known Israeli entertainer Shoshana Damari, a Yemenite Jew, portrays a heroic Druze woman.

Episode two: An Arab official takes a dip in a swimming pool. Nearby, an American Jew complains to an Englishman and an Arab representative. He says that although Jewish refugees are being expelled, the British befriend the Arabs, primarily due to oil interests. "The sequence ends," writes Shohat, "with the Arab character demonstrating exactly how Jewish existence in Palestine will come to an end; he pushes the American Jew into the swimming pool." This scene implies Arabs want to toss Jews into the sea, a term used by Israeli propagandists.

Episode three: The Nazi-Arab theme. An Israeli moves to aid a wounded Egyptian soldier, "only to discover that he is in fact a German-speaking Nazi." Asks the Israeli, "How many more of them are there?" (69–70).

Finis: Following a battle, four heroic Israelis perish. A French UN official, plus an Israeli and Arab arrive at a battle site, a hill. "The Arab argues the defenders did not survive to claim the hill, but the French official discovers the Israeli flag in the hands of the woman fighter, who obviously died when they were about to claim it." Decides the Frenchman, "Hill 24 belongs to Israel."

Scene: Harlem's honey baby, Laura Lewis (Sands), travels around the world. Arriving in Beirut, Lebanon, she speaks Arabic with a friendly desk clerk. At Baalbek's impressive Roman ruins, she poses for photographers. In Byblos, she dines at a seaport restaurant, saying, "Oh, it's so beautiful here."

• A chairlift whisks Lewis up to a Christian monument commemorating the "Lady of Lebanon." Looking out over the Mediterranean, Lewis says, "My interest in both the history and culture of this country is both real and extensive."

• A corrupt African General orders three mute Arab "goons" to threaten Lewis. One Arab tries to kill Lewis. Her friend, Liv (Lockhart) fires back, shooting one.

Note: *Honeybaby* was Ms. Sands' final film appearance; she died of cancer while the film was still in post-production.

Hostage (1986), a.k.a. Colt-Flight 802, Blue Flower/Alpine.

Wings Hauser, Karen Black, Kevin McCarthy, Nancy Locke. EP: James Aubrey. South African actors portray Arabs. PALESTINIANS, WORST LIST

The action occurs in Nairobi. Here, Vietnam veterans exterminate Palestinians belonging to the "The Holy Freedom Party of Allah," a PLO splinter group. Islam is vilified. Aboard a passenger plane, Palestinian Muslim hijackers kill innocents and fellow Palestinians.

Scene: The Zabo home. Palestinian Muslims plan to hijack a plane en route to Nairobi. They want Sobruto, who leads their Holy Freedom Party of Allah, to be released from prison. The Palestinians admire Sobruto's portrait, saying, "Allah be praised." Advises Mr. Zabo, "You may have to sacrifice your lives." Says his daughter, "It's a worthy cause; we are not afraid." The family extends fist salutes, shouting "Sobruto! Sobruto! May Allah be with you!"

• The Palestinians, including Zabo's daughter and his son, Hussein, board the plane. Quips Colonel Tim Shaw (McCarthy), the US ambassador who once served in Vietnam, "I can't tell one from the other. Wrapped in those bed sheets they all look the same to me." Hussein poses as a priest. [See *Wanted: Dead or Alive* (1987), in which an Arab terrorist poses as a rabbi.] He blesses himself incorrectly. Surprised, a nun asks, "What kind of priest are you, anyway?" Among the plane's passengers are Col. Shaw's daughter, Nicole (Locke), and his grandson, Tommy, who needs emergency care at a hospital.

• After the Zabos force the plane to land at an isolated airstrip, Ms. Zabo kills the co-pilot. Tommy's nurse speaks up. The Palestinians shoot her dead. Next, the Zabos toss the two bodies onto the airstrip, warning passengers, "You are hostages of the Holy Freedom Party of God." One woman asks, "What do they want?" Says her husband, "They're absolutely worthless." The Zabos demand the release of Sobruto, plus $25 million in gold. If their demands are not met within 48 hours, they plan to kill one passenger every hour, beginning with Tommy. Says Ms. Zabo, "Tommy is currency for trade, for the glory of the revolution."

• Col. Shaw's residence. "These gangsters piss on the American flag," says Shaw. "Unfortunately, you can't deny an Ayrab a seat on the plane... [Sobruto is] behind a half dozen of these PLO splinter groups. That bastard is behind this [hijacking] operation. My daughter; my grandson." Shaw swings into action, recruiting several Vietnam vets, including his pal Sam Striker (Hauser). They move to save the hostages and crush the Palestinians.

• Sex and Arabs: Among the hostages, a pornographic starlet, Laura Lawrence (Black), and her agent. "I'll try to reason with those fuckin' pigs," says Laura. She approaches a muscular Palestinian, vowing to bed him, provided he "lets the boy [Tommy] go." The Arab agrees. During sex, the camera focuses on Laura's anguished face, revealing tears. Afterwards, the Arab refuses to release Tommy, saying, "You loved it, you bitch!" Retorts Laura, "Loved it? I could have puked."

• Arabs and Christians: Passengers recite the Lord's Prayer; a Palestinian grimaces.

• A miracle man? One hijacker shoots Laura's agent. A white-robed Arab places his hands over the agent's wound. Presto—"the bleeding stopped."

• The Zabo home. Sam Striker kills two guards. Next, he holds hostage Mr. and Mrs. Zabo and their young son. Young Zabo contacts his brother Hussein at the airstrip, pleading they release the passengers. "My beloved brother," he says, "do what he [Striker] asks." The clad-in-black Mrs. Zabo screeches into the phone, "Son, son he threatens our lives." Striker grabs the phone, telling Hussein, "How's it feel to have your family held hostage, you son-of-a-bitch." Next, Striker machine-guns Mr. Zabo. Hoping to save his mother and brother, Hussein opts to free the plane's hostages. His sister intervenes. As she embraces "the cause," she kills him.

• A passenger contests the muscular hijacker; he dies of a heart attack. Abruptly, the Arab shoots him.

• To the rescue, Col. Shaw's Vietnam veterans. They mow down Arabs who guard the plane.

• Inside the aircraft, the pilot is shot. The white-robed Arab saves a passenger's life. A nun grabs a machine gun and kills a hijacker. Then, she blesses herself. A hijacker goes to kill Tommy and is shot. Finally, a grenade blows up Ms. Zabo.

Hot Shots! (1991), TCF. *Charlie Sheen.* CAMEOS, VILLAINS

Arabs as buffoons; rapid-fire anti-Arab slurs.

The movie's final ten minutes reveal the US Navy's "freedom squadron [engaged in a] "great battle." Their assignment? To "knock out the [Arab] nuclear weapons site at Falafel Heights." The Navy pilot (Sheen) directs fellow pilots into "enemy air space." The airmen "spot enemy [Arab] aircraft," shouting "give `em hell."

• "Enemy" pilots wear headgear that lampoons Arab cuisine. Emblazoned on the Arabs' helmets, these words: Toboule, Baklavah, Pita, Hummus, Kabab, Couscous, and Babaganoush. The dense Arab pilots speak gibberish, not Arabic. And, they spout fractured English when saying "burnoose," "shish-ka-bob," "Allahu Akbar," and "Paula Abdul."

• Some bumbling Arab pilots crash their planes into mountains; others smash their jets into each other.

• Final frames. A bomb falls into Saddam Hussein's lap. Iraq's nuclear plant along with Saddam are decimated. Boasts the US pilot, "Sayonara, Saddam." When I saw the film, audiences clapped and cheered during these scenes.

Note: In *Navy SEALS* (1990) and *Hot Shots! Part Deux* (1993), Charlie Sheen terminates Arabs on land; in *Hot Shots!* (1991), Sheen blasts them from the sky.

Hot Shots! Part Deux (1993), TCF. A Jim Abrahams film. *Charlie Sheen, Valeria Golino, Lloyd Bridges, Brenda Bakke.* See *Airplane* (1980) and the *Naked Gun* series. VILLAINS

"Indians on the warpath!" This line alerts a US serviceman of an impending Iraqi attack. Chastised Iraqis function as American Indians. Emulating cowboys, the American protagonists mow down Iraqis. A few scenes poke fun of US politicians, Buddhist monks, and a Japanese diplomat.

Scene: Saddam Hussein's icebox contains "2% Camel Milk" and a box of "Falafel Helper." Abruptly, the "Butcher of Baghdad's" troops capture American soldiers. Barks an Iraqi soldier: "Surrender infidels. You have no chance." In the US, a TV announcer states: We failed to "rescue our hostages from the Middle East."

• Unshaven Iraqi soldiers appear; they don black-and-white kuffiyehs. One slaps an American prisoner, then tortures him with electric shocks, forcing the man to make a false statement. As the serviceman speaks to TV viewers, a cloaked, black-veiled Iraqi woman offers sign language.

• From a US patrol boat, Trooper Harley (Sheen) eradicates Iraqis. An Iraqi officer swallows a live grenade. Whoosh!

• En route to rescuing American POWs, Harley boasts, "There are plenty of bad guys to shoot."

• A flying punching bag and a soaring chicken floor dense Iraqis.

• Harley and Co. invade the Iraqi POW camp. The Americans extinguish scores of Arabs. Emblazoned on the screen, "Bloodiest Movie Ever" and "Body count 287."

Note: Comedies spoofing Saddam Hussein are popular film fare. Many concur that Hussein was solely responsible for the 1991 Gulf War. Yet because of the war, the average Iraqi, not Saddam, has suffered. About 200,000 Iraqi soldiers perished. And, from 1991–1998, primarily as a result of UN sanctions, more than one million Iraqi civilians have died, many of them children. This is why I cannot laugh when Sheen belittles Iraqis in his three *Hot Shots!* films.

Hotel Sahara (1951), UA. *Yvonne DeCarlo, Peter Ustinov, Ronald Culver, David Tomlinson, Ferdy Mayne.* S, SP: Patrick Kirwan and George H. Brown. MAIDENS, EGYPTIANS

WWII. This delightful comedy displays an agreeable Arab couple, a fez-wearing hotel owner, and his lovely fiancée. Bedouins are primitive dunces.

Scene: The Hotel Sahara, somewhere in the North African desert, where "the gentle breeze stirs the palms of the oasis." Regularly, battle platoons from Italy, England, France, and Germany enter, then exit the hotel. Each time a new batch of soldiers arrives, the Egyptians, Emad (Ustinov) and his fiancée, Yasmin (DeCarlo), rearrange the decor. They change clothes, furniture, and loyalties. For example, when Italians pop in, the Egyptians post photos of Mussolini on the walls; when the British enter, down goes Mussolini and up goes Churchill.

• Purrs Yasmin to Emad, "You love me and I love you." Yasmin sings, dances, and swims gracefully in the pool.

• Two British officers, Captain Cheynie (Tomlinson) and Major Randall (Culver), confess to Yasmin, "There isn't one [lady in our English tennis club] that could hold a candle to you, Yasmin. You're like a breath of peace." And, "There's something about this place, a sort of enchantment. No wonder the desert nomads have such quiet dignity, such matchless calm."

• Inside a tent, ill-mannered desert nomads eat with their fingers and haggle over Western goods. One bedouin grabs a rifle, shooting a clock! Another gives a British officer "a goat's eyeball," saying acceptance is an honor; refusal, an insult. The officer gulps it down, nearly puking.

• Brits-as-Arabs. The captain dons bedouin garb; the major wears an Arab maiden's outfit, protesting, "I don't see why I have to be the woman." Says the captain, "You walk behind." Abruptly, a bedouin appears, offering the captain some advice. Suddenly, the captain insists the major lead, saying, "They [the bedouins] make their wives walk in front now—in case of mines!"

• The hotel attendant, Yusef (Mayne), humors the occupants. He initiates parlor games with the Italians, and then hoodwinks a German officer. A German asks, "The Arabs in this part of the desert, are they friendly?" Quips Yusef, "They only cut Christian throats."

• Triumphant American soldiers arrive; the war is over. Smiling, Emad moves to wed Yasmin, sighing, "Everything is as it was, beautiful and peaceful."

How I Won the War (1967), UA. *Michael Crawford, John Lennon.* CAMEOS, EGYPTIANS

Egyptians as properties.

In this stinging satire on British militarism, mute Egyptians appear in four scenes; they feed a goat, guide a donkey, and carry a basket. Plus, they parade in front of a brothel, brandishing an "Out of Bounds" sign. Apprehensive British soldiers wait in the brothel line; some fret that having sex with Egyptian women may inflict social diseases.

How to Marry a Millionaire (1953), TCF. *Marilyn Monroe, Betty Grable, Lauren Bacall.* SP: Nunnally Johnson. D: Jean Negulesco. CAMEOS, SHEIKHS

A blonde bombshell prizes a wealthy Arab.

Scene: The three protagonists want to marry money. One, the blonde heroine (Monroe), dreams of "Arabia"; her illusion reveals a large tent. Inside, she meets an Arabic-speaking sheikh; attending him are harem maidens and slaves. The smiling sheikh presents her with a large chest of riches that "feel real." After accepting the Arab's generous gift, she smiles, purring, "You tell him [the sheikh] from me, I think he's a doll." End of dream.

The Human Factor (1975). A Frank Avianca film. *George Kennedy, Frank Avianca.* P: Frank Avianca. D: Edward Dmytryk. PALESTINIANS

Producer Frank Avianca appears as a Palestinian-American terrorist. In Italy, the Palestinian and several generic villains kill Americans, including six children. The terrorists demand money from the United States and insist that political prisoners in European jails be released.

Scene: Naples, Italy. Masked terrorists invade the home of an American, John Kinsdale (Kennedy), killing his wife and three children. See opening of *The Little Drummer Girl* (1984).

• In Rome, the terrorists crash into the Simpson home, fatally shooting an American couple and their three children. Cut to Kinsdale employing special tracking technologies. He finds out that one of the terrorists is "Arabic"—Paul Kamal Hamshari (Avianca). Kamal's father was a "Palestine professor at Berkeley [teaching] political science and Mideast studies."

• Inside a supermarket, Kamal and his men hold civilians hostage. Kamal uses a woman captive as a shield. Kinsdale shoots Kamal dead. And, he kills all the other terrorists.

The Human Shield (1992), CAN. *Michael Dudikoff, Tommy Hinkley, Steve Inwood, Uri Gavriel, Hana Azoulay Hasfari.* S: Mike Werb, Mann Rubin, SP: Rubin. Filmed in Israel. See *American Ninja 4* (1991). VILLAINS, MAIDENS, WORST LIST

Marines and Kurds liquidate Iraqis.

Scene: Northern Iraq, 1985. Testing his Iraqi soldiers' "combat techniques," a Saddam Hussein look-alike, General Ali Dallal (Inwood), slaughters villagers. Dallal, who shoots a woman clutching her baby, refers to his victims as "pro-Khomeini sympathizers."

• Witnessing the carnage is Marine Captain Doug Mathews (Dudikoff). Doug protests, telling Dallal the US government does not support the slaughter "of innocent people." He and Dallal fight. Doug wins, injuring the Iraqi. But he is jailed.

• Fast forward, Baghdad's airport, August 1990. As civilians depart, Iraqi "bastards" bind and blindfold Doug's diabetic brother, Ben Mathews (Hinkley). The troops haul Ben off to the Abadan chemical plant.

• Amman, Jordan. Doug moves to rescue his brother. A cab driver takes him close to the Iraqi border. Here, a bearded Arab tries to sell Doug "hash, coke, a woman." Doug opts to buy weapons. Next, Doug enters Iraq and meets Lilya (Hasfari), an Iraqi doctor he once loved. When Lilya tells Doug that Dallal is her husband, he registers shock. Later, Doug learns that Lilya married the general to save the then-imprisoned Doug from being killed.

• Doug nabs a jeep and heads for Baghdad. Iraqi soldiers pursue him. Doug tosses some grenades, demolishing them.

• In Baghdad, Doug meets with his Kurdish friend Tanzi (Gavriel). Advises Tanzi: "Insults here can only be washed away in blood." When a US embassy official tries to assist Doug, Iraqis shoot him. Doug kills the assassins.

• At a Kurdish camp, Tanzi's friends shelter Doug. Suddenly, Dallal and his soldiers appear. "There's an old Arab saying," says Dallal, "Things done in a hurry are done in the ways of Satan." Dallal tells the Kurds he will not harm them, provided they deliver Doug. Without warning, the Iraqi "fucker's" men machine-gun Kurdish families; Tanzi, too, is shot.

• In prison, two Iraqis move to shoot Doug. He dumps them and other guards, then escapes. Lilya assists him.

• Doug believes Ben, his brother, is held captive inside a broken-down hotel. The Iraqis set a trap. No matter. Doug machine-guns ten; one Iraqi accidentally kills an Iraqi.

• Dallal's home. Lilya confesses she loves Doug. Screams Dallal, "Bitch." He calls Lilya a "cheap whore," slaps her, then rapes Lilya. Later, Dallal dispatches an aide to kill her. In time, Doug crushes the assassin.

• At the Abadan chemical factory, Doug rescues brother Ben. He also blows up the plant, killing dozens of Iraqis. Plus, Doug torches Dallal. Lilya drives off with the two Americans.

The Hunger (1983), MGM-UA. *Catherine Deneuve, Susan Sarandon.* MAIDENS

Move over Theda Bara, Hollywood's first vamp. *The Hunger* displays Catherine Deneuve as the loveliest Egyptian vampire ever to grace the silver screen. Set in Manhattan's east side, this modern, stylish horror thriller features Deneuve as a bloodsucking Egyptian vampire. The ageless vampire wears an Egyptian pendant, "a symbol of everlasting life." In order to survive, the seductive vampire, who was born in Egypt more than 2,000 years ago, must feed on human blood, once a week. And, she does.

I Cover the War (1937), UNI. *John Wayne, Don Barclay, Charles Brokaw, Major Sam Harris, Frank Lackteen, Abdulla.* SP: George Waggner. VILLAINS

An American newsreel cameraman prevents seditious Arabs from revolting and slaying British Lancers.

Scene: US newsreel cameramen Bob (Wayne) and Elmer (Barclay) arrive in an Arab nation occupied by the British. Here, Arab rebels are terrorizing the British and fellow Arabs. "Welcome to Samari," says Colonel Armitage (Harris), "although why in the world you should come here, I don't know."

• The men check in at the Oasis hotel, telling the manager, Hassan (Brokaw), they are in Samari to photograph rebel leader "Muffadi [and his] fanatic tribesmen." Earlier, Muffadi's men killed three US cameramen. Unknown to the photo-journalists, Hassan is Muffadi.

• Muffadi's main spy is Mustapha (Lackteen), a shoddy beggar with few teeth.

• Believing Hassan, who dons a white suit, is a friend, Bob and Elmer smuggle him out of the British compound. They arrive at the rebel camp; the white-suited Hassan enters a tent, then reappears in Arab garb as Muffadi. His tribesmen shout, "Muffadi, Muffadi." Next, the Arabs nab Bob and Elmer.

• Muffadi and a "horde of tribesmen" ride off to ambush a British patrol.

• Guarding Bob and Elmer are three stupid Arabic-speaking sentries. Bob offers to photograph the Arabs; they smile, then nod. Bob points to a far-off sand dune, telling the Arabs to point their rifles at the distant dune and charge. The dense Arabs dash off; Bob and Elmer escape.

• In time, Bob and Elmer alert the British. Six British airplanes appear; they unleash some bombs, blasting Muffadi's Arabs off the colonial landscape.

Dialogue: Throughout, Colonel Armitage tags the Arabs "the beggars."

Note: Credits reveal that the actor, "Abdulla," portrays Abdul. And "Major Sam Harris" portrays Colonel Armitage.

I Was Monty's Double (1958), Associated British Picture Corp. *M.E. Clifton-James, Marne Maitland.* SP: Bryan Forbes. D: John Guillermin. CAMEOS

In this World War II drama based on facts, British officials enlist the services of an actor (Clifton-James) to pose as General Montgomery. Thanks in part to a shady Arab,

German intelligence agents fall for the ruse.

• Screeching Arab music introduces a souk. An Arabic-speaking German agent hands the Arab proprietor (Maitland) his slacks. The Arab rushes to the back of the shop, locking the door. Taking a pair of scissors, he removes from the trousers, a message revealing the whereabouts of Monty's double. Next, he uncovers a short-wave radio, which is hidden under a sewing machine, and transmits the message to Germany. Soon, German commandos emerge from a submarine. Believing Monty's double is really *the* General Montgomery, the Germans attack. Yet, they fail to assassinate the actor.

I'm All Right, Jack (1959), COL. *Peter Sellers, Marne Maitland.* CAMEOS, VILLAINS

Haughty Arabs appear in this film spoofing the British labor movement. Mr. Mohammed (Maitland) of the "Trans-Berberite embassy" and some shady British plant managers try to swindle an Arab country.

Scene: Mr. Mohammed, an Arab with "an eye for a slick deal," co-hosts a British dinner party; five mute, robed Arabs attend. Seeing Mohammad pilfer some cigars, the Missiles Ltd. Chairman quips, "Mohammed's charm as a diplomat is well matched by his personal integrity."

• Thanks to Mohammed's chicanery, the robed Arabs accept Missiles, Ltd.'s bogus contract. The Ltd. chairman makes a spurious comment, "In supplying your country with arms, the missiles are making their own special contribution to the peace process."

• The Ltd. plant. The British manager delivers to grim employees, an "export or die" speech. Standing next to him are some swindlers: Arabs and Brits. Intent on "getting the export order as soon as possible," the manager pleads with workers to make missiles for Arab nations. The weapons, he says, will "insure this country's healthy trading intercourse with foreign markets." The Arabs applaud his speech. But, irritated, British workers walk away.

Ilsa: Harem Keeper of the Oil Sheiks (1976), Mount Everst Enterprise. *Dyanne Thorne.* X-rated. SHEIKHS

This film's desert sheikh is a kinky, brutal slaver. Arab-German linkage. A suggestion: Fast-forward through explicit frames not related to Arab images.

El Sharif, a depraved oil sheikh, is in cahoots with Ilsa, the German "She Wolf of the S.S." They kidnap, enslave, and torture international beauties. If the women try to flee the palace's harem, Ilsa and the sheikh will see to it that their heads are chopped off.

Imar the Servitor (1914), Majestic. Re-released by Mutual in 1915. *William Garwood.* *NS. Notes from AFIC. VILLAINS

An Arab tries to rape the Western heroine. Arabs vs. Arabs. See *The Gift Girl* (1917).

An American tourist, John Raines, loses his way in the Arabian desert. Fortunately, an Arab slave, Imar (Garwood), rescues John. They become friends. Later, John finds out that his ex-sweetheart has married a not-so-nice "horseman." The brutal horseman mistakenly thinks John's ex has been unfaithful; he beats her.

The poor woman endures more suffering. The Arab chief who dominates the slave, Imar, enters the frame. The Arab tries to rape the Western heroine. Imar intervenes, freeing the woman and safely delivering her to his American friend, Raines.

Finis. Both the brutal "horseman" and the Arab "master are slain."

The Immortal Battalion (1944), a.k.a. The Way Ahead, Eagle-Lion.

David Niven, Leo Genn. CAMEOS

Arab indigents are enveloped by flies.

Scene: Near the end, four well-dressed English women sip tea, discussing the whereabouts of their husbands. Says one, "They must be either in Algeria or Tunis. All Jim writes about are the flies." Cut to an untidy Arab's face and buzzing flies.

• In the street, British soldiers observe idling Arabs.

Soldier #1: What a dump. I'd hate to be an Arab in peacetime.
Soldier #2: How about them harems?
Soldier #1: Haven't seen any yet, nothing but flies.
Soldier #3: If this is the Middle East, heaven preserve us from the Far East.

In the Army Now (1994), HOL. *Pauly Shore, Andy Dick, David Alan Grier, Lori Petty.* P: Michael Rotenberg. See *Back to the Future* (1985), *Iron Eagle* (1986). VILLAINS

In Chad, army reservists from Glendale, California, liquidate Arabs. Credits acknowledge the assistance of the "Department of Defense" and the "Department of the Army."

Scene: Intent on making a quick buck, two Glendale residents, Bones (Shore) and Jack (Dick), enlist in the Army reserves. Their assignment? To oversee a water-purification unit.

• After basic training, the Glendale duo is shipped off to Chad as "part of a UN team." In the desert, Jack suffers from heat exhaustion. Seeing a mirage, he collapses. Bones rushes to his side and warns, You better snap out of it, unless you want "a young Arabic prince to use your skull for an ashtray." Soon, Jack recovers. He and Boone move to kill invading Libyans.

• "Well inside Libya." Arab soldiers nab Jack, Bones, and two more GIs, Fred (Grier) and Christine (Petty). The Libyan commander boasts he is about to "launch chemical weapons against your bases."

• Christine socks an Arab; the GIs escape. BOOM! US forces bomb the Libyan camp. Sighs Bones, "We're not going to be tortured by Baba Ghanouj [a tasty eggplant dish!]."

• The reservists' truck runs out of gas; Bones seeks help from some robed bedouins. Bones speaks mumbo jumbo—"abboud-abboud." Still, the dense Arab gives Bones a camel. In return, Bones gives the Arab the truck, plus $55.

• The reservists spot a "mobile scud launching base," camouflaged by "a camel tent." The Libyan scuds, loaded with "chemical weapons," are set "to fire" at American bases. But these "regular GI Joes" crush the Arabs. Bones contacts his unit, telling them to fire their "laser" weapon at the Libyan base. Says Bones, "the air force will blow the hell out of it."

• Unexpectedly, the Libyans attack the reservists. Shouts Bones, "We've got 60 pissed-off Libyans. In three minutes we're going to be shish-ka-bobs."

• One Arab sneaks up behind Bones; a camel decks him. Then, the camel stomps on the Arab, holding him captive. Bones unleashes a rocket, blowing the Libyans to smithereens. Quips Bones, "Suck on this... Don't mess with the Glendale reservists."

Note: To make certain the film's camel was properly treated, officials with the "Humane Society" were present during the shoot. But no officials were around to check on how Arabs were being treated.

• The producing studio, Hollywood, is owned by Disney.

In the Heat of Passion (1992), Concorde. *Sally Kirkland, Nick Corri, Jack Carter.* W, P, D: Rodman Flender. CAMEOS

A one-liner: Charlie (Corri), a young down-and-out actor, is pursued by a rapist-psychopath. To elude his stalker, Charlie rushes into a TV station, telling the TV talk-show host Sam (Carter) about the threat. Quips Sam, "Oh, this neighborhood. It's getting worse than downtown Beirut."

Independence Day (1996), TCF. *Will Smith, Jeff Goldblum, Sayed Bayedra.* SP: Dean Devlin, Ronald Emmerich. P, D: Emmerich. CAMEOS

In this science-fiction thriller aliens from Mars try to terminate the human race. Moving to ward off the Mars threat, Arab and Israeli pilots launch a counter-offensive.

Scene: Near the end, a one-minute scene. The camera reveals the "Iraqi desert." An Arabic-speaking pilot (Bayedra) delivers a message to British pilots who, in turn, prepare to attack the aliens. Cut to both the Israeli and the Iraqi flag. Preparing to strike the aliens, Israeli, Arab, and British airmen.

Note: While participating at UCLA's "Religion and Prime Time" conference (1 June 1995) a Hollywood producer who prefers to remain anonymous, offered a suggestion as to how soften the stereotype. "Write a screenplay showing aliens attacking planet Earth. Then," he said, "have everybody, especially Arabs, participating, fighting off the bastards. And make the heroes an Arab and a Jew. Show them as a united Semitic force fighting the alien enemy. That, my friend, would do it!" Nearly one year after the producer's comments, the sci-fi thriller *Independence Day* (1996) debuted. All-too-briefly, the camera shows Arab and Israeli "combat units in the Mideast" moving to repel invading aliens.

• In 1986, actor Omar Sharif cited politics as a reason for the stereotype, telling *Cineaste*'s Miriam Rosen, "I think the image will change if they [Arabs and Israelis] make a peace settlement, which I hope they will; then suddenly you will see a film where Arabs are the good guys."[89]

Indiana Jones and the Last Crusade (1989), PAR. *Harrison Ford, Sean Connery, Alison Doody, John Rhys-Davies, Robert Eddison, Alexei Sayle, Kevork Malikyan.* SP: Jeffrey Boam, Chris Columbus, Menno Mevies. D: Stephen Spielberg. Filmed in Jordan. Among the top-grossing films of 1989; one of the 20 highest-grossing films of all time. EGYPTIANS, SHEIKHS

The Mideast, 1938. Stouthearted Indy triumphs over Nazis, unsightly Egyptian Christians, and a pro-Nazi sheikh.

Scene: Italy. Young Indy (Ford), the intrepid archaeologist, arrives in Venice. He moves to locate his father, medievalist Dr. Henry Jones (Connery). Dr. Jones is searching for the Holy Grail, the chalice used "by Christ during the Last Supper." Supposedly, whoever drinks from the Grail will receive eternal life. Suddenly, from nowhere, Egyptian Christians wearing red fezzes charge into a library and beat up Indy. Next, the Egyptians try to burn Indy alive, setting ablaze the library tunnel.

• The chase, Venice's canals. Aboard speedboats, Egyptians pursue Indy; clasping machine guns, they fire away. Indy shoots several, and blows up their boats. Next, he collars the Egyptian leader Kazim (Malikyan), demanding to know why Egyptian-Christians are out to kill him. Explains Kazim, The "brotherhood wants to keep the Holy Grail safe."

• Indy arrives in Alexandria; his friend Sallah (Rhys-Davies) greets him. Cut to Arab hucksters and rambling chickens mingling throughout the souk, a messy place.

• Inexplicably, this brief scene complete with stereotypical images. The camera reveals camels roaming throughout the "Republic of Hatay"; denizens don red fezzes. Hatay's dense, rotund Arab potentate (Sayle) meets with the Nazis and agrees to assist them. The Nazis thank the robed ruler, offering him in return for his cooperation, abundant treasures. But the dumb Arab ruler declines, preferring a Rolls Royce. The Nazis register amazement.

• Arabs vs. Arabs, vs. Nazis. Kazim's Egyptians try to stop the Nazis and their Hatayan accomplices from securing the Grail. Spielberg projects Kazim's Christians as fanatics; crosses are emblazoned on their fezzes and chests.

• In a flash, the Nazis eradicate Kazim's men. Here, again, Spielberg fails to humanize Egyptian Christians, opting not to show them as devout Grail guardians. As Indy and the Egyptian Christians are on the same side and share the same quest, namely, to stop the Nazis from snitching the Grail, why not show Indy and the Egyptians fighting side-by-side against the Nazis? In stark contrast to the Egyptian Christians, Spielberg projects the European Christian Knight guarding the Grail (Eddison) as a saint-like figure.

Dialogue: One line patronizes Indy's Egyptian friend, giving the impression that Sallah is a Third World dumbbell. Sallah tags the German tank "a metal beast." In *The Steel Lady* (1953), an Arab tags the German tank, "The Iron Monster."

The Insider (1999), TOU. *Al Pacino, Russell Crowe, Christopher Plummer, Clifford Curtis.* W: Eric Roth, Michael Mann. D: Mann. Filmed in Israel. CAMEOS, VILLAINS

The film is all about *60 Minutes'* relationship with tobacco whistle-blower Jeffrey Wigand (Crowe). Yet, the movie opens with a ten-minute scene revealing not-so-nice Arabs dwelling in a not-so-nice place.

Scene: Lebanon. Ominous Arab music underscores the action. As credits roll, a blindfolded TV network producer, Lowell Bergman (Pacino), sits in the back seat of a speeding Mercedes-Benz. Cut to images implying turmoil and turbulence: large posters revealing a bearded Arab sheikh; a cannon aimed upward; a machine gun and the Ayatollah Khomeini.

• TV producer Bergman tries to convince Sheikh Fadlallah (Curtis) to appear on *60 Minutes*, "the highest-rated, most respected show in America." Argues Bergman, "Hezbollah does not have a face in America." (In reality, Hezbollah *does* have a face; most press reports wrongly label Lebanon's Hezbollah members "terrorists.")

• The sheikh's bearded, loud-mouthed, Arabic-speaking aide screeches to reporter Mike Wallace (Plummer), move your chair, do not to sit so close to the sheikh. When the man stops shouting, Wallace asks the sheikh, "Are you a terrorist?" "Mr. Wallace, I am a servant of God," says the sheikh. Quips Wallace, "A servant of God? Really! Americans believe that you, as an Islamic fundamentalist, are a leader who contributed to the bombing of the US embassy." Before the sheikh can deny Wallace's accusation, the camera cuts to the US. The following frames focus on a whistle-blower, network news, and tobacco.

Intimate Power (1989), a.k.a. The Favorite, Asconda Films.
F. Murray Abraham, Amber O'Shea, Maud Adams. CAMEOS, VILLAINS
  In Algiers, a French nun is sold into slavery.
  Scene: The 1850s. When a young nun (O'Shea) is abducted from her ship, she asks where she will be taken. Grunts her abductor, "Algiers."
  • Algiers: A grubby jail and a lecherous Arab guard. The nun and other imprisoned women will soon be "bought and paid for."
  • Turkey as Arabia? 99 percent of the action occurs in Turkey. The nun, for example, is whisked off to the Turkish sultan's castle, complete with harem maidens and eunuchs. Yet, the Turkish characters speak Arabic.

Into the Night (1985), UNI. *Michelle Pfeiffer, Jeff Goldblum, Irene Pappas.*
D: John Landis. VILLAINS, MAIDENS
  "Shaheen's boys" invade Beverly Hills. The film's director, John Landis, portrays one of Shaheen's boys. Iranians as Arabs? See *The Hitman* (1991), *The Invincible Six* (1969), *Down and Out in Beverly Hills* (1986).
  Scene: In Beverly Hills, Shaheen's four dark thugs, "all Iranians, Persians, or something," stab a man, then stuff him into the trunk of their gold Mercedes-Benz. Next, they try to assault Diana (Pfeiffer); she runs off, jumping into Ed's (Goldblum) car. They drive off, pursued by the killers. Cut to some Harley motorcycle toughs confronting the "Iranian Gestapo"; they back off.
  • On a boat, Shaheen's boys search for missing emeralds. They trash the place, pistol whip a man, and fondle his female companion's breasts. Plus, they knife a fellow Iranian.
  • A men's clothing store. As Shaheen's boys try on suits, they fondle the breasts of beautiful women.
  • The Beverly Wilshire Hotel. One of the gun-crazed thugs shoots a dog. Cut to a beach house. After ransacking the place, a Shaheen boy shoots a squawking bird. On the beach, the four men catch up with, then drown the lovely Christy, "Miss North America"; she wears a white suit.
  • Ms. Shaheen's (Pappas) mansion. Shaheen's boys crack nuts with their pistol butts. A gong announces Ms. Shaheen's entrance. She's determined to acquire the emeralds. Why? So she can buy up America. Ed and Diana offer her the missing emeralds, in exchange for their safety.
  • At the airport, federal agents surface. Shaheen's boys lose the shoot-out; one even kills himself. Happily, Ed and Diana escape.

Into the Sun (1991), TRI. *Anthony Michael Hall, Michael Paré.* S, SP: Michael Ferris, John Brancato. Filmed in Israel. VILLAINS, WORST LIST

A Hollywood actor and an American airforce pilot blast underhanded Arabs in "their spit of sand." Arabs vs. Arabs. Contemporary high-tech films such as *Into the Sun* and *Iron Eagle* (1986) show "sneaky" Arab soldiers creeping up on American pilots. Anti-Arab scenarios of the 30s, 40s and 50s display creepy desert Arabs slinking up on legionnaires. Basically, the Arab stereotypes are similar; only the settings and costumes differ.

Scene: Before credits, this: "Somewhere over the Mediterranean sea... enemy aircraft." Cut to Arab pilots illegally pursuing two US pilots, Snake and Captain Watkins (Paré). The Americans are ordered, "Do not engage."

• Returning to their base in Sicily, the commanding officer tells his pilots, "I know you'd like nothing better than to blow those assholes out of the sky. They want to provoke an incident [so they can] fuel their propaganda war."

• The pilots attend a party at a posh Italian hotel. Mingling about are air force personnel and mute, bearded Arabs wearing sunglasses and white thobes. Why show robed Arabs attending an air force reception in Sicily?

• A Hollywood actor, Tom Slade (Hall), arrives at the base. Intent on receiving on-the-job flight training, Slade joins Captain Watkins on a special mission. Unexpectedly, Arab jets appear. Shouts Watkins, "[They've] expanded their air space by 200 miles... I have four bad guys and they are not letting go." Watkins is ordered, "Check the bastards." He does. He and Slade down "enemy jets." Yet, one US pilot is killed; Watkins and Slade are "shot down."

• Safely parachuting "in hostile country," Watkins warns Slade, "We're in the middle of the desert... This government has been openly hostile...Those guys torture people for a living."

• Arab vs. Arab. Two unsightly Arab soldiers wearing fatigues come across Slade. They take the actor's money, then go to shoot him. Suddenly, scruffy bedouins arrive; they gun down the soldiers. Slade takes a cigarette from a bedouin, grunting, "Tastes like crap!"

• Watkins and Slade assume the bedouins will safely guide them to the border. Not so. For money, the greedy bedouins deliver the men to an Arab officer, an Arafat look-a-like.

• An Arab missile base. Greeting the two men is Ace, an American mercenary, the Arabs' finest pilot. I work for the Arabs, says Ace, because they pay "a hell of a lot better than Uncle Sam." Next, Arab guards enter Watkins' cell, beating him. See *Iron Eagle* (1986).

• The Arabs force Slade to tape a false confession. Slade reacts by shouting, "You guys (American forces) ought to nuke this fuckin' place off the map."

• The bedouins re-appear. Surprisingly, they kill Arab soldiers and they free Slade and Watkins. Why the change of heart? Earlier, Slade promised them *more* money!

• Arabs-as-buffoons. Arab soldiers try to stop the men from escaping; they fire their weapons; hitting not the American pilots but some gas tanks, immolating themselves! Ignited Arab bodies fill the screen.

• Watkins and Slade fly off in an "enemy" jet. Barks Watkins, "We gotta take out the runway." BOOM! Cut to Snake leading a US rescue mission. Shouts Snake, "It's time to face Mecca, pilgrim."

Note: In *Iron Eagle* (1986), a teenager and a retired pilot wipe out Arabs, destroying their air base. Here, a movie actor and a young pilot blast the base, slaughtering Arabs. Both scenarios are identical. Both reveal devious Arabs violating international air space, capturing and holding hostage American pilots. Both show Arabs torturing US pilots in desert cells. One major difference: *Into the Sun*'s Arab pilots are so inept they employ an American pilot.

Intolerance (1916), Wark Prod. A D.W. Griffith film. Silent. *Lillian Gish, Seena Owen.* See Griffith's *The Fall of Babylon* (1919). MAIDENS

Persians vs. Babylonians. On screen, "Favorites of the harem" for sale. The Hebrews and Babylonians wear similar garb—robes and headdresses.

Scene: Sixth century BC, the Jaffa Gate. Title cards set up the theme: There are "certain hypocrites among the Pharisees." Sighs one man, "Oh, Lord, I thank thee that I am better than other men." And, "If only he thought as we do."

• Appearing is Babylon's Prince Balshazzar, an "apostle of tolerance and religious freedom." His sweetheart, Attarea (Owen), is called "The Princess Beloved." Under Balshazzar's rule Babylon boasts "the first known court of justice in the world, to protect the weak from the strong."

• As in Griffith's *Fall of Babylon* (1919), an auctioneer sells harem maidens at the "marriage market." Note the dialogue, "Money paid for beautiful women given to homely ones as dowers, so that all may have husbands and be happy."

• King Cyrus of Persia conspires with Balshazzar's high priest. Together, they bring down the Babylonian potentate.

Invasion U.S.A. (1985), CAN. *Chuck Norris.* P: *Menahem Golan, Yoram Globus.* SP: Chuck Norris, James Bruner. Not to be confused with *Invasion U.S.A.* (1952), which does not display Arabs. CAMEOS, VILLAINS

A Florida beach. The Golan-Globus movie begins and concludes with Arabs invading the US. Israeli actors Afif Yordi and Tarik Yordi portray two Arab invaders.

Scene: The Christmas holidays. Suddenly, America is assaulted by a "foreign enemy." Uniformed Cuban troops, Soviet soldiers, and Arabs wearing kuffiyehs attack. Taking orders from the Russian leader, the invaders blast homes, shopping malls, and amusement parks, killing scores of Americans.

The Invincible Six (1969), Moulin Rouge. *Stuart Whitman, Elke Sommer, Curt Jurgens, Ian Ogilvy, James Mitchum.* Based on Michael Barrett's novel, *The Heroes of Yucca.* P: Morteza Akavan. D: Jean Negulesco. "Filmed Entirely on Location in Iran." *The Magnificent Seven* (1960) revisited. VILLAINS

Westerners and Iranians vs. Iranians.

Scene: Contemporary Iran, "the desert." Several Western jewel thieves arrive at an empty village. "I wonder what's happened to these people," says Tex (Whitman).

• The camera reveals an empty souk, mosque and a public bath. Suddenly, two survivors emerge: Ahmed, the police chief, and his daughter. Says Ahmed, Soldiers came here; they "captured" and hanged "Malik, the bandit chief." Because our villagers are a "superstitious people," they ran off when the new bandit chief appeared—"Nazar, the mad dog" (Mitchum). Explains Ahmed, Nazar needs to acquire Malik's corpse; "It has something to do with establishing his authority." Supposedly, from Malik's mortal remains comes Nazar's strength.

• "That sleepy-eyed bastard," Nazar, has "maybe a hundred bandits up there." No matter. Tex and his Western pals promise to defend the villagers.

• After Nazar's bandits try to rape "just a girl from the village," a bandit shoots her. Nazar's men charge the village; Tex Inc. mow 'em down.

• At a bath, Malik's blonde "woman," Zeri (Sommer), confronts Tex, the "infidel." Sighs Zeri, "Our [Persian] customs are mixed-up. We often don't say what we mean, or mean what we say." Later, they make love.

• Nazar's bandits capture Tex's buddy, Ron (Ogilvy), an Englishman. Nazar tells Ron, "You're very pretty, I make you a gift to my men."

• At the village, Zeri dances. Suddenly, Nazar Inc. appear. They drop off Ron's mutilated body.

• The bandit's camp. After Nazar slugs Zeri, Tex Inc. destroy the hideout, killing scores.

• Nazar shoots Ahmed; villagers kill Nazar, "the last bandit chief to rule these mountains."

• Inside Malik's amulet, a map revealing the location of hidden "treasures of a lifetime." Unexpectedly, Malik's mother burns the map.

Note: This film was released in 1969, when American-Iranian relations were secure. Not surprisingly, a large poster of Iran's Shah is prominently displayed on a police station's wall. Nearly all the action occurs at a desert village. Yet, a few brief shots display Teheran's museum, complete with the "crown jewels," precious gems and diamonds.

Invitation to the Dance (1956), MGM. *Gene Kelly, David Kasday.*
MAIDENS

Attention US sailors! When visiting Arabia, know this: your lives are in jeopardy. In this movie's animated live-action sequence, "Sinbad the Sailor," an animated Arab woman romances a sailor. The "Sinbad" title is misleading. Actor Gene Kelly never dons Arab garb, nor does he function as Sinbad. Instead, Kelly performs magnificently as a dashing American sailor. In the end, Kelly's wishes turn a young Arab genie and an animated Arab maiden into US navy service persons.

Scene: The souk. A bellydancer fraternizes with several merchants, purchasing goods. Suddenly, an Arab thief surfaces; he runs off with a magic lamp. Seeing a US sailor (Kelly), the thief hands him the lamp, and disappears.

• Abruptly, unsavory Arabs appear, threatening the sailor. The Arabs insist the American stole the lamp. To quell the riotous men, Kelly pays an angry merchant for the lamp.

• Kelly rubs the lamp. Popping out, a boy genie (Kasday) clad in Arab garb. He offers Kelly three wishes.

• Wish #1. Kelly asks the boy to replace his Arab robe and headdress with a US sailor's outfit. The young genie obliges, donning sailor garb.

• Wish #2. Now dressed as a sailor, the boy genie accompanies Kelly to mythical Arabia. Introducing a live action, animation sequence. Kelly performs a novel Sinbad-the-sailor dance; an animated serpent and other animated characters participate. Also, on screen, scores of animated Arab villains. Inside an Arabian palace, lovely and listless animated maidens lounge near a rotund animated emir. Kelly appears; the women perk up. On seeing his harem beauties fawn over the sailor, the emir becomes jealous. He orders two saber-wielding guards to behead Kelly, as well as the boy genie, even his favorite maiden.

• To illustrate the emir's frustrations, the director superimposes on the screen, gibberish, not Arabic. The ruler's animated henchmen toss daggers. Yet, the protagonists escape from the palace. Earlier, the emir's favorite saved Kelly's life. Now, the animated maiden dances with the sailor. Pleased, Kelly kisses the Arab lovely.

• Wish #3. The animated maiden yearns to be released from the emir's domain; Kelly's third wish grants her freedom. Presto! She is transformed into a US sailor wearing navy blue, a WAVE. Smiling, Kelly, the boy, and the maiden exit animated Arabia.

Iron Eagle (1986), Trimark. *Lou Gossett, Jr., Jason Gedrick, Tim Thomerson, David Suchet.* SP: Kevin Elders, Sidney J. Furie. D: Sidney J. Furie. Filmed in Israel, in cooperation with the Israeli government and the Israeli military. VILLAINS, WORST LIST

A retired American air force colonel and a teenager rescue an air force officer and destroy an Arab air base, killing scores.

Scene: Falsely contending USAF colonel Ted Masters (Thomerson) is violating Arab territorial waters, Arabs down the fighter pilot's plane, then imprison him.

• An American air base. Doug (Gedrick), the colonel's son, is informed about the incident. Explains an officer, "Some countries play a little different from us." He tells Doug, "Il Kharem" is using your father, demanding that we lift our "trade embargo."

• The Arab base; Islam equals violence. Sounds of praying Muslims fill the soundtrack. Blasting Americans, an Arab general (Suchet) beats Masters. Repeatedly, the general slugs the airman. He intends to hang Masters later.

• The US government refuses to assist Masters. Doug acts, convincing a retired air force officer, Colonel Chappy (Gossett), to teach him to fly, and to assist with the rescue mission. Affirms Chappy, "There's something about maniacs messing with good men."

• Doug and Chappy fly off to rescue Colonel Masters.

• Abruptly, some Arab pilots sneak up on Doug's F-16 jet. As the soundtrack punches up the Spencer Davis Group's rock song "Gimme Some Loving," Doug terminates the Arabs' ace fighter pilot. Next, he unleashes the devastating "Hades bomb," destroying most of Il Kharem's air base, and the Arab general. Scores of Arab soldiers are engulfed in flames. Screaming, they run off.

• Chappy, Doug, and his injured father, Colonel Masters, return home.

Movies we do not see: In 1973, Israeli pilots flying two American-built Phantom jet fighter-bombers shot down a Libyan civilian plane (Flight 5-A-DAH). The civilian plane was approaching a daylight landing at Cairo International Airport. Due to a navigating error, it strayed over the Israeli-controlled Sinai. 107 people, including one American, were killed. To date, no studio has released a feature film about the incident.

• When Sidney J. Furie's *Iron Eagle* was being shown in movie theaters, members of the American-Arab Anti-Discrimination Committee (ADC) reported that viewers, many of whom wore military garb, stood up and cheered as Jason Gedrick (Doug) demolished Arabs. Ironically, nearly 40 years ago, when the film *None Shall Escape* (1944) was released, some viewers cheered as Jews were being shot. Critics rightly labeled the viewers anti-Semitic "provocateurs." When *None Shall Escape* was being screened there were "disturbances in theaters... deliberately planned and carried out by anti-Semitic elements, particularly in New York and Boston." Bigots focused their attention on a scene showing a Polish rabbi and his flock running from a cattle car "preparing to transport them to concentration camps." A Nazi machine-gunner mows them down. The bigots used this "scene to start applause and consequent disorder in theaters."[90]

• Scenarios showing Americans killing Arabs are money-makers. Roderick Mann reported in the *Chicago Sun-Times* (13 February 1986) that *Iron Eagle* sold "12 million in tickets in two weeks and... finished in the top 10 every week since it opened nationally" (four weeks earlier).

• Writer-director Furie explains how viewers reacted during the previews. "As soon as the [US] planes appeared, they started cheering. The atmosphere was absolutely electric." Mann writes that after reading Furie's screenplay, the film's producer, Ron Samuels, said, "It was just the kind of story I'd been looking for. It reminded me of the old John Wayne westerns."

• An NBC news producer who was in Israel filming a television special about Hollywood's Arabs told me that the producers of *Iron Eagle* used Israeli jets in all the film's bombing raids that bomb Il Kharem, the fictional Arab country. In return, he said, the producers paid the Israeli air force approximately $700 thousand dollars.

Iron Eagle II (1988), TRI. *Lou Gossett Jr.* W, D: Sidney J. Furie. As with *Iron Eagle* (1986) this film was "financed by Israeli producers and shot on location in Israel with the cooperation of the Israeli minister of defense."[91] VILLAINS

As Arabs possess nuclear "missiles capable of reaching densely populated areas," Russians *and* Americans liquidate them.

Scene: Consider the opening statement: "A nuclear warhead has just been tested in their [Arab] desert." Receiving orders to address the situation, US General Sinclair (Gossett) is told, "A few years ago [meaning the original *Iron Eagle* (1986)] you flew in and kicked some hard-core enemy butt. Now we got another one like it, only bigger." Cut to a pilot boasting that he "hosed down Migs [over] Libya in '86."

• An Arab desert base. Cut to a nuclear missile; etched on the missile is the number 39, written in Arabic. Cut to a state department official pointing to an Arab nation, telling pilots, "You've been mobilized to eliminate it [the Arab compound]."

• Americans and Russians launch a joint preemptive strike, destroying the compound. The camera reveals dark-complexioned Arabs and missile 39. In the desert, war: tanks and planes battle.

Note: No more Cold War. An attractive Russian sergeant swoons for an American pilot, and vice versa.

Ishtar (1987), COL. *Warren Beatty, Dustin Hoffman, Isabelle Adjani, Ahron Ipale.* W, D: Elaine May. Original songs: Paul Williams, Elaine May. Filmed in Morocco. VILLAINS, WORST LIST

Arabs vs. Arabs, vs. Americans. "The view of the Arabs [in *Ishtar*] is unexpectedly crude."[92] Two American song writers, tagged the "Messengers of God," elude assassins and a corrupt emir. Islam is mocked.

Scene: Contemporary Morocco. Omar and his Arab colleague uncover an ancient map, which reveals that there are two "Messengers of God," not one (the Prophet Mohammed). Soon, a skirmish erupts; Arabs shoot Arabs. Omar rushes off to Ishtar; he frets that the map discovery may ignite a Holy War, impacting "a few hundred Shiites" and the emir.

• An Arab enters Omar's hotel room, knifing him in the gut. Next, inept CIA agents surface, disguised as Arabs.

• Two New York singer/songwriters, Rogers and Clarke (Hoffman, Beatty), fly off to Ishtar to perform at the Chez Casablanca Club. The men are not seated in the first-class section of an Air Maroc jet, rather, they're squished together inside a cramped prop plane. On arrival, an Arab cabby cheats them. At the hotel, the porter harasses them. Welcome to Morocco!

• Arab food is not edible. A close-up shows Rogers' fingers clutching scraps of greasy food. Shirra (Adjani), Omar's rebellious sister arrives, telling the duo, "Western culture is superior...You are American, from a young country. Ours is an old, devious world." And, "the people have never seen a refrigerator. [Yet], the dome of the palace in Ishtar is gold." (Actually, the vast majority of Moroccans own, or have certainly *seen* refrigerators.)

• Shirra's "communist" cohorts wear battle fatigues; they are the movie's "bad" guys, along with Emir Yousef (Ipale). The ruler tries to kill Shirra. As "Morocco signed a pact with Muamar Khadafi," the emir calls Khadafi "every day." Believing the New Yorkers may be the "Messengers of God," the emir dispatches inept assassins. Also pursuing the men are Shirra's "fanatical Shiites" and the CIA.

• Rogers stares at Moroccans mingling in the souk and quips, "Funny, isn't it? You never appreciate your own country until you leave it." Soon, Arab hustlers surface, tormenting him and Clarke.

• The desert. The duo, and the blind camel they bought from "Mohammed," are lost.

• Clarke spots gunrunners negotiating with a bunch of dense Arab buyers. He tells Rogers: "Just go down there and act Arab." Rogers obeys; he acts Arab; the bedouins gape. Spewing mumbo-jumbo, he auctions off the weapons, easily duping the stupid bedouins. If unkempt Jews appeared in the desert in lieu of scruffy Arabs, would screenwriter Elaine May proclaim: Act Jewish?

• The Americans check out Omar's jacket; inside the lining they find the missing map. In exchange for the "Messengers'" map, the CIA agrees to promote their new record album, and to book the duo in noted nightclubs. Plus, the agency pardons the "reformed" Shirra.

• The songwriters' tune contains dreadful, offensive lyrics. They croon a song, "*I Look to Mecca*," about a romantic rendezvous under a tree in Mecca, Mohammed's birthplace and Islam's holiest city. Surely May knows that the sacred pilgrimage to Mecca is something devout Muslims look forward to making all their lives. Daily, from hundreds of minarets, devout men sing out five calls to prayer. During Ramadan, a time of prayer and reflection, pious Muslims do not eat, drink, or smoke from dawn to sunset. "How would Jews feel," asks American-Arab activist Faris Bouhafa, "if a major motion picture introduced a trite little song smearing Judaism, called: '*Meeting my baby down by the Wailing Wall*.'"[93] See *Aladdin* (1992).

Note: Why does Beatty mock Islam and Muslim Arabs? See his other Arab-bashing scenarios: *Heaven Can Wait* (1978) and *Reds* (1981). Beatty produced, directed, starred in, and helped script both films.

• Morocco was the first country to establish relations with the United States. In 1987, the year *Ishtar* was released, Morocco's King Hassan II visited Washington for festivities marking the 200th anniversary of the US constitution and the Moroccan-American friendship Treaty of 1787. Also, the US postal service issued a stamp commemorating the 1787 treaty.

• Screen credits "acknowledge the kindness and cooperation of his Majesty Hassan II, King of Morocco." I wonder what he really thought of *Ishtar*?

• When *People* interviewed Dustin Hoffman about *Ishtar*, the actor quipped: "All I remember of Morocco is work and diarrhea," he said (25 May 1987). On HBO's *Talk*, Hoffman said his "whole family [was] there, staying at some military outpost." During his TV interview, Hoffman turned to Beatty, asking, "Your bowel movements were okay?" Beatty smiled. As filming in Morocco began the same day Israeli jets bombed Tunisia, the interviewer asked Hoffman, "Did you feel you were in danger at any point?" Sighed the actor, "[Only] when you can't make it to the bathroom."

• From May to August 1987, the American-Arab Anti-Discrimination Committee (ADC) sent scores of letters to Ed Russel, vice president of publicity at Columbia Pictures, and to film critics, protesting *Ishtar's* ethnic and religious slurs. Later that year, *Ishtar* was cited by the National Ethnic Coalition of Organizations (NECO) for advancing negative stereotypes. The film was granted the first-ever "Golden Pit Award." Also, actors Hoffman and Beatty received a "Pit" for their on-screen anti-Arab sentiments, notably their dialogue mocking the sacred pilgrimage to Mecca. In New York, William Fugazy, NECO's honorary chairman, explained that his organization is "dedicated to universal brotherhood and to the advancement, protection, and encouragement of all ethnic groups and races."

• *Ishtar*, a poor imitation of a Crosby-Hope road comedy, cost 40 times as much as *Road to Morocco* (1942). For *Ishtar*, May shot about a half-million feet of film, but only about 10,000 feet of it was used, "a ratio of nearly 50 to 1." During the eight-week shoot in Morocco, the studio employed nearly 1,000 extras. Some of *Ishtar's* budget, "estimated at over $40 million, with $10 million tacked on for promotion," was spent searching for camels. "Several rare blue-eyed camels were needed." Thus, camel trainers were dispatched to look for "a rare blue-eyed camel that would photograph blind." Explains a crew member, "There's nowhere in Morocco to look at camels. They have camel markets, but they're few and far between. So we ended up traveling in increasingly concentric circles around the location trying to bump into nomadic tribesmen who had these camels."[94]

• Though the American government supports the vast majority of Arab leaders, most American films project Arab rulers as immoral caricatures. See *Protocol* (1984).

The Jade Box 1930, UNI. 10 episodes. *NS. Jack Perrin, Louise Lorraine. I could not locate a copy of this serial. VILLAINS, CLIFFHANGERS

A jade box containing a valuable vial that holds the secret to invisibility is stolen and whisked off to the Middle East. Cut to the American heroine, Helen Morgan (Lorraine), appearing in an Arab nation, in the "clutches" of two robed Arabs—"the enemy."

Jericho (1937), a.k.a. Dark Sands, General. *Paul Robeson, Henry Wilcoxon, Wallace Ford, Princess Koula, John Laurie.* This movie was filmed in an unknown Arab country. MAIDENS, SHEIKHS, RECOMMENDED

WWI. A humane African-American doctor befriends Arabs. A black American marries an Arab woman; she gives birth to a baby boy. Actor-singer Paul Robeson stars as a benevolent desert sheikh. Dramatically embellishing the film, the musical score features imaginative orchestrations and ethnic instruments.

Scene: WWI. En route to Europe, a regiment of black soldiers including army corporal "Jericho" Jackson (Robeson). Unexpectedly, Germans torpedo the US ship. A black sergeant accidentally falls, fatally striking his head. Jericho is wrongly accused of murder.

• In France, Jericho stands trial; he is found guilty and sentenced to death. Jericho runs off, betraying the confidence of his white friend and captor, Captain Mack (Wilcoxon). Donning Arab garb, he flees to a North African desert. He recalls a chaplain's advice, "Wise men found truth and righteousness in the desert." Accompanying Jericho is Mike Clancy (Ford).

• North Africa. Jericho and Mile trek across the desert. Feigning to be the "World's Greatest Strongman," Jericho overpowers a strong, but not so clever, Arab.

• Soon after they arrive at a mud-brick dwelling, Jericho meets and falls in love with a lovely villager, Gara (Koula).

• On ascertaining the Arab chief's leg is broken; Jericho assists. He enters a neat-looking Arabesque enclave, attending the ruler's leg. Expressing thanks, the Arab offers Jericho the hospitality and safety of his village. "I think I'm going to like these people," beams Jericho.

• Scenes show Jericho assisting Arab children, saying, "These people need me."

• Speaking "the words of a wise man," Jericho acquires sufficient funds to build a hospital. Next, he unites the "tribes," leading the Arabs through the desert. Cut to a "great caravan," complete with thousands of camels. They head toward valued salt mines.

• When Jericho spots Arab raiders, he shouts, "Assemble the fighting men at once." His Arabs bring down the renegades. Though Mike stops a raider from knifing Jericho, he, himself, is killed. This scene contests the common image of the screen black sacrificing his life for the white protagonist.

• Pleased to live among Arabs, Jericho sings "Deep Desert." The lyrics, in part:

> Deep desert, I'm finding a new world from my native land...
> Oh, Deep Desert, now I know where my place is,
> here in your silent spaces.
> This is my home, Deep Desert."

As the sun sets Jericho and his Arab friends gather around a camp fire; he sings:

Sahara, teach me to reach your history,
holding me with your mystery.

• Suddenly, "a volcano of screaming needles," a sandstorm. Captain Mack arrives in North Africa, determined to nab Jericho. But when Mack learns Jericho is innocent, that the sergeant's death was an accident, his anger turns to friendship. But the Arabs are unaware Mack's intentions have changed. Fearing the captain will harm Jericho, an Arab fires at Mack's plane, killing the officer.

Note: See African-American WWI heroes from Harlem in the 1980s documentary, *Men of Bronze*. See, also, HBO-TV's movie, *The Tuskegee Airmen* (1995), documenting black heroics during WWII.

• Some Hollywood war movies show African-American actors demeaning and murdering Arabs. See Eddie Murphy, Lou Gossett Jr. and Samuel Jackson in *Best Defense* (1984), *Iron Eagle* (1986), and *Rules of Engagement* (2000).

Jerusalem (1996), SYT. Maria Bonnevie, Ulf Friberg. W, D: Billie August. Swedish, with English subtitles. CAMEOS

This film is based on Selma Lagerof's novel about some Swedish Christians who founded a religious colony in Palestine at the turn of the century.[95]

Scene: Palestine. Appearing in the background, elderly white-robed Palestinian workers, veiled Palestinian women, and Palestinian beggars saying "Allah."

• Evening, the souk. This 22-second scene reveals two Palestinians emerging from the shadows and mugging the Swedish protagonist, Ingmar (Friberg). When Ingmar defends himself, the Palestinians beat and knife him in the back. Ingmar loses an eye.

The Jerusalem File (1971), MGM. An R. Ben Efraim Production. Bruce Davison, Nicol Williamson, Daria Halprin, Zeev Revan. SP: Troy Kennedy Martin, Koya Yair Rubin. Filmed in Israel. PALESTINIANS

Palestinians kill Palestinians. Unknown assassins terminate Israeli and Palestinian peace activists. See *The Ambassador* (1984) and *Deadline* (1986).

Scene: Intones the narrator: "Subject: Jerusalem terrorist activities... Arab terrorist attacks [in the old city] have increased 100 percent... group shootings indicate a power struggle between two rival Arab groups [the word, Palestinian, is never mentioned]. A decision to assassinate [the Palestinian] Rifaat has now been reached by his opposition."

• At an outdoor cafe, three Palestinians in a bedraggled Buick sedan drive up and try to kill Rifaat (Revan). They miss, nearly killing Rifaat's American friend, David Armstrong (Davison). David and Rifaat were classmates at Yale. Warns an Israeli Shin Bet officer, Major Samuels (Pleasance), "Arab terrorists are fighting each other, some kind of power struggle."

• Samuels advises David's professor, Lang (Williamson), "A bombing of a coffee shop, and a taxi runs over a mine. A parcel was delivered to a newspaper office in Tel Aviv. These are the sort of Arabs your young friend, David, is in touch with."

• At an excavation site, international students discuss peace. Cut to a 17-year-old Palestinian, seated in a barber's chair. Palestinians wearing dark glasses and Western garb enter the shop, shooting the youth dead.

• Inside a Palestinian's home, Samuels accuses the family of "sheltering terrorists."

As he paces through the house, cut to the evicted occupants. They fear the Israelis will blow up their dwelling. Explains Samuels' aide, the family "say(s) they had no choice." Samuels authorizes the house's destruction, quipping, "Neither have we." The camera does not show the home being demolished, nor do viewers see Palestinians react.

• Back at the archaeological site, sun-drenched students work. Suddenly, a Palestinian sniper appears, wounding a student. Israelis nab the sniper, then toss his body onto a truck. "You know, if that bastard [Palestinian] could shoot straight, I'd be dead," says Barak (Rubin), an Israeli peace advocate. "Some people say this war is going to last 100 years," he says. "We'd like to see it end sooner." Even though three of Rifaat's peace activists have just been killed, the Israeli peace activist Barak insists David contact Rifaat.

• A funeral. Mute Palestinians mourn their dead; four Israelis join them. Cut to Yusef, one of Rifaat's friends. Yusef spots a Palestinian driving a car; he opens the car door. BOOM! The Palestinian driver shoots him.

• Evening, a remote desert area. Israeli and Palestinian peacemakers meet. Barak and Rifaat shake hands, and drink coffee from the same cup.

• Professor Lang asks whether the Israeli-Palestinian meeting went well. Says Major Samuels, "No. The Army found them." Samuels, the professor, and David go to the desert site. Cut to Israeli soldiers and ambulances. Cut to dead students, blankets covering the bodies.

• An ambiguous conclusion. Who shot the peace activists? "There is nothing amateur about this [the shootings]," explains an Israeli soldier. Cut to an Israeli soldier picking up a camera, unloading the film, and handing it to a fellow soldier. Flashback. Several shots show Barak and Rifaat smiling. Arms around each other, they drink coffee. A close-up of a finger on a rifle's trigger, set to fire. Next, shots are heard. Fade to black. As credits roll, freeze frame on the stunned student activists' faces.

Jewel of the Nile (1985), TCF. *Michael Douglas, Kathleen Turner, Danny DeVito, Spiros Focas, Avner Eisenberg, Paul David Magid.* Filmed in Morocco. Credits thank "King Hassan" and Morocco's "Air Force" for their cooperation. SHEIKHS, WORST LIST

Contemporary Arabia. An American brings down evil Arabs. The film contains a plethora of unchallenged smears. Arabs appear as religious fanatics, as messy desert dwellers, as power-crazed buffoons, and as killers of fellow Arabs. Islam is mocked. Blacks are belittled.

Scene: Monte Carlo. Guided by three mute bodyguards, Sheikh Omar (Focas), who pines for blondes, asks novelist Joan Wilder (Turner) to write his biography. He hands Joan a white rose, promising an "exclusive story" as well as a memorable "journey down the Nile." When Joan's publisher spots her client with Omar, she shouts, "Oh, shit!"

• Omar's desert kingdom. Says Joan, there are no roads. Rebuffs Omar, "Why point out the negative?... Feel free to do as you wish here." But when Joan photographs Arabic phrases scrawled on a bullet-ridden wall, Arabs confiscate her film. Explains Omar, "If I wanted the truth, I'd hire *60 Minutes*. The Western press cannot understand the spirit of my good vision."

• Camel-riding bedouins rush into a filthy souk. The rebels engage Omar's black-clad heavies. [As *Jewel of the Nile* is set in present-day Arabia, why show Arabs on camels?

See also *Ishtar* (1987).] Soon, Joan realizes that Omar is a scheming scoundrel intent on ruling the Nile "tribes." See *Protocol* (1984). When Joan asks about screams emanating from the palace dungeon, the Arabs tell her: "Cats."

• Joan's pals, Jack Colton (Douglas) and Ralph (DeVito), find out that the desert-mogul has imprisoned her. They move to free Joan.

• Omar's palace, the middle of a vast desert. Ever since cinematographers began framing Arabia, set designers rigidly displayed isolated desert fortresses surrounded by tents and dirty souks filled with camels, goats, chickens, beggars and hawkers. *Jewel of the Nile's* setting, like *Protocol's*, is similar, with one exception. In lieu of scimitars, the sheikh's black-clad guards possess up-to-date weapons—two tanks and a plane. Arabs manning the hardware, however, are as ineffectual as those who preceded them. From a plane Jack fires at Arabs; scores of Arabs drop. But when Omar fires a shell at Jack, the Arab misses.

• Those Arabs intent on ousting Omar are superstitious, dense, and backward.

• The camera displays in the background, briefly, bellydancers and mute maidens.

• An Arab rebel leader welcomes Ralph and Jack, saying, "We have food, we have drink." Quips Ralph, "You got a toilet?" The rebels direct Jack to run barefoot over burning coals. Next, they perform a knife dance. Underscoring their dance steps, disco music blaring from transistors attached to camels.

• Omar's men capture Ralph and Jack, place them in the dungeon and dangle the duo over a bottomless pit. The splattered-with-goat's-blood dungeon is crawling with rats, and dripping with acid. Asks Jack, "What kind of demented psychopath would do this?"

• Only "the Jewel," a Muslim "Holy Man" (Eisenberg), can stop the ambitious Omar. Yet, producers do not project the Jewel as a devout person. They present him as a clown. In any case, to show Muslim Arabs worshiping a Muslim "Holy Man" is blasphemous. In reality, Muslims, like Christians and Jews, worship the same God, not a "jewel."

• To mesmerize the Arabs, Omar employs special rock concert effects. A mix of sound, light, and video dazzle Arab onlookers. On stage, Omar appears as a God. The ruler dupes the Arabs, walking through what they believe to be real flames. Falling for the ruse, the Arabs gape, swing and sway, rave and rant. This dangerous, grotesque scene implies that reel Arabs are mindless robots. Compare this scene with 1930s stock footage showing Hitler's rhetoric deluding German audiences.

• The Jewel takes center stage, gliding through actual flames. The Arab crowd mutters "ooh's" and "ah's." Drawing knives, they crush Omar's men. Omar, too, is eliminated.

• Jack and Joan wed; the Jewel officiates.

Note: Black stereotypes. Scenes display mumbling blacks who "eat rock shit"; their faces are covered with white and yellow paint. Bare-breasted black women perform a Hawaiian disco dance. Primitive blacks insist Jack fight Hassan, a huge black man who looks like TV's infamous wrestler, Abdullah the Butcher. These portraits do not simply parody caricatures; *Jewel of the Nile's* black images are as hurtful and harmful as the film's Arab portraits.

• Following a live performance of his one-man show, actor Avner Eisenberg told an admirer, Ralph Sutton, that after his performance as the "Jewel," the Muslim "Holy Man," several movie producers approached him, asking the entertainer to portray Arab villains in their films.[96] To his credit, Eisenberg refused.

Dialogue: *Jewel of the Nile's* "Previews of Coming Attractions" were screened in movie theaters and on television. In one promotional preview, Danny DeVito boasts that he will find the "Jewel," declaring: "The only thing that's stopping me is this big shot Ayrab!"

• An Arab is tagged "towel head."

• Watching bedouins dance, Ralph tells Jack, "Look at these guys. No sheep is safe tonight... Why do all these third world cesspools have to be so hot?... [One can] pick up a three-bedroom townhouse for about five or six dollars."

• The screenwriters toyed with Omar's speech, the one designed to stir the masses. They added to his address in Arabic, a compilation of Kirk Douglas movie titles, such as *Lust for Life* (1956) and *Spartacus* (1960).

John Goldfarb, Please Come Home (1964), TCF. *Shirley McClaine, Peter Ustinov, Richard Crenna.* SP: William Peter Blatty. See *Protocol* (1984). SHEIKHS, MAIDENS

Not only does a bumbling oil-rich sheikh lust after the US heroine, he tries to defeat Notre Dame's football team. University officials found this lampoon of their team so insulting, they sued in court. No Arabs, however, attempted to sue producers for the gross caricatures and mocking of Islam.

Scene: Wrong-Way Goldfarb (Crenna), a Jewish U-2 pilot en route to the Soviet Union, mistakenly lands his jet in Sheikh Fawz's (Ustinov) desert kingdom. A reporter named Jenny (Maclaine) joins him. She's out to get the "inside story" on the Arab country. The sheikh spots Jenny and tries to seduce her.

• Giggling maidens snuggle Fawz; he collects them in "shipments." Mumbling gibberish, the ruler drives about the palace in his rocket-shaped sports car. And, he steers a miniature train "made of pure gold." Observing his antics, an owl and a pelican.

• Why do state department officials tolerate dimwitted Fawz's behavior? Because a US "air base [there] is vital to the free world's security." The sheikh will allow the US to have the base, provided Notre Dame's football team travels to his country. Barks Fawz, "We must buy that [Notre Dame] team." Counters Goldfarb, "They're not for sale."

• Shocked, Jenny exclaims, "An Ayrab football team?" Well, why not? Miami's inventive Joe Robbie Stadium is named after the team's former owner, Arab-American Joe Robbie. Two splendid Arab-American NFL quarterbacks are Jeff George and Doug Flutie. And, Denver Broncos' Brian Habib, is a formidable lineman.

• Speaking broken English like a screen Arab, Fawz's son confesses he was ousted from Notre Dame. "I no make [football] team. I not Irish. They not want Arab."

• In the desert, the sheikh's men prepare to play the Notre Dame team, constructing a football field. Fawz approaches Goldfarb, saying, "a good Jewish bedouin" like you is needed to put together an Arab team that will defeat the fighting Irish. On the field, the ruler's clumsy Arabs bump into each other. When told Goldfarb will coach them, they bow. Quips Jenny, "Run it [the football] up the minaret and see who bows to Mecca."

• The players stumble; harem maidens function as cheerleaders; the sheikh smiles.

• The night before the game. Burlesque bellydancers perform for the Notre Dame players. Jenny opts to fix an Arab victory, serving the Irish "stuffed mongoose."

• The game. Rushing onto the field, goats, camels and Arabs clad in flowing red thobes. Cut to the Irish players clutching their aching stomachs.

• State department officials will do anything to secure the air base—even cheat. Instead of penalizing the Arabs for foul play, the US referee, a government plant, penalizes the Irish.

• The Arabs try to employ a "stupid double-hump formation." The Arabs stumble, allowing the Irish to be in scoring position. Abruptly, the call to prayer is announced; the game temporarily ceases.

• The final seconds. The "broad," Jenny, defeats the Irish. Jenny dresses as an Arab player and scores the winning touchdown. Though the Irish tackle her a few yards from the goal line, up gushes a great spout of oil; the black liquid lifts Jenny into the end zone.

Journey Beneath the Desert (1961), a.k.a. L'Atlantide, Compagnia Cinematografica. Italy-France. Dubbed in English. *Haya Harareet, Jean Louis Trintignant, Amedeo Nazzari, Giulia Rubini, Jean Maria Volonte.* EP: Nat Wachsberger. SP & D: Edgar G. Ulmer. MAIDENS, SHEIKHS

Arabs vs. Arabs, vs. Westerners. An Arab woman prefers a Western man to a gracious sheikh. A movie first: A nuclear explosion terminates Arabs.

Scene: The Sahara. Aboard a Delaware-Sudan Mining Company helicopter, three mining engineers: Pierre (Trintignant), John, and Robert. The men spot Sheikh Tamal's (Nazzari) camel caravan advancing toward an "atomic explosion area." But a raging sandstorm prevents them from warning the nomads. Some of Tamal's serfs try to run away. The sheikh's cohort whips and beats some, killing others.

• A violent rainstorm causes the chopper to crash. The three engineers spot Tamal drowning; they save him. The sheikh guides them to a safe place, a cavern that connects to the legendary city of Atlantis. Surprisingly, the city "did not sink into the sea." Unfortunately, it rests in the middle of a nuclear testing zone.

• The men enter the throne rooms of Antinea (Harareet), the last Queen of Atlantis. Cunning Queen Antinea, who is enveloped by robed attendants and veiled maidens, cautions Pierre and his friends, "No man has ever left Atlantis alive."

• A benevolent maiden, Zinah (Rubini), attends a wounded engineer. Earlier, Zinah was captured by the queen's men. Meanwhile, Antinea seduces Robert. Tamal expresses anger; the queen tells him that his lovemaking is too child-like.

• In the dungeon, the queen's henchman Tarath (Volonte) fatally tortures one engineer, John. Armed with rifles and machine-guns, the queen's cohorts also torture Robert and Max, an atomic plant employee. The men fight back, shooting scores of guards. They escape to the river and machine-gun even more Arabs. When Tarath moves to shoot Robert, Tamal kills him, taking Robert prisoner.

• Back at the palace, Antinea insists Robert love her. He refuses, dying in his cell.

• Aware that an A-bomb will soon be dropped over Atlantis, Tamal helps Zinah and Pierre to escape. The couple can save themselves provided they reach the safety perimeter in time, which they do.

• Stock footage. BOOM!—A mushroom cloud igniting the sky. Boulders from the blast crush all denizens of Atlantis, including Queen Antinea and Sheikh Tamal.

Journey into Fear (1975), NWP. *Sam Waterston, Vincent Price, Yvette Mimieux.* CAMEOS, VILLAINS

An shifty Arab pretends to be a "good" Arab.

Scene: Aboard a passenger ship, an American geologist (Waterson) meets an Arab "archeologist [Price] investigating pre-Islamic cultures." Says the Arab, "I think perhaps I should explain. I am an Arab. A good Arab. I am not a terrorist. I do not like war and I bear no animosity towards the Jews." The Arab points to some other passengers, purring, "The American lady and her English husband at the next table are Jewish. They objected to eating with what they called the 'terrorist.' So, they insulted me and moved... If your sympathies are the same," he tells the American, "I would suggest you move now."

• Later, a French woman scolds the American, "Why did you not eat dinner with us? Why did you eat with that smelly old Ayrab?" Believing the Arab is a decent chap, the geologist counters the woman's slur.

Finis: The American learns that the archeologist is not "a good Arab." Rather, the man's real name is Muller—a hired assassin. Muller's assignment? To kill the American!

Judith (1966), a.k.a. Conflict, PAR. *Sophia Loren, Hans Verner, Peter Finch, Jack Hawkins.* SP: John Michel Hayes. S: Lawrence Durrell. Filmed in Israel. PALESTINIANS

Opening frames establish a familiar theme—Nazis and Arabs vs. Israelis. Stock footage of WWII displays German tanks advancing. Fast forward, 1948. Cut to an Israeli declaring, "We are not after [ex-general] Schiller (Verner), the Nazi war criminal; we are after Schiller, the Arab tank expert." Israelis ascertain that Gustav Schiller's is now in Syria advising the Syrian army; they fear Schiller's Syrians will attack Israel; the "Arab tanks will move in."

• A kibbutz on the Syrian border, 1948. Judith (Loren), an Austrian refugee, arrives. Soon, Judith, along with an Israeli mother and her son, take a stroll. Suddenly, an explosion, followed by flames. Palestinians wearing kuffiyehs shoot at the Israelis.

• Judith tells the kibbutz leader, Aaron (Finch), "You seem to have won the fight." Barks Aaron, "If we hadn't, you'd be lying with your throat cut by now." Judith is told that the "Arabs are using heavy tanks," and that Schiller, her ex-husband who betrayed her during World War II, "is teaching them how to use them." Judith decides to help the Haganah find Schiller.

• Says an Israeli officer, "Here we are, one small new nation with one small army, ill-equipped, surrounded by six armies, all very well equipped." (In reality, the Israeli forces in 1948 were well-armed and well-equipped.)

• In Damascus, Aaron tells his Israeli team, "If we are caught we'll be lucky to be shot." Not to worry. Anti-Syrian Arabs wearing thobes and headdresses assist Aaron, enabling the Israelis to nab Schiller.

• Back at the kibbutz, Arab hordes attack. Jewish women and children rush to safety. The Arabs have 1,000 soldiers, a couple of tanks and one plane. Yet, the vastly outnumbered Israelis force the Arabs to retreat. Afterwards, Judith converts, becoming a Jew.

Note: Writes Patricia Erens: "As in *Exodus* and other films set in this period, the enemy is the British, not the Arabs."[97] Not true. Films of the 1960s, such as this one, *Exodus*, and *Cast a Giant Shadow* (1966), show Israelis killing scores of Arabs.

• Though Palestinian-Israeli scenarios show Palestinians and other Arabs killing Israeli innocents, I have never seen a movie showing Israeli soldiers/extremists killing Palestinian innocents.

Juggernaut (1937), Grand National. *Boris Karloff.* D: Henry Edwards. CAMEO

This film concerns a reputable doctor (Karloff) intent on continuing his research. Featured for three minutes are Arab hagglers.

Opening scenes reveal a Moroccan souk; Arab music underscores the action. Cut to Arabs leading a donkey and a camel. Cut to two Arabs, dickering. Argues Arab #1: "Ten shillings. I give you ten shillings. No more." Arab #2 agrees on the price, then abruptly changes his mind, exclaiming, "Ten shillings? Ten shillings is too much... I'll give you six-pence."

The Jungle Princess (1920), WB. Silent. *Juanita Hansen.* VILLAINS

Arabs kidnap Lola, a blonde jungle princess, three Americans, a millionaire, "a fighting Irishman," and a "fighting Missionary." Arabs as non-whites.

Scene: In the jungle, "a roving band of jungle bandits (Arabs)" seize Princess Lola (Hansen), whisking her off to "Kabul's camp." Implying that his Arabs are not white, Kabul, the "trader," advises his men to be wary of "whites" trying to rescue Lola. "Whites are our enemies," he says, "[they] must be disposed of."

• The camera reveals the imprisoned Lola. On screen, this caption: "Morning has its horrors."

• Posing as an Arab, Jack Warren, an American millionaire, enters Kabul's camp. At Warren's side is Pat O'Malley, "a fighting Irishman." They rescue Lola.

• Suddenly, some tigers attack the Arabs. Quips O'Malley, "Well, between the two murdering gangs, I'm for the tigers."

Finis: O'Malley, Warren, and Joe Horton, "the fighting Missionary," liquidate Kabul's Arabs.

Justine (1969), TCF. *Anouk Aimee, Dirk Bogarde, John Vernon, Michael York, Robert Forster, Anna Karina.* Adapted from Lawrence Durrell's *Alexandria Quartet.* Filmed in Tunisia. EGYPTIANS

An anti-Muslim soap opera, with camels. Pre-World War II Alexandria, circa 1938. Egyptian Christians slander Egyptian Muslims. Egypt's Christians and Jews smuggle arms to Jewish "terrorists in Palestine." Children are victims and ragamuffins. Dialogue and images denigrate Islam. The film reflects the novelist Philip Sanford Marden's 1912 view: "The truth is that the present Egyptian people, both the Mohammedan and Coptic, are by education and temperament unfit to administer a government of their own."[98]

Scene: At a seedy club, Egyptians stuff bills inside bellydancers' outfits. Cut to repulsive Egyptian children tormenting Melissa (Karina), a benevolent Greek dancer.

• Presenting Justine (Aimee), a lovely, libidinous Jewish woman married to a wealthy Christian Egyptian banker, Nessim (Vernon). She visits a seedy den; here Egyptian orphans are temporarily sheltered, then sold. "New kids are slipped into here every few months"; Egyptian men are to blame, says the guardian. The men kidnap little girls and turn them into "prostitutes."

• In the desert, Nessim's brother, Narouz (Forster), defies deceitful bedouins, even threatening one. "My people [Christians] tell me you stole these guns," he says. "Tell me the truth." When the bedouin lies, Narouz pulls a knife and cuts off the man's ear. "Every day I'll cut a piece of your flesh," warns Narouz, "until we come to the true part, the part that doesn't lie."

• When Narouz finds out that his brother Nessim is smuggling guns to "[Jewish] terrorists in Palestine," he shouts, "Guns that would keep us [Coptic Christians] alive, you send to the Jews in Palestine?!"

• During a church meeting, Coptic Christians discuss whether they should try to defend themselves against Egypt's radical Muslims. Nessim fears that because of Narouz's anti-Muslim rhetoric, he could be killed. He tells Narouz to leave for Switzerland. Worried that "some Muslim general" would steal his home, Narouz stays in Egypt.

• Trying to save Narouz's life, Nessim visits Pasha, a Muslim leader. Swiftly, Nessim places money inside the Holy Koran; the Pasha snatches the holy book, purring, "I have examined the Koran; it will find an honored place in my library." But, the money fails to placate the Pasha. He tells Nessim Narouz's safety can be guaranteed only if Justine, Nessim's wife, comes to him. Not for prayers, for sex. And never on Tuesdays. "On Tuesdays," says the Pasha, "we hang our criminals from the branches."

• Nessim's residence. Pasha exits his limousine, entering Justine's room. Aware that Justine will sleep with the Muslim, Darley (York) screams, "Selling yourself to that ape!" The slur stands. Earlier, soft, romantic music underscored Justine's bedroom alliances with Darley, the Irishman, and her amour with Pursewarden (Bogarde), the Englishman. This time, however, ominous musical chords imply that sex with an Egyptian Muslim is most unpleasant.

• Apparently, to maintain peaceful alliances between Egypt's Christians and Muslims, several Copts are obliged to kill the "mad" Narouz.

• The British attaché, Pursewarden, refuses to believe an intelligence report stating there is "a conspiracy among the Coptic Christians," that Egypt's Christians support the Jews in Palestine against the British. "The Coptic Christians," says the shocked Pursewarden, "are the only chums we imperialists really have."

• Pursewarden finds out that his Coptic "chums" are indeed sending "sophisticated weapons to butcher John Bull." As a result, "British lads [are] dropping dead all over Palestine." Pursewarden does not say a word about Palestinians being terminated, routed from their homes.

Dialogue: Egyptians as non-Arabs? The movie contends Nessim is a half-breed; though his mother was "Egyptian," his father was an "Arab."

Note: Disrespectful "Moslems" burn "churches." In his diary, Darley, the Irish school teacher, writes that Egyptian civil war is "moments away... If the British were to leave, the Christian minority would be at the mercy of millions of Moslems."

Kazaam (1996), TOU. A Paul M. Glaser film. *Shaquille O'Neal, Francis Capra, Marshal Manesh, Fawn Reed, Anthony Ferar, Juan Gabriel Reynoso, Randal J. Bosley.* S: Glaser. EP: O'Neal. VILLAINS

Americans of Arab heritage appear as gluttonous, greedy gangsters. They brutalize innocents, notably, an American teenager.

Scene: Wearing a flashy Arab costume, the 3,000-year-old genie Kazaam (O'Neal) emerges from a boom box and befriends young Max (Capra). After offering the teenager three wishes, Kazaam tells Max, "I'm your genie... if you've got the itches for a soak of riches." Presto, Arab music gives way to rap. Then, Kazaam delivers enough "junk food" to fill a room.

• Thirty minutes into the film the camera reveals a nightclub. In the background, a neon sign, with nonsensical Arabic lettering. The club's owner? Mr. Malik (Manesh), the movie's one and only readily identifiable ethnic villain. In Arabic, Malik means "owner." The gluttonous Malik, who wears a gold chain, operates as a black marketer. He sits with a stereotypical blonde. Nearby, his aides, Hassem (Ferar) and El-Baz (Bosley). Both Arab-Americans need shaves. Malik spots Kazaam conjuring up gold nuggets and exclaims, "I am really interested in this man."

• Malik tells the African-American heroine Asia (Reed), "I was raised to be interested in everything," notably the business of "pirating [audio] tapes and CD's." Malik intends to market, illegally, a music recording "worth a million dollars." But before Malik can cash in on the "hot tape," Max steals the million-dollar tape, delivering it to fellow teens. Malik confronts Max's father, Nick, who is also in on the deal.

• Ensconced in his limo, the greedy Malik offers Kazaam a plateful of "goat's eyes." Kazaam grimaces. Malik digests the "eyes" as a pig swallows dung.

• Tagged "The Sultan of Sand," Kazaam performs at Malik's club. Cut to Hassem, El-Baz and Foad (Reynoso), slugging Nick's friend. Arab music underscores the violence. Unless Max returns the tape, warns Malik, Nick and his pal will wind up "at the bottom of the lake."

• Malik's club. Again, ominous Arab music. Sitting at a table covered with Arab cuisine, Malik flings food into his mouth. Next, he fingers worry beads, ordering Nick, "I want to talk with you about your son."

• The slobbering Malik kisses Kazaam, purring, "You are the Sultan's gold." Cut to Malik's goons stealing the genie's magical boom box.

• Appearing inside a warehouse are Nick, Max, as well as Malik and his henchmen. Shouts Malik, "I've got the [magical boom] box!" Next, Malik insists that Max make this wish: "Malik to have all the money in the world!" If you refuse, says Malik, "your beloved father will die!" Max hesitates, telling Malik, "If you do that... everyone else will be broke." Malik laughs.

• Hassem and El-Baz close in on the protagonists; Nick slugs them. Abruptly, Malik tosses Max down a deep shaft. Thinking Malik has killed Max, Kazaam acts. The genie overpowers the villains. He turns Malik into a bouncing ball. And, then he tosses Malik-as-ball into a trash bin.

• Fortunately, Kazaam revives Max, telling the boy, "The power is in your heart." Freed from captivity, Kazaam becomes human and dates Asia, the heroine.

Note: See *Aladdin* (1992). Disney's heroic genies never resemble heroic Arabs. In *Aladdin,* the animated blue genie functions as a McDonald's Happy Meal toy. In

Kazaam, kids link the genie's heroics with the L.A. Lakers' center, Shaquille O' Neal. At the same time *Kazaam* was released, audiences could also see Shaq performing on the American Dream Team at Atlanta's 1996 Summer Olympics.

Khartoum (1966), UA. *Charlton Heston, Laurence Olivier.* Filmed in Egypt.
See the *Four Feathers* films. VILLAINS, RECOMMENDED

In 1965, a year prior to the Arab-Israeli Six-Day War, producer Julian Blaustein told NYT critic Vincent Canby that while he was in Egypt filming *Khartoum,* he "was never aware of anti-Semitism." Adding, "I suppose I will never be able to say that back in Beverly Hills" (11 January 1966).

Facts mixed in with fiction. Turbaned Sudanese forces kill British troops and fez-wearing Egyptians. This sweeping historical epic dramatizes the rivalry between British General Charles Gordon (Heston) and Sudan's Mohammed Ahmed (Olivier), an articulate Muslim leader claiming to be the Mahdi. The time, 1880s Sudan, leading up to the siege of Khartoum.

Scene: The Sudan. Boasts the Mahdi, "I'm the expected one, the true Mahdi." (Mahdi means the expected Messiah or the Divine Guide to Salvation). Actor Laurence Olivier, who portrays the Mahdi, speaks with an Indian accent, not an Arab one.

• Responsible for safely removing thousands of British and Egyptians out of Khartoum, is General Gordon. The general believes the Mahdi's men are no match for the British, as they are "armed only with spears and swords."

• Gordon, who dons a red fez with his white uniform, is embraced by Khartoum's Egyptians. Says Sheikh Ali, "We must drink coffee." Sighs Gordon, "It's good to be home." Gordon greets the cheering crowd; he picks up a flower girl, carrying her in his arms. [See *55 Days at Peking* (1963). Here, Heston lifts and carries a Chinese girl.] One Sudanese leader opposes the Mahdi; he also refuses to support Gordon, as the general executed his son.

• The Mahdi's tent. Gordon is told: "The Prophet [Mohammed] speaks to the Mahdi. He has asked me to make Holy War." Warns the Mahdi, "Everyone in Khartoum who opposes the will of Mohammed will die... If Khartoum is sacrificed, all in Islam will tremble and bow." The Mahdi vows to lay siege to Khartoum; "all those who do not accept him" will die.

• In some ways, the Mahdi and Gordon are alike. Both are religious, God-fearing men. When discussing Christianity and Islam, the Mahdi asks, "Is there a difference?" Says Gordon, "I seem to suffer from the illusion that I have a monopoly on God." Cut to Gordon studying the Bible, the Mahdi reading the Koran.

• Gordon tells the Mahdi, "We are so alike, you and I." Pleads the Mahdi, "You are not my enemy. Why should your blood sweeten the Nile?" The men are unable to reach an agreement. Abruptly, the Mahdi's white-robed Sudanese tribesmen charge Khartoum, killing Gordon and his soldiers. Before dying, Gordon tells the Mahdi, "I may die of your miracle, but you will surely die of mine."

Note: In fact, history reveals that the Mahdi's 50,000 Sudanese forces did take Khartoum; they defeated Gordon. The British general was killed in the battle in January 1885. Ironically, the Mahdi died the same year. Though British and Egyptian forces were forced to withdraw from Khartoum, in 1899 they returned, taking over the country. That same year, Egypt and Britain signed an agreement establishing joint sovereignty over the territory. Not until January 1, 1956, did Sudan finally became an independent republic.

A Kid in Aladdin's Palace (1997), Trimark. *Rhona Mitra, James Faulkner, Nicholas Irons, Thomas Ian Nicholas, Taylor Negron, Aharon Ipale.* SP: Michael Part. Filmed in Tunisia. VILLAINS

This children's film pits Arabs against Arabs. An American youth functions as Lawrence of Arabia.

Scene: Aladdin (Ipale) hides the magic lamp inside the "cave of wonders." Meanwhile, his bearded "bonehead brother," Luxor (Faulkner), displays a magic ring, unleashing a wicked spell: "the sleep of a thousand deaths." Unless Aladdin reveals the lamp's location, Luxor vows to kill him.

• A pizza parlor in Reseda, California. Abruptly, the lamp genie (Negron) appears, whisking off to Basra, Iraq, the young protagonist Calvin (Nicholas). On seeing Calvin, Basra's queen exclaims, "Allah works in mysterious ways. If the boy [Calvin] is to deliver us, so be it." Once Calvin is tagged "the deliverer," he begins matching wits with Luxor and his saber-wielding cohorts. The teenager also falls for Princess Schehrazade, and vice versa.

• Calvin dons harem garb; Hassem, a dense Arab, makes a pass at him. Calvin smashes a jug over Hassem's head. Next, Calvin dumps two thugs into large vats of dye.

• The desert, en route to the cave of wonders. Linking up with Calvin and the princess are Ali Baba (Irons) and his three thieves—"Hummus," "Couscous," and "Bob," short for "Kabob."

• Suddenly, the "Guardians of the Dead" charge the protagonists. Only fire can terminate these white-robed bandits. Calvin acts! He places a lighted torch behind a camel's rear. The camel farts, releasing gas, which ignites the flame. Presto. The Guardians are terminated.

• Inside the cave of wonders, Luxor snatches the lamp, entrapping Calvin Inc. As Calvin acts courageously, freeing the group, the reformed Ali Baba places a white turban on the youth's head, saying, "You are my brother." Asked whether he can snatch the lamp back from evil Luxor, Calvin quips, "That's why I'm here, to make the impossible, possible."

• Luxor takes off, magic lamp in hand, on a flying horse. Cut to Calvin Inc. bringing down Luxor's black-robed guards. Calvin mounts a magic carpet, chasing the villain. Mid-air, they duel. Calvin triumphs, dumping Luxor into a pile of camel dung. Employing the lamp genie, Aladdin awakens.

• All ends well. The genie whisks Calvin back to Reseda's pizza parlor. Calvin asks a customer for a date. When she declines, Calvin feels depressed. Not for long. Outside, awaiting Calvin, is the smiling princess. They skip onto the magic carpet and fly off together.

Kid Millions (1934), UA. *Eddie Cantor, Paul Harvey, Warren Hymer, Eve Sully, Jesse Block, Doris Davenport, George Murphy* (in his motion picture debut). EGYPTIANS, MAIDENS

Simple-minded Egyptians are denuded of their heritage. They are no match for one bright street-wise kid from New York—Cantor. While in Egypt to claim his father's treasures, Cantor outwits a dense Arab sheikh intent on murdering him. He also eludes the grasp of an inane Egyptian princess craving marriage.

Scene: As soon as New Yorkers Eddie (Cantor) and Louis (Hymer) arrive in Alexandria, Louis moves to snatch Eddie's $77 million-dollar fortune, left to Eddie by his late father, a 77-year-old Egyptologist. Louis boats to a cohort, "See those [Egyptian] mugs over there. Well, I got it all fixed with those four boys to drag him [Eddie] up an alley and cut him up into a lot of itsy- bitsy pieces."

• In the souk, a pretender's "big trick"; he changes a boy into a dog.

• Dimwitted Princess Fanya (Sully) sucks a lollipop without first removing the paper. The dense princess thinks a barking dog is a bear.

• Fanya's father, Sheikh Mulhulla (Harvey), has "a mere 125 wives." Mulhulla's brother, who once traded a camel for a redhead, has "a mere 30." Mulhulla vows to boil "the infidel" Eddie in oil, boasting, "He'll make fine soup for the camels." Says the sheikh, Eddie's father was an "American dog" who dared ravage my ancestors' tomb.

• Eddie is obliged to kiss Princess Fanya. After the smooch Fanya declares they must wed. Eddie prefers boiling oil. "Go away [Fanya]," he screams, "I can't talk to an idiot."

• Eddie dumps Fanya into a pool, saying, "I like the sheikh; I like his daughter. But I prefer her under water." Eddie yearns for "his gal in Brooklyn," Toots (Davenport). Fortunately for Eddie, Fanya opts to embrace Ben Ali (Block), a fellow Egyptian.

• Mulhulla and Fanya chase after Eddie and his pals. The Americans hide in a tomb area, don mummy masks, then bellow orders to the Egyptians. Believing the "voices" he hears are those of his ancestors, the frightened Sheikh Mulhulla allows Eddie Inc. to depart Egypt with all the treasures.

• Back in New York, Eddie uses his Egyptian loot to open up "a free ice cream factory for kids."

Killing Streets (1991), Israfilm Ltd. A Menachem Golan Production.
Michael Pare, Lorenzo Lamas, Gabi Amrani, Jennifer Runyon. P: Menachem Golan, Stephen Cornwell. SP: Andrew Deutsch. D: Cornwell. Shot in Israel; Israeli actors as Arabs. PALESTINIANS, WORST LIST

Again, producer Menachem Golan vilifies Palestinians. In Lebanon, US marines and diplomats, plus some Lebanese citizens, crush Palestinians. Four Americans and one Lebanese taxi driver kill dozens of Palestinians belonging to the "Guardians of the Oppressed."

Scene: In Beirut, Arab vs. Arab. Off-duty marine Captain Craig Grant (Pare) arrives in Lebanon "to secure the release of US hostages." Craig enters his seedy room in the Pyramid Hotel and goes to bed an Arab woman. Suddenly, several men appear. After shooting the hotel clerk, they kill the woman and beat up Craig, taking him hostage.

• Dayton, Ohio, March 1984. Cut to Chris (Pare), Craig's twin brother. Abruptly, Chris, who coaches the high school basketball team, departs for Beirut to find brother Craig.

• Beirut, rubble everywhere. En route to the American embassy, a dense Palestinian harasses Chris. Cut to Lebanese street children with toy guns playing at war; soldiers wearing fatigues clasp weapons. At the Pyramid Hotel, the Arab informer who set up Capt. Craig's kidnapping tells Chris, "I tell no lies, sir. I tell no lies." Chris punches the liar; the inept Arab pulls a knife on Chris, but kills himself.

• Chris kills a Palestinian, is nabbed and taken to a Palestinian camp. Here, brothers Chris and Craig are held hostage. Palestinians move take the beaten, bloodied Chris to a prison cell. Boasts their leader, who once studied in Ohio for his M.B.A., "America has a pretty face but an ugly heart."

• The brothers are whisked off to a fortress-type facility and told that unless the US frees "twenty-three [Palestinian] brothers held in jails," they will die. A US embassy employee tells Chris not to fret, that there's "no problem." There are "three of us, fifty of them." The Americans move to explode barges, free the hostages, and kill the Palestinians.

• Some Lebanese offer to assist. "The war destroyed our country," says a money-grubbing Lebanese. (The Arab never says what war, exactly. And, he fails to say that in 1982 the Israelis bombed and invaded Lebanon, killing and wounding thousands of Lebanese men, women and children.) Chris asks Sharon Ross (Runyon), a US embassy worker, "You trust this [Lebanese] guy?" Says Sharon, "We pay; he delivers." The Lebanese and his cohorts take Sharon hostage. But when Chris threatens them, they return her.

• Posing as Palestinians, Chris's tiny group frees the hostages. And they obliterate more than fifty Palestinians. Declares Gilad (Amrani), a Lebanese cab driver, "This is my country. Our people must find the courage to say 'no more.'"

• A Palestinian youth is told to kill Capt. Craig; he refuses, Palestinians shoot the boy. Chris enters the frame. He rescues brother, Craig, then kills the youth's assassin.

Note: All-too-often, Israeli producers Golan and Globus [*The Delta Force* (1986), *Operation Thunderbolt* (1977), *American Ninja 4: The Annihilation* (1991)] show heinous Muslim Arabs as anti-Christian, anti-Jewish, religious fanatics who kill Americans, Europeans, and Israelis. Their repetitive and repulsive images serve to stimulate audiences' outbursts of hatred against Arabs.

• Writer Deutsch also penned *Delta Force 3: The Killing Game* (1991).

King Cowboy (1928), FBO Pic. Silent. *Tom Mix, Sally Blane, Frank Leigh, Wynn Mace.* *NS. Notes from AFIC. See *Jericho* (1937). VILLAINS, SHEIKHS

In "El Kubla," Sheikh Abdul's "avaricious" Arabs kidnap Jim and Polly Randall. Cowboy Tom Mix rides to the rescue. But the Arabs nab and imprison Mix. Not for long. The cowboy escapes, and frees the American couple. "Abdul is killed in the confusion." El Kubla's "grateful populace elect" Tom Mix their "new Emir." Mix weds Polly.

Note: *King Cowboy*, a lost film, may be procured from an Austrian film center for about $200. Author Robert S. Birchard recalls seeing "a coming attraction trailer [for it]. The trailer shows Arabs in more-or-less traditional garb, chasing Mix. But the trailer does not really offer any clues as to how the Arab characters were depicted," says Birchard.[99]

King of Kings (1961), MGM. *Jeffrey Hunter.* SP: *Philip Yordan.* A remake of *The King of Kings* (1927). CAMEOS, VILLAINS

In this film about Jesus, the narrator (Orson Welles) falsely states the Roman-appointed leader who slaughters the movie's Jews, Herod the Great, was an "Arab." Significantly, Herod is not falsely labeled an "Arab" in the 1927 silent film, *The King of Kings*.

Scene: Opening frames, Roman soldiers kill scores of Jews. Explains the narrator, "The Jews went to the slaughter." The camera reveals the villain persecuting the Jews, wicked King Herod. Adds the narrator, "Caesar could find no Jew to press Rome's laws on this fallen land... so Caesar named one, Herod the Great, an Arab of the Bedouin tribe as the new, false, and mellifluent King of the Jews." (There is no tribe called "Bedouin." Bedouin simply means "desert dweller.")

• "Herod," intones the narrator, "planted evil seeds from which the forests of Roman crosses grew high on Jerusalem's hills and Herod the Great... made the forests multiply." During the narration, oppressed Jews haul huge wooden poles up hills. Cut to Herod, smiling. Cut to crucified Jewish victims, fixed on crosses. Again, Herod smiles. The camera reveals hundreds of Jewish corpses, stacked like firewood. One body is tossed atop another. As a torch ignites the corpses, Herod smiles.

• A Roman soldier balks at "murdering children"; Herod insists that the Roman start "slaughtering the innocents of Bethlehem."

Note: Writes theologian Father James Swift: "Herod [born about 73 BC] was no 'Arab of the Bedouin tribe.' He was an Idumean, son of the Antipater whose own father, in turn, had been forcibly converted to Judaism during the reign of John Hyrcanus. Grandson of an Edomite proselyte, Herod was a full Jew according to the law [although not qualified to reign]. Herod may have been hated by the Jews, but it was not for ethnic reasons. The politics of his pro-Roman allegiance and his enthusiasm for Greek culture were reason enough for Jews to view him as a destroyer of the tradition."[100]

• The Roman Catholic Legion of Decency advised Catholics not to see the 1927 film.

King of the Wild (1931), Mascot. 12 episodes. *Walter Miller, Nora Lane, Carroll Nye, Boris Karloff.* CLIFFHANGERS, VILLAINS

Arabs vs. Africans, vs. Americans.

Scene: "Rampur," the Algerian desert. Disguised as an Arab, the on-the-run American protagonist, Robert Grant (Miller), seeks sanctuary in Muriel's (Lane) hotel room. Perceiving Grant to be an Arab, the frightened Muriel demands he leave. Pleads Grant, "Trust me." Muriel goes to call for help. Exclaims Grant, "I'm an American." The much-relieved, Muriel allows Grant to stay.

• Evil Mustapha (Karloff), moves to find a hidden diamond mine. Mustapha kidnaps Muriel's brother Tom (Nye). Next, the Arab kills an African chief. And, Mustapha's cohorts incite the "natives" to riot.

• Arabs nab and imprison Muriel. Not for long. She punches the Arab woman guard, dons Arab garb and runs off.

Finis: Grant and Muriel bring down Mustapha and his henchmen, preventing them from acquiring the "vast diamond fields."

Dialogue: Angry Mustapha tells an aide, "Rid the jungle of this dangerous beast (a ferocious tiger) or the wrath of Allah be on your head."

• Most actors portraying Arabs speak broken English.

King of the Wind (1989), MIR. *Frank Finlay, Jenny Agutter, Glenda Jackson, Richard Harris, Ian Richardson, Nigel Hawthorne, Navin Chowdhry.*
SHEIKHS, RECOMMENDED

An Arab boy and his adopted father appear as victims. Europeans beat up bedouins, and abuse a mute boy. Arabs revere Islam.

Scene: North Africa, 1727. The sun rises on a bedouin desert camp; Arabic-speaking men huddle around a pregnant mare. After her colt is born, a mute youth, Acba (Chowdhry), befriends the animal. Explains the boy's adopted father, Achmet (Hawthorne), this colt will be "a gift from our people to the "Bey of Tunis" (Richardson). Achmet notices a white spot on the colt's leg, saying, "This is a sign of Allah's blessing." The Arabs name the colt "Shams," meaning the sun.

• Achmet and young Acba deliver some horses into the Bey's courtyard stables. "The bedouin tribes," Achmet tells the Bey, offer you this "gift of horses."

• Inside the palace, Arab musicians and dancers entertain. The Bey asks Acba a question; the youth does not respond. Explains Achmet, "The boy is mute." The compassionate Bey tells Acba, "Allah grant that through your silence may come wisdom."

• Two years pass. The Arabs return to the palace. The Bey opts to send the young stallion, Shams, to France, allowing Acba to accompany Shams. "May the protection of Allah, the merciful, the compassionate, go with you," says the Bey. Unlike most screen potentates, the Bey functions as a kind, wise ruler.

• Aboard the ship, Achmet discovers that European crewmen are stealing foodstuffs intended for the horses. He tells Acba, "This is not the grain we brought with us; it's full of maggots. They have our good grain in their hold." Adding, "You've been like a son to me, Acba, ever since you were a little boy and your parents were lost in the desert."

• On deck, Acba prays. A Frenchman tags him "a heathen [and] a little Arab rascal." A "good" French sailor intervenes, defending the youth.

• Achmet confronts the ship's captain about the stolen grain; the Frenchman calls the Arab, "You filthy scurvy." Then, the captain grabs a truncheon, delivering a fatal blow to the elderly Arab's head.

• After the ship arrives at La Havre, France, Acba and stricken horse, Shams, are taken to the "Palace of Versailles." At the palace, His Majesty takes a liking to Acba, asking, "Perhaps he could be a riding companion for me." Protests the Lord Cardinal, "That would not be advisable. Your Majesty cannot be seen to associate with an [Arab]."

• Assigned to kitchen duties, Acba befriends a French chef and a blacksmith; he also nurses Shams back to health.

• The chef sends Acba off to the marketplace to buy goods. En route, French youths attack Acba. The boys take the chef's money and run off with Shams. The angry chef thinks Acba is a thief, and fires him.

• An Englishman, Edward Coke (Finlay), spots a Frenchman abusing the displaced Acba and whipping Shams. As Edward loves horses, he whisks Acba and Shams off to his estate. Here, Acba befriends Edward's daughter, Hannah (Agutter). She teaches "Acba to write English."

• Edward wages that Shams will defeat an English squire's top horse. Acba grasps the reins; Shams wins. Next, Edward intends to race Shams at Newmarket.

• Unexpectedly, Edward dies. The bank repossesses his home; Hannah departs. As for Acba and Shams, they are sold to the not-so-nice Williams family. Mrs. Williams slaps

Acba in the face, shouting "Arabian." When her son, Rusty, dumps water on Acba, Shams acts, kicking the bully. Rusty suffers only has a minor head wound. Yet, Acba is falsely accused of nearly killing Rusty; the Arab is dispatched to Newgate prison.

• Hannah convinces an Earl to free Acba and to acquire Shams. "So, this is the Arab boy," says the Earl, "and the Arabian horse you brought."

• At the Earl's stables, Shams mates with a valued white mare. But, Shams disables, permanently, the Earl's prize horse. Forced to leave the estate, Acba rebuilds a damaged hut and cultivates a garden. As a friendly English stable boy provides supplies, Acba survives the winter.

• Finally, the Earl permits Acba to return to his estate. Thanks to Shams, the white mare gives birth to Lath, a superb race horse offering the Earl "hope for the future."

• The Newmarket Race; Queen Catherine and King George in attendance. The horses are off. When Lath falters against the French entry, Acba swings into action. He mounts Shams; they gallop alongside Lath, inspiring the Arabian to finish first.

• Lath's victory brings the Earl needed funds. As for Acba and Shams, they remain on the Earl's estate. Lath is tagged: "the Godolphin Arabian, the first of a line which included some of the most famous horses in racing history."

King Richard and the Crusaders (1954), WB. *Rex Harrison, Virginia Mayo, Lawrence Harvey, George Sanders.* Based on *The Talisman* by Sir Walter Scott. BEST LIST

Arab Muslim heroics. Saladin (Harrison) as a chivalrous leader.

Scene: 1191, Jaffa. King Richard (Sanders) and his knights of the third crusade prepare to invade "Jerusalem and win back the Holy Land."

• Saladin questions why Richard's Christians refer to the Prince of Peace, yet "crusade with the sword."

• Posing as a doctor, Saladin enters Richard's tent and heals the seriously wounded king. Richard's colleagues, Sir Giles Amaury and the Marquis Montferrat, are the villains responsible for Richard's illness.

• Richard thanks the physician, offering gold. Says Saladin, "I accept no gold for Allah's wishes." Richard's friend, Sir Kenneth (Harvey), tells Saladin, "This is chivalry. For one enemy who has never seen the other. My Richard holds your Saladin in equal esteem."

• Lady Edith (Mayo) intends to make a desert pilgrimage. "We shall be quite safe," she says; "Saladin is a man of chivalry." Affirms Richard, "That's true. Saladin directs no attacks on shrines and pilgrims."

• Christians and Muslims prepare to engage in some major battles. Instead of waging war, Saladin, "master of the arts of desert warfare," proposes a one-on-one contest, offering to duel Sir Kenneth. "Total victory goes to the better man," says Saladin. They duel; Saladin wins.

• The triumphant Saladin spares Sir Kenneth, saying, "Peace. Peace. This is a word that everyone should know in every tongue." Next, he invites Sir Kenneth "to share the waters of the oasis." Later, Richard wounds Sir Kenneth. Saladin intervenes, saving the young knight's life.

• Saladin prefers Lady Edith to the "women of Islam." With Edith at his side he intends to create "a world, at least, where beliefs can meet in understanding." Saladin's quest, to "bring eternal peace to east and west." And, "If the Lady goes to him it must be of her own free choice. She will retain her own religion."

• Playing the lute, Saladin sings love songs. Though Lady Edith is touched by Saladin's proposal, she "can never love any man but Sir Kenneth." Saladin understands; "It is a wise man who knows what is not his," he says.

• Austrians, French, and British crusaders battle fellow Europeans and Arab Muslims. Sir Giles, who earlier nearly killed Richard, kidnaps Lady Edith.

• Inside a tent, Saladin's men pray. Giles and his men sneak in, pull their daggers, and stab praying Arabs in the back. Giles' brutal tactics, admits Sir Kenneth, lead to "the persecution of Moslems who do not even bear arms."

• In time, Saladin and his Arabs save Lady Edith from Sir Giles' clutches.

Note: Saladin, the great twelfth-century Muslim commander, was a man of chivalry and honor. His campaigns, note his chroniclers, were waged without bloodshed or hatred. After he liberated Jerusalem from the Crusaders in 1187, impoverished European prisoners were freed without ransom; "widows and orphans were allowed to leave and were offered gifts."[101]

• Most movies do not reveal that in several crusades between the years 1096 and 1270, European rulers and their troops raped and raided their way into the Holy Land and Jerusalem. In *St. Francis and the Foolishness of God*, the invading Christians are described as brutal aggressors. Explain the authors, "The crusades were ruthless, characterized by the plunder and slaughter, not only of Muslims, but also of Jews and any who were considered pagans, including some Christians deemed by the pope to be enemies of the faith." These crusades, say the authors, "constituted a complete reversal of the early Christians' attitude toward war, participation in which was considered inconsistent with gospel ideals... Nowhere in the writings of the early church was violence advocated." But, at "the time of the crusades, in dramatic contrast, *the killings of the Saracens was regarded as a religious act by the Christian church. The crusades were considered a holy war* [emphasis added], commanded and blessed by the church as fulfilling God's purpose on earth. 'Deus vult,' ('God wills it') was the slogan under which the crusaders rallied. Killing was justified by believing the enemy to be less than human; in the words of St. Bernard, 'To kill a Muslim is not homicide.'"[102]

King Solomon's Mines (1985), CAN. *Richard Chamberlin, Sharon Stone, Shai K. Ophir, Herbert Lom, Bob Greer.* P: Menachem Golan, Yoram Globus. CAMEOS, VILLAINS

This Golan-Globus movie shows pro-German Arabs enslaving Africans. Critical of this outlandish 1985 update, Walter Goodman writes in the NYT (23 November 1985), "Can you imagine Deborah Kerr calling somebody a 'cheap-suited camel-jockey?'" Sharon Stone utters the slur, here.

Scene: Arabs and Germans want to nab the heroine's father; the man knows where to find African treasures. Before credits roll, the Arab villain, Kassam (Ophir), "a towel-headed creep" wearing a red fez, plunges steel spikes into a man. Kassam's cohort is Colonel Bockner (Lom), a German.

• Tongola, an African village. Arabs wearing burnooses appear. Says Col. Bockner,

"What animals, what filth. They're sheiss (shit)!" Later, Bockner calls Africans "primitive natives [and] primitive cannibals." Quatermain (Chamberlin) tags an African woman "prune face."

• An Arab holds hostage chained Africans. Barks the whip-wielding Arab, "Black slaves are sold for a hundred bucks. You can own one for life." Quatermain punches the Arab slaver, freeing the Africans.

• Tongola's Africans (not Arabs) attack a train carrying enemy Axis soldiers.

Note: Arab villains do not appear in H. Rider Haggard's classic novel, nor in earlier movie versions of *King Solomon's Mines* (1937 and 1950). Why do producers Golan and Globus insert them?

The King's Pirate (1967), UNI. *Diana Chesney, Doug McClure, Mary Ann Mobley*. Remake of *Against All Flags* (1952). CAMEOS, MAIDENS

Mute Arab women as objects. A dense Arab eunuch.

Scene: AD 1700, Arabia. This tongue-in-cheek swashbuckling adventure features British Lt. Brian Fleming (McClure), who is intent on demolishing a pirate stronghold on the island of Madagascar. Arab music underscores Fleming's actions. Wearing Arab garb, he treks through a souk, observing bellydancers. An attractive, near-naked Arab hooker tries to bed him. He declines. Next, Fleming and the Arab dancers sail off to Madagascar.

• Pirates attack "the state ship of the Emperor of India." Cut to Hassan, "a great man of blubber." Head down, Hassan charges a pirate. Missing, he drops into the sea. The ship's "eight Moorish women" are taken to Madagascar and auctioned off to pirates.

Note: Protests the maidens' elderly Scottish matron, Miss MacGregor (Chesney), "Is it a Christian thing you're doing?" The auctioneer retorts, "Hold your tongue madam, it so happens these persons are Muslims."

Kismet (1920), Waldorf. Silent. *Otis Skinner*. Like *The Thief of Baghdad* (1924, 1940, 1961), *Kismet* has had four set-in-Bagdad incarnations: 1920, 1930, 1944, and 1955. All four movies are based on Edward Knaublach's 1912 play. MAIDENS

Prominent performers appear as admirable Arabs. All four versions depict "common" family members as loving and devoted beings, befriending and marrying royalty. Devoted fathers sacrifice all in order to secure happiness for their daughters. The settings are "peaceful," "romantic," and "fantastic." And, "beautiful Baghdad" appears as "a fabulous old city, the jewel of the Orient." The muezzin calls the faithful to prayer; Islam is revered.

Scene: The 1920 Arab vs. Arab film is not a light-hearted fantasy, rather a serious drama of revenge. The beggar Hajj (Skinner) moves to rescue his daughter Marsinah from the "Harem of the Wazir." The Wazir refuses to free Marsinah unless Hajj slays the kind caliph.

• Hajj kills two Arabs, and is dispatched to the dungeon. After shaking off his irons, Hajj slays Jawan, the evil man who "stole his wife and murdered his son." Next, Hajj drowns the Wazir, whose "rule of blood and oppression struck terror into the hearts of people." As a result of Hajj's heroism, Marsinah weds the wise caliph.

• Seeking forgiveness for his sins and wanting to thank "Allah" for his blessings, Hajj makes the pilgrimage to Mecca.

Note: An Arab wearing a striped robe struggles to move his donkey. Though the Arab pulls the rope attached to his animal, the donkey refuses to budge. Exhausted, the Arab shrugs, picks up the donkey, and carries it off.

Kismet (1930), WB. *Otis Skinner.* MAIDENS

Scene: A faithful repeat of the 1920 film, complete with splendor, romance and conspiracies. Again, Otis Skinner stars as Hajj. The actor was 72 when the 1930 version was shot. The opening reveals worshipers entering the mosque; Hajj prays, "Alms for the love of Allah; for the love of Allah, alms."

• The Wazir will not free Marsinah, Hajj's daughter (Loretta Young), unless Hajj assassinates the caliph. Fortunately, the caliph survives Hajj's botched assassination attempt. Following the Wazir's death, the caliph weds lovely Marsinah. The ruler spares Hajj's life, but the beggar must leave Baghdad.

Kismet (1944), MGM. *Ronald Coleman, Marlene Dietrich, Edward Arnold, Eddie Abdo, Joy Page, James Craig.* MAIDENS, RECOMMENDED

Scene: This rendition offers plenty of perfumed exoticism. Actor Ronald Coleman appears in a dual role, as Hadji, the "king of beggars," and as a wily magician. Marlene Dietrich stars as the seductive Queen Jamilla. Hadji's lovely daughter (Page) weds the caliph (Craig); Hadji captures the queen's heart.

• Seeking to find out whether the people of Baghdad approve of his leadership, the caliph poses as a gardener's son. As soon as he spots Marsinah, he decides to marry her; her social status does not matter.

• Introducing the evil Grand Vizier, Mansur (Arnold); not only does he rob and tax the poor, Mansur tries to bring down the caliph. After praying, Mansur tells his cohorts, "When he stands before the mosque today I want you to send an arrow through his heart." In time, Hadji thwarts Mansur's plans. They duel; the beggar wins.

• Hadji advises the newlywed couple, Marsinah and the young caliph, "May Allah smile on you forever." Also, the caliph is told, "Blessings of the Prophet on your wedding day." At the mosque, a youth and the imam (Abdo) chant prayers in Arabic.

• The joyous caliph mounts a white horse, claiming Marsinah as his bride. And, the queen runs off with Hadji, purring, "You'll be alive when the man-in-the-moon is forgotten."

Note: Most movie souks are unkempt places, revealing goats, camels, and hagglers. Not so with *Kismet*. The film's remarkable market place, a decorative and friendly indoor souk, resembles a classy shopping mall. Appearing are polite, honest, and well-dressed merchants selling first-class wares at fair prices.

• In one of Dietrich's notorious dance numbers, her body, head-to-toe, is painted gold. But the sensuous number was not allowable in *Kismet*. Yet, that same year the infamous dance is featured in the comedy, *Lost in the Harem* (1944).

• *Oriental Dream* was the TV title for this 1944 *Kismet*.

Kismet (1955), MGM. *Howard Keel, Ann Blyth, Dolores Gray, Vic Damone, Sebastian Cabot.* MAIDENS, RECOMMENDED

Scene: On hearing the call to worship, the vagabond father (Keel) and his daughter Marsinah (Blyth), pray together.

• This *Kismet* features a caring father and his faithful daughter. They overcome adversity and go on to wed members of the royal family.

• High points are memorable songs such as "Baubles, Bangles, and Beads," "Stranger in Paradise," and "Baghdad, you must investigate Baghdad."

• The rotund, greedy Wazir (Cabot) continually ignores the amorous advances of his "wife of wives," Queen Lalume (Gray). At the palace, harem nymphets lounge, poolside. After an attractive bellydancer entertains the "royal highness," three pony-tailed Asian acrobats wearing red jump suits perform.

• The Wazir is reunited with his long-lost father; instead of embracing him, the Wazir tosses the old man into prison.

• Palace guards and the Wazir wear crusader-type outfits.

• Neat souks reveal friendly, well-dressed merchants offering stylish apparel.

• Marsinah loves the young caliph (Damone); she threatens to kill herself rather than be forced to join the Wazir's harem.

• After the wicked Wazir is eliminated, Marsinah and the caliph wed. The camera displays an elaborate wedding procession. Also, Marsinah's father, the carefree beggar, and the seductive queen embrace, rushing off to "The Oasis of Delightful Imaginings."

Kiss of Araby (1933), Monarch. *Maria Alba, Walter Byron, Theodor von Eltz, Claude King, Frank Leigh.* SHEIKHS

Desert Arabs fight each other and the British. A sheikh tries to bed the heroine.

Scene: A cafe. British Capt. Randall (von Eltz) flirts with a lovely bellydancer. When the Capt. spots Sheikh Rahman (King), he accuses the Arab of stealing, and has him lashed. Lt. Lawrence (Byron) arrives and stops the beating. Grateful, Rahman tells Lawrence, "May the blessings of the Prophet [he should say "Allah"] fall upon you." Lawrence cautions the Capt., "Treating an Arab chief in such a manner is likely to lead to an uprising."

• The Capt. frames Lawrence, saying the Lt. seduced the C.O.'s wife. Now disgraced, Lawrence tells Sheikh Rahman, "You're the only friend I've got." Affirms the Arab, "In the tents of Al-Rahman, a welcome awaits you. You shall forever be a welcome guest." Donning Arab garb, the Lt. helps the sheikh's good Arabs crush bad ones.

• Screeching bedouins attack Rahman's caravan. Lawrence repels them. Next, the Lt. chases off an Arab intent on harming the heroine, Dolores Mendez (Alba). "We must give this woman safe escort back to the post," affirms the Lt. But an Arab lecher, Caleb (Leigh), clutches Dolores, panting, "As the chief of this tribe I claim her for my wife." In time, the Lt. intervenes.

• Evening. As the Lt. wears Arab garb, Dolores fears him. Lawrence eases her anxieties, explaining, "Haven't you guessed, already. I'm not an Arab!" Sighs Dolores, "Of course." They purr; later, they wed.

• Caleb sneaks into Dolores' tent and again moves to rape her. Lawrence appears; Caleb draws a dagger. Lawrence kills him.

• The jealous Capt. Randall tells some Arab rebels, "We're going to wipe out El Rahman and his band once and for all." British troops arrive, defeating Randall's bad Arabs. Capt. Randall is shot. Before dying, he confesses that he misjudged Rahman, and that he framed Lawrence. As the camera pans Arab corpses, Rahman tells Lawrence, "May Allah bless you."

Kiss the Other Sheik (1968), Concordia. A Carlos Ponti film. Italian, dubbed in English. *Pamela Tiffin, Marcello Mastroianni.* SHEIKHS

An Arab homosexual kidnaps a European man for his male harem.

Scene: A dashing Italian lover-boy, Michele (Mastroianni), smiles; he mistakenly believes he has sold Pepita (Tiffin), his blonde wife, into "Sheikh Mohammad's" harem.

• Scantily-clad Arabs appear inside Sheikh Mohammad's Arabian Nights chamber carrying sacks of gold.

• Unknown to her husband, Pepita has cut a deal with the sheikh; the Arab wants to seduce not her, but her husband. She sets Michele up for the gay sheikh's male harem. Thanking Pepita, the pleased sheikh forks over a wad of cash, plus a Rolls Royce.

• Mute Arab guards kidnap the shocked Michele, tossing him into the sheikh's limo.

• The sheikh's aides are so inept they cannot open the limo's trunk, not even with the key. Pepita asks Mohammad, "Is there more here than sand?"

• The happy Pepita drives off in the Rolls. Her panicked husband, Michele, runs away from the sheikh's all-male harem. Waving sabers, Arabs on horseback chase after him.

La ley del harem (1931) FOX. The studio's Spanish language version of its 1928 film, *Fazil.* *NS Notes are from Alan Gevinson's *Within our Gates: Ethnicity in American Films, 1911-1960* (Berkeley: University of California Press, 1997). SHEIKHS

Arabs vs. Arabs. "Cultural differences" matter.

Summary: Most scenes in this 1931 remake focus not on cultural harmony but on mean and jealous Arabs torturing and killing fellow Arabs. After Prince Al-Hadi rescues the French heroine, Renee, the Arab removes the kidnapper's head—"But not before the appropriate prayers are said." The prince and Renee honeymoon in Paris; for a time they are happy. But Al-Hadi soon becomes "sick of European ways," forcing Renee to return to his desert kingdom.

The Arab maiden, Fatima, moves to bed the prince. Al-Hadi rejects Fatima's seduction proposals; the jealous woman tries to knife Renee. Next, Hassan, an ambitious vizier, murders a guide. He frames Renee and argues that ancient law demands she die, saying, "The woman who has abandoned her husband shall be condemned to death by torture." When Hassan moves to brand Renee with a hot iron, El-Hadi shoots him dead. He and Renee flee. They search for happiness, not in Europe or Arabia, but in a neutral place, the desert. Finis. See *The Sheik's Wife* (1922).

The Lad and the Lion (1917), Selig Polyscope. Silent. *Vivian Reed, Will Machin, Charles LeMoyne, Al W. Filson.* Based on a story by Edgar Rice Burroughs. *NS. Notes from AFIC (pp 494–5). VILLAINS, MAIDENS

Following a shipwreck, a wealthy college student, William Bankinton (Machin), and a lion are cast "adrift upon the shores of Africa." Later, at an Arab village, William meets and falls for the bedouin chief's daughter, Nakhia (Reed). Furious that an Arab woman would dump him for a Westerner, the jealous bandit, Ben Saada (Le Moyne), tries to kidnap Nakhia. William "comes to the rescue." The men struggle; the lion assists, killing Ben Saada.

Finis. William and Nakhia intend to marry; they sail off for America, "where they are reunited with Bankinton's family."

The Lady of the Harem (1926), Famous Players. Silent. *Greta Nissen, William Collier, Jr., So Jin.* D: Raoul Walsh. Based on James M. Flecker's stage play *Hassan.* *NS. Notes from VAR. SHEIKHS, MAIDENS

An Arab ruler moves to seduce a kidnapped blonde. The VAR critic reproved director Walsh for accenting "sex, sex, sex... The Caliph's desire for the heroine is of a nature which will offend many." The critic's comments are on target. Walsh did parade sparsely dressed harem "girls in front of the camera as if they were so many show girls." Adds the critic, there is so much "undressing; [this film] may not get by in the strictly censorial states."

Summary: As the Caliph of Kornassah (Jin) desires "gold and women," especially women, his soldiers abduct Pervannah (Nissen), "a luscious blonde for him." However, when Rafi (Collier), Pervannah's lover, finds out that his blonde precious has been abducted, he enlists some "expert dagger throwers." They attack the caliph's castle. The lecherous caliph gets "a dagger in the back"; Rafi and Pervannah are reunited.

Note: During the time of silent films, some reviewers referred to Japanese actors as Japs. The VAR critic wrote, "So Jin, the Jap, played the Caliph."

• In 1926, the same year *Lady of the Harem* was released, movie theaters were screening Pat Sullivan's animated cartoon *Felix the Cat Shatters the Sheik* (1926). The promotion poster of this cartoon displays an ugly Arab sheikh wielding a saber over Felix's head.

Land of the Pharaohs (1955), WB. *Jack Hawkins, Joan Collins, James Robertson Justice, Dewey Martin, Kermia, Sydney Chaplin, Alexis Mintos.* P & D: Howard Hawks. Filmed in Egypt. EGYPTIANS, MAIDENS

A tyrannical Egyptian pharaoh enslaves innocents.

Scene: Egypt, 5,000 years ago. Pharaoh Khufu (Hawkins), an arrogant and selfish potentate, orders the construction of the Great Pyramid. His objective? To place his remains, along with treasures, linens, and wine, inside the invulnerable, secret tomb. The Egyptians perceive Khufu as a living God. And, they believe life in the hereafter matters most.

• The pharaoh's men kidnap Kushite workers, forcing them to build the Great Pyramid. Khufu promises the Kushite architect, Vashtar (Justice), that after the Pyramid is constructed, he will free the Kushites, allowing them to return home.

• During a funeral, Egyptians sing. Explains the pharaoh, "Each man by his labor will secure a place in the next generation." Cut to enslaved Kushites. What matters most to them is freedom now, not later.

• Flash forward, twenty years. Starving Egyptians and Kushites reflect on the unfinished Great Pyramid; "the stones of the Pyramid are sealed with blood and tears."

• Finally, as the Pyramid nears completion, the Pharaoh selects Vashtar's son, Senta

(Martin), and twelve "priests" to complete the secret tomb. To insure his tomb's location will remain a secret, the ruler proposes to slice the priests' tongues, as well as promising them joyous nights, "food, wine, and the pleasure of women."

• When the bewitching non-Egyptian Princess Nellifer (Collins) speaks, murder, sex, and political intrigue follow. Nellifer's intrigues bring about the demise of three Egyptians: Queen Nallia (Kermia), the loyal Captain Treneh (Chaplin), and the pharaoh. Yet, in the end, wicked Nellifer winds up not on Egypt's throne, but inside the pharaoh's escape-proof tomb.

Finis: A benevolent Egyptian priest, Hamar (Mintos), frees the subjected Kushites.

Note: In one of the movie's pyramid-construction scenes, nearly 10,000 workers dig up and pull 5,000-pound stones from quarries. Next, they place the huge blocks onto ramps leading to the rising pyramid.

The Last Egyptian (1914), Alliance. Silent. *J. Farrell MacDonald, Vivian Reed.* *NS. Notes from VAR (11 December 1914). EGYPTIANS

Lord Roane, an English nobleman, dishonors an Egyptian queen, the mother of young Prince Kara. Years later, the young Egyptian, now King Kara, finds out that "in his veins, together with the blood of kings, there is the blood of a perfidious unbeliever." So, Kara moves to avenge Lord Roane, his mother's betrayer.

During a card game, Kara fleeces thousands from Lord Roane. The king agrees to marry Roane's daughter, Lady Aneth. When she arrives, the ruler dispatches Lady Aneth to his harem. In time, a pure English liberator arrives. He removes Aneth from King Kara's harem, spiriting "her away on his yacht."

Abruptly, Kara's "river pirates" nab and hold Lady Aneth and her Englishman hostage. Not for long. The duo is rescued and "all ends happily." As for King Kara and Lord Roane, they perish. After a "terrific struggle," Roane tosses the Egyptian into a vault. When one of Kara's "discarded" harem favorites sees the Englishman leaving the tomb, she presumes Roane is Kara and stabs him.

The Last Outpost (1935), PAR. *Cary Grant, Claude Rains.* See *Khartoum* (1966), *Lost Patrol* (1934), *The Lives of a Bengal Lancer* (1935). VILLAINS

British soldiers defeat Sudanese "natives."

Scene: WWI. In Turkistan, British soldiers battle Kurdish and Arab "irregulars." Cut to Arabs kidnapping and imprisoning a British officer, Michael Andrews (Grant).

• In the souk, Arab "irregulars" whip women and children. Says a Russian prisoner, "these tribes" are not content unless they "taste blood." Cut to innocents lined against the wall, facing a firing squad. Arabs shoot them. Explains a British officer, the people here "know what butchery is. They're running away from it and I'm helping them."

• The British are told "the natives in the Sudan" are preparing for war. A courageous soldier, Andrews (Grant), is dispatched into the desert to save a besieged fort. Stock footage depicts fierce Sudanese on the move. Cut to the fort's outnumbered troops machine-gunning scores. No matter. The screaming spear-throwing "natives" advance. All seems lost.

• Andrews saves the day. In the desert, he comes across an advancing British column. Andrews tell them about the "native" assault on the fort. Cut to fresh British troops arriving in time to rout the Sudanese.

The Last Remake of Beau Geste (1977), UNI. *Marty Feldman, Michael York, Henry Gibson, James Earl Jones, Ed McMahon.* Co-W, D: Feldman. VILLAINS, SHEIKHS

This spoof of legion films, complete with stock footage from Gary Cooper's movie, *Beau Geste* (1939), presents Arabs as dunces. Mute harem maidens appear.

Scene: North Africa, 1906. Legionnaires ride across the Sahara desert, boasting "Bring on the Arabs... we'll rape their wives and murder the men for liberty, freedom, nobility, fight!" And, "Perhaps for a change we'll murder the wives and rape all the men, for France, for France."

• Near the legion fort. Introducing inept Arabs wearing black turbans, white and black striped pajama-shirts, and baggy pants. Trying to dismount, they fall off their horses.

• While battling legionnaires, Arabs ride camels. Each time an Arab fires his rifle, his camel's bandaged hump deflates. Thus, the Arab dismounts, picks up a portable "Camel Air Pump," and starts pumping air into his camel's caved-in hump. Soon, the hump is restored to its original size. Cut to an Arab horseman; facing the camera, he rattles off a new casualty report.

• On screen, a commercial for used camels: "Let Hawkin hump you!" The black-robed Hawkin hawks recycled camels, saying: "I've got the biggest camel lot in the whole world."

• As the Arabs charge the legionnaires, the clad-in-black "Sheikh Abdul" (Jones) and his cohorts shout, "Akbar!" Next, Arabs enter a tent, extend their arms and bow. Complains the French general, Pecheur (Gibson), "Sheikh, the war is losing money."

• Arabs prepare to attack the legion fort. Advises Abdul, "All right, men, synchronize your hourglasses (each man wears an hourglass wrist watch). We leave in exactly 70,000 grains of sand." Arabs charge the fort; the legionnaires cease firing and march out into the desert. Confused, Abdul shouts, "Hey, come back here! You're supposed to be inside. We're supposed to be outside... Come back and fight, please!" Suddenly, Abdul's men take off. Pleads Abdul, "Wait for me. Wait for me. I'm your leader. How can I lead if you don't wait for me."

• All alone, Abdul sighs, "Oh, I am lost and out of a job." Suddenly, an Arab horseman (McMahon) rides up, saying, "Follow me." "Where? " asks Abdul. To "Hollywood!" says the Arab horseman. Smiling, the two men ride off.

Note: See the Three Stooges as legionnaires bringing down Arabs in the Columbia short, *Wee Wee Monsieur* (1938). Here, Curly, Moe and Larry depart their legion post in a Christmas sleigh. Wearing Santa Claus outfits, they infiltrate an Arab sheikh's hideout, rescuing the legion captain from a bearded tyrant. The men invade the sheikh's harem, don harem outfits and flirt with one of the sheikh's maidens; she has no front teeth.

The Last Samurai (1990), Arrow. *John Saxon, Lance Henriksen, Lisa Eilbacher, John Fujioka, Arabella Holzbog, Foziah Davidson.* P: Tony Carbone. SP, D: Paul Mayersberg. Filmed in Africa. VILLAINS

An unscrupulous Arab gun-runner and a militant African general.

Scene: Africa. The camera reveals the Arabian Nights tent of Haroun Al-Hakim (Saxon). Haroun, who "lives on the phone," confesses to his Western wife Susan

(Eilbacker) that business is not so good. "My genie (his gold-plated telephone) has deserted me... I am so filled with doubts... Allah is taking his powers away from me." Haroun "adores" Susan. Yet, she makes him feel "so helpless." When the naked Susan emerges from a bath, an Arab-clad maid (Davidson), not Haroun, attends her.

• Mumbling gibberish, stereotypical African soldiers attack Haroun's tent, setting it aflame. Next, they kidnap Haroun, Susan, and their Western and Japanese guests, hauling them off to an outdoor jungle prison.

• Haroun, who arranged the kidnapping, meets with the African general. The general refuses to release the prisoners. He demands Haroun provide him with "weapons of mass destruction." Haroun balks, saying he will "authorize" delivery of weapons based upon their earlier agreement.

• The general tells Susan: Your husband set this up because "he didn't want it known around the world he was making deals with scum like me." And, "There are things about your husband that you don't know, Mrs. Hakim, but you're not afraid of the truth are you? Ask him."

• Aware her husband staged the abduction and sells "guns to both sides," Susan berates Haroun: "All that talk of [Arab] honor, what happened to yours? All our lives are at stake because of you," she says. Counters Haroun: " My dear, I made a deal. Right or wrong, I won't go back on it." But, "It was wrong," says Susan.

• When the African moves to hang Haroun's two Japanese friends, Haroun protests: "If you kill these men general, there will be no arms." Counters the general, "Too late. It's too late for conscience, now, Mr. Hakim."

• To the rescue, the Western protagonist, Johnny Congo (Henriksen). Johnny and his friend attack the African camp, freeing all the prisoners including the Japanese. Next, they shoot the general and his men. Exclaims Haroun, "Allah is merciful." But when Haroun moves to assist Johnny, an African shoots him and Johnny dead. "It is finished."

Lawrence of Arabia (1962), COL. A David Lean film. *Peter O'Toole, Alec Guinness, Omar Sharif, Anthony Quinn.* SP: Robert Bolt, Michael Wilson, based on T. E. Lawrence's writings. D: David Lean. SHEIKHS

In 1998, the American Film Institute ranked *Lawrence of Arabia* as the "Fifth Greatest Movie of All Time." Following is an edited version of my essay on the film, from *The Washington Report on Middle East Affairs* (November 1989).

In David Lean's award-winning film, some of the world's most noted screen stars appear as Arabs: Alec Guinness, Anthony Quinn, Omar Sharif. Several memorable Arabs appear in this Oscar-winning epic 216-minute spectacle, filmed in Morocco and Jordan. Telling cinematography reveals spellbinding desert vistas.

Scene: Opening frames reveal two Turkish planes bombing Prince Faisal (Guinness) and his followers. In the desert, the Turks gun down scores of Arab men, women and children. Seeing the slaughter, Lawrence (O'Toole) empathizes with the victims.

• En route to Damascus, Faisal's Arabs come across a ravaged Arab village; mutilated bodies fill the screen. Cut to retreating Turkish soldiers, responsible for the carnage. Fearing the Turkish troops may return and torture the wounded, the Arabs shoot the villagers.

• Lawrence and his bedouins blow up Turkish railroads, destroying their garrisons.

Most scenes display decent Arabs, sustained by the protagonist Lawrence and his British colleagues. Conversely, the Turks, who are in league with the Germans, are projected as villains.

• The Arab leader, Auda (Quinn), leads his men against the Turks, saying, "God be with you." Throughout, devout Arabs request God's blessings. And, Sherif Ali (Sharif), Lawrence's best friend, asks God to have mercy on Turkish soldiers being shelled in Damascus.

Ali: God help them who lay under that.
Lawrence: They are Turks.
Ali: God help them.

• Inside Prince Faisal's tent. No gratuitous harem maidens or bellydancers, here. Instead, an imam reads from the Holy Koran; and Faisal reflects on Arab contributions to society. The Arabs "must gain their freedom," says Faisal, though he fears the British have "a hunger for Arabia." General Allenby confirms Faisal's fears, saying, "We'll let them [the Arabs] drive the Turks out and then move in ourselves." Yet, Lawrence mistakenly believes his British superiors want "Arabia for the Arabs."

• The sincere rigor of the bedouins. Brave bedouins are able to "cross 60 miles of desert in a single day." One bedouin presents Lawrence with a thobe and headdress. Considering Arab garb "a great honor," Lawrence flaunts his white robe, preferring it to his British uniform. And, Lawrence befriends two Arab youths.

• In spite of favorable Arab portraits, shabby stereotypes and historical distortions plague the film. For example, the camera presents feuding, looting Arabs, unable to coexist. And, one dense Arab buys a damaged clock.

• One of the most disturbing scenes occurs as the film begins. A speck appears, eventually becoming a lone rider galloping through the simmering desert heat. Sherif Ali, the approaching rider, thunders toward Lawrence, who is accompanied by a bedouin guide. The two men stand transfixed near Ali's well. Ali greets them by shooting Lawrence's guide dead. The enraged Lawrence shouts, "He was my friend." Then, Lawrence delivers a soliloquy on bedouin blood feuds, saying, "Sherif Ali, so long as the Arabs fight tribe against tribe, so long will they remain a little people, a silly people, greedy, barbarous and cruel, as you are." Ali and Lawrence ride off, leaving the guide's body unattended in the desert heat. As James E. Akins, former US ambassador to Saudi Arabia, writes: "Ali's shooting of Lawrence's guide for drinking water from his well—this is inconceivable." Akins is correct. Hospitality is a sacred duty for bedouins. The killing of the bedouin at Ali's well is not in Lawrence's *Seven Pillars of Wisdom*.

A guide is not killed at the well and, of course, Lawrence does not begin his Arabian adventure with an angry tirade on desert customs that, in reality, would have won him no friends and might have gotten him killed. A similar scene does take place in *Seven Pillars of Wisdom*, but Sherif Ali and a companion peacefully share the well with Lawrence, his guides, and with other bedouins who happen to be watering their camels at the same time. In *Seven Pillars of Wisdom*, the well account is a humorous, rather than a deadly, encounter.[103]

• Several scenes display Arabs contesting Arabs. For example, Auda (Quinn) refuses to permit Ali and his bedouins to drink from his well. Lawrence intervenes and a shoot-out is prevented. And it is Lawrence, not an Arab, who bravely rides back into the desert to rescue a faltering bedouin. Later, when this same bedouin kills an Arab from another group, Lawrence steps in to avoid a "blood feud." The Englishman administers desert justice by shooting the bedouin he once saved.

• Throughout, Auda functions as a dimwitted outlaw. Greed, not honor or love of country dictate his behavior. Early on, Auda took monies from the Turks not to fight them. Only when Lawrence offers the Arab more gold does Auda agree to link up with fellow Arabs.

• Arab women are virtually invisible. One scene, only, projects covered-in-black women; they are perched in a row, atop cliffs; hailing their men with the *zaghreet,* the celebratory trilling sound women make by rippling their tongues on the roofs of their mouths.

• After the victorious Arabs take Damascus from the Turks, the scenario shifts, revealing false and damaging information. Earlier, Lean presented heroic bedouins and sheikhs fighting to liberate Damascus. Now that they occupy Damascus, Lean presents them as untamed animals, stubborn and unreasonable beings who fight among themselves. Even when faced with ordinary tasks, such as operating the city's telephones, hospitals, and water works, nasty Arabs quarrel. Not once does the camera focus on capable sheikhs or the Syrian residents of Damascus, professionals who could easily have restored all basic services. The message here? Arabs are not qualified nor worthy to govern civilized societies. Sighs Ali to Lawrence, "You tried to give us Damascus."

• Two days pass. The feuding Arabs drift aimlessly back to the desert. Abruptly, the camera shows smiling British officers. They ship off to Damascus Western doctors and engineers. Most viewers are not aware that Lean's Damascus scenes are false renderings of history. In reality, the Arabs under Faisal governed Damascus for two years, not two days. The French Army forced them out of Damascus. Affirms British novelist, Gertrude Bell, who resided in Damascus after its liberation: "[Under Faisal's rule] the Arab administration [in Syria] has presented an outward appearance of a national Government; public business has been kept going; tramways have run, streets have been lighted, people have bought and sold, and a normal world has been obtained."[104]

• In summary, though the movie may contain compelling cinematography and engrossing performances, as history, *Lawrence…* receives a failing grade. Throughout, the theme of cultural domination prevails—the civilized British conquering uncivilized folks. After all, the movie concerns a brave Englishman, not a valiant Arab. Lawrence surfaces as an Arabian sun god, uniting the Arabs. His courage and intelligence saves their lives; his strategy crushes the Turks, and he gives them Damascus. Lean and his crew should not be faulted for concentrating on Lawrence, even though he was not a desert savior, but rather an important intermediary between British and the Arabs. But Lean should be soundly criticized for distorting history at the expense of the Arabs. For those viewers interested in more accurate scenarios that depict British and French deceptions at the time of the Arab revolt, see the Discovery channel's 1992 one-hour documentary *Lawrence of Arabia: Great Adventures of the 20ᵗʰ Century,* directed by Christopher Rowley.

Note: "In perpetuating Lawrence's inflated claims to leadership of the Arab revolt," writes Gary Crowdus in *Cineaste,* "the film caters to the same old self-flattering Western prejudices about Third World peoples, those benighted colonial subjects who are incapable of ruling themselves… In actual historical fact… Lawrence's value to the Arab revolt had less to do with his leadership skills or charismatic personality than with his role in supplying arms, equipment, and money. The final drive on Damascus, for example, had less to do with Lawrence's inspirational rousing of the Bedouin tribes than with his means to deliver 2,000 camels at the right time" (XVII: 1).

• *Lawrence of Arabia* is important because it does show Western powers, namely France and England, reneging on their promises for Arab independence. But, writes James E. Akins: "The part [in the movie] I found offensive was the last part: the capture of Damascus and the resulting chaos. The Arabs did conquer Damascus and they ruled it quite well until Faisal was expelled... Nowhere in the film was there any suggestion that the ones who ran Damascus were Arabs."[105] Affirms scholar David Fromkin, "[T]he ruler of Syria was Faisal... On June 6, 1919, [Faisal] called into being a General Syrian Congress." Then, on "26 July 1920 the French occupied Damascus; on July 27 they ordered Faisal into exile." Notes Fromkin, "The French Foreign Minister proclaimed that Syria henceforth would be held by France." [106]

Legend of the Lost (1957), UA. *John Wayne, Sophia Loren, Rossano Brazzi.* SP: Robert Presnell, Ben Hecht. Filmed in "The United Kingdom of Libya." MAIDENS

John Wayne purifies a good-hearted Arab whore, portrayed by Sophia Loren.

Scene: Opening frames display crowded souks. A smoke-filled brothel reveals scantily-clad Arab women dancing with each other.

• Two Western explorers, Paul (Brazzi) and Joe (Wayne), prepare to trek across the Sahara in search of treasures. Abruptly, Arabs toss Dila (Loren) onto the floor. Why? They saw her steal from Paul. Yet, Paul forgives Dila's thievery, allowing her to join the desert expedition.

• The Sahara. Confesses Dila, who never knew her Arab father: "My [Arab] mother taught me only one thing—not to cry. She slapped me every time I cried. 'Men don't buy crybabies,' she said."

• Though Paul and Joe argue, both men attend Dila; her self-image escalates.

• Abruptly, clothed-in-black bedouins appear. The Arabs are not a threat; yet, note the dialogue.

Paul: Did you hear that?
Joe: Yeah.
Paul: Jackals?
Joe: No.
Paul: Men! [*Camel-riding Arabs appear*]

Finis: Mute bedouins assist the protagonists; Joe and Dila embrace.

Legend of the Mummy (1997), a.k.a. Bram Stoker's Legend of the Mummy, Goldbar. *Lou Gossett Jr., Lloyd Bochner, Amy Locane, Eric Lutes, Kahlil G. Sabbagh.* W, D: Jeffrey Obrow. EGYPTIANS, MAIDENS

Reawakened Egyptian queens murder Californians.

Scene: "Egypt 1947, Valley of the Sorcerer." Cut to an Egyptian tomb robber snitching a red jewel. Abruptly, "Queen Tara's tomb is sealed." Soon, the queen's curse takes effect; the thief's face is badly burned.

• Marin County, California. When art historian Abel Treadway (Bochner) translates an ancient inscription, he accidentally restores life to the evil mummy, Queen Tara. Frightened, most of Abel's staff leave his mansion.

• Abel's pal, Corbeck (Gossett Jr.), arrives and explains Tara's deadly curse: "5,000 years ago, Queen Tara was killed by her priests. Her dying breath was a curse [on anyone daring to] touch anything." Sighs Corbeck, "You're cursed even if you talk about what you've seen."

• Abel's cellar. The reawakened Tara emerges from a wooden crate and dispatches deadly scorpions. Thanks to Tara, several people are seriously injured, five others perish.

• Flashback to Egypt. Two young archaeologists, Corbeck and Abel, are told: "Do not enter [Tara's tomb] or their vengeance [will] wither you away." They ignore the warning and enter the queen's tomb.

• Queen Tara wants "her spirit to breathe again." So, she takes over the body of Abel's daughter, Margaret (Locane). Next, she kills Corbeck.

Finis: This mummy triumphs. Queen Tara is resurrected through Margaret's body.

Note: Producers might wish to pattern a mummy movie based on the hit comedy, *Love at First Bite* (1979). Why not show lovely Western maidens willingly embracing gentlemanly mummies? That's what fair heroines do in *First Bite*; they cuddle the debonair Dracula.

Legion of the Doomed (1958), AA. *Bill Williams, Kurt Krueger, Joseph Abdullah, Anthony Caruso, Hal Gerard.* P: William F. Broidy. VILLAINS, WORST LIST

In Algeria, legionnaires vs. Arab "Nazis"; Arabs vs. Arabs.

Scene: The desert. Intones the narrator: "This is Algeria, a lawless land seething with hate, unrest, and turmoil. [The country] is guarded by units of the French foreign legion. [They] live in the shadow of death. Here in Algeria, life is cheap and death is free." Adding, "The towns of Algeria wear yesterday's make-up. This town, like its people, has a great past but no future."

• As an Algerian says, "The sands of time will soon run out for the French," Arabs charge "the legion dogs." Quips a legionnaire, "Maybe they outnumber us three to one, maybe." Boasts Lt. Smith (Williams), "Mm, that's fair odds...[they're not] organized fighters. Someone is training them. They look like Nazis to me, all lined up."

• Captain Marchek (Krueger), explains the Arab attack: "Old Emir Kahn signed a peace treaty with France, [but] some members of his tribe don't go along with it." And, "Berbers, themselves, without a leader, are incapable of a big scale operation." Marchek turns to a lovely woman, warning, "For a French woman, the Berbers have a different kind of death."

• At the Café de Legion, a woman performs the "dance of the seven veils." Cut to an Arab poisoning a fellow Arab. Then, the Arab fires at Lt. Smith, missing from two yards.

• Leading Sheikh Karaba's (Abdullah) rebellious Arabs is Captain Marchek, an ex-Nazi intent on destroying the foreign legion. He boasts, "Under my leadership the Berbers will gain in strength."

• Lt. Smith comes across weapons intended for Karaba's Arabs. "If these rifles would fall into Berber hands," he says, "the (Sahara) sands would run red with blood."

• Smith warns an Arab, "Kill him (Marchak) before he kills you." "You speak the words of Allah!" says the Arab. Believing "a man who betrays his own people cannot be trusted," the Arab knifes Marchak in the back.

• The legion fort. Karaba's screaming Arabs scale the fort's walls. Pulling knives and scabbards, they slaughter legionnaires. Sighs one legionnaire, "They've got us outnumbered." In the end, the legionnaires triumph. Affirms an officer, "One legionnaire is worth five Berbers."

Note: The theme of Islam as a violent faith, surfaces in novelist John Buchan's WWI book *Greenmantle*. Writes Buchan: "Islam is a fighting creed, and the mullah still stands in the pulpit with the Koran in one hand and a drawn sword in the other." The eponym of Buchan's book, a Turkish Muslim "Holy Man" stirs up the "peasants" so they will side with the Germans against the British. The British fear this Holy Man "will madden the remotest Moslem peasant with dreams of Paradise, [putting] a spell on the whole Moslem world." Declares the protagonist, "I saw [in Turkey] what I took to be mosques and minarets and they were about as impressive as factory chimneys."[107]

• The word 'Mohammedanism' is a misnomer; it wrongly implies that Muslims worship Mohammed rather than God.

• No fiction film displays Muslims as distinguished artists.

• The Berbers of North Africa are most numerous in Morocco, where they constitute nearly half the population. The term 'Berber' is applied to various languages and dialects spoken by the Berbers. Most Berber men are bilingual, speaking their own Berber language as well as Arabic, or even French. Yet, imagemakers project Berbers as Arabs, clothing them in Arab garb and having them speak Arabic.

Legion of Missing Men (1937), MON. *Ralph Forbes, Paul Hurst, Ben Alexander, Hala Linda, Roy D'Arcy.* Some stock footage. Hala Linda sings "You are My Romance" and "Song of the Legionnaires." VILLAINS, SHEIKHS, WORST LIST

"Grim, hardy, courageous" legionnaires extinguish the "bloodthirsty" Arabs responsible for ambushing the "20th Marching Company." Inept Arabs are linked with animals.

Scene: Superimposed over Morocco's Atlas mountains, "North Africa, a burning desert empire." Barks the legion commander, "As you know, we're in a state of war with some Arab tribes." Sheikh Ibrahim Al-Ahmed (D'Arcy) is "trying to stir up the hill tribes."

• Legionnaires try to escape "out of Ahmed's territory by night." Says one, "There's something moving on the desert." Abruptly, Ahmed's men pop up from behind cliffs. Screams a legionnaire, "Those monkeys up there!" The Arabs attack, taking the legion's machine guns.

• At Ahmed's camp, a frustrated Arab says, "We have legion guns that shoot many times. But we know not how to put them in one piece." Sighs Ahmed, "Machine guns and no one knows how to use them." To solve the problem, Ahmed abducts a skilled legionnaire.

• In the souk, a dense Arab tries to induce his lazy donkey to sit up. Quips legionnaire Bob Carter (Forbes), "I've shot at Arabs; I've pelted them with machine guns and I've thrown bombs at 'em. But I can't stand by and see even an Arab made a fool of by a jackass." Says his pal, Muggsy (Hurst), "[In England] we used to build a fire under them." Quips Bob, "You're wrong. We should build a fire under the Arab." Cut to Arabs and legionnaires fighting.

• After tagging Ahmed "old horse-face," Muggsy says, "Let's bump off a couple of them AYRABS!" Muggsy says Arabs use "a long curved blade" to pry open their victims. "They shove it between your ribs and twist it—like that." Sighs a legionnaire, We "learned all about torture from the Arabs."

• The Café Royale. Mute Arab dancers appear in the background. But, the patrons focus on the French singer, Nina de Bernay (Linda). Nina finds out that Ahmed is holding hostage, Bob Carter's brother, Don (Alexander). Off Nina goes to Ahmed's camp. Thinking Ahmed is her pal, Nina asks the Arab to free Don. But Ahmed betrays her. Nina tells Don, "I thought Ahmed was my friend. He isn't. He's our enemy!"

• Bob and Muggsy enter Ahmed's camp; Arabs nab them. Ahmed asks, "Do any of you understand the operation of machine guns?" Unless Bob gets the guns firing, Ahmed will torture him and his friends. Bob agrees, then booby-traps all but two guns. He and Muggsy snatch the two workable guns and "pump lead into those Arabs."

• Ahmed's rebels charge the legion fort. Too late. Reinforcements arrive in the nick of time. The outnumbered and "low on ammunition" legionnaires collapse the Arabs.

Dialogue: Muggsy and his pal disguise themselves as Arabs. Asks Muggsy, "Hey, do I look as much like an Arab as you do in that 'Mother Hubbard'?" Barks his pal, "Bloomin' Arabs in back of us."

Note: Actor Ralph Forbes also appears in *Beau Geste* (1926).

Legionnaire (1998), Long Road Prod. Edward R. Pressman Film Corp., Quadra Entertainment. *Jean-Claude Van Damme, Kamel Krifa. SP: Rebecca Morrison, Sheldon Lettich.* S: Lettich, Van Damme. Filmed in Morocco. VILLAINS, MAIDENS

Ferocious desert Arabs vs. outnumbered legionnaires.

Scene: The year, 1925. After 50 minutes, the action shifts to Morocco. Arab music fills the soundtrack as legionnaire recruits stroll through a crowded souk, complete with an Arab snake charmer. Legionnaires visit a seedy club; two go off with Arab prostitutes.

• The legion fort. Explains the captain, French troops are being "slaughtered by the Arabs... the self-proclaimed Arab leader, El-Krim (Krifa) has... destroyed nine of our outposts. The defending legionnaires were all brutally slaughtered and those who did not die immediately were tortured in a despicable manner." A sergeant advises the legionnaire's 60-man rescue squad, "keep one last bullet in your pocket—not for the enemy, but for yourselves."

• Legionnaires trod across the desert; says one, "[The Arabs] are waiting and watching, planning when and how they're going to kill us." As he speaks, the camera reveals El-Krim's camp.

• The legionnaires discover water. They drink; El-Krim's men attack, killing about twenty men. During the battle, legionnaire Alain Lefevre (Van Damme) crushes scores.

• The legion patrol arrives at the besieged legion fort. Abruptly, El-Krim's men attack. Lefevre machine-guns the Arabs. El-Krim's men toss firebombs, igniting the fort. Next, the Arabs nab and torture Luther, Lefevre's African friend. After the Arabs chain the African, they attach him to a horse; the galloping steed drags Luther across the desert.

Just as an Arab is about to slice off Luther's head, Lefevre mercifully shoots his tortured friend.

• The next day. Fearing Arab torture, a wounded legionnaire shoots himself. Again, El-Krim's men charge the fort, killing all the legionnaires but one—Lefevre. El-Krim allows Lefevre to live, saying, "In our culture a man who has courage is valued above all." Pointing to the burned fort, El-Krim warns, "This is what awaits them [your leaders] if they continue invading our country." He and his Arabs ride off.

Note: Producers thank the "Centre Cinematographique Morrocian" for their cooperation.

• One of this film's eight producers is Kamel Krifa.

Legions of the Nile (1960), TCF. Italian. *Linda Crystal.* *NS. Notes from VAR (9 November 1990). Filmed in Rome and Madrid. EGYPTIANS, MAIDENS

The final days of Cleopatra (Crystal) and Mark Antony. "All of the acting" in this quasi-historical Italian spectacle "suffers from the rub-a-dub-dubbing."

The Leopard Woman (1920), Associated Producers, Inc. *J. Parker Read Jr.* Silent. Louise Glaum, House Peters. MAIDENS, EGYPTIANS

Egyptians as inept assassins; Egyptians as Africans.

Scene: Opening frames introduce "Cairo, that city of peculiar mystery and charm, [where] death bows before the whim of Allah." Cut to the British embassy; officials dispatch John Culbertson (Peters) to make an alliance with the far-off Kingdom of M'tela. The camera shows Culbertson trekking through the desert. Cut to enemy agents also intent on forging an alliance with the Kingdom of M'tela. The agents make an offer to the alluring Madame (Glaum). They ask Madame and her safari to follow Culbertson, then kill him before he reaches M'tela. Madame's Egyptian cohort, Chake', volunteers: "I am your slave, Madame. Order me to kill this man."

• Madame searches for an assassin. Off she goes to "The haunt of Ramon Sik, in whose lurking shadows the spirit of evil seeks fresh victims." Here, Egyptian maidens dance, and seedy Arab men grasp Arab women. One Arab rogue tells Madame to employ "That [Egyptian] girl; she is not afraid of man or devil." Protests Chake', "Girl not good. This is man's work." The girl tries to knife Chake'. Madame likes the woman's style, and employs her.

• The Egyptian assassin removes her clothing. Nearly naked, she rushes into Culbertson's bedroom. Placing a knife between her teeth, she lunges at the sleeping Englishman. He awakes, fending her off.

• Culbertson's and Madame's safaris enter M'tela. From this point on, the desert scenes end. The action switches to the jungle, complete with throbbing drum beats, a zebra, and a charging hippo. Surprisingly, in the jungle all Egyptians, including Chake', no longer dress as, nor look like, Egyptians. They don loin cloths and appear as Africans.

• Though Madame loves Culbertson, she orders Chake' to kill him. Chake' enters Culbertson's tent. After he mistakenly plunges a knife into a porter, he is caught and sentenced "to hang."

• Love triumphs. Though his eyes are injured, the smitten Culbertson forgives Madame, embracing her. Also, his mission is a success; M'tela's ruler links up with the

British. And thanks to the now-reformed Chake', a British doctor arrives, restoring Culbertson's vision.

Let It Ride (1989), PAR. *Richard Dreyfuss.* CAMEOS, SHEIKHS

In this comedy, an American wins, an Arab loses.

Scene: A racetrack. Jay Trotter (Dreyfuss), a bettor who often loses, is now winning—a lot of money. Lugging plenty of cash, Jay heads toward a special "back room" to bet on the next race. En route, he sees a really big loser, a white-robed Arab wearing sunglasses. Quips Jay, "God likes me"—inferring, perhaps that God does *not* like the Arab.

• The camera dwells on the melancholy Arab; he stands motionless near large stacks of lost bills. The despondent loser sighs, "*Alekum,*" meaning, "I should have known better."

The Light That Failed (1916), Feature Film Corp. Silent. *Robert Edeson, Jose Collins.* *NS. Notes from AFIC. CAMEOS

Three films are based on Rudyard Kipling's novella, "The Light That Failed."

This first silent screen version of Kipling's romantic war drama focuses on heroic British soldiers. One scene shows Sudanese "tribesmen" killing a near-blind English painter (Edeson).

Percy Marmont starred in the other silent version in 1923.

The Light That Failed (1939), PAR. *Ronald Coleman, Walter Huston, Ida Lupino.* CAMEOS

In this sound version, opening and closing desert-battle scenes display "Soudan's" fuzzy wuzzies fighting British troops.

Scene: The Sudan. Two British soldiers participating in the "Soudan campaign" are artist Dick Heldar (Coleman) and his friend Torpenhow (Huston). Says Dick, "They're [the fuzzy wuzzies] too quiet. It looks like trouble." Affirms Torpenhow, "The wrath of the ignorant, bigoted, and unwashed natives of this country." Anticipating an attack, British soldiers form a circle. Scores of "fuzzy wuzzies" charge, blinding Dick.

• In Port Said, soldiers go to a bar run by a French couple; Arab dancers perform.

• Years pass. Dick returns to the "Soudan." This time, he is killed battling a fresh throng of "unwashed natives."

Note: This post-WWII drama is about a British artist trying to cope with love and the loss of his sight. Why inject "ignorant," "bigoted" caricatures from the "Soudan?"

The Lighthorsemen (1988), Cinecom. *Peter Phelps, John Walton.* CAMEOS, PALESTINIANS

This WWI film tars bedouins and Palestinians.

Scene: Southern Palestine. Australian cavalrymen prepare to contest the Germans and Turks at Beersheba. Appearing in the background, some clad-in-black Palestinian women. Cut to Palestinian baggage handlers and aggressive Palestinian children. An Aussie spots an arrogant Palestinian youth, barking, "Piss off!" Why show Palestinian children as assertive brats? Films seldom present Palestinian boys and girls as normal, fun-loving and helpful children.

• Four armed bedouins wearing red-and-white kuffiyehs pursue an Aussie, firing away at the soldier. Suddenly, the soldier's three friends appear. The bedouins turn tail and run. Apparently, reel bedouins fear a fair fight.

Lion of the Desert (1981) Falcon International. *Anthony Quinn, Oliver Reed, John Gielgud*. P, D: Mustapha Akkad. Filmed in Libya. BEST LIST

Based on historical fact, this fine drama makes a strong statement about occupied peoples seeking self-determination on their own land. The setting is Libya; it could easily be Cambodia, Palestine, or South Africa. The film traces the life of Omar Mukhtar (Quinn), the Libyan leader who struggled for twenty years to free his persecuted people from Italian invaders. Says Mukhtar to an Italian officer, "No nation has the right to occupy another." Throughout, Fascist metal brings down bedouins. Arab Muslims are heroes and victims; Fascists are brutal aggressors.

Note: The film follows the observations of historian Denis Mack Smith, who writes: In Libya, "many grave offenses were committed by the Fascists." In October 1929, for example, Italian generals gave orders that "any [bedouin] leaders taken were to be hanged, and any Italian generals who wanted conciliation were dismissed." General Graziani ordered troops to remove the "whole population of some areas into five concentration camps." Next, Graziani built "a barbed wire fence four meters thick." Subsequently, "the crowding of 80,000 people into these crowded camps resulted in excessive deaths. 20,000 people may have died." Continues Smith, "evidence suggests a real reign of terror, with hundreds of thousands executed, villages sacked or starved into submission, and savage reprisals taken against bedouin communities."[108] According to *Collier's Encyclopedia*, "Foreign observers estimated that during the Italian pacification of Libya (1911–1931), its population was reduced by one-third."

When *Lion of the Desert* was telecast on the History Channel (5 September 1997), history Professor Robert Brent Toplin of the University of North Carolina, told host Sandour Vanocur, that the Italian army even used "poison gas" against the Libyans "quite a lot [and] you don't see that in the movie."

Scene: Frames depict bedouins as freedom fighters and as victims of oppression. To authenticate the Italian occupation, stock black-and-white footage shows Italians invading Libya in 1911, killing bedouins and forcing other Libyans into wired, desert camps. The producer inter-cuts real footage of Italy's 1911 internment camps with his reel footage, showing bedouins entangled in barbed wire.

• General Graziani (Reed) tells his officers to construct in the desert an impenetrable barbed wire wall, 250 miles long, and to place "the bedouins behind barbed wire, in camps and keep them there." "If "there is resistance," he says, "you answer promptly with the old Roman punishment for rebellion—decimation."

• Italian troops raid and ravage villages; food supplies are burned; Koranic tablets destroyed; bedouins are placed in chains and dragged off. Armed with a pistol, one Fascist officer walks behind the Libyan prisoners. Abruptly, he stops. Then, he begins randomly shooting Arabs in the head. Other bedouins are killed in front of a firing squad; still others are shot trying to stop the Fascists from abducting their wives and daughters. As Italian bombs and tanks crush villagers, a bedouin proclaims, "We fight and die here."

• Scenes revere Islam. In the village, Omar Mukhtar (Quinn) instructs children, explaining selected verses from the Holy Koran. "Why do you think we begin every chapter of the Koran with God and the merciful?" Responds a child, "Because one of the names of God is merciful."

• After Fascists kill a villager, Mukhtar returns the man's Holy Koran to his family.

• Before Fascists hang a young Libyan woman, she whispers, "Thank you, God, for the lives you have given us."

• Imprisoned by the Fascists, the 73-year-old Mukhtar asks, "What is the will of wire compared to the will of God?" He asks a guard, "If you would allow me a little water, I could make myself ready for prayers." Prior to being hanged, he says: "From God we came, and unto God we return."

Note: The Italian army recorded, on film, their occupation of Libya. One of the Italian photographs shows the imprisoned Omar Mukhtar in chains.

• Scenes from *Lion of the Desert* illustrate what viewers almost never see—brave young bedouins, such as Ismail. Aware the Fascists will soon capture Mukhtar, Ismail insists Mukhtar take his horse. Later, the Fascists imprison and torture Ismail; he refuses to talk and the Fascists hang him.

The Lion Man (1937), New Realm. *Jon Hall.* SHEIKHS

Based on Edgar Rice Burroughs' book, *The Lad and the Lion*, this film presents a sinister sheikh and his bandits murdering peaceful Englishmen. Arabs also kidnap, then shoot, a graceful English woman. Surfacing as Arabia's champion, an Englishman in Arab garb.

Scene: In London, Sir Arnold Chapman and his son make plans to travel to a "desolate region," a "rotten country." They intend to meet with the villain, Sheikh Yousef Abdul, a desert Arab. Yousef's "palms are not only dirty, but they're very itchy."

• Yousef's desert tent. Puffing his nargelih, the devious sheikh lies, telling Sir Arnold and his companions that he sanctions friendly Arab-British relations. Flashback. Yousef's bandits ambush and kill several Englishmen. Plus, the Arabs abduct Shafia, an English woman.

• The present, morning. Introducing the kidnapped Shafia; she has been Yousef's hostage for many years. Suddenly, Shafia flees the camp, shooting an Arab. Knowing Yousef's men intend to ambush Sir Arnold's party, she tries to warn them. Too late. Yousef's men extinguish Sir Arnold's men. Shafia, too, is murdered. Unknown to Yousef, the son of Sir Arnold survives.

• Fast forward. Arabs call the surviving British youth "Lion El-Din," the Lion Man (Hall). Intending to marry, El-Din asks his adopted Arab father for permission to wed the lovely Leila. Soothing Arabic music underscores the couple's moonlight romance.

• Sheikh Yousef intervenes, demanding Leila wed him. Leila's compassionate father balks; he refuses to force his daughter to marry a man she does not love. The grateful El-Din thanks him, saying, "May Allah smile on thee."

• Yousef invites El-Din to his tent and serves him "drugged wine." El-Din collapses; Yousef takes Leila hostage.

• Soon, El-Din recovers. He rushes into the "infamous creature's" camp, killing Yousef.

• Leila soon learns that El-Din is really not an Arab, rather an Englishman, Sir Arnold's lost son. No matter; she embraces him.

Lion of Thebes (1964), Filmes. *Mark Forest, Yvonne Furneaux.* EGYPTIANS
In Thebes, warring Egyptians vs. Helen of Troy and a sturdy Spartan.
Scene: After the fall of Troy, Helen (Furneaux) seeks a safe haven, fleeing to Egypt. Unfortunately, upper and lower Egyptians are battling each other.
• The smitten pharaoh embraces Helen, dumping his Egyptian princess. Subsequently, killings in the palace escalate. An Egyptian general kills the pharaoh. Another Egyptian nabs Helen, boasting she "will bring us a handsome sum at the slave market."
• Who rescues the distressed Helen from feuding Egyptians? The mighty Spartan (Forest)!
• Egyptian wrestlers challenge Spartan; they lose.
Dialogue: The Egyptian princess complains to Helen about Thebes, "You may have noticed that here life has little value." During the build-up to the Gulf War, Nebraska Senator J. J. Exon was quoted in the *Omaha World Herald* as saying pretty much the same thing: "In the Arab world, life is not as important as in the non-Arab world" (30 August 1990). Later, the Senator apologized for his remark.

Lionheart (1987), WB. *Eric Stoltz, Nadim Salhawa, Gabriel Bryne.* SP: Menno Meyjes, Richard Outten. CAMEOS, VILLAINS
A heroic young English knight, Robert (Stoltz) contests the evil Black Prince (Bryne). Arab "Moslem" slavers are injected; they move to enslave England's "children of God."
Scene: In England, an Arab soldier, Selim (Sawalha), confers with the English prince. Selim wears a cone-shaped hat and a garish red garment. He insists the prince nab and deliver to his "Moslem leader" the "just and righteous children" of England. Not to fret, says the prince, I will sell the children "to the vilest eunuch in Arabia."
• Selim's Arab "slavers" and the Black Prince's cohorts sneak up and seize the children. To the rescue, King Richard and his men. Arriving from the Crusades, Richard's men kill scores of Arabs, terminate the Black Prince's henchmen, and free the children.
Note: The Arabs' outfits resemble costumes lifted from a 1950s Arabian screen fantasy.

Lisa (1962), TCF. *Stephen Boyd, Dolores Hart, Leo McKern, Hugh Griffith, Harry Andrews.* SP: Nelson Gidding. D: Philip Dunne. PALESTINIANS
Palestine as a land without Palestinians.
Scene: Holland 1946. Peter Jongman (Boyd), a Dutch policeman, rescues Lisa Held (Hart) from a Nazi white slaver. Lisa, a 21-year-old survivor of a Nazi concentration camp, tells Peter she wants to work in a mental hospital "in my own country." Peter vows to assist her, saying, "I will help you get to Palestine."
• Tangier, Morocco, a mosque. Cut to a loudspeaker; the call to prayer is transmitted. Another Dutchman, Captain Van Der Pink (Griffith), mocks the prayer call, quipping, "The faithful have been called to prayers, by electrical transcription." Confessing he smuggles weapons, Van Der Pink boasts, "Every man has his price. Take for instance my Captain Ayoob (Andrews). He's an Arab. Every time he takes a cargo into Palestine, he beats his breast because he's betraying his own people. He sold his soul to the devil. That's me."
• At a nightclub, a performing bellydancer fondles a huge snake.

• The souk. Feigning to be blind, a Moroccan beggar functions as a spy.

• Aboard Captain Ayoob's ship. Ayoob, an articulate Palestinian, smuggles Lisa, Peter, and guns into Palestine. The weapons Ayoob carries are for Jewish Haganah fighters.

• Peter, Lisa, and the weapons arrive safely. Nationalistic music underscores the next scene and others. The music swells as Jewish soldiers manning a tank appear; embossed on the tank's side, a white-chalked Star of David.

The Little Drummer Girl (1984), WB. *Diane Keaton, Yorgo Voyagis, Klaus Kinski, Sami Frey, Michael Cristofer.* SP: Loring Mandel, adapted from John Le Carre's novel. PALESTINIANS

On PBS's *Sneak Previews*, critics Siskel and Ebert accurately stated, "[this film] is about Arab terrorists and Israeli intelligence."

Scene: West Germany. Appearing is Michel, a Palestinian student who "makes innocent girls do his dirty work." Tagged "the Gucci Terrorist," Michel and his blonde girl friend blow up an Israeli diplomat, his wife, and child. See *Death before Dishonor* (1987).

• Israeli agents headed by Kurtz (Kinski) nab Michel. Explains one agent, "[One of Michel's girl's] took a bomb aboard a plane. It went up. I guess she never knew." The Israelis place a hood over the "handsome boy's" head, then strip him naked. Though cruelly tortured for "eleven days," Michel refuses to tell his captors about his brother, Kahlil (Frey). "Kahlil makes the bombs; Michel delivers them." Later, Michel's captors explode his Mercedes, killing the Palestinian and his lady friend.

• To catch Kahlil, Israeli agents recruit an American actress, Charlie (Keaton). At first, Charlie believes both sides use people, resulting in needless suffering. She meets Joseph (Voyagis), a sensitive Israeli agent who falls for her. Joseph tells her, "It will end with the assassination of a Palestinian terrorist."

• In Southern Lebanon, Charlie meets a war-weary Palestinian camp commander, Tayeh (Cristofer). Tayeh refers to his Palestinian recruits as "stateless savages." The commander advises Charlie to "go home"; you have "not done anything criminal, yet." Cut to clean-cut Palestinian youths, singing as they run. Next, they practice blowing up cars. Suddenly, the camp Palestinians uncover and kill an Israeli spy.

• Kurtz and his agents receive word that Kahlil will try to kill an Israeli professor who supports peace talks with the Palestinians. A German official tells the Israelis, "It's not our fault you have problems with the Arabs. They have problems with everybody, always." Unknown to Kahlil, Charlie and the Israelis dupe him; working together they defuse Kahlil's "bikini bomb."

• Kahlil believes the bomb he gave Charlie has killed the professor and those attending his lecture, as well. The pleased Palestinian tells her,

> You've done a great thing for us...weep, keep your heart alive...Many Zionist supporters are wounded, many, many civilians...Tomorrow they will read the Palestinians will not wait 2,000 years like the Jews.

• Kahlil and Charlie make love. She notices a missing finger; Kahlil explains its loss. "One day in Beirut I'm in the office; the post comes. I'm in a hurry, I open it. Then, I wake up in the hospital." Advises Kahlil, "Next time before you open a parcel, read the postmark first. If it comes from Tel Aviv, better return it to sender."

• An Israeli squad invades the bedroom, killing Kahlil. Shocked, Charlie screams. Her crying out exemplifies the conflict's insanity. Later, Joseph confesses to Charlie, "I don't know too much any more about right or wrong." His comments summarize a movie that reveals grievances and excesses of Israelis and Palestinians alike.

• In the end, Israelis bomb Tayeh's Palestinian camp; scores are killed including the Palestinian trainees. Next, the Israelis slice the throat of a Palestinian homosexual.

Dialogue: The film does acknowledges the existence of Palestine as an entity, and of Palestinians as a people who merit rights. As Joseph says, "Some on both sides want to come together, Charlie. Want the Palestinians to have a homeland beside us. I do."

Note: Even before the film went into production, news stories revealed that some Israelis were upset with Le Carre's book, saying it was "sympathetic to the Palestinians." For example, one reporter with Israel's widely circulated *Ma'ariv* newspaper said the book was "anti-Israeli." At a Jerusalem seminar about media coverage of conflicts, "Joshua Muravchik, author of a study on news reporting during the Lebanon war, accused Mr. Le Carre' of being anti-Semitic."[109]

Little Egypt (1951), UI. *Mark Stevens, Rhonda Fleming, Stephen Geray.*
MAIDENS, EGYPTIANS

This movie is about a famous Egyptian dancer. Yet, the star is not an Egyptian: the spotlight shines on a lovely American woman posing as an Egyptian.

Scene: For a minute or so, "the friendship of Egypt and the United States" is mentioned, along with talk about a joint Nile reclamation project. Suddenly, the plot shifts, focusing on the Chicago Fair and its star performer, "Little Egypt," Princess Izora (Fleming). Izora performs "ancient Egyptian ceremonial dances; she's "the talk of Chicago, and the sweetheart of thirty million Americans."

• In Egypt, American promoter Mark Cravat (Stevens) considers hiring some Egyptians to work at Chicago's Fair. Cut to "Mahmoud, a two-bit blackmailer." The Egyptian lifts Mark's wallet. Barks Mark, "If there's anything I can't stand, it's a thief."

• The Chicago Fair. Appearing alongside Izora is a bogus Pasha (Geray) and several mute, veiled Egyptian maidens. The Pasha derides his brother-in-law, saying, "May the vultures pluck the eyes from his head."

• A businessman wants to put Izora's "picture in every cigarette pack of his Egyptian Pleasures," with the logo: "Little Egypt brings you Egyptian Pleasures." Historically, this cigarette marketing ploy is accurate. As early as 1900, advertising monies were used to place attractive picture cards in cigarette packs. Cards displaying scantily-clad Arab maidens were commonplace, especially inside American Tobacco Company packs.

• Surprise! Izora, who loves Mark, is not an Egyptian. Only near the conclusion are viewers told that she is actually Betty Lou Randolph of "Jersey City." The Fair's entrepreneurs promote Betty Lou as "Little Egypt" or "Princess Izora" for one reason— to sell tickets!

• Only after Mark finds out that Izora is an American, does he kiss her. In 1893, the real "Little Egypt" featured at Chicago's Fair was really Egyptian. So, why couldn't the producers feature Izora as a bona-fide Egyptian woman?

• Given the Egyptian dancers' popularity at World Fairs, no wonder men flocked to see *Little Egypt*, the American Mutoscope Company's first success. What made "the Mutoscope amusements perfect viewing," writes Professor David Nasaw, was its mechanical crank. Operated by hand, spectators could control performances by the simple turning of the crank. The procedure was explained in an 1897 advertising brochure: "Each separate picture may be inspected at leisure." Thus, viewers could follow each and every movement of Egypt's "Dance du Ventre," a popular amusement that projected the dancer's "attractive, amusing and startling" impressions.[110]

The Living Daylights (1987), MGM/UA. *Timothy Dalton.* Filmed in Morocco. CAMEOS

Dense and slick Moroccans.

Scene: In Tangier, 007 (Dalton) monitors the movements of a Russian. Unexpectedly, a mute Moroccan musician approaches Bond. The Arab plays several instruments, off-key, annoying Bond. But when 007 forks over cash, the Moroccan pockets the money and walks off.

• Believing 007 has killed a famous Russian, Moroccan policemen chase him, firing away. The fleeing Bond nearly floors a Moroccan woman, hanging clothes on a rooftop.

Lola (1969), a.k.a. Twinky, a.k.a. Child Bride, AIP. *Charles Bronson, Susan George.* CAMEOS

Arab marital mores.

Scene: New York City. Introducing Twinky (George), a 16-year-old child bride whose marriage to aging writer Scott Wardman (Bronson) is falling apart. A friend advises Twinky to dump her 38-year-old husband. Twinky reads aloud her letter, "A divorce, Lebanese-style. All you have to do is turn around three times, saying 'I divorce thee, I divorce thee, I divorce thee.'" Final frames. Twinky says, three times, "I divorce thee."

The Lone Runner (1986), TWE. *Miles O'Keeffe, John Steiner, Ronald Lacey, Savina Gersak.* Filmed in Morocco. VILLAINS

Desert Arabs wearing Ku Klux Klan garb vs. the Western protagonist; Arabs vs. Arabs.

Scene: Arabia. Aboard a stagecoach, a passenger from England complains to his British companions about "these people that live under the sand. Their leader is a wild fanatic." Cut to the town's casino, featuring a bellydancer.

• A European becomes ill; an Arab offers to assist, saying, "I have an excellent extract of cactus and camel dung."

• Armed with a crossbow and plenty of explosive-tipped arrows, the heroic lone runner, Garrett (O'Keeffe), gallops through the desert, bringing down Arab villains. Some curs brandish war-paint on their faces; other Arabs cover their faces with Ku Klux Klan-type hoods.

• In the souk, the good Arabs, their white thobes flaring with slatted sunlight, venerate the lone runner. Garrett aids bedouins in need of water. Pointing an explosive arrow into the sand, he fires. Out gushes water! The bedouins express amazement. Garrett's jacket, vest, and boots resemble those cowboy outfits worn by Clint Eastwood in spaghetti westerns.

• Bedouin bandits abduct a blonde European woman. Suddenly, the hood-wearing Arabs attack the bedouins; they grab the blonde and toss her into a wooden cage. One nasty Arab fondles her. Cut to Garrett and his Arab friends; Garrett frees the blonde and crushes the man. Next, he unleashes scores of exploding arrows; the screen reveals lots of dead Arabs.

The Long Kiss Goodnight (1996), NL. *Geena Davis, Samuel Jackson.* SP: Shane Black. P, D: Renny Harlin. CAMEOS

Renegade US intelligence agents frame Arab Muslims for terrorist attacks.[111]

Scene: High-level CIA operatives are angry because Congress has cut funds for their counter-terrorism unit. The agency chief asks the president, "Where is our funding?" Quips the president, "Can you say health care?" Intent on convincing the president to restore funds, the unit's renegades initiate terrorist attacks throughout the country, blaming Arabs.

• Boasts the head agent, "The 1993 World Trade Center bombing. Remember? During the trial one of the terrorists claimed the CIA was involved. We paved the way for the bombing," he confesses.

• The renegade agents intend to set off a major explosion. Rationalizes one agent, "We'll blame it on the Muslims, naturally. Then I'll get my funding."

• The agents dump an Arab Muslim's corpse onto the truck carrying the bomb. Declares the protagonist (Davis), "So, you plant this poor Arab to take the fall." Affirms the agent, "One terrorist on ice waiting to play patsy."

The Long Ships (1964), COL. *Richard Widmark, Sidney Poitier, Rosanna Schiaffino.* VILLAINS, MAIDENS

Vikings slay malevolent Moors. A Muslim woman prefers a Viking to her dark Moorish husband.

Scene: At Barbary's souk, Moors listen to the Viking Rolfe (Widmark) spin a tale about "the great golden bell." Suddenly, Aly Mansuh's (Poitier) troops arrive, whisking Rolfe off to the palace. Aly wants Rolfe to reveal the location of the missing bell, explaining that years ago some Byzantine monks "plundered Islam, [stealing] the treasures of Islam." Affirms Aly's wife, Aminah (Schiaffino), the bell now rests on "Christian land."

• Islam equals violence. Rolfe's Viking friends arrive in Aly's kingdom. Shouting Allahu Akbar (God is great), Aly's clad-in-black soldiers charge the Vikings. The outnumbered Vikings kill scores, but surrender.

• Aly threatens to "sell them (the Vikings) as slaves." As he prays, his Moors whip their Viking captives. Aly wants to show his "power of authority." He orders Aminah to choose a Moor, a man who will sacrifice his life for the ruler. Reluctantly, she selects a soldier, asking him, "Do you believe in Allah?" The Moor nods, then advances toward a mammoth, lengthy steel blade. Aly smiles. On cue, the soldier slides down the huge blade and is split in half.

• Knowing that in order to reclaim the lost bell, Aly needs the Vikings' expertise, Rolfe quips, "You Moors don't make very good sailors." Nods Aly, "We are not sailors, the ocean is not like the desert." Sighs Aminah, "You failed with him (Rolfe), again."

• Aminah begs Aly to love her. Aly walks off. So, she beds Rolfe. Why show "the most envied woman of all Islam" cheating on her husband, bedding a Viking? Racism. In 1964, when the movie was released, producers were probably afraid to show Rosanna

Schiaffino, the white actress portraying Aminah, having sex with a black man, Aly, portrayed by actor Sidney Poitier. Yet, producers willingly perpetuate a stale stereotype showing Aly lusting after, but not seducing a blonde Viking virgin. As the ruler's maidens dress the blonde lass, they sigh "ooh," and "ah."

• Though Aly's men abuse Rolfe's men, the Vikings build a superb ship. Aly Inc. sail off and retrieve the missing bell.

Finis: Abruptly, fresh Viking troops appear, bringing down Aly's men. One Viking kills Aminah. Furious, Aly shouts "Allahu Akbar" and charges Rolfe. They fight; the giant golden bell crushes the Moor.

Looking for Danger (1957), AA. *Huntz Hall, Stanley Clements, Michael Granger, Peter Mamakos, Lili Kardell, George Khoury. Based on a story by Elwood Ullman and Edward Bernds.* SHEIKHS, MAIDENS, VILLAINS

WWII. Arabs and Nazis vs. Americans; Arabs vs. Arabs.

Scene: New York City, "Mike's Hash House." The Bowery Boys, Sach (Hall) and Duke (Clements), spin a tale about how they and "the allies got the situation in hand in North Africa." Flashback. Stock footage displays American soldiers in Casablanca.

• The mythical kingdom of El-Akbar. US soldiers, including Sach and Duke, find out that Sheikh Sidi-Omar's (Granger) "country is [being] overrun by the enemy." The men are ordered to "get a message through to a very good friend of the allies, the Hawk, who is with the Arab underground."

• Disguised as German soldiers, Sach and Duke rush off to Sidi-Omar's palace, intending to warn the ruler about the Germans. Surprise! Sidi-Omar and his Arabs are in cahoots with the enemy Germans.

• Inside the palace, an Arab woman appears in wedding apparel. Other maidens model, then dance. The GIs are warned, "It's sudden death for anyone to look upon the bride-to-be." Perhaps this stale cliché was lifted from an Arabian Nights fable.

• Harem maidens woo Sach and Duke; Arab music underscores the cooing. Protests Sach, "There's gotta be better music than that." The Arab phonograph record is replaced with a "Hep-Cats" single. The GIs and maidens dance the jitterbug; even Arab guards join in.

• Supporting the Allies, Col. Ahmed (Avonde). After Ahmed helps the men escape from Sidi-Omar's "crummy place," he tells the GIs, "You will have the fastest camels [No cars and trucks?] to escort you back to your lines!"

• Pro-Axis Arabs and their German cohorts gather at the "New Moon" restaurant. Cut to Sach eating Arab cuisine, then grimacing: "What a delicious brick; I'll come back tomorrow and get my teeth. If I eat that stuff... you won't have to execute me."

• Sach dons harm garb and approaches an Arab villain. Thinking Sach is really a harem maiden, the dense Arab tries to smooch him!

• Introducing Shareen (Kardell), the heroic Arab maiden; the blonde tells the GIs that she is their contact person intent on crushing the Axis—the Hawk! When Sach Inc. try to warn the Allies, Sidi-Omar appears, imprisoning the trio. The GIs legs are anchored to balls and chains. Shouts an enemy Arab, "Yankee go home." Easily, the men dupe their drunken Arab guard, Mustapha (Khoury), and escape.

• The "Krauts" and Sidi-Omar's Arabs nab them; they go to terminate Shereen, Col.

Ahmed, Sach, and Duke. To the rescue, some GIs. The soldiers assist Sach Inc. Though "outnumbered twenty-to-one," they "snafu the enemy plot." Sach punches out evil Arabs exclaiming, "That ends the hassle in the castle."

• Stock footage displays American paratroopers taking "over in nothing flat."

Dialogue: One Arab is called a "monkey."

The Looney, Looney, Looney Bugs Bunny Movie (1981), WB.

Animated. W: Warren Foster, Friz Freleng. D: Freleng. VILLAINS

Featured in this movie is "Sahara Hare" (1955); it is one of many cartoons edited and spliced into this full length compilation of Warner Bros. classics. The cartoon shows Bugs Bunny humiliating "Mr. Ayrab."

Scene: The Sahara desert. Twenty minutes into this feature film the camera reveals Bugs Bunny taking a bath. Abruptly, the white-thobed, camel-riding "Riff-Raff" (Yosemite Sam) appears, confronting Bugs. Bugs yanks "Mr. Ayrab's" white burnoose, using it to dry his ears.

• Bugs points to "Mr. Ayrab's" thobe, quipping: "Your slip is showing." When Riff-Raff commences firing, Bugs runs off to an abandoned legion fort. Above the fort's entrance, this sign stating: "FOR RENT OR LEASE CALL MOROCCO."

• Continually, Riff-Raff tries to enter the legion outpost. First, he tries to pole-vault into the fort. Wham! The Arab smashes into a wall. Next, Riff-Raff mounts an elephant and charges the fort's doors. Clever Bugs lets loose a wind-up toy mouse. Seeing the mouse, the elephant panics, trouncing "Mr. Ayrab." Finally, Bugs plants some TNT at the fort's entrance. When Riff-Raff charges the fort, boom! The ensuing explosion sends him to directly to hell.

The Lost City (1935), COL. 12 episodes. *William "Stage" Boyd, Gino Corrado, Kane Richmond, George F. "Gabby" Hayes, Eddie Fetherstone.* Columbia also released two feature films that are edited versions of this serial: *The Lost City* (1935) and *City of Lost Men* (1935). CLIFFHANGERS, SHEIKHS, VILLAINS

Three episodes show Arabs enslaving Africans.

Scene: Mad scientist Zolok (Boyd) moves to conquer the world. By unleashing electrical storms, Zolok floods cities and destroys ocean liners and bridges. Also, using a special gadget, Zolok captures normal-sized black natives, then turns the men into giant African zombies.

• Introducing a foul and greedy Arab "slave trader" abusing the black natives, Ben Ali (Corrado). Speaking with an Italian accent, the Arab barks, "I'm looking for slaves, giant slaves."

• Giggling Arab women attend Ben Ali, filing his nails. As the slaver smokes his nargelih, the maidens chant.

• Ben Ali's slavers nab a "white" man, an American named Butterfield (Hayes). To the rescue, the protagonist, Bruce Gordon (Richmond), and his friends, plus some Africans. They charge Ben Ali's camp, killing scores. Ben Ali and Gordon grab sabers and duel; Gordon triumphs. Earlier, Butterfield vowed to bring down the Arab, saying: "Ben Ali's a slave trader. He's here to get the giants from the lost city [and to deliver them] to the slave coast.[But] I'll get my blacks to come back here and wipe out this [Arab's] camp."

Butterfield's true to his word: he, Gordon and the Africans demolish the Arabs.

Finis: Gordon Inc. escape unscathed. As for Zolok, a powerful electrical outburst erases the deranged scientist and his Lost City.

Dialogue: When Gordon's friend Jerry (Fetherstone) dons Arab garb, he sighs, "Wait 'til I get this Arab nightshirt off me."

Note: *The Lost City* serial and both *Lost City* feature films "out of general circulation [because of] the serial's blatantly racist attitudes towards its black characters," writes Roy Kinnard. "When a New York television station attempted to screen *The Lost City* [in the fifties] public outcry was volatile, and the picture was immediately withdrawn."[112] Kinnard, however, says nothing about *The Lost City*'s Arab portraits.

• Discussing how peoples are projected in movie serials, Ken Weiss and Ed Goodgold cite *The Lost City* as one of the most white chauvinist.

> As the hero races toward shrieks coming from the distance, he mentions to his sidekick, "That sounds like a white woman screaming." Later, our hero discovers that Dr. Manyus, the story's scientific genius, has invented a serum that can make a black man white. Awestruck, the hero tells Dr. Manyus, "This is the greatest invention in history." Dr. Manyus smiles modesty and answers, "Science can accomplish anything."[113]

The Lost City (1935), COL. This full-length feature film is one of two made from the 12-episode serial of the same name. VILLAINS

Lost Command (1966), COL. *Anthony Quinn, Alain Delon, George Segal, Claudia Cardinale.* SP: Nelson Gidding. VILLAINS, MAIDENS

1950s Algeria. In this view of the French-Algerian war, Algerians kill women and children; Algerians resisting French rule are called terrorists. In fact, when Algeria emerged from 130 years of French colonial rule on 5 July 1962, at least 300,000 soldiers and civilians, from both sides, had died.

Scene: Vietnam. A Vietnamese commander offers a captured French paratrooper, Mahidi (Segal), special treatment. "So, you are Algerian," he says. Counters Mahidi, "I am a French officer." Says the commander, "Our victory is also a victory for all you Arabs under the heels of the French... Come, you need not feel any solidarity with the French. They will never accept you." Retorts Mahidi, "I prefer to stay with my comrades." Soon, the Vietnamese conflict ends.

• When Mahidi and his paratroopers appear in Algeria, a French soldier stops them, cautioning, "We wouldn't want to find you in a back alley with your throat cut by the wogs, would we?" Mahidi's comrade, Captain Esclavier (Delon), protests the slur, "Don't call them wogs. This officer (Mahidi) is an Arab."

• Later, Esclavier tells Mahidi, "Look, it's a bad situation for you, here [in Algeria]. Why don't you come to Paris and spend your time with me?" Says Mahidi, "Thank you my good friend, but I am staying here. This is my home. There is an Arab saying, 'The courage of your friends gives you strength.'"

• Greeting Mahidi are his parents, his sister, Aicha (Cardinale), and Dr. Ali Ben Saad. "There's been a revolution here," says Dr. Saad. "The yellow-skinned people beat the French. Many Moslems believe we could do the same."

• Cut to Mahidi's younger brother writing "Independence" on a wall. French soldiers spot the youth and shoot him dead. Next, the soldiers destroy the home of Mahidi's parents. Other Algerian youths write "Independence," the French machine-gun them.

• In France, a Frenchman opposed to Algeria's quest for independence tells Colonel Raspeguy (Quinn), "My family has a farm in Algeria. They have been there for 100 years." Next, General Melies dispatches Raspeguy to Algeria, where "a strong band of terrorists" operate. Unknown to Raspeguy, the leader of "the terrorists" is Mahidi, the colonel's comrade in Vietnam. Algerian rebels intend to "push the French back into the sea," says the general. But we will win, and "then we'll give ourselves a treat with all their wives and daughters." Frenchmen listening to his speech cheer.

• On screen, bodies of a French family killed by Algerian farm hands. The French move to avenge "the mutilation." Cut to Raspeguy's soldiers killing Algerian villagers; bodies clutter the roads. "This isn't vengeance," protests a French soldier, "it's pointless slaughter."

• Aicha, who is called "a Moorish whore," says, "It's a bitter war. The Algerians want independence." Captain Esclavier offers to carry her package. Aicha refuses, saying, "In our country, women carry for the men." Quips Esclavier, "And walk behind them."

• Feigning friendship, Aicha uses the captain to smuggle bombs to her brother's fighters. See *Black Sunday* (1977).

• Later, Esclavier finds out that Aicha is a spy. Yet, he promises Mahidi's life will be spared provided she reveals his whereabouts. Believing him, Aicha confesses. The captain informs Colonel Raspeguy, "I promised her we wouldn't kill Mahidi... that we take him alive. Is it a deal?" Nods the colonel, "It's a deal."

• The French kill Mahidi. Esclavier screams at Raspeguy, "You didn't have to kill him." Quips the colonel, "We won, didn't we!" Retorts the captain, "I pity you and your victory. You've turned into an animal."

• As officers decorate the colonel for his victory over the rebels, the camera reveals French soldiers forcing an Algerian to erase "Independence" from a wall. Seeing two Algerian youths writing "Independence" on another wall, the captain smiles.

Note: Recommended viewing is Gillo Pontecorvo's forceful *The Battle of Algiers* (1965, Italian, with English subtitles). This compelling portrayal of the rebellion against the French contains balanced images of the French and Algerians. The film not only allows viewers to empathize with Algerians, the film explains why the Algerians sought to free themselves from French rule. Unlike *Lost Command*, the movie presents some *French* soldiers as terrorists. They shoot civilians on crowded streets, kill innocent Algerian women and children in the casbah, burn Arab houses, and torture prisoners. They even behead one Algerian as he dared say, "Long live Algeria!"

• For a another perspective of the French-Algerian conflict, see noted Egyptian director Youssef Chahine's feature film *Djamila the Algerian* (1958), which depicts French colonizers damaging Algerian innocents, notably a young woman. The Film Society of Lincoln Center honored Chahine during the 1998 New York Film Festival, for his almost half-century of making extraordinary movies at a prodigious rate.

Lost in a Harem (1944), MGM. *Bud Abbott, Lou Costello, Marilyn Maxwell, John Conte, Douglass Dumbrille, the Jimmy Dorsey Orchestra.* See *Ishtar* (1987). SHEIKHS

Two vaudeville performers, Abbott and Costello, along with singer Marilyn Maxwell, resolve intra-Arab strife in "terrible, teeming, Barabeeha."[114] Arab rulers brandish "cats-eyes rings."

Scene: 1940s "Port Inferno." Arab guards "tie a man behind a horse and drag him through the street." Inside the palace, secret passages; a dungeon with skeletons and executioners.

• Barabeeha's rightful heir, Prince Ramo (Conte), approaches Bud and Lou, saying, "Assist me in dethroning my vicious uncle Nimative (Dumbrille) and regaining my kingdom."

• Nimative's desert palace. The lecherous tyrant imports "from America, at great expense, Hazel (Maxwell), a beautiful blue-eyed blonde." Barks Nimative, "Anyone who says she isn't beautiful will have his head cut off." Hazel tags the mesmerizing ruler a "wicked wolf," saying, "He stared at me like I was a porterhouse steak and he was the knife." When Hazel tries to resist the sheikh's advances, he displays "two evil cats-eyes rings," hypnotizing her. Under the ring-spell, Hazel purrs, "You are my master. I wish to become your wife. I love you." Chuckles Nimative, "Very well, my dear, you will become wife number thirty-eight."

• Lou promises Teema, Nimative's star-stuck harem maiden, that he will make her a movie star. But first, she must help him collapse the sheikh. This caper, "I-will-take-an-Arab-to-Hollywood," is similar to the one used in *Beat the Devil* (1954). Here, Humphrey Bogart tells an Arab sheikh he'll fix him up with Rita Hayworth, provided the Arab frees him and his colleagues. *Beat the Devil*'s infatuated sheikh falls for the ruse.

• Unlike typical screen Arabs out to take Western heroines, Prince Ramo woos and weds the blonde, Hazel. Ramo tells Hazel she means more to him than his kingdom.

• Bringing down the sheikh and his cohorts are the courageous "Sons of the Desert," a band of "soft-hearted, quick-witted and sure-footed" bedouins who defend "the meek."

Finis: Arab-as-animal. Nimative is hypnotized. The sheikh is told that he is now a dog. Abruptly, Nimative scurries on all fours, barks, and heads for "the kennel."

Note: Barabeeha's Arabs and magic rings. Explains Ramo, "Whosoever wears those evil rings controls the destiny of the entire country."

• The camera reveals harem maidens lounging in the ruler's "Wives Quarters." When Nimative barks, "Amuse me," bare-chested males as well as half-naked females, rush toward the lens. This scene prompted "The Breen Office [to] express concern about the costuming and dancing of the harem maidens." Breen officials issued MGM a warning,

> Advise the costume department to use extreme care in the designing of these costumes. Make certain that the dance routines performed by these lightly costumed girls be watched closely in order to avoid any suggestive or sensuous body movements. Otherwise they could not be approved under provisions of the Code.[115]

• In their book on Abbott and Costello, Furmanek and Palumbo point out that Breen was "particularly sensitive" about Arab reaction to the film. It was important, Breen told MGM producers, "to avoid any use of the expression, 'Allah be praised,' or any like religious expression that may be taken as a derogatory reference to the religion of

Mohammedans." In spite of the Breen warning, "the film was rejected for showing in Morocco, while several cuts had to be made for showing in Syria."

• Breen's office did convince producers to remove this scene: An Arab fruit monger asking Lou, "Would you like a date?" Lou remains mum. Prods Bud, "Answer the man. He wants to give you a date." Declares Lou, "He don't appeal to me." The scene was "unacceptable because of a 'pansy' flavor," said Breen.

• Accompanying features in the early 1940s were movie musical shorts displaying veiled, scantily-clad harem maidens attending bearded, unattractive sheikhs. Three of Official Films shorts featured tunes such as "Dancing in the Harem," "Sultan's Charms," and "I Don't Like No Gals." In part, the lyrics: "Dancing in the harem every day, you can get an eye full as they sway... look at what they're wearin'... dancin' in the harem with the sultan's wives." And, the "I'm as dumb as they come sultan" croons: "I drive the girls frantic, but I don't like no gals."

The Lost Patrol (1934), RKO Radio. *Victor McLaglen, Reginald Denny, Boris Karloff, Alan Hale.* SP: Dudley Nichols. Based on Philip MacDonald's novel *Patrol.* A 1929 silent version, not discussed here, stars Victor McLaglen's brother, Cyril, and was photographed in the Sahara. This 1934 film was shot near Yuma, Arizona. VILLAINS

Featuring British soldiers vs. Arabs, *The Lost Patrol* was one of 1934's top money-making films. In his review, Gregory William Mank writes, "So powerfully does [director John] Ford build his film that many audiences cheered in vicarious and violent release as McLaglen viciously and maniacally slaughtered the Arabs who finally revealed themselves."[116] See *True Lies* (1994), *Iron Eagle* (1986), *Executive Decision* (1996), *Rules of Engagement* (2000).

Scene: WWI, the "vast Mesopotamia desert... on fire with the sun." Lost in the endless desert, British troops engaged in "fighting an unseen Arab enemy who always struck in the dark, like a relentless ghost." The soldiers wear the "blank look of death."

• Abruptly, an officer is shot. "Blasted Arabs done it," barks the British Sergeant (McLaglen). They "hide like sand flies, never see 'em." The sergeant takes commands of the ten-man patrol. As the men try to find their way back to brigade headquarters, "sneaky Arabs" pick them off. One soldier's fantasy reveals "the joy of killing Arabs." Other soldiers dream of England and the jolly good ol' days.

• Evening. Invisible Arabs shoot the soldiers, dropping them one-by-one. Next, Arabs kill a sentry. After running off the troops' horses, the Arabs "knife in the back" another soldier. The troops spot their tortured comrades strapped to horses. Says one, "Sneaky Arabs. Those dirty, filthy swine."

• Throughout the movie, the Arab snipers' faces are concealed. But near the end, the snipers become visible. The sergeant, now the lone survivor, spots five dark-robed figures surfacing from behind desert dunes. The sergeant grabs a machine gun. Laughing, he mows down the Arabs. Fresh British troops arrive. They ask about the patrol; the sergeant points to several graves in the sand.

Note: The scenario never explains *why* Arabs fight the British... or shows an Arab soldier dreaming of home, being with friends and family.

Love in the Desert (1929), Radio Pictures. Silent (with ten minutes of dialogue during the opening and final frames). *Olive Borden, Noah Berry, Hugh Trevor, Charles Brinley.* *NS. Notes from VAR (8 May 1929). SHEIKHS

Desert Arabs abduct a spoiled American playboy. Arabs vs. Arabs.

Because young Bob Winslow (Trevor) romances too many chorus girls, his wealthy parents decide to ship him off to Arabia. As soon as Bob arrives, Abdullah's outlaw Arabs kidnap him. Suddenly, amour. Princess Zarah (Borden), the daughter of Sheikh Hassan (Brinley), falls for Bob. The enraged and jealous Abdullah (Berry) threatens "a massacre" unless Zarah weds him. But, Zarah prefers Bob. So, Hassan's Arabs fight Abdullah's Arabs. In the end, Bob unites with Zarah. As for Abdullah (Berry), "the vicious turbaned gangster is bumped."

Love in Morocco (1933), a.k.a. Baroud, Ideal. *Rex Ingram, Felipe Montes, Rosita Garcia, Pierre Batcheff.* SP: Peter Spencer. D: Rex Ingram. S: Ingram. *NS. Notes from NYT (20 March 1933). MAIDENS

An Arab woman loves a French officer. Moroccans battle Berbers in the Atlas Mountains. See *The Song of Love* (1923), and *Outpost in Morocco* (1949).

Rex Ingram's first and only sound film, and one in which he himself appears. Ingram's scenario reveals stereotypical images: "The picture is flooded with picturesque types— Spahis, African serving women, beggars, dancing girls, bandits from the desert." Latino performers portray the Arab protagonists.

The Moroccan, Hamed (Batcheff), finds out that Andre, his French friend, loves Zinah (Garcia), his sister. Hamed's father expresses anger, declaring Moorish "custom" demands that "the infidel" Andre be killed. Cut to a Berber "bandit chief" and his renegades attacking Hamed's tribe. Thanks to Andre's heroics, Hamed's men triumph. In battle, the Frenchman earns the "gratitude" of Hamed's father. Thus, Andre may attain Zinah's hand "in marriage."

Note: The NYT reviewer credits Ingram's cameramen for capturing "the dark beauty" of Moroccans.

• In his *Rex Ingram: Master of the Silent Cinema*, Liam O'Leary writes, "Ingram steeped himself in the atmosphere of Morocco and got to know the country and its people intimately. El Glaoui, the great feudal despot of the Atlas," for example, "helped the *Baroud* production in many ways, lending swords, guns and costumes as Ingram required them." While filming, Ingram donned Arab garb "so that he could more intimately mingle with the street crowds without being identified as a European." Ingram would even "sign his name, Bin Aliq Nasr El-Din, which means in Arabic, The Son of the Union of Victory and Religion."[117]

• For its European release, *Love in Morocco* was entitled *Baroud*, meaning "tribal warfare." London's National Film Archive houses the *Baroud* negative.

Loverboy (1989), TRI. *Patrick Dempsey.* CAMEOS

Mute Arabs appear in this comedy about a pizza delivery-boy's bedroom antics.

Scene: Pool side. All the swimmers wear swimsuits. Abruptly, twice, the camera shows three Arabs. The Arabs wear not swimsuits but full-length robes and burnooses. When the young protagonist (Dempsey) spots the fully-clothed men at the pool, he registers shock, and stares.

Madame Rosa (1977), Lira. French, dubbed in English. *Simone Signoret, Sammy Ben Youb, Claud Dauphin, Gabriel Jabbour.* D: Moshe Mizrahi. BEST LIST
   In Paris, an Arab Muslim boy and his beloved friend, an elderly Jewish woman.
   Scene: Pigalle, a dilapidated building. Madame Rosa (Signoret), a Jewish survivor of Nazi concentration camps, struggles to walk up six flights to her flat; Arab boarders assist her. Rosa cares for some hookers' children, earning little money. Her favorite youth is Mohammad (Ben Youb), an ll-year-old Algerian boy.
   • The camera reveals a devout white-robed Arab Muslim, Mr. Hamil, reading to Rosa's children. Mohammad, (Momo is his nickname) asks Hamil, "Why are you always wearing a smile?" Says Hamil, "That is how I found God in my memory, little Mohammad."
   • Unexpectedly, Momo sells "what he loved most in the world," his dog. And, he takes the 500 francs he receives for his pet, and throws the money in the gutter. Upset, Rosa whisks Momo off to Dr. Katz (Dauphin), shouting, "Not even in Auschwitz, they would have done such a thing." She insists that Katz examine Momo for syphilis. "Hold on," says Katz, "I'm surprised to hear such nonsense, Madame Rosa. How can you talk that way? You want me to examine him for syphilis because he's an Arab? Why, of all the old wives' tales. People spread rubbish like that and one fine day you have Auschwitz." Momo cries. Sighs Rosa, "He's not like other children."
   • Rosa decides Momo needs an education; she takes him to a French school. But officials refuse to admit him. Sans a birth certificate, the Arab is considered an outsider. "One thing, sure, when the going gets rough," says Rosa, "the Jews and the Arabs are in the same boat."
   • In a public square, "sensitive" Momo decorates an old umbrella, acquires some puppets and then entertains onlookers. As Rosa is ill, with a weak heart and "high blood pressure," Momo passes a hat, collecting money for the 67-year-old woman.
   • In Rosa's room, Momo does the chores and looks after Rosa's children. "What will become of you without me?" asks Rosa. She tells the Arab boy that he is "handsome," pleading, "Never sell your body."
   • Momo encounters Nadine, an attractive film editor, and Ramon, her lover. And, he befriends Moshe, a Jewish orphan.
   • Mr. Hamil, the Muslim scholar, lugs around a Victor Hugo book. Sadly, he loses his eyesight and memory. And, Rosa dreams of the Holocaust.
   • Suddenly, Momo's absent father appears seeking forgiveness. He was confined in a mental hospital for eleven years. Rosa detests this "sick man"; he killed his wife, Ayisha, a whore. Thus, Rosa protects Momo from this "mental case for a father." When he is told that Rosa raised his son as "a Jew," Momo's father suffers a heart attack.
   • The seriously-ill Rosa pleads with Momo not to let anyone take her away. She tells Momo, "You're the only man I ever loved." He kisses her cheek. Using his wits, Momo prevents Dr. Katz from taking Rosa to the hospital, where she does not want to die.
   • Thanks to Momo's vigilant and tender care, Rosa passes on "in peace, in her Jewish home, a secret room [that is located] in the building's basement." Though Rosa and Momo had "a wonderful time together," Momo mourns, saying, "You can't live without someone to love."

Made for Love (1926), Cecil B. DeMille Prod. Silent. *Leatrice Loy, Edmund Burns, Bertram Grassby, Snits Edwards.* S: Garrett Fort. EGYPTIANS, VILLAINS

This desert melodrama features Egyptian and bedouin villains.

Scene: "Egypt, the Valley of the Kings." A US archeologist, Nicky Ainsworth (Burns), and his Egyptians discover an inner tomb containing two royal lovers, Princess Herath and Aziru.

• Inside a tent, Nicky's fiancée, Joan (Loy), craves amour; Nicky ignores her. Joan drifts off to check out the Egyptian lovers' tomb. Cut to slinky Prince Mahmoud (Grassby), an Arab who "steals from ladies who have died to adorn those who must live." Barks Mahmoud, "This American [Nicky] must be stopped." With Mahmoud is Selim (Edwards), "of the tribe of Twin Bedouins." Selim sees the lovesick Joan, advising Mahmoud, "Behold, a neglected nymph."

• Flashback. Joan and Nicky are now Aziru and Princess Herath. The ruling pharaoh decides to wed Princess Herath/Joan, and dispatches his brother, Aziru/Nicky, to deliver her. But Herath falls for Aziru; they kiss near an oasis. The pharaoh's spy spots them, telling the pharaoh about the embrace. Furious, the jealous pharaoh poisons Princess Herath's drink; she perishes in Aziru's arms. After mourning her death, the pharaoh decides to construct a tomb for the couple, warning, "The curse of Isis upon him who dares disturb their slumber."

• Flash forward. Nicky and Joan now wear Western garb. Nicky examines even more artifacts, ignoring Joan. The really-bored Joan rides off into the desert. Too late, Nicky realizes he's a dunce; he rides out after her.

• A desert camp, complete with dancing maidens and a slimy sheikh. Two bedouins tell their leader that Joan is alone. Appearing from behind sand dunes, the leering bandits approach Joan; their leader snatches her.

• To the rescue, Mahmoud. In time, he arrives to free Joan; she collapses in his arms. Upset at seeing Mahmoud with Joan, Nicky slugs him. Says Mahmoud, "Pig of an infidel—may he perish!" The Egyptian tries to dynamite Nicky.

• As Egyptian women dance, Mahmoud tries to romance Joan. She rejects his advances. Mahmoud tells Joan that she will soon be all his. Why? Because he and Selim intend to kill her beau. Abruptly, Joan pulls a pistol, rushing off to warn Nicky. Mahmoud tries to stop her; Joan slugs him.

• Selim dynamites the inner tomb. Yet, Joan and Nicky survive. As for Mahmoud, "The Curse of Isis" brings him down.

Madhouse (1990), OR. *Kirstie Alley, John Larroquette, Alison La Placa.* CAMEOS

An American woman tags her husband a "Mideast maggot."

Scene: The protagonist's (Alley) sister, Alison, arrives in California, declaring she left her rich husband, Ghadir. When Ghadir phones, Alison shouts, "You Mideast maggot. You towel head! Eat ground glass!" No one counters the slurs.

• Alison returns home; Arab music underscores her actions. She finds hidden inside a pink cherub statue, an intercom, screaming, "That wasn't here before... You two-bit desert rat."

Note: Ghadir, speaks Farsi, a Persian language. Yet, on their *Sneak Previews*, critics

Gene Siskel and Roger Ebert say: "Arabs are fair game" in *Madhouse*. And, such "racism isn't funny" (25 February 1990).

The Magic Carpet (1951), COL. *John Agar, Lucille Ball, Patricia Medina, Raymond Burr, Gregory Gay*. MAIDENS, VILLAINS

This Arabian Nights fable, complete with flying carpet, presents a dashing couple, Ramoth, the prince of Baghdad (Agar), and the gallant Lida (Medina).

Scene: The villains Boreg (Burr) and Ali (Gay) murder Baghdad's king and queen. Cut to a loyal palace nurse rescuing the caliph's son, Ramoth. A magic carpet carries the boy to safety.

• Years later. The grown-up Ramoth assumes the identity of the "Scarlet Falcon," harassing Baghdad's false potentate and his retinue.

• Inside the palace, a large dancing hall filled with harem maidens. Below the hall, a dungeon displaying a wheel of torture. In the desert, a row of wooden chopping blocks reserved for falling heads.

• The film versions of *The Desert Song* (1929, 1943, 1953) show Western protagonists as the heroic "Red Shadow." Not so with *The Magic Carpet*. Here, the dashing "Scarlet Falcon" is 100-percent Arab. Ramoth liberates fellow Arabs, and weds Lida, the lovely heroine.

• Seeking to smooth Lida's complexion, a maiden goes to apply some "lemon or oil" to her face. "No thank you," says fiery Lida. "I have better things to do with my time."

• Battle scenes between Ramoth's Arabs and the Boreg's cohorts reveal properties such as: a magic carpet, boiling oil, knives, and catapulting fireballs.

• In time, the same flying carpet that earlier saved young Ramoth's life appears. Swooping down, the carpet rescues Ramoth from the chopping block. Abruptly, Ramoth showers the Boreg's cohorts with gobs of pepper. The villains retreat.

• Baghdad's denizens rejoice; Ramoth regains his throne. Embracing Lida, he says, "How long I've waited for this... It's not easy to embrace a tigress." Coos Lida, "From now on, you see a lamb."

Note: During one scene the dialogue wrongly labels Persians as Arabs, and vice versa. Damascus is a Syrian city, where Syrian Arabs reside. Yet, the caliph refers to "the Persian caravan from Damascus." Affirms a cohort, "The Scarlet Falcon will attack the Persians."

• When *The Magic Carpet* was scheduled to appear on TNT, *TV Guide* wrongly promoted the movie with this blurb: "A group of desert raiders... trick the cruel Caliph of Islam." The magazine's copy should have stated, the Caliph of Baghdad.

Maid in Morocco (1925), Lupino Lane Comedies. Silent. *Lupino Lane, Helen Foster, Wallace Lupino, Violet Blythe*. D: Charles Lamont. SHEIKHS, VILLAINS, MAIDENS

An Arab ruler called "The high Muck-a-muck of Morocco," tries to seduce the American heroine. Islam is ridiculed.

Scene: In Morocco, ragtime music underscores praying Muslims. A newly married American couple (Foster and Lane) arrive on donkeys, chasing off their Moroccan guides. States the title card: "[The bride's] inexperience cause her to select an Oriental honeymoon—a widow would have known better."

• Moving to abduct the bride is "Ben Hammered the Mighty, Caliph of Ginfez... a glutton for punishment—he has two hundred wives—and is looking for more." Intent on taking the woman, the caliph (Lupino) pulls a curved dagger; his rifle-toting Arabs surround the groom.

• The caliph prepares to bed the American. He dismisses his Arab maidens, shouting, "Off with 'The Thundering Herd' and bring on 'The [American] Charmer.'" In time, the groom intervenes; he and his bride escape the Moroccan ruler and his armed guards, hiding in the palace.

• The groom enters the caliph's harem, "where the sight of a stranger meant 'The End of a Perfect Day.'" Greeting him is the caliph's favorite, "The Queen of the Harem (Blythe)... one of those women who can wear clothes—but she doesn't."

• The chief of the harem notices that the caliph's "favorite wife is in the arms of another Arab, Ali Baba." The caliph threatens to toss Ali Baba to the lions. To protect her sweetheart, the queen embraces the American groom. Thinking the American, not Ali Baba, is her lover, the caliph and his black guards clasp sabers and hatchets, and charge the American.

• Meanwhile, veiled harem maidens clothe the kidnapped American bride in Arab garb. "They have taken me hostage," she tells her husband. "I am to be his new favorite." Not to fear, he says, I have a plan.

• The caliph mistakenly perceives a veiled person to be his new bride. But when he goes for a hug, he discovers that the American has impersonated his bride. Upset, the caliph and his entourage move to kill the groom. The groom rushes off. Approaching a maiden, he lifts her veil, hoping to see his wife. Instead, he gapes at an ugly Arab woman sans teeth.

• Angry Arabs pursue the bride and groom. But when the unruly mob sees an imam atop a mosque; they halt, bow, and pray. The newlyweds flee to safety.

Male and Female (1919), Jesse L. Lasky/Cecil B. DeMille Prod.
Silent. *Gloria Swanson, Raymond Hatton.* CAMEOS, SHEIKHS

Babylon's king tries to "tame" a Christian slave girl.

Scene: On screen, this verse: "I was a King in Babylon, and You were a Christian Slave." The camera reveals London. The British butler Crichton (Hatton), who attends the lovely Lady May (Swanson), dreams he is Babylon's king.

• Crichton's dream sequence reveals a stereotypical throne room. After dancing girls perform for the butler-now-king, attendants deliver to him, Lady May, a "Christian slave girl." Moving to seduce her, the butler-king says: "I'll tame thee, never fear, my pretty, snarling tiger-cat... I saw, I took, I cast you by, I bent and broke your pride." But the enslaved woman chooses to die in the lion's den, rather than hug the butler-king.

The Man with Bogart's Face (1980), TCF. *Robert Sacchi, Franco Nero, Sybil Danning.* SP: Andrew J. Fenady, based on his novel. D: Robert Day. MAIDENS

Mute and subservient maidens appear in this contemporary detective story, complete with a Humphrey Bogart look-a-like.

Scene: Mustafa Hakim's "Blue Fez" nightclub reveals scantily-clad Arab waitresses and bellydancers. Accompanying the dancers, Arab musicians wearing blue fezzes. Detective Sam Marlowe (Sacchi) enters the club and checks out the half-nude Arab women.

Quips Sam, "It looked like a scene from one of those Maria Montez–Jon Hall pictures, except the place reeked of hashish, and so did Hakim (Nero)." The camera shows Hakim smoking a nargelih. He asks Marlowe to help him procure the blue sapphire eyes of Alexander the Great.

• The rich Hakim claps his hands—three well-endowed Arab dancers rush to his side. Smiling, Hakim stuffs bills into their bikini tops. Next, the kinky Hakim orders Cynthia (Danning), his sensuous blonde live-in, to remove her clothing and dance. The embarrassed Cynthia hesitates, then begins stripping. Marlowe heads for the door. Shouts Hakim, "Don't go! The show's just starting." Noting that Hakim enjoys degrading Cynthia, Marlowe tags the Mideast cur "one of the sharks in the sea." Before leaving, Marlowe floors the doorman, a tall and muscular turbaned Arab.

The Man from Cairo (1953), LIP. *George Raft, Leon Lenoir.* EGYPTIANS

This cloak-and-dagger film shows George Raft as an American tourist "at loggerheads with French Intelligence." Among the "gallery of international rogues," two Arabs.

Scene: Algiers. Mike Canale (Raft) searches for a "missing cache of gold." Apparently, back in 1942, $100 million in French government gold disappeared somewhere in the Sahara.

• Arab thugs speaking broken English ["Who got record?" Who get reward?"] collar Canale, tying him to a chair. One Arab slugs Canale; he barks, "You yellow-livered ape."

Finis: Canale nabs the Frenchman behind the $100 million heist. An Arab policeman, Akhim Bey (Lenoir), thanks Canale for his adeptness.

Note: Writes NYT critic H. H. T.:

> The most this tired Lippert Production can offer is a sleazy, authentic-looking backdrop. The murky alleyways, run-down hotels and palm-fringed facades, obviously photographed on the spot, stand in direct, flavorsome contrast [to the] old spy [business] (17 December 1953).

A Man Called Sarge (1990), CAN. *Christopher Pearce, Gary Kroeger, Marc Singer.* EP: Yoram Globus. Filmed in Israel. CAMEOS, SHEIKHS

Producer Globus mocks Islam, smears sheikhs, humiliates children, and equates Arabs with Nazis.

Scene: A US platoon marches "along the burning sands of the Sahara," heading toward Cairo. They intend to link up with the British army. But they are delayed—because their dense Arab guide does not know "where the heck is Cairo."

• In the desert, an Arabesque-Nazi fort. Hoping to mislead the GIs, an Arab posts at the fort's entrance this sign: "RAMADAN INN TOP SECRET COMMANDO RAID." Inside the fort, a dozen-plus Arabs pray. Abruptly, a Nazi officer stomps on their fingers. Cut to celebrating Nazis. Arab musicians play umm-pah-pah music; behind them, a large swastika banner.

• At Bari Bari, a mythical Arab village, a Nazi officer instructs camel-riding Arabs.

• Inside a church, the sounds of a Negro spiritual. Cut to Arab children swaying back and forth. Singing the spiritual are Arab children, a nun, and a priest.

• An American teacher appears, offering Arab girls lessons in sex education. The teacher mentions "masturbation" and "vacuum cleaner parts." The silly Arab girls scream.

• Outside, a latrine. Emblazoned on the toilet seat, "SHEIKS!"

The Man with the Golden Gun (1974), UA. *Roger Moore, Christopher Lee.* CAMEOS, SHEIKHS

This Bond adventure displays oil-rich Arab villains trying to prevent the development of solar energy. An exotic dancer appears.

Scene: Lebanon. In a Beirut bar, 007 (Moore) approaches a mute bellydancer. Earlier, a fellow agent was killed in the arms of an Arab dancer. As 007 moves to remove from the dancer's navel a gold bullet, Arab heavies attack him. Bond plucks the bullet, then floors the Arabs.

• Explains Bond to the villain, "The oil sheikhs will pay you just to keep solar energy off the market."

Note: See Arabs trying to thwart solar energy development in *Power* (1986).

Man of Legend (1971), a.k.a. Il Sergente Klems, Julia Film.

Italian. *Peter Strauss, Tina Aumont, Massimo Serato.* D: Sergio Grieco. Filmed in Tunisia. See *Lawrence of Arabia* (1962), *Lion of the Desert* (1981), and *Jericho* (1937). MAIDENS, RECOMMENDED

"Sergeant Otto of Arabia," known as El-Hajid, helps Moroccan freedom fighters overpower French and Spanish soldiers. Islam is venerated.

Scene: Several years after World War I, circa 1925. A German army deserter, Otto Joseph Clems (Strauss), joins the French Foreign Legion. Legionnaire Otto befriends an Arab, Ahmed, who tells him: "The Spanish and French partitioned my country. [But, we will] fight for independence, and with the aid and guidance of Allah," we will win. Suddenly, Ahmed runs off. Otto refuses to shoot the deserter.

• Fearing the legion may find out he deserted his German unit, Otto also departs. Rushing into the desert, he collapses. Sunrise. An Arab who prays near an oasis spots the near-dead Otto. Though legionnaires are the Arab's enemy, he aids Otto, saying, "The generosity of Abdul Karim is like the desert. It has no limit. Go now." The grateful Otto decides instead to stay with Abdul Karim.

• At Karim's desert village, Otto links up with Moroccan rebels. Now tagged El Hajid, he dons Arab garb and vows to assist Karim's Moroccans.

• Muslims pray: "Allah be with you... be not impatient and trust in Allah, says the Prophet Mohammed."

• As Otto weds Abdul Karim's beautiful daughter, Zeina (Aumont), an imam reads from the Holy Koran. Zeina tells Otto, "You speak like an Arab." Affirms Otto, "I want to be an Arab now."

• Explain Moroccans, we win battles because "of the guidance of Allah." A superstitious Moroccan believes that Spanish cannons are "instruments of the unfaithful," declaring, "Our religion forbids us to use arms of the infidel." The camera reveals a cannon exploding; Moroccans are aflame.

• Abdul Karim asks Otto, "Can you teach my men to use these cannons?" Otto obliges, teaching the Arabs "how to become gunners." Says Otto, "The cannon would not have exploded if shells of the proper caliber had been loaded."

• Two battle scenes. Though outnumbered and outgunned, the Moroccans triumph, defeating a Spanish regiment. Exclaims a French officer, "We do not have just the undisciplined hordes of Abdul Karim, but a German soldier [Otto] who knows military strategy to perfection."

• Explains Abdul Karim, "European colonialism seeks to enslave us without any consideration of the rights of the people to control their destiny. We will no longer live under the tyranny of the oppressor."

• Zeina, too, fires cannons. Quips Otto, "I didn't know Arab women were interested." Retorts Zeina, "I want my country to be free again." She thanks her husband for helping to "organize our women."

Eventually, the French armies triumph. Otto and Abdul Karim are imprisoned. A plane attacks Abdul Karim's village. Cut to several dead Moroccans; among them, Zeina and her young son. Cut to a scrubby cemetery showing El Hajid's grave number: 52342.

The Man with One Red Shoe (1985), TCF. *Tom Hanks.* A remake of the French spoof-thriller, *The Tall Blond Man with One Black Shoe* (1972). CAMEOS

Morocco as a backdrop.

Scene: Initial scenes show Moroccan soldiers murmuring in Arabic; camels appear in the background. Abruptly, two American agents wearing Arab garb kill another US agent.

Note: See *The Man Who Knew Too Much* (1956).

Man of Stone (1921), Selznick. Silent. *Conway Tearle, Martha Mansfield, Betty Howe.* *NS. Notes from NYT (18 November 1921). MAIDENS

Moroccans vs. Moroccans. A British officer falls for an Arab woman.

Summary: Morocco. Presenting Captain Neville Deering (Tearle) "in a drunken state." The broken-hearted officer is upset because his beloved "Lady Mary" (Howe) intends to wed a "richer man." Neville wanders among a group of native travelers. Abruptly, the captain seizes Laila (Mansfield), one of the travelers' dancing girls. Viewers might expect the Arabs to attack the officer. But, no. Instead, the Arabs tenderly carry the captain back to his cot. Later, Laila not only "saves his life"—she falls for him. Unexpectedly, Lady Mary arrives; her "rich fiancé has jilted her." She moves to rekindle her relationship with Neville.

Suddenly, Laila is "taken captive by [Arab] bandits." To the rescue, Neville and his Arab "followers." They bring down the kidnappers, returning Laila "triumphantly back to camp." During Laila's rescue, Lady Mary "is conveniently killed by a stray shot." Neville realizes "he is in love with the native girl and the picture ends with an appropriate embrace."

Note: Interestingly, the same year *Man of Stone*, with its British protagonist wooing an Arab woman, was released, American censors did not allow the British heroine in *The Sheik* (1921) to swoon over an Arab man.

• Some film reviewers refer to Arabs as "natives."

Man about Town (1939), PAR. *Jack Benny, Dorothy Lamour, Eddie Rochester Anderson, the Merriel Abbott Dancers.* SHEIKHS, MAIDENS, CAMEOS

Jack Benny as an Arab sultan surrounded by harem maidens.

Scene: A London theater. Opening night of *Revue*, starring "The Famous Petty Girls." Inside the theater the lights dim and the stage curtain opens, revealing an Arabian Nights setting. The camera reveals plenty of veiled, scantily-clad maidens, all blonde. Slowly, the women remove their veils. Cut to the heroine Diana (Lamour) in chains.

• As the harem maidens (the Merriel Abbott Dancers) dance, Rochester enters the scene. Rochester dons a thobe and headdress, then pokes fun of the dancers' "Oriental" hand gestures. Next, the turbaned Sultan (Benny) appears. Attending him are "sixteen wives" and bare-chested guards clasping swords and feather fans. Benny is tagged, the "New Sultan, Suleiman the Ridiculous."

> Sultan: [*Smoking a nargelih, he boasts of his maidens*] Well, looks like I hit the jackpot. Very nice, very nice.
> Rochester: That's only the freshman team. The varsity's out scrimmaging.
> Sultan: Oh, You mean there's more? [*Attractive acrobatic dancing girls appear*] Well, well. Here comes the varsity team.

Two of the sultan's loyal subjects rush in and kneel; one makes a request.

> Servant: If it's not too much trouble, I'd like my wife back.
> Sultan: Why, of course. Who's got your wife?
> Servant: You have, your majesty.
> Sultan: Oh! Suppose all husbands wanted their wives back, where would I be? Take these men out and have them shot.
> Servant: All right, sultan, you've got us. But I warn you, some husband is going to kill you very soon.
> Sultan: On with the dance.

• Offstage, Rochester quells the anxieties of two irate Englishmen, explaining that the "sultan" does not intend to seduce their wives.

Man of Violence (1970), Miracle. A Peter Walker Prod. *Michael Latimer, Derek Francis.* Filmed in Morocco. CAMEOS, VILLAINS

Arab thugs vs. the British protagonist. Arabs are tagged "wog savages."

Scene: In England, London financier Sam Bryant (Francis) finances an Arab coup. Next, Bryant and some arms merchants move to steal gold worth "30 million pounds." Bryant and "the [Moroccan] general" involved with the coup intend to share the loot. "Do you realize what this [new] regime will mean to me?" says Bryant. "Oil concessions!"

• Boasts Bryant, "A pack of wog savages will use them [his weapons] to kill each other." Quips the protagonist Moon (Latimer), "A pointless revolution killing three-quarters of a million. You were there with the guns at the right price."

• In Morocco, a souk, a hotel, and an amphitheater. Inside the hotel, mute Moroccan musicians accompany a bellydancer.

• At Marrakesh's "Cobano Club," four fez-wearing Arab radicals pull their guns. Firing away, they nearly kill Moon. By mistake, they shoot dead an innocent Arab. Cut to an angry Moroccan crowd pursuing Moon.

The Man Who Knew Too Much (1956), PAR. *James Stewart, Doris Day.* D: Alfred Hitchcock. Remake of Hitchcock's *The Man Who Knew Too Much* (1934). CAMEOS, VILLAINS

Islam is presented as a rigid and unforgiving faith.

Scene: Marrakesh, a busy souk. A vacationing American tourist (Stewart) stumbles into the arms of a fatally wounded British agent wearing Arab garb.

• Inside a crowded Moroccan bus. The tourist's young son accidentally bumps into a veiled Moroccan woman. When the woman's veil drops, an Arab passenger goes to attack the boy. Fortunately, the bus lunges forward. Puzzled, the boy's American father asks a Frenchman about the outraged Arab: "Why was he so angry? It was only an accident." Whispers the Frenchman, "The Moslem religion allows for no accidents."

Note: The 1934 version contains no Arabs; Switzerland's ski slopes are highlighted.

The Man Who Turned White (1919), Jesse D. Hampton Prod.

Silent. *H.B. Warner, Barbara Castleton, Manuel Ojeda, Wedgewood Nowell.* *NS. Notes from AFIC (p 580). VILLAINS

• A dark bedouin coveting the fair Western heroine kidnaps her.

Will the bedouin seduce her?

Or, to prevent a-fate-worse-than-death, will she die at her Western lover's side?

• Action! Ali Zaman (Warner) and his "desert band" raid a caravan. Ali spots his legionnaire "enemy," Captain Beverly (Nowell). Seeing the captain woo the heroine, Ethel Lambert (Castleton), Ali seeks revenge; he abducts Ethel. Soon, Ethel discovers that Ali is not an Arab after all; he is Captain Rand, a legionnaire disguised as an Arab.

• Rand decides to release Ethel. But his comrade, a pure Arab named Jouder (Ojeda), intervenes. Jouder, "lusts for Ethel." Jouder takes her hostage.

• Ali/Rand to the rescue! As the captain truly loves Ethel, he frees her. They run off into the desert; "Jouder's band" closes in on them. "Rand is about to kill Ethel, to save her from Jouder." In time, Legion troops arrive to rout Jouder and his bandits.

Finis: Rand romances Ethel.

A Man and a Woman: 20 Years Later (1986), WB/Films 13.

French, with English subtitles. *Anouk Aimee, Jean-Louis Trintignant, Evelyne Bouix.* D: Claude Lelouch. CAMEOS

Desert bedouins save a French couple.

Scene: "In the heart of the Tenere region." Appearing in the desert is the famous race-car driver Jean-Louis (Trintignant) and his female companion, Francoise (Bouix).

• Evening. Jean-Louis and the heartbroken Francoise drive off into the desert, heading toward the nearest airport. Unexpectedly, Francoise tries to commit suicide. She pulls out the race car's communication wires, slashes the tires, then tosses out all their drinking water. Cut to a French helicopter crew trying to find the couple. A sudden sandstorm thwarts the rescue. But in time, desert bedouins arrive on camelback, saving the couple's lives.

Manhattan Baby (1986), a.k.a. The Evil Eye; a.k.a. Eye of the Dead, Fulvia. *Christopher Connelly, Martha Taylor.* Filmed in Egypt. Notes from VAR (2 July 1986). EGYPTIANS

An Egyptian evil eye amulet plagues the American heroine.

Scene: Egypt. A Western archaeologist (Connelly) uncovers a blue "evil eye." Wham! He "is zapped by it, rendering him blind."

• Back in New York, a "mysterious woman wearing black" gives the archaeologist's teenage daughter, Susie (Taylor), "a matching eye-amulet." Puzzled, Susie's brother asks, "Are Egyptian mummies as menacing as zombies?" Suddenly, the now-possessed Susie releases her "evil extra-sensory powers," causing innocents around her to perish.

• Who is to blame for Susie's sinister deeds? Why, an "ancient Egyptian cult that worshipped the forces of evil," that's who.

• Susie's father tosses the amulet into the sea. Suddenly, Susie is cured.

• Flashback. Again, the camera shows a clad-in-black Egyptian woman handing Susie the blue evil eye.

Note: Children's cartoons also warn viewers to heed mummy curses. In the Pink Panther's, "Pink Sphinx," for example, an inscription warns our hero, "A curse on the one who enters here." Intent on recovering hidden desert treasures, the panther ignores the curse. Entering a dark den, he snitches a large shiny jewel and runs off. Soon, the curse unfolds, changing the Pink Panther into a rat, then a lizard, followed by other unsightly creatures.

Mannequin (1987), TCF. *Andrew McCarthy, Kim Cattrall.* SP: Edward Rugoff, Michael Gottlieb. D: Gottlieb. CAMEOS, MAIDENS

Emmy, a revived Egyptian blonde, refuses to wed an Egyptian camel-dung dealer. Instead, Emmy romances the American protagonist.

Scene: "Egypt, a long time ago"—a three-minute scene. The mother of the liberated Egyptian maiden, Emmhezerah (Cattrall), insists her daughter agree to an arranged marriage. Protests her dressed-as-a-mummy daughter: The man you selected for me "sells camel dung." Emmhezerah prefers "fire." Her exasperated mother sighs, "The Gods have bigger things to [do than] worry about than you." Presto! Emmhezerah vanishes; her mummy wrappings fall to the floor.

• Philadelphia, evening. An up-and-coming department store window dresser, Jonathan (McCarthy), uncovers Emmhezerah; she is now a blonde mannequin. Abruptly, Emmhezerah comes alive, explaining to the surprised Jonathan, "You can call me Emmy. I was born 2514 BC in Upper Egypt. I'll be 4,001 next April. Back there I wasn't allowed to do anything. You know who my parents wanted me to marry?" "Who?" asks Jonathan. "A camel dung dealer," says Emmy. Suddenly, some people enter the store. Seeing them, Emmy promptly reverts to being a mannequin. She becomes human only when she is alone with Jonathan.

• With Emmy's help, Jonathan creates brilliant window displays. Soon, he becomes the city's leading decorator. When Jonathan thanks Emmy, she shrugs, saying, "You saved my life." Abruptly, Emmy becomes human—permanently. Excited, Emmy says to Jonathan, "You're going to have me forever!" They kiss, make love, and plan to marry.

Manon (1949), Discina Int. French, with English subtitles. *Cecile Aubry, Michel Auclair.* CAMEOS, VILLAINS

In Palestine, a white-robed Arab inexplicably shoots a blonde French woman.

Scene: Most scenes take place in post-war Paris. The adulterous Manon (Aubry) brings down her benevolent lover, Robert (Auclair), coercing him to commit murder. Escaping the police, she and Robert stow away on a ship "taking D.P. persons to

Palestine." Cut to Jewish families, who in spite of their hardships, sing. Says the French captain, "I feel sorry for them."

• The ship docks in Alexandria. Two guides escort the Jews, as well as Manon and Robert. They start to move across the desert toward Palestine. Cut to a Rabbi kissing the sand. Says Manon, "This place is like paradise."

• In the desert, near Palestine. Exhausted and needing water Robert says, "We were in Heaven... now we're in Hell." Cut to jackals feasting on the remains of the dead.

• A white-robed, camel-riding Arab spots the Jews. He rushes off to warn his companions. Speaking Arabic, the excited Arab and a dozen or so of his gun-toting white-robed cohorts discuss strategies. They ride off, determined to apprehend the Jews.

• The gun-toting Arabs come across Robert and Manon; one white-robed bedouin raises his rifle and shoots Manon dead.

March or Die (1977), COL. *Gene Hackman, Max von Sydow, Catherine Deneuve, Ian Holm.* S, SP: David Zelag Goodman. VILLAINS, SHEIKHS, MAIDENS

Bedouins vs. legionnaires. Islam and violence. Arabs take Western women.

Scene: France, following WWI. On screen, French citizens welcome home legionnaires. Abruptly, on screen, screeching, clad-in-black desert bedouins. Superimposed over the Arabs this newspaper headline: "ARABS ATTACK IN MOROCCO: LEGION COMPANY MASSACRED."

• French officials meet to discuss how to best nab the "Berber Joan of Arc," a valuable relic buried in the Moroccan desert. The relic is also called the "Angel of the Desert." Archaeologist Francois Marneau (von Sydow) proposes to find and deliver to France "Berber Joan," as well as her tomb's "incalculable fortune in pearls and jewels."

• Legionnaire Major Foster (Hackman) urges Marneau and fellow Frenchmen not to be "graverobbers." Earlier, Foster promised the bedouin leader, El Krim (Holm), that the French would cease excavating. Explains Foster, El Krim's "mission in life is to unite all the tribes of Morocco." His advise is ignored; the French expedition moves forward. See *Jewel of the Nile* (1985), a "unite the tribes" film.

• In Morocco, El Krim's camel-riding bedouins halt a train. The camera reveals two frightened French curators, entrapped in wooden cages. El Krim's bedouins have blinded the men and removed their tongues. "I see you've learned to enjoy watching men suffer," says Foster. When Foster tells the Arab he has "orders" to continue excavating, El Krim retorts, "And I have orders from high authority to stop you... from Allah... You can bring 10,000 trains of legionnaires. You still will not take anything from our homelands. The desert welcomes you, Foster."

• The despondent Foster beds a rotund Moroccan prostitute.

• In the desert, black-robed bedouins observe the Frenchmen working at the excavation site. Cut to several bedouins assisting the French; they are El Krim's spies.

• The French heroine, Simone Picard (Deneuve), intends to smuggle her legionnaire friend out of Morocco. She seeks assistance from a shifty Moroccan, offering him money. The Moroccan takes the cash, then insists she sleep with him. "I don't see many European women here," he pants, "certainly not beautiful European women." The camera zooms in on an anxious and shocked Simone.

• In the desert, vultures and human skeletons. Cut to El Krim's camp. On seeing a suffering legionnaire strung between poles, Foster grimaces. Boasts El Krim, "One of my men became restless." Next, a bedouin spits in the legionnaire's face. Foster's aide shoots the bedouin. Quips Foster, "One of my men became restless."

• Foster warns El Krim, "Devastation will come to Morocco; only you can prevent it." "No man can see that far," says El Krim. "Only the great Allah—Allahu Akbar!". At that, black-clad bedouins emerge from their tents, extending their arms toward the sky. Their loud, garbled sounds, not devout Arabic prayers, jar the soundtrack. As bedouin horsemen flaunt their rifles, black-clad women wail.

• Success! Marneau discovers Berber Joan's tomb. He prepares to take the relic and other treasures to France. Suddenly, surfacing from behind sand dunes, El Krim's bedouins. As all the tribes "are together," they attack. Sighs Foster, the Arabs are "in a holy war." Though Foster's outnumbered legionnaires machine-gun scores, the bedouins triumph. And, Foster dies.

• Seeing Foster's body, El Krim pauses, pays his respects. He warns the few legionnaire survivors, "We will resist all foreigners until we prevail. I let you [legionnaires] live so that what happened today could be known to the entire world."

Maroc 7 (1967), PAR. *Gene Barry, Elsa Martinelli, Cyd Charisse.* Filmed in Morocco. VILLAINS

This movie contends that Westerners are entitled to a valuable artifact that rightfully belongs to Moroccans.

Scene: Western jewel thieves fly off to Morocco. Using leggy Western models as a cover, they move to steal a Moroccan queen's priceless medallion. Emblazoned on the ancient medallion: Marc Anthony and Salena, Cleopatra's daughter.

• Near the airport, the camera shows camels munching straw. Cut to a restaurant; chickens scatter everywhere.

• In the desert, a Western photographer arranges an "exotic" "Bondage-in-Morocco" photo shoot. Though nearly-naked Western models complain about the heat, they pose in front of black tents. In the background, unshaven bedouins attend their goats and donkeys. Suddenly, bedouins on horseback attack. Firing rifles, they surround the models. Next, the ugly bedouins pull some rope, binding the models' wrists. They fasten the models to their horses. Abruptly, the horses drag the women through the desert.

• When the Western protagonist, Simon Grant (Barry), hears a blonde model speaking "Arabic," he asks, "[Were you] born here?" The model laughs, saying "Heavens, no!"

• Determined to protect the queen's artifact, bedouins bury the medallion in a "grave." The heroine, Claudia (Martinelli), warns Simon, "[If the Arabs] find anyone violating the grave, they'll cut him to pieces."

• Simon moves to pilfer the medallion. A bedouin guard intervenes; Simon tosses him over a cliff. Though bedouins shoot at Simon, they miss.

• Surprisingly, Claudia nabs the medallion, then flies off to the South Pacific. Soon, Simon joins her. He and Claudia celebrate a successful theft.

Note: Again, Moroccan officials green light an Arab-bashing movie. See *Ishtar* (1987), *Beyond Justice* (1992), and *Rules of Engagement* (2000).

Mars Attacks (1997), WB. *Jack Nicholson, Richard Assad.* CAMEOS, SHEIKHS

A one-liner slurs the movie's one and only Arab.

Scene: Las Vegas. Mr. Art Land (Nicholson) addresses a group of investors. The only entrepreneur identified by his ethnicity is an Arab (Assad). Land boasts you can get "a return on your investments within five months." The Saudi, who dons a black headdress, raises his hand, and says, "Excuse me, please." Interrupts Mr. Land, "Just a second Sheikh Rag Moolah."

The Mask of Fu Manchu (1932), MGM. *Boris Karloff, Lewis Smith, Myrna Loy.* CAMEOS, VILLAINS

Asians, plus a few Arabs, yearn to rule the world.

Scene: Mute Arabs wearing thobes and kuffiyehs accompany Fu Manchu and his cohorts. Arabs and the evil Asian want to "recapture the world."

Note: Screen Asians function as screen Arabs. In this movie, Asians are depicted as "countless hordes swarming to recapture the world." Among their tools of torture are "Oriental tricks... shattering the strongest courage." Fu Manchu's daughter, Fah Lo See, desperately wants to embrace the Western protagonist. But, he rejects the Asian.

The Masque of the Red Death (1964), OR. *Vincent Price.* P, D: Roger Corman. Based on the story by Edgar Allan Poe. CAMEOS, SHEIKHS

Scene: Prospero's castle. Though a plague ravages the land, the prince stages a grand ball. Attending the gala, his sadistic cohorts. The evil Prince Prospero wears a jet black thobe as well as a black burnoose; he is the only one wearing ethnic clothing. Shouting, "Gifts, gifts for everyone," the prince tosses "diamonds, rubies, and pearls" to his vile guests.

Masquerade (1965), UA. *Cliff Robertson, Jack Hawkins, Roger Delgado, Christopher Witty, Denis Bernard.* SP: Ralph and William Goldman. SHEIKHS

In this cloak-and-dagger yarn Arab royals fight Arab royals. The British move to secure Arab oil, kidnapping a "monster" prince.

Scene: In London, Arab officials are considered backward folks. For example, as British dignitaries bid farewell to "Ramalt's" white-thobed delegation, an official quips, "With all the millions they are snatching from us, you'd think they could afford an Embassy more central." Says another, "Sorry to see them go off?" Sighs his colleague, "Well, hardly. I've been eating off the floor for a week now!"

• British diplomats view a 1943 WWII film showing war hero Col. Drexel (Hawkins) in Arab garb. When Drexel appears, Ramalt's desert denizens cheer. At his side is David Frazer (Robertson), a yank. Reels change; a new film is screened. This one depicts the assassination of pro-Western ruler, King Ahmed. Officials worry that if Ahmed's brother, Ben Said (Delgado), become the new ruler, Ramalt's oil may no longer flow to England. Boasts Ben Said, "Oil is my bargaining power."

• Ramalt's rightful heir is Ahmed's young son, Prince Jamil (Witty). The Brits fear Ben Said may harm the pro-Western youth. Thus, they employ Drexel and Frazer to abduct the teen, and take him to a safe place. Both men care zilch about Arabs; all they care about is securing Arab oil. (More than 60 percent of the world's oil reserves are found in the Arabian/Persian Gulf.)

• Introducing Ramalt, a primitive place; the airport resembles a desert shack. On arrival, Frazer is told to "expect royalty." Cut to Arabs on horseback, waving sabers.

• Prince Jamil, an arrogant twerp, tells Drexel: "You may assist me. I am practically divine." Barks Drexel, I should get "combat pay" for protecting that "little monster." Jamil, a leering "young Genghis Khan," spots a bikini-clad woman sunbathing. "There will come a time when I surround myself with women like that—when I am fourteen," he quips.

Finis: As Ben Said and his cohorts fail to murder Jamil, the "monster" Jamil gains Remalt's throne. The British will continue to receive Arab oil!

A Matter of WHO (1961), MGM. *Terry-Thomas, Marine Benson, Guy Deghy, Ghulam Mohammed.* CAMEOS, SHEIKHS

An American oilman working in the Mideast dies of smallpox. A World Health Organization (WHO) investigator, Archie Bannister (Terry-Thomas), moves to track down the smallpox carrier. Amazingly, oil-rich Arab officials are inserted into this medical-mystery tale. Corrupt Arab diplomats refuse to help the WHO investigator. The movie's chimpanzee is more polite than reel Arabs.

Scene: England, an Arab embassy. A fez-wearing attache (Mohammad) welcomes the WHO fieldworker, Archie. A well-dressed chimp who has "taken a liking to everything English," takes Archie's hat. Expressing concern about a possible smallpox epidemic, Archie asks Mr. Rahman (Benson) whether he may examine the "late minister's" body to see whether smallpox caused the man's death. The robed Rahman objects, saying, "To disturb the remains would be sacrilege." Later, Rahman tells Archie his request is "a direct violation of Moslem burial customs." The Arab dismisses the Englishman; the chimp hands Archie his hat. Quips Archie, "Thank you. You, sir, are a gentleman!" Meaning, of course, that Rahman is not.

• Rahman and his Arab cohorts are tagged "pirates." They conduct shady business with the film's heavies, namely Ivonovich (Deghy). Perhaps, says Archie, the Arabs are "deliberately trying to conceal a smallpox carrier to put over a nefarious oil scheme." Rahman's country has "enough oil to buy the bank of England."

• Archie nabs and runs off with the dead Arab minister's body. Pursuing him in two autos are Rahman's Arabs.

Finis: The lab report reveals the Arab minister was not a carrier. Nor are other Arabs spreading smallpox. In Switzerland, Archie corners the true carrier of the disease, Ivonovich.

Max Dugan Returns (1983), TCF. *Jason Robards, Martha Mason.* SP: Neil Simon. CAMEOS, SHEIKHS

Writer Neil Simon besmirches Arabs.

Scene: Unexpectedly, Max (Robards), the unruly father of Nora McPhee (Mason), appears at Nora's modest home. Abruptly, Max showers Nora with elaborate gifts, including a Mercedes-Benz convertible. Nora's nosy neighbor is impressed and curious about Nora's new-found wealth. She asks Nora, "They raise the teacher's salaries this year?" Explains Nora, "No. I've been doing private tutoring in the evening." Quips the neighbor, "Who ya tutoring? Arabs?" Nora is mum.

The Message (1976), a.k.a. Mohammed, Messenger of God, Filmco International. *Anthony Quinn, Oliver Reed, Irene Pappas.* SP: H.A.L. Craig. P, D: Moustapha Akkad. Two versions. One version is in Arabic, featuring Arab actors. The other version, discussed here, is in English and features an international cast. Filmed in Libya and Morocco. RECOMMENDED

This spiritual drama, which begins in Mecca, AD 610, concerns the Prophet Mohammed. Explains screenwriter Craig, the intent of *The Message*, a film about one of the world's great religions, is to "write against the ignorance of the world."

Scene: Christian religious films feature actors, such as Max von Sydow, Willem Dafoe, or Jeffrey Hunter, portraying Jesus. Here, however, no actor appears as the Prophet Mohammed. In accordance with Islam, the Prophet's presence is conveyed by having someone recite the Prophet's thoughts. Spoken throughout are selected verses from the Holy Koran.

• A vision of the Angel Gabriel tells the Prophet, "You, Mohammed, are the messenger of God." Afterwards, Mohammed goes to the people of Mecca, encouraging them to recognize and embrace one true God. Mohammed tells them to cease worshiping false Gods—the Kaaba's wood and stone idols. As Mecca's merchants acknowledge those idols, they violently object, forcing Mohammed and his followers to leave the city.

• Scenes reveal that Muslims, like Christians, Jews, and others, are persecuted for their beliefs. In Mecca, idol-worshipers whip, torture, and rout from their homes devout Muslims who believe in one God. The clad-in-white Muslims head for Medina, walking across 250 miles of desert.

• During conflicts, Mohammed's faith entreats his Muslim pilgrims to forgive their enemies, and not to seek vengeance. Mohammed's religious convictions are especially revealing near the film's conclusion, when Muslims proceed peacefully into Mecca.

• In the end, Muslims rejoice. Mecca's false idols are destroyed. The Kaaba is transformed into a holy place. Here, the devout now worship one, true God.

Dialogue: Throughout, pious Muslims say: "Mecca is where God spoke to man"; "God is Great"; and, "there are no different races in Islam... all return equally to God."

Metalstorm: The Destruction of Jared-Syn (1983), UNI. *Jeffrey Byron, Kelly Preston, Mike Preston.* VILLAINS

This space-age western shows evil bedouins wearing ape masks.

Scene: The megalomaniac Jared-Syn (M. Preston) moves to become the planet's supreme ruler. How? By "inciting the nomads." Peace Officer Dogen (Byron) worries about how to handle stirred-up nomads, sighing, "It's Holy War all over again."

• Cut to Jared-Syn's mute nomads clad in ape masks and red burnooses. They terrorize innocents. Thousands of nomads move to kill Officer Dogen; he sets them ablaze.

• After Dogen incinerates the burnoosed bedouins, he brings down Jared-Syn.

Miami Rhapsody (1995), HOL. *Sarah Jessica Parker, Gil Bellows.* W, D: David Frankel. CAMEOS

Dialogue targets Arabs: Gwen (Parker) confesses to her live-in fiancé, Matt (Bellows), that her separated parents are unhappy, "They each want one thing, but settle for another." Matt tries to comfort Gwen. "Everybody compromises," he says. "Who doesn't compromise?" Retorts Gwen, "Arabs! Arabs! And Republicans." Retorts Matt, "You're wrong! Arabs live to bargain."

Ministry of Vengeance (1989), Concorde. *Ned Beatty, John Schneider, James Tolkan, Apollonia Kotero, Robert Miano, Maria Richwine, Daniel Radell.* SP: Brian D. Jeffries, Mervyn Emeryys, Ann Napus. From a story by Randal Patrick. PALESTINIANS, WORST LIST

An American minister, a veteran of Vietnam, travels to Lebanon and to terminate a Palestinian who killed his wife and daughter. Islam is slandered. Muslims hate Christians. Arabs vs. Arabs, vs. Americans.

Scene: Rome, Italy. An airport lounge reveals Ali Aboud (Miano) and his "People's Liberation" terrorists slaughtering innocents, including an American minister's family.

• An American paramilitary camp's shooting range. Cut to marksmen firing at cardboard cut-outs of Palestinians; black-and-white kuffiyehs cover the targets' heads. David Miller (Schneider), the minister who lost his family, asks his friend and fellow Vietnam veteran, Colonel Freeman (Tolkan), to help him track Ali Aboud's terrorists in Lebanon. The colonel tags Palestinians "bastards," then says, "You couldn't find a more dangerous place on earth." Yet he accompanies Miller.

• Miller tests his shooting skills. The camera shows a Palestinian's bullet-ridden head. Superimposed over the cardboard cutout is the face of Ali Aboud.

• The Bekaa Valley, Lebanon. As soon as Miller arrives, a Palestinian barks, "Cross worshipper, where you from? Where you going, cross worshipper?" Throughout, Palestinians tag Miller "cross worshipper."

• Miller arrives at a rag-tag Christian mission, complete with chickens and a donkey. Located near the mission is the camp of Aboud's People's Liberation Army. Interestingly, the mission boasts an underground cave and prison cells. Cut to Reverend Bloor (Beatty) comforting Fatima (Richwine). Aboud scarred her face, says Bloor. "[She was] caught in public, unveiled, by zealots. They consider that a sin against Islam."

• Fatima and Bloor track Aboud. Armed with a huge knife, Fatima slices a Palestinian's throat, knifing another in the gut.

• Unexpectedly, Aboud's men charge Bloor's mission. In time, members of a Lebanese "Christian militia" arrive, shooting Aboud's Palestinians dead. Pleads Reverend Bloor to a Palestinian, "This is a church, a holy place. Allah would not approve." The Palestinian shoots Bloor in the back.

• The Palestinians terminate all their mission prisoners. As he shoots a young man, Aboud says, "Without cooperation there is punishment." Delivered to Aboud are Colonel Freeman, Reverend Miller and Zarah (Kotero), a Palestinian woman working at the mission. When Palestinians give Freeman electrical shocks he shouts, "asshole"; and "I heard you Ayrabs like to eat your dates." Miller warns Aboud, "You murdered my wife and daughter. I've come to send you straight to Hell." Sighs Aboud, "Sorry, I don't remember." A Palestinian whips Zarah, saying, "You betrayed your people!" When he moves to rape her, Zarah escapes.

• After Aboud kills Colonel Freeman, Miller frees himself and shoots dead several Palestinians, including Aboud.

• America, Reverend Miller's church. Miller receives a standing ovation from his congregation.

Note: Writes the VAR critic, "The fact that the terrorist [Aboud] is working for the CIA evidently is supposed to mitigate the film's blatant anti-Arab slant, but a racial stereotype is a racial stereotype no matter how you slice it" (15 November 1989).

• During the 1991 Gulf War, a gun club in Edwardsville, Illinois, placed shoot-the-Arab paper targets on their rifle range. For months, club members fired at robed Arabs wearing headdresses and sunglasses.

Mirage (1965), UNI. *Gregory Peck, Jack Weston.* CAMEOS, VILLAINS

An Arab wrestler fights dirty, losing the match.

Scene: In a New York apartment, gun-toting Lester (Weston) corners amnesia victim David Stillwell (Peck). As the men converse, the camera cuts to a TV set displaying a wresting match: "The Arab vs. Lord Percy." Moans the announcer: "The Arab forces Lord Percy into the ropes." While watching the match, the evil-intentioned Lester says, "Look at that; the Arab's got the rope around Lord Percy's neck." Continues the announcer, "A forearm smash to the back by the Arab. Another one. One more. And there's a fist to the ear. Another one." Abruptly, David slugs Lester. Concurrently, David floors Lester; and Lord Percy tosses the Arab to the mat, successfully pinning him. Heralds the announcer: "Boy, the Arab never knew what hit him!"

The moral? Good guys like David and Lord Percy crush the bad guys—Lester and the Arab.

Mission in Morocco (1959), REP. *Lex Barker, Juli Reding, Fernando Rey, Silvia Morgan, Alfredo Mayo.* SP: Brian Clemens. VILLAINS, EGYPTIANS

Scene: A Moroccan beach. Arabic-speaking children flock like vultures over the body of Kennedy, a "top Anglo-American geologist." The kids run off, pawning Kennedy's shoes and cigarette lighter.

• In the souk, the fez-wearing Arab children harass the American heroine, Carol Simpson (Reding), who pleads: "Please go away, I don't want anything. Please. Don't you understand... I don't want anything... No, no, please leave me alone." See *Appointment with Death* (1988).

• A rich prince, Ahmed Mohammed (Rey), appears, chasing off the hagglers. Says Carol, "He's quite charming, isn't he?" Shrugs her boyfriend, Bruce Reynolds (Barker), "Ugh! If you like the type."

• Reynolds tries to find out what happened to Kennedy. He questions one Moroccan about Kennedy's lighter, then asks a bearded Arab merchant on "the street of the Shoemakers" about Kennedy's shoes. Says the cobbler, "I don't deal in stolen goods." Reynolds proffers some bills. "Ah yes, my memory is now returning," purrs the Arab. When Reynolds requests the buyer's name, the crafty Arab sighs, "I am an old man, my memory is not as it was." Reynolds slips him more bills; the Arab says: "Abdul ben Mahar."

• A Moroccan boy, Ali, takes Reynolds to Abdul's flat. "I speak American," boasts the boy. Arriving, they see that Abdul has been fatally knifed.

• An Egyptian major, Salem Narouf, tells his mistress' brother, "I want to help you." Abruptly, the major yanks a sword out of his cane and stabs the man in the back. Cut to the victim's sister trying to kill Narouf; she fails.

• A mosque. The imam chants in Arabic; Muslims pray.

• A nightclub filled with Arabs. On stage, musicians and three bellydancers. Here, Reynolds arm wrestles the Arab champion, Ali Hassan. Reynolds wins. Later, he learns that Narouf killed Kennedy. Why? Because the Western geologist discovered "oil in Morocco."

• Narouf tries to convince Prince Ahmed to link up with him, saying, "A huge oil field in Morocco will change the balance of power throughout the world. It is vital that it should be in Arab hands... We must never let the Western nations become independent of us." The prince balks, "We could work with the West, we have before." Purrs Narouf, "But if this oil were in Arab hands, you would be doing a service to your people, and to yourself, Ahmed."

• Carol arrives at Ahmed's. Instantly, Narouf nabs her. Next, Reynolds enters the room, and shoots Narouf dead.

• Reynolds locates some microfilm that pinpoints the location of Moroccan oil. Thanks to Reynolds, Westerners will oversee Morocco's petroleum. The conclusion implies that Western oil companies, not Arabs, should exercise control of Arab oil.

Mr. Moto Takes a Vacation (1939), TCF. *Peter Lorre, John King.* CAMEOS, EGYPTIANS

Briefly, a view of Egypt and an Egyptian.

Scene: In Egypt, a "young and brilliant" US archeologist discovers the "Queen of Sheba's" crown. The discovery was made, says a reporter, "under the merciless waves of the fierce Arabian sun." Continues the reporter, "Learned men from the far corners of the earth" are present. Interestingly, no "learned" Egyptian archeologists appear at the site; all the "learned men" surrounding the discovery are Westerners.

• An Egyptian prince aids Moto, sharing valuable information with the detective.

Mr. Moto's Last Warning (1939), TCF. *Peter Lorre, George Sanders, John Carradine.* SP: Philip MacDonald, Norman Foster. EGYPTIANS

Port Said, the eve of WWII. An Egyptian conspires with German agents to demolish a French fleet.

Scene: Near the Hotel Khedive's entrance, Egyptian money grubbers torment Western tourists.

• Throughout, a mute Egyptian named Hakim assists German conspirators.

• When a bungling Englishman asks, "Do you know a place with local color?" he's told, "Where tourists find their throats cut?" Gasps the man, "Yes, that's exactly what I mean."

Mistress of Atlantis (1932), a.k.a. L'Atlantide, Nero. French, dubbed in English. *Brigette Helm.* Remake of the 1921 French film. D: G.W. Pabst. MAIDENS

Amour brings down the French hero and an Arab maiden. Arabs vs. Arabs.

Scene: Action occurs in the lost city of Atlantis, which is not hidden beneath the sea, but rather "covered by the sands of the Sahara." See *Journey beneath the Desert* (1961). Bedouins and French soldiers trek across the desert "en route to Timbuktu." Suddenly, black-robed Arabs raiders attack. Black cloth covers their faces; only their eyes are visible. After the clad-in-black Arabs kill white-robed Arabs, they abduct two legionnaire officers.

• Introducing Atlantis, "a godforsaken hole" accommodating the queen's (Helm) 50 mummified ex-lovers. Atlantis's queen, an ex-Parisian can-can dancer named Clementina, holds the two French legionnaire officers hostage. Inside her deadly harem, Arab musicians and sensuous dancers, plus an elderly female sand diviner and a bedouin maiden.

• Flashback. In Paris, as an Arab prince watches can-can dancers, one in particular strikes his fancy—Clementina. The prince gives her a valuable ring; they wed.

• Back in Atlantis, the queen, a cool seductress, moves to romance the French captain; he rejects her. Angry, she convinces the captain's friend, the love-struck French lieutenant, to kill his comrade, which he does.

• Fearing the queen will soon terminate the lieutenant, a bedouin maiden intervenes. Dressing the legionnaire in Arab garb, she says, "Come, I save you." They escape into the desert. Days later, sans water, she perishes; the legionnaire lives.

Modesty Blaise (1966), TCF. *Monica Vitti, Dirk Bogarde, Terrence Stamp, Alexander Knox, Clive Revill.* SP: Evan Jones. D: Joseph Losey. SHEIKHS, MAIDENS

This spoof of the comic strip shows Arabs saving Modesty Blaise, a super-sexy female agent, from Western villains. Opening and closing frames display brave Arabs.

Scene: British diplomats fret that unless "$50 million in diamonds gets through to Massura's ruling sheikh," England "will lose the oil concession," and the pro-British "sheikh will lose his head."

• Explain the diplomats, the sheikh's second cousin has initiated a revolution, and "a couple of his idiot cousins are taking over things." Thus, officials enlist the services of the dazzling agent, Modesty Blaise (Vitti). A British agent tells Modesty that "a woman amongst Moslems has to be particularly careful." Abruptly, Sheikh Abu Tier (Revill) appears, saying, "It's the Moslems who must be careful of Modesty Blaise." Chuckling, he embraces Modesty.

• The sheikh whisks Modesty off to a room filled with dark-robed Arabs. Introducing her as "my son," he explains that after finding this "little girl" in the Sahara, he raised her as his own child. Boasts Modesty, "He made me his son and taught me how to fight."

• A nervous British agent sees the sheikh demonstrate his new "toy"—a missile launcher.

• When European assassins move to terminate Modesty, she "transmits a message to the Arabs." Cut to Abu Tier's desert tent; two youths paint his toenails. When the sheikh receives Modesty's alert, he and his Arabs grab their rifles and charge to the rescue.

• The villains close in on Modesty; she sighs, "This is it!" Suddenly, the sheikh's Arabs arrive: by yacht, pontoon boat, red convertible, galloping out of the sea on horses. Exclaims Modesty, "Here comes the sheikh now!" Soon, Abu Tier's Arabs bring down the villains.

• In the desert, Arab children watch oil dripping from a leaking pipe. Mute clad-in-black Arab women bathe Modesty's colleague, Willie (Stamp). Now wearing Arab garb, Modesty and the sheikh play with the diamonds. "You can ask for anything, anything," says the sheikh. Quips Modesty, "Anything?" The sheikh nods. Says Modesty, "The diamonds?" They both laugh.

Money from Home (1953), PAR. *Jerry Lewis, Romo Vincent, Dean Martin.*
In 3-D. CAMEOS, SHEIKHS

Based on a Damon Runyon tale, this horseracing yarn concerns New York thugs trying to rig a race. Yet, the producers insert a mindless Arab, "The Poojah" (Vincent). The Arab tries to buy our horses, and he tries to seduce the protagonist, Yokum (Lewis).

Scene: New York, a train station. The wealthy Poojah steps onto the platform; several veiled maidens trek behind. Ask news reporters: "Do you take all your wives with you when you travel?" "Are you going to buy the horse that wins?"

• Aboard a train, the Poojah's suite. An aide enters the Arab's harem quarters, saying, "His exalted desires a wife." On cue, several lovely maidens play Arab songs.

• The dimwitted Poojah lounges on pillows, smoking a nargelih. Abruptly, he moves to romance Yokum, who wears harem-garb. The fat Arab chases the disguised Yokum, panting, "You will be among my favorites."

• At a hotel party, New Yorkers mingle in one room. In another room, isolated from the celebration, the camera shows Poojah and his Arabs. When Arab music from the sheikh's room invades the New Yorker's suite, a gangster shouts, "Hey! Tell the manager to clean up them crummy musicians across the hall."

• The gangsters try but fail to fix the horse race. The winning horse and his jockey, Yokum, cross the finish line first. Excited, Poojah asks the horse's owner, "Have you set the price you want for the horse?" The sheikh is told, "The horse isn't for sale." Yokum tags the sheikh, "your worth-less-ness." His friend corrects him, mumbling: "Your worthiness."

Morocco (1930), PAR. *Gary Cooper, Marlene Dietrich.* VILLAINS, MAIDENS

In this sober Western romance, Marlene Dietrich's first American feature, Arabs are backdrops. Briefly, inept Moroccan thugs appear. See *Casbah* (1948).

Scene: When the call to prayer is given devout, white-robed Moroccans kneel and pray.

• Unveiled Moroccan prostitutes beckon legionnaires, and vice versa.

• A down-on-her-luck Parisian entertainer, Amy Jolly (Dietrich), performs in an Arab cafe—a place leading nowhere. Soon, Jolly meets and falls for a legionnaire, Tom Brown (Cooper). The couple run off and make love.

• Brown enters a dark alley. Instantly, two mute Arabs appear from the shadows, try to knife Brown, and fail.

• Brown and his legionnaires march off. Following "their men" into the desert are Jolly, several prostitutes and other Arab women who make up the "rear guard."

Dialogue: When asked whether he worries about "bad" bedouins, legionnaire Brown barks: "Those walking bed sheets can't shoot straight."

Mother (1996), PAR. *Albert Brooks, Richard Assad, Joey Namer, Debbie Reynolds.* SP: Albert Brooks, Monica Johnson. D: Albert Brooks. CAMEOS

Though this comedy concerns a divorced man's relationship with his mother, an Arab dunce appears as a TV installer.

Scene: Several minutes into the film, two "House of Discount" workers appear. The men have just finished installing a TV set in the home of Brooks' mother's (Reynolds). She asks if the installers are married. Nodding his head, installer #2 (Assad) grins, then mumbles, "Hee, hee, hee." Her face expresses puzzlement. Installer #1 (Namer) tells her, "All hooked up and ready to go." She questions the color of the TV picture, asking installer #2, "Does that look green to you?" Again, he grins, then nods his head saying, "Yes, thank you." Furious at his co-worker's behavior, installer #1 shouts at him Arabic. Next, he slaps him on the shoulder, calls him *majnoon* [idiot], and orders him from the room. Confused, the woman asks, "What's wrong with him?" Installer #1 points to his head, "He's mentally ill, ma'am." Again, they discuss the TV's color picture. At last, he convinces her to sign a release form, saying, "Don't bother seeing me out. I will find the door."

Mouse Hunt (1997), DW. *Nathan Lane, Lee Evans.* SP: Adam Rifkin. CAMEOS, SHEIKHS

An auctioneer moves to sell the Smuntz brothers' (Lane, Evans) antique home. Nearly all the bidders are Americans and Europeans. Seated in the front row, however, is a mute, bearded Arab wearing a lengthy headdress that nearly touches the floor. The bidding commences: "The sheikh bids $5 million." In the end, others outbid the Arab.

Mozambique (1965), WAR. *Steve Cochran, Hildegarde Neff, Vivi Bach, Martin Benson.* CAMEOS, VILLAINS

A seedy Ali Baba abducts blondes.

Scene: In Mozambique, "Portuguese criminals smuggle drugs and medicines." An American pilot, Brad Webster (Cochran), and a blonde singer, Christina (Bach), oppose the smugglers.

• "Club Valdez." Cut to Ali Baba, a bearded Arab in sunglasses. The lecherous Arab leers at three Western women.

• Ali Baba requests the blonde (Christina); his cohort steers Christina into a side room. Ali Baba follows and shuts the door. Frightened, Christina stammers, "I think I want to go back to the club." She leaves Ali Baba, telling Brad, "That Arab man, I ran away from him!"

• Christina and Brad swim and smooch. Instantly, Ali Baba, who owns "a very good penthouse in Park Lane," surfaces. Christina is abducted. The cohorts of DaSilva (Benson), the man "with the rich Arab contact," toss Christina inside Ali Baba's car. Pointing to Christina, DaSilva quips, "I hope you won't be too disappointed." Says Ali Baba, "In my youth I used to breed wild Arab horses. I do not intend to be disappointed."

• Observes a DaSilva thug, Ali Baba's "coming across by boat to whet his appetite for blondes, preferably young, preferably new."

• Brad to the rescue. He enters Ali Baba's Arabian nights hideaway and punches out some white-burnoosed Arabs. Next, Brad sees four mute Arab women wearing Indian saris preparing Christina for Ali Baba's embraces. In time, Brad saves her!

Credits state: "The Arab."

The Mummy (1932), UNI. *Boris Karloff, Zita Johann, David Manners, Edward Van Sloan, Bramwell Fletcher.* EGYPTIANS, MAIDENS

Seeking vengeance, the monster mummy Imhotep stalks and murders people. And, believing the heroine Helen is the ancient priestess Amon, his reincarnated darling, the mummy pursues her.

Scene: 1921 Egypt. A British museum's expedition uncovers a 3,700-year-old tomb. Archaeologists fail to heed the inscribed curse: "Death. Eternal punishment for anyone opening this casket." After a young Brit opens the tomb, Imhotep (Karloff) slowly emerges. Watching the dusty mummy creep out of his tomb induces madness; the archaeologist "dies laughing in a straightjacket."

• In England, Dr. Muller (Van Sloan) points out, "Some of the ancient spells are still potent... The Gods of Egypt still live in those hills."

• Imhotep takes on human form. Posing as an elderly Egyptian priest, Ardath Bey, the mummy approaches the half-Egyptian heroine, Helen (Johann). He believes that Helen is the priestess Amon, his ex-sweetheart. Thus, Imhotep moves to "kill her and make her a living mummy like himself."

• Flashback, ancient Egypt. Imhotep's passion for Amon has no limits. He steals Isis's sacred rituals and tries to restore Amon from death. In so doing, he defies Isis's will. Thus, the priests punish Imhotep.

• Back in England, the mummy kills six Englishmen, including a museum guard and two archaeologists. He murders one telepathically.

• "Fight[ing] magic with magic," Dr. Muller stops Imhotep from killing Helen's live beau, Frank (Manners). Muller flaunts not a cross (a Dracula ploy), but Isis's ancient amulet.

• This mummy's powers are too strong for a mere mortal to subdue. Using his telepathic power, Imhotep lures Helen inside his entombment chamber. As he prepares to do "an unholy thing," Helen prays, asking the goddess Isis to save her. Isis acts. A flash of light springs from the priestess's statue. The mummy's special scroll ignites; Imhotep disintegrates.

The Mummy (1959), UI. *Christopher Lee, Peter Cushing, Yvonne Furneaux.* EGYPTIANS

In this remake of Boris Karloff's *The Mummy* (1932), an Egyptian cur appears, directing the mummy down bloody streets.

Scene: An excavation site. Mute Egyptian laborers shift sand and smash rocks. A fez-wearing Egyptian named Mehemet alerts parchment-faced Western archaeologists about an ancient curse, "He who robs the graves of Egypt, dies."

• British archaeologists ignore Mehemet's counsel; they defile Princess Ananka's ancient crypt, snatching treasures. Vows Mehemet, "For this desecration you will be avenged."

• England. Due to Mehemet's ingenuity, Ananka's buried-alive lover, the mummy Kharis (Lee), comes to life. Emerging from "this strange country's" swamp waters, Kharis moves to punish the three tomb intruders. Mehemet's prayer to the "great God, Karnak" requests that the English "unbelievers shall suffer—this I swear!"

• The covered-with-mildewed-bandage-strips Kharis goes to "destroy those who desecrated" Ananka's crypt. Orders Mehemet, "[Kill the] infidels." Kharis dispatches two violators. And, Mehemet fatally stabs a policeman and a passerby.

• Thinking the Western heroine Isabel (Furneaux) is actually Ananka, his long-lost ancient mate, Kharis lumbers after the frightened Isabel.

• Egypt is hostile; England, peaceful. Mehemet tells British archaeologist John Banning (Cushing), "In my country violence is quite commonplace. It doesn't leave the impression that it does in this country."

Finis: Kharis kills Mehemet, then sinks into swamp waters.

The Mummy (1999), UNI. *Brendan Fraser, John Hannah, Kevin O'Connor, Arnold Vosloo, Omar Djalili, Rachel Weisz.* W, D: Stephen Sommers. Filmed in Morocco, Egypt. EGYPTIANS

In this $80 million remake of the 1932 Boris Karloff classic, live and revived Egyptians appear as hostile, sneaky, and dirty caricatures. As *USA Today* critic Susan Wloszczyna points out, "If someone complains of a foul odor, you can be sure an Arab stooge is about to enter a scene" (7 May 1999).

Scene: Egypt, 1290 BC, the "City of the Dead." High priest Imhotep (Vosloo) begins romancing the pharaoh's gorgeous mistress; the potentate catches the couple in the act. Instantly, Imhotep and the ruler's mistress fatally knife the pharaoh. Aware they cannot escape, Imhotep's mistress kills herself. As for Imhotep, pharaoh's guards bury him alive. Before sealing Imhotep's sarcophagus, guards dump flesh-eating scarabs onto his mummified body.

• Fast forward, 1923, the desert. Burnoosed, gun-toting bedouins attack a legion regiment commanded by an American adventurer, Rick (Fraser). Rick's legionnaires terminate scores; hundreds of Arab bodies litter the screen. Before Rick is captured and imprisoned, he manages to gun down a dozen-plus bedouins.

• Cairo, the Museum of Antiquities. The Western heroine, a librarian named Evie (Weisz), and her brother Jonathan (Hannah), discover that the jailed Rick may know the City of the Dead's location. So, they move to free Rick from a Cairo prison.

• The prison courtyard. Unkempt Egyptian guards lead Rick toward the gallows. Cut to Egyptian prisoners cheering; they want to see Rick hang. Evie tries to bribe the Egyptian prison warden (Djalili), an unshaven scoundrel. She offers "500 pounds" for Rick's freedom. The Egyptian cur grabs her leg, saying, "500 pounds and what else? I'm a very lonely man."

• Evie rebuffs the Egyptian jailer, convincing him to free Rick in return for a percentage of whatever treasures they may find in the City of the Dead.

• A boat, en route to the City of the Dead. Black-robed bedouins sneak aboard and attack the Westerner passengers. Cut to some Americans wearing cowboy hats shooting dead the invading bedouins. Sighs one American, "This is a messed up country."

• During a "camel sale," one Western man says, "All you have to do is give him [the Arab] your sisters and he'll be happy." Mounting camels, Jonathan, Rick, Evie, and the Egyptian prison warden trek across the desert. Says Jonathan, "I never did like camels. They smell. They spit." On cue, the Egyptian expectorates. This slimy jailer also snores. Waking up, he shouts, "No more goat soup."

• Arriving at the City of the Dead, Jonathan complains about the foul odor of the burial chamber asking, "Where'd our smelly little friend go to?" The dialogue directly equates the stench with the Egyptian, as the camera swiftly reveals the smelly jailer. A scarab crawls under the jailer's skin, driving him bonkers. When Jonathan sighs, he was "a stinky fellow," the audience where I watched the movie, roared.

• Throughout, mute Egyptian workers function as disposable, frightened props. Salt acid kills several.

• The bedouin leader who befriends Rick near the movie's end, cautions, "You must leave. Leave this place or die." Too late. Imhotep (Vosloo) reawakens. Promptly, the enraged mummy unleashes seven Biblical plagues. Locusts and scarabs fill the screen.

• In Cairo, cut to Imhotep's torch-carrying cohorts. The Egyptians are made-up to look like zombies covered with boils. A mob of zombie-like Egyptians descend on Rick and his friends. As the Egyptians close in, the desperate Rick floors his car's gas pedal. Some Egyptians fall from the moving vehicle; Rick beats up then runs over scores of others. No regrets, here.

• Imhotep recruits some saber-wielding mummies; they charge Rick, Inc. No problem. Rick terminates a dozen-plus of the bandaged assassins. After Rick crushes these baddies, he dispatches Imhotep back into his sarcophagus.

Note: *Entertainment Weekly* noted that *The Mummy* burst "out of its tomb, grossing over the weekend [7–9 May 1999] $44.6 million... the highest grossing non-summer opening in film history" (21 May 1999).

• Though a box office success, several critics criticized Universal for the movie's stereotypes. On "Siskel and Ebert" (12 May 1999) critic David Ansen of *Newsweek* complained of Arab-bashing. Ebert concurred. In *Entertainment Weekly's* "Not So Good" column (21 May 1999), the editors point out *The Mummy's* "negative Arab stereotyping." And *The New Yorker* critic, Anthony Lane, writes:

> Finally there is the Arab question. The Arab people have always had the roughest... deal from Hollywood, but with the death of the Cold War the stereotype has been granted even more wretched prominence. In *The Mummy*, I could scarcely believe what I was watching... So, here's a party game for any producers with a Middle Eastern setting in mind; try replacing one Semitic group with another—Jews instead of Arabs—and THEN listen for the laugh... One could argue that the racism of *The Mummy* is merely period detail, or that the gags slip by so quickly that they don't have a chance to stick. I find, however, that they hang around while the rest of the movie fades (10 May 1999).

• Concerned about the film's stereotypes, Rana Shanawani of Cornell University wrote to Universal. Universal's Claudia Polena had only this to say: "*The Mummy* is escapist entertainment and as such is not intended in any way to be perceived as a realistic depiction of any group of people." Responded Ms. Shanawani, "This is an anti-Arab movie. Please admit it" (*ADC Times*, May 1999).

• Writes Michael Hoffman II, a former Associated Press reporter, in his *Hoffman Wire*,

> *The Mummy* is a racist masterpiece. How is it possible that Hollywood... could make a blockbuster film that is a consummate example of bigotry?... [T]he crude stereotypes of bazaar hagglers and towel heads vs. handsome, robed English and American Lancelots, have been revived... individual Arabs are filthy, greedy, slimy pigs. The Arab masses are mindless, murderous zombies who chant the name Imhotep—though it might as well be Khomeini... A more accurate name for Universal's box office smash [is] *The Dummy*."

Hoffman contends politics may have played a role in the demonization of Arabs, writing, "Universal's President and Chief Operating Officer is Ron Meyer. Universal is owned, in part, by Seagram, whose CEO is Edgar Brofman Jr. Brofman's father runs the World Jewish Congress" (14 May 1999).

• Watching actors perform as dense, sloppy Egyptians such as this one, reminded me of the story of Amr El Bayoumi, a young Egyptian-American working in Hollywood.[118] Bayoumi responded to a Hollywood bulletin calling for: "Extras, Age Open, Middle Eastern and all ethics to play people at an archaeological site in an action adventure film, *Pyramids of Death*." Mused Bayoumi,

> As I neared the production location, I imagined myself on the big screen as an Egyptian diligently excavating for buried artifacts in the hot Sahara sun. Suddenly a tinge of apprehension struck me. I was well aware of the fact that Arabs have been consistently stereotyped by American films and television as fanatic, terrorist, uncivilized and usually inferior."

Would Pyramids of Death be typical? He hoped not, and vowed to investigate before signing on.

On the set, Bayoumi introduced himself to the producer, saying that he was brought up to respect different ideas and customs. In a serious tone, he told the producer, "If this film defames Arabs in any way I will, unfortunately, be unable to participate." The producer reassured him that *Pyramids of Death* would in no way provide a negative image of Egyptians. But as the production crew prepared to begin shooting, the director approached the dark-complexioned extras, explaining that while they may not totally agree, they had to act "stereotypically Egyptian."

The scene began with an explosion inside a cave where Egyptian assistants had been digging. As the Egyptians hastily evacuated the cave, their European archaeologist boss shouts, "Damn it, I said no dynamite!" In broken English, one Egyptian actor-as-laborer grunts an apology. Then, says Bayoumi, the producer screamed: "Hey, you guys aren't dirty enough. Go up that hill and dirty yourselves up." At that moment, the young actress who played the role of the archaeologist's daughter arrived, exclaiming, "Hi there, you Ayrabs." Upset, Bayoumi yanked off his headdress and took the director aside. "That's it… I refuse to contribute to this blatant humiliation of my culture," he said. As he began removing his costume, a grip approached Bayoumi, expressing empathy. "I've been working in this business for a while," he said, "and all you Arabs do in movies is hijack planes and shoot people."

Bayoumi left the set, his mind filled with "associated visions of unclean Arabs." Mused Bayoumi, "How absurd it would be if all Americans were depicted as Charles Manson or Tammy Faye Baker-like characters in the media of foreign lands." Several days later Bayoumi, who was raised in a bicultural environment, said that he " began to understand the root of prejudice more clearly—fear of unfamiliar things, ignorance and misperceptions." When pondering Hollywood's Arab portraits, he offers serious questions:

> Why is it that when some people meet an Arab for the first time they comment, "Oh, do you ride camels a lot?" And, "How many oil wells do you own?" He asks, Why aren't audiences exposed to Hollywood movies that show Egyptian archaeologists in a positive way, men like the renowned Kamal El Malakh? Why not dramatize the lives of the great leaders of history: Ramses, Jamila Bohrait, to name two? Why not reveal the creative genius of Rose El-Yousef and Nobel Laureate Naguib Mahfouz? Why is Hollywood so reluctant to project Arabs fairly?

The Mummy Lives (1993), Global. A Yoram Globus film. *Tony Curtis, Greg Wrangler, Leslie Hardy, Muhammad Bakri.* Filmed in Israel. Israeli actors as Egyptians. EGYPTIANS

Producer Yoram Globus projects Egyptian men as thieves and grave robbers, and Egyptian women as mute, mean mannequins.

Scene: Contemporary Luxor. On screen, pyramids and camels along with bedouins on horseback. Cut to a treasure-seeking newspaper magnate, Lord Maxton. He nears a mummy's tomb bearing the inscription, "Those who defy this sacred place will die." Warns Ali, a worker, "This is an evil place; we must not break the seal." But, of course, excavators break into an ancient crypt.

• Ali snatches the mummy's jewels. Another Egyptian thief, Corporal Fawzi, goes to snitch some gold pieces. Instantly, the mummified hands of Zoth emerge from the sarcophagus, fatally choking the Egyptian. Emerging from the tomb and killing Lord Maxton is the reincarnated Dr. Riad Mohassid (Curtis) "the protector of the dead."

• Dr. Riad cautions Westerners wanting to loot Egypt's treasures, "Get out of my tombs. Get out of Egypt... [you have] no respect for the dead. You dig up our ancestors. You rob us of all of our treasures. You take the remains of my people and you put them in glass cases, in museums, so that people can look at them like circus freaks. You call that research?" If ravaging Egypt is acceptable, says Riad, then I will "go to the British government and ask for a license to steal Westminster Abbey."

• Flashback to ancient Luxor. Dancing concubines draped in white surround the clad-in-black Zoth. Later, Zoth's "favorite concubine," Kia, steals off to Dr. Riad's tent for amour. Guards snatch the duo and bury Dr. Riad alive, as he dared defy "Zoth, God of Vengeance."

• Flash forward. Nightmares frighten the fair heroine, Sandra Barnes (Hardy); she resembles Kia. Sandra's dreams reveal a mummy seducing her. Seeking help, Sandra calls on Dr. Carey Williams (Wrangler).

• The souk presents ugly Egyptians. A beggar and a snake charmer frighten Sandra. Next, repulsive Egyptians accost her. Several mute women in black rebuff Sandra. Sandra runs off; an elderly man chases her. She escapes, descending into a tunnel. Cut to nasty Egyptian women slamming the iron entrance gate, trapping Sandra. Abruptly, unkempt Egyptians fondle and rob her. In time, Dr. Riad rescues Sandra.

• Dr. Riad's serpents terminate all six "grave robbers."

• Thinking Sandra is the 1990s version of his long-lost Kia, Dr. Riad moves to dispatch her to Zoth. Sandra prefers to remain alive. She eludes the reincarnated priest's clutches, igniting a tomb fire. This time Dr. Riad perishes, for good.

Note: The credits list the film's Egyptians as "Thieves."

The Mummy Returns (2001), UNI. *Brendan Frazier, Rachael Weisz, Arnold Vosloo, Adewale Akinnuoye-Agbaje, Oded Fehr, Freddie Boath, The Rock, Patricia Velasquez.* SP, D: Stephen Sommers. Filmed in Morocco and Jordan. EGYPTIANS

This high-tech and high-budgeted movie is yet another cursed, dusty-clothed mummy movie that boosts bigotry by demeaning Egyptians. The film clutters silver screens with even more detestable Egyptians than did its predecessor, *The Mummy*

(1999)—despite the condemnation that movie received from distinguished film critics and Arab Americans alike. Hundreds of evil Egyptians contest a few heroic Westerners and fellow Egyptians. Yet, Universal's stereotypes attracted, not deterred viewers—*The Mummy Returns* earned more than $70 million in its opening weekend (4–6 May), making it the biggest non-holiday opening in movie history. The acceptance of heinous stereotypes in financial blockbusters troubles me profoundly.

Scene: Egypt, 1933. The revived mummy, Imhotep (Vosloo), his long-lost sweetheart, Anch-Su-Namun (Velasquez), and the deadly Scorpion King (The Rock)—a mystical half-man, half-scorpion creature—set out to rule the universe. Assisting them are a knife-for-hire Egyptian, a greedy, disagreeable Egyptian curator, and the curator's dark and sinister looking Arab bodyguard (Akinnuoye-Agbaje). The stereotypical black bodyguard is obsessed with killing Alex (Boath), the protagonist's 9-year-old child.

• Three hirelings move to loot a tomb. The one wearing a burnoose tries to knife Alex. Next, the curator's Egyptian assassins and his bodyguard invade the home of the film's Western champions, Rick and Evelyn O'Connell (Fraser and Weisz). Though Rick, Evelyn, and a good bedouin (Fehr), shoot and knife plenty of red-burnoosed villains, Alex is manhandled and whisked off by the Egyptians. When Evelyn tries to rescue her son, Egyptians try to "burn her" alive. But, the flames burn the inept Egyptians, not Evelyn.

• Numerous scenes show the O'Connells crushing hundreds of Imhotep's Egyptian guards. To insure viewers will identify the guards as Egyptians, the costumer covers them with flaming red-mesh outfits that resemble discarded fishing nets.

• Special effects wizards beef up desert sword fights and fist fights and inject hackneyed Egyptian baddies who pop up everywhere, from London to Thebes. Though outnumbered hundreds-to-two, Rick and Evelyn bring down these funky computer-generated Egyptians, notably flying mummies with sharpened fingernails as long as switch blades. They also terminate undead pygmies, man-eating scarabs, the god, Anubis, and his werewolf-looking canine troops.

• Throughout, computer-generated curs gobble up dense, screaming Egyptians. Non-stop action scenes show the animated heavies wiping out scores of frightened Egyptian guards. Watching dozens of dark-complexioned Egyptians drop made me cringe while the rest of the audience laughed.

• After two hours, this mindless mummy mayhem came to a merciful end—Rick finally dispatches the Scorpion King and Imhotep back into their tombs.

Mummy's Boys (1936), RKO. *Bert Wheeler, Robert Woolsey, Barbara Pepper, Francie McDonald, Mitchell Lewis, Willie Best.* EGYPTIANS, MAIDENS

Presenting a promiscuous "pasha" and his mute wives. Blacks are mocked.

Scene: Filling the screen, this newspaper headline: "Curse of King Pharatine's Tomb." A "curse" is apparently responsible for the demise of ten explorers—they dared enter a mummy's tomb. Dispatched to Cairo to investigate the explorers' deaths are two ditch diggers, Stanley (Wheeler) and Aloysius (Woolsey).

• Cairo's Hotel d'Orient. Appearing are Haroun Pasha's (Lewis) four giggling wives; the pasha "marries them (the black-veiled maidens) wholesale."

• The pasha pursues Stanley. The clever Stanley squirts ink in the ruler's eyes, then he douses the pasha with a fire extinguisher. Cut to laughing hyenas in the desert!

• Later, the pasha sees his wives pampering Stanley and Aloysius; he pulls a knife, chasing the Americans.

• In the souk, a tattoo artist and a conjurer. Stanley hops into the trickster's basket; the Arab thrusts a sword through it. Next, the conjurer directs the rope upwards. See *Kid Millions* (1934).

• Stanley and Aloysius nab the villain, an American archaeologist. Not only did he kill the ten tomb explorers, he stole King Pharatine's jewels. Sighs Egyptian detective Rasheed Bey (McDonald), "You've already accomplished what I set out to do."

• Stanley sees an Egyptian wearing a turban, asking, "Has he got a headache?" Quips the butler, "I can't say sir, he's an Egyptian." "Don't Egyptians have headaches?" asks Stanley. "To have a headache," quips Aloysius, "you've got to have a brain." No one contests the remark.

Dialogue: Blacks are ridiculed. Afraid of ghosts and the darkness, the shivering Catfish (Best) refuses to enter a pharaoh's secret tomb. Barks Stanley, "Well, what about it. They can't see you in the dark. Go on in."

The Mummy's Curse (1944), UNI. *Lon Chaney, Jr., Peter Coe, Virginia Christine, Kay Harding, Martin Kosteck.* Released prior to *The Mummy's Ghost* (1944), this completes the Kharis/Ananka series. EGYPTIANS

In Louisiana, Kharis surfaces from a bayou and terminates innocent Americans. Kharis's cohort, an Egyptian priest, tries to bed the American heroine.

Scene: A monastery. The camera reveals the coffin of the enigmatic Kharis (Chaney). Soon Kharis, who hails from "The Valley of the Seven Jackals," rises. Abruptly, he begins tracking Ananka (Christine), his awakened princess of 3,000 years ago. In the process, Kharis puts into play his deadly one-hand-clutching-the-throat blow, strangling four Americans—a caretaker, Cajun Joe, a female singer, and a doctor.

• Arriving is Ilzor (Coe), an Egyptian high priest armed with a secret formula that brings mummies back to life. Assisting Ilzor is the sex-starved Ragheb (Kosteck). Their task? Return the lovebirds, Kharis and Ananka/Christine, to Egypt. Moans Ilzor, "Non-believing American infidels have driven them into the swamp."

• Ilzor, who detests Americans, tells the one-eyed, limping Kharis, "Anyone who would stand in your way, kill, kill."

• Intending to trap Kharis and Ananka, US government employees drain the swamp. Cautions one, "Too many people, they go to the swamp, they never come out."

• After Ragheb kills Ilzor, he darts off to the monastery. Why? He wants to bed the American heroine, Betty (Harding). To the rescue, Kharis. The mummy terminates Ragheb.

• Rubble drops from a building, crushing Kharis and his long-lost mate, Ananka.

The Mummy's Ghost (1944), UNI. *Lon Chaney, Jr., John Carradine, Ramsay Ames, Robert Lowery.* Sequel to *The Mummy's Tomb.* EGYPTIANS, MAIDENS

Kharis returns to New England. While terrorizing residents, the mummy discovers his reincarnated priestess, a Mapleton college student with Egyptian blood. The priestess' beau, an American student, is unaware she is Kharis's long-lost sweetheart. An Egyptian tries to rape the American heroine.

Scene: The headline of a Mapleton, Massachusetts, newspaper reads: "Mapleton Mummy Returns." Why has Kharis (Chaney) returned to Mapleton? Because Princess Ananka's 3,000-year-old soul dwells within Amina Mansouri (Ames), an Egyptian college student. Seeing Amina with an American student, Tom (Lowery), Kharis panics.

• Amina yearns for Kharis, confessing to Tom, "Something happens to me when I think of Egypt."

• Jealous Kharis terminates three Mapleton citizens—a college professor, a farmer, and a museum guide.

• Arriving in Mapleton to assist Kharis is a salacious high priest, Yousef Bey (Carradine). Bey's role is to brew tanna leaves during "the cycle of the full moon," and to take Kharis and Ananka/Amina back "to their rightful [Egyptian] resting places, in these tombs."

• In *The Mummy's Curse* (1944) an Egyptian priest tries to rape Betty. Here, too, an Egyptian, Bey, tries to seduce the student, Amina. Bey tells Amina, "You cannot escape your destiny." Wanting Amina to become immortal, Bey coaxes her to drink his sacred "tanna leaf brew." In time, Kharis arrives, killing the double-crossing Bey.

• The swamp area. Cut to Mapleton's residents encircling Kharis and Amina. Suddenly, Kharis collapses. At the same time, Amina, also crumbles. Tom, Amina's ex-boyfriend, gasps.

• In the end, the mummified Ananka/Amina is reunited with Kharis. Cut to the happy Egyptian couple descending slowly into a turbid pit.

The Mummy's Hand (1940), UNI. *Dick Foran, Wallace Ford, Peggy Moran, George Zucco, Tom Tyler.* This film has three sequels. EGYPTIANS

The first Kharis feature. Again, an Egyptian priest moves to rape the American heroine. Westerners "seeking a place in archeological history" violate tombs, irking mummies. States the tomb inscription in *The Mummy's Hand*: "A cruel and violent death shall be his fate and never shall his soul rest with eternity."

Scene: The excavation site. Cinematographers employ green-tinted film to accent the exploration scenes. Though the curse states, "Death to whoever enters the unholy tomb," US explorers move forward to unearth a lost princess' coffin. Her tomb is guarded by the princess' lover, Kharis, a deadly mummy. Savvy Egyptian workers run off.

• At a restaurant, Egyptian heavies attack the American protagonists, Steve (Foran) and Babe (Ford). An Arab pulls a knife; Steve drops him.

• Egyptian professor Andoheb (Zucco) brews a special elixir from tanna leaves, keeping alive the 3,000-year-old Kharis (Tyler).

• A full moon; jackals howl. Professor Andoheb dispatches the revived Kharis to crush some people.

• Kharis wants to unite with the American maiden, Marta (Moran). He believes Marta is the reincarnation of his long-lost love. Professor Andoheb, too, wants Marta. After Andoheb forcibly whisks Marta off to the "Temple of Karnak," he straps her down onto a makeshift altar. The lecherous Egyptian professor inserts some tanna leaf fluid into a hypodermic needle, panting, "You shall be my high priestess. I'm going to make you immortal. Neither time nor death shall touch us. You and I, together for eternity."

• In time, Steve and Babe rush into Karnak's temple, rescuing Marta. They also bring down Andoheb and the mummy, Kharis.

• Smiling, the Americans ship off their Egyptian tomb treasures to the US.

Note: I still recall how one Pittsburgh, Pennsylvania, movie theater publicized *The Mummy's Hand*. To attract young viewers, the manager dressed the ticket-taker in mummy garb. Posted in the lobby, an usher in nurse's uniform, complete with a first-aid kit. Though this melodramatic array terrified us, we paid to see the film. At the time, I was only six.

The Mummy's Revenge (1973), a.k.a. The Vengeance of the Mummy, EMB. *Paul Naschy, Riva Otolina, Jack Taylor II.* SP: Paul Naschy. EGYPTIANS, MAIDENS

In this Spanish version of *The Mummy*, actor-director Paul Naschy has a dual role, appearing as the evil eighteenth-dynasty mummy, Amenhotep, and as Assad Bey. An Egyptian reawakens Amenhotep, keeping the mummy "alive," not by administering tanna leaves, but by directing the bandaged prowler to "drink the blood of young virgins and eat the flesh of fellow men."

Scene: Intones the narrator: Amenhotep was a "brutal despot who generated a nightmare of blood and terror. Under his savage rule the warm desert sands turned red with blood."

• In ancient Egypt, Pharaoh Amenhotep tells his sweetheart, Amarna (Otolina), "We'll sacrifice ten virgins." Cut to the pharaoh hurling hatchets into the maidens. Later, Amenhotep pays a price for his barbaric deeds; the pharaoh must "wander the world of the unknown for eternity; the forces of evil are on his side."

• London, the home of US archaeologist, Dr. Landsburg. An English couple admits they sent Amenhotep's sarcophagus to England. They warn Landsburg to keep away, explaining the "tomb has never been violated."

• Unexpectedly, the Egyptian professor, Assad Bey (Naschy), arrives at Landsburg's home. Believing Amenhotep will make him immortal, Bey violates the mummy's resting place, boasting, "The pharaohs of Egypt will control the world!"

• Beware the awakened Amenhotep. The mummy-pharaoh slays several people: Landsburg's manservant, a museum guard, and some policemen. And, on London's dark foggy streets, when the moon is full, Amenhotep slays English virgins.

• In Landsburg's basement, Bey administers unique nourishment to Amenhotep. He also slices dead virgins' throats, then burns incense. Next, Bey pours some blood drippings into a cup, passing the drink onto the mummy.

• The reawakened Amenhotep pursues Landsburg's half-Egyptian daughter, Elena (Otolina). Amenhotep believes that after Elena dies, his ex-sweetheart's spirit will surface. The pharaoh kisses Elena; she disintegrates.

• Earlier, Landsburg reflected on whether he should have married an Egyptian woman, saying, "Some of my friends thought I was insane to marry an Egyptian. I don't know—they could have been right."

• The loss of his daughter, Elena, prompts Landsburg to act. He takes a gun and shoots the mummy. Though bullets do not phase Amenhotep, fire works. Flames engulf the evil pharaoh and Bey.

Dialogue: Contends a Scotland Yard inspector (Dav'ila), "We all know a mummy cannot return to life."

The Mummy's Shroud (1967), TCF. *Andre Morell, John Phillips, Roger Delgado, Maggie Kimberley, Catherine Lacey.* EGYPTIANS, MAIDENS

British archeologists should let sleeping pharaohs rest. Beware those guarding revived mummies.

Scene: 4,000 years ago. A young pharaoh is buried. Flash forward—the early 1920s. Near "the rock of death," Sir Basil's (Morell) British excavation team violates a young prince's tomb.

• After Sir Basil's team enters the burial cave, they discover that the young pharaoh has been preserved in "sand for 4,000 years." Abruptly, a repulsive-looking Egyptian, Hasmid (Delgado), emerges from the shadows. Wielding a knife, the gravekeeper warns, "Death awaits those who disturb the resting place of the pharaoh."

• The archaeologists ignore Hasmid's omen, and whisk the boy mummy off to Cairo. Upset, Hasmid begins mumbling mysterious phrases. Presto! The boy pharaoh's loyal slave, Prem, springs to life.

• Introducing Haiti (Lacey), a ghastly Egyptian clairvoyant sans teeth. Her role? To program Prem so that the slave will kill the Western intruders. Haiti stares into her crystal ball, warning Sir Basil's group, "The spirit of the tomb will journey from death to life and punish you." Cut to the renewed Prem killing four, including Sir Basil.

• In time, an Egyptian policeman appears, saving from Prem's clutches, the British heroine, Miss Preston (Kimberley), and her beau.

• Finally, the avenging slave mummy is eradicated. How? Miss Preston grabs hold of a hexed "shroud" and exclaims "the words of death!" Instantly, Prem crumbles.

The Mummy's Tomb (1942), UNI. *Lon Chaney Jr., Elyse Knox, George Zucco, Turhan Bey.* Sequel to *The Mummy's Hand.* EGYPTIANS

In another popular flick, the vengeful Kharis, who is kept alive by "a strange race of high priests," murders Mapleton's townsfolk and tomb violators.

Scene: Labyrinths of a tomb. Egyptian workers warn American archaeologists, "Effendi, this is an unholy tomb. It means death to whoever breaks the seal." No matter. The explorers crack the seal, profaning Princess Ananka's tomb. Egyptian workers run off.

• The archaeologists dispatch Ananka's body to Mapleton. Cut to Andoheb (Zucco), an elderly Egyptian priest vowing vengeance; he asks Egypt's "secret Gods" for assistance. He sends to Mapleton Mehemet Bey (Bey), a young high priest whom he raised within "the confines of the tomb of Egypt."

• In Mapleton, Bey disturbs Kharis's (Chaney) 3,700-year sleep, then hides the mummy in the cemetery. A howling wolf precedes Kharis's resurrection. Bey assists the renewed Kharis, giving him some tanna juice. Then, he tells Kharis to "carry death and destruction to all those who violated his beloved princess's tomb." The obedient Kharis kills "while the moon is still high in the sky."

• Exclaim anxious Mapleton residents, "A creature that's been buried for over 3,000 years is alive and he's brought death to this town!... We are dealing with the presence of the living dead."

• Dead and live Egyptians lust after Western blondes. Kharis and Bey intend to seduce the American archeologists's clad-in-white girlfriend, Janet (Knox). The bandaged Kharis enters Janet's bedroom. Janet lets loose an unforgettable scream.

• Bey tells Kharis to deliver Janet to him; he wants to make her "a bride of a high priest of Karnak." Hoping to make Janet "immortal," Bey brews tanna leaves. Fortunately, Janet's lover, Stephen (Foran), arrives, shooting Bey.

• Kharis continues stalking Mapleton's residents. Stephen's bullets do not halt the advancing mummy; cremation does. Cut to roaring flames emanating from a mansion. The fire curtails Kharis' assaults—for the time being.

Dialogue: Says a Mapleton resident, Bey is quoting "passages from the Egyptian Bible." Most of Egypt's 65 million residents are Muslims; they read from the Holy Koran. And, Egypt's 10-million-plus Christians read from the Holy Bible, not from an "Egyptian Bible."

Note: In an animated cartoon from the same time, *The Mummy Strikes* (1943), Superman crushes an evil mummy's rampaging sentinels.

Murder on the Orient Express (1974), PAR. *Albert Finney.* D: Sidney Lumet. CAMEOS, SHEIKHS

Why insert a rich white-robed Arab with five wives into a 1930s mystery film? Why tar Turks?

Scene: Aboard the Orient Express. A mute Arab saunters toward his compartments. Behind him, five clad-in-black maidens, with porters lugging lots of bags.

• The train halts at a station in Turkey. Instantly, hordes of beggars appear. As Western passengers re-board the train, Turkish beggars paw them.

• At an Istanbul restaurant, Hercule Poirot (Finney) complains, the "skewers" taste better than the "kebab." Abruptly, Poirot grimaces, dumping his Turkish coffee into a nearby plant.

Note: Director Sidney Lumet's *The Hill* (1965) and *Network* (1976) also deride Arabs.

Murders in the Rue Morgue (1932), UNI. *Bela Lugosi.* CAMEOS, MAIDENS

"Brown" Arab dancers introduce this horror film, based on a story by Edgar Allan Poe.

Scene: A Paris carnival, 1845. To entice the crowd, the barker shouts to onlookers, "See the adorable Arab angels." The camera reveals, on a carnival stage, several skimpily-dressed Arab dancers. Cut to a French woman glaring at the Arab women. She sticks out her tongue and disapprovingly huffs, "Look how brown they are."

Note: The next attraction the camera cuts to: "Apaches."

My Chauffeur (1986), Crown Int. *Deborah Foreman, Penn Jillette, Teller.* D, SP: David Beaird. See *Things are Tough All Over* (1982). SHEIKHS, CAMEOS, WORST LIST

In the back seat of a limo, a moronic, mute, oil-rich Arab ambassador mingles with whores and a street hustler.

Scene: A limo company employs Casey Meadows (Foreman), their first and only female chauffeur. Casey functions as "Dear Abby," generously aiding passengers: a drunken businessman, a rock star, and a young black couple. But when Ambassador Abdul (Teller) arrives, Casey's morality vaporizes. She enjoys watching a con artist ridicule and rip off the Arab.

• Shielded by mute bodyguards wearing sunglasses, Abdul enters Casey's limo. Next, a crook named Bone (Jillette) creeps into the back seat and sits next to Abdul. Bone calls Arabs "Towel heads," "Dune-dumpers," "Camel jockeys," and "Camel farts." His slurs stand.

• Bone preys on Abdul's ignorance. He introduces the Arab to a rip-off amusement entitled, "The Oil Baron and the Dry Well" game. Bone's card game resembles the one where the "pigeon" has to pick the shell with the peanut under it. Bone deals three cards and wins easily, taking all of Abdul's money. The mute ambassador, however, balks when Bone tries taking his ring. Observing Bone con Abdul, Casey smiles approvingly.

• Casey's limo stops in front of a seedy club. Bone tells Abdul, "Even a guy like you can get laid." Several hookers encircle Abdul; he tries to smoke pot, but coughs. Trying to dance, Abdul shuffles like a scarecrow caught in a windstorm. When the Arab's blonde partner pulls the burnoose over his face; everyone laughs.

• The hookers jump into the limo, take Abdul's money, then strip for him. As the women undress, Bone forks over Abdul's money—100-dollar bills.

• The limo returns to Abdul's hotel. Seated in the back seat are near-naked women. Cut to Abdul; his face is covered with lipstick. Bone begins pocketing what remains of the sheikh's money, then returns the Arab's billfold, empty. Amazingly, Abdul smiles. Abruptly, Abdul removes his gold ring, handing it to Bone. Signaling, "I'm okay, you're okay," Bone and Abdul go their separate ways.

• Casey's employers ask about Abdul. Boasts Casey, the evening was "delightful"; the Arab "had a good time."

My Favorite Spy (1951), PAR. *Bob Hope, Hedy Lamarr, Mike Mazurki.*
CAMEOS, VILLAINS, MAIDENS

Tangier is full of assassins, ill-clad children, beggars, and bellydancers.

Scene: The protagonist, Peanuts White (Hope), prepares to visit Morocco. Warns a US agent, "Anyone in Tangier would kill you for the million dollars in this belt. Trust no one!"

• In Tangier, Peanuts and the American agent don Arab garb. The agent cautions, "For this amount of money... anybody in Tangier would slit you up the middle." Cut to an alley. An Arab, knife poised, chases a European.

• Appearing at the airport, Arabs on donkeys. Cut to the souk; rude Arab children surround Peanuts. To escape, he tosses coins in the air; the kids spring for the loot. Shoddy beggars, too, harass Peanuts. He tosses coins; the Moroccans bolt for the change.

• No faucets in Morocco; Moroccan women draw well water. After pouring water into large jugs, the women place the jugs atop their heads and begin walking alongside the highway. Cut to Peanuts, dangling from a speeding fire truck's ladder. As the truck nears the women, Peanuts smashes their water-filled jugs.

Note: No Arab villains appear in *My Favorite Spy* (1942), a sleuth comedy starring Jane Wyman and bandleader Kay Kyser.

My Wife's Best Friend (1952), TCF. *Anne Baxter, Macdonald Carey.* CAMEOS, MAIDENS

Arab women are either submissive or domineering.

Scene: In this romantic comedy, the husband (Carey) complains to his spouse (Baxter), You should be a "helpmate, a plain ordinary wife." She retorts, "A plain, ordinary wife?" Cut to the Arabian desert. Here, the husband appears dressed as an Arab. Trekking behind him is his Arab-clad wife, a servile maiden lugging tons of gadgets. When he whistles, she comes running.

• In another fantasy sequence, the wife appears as a scantily-clad Cleopatra, and her husband, as an Egyptian slave, his head bowed before her.

The Naked Gun: From the Files of Police Squad (1988), PAR. *Leslie Nielsen, David Katz.* CAMEOS, VILLAINS

An American agent floors Palestinians and Libyans.

Scene: This slapstick comedy ridicules Arabs. Before credits roll, Arab music underscores shots of Beirut. Appearing are some mosques and Arab guards parading their camels in front of a building. Cut to a meeting of seven world leaders; they discuss how to best "punish America." Two rulers are "Arabs." Quips Arafat (Katz), "We must rip their entrails out, and [string] them from here to Damascus." Affirms Khadafi, "I say wipe out Washington and New York." Wham! Lt. Frank Drebin (Nielsen) enters the room and punches out the villains, exclaiming: "Don't ever let me catch you guys in America."

• Final frames show an Arab and Jew, plus other "adversaries," hugging each other.

Naked Gun 33⅓: The Final Insult (1994), PAR. *Leslie Nielsen, Raye Birk.* See *Back to the Future* (1985). CAMEOS, VILLAINS

"Arab terrorists" try to kill the Pope. And, a hired assassin intends to blow up the "66th Annual Academy Awards."

Scene: A train station. Several heavies are shooting it out with Lt. Frank Drebin (Nielsen). Among the rogues, a heavily armed Arab terrorist. Abruptly, the shrieking Arab moves to assassinate the Pope; Drebin shoots him.

• Statesville prison. Papshmir (Birk), the villain conspiring with the Arabs "to embarrass the US," meets with an Italian bomber, Rocco Dillon. Complains Papshmir, "My people are very upset." Injects Mrs. Dillon, "They're always upset, they're Arab terrorists." The Arabs, says Papshmir, are prepared to give Rocco "$5 million," provided he builds them a bomb that will blow up the annual Academy Awards ceremony. "If you fail this time," warns Papshmir, "my [Arab] people won't be so forgiving."

• Lt. Drebin learns of the "terrorist threat." "I can't let the bad guys win," he says.

• Evening, the Academy Awards ceremony. Papshmir boasts to his Arab sponsor, "America will be brought her knees by this terrorist act. And give my regards to Mrs. Qaddafi." Meanwhile, Rocco places a bomb inside the "Best Picture" envelope. Thanks to Drebin, when the bomb explodes Rocco and Papshmiri; go up in smoke.

Note: Rocco is never referred to as an Italian terrorist. So, why tag Papshmir and his cohorts "Arab terrorists?"

Naked Lunch (1991), TCF. A David Cronenberg Film. *Peter Weller.* CAMEOS, MAIDENS

In this movie based on William Burroughs' cult novel, among the world's riffraff dwelling in Interzone, "an engorged parasite on the underbelly of the West," are Arabs. Interzone is "a haven for the mongrel scum of the earth."

Scene: 1953. The protagonist (Weller) escapes from his troubled existence and flees to Interzone, a hallucinatory version of Tangiers' casbahs. Interzone, a "strange, surreal landscape, is inhabited by Arabs, mugwumps, half-alien, half-insect creatures, man-sized centipedes, carnivorous typewriters and bizarre humans." Interzone, a center of nightmarish intrigue, also functions as a haven for druggies, homosexuals, and lesbians.

• A resident asks the protagonist, "Did you come to Interzone for the boys? They're very cheap." Another resident points out several veiled Moroccan women to the escapee, telling him they are lesbians—"Fedela's lovers."

• Arab music underscores Interzone's casbah scenes. Mumbling Moroccans pop up inside narrow alleys; they grind raw meat and sell trinkets. Other Moroccans lead their camels along the highway.

National Lampoon's Vacation (1983), WB. *Chevy Chase, Beverly D'Angelo, Eddie Bracken.* CAMEOS, VILLAINS

Got problems? Blame the Arabs!

Scene: Finally, the vacationing Griswold family arrives at California's incredible amusement park, Walleyworld—only to find it closed. Incredulous and frustrated, the family breaks in.

• The park's alarm system goes off. Frightened that someone is violating his celebrated park, Roy Walley (Bracken), the owner, along with some policemen rush over to the entertainment complex. Screams Roy: "What's going on?... Is it Arabs?"

Navy SEALs (1990), OR. *Charlie Sheen, Michael Biehn, Joanne Whalley-Kilmer, Dennis Haysbert, Nicholas Kadi.* P: Brenda Feigen, Bernard Williams. SP: Chuck Pfarrer, Gary Goldman. D: Lewis Teague. See *True Lies* (1994). PALESTINIANS, MAIDENS, WORST LIST

Arabs snatch US-made Stinger missiles and hold hostage an American helicopter crew. To the rescue, seven Navy SEALs (an acronym for Sea, Air, and Land). They throttle scores of Palestinians. Amazingly, early on, an American reporter of Lebanese descent refuses to help the SEALs nab the terrorists, declaring, "I'm a journalist."

Scene: The eastern Mediterranean. Supposedly, some good Arabs aboard a ship are in danger, they are "taking gunfire." Unaware the Arabs have set a trap, the Americans answer their call for help, dispatching a US helicopter crew. Abruptly, Palestinians wearing kuffiyehs appear. They kill one crewman, taking the Americans hostage.

• Inside an Arab dungeon, bloodied US servicemen are bound to chairs. Cut to a US rescue team, lead by Hawkins (Sheen) and Curran (Biehn). They free the Americans and terminate the Palestinians. But the Palestinian, Ben Shaheed (Kadi), "a piece of shit," gets away. Exclaims Hawkins as he dynamites the Arab stronghold, "I hope these fuckers paid their gas bill." The movie screen shows scores of Palestinians, aflame. Boasts Hawkins, "I got everything in the room, every thing but the onions... I vaporized hostiles."

• In Washington, DC, Israelis and SEALs work together, mapping an attack that will terminate those Palestinian "assholes" that have " a warehouse full of [Stinger] missiles." Someone suggests that a "half-Lebanese woman reporter," Claire (Whalley-Kilmer), might be able to assist them. Says another SEAL, "[She's] not going to give us anything."

• Off the Syrian coast; a ship bound for Lebanon. Intending to bring back the stolen US missiles, the SEALs board a ship manned by Arabs. Blending with the ship's sheep and goats are huddled Arabs. The camera reveals Arab terrorists. Barks the lying captain, "This is a merchant ship; no missiles." Instantly, the SEALs shoot several terrorists. One Palestinian grabs a woman passenger, using her as a shield.

• Back in the US, Hawkins takes Claire to dinner, saying "Beirut" is a "shithole filled with ragheads." Says Claire, "I'm half-Lebanese." Continues Hawkins, "I was mocking your heritage and now we're having dinner." Claire not only fails to contest the "ragheads" slur, she also refuses to tell Hawkins where Shaheed's Palestinian terrorists are based. This slanderous scene, especially, reveals prejudice in its implication that because of her heritage, she is lenient toward terrorists. Would the writers use similar dialogue had Claire been projected as an American-Italian reporter? Only after Claire watches a TV report showing nasty "Algerians" attacking a civilian aircraft, does she assist the SEALs.

• Israeli radar is employed, directing the SEALs safely to Beirut, the "asshole of misery." The camera reveals exploding bombs, fires, and a sign stating "God kills." Disguising themselves as Palestinians, SEALs don checkered kuffiyehs. Before he shoots a seriously wounded SEAL, a Palestinian grunts, "Your God can't help you, now."

• Let's go SEALs. Barks Hawkins, "Let's go tag 'em and bag 'em... We [Americans] go in there, hit 'em [Arabs], and forget 'em." Cut to a sloppy, obese Arab watching Francis [the talking mule] on televison. After the SEALs crush one Arab villain, "Mohammed," some Palestinians kill an African-American SEAL, Graham (Williams). Screams Hawkins, "I'll get the scumbag [Shaheed], I want to get the fucker on his knees... waste that fucker." In the background, screeching Arab women.

Finis: In Beirut, Hawkins slices Shaheed's throat. At the movie theater where I saw the film, viewers stood and cheered.

• The SEALs nab a Mercedes from two Arabs and drive to the coast, anxious to board their awaiting submarine. Checking out the sub's rendezvous spot, one SEAL laments, "It looks the same. It all looks the same." My thoughts exactly: Movies demonizing Palestinians all look "the same."

Dialogue: Palestinians are tagged "cheese-dick," "fucker," "rag heads," "scum bag."

Note: In the credits, the producers extend thanks to the department of defense and the navy. Their acknowledgment is false. Only a retired SEAL, Chuck Pfarrer, provided the producers with technical advice.

In May 1989, Orion Pictures submitted this script to US naval authorities, seeking approval. The navy objected to the scenario's gratuitous and random violence, pointing out that "SEALs would not fire 'make sure' rounds into each of the [Arab] bodies... that is murder. They would not hurt or kill anyone unless 'deadly force' were authorized." Explains Phil Strub, the Pentagon's liaison with Hollywood, "We cannot recommend navy or department of defense production support of a film which depicts Navy sailors on covert operations in the Middle East killing with abandon."[119]

• On 12 September 1990, J.P. Mitchell, assistant chief of information to the US Navy, responded to my letter of concern about images of Palestinians in *Navy SEALs*:

The Navy did not formally cooperate with Orion Pictures... Quite recently the Navy denied support to another SEAL movie... not only because of the inaccurate portrayal of the Navy SEAL community but also because of the negative portrayal of Arabs in the Middle East. The Navy remains sensitive to stereotypical portrayals in productions requiring formal cooperation.

• Writes Caryn James in the NYT, "What will Teen-Age Mutant Turtles be when they grow up? On the evidence of *Navy SEALs*, they are perfectly suited to be members of an elite navy commando team. The men who fight Middle Eastern terrorists in this new action film are a mere step away from the adolescent Turtles in maturity and complexity of character" (20 July 1990). In spite of the criticisms, *Navy SEALs* has grossed much more than $22 million since its release.

• Some newspaper ads for this film stated: "GET AN OFFICIAL 'NAVY SEALS' HAT BY MAIL. Only $5.00 with Pepsi purchase. Details at participating 7-Eleven stores."

Nefertiti, Queen of the Nile (1961), a.k.a. Nefertiti, regina del Nilo, Colorama Features. Italian/American. *Jeanne Crain, Vincent Price, Edmund Purdom.* EGYPTIANS, MAIDENS

Scene: Thebes 2,000 BC. The high priest (Price) insists his daughter Tanit/Nefertiti (Crain) fulfill her destiny and wed a kind but mentally unstable pharaoh, Amenophis. Fearing that if she disobeys her father, he will murder the man she truly loves, the sculptor Tumos (Purdom), Tanit agrees.

• During the purification service, Tanit changes her name to Nefertiti. The elderly pharaoh observes that his bride, Nefertiti, loves not him, but Tumos. Thus, he does not consummate the marriage.

• In the palace's romance den, scantily clad Egyptian couples make love.

• Tumos sculpts a bust of Nefertiti, then uses strength alone to crush a lion.

• Aware Thebes' conniving priests are corrupt, the wise pharaoh rids the palace of the rascals, including Nefertiti's father. Plus, he banishes all false gods.

• The "Revolt of the High Priests." Seeking vengeance, the priests murder the pharaoh's one loyal minister. Despondent and seriously ill, the pharaoh commits suicide.

• Nefertiti and Tumos garner support from the army. Together, they collapse the mutinous priests. Nefertiti's evil father also dies, at the hand of his spurned ex-mistress.

• Nefertiti rules. Reluctantly, she renounces her love of Tumos.

Network (1976), UA. *William Holden, Faye Dunaway, Peter Finch.* SP: Paddy Chayefsky. D: Sidney Lumet. CAMEOS, SHEIKHS, WORST LIST

Arab oil conglomerates seek control of an American TV network. Arabs are projected as "medieval fanatics [who are] simply buying us." Chayefsky received the Academy Award for this screenplay. To my knowledge, no major critic, studio executive, or performer protested Chayefsky's prejudicial Arab colloquies.

Network is about the business of television and the fact that US businessmen motivated by greed will put anything on the tube in order to receive ratings and profits. In Chayefsky's scenario a newsman, Howard Beale (Finch), delights in smearing Arabs. He shows his viewers a news clip of OPEC ministers deciding "how much to increase the price of oil." On screen, stock footage of Saudi Arabia's minister, Sheikh Yamani. Beale tells his viewers, "I want you to get up out of your chairs, go to your windows, stick your head out and say, 'I'm mad as hell and I'm not gonna take this anymore.'"

• Later, Beale warns his audience that the Saudis intend to take over his network, UPS-TV. UPS, explains Beale in a highly charged emotional speech,

> is controlled by CAA, the twelfth largest company in the world... Somebody's buying up CAA, somebody called the Western Funding Corporation. They're buying it for the Saudi Arabian Investment Corporation. They're buying it for the Arabs." The Arabs, predicts Beale, "are going to own what you read and what you see. Not a single law in the book to stop them. We all know Arabs control $16 billion dollars in this country. They own a chunk of Fifth Avenue, 20 downtown pieces of Boston, part of a port of New Orleans, an industrial park in Salt Lake City. They own big chunks of the Atlanta Hilton, the Arizona land and cattle company, part of a bank in California." And, "they control ARAMCO, so that puts them in EXXON, Texaco, and Mobil Oil. They're all over: New York, Louisville, St. Louis, Missouri. And that's only what we know about them; there's a hell of a lot we don't know about because all of those Arab petrodollars are washed through Switzerland and Canada and the biggest banks in the country... Right now the Arabs have screwed us out of enough American dollars to come right back and with our own money buy General Motors, IBM, IT&T, AT&T, DuPont, US Steel, and twenty other companies. Hell, they already own half of England. So listen to me, the Arabs are simply buying us. There's only one thing that can stop them—you, you. So, I want you to get up now, out of your chairs and go to the phones... By midnight tonight I want a million telegrams in the White House, [saying] 'I'm mad as hell and I'm not going to take this anymore. I don't want banks selling my country to the Arabs. I want the CAA deal stopped now.'

Cut to members of his studio audience applauding thunderously.

• A CAA executive explains his company's proposed deal with the Arabs, saying that his corporation "has $2 billion in loans with the Saudis... We need that Saudi money bad." The executive tries to convince Beale there's nothing wrong in selling out to the Arabs. "The Arabs are taking billions of dollars out of this country and now they'll have to give it back," he says. Beale, however, remains firm. Following the CAA meeting the victorious newsman goes on the air and tells viewers, "Last night I got up here and asked you people to stand up and fight for your heritage and you did. Six million telegrams were sent to the White House. The Arab takeover of CAA has been stopped. The people spoke. The people won. It was a radiant eruption of democracy."

Note: Would it be acceptable for Chayefsky to label Israelis "medieval fanatics" who control US media, who are "buying us"? Why did producer Gottfried and director Lumet sanction Chayefsky's anti-Arab diatribe? "Before Sidney Lumet went into rehearsal with *Network*, that script was just the way he wanted it, just the way I wanted it," boasts Chayefsky, "and just the way Howard Gottfried, the producer wanted it."[120]

• Americans fed up with Hollywood's anti-Arab scenarios should consider emulating Howard Beale's plan-of-action. If more "people spoke" up, notably Arab-Americans, if they were "to stand up and fight for [their] heritage," and if they were to become "mad as hell" and decide not "to take this [Arab-bashing] anymore [and] send six million telegrams" to the White House protesting Hollywood's Arab portraits, perhaps a "radiant eruption" of humane Arab images would appear on movie screens. And, like Howard Beale, Arab-Americans could claim: "The people spoke. The people won."

• At the March 29, 1978 Academy Awards ceremony, Vanessa Redgrave accepted the award for Best Supporting Actress for her role in *Julia*. While at the podium, Redgrave tagged demonstrators protesting her pro-Palestinian politics as "a small bunch of Zionist hoodlums." Not only did the audience boo the actress, later, Redgrave was denounced by Paddy Chayefsky.

• Contrary to Chayefsky's blustering racist tirade in *Network*, consider the facts about who is "buying up" this country: According to department of commerce reports, during 1980 approximately "90 percent of direct foreign investment in the US was accounted for by the Netherlands, the United Kingdom, Canada, Germany, the Netherlands Antilles, Japan, Switzerland, and France." As for OPEC's seven Arab nations, "together [they] accounted for less than one percent of the total."[121]

• In December 1977, one year after *Network* was released, CBS-TV's *60 Minutes* telecast a segment entitled, "The Arabs are Coming." This news program perpetuated the myth that Arabs are invading and buying up England.

Never Say Never Again (1983), WB. *Sean Connery, Kim Basinger, Barbara Carrera.* SP: Lorenzo Semple Jr. P: Jack Schwartzman. Remake of *Thunderball* (1965), in which no Arabs appear. See *Black Sunday* (1977) and *Nighthawks* (1981). CAMEOS, MAIDENS, VILLAINS

The dazzling Fatima Blush (Carrera) appears not as Bond's (Connery) love interest, but as an Arab nuclear terrorist aiding SPECTRE. Fatima intends to detonate two nuclear bombs in the West. She fails; Bond shoots her dead.

• The chief villain's henchmen nab the blonde, blue-eyed heroine, Domino Petachi (Bassinger), tying her to an outside pole. Instantly, scores of unshaven, gun-toting, sword-wielding bedouins on horseback appear. Screaming, they encircle Domino, threatening to—can you imagine? The lecherous auctioneer strips Domino; then asks glaring bedouins to bid for the blonde. Primitive-looking bedouins, sans teeth, begin bidding. The Arabic-speaking bedouins haggle over the price of the blonde. Cut to the frightened Domino. In time, Bond enters the frame. He smashes the bedouins and frees Domino. As they ride off, a missile launched from a nearby submarine lands in the square, blowing up the screeching Arabs.[122]

The Next Man (1976), Artists Ent. *Sean Connery, Cornelia Sharpe, Albert Paulsen, Adolfo Celi, Charles Cioffi.* S: Morton Bregman, Alan Trustman. SP: David M. Wolf, Mort Fine. VILLAINS, PALESTINIANS

Arabs opposing peace kill Americans; Palestinians kill Israelis. Saudi Arabia's ambassador wishes to sign a mutual assistance pact with Israel. He proposes to provide free oil and its by-products to poor nations. Intent on killing him are Palestinians and Syrians, and a Western assassin.

Scene: New York and Moscow. Declare some diplomats: Three Arabs leading "a faction within the oil-producing states" pose a threat to the West. As credits roll, viewers see those three Arabs being terminated. In London, assassins toss one Arab and his wife onto the street. Next, an assassin in Riyadh's souk shoots a Saudi. In New York, Nicole Scott (Sharpe) kills a Kuwaiti, Al Sharif (Celi). Nicole's next target? The Saudi ambassador to the UN—Kahlil Abdul-Muhsan (Connery).

• New York. Ambassador Kahlil and his friend, Colonel Hamid (Paulsen), arrive at the UN. Addressing the General Assembly, Kahlil says OPEC should be disbanded, and that the Arabs should establish a "direct dialogue with Israel so we can create a Palestinian state." He proposes to make Israel a member of OPEC, "a full partner." Most UN members applaud. Expressing outrage are representatives from Iraq, Kuwait, and Syria.

• The Syrian diplomat, Fouad (Cioffi), berates Kahlil, saying that the Palestinians will never talk peace with Israel.

• Outside, angry Arab-American protestors attack Kahlil's car. Their signs state: "Arabia for the Arabians" and "Palestine Liberation Forever."

• Arab diplomats warn Kahlil: "Don't break up OPEC" and "When you speak at the United Nations again, do not speak of peace with the Israelis." Says Fouad, "You frighten me. Is it not better to have a gun in our hand and face the enemy? There will be killings."

• Kahlil says the Palestinian refugees are suffering not because of the "Jews," but because of the Arabs. "I'll never support [Palestinian] terrorism," Kahlil tells the "bastard" Fouad. Cut to stock footage, carnage resulting from "a wave of [Palestinian] terrorist attacks" in Israel. On this school bus, says a newsman, "23 children" were killed.

• The ambassador flies off to the Bahamas; terrorists attack, failing to kill Kahlil. Cut to the Saudi Arabian consulate in New York. Terrorists set several bombs, killing "at least fifteen people." Among the victims, a New York policeman protecting Kahlil.

• Inside Kahlil's car, Colonel Hamid tells Nicole, "Do it now"; kill Kahlil "now." Nicole shoots Hamid, then she kills Kahlil.

A Night in Casablanca (1946), UA. *The Marx Brothers, Charles Drake.* CAMEOS, VILLAINS

Morocco is backward and its citizens shady.

At the Hotel Casablanca, the Marx brothers tangle with post-war Nazis intent on nabbing hidden treasures. "In the last six months," fez-wearing Nazis posing as Moroccan waiters, "murdered "three [hotel] managers."

• Since there are no cars, Chico runs "The Yellow Camel Company" and "The Checker Camel Company."

• A Moroccan confronts Groucho, shouting, "You buy! You buy!" As the Arab flaunts various garments, Chico intervenes, saying, "Scram! Get outta here." Advises Chico, "You gotta be careful of those guys. They take you to the cleaners."

• After a Moroccan uncovers the Nazi hideout, he approaches the Western hero, Pierre (Drake). Quips Pierre, "All right, all right, what do you want?" The Arab rubs his hands together, purring, "Not so quick my friend... It costs money!" As Pierre lacks funds, the Moroccan walks off. Grumbles Pierre, "I'll get what I want from that rat without money."

Nighthawks (1981), UNI. *Sylvester Stallone, Rutger Hauer, Billy Dee Williams, Persis Khambatta, Nigel Davenport.* MAIDENS, CAMEOS

New York City policemen vs. a German assassin. Producers insert a Moroccan female terrorist, making the Arab-German connection.

Scene: In Paris, Hammad and a Moroccan terrorist named Shakka (Khambatta), locate a plastic surgeon for their cohort, the global assassin, Wulfgar (Hauer).

• In New York, detectives Deke (Stallone) and Matt (Williams) are assigned to track Wulfgar and Shakka. Though Shakka appears throughout the movie, she seldom speaks.

• Officers caution Deke to be wary of Shakka. Explains the city's security chief (Davenport), Shakka was "born in Tangiers, Morocco of wealthy parents, a spoiled broad who kills without provocation." The chief's profile of Shakka is on-target—she shoots him dead.

• Inside a Roosevelt Island cable car, Shakka and Wulfgar hold hostage families of UN officials, plus some New York commuters. States a TV newsman: The terrorists' "hostages" remain "250 feet above the East River in a cable car."

• Deke and the police arrive. Shakka and Wulfgar mingle with their captives, eluding the cops. Suddenly, Shakka hears a voice describing her as a heartless killer. Angry, she reveals herself, shouting, "You scum." New York police snipers shoot her dead.

• The hostages are rescued; Deke eradicates Wulfgar.

Noises Off (1992), TOU. *Carol Burnett, John Ritter.* Based on the stage play by Michael Frayn. CAMEOS, SHEIKHS

In this farce, stage actors belittle Arabs.

Scene: The camera reveals some actors rehearsing a Broadway-bound play. One actor (Ritter) declares it's high time they began to conduct business. "Someone's coming at four o'clock. In fact, Arab. Oil. You know," he quips. Throughout, cast members don Arab garb. One actress dons a black sheet; an actor wears a white sheet. Seeing the Arab-clad cast, an observer exclaims, "Who are these people?" Sighs the housekeeper (Burnett), "We get them all the time. They're just Arab sheikhs." As the housekeeper removes the cast members' sheets, she jests, "Arab sheikhs? They're Irish linen sheets off my own bed."

Nostradamus (1994), OR. *Tcheky Karyo.* SP: Knut Boeser. CAMEOS, VILLAINS

Saddam Hussein appears in this drama set in the 1500s.

Scene: Final frames reveal Michel de Nostradamus (Karyo) anticipating for planet earth horrifying events. Stock footage displays Hitler, Nazi storm troopers, the assassination of President John F. Kennedy, and starving African children. Cut to Saddam Hussein. Smiling, Saddam extends his arms. Next, the camera shows Kuwait's flaming oil fields.

Not Quite Paradise (1986), a.k.a. Not Quite Jerusalem, Acorn.

Joanna Pacula, Sam Robards. SP: Paul Kember. P, D: Lewis Gilbert. Filmed in Israel. "The producers gratefully acknowledge the assistance of the "Israeli Ministry of Defense, the Israeli Film Center," and "Kibbutz Elot, Kibbutz Grofit." PALESTINIANS

As Palestinian terrorists appear, life on a kibbutz is momentarily interrupted.

Scene: Superimposed over a desert kibbutz, this message, "A kibbutz is an agricultural settlement in Israel... This is the story of some of them." Cut to an Israeli truck driver carrying several volunteers; he dodges an Arab and his camel. The Arab yells.

• Jerusalem, a cafe. Introducing an American, Mike (Elliott), who loves an Israeli, Gila (Pacula). Says Gila, "I wouldn't want to live in the city. City people have no quality of life." Cut to two scruffy Palestinians, seated behind them.

• Gila, who wears blue-frayed shorts with a matching top, rides horses and drives a tractor. She attacks a haystack with a pitchfork, shouting that "[Cows] eat straw like they were Yemenites." Later, Gila and Mike visit a burial site. Gila refers to the "graves of people," including her brother, "who died saving the kibbutz."

• Just prior to the film's conclusion, five Palestinians wearing Western clothing feign their car is not functioning. When an Israeli military vehicle pulls up to assist, the Palestinians shoot a soldier. Next, Israelis kill a Palestinian. An Israeli helicopter appears; a second Palestinian is shot. Three Palestinians run off; two Israelis in a jeep track them. The Palestinians come upon the kibbutz, threatening Mike, Gila, and others.

• At the kibbutz, the Palestinians hold hostage innocents from several nations. Israeli troops arrive; shots are fired. Silence. Finally, Israeli soldiers emerge dragging a dead Palestinian's body; blankets cover two other bodies. Fearing Gila may be dead, Mike lifts one blanket. He sighs in relief: a Palestinian man. Mike lifts the other blanket: a Palestinian woman. Again, he sighs.

• The volunteers prepare to leave. Not Mike. Instead of returning to medical school, he will remain on the kibbutz with Gila.

Note: Credits list Palestinians as "The Terrorists"; Israelis are listed as "The Volunteers," "The Kibbutzniks," and "The Visitors."

The Nut Farm (1935), MON. *Wallace Ford, Betty Alden, Oscar Apfel.* SHEIKHS, VILLAINS

Spoofing Arabs makes for good box office returns!

Scene: Some Hollywood agents hoodwink a naive couple, Helen and Bob Bent (Alden, Apfel). The sly agents convince the Bents to invest in *Scorching Passion*, a movie parodying *The Sheik* (1921). The agents take a script and read to the Bents, "They are fleeing across the desert pursued by bedouins; the foreign legion comes to the rescue. [Our film] is about desert passion and camels across the desert."

• The agents arrange a bogus screen test for star-struck Helen. Immediately, they declare she will portray the sheikh's Western sweetheart in *Scorching Passion*. Helen rejoices. Thinking she will soon become a celebrated actress, Helen persuades Bob to fork over their life savings—$40,000.

• The studio set. The actor portraying *Passion's* sheikh grasps Helen, "The bedouins are coming! I've got to kill you darling," he sighs. In time, Helen exclaims, "The foreign legion. We're saved."

• After *Passion's* disastrous premiere, a legitimate movie mogul points out the audience "laughed all through the desert scenes." His comment prompts Helen's cousin, Willie Barton (Ford), to acquire *Passion's* screen rights. Thinking their film is a dud, the agents sell.

• The Bents have the last laugh. Willie's astute editing turns the movie into a smashing box-office comedy hit. Impressed with the fresh farce, Monarch Pictures' executives give the couple $90,000.

Nyoka and the Lost Secrets of Hippocrates (1966), REP. *Kay Aldridge, Lorna Gray.* This feature film was assembled from the movie serial *Perils of Nyoka* (1942). VILLAINS

Off and Running (1992), OR. *Cyndi Lauper.* CAMEOS, SHEIKHS

The "Florida Racing Commission" moves to auction off a "champion stallion." Everyone participating at the auction wears Western clothing—except for two Arabs in burnooses. One Arab sports a beard and wears dark glasses. Bids for the stallion start at "$20 million." Though the Arabs up the ante to $27 million, they lose the horse to another bidder. See *Let it Ride* (1989).

Office Space (1999), TCF. *Ron Livingston, Ajay Naidu.* S, D: Mike Judge. CAMEOS, VILLAINS

A one-liner.

Scene: An American software engineer (Livingston) tries to convince his co-worker (Naidu) to rig the computers in order to steal from their cold-blooded employer. The co-worker balks, fearing he may be caught and severely punished. The engineer tells his friend not to worry: "This is America... this isn't Riyadh. You know, they're not going to saw your hands off here."

Note: Though the Saudi criminal justice system does sanction amputations for theft, the Saudis never *saw* a criminal's hand off; they surgically amputate it, and only after three proven offenses. And, the thief must either confess, or there must be two actual witnesses who saw the theft of a significant amount determined by the court. Usually judges seek mitigating circumstances in order to reduce the sentence. Should the thief repent and offer to make amends, God (Allah) is All Forgiving toward the person.[123]

Oh God! You Devil (1984), WB. *George Burns.* CAMEOS, PALESTINIANS

The Prince of Darkness (Burns) intends to acquire some new clients. Singing "That ol' Black Magic," the Devil boots up his computer. This message flashes: "Today's Best Bets." Appearing on the laptop's screen, Yasser Arafat. Sighs the Devil, "Huh, Huh. Computer's on the blink again. I've had this guy for years." Next, Idi Amin emerges. "Him, too," whines the Devil.

Oil (1977), Spectacular. *Ray Milland, Stuart Whitman.* CAMEOS, MAIDENS

Apathetic Arabs and dancing maidens.

Scene: A mythical Arab nation. The Western villain tries to persuade a small oil-rich Gulf country to lower oil prices. The Gulf Arabs refuse to comply. Abruptly, their oil wells are set ablaze, endangering the country. Enter the Western protagonist (Whitman). He and his six non-Arab colleagues begin battling the Sahara oil field fire. As they struggle with the raging flames, Arabs appear, dawdling in the background.

• At a restaurant, bellydancers perform.

Old Mother Riley (1952), a.k.a. Old Mother Riley's New Venture, Renown. *Arthur Lucan, Kitty McShane, Sebastian Cabot.* SHEIKHS

A rotund, sloppy, illiterate sheikh makes a fool of himself.[124] Harem maidens accompany the Arab.

Scene: In the lobby of a London hotel, the manager, Mother Riley (Lucan). Abruptly, Arab music underscores the arrival of Sheikh Abdul Shish-ka-bob (Cabot). Trotting behind Abdul is a bespectacled assistant and several maidens speaking gibberish. When asked a question, "His Excellency" shakes his head, "No," then speaks, "Yes." Why all the confusion? Abdul "speaks hardly any English."

• Mother Riley steers Abdul and his Arabs to the elevator, saying, "Follow me, your disgracefulness." Even the hotel waiter complains about "these foreigners."

• The dinner table. When it comes to "eating Western" cuisine, the sheikh displays bad manners; he drinks from his finger bowl. Though Mother Riley knows nothing about Arab food, he tries to emulate the ruler's eating habits. As the two men waste their meals, the other diners, too, behave outrageously. Soon, a food fight breaks out.

• Abdul finds out that someone stole the "Hula Diamond"; everyone panics. Clasping their hands, the sheikh's Arabs run around and around and around the room. Concurrently, Abdul and Mother Riley mumble gibberish. No one uncovers the diamond. Abruptly, the Arabs disappear from the hotel.

Omar Khayyam (1957), PAR. *Cornel Wilde, Debra Paget.* CAMEOS, VILLAINS

Scene: Eleventh-century Persia. The Persian characters, settings, costumes, and plot are interchangeable with Arabian fantasy features. Persia's celebrated poet-mathematician, Abu'l-Fath Umar Khayyami ibn Ibrahim, a.k.a. Omar Khayyam, brings down the wicked vizier and hashish addicted assassins, the "Hashshasheen."

• The movie's "Syrian [guard] has a split tongue; he's dumb."

Note: In Mutual's silent film, *The Rummy Act of Omar K. M.* (1916), the Western protagonist dreams he is Omar the poet. Presto. He is promptly transformed into Omar and whisked off to the Middle East.

One Arabian Night (1920), a.k.a. Sumurun. E. L. Film. Germany.

Silent. *Ernst Lubitsch, Pola Negri, Paul Wegener, Carl Clewing, Jakob Liedtke, Jenny Hasselquist.* D: Lubitsch. SHEIKHS

In the early 1920s, even noted German filmmakers projected vile Arabs intent on injuring Westerners. A severe sheikh abducts a beautiful performer; the Arab kills her and his own son.

Scene: Baghdad's desert souk reveals dogs, snake charmers, jugglers, and slave merchants. At the palace, guards brandish whips; maidens and eunuchs attend the potentate (Wegener). As he is consumed with jealousy, the ruler "never sleeps."

• Not only do maidens mock the "Head Eunuch," they tag all eunuchs, "the pompous keepers of the harem."

• Zuleika (Hasselquist), the sheikh's "favorite," runs off with the merchant, Nur-al-Din (Liedtke). The angry sheikh demands a fresh maiden to replace her. He dispatches the slaver Achment to kidnap Yannaia (Negri), a dancer touring the kingdom. The moral here? Western performers should avoid Arabia!

• Achmet obeys, stealing Yannaia from her troupe. Palace maidens prepare the virgin for seduction.

• Suspecting that his son may also be attracted to Yannaia, the ruler arranges for Yannaia's death, then kills his son.

• Yannaia's traveling companion, the dwarf Yeggar (Lubitsch), learns of her death and kills the sheikh.

Note: Here, from MPW (10 August 1918), are some captions emblazoned on the film's publicity posters: The Dancer, "The wild desert dancer"; The Sheikh,"Lord of a hundred wives—swift to wrath"; The Eunuch, "Keeper of the hundred jealous wives in the mighty sheik's harem"; Harem Keepers "guard veiled lives, beautiful wives... none but the mighty sheik may pass their frowning portals. Intrigues... murders, the kiss of sword and scimitars."

One Stolen Night (1923), Vitagraph. Silent. *Alice Calhoun*. Based on the magazine story, "The Arab." S: D.D. Calhoun. *NS. Notes from VAR (1 February 1923). SHEIKHS

As with early sheikh scenarios, the "sloppy, maudlin sentiment" of *One Stolen Night* features "the same love sick American girl tourist Dianith (Calhoun) who ventures out on a moonlit night, after visiting an Arabian camp in disguise as a native woman." The heroine falls for an "Arab" horseman; "there are hectic love scenes." Suddenly, desert outlaws interrupt the romance, whisking the girl off to their camp. The bandits deliver trembling Dianith to a "fat black chieftain, an ogre, a horrid brutal brute."

• In time, the Arab horseman "of the love scene" recovers from his wounds and rescues Dianith. The "horde of pursuing tribesmen" fail to catch the couple.

• In the final frames, Dianith discovers that her heroic "Arab" horseman is actually "a disguised white man," the very gentleman she "was engaged to several years before." He approaches her wearing "the shirt and pants of civilization." But, she insists he change "into his [Arab] disguise." Dianith, too, dons her "trick native clothes." Clad in Arab garb, they go "forth into the desert for a regular sentimental wooing."

Note: From the beginning, heroic desert "Arabs" who won the affection of Western maidens were in fact, Americans or Europeans. See especially *The Sheik* (1921) and *The Shriek of Araby* (1923).

One Stolen Night (1929), WB. Half dialogue. *Betty Bronson, William Collier Jr., Otto Lederer, Harry Schultz*. S: D.D. Calhoun. SP: Edward T. Lowe. *NS. Notes from VAR (6 May 1929). Remake of *The Arab* (1923). SHEIKHS

In the Sudan, young Jeanne (Bronson) and a disgraced British cavalry officer link up with a with a touring vaudeville troupe—"the wild tempered Blossoms." The officer falls for Jeanne. But, Arabs kidnap her and sell Jeanne to a nearby sheikh (Shultz). Amazingly, when the sheikh sees that Jeanne "had stained her skin," that she is actually "white," he tosses her out.

Note: Theme song, "My Cairo Love," Sam Fox Pub.

Operation Condor (1997), a.k.a. Armor of God II: Operation Condor (1991), Rel. MIR. *Jackie Chan, Carol Cheng*. SP: Chan, Edward Tang. D: Chan. Filmed in Morocco. Dubbed in English. VILLAINS, WORST LIST

Jackie Chan, a martial arts superstar, crushes an Arab money-grubber and bedouin slavers and brings down Arab buffoons. Islam is ridiculed.

Scene: Italy. The UN wants to recover 240 tons of stolen gold, hidden somewhere in the Arabian desert. Cut to two hook-nosed Arabs wearing checkered headdresses that resemble tablecloths pinched from a pizza parlor. The dense Arabs speak fractured English; characters tag them "pigs" and "vampires." One Arab calls his cohort an " idiot!" Abruptly, the Arabs invade the blonde heroine's home, demanding she reveal a map pinpointing the gold's location. Chan arrives, flooring the duo. "Gold always attracts the scum," he says. Retort the "Soldiers of the Faith" Arabs, "We will never give up the struggle for the holy battle." The two simple-minded Arabs try to commit suicide, but fail.

• In the desert, a crucified figure on a cross. Cut to camels and Arabs. Arab music underscores the appearance of a shady fez-wearing innkeeper. The Arab, who speaks with an Indian accent, fleeces Chan and his female friends, an Asian lovely and a "young and glorious Aryan blonde."

• Suddenly, the two inept Arabs appear, ransacking the protagonists' rooms. On hearing Chan approach, they dash for the outside balcony and instantly fall, twice, to the ground.

• The greedy Arab innkeeper visits the guestrooms, offering chocolates. There's a catch. In return for the chocolates, he demands money. In the background, Arabs clad in traditional garb dance.

• Some generic villains arrive and rough up Chan. The innkeeper offers to give Chan's blonde friend a gun, provided she forks over cash. "Pay me. No money, no shoot," he wheedles. Next, the heavies corner the innkeeper, demanding he tell them Chan's whereabouts. Says the Arab, "I like pay first. No money, no talk." The hoods rough him up; the Arab talks, shouting, "May the Gods punish you!"

• Islam and violence: Arabs pray. Cut to camel-riding black-clad "desert bandits" attacking Chan, Inc. The bedouins kidnap Chan's two female companions.

• At a desert stronghold, robed bedouins huddle around a campfire. An auctioneer, whip in hand, proceeds to auction off maidens, displaying Chan's lovely blonde and Asian friends. Abruptly, scruffy Arabs bid on the two women—"150 camels." In time, Chan arrives, flooring "the sheikh in the sunglasses." And, he punches out scores of bedouin slavers. Suddenly, the tents collapse, trapping inept bedouins. Chan runs off with the maidens.

• In the desert, the two dense Arabs corner Chan's party. Says one, "Praise Allah for delivering you to us, again." The Arabs snatch the treasure map, but cannot read it. Chan acts, shoving the duo down a huge sand dune. One screams, "Allah have mercy!" Says Chan, "We don't ever want to see you, again." Yet, the two appear one more time. As they fight over a canteen of water one sighs, "The Gods must be angry with us."

Finis: Chan discovers the missing gold and crushes the villains.

Note: Chan's film avoids stereotyping Germans. Assisting Chan Inc. is Adolf, a German WW II veteran.

• While watching *Condor*, I was reminded of lyrics from the satirist Tom Lehrer's "National Brotherhood Week": "To hate all the right folks is an old established rule." At a time when the motion picture industry is trying to curb biases, why is Miramax, a subsidiary of Disney, teaching viewers to look down on Arabs? What prompted the studio to re-release this fifth-rate 1991 movie? Could it be anything other than money? Contends Dick Feagler, some Disney moguls go to work in the morning whistling, "Hi-ho, hi-ho, we pander to our dough."

• Throughout the world, Jackie Chan's films are well-received, especially in America. Forty-seven states boast Jackie Chan fan clubs. Club president Joy Al-Sofi, who has seen all of Chan's 30-plus features, told me she was shocked to discover so many Arab stereotypes in Condor. This "was not a typical Chan movie," said Ms. Al-Sofi. Jackie "is a popular figure in the Middle East. He would never intentionally hurt anyone." She went on to cite the fan club's motto, which Chan, himself, wrote: "To foster international friendship and understanding through a common interest."[125]

• Disney President Michael Eisner has said: "We are proud that the Disney brand [of movies] creates... family entertainment."[126] Yet, Disney is the same studio that projected Arabs as hook-nosed buffoons in *Aladdin* (1992), as "desert skunks" in *The Return of Jafar* (1994), as asinine desert caricatures intent on destroying American troops with chemical weapons in *In the Army Now* (1994), and as fodder for American soldiers in *G.I. Jane* (1997).

Disney also belittles Americans of Arab heritage in two films: *Father of the Bride Part II* (1995), and *Kazaam* (1996). In the movies, Arab-Americans appear as hooked-nose, sleazy money-grubbers and hoggish thugs. Certainly, Disney's stereotypes hurt innocents, especially children. A barrage of ugly images causes feelings of apprehension, vulnerability, and estrangement, even denial of one's heritage. The studio should heed Senator Bob Dole's advice. During his meeting with imagemakers, Dole urged they "choose excellence over exploitation." There is a yearning, he said, "for movies that help us raise our families instead of hurting us, movies that raise our vision of life instead of dragging us down."

Operation Eichmann (1961), AA. *Werner Klemperer, Oscar Beregi Jr.* SP: Lewis Copley. D: R.G. Springsteen. CAMEOS, VILLAINS

Two Israeli agents enter Kuwait. They intend to flush out Eichmann, who is using an alias. How? By bribing a Kuwaiti policeman with "vast sums of money." The camera reveals Kuwait's uniformed chief of police (Beregi Jr.), whom the Israelis bought off, entering Eichmann's arabesque flat. His comments falsely imply the Kuwaiti hate Jews. The policeman tells Eichmann, "I'm here to protect your life. An official in my department has received a report branding you as a Jew. As a Jew [living in Kuwait] you will be assassinated in 24 hours." Eichmann protests, insisting that he is German. Whether you are Jewish or German, "Herr Eichmann," your life is in danger, says the policeman. He threatens Eichmann, "I regret we have many impoverished people to whom money has greater value than life." Abruptly, Eichmann departs for South America.

Note: Eichmann never resided in Kuwait. In their e-mails of April 26, 2001, noted Middle East history scholars, Joel Beinin of Stanford and Jill Crystal of Auburn, told me they never read anything about Eichmann being in Kuwait. Two respected Jewish Zionist historians make no mention of Eichmann ever being in any Arab country, yet alone Kuwait. See Aharon Cohen's, *Israel and the Arab World* (1976), and Howard M. Sachar's *A History of Israel* (1996). Crystal and Beinin both point out that the British would not have let Eichmann into the country; Kuwait was a British protectorate until 1961.

Operation Thunderbolt (1977), A Golan-Globus film. *Klaus Kinski, Assaf Dayan, Yehoram Gaon, Sybil Danning, Gila Almagor, Hi Kelos.* SP: Clark Reynolds. P: Menachem Golan, Yoram Globus. Primarily, an Israeli cast. Filmed in Israel. The film received the Israeli government's stamp of official approval. PALESTINIANS

Israelis vs. Germans and their Palestinian cohorts. This Golan-Globus film is based on the actual 4 July 1976 raid by Israeli commandos, in which Israelis rescued 104 hijacked passengers from an Air France passenger plane. On screen discussing the hostage crisis, real officials such as Yitzhak Rabin and Moshe Dayan.

Scene: Aboard a French jetliner. A boy seated across from two dark-complexioned Palestinians warns his mother, "They look like Arabs." "So what dear, they're tourists just like us," she says. Sighs the boy, "I don't trust them." One Palestinian offers the boy "dates, candy." Quips the boy, "No, thank you. " Abruptly, the Palestinians pull guns and hijack the plane.

• An Israeli tells a German passenger, "They [the skyjackers] kill us like Nazis."

• Libya allows the hijacked plane to land. As the plane is being re-fueled, several robed Arabs greet the two main German terrorists (Kinski, Danning). Says one Arab, "President Khadafi sends you his regards." And, "God be with you."

• After the plane lands in Entebbe, all passengers with Jewish names, 104 including the crew, are whisked off to a separate area. The terrorists also target American-Jews. Non-Jews are allowed to leave.

• Cut to Amin, the Palestinian leader; he claims no harm will come to anyone. All we demand is "43 [Arab] freedom fighters" be released from prison. Now, "It's up to Israel."

• An American (Kelos) whispers to a journalist, "I tell you, if these Jews give in [to the terrorists' demands] we've all had it. There'll be a national epidemic of skyjacking." Sighs the journalist, "What else can they do? In less than an hour, they're going to start killing people one by one."

• The Israelis launch a successful rescue mission, killing the skyjackers. Next, they blow up Uganda's planes. Sadly, three hostages are killed. And one passenger is reported missing: Dora Block was removed from a hospital, kidnapped, and never heard from again.

Note: The retelling of this successful Israeli operation surfaced, in various forms, on all three US TV networks. On 11 September, CBS-TV presented a one-hour reenactment in documentary style, *Rescue at Entebbe: How They Saved the Hostages.* Two months later, ABC-TV presented *Victory at Entebbe*, a two-hour docudrama featuring Elizabeth Taylor in a cameo role. Six months later, NBC-TV presented a three-hour drama, *Raid on Entebbe*, starring Charles Bronson, Peter Finch, and Martin Balsam.

Our Man in Marrakesh (1966), a.k.a. Bang, Bang You're Dead!

AIP. *Tony Randall, Senta Berger, Terry-Thomas, Wilfrid Hyde-White, Herbert Lom, Gregoire Aslan.* SP: Peter Yeldham. D: Don Sharp. Filmed in Morocco. VILLAINS

Scene: As Moroccan musicians pound their drums, Moroccan assassins knife a Westerner in the back. Credits roll.

• Arriving in "very hot" Marrakesh are six Western tourists, including Andrew (Randall), an American architect, and Kyra (Berger), an attractive CIA agent. One of the tourists intends to fix an upcoming UN vote; he has $2 million to pay off Mr. Casimir (Lom), the "most dangerous and the most powerful man in Morocco."

• Casimir's men knife a Western agent in the back, then dump the man's body in Andrew's hotel room. Andrew and Kyra hide the body and drive off. Casimir's gun-toting Moroccans pursue them, firing away. "Something like this could not happen in

New York or Boston," says Kyra, "but we're in Morocco."

• Casimir's thugs knife Kyra's colleague in the back, prompting her and Andrew to leave Marrakesh. Soon, their car collapses. To the rescue, a friendly Moroccan truck driver, Achmed (Aslan).

• Rifle-toting bedouins surround the couple, whisking them to the castle of El-Caid (Terry-Thomas). El-Caid offers them hospitality and needed assistance.

• Final frames show Moroccans contesting Moroccans. El-Caid, Achmed, and their men bring down Casimir's villains, tossing a few into a pool. And, Andrew and Kyra nab Mr. Arthur Fairbrother (Hyde-White), the $2-million dollar man. Now, the upcoming UN vote is safe.

The Outing (1987), a.k.a. The Lamp, HIT. *Deborah Winters.* P, D: Warren Cheney. VILLAINS, MAIDENS

After 3,000 years, a lamp genie kills fifteen Americans, mostly teenagers. Deborah Winters portrays three women: "Eve," "Young Arab woman," and "Old Arab woman."

Scene: Houston, Texas, a foggy evening. Three local thieves break into the home of an elderly Iraqi-American woman. The thugs rob the "old witch," then kill her. In the home, they come across "an old artifact from the Middle East," something "out of the Arabian Nights going back to 3,500 BC." Also, they find a dusty lamp, hidden inside an old chest. They rub the lamp. Out pops a gigantic, luminous, green jinn. Wham! The malevolent jinn slays the three crooks.

• A Houston school teacher, Eve Farrell (Winters), presents her class with a unique definition of the word, genie: "Every myth has an origin, a beginning somewhere. [There was] no magic lamp, [but there was] an evil spirit called a jinn. Hence our word, genie."

• Spotting the stolen lamp inside the museum, a teen grabs it. Wham! The jinn pops up and begins murdering adolescents. His foul deeds are attributed to an ancient curse. Explains the museum's curator, five years ago an Iraqi-American woman and her mother brought the lamp to the United States. When the ship sank, all perished, except the two women.

• Bringing even more "death and destruction," the jinn crushes the curator and other adolescents.

Finis: The teacher, Eve, smashes the lamp, eradicating the evil jinn.

Outlaws of the Desert (1941), PAR. *Bill Boyd, George Lewis, Duncan Renaldo, Luli Desti, Jean Phillips, Brad King, Andy Clyde, Joan Del Val, Forest Stanley, Mickey Eissa, Jamiel (Action in Arabia) Hasson.* SP: J. Benton Cheney, Bernard McConville. See *Perils of Nyoka* (1942). VILLAINS, SHEIKHS

In Arabia, Hopalong Cassidy and his cowboys bring down desert Arab "Injuns."

Scene: The US, a ranch. As Major Crawford wants to purchase some "Arabians," he asks Hoppy (Boyd) and his friends, plus Mr. and Mrs. Grant, and their daughter Susan (Phillips), to travel with him to Arabia. Their horses make fine "studs," says the major. Cautions California (King), "There's no telling what we'll find in the desert."

• Arabia's souk. Cut to camels, veiled women, and an Arab vendor trying to bilk Susan. "I won't pay any more than five dollars," she insists. Later, Susan quips, "Don't they ever drink anything but coffee in Arabia?"

• Hoppy, California, and Johnny (Clyde) ride off into the desert to visit Sheikh Suleiman (Renaldo). Abruptly, they spot menacing Arabs attacking a camel caravan. To the rescue, Hoppy's Group. The cowboys run off the Arab bandits. The caravan leader, Yussef (Lewis), thanks Hoppy for "driving away the evil ones."

• Sheikh Suleiman's camp; one cowboy tags Suleiman's headdress a "bed sheet wrapper." And, Johnny says the sheikh "looks like an Injun friend of ours back home, Lone Eagle." Cut to California smoking a nargelih. Coughing, he asks, "Wonder where he (Suleiman) keeps his harem?"

• Mr. Grant (Stanley) presents Suleiman with a gift—a Palomino stallion. As Suleiman refuses to accept any payment, he gives Mr. Grant two Arabians. "We of the desert never forget those who help us at the risk of their own lives," he says. "Go in peace."

• Unexpectedly, El Kader (Del Vel) and his bandits attack Suleiman's camp. Hoppy and his pals outsmart the charging Arabs; El Kader retreats. Next, El Kader's "cutthroats" kidnap and hold hostage Mr. Grant and Susan. Not for long. Hoppy and his cowboys rescue them. Says Sheikh Suleiman, He (El Kader) is a "half-breed dog of a slave-trader, a thief, and a murderer. May the jackals defile his grave."

• Suleiman believes El Kader's bandits will charge again. The sheikh proposes to Hoppy that they gather their men and strike El Kader first. Hoppy disagrees, convincing Suleiman to accept his plan of attack. Their conversation illustrates that Cowboys know best:

> Hoppy: That's going to cost the lives of a lot of your men, isn't it?
> Suleiman: What is written is written.
> Hoppy: I have an idea how we might lead them into a trap and smash 'em in a hurry. It's a trick our Apache Indians sometimes used to surprise their enemies. They lead the enemy to believe everyone was asleep and that the camp was unguarded.

• Hoppy's ruse works. Suleiman fatally stabs El Kader. And, the cowboys rout the bad Arabs. Boasts Johnny, "This sure reminds me of round-up time on the 'ol Bark Wing."

• Back at the Grant ranch, the camera reveals California clad in harem garb. Impersonating a bellydancer, California performs for his cowboy friends.

Note: To illustrate similarities between some Chinese and Arab villains, cinema teachers may wish to screen and discuss *Outlaws of the Desert* and *Outlaws of the Orient* (1937), depicting cowboy Jack Holt in Gobi's oil fields, battling Ho-Fang, an evil Chinese war lord.

Outpost in Morocco (1949), UA. *George Raft, Marie Windsor, Akim Tamiroff, Eduard Franz, Erno Verebes.* Filmed in Morocco. Made in cooperation with "the French government" and the "French Foreign Legion." See the Geste films and *The Song of Love* (1923). MAIDENS, VILLAINS

Legionnaires kill Arabs. A lovely Arab princess loves a Legion officer. But, the scenario does not allow a wedding.

Scene: A nightclub in Bel-Rashad, Morocco. Princess Cara (Windsor), the emir's daughter, becomes smitten with Captain Paul Gerard (Raft). As they tango, Cara utters the film's theme—"You and I are worlds apart."

• An Arab enclave. The emir (Franz) plays chess with his daughter Cara. The emir, who hates the French, boasts that he will soon remove all legionnaires from Morocco.

Cara tells him that peace is best. Sighs the emir, "Sending you to Europe wasn't wise."

• The emir's men attack a legion squad, slaughtering legionnaires. Dead bodies clutter the fort. Quips a grieved legionnaire, Moroccan snipers are "like sand fleas." Vows Captain Gerard: "I've got to make those [Moroccan] butchers pay for what they've done."

• Inside the fort. As Gerard and his outnumbered legionnaires are trapped, they are obliged to ration what little water remains. Unable to resist a drink, Bambouie (Verebes), Gerard's Moroccan aide, steals a cup. The penalty for stealing? Death! Interestingly, not one Frenchman snitches a drink, implying legionnaires are both tougher and more honest than Moroccans.

• The legion water supply is depleted. Lieutenant Glysko (Tamiroff) recites the Lord's Prayer. Suddenly, rain, lots of it. Apparently, God favors legionnaires.

• Disobeying her father, Cara rides off to warn Gerard's men of the emir's impending assault. Anticipating the Arab attack, Gerard and his legionnaires plant dynamite outside the fort's perimeter. The emir's charging Arabs approach the fort. Boom! The explosion blows to smithereens the Emir's "butchers" and lovely Cara.

Finis: Arab potentates gather around victorious French officers. Declaring loyalty and friendship to France, the Arab rulers turn in their rifles.

Overseas (1992), Aires. French with English subtitles. *Nicole Garcia, Marianne Basler, Brigitte Rouan.* Filmed in Tunisia. RECOMMENDED

Arabs as oppressed peoples. Tragedy strikes a French heroine and her Algerian lover.

Scene: French-ruled Algeria, 1946, 1949, and 1957. French colonialists who are willing "to die for the love of France" mock native Algerians.

• Outside a French-owned winery, the camera pans mute Algerians; some stand in a row; others work. The pregnant French owner tells one Algerian worker, "My husband thanks you; the winery is doing fine." Says the Algerian, "Because of you, Madame." Later, when the Algerian uprisings escalate, the winery worker alerts her, "You must leave before they kill your husband." She ignores his warning; the woman and her husband are shot dead. Cut to a raging fire; the winery is destroyed.

• A wealthy Frenchman learns that Lakhdar, an Algerian youth who was "like a son" to him, has "joined the rebels." The angry Frenchman beats the boy. Algerian workers and the man's maid, Zohra, are silent.

• French soldiers arrive at a French villa. For protection, they place sandbags and a siren at the villa. Concurrently, a French youth wearing fatigues and his Algerian friend play at war.

• One French woman, a nurse, aids elderly Algerian women. She also tends a young Algerian man brutally beaten by French soldiers. Later, she falls in love with a striking rebel; they make love. Though French soldiers have surrounded the nurse's villa, her Algerian lover tries to break through and see her. French soldiers kill him; she weeps.

• The following dialogue illustrates how the movie's colonialists view Algerians:

[Arab rebels are] spoiling our fun.

If only I could leave this dump [Algeria].

He used to be pro-French. Damn [Arab] turncoat.

We won't let the damn Arabs step on us. They can't run this country without us; they fight among themselves.

Don't forget the cultural differences.

Arabs have no guts. Tickle them and they squeal.

This is our country. There's only one solution; ship 'em out to sea and open the bilge!
   [*Laughter*]

Paradise (1982), Avco Emb. *Phoebe Cates, Willie Aames, Tuvia Tavi.* SP, D: Stuart Gillard. Filmed in Israel. SHEIKHS, MAIDENS, WORST LIST

Two teenagers and some chimpanzees slay a sinister sheikh. Uncivilized, anti-Christian Arabs are murderers, lecherous slavers, and ravishers of white women. Arab women appear as ugly, cackling caricatures who prod the Western heroine. See Western teens eradicating Arabs in *Sahara* (1983) and *Iron Eagle* (1986).

Scene: Baghdad's souk, 1823. Depraved Arabs are selling women into slavery.

• Arab Muslim bandits are threatening to kill Christians. Thus, an English couple and their teenage daughter, Sarah (Cates), depart Baghdad. They link up with a camel caravan en route to Damascus. Among the traveling pilgrims, young David (Aames), his missionary parents, and some bellydancers.

• Appearing is Sheikh Abdul Aziz (Tavi), "the jackal," and his saber-wielding desert cohorts. The Arabs attack the caravan, massacring the pilgrims. Assessing his prey "much like the hawk looks upon the sparrow," the jackal detaches David's mother's head.

• David and Sarah run off into the Sahara. "If he [the jackal] kills me," says Sarah, "I'll be lucky."

• The jackal tracks the youngsters and nabs Sarah. The Arab whisks her off to his desert camp. Surrounding and prodding Sarah, who wears a white negligee, are grimy Arab women.

• Savoring her fair body, the jackal touches Sarah's breast, demanding, "You come to me." To the rescue, young David and two ingenious chimpanzees, Doc and Eve. Later, Sarah tells David, "This ugly woman came into the tent and I thought, oh, no, not another one!"

• The chimp, Doc, dons a burnoose and acts like a reel Arab. I wonder how viewers might have reacted if the chimp had donned a yarmulke and acted like a reel Jew? Would this be considered amusement? (See also *Cannonball Run II* (1984), in which a chimp smooches a sheikh.)

• Again, the jackal's desert bandits attack the teens. Yet, Sarah and David repel the Arabs. How? By dropping coconuts on their heads. Using a hand-made bow and arrow, David kills the jackal. "It's all right," he tells Sarah, "he's dead."

• The young couple approach a city. Says Sarah, "There are people down there." Sighs David, "Civilized people."

Note: Writes critic Tom Shales in the *Washington Post*, "The [film's] two adolescents are left stranded in 1823 Baghdad when a nasty sheik, played as an offensively stereotyped Arab by [Israeli actor] Tuvia Tavi, massacres an entire village all because little Phoebe didn't respond to one of his slimy overtures. The rest of the film consists of his chasing her all over the desert with a single-mindedness that is totally bewildering" (10 May 1982). In his NYT review, Vincent Canby does not acknowledge the movie's stereotypes; nor does Canby mention the Israeli connection. Instead, he writes, Paradise is "without doubt, the best camel movie of the year" (10 May 1982).

Party Girl (1995), Party Pictures. *Parker Posey, Omar Townsend.* Made for less than $1 million by first-time filmmaker Daisy von Scherler Mayer. SP: Harry Brickmayer, Mayer. RECOMMENDED

In this charming tale, a Lebanese vendor/teacher gets the girl!

Scene: Present-day Manhattan. Perky Mary (Posey) loves to party, party, party. But after she meets and falls in love with Mustafa (Townsend), a handsome Lebanese immigrant running a falafel stand, Mary's priorities soon change. Several telling scenes reveal the couple, Mary and Mustafa, at his falafel stand, sharing thoughts and chuckles.

• When Mary approaches Mustafa, Arabic music is heard in the background. "Do you like this kind of music?" asks Mustafa. "Sure," says Mary. She orders a falafel sandwich and *babaganush* (an eggplant dish). Speaking Arabic, they introduce themselves.

• Explains Mustafa, "In Lebanon I was a teacher, but here I'm just a vendor." He intends to resume teaching once his English improves. Mary feigns speaking Arabic—a genuinely funny moment prompting Mustafa to laugh. She asks Mustafa to teach her "some Arabic"; he invites her to dinner. She accepts.

• While working at a local library, Mary blunders. "I can't really do anything," she tells Mustafa. But, Mustafa helps Mary overcome anxieties and build self-confidence. He brings her flowers and tells her stories, such as the myth of Sisyphus.

• Regularly, Mary goes to the falafel stand, seeking to win Mustafa's affections, which she does, eventually.

• Evening, the library. Mary and Mustafa kiss and make love.

• To show Mustafa she truly cares for him, Mary covers her face with a veil and performs a humorous Arab dance, chanting, "Na, Na, Ni Na."

• Thanks to Mustafa's love and guidance, Mary now excels at the library. Plus, she makes plans to attend college.

• Hal Roach's comedy *Sons of the Desert* (1933) asserts that Americans can don Arab garb and party respectfully with one's friends without being insulted. Here, comedians Laurel and Hardy attend the annual "Sons of the Desert" gathering in Chicago. During the Masonic-like convention scenes, the camera shows "typical" Americans, such as the fez-wearing participants, and some hula and bellydancers, enjoying themselves.

Passion in the Desert (1998), Fine Line. *Ben Daniels, Nadi Odeh.* SP, P, D: Lavinia Currier. Filmed in Jordan. The producers thank Crown Prince Hasan of the Hashemite Kingdom of Jordan for his cooperation. VILLAINS, MAIDENS

How does a French soldier survive, alone, in the Egyptian desert? He befriends Simoon, a leopard, that's how. And, the leopard protects him, killing warring bedouins.

Scene: 1798. Superimposed over the sphinx: "Napoleon's struggling army pursues Mameluke warriors deep into the Egyptian desert." Suddenly, bedouins attack a French regiment. After the Arab leader is shot, bedouins retreat. As the camera pans the dead and wounded, a French soldier, Augustin Robert (Daniels), says, "The bedouins will be behind us like jackals."

• Alone, and in need of water, the surviving Augustin comes across a desert tent. On entering, he sees a veiled bedouin bride (Odeh). The frightened woman calls for help. When the French soldier tries to muzzle her, she pulls a knife, cutting his face. Augustin clips her hair, then runs off. Three Arabic-speaking bedouins arrive, vowing vengeance.

They track Augustin, who runs off and hides in some caves. The bedouins hesitate to enter the caves, saying, "Night is coming. Let the Jinn (the leopard) destroy him."

• Morning. A bedouin sneaks up on Augustin and goes to knife him. Abruptly, the leopard gobbles the Arab, then cuddles the Frenchman. The message here? A reel leopard favors a Frenchman, not an Arab.

Note: Credits state three Arab actors portray the bedouins: Habis Hussein, Tasheen Kwalda, and Ismael Al-Hamd.

Passport to Suez (1943), COL. *Warren Williams, Eric Blore*. CAMEOS, EGYPTIANS

Alexandria, WWII—a setting for British heroics. Briefly, Egyptian waiters wearing fezzes appear.

Scene: The British protagonist, the Lone Wolf (Williams), prevents Germans from acquiring secret "Suez" plans.

• A dark, dense Egyptian wearing baggy pants sees the Lone Wolf's valet (Blore) pop open an umbrella. Frightened of the device, the Egyptian screams and runs off.

Patriot Games (1992), PAR. *Harrison Ford, Anne Archer*. CAMEOS, PALESTINIANS

British agents and an ex-CIA agent (Ford) battle Irish terrorists, a rogue branch of the IRA. Yet, Arab terrorists are injected—and instantly annihilated.

Scene: Surfacing in the Libyan desert, Irish and Arab terrorists wearing red-and-white checkered kuffiyehs. At the rifle range, an Arabic-speaking instructor barks out commands, directing the renegades to sharpen their skills.

• CIA headquarters. A satellite photo displays terrorists: Palestinians, Libyans, and Syrians. The "arms dealer that supplies Khadafi," points out a CIA agent, has "Syrian registry." The satellite scan reveals "Libyan bases"—a haven for Irish extremists and "the PLO."

Why say "PLO?" Producers of this film never call the IRA a terrorist group. Rather, the producers clearly state their film's villains are IRA offshoots. As the "PLO" is the legitimate organization representing Palestinians, why toss out a false terrorist tag? Easily, the producers could have employed more accurate terms, e.g., Palestinian extremists, or a rogue branch of the Palestinian Front for the Liberation of Palestine (PLFP).

• Fiction and reality. In the movie, American forces bomb the Libyan camp. Satellite-transmitted photos show Palestinian and Irish "terrorists" being decimated. These scenes reminded me of video arcade games—the victims are non-entities. *Patriot Games* was released just after the Gulf War, and it echoed that war's sanitized TV coverage, in which Iraqi victims were presented to viewers no differently than fallen objects from video games.

Note: Movie studios, film critics and trade publications. Consider this incident. In his 8 June 1992 review of *Patriot Games*, VAR critic Joe McBride criticized the film for displaying the Irish as terrorists. Disturbed by McBride's critique, Paramount threatened to pull $100,000 worth of advertising. To placate Paramount, editor Peter Bart considered replacing McBride, a VAR staff critic for nearly 20 years.[127]

Patton (1970), TCF. *George C. Scott, Karl Malden.* SP: Francis Ford Coppola, Edmund H. North. Winner of seven Academy Awards, including Best Screenplay. This biographical WWII drama renders tribute to the late General George S. Patton Jr. Filmed in Morocco. See Coppola's *The Black Stallion* (1979) and *The Black Stallion Returns* (1983). CAMEOS, VILLAINS

In a military drama intent on being factual, pillaging Tunisians are equated with vultures.

Scene: North Africa, "Kasserine Pass, Tunisia 1943." Credits roll; a vulture perches on a cliff. Cut to a Tunisian boy trying to yank a ring off a dead US soldier's hand. Methodically, unkempt Tunisian men, women, and children strip dead American soldiers of their socks, shoes, and trousers, depositing the GI's clothing atop camels and donkeys. Cut to General Omar Bradley's (Malden) jeep pulling up; several untidy Tunisians run off. Though the Tunisians are in "need of food and clothing," Bradley correctly censures them, barking, "They strip our dead even before we can bury them." Again, vultures fill the frame; a soldier shoots them.

Considering Patton's nearly three hour [2:51] running time, why did Coppola insert scenes showing vultures and Tunisians hovering over dead American soldiers?

• In Carthage, General George S. Patton (Scott), looking over ruins at an ancient battleground, declares, "The brave Carthaginians defending the city were attacked by three Roman legions and massacred. *Arab women* [emphasis mine] stripped them of their tunics and their swords and lances. The soldiers lay naked in the sun, 2,000 years ago." The "Arab women" line is pure fiction, reinforcing the stereotypes from the opening scene. Supporting my contention that Coppola's line is 100 percent fiction are three military historians: Colonel Cole Kingseed, US Military Academy, West Point; Douglas Bittner, Marine Command and Staff College, Quantico, VA; and Glenn Robinson, Naval Postgraduate School, Monterey, CA. All three concur that at the time of the Punic wars, there were no Arabs in North Africa. "The dialogue used in this part of the movie was pure fiction," writes Kingseed. In this Carthage scene, explains Kingseed, Patton "is referring to the battle of Zarna, in which the Roman legions under Scipio Africanus defeated Hannibal in the final battle of the Second Punic War in 202 BC. Assures Robinson, "Patton was certainly wrong to speak of Arabs in Carthage 2,000 years ago. The great sweep of Arabs across North Africa did not come for another 800 years or so," during the eighth and ninth centuries.

• What *Patton* and other North African war movies do not reveal: Two military historians, professors Douglas Porch and Donald Bittner, shared the following information with me. During WWII, the French Army in North Africa was largely an Arab army. The Fourth Moroccan Mountain Division (4ᵉᵐᵉDMM); the 1ˢᵗ/3ʳᵈ Algerian Infantry Division, and the Second Moroccan Infantry Division fought bravely in the Lori Valley. Though feelings of anti-Colonialism existed, the Arabs were unfailingly pro-Allies.

The Pelican Brief (1993), WB. *Julia Roberts, Denzel Washington, Stanley Tucci, John Heard, Sam Shepard.* SP: John Grisham, Alan J. Pakula. CAMEOS

Into this all-American political murder mystery, the writers insert a slick, mostly mute Arab terrorist named Khamel (Tucci); he speaks seven lines. Khamel kills American dignitaries, notably two Supreme Court justices. The American villains, lead by an oil tycoon from Louisiana, direct Khamel to eradicate the justices and to kill the heroine, investigative journalist Darby Shaw (Roberts).

Scene: Evening, the east coast shore. Khamel docks his rubber raft, then hops into a pick-up truck and drives off. Cut to the residence of Supreme Court Justice Rosenberg (Cronyn). Khamel shoots the justice and his male nurse. Cut to ruby-red blood splattered over the bed's white sheets.

• After meeting with Darby, her law professor, Thomas Callahan (Shepard), gets ready to drive off. He turns the key and his car blows up, killing him.

• Khamel enters a movie theater. He munches popcorn, then takes a rope and strangles Justice Jenson.

• The concerned US president believes the killings are taking place because immigration officials "let foreign terrorists in [the country] again." Cautions a TV reporter: "The French authorities, while watching footage of airport arrivals, thought they recognized Khamel, the terrorist. According to White House unnamed sources, the Middle East terrorist known as Khamel may be one of those who carried out the assassination of Judges Rosenberg and Jenson."

• Darby asks Callahan's friend Gavvin (Heard) for assistance. Abruptly, Khamel enters Gavvin's room and shoots him dead. Cut to spattered blood on the TV set. Cut to Khamel; he munches a bedside chocolate.

• Dressed as Gavvin, Khamel dons a red baseball cap and meets Darby at a crowded river walk. Khamel moves to kill Darby. Unexpectedly, the Arab is fatally shot.

Note: Given this is an all-American scenario, why inject an Arab terrorist? The Louisiana oilman behind the killings wanted new Supreme Court justices, judges that would allow him to continue drilling in the marshlands. He did not care about his company's oil slicks killing off pelicans and other animals; Justices Rosenberg and Jenson, however, did care. They intended to prevent him from drilling. Though the US president's right-hand man knew about this ploy, he did nothing to stop the violence.

• Fortunately, one scene from Grisham's book is not included in the film. Writes Grisham, "Four Arabs noisily filled a table [in a crowded bar]... yakking and jabbering."

A Perfect Murder (1998), WB. *Michael Douglas, Gwyneth Paltrow, David Suchet, Viggo Mortensen.* SP: Patrick Smith Kelly, based on the play *Dial M for Murder* by Frederick Knot. P: Peter McGregor Scott. D: Andrew Davis. RECOMMENDED

A remake of the 1954 thriller *Dial M For Murder*. The screenplay updates the action from *Dial M's* 1950s London to *Perfect's* 1990s Manhattan. David Suchet plays a bright, soft-spoken Arab-American detective, Mohamed "Mo" Karaman.

Scene: At New York City police headquarters, detective Karaman shows compassion for the heroine, Emily (Paltrow), a multilingual translator with the UN. Karaman questions Emily about the death of a man she claims she killed in self-defense. The victim, says Emily, was trying to kill her. Abruptly, the phone rings. Karaman is told his wife is on the phone and that the call is important; he lifts the receiver. Speaking Arabic with her, he discusses the condition of their one-month infant. Concerned, Emily also speaks Arabic, asking Karaman whether his son is all right. "Colic," sighs the detective.

• Final frames. Karaman deduces that Emily is not a murderer. He knows she acted in self-defense, and that her husband Steven (Douglas) is the villain behind the attempt on her life. Karaman comforts Emily, saying in Arabic, "Allah ma cum (May God be with you.) In English, Emily replies, "And you, as well."

Perils of Nyoka (1942), a.k.a. Nyoka and the Tigermen, REP. 15 episodes.

Kay Aldridge, Lorna Gray, Clayton Moore, Robert Strange, Charles Middleton, George Renavent, George Lewis, Ken Terrel, John Bagni. Republic studios later edited the *Nyoka* serial, making it into a full-length feature entitled *Nyoka and the Lost Secrets of Hippocrates* (1966). Many television stations purchased and telecast the 1966 feature. CLIFFHANGERS, MAIDENS, VILLAINS

In this Arabian desert shoot-em-up, the American heroine brings down the Arab femme fatale. White-robed Arabs battle stripe-robed Arabs.

Scene: Resembling screen Indians, "bad" Arabs appear wearing war-paint on their faces. The dialogue emulates and at times embellishes Cowboys-and-Indians scenarios. For example, an evil Arab tells his cohorts, "You take some of the men and encircle them." One "good" Arab says, "[We are] greatly outnumbered." The Arabs refer to the American protagonist, Dr. Larry Grayson (Moore), as the "White Chief."

• In the desert, the heroine, Nyoka Gordon (Aldridge), and her Americans friends plan to locate the long-lost "Golden Tablets of Hippocrates." The inscriptions, which only Nyoka can translate, are invaluable; they will reveal "medical knowledge to aid humanity," even the cure for cancer. Should they uncover the tablets, Nyoka plans to establish "a chain of cancer clinics." Opposing Nyoka is the Arab femme fatale, Vultura (Gray), and her Arab henchmen. They want the tablets' treasures for themselves.

• Interestingly, Nyoka is called "Queen of the Jungle." Yet, all the episodes are set in the Arabian desert. And, episode one is entitled "Desert Intrigue."

• Attending Vultura is the nefarious killer Cassib (Middleton), plus a huge gorilla called "Satan" and many sword-slinging Arabs. Vultura tags Nyoka's Americans "the white infidels," as does Cassib, who shouts: "The white infidels are attacking us."

• Aiding Nyoka is her dog Fang. Also, assisting Nyoka is her father, Professor Gordon (Strange), Larry Grayson, and some good Arabs. Nyoka's bedouins "hate her [Vultura] as much as they worship Nyoka."

• Throughout, the camera reveals slashing sword fights between Vultura's Arab curs and Nyoka's pals. Meriting special attention are the following action scenes. In episode one, see Fang outwit the Arabs. Episodes thirteen and fifteen show Vultura mounting a desert chariot and trying to burn Nyoka at the stake. Vultura's palace hideout, the "Desert Temple," displays a unique shrine—the "Shrine of the Evil Birds." Warns Professor Gordon, "Every dark passage" will be swarming with Arabs. The avaricious Vultura appears inside her temple, clasping the precious tablets. Unable to decipher the tablets, Vultura opts to pry its message from Nyoka with Arab torture. Final frames reveal lots of fight-to-the-finish scenes between America's Nyoka and Arabia's Vultura. Guess who wins!

Dialogue: Constantly, Arabs are tagged "Ayrabs."

Note: Actress Theda Bara presents the Arab woman as Vamp(ire) in 1917; Here, 25 years later, Lorna Gray projects the Arab woman as Vulture(a).

• The plot of the serial *The Tiger Woman* (1944) is similar to the Nyoka scenario— with major exceptions. There are no vile Arabs in Tiger Woman. Also, the serial does not pit Indian against Indian. Instead, the Tiger Woman and her Anglo and Indian friends contest generic criminals.

• The Republic serial *Adventures of Captain Marvel* (1941) pits good Westerners against bad ones. Westerners manipulate bearded nationals who resemble, ever-so-slightly, screen Egyptians. The sword-flaunting nationals wear robes, cloaks, and cone-shaped turbans. And, their sashes contain curved knives. Plus, their underground tomb displays two huge sabers attached to a wall, and a dangerous gold weapon, the "Scorpion." The robed nationals tag Westerners "alien whites," and "white infidels." If violators dare enter the sacred "Valley of the Tombs," the nationals vow to activate a curse, arousing "all the tribes against them."

Perils of Pauline (1967), UNI. *Pat Boone, Pamela Austin, Rick Natoli, Aram Katcher.* SP: Albert Beich. SHEIKHS

Not one Arab appears in Betty Hutton's *Perils of Pauline* (1947). Fast forward 20 years to *Perils of Pauline* (1967), a film displaying foul Moroccans, notably a disgusting, horny prince with a penchant for blondes. The 1967 version should be labeled, *Perils in a Harem.*

Scene: Pauline pops up in Casablanca, "far from home." Cut to a souk, then a mosque.

• The palace. Bored with firing shots at dummy targets, Prince Benji (Natoli) tells his British teacher, "Let's shoot a guard." His anxious teacher grabs the gun. "I'm the royal prince," barks Benji, "and you're not to touch me. I'll slice your ear off."

• Told to behave, Benji protests, "I'm sick of morals." He orders guards to "throw [his British teacher] over the wall and send him into the jungle." They obey.

• When the prince's fresh tutor, Pauline (Austin), arrives at the palace, he exclaims, "Is she blonde? From America? I saved up my allowance and sent away for her. I've started my own harem."

• Benji makes a move on Pauline, warning, "You'll be engaged to me or I'll cut your head off." Armed with a blade, he pursues her. "It's very bad manners," says Pauline, "to threaten your teacher with a scimitar." Says Benji, "I'm your prince and you'll do as I say." He releases two leopards, directing them to catch her.

• Pauline refuses to kiss Benji. The angry prince hits a switch, dispatching her through a trap door and into shark-filled waters. Shouts Benji, "Why don't you scream? My other tutors did. They always screamed. It's more fun."

• In time, Benji's father, the king (Katcher) saves Pauline. "What are you doing playing with my sharks?" he asks Benji. And, "You'll have your harem when you're eighteen, and not before." Vows the king, "He won't bother you, again, or I'll cut off his hand."

• Upset, Benji entombs his father within a brick wall. Shouts the trapped king, "All right. You can have your harem." Benji snatches his father's royal ring, and runs off declaring, "I don't want your old harem, I'm stuck on teacher."

• Finally, Benji grabs Pauline, then has her "bathed and oiled." Wearing harem garb, Pauline appears in the youth's "Den of Sin"; blindfolded Arab musicians perform. Immediately, Benji tries to bed Pauline. She tosses pillows, eluding his grasp. Next, Pauline hops into a convertible and drives off through a souk filled with sheep. After crashing the car into an Arab's shop, Pauline rolls herself up in a rug to hide.

• An Arab haggler spots Pauline; he buys the carpet and places her atop his camel. The Arab promises to free her. He lies, telling a pal, "American girls bring a fortune in the Congo."

• The freed king tells Benji, "Brick me up, you gangster? You're under house arrest and no harem until you're 35." Abruptly, Pauline's Western suitor, George (Boone), arrives in Morocco. George moves to rescue his orphanage suitor. "Produce Pauline at once," demands George, "or you'll lose your oil and your country."

Finis: The prince hires an Englishman, the "white hunter." Benji offers the hunter a fortune, provided he nabs and delivers Pauline to the palace. Sighs George, "That kid's the worst delinquent since Ivan the Terrible."

Pharaoh's Curse (1956), UA. *Mark Dana, Ziva Rodann, Diane Brewster, Alvaro Guillot.* P: Howard W. Koch. EGYPTIANS, MAIDENS

An Egyptian drinks the blood of Westerners. Ignoring tomb warnings, Anglo-American archaeologists violate a pharaoh's sarcophagus, initiating this curse: "Beware. Flesh of my flesh shall creep into the body and eat of the flesh of thy spirit."

Scene: A Cairo military post. After Westerners desecrate a sacred tomb, Egyptians rebel, contesting British soldiers. The mob's actions prompt a surviving British soldier to say, "They butchered us proper, they did. They cut Johnny's tongue out. You'd think this was the dark ages instead of 1902."

• To halt the "native uprisings against the Crown," a British general enlists the help of Captain Storm (Dana). Storm's three-man squad's objective? To march off into the Valley of the Kings and stop the Western archaeologists from digging. Joining the soldiers is Simira (Rodann), a reincarnated "cat goddess." Soon, she links up with her brother, Numar (Guillot). Quips a British soldier, "That beautiful Simira, she's a walking nightmare."

• The Valley of the Kings. Storm's squad arrives "too late"; archaeologists unearth the slumbering king's mummy. Soon, Numar notices he's becoming less human; he grips his face and runs off. Meanwhile, the renewed mummy functions as an unstoppable robot. Says the camp doctor, "There's nothing in the medical books on this one."

• The mummy king's underground chambers collapse. Abruptly, the mummy king invades Numar's body. Now, Numar acts as the murderous mummy; he vows to draw and drink the "blood from the living [archaeologists] until the last intruder shall be no more."

• On learning about Numar's transformation, Storm muses, "Are you asking me to believe that a man who's been dead 3,000 years has the power to transfer his soul into the body of another human being?"

• Numar fails to kill the British soldiers. Amazingly, his mummified body turns to dust. British soldiers and archaeologists seal the king's coffin. As for Simira, Storm reasons she was indeed an authentic cat goddess, masquerading as a human.

The Pharaoh's Woman (1960), UNI. *John Drew Barrymore, Linda Crystal, Armando Francioli, Pierre Brice.* EGYPTIANS, MAIDENS

Feuding Egyptians move to nab the throne and a beautiful princess.

Scene: Though cousins Skaku (Barrymore) and Ramsis (Francioli) rule, respectfully, Upper and Lower Egypt, they "hate each other."

• Following a really big battle, the camera shows ravaged villages. And, Egyptians rape Egyptians. Fast forward. In the background, plenty of slave girls and Oriental dancers.

• After his forces triumph over cousin Skaku's, Ramsis feigns forgiveness, telling Skaku, "Do you forget we are of the same blood. Sit on your throne." Before Skaku can move toward the throne, Ramsis's archer dispatches an arrow, piercing Skaku's heart.

• Ramsis, however, fails to secure the heroine, the lovely Princess Akis (Crystal). The princess rejects the despot, embracing instead the court physician, Amosi (Brice).

Pirates of Tripoli (1955), COL. *Patricia Medina, Paul Henried, Maralou Gray, John Miljan.* S, SP: Allen March. VILLAINS, SHEIKHS

European pirates crush Arab "roaches." Savage Arabs threaten Tripoli's princess. This sixteenth-century swashbuckling tale presents saber duels and battles on land and sea. Why are Tripoli's champions pirates and not Arabs?

Scene: After "Majek, the Bey of Tunis" (Miljan) invades Tripoli, he moves to kill Karjan (Medina), "the beautiful princess." Though Majek's Arab prisoners "beg for mercy," he hangs them "in the public square."

• The princess escapes to a safe place—the "Inn of the Golden Feather." Here, Spanish and British "pirates" rule.

• Majek dispatches Arab assassins to locate the princess. Though the inept killers find Karjan with the pirates, they fail to kill her. Opting to assist lovely Karjan is the pirate, Edri Al-Gadrian (Henried).

• The Arabs offer gold to Rhea (Gray), a French maiden, provided she betrays Edri's pirates. She does. Abruptly, she is rewarded. How? An Arab plunges a knife into her stomach, retrieving the gold.

• Edri and his men are whisked off to Tripoli and imprisoned. Inside the palace dungeon. Majek's "torture master" whips the bold pirate. When some prisoners try to escape, the Arabs nab and dump boiling oil on them.

Finis: Edri and his pirates escape their cells and crush Majek and his Arabs. Plus, Edri kisses the princess.

Dialogue: Pointing to dead Arabs, Edri says: "Take those two roaches out!"

Costumes: The non-Arab pirates don brocaded shirts, high boots, and black eye patches. Princess Karjan and her attendant wear full-length yellow and red skirts, and low-cut white blouses, exposing their breasts.

Note: In 1951, four years prior to the release of *Pirates of Tripoli*, the US helped establish the nation of Libya. At the time, the Libyan people were still haunted by horrific memories of the brutal Italian conquest. Citing Libya's pro-American feelings, Henry Villard, the first American representative dispatched to the newly created state, wrote: On account of "its usual respect for liberty and independence [and] its anti-imperialist" record, "America's reputation in Libya was higher than anyone else's."

Eighteen years later, in 1969, Muamar Khadafi seized power from Libya's aging King Idris. Khadafi closed America's air base. In 1981, US Navy jets shot down two Libyan jets. In 1987, Vice President George Bush called Khadafi a "mad dog." In 1989, two American F-14s shot down, 70 miles off Libya's coast, two Libyan jets.

Play Dirty (1969), UA. *Michael Caine, Nigel Davenport, Harry Andrews, Nigel Green, Aly Ben Ayed, Moshen Ben Abdullah, Mohammed Kouka, Vivian Pickles.* VILLAINS

In this WWII drama Arab homosexuals assist the Allies and pro-German Arabs attack them.

Scene: Circa 1942, the North African desert. British Captain Douglas (Caine) briefs his squad—a group of multiracial mercenaries. The squad's objective? To destroy a vital German fuel depot. Among the hirelings is a Tunisian demolitions specialist, Sadok (Ben Ayed).

• At a local bar, a bug appears in Douglas' whiskey glass. Noting the bug, a mute Arab bartender shrugs, removing the insect with his fingers. Douglas does not drink the whiskey.

• Two cuddling Arabs, Assine (Kouka) and Hassan (Ben Abdullah), help guide Douglas' patrol. The Arabs hold hands, giggling. Says Douglas, "Are they always so friendly?"

• The patrol spots Arabs; Assine moves to ascertain whether they are friendly. Squad member Leech (Davenport) advises Douglas how to interact with these Arabs, "If they offer you tea, drink it. If they offer you food, eat it." Douglas smirks.

• Leech notices that the so-called friendly Arabs possess a German radio. Abruptly, one Arab goes for his rifle; Leech grabs his pistol, terminating the Arab. Later, British soldiers spot the dead Arabs. Barks an officer, "Get these corpses buried, they're beginning to stink."

• Douglas' men ambush some Germans, taking only needed supplies and rifles. Yet, the Tunisians, Assine and Hassan, prowl the dead Germans for jewelry, watches, and rings. See Tunisians looting dead American soldiers in *Patton* (1970).

• Douglas' hirelings abduct a German nurse (Pickles). As Hassan is wounded, the men use medicines from the nurse's Red Cross truck to treat the injured Hassan. When Hassan sees three hirelings trying to rape the nurse, he shoots one in the butt—a harmless wound.

• The patrol must move forward. They leave behind the wounded Hassan and the German nurse. Assine kisses Hassan on the forehead, then gives him a pistol.

• Surprisingly, Colonel Masters betrays his fellow mercenaries. He tips off a double agent, who in turn tells the Germans the exact location of Douglas' men. Still, Douglas' patrol manages to blow up the German oil dump. In the end, all the mercenaries perish.

Note: While attending a 1999 academic conference in Oxford, I discussed the pervasive Arab stereotype with a Middle East studies professor from London. He confided that he, too, was guilty of advancing misperceptions, saying that during WWII, British soldiers, himself included, used to sing "Farida, Queen of the Wogs," "The Whore of Jerusalem," and other such songs.

Point of No Return (1993), WB. *Bridget Fonda, Richard Romanus, Joe Garcia.* SP: Robert Getchell, Alexandra Seros. CAMEOS, VILLAINS

A remake of the French film *La femme Nikita* (1991), which had no Arabs. Here, producers inject an Arab nuclear rogue and his cohorts.

Scene: Near the conclusion, the heroine, Maggie (Fonda), receives orders to kill "one of the richest men in the world," Fahd Bahktiar (Romanus). Maggie is told to terminate

Fahd because he is "peddling nuclear information in the Middle East."

• Maggie poses as Fahd's blonde girlfriend. Isn't there a blonde in almost every screen Arab's life? Disguised as a blonde, Maggie dupes the guards and enters the Arab's house. She confronts Fahd and threatens to shoot him unless he displays on the computer screen his valuable "nuclear program." Fahd hesitates, then suggests a bribe, offering Maggie "anything" provided she does not destroy the disk holding his nuclear data. Maggie uncovers and demolishes the nuclear evidence.

• When Fahd tries reasoning with Maggie, he implies all Muslims are Arabs. Says Fahd, "You think the Arabs should be the only people on this planet not to have this [nuclear] technology? Is that what you think?" he says. "You think you can keep 800 million people [Muslims] in the fourteenth century forever?"

• Maggie runs off. Shouts Fahd to his guards, in Arabic, *Imshe! Imshe!* [Go! Go!] One of Fahd's henchman is named Hassan (Garcia).

Port Afrique (1956), COL. *Pier Angeli, Phil Carey, Rachel Gurney, Richard Molinas, Eugene Deckers.* VILLAINS

In Morocco, some "dirty" Arabs try to kill an American air force veteran.

Scene: At a Moroccan cafe, flamenco dancers and musicians perform. Arabs wearing fezzes are doormen and waiters. Outside, veiled and haggard-looking Arabs parade donkeys, encircling Westerners.

• Introducing Diane (Gurney); she is the villain who has just "hired the Arabs" to murder WWII veteran Rip Reardon (Carey). Outside, her assassins wait for Rick. Diane pours a drink, saying, "It's a foul country, makes everyone venomous, too."

• The alley reveals Diane's two "dirty" Arabs. They fail to kill Rick. The police arrive, describing one Arab as "a small time cut-throat from a slum area of the casbah."

• A Frenchman, Colonel Moussac (Deckers), supervises all investigations. Yet, he respects the expertise of Moroccan Captain Abdul (Molinas).

Credits state: "First Arab" and "Second Arab."

Port Said (1948), COL. *Gloria Henry, William Bishop, Robin Hughes, Lester Sharpe, Ian MacDonald, Martin Garralaga, Jay Novello, Richard Hale, Steven Garay, Joseph Malouf, Edgar Barrier.* SP: Brenda Weisberg. Note the song, "Fatima Brown," a tune about a "bubbly" bellydancer. Music and lyrics by Allan Roberts and Lester Lee. EGYPTIANS, MAIDENS

A wicked Egyptian and an Arab midget.

Scene: The American author Leslie Sears (Bishop) rushes off to Port Said to meet with his WWII buddies, Greg Stewart and Bunny Beacham (Hughes). At Port Said's Hotel Silwa, the Egyptian porter (Garralaga) is both helpful and amusing. The hotel clerk, Taufik (Novello), on the other hand, is a scoundrel. When Sears asks Taufik about his pal, Stewart, the Egyptian purrs, "There's no reason to be alarmed, I assure you." Cut to the villains, Jakoll's (MacDonald) curs, tossing Stewart's body into the canal.

• At the Café Dalaga, Egyptians, Europeans, and US sailors sing along with the pianist, Bunny Beacham. Abruptly, Ali, an Egyptian midget, pushes the piano closer to patrons' tables. Bunny sings "Fatima Brown":

Her snake number was sure a cutie...
She's got wiggles, she doesn't spare 'em,
Sheikh would leave his harem
[To be] with little Miss Fatima Brown.

• A bright Egyptian police officer, Lt. Zaki (Sharpe), meets with Sears. He explains that his friend Stewart is dead. Concurrently, Gila Lingallo (Henry) checks in at the Hotel Silwa. The clerk, Taufik, gives the European villain, Jakoll, Gila's room key. Jakoll intends to kill her.

• Gila's helpful companion, Paolo (Barrier), is in Egypt for revenge; he wants to snare the Nazi collaborators, Jakoll and his cohort, Mario (Hale). During the war, Mario betrayed Paolo and his wife, turning them over to the Gestapo. After the Nazis tortured and killed Paolo's wife, they rewarded the informer, Mario, with jewels and paintings.

• Bunny discovers that his employer, Signor Tacca (Geray), is also in cahoots with the villains. Instantly, Jakoll knifes Bunny in the back.

Finis: At the Rameses Theater, Jakoll is terminated. His cohorts, Mario and Tacca, are arrested. As for the protagonist, Sears, he embraces Gila.

Power (1986), TCF. *Richard Gere, Julie Christie, J.T. Walsh, Denzel Washington, Tom Mardirosian, Gene Hackman.* SP: David Himmelstein. D: Sidney Lumet. CAMEOS, SHEIKHS

Unscrupulous oil-rich sheikhs buy a US politician, in order to prevent America from developing and using solar energy.

Scene: Media consultant Pete St. John (Gere) is a hired gun who will work for anyone—except politicians linked with Arabs. Pete's wizardry enables a Central American politician, one that Arabs do not fancy, to emerge the winner in his country's election.

• Two Arabs appear inside a limousine; they wear suits and white headdresses. One (Mardirosian) complains to public relations specialist Arnold Billing (Washington) about American elections. We "have spent considerable sums" to stop this man from being elected. Oil "prices keep falling," moans the Arab. "Now, we have senators and congressmen talking about solar energy, windmills... Your elections are important to us. I don't want his Majesty upset with another failure, yours or mine."

• Arabs manipulate a senatorial candidate from Ohio, Mr. Cade (Walsh). Because of Arab pressure, Cade opposes "the solar energy bill."

• St. John's phone is tapped. The suspected culprits? Billing and/or the Arabs. Billing warns St. John, "If you tried to screw us, something bad could happen to you."

• Billing forces a senator who supports the development of solar power to resign. The senator's wife owes the Arabs "$380,000." Apparently, the Arabs gave her the money to convince her husband to kill the solar bill.

• Thanks to St. John, the Arab-backed anti-solar candidate, Cade, loses the election. St. John's ex-wife Ellen (Christie) assures him the solar bill will now pass, pointing out, "Do you know what the real story is? Foreign influence in American elections."

Note: Power's theme, Arabs obstructing solar energy development, is a real whopper. For decades, Arabs and Americans have worked together, developing solar energy into a cost-effective and realistic alternative for the future. Interest in solar energy research began in the Saudi Arabia in the 1960s. In the mid-70s, the Saudis funded a solar power system for the Terraset school in Reston, VA as an example of "urban social technology." In 1977, Saudi government officials signed a Program Agreement for Cooperation in the Field of Solar Energy with the United States (SOLERAS). The program is under the auspices of the Saudi-Arabian-United States Joint Economic Commission. Collectively, Saudi and American scientists take the sun and convert its energy into solar power.[128]

• The film's two Jewish-American characters help bring down Arab supporters, Cade and Billing. In the film, Philip Aarons, a pro-solar, pro-environment history professor from Ohio, defeats Cade. And the yarmulke-wearing Ralph, a computer whiz in a wheelchair, uncovers the Arab connection, revealing that Billing's major client is AMERABIA. Note the resemblance of AMERABIA to ARAMCO, the American Arabian Oil Company.

• When it comes to backing candidates, Washington DC's Arab lobby is considered to be virtually impotent. Conversely, the Jewish lobby, notably, the American Israel Public Affairs Committee (AIPAC), is one of DC's most influential special interest groups.

The Power of the Sultan (1908), Selig. Silent. *NS. SHEIKHS
The first feature to be filmed in Los Angeles.

The Prince of Egypt (1998), DW. Animated. *Voices of Val Kilmer, Ralph Fiennes, Helen Mirren, Michele Pfeiffer, Martin Short, Steve Martin, Patrick Stewart.* P: Penney Finkleman Cox, Sandra Rabins. SP: Philip LaZebnik. D: Simon Wells, Brenda Chapman, Steve Hickner. See Cecil B. DeMille's *The Ten Commandments* (1956). EGYPTIANS

Evil Egyptians enslave heroic Hebrews. Moses and his followers worship the one true God; Egyptians bend before false Gods. This 97-minute animated-musical version of the Exodus story, budgeted at $80 million-plus, highlights Hebrews fleeing from Egyptians to the Promised Land.

Though the Exodus story portrays Egypt's pharaoh and his Egyptians as heinous villains, DreamWorks, more so than any other studio documenting Moses' liberation, softens harsh Egyptian images, humanizing some antagonists. For this film, Jeffrey Katzenberg consulted with hundreds of scholars, theologians, archaeologists, Egyptologists, and biblical experts, including members of the Muslim and Arab community. Thanks to my friend, Don Bustany, I was invited to the screening of the "in-progress" film (6 December 1996). Among those viewing this version of the film were Bustany and Muslim scholar Maher Hatout. Afterward we saw the rough cut, Katzenberg called us into his office, requesting our opinions and insisting we "be blunt." I told him, "This is yet another film America's Arabs and Muslims will *not* want their children to see." Katzenberg, who is Jewish, was taken aback by my comment, so much so that he asked me whether I was the kind of parent who would deny my children access to movies such as *Schindler's List.* Outraged at his ridiculous accusation, I told him my children knew and cared more about racist images than he did. A heated discussion took place. Before leaving his office, I challenged Katzenberg to invite me back to DreamWorks for a "sensitivity session," so that I might explain to him and his staff members how Hollywood's omnipresent Arab stereotypes impact America's Arabs and

Muslims. To be honest, I never expected to hear from him. Yet, a few weeks later, on 18 December I received a letter from producer Penney Finkelman Cox stating, "We would like to take you up on your offer to conduct an in-house sensitivity session on Arab and Muslim issues in relation to *The Prince of Egypt*."

Two months later, in February 1997, I went to Los Angeles and met with Katzenberg, producer Cox, and other *Prince of Egypt* staff members. They hosted a give-and-take stereotyping session, lasting for nearly three hours. Subsequently, I came to develop an excellent working relationship with Katzenberg. I came to respect his integrity, and his willingness not to vilify peoples. He invited me to two additional screenings, one in November 1997, the other in June 1998. Before and after each showing, we exchanged opinions about the film's Egyptian images. As a result, prior to the film's December 1998 release, the studio made several additions and alterations.

To me, the most important change occurred in the Angel of Death sequence, in which God smites Egypt's first-born. In order for viewers to empathize with Egyptian victims, Katzenberg and his animators re-worked this sequence. Also, Katzenberg presents Egypt's queen, albeit briefly, as a beautiful, intelligent woman, devoted to her sons, Moses and Rameses. And the movie's desert scenes focusing on the Midians are fun-filled and heart-warming.

To their credit, the producers project a humane, though seriously flawed pharaoh. No other Exodus feature film displays such a three-dimensional pharaoh. Here, Rameses and Moses appear as loving brothers. As Katzenberg told *Time* magazine reporter Kim Masters, he and his colleagues were so impressed with the majesty of Egypt's pyramids that "we found ourselves not wanting to simply portray Rameses as the bad guy" (14 December 1999).

As to be expected, not all suggestions from consultants, myself included, were embraced. For example, from the very first screening I urged Katzenberg to omit violent scenes showing Egyptian guards tossing the Hebrew children to crocodiles, explaining, "It's historically inaccurate, you know, it's not in the bible." I continued, "You don't need it. The scene is overkill. Look, you show the Egyptian guards with scythes snatching the Hebrew babies. Doesn't that convey your message, Isn't that enough?" Besides, "Those crocodile-baby scenes will frighten young viewers." Yet, Katzenberg and his producers opted to keep the two crocodile sequences.

Scene: The construction site of Egypt's monuments. Egyptian guards whip laboring Hebrew slaves. One dark-complexioned Egyptian worker assists a fallen Hebrew. Unfortunately, the producers did not include more footage showing Egyptian laborers working alongside the Hebrews. Even though the film's Egyptians are not slaves, they, too, are obliged to labor and suffer under pharaoh's rule.

• The pharaoh's guards move to assassinate the Israelites' first-born. Cut to the baby Moses (Kilmer) being placed in a basket and sent down river. The baby is rescued by the pharaoh's wife (Mirren). The queen loves and cares for Moses, raising him as she does her own son, Rameses (Fiennes).

• Initial scenes show Rameses and Moses, his adopted brother, as devoted brothers. They act as mischievous young men, engaging in chariot races, dropping water balloons to harass the court magicians.

• The dream sequence. Moses becomes concerned about his true identity. He falls asleep, dreaming of pharaoh's genocidal campaign against the Israelites' first-born.

Abruptly, the hieroglyphic wall drawings come to life. Pharaoh's marching men function as fascists. Armed with scythes, they snatch the Hebrew babies from their mothers' arms. Moses awakens; the dream becomes reality. Clasping a torch he views wall paintings that show the Egyptian guards tossing the babies to crocodiles. Moses confronts the pharaoh (Stewart). "The Hebrews grew too numerous," says the ruler, "they might have risen against us... sacrifices must be made." Later, Rameses tries to find out why Moses is troubled; Moses runs off into the desert.

• In the desert, a camel helps save Moses' life. He soon links up with the Midians, befriending Jethro, the High Priest, and his daughter, Tzipporah (Pfeiffer). Soon, Moses and Tzipporah wed. As described in the studio's November 1996 board outline, this desert scene featured ugly bedouins trying to rob the Midian women. But the film displays no bedouin villains; instead, two generic thieves surface, briefly. Moses chases them off.

• Following God's will, Moses returns to Egypt. He warns Rameses, now the pharaoh, "The God of the Hebrews... commands that you let his people go." Moses' demands hurt and anger Rameses. As pharaoh, he insists on carrying on the legacy of his father, refusing to become "the weak link." Though Rameses breaks with Moses, both men pause for a moment to reflect on the past. Asks Rameses, "Why can't things be as they were before?" Flashback. Moses sees the crocodiles devouring the Hebrew children.

• Rameses refuses to honor Moses' request. Thus, God punishes the Egyptians. Swarms of locusts attack; an "Angel of Death" snuffs the lives of Egypt's first-born, including Rameses' son. When Rameses son dies, the camera fails to reveal the boy's father's grief. Instead, Rameses emits an ugly grimace. Cut to Moses, crying.

• Final scenes show Moses and the Hebrews departing Egypt. Suddenly Rameses' army attacks; the Red Sea parts and all the Egyptians except for Rameses perish. Cries the anguished Rameses, "Moses, Moses, my brother."

The Prince Who Was a Thief (1951), UI. *Tony Curtis, Piper Laurie, Don Randolph, Frank Lackteen, Peggie Castle. See Son of Ali Baba (1952).* MAIDENS

Moroccans vs. Moroccans. Good-natured Arab thieves bring up the boy, Prince Hussein (Curtis) of Tangier. Opposing Hussein and his Arabs, evil Prince Mustapha (Randolph) and his cohorts. As the NYT reviewer put it, Tony Curtis "is surrounded by burnoosed Moslems " (4 July 1951).

Scene: Opening scenes reveal swordplay, "a magic carpet endowed by rainbow hues," voluptuous women, and an extraordinary jewel, "the "Pearl of Fatima."

• The lovely Moroccan street urchin Tina (Laurie) steals the precious "Pearl of Fatima." Unless the stolen pearl is recovered and returned to its Algerian owners, the Algerians vow to attack Tangier and set the city aflame.

• Moroccans suffer under the rule of "Prince Mustapha, the Imposter." Mustapha and his retinue "squeeze gold from their people."

• Boast Prince Hussein's foster parents, "He's so handsome; he has the look of eagles in his eyes, the brow of lions, the speed of stallions in his loins."

• Mustapha's palace guards pursue Hussein. Abruptly, Hussein halts and gives coins to a blind man (Lackteen). The prince also stops to help a fellow Tunisian lift a heavy package.

• Tina saves Tangier; in time she discloses the stolen pearl. Hussein and his courageous thieves crush Mustapha and his cohorts. Showing mercy, the rightful Prince of Tangier spares the villains' lives.

• Regaining his throne, Hussein rejects the advances of Princess Yasmin (Castle), opting to wed Tina, the commoner. Says Hussein, she is "the most beautiful Princess in all Islam, more beautiful than the dawn."

Dialogue: Characters tag Arabs "sons-of-she-camels" and "jackals." Also, characters say, "By the sword of Allah," and "By the beard of the prophet."

Note: A commoner captures the ruler's heart. See *Kismet.*

A Princess of Bagdad (1913), Helen Gardner Pictures. Silent. *Helen Gardner, Robert Gaillord.* Produced in Gardner's studio, Tappan-on-the-Hudson. *NS. Notes from AFIC. MAIDENS, SHEIKHS

Once he has the money, a caliph allows his daughter to wed a humble youth.

This scenario is somewhat like an Aladdin and Ali Baba tale. Here, Baghdad's Princess Ojira falls for a commoner, the son of a cobbler. But Ojira's father, the caliph, disapproves of the arrangement, imprisoning the youth. The boy's father, Seyn, intervenes. Unexpectedly, he uncovers a cave of treasures, offering the caliph his newly-found riches. Pleased, the caliph frees Seyn's son, permitting the youth to wed his daughter, Princess Ojira.

Princess of the Nile (1954), TCF. *Debra Paget, Jeffrey Hunter, Michael Rennie, Michael Ansara, Lee Van Cleef.* EGYPTIANS, MAIDENS

AD 1249. An Egyptian couple helps Egyptians crush bedouins.

Scene: In the desert, Egyptian Princess Shalimar (Paget) and Prince Haidi (Hunter), the Caliph of Baghdad's son, battle warring bedouin bandits.

• At the palace, harem maidens comfort Shalimar's benevolent father, Rama Khan (Rennie). Meanwhile, Khan's two-faced advisors move to oust the ruler. Soon, the scheming counselors take control, oppressing peoples. Cut to Hakar (Van Cleef), an evil counselor lusting after Shalimar. The princess rejects him, for she loves Prince Haidi.

• Not only does Shalimar excel with a scimitar, her dance solo is exceptionally animated.

Finis: Aided by heroic partisans, Shalimar and Prince Haidi rout counselor Hakar and his conspirators. Shalimar's father, Khan, regains the throne.

Note: Major stars, Debra Paget and Jeffrey Hunter, portray brave Arabs. See *Flame of Araby* (1951).

Princess Tam Tam (1935), ARYS. *Josephine Baker, Albert Prejean.* Filmed in Tunisia. MAIDENS, RECOMMENDED

Josephine Baker appears as Tunisia's Eliza Doolittle. Baker stars as Alwina, which in Arabic means "small source." This French film with English subtitles present a sincere and loving Arab woman.

Scene: In France, Max (Prejean), a bored writer, plots to make his wife Lucie jealous. Max meets with his friend Coton, convincing him to travel to Tunisia, where Max plans to write a book. As Max puts it, "Let's go among the savages, the real savages."

• Tunisia. Near desert palm trees, Alwina attends sheep. Cut to Max and Coton relaxing at an outdoor cafe. Abruptly, a vendor collars Alwina for stealing oranges. To the rescue, Max and Coton; they befriend her.

• The "ruins of Dougga," an ancient Roman city. As Alwina dances, playful Tunisian children admire her performance.

• Max meets with his European friends, asking them to mingle with Alwina. One woman refuses, "You wouldn't subject us to that savage's company," she says. Chimes in her companion, "Ugh! A bedouin!" Adds another, Alwina smells "like a wild animal."

• Aware she is being mocked, Alwina snatches a salt shaker and fills it with pepper. The Europeans get pepper, not salt, and are obliged to cough up their meals. Max chuckles. Coton advises, "If you were less intent on your savage, you'd write more."

• In order for Max to pen a really convincing "interracial story," he and Coton begin to "polish and educate" Alwina.

• Note the dialogue.

Max: That little animal moves me. She's so naive.
Coton: You must civilize her.
Max: How?
Coton: Teach her to lie!

• Several scenes show the Frenchmen teaching Alwina piano and math. Also, she learns to how to walk with shoes, and to sail. Thinking Alwina has become sufficiently civilized, they leave for Europe. Max boasts that everyone will think her the "Black Princess of Parador."

• France. Bored with her stuffy surroundings, Alwina runs off. Entering a seedy nightclub, she sings and dances. Later, at Max's formal reception, a jealous guest slips the "Black Princess" too much champagne. Thus, when Alwina hears the band belt out some rhythmic drum beats, she strips, all the way down to her slip. Dancing sensuously, she becomes "a sensation."

• Concerned that Max's European learning lessons may eventually tarnish Alwina's purity, as well as break her heart, a wise Indian Maharajah approaches her. He tells her that if she seeks true happiness to leave, that "civilized" France is really not so civilized.

• The Tunisian countryside. The smiling Alwina appears alongside her husband, Dar, a fellow Tunisian. They embrace their child.

Note: Seeing Dar, Coton says: "He reminds me of a crocodile!" At times, characters tag Alwina a "savage."

• At the time *Princess Tam Tam* was produced, Hollywood's filmmakers were presenting blacks as simple-minded caricatures. But this French-made film and several other European scenarios contested the stereotype, offering fresh portraits. See *Jericho* (1937).

Prison Heat (1993), CAN. *Uri Gavriel, Gabi Shoushan, Rebecca Chambers.*
D: Joel Silberg. Filmed in Israel. CAMEOS, VILLAINS

Though the action takes place in a Turkish prison, this soft-porn Cannon film presents Israeli actors as Arabs running a white slavery ring. Aiding the Arabs are vicious Turkish Muslims who abduct and abuse American women. This detestable film makes Oliver Stone's Turkish prison in *Midnight Express* (1978) seem almost a playground.

Scene: At the Turkish border, Turkish guards frame lovely American tourists, Bonnie,

Colleen, and Audrey. When the women enter Turkey, the Arabic-speaking border guard plants drugs in their van. Thus, the women are hauled off to a Turkish cell. Next, the guard calls Saladin (Gavriel), the Turkish warden, who boasts, "I'm sending you some fresh meat." Inexplicably, this Turk also speaks Arabic, saying "*Shookran*" [Thank you].

• In prison, one woman suggests a Turkish worker may help them. Warns an American, "She would sell her own mother." An Arab businessman, Akim (Shoushan), enters Saladin's office. The Arab gives the warden a fistful of bills, chuckling, "There are more where those came from if the honorable sheikh is happy." Affirms Saladin, "He will be. They [the fresh American women prisoners] are being prepared, now." "*Ma'ssalameh* [Goodbye]," says Akim. Saladin responds, "*Ma'ssalameh.*" Akim also says, "*Yallah, yallah*" [hurry, hurry]."

• Saladin brutally rapes Bonnie. She takes a shower, then throws up. Saladin rapes the bruised woman again; this time Bonnie tries to commit suicide.

• One woman prisoner is near death. She advises fellow inmates to try and escape, that she was once "sold to a white slaver that runs brothels up and down the Middle East." She raises her skirt, revealing an "S" branded onto her leg. As soon as the woman dies, the camera cuts to a mosque; the muezzin chants "Allahu Akbar" [God is great].

• Saladin summons Bonnie to his office, purring: "Permit me to introduce my friend, Akim, from Beirut." Barks Saladin, "She is yours." Off camera, Akim rapes Bonnie. Next, Akim tries to brand her with the "S." In time, the American prisoners arrive, vanquishing the two abusers.

• In the end, the Americans terminate the prison guards, then escape to freedom.

Prisoner in the Middle (1974), a.k.a. Warhead, Worldwide.

A Buddy Raskin Film. *David Janssen, Karen Dor, Joan Freeman, Chris Stone, Eddy Muktar, David Semadar.* SP, P: Raskin. Filmed in Israel. PALESTINIANS, WORST LIST

Palestinian rapists and nuclear terrorists slaughter Israeli children. An American colonel and Israelis demolish Palestinians. Injected into the scenario is the myth that Israelis do not have nuclear weapons.

Scene: Jerusalem. On screen, anAmerican B-52 bomber "accidentally jettisoned a new top-secret nuclear weapon over the Jordanian desert, near [the] Israeli border." Instantly, Colonel Stevens (Janssen), on leave in Israel, moves to locate and "deactivate" the warhead.

• As credits roll, the camera reveals a desert road, a bus carrying Israeli school children happily singing along in Hebrew. Cut to their escorts, Liona, an Israeli army officer, and her colleague. One child holds a stuffed animal. Without warning, a rocket hits the bus. Cut to bloodied bodies. All but Liona perish. Appearing atop a desert dune are the villains—Palestinians wearing kuffiyehs. Liona fires three times, killing three. The fourth Palestinian, Malouf (Muktar), runs off. "A bus full of children would still be alive if it wasn't for Malouf." Liona picks up the child's burned doll and cries. See *Wanted: Dead or Alive* (1987) and *Death before Dishonor* (1987).

• At an Israeli Army Firing Range, the Major (Stone) says they will "go after Malouf in Jordan." Two soldiers, Namoi (Freeman) and Liona, wear micro-mini outfits. Namoi, a blonde, is the unit's "Best Marksperson." Soon, she kills several Palestinians. Before they begin to track Malouf Inc., the Israelis pray.

• Israeli squad members appear in the desert. One hails from "Trenton, New Jersey"; another called "rabbi," carries the Holy Torah. When a soldier proposes getting "hash" from bedouins, his pal retorts, "Nah, those bedouins are too busy making love to their sheep to do business with you." Major Stone spots tank tracks and chuckles, "One thing about Arabs, they never change their schedules."

• No sooner does US Colonel Stevens locate the nuclear warhead, Malouf and men capture him. Grunts Malouf, "You may consider yourself a prisoner of the Palestine Liberation Army [PLA]." [Note the resemblance to the Palestine Liberation Organization (PLO).] Malouf boasts that his PLA will use the weapon against Israel: "One bomb, no Jews." And, "We of the Palestine Liberation have an understanding with airlines. We Arabs are not so ignorant."

• Fifteen dense Palestinians try but fail to lift the warhead onto the back of a pickup truck. Sighs Malouf, "What they lack in brains they make up in courage." Note the comments made by observing Israeli soldiers.

Soldier #1: Maybe they're trying to put up a gas station.
#2: Just like Arabs. They put up a gas station and forget to put in the roads.
#1: There are plenty of roads around here.
#2: Sure, right in the middle of nowhere.
#3: Yeah. If you're a camel.

• The Israelis attack, killing scores of Malouf's men, some of whom ride camels. Cowardly Palestinians run off. Perhaps to show empathy for Israeli casualties the camera reveals a funeral; comrades mourn and pray. In the foreground, the body of a Palestinian. No one mourns for him.

• Malouf eats with a knife, claiming his Palestinians will "attack [the Israelis] from behind." He holds a female Israeli soldier hostage. Leering at her is Hassan [Semadar], Malouf's sex-starved cohort. Hassan, who resembles a glob of grease, rips off the woman's shirt. Seeing her breasts, he gapes. Says Malouf, "I will leave the Jew for your pleasure." As Hassan draws near, the woman begs, "Please, don't." Her screams are amplified on the soundtrack. Appearing on screen, rotating images of the brutal rape.

• Eventually, the Israelis secure the warhead. Colonel Stevens advises them, "You don't want that thing. So long as you don't have it you're the little guy in the neighborhood being picked on by the big Arab boys." And, "You don't possess that bomb and you're the underdog. That means help from my country. You come marching in there with Big Bertha and you'll be cast in the role of a heavy. Then nobody's gonna help you." Cautions Stevens, "The nuclear club is a very exclusive organization. We'd like to keep it that way."[129]

• Major Stone tells Stevens, "Colonel, you can stay here and take your chances with the Arabs, or you can come with us [Israelis] and fight." The Israelis have only six men and one woman. But, Malouf boasts "30, 40 Arabs." Declares Stevens, "I go where the bomb goes." He grabs a machine gun, and helps Israelis kill Palestinians. Quips Stevens, "There will be six or seven of them [Arabs] for every one of us." I'm told "that's just about right for your people." Affirms an Israeli soldier, "I'll have eight."

• Palestinians tie an Israeli prisoner's arms to two horses; the man is torn apart.

• At a deserted fort, Israelis hide out. Hassan checks the abandoned fort. Failing to see the hidden Israelis, he beckons fellow Palestinians to enter. Wham! Israelis swat them, like flies. Stevens kills several, including Malouf. Blood stains appear on the rabbi's Holy Torah.

• In Jerusalem, Stevens approaches the Wailing Wall, recalling the words of an Israeli woman soldier. Her image is superimposed on the screen; she says, "Some day death will touch you personally, and you will feel the pain."

Prisoners of the Casbah (1953), COL. *Gloria Graham, Turhan Bey, Cesar Romero, Nestor Paiva.* D: Sam Katzman. MAIDENS, VILLAINS

Algerians vs. Algerians. Brave Ahmed overpowers the evil vizier, "desert bandits," and Marouf, king of the thieves.

Scene: Palm trees shade Princess Nadja (Graham), "the most spoiled child in Islam." As she bathes at the oasis, scantily-clad maidens attend her. Ahmed (Bey) arrives, but he refuses to pamper her. Nadja punishes him. A horse drags the bound Ahmed across desert sands.

• Intending to kidnap Ahmed and Nadja, the vizier's (Romero) men enter a secret casbah, "a refuge for thieves and murderers." Here, the doublecrossing Marouf (Paiva), "king of the thieves," betrays Ahmed. But, another thief kills the "traitor" Marouf.

• A screen first: "European guard dogs" protect palace passageways. In her bedroom, Nadja plays a flute; abruptly, a snake pops up from a basket.

• To save Nadja, Ahmed enlists the help of the casbah's denizens. Together, they attack the palace, crushing the vizier and his cohorts. A reformed Nadja captures Ahmed's heart.

Treatment of Islam: An Arab guard spots a fellow Arab drinking, protesting, "You're not a good Moslem, drinking wine when the Prophet forbids it." Then he, too, begins guzzling booze, laughing, "Neither am I."

Dialogue: An Arab is tagged "jackal" and "son-of-a-dog."

Note: Producer Sam Katzman's credits list Arabs as: "Thief No. 1," "Thief No. 2," "Thief No. 3," and as "Slave Girl No. 2," "Slave Girl No. 3."

Private Worlds (1935), PAR. *Claudette Colbert, Charles Boyer, Nick Shaid.* SP: Lynn Starling. D: Gregory La Cava. CAMEOS, RECOMMENDED

Though only two scenes reveal a seriously-ill Arab, I highly recommend this medical drama.

Two gentle and caring physicians, Jane Everest and Carles Monet (Colbert, Boyer), attend patients in a mental hospital. Dr. Everest examines one bedridden patient, the "Arab," (Shaid) who is not "responding to treatment." On hearing the elderly man speak, very softly, Arabic, Dr. Everest says, "Poor lovely soul. If we could only understand what he is trying to tell us, we might be able to help him." Adds a sympathetic nurse, "It's a shame he couldn't end these days in his own homeland." Sighs Everest, "He'll soon be home."

Later, the hospital's director, Dr. Monet, rushes to the Arab's bed. The Arab is singing traditional Arab songs. Explains the nurse, "This is the Arab, Dr. Monet; he's been going on like that all day, as though he was trying to ask us something. No one around here understands his language." Says Monet, "I understand Arabic." The doctor speaks Arabic with his patient, explaining to the nurse, "He's asking for someone… he's dying." Monet and the Arab converse in Arabic. The Arab now seems at peace. He stops singing, telling Monet, "*Assalamu Aleikum* [Peace be upon you]." Dr. Monet stays with his patient until the lights go dim and the Arab dies. Dr. Everest arrives as the Arab passes away; she bows her head.

The Prodigal (1955), MGM. *Lana Turner, Edmund Purdom, Louis Calhern, Neville Brand.* MAIDENS, VILLAINS

Hebrews vs. Syrians. 70 BC. Loosely based on the prodigal son story, this film shows devout Hebrews worshiping Jehovah. Opposing the Hebrews are Syrian heathens idolizing the High Priestess of Asarte. See *The Ten Commandments* (1956) and *The Prince of Egypt* (1998).

Scene: In Jaffa, a pious Hebrew cautions that Syrian "infidels [frequent] an unholy temple in Damascus with its 500 women... women who will do anything for a silver coin, painted women serving painted graven images." When Micah (Purdom), the young Hebrew protagonist, arrives in Damascus and spots the city's golden haired priestess, Samarra (Turner), he becomes smitten. He moves to Syria.

• To woo Samarra, the "infidel," Micah purchases a lavish dwelling in Damascus. Cut to a huge spinning wheel, and gamblers placing bets. Attached to the wheel are scantily clad maidens. Inside tents, lovers improvise. In the slave market, Syrian guards whip innocents. And, women are auctioned off for "ten pieces of silver." Damascus appears as a not so pleasant place; Syria's high priest, Nahreeb (Calhern), starves the people.

• Syrians believe the goddess Samarra belongs "to all men." When she appears, Syrians bow. One young Syrian even sacrifices himself before the High Priestess' altar.

• Nahreeb is intent on forcing Micha to "renounce his faith"; the ruler dispatches the "desert tribes" to attack the Hebrew's home. As a result, not only does "the unholy infidel" lose his fortune, Micha is whipped and enslaved by Nahreeb. The Syrian will release Micah, provided the Hebrew confesses to "the people of Damascus that his God is a false God." Micah refuses.

• Micah escapes; he returns to his father's home, promising, "I would rather be a servant in my father's house than a king in Damascus."

• Cut to the maiden Samarra worshiping the High Priestess of Asarte. Samarra refuses to embrace Micah's God. Thus, she and other heathens perish. Among the survivors are those Syrians who suffered under Nahreeb's rule; they destroy Asarte's temple.

Note: Most Syrian villains don Crusader-type outfits; they do not look like screen Arabs. Only the dialogue labels them as "Syrians" who worship "false Gods."

Professor Beware (1938), PAR. *Harold Lloyd, Phyllis Welch, William Frawley.* EGYPTIANS, CAMEOS

Scene: The fleeting opening scene takes place in Egypt, circa 3000 BC. An Egyptian villain delivers a knock-out punch, flooring the protagonist, Neferus, who drops into a tomb. Several Egyptians move to seal Neferus inside, permanently. Cut to Anebi, Neferus' betrothed. She screams.

• The rest of the story occurs in the US, circa 1930. While studying ancient Egyptian tablets, an Egyptologist named Lambert (Lloyd) locates data documenting young Neferus's tragic death. Suddenly, Lambert begins to believe that he is the reincarnated Neferus. For example, though Lambert loves Jane (Welch), he avoids her, fearing Jane may be the reincarnated Anebi. Lambert worries that if he dares smooch Jane, he will perish, just like Neferus. Finally, common sense prevails. Lambert and Jane dismiss all their reincarnation anxieties and embrace.

Project Z (1987), Lion Pacesetter. *Annabel Littledale, Michael Hale.* Filmed in Tunisia. RECOMMENDED

When British thugs hold British youths hostage, a brave young Tunisian and his Arab friends come to the rescue.

Scene: The Tunisian desert. Arab music underscores opening frames. Arabs on camels appear from behind the sand dunes, surrounding two British youths who are "lost in a sandstorm." The music swells; the camera closes in on the Arabs, giving viewers the impression they will attack the lost duo. The British youths smile, saying, "They're friends." Cut to the Tunisians providing them with water and fresh fruit, then guiding them to safety.

• A British spy and his cohorts scheme to steal plans for a top-secret vehicle. They also move to harm the two British youths. Cut to a "nice" Tunisian named Ahmed and his Arab companions; they chase off the villains.

• After Ahmed saves the protagonist, Mr. Knight, he finds in the desert a missing British schoolgirl and shoots a pistol out of the British villain's hand.

• Thanks to Ahmed, the British spies fail to pilfer plans for the secret vehicle. Throughout, Ahmed refers to the two British youths as his "brothers." In the end, they are "sorry to see him go."

Protocol (1984), WB. *Goldie Hawn, Chris Sarandon, Richard Romanus, Andre Gregory.* SP: Buck Henry, P: Anthea Sylbert. EP: Goldie Hawn. Filmed in Tunisia. SHEIKHS, MAIDENS, WORST LIST

Protocol's messages include: American politicians should not consort with Arab leaders. Oily Arabs will do anything to bed blondes; they are cruel, crooked, carnal, and crude womanizers.

Some Jewish leaders protested the film's stereotypes. Paul R. Zilsel of KADIMA, the Seattle affiliate of the New Jewish Agenda, wrote to producer Anthea Sylbert, saying, "We are a Jewish organization that is deeply committed to working for better understanding between Jews and Arabs and a just peace in Israel/Palestine. What we need [to see] is not derision and contempt, but mutual respect." Said Henry Siegman, executive vice president of the American Jewish Congress,

> Americans looking at Israel have not found it difficult to identify with its travails and its accomplishments... By contrast, when Americans look at the surrounding Arab societies, they do not generally experience a similar sense of empathy and likeness. To the contrary, these societies, their cultures and their values evoke a sense of strangeness, of otherness in most Americans.

And Laurence Pope of the foreign service office affirmed,

> Siegman is right. One consequence [of screen portraits] is that Arab and Muslims, their cultures and their values are fair game for racial stereotyping and bigotry of the crudest kind. That ought to make us think—not about the movie business, which is only out to make a buck, but about fairness, and our own values.[130]

Bob Cohn, editor of St. Louis' *Jewish Light*, said at a St. Louis Jewish Center Film Festival, "Would we Jews laugh at a Hasidic Rabbi abducting women; at *Protocol* and other Hollywood films with similar themes perpetuating the... myth of Jewish men raping German women?"[131]

Scene: Appearing is Sunny Davis (Hawn), a blonde Washington, DC, cocktail waitress. She sees an Arab assassin about to shoot Othar's emir (Romanus); instantly, she bites the radical's hand, saving the ruler's life. This Arab emir, who presents Rolls Royces as Santa doles out toys, offers Sunny a Rolls; she refuses.

• The smitten emir wants Sunny for his bordello. Cut to state department officials musing that if Sunny beds the emir, America will receive in return, a "strategically located" military base in Othar's "spit of sand." See *John Goldfarb, Please Come Home* (1964).

• Sunny escorts the emir's Arabs to the seedy Safari Club; the menu displays ham as the main course. The lecherous Arabs ogle Sunny. Islam is mocked. Nawaf (Gregory), a Muslim religious leader, does everything a good Muslim does not do. He surrounds himself with hookers, gulps booze, then falls onto the floor chanting, Allahu Akbar (God is Great). A fight breaks out, followed by an orgy.

• State department officials hoodwink Sunny, saying she has been appointed to serve her country in Othar as a goodwill ambassador. They fail to tell Sunny the truth: She is going to Othar to become a concubine in the emir's harem.

• Off to Othar goes naive Sunny. Black-clad ululating women appear; they are framed to sound like a chorus of screeching camels. Cackling like crows, the clad-in-black women fawn over Sunny. The demure appearance of Arab women as mute, uneducated objects in black distorts. Highly educated Gulf business women, for example, are actively engaged in helping to build the economies of their countries. In two of Saudi Arabia's major cities, Jeddah and Riyadh, 6,000-plus commercial licenses are issued to professional women. Though a quarter of a million of working women still face "unusual challenges—they cannot drive, nor may they have any direct contact with male workers"—they make full use of technologies. Many business dealings are done over the phone, by fax, and e-mail. Other working women teach, function as nurses, and get into "accounting, banking, or journalism."[132]

• At the emir's secluded desert palace, Sunny is served Arab cuisine; she grimaces. She prefers "tuna salad." Arab soldiers grunt and ogle her. Feeling trapped Sunny shouts, "I want to see a school, a hospital, a daycare center."

• Some of Othar's Arabs revolt. Storming the palace, they fire at fellow Arabs. Why this uprising? Because their emir wants to wed Sunny!

Finis: Sunny escapes Othar. Back in Oregon, she runs for office and is elected to Congress. In the nation's capitol, reporters tag Sunny's safe return, "Sunnygate." When Sunny appears before a Senate committee, she cites the Declaration of Independence, advising the senators to avoid Arab dignitaries. Declares Sunny, we should think twice before "inviting foreign bigshots to the White House."

Dialogue: Mingling with Othar's Arabs at the Safari Club are hookers, motorcyclists, Japanese businessmen, and homosexuals. Quips a cop, "I guess it's one of those gay-Arab-biker-sushi bars." Seeing an Arab guard wearing a kuffiyeh, Sunny says: "I have the napkins that match your hat."

Note: Prior to *Protocol*'s release, Ron Lahoud, a legal affairs staff assistant with the American-Arab Anti-Discrimination Committee (ADC), arrived on the set to portray one of the "Arab-looking" extras. Costumers placed a scruffy T-shirt on Lahoud's head to simulate a kuffiyeh; he was directed to "look sinister." Upset, Lahoud contacted ADC; the organization lobbied Warner Bros. to make major alterations in the movie. Yet, the studio kept the scenario intact, agreeing to make only two minor changes. The studio changed the country's name to Othar, from el-Ohtar, which, spelled backward, is rathole. Though not significant, this minor agreement marked the first time Arab-Americans successfully negotiated changes with a Hollywood studio. See *Executive Decision* (1996).

Ironically, following pre-release protests by the ADC, producer Anthea Sylbert wrote to the organization, saying, "*Protocol* will be a film you will not be ashamed to take your children to." Affirmed Goldie Hawn, "I've got kids, and I want them to make movies families can see. I feel the responsibility to the people who see my films."[133] On 27 January 1987, three years after *Protocol*'s release, the American Committee for the Tel Aviv Foundation honored Hawn in Los Angeles for her patronage of Israel's Tel Aviv Cinematheque.

• Prior to, during, and after the filming of *Protocol*, Americans of Arab heritage and others criticized Goldie Hawn and her colleagues for perpetuating Arab stereotypes. Responded Hawn, "The one thing my dad always said to me was maintain a sense of humor about yourself. Some people [meaning Arab-Americans] don't have the same sense of humor, I guess."[134]

• *Protocol* was filmed in Tunisia. Tunisian film producer Tarek Ben Ammar, who acted as a go-between for executive producer Hawn and producer Sylbert, tried to convince them to eliminate scenes mocking Islam and Arabs. "The use of stereotypes is first-degree simplicity and dangerous," he said. Ammar's concerns were ignored.[135]

Puppet Master II (1990), PAR. *Elizabeth MacClellan, Collin Bernsen, Steve Welles.* CAMEOS, EGYPTIANS

An evil Egyptian is responsible for dispatching deadly puppets to kill people.

Scene: The camera reveals the diabolical puppet master contemplating his creepy puppet creations. He recalls his younger days, when he first discovered the dark arts. Cut to a wall poster stating: "1912 Cairo Exposition." Abruptly, a flashback to Egypt, circa 1912. On screen, a souk, a camel, some pyramids, and the exposition grounds.

• Inside one of the exhibition's tent, a young puppeteer's marionettes are performing "Faust." Arabs in attendance are bored with the performance. Cut to a bearded Cairo sorcerer; he wears a dark headdress. Eyes flashing malevolently, the evil Egyptian glares at the puppets. Suddenly, the impresario's marionettes burst into flame.

• Inside the sorcerer's tent, the Egyptian shows the young puppet master one of his demonic puppets, covered with green scales. "It's horrible," says the puppeteer, pulling away. "Its design reflects my taste," replies the Egyptian. The sorcerer offers to teach the puppet master how to create similar "horrible" puppets. At first, the young impresario balks, saying, "I'm an artist, not a sorcerer." The Egyptian reminds him that his last show failed, that he should "think of the children." The puppeteer relents, falling under the Egyptian's spell.

• Flash forward. Soon—all because of a vile Cairo sorcerer—the young impresario's puppets slay everyone in sight, even children.

Puppet Master III: Toulon's Revenge (1991), PAR. *Guy Rolfe, Walter Gotell.* CAMEOS, EGYPTIANS

Appearing once again is the Egyptian sorcerer from *Puppet Master II.*

Scene: Berlin, 1941. Toulon, the puppet master, eludes pursuing Nazis, telling his puppets, "Look my friends, I got us home."

• Prior to the conclusion, flashback to 1912. Toulon recalls his encounter with the Egyptian sorcerer. The camera reveals the pyramids, and an Arab atop a camel. Cut to the poster: "1912 Cairo Exhibition." The Egyptians promote Toulon as "Europe's Greatest Puppet Master." As Toulon's puppets perform, the Egyptian occultist, eyes glaring, appears. This flashback serves to remind viewers that an evil Egyptian taught Toulon "the black arts."

Pursuit to Algiers (1945), RKO. *Basil Rathbone, Nigel Bruce.* CAMEOS, EGYPTIANS

A one-liner points to an Egyptian thief.

Scene: Holmes and Watson are protecting a Ruritanian king from non-Arab shipboard assassins. Yet, Holmes is warned, "Then there's this Egyptian fellow, Hassan. He's been suspected for years by the police in two continents as the largest receiver of stolen goods."

Note: In Sherlock Holmes' *Dressed to Kill* (1946), the master sleuth contests three villains, including Hamid, a deadly knife-thrower. With the exception of his name, and the reference to Islam, "Mohamet's coffin suspended between heaven and hell," Hamid performs like his criminal British cohorts.

Putney Swope (1969), Cinema V. *Arnold Johnson, Mel Brooks, Antonio Fargas.* SP: Robert Downey Sr. CAMEOS

This dark satire knocks nuns, orphans, blacks, liberals, and Arabs.

Scene: "Truth and Soul, Inc.," a Madison Avenue ad agency, is run by an African-American, Mr. Swope (Johnson). One of Swope's employees is tagged "the Arab" (Fargas). The Arab, who wears sunglasses and a headdress, tries to seduce the firm's secretary.

• Noting his North African garb, someone asks the Arab, "Who do you think you are, Lawrence of Nigeria?" A friend asks Swope, "Where you been, man?" Quips Swope, "Mecca."

• In the end, Swope gives all his employees, except the Arab, a share of the firm's profits. Furious, the Arab tosses a torch, igniting a container holding wads of money.

Note: Why tag an unruly employee "the Arab?" No other characters are so labeled.

The Queen of Babylon (1956), a.k.a. The Courtesan of Babylon and Semiramis, TCF. *Rhonda Fleming, Ricardo Montalban, Roldano Lupi, Carlo Ninchi.* MAIDENS

Evil Assyrians vs. Assyrians, a Chaldean clan, and Babylonians. The lovely Semiramis, a Babylonian farm maiden, becomes queen of Babylon.

Scene: Ninth century BC. Assur (Lupi) and his Assyrian troops conquer Babylon (present-day Iraq), suppressing its peoples.

• Assyrian soldiers move to capture Amal (Montalban), a wounded Chaldean freedom fighter. On seeing the injured soldier, Semiramis (Fleming) hides Amal in her farm, nursing the warrior back to health.

• An Assyrian soldier finds out that Semiramis has sheltered Amal. Furious, he beats her. Semiramis and other Babylonians are marched off and imprisoned in the palace dungeon. Soon, the Babylonian women emerge from the prison wearing harem garb; they perform dazzling dances for the Assyrian ruler and his men.

• To prevent fellow hostages from being tortured, Semiramis agrees become a royal concubine; she will wed the Assyrian King Assur (Lupi). But the king's cousin, Prime Minister Sibari (Ninchi), poisons Assur. Sibari then moves to burn Semiramis at the stake.

• In time, the invigorated Amal and his Chaldean comrades attack the castle, crumbling Sibari and his cohorts. Amal installs Semiramis upon Babylon's throne, declaring: "The tyranny of Assur the Assyrian has been destroyed. Law and justice has been restored."

Note: This movie's Assyrians, Babylonians, and Chaldeans look alike. Antagonists and protagonists wear Crusader-type breastplates and helmets.

Queen of the Jungle (1935), Screen Attractions. 12 episodes. *Mary Kornman, Reed Howes*. In late 1935, the studio edited this serial, releasing it as a feature film with the same name. CLIFFHANGERS

Brave Arabs appear for about three minutes. See episodes 9, 10, and 11.

Scene: Appearing in Africa is the heroine, Joan Lawrence, or the Jungle Woman (Kornman). She was reared and adopted by natives.

• Assisting Mr. Lawrence and Joan's beau, Dave (Howes), is an Arab leader, fluent in three languages, Arabic, Swahili, and English. The Arab and his five aides help Mr. Lawrence find Joan, his "lost daughter." Joan, along with her father and Dave, set out to locate "the greatest radium deposit in the world." Opposing them are jungle natives, Western criminals, sorcerers, and high priests.

• Episode 11. After the Arab locates Joan and Dave, his Arabs shelter the couple from the villains, then give them horses.

• The final chapter. Episode 12 begins with this screen credit: "Befriended by a peaceful tribe of Arabian hunters…" Cut to the jungle chieftain about to terminate Dave, Joan, and Mr. Lawrence. Arabs to the rescue; they arrive in the nick of time, saving the protagonists' lives. The Arab leader shoots the chieftain; his men bring down all the other culprits.

The Queen of Sheba (1921), FOX. Silent. *Betty Blythe, Fritz Lieber, Nell Craig, George Raymond Nye*. *NS. Notes by Harry Lee Holland in MAG (892–94). MAIDENS

A genuine Arab heroine; no Arab villains. Israelites vs. Israelites.

The tenth century BC. Sheba's kingdom, "located on the southwest tip of Saudi Arabia (today's Yemen)." The biblical queen of Sheba (Blythe) rules in golden splendor over the southern rim of the Arabian peninsula. Chaperoned by slaves, Queen Sheba presents "four white Arab steeds" and other gifts to Judea's King Solomon (Lieber). Why is Sheba so generous? She wants Solomon to become her "ally." One of Solomon's wives, Vashti (Craig), disputes Sheba's claim that her steeds are "the fastest in the world." To prove her point, Vashti challenges Sheba in a "chariot race." Sheba wins, beds Solomon and then returns home to give birth to their son. When the boy is four years of age, Sheba sends him to Solomon, his father. But Solomon's brother Adonijah (Nye) considers the youth a threat. Thus, he kidnaps the boy and moves to overthrow Solomon. Sheba learns "of the revolt [and] leads her army," rescuing her son and Solomon. Sheba and the boy return safely home.

Note: In *She* (1925), Betty Blythe starred as Ayesha, a 2,000-year-old queen who maintains her beauty by "bathing in fire." Blythe also appeared in *Chu Chin Chow* (1925), "a lavish Arabian fantasy." The *Chu Chin Chow* of 1934, a talkie, features Anna May Wong.

The Queen of Sheba (1953), Oro. *Leonora Ruffo, Gino Cervi, Franco Silva.* Italian, dubbed in English. MAIDENS

Unlike the 1921 *Queen of Sheba*, this version presents Arabs as idolaters ("holy hyenas") and war-mongers who despise Christians and Israelites.

Scene: Intones the narrator, Sheba's (Ruffo) "Arabian desert" is "a strange nation. [The people are] on a path of death and destruction." The Arabs trod a destructive path, says the narrator, because they want to reach "the walls of Jerusalem." In Jerusalem, the camera reveals the peacemaker, Solomon (Cervi). He proposes not "war and hate," rather "peace and love."

• When Solomon visits Sheba's desert kingdom, he sees high priests worshiping not "God," but an inane "stone idol" that bans "human love." Though Solomon falls in love with Sheba, they cannot wed until the "mountain speaks."

• Sheba's evil general Kabael (Silva) crucifies innocents on crosses.

• As Sheba's ladies-in-waiting entertain fellow maidens, the queen bathes in gazelle's milk.

• A wrestling match. "Babu, the Assyrian Tiger" vs. "Eli," the Israelite. Sheba's attendants bet on Babu. Eli triumphs.

• Sheba loves Solomon. But, thinking he has betrayed her, she declares war, attacking "Jerusalem, the heart of Israel." Easily, the Israelites defeat "Sheba's hordes."

• Finally, "the mountain speaks"; Sheba may wed Solomon. Unexpectedly, an avalanche. Scores perish in the "Valley of Silence."

Dialogue: Sheba's men are tagged "a pack of dogs," and "holy hyenas."

Quick Change (1990), WB. *Bill Murray, Geena Davis, Tony Shalhoub.* SP: Howard Franklin. CAMEOS

Never hail a cab driven by a mindless Arab.

Scene: New York City. Rushing to reach the airport, Grimm (Murray) and Phyliss (Davis) flag down a cab. The driver (Shalhoub) listens to Arab music, which annoys Grimm. "To the airport, please," says Grimm. The driver responds to Grimm's request, speaking Arabic. Why in Arabic? Because this cabby does not understand or "speak a word of English." Upset, Grimm and Phyliss shout at the driver: "To the goddamn airport! What da ya got, shit in your ears?" The confused dense cabby speeds through a red light; Grimm and Phyliss rush out of the cab.

• Some policemen arrive; they ask the driver about his two passengers. In Arabic, the cabby mumbles, then begins to cry. Next, he falls to his knees, begging the officers to arrest him. Though one officer "knows the [Arabic] language," he and his pal opt to cuff the dispirited cabby.

Note: Why not present a real New York Arabic-speaking cabby? Most speak two or three languages, including English.

Radio Patrol (1937), UNI. 12 episodes. *Grant Withers, Frank Lackteen, Dick Botiller, Mickey Rentschier.* CLIFFHANGERS, EGYPTIANS

Radio Patrol vs. a US industrialist and Egyptian-Iranians. Every episode shows Egyptian-Iranian villains attempting to steal our "secret formula for flexible [bulletproof] steel." Should they secure the formula, the Egyptians-Iranians would become "masters of the universe."

Scene: In the United States, two "Egyptian representatives of the Iranian government," Zutta (Botiller) and Thata (Lackteen), exit the "Iranian embassy." They meet with and offer the inventor of flexible steel, Mr. Adams, millions for his formula. Retorts Adams, "The secret of flexible steel controls the peace of the world. I'd be a traitor to mankind if I turned it over to you at any price."

• The Egyptian-Iranians drive to an American city resembling an Arab screen souk—the "Egyptian Quarter." Cut to the villains about to leave the "Cairo Hotel." They nab an American, roll him up into a carpet, then toss their hostage onto a "Cairo Rug Company" truck.

• A typical American boy, Pinky Adams (Rentschler), observes Arab-Americans wearing Arab garb walking through the "Egyptian Quarter" and patronizing Egyptian-Iranian shops. Pinky asks this serial's hero, Radio Patrol's Pat O'Hara (Withers): "Is this Chinatown?" Grunts O'Hara, "This is the Egyptian Quarter. There's some places in here that make you think you're not even in America." Abruptly, O'Hara begins beating up two Egyptians.

• Aware that an American businessman is keenly interested in "Egyptology," Thata gives him a gift, "a mummy's tomb from the museum of Iran." Purrs Thata, "This is in appreciation for our friendly relations." Then Thata pulls a gun and pistol-whips the American. The message here? Beware an Egyptian-Iranian bearing gifts.

• Thanks to O'Hara's heroics, Thata perishes. Sighs the American businessman, "Many people hated him (Thata). He deserved to be killed. I wish I had done it... He is the man who destroyed my mind."

Finis: O'Hara's men round up Egyptian-Iranians and other crooks. And, the secret steel formula remains secure.

The Rage of Paris (1921), UNI. Silent. *Jean DuPont, Jack Perrin.* *NS. Notes from NYT. CAMEOS, VILLAINS

The heroine, Miss Du Pont, rushes off to Arabia. She intends to link up with her ex-sweetheart. Though her cruel husband tracks her, he "is killed in a sandstorm by an Arab who seeks to steal his camel to escape the storm."

Raiders of the Desert (1941), UNI. *Richard Arlen, Andy Devine, Maria Montez, Turhan Bey.* SHEIKHS

Mr. Jones' pals have "fun" trouncing a sheikh's undesirable Arabs.

Scene: A New York harbor. The protagonists, Hammer (Arlen) and Dick (Devine) steal aboard a ship. Quips a crew member, "We ain't goin' to California, we're goin' to Arabia!"

• Arabia. As soon as passenger Alice Evans (Montez) departs the ship and touches Arab soil, hagglers harass her. Alice seeks safety at "Libertahd," a walled, modern US-type city complete with hair salon, movie theater, clothier, and medical building. Greeting her is Mr. Jones, the city's founder, who explains, "These people were slaves to their rulers." The camera reveals evil Sheikh Khalifa's (Bey) tent camp, outside Libertahd.

• The newly-arrived Dick cautions Abdullah, his cab driver, "This better be a beautiful trip, yahoodie." In Arabic, yahood means Jew.

• Sheikh Khalifa, a "dark and evil man," intends "to take over the city." The sheikh warns Mr. Jones, "Give up this wild scheme, this modern metropolis is in the middle of the desert." Retorts Mr. Jones, "[Why don't you treat your fellow Arabs] as civilized human beings instead of as slaves. Why keep your people ignorant and uneducated?"

• An Arab moves to knife Mr. Jones in the back. Wham! Hammer floors the assailant. Next, Hammer and Dick punch out two more Arabs. Dick tags Arabs "nitwits" and "Ayrabs."

• Hoping to assist Libertahd's residents, two of Jones' Western supporters drive off to deliver needed weapons to the city. Khalifa's Arabs kill them, securing the guns.

• Khalifa's men hide the stolen weapons in Ahmed's shop. Moments later, Dick and Hammer check out Ahmed's. Quips Dick, "There's something in those sacks besides coffee." He and Hammer slug the Arab guards, and run off with the guns.

• Arab vs. Arab. Pro-Western khaki-clad troops ride up to a nearby mountain top, dismount and machine-gun Khalifa's Arabs.

• After Khalifa is captured, Dick, Hammer, and Mr. Jones' Arabs link up, terminating the sheikh's remaining cohorts. Quips Hammer, "It was a lot of fun while it lasted."

Raiders of the Lost Ark (1981), PAR. *Harrison Ford, Karen Allen, John Rhys-Davies.* SP: Lawrence Kasdan. D: Steven Spielberg. Filmed in Tunisia. See Spielberg's *Indiana Jones and the Last Crusade* (1989). EGYPTIANS

Egypt, 1936. Good and evil Egyptians appear in this action adventure thriller. Archeologist-adventurer Indiana Jones tangles with dastardly Nazis and their Egyptian cohorts. *Raiders of the Lost Ark* was selected by the American Film Institute (AFI) as one of America's best 100 movies. The movie was not only one of 1981's top ten money-making films, it is also one of the biggest blockbusters of all time.

Scene: Introducing an Egyptian cur boasting a patch over one eye; he and his cohorts spy for the Nazis.

• Throughout, scenes reveal Egyptian beggars and laborers.

• A huge black-masked Egyptian confronts Indy (Ford). The action-site resembles a set for a Hollywood Cowboys and Indians shoot-out. The tall Egyptian swishes his huge saber; Indy casually draws his gun and shoots him dead. Audiences roared. This shoot-'em-up scene is embraced by notables such as Oprah Winfrey. The action clip was featured on Oprah's 16 June 1998 CBS-TV special, commemorating the AFI's top 100 films. One year earlier, in March 1997, Oprah interviewed Harrison Ford on her show. My friend, Michael Singh, who saw this segment, heard Oprah telling Ford, "My favorite movie scene" of all time is where "you shoot that Arab." Oprah chuckled, then emulated in part, the shoot-'em-up. Next, she showed viewers the actual clip of Indy shooting dead the Egyptian. The studio audience applauded.

• Evil Egyptians attack. Indy's spunky female companion Marion (Allen) grabs a frying pan, flooring several Egyptians, shooting others.

• Says Indy's Egyptian ally, Sallah (Rhys-Davies), "You're my good friend." Briefly, Sallah introduces Indy to fellow Egyptians, saying, "These are my friends. These are my family."

• Indy's love interest, Marion, is attractive, outspoken, and active. Conversely, Sallah's wife is mute, passive, and homely.

• Sallah directs Egyptian youths to rush into a coffee house; the boys rescue Indy from the "enemy." Later, villagers protect Indy from the Nazis. As Indy rides off on a white horse, Egyptian villagers cheer! Later, Sallah rescues Indy from a snake pit.

Note: *Raiders of the Lost Ark* focuses on evil Germans trying to unearth the long-lost Ark of the Covenant. Supposedly, the army that possesses the Ark will become invincible. Does it make any sense for director Spielberg to show Indy and Marion beating up and killing Egyptians?

• Filmmaker George Lucas "takes seriously the notion that entertainers have an obligation to promote positive moral values in their works. Talking earnestly about what artists 'teach' with their creations," Lucas "criticizes himself for the scene played for laughs in *Raiders of the Lost Ark* where Indiana Jones drops his bullwhip and casually guns down an Arab swordsman."[136]

Raiders of the Seven Seas (1953), UA. *John Payne, Donna Reed.*
CAMEOS, MAIDENS, SHEIKHS

A swashbuckler and his pirates overpower a Spanish fleet. Appearing briefly is an obese Moroccan sultan and his docile maidens.

Scene: Opening frames display a Moroccan palace and a fat sultan possessing "the finest taste in the world and the most ungenerous mind." Watching his harem maidens parade, the sultan barks, "Now, which ungrateful baggage" dared dally with my "red-bearded captain?" (Payne). The sultan suspects the captain has seduced "a pretty young flower that he was about to wed." The ruler tells palace guards to nab the rogue. Abruptly, the captain departs, stating that "Tangier has become a coast to avoid." Later, after the rogue falls for a Spanish countess (Reed), he declares, "The sultan's harem has just faded from my memory."

The Razor's Edge (1946), TCF. *Tyrone Power, Ann Sheridan.* SP: Lamar
Trotti. CAMEOS, VILLAINS

Protagonist Larry Darrell (Power) moves to assist a despondent friend, Sophie MacDonald (Sheridan). As Sophie lost her husband and child in an auto accident, she uses drugs and alcohol, turning to lowlifes. Among the brutes abusing her are Arabs.

In this four-minute scene, Arab music underscores the action. In Paris, Larry enters a seedy club. Near the door, a bearded Arab smokes a pipe. Cut to a woman lounging near a fez-wearing Arab. A tall Arab waiter appears, followed by another woman lounging with another fez-wearing Arab. Larry spots the drunken Sophie reclining on a couch; seated next to her is an ugly Arab. Larry rushes to her side, saying, "Come Sophie, let's get out of here. Come along, Sophie." Too drunk to stand, Sophie falls to the floor. "Come with me now," insists Larry. Abruptly, Sophie's Arab escort intervenes, smashing his lit cigarette into Larry's neck. A fight ensues. The club's Arabs, including a thug tagged Ali Hassan, join in. Arab music swells as Arabs pummel Larry, then toss him outside into the rainy street.

Reds (1981), PAR. *Warren Beatty, Diane Keaton.* Co-W, P, D: Beatty. Beatty won the Academy Award for Best Director. At times, Beatty mixes reality with fiction, interviewing people such as writer Henry Miller. CAMEOS, VILLAINS

1917. This romantic revolutionary tale about the American journalist John Reed runs 195 minutes. Still, actor, producer, director, and co-writer Beatty manages to set aside five minutes of footage to vilify Islam. Beatty projects Arab Muslims fanatics who hate America and declare a "Holy War."

Scene: Captivated by the 1917 Bolshevik uprising, John Reed (Beatty) hurries off to Russia. Asked to assist Bolsheviks, Reed travels to "the Middle East." His objective? To "inspire a revolution among the peoples." Cut to screaming bedouins wielding sabers. In the background, camels and tents. Filling the screen, Uncle Sam's effigy, aflame.

• A mosque, decorated with hammer and sickle banners. As Reed addresses the crowd, unruly Arab Muslims wave their sabers, shouting "Jihad" (Holy War). "What's that [screaming] for?" asks Reed. "They are supporting your call for a Holy War of Islamic people against the Western infidels," explains a devious Muslim. Obviously, the Muslim translators dupe Reed, altering his speech. Reed never once calls for a Holy War.

Note: One fact remains constant. Whether the year is 1917 or 2001, the vast majority of Russians are Eastern Orthodox Christians. Interestingly, Beatty does not display Orthodox fanatics torching Uncle Sam in 1917. Nor does he show hammer and sickle banners draping a Russian Orthodox church. Such false anti-Christian scenes would be as defamatory and as inaccurate as Beatty's anti-Muslim footage.

Renegades (1930), FOX. *Warner Baxter, Myrna Loy, Noah Berry, Bella Lugosi.* P: William Fox. D: Victor Fleming. *NS. Notes from *Harrison's Reports* (25 October 1930). SHEIKHS

Four brave Western Christian legionnaires with questionable pasts "redeem" themselves by crushing the Arab Muslim enemy. The motif of a few legionnaires routing scores of white-robed bedouins surfaces especially in films from the late 1920s to the early 1930s.

Scene: In Morocco, Eleanore (Loy), a female agent reminiscent of Mata Hari, is a German spy. She manages to obtain valuable information from Deucalion (Baxter), a French officer. Disgraced, the officer joins the legion.

• Fast forward. The treacherous Eleanore has now "becomes the chattel of the Arabs"; she supports Marabout (Lugosi), an Arab sheikh relishing torture of Western women.

• In the throne room, a black slave fans Marabout. The sheikh's cohort enters, refusing to torture prisoners-of-war.

• The clad-in-harem garb Eleanore threatens to love another man. Marabout laughs at her, saying, "We [Arabs] don't fight over women. If I get tired of you, I give you back to him. What do I care?"

• Four legionnaires with a past, including Deucalion, link up with the sheikh. The legionnaires assemble an Arab army to fight fellow Frenchmen. The sheikh vows to exterminate the French and torture the survivors. Just in time, Deucalion remembers that he is still a Frenchman. Deucalion "turns his machine guns against the sheikh's Arabs, routing them."

Finis: The four previously disgraced men receive medals of bravery.

Requiem for a Secret Agent (1965), Intercontinental. *Stewart Granger, Georgia Moll.* S, SP: Sergio Sollima. Shot in Morocco. VILLAINS, MAIDENS

This spy drama shows Moroccan lowlifes assisting European thugs.

Scene: In Tangier, a mute Moroccan wearing dark glasses tracks a British agent, John O'Brien. In a public square, two Moroccan vendors approach O'Brien. One tries to sell a trinket for "20 dinars." O'Brien says, "No." The Arab insists, finally getting his asking price. O'Brien sighs, then watches male dancers perform. Abruptly, he turns and shoots his Moroccan pursuer.

• A club displays Betty Lou (Moll), an Arab stripper. When Betty Lou removes her black attire, scenes of a bullfight are superimposed over her midriff.

• O' Brien arrives at his European chief's office. He sees, sprawled over a desk, his dead boss, a knife in the gut. O'Brien goes to leave; Alexi, a Polish assassin, shoots him.

• Cut to marines guarding the movie's super-agent, the "old man." Concerned about the deaths of O'Brien and his boss, the old man says, "Our agents know all about Chinese, Russian, and Cuban espionage. However, this time we're up against something different. In Morocco we're fighting against... a private network of mercenaries who sell themselves to the highest bidder... We have only one possibility in fighting these SOBs—John Merrill (Granger), better known as 'Bingo.'"

• As soon as Bingo arrives in Tangier he teams up with a British agent, Eric. They go and watch Betty Lou perform her strip act. When Bingo goes to the dancer's dressing room, he spots two of Alexi's cohorts; he shoots them. Later, Alexi fatally tosses Betty Lou down the steps.

• Moroccan thugs appear, cornering Bingo and Eric. One Moroccan wields a heavy chain, another clasps a knife. Their leader, who boasts a scar over one eye, barks orders in Arabic. The Arabs close in, preparing to damage Bingo. Instantly, he drops them.

• Bingo meets with El-Bar, the chubby Moroccan who dispatched the thugs. Wham! The agent punches him out as well as more Moroccans.

Finis: Bingo brings down all the villains.

The Rescuers (1977), Disney. Animated. *Voices of Bob Newhart, Eva Gabor.* CAMEOS

Gallant rescuers, all mice, best an evil witch.

Scene: The UN lobby. Arabs clad in thobes and fezzes are among the delegates reviewing the day's schedule. Cut to an international gathering of mice, including a white-thobed Arab mouse speaking French. The mice pop up from the delegates' briefcases, then proceed to their annual "Rescue Aid Society" meeting.

• The "Rescue Aid" mice, including Arab and Turkish ones, come from "all corners of the globe." The international group of mice agree to rescue an orphan girl held captive by a swamp witch. Bernard and Bianca are selected to free the girl, which they do.

Note: In the sequel, *The Rescuers Down Under* (1991), Bernard and Bianca rescue an Australian youth. Among the "Rescue Aid" members, a white-thobed Arab delegate.

The Rest Cure (1936), a.k.a. We're in the Legion Now (1937), Grand National. *Reginald Denny, Vince Barnett, Esther Ralston, Eleanor Hunt, Claudia Dell, Franciso Maran, Robert Frazer.* The first independent American movie shot in color. VILLAINS

Affable crooks and their legionnaire pals liquidate burnoosed Arab "natives." Arabs try to nab Western maidens. Producers use stock newsreel footage of desert Arab villages.

Scene: The American gangsters, Dan Linton (Denny) and Spike Connover (Barnett), join the Foreign Legion. As they peel onions in "El Jazir," Morocco, Spike quips, "No wonder the Ayrabs can't stand up to them."

• In the souk, Arab merchants haggle. One tries to swindle Louise (Ralston), a legion officer's wife. The Arab demands "100" for an item; Louise pays only "50." When Louise tells her husband that El Jazir is "colorful," He retorts, "[It's] colorful in Hades, too."

• Arabs as non-whites: Spike spots Honey (Hunt), a US entertainer, sighing, "This is the first white woman I've seen in months."

• Dan notices that some of Abdul's "natives" are about to abduct Honey and Louise. He warns, "Here comes trouble." Counters Abdul, "Surround the infidels and carry them off." But thanks to Dan and Spike, Abdul's brigands fail.

• Armed with nitroglycerine and brandishing rifles, Arabs on horseback charge the legion post. They intend to "blow... to *shaitan* [Satan]" the heroines and the legionnaires. But, a dense "native" mistakenly dumps the "nitroglycerine bomb"into Abdul's camp. Boom! The explosion terminates Abdul's Arabs.

• Treatment of Islam: The villain, Abdul Ben Abou (Maran) moves to murder Captain Henri Rillette (Frazer). Boasts Abdul, I have "rifles and ammunition for the faithful... Pass the word among the faithful... Allah be praised."

Note: Metropolitan Picture's also released a Spanish language version of this movie, entitled, *De le sartén al fuego* (Out of the frying pan, into the fire). The Spanish version was "shot simultaneously with *The Rest Cure* and screened in Mexico as *La legion extranjera.*[137]

The Return of Chandu (1934), Principal. 12 episodes. *Bela Lugosi, Maria Alba.* CLIFFHANGERS, MAIDENS, EGYPTIANS, RECOMMENDED

The same year *The Return of Chandu* was released, the studio edited this serial, transforming it into two one-hour feature films. The first feature, also titled *The Return of Chandu* (1934), is comprised of footage extracted from the first part of the serial; the second feature, *Chandu on the Magic Island* (1934), is composed of scenes from the latter half of the serial. See my notes on *Chandu the Magician* (1932).

A lovely Egyptian weds the American champion.

Scene: The action occurs on the Magic Island of Lemuria and in Beverly Hills, California. The Black Magic Cult of Ubasti is determined to nab and terminate the beautiful Egyptian heroine, Princess Nadji (Alba). The Ubasti believe that once Nadji is extinguished they can conquer the world. Standing in their way is Frank Chandler, a US magician known as Chandu (Lugosi). As Nadji's beau and protector, Chandler staves off the "man-eating dark savages."

• Nadji explains that someone in Egypt tried to kidnap her. Assures her American hostess, "Remember, you're in California now, not in Egypt. Nothing can harm you here." Abruptly, Ubasti villains move to abduct the princess.

• The spear-wielding Ubasti nab and whisk Nadji off to their Magic Island. She tells her kidnappers, "I am a princess of Egypt. I shall not cry for help."

• The kidnaped Nadji realizes the Ubasti are also intent on killing her beau, Chandler. The princess meets with the Ubasti grand priest, offering to sacrifice her life provided he frees Chandler and his American friends.

• Chandler escapes. Entering the "Gods of Black Magic" chamber, he frees his beloved Nadji. Next, Chandler recites an ancient chant. Presto. The chamber walls collapse, crushing the Ubasti priest and his cohorts.

Finis: The reunited couple returns to America; their engagement is announced. Reporters flock around the cheerful duo. Later, Chandler and Nadji are alone; they kiss.

Return of the Killer Tomatoes! (1988), NL. *John Astin.* CAMEOS

The movie begins with a flashback of anxious citizens, including a white-thobed Arab armed with a sword, chasing off the huge attacking tomatoes. This same scene appears near the end of *Attack of the Killer Tomatoes!* (1977).

Return of the Pink Panther (1975), UA. *Peter Sellers.* CAMEOS

Muslims revere a diamond.

Scene: Opening frames of this fourth *Panther* film displays the mythical kingdom of "Lugash." Cut to a mosque; the imam calls the faithful to morning prayer. Cut to the interior of the Royal Museum. "For over a thousand years," explains a thobe-wearing guide boasting a red fez, "our nation's religious symbol" has been "the Pink Panther, the largest and most famous diamond in the world."

• Mute bellydancers perform.

Finis: After Inspector Clouseau (Sellers) recovers the stolen "Panther" diamond, he is "decorated by General Wadafi." Note the resemblance to Khadafi.

Note: Among the settings, a souk, nightclub, desert fort, and hotel. Scenes in Lugash's hotel are accompanied by "As Time Goes By," the classic tune from *Casablanca* (1942).

Ride 'Em Cowboy (1942), UNI. *Bud Abbott, Lou Costello.* CAMEOS

See *Arabia* (1922). Ella Fitzgerald croons, "A Tisket, A Tasket."

Oriental music complements cowboy Lou Costello's dream. In the dream, a vulgar mystic wearing a turban asks Lou, "Would you like to have your palm read?" Lou nods. Laughing, the man soaks his brush in red paint, paints Lou's hand red, then vanishes.

Note: American Indians appear as knife-wielding buffoons.

Riding the Edge (1989), Kodiak. *Lyman Ward, Raphael Sparge, Catherine Mary Stewart, Asher Sarfati.* D: James Fargo. VILLAINS, MAIDENS, WORST LIST

An American teenager vs. Arab terrorists. Mostly, Israeli actors appear as Arab villains. Director James Fargo portrays Tarek, the main Arab terrorist. Also see US teens liquidating Arabs in *Iron Eagle* (1986) and *Paradise* (1981).

Scene: Arabia's desert. As the sun rises, the call to prayer is heard. Cut to "Raycor International," an American research lab guarded by Arabs. Working in the lab is Dr. John Harmon (Ward), a specialist whose "microprocessor [enables] solar satellites to work." Explains a Raycor executive, "The country that flies the first operational satellite is going to have enormous geopolitical power." Suddenly, Arab terrorists wearing fatigues and white burnooses invade Raycor, killing the guards. The leader, Tarek (Fargo), whisks off Dr. Harmon.

• In America, a Raycor executive asks, "Are we going to give in to these terrorists, or are we going to let John Harmon fry?" Dr. Harmon's teenage son, Matthew (Sparge), volunteers to act as Raycor's courier. Sighs Mrs. Harmon, "He's only a boy."

• Matthew arrives in Arabia, carrying the special "chips" that Tarek demanded. Cut to an Arab assassin. Abruptly, Maggie (Stewart), "an American customs agent," kills him. Next, Dean Stratling, a double-dealing Raycor executive, welcomes Matthew. Dean, too, wants the "chips"; he intends to sell them to an East German heavy.

• At an Arab restaurant, a bellydancer performs. Observing her moves is Captain Moussa (Sarfati), a decent but inept Arab.

• Donning Arab garb, Matthew and Maggie hop into a limo and head for Tarek's desert camp. As their car maneuvers through the souk, complete with vendors, animals, and dancers, Arabs gape at the couple. Boom. An Arab sets off a car bomb.

• The souk displays a unique hawker. After exhibiting two live white rats, the Arab places them inside his white pantaloons. Abruptly, his pants turn blood red. Then, the Arab brandishes before his audience—two dead white rats.

• Inside a crowded tent, a "Holy Man" requests money. A woman passes a basket.

• Ruthless Tarek tosses innocents off a helicopter.

• Matthew hops onto his motorcycle as the Lone Ranger would mount Silver. He rides off to rescue his father. Maggie assists him.

• Matthew's cycle needs some petrol. Not only does a scruffy Arab attendant use an antiquated hand crank to fill the gas tank, but he also overcharges Matthew.

• Matthew accidentally breaks a worthless pot. A hideous Arab woman screams, demanding 150 dinars (at least $150). The woman, thanks to Maggie who knows "how to deal with these people," settles for 25 dinars.

• A boat en route to the terrorists' camp. Three Arabs try but fail to kill Matthew. In time, Matthew saves a boy from drowning.

• Pointing to a cafe, Maggie cautions Matthew, "They won't serve women without a hassle." Maggie, a student of "ethnology," explains her vocation: "[It's] the study of technologically primitive societies... [just] look around you. I'm in heaven."

• At Tarek's camp, Maggie employs karate and floors several Arabs. Matthew drops other terrorists. He and his father ride off on the cycle. Warns dad, "There are more than a dozen men out there. We won't get very far." Yet, they escape. How? Because the boy who nearly drowned sets off an explosion, puncturing a huge dam. All the Arab villains perish.

Note: While perusing *TV Guide*, I came across this synopsis of *Riding the Edge*: "A high-school student ventures to Africa to rescue his dad from terrorists." Though this description said Africa, not Arabia, I decided to review this movie because of three key words: "high-school student," "rescue," and "terrorists."

The Road to Love (1916), PAR. Silent. *Lenore Ulrich, Colin Chase, Herschell Mayall, Joe Massey.* MAIDENS, SHEIKHS

Local and national censorship boards prohibited interracial romances, yet *The Road to Love* presents the American hero marrying an Arab woman. From the beginning, right after movie boards were established, they dictated that the Western white hero could not wed the "colored" other—Indians, blacks, Mexicans, or Arabs. In the real world, in 1909, a US district court in St. Louis, Missouri, ruled Arabs ineligible for naturalization on the grounds they were non-white. The circuit court of appeals of the same district, however, reversed the former decision in the same year and the reversal was later upheld in the circuit court of appeals in New York City.[138]

Scene: In Algeria, American adventurer Gordon Roberts (Chase) swoons over Hafsa (Ulrich), the daughter of wealthy Sheikh Malik (Mayall). Suddenly, Arab slavers seize Gordon. They try selling him to the highest bidders.

• Hafsa tries to free Gordon. But, the slavers grab and place her, too, on the auction block. At the next day's auction, Sheikh Ibrahim (Massey) orders bearded Arabs to remove Hafsa's veil. Impressed, onlookers gasp.

• Introducing a jealous maiden, Leila. Envying Hafsa's beauty, Leila has Ibrahim, an ugly, white-bearded, lecherous old sheikh, buy the enslaved Hafsa.

• When Sheikh Malik learns of his daughter's fate, he blames Gordon, warning, "Dog of an American, deliver to me my daughter—before I kill you."

• Unexpectedly, Leila encounters Hafsa's father. She soon realizes that Sheikh Malik is her former spouse. Shouts Leila, "It's Malik—my husband! Then Allah forgive me—the girl is my daughter, too—my Hafsa!" The enlightened and reformed Leila convinces Malik to accept Hafsa's betrothal to Gordon. "If she loves the American," she says, "let him take her away to a Christian marriage, to save her from Sheikh [Ibrahim]."

• Gordon and Hafsa ride off together. On screen: "And the faithful Koran leads them to safety."

Note: One of the most "provocative cultural images" in the nineteenth century was Hiram Powers' *The Greek Slave* (1843). This American artist's sculpture was "a Grecian maiden, made captive by the Turks, and exposed for sale in the Bazaar of Constantinople." To make certain "the very, very naked" manacled-in-chains statue would be accepted in Europe and in America, Powers placed "a Christian cross upon the clothes piled beside the maiden."[139]

Road to Morocco (1942), PAR. *Bob Hope, Bing Crosby, Dorothy Lamour, Anthony Quinn, Dona Drake.* Filmed in Paramount's back lot. SHEIKHS, MAIDENS

This wacky spoof shows American entertainers romancing an Arab lovely. A sheikh and his quarrelsome desert nomads appear as buffoons. Quips the film's talking camel, "This is the screwiest picture I was ever in."

Scene: Introducing mythical Karamesh, complete with mirages, magic rings, and morons.

• Two shipwrecked performers, Lucky and Jeff (Hope and Crosby), sing five songs. Note some of the lyrics: "For any villains we may meet, we haven't any fears... Where they do the dance of the seven veils... where men eat fire and saw their wives in half."

• Princess Shalmar (Lamour) believes in a silly "written in the stars" prophesy, contending that her new husband will die a week after their marriage. Thus, Shalmar decides to wed Lucky in lieu of her intended beau, Kassim (Quinn), "the Desert Sheikh."

• When Shalmar meets Jeff, however, she falls for him and dumps Kassim. Hot-tempered Kassim abducts Shalmar and tries to force the maiden to wed him. Kassim also dispatches Lucky and Jeff into the desert, expecting them to perish. Abruptly, desert Arabs appear. They try to cut off the entertainers' heads.

• Inside the wedding tent, desert swordsmen and a bellydancer. Says Kassim to rival Arabs, "We will all be like brothers." Lucky and Jeff arrive, spoiling Kassim's Arab unity plan.

• To save Shalmar from "that wolf, Kassim," the entertainers humiliate Arabs. First, they pass dense bedouins a leaking goblet. Next, they place gunpowder inside the Arabs' cigarettes. The bedouins inhale—Poof! They also pull some matches and administer hotfoots, prompting the nomads to grab their feet and screech. Instantly, white-robed Arabs blame black-robed Arabs for all the pranks. Says one, "You trying to make fools of us!" They Arabs fight; the tent collapses, covering them. This melee is labeled a "sort of an Arabian Gestapo."

• After eluding Kassim, Shalmar, Lucky, and Jeff appear on a raft, gliding to a safe place. Sharing the raft with them is Mihirmah (Drake), a sexy Arab maiden pining for Lucky.

Dialogue: Lucky warns Jeff that Kassim, a tough guy with nasty Arab agents, may track them. Scoffs Jeff, "Let 'em try Brooklyn!" Often, the duo say: "It's a strange country."

Note: Considering that most Moroccans and other North African Arabs sided with the Allies during WWII, why does *Road to Morocco* mock Arabs? Why the line, "Arabian Gestapo?" Even some 1940s cartoons belittle Arabs. An early 1940s Popeye cartoon, for example, lampoons sheikhs. Popeye sings, in part: "And I make Arab sheikhs as my slaves."[140] Interestingly, after the Allies landed in North Africa, Bob Hope visited Morocco and poked fun of Arab women. As he addressed American soldiers, Hope joked, "I tried to find a few [Dorothy] Lamour's over here. But they all wear their sarongs a little higher... under their eyes. Boys, don't ever lift one of those napkins. I did, and... what I saw! A B-bag with legs."[141]

• How many Americans know that in 1777, Morocco became the first country to recognize the new United States of America? Since 1778, the treaty of friendship between the two countries has been uninterrupted. One example of this long-lasting friendship took place in 1977, when Morocco's King Hassan gave Voice of America (VOA) officials approval to build in Morocco the largest radio transmitter in the non-communist world.

Road to Zanzibar (1941), PAR. *Bing Crosby, Bob Hope, Dorothy Lamour, Una Merkel.* CAMEOS

In South Africa, an Arab slaver sells an American woman to the highest bidder. Promptly, one Arab bids for a lovely Brooklyn entertainer (Lamour). Desperate to save her, her fellow entertainers (Crosby and Hope) give the Arab a wad of cash, rescuing the woman. Soon, the duo find out the joke's on them. They were duped. Lamour's girlfriend (Merkel) staged the woman-for-sale auction. Cut to Merkel sharing the entertainers' money with the Arab trader.

Roaring Fire (1982), NLC. *Sonny Chiba, Abdullah the Butcher.* CAMEOS

In Japan, the wrestler Abdullah the Butcher meets and befriends martial arts hero Sonny Chiba. Their friendship is short-lived.

Scene: Near a swimming pool, Abdullah chases after Chiba, but Chiba is too quick. The exhausted Abdullah cannot keep pace.

• Later, Abdullah tells Chiba, "Me. You. Longtime friends. We'll be good sportsmen." The men embrace. Impressed, Chiba's aide says, "A black follower [Abdullah is from the Sudan] for him [Chiba] will be good."

• When some gunmen move to kill Chiba, Abdullah intervenes. While fending off the villains, Chiba's "black retainer" is killed.

The Robe (1953), TCF. *Richard Burton, Jean Simmons, Victor Mature, Michael Ansara.* CAMEOS, VILLAINS

This drama about Christ's crucifixion focuses on a Roman tribune (Burton), his Christian lover (Simmons), and a Greek slave (Mature). Yet, the producers inject a deluding, greedy "Syrian" (Ansara).

Scene: Palestine. A Roman seeking to possess Jesus' robe offers to pay any price for the garment. Attending him is an untrustworthy "Syrian guide." The Syrian acts as Judas, doublecrossing anyone for "gold." Behind the tribune's back, the Syrian quips, "These Romans drink like pigs, but they pay well." The Syrian tells his Roman employer that "people called Christians pay well, in gold, generously." Thus, he suggests cheating them. Disgusted with the Syrian's unethical behavior, the Roman threatens dismissal. Quips the Syrian, "Oh, you won't get rid of me so easily. [The Christians] might pay me well to know who you are. You are the man who crucified Him. You are His murderer, so they'll say." The Roman slugs the Syrian, who runs off.

• Inside a courtyard Christians gather to hear the Apostle Peter speak. Suddenly, Roman soldiers appear, killing the Christians. How did the soldiers know where to find the Christians? Who blabbed to them? Cut to the smiling "Syrian," watching the slaughter.

Robin Hood: Men in Tights (1993), TCF. *Cary Elwes, Richard Lewis, Dave Chappelle, Isaac Hayes.* P, D: Mel Brooks. CAMEOS

This funny fable spoofing *Robin Hood: Prince of Thieves* (1991) contains harmless visual and verbal puns. Appearing are Robin Hood and his men, Maid Marion, some blacks, a rabbi, a Muslim Moor, and an abbot. Producer Brooks presents as Robin's sidekick, the Moor, "Ahchoo" (Chappelle), son of "Ahsneeze" (Hayes).

Scene: Arab music underscores shots of "Khalil Prison: Jerusalem." Two Saracen guards, "Mukhtar" and "Falafel," toss Robin into a dungeon. Employing a "tongue" stretcher, the guards "torture" Robin. Anticipating trouble, a guard exclaims, "Oh, by the love of Allah."

Note: Arab-American actor, Richard Assad, portrays one of the guards.

Robin Hood: Prince of Thieves (1991), WB. *Kevin Costner, Morgan Freeman, Mary Elizabeth Mastrantonio.* See *Lion of the Desert* (1981). CAMEOS, BEST LIST

Following the third Crusade, the legendary hero Robin Hood (Costner) returns to England, leading his men against the Sheriff of Nottingham. Aiding Robin is a dignified Saracen warrior with superior judgment, Azeem (Freeman).

Scene: Twelfth-century Jerusalem, a dungeon. Ottoman prison guards speaking Arabic approach a prisoner. "Cut off the infidel's hand," barks a guard. Cut to Robin, rescuing the Moor, Azeem. Vows Azeem, "You saved my life, Christian. I will stay with you until I have saved yours." The two men travel to England.

• Sherwood Forest. Before praying, Azeem, who "fights better than twenty knights," says, "No man creates my destiny." As Robin's men are puzzled by Azeem's faith, he explains that as a Muslim "it is vanity to force other men to our religion." Asked why his skin is dark, Azeem declares, "Allah loves wondrous variety."

• Azeem refuses to drink alcohol, saying, "I must decline. Allah forbids it."

• Throughout, the Muslim functions as a champion. Among his feats: employing a telescope, delivering a breech baby, and initiating gunpowder into a decisive battle. Grateful for the Muslim's loyalty, Robin says, "You, truly, are a great one. You're an honor to your country."

Finis: Azeem saves Robin's life. As "the wicked witch" is about to murder Robin, Azeem enters the frame, killing her. Before returning to the Mideast, Azeem dons a robe and headdress, participating at Robin and Maid Marian's wedding festivity.

Note: Some nasty barbs are directed at Azeem; one man calls the Saracen a "savage," another tags him a "barbarian." Yet, Robin counters the slurs, telling his men to treat Azeem as an equal, which they do. See *Ivanhoe* (1952). Here, the champion (Robert Taylor) contests prejudicial barbs aimed at a lovely Jewish maiden, Rebecca (Elizabeth Taylor).

Robinson Crusoe (1916), WB. Silent. *Robert Patton Gibbs.* CAMEOS, VILLAINS

In this children's film, the first with the Arab-as-slaver motif, a Moroccan enslaves Robinson and an African befriends him.

Scene: In England, Crusoe addresses youngsters, weaving a tale about his journey to Africa. En route, he says, he and his shipmates were ambushed by pirates and "sold as slaves in Morocco. "[I became] the personal slave to a Moorish sea captain," says Crusoe.

• Flashback. Stranded on an island, Crusoe befriends "Friday," an African. "I named him Friday," he says, "because no friend could be more faithful than he."

Note: A decade later *Robinson Crusoe* (1927), narrated by "Uncle Don," was released. In 1936, the movie was reissued. Uncle Don's *Robinson Crusoe* films do not display Arabs.

Rock-a-Bye Baby (1958), PAR. *Marilyn Maxwell.* CAMEOS, MAIDENS

A Hollywood movie actress Carla (Maxwell) goes to off to Cairo to star as "the white virgin of the Nile." Her desert movie set displays a camel in the foreground. Arab music underscores the lyrics of "White Virgin of the Nile." Cut to Carla and scantily-clad dancing Egyptian maidens gliding onto the set and singing, "Ya, ya, ya, ya, ya."

Note: The tunes are by Harry Warren and Sammy Cahn.

Rollover (1982), WB. *Jane Fonda, Kris Kristofferson.* P: Bruce Gilbert. SP: David Shaber. Shaber also penned *Nighthawks* (1978). See *Protocol* (1984). SHEIKHS, WORST LIST

The movie scapegoats hirsute Arabs, fueling bigotry and hatred with images reminiscent of Nazi cinema's Jewish portraits, which falsely presented Jews as financial conspirators.

Rollover's message? Beware sinister, funny dressing, finger-licking Saudis in Rolls

Royces. Launching an "economic conspiracy," the "greedy" Saudis take control of our banks.

Scene: American financial experts fret about the economy. Says one, "The concentration of wealth is in the hands of one group. These [Arab] people are unpredictable. They can't let that kind of money sit that long [in our banks] without getting interest."

• The Saudi desert; a sandstorm. To help resolve America's "illusion of [economic] safety," Lee Winters (Fonda), a petrochemical widow from Texas, and Hubbell Smith (Kristofferson), a bank troubleshooter, meet with the Saudis to request some loans. Inside the Arabs' large tent, camels and Saudis. Abruptly, the Saudis remove their shoes and begin eating. Using their fingers they munch on greasy chunks of roast lamb. Repulsed by such behavior, Lee whispers to Hubbell, "I feel like a beggar asking them for alms, and I hate it." Affirms Hubbell, "You and the rest of the world."

• Next, the Americans enter a Saudi palace, anxious to discuss the loans. Cut to more than twenty robed Arabs bowing to Mecca, and praying. In lieu of respecting praying Arab Muslims, Lee registers shock, barking at the praying Saudis, "I thought we had an appointment."

• Two Americans, apparently, were murdered by Saudis. One victim is Lee's husband, who knew all about "Arab Eurodollars and secret Arab financial systems."

• American bankers contend "Arab money" is gobbling US companies. As a result, the dollar is collapsing. Noting the Arabs are also withdrawing funds, one US banker moans, "The Arabs yanked every penny they had with us. [People] across the world are seeing their life savings becoming worthless in a matter of hours." He warns because of the Arabs, we will soon witness "a bankrupt world, a world-wide depression."

• The Saudis act, withdrawing all their "worthless paper money" from American banks. Promptly, they transfer their dollar deposits into gold. Their withdrawals serve to destroy the world's financial systems. Subsequently, social anarchy. The Saudis bring about the end of the world. Or, as one sinister Arab tells Lee, "The end of the world as you know it." As the Saudi speaks, frames reveal "the world teetering on the edge of anarchy." As the Pope prays, the world's angry unemployed commit violence.

• The final shot displays a mosque, implying Saudi Muslims are to blame for a "bankrupt world."

Note: Arabs bringing monies into the US during the 1970s and '80s were often perceived not as individuals who stimulated American businesses, but as foreign predators, intent on expropriating our land. For example, some media systems perpetuated the myth that oil-rich Arabs were buying America's farmland. Yet, during the 1970s, department of commerce figures revealed that Arabs owned less than 1 percent.[142]

The same year *Rollover* was released, *Time* magazine's 25 January 1982 issue reproduced the film's message. The magazine's essay entitled "Beware Saudi Investors." Beneath the word "POWER," there appears a photograph of an Arab sheikh, followed by this caption: "Oil is king. Those who have it have the power to shape events across the world." *Time* watches "the volatile, oil-rich kingdoms of the Middle East. It brings you closer to the distant rulers... that have the power to change the way we live."

• In the early 1980s what did Jane Fonda think about Arabs, the Middle East? Soon after *Rollover*'s release, Fonda told Copley News Service correspondent Nancy Anderson, "We have allowed the Arabs to have control over our economy." And, "If we aren't afraid of Arabs, we'd better examine our heads. They have strategic power over us. They are unstable, they are fundamentalists, tyrants, anti-woman, anti-free press. That we have to depend on them is monstrous."[143] One year later, Fonda said: "I love Israel and I think it represents to the United States what a true ally should be."[144]

• In its 1996 report to the Senate Intelligence Committee, the CIA identified Israel as one of six foreign countries with "a government-directed oorchestrated clandestine effort to collect US economic secrets." In 1996, "US Ambassador Martin Indyk complained privately to the Israeli government about heavy-handed surveillance by Israeli intelligence agents, who had been following American embassy employees in Tel Aviv and searching the hotel rooms of visiting US officials."[145]

Romance in the Dark (1938), PAR. Based on the play, "The Yellow Nightingale." *Gladys Swarthout, John Barrymore.* EGYPTIANS, MAIDENS

The Hungarian heroine appears as a Persian-Arab.

Scene: Auditioning for Zoltan Jason (Barrymore), a famous opera manager, is a lovely Hungarian peasant singer, Ilona Boros (Swarthout). To secure the job, Ilona passes herself off as a "Persian" princess. The ruse works; Zoltan books the "Persian" to star in the opera *1001 Nights.*

• A Budapest theater; Ilona's debut. The stage setting reveals the Arabian desert, palm tree and oasis, plus robed bedouins and scantily-clad harem maidens. The clad-in-Arab garb Ilona sings the romantic ballad, "Blue Dawn," receiving a standing ovation. Suddenly, her audience is told that Ilona is not really an Oriental princess; they boo!

• Moments later, however, the audience applauds Ilona. They accept her for who she truly is—a magnificent Hungarian vocalist.

Rosebud (1975), MGM/UA. *Peter O'Toole, Richard Attenborough, John V. Lindsay, Peter Lawford, Cliff Gorman, Yosef Shiloa, Raf Vallone, Isabelle Huppert, Kim Cattrall.* SP: Erik Lee Preminger. P, D: Otto Preminger. Based on the novel by Joan Hemingway and Paul Bonnecarre. Made in Israel. PALESTINIANS, WORST LIST

Otto Preminger and his son, Erik Lee, glorify Israelis and vilify Palestinians. This movie, like nearly all Palestinian scenarios, reveals no humane Palestinians. Instead, the producers show Americans, Europeans, and Israelis contesting evil Palestinians. Members of the Palestinian Liberation Army (PLA), known also as Black September, function as unrelenting caricatures. Aboard a yacht, the Palestinians murder several crewmen. And, they terrorize five young women, daughters of internationally prominent figures.

Scene: Aboard a yacht. The PLA leader uses an ice pick to puncture the heads of crew members. One woman unable to endure such brutality pleads, "Let them kill me."

• A Palestinian terrorist places hoods over the kidnapped women, then photographs them, naked. Next, he drags them off, dumping the women inside a Corsican farmhouse cellar. The PLA propose to release their hostages provided world nations place "a total boycott on all exports from Israel." They offer the parents of the women a lame excuse, saying, "We have no other way to call attention to our plight."

• The kidnapped victims' concerned fathers watch a BBC-TV newscast. Intones the announcer, "In Beirut, Yasser Arafat, the leader of the Palestine Liberation Organization, has denied any knowledge or involvement of the kidnaping." Arafat's statement prompts an Israeli to tag the PLO leader a liar; the Israeli says the PLO approves of the kidnaping.

• Who can nab these evil Palestinians? Cut to CIA agent Larry Martin (O'Toole), who quips, "The Palestinians need public opinion on their side."

• Complains Mr. Freyer, a German, whose daughter is held hostage, "This entire fiasco was brought about by Israel and the intrigue of the Jews." Counters an Israeli agent named Hamiekh (Gorman), "That seems to ring an ancient bell in my head. Blame everything on the Jews, right?" The German is silent.

• The man leading the PLA kidnappers is Edward Sloat (Attenborough), an Englishman who dons a kuffiyeh. Declares Sloat, "I want the elimination of Israel." Cut to an Israeli; he points to some comic books that reflect Sloat's "anti-Semitism." Explains the Israeli, "The [comic book] hero, a devout Muslim, changes from country to country. Algerian in Algeria; Egyptian in Egypt, and so on. But the villain is always the Jew." Continues the Israeli, The Palestinians are ruthless. During the "communist revolution in Iraq every rich family was lined up [by the PLA] and shot."

• The hostages are whisked off to Lebanon. Here, one of Sloat's young Palestinians takes a gun, points the weapon to his head and fires. Sighs Sloat, "He was one of my best men. He survived a suicide mission." Adding, "When one of my men go on a mission, he's dead. I cannot afford survivors."

• After killing a Palestinian, Marin warns Sloat, "Release the girls and you can have what the Palestinians urgently wish to have—negotiations with Israel." Sloat refuses to negotiate. He prefers a "holy war"; cut to Sloat and his Palestinians, praying.

• Martin and Israeli paratroopers land in Lebanon; they rescue the hostages and collar Sloat and his Palestinians. Sloat is delivered to the Israelis. Demanding to be released, Sloat orders Black September, labeled here as a communist organization, "to kidnap scores of children from every country and kill them, one by one."

Finis: Abruptly, Palestinian skyjackers appear on a commercial airline that is low on fuel. A bearded Palestinian places a pistol near the flight attendant's head, pulls a grenade pin, and issues a warning. Unless the Israelis release Sloat and his Palestinian cohorts from prison within the next four hours, he "will destroy this plane and everyone on it." Credits roll.

Dialogue: Palestinians are called "bastards" and "these animals." Writes Michael Medved, "Wouldn't it be strange if there weren't Arab terrorists in movies?"[146]

Note: New York City's Mayor John V. Lindsay portrays a US senator.

Rough Cut (1980), PAR. *Burt Reynolds, Leslie-Anne Down.* CAMEOS, MAIDENS

Westerners pose as stereotypical Arabs.

Scene: This romantic caper features a jewel thief and a Scotland Yard agent. The couple moves to acquire new passports. The thief (Reynolds) proposes to initiate the "Pakistani-Arab caper." Cut to the thief wearing "something exotic"—a thobe and headdress. His cohort, the agent (Down), wears a black abaya. When passport officials question them, the thief speaks with an Arab accent. "I'm doing Peter Sellers doing Omar Sharif," he boasts. To convince the custom officials they are really Arabs, he barks at the black-clad agent, "Lower your veil!" Immediately, she feigns obedience, dropping the veil. The ruse works.

Rules of Engagement (2000), PAR. *Samuel L. Jackson, Tommy Lee Jones, Ben Kingsley, Bruce Greenwood.* SP: Stephen Gaghan. D: William Friedkin. Filmed in Morocco, in cooperation with the Moroccan government. VILLAINS, WORST LIST

This movie, one of the most blatantly anti-Arab scenarios of all time, is based on a story by former Secretary of the Navy James Webb. It was produced in cooperation with the US Department of Defense (DOD) and the US Marine Corps. The film, a gross defamation of the Yemeni, encourages viewers to hate Arab Muslims. Audiences embraced *Rules of Engagement*; it was number one over the opening weekend (7–9 April 2000), grossing $15 million. In some theaters viewers cheered as the marines gunned down the Yemeni.

Scene: On screen: "San'a, [sic] Yemen."[147] Ten minutes into the film, the camera reveals scores of violent Yemeni demonstrators outside the American embassy. A chanting mob of veiled women, bearded kuffiyeh-clad men with missing teeth, and unruly children toss rocks, throw firebombs, and brandish anti-US banners, written in Arabic. All raise their fists. Positioned away from the crowd of protestors, some Yemeni snipers appear on rooftops; they fire away at the Americans trapped inside the embassy; bullets narrowly miss the US ambassador (Kingsley). To the rescue, Marine Colonel Childers (Jackson). Three helicopters deliver the marines to the embassy compound. Abruptly, Yemeni snipers begin firing. Three marines are fatally shot—the camera displays the bloodied marine casualties. Incessant firing from the Yemeni endangers the rescue mission. As Childers and his men are pinned down, the colonel orders his marines to open fire. Questions a captain, "Are you ordering me to fire into the crowd?" Affirms Childers, "Yes. Waste the mother-fuckers!" Bodies of 83 dead Yemeni fill the screen. As several rooftop Yemeni snipers fire at the marines and riddle the American flag, viewers assume the snipers killed three marines, that the angry civilian demonstrators were unarmed, innocent victims. This scene lasts 15 minutes.

• North Carolina. Believing Childers acted irresponsibly by killing innocents, the Marine Corps moves to court-martial this "warrior's warrior." Childers' friend, Colonel Hodges (Jones), decides to defend him. Cut to National Security Advisor William Sokal (Greenwood); he views an embassy video revealing the armed Yemeni crowd demonstrators shooting at the marines. Though the tape affirms Childers' innocence, Sokal wants a fall guy. He destroys the video.

• In search of the truth, Colonel Hodges travels to Yemen. He meets and empathizes with a victim of the marine attack—a wounded Yemeni girl with only one leg. Next, he chats with three Yemeni, including a doctor. All the Yemeni lie, telling Hodges the demonstrators did not fire at the marines as they were unarmed, assuring Hodges the crowd had no weapons. The doctor points to casualties of the shoot-out, dozens of wounded Yemeni children waiting to die. The one-legged girl calls Hodges "killer." Pausing after seeing the hurt children, Hodges thinks Childers may be actually be guilty of killing and wounding innocents. Later, in the souk, some Yemeni men surround Hodges, threatening violence. He escapes and rushes back to the states.

• Flashback to the embassy compound. Footage reveals an unruly crowd of protesting Yemeni, armed with weapons, shooting the marines. The innocent Childers correctly explains the slaughter, saying he had no choice but to fire as all the Yemeni were armed, and they were shooting at his marines. What does this flashback footage imply? First, that the Yemeni, including women and children, deserved to die; they brought it on themselves. Secondly, Childers' actions are justified and praiseworthy. After all, his rescue mission was a success. He rescued embassy personnel from the firing Yemeni mob. And, by killing the Yemeni he saved marine lives.

• The courtroom. Hodges displays two audiotapes; one tape was found inside the American embassy, he uncovered the other tape while visiting the Yemeni children's clinic. Hodges plays the tape. Intones the Arabic speaker: "[This is a] declaration of Islamic Jihad against the United States... We call on every Muslim who believes in God ... to kill Americans and their allies, both civilian and military. It is the duty of every Muslim, everywhere... to kill Americans is a duty."

• A three-minute flashback reveals the angry Yemeni crowd of civilians outside the embassy. Gun-toting Yemeni men, women, and children [including the crippled girl], shoot at the marines. Childers visualizes their attack. No wonder he said: "Waste the mother-fuckers!"

• The film's message? Colonel Childers' made the correct call; his order to kill 83 Yemeni is justified. This movie's Yemeni are, after all, hateful marine-killers and anti-American terrorists.

Note: No such violence directed at American marines has ever occurred at a US embassy in Yemen, a nation with whom the US has had diplomatic relations for decades. Yemen, population 16 million, sits on the southeastern tip of the Arabian peninsula. Sana'a boasts some of the world's most beautiful architecture.

• US advisors and the use of American military equipment play a role here. Several questions need to be addressed. Why did the DOD and the US Marine Corps cooperate with producers of *Rules of Engagement* and help slander Arabs? What, exactly, was the extent of the DOD's "cooperation"? Did the DOD provide technical advisors for free, and free equipment as well? Annually, how much taxpayer money is spent to fund DOD's film offices? What about the use of federal property, federal personnel? One way to answer these questions and others is to ask congresspersons with the Armed Service Committee, as well as those serving on the Senate Relations Committee, to request from the General Accounting Office (GAO), detailed reports stating exactly what kind of cooperation DOD extended for *Rules of Engagement.* To expedite the GAO review, activists should view *Rules of Engagement* with their respective congresspersons.

Troubled by the DOD's involvement with *Rules of Engagement,* Nihad Awad, executive director of the Council on American-Islamic Relations (CAIR), penned a missive to James Desler, DASD (PA). In Desler's letter of 11 April 2000, he responded to Awad's concerns:

> While we review scripts that have been submitted to us, we focus on... namely the depiction of US military personnel, missions, and equipment... we cannot serve as arbiters of moral or social probity over the entire script... [But] we do give consideration to the context of the overall film. We would not provide assistance to a production that we believed implicitly or explicitly encouraged audiences to believe that untoward behavior of ethnic or religious characters on the screen would be generalized to include all members of the group in reality.

Since 1980, the DOD has been actively involved with motion pictures vilifying Arabs. What's happening, here? Assuming that screenplays are given to the military in advance are there any guidelines that enable those reading the scripts to approve/disapprove movies that denigrate peoples? Perhaps all copies of notes and memos, etc. pertaining to the DOD movies should be submitted to the GAO. The GAO review should examine the files that contain the names, titles, and ranks of those individuals responsible for reviewing the screenplay[s].

• How will audiences in Yemen and other Arab nations view this film? How will American servicemen stationed in the Middle East react? Will they invite their Arab co-workers and friends to watch the film? And, why did the Moroccan government cooperate with the producers?

• On 30 March, Paramount Executive Vice President Blasie Noto wrote to the American-Arab Anti-Discrimination Committee's (ADC) Hussein Ibish, saying, "*Rules of Engagement* is not anti-Arabic, anti-Moroccan, or anti-Yemenite but rather anti-extremist. This film is not a negative portrait of any government or people."[148]

• Some movie reviewers were outraged at the film's stereotypes. Writes the *Toronto Sun* critic, "Little attempt is made to humanize the Yemeni. On screen... they are stock villains, human cattle ready for herding and slaughter to demonstrate the right and might of the U.S. policeman's role."[149]

• For his scenario, former Secretary of the Navy James Webb chose an attack on an American embassy "because it could happen." Originally, "the locale was to be South America, but that became too topical." He selected Yemen, he said, "because it is sufficiently remote. I mean we don't get up every morning and ask 'How are things in Yemen?'"[150]

Saadia (1953), MGM. *Cornel Wilde, Mel Ferrer, Rita Gam, Wanda Rotha, Michel Simon, Cyril Cusak.* W, P, D: Albert Lewin. Shot in "French Morocco," with the authorities' "generous cooperation." MAIDENS, VILLAINS

An Arab woman is "possessed of devils," but a French doctor saves a Moroccan woman from the sorceress' black magic. The doctor also contains a plague. Though some stereotypical characters appear, the film also reveals caring Moroccan parents, courageous and devout villagers, a brave woman, a benevolent prince, and a pious Muslim leader.

Scene: States the narrator, Morocco is "a land of strange and haunting contrasts. Here, the primitive camel and the gasoline truck take on fuel side by side." Concurrently, the screen displays a vehicle at a gas pump; nearby, camels drink water.

• Continues the narrator, Prince Lahssen (Wilde) was "educated in France. He brings his Western knowledge to the service of his country. Through crowded streets and noisy market places, he drives his modern motor car [a white convertible] to the ancient gates of the walled town."

• The prince visits a village hospital managed by Henrik (Ferrer), his French friend. The doctor's "greatest struggle" is to win the villagers' trust. Some superstitious villagers will not visit the hospital; they fear Fatima (Rotha) is "possessed of devils" and will inflict them with her spells and curses. As Fatima envies Henrik's popularity and skills, the sorceress threatens to employ black magic and kill him. The Frenchman does not fret. "Before long, Henrik's medicine will give her competition."

• Henrik aids a plague-stricken Moroccan youth. Knowing he will die, the boy tells his mother, "I love you."

• Since childhood, Saadia (Gam), the village dancing girl, who is now ill, has been under Fatima's spell. Fatima warns the ailing Saadia (which means beautiful in Arabic),

"If you return to me, no harm will come to him [Henrik]." Fatima meets with Henrik, saying, "I warn you, when the moon is full, the devil whose name you have spoken, will strike you."

• Saadia is dying, supposedly from Fatima's "evil eye." But thanks to Henrik's skills, he conducts a successful appendectomy and she survives. Grateful, Saadia begins to assist Henrik, working in the hospital.

• The angry Fatima employs witchcraft. Suddenly, villagers are stricken with bubonic plague. In time, a full moon appears; soon evil spirits overpower the sorceress. Explains the narrator: "The demon she had invoked took possession of Fatima. She was literally possessed by devils."

• Fearless villagers assist plague-afflicted patients. Cut to a plane from Paris carrying "a new vaccine" to curb the plague—it crashes. Appearing at the crash site, "the one tribe in Morocco that creates difficulty." The Moroccan bandits run off with the valuable serum. Quips a French officer: "They'll hold the cargo for ransom." The bandit leader, Bou Rezza (Simon), a ruthless cur who hates the villagers, would like "nothing more than to see them die—like rats!"

• Hoping to retrieve the serum, Saadia rides off to Rezza's hideout. She enters his tent. Cut to scraps of food dripping down Rezza's fat face. He grabs Saadia and kisses her. Saadia knifes him in the gut, then wipes her face. In the nick of time she arrives with the serum, saving the stricken villagers.

• Intent on avenging their leader's death, Rezza's bandits ambush Henrik's search party. Henrik tries reasoning with the men, saying, "French and Moroccans have fought side by side on the same battlefields for two wars." Not in this film. Cut to French troops crushing the bandits. During the battle, Prince Lahssen is seriously wounded.

• Though a novice, the stricken prince has sketched numerous drawings of Saadia; he loves her. A wise holy man, Khadir (Cusak), appears, advising, "Without love, one can do nothing great in this country." To save the prince, he calls on fellow villagers to renew their faith, to "pray" for the prince's recovery "with all your souls."

Finis: The prince recovers and marries Saadia. Cut to the wedding celebration, complete with traditional Moroccan dancing and music; entertaining the guests are acrobats and skilled horsemen.

Treatment of Islam: The holy man approaches some French officers, saying: "We [Muslims] are calling on our God. If you want to help us, pray to yours. He is one and the same."

Note: The NYT, VAR, and *Film Daily* critics label the movie's Moroccans, "natives."

• The movie could have featured an Arab-American doctor attending Moroccans. Consider, for example, the accomplishments of North Carolina's Dr. George Hatem, one of the most celebrated physicians in China. Dr. Hatem, who cured millions of venereal disease sufferers, also played a major role in helping to eradicate leprosy and prostitution in that country.

Sabrina (1995), PAR. *Harrison Ford, Julia Ormond, Ronald L. Schwary.* D: Sidney Pollack. CAMEOS, SHEIKHS

Briefly, sheikhs appear; the protagonists share fine Arab cuisine.

Scene: Well-dressed guests mingle at a lavish gathering hosted by the wealthy Larrabee family. Opting not to join the festivities is Linus Larrabee (Ford). He talks business with

Japanese entrepreneurs and two robed Arabs. The credits reveal that the film's executive producer, Ronald Schwary, portrays one of the sheikhs.

• At a fine Moroccan restaurant, Linus romances the chauffeur's daughter, Sabrina (Ormond). Soft Arab music underscores amour. A polite, fez-wearing waiter attends the couple, serving trays of scrumptious cuisine. Says Sabrina, "My favorite food."

Note: No sheikhs surface in the original *Sabrina* (1954).

Sabu and the Magic Ring (1957), AA. *Sabu, Robin Moore, Daria Massey, George Khoury.* SP: Sam Roeca. D: George Blair. The producers made this feature out of two half-hour television pilots. VILLAINS

Scene: An elderly storyteller relates a fantasy. He talks about a stable boy (Sabu) who uncovers a magic ring. Flashback. Sabu rubs the ring. Presto! Appearing is the "slave of the ring for 5,000 years."

• Introducing this movie's villains: an evil magician, a power-mad vizier, and hired assassins. They intend to poison the benevolent caliph and to "triple the taxes."

• Aiding Sabu, who plays himself, is a lovely princess (Massey) and the ring genie. "Command and I shall obey," says the benevolent genie.

• For a time, the vizier and the magician have the upper hand; they even manage to abduct the princess. And, as a goose swallows "the enchanted ring," Sabu is rendered helpless. The vizier's henchmen nab the youth, whisking him off and then torturing him in the palace's underground chamber.

• In the desert, the vizier's assassins murder a Damascus prince. And, a fakir betrays Sabu for money. Cut to the evil vizier turning a beautiful bird into stone.

Finis: Sabu and the good caliph crush the vizier's cohorts. The ring genie rewards Sabu and his beloved princess, not with treasures, but rather with "the greatest blessing of all—happiness."

Treatment of Islam: Quips a character, the assassins "respond to the call of gold as the faithful answer the call to prayer."

Dialogue: Sabu is called a "dog monkey." Arab rogues are tagged "greedy dogs who lust for power," and "swine of the alleys."

The Sad Sack (1957), PAR. *Jerry Lewis, Phyliss Kirk, David Wayne, Peter Lorre, Liliane Montevecchi, Michael Ansara.* VILLAINS, MAIDENS, WORST LIST

During WWII, Jerry Lewis clobbers inept Moroccans. Arabs vs. GI's and legionnaires. Arabs kidnap a beautiful Mexican dancer.

Scene: Midway through this 1957 movie, Private Bixby (Lewis) and his Army pals ship off to Morocco, a place with "sandstorms and pretty girls." Boasts a Moroccan sign outside a nightclub: "60 Dancing Girls 60." The GIs rush in, then promptly rush out, grumbling, "Sixty dancing girls? Ha!… Well, at least they were telling the truth about their ages."

• A hook-nosed Arab's camel remains transfixed in the middle of a road, halting an Army jeep. Bixby approaches the Arab, speaking gibberish. The dense Arab nods, kisses Bixby's hand, and removes his camel.

• At the "Pink Camel Club," Bixby meets and falls for a Mexican performer, Zita (Montevecchi). Abruptly, the club owner, Ali, nabs and holds Zita hostage. Ali also provides the Arab rebels contesting Americans with "rapid fire" guns.

• When a soldier asks Bixby how he traveled from Ali's club back to the army camp, he quips, I hitchhiked—on "three ox carts, two camels, and a burro."

• At the "Pink Camel," Bixby meets up with knife-wielding, gun-running Arabs. The Arabs try to reassemble a stolen US weapon, the "R-2 Cannon." They fail. Thinking these Arabs are decent folk, Bixby offers a helping hand; he assembles the R-2. See *I Cover the War* (1937) and *Back to the Future* (1985).

• In the desert, Arabs drink coffee and smoke nargelihs. They also hold Bixby and Zita hostage. One Arab cracks a whip, threatening Zita, "You going to talk?"

• Later, prisoner Bixby convinces the dense Ali to do 50 push-ups. And, he tags the Arab, Abdul (Lorre), "You fat ant-eater." When fellow GIs move to eat Arab cuisine Bixby warns, "They're stuffed with goat's eyes, we had 'em for supper." The GI gasps, spitting out the food.

• Before legion reinforcements arrive, Zita, Bixby, and his GIs trounce about two dozen Arabs. Reclaiming the R-2 weapon, Bixby parades Ali's Arabs through the desert. Barks Bixby, "Keep in step." Later, Bixby is awarded "The Foreign Legion Medal of Gallantry."

Note: Michael Ansara portrays an Arab villain, Moki.

Sahara (1919), A.J. Parker Read Prod. Silent. *Louise Glaum, Matt Moore, Edward Stevens.* *NS. Notes from NYT (30 June 1919) 16. VILLAINS

This "Wild East" Arabian Nights melodrama contains desert sand storms, camels, "dashing horses," beggars and "picturesque Arabs" wearing flowing robes, bloomers, and turbans. The film review does not specify the actual role of Sahara's "picturesque Arabs."

Sahara (1943), COL. *Humphrey Bogart, Rex Ingram, Bruce Bennett, J. Carroll Nash.* SP: John Howard Lawson. RECOMMENDED

The first American feature to sanction the UN. Based on the 1942 fall of Tobruk, the scenario displays a courageous tank crew comprised of American, British, French, and Sudanese soldiers. In the Libyan desert, a Sudanese corporal sacrifices himself in order to save his American friends, trapped by German troops.

Scene: A uniformed Sudanese corporal, Tambul (Ingram), who is part of an Allied tank crew, leads the patrol and their tank, Lulubelle, to an oasis. But the well is practically dry. Still, the patient Tambul draws the remaining water drops. At Tambul's side is Waco (Bennett), a soldier from Texas. Note the dialogue:

> Waco: The boys tell me you Muhammadans have as many as 300 wives.
> Tambul: No, the Prophet tells us that four wives are sufficient.
> Waco: That sounds all right. You got four, huh?
> Tambul: [*Smiling*] No, I only have one.
> Waco: [*Astonished*] What's holding you back?
> Tambul: Well, if you had this law in Texas, would you have four wives?
> Waco: No, my wife wouldn't like that.
> Tambul: It is the same with me. My wife, she would not like it.
> Waco: You sure learn things in the army.
> Tambul: Yes. We both have much to learn from each other.
> Waco: Yeah!

• The tank crew's German prisoner escapes. He runs toward his 500-plus thirsty comrades, intent on telling them the well is dry, that they should attack the outnumbered Americans. Before he can warn his comrades, Tambul catches up with the German, killing him with his hands. Believing the well contains water, and that the Americans will blow up the well if they attack, the German soldiers hold their fire. Yet, when Tambul moves to rejoin his unit, the Germans shoot him.

• Midway through the film, an Arab scout appears with the German army. The robed rogue leads an "advance party" to the oasis; the Americans shoot the Arab.

Note: For this film, writer Lawson and producer Korda consulted with the US Office of War Information (OWI). As a result, the scenario humanizes the Italian prisoner, Giuseppe (Nash). Giuseppe appears as a victim of fascism, not as a fascist.[151]

• In August 1995, Showtime telecast its version of *Sahara*. In this admirable sequel, actor Robert Wisdom portrays Tambul. The TV version offers scenes not included in the 1943 film. Writer David Phillips, for example, presents Tambul as a devout Muslim. When US soldiers ask Tambul whether he can find water, the Sudanese says, "Allah is my guide. I can only try." Inside the well, Tambul spots water drops, saying, "Allah be praised." Also, the TV movie offers a moving prayer scene, reflecting commonalities among faiths. No sooner does Tambul report the well is dry, he places his prayer rug onto the sand, kneels and recites prayers in Arabic. Observing the Sudanese's actions, an allied soldier blesses himself.

Sahara (1983), CAN Golan/Globus. *Brooke Shields, Lambert Wilson, John Rhys-Davies, Horst Buchholz, Ronald Lacey, John Mills.* S: Menahem Golan. SP: Leslie Stevens, James A. Silkes. Filmed in Israel. SHEIKHS, VILLAINS, MAIDENS, WORST LIST

1920s Morocco. Golan and Globus's "Brooke of Arabia" camel opera displays Arabs and Germans fighting Americans and Arabs. Bedouin women appear as ugly screeching, superstitious caricatures. Primitive Arabs move to rape Shields; she demolishes them.

Scene: An American auto-heiress, Dale (Shields), promises her dying father that she will enter and win an upcoming desert race, driving the car he designed. Dale flies off to the Sahara. Here, she disguises herself as a boy, and enters the treacherous auto race.

• Arabs vs. Arabs. The camera presents the pro-German, Sheikh Beg (Lacey); Beg dispatches a leopard and panther to collar "nomads of the desert." The sheikh's cohorts shoot the nomads, then enslave women and children.

• Some clad-in-black horsemen nearly collide with Dale's car. Shouts Dale, "What kind of place is this? Who are these people?" Explains a friend, "They come up from the desert to buy women." As Dale wonders, "To buy women?"—the horsemen abduct a bellydancer.

• The rotund Sheikh Rasoul (Rhys-Davies) lusts for Dale; he abducts her. After dismissing some of his over-eager bedouin women, Rasoul moves to rape the "blue-eyed-demon," panting, "You are my slave." Dale bites Rasoul's hand, screaming, "You pig! Get away from me, you dirty pig!"

• Introducing the German heavy, Von Glessing (Buchholz). The German delivers a machine gun to Sheikh Beg, who butchers fellow Arabs in their tents.

• Rasoul again tries to bed Dale. To the rescue, Rasoul's dashing nephew, Sheikh Jaffar (Wilson). He tells his uncle, "I claim the girl. She is mine by law, if I marry her." Cautions Rasoul, "She is an infidel, a blue-eyed demon."

• Upset, Rasoul kidnaps Dale's racing companions, then buries them in the sand. Only their heads are visible. Insects swarm over their faces; they scream. Suddenly, Sheikh Beg and his bandits prepare to attack Rasoul's camp. Dale to the rescue; she places gobs of dynamite beneath the sand. When Beg goes to fire his maneuverable machine gun, Dale sets off the dynamite, destroying the weapon. Beg's Arabs retreat.

• Beg manages to kidnap Dale, tossing her into a leopard's cage. Thinking Dale is really a witch, Beg's clad-in-black bedouin women declare, "They say you are an evil power capable of possessing a man's soul." The cackling, pawing bedouins rip off "demon" Dale's clothing. Pleads Dale, "Leave me alone."

• The "good" Arabs triumph! Rasoul and Jaffar crush Beg's ghastly bedouins. The freed Dale enters the desert race and—surprise!—she wins.

• Ninety-nine percent of *Sahara's* frames display grotesque desert Arabs. Perhaps Golan and Globus felt guilty about projecting so many heinous images, as they end the movie showing Dale riding off into the desert sunset with Sheikh Jaffar.

Treatment of Islam: Germans ask Sheikh Beg to pay for arms shipments. Says the sheikh, "[First,] prayers must be said and the women must be pleasured."

Dialogue: An Arab tags an Arab, "You son of a flea-bitten goat."

Sahara Heat (1989), First Cinema. Italian, dubbed in English. *Fiona Gelin, Enzo Decaro, Yves Collignon.* Filmed in Morocco. CAMEOS, VILLAINS

Desert heat drives a British woman to be immoral.

Scene: In Tunisia, an attractive British photojournalist (Gelin) and nymphomaniac sleeps around. When she dances in a seedy cafe, Tunisians gape. Like predators, they ogle as she makes love to a European.

• A Tunisian offers to assist the journalist, giving her a "magic talisman." Advises the Tunisian, "If you give it to the man you love, he'll be true to you for life." The talisman helps cure the reporter of nymphomania. Abruptly, she departs Tunisia. She flies off to England and is soon reunited with her loving husband.

St. Elmo's Fire (1985), COL. *Rob Lowe, Judd Nelson, Demi Moore.* CAMEOS, SHEIKHS

Gang-banging Arabs are injected into this movie about college graduates coping with real-life crises.

Scene: Late evening. The unsettled heroine (Moore) makes a phone call, asking her male buddy for immediate assistance. "I've been cooking for these Arabs all night," she sighs, "I don't understand Arabic, but [from] what they're saying, I feel it's a gang bang."

• Her friend rushes to the Arabs' hotel suite, grabs the girl and exits. The room's four robed Arabs wearing headdresses pay no attention to the departing duo. Says the woman's friend, "They didn't look like gang bang to me." Relieved, the excited heroine rushes to a phone and calls "a hot Jewish guy for good coke."

St. Ives (1976), WB. *Charles Bronson, Jacqueline Bisset, John Houseman.* CAMEOS, SHEIKHS

Scheming sheikhs are linked with shady US businessmen.

Scene: The protagonist (Bronson), an ex-crime reporter, is hired by an American millionaire (Houseman) who wants the ex-reporter to recoup some stolen journals.

• The millionaire describes an unscrupulous ploy involving Arabs. "International Electronics," he says, "is bribing the Arabs to buy their products." Cut to three shady-looking businessmen discussing an order worth "$100 million-plus." Says the millionaire, "The man in the middle is Sheikh Amani." Once the deal goes through, Amani (who wears a burnoose, thobe, and sunglasses) will receive a "minimum $4 million."

Note: Amani sounds like Yamani, Saudi Arabia's Oil Minister.

The Saint's Double Trouble (1940), RKO. *George Sanders.* CAMEOS

Scene: Superimposed over a souk, "Cairo." Inside an Egyptian "Express" office, Fernack the smuggler stuffs a mummy with stolen diamonds.

Note: Remaining scenes are set in the US. Here, the stuffed mummy surfaces in a professor's study.

Samson against the Sheik (1962), Medallion. Italian, dubbed in English. *Ed Fury.* SHEIKHS

The "infidel," Samson, trounces anti-Christian Arabs. Islam is ridiculed; Arab Muslims worship a "sacred obelisk."

Scene: During the crusades, the courageous Samson (Fury) contests invading Arab Muslims wearing red, white, and multi-colored burnooses. The camera reveals the Arabs desecrating Spain's religious sites, e.g., the "shrine of the Virgin Mary." See *El Cid* (1961).

• In Arabia, Spanish soldiers bring down the Arabs' "symbol of power," their "sacred obelisk." A sheikh, accompanied by harem maidens and his effeminate vizier, vows revenge.

• The Arabs nab Samson; the sheikh's wife frees him. Angry, the sheikh kills her. The chess-playing sheikh moves to acquire a fresh woman, Isabella, a Spanish maiden.

• In Spain, plenty of Arab invaders attack a convent. As they shatter stained-glass religious figures, nuns scream. Next, they kidnap Isabella.

• Moving to free Isabella from the sheikh, Samson punches out mute Arabs.

• Thanks to Samson's heroics, the sheikh agrees to release his Spanish prisoners, including Isabella. Samson decides to lift up and return the Arabs' huge "sacred obelisk" back to its rightful place. Sighs the sheikh, "Infidel hands debased it... infidel hands shall raise it."

Sands of Beersheba (1966), AIP/Landau Unger. *Diane Baker, David Opatoshu, Tom Bell, Paul Stassino, Didi Ramati.* W, P, D: Alexander Ramati. Adapted from Ramati's book, "Rebel Versus the Light." Filmed in Israel. PALESTINIANS, MAIDENS, WORST LIST

In this 1966 filmed-in-Israel movie, Palestinians vs. Palestinians, vs. Israelis. Film as propaganda.

Scene: The Negev Desert, Israel, 1949. When Salim (Blassino), a Jew-hater, and his Palestinian cohorts spot a near-empty Israeli bus they plant a mine in the road, hoping to explode the bus on its return trip, when more passengers are seated. Chuckles one Palestinian rogue, "Good. Better twenty than two [passengers]. I can hardly wait."

• Introducing Susan (Baker), a gentile from Denver whose American-Jewish lover was killed during the 1948 war. In a nearby Palestinian village, Susan approaches women drawing water from a well. Seeing her, all but one Palestinian retreats. Cut to Palestinian men dancing, others drinking coffee. Instantly, all rush from the square; Salim's men are coming to raid the village.

• Palestinians, even Salim's father, tag Salim's men "terrorists." Yet, not one villager dares oppose Salim. Even a Palestinian soldier, "[a] traitor, who works with the Jewish police," balks. Only Daoud, Salim's father (Opatoshu), takes a stand against his son. Daoud "only wants to live in peace; [he] doesn't want anyone to get killed." Salim, however, is determined "to drive the Jews [away]."

• Daoud tries to convince villagers to oppose his son; he fails.

• The village square. Daoud, alone, confronts Salim, declaring, "You've learned to hate." Says Salim, "We'll keep on killing until there are no Jews left in Palestine... You're an old man."

• Salim's men shoot the Palestinian who works with the Jewish police. No empathy is shown for the victim. Villagers do not pray, nor do they bury the Palestinian. Instead, they trod past his body.

• Susan meets up with Dan (Bell), a British military strategist running guns for the Israelis. Dan prepares to drive off in a military truck; Susan wants to tag along. Warns the bus driver, "Arab scavengers may be in the desert, that it would be too dangerous to drive." Amos, Dan's friend, opts to take Susan in his jeep.

• The desert. The mine Salim's men had planted explodes, seriously wounding Amos. "Who did it, the Arabs?" asks Susan. Corrects Dan, "Arab terrorists."

• Dan delivers the wounded Amos and Susan, to Daoud's village. Fearing Salim may harm him, should he assist a Jew, the village leader refuses to help Amos. Salim's sister, Naimia (Ramati), however, tends to the injured Amos saying, "You're in a friend's house." When Amos dies, Daoud says, "My wife, killed by a Jewish mine; this Jew killed by an Arab mine." The Palestinians bury Amos; speaking Hebrew, Dan prays.

• Dan's truck will not start, so he and Susan stay with Daoud. Soon, Dan and Daoud bond. Says Daoud, "When your [Israeli] factory opened, I bought some bags of potash from your factory. That's how I grow tomatoes in the desert. My father, my grandfather, my great-grandfather, they never grew tomatoes."

• Salim and his four men ride into Daoud's courtyard. When Salim learns that Amos is buried next to his mother he shouts, "I will dig his body and throw it to the dogs. No Jew will profane the earth where my mother is buried."

• Father vs. son, vs. fellow Palestinians. Daoud and Dan get some guns and begin shooting dead Salim's Palestinians. And, Naimia berates her Palestinian fiancé, calling him a "bandit." Also, Naimia refuses to aid a wounded Palestinian.

• Salim's Palestinians battle Daoud and older Palestinians. Finally, Salim and his cohorts, including Naimia's fiancé, are fatally shot.

Finis: Susan and Dan drive off in the truck; the vehicle carries weapons intended for Israeli fighters. And, Susan decides she belongs in Israel.

Sands of the Desert (1960), Associated British Prod. *Charles Drake, Peter Arne, Derek Sydney, Alan Tivern, Harold Kasket, Susan Branch, Peter Illing, Neil McCarthy.* See *Harum Scarum* (1965). SHEIKHS

Charlie-of-Arabia shakes, rattles, and rolls, ridiculing desert Arabs.

Scene: Mythical Benadeen. Two Arabs crouching behind a sand dune ignite a British recreation facility, Blossom's Bedouin Holiday Camp.

• In London, Blossom executives tell their not-so-bright employee, Charlie Sands (Drake), to repair Benadeen's damaged camp. They caution Charlie about the country's "flies."

• Presenting Benadeen's inept airport custom officials. Their hands are glued onto mustard plaster sheets.

• Charlie and Janet (Branch), the Western heroine, enter an office to acquire a building permit; no one attends them. The Arab workers are sound asleep. Janet whispers something about a "bribe." Suddenly, one Arab wakens! Grabbing Charlie's money, he stamps the permit, then falls back asleep.

• Charlie hires a bodyguard, the huge Hassan (McCarthy). The dense Hassan aches not for a woman, rather "a nice and fluffy donkey." He calls Charlie, "Master."

• Introducing Sheikh El Jabez (Arne), "the wolf of the desert"; El Jabez alone knows "there's oil in them thar dunes." The sly Arab wants to nab and tap into all that oil hidden beneath Benadeen's sand. He moves to stop the Blossom camp from being repaired, telling his cohorts, Mamud and Mustafa (Sydney, Tilvern), to bump off Charlie.

• On a bus, an Arab woman removes her veil. Seeing her ugly face, the repulsed Charlie puts the woman's veil back in place. As the bus chugs along, parts break off. Suddenly the driver disembarks and leaves; the passengers remain seated. "Master" Charlie takes the wheel. Only Charlie knows how to drive a vehicle.

• Mamud and Mustafa spot Charlie at a cafe. After saying "Peace be with you," the Arabs dump some poison in Charlie's drink. And, they abduct Janet.

• El Jabez's tent. Held hostage, Charlie and Janet watch Arab maidens dance. Bored with the performance, El Jabez, yawns. Suddenly, the blonde Janet takes center stage. She wiggles. Excited, El Jabez howls his "betrothal to Miss Janet Browne."

• "It's common knowledge," a Brit tells a sheikh, "Your tribes have been enemies for years." To prevent further strife, Charlie intervenes. He finds a missing person—El Jabez's daughter. Charlie delivers the long-lost woman to Sheikh Ibrahim, who, in turn goes to El Jabez, saying, "I bring you your long-lost daughter." Thanks to Charlie, peace among the tribes is restored. And, Hassan gets his donkey.

Finis: The new and improved Blossom Camp opens. Charlie opens the faucets; out comes neither water nor sand, but oil.

Note: In this film, untidy Arabs toss melons at each other. Charlie's hotel contains cobwebs, dirt, dust, flies, and a collapsing mattress. Scenes show dirty villages. Inside the souks are tents, goats, donkeys, camels, a horse and buggy, and a broken-down bus.

• In Abdullah's (Kasket) "courtyard of delights," charming women pamper and bathe Charlie. Purrs Abdullah: "These and others will administer your every want." Sighs Charlie, "I feel like Aladdin." Awaiting Charlie in the "sleeping room," however, is an old, obese maiden.

• In Sheikh Ibrahim's (Illing) tent, several unshaven Arabs, sans teeth, grab chunks of meat from a huge bowl; then begin chewing like starving animals. When told, "Take the sheep's eye," Charlie grimaces.

The Saracen Blade (1954), COL. *Ricardo Montalban, Michael Ansara.*
P: Sam Katzman. CAMEOS, SHEIKHS, MAIDENS

This set-in-Italy tale features an evil sheikh. Tagged a malevolent "devil" slaver, the brutal sheikh scars an Arab maiden.

Scene: Thirteenth century Italy, Sicily. Pietro (Montalban) duels, in jest, with his father. Nearby, two robed Arabs bet on the outcome.

• The Italian Count Siniacola (Ansara) betrays Pietro, turning the swashbuckler over to the Turks. Boasts a Turkish soldier, We'll get "500 dinars on the slave market" for him.

• Inside a sheikh's posh tent. A black slave whips an Arab maiden, Zenobia. Pietro intervenes, stopping the beating. "Why do you interfere?," demands the ugly sheikh. Says Pietro, "What has she done?" The sheikh points to a knife wound on his face. "This. I am not any man. I am Haroun and the wound is to my pride." Pietro offers to take the lash, in lieu of the woman. Barks the sheikh, "If I can't get value from you as a slave, at least I'll make an example of you to the others."

• Zenobia begs the sheikh to free Pietro. The Arab agrees. He takes all her jewelry, even yanking off her ring. Vows the sheikh, "He will be free."

• In Italy, Zenobia wears "a veil after the manner of Moslem women." She tells Pietro's betrothed, "If ever you thought me a woman loved by Pietro or any other man, you will not think so now." Zenobia removes her veil, the camera reveals her knife-marked face. When asked, "Who did this to you?" Zenobia says, "A devil named Haroun."

Scanners (1981), Avco. *Stephen Lack, Jennifer O'Neil, Patrick McGoohan.*
W, D: David Cronenberg. CAMEOS, SHEIKHS

Are sheikhs responsible for the deaths of innocents?

Scene: In this sci-fi horror film, a speeding van smashes into a school bus full of scanners, referred to as "social outcasts." Machine-gun fire from the van tears into the scanners' bus. Suddenly, the out-of-control bus crashes through a record store window, falling on its side. Immediately, the camera cuts to several of Frank Zappa's "Sheik Yerbouti" record albums—all displaying a mustachioed Arab, wearing a white headdress.

Note: Why this juxtaposition? Why show, after innocent bus passengers are killed, so many album covers displaying a burnoosed Arab?

Scorpion (1986), Crown International. *Tonny Tulleners, Don Murray, Bart Baverman.* SP, P, D: William Riead. PALESTINIANS

Palestinian "terrorism" explodes in Los Angeles. Palestinians target American civilians, diplomats, and military leaders. Surfacing is ex-karate champ Tonny Tulleners (Scorpion); he extinguishes the villains.

Scene: Outside the DIA [not CIA] office are flags from England, France, the US, and Israel. On learning Palestinian terrorists have skyjacked a passenger jet in Los Angeles, the DIA contacts Scorpion (Tulleners).

• Washington, DC. Intones the Senate Sub-committee chief: "The President has just signed a policy directive endorsing the principle of preemptive strikes and reprisals against terrorists in the United States and abroad... The policy was triggered by the truck bombing in Lebanon that killed 241 Marines." And, "The potential American targets are individual diplomats, servicemen overseas, and most of us in this room. The [Palestinian] terrorist network has spread to the United States." Affirms General Higgins, "What concerns us is the sudden swing away from attacks on government property to attacks on individuals." Committee members view newsreel footage revealing Palestinians blowing up three passenger planes in a desert. Warns one observer, "A dangerous terrorist, Hamis, is headed toward Los Angeles. [His] suicide group [was] formed to launch suicide attacks against the West."

• Hamis and three cohorts have hijacked a passenger jet; the plane, with 132 passengers aboard, remains on the ground in Los Angeles. See *Wanted: Dead or Alive* (1987), *Hostage* (1986), and *The Delta Force* (1986).

• As one Palestinian struts down the plane's aisle, he shouts and hits passengers. Three Palestinians sport beards and moustaches; a mute woman wears fatigues. Their leader, Hamis, threatens to "blow this thing to hell and back." A frightened passenger, an American mother, cuddles her child. Scorpion appears. He promptly rescues the passengers. Then, he crushes all the hijackers.

• Earlier, the DIA jailed "a bad-ass terrorist" called Faued. The DIA tried to convince Faued to inform on other terrorists. But the sly Faued never intended to tell the DIA "who's who in the terror network in the United States." Instead, Faued duped the DIA. He paid someone to impersonate him, then had the imposter and his wife killed.

• The freed Faued boards a ship and begins terrorizing passengers. In time, Scorpion arrives; he brings down the villain.

Note: Credits state: "1st, 2nd, 3rd terrorist"—portrayed by Duke Jubran, Ali Barak, and Nagwa Abou-Seif.

Sea of Sand (1958), UI. *Richard Attenborough, John Gregson.* Filmed in Libya. CAMEOS

"Ayrabs" appear once; sitting near a dirt road they watch Allied jeeps drive by.

Scene: War-time Libya. After a British patrol blows up a Nazi petrol dump, a soldier grabs a handful of sand, griping, "Thousands of miles of rotten soil." Quips his pal, "The Ayrabs get a living out of it." Retorts the soldier, "They can have it!"

Note: Invisible Libyans. Stated in the credits: "The producers wish to acknowledge with thanks the assistance given by the Government of the United Kingdom of Libya." Yet, Libyans do not assist British soldiers.

Secret Service in Darkest Africa (1943), a.k.a. Manhunt in the African Jungles, REP. 15 episodes. *Rod Cameron, Joan Marsh, Lionel Royce, Kurt Kreuger, Frederic Brunn, Duncan Renaldo.* CLIFFHANGERS, VILLAINS

WWII. All episodes show Arabs aligned with Nazis. In Casablanca, Arabs and a few Nazis confront Allied agents, notably US Secret Service agent Rex Bennett (Cameron) and reporter Janet Blake (Marsh). All episodes show Rex and Janet crushing Arab villains; Janet excels at shooting Arabs dead. Also, each episode displays a chained-to-a-wall "good" Arab—Sultan Abou Ben Ali (Royce) utters a few sentences. Also assisting the US agents is Zara, a French dancing girl.

Scene: Casablanca. In episode one, Rex asks the sultan, "Will the North African tribal leaders support the United Nations or the Axis?" Replies the Arab, "They'll follow the precepts of the Prophet." Standing in front of the Sultan Abou Ben Ali's limousine are mute bodyguards with raised sabers. Cut to the sultan being held hostage by the evil Baron Van Rommler (Royce). Throughout the serial, the Baron impersonates the sultan. Islam is mocked.

• Rex and Janet continually battle two German leaders, the Baron and his cohort, Wolfe (Brunn). And, the agents contest the Arab villains assisting the Nazis, "Feisal" and "Hassan," as well as nearly "all the natives in North Africa."

• Moving to convince the Arabs to link up with German forces, the Baron exploits superstitions. He snatches the Arabs' "Dagger of Solomon," then forges an ancient scroll. Cut to Rex describing the "Dagger of Solomon" as an archaic "Moslem" weapon. "It's an ancient symbol revered by all Moslems," says Rex. "The Arabs believe that when the dagger is found and the tomb is opened, they will find a message, which will guide their cause in war and peace." Meanwhile, Hassan's Arabs try to sink American military ships carrying shipments of blood plasma intended for Allied forces.

• Several episodes present Arabs as inept buffoons. The camera shows Arabs blowing each other up, knifing, and even shooting one another. Often, a radical Arab conspiring with the Nazis does a "*Sieg Heil*" salute; he calls Wolfe "our master."

• In episode seven, Janet asks Arab rulers, "Am I to tell my leaders these attacks [by the Germans] mean the people of North Africa [Arabs] are pro-Nazi?" No Arab replies.

• Foiling a Nazi plot, Janet stops "the Moslem tribes" from joining the Germans.

• In the end, Rex frees Sultan Abou Ben Ali, the "good" sultan who was chained by the Nazis. Says the sultan to Rex, "I owe you my life and my freedom."

• Ironically, after they display scores of villainous Arab-loving-Nazis, the producers conclude the serial with this declaration: Arabs will not "follow the sign of the Swastika."

Note: This Arab-bashing serial was released in 1943, during WWII.

Serpent of the Nile (1953), COL. *Rhonda Fleming, Raymond Burr, William Lundigan, Michael Ansara.* P: Sam Katzman. Some of the movie sets used in this film are from Rita Hayworth's *Salome* (1953). EGYPTIANS, MAIDENS

Scheming Cleopatra betrays a humdrum Anthony.

Scene: Cleopatra displays not a morsel of affection for Anthony. Cleopatra's (Fleming) "first [and only] love" is Egypt. Thus, the cunning queen moves to eliminate Anthony (Burr). With Anthony out of the way, she plans to place her son on Rome's throne. So smitten is Anthony, that he fails to see "only an idiot would underestimate her."

• Cleopatra manipulates the dense Anthony. She wants her son by Julius Caesar to rule; the youth has "Roman blood and Egyptian blood."

• At the palace, scantily-clad maidens giggle as wrestlers duel. There is also a novel entertainer, "The Metallic Paint Dancer." Onlookers refer to her as "the golden wench."

• Though the Egyptian "people grow hungry," Cleopatra boasts that Egypt is a prosperous nation. Her servants provide guests with ample wine and elaborate feasts.

• Anthony's loyal lieutenant, Lucilius (Lundigan), confronts Cleopatra, saying, "Egypt is nothing; it is a shell. This is no country of unlimited wealth. These celebrations are to impress Anthony while your people starve."

• Feuding Egyptians kill Egyptians. The Egyptian Captain Florus (Ansara) assists his queen. Florus kills Cleopatra's sister and her cohort. Next, the captain sends off some guards to knife Lucilius as he sleeps; the Roman awakens and kills the Egyptian soldiers.

• The noble Roman, Lucilius, and the sly Egyptian, Florus, duel. Lucilius triumphs!

• Octavius's Roman legions arrive in Alexandria. Chariots clash! Egyptian troops succumb to superior Roman forces. The depressed Anthony commits suicide. Cleopatra's political ambitions are thwarted. The queen draws a poisonous snake to her bosom and expires.

Dialogue: Lucilius tells Cleopatra, "A serpent can be trusted more because we [Romans] know how to defend ourselves against its venom. There's no defense against you." See Theda Bara's *Cleopatra* (1917).

The Seven-Per-Cent Solution (1976), UNI. *Nicol Williamson, Robert Duvall, Vanessa Redgrave.* SP: Nicholas Meyer. P, D: Herbert Ross. Adapted from Meyer's novel. CAMEOS

A one-liner vilifies Islam. Emulating the actions of an ugly screen Arab, a Turkish man abducts Western women.

Scene: Circa 1890. When one of the hospital's "Sisters of Mercy" is murdered, Sherlock Holmes (Williamson) emerges, saying, "Ritual slaying. Throat slit, left to right. Common in Muslim rites and practices. Sharp, curved blade."

• Exiting a carriage, a fat Turkish "Pasha," wearing a red fez. His several clad-in-black wives trod behind him. Suddenly, the Pasha, "[who holds] a peculiar fascination for women with red hair," kidnaps, for "his harem," the heroine (Redgrave). Warns Holmes, "She's being taken out of the country against her will." Holmes and Watson to the rescue. On a train bound for Istanbul, they confront the Pasha's entourage, freeing the clad-in-harem-garb Redgrave.

Note: Meyer's book does not contain such stereotypical characters as the pasha and maidens, yet he injects them here. This movie mystery focuses on Holmes' attempts to kick his heroin addiction. And, the subplots address Holmes' nemesis, Dr. Moriarty, Sigmund Freud's heroics, and discrimination directed at Jews.

The Seventh Coin (1992), Orbit/Castle Hill. *Peter O'Toole, Alexandra Powers, Navin Chowdry, John Rhys-Davis, Arie Elias.* SP: Michael Lewis, Dror Soref. D: Soref. Filmed in Israel. PALESTINIANS, RECOMMENDED

Israeli filmmaker Dror Soref humanizes Palestinians. In Jerusalem, a street-wise Palestinian and a young American tourist fall in love.

Scene: Credits roll; the camera reveals devout Muslims, Christians, and Jews. In the souk is Salim Zouabi (Chowdry), a Palestinian Muslim who steals so he may support his grandfather, Fouad (Elias). After Salim grabs a shopper's purse, he then snatches and runs off with an American girl's camera case.

• Fouad's home. The elderly Muslim prays. Knowing Salim's monies stem from the boy's pilfering, Fouad refuses to eat. "If I do not steal," argues Salim, "how do you live?"

• The British villain, Emil (O'Toole), moves to acquire a priceless seventh gold coin, which was taken from a 1947 Masada dig. Believing Fouad possesses the seventh coin, Emil sends two generic thugs to Fouad's residence. The men beat Fouad to death. The elderly Palestinian manages to hide the coin inside the stolen camera case.

• Salim arrives home. Seeing his dead grandfather, the youth grieves. His Palestinian friends comfort him.

• Approaching Salim is a bright American tourist, Ronnie (Powers). She offers to give him a one hundred dollar bill, on one condition—he forks over her friend's camera case. Ronnie goes to snatch the case; she fails. Quickly, clever Salim takes her money. Later, they find the gold coin; Emil's thugs arrive, chasing the couple. Twice, Salim helps Ronnie elude the villains. The youths find sanctuary in an underground sewer.

• Leaving the tunnel, Ronnie and Salim hold hands. Salim decides to return Ronnie's money. Then, he boosts her confidence, convincing Ronnie that she is indeed quite "pretty." After teaching her how-to-survive-on-the-street tactics he exclaims, "You make a good thief." Later, as Salim mourns his grandfather, Ronnie comforts him.

• Upset at his hirelings' failure to procure the coin, Emil kills them.

• Ronnie tells Salim he is handsome, brave, and smart. She props the Palestinian's hopes, prompting him to say, "One day I become a teacher, and I help my people. I help my people [and] your people, like you and me. We are friends, yes!" Affirms Ronnie, "Very good friends." They kiss. Moving to make love, they begin to undress. Suddenly, a friend appears, interrupting their embraces.

• Emil moves to kill Salim. But Ronnie dupes him, saving Salim's life.

• Emil pursues Ronnie and Salim. After Emil wounds Salim, he moves to extinguish the Palestinian and Ronnie. In time, Israeli Captain Gail (Rhys-Davis) arrives, shooting Emil dead. Ronnie and Salim kiss.

Finis: Salim reunites Ronnie with her tourist companions. Seeing the about-to-return-home Americans embrace the long-lost Ronnie, Salim walks off. Ronnie searches for him, calling "Salim." Off in the distance Salim whispers, "Until we meet again, my dear."

The Seventh Voyage of Sinbad (1958), COL. *Kerwin Mathews, Kathryn Grant [Crosby].* Special effects: Ray Harryhausen. VILLAINS

In this adventure fantasy, Sinbad, Baghdad's caliph, and Princess Parisa, the caliph's lovely daughter, oppose the evil wizard Sokurah and some fierce creatures.

Scene: The wizard demands Sinbad (Mathews) rush off to the magic isle and acquire "the [boy] genie of the lamp." This amiable young genie, "whose powers are invincible, will not evoke harm."

• When Sinbad refuses the wizard's request, Sokurah reduces Princess Parisa (Grant) to miniature-size. Thus, Sinbad is obliged to sail off to the magic isle. Sighting land, Sinbad tells his men, "May Allah grant you to find food and water."

• Accompanying Sinbad are recently released prisoners. When the men uncover treasures on the magic isle, several turn against Sinbad. Abruptly, one ex-prisoner falls from a cliff. Sinbad sighs, "Allah knows many ways of dealing with hungry men."

• Ray Harryhausen's telling special effects. Sinbad duels a skeleton. He also contests some snake ladies, a colossal one-eyed cyclops, a giant Roc, a two-headed bird of prey, and a fire-spitting dragon.

• Now released from the lamp, the boy genie chooses to side with Sinbad and his men. Together, they crush the wicked wizard. Cut to Sinbad and Parisa sailing off into the sunset.

The Shanghai Gesture (1941), UA. *Gene Tierney, Victor Mature, Walter Huston, Ona Munson.* EGYPTIANS

Western women should avoid fez-wearing Egyptians. In a Shanghai casino an Egyptian, tagged "a thoroughbred mongrel," dooms a British mogul's daughter.

Scene: Shanghai, Madame Gin Sling's (Munson) gambling place, "a modern Tower of Babel." Describing himself as a "poet of Shanghai and Gomorrah," Dr. Omar (Mature) purrs to a lovely blonde in distress, "Allah be praised for always providing new women."

• When asked who buys the drinks, Omar boasts, "I can say with pride that I've never paid for anything in my life." Some money drops into Omar's hands; he bows, then exchanges the bill for gold, saying: "Allah, Allah, Allah is great."

• Arriving is Sir Guy's (Huston) missing daughter, Polly (Tierney). She calls the slick Omar "the tent maker," saying "[he should cease] playing at being the Caliph of Baghdad."

• As fragile Polly cannot cease gambling, she begs Omar, her unscrupulous lover, to help her; "otherwise I'll be here for good," she says. But Omar, "who trades on the weakness of others," exploits her addiction. Not only does he snatch Polly's costly necklace, but he also convinces her to continue at the gambling tables. Omar deceives her, saying, "[Casino personnel] buy and sell everything in an honorable manner."

• Sir Guy enters the casino. The anguished Polly mocks her father. Pointing to Omar she shouts, "How do you like him, dad?" Sir Guy grimaces.

• Concluding scenes show a seriously ill Polly as an alcoholic. Omar remains apathetic.

Note: Why place an Egyptian cur in a Shanghai casino?

Shark (1969), a.k.a. Maneater, Heritage-Cinematografica. *Burt Reynolds, Barry Sullivan, Enrique Lucero.* D: Samuel Fuller. Filmed in Mexico. MAIDENS, VILLAINS

This treasure-hunting tale shows Arabs as street urchins and plump thugs. Also appearing, a corrupt Sudanese police inspector and a covetous Arab mother.

Scene: Sulibar, a Sudanese "hell-hole and pig sty." Opening frames imply Arab mothers do not care about their children. After sharks kill a diver named Mohammed, the camera reveals Mohammed's mother and other relatives. Anna (Pinal), the Western heroine, approaches the women, including the boy's mother, with a wad of bills. Displaying not tears but greed, the mother grimaces, then abruptly licks her thumb and begins counting the money.

• The Western gunrunner, Caine (Reynolds), asks Anna, "What's a nice girl like you doing in a place like this?" Cut to the souk. Unkempt "superstitious" Arabs mingle with sheep, chicken, and donkeys. Goats accompany a fat, mute Arab bartender. A car breaks down; three Arabs push it.

• Needing some booze, Caine gives the chubby bartender his watch in exchange for two drinks. An Arab youth snatches the timepiece and runs off. Later, the boy returns the watch.

• Thinking Caine may thwart his treasure-hunting business, Mallare (Sullivan) dispatches "a big, fat stinking whale and his [Arab] boys" to beat up the American. Wielding broken bottles and clubs, "Fatso's" hoods charge Caine; he floors them. One

Arab grabs a "kid" for protection, nearly killing him. See *Navy SEALs* (1990) and *True Lies* (1994). Here, too, cowardly Arabs use innocents as shields.

• Mallare decides he and Caine should team-up; soon they uncover sunken treasures. Enter Barok (Lucero), Sulibar's corrupt Sudanese police chief. He demands the men fork over all the discovered gold. If not, he threatens to kill them. Caine acts, dumping Barok to the sharks.

She (1917), FOX. Silent. *Valeaka Suratt, Ben L. Taggart, Miriam Fouche.* Based on Sir H. Rider Haggard's book. EGYPTIANS

An Egyptian as victim.

Scene: Egypt, 350 BC. The pharaoh's daughter, Ustane (Fouche), convinces her lover, the priest of Isis, to wed her.

• The couple run off to the "coast of Africa." Here, they are greeted by Ayesha (Suratt), a woman with "mystic power," and Ayesha's non-Arab cohorts.

• Ayesha, who is called "She-Who-Never-Dies," moves to seduce Ustane's husband. As the Egyptian rejects Ayesha's advances, she strikes the newlywed dead. Ustane vows to avenge her husband's death.

• Flash forward to England, 1885. Leo, the protagonist, uncovers letters verifying that he and the ill-fated Egyptian couple are, in fact, related.

• Vowing to strike back, Leo travels to Africa, and promptly dupes Ayesha, encouraging her to strut through the roaring "Flame of Eternal Life." This walk-through-fire, purrs Leo, will make you beautiful and immortal. Ayesha believes him, takes the fire-walk, and emerges from the fire as an ugly ape.

Note: Hollywood released other silent *She* movies, in 1908, 1911, and 1925. Actress Marguerite Snow appeared in the 1911 *She*. See my analysis of *She* (1925). See, also, *The Vengeance of She* (1968).

She (1925), Lee-Bradford Corp. Silent. *Betty Blythe.* Seven versions of *She* were filmed between 1900 and 1930. CAMEOS

No evil Arabs in this production. Arab curs do, however, appear in *She* (1965) and in *The Vengeance of She* (1968).

Scene: The action occurs off Libya's coast. Cut to the home of the veiled "She" (Ayesha), "[a] queen whose days and loveliness do not fade." Inside Ayesha's quarters are Egyptian statues, and Egyptian drawings decorate the walls.

• Surfacing briefly is "Mahomet, an Arab dragoman."

She (1965), MGM. *Ursula Andress, John Richardson, Peter Cushing, Christopher Lee, Rosenda Monteros.* SP: David T. Chantler. D: Robert Day. CAMEOS

Bellydancers and bedouin bandits are inserted in this 1965 version of H. Rider Haggard's story about a 2,000-year-old temptress.

Scene: Palestine 1918, the end of WWI. Arab music underscores the action at a club. Rowdy British veterans, soldiers, and Arabs cheer an attractive bellydancer. Appearing is a shady-looking Arab wearing a red and white kuffiyeh. The Arab brings to his table, the lovely Ustane (Monteros). One British veteran, Leo Vincey (Richardson), moves in on Ustane, convincing her to jilt the Arab. She agrees; they leave the club. Two veterans begin mingling on stage with the dancers. Soon, a friendly brawl breaks out.

• In a dark alley, Ustane and Leo kiss. Suddenly, two Arabs surface from the shadows; they floor Leo. Cut to Billali's Arabian Nights abode. Though Billali wears a black robe and burnoose, neither he nor Ustane are Arabs. They hail from the secret city of Kuma. Cut to "She" (Andress), who persuades Leo to make the treacherous journey to Kuma.

• Leo convinces his two British friends to join him; they trek across the desert. For no clear reason, camel-riding bedouins attack. The three Brits kill several, and the surviving bedouins retreat. Remaining scenes display no Arab scharacters.

She's a Sheik (1927), PAR. Silent. *Bebe Daniels, Richard Arlen, William Powell, Paul McAllister.* *NS. Notes from De Witt Bodeen's review in MAG (972–73). MAIDENS, SHEIKHS

Arabs vs. Arabs, vs. legionnaires. The heroine, who is half-Arab, spots the Frenchman she wants, and she takes him. See *The Sheik* (1921).

Summary: In this parody of *The Sheik*, Zaida (Daniels), the Arab-Spanish granddaughter of Sheik Yussiff (McAllister), appears as a "hot number." The lovely Zaida rejects Arab suitors, opting to romance a dashing legionnaire, Captain Colton (Arlen). When Colton balks, she kidnaps him, whisking the captain off to her tent. Here, she places Colton in a cage "formerly occupied by her pet leopard." Before she begins romancing the legionnaire, Zaida arranges for him to be "sufficiently tamed, bathed, and freshly barbered." Writes De Witt Bodeen: "Like Valentino in *The Sheik*, Zaida's motto is: "When I see a [Christian] man I want, I take him."

Though the Arab chieftain Kada (Powell) proposes amour, Zaida rebuffs him. Thus, they fence. Zaida "skillfully rips off Kada's flowing garments with her rapier." Upset, the spurned Kada convinces some "renegade tribesmen" to charge "the outnumbered French garrison forces." Zaida and her all-too-few followers seem doomed. Unexpectedly, two wandering Western showmen arrive at Zaida's camp. The entertainers bring out a movie projector and "project a film they have of attacking 'good' Arabs" about to rescue them. When Kada's dense tribesmen charge the camp, they see this film, displaying scores of attacking Arabs. They fall for the reel ruse, believing the movie Arab army is real. Terrified, they "retreat in disorder." After Kada's "regulars are completely routed," Zaida runs off to seduce the "handsome captain."

Note: Religion. States one critic, in VAR (23 November 1927), "[Zaida] would marry only in the Christian faith, declining to choose from the swarthy brethren among whom she had always lived."

The Sheik (1921), PAR. Silent. *Rudolph Valentino, Agnes Ayres, Adolphe Menjou, Walter Long, George Waggner.* Adapted from Edith M. Hull's novel. Shot in Yuma, Arizona. After *The Sheik*, Valentino became an international idol. SHEIKHS, MAIDENS

Desert dramas display Arabs living in an "old" world. Bellydancers appear as exotic maidens. Producers present an Arabian stallion, "Jahad." (Note the resemblance to Jihad [Holy War].) Arab slavers auction off Arab women to the "Lords of Harems." Sheikhs romance Western heroines; saber-wielding desert Arabs furiously fight fellow Arabs to secure the light-complexioned heroines. Should the woman be abducted and whisked off to a lecherous sheikh's enclave, no problem. At the last-minute, the dashing Western hero will rescue her. In preparation for amour, mute Arab women attend, bathe, and dress the kidnapped civilized woman of the West.

Even before the Production Code, reel Western women did not engage in hanky-panky-with-Arabs. However, the fair heroine could love an Arab, provided the robed sheikh turned out to be a Westerner, disguised as an Arab. In films like *The Arab* (1915), producers refused to assimilate "colored" Arabs in their movies. To curb audiences' real or imagined fears, they displayed Arabs as nonassimilable beings. States the Motion Pictures Producers and Directors of America, Inc., Production Code, (1930–34): "Miscegenation (sex relations between white and black races) is forbidden." As some Code executives believed Arabs to be nonwhite persons, it became unthinkable for producers to show a white Western woman loving a dusky-skinned, swarthy Arab. Like brown Indians and black Africans, dark Arabs, too, could not be bonded with "white" heroines.[152]

Scene: In the desert, Islam is revered. Frames reveal a mosque, the imam calling the faithful to prayer, "Allah is Allah—there is no God but Allah." Sheikh Ahmed Ben Hassan's (Valentino) Arabs bow and pray to "Allah." Affirms one, "All things are with Allah."

• Women as property. On screen, this message, "An ancient [Arab] custom." Cut to "a marriage market, where [mute] wives are bought by wealthy men." When the attractive Zilah is offered for sale, an Arab protests, declaring he loves her. Ahmed comforts the man, saying, "When love is more desired than riches, it is the will of Allah. Let another be chosen." Yet, the other women are dispatched "to the harems of the rich merchants to obey and serve like chattel slaves."

• Biska, "a city of adventure." Here, the new (the West) rubs elbows with the old (Arabia). A beggar receives money from Westerners.

• The inquisitive English heroine, Lady Diana (Ayres), borrows a dancing girl's costume and sneaks into Biska's "casino [which] is closed to all except Arabs." Inside the casino, a "marriage gamble" game. "Brides are won on the turn of the wheel." Abruptly, Ahmed sees through Diana's disguise. The Arab berates Diana for intruding. Yet, he desires her.

• "Dawn with the Arab under the lure of the defiant English girl." Ahmed climbs the trellis to Diana's balcony, serenading her with the song, "Beautiful Dreamer."

• Diana rides into the desert. Ahmed abducts her, holding her captive in his desert tent. "Her exultant dream of freedom ended—a helpless captive in desert wastes." See *Harem* (1985), *Protocol* (1984), and *Sahara* (1983).

• A "savage sandstorm." Ahmed moves to seduce Diana; she tries to kill herself.

• Weeks later, Ahmed's French friend, the novelist, Dr. Raoul de St. Herbert (Menjou), visits with the sheikh. Seeing the captive, Diana, Raoul berates Ahmed, saying, "Does the past mean so little to you that you now steal white women? You might have spared her... the humiliation of meeting a man from her own world." Raoul insists Ahmed restore "Mademoiselle to her people." Counters Ahmed, "When an Arab sees a woman he wants, he takes her."

• In the desert, Sheikh Omair's (Long) "barbarous" bandits spot Ahmed's Arabs escorting Diana. After killing the Arabs, they abduct Diana.

• Omair's quarters. The debauched "black native" Omair creeps toward Diana;

she pleads for death, saying, "Do not let me fall into their hands."

• On learning Omair has kidnaped Diana, Ahmed rouses his men. They attack Omair's stronghold, killing scores of people.

• Omair's boudoir. "Bring forth the white gazelle," barks Omair. The anxious Diana enters; he goes to rape her. Abruptly, Omair's jealous mistress pulls a knife. At the same time, Ahmed arrives, saving Diana. But one of Omair's cohorts shoots Ahmed.

• Inside Ahmed's tent. Diana and Raoul tend the seriously injured sheikh; he may not recover from his wounds. Outside, praying Arabs resolve that Ahmed's fate "rests with Allah."

• At this life-or-death moment, an unexpected surprise. The burnoosed Ahmed is not really an Arab, but a super-powerful Englishman: "Viscount Caryll, Earl of Glencaryll." Note the dialogue:

Diana: His hand is so large for an Arab.

(Note: How small or large should an Arab's hand be?)

Raoul: He is not an Arab. His father was an Englishman, his mother a Spaniard.

• Explains Raoul to Diana, many years ago a desert sheikh found Ahmed's mother and father, deserted by their escort, "left to die in the desert." When Ahmed's foster father passed on, the young sheikh returned home from Paris, "[where he was studying] to assume leadership of the tribe." Diana rejoices. Now, marriage is possible, not with Sheikh Ahmed, but with the Viscount Caryll, Earl of Glencaryll. Affirms the NYT reviewer:

And you [film-goers] won't be offended by having a white girl marry an Arab either, for the sheik isn't really a native of the desert at all. Oh, no; he's the son of a Spanish father and an English mother who were killed when he was a baby so the old sheik could raise him as his son. These Arabian romantic movies, you know, never have the courage of their romantics (7 November 1921).

Note: Consider *The Sheik*'s impact on Arab audiences. No Arab heroes appear. Thus, Arab audiences may cheer the European protagonist. Consider how American audiences might react if an Egyptian filmmaker produced *The American Cowboy*, a movie adapted from a Korean novel. Would audiences be pleased to see the cowboy hero being portrayed by a Bulgarian? Would they applaud if the film's cowboy champion turned out to be not an American, but a Romanian Earl in disguise?

• *The Sheik*'s record-breaking popularity enabled Paramount to make $3 million-plus on the film. Studio ads spurred viewers to "see the auction of beautiful girls to the lords of Algerian harems." Writes Shulman, Valentino's biographer, "Police sought hundreds of runaway girls whose destination was reputed to be the Sahara. Sighing in their kitchens, parlors and bedrooms, American women longed for burning sands."[153]

• Following *The Sheik*'s success, silent Arabian shorts began parodying the desert dramas. For example, *Whistling Lions* and *Two Arabian Sights* (1927) reveal dense, unkempt, and lecherous sheikhs rejecting their own women, preferring to kidnap, adding to their harems and seducing "a new favorite"—the fair western heroine. In *Whistling Lions*, the American protagonist rescues his sweetheart from the clutches of a dense, pint-sized Egyptian potentate. When a lecherous desert sheikh, Hassan Ben Homemuch, "[who loves women] but not his own," spots Lotta Gelt in the souk, he tries smooching the American. Hassan grabs Lotta, "[who runs] a boxing gymnasium at home"; she decks the Arab with a single punch.

Among the feature films spawning sand and sheikh dramas are *Arabian Love* (1924); *The Arab* (1924); *Song of Love* (1923, 1928); *Burning Sands* (1929); *The Son of the Sheik* (1926); *The Shriek of Araby* (1922); and *She's a Sheik* (1920). Even Will Rogers donned Arab garb, spoofing Valentino in a 1920 movie, title unknown.

The sheet music industry fused itself onto the cash wagon. Consider Ted Snyder's 1921 song, *The Sheik of Araby*:

> I'm the Sheik of Araby.
> Your hearts belongs to me.
> At night when you're asleep,
> Into your tent I'll creep.

• From MPW (22 October 1921), emblazoned on the movie's poster: "When an Arab sees a woman he wants he takes her!" Ancient Proverb of Arabia. Some women fainted during passion scenes, prompting local censor boards to criticize Hollywood's morals. Publicity posters and newspaper ads encouraged females to: "Shriek—For the Sheik Will Seek You Too!" Even before promotions for *The Sheik* were distributed, some Americans mispronounced the word "sheik," speaking it to rhyme with "shriek," not with "shake." Also, ladies' fashions mirrored the film's burnooses and thobes.

• Capitalizing on the movie's "Great Lover" notoriety, Canada's Julius Schmid marketed a condom, "Sheik." Each of the entrepreneur's "3 for 50 cents" packet displays a robed Arab atop a stallion.[154]

The Sheik Steps Out (1937), REP. *Ramon Novarro, Lola Lane, Stanley Fields, Robert Coote, Jamiel Hasson.* S, SP: Adele Bullington. SHEIKHS, RECOMMENDED

Does this comedy-with-ballads show a sheikh marrying a fair American? No! In the end, the groom's true identity is revealed; he is not an Arab, rather a "Spanish Nobleman."

Scene: The desert. Devout Arabs on horseback sing, in part, "And like the faithful followers of Allah, Allah be praised. I ride with the wind."

• Introducing mythical Tamareed. Here, Sheikh Ahmed Ben Nesib (Novarro), breeder of the world's fastest horses, greets Ms. Flip Murdock (Lane), a rich, spoiled American. For amusement, Ahmed feigns being a poor, native guide. Flip decides to employ him.

• In the souk, Flip and her father move to buy some souvenirs. All the merchants are honest and friendly.

• Boasting, Flip makes a wager with an English nobleman, Lord Byington (Coote), that she will find a horse that is faster than any steed he owns. Flip promptly trys to acquire Ahmed's fine horse, "Mad Chestnut."

• Ahmed wants to teach the ill-mannered Flip some manners. Thus, he stages an all-in-fun kidnapping party. When Ahmed's hired Arabs close in on Flip, Ahmed shows up, rescuing her. Their romance blossoms in the desert moonlight.

• Islam is respected. Wearing Arab garb, Flip and Ahmed exchange wedding vows then sign the marriage contract. The mosque's imam chants in Arabic. Flip tells Ahmed, "It's all so beautifully strange."

• Soon, Flip finds out that Ahmed staged the kidnapping. Upset, she rushes off to Paris, intending to wed Lord Byington. During the wedding ceremony, Flip refuses to say, "I do." Quips an observer, "She's in love with an Arab!" Suddenly, Ahmed appears. He snatches Flip from the altar; they run off. The altar abduction ploy predates by 30 years *The Graduate*'s (1967) famous finale, in which Dustin Hoffman whisks Katherine Ross away from her intended.

Finis: Flip kisses Ahmed; they advance toward their honeymoon suite. Suddenly, Ahmed exclaims: "[I am a] Spanish Nobleman; my foster father was a great desert chieftain." See Valentino's *The Sheik* (1921), in which the Western heroine also ascertains that her Arab lover is not an Arab, that his father was an Englishman, his mother a Spaniard.

Treatment of Islam: Says Abu Saal (Fields), "By the sacred tooth of the prophet." And, "By the beard of the prophet."

Dialogue: When Flip mocks Arabs, Ahmed counters, saying, "Mademoiselle might learn that sheikhs resent being called mules." Others blemishes are not challenged. Flip says, "They [the Arabs] all look alike to me." A French officer tells Flip, "We have learned to be wary of all Arabs, Madame."

Note: Why reveal in the final seconds that Ahmed is a Spaniard?

The Sheik's Wife (1922), Vitagraph. Silent. *Emmy Lynn, Marcel Vibert, Albert Bras.* Filmed in Algiers. Release of a French film. *NS. Notes from VAR. SHEIKHS, RECOMMENDED

One year after *The Sheik* (1921), this French movie, *The Sheik's Wife*, presents an English lady happily married to an educated sheikh. Writes a NYT critic, "the girl is not a young innocent whom the Arab takes advantage of." Though she confronts "a clash of customs and mental habits," her sheikh is "a rather heroic figure" (6 March 1922).

Summary: Estelle Graydon (Lynn), an attractive English woman, meets the son of an Arab sheikh, the Oxford-educated Hadjid Ben-Khedin (Vilbert). They fall in love, and marry. Whisking Estelle off to their desert home, Hadjid vows that she will be his one and only wife. All is well until Estelle gives birth to a girl. Abruptly, Hadjid's father, Cassim (Bras), insists his son find another woman. Explains Cassim, according to the tribe's "ancient custom," Hadjid must take a "second wife so that a son may be born to him." When Estelle finds out about the proposed "breach," she runs off with their little girl. However, Hadjid intercepts them, bringing them back to the village.

Promptly, Estelle's former suitor as well as British troops intervene. Cassim's men engage the British; Hadjid is captured. As Hadjid "promises to go forth into the desert and create no further trouble," a British officer releases him.

Finis: The reformed, contented Hadjid and his wife, Estelle, are "seated by a stream with their child."

Note: Some European producers depicted Arabs marrying Westerners. See *Jericho* (1937).

The Sheltering Sky (1990), WB. *Debra Winger, John Malkovich, Eric Vu-An.* Based on Paul Bowles' 1949 novel. Shot in Morocco and Algeria. MAIDENS, VILLAINS, WORST LIST

Tangier. Foul Arab women prowl the shadows. Mute whores appear as objects in black. Lurking outside tents, they trek across the desert. Functioning as immoral seducers of women, Arab men threaten Westerners and accommodate annihilators. North Africa appears as a filthy, inhospitable area, complete with dark alleys and terrifying desert sandstorms. See *Naked Lunch* (1991).

Scene: This post-WWII scenario concerns Kit Moresby (Winger) and Port Moresby (Malkovich), a disaffected New York couple. They journey across the Sahara desert, drifting toward emptiness. Along the way, the couple encounters unkempt, unethical Arabs. For example, a greedy Arab clerk refuses to assist the duo until they fork over money. An Arab woman dances, as if possessed. Arab shoe-shine boys fight each other. Other kids aggressively pursue Westerners, demanding "tips" for baggage handling. The children harass an American visitor. Abruptly, he tosses coins in the air; the youths scramble.

• Kit and Port Moresby tell an Arab customs official they may stay a while. Replies the Arab, "A year or two? In this place?... [with] no four-star restaurants?"

• The couple spends time at the "Grand," a hotel without electricity or water. "From now on," they're told, "there's nothing with running water, nothing at all." Cut to swarms of flies, tagged "black snow," appearing in their soup, buzzing around their meals.

• Prostitutes and thieves surround the visiting couple. The Moresbys face more difficulties. Arriving at a new village, an Arab tells Kit, "I have a wonderful room for you." When Kit sees the room, she gasps, "It does have a smell of its own, doesn't it."

• A cloaked, unshaven pimp escorts Port to bed a seemingly naive whore. The Arab woman disrobes, then suddenly lunges for Port's wallet. When Port tries to recover his money, the woman abuses him. Arab men enter, chasing off Port.

• Stricken with fever, Port is near-death. Mute Arabs encircle him; musicians perform—for money. Not one Arab moves to call a doctor, not one Arab tries to comfort Port. Finally, he is taken to a sanitized French fort. Here, Port receives proper medical care, but he dies.

• Alone, the despondent Kit becomes "lost." She permits a bedouin, Belquassim (Vu-An), to bed her, violently. Belquassim functions as a sexual predator; he seizes Kit's wedding ring, handles her roughly, then ravishes her.

• After Belquassim's camel caravan arrives at a village, he hides Kit away in a private roof-top shack. Soon, Belquassim visits Kit. Removing his ink-blue burnoose, the bedouin beds, again, the unresponsive Kit. The "copulation on the cot" implies Arab men are barbarians. Continually, Belquassim and his ugly bedouins abuse Kit, leaving her alone to die. Regrettably, Kit intends to slowly commit suicide.

• The seriously ill Kit makes an effort to help herself, requesting soup. An Arab woman delivers the soup; Kit pays her server with foreign bills, worth much more than Arab currency. Thinking Kit has cheated her, the dense woman and her cohorts screech, then chase Kit.

Finis: Kit is looked after at a French hospital. But, she rushes off, returning to the Grand Hotel, where she becomes "lost," again.

Note: Writes Caryn James in the NYT (27 January 1991): the American heroines, in movies such as *The Sheltering Sky* and *Not Without My Daughter* (1991), "wake to find themselves being assaulted." In *The Sheltering Sky*, the grief-stricken American, played by Debra Winger, "gives herself over to a mad sexual adventure and escape into a harem." Says James, "The image of the turbaned tribesman creeping over the sand to attack the

American woman is part of the eroticism and danger that imbues *The Sheltering Sky*, it is a cliché." Continues James, "The same image is just one more nasty stereotype in *Not Without My Daughter*." In *Not Without My Daughter*, the Mideast Muslim male kidnaps his American wife (Sally Field) and their daughter, and imprisons them in Iran. He slaps his wife's face, breaks an holy oath sworn on the Qur'an, then boasts, "I'm a Muslim... Islam is the greatest gift I can give my daughter."

• Kate Higgs Khalilian writes in *Newsweek* (5 August 1999):

> Don't believe the [movie] myth that only two people from the same culture are suited for each other. I'm American and my husband is from Iran. Nationality aside, we're not very different. His family engages in the same kind of family drama as mine. We find humor in the same kinds of things. We share beliefs about how to raise our children. Most important, we love each other. We've been married for 13 years and have a very strong relationship.

Sherlock Jr. (1924), Metro. Silent. *Buster Keaton, Kathryn McGuire, Ward Crane.* P, D: Keaton. See *So This Is Paris* (1926). SHEIKHS

A dandy is tagged "The Sheikh."

Scene: Keaton, who works as a moving-picture operator in a small town theater, studies to be a detective. He and "the local sheikh," a ladies' man sporting a moustache and a three-piece suit, vie for the heroine's affection. Desperate to win the heroine, the sheikh steals her father's watch. Next, the sheikh pawns it, framing Keaton for the theft. In the end, the sheikh's ruse is discovered. Keaton gets the girl.

Note: As early as 1924, producers used the word "sheikh" as a synonym for rogue.

Ship of Fools (1965), COL. *Vivien Leigh, Simone Signoret, Jose Ferrer.* P, D: Stanley Kramer. CAMEOS, VILLAINS

A one-liner links Arabs with a Nazi disciple.

Scene: Aboard the German ship Vera, en route to Bremerhaven, circa 1931. One passenger, a despicable believer of Hitler's new order (Ferrer), boasts that Arabs also abhor Jews. "The Arabs are my kind of people," he proclaims.[155]

Shoot the Moon (1982), MGM. *Albert Finney, Diane Keaton.* CAMEOS

Scene: The action focuses on a separated California couple. As Keaton prepares a sandwich in the kitchen, Finney appears and asks what she [his ex-wife] is doing. She says, "[I am making my lover] Frank's lunch. He loves Syrian bread." Quips Finney, "What is he, an Arab?" She repliess, "no," and leaves the room. Finney grabs the Syrian bread, sniffs it, then tosses it into a bowl.

Note: Most Americans love Syrian/Pita bread!

Short Circuit (1986), TRI. *Ally Sheedy, Steve Guttenberg.* CAMEOS, SHEIKHS

Arabs are singled out as procurers of robots capable of launching "25-megaton bombs."

Scene: In the US, robed Arabs appear in four scenes, wearing sunglasses and headdresses. After they surface at a military reviewing stand, the camera shows the "most sophisticated robots on planet Earth" destroying tanks and jeeps. Cut to Arabs, applauding. The robots are said to function well in "burning deserts."

Note: Why are members of the international community absent?

Shout at the Devil (1976), AI. *Lee Marvin, Roger Moore, Ian Holm.*

An American, Englishman, and Arab join forces to bring down vicious Germans.

Scene: In East Africa, prior to WWI, an Arab mute, Mohammed (Holm), functions as a second banana. Wearing a red fez, Mohammed is the steadfast friend of Flynn (Marvin), the Irish-American protagonist.

• Scenes show Mohammed fighting alongside Flynn, helping him crush the German villains. Later, in Tanganyika, Germans kill Mohammed.

Note: Mohammed does not speak, as the Germans try but fail to hang him.

The Shriek of Araby (1923), Mack Sennett Prod. Silent. *Ben Turpin, Katheryn McGuire, Dick Sutherland.* Notes from NYT (11 June 1923). SHEIKHS, MAIDENS

Arabs vs. Arabs. In this parody of *The Sheik* (1921) an American routs an "atrocious" sheikh and his cohorts, then gets the fair heroine.

Scene: Turpin appears as a movie usher; he stands outside the Palace theater that is screening the movie *The Sheik*. Turpin, who is nicknamed the Shriek, promotes the movie by "putting on the Sheik's raiment." Suddenly, he dreams he is an Arab sheikh, living in "Arabia."

• Turpin's dream. When the clad-in-Arab-garb usher arrives in the desert, robed Arab horsemen whisk him off to a tent. Here, the villain "Mahomet" barks to an executioner wielding a huge saber: "Make him a foot shorter." In time, a dashing prince arrives. The villains fail to sever "the Turpin head from the Turpin torso."

• Says the prince to his Arabs: "He [Turpin] shall take my place while I am away in Baghdad." Abruptly, veiled maidens bow before Sheikh Turpin. As they lower their heads, Sheikh Turpin quips, "I'm starting to enjoy this."

• The sheikh encounters a lovely American artist (McGuire); she is "painting pictures in the desert." He whisks her off to his tent. Demanding she be "his wife," he orders Arab maidens to prepare her for the "wedding." Suddenly, Mahomet rushes into the tent and rescues her. Or does he? Declares Mahomet, "I saved you because I must have you for myself." Sheikh Turpin and his Arabs attack; Arabs fight Arabs. Turpin saves the girl from Mahomet's clutches.

• Later, back at Turpin's tent, she "learns to love him." They kiss, and decide to stay "together until this desert freezes over."

• The camera introduces a black-bearded lecherous Arab, "the bandit king—He likes Eastern sweets!" Says Mahomet to the bandit, "She'll [the American] be the prize of your harem." After the bandit kidnaps the American lovely, he not only tries to seduce her, but he forces "her to do washing during the day." Sheikh Turpin comes to the rescue. The "brutal schemer" and Mahomet, his cohort, "are shot forth into the harem's swimming bath, where they are drowned."

• The film concludes as it began, outside the Palace movie theater. The clad-in-Arab-garb Turpin, sits atop a horse, still dreaming. A policeman wakes the usher.

Note: Comic moments. From his tent, Turpin makes a phone call: "Camel 4-1904!"

In the desert, Turpin rides an ostrich; a magician named Presto conjures up a trout-filled lake. And, Turpin reads a paper, "The Daily Camel."

The Siege (1998), TCF. *Denzel Washington, Tony Shalhoub, Annette Bening, Bruce Willis, Sami Bouajila.* P: Lynda Obst, Edward Zwick. W, D: Zwick. VILLAINS, PALESTINIANS

Arab Muslims as terrorists. Arab immigrants along with Arab-American auto mechanics, university students, and a college teacher terrorize and kill more than 700 New Yorkers. The extremists destroy the city's FBI building, killing scores of government agents. They blast theater-goers, detonate a bomb in a crowded bus, and try to murder school children.

Points out Roger Ebert, in the *Chicago Sun-Times* (6 November 1998):

The prejudicial attitudes embodied in the film are insidious, like the anti-Semitism that infected fiction and journalism in the 1930s—not just in Germany but in Britain and America." And, "There is a tendency to lump together 'towelheads' (a term used in the movie)... Given how vulnerable Arab-Americans are to defamation, was this movie really necessary?

Richard Schickel, of *Time,* also cites the film's stereotypes, noting that the producers single out Arab Muslims, the "easiest-to-despise of all groups" (9 November 1998).

Washington Post reporter Sharon Waxman questions how viewers might react had the villains not been Arabs.

A nefarious rabbi exhorts his extremist ultra-Orthodox followers to plant bombs against Arab sympathizers in America. Innocents are killed and maimed. Or how about this: A Catholic priest has molested an altar boy. The church refuses to hand him and other offenders over to the police. The FBI starts rounding up clerics in an attempt to ferret them out...[P]rovocative narrow-minded scenarios suggesting every Catholic was a pervert or IRA member, or every Jew was a terrorist, would certainly spark protests from Jews and Catholics... Would Hollywood choose to portray them in the first place?[156]

Since *Black Sunday* (1977), eighteen Hollywood motion pictures have displayed Arab Muslims invading America and liquidating innocents—from California to Indiana to New York. See this writer's Op-Ed essay.[157]

Background information. In mid-March of 1998, prior to the film's release, Washington, DC's Council On Arab Islamic Relations (CAIR) called me, requesting I review a copy of the *The Siege* screenplay, then titled *Martial Law,*[158] which producers Obst and Zwick had sent them.

I concluded my analysis in early April. Then, I traveled, along with two CAIR officials, to New York City where we met with the film's producers. We expressed serious misgivings about the screenplay. Given how vulnerable Arab and Muslim Americans are to defamation, especially children, why single them out as terrorists, we asked. We pointed out that as numerous Arab-American families reside in Brooklyn, why show American tanks and infantrymen streaming across the Brooklyn Bridge? Why show our soldiers conducting house-to-house searches in Arab-American neighborhoods? We explained the film offered gross and harmful distortions, that it certainly did not accurately reflect the world's 1.1 billion Muslims and Arabs. We cited a 1995 *Los Angeles Times* report, which stated that of 171 people indicted in the United States "for terrorism and related activities... 6 percent were connected to Arab groups." The greatest threat to our country, we told the producers, comes not from outside forces, rather from domestic terrorism.

At one point during our New York meeting, Zwick insisted his film offered fair and balanced portraits. He cited Tony Shalhoub's portrayal of a decent Arab-American FBI agent. Having one "good" guy, I countered, will not change the movie's violent, monolithic view of Arabs and Muslims. Though Shalhoub's character is a good one, it could never offset all those scenes that show Arab Muslims murdering men, women, and children.

Zwick's Shalhoub comment reminded me of how producers once tried to justify their hostile depictions of Native Americans. Back then, in movies displaying scores of savage Indians massacring settlers, moviemakers pointed to the presence of Tonto.

Repeatedly, we stressed to Obst and Zwick that they should not link Islamic practices, e.g., reciting prayers from the Holy Koran, the ritual washing before prayer, the call to prayer, and supplication, with terrorism. We also asked them not to project as terrorists, Arab immigrants, a college professor, and Brooklyn's Arab-American auto mechanics. And, we requested they not selectively frame nor refer to Mideast Palestinians and Muslim religious leaders as perpetrators of terror in the US, Israel, Saudi Arabia, and/or Lebanon. They ignored our requests. Later Zwick admitted, "We made the movie we wanted to make... I made extremely minor changes."

As I firmly believed Zwick's minor edits would not suffice, I again reiterated my concerns, writing several letters to the producers, dated 3, 5, and 15 April. I explained to Obst and Zwick that *The Siege* might advance hatreds, and asked them to consider changing the major plot line linking violence with religion—Muslims and Islamic prayers. Also, I offered several fresh alternatives for their consideration, suggesting they consider replacing the movie's Arab Muslim villains with other groups: multi-cultural terrorists, radical militia men, military extremists, even right-wing government agents.

Ignoring these and other suggestions, Zwick and Obst moved forward with the movie production and vilified Arab Muslims. Thus, CAIR and other Arab and Muslim organizations began conducting press conferences, contesting the film's stereotypes. When the film opened on 6 November 1998, America's Arabs and Muslims demonstrated in front of movie theaters, citing the film's heinous portraits. Nearly all network television reports featured cast members and Zwick promoting the film. CNN-TV's *Newstand*, however, provided viewers not with movie hype, but rather with a balanced 20-minute report, featuring Zwick and myself (10 November 1998).

Leading newspapers, e.g., *The New York Times* and *The Washington Post*, also offered thorough pro and con Op-Ed essays. Note how Zwick concludes his *New York Times* Op-Ed essay: "So, I'm sorry I offended anyone. But I'm really not."[159]

Scene: Dhahran, Saudi Arabia. Stock footage of an American military building exploding. Cut to the desert; Israelis kidnap an Islamic religious leader linked to terrorism.

• In New York City, ominous music underscores praying Muslims. The call to prayer echoes to One Federal Plaza, FBI headquarters.

• Inside a city bus, passengers are held hostage. FBI agent, Hub Hubbard (Washington) pleads with the Arab Muslim terrorists to let the elderly go. But the Arabs blow up the bus, killing scores. Bodies litter the screen. Thrice, law-enforcement officials link this make-believe tragedy with a real tragedy, saying, It's "the worst terrorist bombing in the United States since Oklahoma City." Later, an FBI agent mentions "[that] Hamas is raising so much money here [in the US]."

• "Using a student visa," Ali Waziri, an Arab Muslim terrorist, gains entry into the United States. Hub and FBI colleague Frank Haddad (Shalhoub) track Ali. Cut to Hub asking Elise (Bening), a CIA agent, "[whether] there is a [Muslim] terrorist cell operating in Brooklyn." Amazingly, Elise says, "Yes!" And, "They're speaking Arabic." Hub tells his agents to "turn the heat up, [check] student organizations and *anyone critical of this country.*" [emphasis added] One Arab suspect hails from "Ramallah, the West Bank."

• The FBI agents move to nab a Palestinian-American professor; he teaches Arab Studies at Brooklyn College. And, his "brother blew up a movie theater in Tel Aviv." Note the dialogue, labeling Palestinians as terrorists: "[One Palestinian] bombed the market [in Tel Aviv]. [He] spent two years in Israeli jails during the intifada [uprising]."

• Beirut, Lebanon; stock footage of a burnt building. An FBI agent, Sheikh Ahmed bin Talal, says an Iraqi "is responsible for bombing the American barracks."

• Arab vs. Arab. Expressing anger, Frank tells Hub, "I'll tell you what [a Palestinian Muslim's] people did to my village in Lebanon."

• Arab Muslim terrorists bomb a crowded Broadway theater; scores are killed; others are seriously injured, including the "city's cultural leaders."

• Inside a classroom, an Arab terrorist holds young school children hostage. He moves to set the bomb. Hub enters the school room, defuses the bomb, shoots the Arab dead, and saves the kids.

• A "Syrian" man confides in the FBI, telling the agents about some suspicious-looking Arabs. "There are three of them. All day long they watch TV," he says. "All they eat is pizza. All day long, pizza, pizza." Cut to Hub and his men barging into a filthy room, terminating the three terrorists. Following the shootings, the camera cuts to a mosque.

• "Towel Arabs" bomb One Federal Plaza's FBI building, killing nearly all of Hub's colleagues and friends. Affirms a New York police officer, "Definitely Arab types."

• "They're [Arab Muslims] attacking our way of life," says the US chief of staff. Demands a senator, "Find out who they are and bomb the shit out of them."

• Brooklyn's Arab-American neighborhoods. As martial law is declared, American soldiers round up America's Arabs and Muslims, placing them in detention camps, behind barbed wire. The interred are mute, and they look alike. Most are dark, and in need of a shave; some don kuffiyehs. Zwick also stereotypes a US general (Willis); the officer functions as a dense and insensitive radical.

• Tariq Husseini's garage. FBI agents terminate Arab-American auto mechanics, all terrorists.

Finis: After the main terrorist, Samir (Bouajila) prays, he moves to kill peaceful American demonstrators. Elise tries to stop the Arab; Samir shoots her. Hub arrives, shooting Samir dead.

Note: In HBO's "Making of *The Siege*" special, producer-director Zwick said his movie is "based on truth, rather than a [fiction] thriller." On 4 November 1998, actor Denzel Washington told a CNN reporter, "This is not a stereotypical view of any group of people, by any means." Two days later, (6 November), Washington echoed Zwick's thesis: *The Siege* is not fiction, he said, "unfortunately, we're imitating life." NBC's *Today* host Matt Lauer said, "[The film] does not paint all Arabs as suicide bombers." Lauer told Washington, "You're getting some heat from Arab groups." Washington frowned, replying, *"[In] certain countries, they wouldn't even be allowed to do that"* [emphasis added]. Not only does Lauer fail to contest Washington's slur, he makes a major error. He should have said, you're getting "heat" from Arab Americans, not from "Arab groups." Also, Lauer's sloppy and biased *Today* segment excluded individuals critical of the film.

• Reminiscent of *The Siege*'s nightmare scenario, in March 1999, the US military conducted "Urban Warrior" exercises in Monterey and Oakland, California. The military employed some actors to portray disloyal Arab Americans. The actors as Arab Americans were told to appear in crowded urban areas, harass the Marines, and then stop them from tracking "terrorists."

• Concerned that some viewers might perceive *The Siege* as fact, not fiction, America's Islamic communities opened their mosque to those wanting to learn the truth about Islam. While most people were sympathetic, some moviegoers responded with foul language, or even more. Outside one theater, Yama Niazi, president of the Islamic Society of Santa Barbara, observed a young Muslim woman passing out leaflets about Islam—a passerby spit on her.[160]

• To help attract audiences, CNN's *Showbiz Today* ran one-page ads in major publications, e.g., *Entertainment Weekly*. The CNN ads, which promoted *The Siege*, informed readers that if they correctly answered several trivia questions, they could "Win a 3 Day, 2 Night Trip to New York City."

Sign of the Gladiator (1958), a.k.a. Nel segno di Roma, AI. *Anita Ekberg, George Marchal.* CAMEOS, MAIDENS

Betrayed by her Persian minister, a Syrian Queen romances a Roman General.

Scene: AD 217, Palmira. A captured Roman general (Marchal) wins the heart of Syria's Queen Zenobia (Ekberg). Mute Syrians appear in the background.

• In return for some Roman money, Syrian mercenaries betray a lovely virgin.

• The concerned queen says, "My people are suffering. If only I could help them."

• Queen Zenobia's advisor, a doublecrossing "Persian," moves to nab the throne. He fails; his Persian soldiers cannot overcome Roman and Syrian troops.

Silver Bears (1977), COL. *Michael Caine, Cybill Shepherd, Jay Leno.* CAMEOS

Scene: Dubai appears as a backward place; men ride bikes and horse and carriages. Veiled women in black trudge along dirt roads. Such images are counterfeit. In reality, much of Dubai is as upscale as Beverly Hills.

• Dubai, a place for international chicanery, hosts a smuggling center. Cut to a warehouse; inside, silver is illegally transported to the West.

Note: At the time *Silver Bears* was released, US-Iranian relations were at an all-time high. Could this explain why the film's beautiful Iranian woman (Stephanie Audran) marries an Italian Prince (Louis Jourdan)? Their gorgeous Iranian home looks like a French chateau.

Sinai Commandos: The Story of the Six Day War (1968), a.k.a. Sinai Commandos, Ran, Gillman Film Corp. *Robert Fuller, John Hudson, Joseph Shiloach, Esther Ullman.* SP: Jack Jacobs. P, D: Nussbaum. Filmed in Israel following the Six Day War. VILLAINS

Israeli and American filmmakers tar Arabs. Israeli actors portray vile bedouins.

Scene: The narrator's statement misleads viewers into thinking Egypt, not Israel, launched the 1967 war: "The armed forces of the Arabic Countries unite for an attack against Israel with the aim of total destruction."

• Israeli Captain Uri Litman (Fuller) and his soldiers move into Egyptian territory. The squad's mission? To wreck an Egyptian radar installation.

• The Israelis discover some mute, scruffy, bedouins smuggling hashish. They kill a few, then bind the arms of others. Argues an Israeli, "We are going to kill them; we have to kill them." Injects Lieutenant Kramer, "Whoever kills them is an executioner, not a soldier."

• After the Israelis depart, the bedouins escape, warning Egyptian troops.

• The Israelis capture Egyptian Captain Halil (Shiloach), a Jew-hater. Yet, Halil assists the soldiers. In time, the Israelis blow up the radar station, ensuring a successful Israeli attack.

• To help make this fiction film appear factual, German producer/director Nussbaum uses actual stock footage. This black-and-white combat footage, which was shot during the 1967 Six Day War, depicts Israeli troops battling and crushing Egyptians and other Arabs.

Sinbad: The Battle of the Dark Knights (1998), FM Entertainment. *Richard Grieco, Mickey Rooney, Lisa Ann Russell, Dean Stockwell.* SP: Alan Mehrez and Elvisto Restaino. P, D: Alan Mehrez. Filmed in Jordan. MAIDENS

Appearing is a dense Anglo-looking Sinbad (Grieco) intent on bringing down evil Bophisto's (Stockwell) dark knights. Sinbad needs assistance from a clever magician (Rooney). Most likely, the generic settings and costumes will mislead young viewers into thinking this movie has nothing to do with Arabia or Arabs.

Scene: The wise magician tells Sinbad, "[Your mother was] queen of the desert gypsies." Sinbad moves to protect "Araby" from the evil knights; he battles the dark knight, and loses. The evil knight's villains advance, crushing the sultan's men.

• The dark knight holds Princess Shalazar (Russell) hostage. Cut to a revived Sinbad. Wearing a flowing white caftan, he and his multi-cultural warriors march off determined to rid the sultan's kingdom of Bophisto's tyrants.

Finis: Sinbad triumphs. He and his aides free the imprisoned sultan and lovely Princess Shalazar.

Note: Another non-Arab Sinbad trounces Arab villains. See International Family Classics' 50-minute animated *Sinbad* (1993). Here, the Anglo-looking Sinbad speaks with an Indian accent. Opening frames display a donkey besting two bearded Arabs, tossing one. Often, this Anglo Sinbad defeats nasty Arab villains, notably the devious, hook-nosed cur, Kubin, and the lecherous sheikh, Farzuma. The Arab ruler kidnaps a girl-child, Sinda, boasting, "You will be wife 513, little girl." To the rescue, Sinbad! He smashes Farzuma, frees the girl, and later, after she is all grown-up, Sinbad marries her.

Sinbad and the Eye of the Tiger (1977), COL. *Patrick Wayne, Jane Seymour, Taryn Power, Damien Thomas, Kurt Christian, Margaret Whiting.* SP: Beverly Cross. Special effects: Ray Harryhausen. Filmed in Jordan. MAIDENS

In this entertaining Arabian Nights fantasy, Sinbad and Kassim, Baghdad's "good" prince, contest "the witch" Zenobia, and Rafi, her dense son.

Scene: Baghdad's denizens are pleased; the rightful heir to the city's throne, Prince Kassim (Thomas), is about to be crowned caliph. Abruptly, Kassim's stepmother Zenobia (Whiting), an evil sorceress wearing a black cloak and black veil, conjures up "from hell... the spirits of the underworld." Presto! The evil "spirits" begin to transform Kassim into a baboon. Zenobia's "black witchcraft enables her to be as cunning as a snake, as malicious as a shark."

• Zenobia's son, Rafi (Christian) offers Sinbad (Wayne) and his men the hospitality of his tent. As he watches performing bellydancers, Sinbad notices someone poisoning his wine.

• Sinbad falls for Princess Farah (Seymour), Prince Kassim's sister. Purrs the sailor, "For him (Kassim), I risk my life, for you I would give it." Sinbad and his crew set sail; they pass along the Arctic, "[the] coldest region of the world," encountering icebergs and snowstorms.

• The sorceress' curse—"secrets of darkness [and] the forces of hell"—takes effect. Now, poor Kassim looks and acts as a baboon.

• Introducing the Greek [not Arab] philosopher Melanthius, "the wisest man in the world." He helps Sinbad free Kassim from Zenobia's sinister spell.

• Surprisingly, a giant troglodyte opts to befriend, not fight, the brave Sinbad.

• Ignoring her brother's appearance, Princess Farah plays chess with the baboon-looking Kassim.

• Sinbad moves to shatter the witch's curse; he brings down three vulgar ghouls, a giant bee, an immense walrus, and finally, Zenobia. Ray Harryhausen's effects are impressive; he changes the sorceress into a bird, a one-inch figure, even a saber-toothed tiger.

• Thanks to Sinbad's heroics, Prince Kassim's baboon features instantly begin to evaporate. Moments later, the Prince becomes his former self—a human being. Expressing gratitude, Princess Farah embraces Sinbad.

Note: The camera presents Petra, a city in Jordan. Yet, characters call Petra a "Greek" island.

Sinbad the Sailor (1947), RKO. *Douglas Fairbanks Jr., Maureen O'Hara, Anthony Quinn, Walter Slezak.* VILLAINS

The action in this fun-filled fable takes place in Basra, Iraq. Sinbad vs. a nasty Arab and an evil Mongol.

Scene: In search of Alexander the Great's lost island of gold, the legendary adventurer, Sinbad (Fairbanks Jr.), sails the seas. After a while, Sinbad meets up with the wealthy Emir of Daibul (Quinn) and his Mongolian accomplice, Malik (Slezak).

• Aboard the emir's ship residing in the women's quarters is Princess Shireen (O'Hara); surrounding the princess are mute, attractive harem maidens.

• The emir's men whip slaves at the oars, tossing the weak ones overboard. Intent on holding "the earth in his arms," Malik poisons the ship's water supply; dead bodies appear on deck.

• Warns the emir, if any man dares cast "eyes on the unveiled women of Daibul," off goes his head.

• Daibul's smitten emir proposes to reward the beautiful Shireen with riches, provided she beds him. The princess refuses, opting to wed Sinbad, the man with the rose.

• At last, the emir's crew uncovers Alexander's gold treasures. But, the emir and treacherous Malik are crushed. As for the newly-married Sinbad, he reunites with his father.

Treatment of Islam: An imam beckons the devout; Arabs kneel and pray.

Note: Some viewers may mistakenly think Sinbad and his men are Asians, not Arabs. Why? Because they wear instead of Arab garb, Oriental-looking outfits, a potpourri of Indian and Chinese garb.

Sinbad of the Seven Seas (1989), CAN. *Lou Ferrigno, Alessandra Martines, John Steiner, Yehuda Efroni.* Dubbed in English. Supposedly, the film is based on Edgar Allan Poe's 1845 elaboration of the "Arabian Nights." MAIDENS

Scene: A mother reads the Sinbad story to her daughter. "The people of Basra were the happiest people in all the world," she says, "because they were ruled by a kind and wise caliph." Cut to joyous Arabs preparing to celebrate a wedding.

• Flashback to the ancient city of Basra. Suddenly Jaffar casts a spell, transforming Basra into a "Kingdom of Evil." Now, it's up to Sinbad, "the greatest prince of the seas," to save the people and defeat the villain.

• Cut to the "darkest corner of the royal palace"; here, the clad-in-black Jaffar casts another evil spell, conjuring up black clouds. Soon, Basra's residents, including the caliph and his guards, fall victim to the wizard's curse.

• The palace's underground torture chamber contains branding irons and a water tank, filled with hungry piranha. Cut to Jaffar dispatching cobras to terminate Sinbad. But, the sailor befriends the snakes.

• Muscle-bound Sinbad goes to help a young prince regain his throne. He also seeks to release Basra from Jaffar's spell. To succeed, Sinbad must retrieve five magic gems. He sails across the seas, from Basra to the Amazon, and then to the "Isle of the Dead." Accompanying and assisting him are Prince Ahmed (Efroni), a Chinese soldier of fortune, a Viking, "little Puchi," and a "bald cook."

• During the journey, Sinbad's men contest ghosts, ghouls, and armor-plated fighters.

• Jaffar sees the courageous Princess Alina (Martines), "[a woman] as beautiful as a blushing rose." Instantly, he casts a spell over her. Though Jaffar tries to control Alina's mind and body, the princess resists, declaring she will never wed him, even if he is "the last man on earth."

Finis: Sinbad acquires the sacred gems. Jaffar collapses. And, Basra is restored to its previous blissful state. Prince Ahmed weds Princess Alina; Sinbad marries the lovely Kyra. The couples intend to "live happily ever after."

The Singing Princess (1967), Trans-National. Animated. *Voices: Julie Andrews and Howard Marion-Crawford.* SP: Nina and Tony Maguire. P, D: Anton Gino Domeneghini. Grand prize winner, the International Children's Festival. This animated film was originally released in Italy in 1949 as *La Rosa di Baghdad.* VILLAINS

This animated fantasy displays benevolent and villainous Arabs. The film's message seems to be: "Once more, love triumphs over hate, right over wrong, good over evil." When Princess Zeila (Andrews) sings "Sunset Prayer" and other songs, youngsters may wish to sing along.

Scene: Intones the narrator (Marion-Crawford), "Sunny and smiling Baghdad... [is] the greatest city of all the Orient. [The inhabitants are] a simple, honest and industrious people who lived happily under the wise and gentle rule of Oman the Third, the greatest and kindest of all the Caliphs."

• Omar and his advisors "fight for what his right." Siding with him are Amin, a genie, a beggar woman, and citizens of Baghdad. Opposing Omar are two super-villains, a one-toothed wizard and Sheikh Jaffar—"the name of Jaffar strikes terror."

• Cautions the narrator, "The sinister shadow of the malevolent magician," Jaffar, menaces the Princess Zeila, "the rose of Baghdad."

• Jaffar intends to wed the princess so that he may rule Baghdad. He enlists the evil wizard's help; supposedly, the wizard's magical ring "will compel" Zeila to love him. Cut to the wizard's mountain retreat. Declares the one-toothed villain, "In the name of Satan, my master, hearken these spirits of darkness."

Finis: Eventually, Amin brings down Jaffar and most of his evil-doers. Plus, he weds Princess Zeila. Unexpectedly and without warning, the one-toothed wizard appears, killing Amin. Intones Amin, after his deliverance, "Allah is watchful and ever merciful towards those who fight for the right."

Note: The wizard's magic cloak, which enables him to fly, is made "from the wings of bats, owls, and vampires."

Siren of Bagdad (1953), COL. Sam Katzman Prod. *Patricia Medina, Paul Henreid, Hans Conreid, George Keymas, Michael Fox, Charles Lung.* S, SP: Robert E. Kent. MAIDENS, SHEIKHS

Arabs kill Arabs and enslave women. A mighty princess and prince.

Scene: Near Baghdad, a desert tent. Arabs applaud the skills of Kazah (Henreid), a traveling magician. Kazah changes his friend Ben Ali (Conreid) into a blonde woman. Next, he makes beautiful women "vanish."

• Atop a sand dune, two clad-in-black Arabs observe Kazah's group. Next, they ride off to brief the tyrannical bandit, El-Malid (Lung), about the magician and his troupe. Barks El-Malid, "On your horses; we attack at once." Waving sabers, the marauders charge Kazah's caravan, carrying off three dancers. Sighs one survivor, "Those thieves have stolen all our girls."

• Baghdad's slave market. Kazah spots an Arab slaver hawking his dancers. Instantly, he frees the women, killing the guards.

• Introducing the evil vizier Soradin (Keymas), and the "harem happy" sultan who is referred to as an "empty-headed old fool." These two scoundrels smuggle cargo and enslave women. The "drooling" sultan purrs, "My harem is a bit overcrowded. I think I should throw out some of the fat ones."

• Royalty in disguise. Appearing is the "good" deposed sultan Telar (Fox); he poses as a merchant. The sultan's daughter, Zendi (Medina), Baghdad's true princess, poses as a beggar. To save Baghdad, Zendi tells her father she will wed the lecherous bogus-sultan. The princess's lover, the magician Kazah, objects. He moves to invade the palace.

• The bogus-sultan's throne room. Thinly-clad dancers perform. Nearby, posh harem quarters. Cut to Kazah unleashing some ropes over palace walls. He, Telar, and their comrades attack, cancelling the bogus-sultan's men.

• Next, Kazah confronts and crushes El-Malid and his bandits. Employing magic, he convinces El-Malid's men that he can make people disappear. To demonstrate, Kazah locks El-Malid in a box. Next, he employs a slight-of-hand trick. Presto! El-Malid vanishes. "Gone before our very eyes," says one Arab. "It is the will of Allah!" Fearing Kazah will also make them disappear, the dense bandits rush off into the desert. Earlier, an Arab who observed Kazah's magic, said, "By the grace of Allah who rules our destinies."

• Kazah and Zendi embrace. And, Telar, the true sultan, is restored to the throne.

Dialogue: Arabs are called "pigs."

Sirocco (1951), COL. *Humphrey Bogart, Marta Toren, Lee J. Cobb, Everett Sloan, Zero Mostel.* SP: A.I. Bezzerides, Hans Jacoby. Based on *Coup de Grace* by Joseph Kessel. VILLAINS

This gunrunning drama's Syrian heavies shoot Humphrey Bogart dead. Syrians appear as terrorists, traitors, liars, and as killers of Frenchmen. Not a single frame shows French soldiers killing Syrians. Instead, the movie's Frenchmen appear as victims.

Scene: On screen, "Damascus 1925." Blazing fires; Syria at war. Some rebellious Syrians deliver two Western reporters to their leader, Emir Hassan (Stevens). Hassan tells the blindfolded men, "You want to know why the Syrians fight. You may tell your people we fight because they [the French] have invaded our country. They want to govern us, tell us what to do. We want to govern ourselves. We want Syria for ourselves. We fight to throw out our enemies... And we will win because God and justice are on our side." Cut to General La Salle (Sloan), affirming, "We [French] are here because of a mandate."

• The souk reveals some ragged Syrians; goats and a camel munching lettuce. Suddenly, an angry Syrian socks the camel. See *Road to Morocco* (1942) and *Blazing Saddles* (1974).

• Syrians pop up from the shadows and shoot French soldiers. La Salle issues a proclamation: "From today on, for every Frenchman murdered we will execute five Syrian hostages. That's a language they should understand." But, Colonel Feroud (Cobb), manages to convince his general to retract his edict.

• An American, gun-runner Harry Smith (Bogart), a man "without morals" and without "political convictions," smuggles weapons to the Syrians. Smith and his sidekick, Nasir Aboud (Dennis), visit a local cafe; they watch a bellydancer perform. Outside, a benevolent-looking Syrian beggar sells flowers to French soldiers. Soon, the beggar enters the cafe, and tosses grenades at French patrons, killing most of them. Grunts Smith to Aboud, "You and your Syrian patriots... they almost got me."

• Damascus' disagreeable Syrians. A Syrian hawker moves to sell Smith some jewelry;

willing to do anything to close the deal, a sly merchant even offers to dispatch a "boy" to steal a bracelet. Cut to a French soldier berating a Syrian man; the Syrian has "three wives and eleven children."

• A French officer delivers a peace proposal to Hassan. How does the emir respond? He order's the officer's throat cut; the Frenchman's body is "found in an alley." Shouts General La Salle, "You can't trust these [Syrian] people, colonel. They're fanatics! They want war!"

• The French officers find out that Smith sells munitions to the Syrians. Cut to Smith and several unkempt Arabs hiding out "in a filthy hole."

• Some clumsy Syrians try to start their getaway bus's engine; they fail. Smith appears, saying, "Maybe I can help." Smith separates a few wires—the engine starts. But French soldiers arrive on the scene, thwarting the Arabs' escape.

• Seeking protection from the French, Smith rushes to his Syrian procurers. They refuse to assist the American saying, "I am sorry, Mr. Smith. We cannot help you. We have no further use for you." Smith registers shock, as if to say, where is Syrian loyalty? He retreats to "the filthy hole," giving some coins to a Syrian almsman. The Syrian returns one coin. Puzzled, Smith says, "Since when are you giving back money? What are you up to?" Abruptly, some French soldiers nab Smith, delivering him to Colonel Feroud. The colonel vows to release Smith, provided he discloses the emir's hideout. Cautions Smith, "When you get down there nobody can protect you."

• Cut to the emir's headquarters, "ancient Roman catacombs." The emir's Syrians hold Colonel Feroud hostage. Aware that the Syrians plan to murder the colonel, Smith advises the general, "They (the Syrians) like money... You never know about these characters, you never know."

• Smith enters the catacombs with monies, telling a Syrian, "I'm not going to start with 5,000 and let you work me up to eight or nine. I'll lay my cards on the table. 10,000. That's my offer for the colonel." Muses the Syrian, "I see."

• Hassan decides to order his Syrians to slice the colonel's throat. Suddenly, a fez-wearing Syrian appears, whispering to the emir, Smith's cash offer of "10,000," provided they release the colonel. Note the dialogue:

Hassan: For 10,000 pounds I can kill a lot of Frenchmen.
Feroud: You'll also kill a lot of Syrians... I want to arrange a truce.
Hassan: You're a fool.
Feroud: I come to talk of peace and understanding and you call me a fool?
Hassan: Yes, colonel. I respect you, but you are a dreamer and a fool.

• Hassan takes the 10,000 pounds, releasing Feroud. As Smith's cover is blown, the emir no longer needs him. One of the Syrian's assassins tosses a hand grenade, blowing Smith to smithereens.

Note: Contrasting images. In *Sirocco* (1951), Syrians under French occupation appear as terrorists. In *Sword in the Desert* (1949), Jews under British rule appear as freedom fighters.

• Writes Bosley Crowther in the NYT, "[the] shadowy shots of sloppy Syrians lying around in dingy catacombs... [are] no more suggestive of Damascus than a Shriner's convention in New Orleans, on which occasion you would see more fezes that ever show up in this film" (14 June 1951).

Slave Girl (1947), UNI. *Yvonne DeCarlo, George Brent, Broderick Crawford, Albert Dekker, Lois Collier, Carl Esmond.* P: Michael Fessler, Ernst Pagano. MAIDENS, SHEIKHS

Libyans vs. Libyans. US sailors trounce Libyans. The attractive Yvonne DeCarlo stars not as an Arab lovely, but as a Venetian heroine. Arab women as subservient caricatures. See *Tripoli* (1950).

Scene: Narrating the film, Lumpy, a talking camel with a Brooklyn accent. Lumpy describes "Tripoli" as "a land of intrigue and violence," a place where "girls cover up their faces." Cut to the souk. Mingling about are merchants, beggars, and a nasty Arab slaver selling women. "Let us consider the foreign wench," he barks.

• Arriving in Tripoli are two Americans, Matt Claiborne (Brent) and Chet Jackson (Crawford). Their objective is to buy the release of US sailors, held hostage by the Libyan pasha (Dekker).

• A club featuring bellydancing. Here, Chet accidently touches an Arab woman. Suddenly, a ruckus occurs. The dancer's Arab friends nearly kill Chet.

• The palace, pool side. The pasha sits on ornate pillows, smoking a nargelih. Two dozen svelte, half-naked dancers entertain him. Cut to the palace prison, holding the ten US sailors.

• Matt and Chet move to offer the pasha a chest of gold. In return for the gold, the pasha shall free the sailors. The two men hire an Arab to guard the gold chest. Still, they fret no Arab is trustworthy. They chain the man to a chair, right next to the gold. Smirks the Arab, "You pay, I sit."

• Chet returns from shopping in the souk. He brings into the room "junk," and an Arab maiden named Aleta (Collier). Purrs Aleta: "I belong to him. I work for him. I wash his clothes. I wash him." Affirms the chained Arab, "That is the custom."

• Presenting the clad-in-black villain, El-Hamid (Esmond). He not only hoodwinks the pasha, he betrays the American sailors, as well. Double-dealing El-Hamid turns the sailors over to a desert leader, saying, "The [US] government will pay more gold for them. They're yours, to be used as slaves until they are ransomed."

• Appearing is lovely Franchesa (DeCarlo), the pasha's unwilling bride-to-be. She berates El-Hamid, saying, "But you gave your word!" Retorts El-Hamid, "What good is one's word when given to a foreigner?" Franchesa: "So, there is no difference between you and the pasha."

• The pasha tries wooing Franchesa, purring, "Remember, my dear, in this land a bride is weak, docile, and most agreeable to her master's wishes." And, "In my philosophy, one's word given to a woman is as binding as one's word given to a camel." Marry me, he warns, or I'll dump you onto a flaming couch.

• Matt, too, falls for Franchesa; "You do not look like a native," he says. "You do not talk like a native." Matt's hunch is correct; she has Venetian roots. Explains Franchesa, "My family and I were voyaging to France" when the pasha's men took our ship. "They killed my family [and] brought me here as a slave girl."

• Chet and Matt return to their room; the gold chest is gone! So, the pasha tosses the duo in prison. Chet's maiden, Aleta, rescues them and helps free the sailors. Outnumbered twelve to one, the Americans liberate Franchesa. Next, they release some Arab prisoners and then trounce the pasha's burnoosed bullies. Note the dialogue:

Sailor #1: [I don't like] paying tribute to a flea-bitten bunch of pirates.
Sailor #2: I don't like Tripoleans.
Sailor #1: Me neither.
Sailor #3: Nor me.
Sailor #1: I hate 'em. Let's go get 'em." [*They rout the Arabs*]

• As the sailors, along with Matt, Chet, and Franchesa depart from Tripoli, they spot the pasha's Arabs fighting El-Hamid's Arabs. Troops on both sides wave sabers, charge each other, and perish. The camel, Lumpy, appears. At his side is a veiled camel. "A very satisfactory conclusion," says Lumpy.

Slavers (1977), Lord. *Trevor Howard, Ron Ely, Ray Milland, Cameron Mitchell.* See *Ashanti* (1979). SHEIKHS

Scene: Africa 1884. Appearing atop a white horse is Sheikh Hassan (Milland), a depraved clad-in-black slave hunter. Nearby, Hassan's mute Arab guards, wearing white thobes. Hassan directs African hirelings to burn villages and to kidnap and chain other Africans.

• Hassan's amuses himself by freeing an enslaved African. The slave dashes off, trying to swim to safety. Hassan takes up a rifle, shooting the African dead.

• Repulsed by Hassan's actions is a "compassionate" Western slaver, Alec Mackenzie (Howard). Note the dialogue:

Hassan: May Allah make this a happy day! [Arab violence often precedes or follows the ` word, Allah.]
MacKenzie: It seems Allah took the day off.
Hassan: You can't hold me responsible for all Arabs.
Mackenzie: If you're really bored, why don't you try shooting fish in a barrel!

• Though Westerners and one African appear as slavers, this movie certifies that only Arabs are ruthless. For example, an exhausted African slave goes to take a sip of water. Wham. An Arab guard pulls his scimitar, removing the slave's hand.

• Hassan doublecrosses his Western cohorts, killing DaSilva (Mitchell).

• Mr. Hamilton (Ely) protests the enslavement of Africans. Says a European, "We'll have to sell you to an old Arab woman, who'll put you in a cage and feed you till you burst."

Note: The epilogue reveals that months later, all the villains perished.

Slaves of Babylon (1953), COL. *Richard Conte, Michael Ansara, Terrance Kilburn, Leslie Bradley, Maurice Schwartz.* P: Sam Katzman. VILLAINS

This pseudo-biblical drama reveals Babylonians (Iraqis) holding Israelites hostage. The Israelites and Persians rout Babylonian heathens, freeing enslaved Israelites.

Scene: Sixth century BC. On screen, the Holy Bible's "Book of Daniel." Cut to Babylon's King Nebuchadnezzar (Bradley) and his son Balshazzar (Ansara); they plan to destroy Jerusalem.

• With the exception of Daniel (Schwartz), the Babylonians whip and enslave all Israelites; the Star of David is emblazoned on the prisoners' robes.

• Nebuchadnezzar believes that no Babylonian is qualified to run the country. Thus, he moves to recruit Daniel. Demands the king, "Stop praying to your God." Counters Daniel, "Set our people free."

• Miracles. Daniel's God saves him from the lions; God also rescues captured Israelites from raging flames.

• A bellydancer functions as a Babylonian spy; she moves to assassinate the wise Persian ruler, Cyrus (Kilburn), but fails.

• The siege of Babylon. Persians and Israelites rout the Babylonians. Cyrus, the Persian conqueror, grants the Israelites freedom to return to Jerusalem, to rebuild the city.

Note: With the exception of names, costumes, settings, technologies, and time periods, images of present-day Iraqis and yesteryear's Babylonians are quite similar. Many biblical films present Babylonians as villains opposing the Israelites; contemporary films display Iraqis as culprits contesting Israelis.

Snake Eyes (1998), PAR. *Nicholas Cage, Gary Sinise, Eric Hoziel.* SP: David Koepp. P, D: Brian De Palma. CAMEOS, PALESTINIANS

Palestinian as terrorist.

Scene: Atlantic City. At the Millennium hotel and casino, 14,000 patrons, including the US Secretary of Defense, watch a heavyweight boxing match. Suddenly, an unknown assassin's bullets kill the Secretary.

• Moments later, US Navy Commander Kevin Dunne (Sinise) identifies the assassin. Dunne reveals a photograph of the murderer, 37-year-old Tariq Bin Rabat (Hoziel), a mute, unshaven Palestinian who has been living in the US for the past six years. Dunne tells the press that Rabat has "been linked to a series of threatening letters written to various defense secretaries, expressing outrage over the sale of missile systems and other weapons to Israel."

• Explains Dunne to his friend, "This guy, Rabat, he's a well-known nut case. It's clear he was ready to die for his cause. That's a suicide note. You know, 'I fly into the arms of Allah' and shit like that. He was all worked up about our nuclear sales to Israel."

• Flashback. The camera shows Dunne instructing Rabat to kill the defense secretary. Seconds later, Rabat shoots the secretary dead. Cut to Commander Dunne killing Rabat, a "known terrorist." Quips Dunne's cohort, "One less terrorist in the world." Later, Dunne, the villain behind the assassination, kills some of his accomplices.

• Asked to explain the killings, Dunne says the secretary was eradicated because he refused to fund some advanced weapons systems. During the Gulf War, argues Dunne, a new and improved defense system would have saved American lives, adding, "an Iraqi missile" hit our vessel, "28 crew members drowned."

Note: Why inject a mute Palestinian killer as assassin?

• In 1950, United Artists released *Conspiracy in Teheran*, a.k.a. *The Plot to Kill Roosevelt.* In the film, a wealthy pro-Nazi Persian conspires with some arms merchants intent on assassinating the US President. In time, a British war correspondent foils the assassination; his actions prevent the continuation of the war.

So This Is Paris (1926), WB. Silent. *Monte Blue, Patsy Ruth Miller, Lilyan Tashman, Andre Beranger, Myrna Loy.* D: Ernst Lubitsch. See *Sherlock Jr.* (1924). SHEIKHS

This comedy pokes fun at European women who are preoccupied with desert Arabs. Husbands feigning to be Arab sheikhs are mocked.

Scene: The swooning French maiden, Suzanne Giraud (Miller), reads of intrigue in "hot Arabian romances." As soon as her husband, Paul (Blue), arrives, she kisses him, saying "My sheikh!" Laments Paul, "[the] crazy books our wives read while we are away."

• The Giraud's neighbors, Maurice and Georgette Lalle (Beranger, Tashman), try to spice their humdrum relationship. They don Arab garb and act out a harem scene, performing the "Dance of the Forbidden Fruit." Trying to behave as a savage sheikh, the nearly-naked Maurice approaches his semi-nude wife Georgette, reclining on the bed. He pulls a knife and then feigns stabbing Georgette. Shedding tears over her body, the frail Maurice collapses, exhausted.

• Maurice flops as a sheikh; he lacks sufficient strength to carry his wife. The disappointed Georgette lifts Maurice, tosses him onto the bed, and angrily departs. Even the piano player jests, "After seeing you (Maurice) as a sheikh, I've gained back my lost confidence."

Soft Cushions (1927), PAR. Silent. *Douglas MacLean, Sue Carol, Richard Carles, Albert Prisco, Albert Gran.* Boris Karloff has a minor role. *NS. Notes from NYT (19 September 1927). SHEIKHS, MAIDENS

Summary: This light-hearted comedy displays a sultan (Gran) out to wed Joy-El (Carol), a bright slave girl. Also moving to win her heart is a "Young Thief" (MacLean) with a sense of humor. The young man's humorous story "saves his head from the executioner's blade." The Wazir is tagged "the sublime pet of the universe."

• Appearing is the Grand Vizier (Prisco), a slave dealer (Carles), "a fat thief," and "a lean thief," plus an executioner.

Treatment of Islam: Islam is mocked. The young thief comes up with sufficient gold to purchase Joy-El; he rushes off to the slave market, examines the slaver's scales, and doubts their accuracy.

• Exclaims the slaver, "Allah knows these scales are true." Retorts the young thief: "Allah knows that they are crooked, so we are quits about Allah."

• Eventually, the young thief and Joy-El, a woman who boasts "independence in her bearing," unite. And, they triumph over the film's villains.

The Soldier (1982), EMB. *Ken Wahl, Alberta Watson, Klaus Kinski.* W, P, D: James Glickenhaus. Filmed in Israel. CAMEOS, PALESTINIANS

Russian radicals and Palestinians vs. Israelis.

Scene: Renegade KGB agents steal some plutonium; cut to Arabs planting a nuclear bomb in Saudi Arabia's Ghawar oil field. The agents issue a warning: If the Israelis do not withdraw from the occupied West Bank within "96 hours," they will detonate the weapon, destroying this rich Saudi oil field that contains half the world's supply of crude. Thinking the Israelis will not return the West Bank, the US briefly considers dispatching American troops to Israel.

• Mossad headquarters, Tel Aviv. Israeli soldiers drag a Palestinian prisoner along the floor, chain him to a wall, and beat him. Abruptly, the officer in charge, Susan Goodman (Watson) takes her pistol and shoots the prisoner through the head—not really. She in fact fires a blank. Her so-called prisoner is really an Israeli, "the best double agent they've ever had," posing as a Palestinian. Susan succeeds in duping her real Palestinian prisoner;

he believes she shot a fellow Palestinian.

• Susan tells the frightened Palestinian, "I want the people who stole the plutonium. Give us two more terrorists. We'll turn you over to our plastic surgeon and you can start a new life, OK?" She hands the scrubby prisoner several photographs of suspected Palestinians. Fearing for his life, the Palestinian identifies them.

• In the end, the Russians defuse the bomb. Israel maintains the West Bank.

Note: The line uttered in *The Soldier*, "the world as we know it, would end," is also spoken in *Rollover* (1981).

• On 9 May 1997, a UN human rights committee, the Committee Against Torture, denounced interrogation methods practiced on suspected Palestinian terrorists by Israel's General Security Service. The UN committee said that Israel should immediately halt its interrogation methods, e.g., prolonged sleep deprivation, violent shaking, death threats, and loud music. Amnesty International, a London-based human rights group, welcomed the committee's conclusions.[161]

Solomon and Sheba (1959), UA. *Yul Brynner, Gina Lollobrigida, George Sanders, David Farrar, Harry Andrews.* EGYPTIANS, MAIDENS

This biblical epic shows Israelites crushing Egyptian pagans. Sheba functions as a sensual, compassionate, and intelligent queen.

Scene: Israelites defeat, in a major battle, warring Egyptians. King Solomon's (Brunner) brother, Adjonah (Sanders), recounts the conflict, "The Egyptians were on the prowl, again. They sought to trap me, to rush in our camp and kill us while we slept. But we were not sleeping."

• Cut to Egyptian soldiers charging into Adjonah's camp. Promptly, Israelite soldiers repel the Egyptians, killing scores. One Egyptian shouts, "Sound the retreat." Later, Adjonah drinks wine, declaring, "Let me cleanse my mouth with the stench of the Egyptians."

• Egypt's Pharaoh (Farrar) muses over fresh strategies. He meets with Yemen's Queen Sheba (Lollobrigida) and her advisor, Baltor (Andrews). Note the dialogue:

Sheba: In spite of our eternal hatred, we [Yemen] now have friendly relations with Israel.
Baltor: Israelites should be feared as they have no slaves, believe in only one God, and teach all men to be equal.
Sheba: What a foolish idea. If that idea reached our people the Queen of Sheba will soon come crushing down from her throne.
An Egyptian: We will drive them into the sea.

• Sheba agrees to help crush the Israelites. She plans to seduce then destroy Solomon. Immediately, the queen dispatches gifts to Solomon—horses, silks, and gold. The pleased Solomon explains to Sheba how much his people have accomplished, "Only four years ago it was barren. It is a joy to make things bloom, to bring water from the mountains."

• Solomon's harem maidens approach; they do not please him. The king wants Sheba. Later, his jealous female attendants stone Sheba.

• Solomon proposes marriage to Sheba. Abruptly, the queen dons a skimpy bellydancer's outfit, performing an erotic dance for Yemen's "God of Love." Onlookers are so emotionally charged by the dance, they rush to participate in an orgy.

• Believing the Israelites are now vulnerable, the pharaoh's army attacks. During the battle, however, the Israelites' sun-lit swords blind the charging Egyptians; unable to see, scores of Egyptian soldiers descend over a cliff.

• Fearing her beloved Solomon may be killed, Sheba converts. Embracing Jehovah, she prays to her husband's God.

• Ambitious Adjonah wants his brother, Solomon, dead; he sends two men to kill him. When they fail, Adjonah fights Solomon and is killed.

Note: No Hollywood movie shows Arabs making barren land fertile, or making deserts bloom. Palestine, especially, was noted for its orange groves and olive orchards. See Sami Hadawi's books, notably *Bitter Harvest* (New York: Caravan Books, 1979).

Son of Ali Baba (1952), UNI. *Tony Curtis, Piper Laurie, Hugh O'Brien, Victor Jory, Susan Cabot, Morris Ankrum.* MAIDENS

This fantasy fable, complete with ornate palaces and harem chambers, shows Persians collapsing an evil caliph and his Arabs. The movie presents the Arab city of Baghdad as a Persian city. Also, advancing the Arab-as-Persian myth, Arabia's 40 thieves, including Ali Baba (Ankrum) and his son, Kashma (Curtis), appear as Persians,

Scene: Giggling mute harem maidens fawn over the handsome Persian protagonist, Kashma. And, an "Egyptian" bellydancer provides entertainment.

• Adorned in raiments of splendid gossamer is the heroine, Princess Azura of Morocco (Laurie). Aiding Azura is the courageous woman, Taha (Cabot), an expert archer.

• Observes Kashma, "The promises of the [Arab] caliph [Jory] are as black as the dried blood in his torture chamber." Cut to the caliph's underground torture chamber, complete with stretching rack and lash. Here, Kashma's father, the imprisoned Ali Baba, pleads with his captors, "Put an end to your fiendish torture."

• Baghdad's troops, led by vile Hussein (O'Brien), torch Ali Baba's Persian village. Interestingly, during the 1991 Persian Gulf war, which took place 39 years after the movie *Son of Ali Baba* debuted, Baghdad's Hussein torched Kuwait's oil fields.

• Hussein moves to harm Princess Azura. To the rescue, Kashma. Aided by the 40 "Persian" thieves and the "Persian Imperial Military Academy" cadets, young Kashma and his father, Ali Baba, bring down Baghdad's evil caliph and his cohorts.

Finis: The Persian "shah" appoints his "old and trusted friend," Ali Baba, ruler of Baghdad. Declares Ali Baba, "Freedom is a treasure beyond price."

Note: This film's Arabs and Persians wear armor and steel-pointed helmets; their medieval costumes seem more suitable for Robin Hood and King Arthur tales.

The Son of Cleopatra (1964), Seven Film. Italian. *Mark Damon, Livio Lorenzon.* Filmed in Egypt, in cooperation with the Egyptian government. Egyptian actors appear. EGYPTIANS, RECOMMENDED

Cleopatra's half-Roman son and his Egyptian companions drop cruel Romans.

Scene: Appearing is a "man fighting for the just cause of his people," the heroic El-Kabir (Damon). Tagged "the phantom of the desert, " El-Kabir wears a black mask. When Roman troops lash Egyptian slaves, El-Kabir's men sweep down from sand dunes, smashing the tyrants. El-Kabir spares some Romans, telling them to warn the Roman ruler, Petronius, that "his time is running out in the land of the pharaohs."

• Villagers and children cheer El-Kabir's men. Says one, "The Gods have answered our prayers." El-Kabir's soldiers kneel and pray for peace.

• Roman soldiers capture Uru, El-Kabir's "adopted" brother. They drag Uru to the palace dungeon and pour boiling water over his body, killing him.

• El-Kabir's men attack the palace, freeing Egyptian slaves. Next, the champion takes prisoner, Petronius's blonde, blue-eyed daughter, Lydia (Lorenzon), and other Romans. El-Kabir treats his Roman prisoners as VIPs. Meanwhile, the tyrant Petronius ignores Caesar's proclamation, stating, "The people of Egypt have the right to rebel against slavery, and any form of oppression that would deny them the dignity of their culture." Petronius shows no mercy, abusing Egyptian elders and their daughters.

• A Roman soldier fatally stabs El-Kabir's lady friend, Maraway.

• Imprisoned Egyptian women, their hands and feet bound to wooden poles, are delivered to Petronius. The ruler dispatches Roman chariots armed with blades fixed to their wheels, to encircle the women. The wheel-blades cut into their feet. To the rescue, El-Kabir and his men. They free the bound women and bring down Petronius.

• The respected Roman commander, Octavian, arrives in Egypt. He and El-Kabir bond. As peacemakers, they prevent further bloodshed.

• El-Kabir confesses that he loves Lydia, sighing, "All I can offer you is the desert." Lydia smiles; they ride off together.

A Son of the Desert (1928), American Rel. Silent. *William Merrill McCormick, Marin Sais, Robert Burns.* D, W: McCormick. *NS. Notes from AFIC. See *Outlaws of the Desert* (1941). SHEIKHS

Cowboys and Arabs.

Summary: In Arabia, an art student, Helen Dobson (Sais), offers to paint "the portrait of Sheik Hammid Zayad" (McCormick). Zayad refuses Helen's request, explaining "[that] the custom of the country does not permit it."

• Later, Helen receives an invitation to visit the sheikh's camp, where she will be allowed to view some of Zayad's "treasures." Helen's cowboy friend from Texas, Steve Kinard (Burns), who procures horses for Zayad's Arabs, warns Helen to stay put.

Son of the Pink Panther (1993), UA. *Roberto Benigni, Herbert Lom, Shabana Azmi, Debrah Farentino.* S, SP: Blake Edwards. Filmed in Jordan. VILLAINS, MAIDENS, WORST LIST

Arabs kill Arabs. Bringing order out of chaos, French Inspector Clouseau woos and rescues a kidnapped princess and crushes Arab villains.

Scene: "High spirited" Princess Yasmine (Farentino) appears at a gaming table. Without warning, mercenaries kidnap and whisk the half-American princess off to war-torn "Lugash."

• Those responsible for the princess' abduction are General Jaffar and Lugash's queen. The villains intend to capture the throne, demanding Yasmine's father cease governing. Should he refuse, they vow to kill Yasmine. The queen speaks with an accent; her general is a bonafide two-timer who seduces other women.

• Arab music underscores a civil war hovering over desert sands. The camera displays the king's Arabesque abode, a desert fortress, and a bar, "Omar's Oasis."

• Arriving at Omar's Oasis is Clouseau (Benigni). Abruptly, a bellydancer shoves Clouseau's face to her navel. Speaking broken English, the dancer asks the Frenchman to ink her navel. "Oh, quickly," she purrs, "I must finish dance or Omar cut off my nipples."

Immediately, Omar appears, knife in hand. To escape Omar's wrath, she resumes dancing. A brawl occurs. Arabs punch, knife, and shoot each other.

• Arabs vs. Arabs, a desert fortress. Arab troops wearing khaki uniforms attack. They gun down the general's Arabs, who are wearing headdresses, black-and-white kuffiyehs.

• Clouseau asks Yasmine, "How is it being a princess?" Sighs Yasmine, "It's not much fun." Thanks to Clouseau's brave actions, the princess is freed, the wicked queen and her general are brought down, and order is restored to Lugash.

Note: *Son of the Pink Panther* was filmed in Jordan. Why did Jordanian officials endorse this "shoot-up-the-Arabs" venture? Didn't anyone read the screenplay?

• In the credits, the producers offer "Special Thanks to Professor Seif W. Romahi, Applied Science University, Amman, Jordan."

• Also, this novel credit: "Burly Arab."

A Son of the Sahara (1924), First National. Silent. *Claire Windsor, Bert Lytell, Rosemary Theby, Montagu Love*. *NS. Notes from NYT (21 June 1924). Filmed in "Biskra," Africa. Based on Louise Gerard's 1922 book, *A Son of the Sahara*. SHEIKHS

Films from the 1920s do not usually show Western women loving dark Arabs. Instead, fair heroines embrace white Westerners clad in Arab garb.

Summary: In Arabia, Prince Cassim (Lytell), a Frenchman raised by Arabs, meets up with Barbara (Windsor), the daughter of a French officer. Instantly, Cassim proposes marriage. Lovely Barbara thinks Cassim is an Arab; she rejects him.

• Cassim directs his "Arab hordes" to attack the French fort because the French captain called him "black," and because Barbara mocked him. The angry Cassim whisks Barbara off to his harem. Here, the maiden Rayma (Theby) "eyes her with bitter scorn." Next, Cassim delivers Barbara to the slave market's auctioneer. In time, French troops arrive, saving the heroine.

Finis: Only after Cassim's French heritage is certified does Barbara express excitement. Immediately, she embraces Raoul (Cassim's French name). Concludes the scenario, the French couple "find happiness together."

Note: In desert scenarios, when Western men wearing Arab garb kidnap Western heroines, all ends happily. But, when Arabs kidnap Western women, scores of Arabs are killed. Plus, the Western heroines are rescued and embraced by Western heroes. See *Jewel of the Nile* (1985).

• Note the NYT critic's comment about *Son of Sahara's* director, Edwin Carewe:

That Mr. Carewe should have insisted the Sheik weeping copiously on one or two occasions is a mistake, for the average Sheik would, we imagine, be able to keep control over his emotions, even if they represented acute affection, rather than make a display of himself by having tears running down his cheeks.

Son of Samson (1960), Dubrava Film. Italian, dubbed in English. *Mark Forest, Chelo Alonso*. EGYPTIANS

Egyptian heroics; Persians oppress and enslave Egyptians.

Scene: Egypt. Intones the narrator, "More than 3,000 years ago in the eleventh century BC, the conquering Persians plundered the country's wealth and enslaved its people." The invaders brought "suffering and devastation upon the unprotected people of the Nile" for one reason—to please their queen, the beautiful, but wicked Smedes.

• Some Persians sell Egyptian women into slavery; others bury Egyptians alive. Persian soldiers also brand Egyptians at the stake "with fire until they turn to ashes."

• Who will "liberate the Egyptians and smite all their oppressors?" The blind Egyptian, known as "Maciste, the Son of Samson," that's who. Maciste handles huge "rocks as though they were pebbles."

• An Egyptian boy watches Persians beat up his father; the brave youth charges the soldiers. As Maciste intervenes, the boy is reunited with his father.

• Earlier, the pharaoh's son saved Maciste's life. Now, the Persian queen, Smedes, entraps the young Egyptian. She places a "necklace of forgetfulness" around his neck, enabling her to control him, temporarily. The queen also embellishes the palace with secret panels, crocodiles, and a "cell of death"—its walls crush trapped victims.

Finis: Maciste collapses the evil queen and her Persian cohorts. He also saves his Egyptian friend, restoring the latter to his rightful place on the throne.

Note: The film offers a familiar torture ploy—fixed blades attached to chariots' wheels maiming innocents.

Son of the Sheik (1926), UA. Silent. *Rudolph Valentino, Vilma Banky, George Fawcett, Bull Montana, Agnes Ayres, Mantague Love.* Adapted from E.M. Hull's novel. Filmed in Yuma, Arizona. A sequel to *The Sheik* (1921). Also, see *Lawrence of Arabia* (1962). SHEIKHS, MAIDENS

This European desert romance drama features two heroic Englishman steering good Arabs against bad ones. In this, his final film, Valentino has a dual role. He appears as young Sheikh Ahmed, and as Ahmed's father, Sheikh Ahmed Ben Hassan.

Scene: Screen credits reveal Yasmin (Banky), the French heroine, and some Arab cutthroats, notably the knife-thrower, "Ghabab, the Moor" (Love), "[whose] crimes outnumber the desert sands."

• At the Café Maure, cut to mute and heavily made-up Arab whores, smoking.

• Young Sheikh Ahmed (Valentino) informs his father, Ben Hassan (Valentino), "When the time comes I'll select my own bride." Later, Ahmed meets and embraces Yasmin, the French dancing girl. Purrs Ahmed, "Why fear me, dearest? Love such as mine can do no harm." Cut to Yasmin's cruel father, Andre (Fawcett). He wants Yasmin to wed Ghabab. Yet, when Ghabab touches Yasmin, she despairs.

• A desert trap. Believing he will meet and romance Yasmin, Ahmed rides off to a secluded spot in the desert. Abruptly, Andre and his mountebanks appear from the shadows, taking Ahmed hostage. Continually, they lash Ahmed, demanding "10,000 francs" for his release. In time, Ben Hassan's men arrive, freeing the tortured Ahmed.

• Though an Arab thief was the culprit who deceived Ahmed, he mistakenly believes Yasmin betrayed him. "Her [Yasmin's] mission in life is to lure men into lovely ruins," says the thief. "[Then we (swindlers)] rob and torture them." Believing the charlatan, Ahmed bursts into the Café Maure, whisking Yasmin off to his desert camp. "Not a knife had been thrown—so far."

• He threatens to take Yasmin, saying, "An eye for an eye—A hate for a hate—That is the law of my father."

• Cut to Ahmed's parents villa. Appearing is Diana (Ayres) and her husband, Ben Hassan, "The Sheik—English born—Sahara bred—undisputed ruler in this sea of sand." Diana reads from her cousin Clara's letter, "I hope the desert is as romantic as it has been pictured. I am mad to see it."

• Ben Hassan meets with his son, advising, "No matter what she has done, Ahmed, you must free her at once." Ahmed obeys; releasing Yasmin he sighs, "I love her." When Ahmed learns the truth, that Yasmin was not responsible for his capture, he rides through a sandstorm intent on penalizing Andre's cutthroats.

• Ahmed barges into the "Den-of-Thieves" dance hall. A rip-roaring fight occurs. Ahmed and his father, Ben Hassan, punch out upwards of 30 knife-wielding Arabs.

• As Ghabab runs off with Yasmin, she shouts to Ahmed, "My heart has always been yours." Ahmed and Ghabab draw swords; Ghabab is killed. Ahmed takes Yasmin in his arms.

Note: No Arab amour, here. In *The Sheik* (1921) an Englishman in Arab garb falls for Diana, an English lady. In *Son of the Sheik*, Ahmed, the Englishman, pines for a Frenchman's daughter. Also, critics fail to note that both *The Sheik* and *Son of the Sheik* display not beautiful Arab heroines, but rather courageous European women who marry brave Englishmen. And, both films present Arab women as mute jealous assassins, as wives for sale, and as prostitutes.

• An Arab calls his friend, "Son of an owl." Retorts his friend, "Nay, my mother was no owl—only a little cuckoo."

• Many of this movie's Arabs function as lechers and crooks, belittling Arab women. Note the dialogue:

The Arab: What's your wife's name?
His friend: I don't know her name. When I want her, I whistle.

Treatment of Islam: An Arab is tagged "Ramadan," the name for Muslim Holy days.

Son of Sinbad (1955), RKO. *Dale Robertson, Sally Forest, Lili St. Cyr, Vincent Price. Kim Novak* makes a fleeting appearance. MAIDENS

Gallant Arab women collapse the Tartars. Sinbad (Robertson) and Omar Khayyam (Price) offer only modest assistance. No Arab villains.

Scene: "If a mortal man can save Baghdad, it is he [Sinbad]." Yet, Sinbad needs help from Omar Khayyam, and from some expert archers—the 40 thieves' gifted daughters.

• Throughout, the Arab heroines wear silk pantaloons. The camera also reveals, up close, the rotating navels of sensuous swivel-hipped dancers. These navel close-ups were too revealing, as the *Son of Sinbad* was condemned by the American National Legion of Decency (ANLD) on grounds that it contained "grossly salacious dances and indecent costuming." States an ANLD document, *Son of Sinbad* is "an incitement to juvenile delinquency; it is especially dangerous to the moral welfare of youth."[162]

• The evil potentate, Tartar Tamarlane, perches the skulls of his human victims on spikes, then hangs them from palace walls.

• Instead of acting as a warrior, this Sinbad functions as a "love-plagued parrot." He cares only about seducing every maiden he meets. When lovely Ameer (Forest), who falls for Sinbad, insists the sailor cease his constant panting, Sinbad huffs, "Have you forgotten that I am Sinbad, the son of the greatest authority on women that ever lived?"

• Armed with arrows and bows, 40 or so Iraqi women swing into action, crushing the invading Tartars. Soon, they liberate Baghdad. Sinbad offers some help; he gains an explosive formula, then creates some secret "Greek Fire," expediting Tamarlane's demise.

Dialogue: An Arab beggar out to secure baksheesh feigns blindness, telling Omar Khayyam, "You look like the father of an expectant camel."

Treatment of Islam: Exclaims Sinbad, "May the prophet strike me dead!"

Son of Tarzan (1920), National Film. Silent. 15 episodes. *Kamuela Searle.* *NS. This 1920s movie serial was released in 1920 as a full-length feature film, also entitled *Son of Tarzan.* CLIFFHANGERS, VILLAINS

Summary: "Back in the jungles of Africa, the son of Tarzan, Korak, frees the white girl, Meriem, from her own captors, a horde of evil Arabs," writes Jim Harmon.[163]

Son of Tarzan (1920), Jungle Pictures. Silent. *Kamuela Searle.* P: Demsey Tabler. SP: Edgar Rice Burroughs. Based on the movie serial, *Son of Tarzan.* SHEIKHS, WORST LIST

In the African jungle, Tarzan, Korak, his son, plus an ape and an elephant, terminate Arabs. A ghastly sheikh kills the wife of a French officer. The sheikh also abducts and abuses the dead French woman's daughter.

Scene: Sheikh Amor Ben Khatour approaches Captain Jacot, a French officer, demanding Jacot free his imprisoned brother. Not only does the outraged captain refuse to take Khatour's bribe monies, but he also slugs the sheikh. Snickers the Arab, "Amor Ben Khatour never forgives."

• States the title card, "The sheik swore vengeance and when Capt. Jacot's wife and baby come to join him in Africa..." On screen, desert Arabs appear, attacking Jacot's escort party. Evil Ben Khatour shoots Jacot's wife, then rides off with Jeanne, the officer's little girl. Ben Khatour "cruelly abused her [Jeanne] in childhood."

• A few years pass. Cut to Ben Khatour sitting next to an ugly Arab woman who puffs a nargelih. Jeanne, now ten years of age, clutches a homemade doll. Khatour calls her, Meriem. Functioning as a child-slave, Jeanne goes to place some tobacco into the Arab's pipe. But, the girl stumbles, falling down. "Child of evil," shouts the sheikh. Ben Khatour grabs and tears the girl's doll apart. Next, he pulls Jeanne's hair, and tosses her to the ground.

• To the rescue, Akut, "the human ape" and Korak (Searle), Tarzan's son. Korak slugs the sheikh, running off with Jeanne.

• Khatour's Arabs search for and eventually discover Korak; they shoot him. Jeanne is returned to Ben Khatour. The sheikh kicks and binds the girl; then he yanks her hair and again throws Jeanne to the ground.

• Ben Khatour's Arabs and some "Swedes" kidnap Jane, Tarzan's mate. The Arab pulls a knife, threatening Jane. In time, Tarzan (Tabler) appears, flooring the Arab.

• After Korak's wounds heal, he asks about Jeanne. He finds a note, stating, "then came the Arabs and took her away." Korak springs to action.

• Boasts Ben Khatour to enslaved Jeanne, "I have sold you to Hamid the Black!" The Arab grabs a branding iron, thrusting the weapon toward the girl's face. He exclaims, "The brand of Amor Ben Khatour." Korak arrives, freeing Jane and killing Ben Khatour.

• "The killing of the Sheik moves the Arabs to wreak vengeance on the son of Tarzan." The sheikh's cohorts capture Korak; the Arabs tie the youth to a tree and light a fire. Next, they pierce Korak's body with spears. Abruptly, Tantor the elephant appears, whisking Korak off to safety.

Finis: In England, two happy European couples mingle. The camera reveals Lord and Lady Greystoke (Tarzan and Jane); along with Korak and Jeanne. And, Captain Jacot, Jeanne's "real [French] father," is reunited with his long-lost daughter.

Note: The unsightly Arabs in this film continually abuse and kill innocents. Yet, a few frames reveal Ivan Paulovich, Tarzan's arch-enemy.

The Song of Love (1923), First National. Silent. *Norma Talmadge, Joseph Schildkraut, Edmund Carewe.* *NS. Notes from NYT (24 February 1924). Based on Margaret Peterson's 1922 novel, *Dust of Desire.* MAIDENS, SHEIKHS

An Arab woman rebuffs a sheikh, opting to romance a Frenchman.

Summary: The Algerian desert. Norma Talmadge, who appears as Noorma-hal, an Arabian dancing girl, "certainly does face the camera in a state of undress." Noorma-hal's performances at a gambling house attract scores of Arabs and Frenchmen.

As soon as the lecherous Sheikh Ramilak (Carewe) enters the casino, he tries to seduce Noorma-hal. This nasty sheikh intends to become the "king of North Africa." To do so, he plans to extinguish French forces. Contesting the sheikh is Vaiverde (Schildkraut), a dashing French secret agent who woos and captures Noorma-hal's heart.

Posing as an Arab, the Frenchman halts the fanatic sheikh's uprising. When the sheikh's rebels charge the French garrison, they are defeated; Ramilak perishes. Now that the lovely Noorma-hal has saved Vaiverde's life, she eases into "the [French] hero's arms."

Song of Scheherazade (1947), UNI. *Yvonne De Carlo, Jean-Pierre Aumont, Rex Ravelle, Robert Kendall.* See *Tangier* (1946). CAMEOS

Morocco as a Spanish port. Though Rimsky-Korsakoff's opera "Scheherazade" focuses on Fatima, a bright and lovely Arab, this film presents a Spanish maiden as his muse.

Scene: The year, 1865. Russian naval cadets, including Rimsky-Korsakoff (Aumont), arrive in Morocco. Cut to Flamenco dancers. When Rimsky-Korsakoff spots Cara (De Carlo), a Spanish maiden, he becomes smitten.

• Cara's wit and beauty spark the composer to pen "Scheherazade." He sees to it that Cara will portray the lead, Fatima.

• Fast forward. Inside a Russian opera house, Cara appears as Fatima, dazzling the cheering Russians.

Note: Cara's family employs Hassan (Kendall), "the little Arab boy." Hassan fetches various items for the family and drives the carriage.

Sorcerer (1977), UNI, PAR. *Roy Scheider, Amidou, Ramon Bieri.* SP: Georges Arnaud, Walon Green. D, P: William Friedkin. Remake of *The Wages of Fear* (1952), in which no Arabs appear. PALESTINIANS

One of this film's four tragic fugitives is a Palestinian; the brief opening scene displays the Palestinian in Israel as a bus bomber. Remaining frames present the Palestinian as a reformed, courageous man.

Scene: In Jerusalem, three men wearing yarmulkes board a bus. Moments later, as the bus passes a building, a huge explosion. The men flee to an upstairs flat, removing their yarmulkes. Speaking Arabic, they hug each other. Israeli soldiers arrive; they kill and capture all the bombers but one; Kassim (Amidou) escapes.

• Cut to a squalid Central American village. Here, Kassim and three other desperate criminals labor for a petrol company. One day, the workers are given an opportunity to leave the country. All they need do is deliver some nitroglycerin to an endangered site, nearly 300 miles away. The nitroglycerin is desperately needed to put out a raging oil fire. The company promises volunteers new identities provided they successfully manage to steer two nitroglycerin-filled trucks over rough jungle trails to the fire site. Kassim and three others volunteer.

• When Kassim finds out an assassin has killed his companion, a benevolent elderly truck driver, he promptly moves to apprehend the slayer.

• Scenes show Kassim as the ultimate team player. Steering the truck along treacherous terrain, the Palestinian earns the friendship of his Parisian partner, Serrano (Bieri).

• As a huge tree blocks the truck's path, three of the four volunteers become disheartened, opting to call it quits. Not Kassim. "I think I can clear it," he says. Kassim supervises the clearing-up process. After gathering rocks, he tosses some dirt into a bag. Next, he adds a touch of nitroglycerin. Single-handedly, Kassim explodes the giant tree, opening the road.

• Feeling confident, Serrano and Kassim approach the fire site. Suddenly, one of the truck's wheels spins off. The truck falls down a hill, setting off the nitroglycerin and killing the two men.

Sorority House Massacre 2 (1992), New Horizons. *Robyn Harris, Melisa Moore.* CAMEOS

Decadent Arabs.[164]

Scene: In this gore-galore movie, a murderer's ghost haunts a mansion, threatening coeds. Cut to topless dancers performing in a bar. Among the gaping spectators, two Arabs, wearing business suits, dark glasses, and headdresses. They puff nargelihs, mutter gibberish and shout: "Take it off, baby."

Note: Credits bill the duo: "Abdul" and "Schmabdul."

South of Algiers (1953), a.k.a. The Golden Mask, UA. *Van Heflin, Wanda Hendrix, Eric Portman, Jacques Francois, Marne Maitland, Alec Mango, Marie France, George Pastell.* SP: Robert Westerby. Filmed in Algeria. VILLAINS

Arabs vs. Arabs, vs. Westerners.

Scene: In Tunis, a policeman directs cars, not camels. Date trees line neat streets.

• The souk reveals craftsmen at work, an exotic bellydancer, and musicians. Cut to a shady Arab guide, Thankyou (Maitland), telling his employer, archaeologist Dr. Burnet (Portman), "To fix this car will cost you $1,200." Replies Dr. Burnet, "Show me the bill." Sighs Thankyou, "800 francs." Later, Thankyou says, "Oh what a wonderful bargain, sir. [It costs] only 39,000 francs for each one [goat]." Burnet gives the Arab only "32,000" per goat.

• Dr. Burnet, his daughter, Anne (Hendrix), her fiancé, Jacques Farnod (Francois), and writer Nicholas Chapman (Heflin) are intent on locating the lost Roman tomb of Marcus Manilus. His tomb, they believe, contains a mask, worth millions. Before their camel caravan departs, they are warned, Watch out for "the bandit, Mahmoud" (Mango).

• Appearing is Yasmin (France), a young Arab girl, "[whose] parents are dead." When Yasmin's caring brother tries to sell their donkey, she sobs. Chapman intervenes, giving the youths needed monies—"2,000 francs." "[As the two] young Arabs know every inch of the desert," they and their donkey link up with Chapman's expedition.

• A sandstorm. Lurking in the background, Mahmoud's sinister henchmen.

• Burnet's group enters a friendly Arab village; Arabs perform traditional dances. And, they provide the Burnet party with needed water and food. Seeing Arab food, Chapman grimaces.

• Suddenly, staggering into the village is a wounded Camel Corps soldier. Explains the soldier, Mahmoud's bandits just killed five corps soldiers.

• The Westerners manage to uncover Moloch's much-sought-after mask. Pants their greedy guide, Hassan (Pastell), "This treasure should be sold, not placed in a museum."

• Mahmoud's bandits surface from the shadows. The Arabs whip the Westerners; they kill Hassan and fellow Arabs. As Mahmoud annihilates innocents, he screams in Arabic.

• To the rescue, Camel Corps members riding white horses. They bring down Mahmoud's bandits, freeing the Burnets.

Note: Movie credits thank "the Algerian government" for their cooperation.

Spawn (1997), NL. *Michael Jai White, Martin Sheen.* SP: Alan Mc Elroy. Based on the comic books by Todd McFarlane. CAMEOS

Arabs as disposable victims.

Scene: Hong Kong, a military air base. Cut to hired assassin Lt. Col. Al Simmons (White). He works for a sinister government agent, Jason Wynn (Sheen). Simmons barges into the flight control room and mows down several military men. Next, Simmons targets three Arabs emerging from an airplane. When one Arab, the "leader of the Algerian Revolutionary Front" smiles, BOOM! The clad-in-Arab-garb leader and "26 innocent civilians" perish. Credits roll.

• The TV announcer declares that an Arab-Israeli peace summit was "disrupted by bomb threats from the Christian Coalition."

• A ritzy gathering. Robed Arabs warmly greet the diabolical agent, Wynn.

Speed Zone (1989), OR. *John Candy, Jamie Farr.* SP: Michael Short. See *Cannonball Run* (1981), *Cannonball Run II* (1983). CAMEOS, SHEIKHS

A stupid, lustful sheikh pops up as a "cannonballer."

Scene: Wearing a gold-braided robe and white burnoose, the sheikh (Farr) makes a fool of himself. Before a major cross-country race begins, a reporter tries to interview the sheikh. The reporter asks the Arab some questions. Instead of answering the questions, the Arab repeats them.

• At a pre-race party, the Arab tries to pick up a busty bodybuilder. "I am a man with a lustful appetite," he boasts. Alas, the sheikh cannot hold his liquor; passes out.

• The Arab continues to ogle the bodybuilder, quipping, "A great body is a terrible thing to waste. I give up racing."

Sphinx (1981), WB. *Frank Langella, Leslie-Anne Down, John Gielgud, Vic Tablian, Martin Benson, Nadim Sawalha.* SP: John Byrum. Filmed in Egypt; banned in Egypt. EGYPTIANS, WORST LIST

Egyptian tomb violators kill fellow Egyptians, including family members. And, Egyptians try to rape and murder the US heroine. In the souk, a prison cell and inside a tomb, the lovely American is obliged to scream for help.

Scene: Cairo, 1980s. Harvard-educated Egyptologist Erica Baron (Down) travels to Egypt seeking to purchase artifacts for a Boston museum. Also, she wants to trace the life of Seti, the pharaoh. Baron also intends to investigate a Seti confidante, Menephta, an extraordinarily cruel but talented architect. A flashback to 1301 BC reveals Menephta nabbing the violator of Seti's tomb; horses pull the thief apart, wishbone style.

• Erica strolls in the souk. Instantly, ugly Egyptian children mob her, begging for cigarettes. One boy pinches her buttocks. No one speaks English. The souk scenes distort. The majority of Khan Khalili souk merchants speak more than one language, especially English. While some Egyptian children may ask tourists for baksheesh (tips), explains actor Frank Langella, but they are never "threatening." This writer and his friends, many of whom lived for a time in Cairo, never saw, nor knew of a single case whereby an Egyptian boy grabbed an American woman's butt.

• Erica visits the shop of Abdu (Gielgud), an unethical antiquities dealer. Abruptly, Egyptian thugs rush in. They grab a saber, killing Abdu, and molest Erica.

• Shocked and afraid, Erica rushes back to her hotel and hides her money.

• A tiny prison cell. Here, a shabby Egyptian police sergeant attempts to rape Erica. As he slowly strips Erica, he paws her body. Erica sobs. To the rescue, Ahmed (Langella), an Egyptian-Italian in charge of the UN antiquities division. "Are you still enthralled with our magnificent traditions?" asks Ahmed. He warns Erica to leave Egypt, "A Harvard student went out into the desert and disappeared, never heard from again."

• In Luxor, Ahmed and Erica make love. "You'll have one happy experience from Egypt to remember," he sighs.

• Erica uncovers an Egyptian smuggling ring. But the thieves nab her and then move to bury Erica—alive! She screams. Ahmed's friend, Gamal (Sawalha), tries to save her, but his fellow Egyptians kill him. Again, Ahmed rescues Erica. Only this time, he murders his Uncle. Sighs Ahmed, "Egypt's one great national resource—death!" Depressed at having to crush a relative, Ahmed decides not to wed Erica. Instead, he kills himself.

• In the end, Erica comes to realize that for hundreds of years, Egyptians like Ahmed's uncle, and not Western archaeologists like herself, are to blame for pilfering Egypt's tombs.

Note: Points out actor Frank Langella, "The Egyptians were terribly concerned that they would be portrayed as evil, ignorant, and so on."[165]

• Egyptians should be concerned about their image in Hollywood films. After *Sphinx's* film crew ceased shooting in Egypt, the producer injected an offensive and

> improbable scene [which] shows an Egyptian policeman trying to rape the female lead [Down] inside, of all places, the police shed at Saqqara, a busy archaeological tourist attraction which almost no foreigners visit. [Unknown to Egyptian authorities, this rape] scene was added to the scenario. The producer shot the rape scene in Europe, adding the Egyptian footage later[166]

• US producers complain about Egypt's bureaucracy, saying Egyptian officials move too slowly, taking way too much time before approving screenplays. Thus, some producers are reluctant to film in Egypt, even when their stories are set there. Affirms Egyptian producer Ahmed Sami, "Antique and obsolete equipment and the snail's pace of the bureaucracy hurt us. Approval is supposed to take one month but ninety percent of the time it takes longer." In the film business, "time is really money, and Egypt is the loser," says Sami.[167]

• In his NYT review (11 February 1981), Vincent Canby writes, "The film's attitude toward Egypt suggests the British Empire in mid-nineteenth century." St. Louis KSDK-TV 7 critic Joe Pollack comments that *Sphinx* is a "morass of nonsense. When Charlton Heston did *The Awakening* (1980) a few months ago, I thought we'd reached a new low in Egypt films. But I was wrong, again. Not even pyramid power can save this turkey" (7 March 1981).

Spy Hard (1996), HOL. *Leslie Nielsen.* CAMEOS, VILLAINS

Arabs as terrorists.

Scene: Before credits roll, Agent WD-40 (Nielsen) receives a recorded message alerting him that "an international arms dealer [General Rancor] has brokered a deal to sell a Scorpion missile to a Middle Eastern terrorist cell." While listening to the message, Nielsen checks out two photographs; one shows Yasser Arafat with the dangerous arms merchant, the other reveals the mercenary fraternizing with Saddam Hussein.

The Spy Who Loved Me (1977), UA. *Roger Moore, Barbara Bach, Richard Kiel, Edward De Souza, Nadim Sawalha.* EGYPTIANS, SHEIKHS, MAIDENS

Typically, Bond films exhibit Arab and non-Arab women as sexual playthings. Here, an Egyptian gives his woman to 007.

Scene: Intent on squashing a nuclear terrorist, James Bond (Moore) flies off to Egypt. On entering a desert tent, Bond asks his Cambridge-educated pal Sheikh Hosein (De Souza) for assistance. Bond notes that three scantily-clad Egyptian women are pampering Hosein. Quips 007, "I never had any problems knowing what you were going to do [after graduation] Hosein." Retorts the sheikh, "We don't only have oil, you know." The comment is a fabrication. Egypt, one of the world's poorest nations, has no oil.

• The myth: Arabs view women as disposable items. Bond tells Hosein he wants to discuss with him a most private matter; the sheikh claps his hands; the three women promptly exit. Hosein asks 007 to stay a while, offering him everything from "sheep eyes" to a "vodka martini" and "a bed for tonight." Bond refuses, saying he must leave. Hosein claps his hands. A beautiful, Egyptian woman emerges; 007 remains.

• Bond rushes off to Aziz's (Sawalha) Cairo flat. A seductive Egyptian woman embraces 007, saying, "Aziz asked me to entertain you while you are waiting. If there's anything you would like, anything at all." Suddenly, an assassin's bullet meant for Bond kills the woman.

• Egyptian folk dancers perform at a club owned by "Max Kalba."

• In Luxor, the villain, Jaws, swings a wooden club at Bond, missing. The club hits a large pole supporting some scaffolding. Instantly, tons of rubble fall, crushing Jaws. Bond checks out the debris, dusts off his hands, cracking, "Egyptian builders."

Note: *The Spy Who Loved Me* presents no Egyptian heavies. Bond even speaks some Arabic. Credits label Hosein's harem maidens, "Arab beauties."

Stanley & Livingstone (1939), TCF. *Spencer Tracy, Sir Cedric Hardwicke, Nancy Kelly.* SP: Philip Dunne. CAMEOS, SHEIKHS

Inserted are brutal Arabs enslaving Africans. See *Anthony Adverse* (1936).

Scene: On learning that Stanley (Tracy) is off to Africa, Eve (Kelly) tells a reporter, "That's where the slave buyers go, isn't it? They (the Arabs) hate the whites for trying to stop the slave trade. And worst of all, they hate Dr. Livingstone (Hardwicke)."

• In Kenya, Africa, a robed Arab posts a sign, announcing the departure time of Stanley's group. Cut to a "slave caravan" and shackled slaves struggling "through this country." The slaves' hands are tied behind their backs and ropes are fastened around their necks. Arabs wearing white thobes whip the Africans.

Finis: Stanley and Livingstone "drive away the [cruel Arab] slave trader."

Note: Livingstone ponders Africa, "White men have seen Africa only through the eyes of ignorance," he says. "And that means through the eyes of fear... fear of the unknown." Fittingly, his statement delineates how some filmmakers see Arabia.

Stargate (1994), MGM. *James Spader, Kurt Russell, Alexis Cruz.* EGYPTIANS, MAIDENS

An ode to freedom. In this science fiction fantasy, brave Egyptian look-a-likes link up with Americans. Together, they contest a despotic alien force, one which enslaves, oppresses, and terrorizes villagers. The US protagonist falls for a bright "Egyptian" maiden.

Scene: Dr. Daniel Jackson (Spader), a maverick Egyptologist, and Colonel Jack O'Neil (Russell) a military commander, pass through a star gate, arriving on a distant desert planet. The planet, complete with an exact replica of Giza's great pyramid, resembles ancient Egypt. Even the "natives," who wear robes and head scarves, look like Egyptian nomads.

• The desert leader invites the Americans to dinner. He explains that an immortal alien, the Sun God Ra, forbids them to read or write. Ra, a vampire, who came to earth 10,000 years ago, he says, possesses the body of a youth. To sustain himself, he and his armed guards wear animal masks.

• As a gesture of friendship, the leader gives Skaara (Cruz), his beautiful daughter, to Dr. Jackson, who, after hesitating, takes her. The daughter, an atypical reel Egyptian, can translate an ancient dialect. Meanwhile, O'Neil befriends a young boy, giving the youth his cigarette lighter.

• Suddenly, Ra's massive pyramid spaceship attacks. Floating above the planet, the monstrous pyramid plane bombs the village, killing scores; some Americans are captured.

• Though Ra's forces outnumber the villagers, they revolt, freeing the imprisoned Americans from Ra's grasp.

• Ra moves to escape in his spaceship; an atomic blast destroys him.

• All but one American chooses to return home through the star gate. Dr. Jackson decides to remain in ancient "Egypt" with Skaara, the woman he loves.

The Steel Bayonet (1957), UA. *Leo Genn. P, D: Michael Carreras.*
CAMEOS

This WWII movie displays Tunisians as unprincipled merchandisers.

Scene: Tunisia, 1943. British soldiers battle the Germans. Yet, "Mahomet," their guide, is nowhere in sight. The white-turbaned Tunisian runner is away from the front line, busy selling fellow Tunisians "second-hand tea leaves." Later, a soldier warns Mahomet that if they catch onto your game, "they're gonna slit your throat from ear to ear."

• A ragged Arab villager hands two British officers an egg. The officers run the Tunisian off. Quips one, "They hang on, these wog farmers, don't they?" His pal says, "You can't blame them; it's not their war." The use of "wog" is not disputed.

The Steel Lady (1953), UA. *Rod Cameron, Tab Hunter, Frank Puglia, John Abbott, Christopher Dark, Carmer d'Antonio. SP: Richard Schayer. S: Aubrey Wisberg.*
SHEIKHS

Post-WWII Sahara. Four Americans shoot marauding Arabs. Islam is derided.

Scene: Americans working with Trans-Africa discover oil. They are warned, "That 50 miles of Khalifa is taboo [the] old Sheikh has a mad-on against all foreigners, [because of] something that happened during the war." The men opt to board their plane and fly off.

• A sandstorm surfaces; the plane crashes in the Sahara. All seems lost until the men see a flag perched atop an abandoned German tank, "The Steel Lady." Says one, "[The storm] uncovered that flag, or the Arabs would have pots and pans long ago."

• Inside the tank's secret compartment, a fortune in jewels belonging to the Arabs. Syd Barlow (Dehner) finds the treasures, but tells no one. The men repair the tank, and head across the desert. Spotting them is the villain, Mustapha El-Melek (Abbott), a University of Rabat graduate.

• Quips El-Melek, "The Iron Monster" is coming. Says his nephew, Sheikh Taras (Puglia), "And the treasure of Khalifa is moving along with it." "If it is Allah's will," replies El-Melek. Adding, "But one thing is certain, it is the same monster that accompanied the German raiding party I guided into Khalifa many years ago." Says Taras, "Let us see what Allah has done for us. Assemble the men. We will capture the monster and its keepers."

• The tank stops at an oasis. Suddenly, Arab maidens appear, including a bedouin bellydancer (d'Antonio). Proclaims Monohan (Cameron), "I wasn't expecting that."

• Ponders Taras, "The answer to where the jewels are now seems to have been stolen among the other mysteries of the Sahara." Sly Taras calls the Americans, "my friends," then advises them to leave the oasis, saying "[desert bandits] are many and ruthless. [And] as the Prophet says, evil is the wind that brings blessings to no one."

• Taras questions whether the Arabs can trust the Americans. "Not entirely," says El-Melek, "but for the good of their souls we'll soon make sure."

• In exchange for the tank, Taras offers Monohan four horses, a camel, and a tent. "My son and I will be on hand to wish you the blessings of Allah," he says. Cut to El-Melek's cohorts searching the tank for the missing jewels; they find one gem. "My suspicions are confirmed," says Taras. He wakes the sleeping Americans, barking, "Surrender what we seek and you will be allowed to leave as promised, with Allah's blessing." Abruptly, Barlow socks an Arab; he and his buddies rush into the tank and drive off.

• The four men encounter one of Taras's Arabs, a liar who says that some desert bandits killed off his patrol. "It will seem by Allah's mercy I still live," he says, directing them to a nearby oasis.

• Taras's cohort slinks towards the tank. An ailing crew member, Billy (Hunter), sees him. Aware Billy's spotted him, the Arab says, "It is written that the sick and wounded are under Allah's protection... Don't force this sin upon me." Yet, the Arab kicks Billy. Billy fires some shots, warning his friends. The tank crew departs; a bullet hits the tank's water tank.

• The tank rests motionless in the desert. Suddenly, El-Melek's Arabs encircle the greatly outnumbered Americans. In time, a rescue plane appears, saving the Americans. But, Barlow, the jewel thief, stays behind and shoots-it-out with El-Melek's Arabs.

• Monohan decides to deliver the jewels to the Arabs; his pals balk. Not to fret, says Monohan, more riches will gush forth. In return for the jewels, Taras' Arabs allow Monohan Inc. to drill for oil.

Dialogue: Arabs as American Indians. Noting that Arabs dwell in the Sahara, one American says, "This is bandit area, worse than Arizona Apache."

Step Lively (1944), RKO. *George Murphy, Gloria De Haven.* Songs by Sammy Cahn and Jule Styne. Based on the Broadway hit, *Room Service, Step Lively.* CAMEOS, MAIDENS

Actors appear as Arab caricatures in a stage musical.

Scene: A theater stage. About to debut, the musical comedy, "A Lovely Evening." On stage, six bearded actors-as-Arabs wearing tall turbans. In the background, palm trees and a village. One Arab character waves a rug and presto—rushing from a stage tent are a dozen veiled and scantily-clad harem maidens wearing jeweled fezzes.

Actor George Murphy appears in Arab garb, equating the Arab maidens with Salem's witches. He sings, in part:

But today the witches got a racket; they wear a turban and a jeweled jacket. And pretty soon they're with the upper bracket clan. Yeah, man... Talented fortune tellers no longer hide in cellars; no doubt you've met the lady with the crystal ball. But now I want to introduce the queen of them all.

Gloria De Haven appears in Arab garb. Arab music underscores magic scenes: As a rope elevates towards the ceiling, water suddenly flows from the six Arabs' turbans. And, instead of showing snakes rising from three straw baskets, emerging are three women wearing tight-fitting snake-like clothing.

Storm Over the Nile (1955), COL. *Anthony Steel, Laurence Harvey, Ferdy Mayne, Christopher Lee.* Filmed in Sudan. Remake of *Four Feathers.* The producers use footage from Korda's *Four Feathers* film. See the Geste films and the *Four Feathers* listings. VILLAINS

British heroics in the Sudan. Arabs vs. Arabs, vs. the British.

Scene: "1885—Rebellious Army of dervishes enslaved and killed thousands of defenseless natives in Sudan. General Gordon appealed for help from England—none came."

• As Harry Faversham (Steel) refuses to fight in the Sudan, his three British friends present him with a white feather, symbolizing cowardice. Later, Harry does go to the Sudan. His face is "tanned" by Dr. Haraz, a proficient Arab. Haraz also teaches Harry how to act like a mute tribesman. Once Harry is branded, his disguise is complete. He dons a white turban and thobe, helping the British defeat the dervishes.

• Attacking dervishes shout, "Allah, Allah!" And, they toss flaming wooden spears into British tents. After capturing British soldiers, they bind them to horses; the horses drag the men through the terrain. Sighs a soldier, "they'll kill them [the prisoners] out of pure joy!"

• At British headquarters, soldiers contemplate whether comrades are dead or in prison. "They're better off dead," says one. "The Arabs take them [and] it's a long time dying... We've been slaughtered like cattle."

• Arabs, and the disguised Harry, toil as part of a "convict gang." Cut to a crowded dungeon. Here, guards kick and whip the British captives.

• The dungeon reveals British prisoners, chains fastened to their necks. Enter Harry. He uses a file to remove the chains. The soldiers escape.

• The decisive battle. Thousands of dervishes charge. Due to Harry's bravery, the British are well prepared for the attack, defeating the dervishes.

Striptease (1996), COL/Castle Rock. *Demi Moore, Burt Reynolds.* SP, D: Andrew Bergman. CAMEOS, SHEIKHS

A one-liner refers to a wealthy "Arab sheikh."

Scene: A Miami strip club. Having lost her job and custody of her daughter, the protagonist (Moore) moves to acquire needed monies. Two strippers, including an African-American, try to comfort her. Note the dialogue:

Dancer 1: The judge will see the light, he has to.
Moore: Oh yeah, it's expensive, I'll tell you that. It's going to cost me $15,000 for
        this appeal and there's not even a remote chance I can make that in six weeks.
Dancer 2: You're going to have to dance day and night, and hope that some Arab sheikh
        shows up!

Sudan (1945), UNI. *Maria Montez, George Zucco, John Hall, Turhan Bey.* EGYPTIANS, MAIDENS, RECOMMENDED

Egyptian commoners supporting their queen depose a tyrannical ruler and his slave traders. Maria Montez appears as Queen Naila, a superb dancer and horsewoman.

Scene: After the evil counselor Haradef (Zucco) murders Queen Naila's father, Haradef sells Naila into slavery. Vowing to avenge her father's death and to regain the throne, Naila moves to free herself and the slaves. See *Flame of Araby* (1951).

• Palace guards prepare to deliver chained women to the slave markets, branding them with the letter "S." Naila escape the slavers. Later, she enters a horse race, defeating all the male riders.

• Posing as a commoner, Naila dances in a public place. Egyptians cheer.

• Two men vie for Naila's hand; Marab (Hall), the thief, and Herua (Bey), the slave. No feuds here; both men focus on the queen's safety. The "skilled in statecraft" Naila, risks her life to save Herua, the man she loves.

• Barks Haradef, "Escaped slaves and those who help them will be torn apart by wild horses." Not so. Cut to Naila and her Egyptians bringing down the villain.

Finis: Naila and Herua ride into the sunset; the song, "Proud and Free," underscores their freedom. Note the lyric, "Riding forever for liberty, we're free."

Suez (1938), TCF. *Tyrone Power. Loretta Young, Annabella, Maurice Moscovitch, J. Edward Bloomberg.* SP: Julian Josephson and Philip Dunne (*True Confessions*). In his autobiography, Dunne describes the film as "pretty bad."
EGYPTIANS

Egypt, 1850s. Egyptian and Sudanese workers appear in the background, shifting sand. French architect, Ferdinand de Lesseps, is credited with building the Suez Canal. No mention is made of Egypt's historic role in the development this important waterway. Yet, "The idea of connecting the Mediterranean with the Red Sea dates back to... the time of Seti and Ramses II. The ancient Egyptians constructed a boat canal from the Nile to the Red Sea in about 1300 BC." Their goal? To "supply Arabia with wheat and food... In about 600 BC, at the time of the Pharaoh Necho II," the canal was extended to Suez.[168]

Scene: In this love story, consider the key question: Will the diplomat Ferdinand (Power) wed Countess Eugenie De Montijo (Young) or Toni Pellerin (Annabella)?

• Some scenes show Ferdinand "cultivating" Egypt's Prince Said Pasha (Bloomberg), son of Mohammad Ali (Moscovitch). The Frenchman teaches the always-being-fanned-by-slaves Said, how to fence, how to ride, and when dining, how to use utensils instead of his fingers. The countess calls Said, Ferdinand's "fat friend."

• Initial frames project rotund Said as an uncouth person. Later, Said appears as a visionary; he supports the canal's construction. As Ferdinand's staunchest patron, Said empties his treasury to assist the diplomat.

• Posing as Egyptians, Turkish renegades dynamite the hills encompassing the canal, killing hundreds of Egyptian workers.

Treatment of Islam: Often, the countess calls her donkey, "Hassan." The donkey scenes "were deleted in India because Hassan, the revered grandson of the prophet Mohammad, was a martyr still mourned in India for ten days every year." See the AFIC commentary on *Suez*, Record 1535.

Note: Fifty years prior to the construction of the canal, Napoleon Bonaparte and his army landed at Alexandria (1 July 1798). Napoleon's invasion was the first conquest of a Muslim country by a European army since the Crusades. From here on, European interest in Egypt expanded.

The Sultan's Daughter (1943), MON. *Ann Corio, Irene Ryan, Eddie Norris, Charles Butterworth, Fortunio Bonanova.* OS: Milton M. Rasion, Tim Ryan, Gene Roth. Freddy Fisher's orchestra plays, "The Sultan's Daughter." MAIDENS, SHEIKHS

Arabs vs. Arabs, vs. American entertainers. Oil and the Arab-German connection. Arab women hug Americans. See *Ishtar* (1987), *Road to Morocco* (1942).

Scene: Mythical "Araban," circa WWII. On screen, this book: "Phony Phables." Intones the narrator, "At the palace, filled with harem maidens, the sultan rules with an iron hand."

• Appearing is Araban's Grand Vizier, Kuda (Bonanova). This "bad boy," who gets things done in a "sort of underhanded way," plans to snatch the sultan's oil fields. His cohorts conspire with Baron (Roth), a German government agent.

• Kuda makes a move on the sultan's daughter, Princess Patra (Corio). But Patra pines for Jimmy (Norris), a Broadway dancer who, along with his pal Tim (Ryan), is stranded in Araban. "You're not a princess," purrs Jimmy, "you're a queen." Says Patra, "I never knew the oil business could be so nice." Later, Patra tells Kuda, "I will not lease the oil lands to anyone but Americans."

• The sultan, tagged "wolf of the desert," collects women for his harem. Eventually, the ruler realizes the Baron is up to "no good, [that] he's working against the interests of our country." Suddenly, Kuda's Arabs attack. Waving sabers, they pursue Jimmy and Tim, shouting, "off come your heads."

• The "Seven Veils Cafe, a dive." To the tune of "Yankee Doodle," Jimmy and Tim punch out Nazi-sympathizing Arabs. "Those [Arab] guys are a couple of fakirs, phonies."

• In the souk, Patra's girl friend from Brooklyn, Irene (Ryan), haggles with a merchant.

Irene: You bandit, you robber! How much?
Arab: A thousand drachmas.
Irene: I'll give you 40 drachmas.
Arab: Forty drachmas? You insult me; you insult my mother; you insult my ancestors.
    [*Pause*]. All right, I'll take it.

• Kuda kidnaps and imprisons the sultan. But, Jimmy and Tim free the ruler, then collar and imprison Kuda.

Finis: Araban's two maidens are united with their American sweethearts. Irene hooks up with Tim; Patra embraces Jimmy. Swoons Jimmy to Patra, "I'd like to make love to you." Cut to the sultan's harem maidens jiving to jazz music. The Arab musicians play some country and western tunes, prompting the Arabs to tap dance and dance the jitterbug.

Sundown (1941), UA. *Gene Tierney, Bruce Cabot, George Sanders, Marc Lawrence, Carl Esmond.* Filmed in Kenya. MAIDENS, VILLAINS

The half-Arab heroine captivates the British commander, helping him crush Arabs who conspire with Nazi agents.

Scene: A British East African outpost. At a train station, Arabs on camels greet the arriving Zia (Tierney); the "lovely, intelligent" woman dons western garb. She and the Arabs trek across the plains, arriving at Zia's father's village, now occupied by British forces.

• Seeing Zia, an Italian prisoner-of-war exclaims, "From Cairo to Zanzibar she has a network of stores. They all belong to her. The largest trading network in all of Africa. They are in every village and she runs them."

• Introducing Kuypens (Esmond), a Nazi spy generating "native [African] uprisings" against the British. Alongside the German is his Arab cohort, Abu Hammud (Lawrence). The Arab, "[who] is rotten clean through," spits at a British officer.

• Soon, Zia finds out that Kuypens is a Nazi spy, and that a German-inspired uprising will soon occur. She rushes off to warn the British major, Coombes (Sanders). But, Kuypens nabs and holds Zia hostage. And, Major Coombes is killed.

- In time, British forces arrive at the village, squashing the renegade "natives," and dispensing with Kuypens and Hammud.
- Several scenes show that British Commissioner Crawford (Cabot) is attracted to Zia. Yet, Crawford never once moves to embrace Zia. Only when Crawford learns that Zia "was reared as an Arab girl by Abu Khali (her father), [and that] she's only half-Arab, her mother was French" does he openly display affection.
- London, a bombed-out church. Crawford and Zia listen to a bishop's sermon, acknowledging the courageous Major Coombes.

Note: In this 1941 movie, why did producers inject a "rotten" Arab as a Nazi aide? And why did they present Zia as being only half-Arab?

Superman III (1983), WB. *Christopher Reeve, Richard Pryor.* SP: David and Leslie Newman. CAMEOS, SHEIKHS

The scenario concerns the Man of Steel, a megalomanic, and a computer virtuoso. Yet, a one-liner demeans Arabs.

Scene: Smallville, USA. Richard Pryor poses as an US Army Colonel. He lectures residents of Smallville, saying, "America leads the world in high-grade plastics. And do you know why? Because we got the greatest chemical plants in the world. We cannot afford a chemical plastics gap." The camera offers a close-up of the colonel, warning, "Listen to me. Do you want some Arab in a white robe telling you that their plastics can whoop our plastics?" All together, Smallville's residents shout: "Noooooooooooooo!"

Surrender (1987), CAN. *Michael Caine.* CAMEOS, VILLAINS

Gulf Arabs whip women.

Scene: This romantic Cannon comedy focuses on a bestselling author (Caine). As the writer is being swindled by his former wife, he threatens flying off to "Kuwait." Says his attorney, "This is the craziest thing I ever heard of. Selling everything and going to Kuwait. Why the hell Kuwait?" Retorts the writer, "Because women can't vote there. And they flog them!"

Sweet Revenge (1987), Motion Picture Corp. *Nancy Allen, Martin Landau.* CAMEOS, SHEIKHS

Kinky sheikhs try to buy American women.

Scene: In the Far East, a Los Angeles TV-reporter (Allen) investigates the villain's (Landau) white-slavery ring. Cut to the white-slave trader's annual "spring auction," revealing scores of lovely women. Bidding for the abducted models is an Arab. Also, a brash Texan and two mute Arabs surface; the Arabs wear red and white kuffiyehs.

Note: Arabs, only, are singled out by their ethnicity.

The Sword of Ali Baba (1965), UNI. *Peter Mann, Jocelyn Lane, Frank Puglia, Frank DeKova, Gavin MacLeod.* S, SP: Edmund L. Hartmann. Footage from the 1944 *Ali Baba* is used here. I suggest viewers skip this 1965 tale. Instead, see *Ali Baba and the Forty Thieves* (1944). MAIDENS

Ali Baba (Mann) and his thieves return to Baghdad and oust "swiftly and surely, the

Mongol tyrants." One Arab cur appears, Princess Amara's (Lane) father, Cassim (Puglia).

Scene: As children, Amara and Ali Baba pledge everlasting love.

• When Ali Baba is told, Baghdad's "brave men died for freedom," the boy affirms, "I will never fail you or Baghdad, father."

• Years later. Cassim betrays the ruler, delivering him to the Mongol tyrant, Hulagu Khan (MacLeod). Next, Cassim tells his grown-up daughter, Amara, "Once you are married to Hulagu Khan, my position in his court will remain safe." Amara refuses to wed the Khan, saying, "I will not be treated as a slave."

• Inside the 40 thieves' den, Old Baba (DeKova) tells one of his thieves, Ali Baba, "If Allah had granted me a son, I would have wished him in your image." Advises Old Baba, "Return to Baghdad. You cannot escape your destiny. Rouse the people. They must throw off the Mongol yoke. Allah be with you."

• Ali Baba and his people crush Cassim, the Khan, and his Mongol cohorts. Princess Amana and Ali Baba together rule Baghdad.

Sword in the Desert (1949), UNI. *Dana Andrews, Marta Toren, Jeff Chandler, Stephen McNally, Liam Redmond.* D: George Sherman. P, SP: Robert Buckner. PALESTINIANS

Hollywood's first fiction fable about strife in Palestine. The stale cliché—a land without a people—is perpetuated. This movie's Palestinians are practically invisible; they surface for about fifteen seconds. Yet, all the action is set in British-supervised Palestine, late 1947. The word, "Palestinian," is never spoken. Members of the Jewish underground are tagged "freedom fighters." Assisting them is an American sea captain; he smuggles Europe's Jews into Palestine. Upper-lipped British soldiers appear as villains.

Scene: The myth, no Palestinians ever lived in Palestine, is established. Initial scenes show Palestine as belonging to Jewish refugees, not to resident Palestinians. For example, the camera reveals Jewish refugees and their families departing a merchant ship. Next, David (McNally), a Jewish underground leader, tells Matt (Andrews), an American sea captain, the people you bring here are "survivors of concentration camps." "[This is] their last hope. Don't these people mean anything to you, captain,… as human beings?" The camera cuts to a woman refugee joyously crying, an elderly man kissing the ground. Another refugee says, "We're home, now." Affirms David, "They are indeed, home."

• Mute Palestinians. A truck carrying Jewish "illegals" drives by some Palestinians and goats straddling their side. An elderly Palestinian looks up at the truck and spits. Later, the camera shows three Palestinians selling watermelons.

• A member of the Jewish underground, Kutra (Chandler), is asked how things are going. "The Arabs are growing stronger every day. They'll try to wipe us out before the British leave," he says. Adding, "God save Israel!" Affirms David's sweetheart, Sabra (Toren), "I'm a Jew and this is my country. [The British] have occupied my country." Members of the Jewish underground who contest British soldiers appear as triumphant, heroic liberators. Interestingly, not one Palestinian says, "[I am a Palestinian; the British (and the Jewish "illegals")] have occupied my country."

• Kutra warns refugees that the road "is guarded by the British and their Arab spies." Seeking to dupe the British, two "illegals" dress as Arabs. British soldiers stop and question the duo, asking whether they have spotted any "illegals." To convince the British guards they are indeed Palestinians, one spits. The soldiers let them pass.

• Wearing Arab garb, David flashes a business card stating, "Ahmed the Great, Fortune Teller, Magician." The disguised David moves to free illegals imprisoned by the British. To induce a soldier he is truly Ahmed, the Arab, David speaks fractured English, saying, "What you want. We not politicians… we not fight!"

Finis: In Bethlehem, British soldiers sing Christmas carols. One says, "This is where our faith began. Peace on earth, goodwill to men." During the singing, not one of Bethlehem's thousands of Palestinian Christians appear.

Note: *Every Time We Say Goodbye*, a 1986 Tri-Star film with Tom Hanks surfaced nearly four decades after *Sword of the Desert*. The scenario of *Every Time We Say Goodbye* focuses on an American pilot who loves an Israeli woman. Filmed in Israel by Israeli filmmakers, this movie also fails to display Palestinians in Palestine. Though the action is set in Jerusalem, 1942, no Palestinians appear. Actually, viewers may perhaps spot, for a second or so, a Palestinian couple sitting in the back of a moving truck.

Table for Five (1983), WB. *Jon Voight, Richard Crenna.* SP: David Seltzer P: Robert Schaffel. Filmed in Egypt. CAMEOS, EGYPTIANS

Unhygienic Cairo.

Scene: Jon Voight appears as a divorcee intent on establishing a good rapport with his three children. A summer cruise ship takes the family to Athens, Rome, and Cairo. When touring Rome and Athens, the camera offers lovely views of the Coliseum and the Parthenon, as well as charming outdoor cafes and fine restaurants. Conversely, as soon as the family arrives in Egypt, displeasing images of contemporary Cairo fill the screen. The camera does not show the family dining at an elegant Nile restaurant. Instead, they visit a seedy souk cafe—swarms of flies annoy them. The flies buzz the table, buzz their clothing, then buzz, buzz their faces. To make certain viewers see the buzzing flies, a close-up reveals a fly crawling toward an envelope. In the background, a fat Egyptian, wearing a red fez, munches his meal.

• At the souk, mute Egyptians are enveloped by chickens, donkeys, even camels.

Tale of the Mummy (1998), Carousel. *Jason Scott Lee, Christopher Lee.* SP: Roger Mulcahy and John Esposito. D: Mulcahy. EGYPTIANS

This monster mummy is "a Greek heretic."

Scene: Valley of the Kings, 1948, the Turkel expedition. On ascertaining a mummy's tomb has been discovered, a crowd of fez-wearing Egyptian workers cheer. Nabil, the Egyptian youth who uncovered the tomb, guides Western archaeologists to the entrance. Though the curse states, "avoid the place," the three archaeologists move forward. Instantly, they perish.

• Fast forward to the identical tomb site. Working away, the British "1999 KV-6 Expedition." Here, too, laboring Egyptians cheer the discovery. Though the British crew is warned that a fate worse than death awaits, they ignore the curse and violate Talos's tomb. When one Britisher snatches a powerful amulet, he dies.

• London, three months later. Displayed at the British museum are mummy Talos's discarded, dusty bandages. Not for long. Soon, Talos's dusky gauze roll unravels, taking flight. And, Talos proceeds to bump off upward of a dozen people, even a dog. Why such behavior? The legend goes that 3,000 years ago Talos had all his organs removed; now he needs to replace them. Using his victims' body parts, the mummy restores himself with fresh organs.

• This film's Talos, who is tagged "the Dark Prince [and] a mad foreigner," is actually "a Greek heretic exiled from homeland for performing acts of sorcery."

Finis: The revived Talos now prowls planet earth not in shifting white bandages, rather as a policeman.

Tales from the Darkside: The Movie (1990), PAR. *Christian Slater.*
CAMEOS, EGYPTIANS

Do not revive an ancient Egyptian mummy.

Scene: In of the film's segments entitled, "Lot 249," an American college student removes bandages from a 3,000-year-old mummy. The unraveled mummy kills two students.

The Tales of a Thousand and One Nights (1922). Silent. Filmed in North Africa. See Mr. Magoo feature-length cartoon, by the same title. SHEIKHS, MAIDENS

This 1922 movie presents stale themes and portraits, e.g.,. Arab father vs. his son. Arab traders are unscrupulous, greedy shylocks. And, Arab men take their women. Also, Arab women function as harem maidens and as vindictive, ruthless vamps. Yet, Islam is revered. Devout Arab Muslims believing in "God" triumph over Arab pagans.

Scene: Inside an Arabian castle, lovely Schehrazade spins for the sultan, a love story about Princess Gul-Y-Hanur and Prince Abbas.

• Flashback. A sea storm destroys Princess Gul-Y-Hanur's ship; all drown except the princess. Waves deliver her to a unique kingdom ruled by a jaded Arab sultan.

• Safely ashore, the princess prays, "Allah is Allah and Mahomet is his prophet."

• The pagan sultan and his followers appear, worshiping an idol, the "Great God, Nardon." Yet, a few of the sultan's men do not worship this false God. Instead, Prince Abbas and his tutor, Ibrahim, surface as devout Muslims. Explains the prince to Gul-Y-Hanur, "Thy beauty is as the jewels of heaven. People embrace the faith of Allah."

• Ugly Arab traders invade the sultan's domain. Abruptly, they begin fighting among themselves. Next, they pillage "the town of the dead. When the heathens "threaten to kill devout Muslims," they turn to stone. Arab horsemen arrive, riding off with "rich booty."

• Stroking his beard, the sultan orders the princess, "Goest thou now to my harem where my slave will attire thee to await my coming." When Gul-Y-Hanur tries to escape, she is caught, given 50 lashes, and taken to the harem "to await the sultan's pleasures."

• Prince Abbas declares his love to the princess, saying, "Thy beauty is as the jewels of heaven." Reading from the Koran, Abbas and Ibrahim pray to "Allah." A miracle prevents the sultan from removing Abbas's head.

• Performing "The Dance of the Knife of the Death" is the sultan's favorite, the "High Priestess." Accompanied by maidens, the priestess flashes a knife.

• Moving to kill the princess are the ugly sultana and the vizier, an evil cone-headed, "half-man." Sultana commands her slaves to bury Gul-Y-Hanur, alive.

Finis: Abbas and Gul-Y-Hanur escape the sultan's grasp. Happily reunited with her joyous father, the princess says, "Oh joy of my heart." "Blessed be to Allah. Take thou my throne. It is the will of Allah," says her father. Affirms Prince Abbas, "[The] people embrace the faith of Islam." The devout Arab Muslims, Abbas and the princess, wed.

Dialogue: One Arab barks to another, "Silence, thy foal of a camel."

Tangier (1946), UNI. *Maria Montez, Preston Foster, Sabu.* See *Song of Schehrazade* (1947). CAMEOS

Tangier, Morocco, a city sans Arabs.

Scene: In Tangier, Maria Montez moves to track a Nazi. Montez appears as a Spanish dancer, performing at a Moroccan nightclub. Spanish musicians and dancers also perform. And, Sabu portrays Pepe the "interpreter," a likeable Spaniard who may secure "a camel or donkey," or who could sell a "Moroccan prayer rug, cheap." In Tangier, no one speaks Arabic, everyone speaks Spanish. The police car is labeled "Polica."

• Two three-second scenes imply some Moroccans may actually reside in Tangier. Initial frames show a mute Arab boy in front of a hotel, begging. And, when a fortune teller hands Montez a note, she moans, "It's in Arabic!"

Tangier (1983), Shapiro Glickenhaus Ent. *Ronny Cox, Adel Frej.* VILLAINS

Morocco's seascapes, souks, hotels, and cafes, complete with camels and sheep, serve as a backdrop for British agents. Appearing, briefly, Moroccan thugs and a friendly cabby.

Scene: A British agent (Cox) moves to nab a British spy; the spy wants to "sell the Mediterranean network to the Russians."

• Ahmed (Frej), a Moroccan cabby, befriends the agent. Promptly, the spy's cohort shoots Ahmed.

• Watermelons as snare! The spy dispatches some shady Moroccans to ambush the protagonist. The Moroccans dump dozens of watermelons onto the road, halting the British agent's cab. Instantly, some knife-wielding Arabs close in; the agent rushes off. What happens to all those smashed watermelons? Well, a melon fight! Arab youths pick up melon chunks, tossing the broken chunks at each other, and at others.

Tangier Incident (1953), AA. *George Brent, Mari Aldon, Dan Seymour, Dorothy Patrick.*

A Moroccan policeman prevents Russian communists from acquiring atomic secrets. Tangier as a threatening place.

Scene: Tangier's keen police inspector, Mr. Rabat (Seymour), wears a tarboosh. And, he helps Western agents intercept three shady atomic scientists intent on selling the "secrets to communist Russia." The inspector's actions help prevent "all civilization [from] going down the river for keeps."

• Appearing are mute Moroccan waiters wearing huge fezzes. And, feigning to be honest, a shifty Arab guide wearing a striped robe convinces tourists to pay for services they never received. "Would you mind please," he purrs with outstretched hand, "taking care of this situation?"

• Someone warns Steve (Brent), the American agent, "How long will it be before I find your body in one of Tangier's dark and narrow alleys?" Steve cautions Nadine (Patrick) the US heroine, "Walking the streets of Tangier at night can be very dangerous."

Tank Force (1958), COL. *Victor Mature, Leo Genn, Luciana Paluzzi.* SP: Richard Malbaum. Originally titled *No Time to Die.* CAMEOS, EGYPTIANS, SHEIKHS

In the Egyptian desert, a decent German soldier and a brave Italian woman. And, Arabs and Nazis torturing American soldiers. See *Death before Dishonor* (1987).

Scene: A Gestapo officer tells "the sheikh" he will pay plenty to him and his Arabs, provided they retrieve and deliver four Allied prisoners. Boasts the sheikh, "We shall find these four men. In the desert, I know everything that happens... Money is of no importance. But I'll take it, of course. What interests me more is the friendship of Germany."

• Seeing Arabs appear atop distant sand dunes, an Allied soldier screams: "Look, Sarge. Ayrabs!"

• The sheikh's men find the soldiers; instantly, one of the sheikh's Arabs slits a sleeping Australian's throat.

• A Gestapo agent tries to force US Sergeant Thatcher (Mature) to reveal tactical information. The sheikh intervenes, saying, "Our desert methods are much more effective." Cut to Mustapha. The Arab pushes Thatcher's hands inside a vice, slowly crushing his fingers.

Note: As this WWII drama is set in Egypt, why are Egyptians not shown fighting alongside the Allies, opposing the Germans?

• This film was released two years after Britain invaded Egypt; producers thank for their cooperation, the "British War Office."

Tarzan of the Apes (1918), Hollywood Film Ent. Silent. *Elmo Lincoln, Enid Markey, George B. French.* SHEIKHS

Arabs enslave Africans.

Question: How did Tarzan become "King of the Jungle?" Answer: In 1897, his English parents, Lord and Lady Greystoke, traveled to the African jungle. Question: Why did Tarzan's parents journey all the way to Africa? Answer: "[To] suppress Arab slave trading." Notes specialist Irwin Porges, "Derived from a language Burroughs had invented from a fictional tribe of anthropoid apes, the name Tar-Zan meant 'white skin.'"[169]

Scene: This is the first Tarzan feature film, appearing only four years after Edgar Rice Burroughs published his first "Tarzan" tale. States the opening title card: "Lord Greystoke was summoned by the government to suppress Arab slave trading in British Africa."

• Brutal, bearded Arab slave traders whip black slaves. They also capture and hold hostage, Greystoke's good friend, the English "Sailor Binns" (French). The Arabs force the imprisoned Binns to endure "ten years of agony."

• Appearing on screen, the title card: "The return of the Arabs." Cut to Arab villains brandishing rifles; they pursue Binns through the jungle. Binns meets up with Boy Tarzan; they rush through the woods, hoping to reach England.

• Arabs, including one armed with a shotgun, shoot at the duo. They miss; Boy Tarzan escapes.

Dialogue: When Tarzan woos Jane he becomes overly amorous. Entreats Jane, "Tarzan is a man, and men do not force the love of a woman." Tarzan minds.

Note: Africans appear as stereotypical primitive spear throwers, and as kidnappers waging " a council of war against whites."

• See other Tarzan features demonizing Arabs: *The Son of Tarzan* (1920), *Tarzan the Fearless* (1933), *Tarzan's Revenge* (1938), *Tarzan's Desert Mystery* (1943), and *Tarzan and the Slave Girl* (1950).

Tarzan the Fearless (1933), Principal. *Buster Crabbe, Frank Lackteen.* 15 episodes. P: Sol Lesser *NS. CLIFFHANGERS, VILLAINS

Summary: In this serial, Arabs enslave whites and blacks. Although I could not locate a video cassette of the serial, I did manage to acquire a copy of producer Sol Lesser's feature, *Tarzan the Fearless* (1933), see below. Lesser's 85-minute film is adapted from his serial, which was released in the same year.

Tarzan the Fearless (1933), Sol Lesser Prod. *Buster Crabbe, Jacqueline Wells, Julie Bishop, Mischa Auer, Frank Lackteen.* S: Edgar Rice Burroughs. See *Tarzan's Desert Mystery* (1943). VILLAINS, MAIDENS, EGYPTIANS

Arab slavers vs. Tarzan, vs. Africans. Tarzan upends slavers and Egyptian look-a-likes. Arabs kidnap the Western heroine.

Scene: Look-alike Egyptians appear, trapping a fawn; Tarzan (Crabbe) frees the animal. The Egyptians rush off to a secret cave; they are protecting the "largest emerald in the world."

• Arabs perceive Westerners as "aliens." The heroine, Mary Brooke (Wells), and her father are imprisoned by the Egyptians. Cut to a Sphinx look-a-like, the "God of the Emerald Fingers." The Egyptians move to sacrifice Mary and her father; Tarzan saves the duo.

• Cut to Abdul (Lackteen) the slaver whipping his African prisoners. After he kidnaps Mary, Abdul boasts to his wife about "the white pearl." Wife gloats, "[This woman] will bring us a fortune in gold." The Arabs cover Mary with a black cloth and whisk her off.

• An Arab leader's camp, the camera reveals African men and women in chains. Abdul presents Mary to his chief, "Here is the white pearl I promised, master." Mary screams.

• Tarzan hears Mary's cry. Howling his trademark jungle cry, he proceeds to crush all the Arab slavers. Mary joins in, slugging Abdul's wife.

Note: This full-length 85-minute feature has "an unresolved ending." Producer Lesser wanted to supplement this *Tarzan the Fearless* feature with a "to-be-continued serial, eight two-reel episodes, that were designed to follow in sequence." But, movie distributors balked at this idea. Thus, "in many theaters only the feature [*Tarzan the Fearless*] was shown, [leading to] unfavorable comment by viewers."[170]

• In *Tarzan's Desert Mystery* (1943), an American showgirl sings "Boola Boola" to a sheikh's son.

• Some television episodes from the 1966-69 TV *Tarzan* series offer similar Arab portraits TV's Tarzan (Ron Ely) also crushes Arab villains enslaving Africans.

• Johnny Weissmuller appears in nine "Jungle Jim" features, 1948-1954. Not one of his "Jim" movies displays Arab culprits. Most scenarios show Jim battling Nazis.

Tarzan and the Leopard Woman (1946), RKO. *Johnny Weissmuller, Brenda Joyce, Johnny Sheffield.* S, SP: Carroll Young. CAMEOS

Scene: Arab music underscores the establishing shot—mythical Zambezi. Mulling about the souk, Arabs and camels. A crowd watches Tarzan (Weissmuller) wrestle an Arab strongman, "Tongol the Terrible." Tarzan lifts Tongol above his head, then twirls and dumps the Arab into the crowd. The defeated Tongol shakes Tarzan's hand, "Your strength is that of ten men, my friend... Again, you have defeated Tongol the Terrible." Sighs Tongol, "With Tarzan, Tongol is not so terrible." In the background, a large Arab poster of Tongol.

• In the souk, as Jane (Joyce) converses with two friendly fez-wearing Arab merchants, a flute player coaxes a snake out of a basket.

• A few Arabs help escort four maidens through the jungle. Suddenly, the evil leopard men strike, killing the Arab guides, sparing the maidens.

Note: The rotund Sheikh Ibn-Ben-Abou, "The Scourge of the Desert," was featured in some 1938 Joe Palooka newspaper comic strips. In one strip, desert Arabs arrange for Joe Palooka to box the Arab champ. Joe KO's the Arab.[171]

Tarzan and the Slave Girl (1950), RKO. *Lex Barker, Vanessa Brown.* P: Sol Lesser. CAMEOS, EGYPTIANS

Lionian slave-traders vs. Tarzan.

Scene: Tarzan pursues the wicked "Lionians," men wearing cone-shaped hats and pajamas. After the villains kidnap African natives and Jane (Brown), they whisk them and some "slave girls" off to an ancient "Egyptian city somewhere across the jungle and over the mountain." The city boasts enormous crypts, mummy cases, a lion's pit, and harem quarters.

• Supposedly, the captured maidens are to breed with the city's seriously ill Egyptian inhabitants. But when the Lionian slavers arrive, the Egyptian High Priest admonishes them, ordering, "Return these women to their homes."

• To the rescue, Tarzan and a Western doctor. Arriving in the Egyptian city, the physician detects the residents' ailments. Promptly, the doctor administers an antidote to the prince's son. He recovers, as do, eventually, all the ill Egyptians. The revived prince says of Tarzan and his cohorts, "These are good people. Our sufferings are cured." As for the slavers, Tarzan overpowers the Lionians, freeing the maidens.

Tarzan the Tiger (1929), UNI. Silent. 10 episodes. *Frank Merrill, Natalie Kingston, Lillian Worth.* CLIFFHANGERS, VILLAINS, WORST LIST

Arabs vs. Arabs, vs. Tarzan. Eight of the 10 episodes display Tarzan (Merrill) battling Arab "raiders" and slavers, namely the nomad chief, Ahmet Zek.

Scene: Mythical Opar, complete with sandstorms, filthy streets, camels, donkeys, and slavers. Ahmet's scrubby Arabs appear, whisking Tarzan's Lady Jane (Kingston) off to a "slave mart." They kidnap Lady Jane not once, but four times. During each abduction, Arab music underscores her plight.

• Unlike Lady Jane, a woman "noble of birth, " Arab women function as mute objects, worth little. The Arab women sold on the auction block accept enslavement.

• The slave mart. Clasping bills, ugly Arabs bid.

• Lord Greystoke's mansion. Resembling, shadowy creatures, Ahmet's nomads prowl the mansion. Suddenly, Ahmet, "against whose traffic in slaves Tarzan has waged relentless war," creeps into Lady Jane's bedroom. The clad-only-in-a-negligee Lady Jane awakens. Seeing Ahmet approach, she collapses.

• Ahmet threatens Lady Jane, "You will become one of my wives! Or, [you will] be sold in slavery to the highest bidder." Soon, Ahmet vows to violate Jane. Mohammed, Ahmet's aide, appears, promising he will release Lady Jane—on one condition— if she sleeps with him.

• At the slave mart, a ghastly Arab purchases Lady Jane, "the fairest that has ever graced the auction block." Suddenly, Tarzan attacks. Riding atop a charging elephant, Tantor the Terror, they crash through the city gate, rescuing Lady Jane. Instantly, Tantor tramples the Arab procurer; Tarzan screams the "jungle cry of victory."

• When Ahmet is killed, Mohammed rejoices.

Dialogue: Evil Abdullah, "the sand diviner," contends that those reading "from the yellow sacred sands... are thrice blessed."

Tarzan's Desert Mystery (1943), RKO. *Johnny Weissmuller, Johnny Sheffield, Nancy Kelly, Robert Lowry.* P: Sol Lesser. SHEIKHS

The Western heroine dupes Arab buffoons. And, she prevents intra-Arab strife, protecting bedouins from the Nazis.

Scene: As American soldiers stationed in Burma are stricken with malaria, they are in need of a rare cure-all herb. Running off to find the "fever medicine" are Tarzan (Weissmuller), Boy (Sheffield), and Cheta. Checking out "the great desert" Tarzan says, "Desert not good place. Jungle much safer than desert."

• En route across the desert they encounter Nazis, bedouins, and Connie (Kelly), a USO entertainer. Connie's mission? To deliver a secret message from Prince Amir, a Yale graduate, to his classmate, Prince Selim (Lowrey).

• Pretending to be "the mystic lady," Connie dons Arab garb and employs a sawing-the-body-in-half stunt. Following her act, one dense Arab tries to cut, literally, his two wives in half. Quips Connie, "Rub your lamp and let's move on to Bir Harari."

• En route, Tarzan comes across an Arabian stallion, a horse he intends to offer as a gift to Prince Selim. But, after they arrive in Bir Harari Nazis begin calling Tarzan a horse thief. Dense Arabs believe the Nazis, placing Tarzan in jail, not far from a "camel driver's hut."

• In the souk, Cheta performs; Arabs applaud. Meanwhile, Connie delivers Amir's note to Prince Selim. As the prince reads that the Nazis intend to "to gain control of the whole country," a German surfaces, fatally knifing Selim.

• The Nazis blame Connie for Selim's death. Selim's Arabs, a people Connie risked her life to save, commence screaming. They next move to hang Connie. Cheta rushes off to the imprisoned Tarzan, handing him several stolen burnooses. Tying the headdresses together, Tarzan escapes. In the nick of time, he saves Connie from an angry Arab mob.

• As Cheta plays with a burnoose, Tarzan warns the Arab elders that the Germans are "arming border tribes," and that they intend to crush their ruler, Selim's father. A grateful elderly sheikh tells Connie, "In risking your life to bring Prince Amir's message, you avoided bloodshed between his tribe and mine. I, and my people, will be forever grateful to you."

Note: When asked why he presented Africans fighting off Nazis in *Tarzan's Desert Mystery*, producer Sol Lesser said, "[Because] the State Department asked [me] to work it in." Government officials also asked Lesser to include heroic Africans in his film. Explains Thomas Cripps, "[During WWII] the new African-American presence [in film] was everywhere."[172] Interestingly, the government did not ask Lesser to show heroic Arabs in *Tarzan's Desert Mystery*, nor in *Tarzan Triumphs* (1943).

• No Tarzan movie shows Arabs alongside Tarzan, helping him bring down Nazis, notably RKO's release *Tarzan Triumphs* (1943), starring Johnny Weissmuller. In this film, "Nazis are [again] on the prowl." But instead of showing pro-American Arabs linking up with Tarzan to crush the Germans, Lesser presents as Tarzan's helpers, bare-chested, generic villagers.

Tarzan's Revenge (1938), TCF. *Glenn Morris, Eleanor Holm, C. Henry Gordon, Hedda Hopper.* SP: Robert Lee Johnson, Jay Vann. P: Sol Lesser. SHEIKHS, WORST LIST

A foul, wealthy sheikh, surrounded by wives and harem maidens, appears in initial and closing scenes. The gruff Arab kidnaps an American woman.

Scene: Americans aboard the SS Congo Hope travel to Africa, intending "to bring back rare animals for a zoo." On hearing Arab music emanating from Sheikh Ben Alleu Bey's (Gordon) cabin, a passenger says, "He acts like he owns the boat." Affirms the Captain, "It's quite possibly he does. His Excellency owns a lot of property in this country."

• Bey's cabin is reminiscent of an Arabian Nights palace. Cut to Bey reclining on soft cushions and smoking a nargelih; scantily-clad dancers entertain him. Bey is "well educated, Oxford. He just came back from Paris. Lives like a king; he has a palace in the jungle," says the Captain. And, "I understand he has some 100-odd wives."

• The inquisitive Ellen (Holm), an adventurer's daughter, peers into Bey's cabin. The Arab spots her, dispatching a servant to present "the lady" with a ruby. Ellen returns the gift.

• The ship docks. Ellen registers shock; Bey is beating a baggage handler with his cane. The angry Ellen acts; she grabs Bey's cane and smacks him, saying, "Who do you think you are?" Enraged at Ellen's behavior, Bey departs, vowing revenge. Harem maidens follow.

• Arabs-take-women. Bey's "natives" kidnap Ellen. To illustrate purity, the abducted heroine wears a white swim suit.

• Bey's jungle palace. Huge wooden doors open; revealing Bey shouting, "Bring the girl here." Cut to maidens dancing around a huge pool; Africans fan the jungle nabob.

• After Bey's maidens dress Ellen in a jeweled robe; she is dragged to the Bey's side. Taking his rod, the Arab beats a servant. And, he threatens Ellen, daring her to take the cane and to strike him, as she did earlier. Bey offers her some wine; Ellen tosses liquid in his face.

• To the rescue, Tarzan (Morris). He saves Ellen from the Arab's clutches.

Temptation (1946), INT. *Merle Oberon, George Brent, Charles Korvin, Arnold Moss.* I could not view *Temptation* (1923), with Pola Negri. See Barbary *Sheep* (1917). EGYPTIANS

An Egyptian black guard defiles the British heroine.

Scene: Cairo 1897. Newly married Ruby (Oberon) is tired of her Egyptologist husband, Nigel (Brent). And, she is bored with "Egypt and the heat and the flies." Plus, she has "been cheated by every rug merchant in the bazaar."

• Seeking advice, Yvonne, a young French woman, meets with Ruby. Yvonne confesses that an Egyptian dandy and Oxford graduate, Mahmoud Baroudi (Korvin), is blackmailing her. Seeking excitement, Ruby opts to approach Baroudi, "a name out of a thousand and one nights," to request he cease blackmailing Yvonne. Baroudi gives to Ruby, Yvonne's love letters.

• This clever fez-wearing Egyptian has "an instinct for women." When Ruby's husband, Nigel, departs Cairo to engage "in a British museum expedition," Baroudi seduces Ruby. He assures her he is in love; Ruby falls for the ruse.

• Baroudi's interests are monetary; soon, he manages to persuade Ruby to kill Nigel for the inheritance monies. Should she fail, he threatens to dump her for an American heiress. Thus, love-sick Ruby begins feeding Nigel small doses of poison. Barks Baroudi, "Finish it, quickly!

• Suspecting foul play, Ruby's devoted maid says, "You've changed." She advises, "Horrid. This man, Baroudi. He will destroy you." And, in fact, he does.

• In time, Ruby ceases poisoning Nigel. She delivers to Baroudi all the money she has, plus her jewels. The Egyptian's not satisfied, saying, "You can have me as your partner or as your enemy. Make your choice." Realizing the seedy Arab does not love her, she poisons him.

• Fearing Nigel may find out that she slept with, then killed Baroudi, Ruby sets up an accidental death for herself.

Note: Opening and closing scenes reveal a decent Egyptian policeman, Captain Ahmed (Moss). The captain befriends both Nigel and Ruby; he also prevents Nigel from learning about Ruby's unfaithfulness. He keeps secret, Ruby's affair with Baroudi.

The Ten Commandments (1923), PAR. Silent. *Theodore Roberts, Charles de Roche, Richard Dix, Estelle Taylor.* Cecil B. DeMille's precursor to his 1956 *Ten Commandments* was considered the *Titanic* of its time; the film boasted a $1.4 million budget, four times the typical film budget for the era. Discussed here is part one, the Moses and the Exodus story. EGYPTIANS

Moses frees suffering Israelites from brutal Egyptians. To help authenticate the Exodus tale, DeMille displays on the screen, citations from the Bible: "And the Egyptians made the children of Israel to serve with rigeur. And made their lives bitter with hard bondage, in mortar and in brick, and in all manner of service in the field..." (Exod. 1:13–14.)

Scene: Israelite slaves tow the massive Sphinx. Brandishing whips, the Egyptian heathens show no mercy. The weight of a huge boulder crushes one Hebrew. Barks a soldier, "Kneel to the King of Kings, the conqueror of conquerors. Kneel to the mighty Pharaoh, dogs of Israel." As the Pharaoh and his entourage pass, persecuted Israelites kneel.

• Miriam, Moses' sister, prays, "Lord God of Israel, see the affliction of my people which are in Egypt" (Exod. 3:7).

• Pharaoh's young son whips Moses, threatening, "Moses has tormented us already with nine plagues. Let us slay him before the tenth."

• Egypt's first-born male children perish, including the pharaoh's son. The pharaoh pleads to Egypt's sundry "Gods, Show that ye are stronger than this God of Israel and call back life into the body of my son." Silence; the boy remains still.

• Moses asks the pharaoh, "Let my people go." Still, the ruler refuses. On screen, "That night all the hosts of the Lord went out from the land of Egypt. And they despoiled the Egyptians of jewels of silver, jewels of gold and raiment." Exod. 12:31-46.

• The pharaoh calls the Israelites "these dogs of Israel." And, "This day shall Israel be ground under the chariots of Egypt." The ruler tells his Egyptians, "Fear not this God of Israel—follow and destroy them." Utilizing chariots, the pharaoh's soldiers pursue the fleeing Israelites. Seeing the Egyptian army close in, Moses calls on God for assistance, telling his people, "Fear not to pass through the deep waters—for the Lord fighteth on our side." Abruptly, the Red Sea waters divide. The Israelites pass safely; the rushing waters engulf the pharaoh and his army.

Note: States a NYT review (27 December 1923), "It's a great picture for the Jews. It shows the Bible made them the Chosen People and also [on the statement of a Catholic] it will be as well liked by the Catholics for its Catholicity."

The Ten Commandments (1956), PAR. *Charlton Heston, Yul Brynner, Anne Baxter.* P: Cecil B. DeMille. Three hours and thirty-nine minutes. EGYPTIANS

Like its 1923 predecessor, this biblical drama shows Moses releasing the Hebrews from Egyptian slavery and leading them to freedom. Especially impressive are two scenes—the writing of the sacred tablets and the parting of the Red Sea. The film received an Oscar for special effects. As this 1956 movie, *The Ten Commandments*, appeals to millions of viewers, on Easter Sunday, ABC-TV annually telecasts the movie in its entirety.

Note: Pre-dating DeMille's 1923 and 1956 *The Ten Commandments* is Vitagraph's 1909 five-reel silent movie, *The Life of Moses*, which some critics and historians consider to be America's first feature-length motion picture. In *The Life of Moses*, Egyptians also persecute "the children of Israel." The pharaoh orders to be killed, all male children born to the Israelites. God's reprisals against the Egyptians are revealed in the plague scene, in which all Egypt's first-born male children perish. And, as described in the Bible, Moses frees the Israelites from Egyptian bondage, leading them to the promised land.

Ten Tall Men (1951), COL. *Burt Lancaster, Jody Lawrence, Gerald Mohr, Nick Dennis.* SP: Ronald Kibbee, Frank Davis. VILLAINS, MAIDENS, SHEIKHS

Dense Arabs vs. legionnaires, vs. Arabs. The Arab heroine woos a legionnaire.

Scene: Superimposed over sand dunes: "The Sahara—Land of the Foreign Legion."

• Introducing the villains, Sheikh "Hussin's boys," who wear black-and-white striped robes. Hussin's men approach an Arab riding a donkey. At the rider's side, two legionnaires disguised as Arab women; the bandits try to seize them. Abruptly, the

legionnaires shed their Arab women's garb, hauling off the Arabs.
- Tarfa, the legion fort. For legionnaires, "[Hussin's] Riffs employ special slow deaths." Says a legionnaire, adding, "A dead Riff is a peaceful Riff."
- Affirms Sergeant Mike Kincaid (Lancaster), Hussin (Mohr) "talks peace with the French, then he slaughters them. You can't make a deal with that lying rat.".
- A Riff prisoner confesses to Kincaid that Hussin's men intend to attack Tarfa. Abruptly, Kincaid and twelve legionnaires terminate upward of 30 Arabs.
- Presenting Mahia (Lawrence), a seductive Arab woman. Mahia is summoned to wed Hussin, a villain demanding "obedience." Mahia balks, then agrees to the wed the tyrant, saying that "a marriage of state brings the tribes together... Two tribes that have always been enemies shall be united in friendship with this marriage."
- To prevent Arab unity, Kincaid and his men kidnap Mahia. And, they kill Arabs.
- The legionnaires come across a sturdy safe that the Arabs "couldn't crack." Boasts the dexterous Mouse (Dennis), "You gotta be civilized to crack a safe."
- Legionnaires dupe gullible Arabs. Kincaid's legionnaires remove their uniforms and then stuff their outfits with straw. Next, they place the uniformed straw dummies atop horses. Pursuing Arabs spot the stuffed uniforms; thinking the straw dummies are real legionnaires, the Arabs gallop after them. In Geste films, legionnaires dupe Arabs by bolstering plenty of dead bodies at the fort.
- Hussin's men nab Kincaid and his legionnaires. To the rescue, Mahia. She prevents Hussin from torturing Kincaid with "hot coals." Yet, her wedding ceremony commences, complete with bellydancing.
- Again, legionnaires outwit Arabs. After Kincaid and his men don Arab garb, they hurl insults at Hussin's men. The disguised legionnaires make fun of Mahia's white-robed Arabs, upsetting them. Instantly, Mahia's Arabs begin fighting with Hussin's dark-robed Arabs.
- As soon as Hussin, the "cockroach," is crushed, Mahia rushes into Kincaid's arms. Back in Tarfa, the camera reveals "the bringing of peace ceremony." Victorious legionnaires celebrate. Smiling, Kincaid kisses Mahia.

Note: See the duping Arab scene in *Road to Morocco* (1942).

The Tents of Allah (1923), Encore. Silent. *Monte Blue, Mary Thurman, Macey Hallam.* See *Tripoli* (1950), *Wind and the Lion* (1975). *NS. Notes from AFIC.
VILLAINS, SHEIKHS

Arabs vs. the US Marines. Moroccans kidnap and torture Americans.

Summary: Tangier, Morocco. "A battleship and the marines are sent into the desert [to rescue the] niece of the American Consul." The woman (Thurman) is held hostage "by some of the natives." Moroccans kidnapped her because she incurred their anger by committing "a breach of etiquette on a feast day of the natives." And, the evil sultan (Hallam) holds hostage, a former US Navy officer and his Moroccan wife.

The marines to the rescue, notably the navy officer's half-Arab son (Blue). The young marine demonstrates heroics. Abruptly, he delivers his Moroccan mother and American father "from the sultan's hands." Final frames show the "boy and his mother riding into the desert."

Terminal Entry (1986), Intercontinental. *Yaphet Kotto, Paul Smith, Mazhar Khan, Eddie Albert, Kavi Raz, Kabir Bedi.* SP: Mark Sobel, David Mickey Evans. D: John Kincade. See *The Siege* (1998). VILLAINS, WORST LIST

Arab Muslims invade America; American forces terminate them.

Scene: As Arabs are "planning mass assassinations in this country," Captain Jackson's (Albert) troops move out, tracking and killing four gun-toting Arabs.

• Cut to a TV screen displaying the kuffiyeh-clad Mahadi (Raz). The white-robed Arab warns American viewers, "We have 250 freedom fighters in the United States. We seek martyrdom, death is a salvation to us." Mahadi's Arab Muslims intend to "eliminate all key political and military figures [in the US]."

• Commenting on whether Mahadi's Arab suicide squads will inflict casualties, Captain Jackson boasts, "[My men] killed eleven—with the four Abdulies that the Colonel and I zapped this morning... total up to 22."

• Colonel Stewart (Smith) and Jackson blow up an Arab suicide driver. Notes Jackson, "They're bringing the war to us." Next, Jackson's men attack Mahadi's base, killing scores of Arab Muslims.

• Accidentally, some American teenagers hack into the terrorist's satellite. The teens see, on screen: "Terminal Entry." Believing "Entry" to be a just clever game [See *War Games* (1983)], the youths direct the Arabs to bomb seventeen-plus US targets. As a result, the nation is "thrown into a state of turmoil." Arabs kill a Russian peace delegate, and they blow up a Los Angeles oil refinery. Next, the television screen displays destroyed American cities. Intones the announcer, "Across the country seemingly unlimited acts of terrorism have occurred simultaneously. The known death count is now into the thousands... our nation is placed under martial law."

Finis: Mahadi's terrorists move to extinguish the teenagers; Jackson's troops drop the Arabs. Dead bodies litter the screen.

Terror in Beverly Hills (1988), AIP/A Peacock film. *Frank Stallone, Cameron Mitchell, Lysa Hayland, Behrouz Vassoughi, Shahurad Vassoughi, William Smith.* EP: Moshe and Simon Bibiyan. SP, D: John Myhers. Filmed in Israel. See *Terror Squad* (1987). PALESTINIANS, WORST LIST

This made-in-Israel film presents an ex-Green Beret, now a Los Angeles policeman killing Palestinians as well as Arab-American fanatics. Why? Because they kidnapped his wife and son, as well as the US president's daughter.

Scene: Israel. The muezzin calls the faithful to prayer. Cut to two "suspicious looking" Palestinians, Abdul (B. Vassoughi) and Mohammad (S. Vassoughi), boarding a plane for Los Angeles. The flight attendant asks Mohammad to buckle up; he grunts, "Don't touch me, infidel!" As Mohammad heads for the rest room a passenger barks, "Filthy Ayrab!" Arriving in Los Angeles, the Palestinians are welcomed by Arab-American terrorists [See *Wanted: Dead or Alive* (1987)].

• In Beverly Hills, the Palestinians park their van, then enter a swank clothing store. They shoot shoppers and sales clerks, then capture and run off with Margaret (Hayland), the president's daughter. She will die in "12 hours," they warn, unless America orders "Israel to release 55 [of their] political brothers."

• A warehouse, on the outskirts of town. The Palestinian binding Margaret to a chair spits in her face. Suddenly, he begins fondling her body. Next, his cohort tries to rape her. Yells Margaret, "What are you doing to me?"

• To the rescue, the Los Angeles Police Department's Hank Stone (Stallone). Stone, an ex-Marine and a TV crew rush off to the warehouse. A Palestinian tells them, "We are all prepared to die."

• When Stone's pal goes to save Margaret, the Palestinians nab him. They beat the man, then shoot him dead. Says Stone, "[Abdul] kills and he likes it."

• Meanwhile, Arab-American radicals kidnap and hold hostage Stone's wife and son. The LAPD takes action: An African-American police officer empties his shotgun, boasting to an Arab-American thug, "You've made my day!"

• In the end, all the villains, the Palestinians imprisoning Margaret as well as the Arab Americans holding Stone's wife and child hostage, are killed. Declares Stone, "It's all madness."

Note: An ad for *Terror Squad* states: "They brought terror to our streets. Only one man could stop them."

• In the credits, producers thank the Israeli Government.

• In Mario Puzo's book *The Fourth K* (New York: Random House, 1990), Yabril, a Palestinian, kidnaps, then kills Theresa Kennedy, the US president's 23-year-old daughter. Like *Terror in Beverly Hills'* Abdul, Puzo's Yabril demands that Palestinian prisoners be released from Israeli jails. The Palestinians also assassinate the Pope on Easter Sunday. Says Yabril, "If you cannot throw a bomb into a kindergarten, then you are not a true revolutionary."

Terror Squad (1988), Manson Int. *Chuck Conners, Kavi Raz, Joseph Nasser.* SP: Chuck Rose. P, D: Peter Maris. See *Terminal Entry* (1986), *Wanted: Dead or Alive* (1987), *Back to the Future* (1985). VILLAINS

In the US, Libyan terrorists hold high school students hostage. Warns a student, "[Arab] terrorists are attacking Indiana." Says a school teacher, "Terrorists in Indiana? I never heard of such a ridiculous thing in my life."

Scene: Outside an Arab university, screaming Arab youths flaunt signs: "Death to the American Dogs," "Death to the Great Satan," and "Death to America." The students ignite the American flag. Then, they shout "die, die," as they burn Uncle Sam in effigy.

• Kokomo, Indiana. The camera reveals three Arab terrorists—"Mohammed is the chosen one for the [suicide] mission." Declares a TV announcer: "Terrorist attack at the Black River nuclear power plant." The Libyans kill two plant guards. Next, the inept terrorists mistakenly blow up their own van instead of the nuclear plant.

• The Arabs rush off, killing several policemen. They run over a handicapped man, and then machine-gun scores of innocent bystanders, including a student. Using grenades and rockets, they blow up pursuing police cars.

• After Mohammed is fatally shot, Yassir (Raz) and Gemal (Nasser) invade the high school, holding a teacher and six students hostage. "We're here to avenge your government's bombing of our country. We're not here to hurt students," says Yassir. "We are peace-loving people." But then the reel Arabs kill "in cold blood," a student and Gus, the black janitor. Says an anxious student, "[They] are going to pick a name and kill one of us like they did on that ship, Achille Lauro." The students address the Arabs as "camel-jockeys," "asshole," "son-of-a-bitch," and "bastard." The slurs stand.

• "I have to go to the bathroom," says an attractive blonde student. Responds Yassir, "Gemal will go with you." Smiling, Gemal beckons the girl to follow him. She remains seated.

• Kokomo's police surround the school. Intending to escape, the Arabs jump onto a high school bus, taking the girl, Jennifer (Brennan), with them. To the rescue, a student with a hand made bow and arrow. The arrow drops Yassir.

• Jennifer heads for the bus door. Abruptly, Gemal appears. He grabs her leg. But, Johnny (Calvert) arrives, punching Gemal. Then, Gemal socks Johnny. Jennifer acts! She grabs Gemal's gun and shoots him dead. As soon as she and Johnny exit the bus, it explodes.

Finis: Sums up Kokomo's Police Chief (Connors), "Those god-damn [Arab] terrorists nearly destroyed my town, and [they] killed a lot of innocent people."

Note: *Terror Squad* failed to receive a theatrical tryout, going directly to cable and home video.

• Interestingly, the story line for *Demolition High* (1996) is similar with one major exception—no Arab villains appear. In *Demolition High*, anti-US government militia members attack a military installation, then occupy a small town's high school and terrorize students. The movie does not tar any ethnic or minority group, presenting only generic villains.

Thais (1914), Loftus. Silent. *NS. MAIDENS

Thais (1917), Goldwyn. Silent. *Mary Garden*. *NS. Notes from AFIC (917). Based on Anatole France's novel *Thais*. A French silent was also made in 1911. MAIDENS, EGYPTIANS

An Egyptian and her Roman beau convert to Christianity.

Summary (of both *Thais* films): In Alexandria, the dashing Roman, Paphnuce, romances Thais, a "notorious [Egyptian] courtesan." Soon, lovely Thais' affection for Paphnuce "cools"; he decides to convert, becoming "a monk." Later, Paphnuce convinces Thais to forsake "her wicked ways." Thus, the Egyptian woman, too, converts, becoming "a member of the White Sisters." At "the Christian retreat," the now nun, Thais, is "purged of sin." Then, she dies in Paphnune's arms.

The Thief of Bagdad (Overview). In considering all the versions of this film, I suggest the reader skip MGM's 1961 film, shot in Tunisia, and starring Steve Reeves. Skip, also, the 1978 TV-movie, *The Thief of Bagdad*, with Roddy McDowell and Peter Ustinov.

Love and faith conquer evil. The Oriental versions of this John Doe fable show an Arab "thief" wedding a courageous princess. Plus, the commoner crushes Mongol invaders and evil Arab viziers. With an unprecedented budget of $2 million, the largest budget of any film at the time, the 1924 movie, featuring only Arab heroics, remains magical entertainment. Only the 1924 feature displays the following: devout Muslims appear and Islam is revered; the thief accepts humility; the thief earns the imam's respect and he embraces the Holy Koran.

The 1940 and 1961 films display Arab knaves, not Mongol villains. The films display no mosque scenes, no "Holy Man." Currently in production, *Return of the Thief of Bagdad* (2001).

The Thief of Bagdad (1924), UA. Silent. *Douglas Fairbanks Sr., Charles Belcher, Julanne Johnston.* P, SP: Douglas Fairbanks Sr. S: Elton Thomas. D: Raoul Walsh. BEST LIST

For the premier, the owner of New York's Liberty Theater gave his movie palace a Mideast setting, "[complete] with drums, ululating vocal offerings, odoriferous incense, perfume from Bagdad, magic carpets and ushers in Arabian attire, who, during the intermission made a brave effort to bear cups of Turkish coffee to the women on the audience," as reported in NYT (19 March 1924). And the lobby of Cleveland's Stillman Theater was transformed into an Arabian Nights setting, states MPW, featuring "Oriental stuffs and rugs... a magic carpet... as well as a huge life-size mechanical elephant" (24 January 1925).

Scene: The tale begins on "A street in Baghdad, dream city of the ancient East." A clad-in-white-robe Holy Man (Belcher) advises a young boy. The imam points to the sky where a cluster of stars reveals this message, "Happiness Must Be Earned." Final frames repeat the stars visual. Appearing on screen, this title: "Praise be to Allah—the Beneficent King—the Creator of the Universe—Lord of The Three Worlds! The Koran." Cut to reverent worshipers proceeding toward a mosque, responding to the muezzin's call to prayer.

• This *Thief of Bagdad* production displays no Arab villains, only Mongol heavies.

• As "custom dictates," the ruler allows the princess, his daughter, to select her mate.

• At first, Ahmed the thief (Fairbanks Sr.) mocks devout Muslims, especially the imam. Later, he realizes his errant ways and moves to rescue the princess (Johnston) from the Mongols' clutches.

• Before Ahmed may gain the princess' love, advises the imam, he must save Baghdad from the Mongols. The imam tells the princess that the brave Ahmed will face incredible dangers, saying, "You must pray for him."

• Mounting a winged horse, Ahmed flies off to a cavern, complete with enchanted trees and a flaming cave. Here, he confronts a huge dragon and sea spider.

• Two imaginative, memorable sequences: The flying carpet race over Baghdad; Ahmed riding a winged horse en route to "the Citadel of the Moon."

• Most likely, 1920s audiences cheered this film's Arabs. The final scene shows Ahmed magically summoning a vast clad-in-white Arab army. The Arabs bring down the Mongol villains. Next, Ahmed repents. Accepting "God," he goes to the mosque and embraces the imam.

Finis: Ahmed and the Arab princess fly off on a magic carpet.

The Thief of Bagdad (1940), UA. *Jon Hall, John Justin, June Duprez, Sabu, Conrad Veidt, Miles Malleson, Rex Ingram.* VILLAINS, MAIDENS

Arabs vs. Arabs. Among the villains intent on suppressing the people of Basra and Baghdad are the magician Jaffar (Justin) and his Arab guards, the wicked vizier, and a black sorcerer extraordinaire (Veidt). See the magician, Jaffar, in Walt Disney's *Aladdin* (1992).

Scene: The villain, Jaffar, moves to snatch the throne from the Sultan of Basra (Malleson). Jaffar also intends to marry the princess (Duprez), "[whose] beauty is as the sun and the moon." The magician condemns opponents to "The Death of A Thousand

Cuts," he turns a boy, Abu (Sabu), into a dog. Jaffar also casts a spell on the princess. To break Jaffar's evil trances, Prince Achmed (Hall) must crush sea monsters, a huge spider, and sword-wielding skeletons.

• The princess, who loves Achmed, refuses to wed Jaffar telling her father, "No, never, never, never... never while I live. I shall never marry him. I would rather die." "If you don't want to," affirms her father, "you shant. Not while I"m alive."

• The camera reveals the toy-crazed sultan's gleaming marble "Palace of 1,000 Toys," complete with mechanical play things, such as a flying horse. Abruptly, Jaffar creates and directs a mechanical six-armed dervish "toy," the dancing Silver Maid, to fatally stab the ruler.

• Suddenly, an immense Djinni (Ingram), who has been imprisoned in a bottle for 2,000 years, appears. At first, the Djinni threatens the youth, Abu. Later, he grants the boy three wishes. Abu and the Djinni, along with some white-bearded patriarchs from the "land of the golden tents," help the princess shake off Jaffar's evil trance.

Finis: In time, Abu enters Baghdad, rescuing Achmed from the chopping block. Riding atop a flying magic carpet and armed with a crossbow, Abu drops Jaffar. The magician's evil powers no longer threaten innocents. Achmed and the princess are reunited.

Note: After the 1940 version of *The Thief of Bagdad* was released, producers distributed many new films about Arabian adventures, complete with Arab wizards such as Sokurah, Koura, Zenobia, and Alquazar. See: *The Seventh Voyage of Sinbad* (1958), *The Golden Voyage of Sinbad* (1973), *Sinbad and the Eye of the Tiger* (1977), and *Arabian Adventure* (1979).

The Thief of Bagdad (1961), MGM. *Steve Reeves.* VILLAINS

Summary: Though the story line is similar to earlier versions, this writer does not recommend the 1961 adaptation. Here, Baghdad's thief, Karim (Reeves), discovers the enchanted blue rose, and wins the princess's hand. Next, he brings down scores of Arab villains. Perhaps this 1961 production of *The Thief of Bagdad* should be titled *Robin Hood of Bagdad*. The character's costumes lead viewers to believe the film is set in medieval England, not Baghdad. Male actors wear white jogging outfits, blue stocking caps, cone-shaped hats, black berets, fencing masks, steel helmets, armor-meshed collars, and long red coats. The women don white togas. Even the music implies this film is a medieval drama; romantic choral chants underscore the action.

Thief of Damascus (1952), COL. *Paul Henreid, Elaine Verdugo, John Sutton.* P: Sam Katzman. MAIDENS

Damascus, AD 634. Persians vs. Arabs.

Scene: Following orders from their wicked potentate, Khalid (Sutton), the Persian army occupies Damascus. The troops attack, killing and injuring Syrians. Inside a palace's harem quarters, scantily clad Arab women tend to wounded Syrian soldiers.

• While the Persian ruler tortures Syrian prisoners, the Persian General, Abu Andar, (Henreid) opts to overthrow Khalid. Assisting Andar is Ali Baba and his Arabs. The Arabs enter Damascus, hidden in large olive jars.

• Appearing is a trusty Arab merchant, Ben Jammal. While he works in a back room,

Ben Jammal tells customers to "put a coin on the table and take what you wish." To help free Damascus from Khalid's rule, Ben Jammal and his family "work day and night," making weapons of Damascus steel.

• Persian men take their women. The ruler tells the Arab Princess Zafir (Verdugo), "Khalid takes what he wants, my dear. You will become Khalid's queen." Zafir, "who dances with the grace of a fawn," refuses to embrace the Persian. "The vultures will pluck your eyes before you will find me a reward, Khalid," she says. "I am not a slave to be bought and sold."

• The city square; a Persian executioner chops heads off Syrian patriots.

• General Andar directs his outnumbered Syrians to battle Khalid and his cohorts. Armed with weapons made of "the most wonderful [Damascus] steel," Andar and the Syrians liberate the besieged city, crushing the Persian invaders.

• After rescuing Zafir from Khalid's clutches, Andar moves to woo and wed the princess.

Treatment of Islam: Characters say: "Allah watches over all"; "May Allah watch over you both."

Dialogue: Persians are tagged "jackasses," "infidels"; Khalid is labeled "son-of-a-pig."

Note: The film features stock characters such as Schehrazade, Sinbad, and Ali Baba. And, familiar settings, e.g., the "Open and Close, Sesame" cave and Ali Baba's cave. Amazingly, Persian soldiers wear armor vests and pointed steel helmets. Producer Sam Katzman extracts battle-scene footage from the movie *Joan of Arc* (1948), and uses the stock footage here, lending an explanation as to why the *Thief of Damascus* costumes resemble outfits used in medieval dramas.

Things Are Tough All Over (1982), COL. *Richard "Cheech" Marin, Tommy Chong.* SP: Richard "Cheech" Marin. SHEIKHS, WORST LIST

Cheech and Chong portray rich, repulsive, ridiculous, and ribald Arab Muslim brothers; one weds a camel.

Scene: Chicago. The camera reveals two perverted Arabs, Prince Habib and Slyman (Chong, Cheech) mumbling gibberish at their sloppy "Mekka Car Wash." Note the resemblance of Mekka, to the holy city, Mecca. Featured inside their tent are a bellydancer and a snake. The Arabs also own "Magic Carpet Rent-a-Car" and a useless nightclub. The club's interior has too much space, too few customers.

• As Prince Habib munches on some "kish-ka-bob," he pulls a knife and cleans his filthy toenails.

• Whenever Habib thinks about killing someone, he quickly produces his prayer beads and mutters mumbo-jumbo. Cautions Slyman, "[Don't kill anyone,] you won't get your green card."

• The Arabs' "mother messed around with a goat herder."

• Slyman mocks Habib's behavior, "You do not make joke. You are a joke."

• Some Arab financiers provide the two Arabs with a limo; hidden inside is $5 million—cash. The hapless drivers, Habib and Slyman, drive to Las Vegas. Unexpectedly, the limo runs out of gas. Barks dense Habib, "kill" it.

• On arrival in Las Vegas, the two Arabs dress in drag. After viewing a pornographic movie, Habib and Slyman try to seduce two French streetwalkers (who are portrayed by the comedians' real-life wives, Shelby Fiddis and Rikki Martin). First the two French women deride the Arabs. Then, they dump the sexually repugnant duo, saying, "Those guys. What a drag!"

• Inside a movie theater. Flashback. The perverted Habib recalls his rapport with a camel and begins masturbating. Warns Slyman, "Point that stupid thing, ding-dong, away. You want to go blind?"

• Dialogue:

Habib: I'm so hungry I could eat a camel. Two camels... She's even uglier than my wife. Or my camel.

Slyman: Your first wife was a camel!... May the fleas of a thousand camels nest in your beard.

Note: Writes a VAR critic, "Middle Easterners are also played to the hilt of greedy vulgarity, by Cheech and Chong" (8 August 1982).

The 13th Warrior (1999), TOU. *Antonio Banderas, Omar Sharif.* D: John McTiernan. Based on co-producer Michael Crichton's 1976 novel, *Eaters of the Dead,* which in turn is based on a real-life story about a highly cultured Arab Muslim from Baghdad. BEST LIST

This old-fashioned, rousing historical action film presents a bona fide Arab champion, Ahmed Ibn Fahdlan (Banderas). Ahmed travels to an unnamed northern land, befriends the blue-eyed blonde heroine, and helps Nordic warriors defeat "a terror that must not be named." The Norsemen tag Ahmed "friend," "Arab," and "little brother."

Scene: Tenth Century. Departing Baghdad is Ahmed, accompanied by some Arabs and the veteran courier Melehisidek (Sharif). Abruptly, in the desert, Tartars attack. But, when they spot a ship filled with Nordic warriors approach the shore, the Tartars retreat.

• Ahmed and Melehisidek meet with the Norsemen, ascertaining that "an ancient evil," a mysterious marauding tribe, threatens the northland's villagers. To contest this terror, thirteen men are to be chosen; at least one of them cannot be from the North. Thus, Ahmed is drafted. Melehisidek advises Ahmed, "Go with God." As Ahmed rides a white horse, a small Arabian, the northland warriors poke fun of the horse's size. Instantly, Ahmed mounts the swift horse, demonstrating that his Arabian can move faster and jump higher than any of the Norsemen's big stallions.

• Montage; Ahmed begins learning from immersion, the Norsemen's language. Regrettably, these Norsemen cannot read nor write. Thinking Ahmed does not understand their language, one Norseman slurs the Arab's mother. Retorts Ahmed, "My mother was a pure woman from a noble family." The shocked warrior asks, "Where did you learn our language?" Says Ahmed, "I listened." Next, Ahmed teaches the Nordic leader how to "draw speech"; e.g., write in Arabic. When the leader says, "Arab, speak what I draw," Ahmed, writes, "There is only one God and Mohammad is his prophet." Only Ahmed is monotheistic; the Nordic warriors have many gods.

• Their ship arrives at a Norseman's farm house; Ahmed and his friends come across beheaded northland victims, their bodies eaten by the attackers. Ahmed throws up, saying, "I am not a warrior." Counters a Norseman, "You soon will be." To defend himself, a warrior gives Ahmed a Nordic sword. Yet, because of its weight, Ahmed fails to cut anything with it. Swinging the weapon, he falls to the ground. Determined to excel, Ahmed grinds down the heavy sword, making into a fine, manageable scimitar.

He soon demonstrates his swordsmanship.

• Hundreds of torch-carrying clad-in-bear-garb villains emerge from the fog, intent on destroying the village. Sighs Ahmed, "Allah be merciful." Ahmed spots a running child; she appears directly in the attackers' path. The Arab mounts his white horse, rescuing her.

• The village under siege. The beast-like attackers move to trample every body in their path. During the battle, Ahmed discovers the true identity the bear-like invaders, exclaiming, "[I killed] a man." Affirms a warrior, "The claws, the headdresses; they want us to think they are bears."

• Asks a Norseman, "How do you hunt a bear?" Ahmed and he come to the conclusion that like bears, the attackers hide in caves. Ahmed directs his friends into and out of the villains' caves.

• Inside the caves, the vastly outnumbered northmen and Ahmed crush the villains, including the "mother." Yet, the leader survives. As he is fatally wounded, the Nordic champion asks Ahmed to kindly "draw a story of his deeds so he might be remembered."

• Back at the village, Ahmed warns, "Prepare yourselves." Before the final battle, Ahmed kneels. Praying to Allah he says, "Merciful father... I pray thee, God." His Nordic friend looks on, expressing sympathy, even awe.

• The final battle. The wounded Nordic champion terminates the bear-clad leader; all the attackers retreat.

• Ahmed prepares to depart; the Arab has earned the respect and friendship of his northland comrades, and vice versa. Arab music underscores farewells: "Goodbye Arab," and, "Goodbye Northman."

Finis: No clash of civilizations here. Instead, Arab and Aryan appear as friends. These courageous men have gleaned much from each other. During the film's final frames, the camera shows Ahmed documenting his northland journey. He writes in Arabic, "Praise be to Allah, merciful and compassionate."

Note: Unlike other Viking-Arab films, e.g., *The Long Ships* (1964), *The 13ᵗʰ Warrior* advocates tolerance and respect of other religions and races. No Arabs and no northmen appear as fanatics; they do not move to rape maidens; no one ridicules another's faith.

• Michael Crichton drew the inspiration "for the story from parts of a [true] historical account written by Ahmed Ibn Fahdlan." Explains Crichton, in the Disney press packet for the movie, "In the tenth century, Ibn Fahdlan was traveling to Central Asia and came across a group of Norse warriors... he is one of the few who wrote detailed eyewitness accounts of these people." Crichton assembled as much as he could "into English and used that as the basis for the first three chapters of the story." He explains, "The way Fahdlan described the Norse warriors was very compelling and it led me to learn more about them. [At the time,] Baghdad was one of the major founding centers of civilization."

1001 Arabian Nights (1959), United Production of America.

Animated. *Voices: Jim Backus, Hans Conried.* A Mr. Magoo cartoon feature. MAIDENS

Released during the 1959 Christmas holidays, this oft-told tale displays a benevolent giant green genie. Seeking the magic lamp are Baghdad's heroes and villains. The Wazir, especially, appears as an ominous caricature complete with razor-sharp teeth. The Wazir's grotesque appearance and eerie behavior may frighten some child viewers.

Scene: In Baghdad, three veiled maidens from Damascus move to wed Aladdin. The women chase after him, shouting, "Choose me."

• Princess Yasminda learns that her father, the sultan, needs funds (he sold half his camel stock). "I'm willing to do anything for you, father. I'll marry the Wazir," she says.

• Not only does the wicked Wazir rob the sultan's treasury, he tries to eradicate Aladdin, and secure Yasminda. Assisting him are comical bats, snakes, spiders, and rats. Plus, the Wazir possesses a magic flame and a tailor-made flying carpet.

• When Baghdad's citizens are told that Yasminda is being forced to wed the Wazir, they mourn. To the maiden's rescue, Abdul Aziz Magoo/Uncle Ben. Promptly, he moves to oust the Wazir. Cut to palace guards about to remove Aladdin's head; Abdul Aziz rescues the lad.

• Abdul Aziz Magoo outfoxes, then brings down the Wazir. Aided by a jolly green giant genie, Abdul Aziz arranges for Aladdin to marry Princess Yasminda.

• Cut to an anxious shark desperate for some Pepto-Bismol. Trying to stomach the foul taste of the Wazir, the ill shark moans and groans.

Note: Screen images have a lasting impact on some children. For example, back in 1982, I employed a college senior to type the initial draft of my book, *The TV Arab*. From time-to-time, we talked about the stereotypes. One afternoon, she confided in me, saying that when she was a young girl, her parents took her to see this Magoo movie, *1001 Arabian Nights*. She admitted, "I was so terrified by that bearded, needle-nosed Wazir, that I kept my eyes shut, tight. And when the really scary parts appeared, I hid under my seat." Following the screening, a girl friend gave her an Arabian Nights coloring book, based on the movie. She never even risked looking at the book, saying, "I was so afraid of anything Arabian."

• From 1904–7, the New York Herald newspaper displayed the comic strip, "The Wish Twins and Aladdin's Lamp." In the strip, ten-year old American twins acquire the fabled lamp, and use the lamp to satisfy childhood wishes, e.g., running a candy store, playing pranks on adults.

A Thousand and One Nights (1945), COL. *Cornell Wilde, Evelyn Keyes, Adele Jergens, Phil Silvers.* A remake of Korda's, *The Thief of Bagdad* (1940). MAIDENS

In this romantic parable, Arabs and a female genie bring down an Arab villain. Aladdin, the legendary poor boy of the streets, weds the royal princess.

Scene: Cautions a sorcerer, "[In Baghdad,] evil broods over the palace of the sultan." The wise sultan's dominion is menaced by his twin brother, Hajji.

• As soon as she appears, the personable, diaphanously clad genie, Babs (Keyes), begins wooing Aladdin (Wilde). Yet, Aladdin pines for Princess Armina (Jergens). Female genies are not unique in Arabian Nights scenarios. I recall a *Three Stooges* short displaying three femme fatales emerging from a magic lamp and crushing Arab "buzzards."

• Near the souk's slave market, Aladdin performs; "[his] songs are a legend throughout the east." Aladdin sings not for money but "for the joy of it." He purrs to onlookers, "The time is nigh for you to buy, beauty for sale... If you buy one of these maidens, you"ll have a chance to peek behind every veil." As Aladdin sings, his sidekick, Abdullah (Silvers), picks pockets. When playing gin rummy, Abduallah uses "loaded dice."

• To make certain "no man may gaze upon the Princess Armena and live," the sultan's men clear the streets.

Finis: The sultan brings down Hajji, his evil twin brother; Aladdin captures Armina's affections. In lieu of imprisoning or killing Hajji, the sultan plays chess with him. Two decades later, a nearly identical scene transpires in *Harum Scarum* (1965). Here, too, a forgiving sultan plays chess with his not-so-trustworthy brother.

Treatment of Islam: Inside the palace, a religious leader recites litanies. The pious sultan kneels and prays. The palace features the maidens' quarters, and a grand hall filled with lovely dancers.

Note: Persian as Arab? The film an Arabian Nights tale; the city, Baghdad; and the ruling sultan, an Arab. Yet, Hajji, the sultan's twin brother, is called "the best swordsman in Persia."

A Thousand and One Nights (1968), Domino Film. Italian. *Raf Vallone, Luciana Paluzzi, Jeff Cooper, Ruben Rojo.* D: Joe Lacey. Filmed in Spain.
MAIDENS

Arabs and a female genie vs. Arabs.

Scene: This tongue-in-cheek fantasy is set in Grenada. Representing "good" is Mizziana (Paluzzi), a lovely 400-year-old female genie, along with Omar (Cooper), Ali (Rojo), and their followers. Opposing them are Hixam, an evil vizier, and his black-cloaked Arabs. The settings include a souk, harem quarters, and a torture chamber.

• Hixam strikes, murdering Omar's father, a benevolent sultan. Vowing to avenge his father's death, Omar moves to collapse the vizier. Too late. The vizier's men nab Omar.

• To the rescue, lovely Mizziana, a "third class genie." She pops out of her bottle apologizing. Declaring her powers only work twice, daily, she sighs, "I can only make a miracle every five minutes."

• In time, Mizziana conjures up "invisible warriors." They clobber Hixam's forces. Concurrently, Omar duels and defeats Hixam.

• Love conquers all. Mizziana foregoes an eternity of youth, opting to wed Omar, Grenada's rightful vizier.

Treatment of Islam: Characters say, "May Allah go with you"; "Allah had a hand in all of this." Yet, one character says, "By the beard of the prophet."

Dialogue: A dense Arab guard is tagged "hippopotamus." When the guard spots the clad-in-harem-garb Ali, he makes a pass at him.

1001 Rabbit Tales (1982), WB. An animated Bugs Bunny feature.
VILLAINS

No champions, only animated villains: an ugly green genie, a stupid guard, a menacing sultan, and his "spoiled-rotten" son.

Scene: Featured in this animated movie, complete with flying carpet duels, is an ornate desert palace, an oasis, and a cave filled with treasures. Sultan Sam (Yosemite Sam), who appears as a "pinhead potentate," tags his cohort the "son of an unnamed goat."

• Sultan Sam's son, "crabby Prince Abadaba," insists that Bugs Bunny serve as his storyteller. Exiting the palace is an about-to-be-exiled storyteller; he cautions Bugs, "That rotten kid [Prince Abadaba] in there doesn't need a storyteller; he needs an exorcist."

• Abadaba, a "spoiled-rotten, loud-mouthed cry-baby," points a saber at Bugs' throat, threatening to boil him in oil.

• After Daffy Duck links up with Bugs, they uncover a cave and discover the magic lamp. Out pops a vile green genie. Instantly, the evil genie attacks Daffy. Next, Hassan, a huge, dense Arab guard with only a few teeth appears. Wielding an extra-large saber, Hassan chases after the duo, shouting, "Hassan chop! Hassan chop!"

• Daffy and Bugs manage to avoid being nabbed by Hassan and the sultan. They return safely to the good ol' USA!

• Sultan Sam decides to seek out and employ fresh readers to entertain his son, the spoiled Abadaba. The sultan considers kidnapping and whisking off to his Arabian palace, "some storytellers from Hollywood."

Three Kings (1999), WB. *George Clooney, Mark Wahlberg, Ice Cube, Spike Jonze, Cliff Curtis, Said Taghmaoui.* W, D: David O. Russell. P: Charles Roven.
BEST LIST

This anti-war movie helps erase damaging stereotypes, humanizing a people who for too long have been projected as caricatures. Following the Gulf War and Operation Desert Storm, four US Army rogues set out to retrieve a fortune in Kuwaiti gold bullion, stolen by Saddam Hussein. Along the way, they try to prevent Saddam's soldiers from killing Iraqi rebels. President Bush's decision to pull US troops out of Iraq, goes the scenario, is criticized, as it caused numerous deaths, leaving Iraqi rebels vulnerable to Saddam's wrath. On 15 February 1991, President Bush encouraged Iraqis to fight Saddam, saying the US would assist them. One week later "Voice of Free Iraq" repeated his message.

Background note: In March 1996, several Arab-American and Islamic organizations met with Warner Bros. (WB) executives in Burbank, California, to express concerns about stereotypical Arab Muslims in the studio's film *Executive Decision* (1996). Following the meeting, WB issued a statement, declaring it shared "the goal of increased understanding and sensitivity in the portrayal of Muslims and Islam to audiences throughout the world."

Intent on fulfilling its commitment, in July 1998, WB's legal department contacted me, requesting I examine the *Three Kings* screenplay, which I did. Afterward, I wrote, saying WB needed to make numerous script changes. I pointed out that about 100 of the 136 script pages had Iraqis killing Iraqis, plus GIs killing Iraqis. "I strongly advise WB not to produce this film," I wrote. "It perpetuates hurtful and harmful images of Arabs and Muslims." Months later, I was informed that WB was moving forward with the film. I was asked whether I would be willing to serve as a consultant. My role, as clarified by producer Charles Roven in his 15 December 1998 letter,

[would be] to function as a consultant on this film—helping to enrich the various Iraqi characters and [helping us] stay away from damaging stereotypes. Your specific area of expertise would be in helping us portray the Iraqi characters as more fully developed characters and making sure, whenever possible, that we stay away from uncomfortable stereotypes.

Initially, I was reluctant to sign on, thinking my input would not be seriously considered. But, I was impressed with Roven's candor and sensitivity. Also, I was being given an opportunity to address screen stereotypes; I accepted the consulting position. My early anxieties were soon put to rest. Obviously, not all of my suggested edits and additions were implemented. Yet, my one-year working relationship with Roven and his colleagues was exemplary. To the studio's credit, Roven, director David Russell, and co-producer Doug Segal worked diligently, attempting to avoid perpetuating the "seen one, seen 'em all" cliché. They made significant alterations to the screenplay, revealing a failed US policy that allowed Saddam Hussein's Republican Guards to advance the suffering of those courageous Iraqi rebels opposing him.

Numerous scenes reveal Iraqi rebels assisting the movie's American soldiers, and vice versa. Roven deleted some objectionable scenes; e.g., an Iraqi woman exposing her breasts; Iraqi soldiers eating animals. To project dignified rebels, new scenes were added. Subsequently, viewers could see a wide range of Iraqis—devout Muslims, children, and freedom fighters. Islam is revered. Women wearing black, such as the Iraqi rebel leader's wife, are projected as real people, not as mute, faceless objects.

Scene: March 1991. The Iraqi desert. A truce has been declared; Iraqi soldiers surrender. US Major Archie Gates (Clooney) and his men recover a map from a prisoner's ass [a cheap laugh] leading to Kuwaiti gold bullion hidden in a nearby village.

• Mjr. Archie Gates, Sgt. Troy Barlow (Wahlberg), Chief Elgin (Ice Cube), and Vig (Jonze) ride off to retrieve the loot. Arriving at an Iraqi village, they spot Republican Guards harassing anti-Saddam civilians. Because Saddam's followers help Archie and company haul off the gold, he and his pals opt not to get involved in the Iraqi vs. Iraqi struggle. The rebels ask the Americans not to leave. As Gates moves to depart, an Iraqi rebel berates him, "We're fighting Saddam and dying, and you're stealing gold." Gates sighs, explaining that the US has abandoned all those Iraqis opposing Saddam. But when a Saddam clone suddenly shoots an unarmed Iraqi woman, the GIs change their minds and shoot some Republican Guards dead. The Iraqi rebel leader, Amir (Curtis), shakes hands with Gates. Next, the GIs shoot more baddies, free imprisoned Iraqi rebels, and ride off to safety—so they think.

• Angry that the GIs nabbed their prisoners, the Republican Guards launch a missile, which destroys Gates' vehicle holding the stolen gold. To the rescue, devout Iraqi Muslims. They assist the wounded men, finding shelter for Gates, Vig, Chief Elgin, and the rebels.

• Inside a cave, Muslims pray. Chief Elgin joins them, twice. Acknowledging their prayers, Gates blesses himself, saying, "Amen."

• Republican Guards capture Sgt. Barlow; he is bound and questioned by Capt. Said (Taghmaoui), a Bowling Green State University graduate. The dialogue reveals that both men are fathers. And, that during the war American bombs crippled Said's wife, killing his young son. Flashback: Barlow imagines his home, wife, and child being blown up. Flashback: Rubble from US bombs destroy Said's home, crushing his son as he sleeps in his crib. (This flashback was added per my suggestion, by Roven and Russell.)

• Initially, the Barlow-Said scenes suggest that the men, despite their differences, will bond. Not for long. Said asks Barlow why the US bombed Iraq, killing so many people. Explains Barlow, the bombing had nothing to do with oil, rather the US bombed Iraq to free Kuwait. At this point, Said's personality alters. The Iraqi becomes hostile; pours oil down Barlow's throat. In time, Gates and his men arrive, rescuing Barlow. I objected to the oil-guzzling sequence, saying Said should not behave so violently. Repeatedly, I asked the producer and director not to display Said as an unrestrained Iraqi, rather to present the men as being more alike than different.

• The Americans shout several times, "Saddam is Coming!," thus duping some Republican Guards to run off. Most Iraqis fall for the ruse and head into the desert, shedding their clothes and tossing their weapons. This scene makes the Iraqi troops look stupid and cowardly. Later, however, a brave Iraqi surfaces. When Gates asks an Iraqi rebel whether he will seek safety in Iran, the soldier replies, "No, I will stay here and fight Saddam."

• Abruptly, Republican Guards shoot and kill Vig, and they seriously injure Barlow. Gates reacts, pumping scores of bullets into the Iraqis. As the scene was overkill (a few shots would do), Russell agreed to omit some of the bang-bang-you're dead frames.

• Throughout, differences between Iraqi rebels and the Americans are respected, not belittled. The GI's, who escort dozens of Iraqi rebels to safety across the Iranian border, are no longer selfish mercenaries. They have changed for the better, showing compassion for their fellow man. To illustrate, they bond with the rebels. Chief Elgin dons a kuffiyeh. He, Gates, and the Iraqis respectfully carry Vig's body to a religious site. Earlier, Vig befriended Iraqi twins, two decent ordinary hair dressers. Believing a Muslim saint opens access to heaven, Vig makes a dying request—to be buried in a Muslim shrine village. And, he is.

Note: President Bill Clinton and critic Robert Ebert addressed the movie during a special edition of "Roger Ebert and the Movies," broadcast by UPN-TV (28 February 2000). Said Ebert, "[It was] one of the best movies of the year."

> Clinton: I loved *Three Kings*... I loved it.
> Ebert: Movies like *Three Kings* help us to empathize with other people so that we can see things from more than our own point of view. I think that's the most valuable thing a movie can do.
> Clinton: I loved that aspect of *Three Kings*. The biggest problem in human society is fear and distrust and dehumanization and violence against the Other. And that is a big problem. So, what we have to learn to do... is to actively celebrate our differences. And the only way you can do that is to be secure in the knowledge that your common humanity is more important than your most significant differences.
> Ebert: And movies can help do that.
> Clinton: And movies can help do that. That is really, really important.

• Muslim and Arab-Americans acknowledged the movie's telling Iraqi portraits. "We're happy that for once we are not stereotyped by Hollywood... It shows the Arab and Muslim and their complexity, with feelings and normal aspirations," said Dr. Hala Maksoud, President of the American-Arab Anti-Discrimination Committee. Affirmed Salam Al-Marayati, Director of the Muslim Public Affairs Council [MPAC], "For the first time on screen, you see the human face of the Iraqi people." Al-Marayati was so pleased with the producers' efforts to project an authentic image of the region and its people that prior to the film's theatrical release, 30 September 1999, the MPAC invited its members and others to attend a special Warner Bros. screening of *Three Kings* at the Steve Roth Theater in Burbank, California.[174]

• Two Arab-American specialists assisted producer Roven, helping him with the movie's Arabic dialogue, slogans, and Islamic prayer scenes.

The Three Musketeers (1933), Mascot. 12 episodes. *John Wayne, Edward Piel, Elaine Corday, Raymond Hatton, Francis X. Bushman Jr., Jack Mulhall.* This serial was edited and released as a feature film, *Desert Command* (1948). CLIFFHANGERS, VILLAINS

Producer Nat Levine's version of the Alexandre Dumas story displays Arabs as "brown devils." In the Sahara desert, American legionnaires crush bedouins.

Scene: The desert D'Artagnan, Tom Wayne (Wayne), rescues three legionnaires from treacherous Arabs—a "one-sided scrap." The rescued legionnaires, Clancy, Renard, and Schmidt (Mulhall, Hatton, and Bushman, respectively), hail from Brooklyn.

• Wayne flies off, gunning down bedouins from a plane. Barks the Arab tagged "Devil of the Desert," El Shaitan, literally, Satan (Piel), "A band of our horsemen has been cut to pieces by an American flyer with a machine gun."

• The American heroine (Corday) spots prowling desert Arabs, fearing for her life. As they encircle her, she sighs to Wayne, "What can we do against all those Arabs?"

• El Shaitan's "merciless desert cult" is beaten; they are unable to defeat heroic legionnaires. The bodies of dead bedouins fill the screen.

• Drums beats summon El Shaitan and his cohorts to "The Devil's Circle," their secret meeting room. Cut to the souk; Wayne and the legionnaires punch out charging Arabs.

• In episodes three and five, bedouins try to knife Wayne in the back. Similar knife-in-the-back ploys are employed in *The Desert Hawk* (1944).

• In episode eleven, two dense Arabs examine Wayne, checking to see whether he is dead. One Arab places his gun on the ground; Wayne jumps up, dropping both men.

• Dressed in Arab garb, the legionnaires permanently bring down the bedouins. After the legionnaires shoot El Shaitan, the bedouins supporting "The Devil's Circle" run off. With one hand, a legionnaire munches a leg of lamb; with the other he socks a bedouin.

• One legionnaire directs some bedouins to a tent, then collapses the tent on them. Another legionnaire shouts: "Those brown devils are after her [the heroine]."

Treatment of Islam: When bedouins see the legionnaires of Brooklyn, they scream, "Look, unbelievers," "drive the unbelievers from our land," and "death to the unbelievers."

Note: Several scenes from this movie serial remind me of the animated cartoon, *The Three Musketeers*, telecast in 1991 on WGN-TV. The cartoon, an altered version of the Dumas classic, also reveals Arab villains. Here, the three musketeers battle evil Prince Abdul and his cohorts, plus Abdul's clad-in-Arab-garb monkey. On learning that Abdul and his Arabs have robbed the King's treasury, the three musketeers ride off to Abdul's palace, routing him and his bandits. Seeing two Arabs without weapons, a musketeer tosses his sword then slugs them, boasting, "Now it's an even match, two against one."

3 Ninjas (1992), TOU. *Michael Treanor, Chad Power.* CAMEOS

Opening frames show an FBI agent wearing reel Arab garb. The agent moves to purchase American missiles from a shady arms merchant.

Scene: A white limousine pulls into a warehouse. The driver opens the back door and out pops the clad-in-Arab garb FBI agent. He wears a white headdress and dark glasses, sports a moustache and speaks with a thick accent. The agent/Arab opens his briefcase, revealing money. The weapons dealer approves of the amount. Abruptly the agent/Arab says, "It is a pleasure to do business with you, Mr. Snyder. Now, on behalf of the people of my country [the Arab accent stops here] I'd like to say you're under arrest," he says. The agent flaunts his FBI badge; the villain punches him out.

Note: Why show the FBI agent as an Arab? The reader interested in FBI scams should see my comments on the FBI's ABSCAM in my book *The TV Arab.*[173] A major 1980 news event engendering a host of Arab jokes was the FBI's ABSCAM [Arab Scam] caper; attempting to ensnare slippery US politicians, FBI agents posed as Arab oil sheikhs.

Three Spare Wives (1961), UA. *Robin Hunter, Susan Stephen, Ferdy Mayne, Golda Casimir.* SP: Eldon Howard. MAIDENS

In this British comedy, mythical Ishram appears as a primitive and violent place with oil. "Ishram is sitting on a lake of oil... 700,000 barrels." According to "Ishramic law," women are chattel. A happily married Brit gets stuck with an outlandish inheritance— Uncle Ben's three Arab wives. The British protagonist and his wife vs. Ishram's submissive Arab women.

Scene: Opening scenes display uncivilized "Ishram." As the call to prayer is chanted, the camera displays camels trotting on dirt roads, a woman with a jug on her head, and a mother poking her child. Intones the narrator, "All nature seems to slumber." And, "The natives are noted for their hospitality." Abruptly, a jeep filled with Arabs speeds past a shop owned by Benjamin Bull. An Arab tosses a grenade, blowing up the store and Uncle Ben.

• Looking forward to being reunited with his wife, Susan, a Brit named George (Hunter) prepares to leave Ishram. Unexpectedly, delivered to George are Uncle Ben's household effects—three veiled, scantily clad maidens. The babbling women, who flaunt bare midriffs and expose their navels, will accompany George to England.

• George's Uncle Ben "had fifteen [wives] at one time, but he lost the others playing cribbage." How can this be? Well, in Ishram "wives are property... they can be bought and sold." And, "[the] law says that wives must walk in the shadow of the master." Women, however, do have the right to "approve or disapprove the buyer." The women, however, do approve of George. He balks, "I can't take three wives back to England." But George is warned that if he fails to follow Ishram's laws, "they'll cut off both your ears and give them to wife number three. Or, they'll cut off your head." Thus, George acquiesces.

• England, the airport. George appears before the customs agents claiming his wives as "household effects." An official examines Fatima (Casimir). George explains, "[she is a] work of art." Then, he frowns, telling the agent that his other wife is simply an "ancient relic."

• The three Arab women enter George's flat. Seeing Susan's mother (Stephen), they bow. Sighs George, "I don't want them here. But how can I get rid of them?"

• Arriving at George's flat is the bearded Fazim Bey (Mayne), a stereotypical Arab negotiator. Bey smokes a nargelih and speaks broken English. Sitting on the floor, he and the women munch "chocolates." The chocolate-addicted maidens, who address George as "Master," demand more chocolates. When George balks, Bey cites Ishramic law: "If wives complain, he loses all his money, his ears, his head, his..." Pleads Susan, "Get rid of the women." George obeys, moving to "get rid of his three Ishramic wives."

• States a newspaper headline: "Harem Comes to Wimbledom." A British "foreign office representative" visits George's flat, trying to budge the wives. He fails. Insist the Arabs, "We not go back to Ishram; Ishram stinking country." To the rescue, George's friend Rupert. He offers to wed all three maidens. George rejoices; the women "approve" of Rupert.

• Suddenly, Jocko Pyle, a sly and successful Scotsman who resides in Ishram with his five Arab wives, arrives. Jocko succeeds in nabbing from George, the deed to Uncle Ben's oil office in Ishram.

• The pleased Jocko flies off to Ishram; instantly, he sets up a brand-new "Pyle Oil" office. Intones the narrator, "The natives are noted for their hospitality." Soon, the on-screen action duplicates opening frames. A jeep filled with Arabs appears. An Arab tosses a grenade, igniting the office and Jocko.

Note: Note the similarities, Ishram and Islam.

The Thrill Chaser (1923), UNI. Silent. *Hoot Gibson, Billie Dove, Abdul Bey, William E. Lawrence.* S: Elmer Davis. *NS. Notes from VAR (17 January 1924).

MAIDENS, SHEIKHS

Dainty Prince Ahmed exploits cowboy Hoot Gibson's rough-and-tough talents. The Arab heroine rushes into the cowboy's arms.

Summary: Gibson surfaces on a Hollywood set, performing stunts as a movie actor's double. Appearing on the set is Ahmed (Lawrence), an Arabian Prince. The Arab admires the way Gibson takes punches without flinching. Fearing some Arabs in his kingdom may slug and injure him, Ahmed hires Gibson. Says a colleague, "[It's a] good plan for him to have a double in his native country." Ahmed and Gibson rush off to Arabia. Here, Ahmed lets Gibson "take all the slams [while he receives] all of the glory." In the end, Gibson turns the tables on Ahmed. The cowboy elopes with Olala (Dove), the ruling sheikh's daughter.

Thunder over Tangier (1957), REP. *Martin Benson, Lisa Gastoni, Adeeb Assaly.* CAMEOS, VILLAINS

Arab and German counterfeiters vs. British agents.

Scene: WWII, a Tangier souk. Arab music underscores the action. The Arab villain, Darracq, and his German cohorts kill an Arab counterfeiter. Aiding them, an Arab cab driver.

Note: Credits state: Adeeb Assaly as the "Lean Arab."

• When *Thunder in Tangier* appeared in movie theaters, *Passport to Danger*, a syndicated TV series starring Cesar Romero, surfaced on television screens. One half-hour episode of *Passport to Danger* is set in Tangier, which is described as "a squalid, Moroccan seaport where violence is a way of life." Appearing in the episode is Marija, a brave Arab woman. Believing Tangier is much different than the West, she says, "The people [here are] quicker to hate and quicker to love." Later, Marija sacrifices her life, saving the Western protagonist.

Timbuktu (1959), UA. *Victor Mature, Yvonne De Carlo, John Dehner, Leonard Mudie.* SP: Anthony Veiller. *NS. Notes from VAR (15 October 1959). VILLAINS

Legionnaires and an American quash "[Arab] tribes of the French Sudan, about the time France was falling to the Germans." A sly Arab watches tarantulas devour a young man.

Summary: An Arab uprising threatens the emir's (Dehner) country, and Timbuktu's French garrison. To quell the "natives," the protagonist, Mike Conway (Mature), safely delivers a Muslim "holy man," Mohamet Adani (Mudie), to Timbuktu.

Time After Time (1979), WB. *Malcolm McDowell, David Warner.* SP, D: Nicholas Meyer. See Meyer's *The Seven-Per-Cent Solution* (1976). See also *True Colors* (1991). CAMEOS, SHEIKHS, PALESTINIANS

Film as propaganda? Palestinians shoot Israeli schoolchildren. And, oily Arabs own "London"; see *Chapter Two* (1979); Neil Simon also targets Arabs in London.

Scene: San Francisco, 1979. Note the dialogue:

Person one: She wants to know if London is really crawling with Arabs.
Person two [*confused*]: Arabs?
Person one: She wants to marry into oil.

• London. Unexpectedly, Jack the Ripper (Warner) uses H.G. Wells' (McDowell) time machine, rushing off to modern San Francisco. Wells follows him; they meet in a San Francisco hotel room. Ripper tells Wells that he feels very much at "home" in America's violence-ridden society. To enforce his thesis, Ripper clicks on the TV set. Abruptly, the news anchor states: "Palestinian terrorists carried out their threat and began shooting the first of five of 106 Israeli school children held hostage for eighteen days in a secret..."

Note: No such heinous act ever took place. There is about as much truth in the fictional statement made by the film's news announcer as there is in having the news anchor say: Israeli terrorists began shooting the first of five of 106 Palestinian school children, and so forth.

The Time of Your Life (1948), UA. *Jimmy Cagney, William Bendix, Pedro de Cordoba.* W: Nathaniel Curtis. Based on William Saroyan's stage play. CAMEOS

An "Arab" by any other name. Georgette and Jack Ayoub suggested I view this film, as the credits display the words, "Arab philosopher."

Scene: Continuously, interesting characters frequent Nick's (Bendix) saloon restaurant and entertainment palace. One such character is tagged "the Arab" (de Cordoba); he wears a wrinkled black suit. When a customer inquires about the man, Nick shrugs, "I don't know what his name is but we call him the Arab."

• "The Arab" utters three short sentences; and, he helps Nick fend off a bully.

Time Walker (1982), New World. *Ben Murphy, Nina Axelrod.* EP: Robert A. Shaheen. EGYPTIANS

Descending from outer space, a rampaging alien "mummy" wreaks havoc, killing students. How does this clad-in-mummy-garb creature terminate folks? He infects them with his deadly green fungus touch.

Scene: Stock footage of several Egyptian locales. Abruptly, Western archaeologists uncover a mummified alien "resting" in King Tut's tomb. The explorers consider how this outer space traveler came to reside in Tut's tomb. Apparently, centuries ago, after its "deadly [green] touch" terminated Tut, the Egyptians acted, killing and burying the alien.

• Curious about his alien-mummy discovery, noted archaeologist Doug McCadden (Murphy) whisks the bandaged being off to "The California Institute of the Sciences." When associates examine the creature, they mistakenly administer an overdose of radiation rays, promptly reviving the alien. Abruptly, the alien-mummy's lethal green fungus, dormant for 3,000 years, emerges from the sarcophagus. The green slime destroys human flesh.

Tin Pan Alley (1940), TCF. *Betty Grable, Alice Faye, Billy Gilbert.* Later remade as *I'll Get By* (1950). See *Coney Island* (1943). SHEIKHS

This 1940s musical features a rotund, sissyish sheikh (Gilbert). Attending the ruler, scantily clad maidens. Lounging on soft pillows, the sheikh romances two of his wives (Grable and Faye)

Scene: Circa 1917, a theater. On stage, performers prepare to entertain audiences with the hit musical, "The Sheik of Araby." The stage curtain rises! Arab music underscores the entrance of two dozen harem dancers wearing see-through pantaloons. Two semi-nude blacks wearing turbans perform as eunuchs, and tap dance, vigorously. Cut to the bored, effeminate sheikh; he munches grapes, and pokes fun of wiggling maidens. Instantly, his two wives (Grable and Faye) perk him up, singing and dancing to "The Sheik of Araby." Slithering up to the sheikh his wives croon, "When you play Sha-hare-a-zaddy, you're my great big Baghdad-daddy." Dazzled by such sensuality, the sheikh collapses.

Note: In *She's Working Her Way through College* (1952), an ex-burlesque dancer portrayed by Virginia Mayo, enrolls at Midwest State University. Here, she stars in some college variety shows, performing femme fatales such as Queen Cleopatra. As Cleopatra, she and her classmates wearing Egyptian garb, sing, "She's Working Her Way through College" (lyrics by Sammy Cahn). Goes the tune,

> And Cleopatra, when she used to walk into a school room made all the young Egyptian boys forget about the pool room... the only easy mark she made was Antony... She failed in every subject, couldn't get above a D.

The camera reveals several Egyptian-clad maidens surrounding Antony (played by Gene Nelson). Antony sips some nectar and passes out. Croons Cleopatra, "As soon as he's cold, I'll take his gold. Too bad the lad [Antony] didn't live to grow old." Smiling, Cleopatra runs off with the gold.

Titanic (1998), TCF. *Leonardo DiCaprio, Kate Winslet.* W, P, D: James Cameron. CAMEOS

The telling book, *Titanic: Women and Children First* (New York: W.W. Norton & Co., 1998), contains personal interviews with Titanic survivors and their families, as well as the most up-to-date passenger list yet published. Point out authors Judith B. Geller and John P. Eaton, "officially there were 154 Syrians on board the Titanic [when it sank], and 29 were saved: four men, five children, and twenty women." All but four "Second Class"

Arab travelers were ticketed "Third Class." Yet, writer-producer-director James Cameron omits this reality. Also, instead of highlighting "one of the three Arab weddings that took place" aboard the ship, Cameron presents a make-believe Irish wedding.[175]

Scene: As the Titanic sinks, the camera reveals for a few seconds only, an Arabic-speaking Syrian man and his family. The man exclaims "Yallah Habibi" (Hurry, my love).

Note: Another sunken ship thriller is the TV movie, *Britannic* (2000), set in June 1916, two years into WWI. One scene reveals several passengers at dinner, questioning the war's purpose. Quips a British military doctor, "What are we really fighting for? Arabia's oil." The physician's statement makes no sense. Only in 1933 did Western companies begin exploring the Saudi deserts for oil. And, oil was not discovered until 1939, two decades after the war.

To Live and Die in L.A. (1985), MGM/UA. *William Dafoe, William L. Petersen.* CAMEOS, VILLAINS

In Los Angeles, an Arab Muslim moves to assassinate the US president.

Scene: Before credits roll, the camera reveals police cars escorting the president's limousine. Cut to the hotel housing the President, evening. A secret service agent (Petersen) guarding the president spots a strolling waiter near the president's suite. Suspecting the waiter might be up to no good, the agent charges up the stairs, heading for the roof. En route, he spots a dead security guard. On the roof, the agent confronts the waiter. Several dynamite sticks are affixed to the Arab's waist. Asserts the Arab, "I'm ready to die. Death to Israel, and America, and all the enemies of Islam." Abruptly, the Arab lowers himself to the building's edge, declaring, "I am a martyr. I will bomb myself on you and all the enemies of Islam." When the Arab jumps to his death, screaming "Allahu Akbar," the dynamite explodes. Credits roll. From here on the film focuses on the agent tracking his partner's killer.

Tobruk (1967), UNI. *Rock Hudson, Nigel Green.* SP: Leo V. Gordon. CAMEOS, VILLAINS

The Libyan desert, WWII. The Allies battle Rommel's Africa Corps. History is falsified; clad-in-black bedouins assist the Germans.

Scene: The souk reveals unkempt Arabs and donkeys.

• British, Canadian, and Jewish commandos pose as German officers. Seeing armed bedouins surface atop sand dunes, two British soldiers say, "Look at 'em. I wish I had me rifle... Wouldn't be the first time they attacked a column, an English column, colonel."

• Feigning to be a German officer, Major Craig (Hudson) approaches the bedouin leader. In exchange for weapons, the Arab offers to give Craig two British prisoners. "Trust an Arab to argue," quips a British colonel (Green). Craig refuses to deal. Instantly, he and his commandos fire away; the sword-wielding bedouins rush off.

Note: To support my contention that *Tobruk* distorts history, I approached several authorities, asking about Libya's loyalties during WWII, notably history Professor Raymond Callahan, at the University of Delaware. In a personal letter (7 December 1993), Dr. Callahan explained Libya's pro-British policy. Military historians recognize that "The Libyan population were mostly adherents to the Senussi sect whose leadership was ferociously anti-Italian and therefore pro-British." After the war, writes Callahan, the British showed their appreciation, making Libya's "Senussi leader, Idris I, into a King."

The Tomb (1985), Trans World. *Cameron Mitchell, John Carradine, Richard Alan Hench, Michelle Bauer.* EGYPTIANS, MAIDENS

In this low-budget film, complete with racial slurs, a fiendish Egyptian princess terminates Californians.

Scene: Professor Howard Phillips (Mitchell) violates Princess Nefratis' (Bauer) crypt. In the past, this demon Egyptian princess "drank the blood of the living so that her dark energy would never die." Now that Phillips has reawakened Nefratis, the princess intends to avenge those who ran off with her sacred treasures. Employing laser-like skills, Nefratis travels to California and murders several people.

• Ancient amulets keep Nefratis alive.

• An American pulls a knife on an Egyptian guide, warning, "How about a little filet of Ayrab?"

Finis: Declares the protagonist, David Manners (Hench): "Man's courage is pitted against her [Nefratis'] evil powers in a battle of will against [Egyptian] mysticism."

Dialogue: Egyptians are tagged "camel humper," "raghead," and "towel head."

Note: Appearing in the film is a musical group called, "Pharaoh and the Mummies." Members of the band wear fezzes, and cover themselves with bandages. A mummy band is also featured in *Abbott and Costello Meet the Mummy* (1955).

The Tomb of Ligeia (1965), Alta Vista. *Vincent Price, Elizabeth Shepherd.* SP: Robert Townsend. D: Roger Corman. Based on Edgar Allan Poe's story. CAMEOS, EGYPTIANS

Mysterious Egyptian eyes.

Scene: Circa the late nineteenth century; the English country home of Verden Fell (Price). Not only do Fell's eye problems cause him to wear dark glasses, the man is haunted by his first wife's ghost. The camera shows Fell displaying to an attractive woman, one of his unique artifacts. Says Fell, "[This] wax [bust of an Egyptian is] a reproduction. You see I am loathe to open ancient tombs, rob a nation of its treasures and call it archaeology." Glaring at his Egyptian reproduction, Fell continues, "Twentieth dynasty, you can tell by the eyes. The eyes, they confound me. There's a blankness, a mindless sort of malice in some Egyptian eyes. They do not readily yield up the mystery they hold."

Torn Apart (1990), Castle Hill. *Cecilia Peck, Adrian Pasdar, Machram Huri, Arnon Zadok, Michael Morim, Amos Lavi.* SP: Marc Krystal. Made in Israel. PALESTINIANS, MAIDENS

An Israeli soldier and a Palestinian school teacher fall in love. Palestinians vs. Israelis, vs. Palestinians. The film presents humane Palestinians, Mahmoud Malek, Professor Mansour, and Jamilah. Regrettably, like *Hanna K.* (1983), it received limited distribution; the film was not screened in many theaters. No movie theater in St. Louis, Missouri, screened *Torn Apart.*

Scene: Jerusalem. A Palestinian family, the Maliks, move into their home, alongside a Jewish family, the Arnons. A young girl, Laila Malik (Peck), and a young boy, Ben Arnon (Pasdar), vow to be "friends forever."

• Laila's father, Mahmoud (Huri), encourages her to get an education, saying, "an education holds the future of the Arab world." When Laila's militant cousin, Fawzi (Lavi), arrives from Jordan, he brandishes a "marriage contract." Mahmoud refuses his offer, declaring that Laila will select her own man.

• The Palestinians talk politics. "What kind of man blows up a school bus?" asks Mahmoud. Retorts Fawzi, "My land, your land, was taken by Jews. How can you sit here and write about peace?"

• Flash forward, a decade later, 1973. Israelis talk politics. The grown-up Ben, now an Israeli soldier, tells his father, Arie, "You know what we're doing in the occupied territories? We're searching fruit baskets for bombs. For bombs, hell, it's old women and children." And, "These Arabs in the territories. They're suffering. They're suffering in our hands. They're suffering in my hands." Counters Arie, "The Arabs can lose a hundred wars and they'll still be here. We lose one and our dream is over."

• Laila's father, Mahmoud, who is confined to a wheelchair, writes of peace and "brotherhood." He says Palestinians should accept Jews as "equal citizens; the Jews improved our lives." Rebuts Laila, "They wanted your vote." Citing poor economic conditions and preferential treatment for Israelis, Laila says, "I cannot be happy with what you got in '48. A Jewish girl, my age, she makes good money for the work she does. She has no [military] curfew... she is not treated with disrespect in her own country. Why should I be?" Laila, who teaches at an all-girl grade school and plays the lute, is also a peace activist. She picks oranges with her Israeli friends, and places flowers on Ben's father's grave.

• Cut to a sea shore; a Palestinian youth is drowning. As not one of the reel Palestinian beach-goers can swim, Ben plunges in, rescuing the boy. Later, Mr. Arnon berates his son, saying he should have let the Arab drown. You're "out of control," he shouts. Laila's family will "kill both of you." Counters Ben, "You taught me to care." Sighs his father, "You love an Arab girl, so we can all go hang. Now you go hang. You're on your own."

• The Palestinian youth that Ben rescued from the sea steals his army pistol. Seeing Israeli soldiers approach, the boy shoots. Ben tries to convince the Palestinian to surrender. The youth refuses; Ben kills him, in self-defense.

• Israeli soldiers harass Ben, warning him to avoid Palestinian women. Laila, too, is harassed. Bark Palestinians, "[Have you] been with an Israeli soldier?" Confesses Laila, "Yes. Ben Arnon." Protests her father, "I am not a conventional man... but in our society everything is against this. Differences are not so easily torn away. I forbid you to see him again." Counters Laila, "I believed in what you and your work have stood for, about peace, faith, the future. Now that I can make them real, you're ashamed of me?" " No," insists Mahmoud, "afraid." Says Laila, "I am not afraid." Later, Mrs. Malik warns Laila that her Uncle Fawzi and his son, Moustapha (Morim), intend to murder Ben.

• A Palestinian wedding. Here, Palestinians dance the dubke. There are similarities between the Arab dubke and the Jewish dance, the horah. During both dances men and women gracefully wave their arms, and sway their hips. As my colleague Ray Hanania says, it's a frenzied combination of a conga line and the hokey-poky. Also, early movie shorts [Thomas Edison's *Arabian Jewish Dance* (1903)] reveal the national dances of Arabs and Jews are similar.

• A Jewish celebration; Ilana Arnon's wedding. Frustrated at being separated from Laila, Ben leaves his sister's wedding and goes to Laila, proposing marriage, "This is my home. Your home. But never our home." They decide to leave for New York.

• Laila's friend, Professor Mansour (Zadok), assists the couple, giving them an escape vehicle, a jeep. Says Mansour, "Who has claim to this land? Both do. See the building rods. To a Jew it's bad construction. To an Arab, it signifies where the next generation will add another level on the top of the building so the whole family will all be together." Continues the professor,

You've no doubt seen other Arab influences on Jewish culture, architecture, the food, music. More important, however, are the personal similarities. The Palestinians are a small race of educated, ambitious, financially astute nomads. Sound familiar? We are engaged here, my friend, to keep hold of our identity, to live beside the Jews. Now, if we fail, we are lost. Both of us.

• Violence. Moustapha arrives from Jordan, slicing Professor Mansour's throat. Instantly, Israeli soldiers shoot Moustapha dead. Cut to a West Bank marketplace, Mansour's funeral. Palestinians demonstrate; an Israeli soldier prevents his comrade from beating a Palestinian youth. Israeli soldiers fire in the air; they do not shoot at the demonstrating Palestinians; nor do they club them.

• When Ben and Laila arrive, they are immediately "torn apart" by the mob. Laila rushes toward her father and is fatally shot. The camera does not show the individual firing the weapon. The most likely suspect is a Palestinian, one opposing Laila's marriage with Ben. Grieving, Ben calls Mahmoud "Papa," then takes Laila in his arms and reads from a letter Laila penned, years ago: "I know there will be peace some day, too. Because our families did what everyone said can't be done. We shared the land." Earlier Ben said, "Good coffee." "Arab coffee," affirmed Laila. "My mother made this."

Note: A few scenes show Palestinians initiating and commiting violence against fellow Palestinians and Israelis. For example, a Palestinian mob attacks Ben; and, two Palestinian militants kill Mansour.

• Three Israelis surface as decent folk, Ben, Ilana, and Ben's Army friend. Only in self defense do Ben and other Israeli soldiers use force. But, Ben's father appears as a disagreeable character.

• When movies show Palestinians and Israelis bonding, despair or death usually follow.

Trapped in Tangier (1960), TCF. *Edmund Purdom, Genevieve Page.* *NS. Notes from VAR (6 June 1960). VILLAINS

In Tangier, a federal agent pursues "an international dope ring."

Summary: When an American agent (Purdom) goes after an international dope ring, he unexpectedly falls for the leader's "adopted daughter."

Treasure of the Lost Desert (1983), A&Z Comp. *Bruce Miller, Susan West.* W, P, D: Tony Zarindast. Filmed in Yemen. See *Wild Geese II* (1985). VILLAINS

An Arab-American Green Beret captain vs. Arabs and an Asian.

Scene: As US soldiers jog, the narrator says: "The Middle East... a place where one's brother is often his enemy, and the end of one war is merely the beginning of another." Cut to Captain Claude Servan, an Arab American, born in Dubai.

• Servan recruits some Green Berets. Their mission? To prevent "Eagle," an evil Asian, and his Arab cohorts from "financing a coup."

• A rotund bellydancer performs at the "Shish-Ka-Bob Cafe."

• After trying to rape a woman, an ugly Arab sticks a pitchfork into an Arab-American recruit. Next, he knifes a fellow Arab in the back.

• The Green Berets terminate the Eagle and his Arab cohorts.

Trenchcoat (1983), BV. *Margot Kidder, Robert Hays.* SP: Jeffrey Price, Peter Seaman. CAMEOS, SHEIKHS

A vacationing court stenographer becomes involved with international intrigue and murder. Arabs are tossed in as dense druggies and ugly abductors.

Scene: In Malta, a limousine holding three robed Arabs pulls alongside a vacationing American stenographer, Mickey Raymond (Kidder). Abruptly, the Arabs grab and toss Mickey onto the back seat, and begin grilling her about drug deals. One Arab grips a hypodermic needle, giving Mickey a shot of Sodium Pentothal. Next, a really fat Arab places his foot on Mickey's neck, warning her to confess she's behind the drug deal, or else. Quips Mickey, "You have bad breath." Affirms another Arab, "It's working." To the rescue, Mickey's friend. He crashes his car into the Arabs' limo; Mickey runs off.

• Mickey tells a fellow American (Hays) about the Arabs who kidnapped her. "They think Ortega [a man who was just killed] gave me ten kilos. He didn't."

• On their boat, the Arabs discuss doing drugs. One Arab lights a nargelih. "Let us share into smoke, it will put our minds to rest," he says. Boom! The boat explodes; the Arabs die.

Tripoli (1950), PAR. *John Payne, Maureen O'Hara, Howard DaSilva, Philip Reed, Grant Withers, Alan Napier, Alberto Morin.* SP: Winston Miller. See *Harem Scarum* (1965). VILLAINS, MAIDENS, WORST LIST

In the Libyan desert, US marines wipe out "them Ayrabs." This film, complete with treacherous, inept, and ugly Arabs, is loosely based on an incident that occurred in 1805.

Scene: Opening credits state: "The Mediterranean. The United States was at war. The Tripoli pirates had challenged our right to freedom of the seas, attacking our merchantmen and demanding tribute for safe passage... Our answer was to send warships to blockade the enemy's capitol port of Tripoli, bottling up the pirate fleet." See *Patriot Games* (1992).

• Brother vs. brother. Once upon a time, the Libyan pasha (Reed) "was friendly to the United States, but he was overthrown by his brother Yousef" (Napier). To regain his throne, the pasha agrees, albeit reluctantly, to assist marine Lieutenant O'Bannon (Payne). As the lieutenant begins recruiting Libyan "natives," he spots Countess D'Arneau (O'Hara) playing chess with the Pasha, and winning. O'Bannon is smitten.

• The marines and the pasha's "natives" plan to attack Yousef's fortress in Derna. To do so, they must trek across the desert for 30 days. The pasha's Arabs refuse to budge. Why? They want money for their services. US Sergeant Derek (Withers) questions whether the marines should trust Arabs. Quips O'Bannon, "I don't care what they look like, as long as they can fire a gun." Says the sergeant, "They'll fire a gun. The question is, which way?" Suspecting betrayal, Derek gives the Arabs only half the money, promising the rest after the battle.

• Arab as cheater. A Libyan tells the sergeant to pay for thirteen sheep. The sergeant counts only twelve, sighing, "[I must] keep my eye on them, these guys... see double."

• When Sgt. Derek is told that eight rumpled Arab women, "all wives," will travel with them, he asks, "Are you sure?" Affirms a pal, "I seen 'em sir, must be!"

• O'Bannon wants the countess to bunk with veiled, scantily-clad Arab maidens. Protests a colleague, "She's no ordinary camp follower. You can't send her back with those women. Whatever you think of her, she's a lady."

• Captain Demetrious (Da Silva) and his men appear, offering assistance. The lieutenant asks Demetrious his nationality. He boasts: "Greek... now, American!"

• The gutless pasha insists on "going back." He says the desert has no water wells. To illustrate marine toughness, O'Bannon slices his men's water bags.

• Three of Yousef's men sneak into camp, convincing the pasha to doublecross the marines, and to link up with Yousef to "fight the common enemy, [the American] infidels." The pasha's advisor asks, "Can your brother [Yousef] be trusted to keep his bargain?" Quips the pasha, "No! But then, neither can I. You merely do what's best for yourself."

• In time, the countess warns O'Bannon about the pasha's doublecross; the Arabs fail to ambush the marines and Demetrious's men. Again, the underhanded pasha switches allegiances, opting to link back up with the marines. Together, they attack Yousef's forces at Derna's fortress.

• Sergeant Derek and Demetrious shoot scores of Arabs. Note the dialogue:

Derek: Shouldn't we wait until they turn around? Don't shoot 'em in the back!
Demetrious: Why not, it's easier!
Derek: Yeah!

• The marines hoist the American flag over Derna's fortress. As the marine battle anthem accents the soundtrack, the countess and Lieutenant O'Bannon kiss.

Note: In lieu of Demetrious, why didn't the producer feature an Arab champion who assists the marines? Why not display an Arab princess, not a European countess, as the heroine? And, why not present the pasha and his men as pro-American, loyal to the marines?

Tripwire (1990), CineTel. *Terence Knox, David Warner.* CAMEOS, PALESTINIANS

Palestinians and a German terrorist vs. Americans.

Scene: A Western intelligence agent (Knox) pursues "the [world's] most dangerous terrorist," a German assassin (Warner). "Around 1969 [the German] was trained in the Middle East by forces of the Popular Front for the Liberation of Palestine."

• At a gun shop, the agent slugs "Moustaffa," one of terrorist's Palestinian cohorts. Next, the agent's aide shoots dead the Palestinian.

• A bearded Arab with an accent delivers to the German assassin cocaine worth a half million. In return for the drugs, the Arab requests "ten cases of state-of-the-art munitions."

Troma's War (1988), Troma Film. *Sean Bowen.* CAMEOS, VILLAINS

Intent on controlling the US, Arab, German, and Latino terrorists prepare to infect Americans with the AIDS virus. Several Americans crush the curs.

Scene: A tropical island. After a plane crashes, the camera displays bearded Arab terrorists wearing white burnooses. The Arabs move to "create chaos" by smuggling into the US via a "mass infiltration system," the AIDS virus. An American who survived the crash spots one of the lurking terrorists, shouting, "He looks like an Ayrab!" A fellow survivor screams, "There's another one!"

• Abruptly, a Vietnam veteran appears, crushing the mute Arab. He tosses the Arab's blood-soaked body into the woods, boasting, "You don't murder vermin, you exterminate them!"

• A shady American joins the assassins and mocks Islam, saying: "Allahu Akbar." Next, he blows a kiss, saying, "This to Allah, to Allah."

Trouble in Morocco (1937), COL. *Jack Holt.* *NS. Notes from VAR (17 March 1937). See *I Cover the War* (1937), John Wayne's serial *The Three Musketeers* (1933), and *Action in Arabia* (1944). VILLAINS

An American reporter and legionnaires kill gun-running "desert-tribes."

Summary: As an American war correspondent (Holt) is mistaken for a New York gangster, he winds up in Morocco, a member of the foreign legion. Here, the reporter/legionnaire comes across "an arms-smuggling plot along the Moroccan front." He engages in "actual combat with the desert tribes." Thanks to his heroics, marooned legionnaires escape from nasty bedouins. In the end, the outnumbered legionnaires acquire "two small armored tanks," machine-gunning the bedouin "desert-tribes."

True Colors (1991), PAR. *John Cusack, James Spader.* SP: Kevin Wade. P: Herbert Ross. CAMEOS, VILLAINS

The producer links an American swindler with Lebanese lobbying. See also *Time After Time* (1979), and *Chapter Two* (1979).

Scene: Minutes into the film, a law student without money (Cusack) tells a whopper to his friend (Spader), saying he will vacation in London. Says his surprised friend, "London! Christmas in London! That's not bad. Plum pudding and Marley's ghost." Sighs the student, "Oh, I don't know. Mostly Arabs and rain." The slur stands. Question: Would the producers allow the student to quip, instead, "Mostly Jews and rain?"

• Fast forward, years later, Capitol Hill. The graduated-from-law-school-student prepares to enter the court room. He advises his aides on how to nail a culprit who has arranged unethical "pipeline contracts." Advises the young attorney, "Hammer Standish as he starts twisting his watch... Every time he takes the Fifth, or he pulls one of those 'I can't recall,' he's twisting his watch... Same with those bullshit answers [he gave] on Lebanese lobbying. You see him twisting his watch, come down hard. He's lying to you."

True Confessions (1981), UA. *Robert DeNiro, Robert Duvall, Ed Flanders.*
SP: Joan Didion, John Finley Dunne. CAMEOS

Calculated slur?

Scene: 1940s Los Angeles. This movie is about an-up-and-coming monsignor (DeNiro) with the Roman Catholic Church, and the priest's relationship with colleagues and his detective brother (Duvall). At one point, the priest moves to convince the church's lawyer (Flanders), to accept a shady developer's contribution for a much-needed church project. The attorney balks, then finally he accepts the priest's argument, approving the deal. Beaming at his priest, the lawyer quips, "Looks like a leprechaun, thinks like an Arab."

Note: After Victor Ayoub, professor emeritus at Kenyon College, detected this one-liner, he wrote to me (24 March 1990) commenting:

> I am willing to overlook such slurs, if they come from the pen of `hacks' on the grounds that it reflects such a lack of imagination and dignity to be beneath contempt, and public censure would only give them undeserved credit. I refuse to bring my sensitivities, as well as my sensibilities, down to their level. [But] the [True Confessions] screenplay was written by Joan Didion and John Finley Dunne, neither of whom can be classified as `hacks' and both of whom belong to the mainstay of contemporary liberal-minded, literary culture. It is based on one of Dunne's novels. The movie's setting is Los Angeles in the 1940s. The moment I heard the line I reacted to it as an anachronism. The characters are part of the Irish community. I doubt that any Irishman in the 1940s would have known what an 'Arab' was to imagine that the name would fit into such a line, in that setting. On the assumption that it is in the text of the novel, the line, in that [1940s Los Angeles] setting, would have likely read as `Smiles like an elf; thinks like a Jew.' Of course, that would be a use reflecting a sentiment not allowable for a populist medium like movies... So, the chic bigotry of the liberal literary and political mainstream supplied the perfect way to retain a clever line. In effect, using a line that would have been out of place at that time, leaves no doubt that it was a calculated, manipulative, substitution of 'Arab' for 'Jew,' whether it was in the original novel or not. It should have been beneath the dignity of writers like Didion and Dunne to cheapen themselves that way.

True Lies (1994), TCF. *Arnold Schwarzenegger, Jamie Lee Curtis, Tom Arnold, Tia Carrere, Art Malik.* P, W, D: James Cameron. *True Lies*, a remake of a French film about a spy leading a double life, boasted a budget of more than $110 million. Perhaps the use of a Harrier jet and other ultra-tech devices prompted producer-writer-director James Cameron to say, "I think the nature of how we create movies is really changing now." The studio thanks for their cooperation, the US "Department of Defense" and "United States Marine Corps Aviation." PALESTINIANS, WORST LIST

Institutionalizing the Arab stereotype. Make no mistake, Cameron's *True Lies* is a slick film perpetuating sick images of Palestinians as dirty, demonic, and despicable peoples. The reel portraits are so remote from reality as to give normal viewers the willies.

Cameron presents Palestinian Muslims as fanatical kuffiyeh-clad terrorists. Stalking America, the Palestinians plant nuclear bombs, detonating an atomic bomb in the Florida Keys. Although the stale Arab-as-nuclear-terrorist image is a familiar one, *True Lies* is the first feature showing Arabs exploding a nuclear bomb inside the US. Since the thriller *Trunk to Cairo* (1966), films such as *Delta Force 3: The Killing Game* (1993),

Wrong Is Right (1982), *Operation Thunderbolt* (1977), *Wanted: Dead or Alive* (1987), *Back to the Future* (1985), *Terror in Beverly Hills* (1988), *Black Sunday* (1977), *Invasion USA* (1985), and *The Siege* (1998) have displayed detestable Arabs invading the US, trying to nuke, poison, and terrorize citizens from Miami to New York, from Indiana to Los Angeles. Also, reel Arabs try to nuke Tel Aviv. Cameron labels his Palestinian terrorist group,"Crimson Jihad." Crimson, meaning red, implies blood. The root of "crimson," states the Oxford dictionary, comes from the Arabic language. Yet, Cameron misuses the word, "jihad," wrongly implying that jihad means violence.

Scene: In Switzerland, US special agent Harry (Schwarzenegger) attends a posh· party, complete with "boring [Arab] oil billionaires." Harry's mission is to ascertain the identities of villains transporting nuclear weapons. Stealthily, Harry taps into a computer; the screen displays Arabic writing. Arab thugs arrive, but fail to thwart Harry's efforts.

• Harry moves to prevent the "dirty" Crimson Jihad from blowing up American cities. The extremist Palestinian group has plenty of connections "in this country." Jihad, which smuggles nuclear weapons "out of a former Soviet country," Kazakhstan, issues a warning: Unless the US government withdraws its troops from Arab nations, they'll detonate, one-by-one, six nuclear weapons over American cities.

• Thinking his wife, Helen (Curtis), is having an affair, Harry becomes depressed. To help cheer Harry, his agent partner, Gib (Arnold), arrives, exclaiming, "We're gonna catch some terrorists and we're gonna beat the hell out of 'em. And you'll feel a lot better." Gib's message is frighteningly clear: Feel gloomy? Pulverize an Arab!

• Harry and Gib go to work; they flip though mug shots of unshaven men with Arab names. Abruptly, TV newscasters warn citizens: Arabs are blowing up cars and killing innocents. Viewers are told, "They [the Arabs] can go anywhere in the United States. There's nothing, no one to stop them."

• Arabs function as mad murdering machines and as blundering dunces, nothing much in between. Trying to launch a missile, the Palestinians kill one of their own. When a bumbling terrorist tries to videotape Jihad's leader, Aziz·(Malik), the camera's battery goes kaput. Aziz, who is tagged "sand-spider," shouts, "Get another one, you moron." When Harry and Gib spot Arab assassins in Washington, DC, they quip, "Beavis and Butt-head." Cut to Arabs trying to shoot Harry; they shoot each other. A truck driver mistakenly runs over a fellow Arab.

• In the restroom, Harry punches out several Palestinians. Then, he stuffs one Arab's face inside the urinal. Cut to Harry atop a horse, pursuing an Arab Muslim terrorist through a Marriott hotel. The script originally called for Harry to "chase a gang of Islamic terrorists on horseback through the Reflecting Pool near the Washington monument." The proposed scene, however, was rejected by the National Park Service. Seeking to overturn the park service's decision, the studio appealed to Jack Valenti. Even Arnold Schwarzenegger got into the act. He called on his brother-in-law, Sargent Shriver, who then appealed "directly to Interior Secretary Bruce Babbit. "Sorry," said Babbit, "no horses permitted in the pool."[175]

• Arabs abuse women. Jihad's leader, Aziz, smacks the villainess Juno (Carrere), calling her a "whore [and] sharmoota, stupid bitch." Later, in a hotel elevator, Aziz nabs and holds hostage, an attractive African-American woman.

• Near the Florida Keys. The Palestinians take two prisoners: Harry and his wife,

Helen. The Arabs gather round some nuclear warheads, setting one to explode. If Harry fails to escape in time to warn Floridians, the bomb will detonate—"two million people will die."

• To the rescue, Helen. She grabs an Uzi and slugs Palestinians. Abruptly the Uzi drops from her hands. In slow motion, the Uzi descends down the steps, firing away.

• After Harry eludes Jihad's Arabs, he alerts Floridians in the nick of time. Cut to Jihad's nuclear bomb exploding far, far, far away! No one is injured.

• Harry receives official orders to extinguish Jihad's Arabs—"Okay marines, it's time to kick [Arab] ass." This line is disturbingly familiar. Movies such as *Navy SEALs* (1990), *Iron Eagle* (1986), *The Delta Force* (1986), and *Death before Dishonor* (1987), as well as others, show members of the US Navy, Air Force, Army, and Marines kicking "Arab ass."

• Moving to escape, Palestinians drive a van across a damaged bridge. Helen manages to free herself from the Palestinians. Suddenly, the speeding van tatters over the bridge's edge, killing the Arabs. The audience watching the film with me, roared.

• Inside a hotel, scores of Palestinian bodies litter a room.

• Amazingly, Aziz finds and holds hostage Harry's son. Furious, Harry flies off in a jet and attaches the villain to a missile. Harry launches the Palestinian into space.

• Final frames emulate the opening scene, "a ballroom laden with opulence and grandeur." But this time, writes critic Vicki Roland,

> the elite in attendance are Americans, Asians, Africans, French-speaking people, and no Arabs; [emphasis added] no dark, unshaven men wearing kuffiyehs. The film's message is clear: When the world is rid of Arabs, we will at last be safe.[177]

Dialogue: Helen asks Harry, "Have you ever killed anyone?" Quips Harry, "Yeah, but they were all bad." Throughout, Arab "terrorists" spout out "Allahu Akbar" (God is Great) and "Bismallah" (in the name of God). And, cowardly Palestinians scream, "Yallah, Yallah!" (Hurry, Hurry!).

Note: Why does a respected international movie star such as Arnold Schwarzenegger slaughter Arabs as an exterminator swats flies? After watching Schwarzenegger dispatch upwards of 64 Palestinians, I stopped counting. Did the actor ever pause to consider this film's impact on Arab-Americans, their families? As soon as the film was released, Schwarzenegger appeared on television with CBS-TV's Paula Zahn, telling her, "The most important thing to me is my family." He explained that as a concerned parent, he carefully monitors what films his three young children may or may not see. When asked by Zahn whether he'll take them to see *True Lies*, he responded, "When they grow up, they can see it." Following her interview, Zahn smiled, saying, "Well, *True Lies*, really, was great fun!" (25 July 1994).

• Sadly, moviemakers, audiences, and film critics applauded *True Lies'* status quo stereotypes. Explains Schwarzenegger, as a guest on CBS: This Morning, "So many people are excited about it... and what made me really happy with the film were the reviews, that the critics were one hundred percent behind this movie... the *New York Times*, to the *Wall Street Journal, Newsweek, People* magazine" (7 July 1994). Many critics gave *True Lies* a "thumbs up." "A Heck of a Ride" said *Good Morning America's* Joel Siegel; "There's something for everybody," wrote Richard Corliss of *Time*. Sighed CBS-TV's Gene Siskel, "The terrorists are totally boring." And, "He [Schwarzenegger] just might as well be working in a carnival, knocking off stuff with a BB gun!" Syndicated columnist Russell Baker, however, was not enthused, writing, "Schwarzenegger... slaughters multitudes for a laugh... the murdered villains are Arabs, apparently the last people except Episcopalians whom Hollywood feels free to offend en masse." Watching "two hours" of the kind of "violence," says Baker, "is vulgar, immoral and disgusting."[178] Point out Don Bustany and Salam Al-Marayati in their *Los Angeles Times* "Counterpunch" essay,

> [If Schwarzenegger] wore jeans instead of a tux, carried a six-gun instead of a Beretta, rode a palomino instead of a Harrier jet, and killed 'Redskins' wearing feathers instead of 'brown skins' wearing beards (and kuffiyehs), we'd have a classic and racist cowboy and Indian movie.[179]

Outside a Washington, DC, movie theater, marchers protested *True Lies.* They carried placards stating: "Hasta La Vista Fairness," "Reel Arabs are not Real Arabs," and "Open Your Eyes and Terminate the Lies." Yet, criticism, protests, and declarations did not adversely effect ticket sales. *True Lies* topped box office charts, pulling in $62 million in just two weeks. Because of the movie's striptease, performed by Jamie Lee Curtis, some women's groups thought the film was sexist. Not so, says Tammy Bruce, president of the National Organization for Women's Los Angeles chapter: "Compared to the Arabs, women come off relatively well in this one."[180]

• Troubled with *True Lies* stereotypical images, radio personality Casey Kasem shared with me a copy of his 3 August 1994 letter that he sent to key individuals associated with the film, such as James Cameron and Arnold Schwarzenegger. No one responded to Kasem's missive. In his letters, Kasem writes, "In the future, I hope you'll aim for balance in your depictions... I presume it was inadvertent or unintended racism, but believe it: that's what it was—racism." Kasem said *True Lies* was "an insult to anyone's intelligence. We're trying to make people more sensitive to the fact that when you vilify one group, you vilify all groups."

• FOX brought in and paid the Humane Society to oversee *True Lies'* treatment of animals. The studio also invited critics to pre-release showings. Yet, the studio refused to consult with or to meet with America's Arab and Muslim specialists. Nor were the specialists allowed to attend pre-release showings.

• Soon after *True Lies* debuted, the studio made a feeble attempt to placate concerned viewers. They added to the movie, this disclaimer: "This film is a work of fiction and does not represent the actions or beliefs of a particular culture or religion." Fox spokeswoman Andrea Jaffe states in VAR that the disclaimer "cost us some money, and required an extra day's work on the picture" (1 July 1994). The disclaimer appears after the movie, at the very tail end of the credit roll. I was the only one who remained in the movie theater to read it. Some say disclaimers are more effective when placed as the film begins. But I believe, regardless of whether disclaimers appear at the beginning or end of a movie, they are 100 percent worthless. Explains my friend and colleague, Dr. Carlos Cortés:

> Prior to the 1977 network TV showing of The Godfather Saga (a revised and expanded version of two films, The Godfather (1972), and The Godfather: Part II (1974), a solemn voice intoned the following words as they appeared on screen: 'The Godfather is a fictional account of the activities of a small group of ruthless criminals. It would be erroneous and unfair to suggest that they are representative of any group.' This disclaimer regarding Italian-Americans became a model for future disclaimers. Modified disclaimers began appearing in films stereotyping Cuban-Americans and Chinese-Americans, e.g., Scarface

(1983) and Year of the Dragon (1985). While such words could do little to mitigate the impact of these movie textbookswrites (in fact, howls of laughter in movie theaters during the disclaimers suggest the warnings may have done more harm than good), the disclaimers did serve as an admission that feature films do, in fact, teach and influence learning about ethnicity and ethnic groups."[181]

• Ignoring the Arab proverb, "Your freedom ends when it trespasses on the freedom of others," director James Cameron tars a whole people. He pleads not guilty to the charge that *True Lies* vilifies Arabs, quipping, "I just needed some convenient villains."[182] "It could [have been] anybody. I could have picked Irish terrorists." Yet, Cameron goes on to say that anyone who resorts to terrorism, regardless of their ethnic or religious background, is morally wrong, and therefore, Arabs are fair game as bad guys in any film.[183] Reporter Nicci Gerrard asked Jamie Lee Curtis whether she felt the film was objectionable. Said the actress, "It's just a funny film. It's funny. It has no ramifications for me. It's funny, funny, just funny."[184]

• Movie credits thank for their cooperation, the "Mayor of Washington, DC," "Department of Defense," and "United States Marine Corps Aviation." Question: Does the cooperation of the mayor and the US military mean they concur with Cameron's statement that this film "is exactly like a military maneuver"?

• Some viewers recognize that movies help shape attitudes. For example, in the fall of 1993, hate crimes were on the rise against Arab and Muslim Americans. In fact, the town of Natchez, Mississippi, was planning a "National Security Exercise Day," featuring a mock terrorist attack by a fictitious group called "Arabs against Americans." The military exercise was planned statewide; Natchez's directive came directly from the Mississippi State Emergency Management Agency. Later, to their credit, Natchez's mayor and the Agency director changed the name of the mock terrorist group to "Anyone against America." Also, they sent a letter-of-apology to the American-Arab Anti-Discrimination Committee (ADC).[185]

Trunk to Cairo (1966), A Menachem Golan Prod. P, D: Menachem

Golan. Audie Murphy, George Sanders, Marianne Koch, Gila Almago, Eytan Priver. Made in Israel. Completed in 1966, released in the US by AI in 1967. EGYPTIANS

Israeli producer Golan shows Americans, Germans, and Israelis overpowering and killing Egypt's "atomic" terrorists. Islam is presented as a hateful and violent religion.

Scene: Near an Egyptian beach, a car explodes killing a German couple. Cut to the murders—a smiling Egyptian and his three cohorts. Later, Israelis are blamed for the killings.

• Cairo's International Airport. Producer Golan frames the airport in a pre-aviation era, revealing a horse and buggy, and one bus, even though in reality, modern taxis are available.

• Traveling to Cairo is US secret agent Mike Merrick (Murphy). The Israelis enlist Merrick's help; they need to ascertain why they are being framed for murdering Germans. Cut to Egyptian heavies trying to bump off Merrick.

• A Cairo nightclub features bellydancers and Egypt's real radio and television vocalist, Yasmin (Almago). Viewers are lead to believe lovely Yasmin is an Egyptian heroine. Not so. Yasmin works with Israeli intelligence.

• Inside a desert factory, Professor Schlieben (Sanders) directs German scientists to make missiles capable of carrying "atomic warheads." When Merrick meets Schlieben, he warns, "Capped with a nuclear warhead, these missiles could wipe a small country right off the map."

• Schlieben's daughter, Helga (Koch), fears that once the weapons are operational, the Egyptians may launch them. "Let them make it themselves," she says. Her father says, "They can't. They're too backward, isn't that right?" Nods Merrick, "Oh yes, that's right, professor."

• On learning Yasmin is an Israeli agent, an Egyptian officer shoots her. The dying Yasmin tells Merrick, "[I] couldn't shoot first." But Merrick has no qualms about firing first; he shoots more than fourteen Egyptians.

• In Rome, Helga convinces her father to terminate the missile project. He agrees, saying several times, "I will never go back to Egypt. "In the end, though the German scientist, Schlieben, directed the missile project, the Israelis pardon him. Merrick and Helga fall in love.

Finis: Cut to the destroyed missile plant; scores of dead Egyptians litter the desert.

Treatment of Islam: Even in the mid-60s, producers such as Golan presented Muslim leaders as hateful, hypocritical anti-American beings. For example, Golan shows Egyptian soldiers tracking Merrick; the American seeks sanctuary in a mosque. Inside, he meets Imam Mohammad, asking, "We [you, me, the Israelis] want the same things, don't we? Who are you, anyway?" Feigning friendship, the imam says, "Holy Islam Freedom Fighters. The Egyptians have assassinated our leaders in Baghdad; they enslaved our brothers in Syria; they used gas against our people in Yemen and they won't hesitate to use atomic weapons." Interestingly, no Arab nation possesses atomic bombs; the only country in the region armed with nuclear weapons is Israel. Continues the imam, "We, the Holy members of Islam must prevent that... May the blessings of Allah be unto thee, and peace be on your soul." Suddenly, the imam's voice and behavior alters. He directs fellow Muslims, "Please accompany the gentleman to the roof. Let him die like a friend. No pain, for he's our friend. We, Arab patriots, hate Arab dictators, hate German scientists, hate Israeli spies." Says Merrick, "But I'm an American." Shouts the imam: "And we hate Americans above all!" As the imam prays, the camera pans to hundreds of weapons. Posing as an Arab woman, Merrick escapes from the mosque, grumbling, "Allah be praised."

Tuareg, The Desert Warrior (1984), ASPA Productions. *Mark Harmon.* Filmed in Israel, Spain, and Italy. VILLAINS, SHEIKHS

Arab vs. Arab.

Scene: The desert nation of "Aramy." Says Tuareg, "Hospitality is the first commandment of the Tuareg the first law of the desert." Abruptly, Aramy's soldiers violate the "law," abducting Tuareg's guests. Enraged, Tuareg tracks and kills the Arabs.

• Aramy's corrupt sheikh dispatches fatigue-clad soldiers to assassinate Tuareg; they fail. More soldiers begin trekking through the desert in cars and jeeps; Tuareg rides a camel.

• Only after Tuareg brings down about twelve Arab soldiers, is he captured.

• Aramy's military stronghold. Soldiers torture Tuareg; but not for long. The near-dead warrior musters ample fury and slays the sheikh's men. Single-handedly, he blows up the base.

• The clad-in-black Tuareg is as adept with a sword as he is with a rifle. Arabs challenging him die.

• The victory celebration. Though Tuareg could easily terminate Aramy's base sheikh, he withdraws. To him, such a violent act would be dishonorable. Bewildered by Tuareg's compassion, the over-wrought sheikh suddenly clasps his aching bosom and dies.

• Tuareg returns to his desert abode; his wife and son greet him.

20,000 Leagues under the Sea (1916), UNI. *Allan Holubar, Jane Gail.* Silent.

My analysis of this non-Arab film illustrates that because so many movies vilify Arabs, some Arab-Americans families are desperate, yearning to discover and view a film with their children that displays heroic screen Arabs.

In August 1999, my friend, Dr. Samir Farra of Richmond Hills, Georgia, was at home, watching on television, the silent 1916 film version of the classic *20,000 Leagues under the Sea*. Afterwards, Samir phoned me, excitedly boasting that he, his wife, and two teenage daughters saw "courageous Arabs. It was terrific, terrific. Do you know about this film? Can you get it?" he asked. Instantly, I purchased the movie. While viewing the film, I, like Samir, was excited, thinking the protagonists were Arabs from Arabia. Surprise. During the final frames, the on-screen subtitles reveal the protagonists are Indians from India. When I told Samir, he sighed, "I must have walked out of the room, just when those subtitles came up."

Viewers such as Samir may perceive Indians as Arabs because movie-land offers stereotypical "seen one, seen 'em all" portraits of the Near and Middle East "Other." After all, *20,000 Leagues under the Sea* displays familiar Mideast settings and costumes. The film's protagonist, a bearded prince, wears a turban and pointed shoes. The camera displays a souk, complete with goats, sheep, and a snake charmer, plus an Arabian Nights castle complete with a bathing pool, ornate pillows, and feather fans. And, the film reveres Islam. When the prince links up with his missing daughter he says, "Allah be praised; it is my child... I prayed to Allah."

Refreshingly, Indians appear as bright, courageous victims. And, instead of showing a coarse dark-complexioned "Other" moving to seduce the Western blonde, the movie displays an uncouth Western drunkard intent on raping an Indian princess. To spare her daughter from watching the Western man take her, the princess kills herself.

24 Hours to Kill (1966), SA. *Lex Barker, Mickey Rooney, Walter Slezak, Michael Medwin, Helga Sommerfield, Hans Clarin, Shakib Khouri.* Filmed in Lebanon.

Nadia Gemal, the noted Lebanese dancer who entertained audiences at Beirut's Phonecia Hotel for decades, appears momentarily as Mimi, "a dancer with a seventeen-jewel movement." VILLAINS

Lebanese smugglers terminate an American swindler.

Scene: When a Transcontinental plane encounters engine problems, an elderly Arab woman panics and seizes the pilot, Jamie (Barker). Yet, Jamie manages to safely land the plane in Beirut. An unhappy US crewman asks, "Why did you bring me to this dump?"

• In Beirut, Malouf's (Slezak) Lebanese gold smugglers, called "carpetbaggers," toss a fellow Arab in front of a speeding truck. Why? Because he failed to nab Norman Jones

(Rooney), the plane's US purser. Several years ago Jones ran off with Malouf's gold. Barks Malouf, "I've lost face, and that I will not tolerate."

• Malouf's Lebanese move to kidnap Louise (Sommerfield), a Transcontinental flight attendant. They intend to exchange Louise for Jones. Jamie and his pal Tommy (Medwin) foil their attempt. Jamie confronts Jones, who says, "They're trying to kill me." Thinking he is guiltless, Jamie says, "Jones doesn't deserve a knife in the back."

• Though the Lebanese botch several kidnapping attempts, Jones is finally nabbed. Malouf slaps Jones' face, saying, "Welcome to Beirut," then demands the purser return the gold; Jones refuses.

• As the fez-wearing Malouf is tagged "a collector of beauty," the camera reveals an attractive blonde driving his Rolls Royce. In the back seat, a lovely redhead pours him champagne. But Malouf never makes a move on his beauties—not once.

• Malouf boasts that years ago his grandfather set up the smuggling firm. "He used camels to run hashish. I moved onto gold and use the national airlines, transporting gold from Hong Kong to India."

• After Malouf's men gag Jones, one fatally knifes the purser in the gut.

Treatment of Islam: When Malouf learns Jones is dead, he sighs, "Allah disposes... As we say in the East, man proposes, Allah disposes." Cut to the repaired Transcontinental plane departing Beirut.

Note: Hollywood films displaying ugly Arab stereotypes receive assistance from some Arab governments and businesses. For example, with *24 Hours to Kill*, the credits thank the "Lebanese Tourist Office [and] Middle East Airlines."

Two Arabian Knights (1927), The Caddo Company. Silent. *William Boyd, Mary Astor, Boris Karloff*. D: Lewis Milestone. *NS. Notes from NYT (24 October 1927). VILLAINS

Turks as Arabs. Two American soldiers bring down robed villains.

Summary: In this WWI romantic comedy, two GIs "scale walls, invading a Bey's palace somewhere in Turkey." First, the soldiers save the heroine, overpowering the Bey's soldiers. Next, "the Americans [escape by] helping themselves to the white cloaks of their victims."

Note: In 1929, at the first-ever Academy Awards ceremony, Lewis Milestone was awarded an Oscar for his direction of *Two Arabian Knights*.

Two Nights with Cleopatra (1954), Rosa Film. Italian. *Alberto Sordi, Sophia Loren*. EGYPTIANS

This racy Italian comedy features a 19-year-old Sophia Loren in a dual role, portraying a lusty Cleopatra and a blonde slave girl.

Scene: To cure her insomnia, the vivacious Queen Cleopatra (Loren) beds a different suitor, nightly. To uphold her reputation, her lovers are poisoned soon afterward.

• The camera projects typical reel settings, e.g., the dungeon, throne room, and bathing pool. The slave markets are filled with harem maidens; auctioneers hawk the women, barking, "Slaves for sale"; "Fresh slaves."

• No Egyptian–Roman battles, here. Though some Egyptian officers and Cleopatra's advisor conspire to terminate the queen, they fail.

• Loren goes skinny dipping in the palace pool.

Two Women (1960), EMB. Italian, with subtitles. *Sophia Loren, Eleanora Brown.* D: Vittorio De Sica. SP: De Sica, Cesare Zavattini. Loren received an Academy Award for her performance. CAMEOS, VILLAINS

WWII Italy. An Italian mother, Cesira (Loren), and Rosetta (Brown), her twelve-year old daughter, seek shelter inside a bombed-out church. Abruptly, the women are brutally raped; not by the Nazis and not by the Allies, but by a howling horde of Moroccan troops.

Scene: War-torn Italy. Aware the Allies are arriving, Cesira and Rosetta walk toward Rome. Jeeps filled with Moroccan soldiers drive pass them. "I wonder who they are?" asks Cesira. "They're Allies, mama," explains Rosetta.

• The women pause to rest "in a holy church." Suddenly, threatening shadows of Moroccans fill the frame. Rosetta screams, "Mama!" The Moroccans grab and rape Rosetta; then they rape Cesira. When Cesira tries to resist, a Moroccan slams her head to the church floor.

• Later, an Italian truck driver gives the battered women a lift, telling them, "At Valecorsa this morning they [the Moroccans] raped half the village."

Note: Though the rape may reflect the film's theme—the demise of morality, innocence, and faith—why are Moroccans singled out as violators of humankind?

• Omitted from the scenario is this fact: From November 1943 through August 1944, the 2nd Moroccan Division and the 3rd Algerian Division [beginning January 1944] distinguished themselves in battle, fighting Axis forces in Italy.[186] Historian J. Lee Ready writes of Moroccan heroics: "[During WWII,] Moroccans had fought in most of France's campaign of the war and had proven themselves to be superb soldiers in every affair... When France declared war on Germany in 1939 many Moroccans volunteered, serving in their own units with French officers." In 1940, when Germany invaded Belgium, Moroccan troops and French forces went north to help repel the invader. Ready continues, "Other Moroccan troops were in central France when the Germans attacked that region on 5 June." And, "on the 22nd it was all over. About 15,000 Moroccans had been killed or captured." ["The Moroccans had been the first allied troops to liberate a department of France."] In November 1942, when US forces landed on Moroccan beaches, the Moroccans joined the Americans, and together, they moved "to take Tunisia from a German-Italian army." After the Allies invaded Italy [3 September], they "needed help." Troops with the "4th Moroccan division" linked up with anti-German forces and helped capture "three mountains in three weeks. On 6 January 1945 in deep snow the 4th Moroccan Division beat back a German attack."[187]

Tyrant of Lydia against the Son of Hercules (1963), F.I.A. An Italian-French production, dubbed in English. *Gordon Scott.* CAMEOS, VILLAINS

Fourth Century, BC. Hercules' son crushes bedouin slavers.

Scene: Bedouins-for-hire armed with knives appear from behind bushes and attack the heroine, "Princess Cory," and her white-robed maidens. To the rescue, the son of Hercules (Scott). He stabs about twelve bedouins, warning the princess, there are "many robbers in these hills."

• Money-grubbing bedouins, armed with knives and bows and arrows, intend "to kill the country's [Lydia's] ambassadors." The bedouin "archers" strike the "ambassadors, swooping down on them like vultures." Shouts the bedouin leader, "Don't stop until everyone is dead." Later, the aide to the leader of the bedouins, kills him.

• Mistakenly thinking that Princess Cory is "a slave girl running away from her master," a greedy bedouin says, "Let's take her with us. The merchant will pay well for her."

• The slave market; Arab music underscores the action. A black-robed bedouin, brandishing a whip, delivers the princess and her maidens to the auctioneer, a "Phoenician merchant." Cut to a scruffy bedouin examining one of the enslaved women. He barks, "I want to see the soles of her feet, if they're flat-footed you can't get 'em work!" Abruptly, a conspirator appears, whisking off the princess.

Finis: In time, Alexander the Great's army appears, bringing down those intent on crushing him. Princess Cory and the son of Hercules rule.

Note: No Arabs surface in the Italian-French film *The Beast of Babylon against the Son of Hercules* (1964), a.k.a. *Goliath, King of the Slaves*. In the 1964 film, actor Gordon Scott appears, again, as the son of Hercules, the "mightiest of mortal men," righting wrongs. Villains and heroes don medieval costumes: huge helmets and armored breast plates.

Under Siege 2: Dark Territory (1995), WB. *Steven Seagal, Eric Bogosian.* CAMEOS, VILLAINS

Ex-navy SEAL Casey Ryback (Seagal) vs. non-Arab mercenaries. Yet, the mercenaries are funded by "Mideast [desert] investors."

Scene: "Million-dollar-mercenaries" hijack a passenger train en route to Los Angeles. Aboard the train, the camera shows ex-Pentagon employee Dane (Bogosian) and his cohorts securing "satellite transmission equipment," capable of releasing weapons of mass destruction. "God, Allah, and the winds willing," Dane intends to decimate "Washington and the eastern seaboard as well."

• A cohort tells Dane, "We have our investors on the line." The computer screen reveals the word, "MIDEAST." Dane communicates with his Mideast backers, telling them, "Gentlemen, how's the weather out there? Sunny and sandy I hope." Adding, "[Now it's] demonstration time." Dane acts. Cut to his computer screen revealing a Chinese "chemical weapons plant." The plant explodes; thousands die.

• One of Dane's Arab "customers" requests "a small personal favor," asking Dane to "blow up an airplane." Dane balks; advises a cohort, "He says he'll pay us an additional hundred million dollars." Smiling, Dane says, "Tell him his ex-wife is history as soon as the money is deposited in our account." Promptly, Dane's Arab customer deposits the money. Cut to the computer screen, revealing the jet carrying the Arab's ex-wife. "Boom," says Dane. The plane explodes.

• Washington, DC's War Room. Explains a navy officer, "[Dane's terrorists have] an extensive network of contacts: North Korea, here in the States, in particular in the Middle East." These terrorists may be able to blow up Washington, DC, he warns; "[they] have the money and the moxie to pull it off."

Note: See *Crash Dive* (1996). Here, Eastern European terrorists move to blow up New York City. When the terrorists take over a American nuclear submarine, an ex-navy SEAL (Michael Dudikoff) moves to stop them. Cut to an anxious US admiral. Note the dialogue, stating that Middle East villains are masterminding the operation.:

Adm: What da ya got from Interpol on these people?

Aide: They're all part of a movement, tied to a radical Middle Eastern terrorist group, a well-funded, organized Op. Their M.O. isn't money, it's domination of the free world, by any means necessary. They'd use a nuclear bomb without a second thought.

Adm: So they plan to nuke us, whether we pay them or not.

Aide: I'm afraid that's what we must assume.

Under Two Flags (1912). Silent. *William Garwood.* *NS.

Under Two Flags (1916), FOX. Silent. *Theda Bara.* *NS.

Under Two Flags (1922), Universal–Jewel. Silent. *Priscilla Dean, James Kirkwood.* *NS. Notes from De Witt Bodeen in MAG (1169-71), relating only to the 1922 version. MAIDENS, SHEIKHS

Summary: British heroics in Algiers. Arabs vs. Arabs, vs. legionnaires. Based on the 1867 novel *Under Two Flags,* by Ouida (pseudonym of Louise De la Ramee). As soon as Victor (Kirkwood), an English nobleman, joins the French Foreign Legion, the shady "Sheik Ben Ali Hammed" (Davidson) sets him up for a crime he did not commit. Thus, Victor is jailed and sentenced to die. Appearing is the regiment's "mascot," Cigarette (Dean), a "loveable, gutsy" half-Arab, half-French maiden. When she finds out the Hammad framed Victor, she rides ride "like the wild wind," saving the Englishman from "the firing squad." She also prevents Hammed from destroying "the city of Algiers." Hammed and his cohorts pursue Cigarette. They, in turn, are chased by "the French Cavalry." Arriving at the fort, Cigarette "rushes to Victor as the order `Fire' is given." Tossing herself in front of her beau, "she takes the bullets" meant for him. Cigarette "dies with his kiss upon her lips." The cavalry apprehends Hammed and company.

Note: A familiar theme: An Arab woman rides across the desert and saves the legion regiment from warring Arabs, sacrificing her life to save the Westerner she loves.

Under Two Flags (1936), TCF. *Ronald Coleman, Claudette Colbert, Rosalind Russell, Onslow Stevens, Francis McDonald.* See *The Four Feathers* (1977), *Outpost in Morocco* (1949). MAIDENS, VILLAINS, SHEIKHS

Arabs vs. Arabs, vs. legionnaires.

Scene: The desert is labeled, "land of eternal mystery, primitive, barbaric." The camera reveals barking dogs, snake charmers, sleeping Arab hagglers, and women carrying water jugs. Goes this scenario, Algeria's only link to the world is "the camel train."

• Seeing an unkempt Arab leer at Lady Venetia (Russell), legionnaire Victor (Coleman) warns the lady, "Just a moment, better give me your jewelry." Quips another legionnaire, "Turn your back for one minute and they'll swindle you."

• Inside the legion fort, a formal dance. Westerners don tuxedos and gowns, ugly Arabs peer in from outside.

• A legionnaire describes Arab torture. He saw his two comrades buried in the sand up to their necks. "Bare heads, sun, water out of reach, tortured, poor devils. They cut 'em to bits," he says. Affirms Cigarette (Colbert), the French-Algerian cafe hostess, "I even shot them so the Arabs could not take them alive."

• The pro-British Sheikh Husson (McDonald) is killed by the rebel, Sidi-Ben Youssiff (Stevens). As a result, legionnaires fear the "tribes will unite, and go the other way to join the rebels." Says one, "[This is] a gruesome way to declare war."

• The legion oath is, "All for one, one for all." Inside the fort, this plaque: "V Battalion massacred on this spot, 1870." Cut to about twenty nearly-out-of-ammunition legionnaires. They hold off thousands of screaming bedouins. Trying to draw "the battalion into a trap," bedouins pop up from behind sand dunes, circle the fort and fire.

• Cigarette fails to capture Victor, the English hero; she is shot leading French troops against the bedouins. Citing her bravery a Legion officer intones, "She prevented the revolt of all the Arab tribes."

• Though Sergeant Victor and Sidi-Ben Youssiff studied at Oxford together, "[the] old classmates meet in the heart of the desert as enemies." Abruptly, Victor crushes Youssiff. Reinforcements arrive, routing the charging bedouins.

• In the end, Victor unites with Lady Venetia.

Underground Aces (1980), Filmways. *Samuel Z. Arkoff, Melanie Griffith, Frank Gorshin, Audrey Landers, Randy Brooks, Dirk Benedict, Kario Salem, Robert Hegyes, Sid Haig.* SHEIKHS

A young sheikh weds the American heroine; oily Arabs are ridiculed.

Scene: Appearing at an exclusive Beverly Hills Hotel is Sheikh Yamani (Salem) and his mute bodyguards. The hotel parking lot attendant, Chico (Hegyes), notices that the young sheikh is attracted to a lovely blonde, Ann (Landers). Chico decides to aid the shy ruler.

• Chico and his fellow attendants, Ali (Brooks) and Pete (Benedict), function as Yamani's tutors. They teach him how to shave, then dress the Arab in Western garb. Yamani poses as Bernie, an attendant. When asked why his bearded mute guard, Fouad (Haig), always looks downward, the sheikh says: "It is forbidden for Fouad to look upon my countenance."

• Yamani balks at asking Ann for a date, offering as an excuse this stereotypical tale: "Well, it's a lot different where I come from," he says. "You see, in my country, my father rode into my mother's house on a spirited horse and stole her from her betrothed. Yes, there was a bloody battle, her brothers against my father's brothers. Two deaths."

• Posing as an Arab Muslim, Chico feigns praying, speaking gibberish. Cut to some businessmen imitating Chico's garbled murmurings. Next, Fouad and Chico don Arab garb and drive off in Yamani's Cadillac. They intend to procure a prostitute for a non-Arab hotel guest. When two hookers spot them, they yell, "You rag head faggot! Hey, go play with your camel."

• Suddenly, a pimp appears clad in cowboy garb. He calls the Arab-clad duo, "rich bastards," adding, "You know what I hate is people who make me wait. And I'm waiting every damn day at that gas pump. I'm hurtin', America's hurtin'. We're spending so much damn money at your gas pumps we ain't got nothin' left to get down with." He shouts, "No gas, no ass!" Joining in are the pimp's three cowgirls. They too, chant: "No gas, no ass."

• Yamani drives off in his limo, crashing immediately. This sheikh cannot drive; "[he] always had a chauffeur."

• Ann falls for Yamani. Yet, she decides to marry a graduate of Harvard, a man insisting she be a "virgin." Hmm, usually a reel Arab initiates the "virgin" request.

• Alone with Ann, Yamani asks, "Do you love me?" "Yes," she whispers. They kiss.

• A hotel party. Fouad thrusts his saber into a large round ball, angering the hotel manager. He fires Chico and all the attendants. Yamani intervenes, telling the manager, "I will do whatever is necessary to see that my friends, all of them, will retain their jobs." The sheikh buys the hotel. Chico, Pete and the guests cheer.

• The wedding ceremony. Ann hesitates saying "I do" to the Harvard man. Chico and cronies hit the fire alarm. All but Ann rush off. Suddenly, Yamani appears riding a stallion. He embraces joyous Ann; they ride off to the beach.

• Two women spot Fouad. Whispering "oil" they whisk him away.

The Undying Flame (1917), a.k.a. The Severed Scarabs and the Scarabacus, PAR. Silent. *Madame Olga Petrova, Edwin Mordant, Herbert Evans, Mahlon Hamilton.* *NS. Notes from AFIC. EGYPTIANS

A tyrannical Egyptian pharaoh. Everlasting love triumphs.

Summary: An Egyptian princess (Petrova) falls in love with a Shepherd youth (Hamilton). Declaring eternal devotion, they break a scarab. Each keeps a broken half, pledging "their souls will be reunited in death." But an evil pharaoh (Mordant) insists the princess wed the temple architect (Evans). The pharaoh nabs and buries the Shepherd boy, alive.

Flash forward, a British desert garrison. British Captain Harry Paget declares his love to Grace Leslie, the commander's daughter. Alone in the desert, the couple sees that "each possesses a piece of the broken scarab."

The Unfaithful Odalisque (1903), AM&B. Silent Short. Camera: Arthur Marvin. *NS. Notes from AFIC. SHEIKHS, MAIDENS

As early as 1903, screen sheikhs enslaved and abused women.

Summary: The "Harem." Here, a woman dressed in Arab garb reclines on a sofa, fanning herself "next to a palm tree." An angry "turbaned" Arab potentate appears, "accusing her of some action she denies." The sultan summons a "Nubian slave" to whip the woman. Grasping a "cat-o'-nine-tails," the slave lashes the maiden. Next, the potentate vigorously whips her.

Note: Similar images surface nearly a century earlier in George Byron's 1813 Oriental story, *The Giaour, A Fragment of a Turkish Tale.* Byron writes of a Christian "unbeliever," a young Venetian male, who avenges the death of his sweetheart, "a female slave... locked in the grip of Islamic despotism." A "vile Musselman" throws the maiden "into the sea." And, interestingly, *Father Bombo's Pilgrimage to Mecca* (1770) by Hugh H. Brackenridge and Philip Freneau is considered to be "the first American novel."[186]

The Unholy Garden (1931), Samuel Goldwyn. *Ronald Colman, Fay Wray.* *NS. Notes from NYT. Based on a story by Ben Hecht and Charles MacArthur. CAMEOS, MAIDENS

Summary: The action occurs in "Orage, in the Sahara, where murderers and thieves feel that they are in sanctuary from the law." Appearing as a "Native dancer," the actress, "Nadja."

The Unknown (1915), PAR. Silent. *Richard Farquhar, Dorothy Davenport.* D: George Melford. VILLAINS, CAMEOS

The first legionnaires-kill-bedouins film.

Scene: In Sidi Bel Abbes, Algeria, two British legionnaires court the American heroine.

• Initial frames state: "The Foreign Legion in Algeria is a sanctuary where men who have met misfortune or disgrace may redeem their past by bravery and honorable service." In this case, "honorable service" means heroic legionnaires will terminate evil bedouins.

• Declares the heroine, Nancy Preston (Davenport): "I'm crazy to see an Arabian dance hall." Nancy tips a local guide and rushes off to a cafe. See *The Sheik* (1921). Inside the only-men-are-allowed-hall, are Arab patrons, musicians, and one Englishman, Lou Tellegen (Farquhar). Also present is lovely Ourida, the local dancer; she wears a white-laced dress.

• Suddenly, an Algerian tries to force himself on Nancy. Tellegen intervenes. The Arab's robed cohorts beat up Tellegen. But when the Algerians see two legionnaires approaching, they run off.

• The legion fort. An Arab delivers a wounded Arab, explaining, "Bedouins robbed his caravan in the desert." Instantly, the commander dispatches a six-man squad, including Tellegen, to "get the thieves."

• Cowboys and Indians. Bedouins on horses appear from behind sand dunes. Firing away, they encircle Tellegen's legionnaires. In time, reinforcements arrive; the "thieves" are defeated.

Finis: Tellegen and Nancy ride off into the desert sunset. When's the last time audiences saw amorous Arab couples riding off as the sun sets?

Unsettled Land (1987), a.k.a. Once We Were Dreamers, Hemdale.

A Belbo film. *Kelly McGillis, John Shea, Amos Lavi, Motta Shirin, Arnon Zadok, Christine Boisson.* SP: Benny Barbash. D: Uri Barbash. Made in Israel, "with the assistance of the Israel fund for the promotion of quality films. Ministry of Education and Culture." PALESTINIANS

Jews vs. Jews, vs. Palestinians; Palestinians vs. Palestinians. One brave, peace-loving Palestinian appears; Palestinians militants initiate violence.

Scene: 1918, following WWI, in Palestine. Initial frames display two messages. "[As] everywhere in Eastern Europe violence erupts directed against the Jews, [a group of Jews] set out to forge a utopian society in the land of their forefathers." The next message advances a stale myth. Intones the narrator, "[In 1919], a people without a land [are] returning to a land without a people [Palestine]."

• Among those Jewish immigrants settling in 1919 Palestine are an Austrian doctor (McGillis) and her lover, a violinist (Shea). The couple purchased their land from an Arab in Beirut. Yet, they fear local Palestinians will prevent them from farming the fertile soil.

• Upset at having Jews as neighbors, bedouin farmers steer their sheep to trod on the immigrants' land. Later, Salim (Shirin) and his Palestinian militants attack the immigrants.

• Muhamad (Lavi), a Palestinian, and Amnon (Zadok), a Jew, are friends. Earlier, a Jewish doctor, a recent immigrant, treated Muhamad's daughter, saving her life. The men decide that unless they act to stop the violence, "the British and the French [imperialists] will all be here. There will be no victors." Affirms a Jewish immigrant, "This place belongs to us and them."

• The Arabic-speaking Muhamad presents a peace proposal to Palestinians. They all opt for peace, saying, "Let us divide the land between us [Palestinians] and them [Jews]."

• Suddenly, Salim's Palestinians kill two Jewish immigrants. Cut to a wounded Muhamad displaying a blood-stained cloth containing the Palestinian killers' hands. Furious that Muhamed murdered fellow Palestinians, Salim declares a "blood feud." Jewish immigrants also feud, causing the death of a fellow Jew.

• A pause in the action, revealing Semitic unity. Making the most of an out-of-tune violin, Muhamad and Amnon sing a traditional folk song, in Arabic.

• As Muhamad and Amnon leave the compound, assassins appear, killing them. Later, the camera reveals a peaceful setting—Jewish immigrants working the land.

Note: Credit Israeli actor Amos Lavi for his telling portrayal of Muhamad.

• Scenarios seldom show common interests; e.g., scenes displaying Arab and Jewish business leaders working together with "Builders for Peace," an organization advancing investment and economic growth in the West Bank and Gaza Strip.

• Recommended viewing is the Israeli film, *Hamsin* (1982), produced with help from the Fund for the Promotion of Israeli Quality Films. Featured are Palestinian and Jewish militants. Note the dialogue:

Abed: Jews are eyeing our land.
Khalid: It's the government, not the [Jews of the] village.

Set in "Galilee, Israel, 1982," the plot focuses on two young men—Gedaliah, the Jewish land owner, and Khalid, his Palestinian worker. Both seek peace. In spite of unfair government actions, they are determined to maintain their friendship. When Israelis threaten Khalid, Gedaliah intervenes, saying, "I don't want any violence here." Yet, mutual trust soon dissipates. Prejudice, peer pressure, and the quest for control of fertile farm land, escalate tensions. Unexpectedly, Palestinian militants destroy Gedaliah's farm. Israeli militants who tag Gedaliah "Arab lover," brutally beat young Palestinians. Boasts one Israeli, "I'd tear the bastards apart." Sadly, in the end, after Gedaliah sees Khalid sleeping with his sister, the Israeli loses control of his emotions. The angry Gedaliah sets a wild bull loose, intentionally killing his friend, Khalid.

Unveiled (1994), Olivar. *Lisa Zane, Martha Gehman.* Filmed in Morocco.
MAIDENS

Unsafe Morocco; mute maidens.

Scene: Instead of taking her father's advice and going to a drug rehabilitation center, Stephanie (Zane) runs off to Morocco, residing with her friend, Ellen (Gehman).

• Stephanie goes alone to a crowded souk, complete with vendors, snake charmers, and mysterious-looking Arabs. Suddenly, she cannot find her way out. Moroccans jostle her. Fearing souk Arabs may one day harm her, she and Ellen hire as their protector, "Moon," a young Moroccan boy.

• When Ellen says, "There are amazing things to do and see in Morocco," the camera cuts to fashionable hotels, cocktail lounges, and casinos. Impressed with an attractive Moroccan bellydancer's graceful movements, Stephanie, too, gets up and dances.

• A dimly lit room. Three mute Moroccan women prepare Stephanie to be seduced by her lover, Jeremy. Hauling water jugs, the women bathe her.

• Ellen disappears. A fellow American blames Stephanie. Two assertive and inept Moroccan policemen also accuse her. But, thanks to Moon, the police back off.

• Stephanie decides a drug rehabilitation center in the US is a much better, a much safer place, than Morocco. She returns home.

Up the Academy (1980), WB. A Marvin Worth/Danton Rissner Prod. *Ron Leibman, Ralph Macchio, Wendell Brown, Tom Citera.* D: Robert Downey. VILLAINS, MAIDENS

At the Sheldon R. Weinberg Military Academy, four youths, including a rich Arab, contest Liceman, their sadistic instructor. Repulsive stereotypes are displayed in this, MAD magazine's sloppy movie that fails to emulate the success of *National Lampoon's Animal House.*

Scene: The Arabian desert. Surrounded by white-robed Arabs and plenty of veiled wives, an anxious sheikh bids farewell to his son Hash (Citera).

A maiden: Be a good boy in America.
Hash: I will, mother.
Sheikh: That is not your mother. [*He points to another veiled wife.*] This is your mother.
Hash: Sorry, the veils confuse me.
Sheikh: Me too; she was supposed to be your mother.
Hash: When I am sheikh, I will abolish veils.
Sheikh: You will never be sheikh as long as you have the heart of a petty thief.
Hash: I am not a thief.
Sheikh: Then give me back my wallet, you little putz. [*Hash does so, then lifts his father's gold watch.*] A million dollars has been placed in your account.
Hash: But what will I do the second week?
Sheikh: [*Seeing his watch is gone, the sheikh shouts.*] I hope you have a forced landing in Israel.

• The Military Academy. Note how the boys are nicknamed. Hash shares a room with Chooch (Macchio), the son of Italian gangsters, and Eisenhower (Brown), "a jive-ass nigger." Officer Liceman (Leibman), calls the burnoose-wearing Hash, "Punjab" and "Swami," telling Hash, "[take] that filthy rag off your head. You stand out like a turd in a punch bowl."

• Hash bows in prayer before two cans of motor oil.

• Hash, who speaks with a British accent, is an active thief. He purloins pool balls and gold candlestick holders. Abruptly, Hash takes his pals for a joy ride in his Cadillac. When they run out of gas, Hash pulls out his "Bank of Arabia credit card."

• Displayed at the Academy's annual faculty-student soccer game is a giant-sized photograph of Liceman clad in a bellydancer's outfit.

Finis: Hash and his friends win the soccer match, triumphing over Liceman and his cohorts. Watching the match is Sheikh Amier, Hash's father. At the sheikh's side are eight veiled maidens wearing purple outfits.

• Credits acknowledge the cooperation of: "The 92ⁿᵈ Corps of Cadets of St. John's Military School, Salina, Kansas."

Utz (1992), Viva Pictures. *Armin Mueller-Stahl, Peter Reigert.* CAMEOS, SHEIKHS

An Arab sheikh collects dwarfs.

Scene: An elderly man, Utz (Mueller-Stahl), who gathers porcelain figurines, strolls along with an admirer, Fisher (Reigert). Note their conversation:

> Fisher: I once met a man who was a dealer in dwarfs.
> Utz: Dwarfs, you say. Where did you meet this man?
> Fisher: On a plane to Baghdad. He was going to view it to offer a client. He had two clients; one was an Arab oil sheikh, the other owned hotels in Pakistan.
> Utz: And what did they do with these dwarfs? ·
> Fisher: They kept them. [*The bearded Arab appears, wearing a gold and white thobe*]. The sheikh liked to set his favorite dwarf on his forearm, and his favorite falcon on his dwarf's forearm.
> Utz: And nothing else.
> Fisher: How could one know?
> Utz: You are right; these are things one could not know.
> Fisher: Nor would want to.

Valley of the Kings (1954), MGM. *Robert Taylor, Eleanor Parker, Kurt Kasznar, Victor Jory, Carlos Thompson.* Filmed in Egypt. EGYPTIANS

Egyptian sidekicks as villains; bedouins as devout Muslims; Islam and Christianity are revered.

Scene: Egypt, circa 1900. American archaeologist Mark Brandon (Taylor) assists Ann Mercedes (Parker) in locating "the tomb of the [eighteenth dynasty] pharaoh, Ra-Hotep." The protagonists believe that Ra-Hotep's crypt contains significant "evidence in it that the Old Testament's account of Joseph in Egypt is true."

• At the dig site, Egyptians swing picks and shovels, hauling dirt. Mark spots a worker stealing a relic; he socks the Egyptian, twice. Says Mark, "[He robbed] his co-workers... Whenever anyone digs up an antiquity, everybody in his squad gets a bonus."

• A shady Cairo antiquities huckster tries to sell Ann a bogus bracelet, claiming it "belonged to Cleopatra." "All I ask," says the Egyptian, "is a fraction of its value." Confronting the dealer is the sinister Hamed (Kazznar) and his cohorts. The Egyptian conspires with a corrupt Westerner (Thompson); they rob tombs and then smuggle valuable artifacts out of the country. Sensing the antiquities dealer is a cheat, Hamed knifes him in the gut.

• At St. Catherine's Monastery, Mark and Ann befriend a benevolent Egyptian priest. Compare this humane priest with radical Egyptian priests in *Raiders of the Lost Ark* (1981).

• Sailing the Nile in a felucca (a type of sailboat), Egyptians sing in Arabic. Mark, too, sings along, in Arabic. Ann smiles. Evening at the camp, another sing-a-long session. This is a rare screen moment—the Western hero happily singing Arab songs in Arabic, with Arabs.

• Though "no unfriendly tribes" appear here, Mark does cross swords with one desert bedouin, and wins.

Finis: Mark and Ann bring down Hamed and his cohorts. And, they uncover "[the] tomb of the first ruler who believed in [one] God." Thus, they verify that Joseph was indeed in Egypt and did in fact influence Ra-Hotep.

Treatment of Islam: In the desert, devout bedouins pray. A bedouin chieftain (Jory) appears, challenging Ann and Mark's motives for unearthing the crypt. Explains Ann, "We seek not to plunder. We hope to find a tomb with evidence that confirms our Bible. That should mean as much to you as to us; our prophets are yours." Affirms Mark, "Your Koran accepts a lot that is in our Bible." The bedouin leader concurs, "If they are telling the truth," he tells his men, "we will serve Allah by helping them."

The Veils of Bagdad (1953), UI. *Victor Mature, Mari Blanchard, Guy Rolfe, Leon Askin, Virginia Field.* S: William R. Cox. MAIDENS

In Baghdad, Arabs vs. Arabs. Arab women are intelligent and courageous.

Scene: The ruler of the Ottoman Empire, the benevolent "Suleiman the Magnificent," reigns "over half the world," including ancient Baghdad, 1560. Opposing Suleiman is the ambitious pasha (Askin) and his cohorts, the hill tribes, and an evil vizier, Kasseim (Rolfe).

• The vizier's caravan is "set upon by bandits." Riding to Kasseim's rescue is the burnoosed Antar (Mature). Grateful for Antar's assistance, Kasseim offers him a post with Pasha Hammam. Antar accepts; they ride off.

• Inside the palace hall, acrobats and harem maidens attend the pasha. Antar soon discovers the pasha and Kasseim are scheming tyrants; the two men intend to link up with the "Venetian Republic's" forces and overthrow Suleiman. The villains also seek to bribe "Mustapha the Wild" and his renegades.

• Antar enlists the help of Kasseim's wife, Rosanna (Field). The anxious Rosanna warns Antar, "Know that Kasseim is not a normal man. He breeds destruction, treachery." And, "Do I look like a woman who should live with such a person?"

• The souk displays honest merchants and a few wrestlers. Here, pasha's palace guards whip innocents.

• Antar falls for a dancer who performs at the Crescent Moon, Selima (Blanchard). Lovely Selima hails from the Arab village, Abu Kharum. Not so long ago, she tells Antar, Kasseim's men massacred Abu Kharum's villagers, including her father. Seeking to "avenge" her people, she intends to kill Kasseim and the pasha.

• Introducing the rebel leader, Kafar. Antar advises Kafar to be patient, not to take many risks. Before attacking Kasseim, says Antar, you must first have some "knowledge of medicine, navigation, and the arts of war and politics."

• As Selima dances, lecherous Kasseim pants, "She looks like a wild, untouched gazelle of the hills."

• Kasseim gains the support of Mustapha's hill tribes, the pasha's guards and some Venetian "unbelievers." Together, they move to "overthrow Suleiman the Magnificent."

• Inside the pasha's palace dungeon. The pasha, who derives pleasure from torturing prisoners, tells the rebel, Kafar, "[We have] playthings, all sizes and designs for every part of the body." He boasts, "I've kept a man alive a year by using the doctors, you see. Patch them, break them up again. Somehow they do not even go mad."

• To the rescue, Antar and friends. They free Kafar. Next, they crush the pasha's guards and bring down Kasseim. In the end, "Antar the Great," with Selima at his side, is declared "Prince of Baghdad."

Treatment of Islam: Antar says, "Allah be with you." Conversely, the Captain of the Guard says, "By the prophet's beard, preserve me from a chattering woman."

Note: This "murky" film, says Bosley Crowther in his "unpublished" NYT review, "[is] a run-of-the-back-lot-Baghdad-shows."[189]

The Vengeance of She (1967), SA. *John Richardson, Olinka Berova, Noel Willman, Derek Godfrey, George Sewell.* Rel. TCF. Sequel to *She* (1965). VILLAINS

A scheming Arab, intent on ruling the world, seeks immortality.

Scene: Carol (Berova), the French heroine known as Ayesha, fears that an evil Arab from "Kuma, the Lost City," Men Hari (Godfrey), is using his power to dispatch her to Kuma. Men Hari dons a white headdress, sports a goatee, and chants, "Look now across the ages, Ayesha."

• Sighs Carol, "I see strange faces, always calling me, Ayesha." Hoping to dodge her disturbing nightmares, she and Dr. Philip (Judd) board a private ship.

• Men Hari is intent on nabbing Carol because Kuma's immortal king, Killikrates (Richardson), has promised the Arab immortality, provided Men Hari delivers Kuma's lost queen to him. Affirms Killikrates, "She must come as you promised me, or I will never give you the immortality that you so much desire."

• In Arabia, Carol is besieged by begging children. Friendly Kassim (Morell) arrives, chasing off the beggars. He asks Carol, "Are you in trouble? Perhaps I can help you." Kassim, who possesses "a certain psychic ability," takes Carol to his home, vowing, "I will help you break that grip [of Men Hari's]."

• Killikrates orders Men Hari to "deal with" the Arab, Kassim. "It is not so simple," says Men Hari, "[Kassim is] a scholar and a mystic." Insists Killikrates, "Go forth and destroy him." Cut to Men Hari unleashing a terrible windstorm, killing Kassim.

• In the desert, Carol collapses. Abruptly, two ugly Arabs appear. One Arab purchases Carol. He fondles her face, laughs, then binds her. The Arab then mounts his horse, forcing Carol to trudge behind.

• Philip and his friend Harry (Sewell) search for Carol. Arriving at a desert oasis, the in-need-of-water Harry begins drinking. An Arab creeps behind Harry, drowning him. When Philip confronts the Arab, the murderer flees.

• Finally, Philip links up with Carol. They enter Kuma's Egyptian-looking temple. Greeting them is Kuma's high priest, ZaTor (Willman). Cautions ZaTor, "[Men Hari would] sacrifice his soul so he might conquer the world."

• ZaTor meets with Killikrates, explaining that Men Hari deceived him, that Carol is not really Kuma's Queen, "Ayesha." Instantly, Men Hari stabs ZaTor. "I had the world, eternity here in my hands," he shouts. Next, Men Hari goes to knife Philip. Killikrates intervenes, saying, "You have betrayed me." On cue, Killikrates' guards kill Men Hari. Knowing he will never be united with the real Ayesha, the despondent Killikrates walks into flames; the temple collapses. Carol and Philip depart, unscathed.

The Vigilante (1947), COL. 15 episodes. *Ralph Byrd, Robert Barron, George Offerman Jr., Ramsay Ames.* CLIFFHANGERS, SHEIKHS, RECOMMENDED

An Arab and the American protagonist defeat the Arab villain and American gangsters. "Good" Arabs surface in most episodes. In 1947, when the serial was released,

"The Vigilante Fighting Hero of the West," was a comic book hero, part of the *Action Comics* series.

Scene: Supposedly, some valuable pearls are cursed. The pearls, referred to as "The curse of the 100 tears of blood," follow Arabian white stallions wherever they tread. This time, the pearl curse tracks the stallions to an American ranch.

• At the ranch, a devout Arab Muslim ruler, Prince Hamil (Barron), presents five Arabian horses to rancher George Pierce (Talbot). The prince is unaware that Pierce and his X-1 gang, along with the ruler's aide, Hamid, intend to snitch the precious pearls.

• As soon as Hamid steals the "blood-red pearls," the Arab perishes. Sighs Prince Hamil, "[There has been a curse on these] perfectly matched red pearls for a thousand years."

• Throughout, Prince Hamil and the disguised Vigilante, who is actually undercover agent Greg Sanders (Byrd), work together to capture the gangsters. Kissing the heroine's (Ames) hand, Hamil says, "Miss Winslow, I will add my prayers to the providence which protected you tonight."

• Prince Hamil saves the Vigilante's life. And, the Arab rescues the Vigilante and Stuff (Offerman) from several gangsters.

• When the prince finally discovers the blood-red pearls, which were secretly hidden in the horses' hooves, he pours acid over them, thus ending the mysterious "curse."

Finis: The Vigilante, the prince, and his "most trusted" Arab associates, bring down the main villain, rancher George Pierce. And, they collar Pierce's X-1 hoodlums. The Vigilante tells Hamil, "Thank you, my friend."

Dialogue: Arabian is pronounced: "Ar-a-bay-yan."

Note: See *Queen of the Jungle* (1937).

Wanted: Dead or Alive (1987), New World. *Rutger Hauer, Gene Simmons, Robert Guillaume, Mel Harris, William Russ, Susan McDonald, Jerry Hardin.* SP: Michael Patrick Goodman, Brian Taggert, Gary Sherman. D: Sherman. PALESTINIANS, WORST LIST

Palestinians and Arab Americans vs. Americans. This theme— Arabs and Arab-Americans killing innocents in the US—surfaces in movies-made-for-television, e.g., *Under Siege* (1992) and *Path to Paradise* (1997), and in feature films, e.g., *True Lies* (1994), *Invasion U.S.A.* (1985), *Black Sunday* (1977), *Terror In Beverly Hills* (1988), and *The Siege* (1998).

Set in Los Angeles, *Wanted: Dead or Alive*'s Arab-Americans and Palestinians murder a rabbi, and extinguish more than 200 men, women, and children. Plus, they move to release poison gas [See *Executive Decision* (1996)] into the atmosphere, exterminating millions in Los Angeles. Eliminating the culprits are members of the CIA and the Los Angeles Police Department, and a bounty hunter.

Scene: Los Angeles International Airport. After a rabbi embraces a rabbi ominous Arabic music underscores the next scene. Posing as a rabbi is a Palestinian terrorist, Malak Al Rahim (Simmons). Malak slices the real rabbi's throat.

• A Los Angeles movie theater. After setting a bomb, Malak approaches a clean-cut family; he feigns friendship with a little girl holding her doll. Next, he and his Arab-American cohorts ignite the bomb; 138 people, including the family, perish. Aiding

Malak are Arabs wearing kuffiyehs and American-Arab students attending the University of California, Los Angeles (UCLA). One UCLA student, Abdul Renza, acquired the explosives.

• Outside the ravaged theater, cut to the child's burnt doll. Says the TV announcer, "Possible identification of some of the bodies may be impossible."

• Bounty hunter Nick Randall (Hauer) intends to "blow this scum-bag [Malak] away." Randall is warned, "[Malak] killed thousands of people in the Middle East and Europe. [He] is an animal. He doesn't get scared, he gets even."

• Seeing an Arab student driving a Mercedes 450 SL, a CIA agent quips, "Isn't it nice to have money?" Cut to "Amir's Falafel" restaurant; Randall kills a terrorist.

• Following the declaration that "in just 36 hours," Malak's car bombs and shootings have "created chaos, 173 people" in Los Angeles are dead; the camera reveals an Arab-American Bomb Factory. Pleased that 50 more bombs are being produced, Malak boasts, "Bhopal, India, [will] look like a minor traffic accident."

• Amir's restaurant. Arab-American "desert dwellers," who are also tagged "animals," shoot the CIA agent's knees. Next, they slice his throat. See the power saw scene in *Death before Dishonor* (1987). Next, the terrorists explode Randall's boat, killing his friend and his girl. The police officer, Philmore Walker (Guillaume), embraces Randall.

• Randall enters Robert Aziz's home, a dump. Previously, Aziz set off several car bombs. Randall nabs and tosses Aziz inside a foot locker, sealing it shut. Fearing suffocation, Aziz puts a gun to his mouth and shoots himself. At the home of another Arab American, policemen collar Malak's accomplices.

• At a chemical plant, Arab Americans wearing headdresses move to explode the factory. Malak honks the truck's horn; abruptly, scores of Arab Americans pop out of large steel barrels. The barrels also contain dynamite. Someone points out that should the plant explode, Malak and his cohorts will also die. Such information fails to faze a female terrorist; she insists they blow up the factory. Not Malak; he shoots her and runs off.

• Randall shoots some Arab Americans, then corners Malak. "I am not a criminal; I am a soldier [and] I deserve to die like a soldier," says Malak. Quips Randall, "You're no soldier; you're a fly in a piece of shit." Randall stuffs a grenade inside Malak's mouth and pulls the pin.

Note: On 30 January 1987, movie critic Michael Medved, co-host of *Sneak Previews*, wrote to this writer, saying:

> My specific objection to Wanted: Dead or Alive centered on its depiction of Arab Americans. They are shown to be active supporters of a bloody vicious terrorist kingpin. This disturbed me precisely because it bears so little connection with reality. ... "Instead of creating hysterical fantasies about a secret underground network supporting Arab terrorists in America, we should all be thankful that the more than two million Arab Americans have been such decent and law-biding citizen of this country. [My] fear is that crude Arab-bashing in movies and on TV—particularly when directed at Arab Americans—helps to create the atmosphere that makes this sort of crime [the death of Palestinian-American Alex Odeh in Los Angeles, murdered by Jewish terrorists hiding in Israel] possible.

• A possible link between screen images of falafel vendors and real images. At the time *Wanted: Dead or Alive* was screened in movie theaters, the words, "Go home, camel," were scrawled outside the home of an Arab-American couple in Chicago; two brothers were beaten and jailed in Flint, Michigan, on false charges of being members of a "Kadafy hit squad." Also, in Washington, DC, the United States Information Agency (USIA) tried to persuade District of Columbia officials to force Mohammed Nassiri, "a falafel vendor of Middle Eastern or Palestinian origin," to relocate. As Nassiri's food stand was located directly "in front of the main entrance of the USIA building," some administrators considered him to be a "possible threat to personnel or physical security." Even USIA director, Charles Z. Wick, intervened, asking DC overseers to remove Nassiri. To their credit, city officials took no action.[190]

• A press release for the film states, "Terrorism has never hit home until now."

• Political films elicit controversy. Consider *Michael Collins* (1996); it took director Neil Jordan twelve years to get his film about the Irish Volunteers, which became the Irish Republican Army (IRA), produced. Even before its United Kingdom release in November 1996, the film was attacked by some English journalists, saying that it had a pro-IRA stance and that it offered a biased account of Anglo-Irish history. The (London) Times dismissed the film as "an anti-British travesty." "Two hours of sheer lies," declared the *Financial Post*. The *New Statesman* labeled it "a deceitful piece of propaganda." Yet, as *Michael Collins* is on-screen Irish history projected with an Irish viewpoint, the film became a national event in Ireland. "[To] counteract the conventional cinematic portrayal of IRA members as inhuman, cold-blooded, even psychotic killers," most Irish assassins appear as devout Catholics, even praying in church before killing English agents. And, the Irish allow a British agent, "caught unawares by three IRA gunmen during his morning exercises," to say his prayers before shooting him. "Despite violent language and scenes, Ireland's national censor passed the film with a PG (Parental Guidance) rating, thereby enabling young children to see it. Thus, in Ireland, *Michael Collins* received overwhelmingly favorable critical response."[191]

War Birds (1988), Skylark. *Jim Eldert, Curly Howard, Bill Brinsfield, Sahid Farid.* W, D: Ulli Lommel. Song "12 O'Clock" by Denny Densmore. VILLAINS, SHEIKHS, WORST LIST

Arabs vs. Arabs, vs. US marines, airmen, and Vietnam veterans. Should Arabs oppose a US air base in "Arabia," bomb 'em.

Scene: In "El Alahaim," Arab insurgents slaughter fellow Arabs. Brandishing red flags, Arabs kill an 11-year-old boy, then abuse and kidnap a young Arab woman.

• The War Room, Washington, DC. A map of El Alahaim, reveals the desert, some oil fields, a walled-in palace, and a souk. Quips a US officer, "[This country is] the last place on earth I'd rather be. [But] we need a new base in the Mediterranean." And, Sheikh Ali Hadhi will give us one, provided "we knock off the rebels." Says a colleague, "Two F-16s" should do it.

• El Alahaim's oil fields. Captain Selim (Farid) plans to set a trap for the US pilots. Says his cohort, "We will give the Americans a welcome party they will never forget."

• The F-16 pilots fall for Selim's "fuckin' trap"; the Arabs kill Jim Harris, a dare-devil ace from Oklahoma. Selim's men also bring down Sheikh Ali's Arabs. The rebels move to nab "souvenirs, pieces of the war plane [and] the balls of the American pilot, if there are any left."

• Americans assemble a new attack team. Quips Costello (Eldert), a CIA-trained ex-marine, "We're dealing with a bunch of nuts!" Selim sets another ambush, ensnaring

Costello, who is tagged an "American pig."

• A bearded Arab rebel places a huge knife at Costello's throat. Told to talk, Costello shouts, "Go to hell" and spits in the Arab's face. So, the Arabs opt to torture him. They go to stretch Costello, permanently, tying him to two tanks. In early films, screen Arabs employed a similar stretching-of-limbs ploy, binding the Western protagonists to horses.

• American planes to the rescue. Though ten MIG fighter planes chase off the US planes, two US jets return, shooting down the MIGs. Leading the attack, Kansas' Billy Hawkins, one of our "best fighter pilots." Billy and crew destroy Selim's desert air base [See *Iron Eagle* (1986)]. Afterward, Billy says, "This is hell down here guys, never seen flames as vicious as those."

• Sheikh Ali's men arrive at the base, obliterating what remains of Selim's Arabs.

• Proclaims a triumphant American airman, "What a historic moment. Our jet touching down on the future home for our Air Force." Cut to a tent. Inside, a bellydancer entertains the smiling Costello.

Waxwork (1988), Vestron. *Zach Galligan, Deborah Foreman.* CAMEOS, EGYPTIANS

Deadly mummies slay college students.

Scene: Inside a wax museum, bogeymen, including two mummies, come alive.

• Appearing from behind Anubis' statue is a really mean mummy; he crushes a student's head. Next, the mummy kills an elderly man.

• Checking the museum, the students come across the second mummy. Abruptly, the entombed mummy reaches up and seizes the youths. Then, he closes the crypt!

West Beirut (1998), 3 Productions—Douri films. Arabic, with English subtitles. *Rami Doueiri, Mohamad Chamas.* D: Ziad Doueiri.

Director Ziad Doueiri, an Arab American, offers a compelling view of Lebanon's civil strife, sans stereotypes. Doueiri shows Lebanese teens coping with violence in divided Beirut of the 1970s.

Scene: Two Muslim boys, Tarek and Omar, share thoughts about life with their friend, a Christian girl, May. Though the craziness of the civil war invades the teens' homes, threatening them as well as their neighbors and families, the youths refuse to allow themselves to be drawn into the spiraling hostility. Instead, their actions serve to illuminate the human spirit. Despite religious differences the three adolescents get along.

Note: *West Beirut* displays understanding between Muslims and Christians. For example, Muslims, like Christians, use prayer beads, mostly plain ones with no decorations. Wartburg College Religion Professor Fred Strickert, points out that Bethlehem's mosque of Omar is located next to Manger Square. After the time of Mohammed, the Great Caliph Omar, made sure Bethlehem's Christian Patriarch knew of his forthcoming visit. The wise Patriarch invited Omar to pray near the eastern end of the Nativity Church. For centuries, that is where Muslims gathered for prayer. Recognizing Christian tolerance, Omar guaranteed the safe passage of all Christians in the Holy Land. Since then, during Bethlehem's Christian evening services, the Christian Patriarch has invited the city's Muslim leader to join in during the procession to the Nativity Church. Together, they embrace peace on earth, good will to all.[192]

• In June 1998, Doueiri's *West Beirut* received the Biennale award, presented by Constantine Costa-Gavras in Paris.

West of Zanzibar (1954), UI. *Anthony Steel, Sheila Sim.* CAMEOS, VILLAINS

Arab slavers vs. Africans. Africans, not Arabs, are denigrated.

Scene: In East Africa, a British ranger (Steel) tracks renegade "native tribes" smuggling ivory. The film's narrator, however, does not fault nor does he focus on thieving native tribes. Instead, he cites wicked Arab slavers. Declares the narrator, "[Not so many years ago, the Arabs, forced poor Africans to sell their ivory.] Tribesmen [were] torn from their homes to serve in the palaces and harems in Arabia."

• Quips an angry Englishman, "[When it comes to stealing white] ivory, the law punishes the foolish Africans while the tempters [Arabs] escape." Affirms an African Chief, "My people have tasted the money of evil." Cut to Arabs dumping plenty of stolen ivory aboard their dhows. Before the Arabs can whisk the ivory off to Abu Dhabi, the British ranger nabs them.

Note: For more information, see "TV Arabs," *Voice*, London, April 1980.

• See MGM's *West of Zanzibar* (1929); In that version, Africans are vilified. The camera shows Africans about to immolate an innocent woman. Quips the Anglo protagonist, "It's a lovely custom. When a man dies they always burn his wife or daughter with him. That's the law of the Congo."

What the Moon Saw (1990), Boulevard. Australian. *Andrew Shepherd, Murray Fahey.* EP: Peter Boyle. RECOMMENDED

Sinbad serves as a role model.

Scene: The protagonist, an Australian boy named Steven (Shepherd), regularly goes to the theater to watch his movie hero Sinbad perform in "Sinbad's Last Voyage." One day, Steven falls asleep. Presto, the boy imagines himself to be Sinbad, "the beloved hero of the people."

• Functioning as Sinbad, "the conqueror of evil," Steven contests an evil enchanter named Bong, and his aide, Bing Bong. Resembling Fu Manchu, Bing Bong was "born in the shadows somewhere in the East"; his brother was "the devil's magician."

• Bing Bong kidnaps the lovely Morgana. Yet, all ends well. Steven-as-Sinbad, along with his trusty assistant, Ali (Fahey), bring down the villain, rescuing Morgana from "the evil enchanter's" clutches.

Where Do We Go from Here? (1945), TCF. *Fred MacMurray, Gene Sheldon, June Haver.* CAMEOS

An Anglicized genii joins the marines.

Scene: This musical comedy features a bumbling, well-meaning two-thousand-year-old genii. Popping out of a glass lamp, the genii, Ali (Sheldon), greets his new master, Bill Morgan (MacMurray). Morgan is frustrated; He wants to serve in the military but cannot because he is classified 4-F. Ali to the rescue.

• Ali examines his erratic time piece, then grants Morgan's request to serve in the armed forces. But Ali fails to dispatch Morgan to WWII locales. Instead, Morgan is first sent to Washington's Valley Forge, and then Morgan surfaces on Columbus' ship, the Santa Maria.

• Finally, Ali gets his act together; He places Morgan where he wants to be—with the United States Marines. Ali, too, enlists, becoming a marine. He and Morgan march off in a parade.

Note: Only once does Ali don Arab garb—when he appears from the lamp.

Where the Spies Are (1965), MGM. *David Niven, Cyril Cusack, Paul Stassino, Eric Pohlmann, Riyad Gholmeih.* Filmed in Lebanon. See *Masquerade* (1965). SHEIKHS

Good Arabs and brave Englishmen vs. foul Arabs and Russians.

Scene: London. British intelligence officials dispatch to Lebanon, Dr. Love (Niven), a mild-mannered physician. Officials tell Dr. Love not to worry, that Beirut's "weather is great; night life, fabulous; and the food is first class." Dr. Love's assignment? Find Rosser (Cusack), a missing English agent, presumed dead.

• In Rome, Dr. Love watches a passenger jet take off. Suddenly, the jet explodes. Dr. Love sighs, as he was booked to be on the downed plane.

• In Beirut, a Lebanese cab driver (Gholmeih) delivers Dr. Love to a posh hotel, complete with nightclub, band, and dancers. Later, after an Arab cabby pockets the fare, he tells Dr. Love about the missing agent, Rosser.

• Introducing Farouk (Pohlmann), the cabby's brother. Now, he drives Dr. Love around Beirut. "Want me to buy car for you? I get darn good price," boasts Farouk. The cabby balks at taking Love's money, "No. No, it's been a pleasure," he says. Only after Love "insists" does Farouk acquiesce, accepting no more than the correct cab fare.

• British intelligence receives a Telex—"Assassination Prince Zalouf at Byblos; Nationalists then seizing British Oil." Sighs an official, "[We only have] two or three men [in Lebanon] to save half the oil supply in our country. We depend on Prince Zalouf for almost half our oil consumption." The official's statement misleads. Lebanon is not now, nor has it ever been, an oil-rich country.

• Appearing is the sly Dr. Simmias (Stassino), the Arab responsible for Rosser's death. Dr. Simmias also arranged for the Rome jet to explode. Now, he conspires with Russian agents to assassinate Prince Zalouf. Simmias tells an assassin, "[Your act] will be a major military defeat for Britain. You are not merely an assassin, you are a military army."

Finis: Beaming, Prince Zalouf appears in a parade; Lebanese onlookers cheer. On cue, Dr. Love nabs the assassin. And, British authorities collar Dr. Simmias.

The White Man's Law (1918), a.k.a. The Unforgivable Sin, PAR.
Silent. *Sessue Hayakawa, Florence Vidor, Jack Holt.* *NS. Notes from MPH. MAIDENS

Summary: In Sierra Leone, an Englishman, Sir Henry Falkland (Holt), takes advantage of Maida (Vidor), a French-Sudanese woman. After seducing the woman, Sir Henry shuns Maida. And, he tries to drown an Oxford-educated Arab, John A. Ghengis (Hayakawa). Fortunately, local villagers find out that Sir John is a culprit. Exposed, the distraught Englishman shoots himself. As for Maida and Ghengis, they marry.

The White Sheik (1928), a.k.a. King's Mate, British Independent Pictures.

Silent. *Lillian Hall-Davis, Warwick Ward, Jameson Thomas.* *NS. Notes from NYT (9 December 1929). Filmed in Morocco. See *Bolero* (1984). SHEIKHS

In Fez, Arabs fights Arabs, in order to gain the British heroine's affection.

Summary: As the heroine (Ward) reads E.M. Hull's book, *The Sheik*, she becomes fascinated with "what she presumes to be a legendary person known as the White Sheik."

Cut to Morocco. Here, after watching "hosts of Arabs on their fast horses," the heroine comes to believe her dream sheikh is "alive and kicking." Regrettably, "he [the counterfeit Arab-lover] is ready to fall in love with the first pale-faced screen actress that comes his way."

The White Sheik (1951).

A Federico Fellini Prod. Italian, with English subtitles. *Alberto Sordi, Brunella Bovo, Giulietta Masina.* Remade as *The World's Greatest Lover* (1977). SP, D: Fellini. SHEIKHS

Beware counterfeit sheikhs. Western women should stick with Western beaus.

Scene: Photographs of the White Sheik (Sordi) and his entourage appear weekly in Italian magazines, the *fumetti*. The magazines are enormously popular, offering consumers exciting escapist tales through the use of exotic photographs. For many Italians, especially the newly wedded Wanda (Bovo), the fantasy images of Arabs that appear in the *fumetti* are believable, and much more exciting than everyday realities.

• As soon as Wanda arrives in Rome she darts from her honeymoon suite and links up with the White Sheik's troupe. Off they go to the countryside for a magazine shoot. The crew begins discussing how to best shoot a "rape scene." The director prepares to photograph a camel, bellydancers, harem maidens, including Wanda in maiden garb, and "Oscar, the heartless bedouin, the scourge of the East." The director shouts action; the actors-as-bedouins move to attack "the beach of the Lost Harem to destroy the White Sheik."

• Wanda's extravagant admiration for the White Sheik prompts her to dress as his concubine. Abruptly, the Italian actor clad-in-sheikh garb moves to seduce her. He takes Wanda sailing, spinning false tales. After eliciting Wanda's sympathy, the phony sheikh goes to bed the now-vulnerable woman. In time, the White Sheikh's wife surfaces, shattering Wanda's illusions about the two-bit sheikh's whopping stories. Though heartbroken, Wanda comes to realize the White Sheik is a fake, not at all what she had imagined him to be. Soon, her false illusions melt into reality.

• At St. Peter's Square, the no longer disillusioned Wanda happily reunites with her Italian husband. The sensible Wanda gazes at her spouse purring, "You are my White Sheik."

The White Sister (1923), Inspiration Metro.

Silent. *Lillian Gish, Ronald Colman, Gail Kane.* Based on Francis Marion Crawford's novel/play of the same name, this film was the first American feature produced in Italy. Two other versions were released: an earlier silent film in 1915 and MGM's 1933 sound film with Clark Gable and Helen Hayes. CAMEOS, VILLAINS

In this post WWI set-in-Italy romance drama, bedouin "bandits" kidnap and hold hostage an Italian officer.

Scene: Unexpectedly, Donna Angela's (Gish) beau, Captain Giovanni Severi (Coleman), is ordered to depart Italy and "command an expedition in [North] Africa." Later, when Donna Angela is informed that Giovanni is dead—"the Italian government failed to find the Arab bandits"—she decides to "work in a hospital and to become a nun."

• Cut to the Arabian desert, complete with a camel caravan, tents, and Arabs. The camera shows the imprisoned Giovanni behind prison bars. Outside, desert Arabs pray, "giving thanks to Allah."

• As Donna Angela believes Giovanni is dead, she prepares to "become a bride of the church." Cut to the Arab desert. Giovanni escapes. He punches out his bedouin guard, puts on bedouin's white thobe and rides off. On screen, "Giovanni struggles for liberty across the desert wastes."

• Too late, Giovanni arrives in Italy. Donna Angela will not marry him; she refuses to "break her vows to the church." Later, the broken-hearted Giovanni dies.

Note: Credits state that "Sheik Mahomet," a real Arab, portrays the "Bedouin Chief."

Who's Afraid of Virginia Woolf? (1966), WB. *Richard Burton, Elizabeth Taylor, George Segal, Sandy Dennis.* SP, P: Ernest Lehman. D: Mike Nichols. Based on the play by Edward Albee. Taylor and Dennis won Academy Awards for their roles. CAMEOS, VILLAINS

A one-liner tars Arabs.

Scene: Evening, outside a college tavern. Following a bitter verbal exchange between university professor George (Burton) and his wife, Martha (Taylor), George says: "It's all right for you [to hurt me]. You can go on like a pumped-up Arab, slashing at everything in sight, scarring up half the world if you want to. But let someone else try it, oh no!"

Wholly Moses! (1980), COL. *Dudley Moore.* CAMEOS

This harmless satire displays a not-too-alert bus driver, Mohammad. See *Quick Change* (1990).

Scene: Israel. When mute Mohammad, an absent-minded bus driver is introduced to his passengers, his eyes switch back-and-forth from the highway to the tourists. Subsequently, the bus begins zigzagging. Finally, the bus comes to a safe stop. The passengers walk about, then re-board the bus. Mohammed drives off, leaving behind the protagonist (Moore). Fortunately, the protagonist manages to catch up and board the bus.

Wild Geese II (1985), WB. *Scott Glenn, Barbara Carrera.* SP: Reginald Rose. CAMEOS, PALESTINIANS

The Arab-American protagonist, "born and raised in Pittsburgh" vs. cruel Palestinians. This film is dedicated to "Richard Burton." See *The Siege* (1998).

Scene: In Berlin, Arab-American John Haddad's (Glenn) mercenaries move to free arch-Nazi Rudolf Hess from Spandau prison.

• A German terrorist appears, warning Haddad, "[You are] a man who hurts Palestinian commando units in Lebanon so badly that they have an attractive price on your head." And, "Your Palestinian friends have been good to us and it will please us to do them a favor [to turn you over to them]." Retorts Haddad: "I want the Palestinian price on me lifted." Quips the German, "When Hess is delivered, I'll have the price on you lifted."

• Two Palestinians try to kill Haddad; they are shot.

• Flashback. Haddad graduates and marries his high-school sweetheart; they have a child. Soon, Haddad and his "Lebanese family" move from Pittsburgh to Beirut. In Lebanon, he studies medicine at the American University of Beirut. Abruptly, "in a village south of Beirut," Palestinians shoot dead Haddad's "wife and three-year-old daughter, his mother and father." This is why, contends this scenario, Haddad "went to war" against the Palestinians.

• Among Haddad's mercenaries are two Arabs, Jamil and Joseph. An IRA hireling protests having to work with Arabs, saying, "I don't share a room with any wogs... I said wogs, Ayrabs. Them bastards!" A British hireling counters the slurs.

Note: Appearing briefly is "El Ali," a rotund Arab operating a cafe: "[The Arab is] a man of all trades, schemes, skulduggeries, a procurer of the unprocurable." After Haddad drinks El Ali's Arab coffee, he makes a sour face quipping, "[El Ali is] a server of the undrinkable."

The Wind and the Lion (1975), UA/MGM. *Sean Connery, Candice Bergen, Brian Keith, Nadim Sawalha, Simon Harrison, Polly Gottesman, Steve Kanaly.* SP, D: John Milius. SHEIKHS

Tangier, circa 1904. Loosely based on a true incident. Moroccans vs. Moroccans and Westerners. When Americans are kidnapped, the American president, Teddy Roosevelt, dispatches the marines. In stark contrast to movie-land's stereotypical Moroccans, the Moroccan, Raisuli (Connery), appears as a heroic figure, as "a Robin Hood of the Rif."

Scene: Morocco. Brandishing swords and guns, Raisuli and his followers crash into a European estate; the Arabs slash art works, and kill Westerners and their Moroccan servants. Raisuli's men also kidnap Mrs. Eden Pedecaris (Bergen), an American widow, and her two children, William and Jennifer (Harrison, Gottesman).

• Promptly, the US Consular's office sends a report, advising Washington, "This act of barbarous criminality appears perpetuated by Raisuli. There exists alarming prospects for all foreigners in Morocco. Request warships."

• Declares President Roosevelt (Keith), "[This Raisuli has no] respect for human lives; he is an Arabian thief [who is] holding me up like a common desperado.[I am] not a man to stand by and condone barbaric acts." Raisuli rebuts Roosevelt, "I am a true defender of the faithful and the blood of the Prophet runs in me." No matter. Instantly, Roosevelt dispatches "the Atlantic squadron."

• Raisuli's Arabs rummage through Eden's suitcase, poking fun of her garments. The angry Eden tosses a shoe; the Arabs run after it and scuffle.

• Young William idolizes Raisuli. Covering his head with a white cloth, the boy displays a knife, telling his mother, "He has a way about him; he sure has a way."

• Raisuli explains to Eden why he kidnapped her: I want to "embarrass" my uncle, the sultan. "[The sultan is] the bought dog of the European armies... I am the true defender of the faithful. And the blood of the Prophet runs through me. And I am nothing but a servant to His will."

• The "Palace of the Bashaw." Surrounded by guards, the Bashaw, who is the sultan's nephew, acts as a stereotypical screen sheikh. Reclining on his couch, he eats, drinks, and puffs a hookah. Arriving is Mr. Gummere (Lewis), an American diplomat. He asks what the Moroccans intend to do about the kidnapped Americans. The bored Bashaw passes the buck, telling the official it's best to visit Fez, to discuss the kidnapping with the sultan.

• Gummere seeks advice, asking, "What would please the sultan? Gold? Another carriage?" "Lions," says the Bashaw. Cut to "Fez, the Seat of the Sultan." Two caged lions are "delivered by camel [to the sultan]." Camels, not trucks, are used to transport the lions. Why? Because the dense sultan refuses to build roads.

• The pompous sultan treats blacks as inferiors; his black slaves hold aloft the ruler's decorated palanquin. The inept, giggling "exultance" anxiously grabs and test-fires a machine gun. Bullets scatter everywhere; aides and guests run for cover. Gummere arrives, asking the sultan to rescue Eden and her children. Screeches the sultan, "You cannot talk to a defender of the faithful in this manner. Foreigners do not understand."

• Curious, Eden asks Raisuli, "Do you pray, often?" Explains Raisuli, "I pray to Mecca, five times a day." Quips Eden: "Is that so? I wonder how you find time. You are so busy cutting off men's heads and kidnapping women and children." Sighs Raisuli, "If I miss the morning prayers, I pray twice in the afternoon. Allah is very understanding."

• Raisuli's Arabs bow, then pray, saying, "Allahu Akbar." Explains Raisuli to Eden, "[I am not a] barbarous man. I am a scholar and leader of my people." He reminds Eden that four men "dishonored" him, yet he released two. As for the others, he removed their heads. "A barbarous man would have killed them all," he says.

• Raisuli provides Eden with a private tent. When he suspects she fears he may seduce her, Raisuli laughs. Morning, the two play chess. He explains, "I prefer to fight the European army but they do not fight as men; they fight as dogs. Men prefer to fight with swords so they can see each other's eyes. They [the Europeans] use guns."

• Raisuli's friend, Sherif (Sawalha), and his men enter the camp; Raisuli warmly welcomes them. Sherif displays a tongue, taken from the mouth of an opposing Arab. Next, all the Arabs ride off to a walled desert castle.

• In Tangier, Marine Captain Jerome (Kanaly) proposes the marines seize the Moroccan government, "at bayonet point."

• The castle, evening. Eden bribes a cackling Moroccan to help them escape. She gives the sly Moroccan some jewels; they ride off into the desert. Noon; the Moroccan doublecrosses Eden, delivering her and the children to a band of blue-robed leper-ish Tuareg outlaws, nomadic descendants of Berbers and Arabs, who move to abuse Eden and the children. Suddenly, Raisuli appears. He shoots the outlaws, rescuing the Pedecaris family.

• Raisuli tells Eden that they are his guests, and safe from harm. Exclaims Eden, "Why, then, you're just bluffing them [the US government], you've never had the intention of killing us?" "Raisuli does not kill women and children," he sighs. "It's a silly question."

• Waving the American flag, Captain Jerome's marines charge the Bashaw's residence. The Marines kill mute Moroccan guards, and nab the hookah-smoking Bashaw.

• Evening. The "Lord of the Rif" tells Eden, "I trusted my brother... he betrayed me. [He went with the Germans,] and I was sent to a prison dungeon on the edge of the sea."

• Raisuli decides to free Eden and her children. His men "sing [in Arabic] to God." But as Raisuli prepares to turn over his "hostages" to the marines, the Bashaw's men, plus German troops commanded by his deceptive brother, ambush him.

• Raisuli is imprisoned and tortured. Affirms Eden, "I intend to free the Raisuli." Captain Jerome concurs, "We'll throw in with ya."

• Inside the compound, the marines terminate the German squad and the Bashaw's Arabs; Eden shoots the Bashaw dead. Cut to Raisuli and Sherif's men entering the compound. German cannon fire kills scores, but "good" Moroccans manage to penetrate the fort. Assisting the marines, they crush the villains.

• Eden releases the bound Raisuli. Abruptly, he confronts his brother, who wears a German uniform. They grab swords, and duel. Raisuli triumphs, sparing his brother's life. Eden and the children pause, acknowledging his gallantry. Raisuli and his men ride off.

• Reading Raisuli's letter about the incident, President Roosevelt, too, acknowledges the Arab's bravery. The camera reveals the Moroccan sea coast. Sunset. Raisuli and his friend Sherif are rejoicing.

Note: In Tangier, on 18 May 1904, Raisuli actually kidnapped Mr. Ion Perdicaris, a wealthy Greek-American businessman, "about sixty years of age," and his companion, "Cromwell O. Varley. [But] No one [was] shot at the villa—no one." Though both men "were well treated" and eventually released, President Roosevelt was outraged, threatening intervention. That same month, "the Americans sent six heavy cruisers" to Morocco. "[The] American invasion of Tangier by American soldiers had its amusing side. Roosevelt discovered but kept secret that Perdicaris was 'indeed a Greek subject' and had 'therefore forfeited his American nationality.'" In the end, Sherif Moulai Ahmed Ben Mohammed el Raisuli benefitted from the president's actions. As for Raisuli's "old enemy Sidi Abderrahman, [he was] removed and [Raisuli] promptly stepped into his job as Caid of Tangier. He also pocketed a ransom of seventy thousand dollars." In 1923, two years before his death, writer Rosita Forbes interviewed Raisuli. This Moroccan, she writes, "constructs an image of a patriot and defender of the weak, a Robin Hood of the Rif."[193]

The Wizard of Bagdad (1960), TCF. *Dick Shawn, Diane Baker, Barry Coe, Michael Burns, Leslie Wenner, Don Beddoe.* P: Sam Katzman. EGYPTIANS

This set-in Baghdad satire has Iraqi bedouins contesting treacherous Egyptians. Appearing is a genie and his talking horse; the horse speaks with a Bronx accent.

Scene: The genie, Ali-Mahmud (Shawn), rides atop a magic carpet singing, "Eni Menie Genie." Throughout, Ali-Mahmud gapes and gapes at harem maidens' midriffs. An Iraqi woman is mistakenly tagged, "My Persian pearl."

• The camera shows Princess Yasmin and Prince Husan as childhood sweethearts.

• Flash forward. The palace displays scantily-clad harem maidens. The evil Wazir moves to corner Yasmin (Baker); She rejects the villain.

• Though Husan (Coe) wins a wrestling match, Egyptian villains dispatch him to the palace dungeon. In time, the genie Ali-Mahmud arrives, freeing Husan from the chopping block.

• Ali-Mahmoud and Husan enlist the help of brave Iraqi bedouins; together, they bring down the Egyptian invaders. The genie's talking horse kicks an Egyptian over the palace wall.

• In the harem, scantily-clad maidens coddle Ali-Mahmoud and his talking horse.

• Hasan finally comes to find out that lovely Yasmin is his childhood sweetheart; they unite and rule Baghdad.

Note: Some early 1960s movies presented young starlets, such as Diane Baker, as stunning Arab heroines.

• Egyptian heavies wear unconventional garb—red medieval outfits, complete with steel-pointed helmets and armor mesh.

Dialogue: An Arab is called a "treacherous toad." Maidens are tagged "lazy, useless girls."

Women on the Verge of a Nervous Breakdown (1988), OR. Spanish with subtitles. *Carmen Maura, Maria Barranco.* W, D: Pedro Almodovar. Academy Award for Best Foreign Language Film. CAMEOS, VILLAINS

A distraught woman tries to cope after her long-time lover abandons her. Yet, the protagonists often refer to Arab Muslim terrorists.

Scene: In Madrid, three Arab Muslim terrorists plan to hijack a plane en route to Switzerland. The Arabs deceive a lovely model, Candela (Barranco), who inadvertently permits them to stay in her flat. During the weekend, she even allows one of the "Shiite terrorists" to make love to her. Explains Candela to her friend, "[One day] he showed up with two more Shiites... all three just moved in... I noticed something weird about them and he confessed they were Shiite terrorists. They had weapons [and] they were planning to attack somewhere." Sighs Candela, "That's when I realized he didn't love me... I was a hostage in my own house."

• Later, the naive Candela confesses, "Men keep taking advantage of me. Look how the Arab world treated me... I wouldn't want to be with a man right now." Candela worries that "the cops" will find out about her housing the "terrorists" and then jail her "for collaborating." To her relief, the police prevent the Shiites from hijacking Madrid's "ten PM flight to Stockholm... taking it to Beirut to free some Shiite prisoners." Declares the TV announcer: "A group of Shiite terrorists were captured here in Madrid today."

• After watching television, Candela removes the terrorists' clothing from her apartment. Immediately, she empties their belongings atop a garbage dump.

Won Ton Ton, The Dog Who Saved Hollywood (1976), PAR. *Art Carney, Madeline Kahn, Ron Liebman.* See *World's Greatest Lover* (1977). CAMEOS, SHEIKHS

In this parody of "Sheik" films white-robed Arabs fight black-robed ones.

Scene: A movie poster promotes the silent film, *The Fighting Sheik.* Actor Ron Liebman stars as the Arab potentate. The poster reveals the white-robed actor atop a white horse, pointing a scabbard at a black-clad Arab.

• The actor's Hollywood abode resembles an Arabian Nights movie set, complete with decorative pillows and Oriental carpets. The actor's servants wear Arab garb. And, two live camels frame the entrance-way.

• Inside a movie theater, the actor watches himself perform as the "fighting sheik." The film shows him romancing beautiful maidens and crushing black-robed Arabs.

The Wonders of Aladdin (1961), MGM. *Donald O'Connor, Vittorio DeSica, Noelle Adam.* Filmed in Morocco. MAIDENS

This Arab vs. Arab tale, complete with magic carpet, displays some not-so-nice Arabs. Baghdad's Grand Vizier, "the father of 27 sons," lusts after the princess (Adam).

Opposing the vizier and his evil magician are Aladdin (O'Connor), his sidekick, Omar, a heroic prince, a lovely princess, a benevolent sultan, a blind beggar, slave girls, bellydancers, and scores of half-naked Amazon women; plus, a white-haired red-robed Anglo genie (DeSica). Speaking with a thick European accent, the genie looks like an elegant Italian opera singer.

Scene: Aladdin's mother, a selfless woman, serves her son soup; taking none for herself.

• As the princess and her maidens bathe, men bearing jewels arrive, blindfolded. Says the princess, "[If they see us,] my father would have them beheaded."

• The vizier opens a trap door; his screaming victims go hurtling down into a lion's pit. Cut to the evil magician; he creates life-size female mannequins, one of which doles out embraces of death. A similar mannequin-as-assassin ploy is used in *The Thief of Bagdad* (1940).

• In the desert, the Amazon women collar Aladdin and Omar. Aladdin is selected to spend the night with the leader. Aladdin's joy turns into sorrow when he ascertains that come morning, "the one she chooses" is usually "made into a kerchief." But, the Amazon leader and her women spare, then aid, Aladdin

• Throughout, the Amazon women wear skimpy red and silver swimsuits, prompting Eugene Archer to write "[*The Wonders of Aladdin* not only features a] multitudinous display of pulchritude [but offers] the sleaziest chorus of bellydancers since Sally Rand abandoned burlesque."[194] The American Legion of Decency cautioned producers that Arabian fantasies such as *Aladdin and His Lamp* (1952), *Thief of Damascus* (1952), *The Veils of Bagdad* (1953), and *Adventures of Hajji Baba* (1954), display an abundance of suggestive costumes and dances.

• The princess' loyal guards attack. Quips one of the vizier's henchmen, "Royal horse guards fighting bravely and intelligently. I thought I'd never live to see that." As soon as the vizier is crushed, the prince and princess embrace. As Aladdin and his lady friend fly off on a magic carpet, the heavenly red-robed genie soars upward through the clouds.

Note: During the filming in Tunis, Muslims rioted over the use of a mosque.

The World's Greatest Lover (1977), TCF. *Gene Wilder, Carol Kane.* SP, P, D: Wilder. SHEIKHS

This fun-filled odyssey, complete with a telling conclusion, spoofs desert Arabs.

Scene: Inside a movie theater, the lovely Anne (Kane) watches an ugly, bearded Arab torturing the bound Western protagonist. When the movie Arab wields a ball and chain, bloodying the screen hero, Anne shudders.

• The film studio auditions performers; they are in need of actors to portray Arabs in a forthcoming desert film. Most performers who audition are inept. One falls off his horse; the other has really bad breath, flooring both the leading lady and the director.

• The director selects to portray a desert sheikh, the actor Valentine (Wilder). He teaches Valentine how to dress and how to act "Arab." Abruptly, a crew member yanks a checkered tablecloth from a nearby table. Representing a burnoose, the cloth is placed atop Valentine's head.

• Appearing before the camera as a screen sheikh, Valentine gallops onto the shooting set. Sitting atop a white horse, he takes in the desert oasis setting, complete with beautiful dancing girls and legionnaires. Unexpectedly, Valentine ignores his scripted lines, shouting instead, "This is fake. This is not real life." Deciding all this Hollywood Arab movie stuff is "fake," Valentine rides off the set.

Note: Perhaps one day, actors called on to portray stereotypical Arabs will be as spirited as Valentine, and exit shooting sets declaring, "This is fake."

Credits state: "Arab Wrangler" and "Slave Girl #2."

Wrong Is Right (1982), COL. *Sean Connery, George Gizzard, Robert Conrad, John Saxon, Katherine Ross, Henry Silva, Hardy Kruger, Ron Moody, Jennifer Jason Leigh, Leslie Nielsen, Robert Webber, Rosalind Cash, Dean Stockwell, Tony March.* SP, P, D: Richard Brooks. Based on the novel, *The Better Angels,* by Charles McCarrey. Filmed in Israel. PALESTINIANS, SHEIKHS, WORST LIST

WWIII is imminent. In the US, Arab students and Palestinian fanatics implant plastic bombs into their bodies, then blow up themselves and innocent Americans. The Arab villains insist the US president resign. If not, they intend to unleash two atomic bombs over New York City. An irrational oil-rich Arab potentate supports a Palestinian terrorist who hate Jews.

Scene: Appearing in "Hagreb," Arabia, a desert with oil wells, is Patrick Hale (Connery), a globe-trotting reporter for the World Television Network (WTN). Accompanying Hale is undercover agent Sally Blake (Ross). They plan to meet with King Awad (Moody). Cut to Awad fraternizing with Rafeeq (Silva), "the world's bloodiest terrorist"; Rafeeq leads fanatics called, "The Eye of Gaza." En route to see Awad, Patrick and Sally encounter several bearded Arabs, toting guns. The screeching Arabs, who wear red and white checkered kuffiyehs, are pummeling a car belonging to a European arms merchant, Helmut Unger's (Kruger). Why are the Arabs behaving so violently? Because Unger's auto crushed a camel. "Death to America," shout the Arabs; "Death to the Jews." Quips Sally, "God bless oil!"

• Outside the US Embassy, Arabs flaunt signs and scream, "Leave us Yankees"; "Go Home We Don't Want You"; and "Stay out of our country." Fending off the mob, guards toss a tear gas canister, then fire their weapons.

• Claiming Sally Blake's pal "was an Israeli secret agent," Arab terrorists kill him and Sally. Says an Arab, "The terrorist Jew dies by his own bomb. No question. No question."

• Washington, DC, Office of President Lockwood (Gizzard). The President watches a TV newscast showing demonstrating Arabs shouting, "We don't hate the American people. Except the Jews. And President Lockwood."

• Cut to Texas. Standing atop a truck is the rabble-rousing Senator Mallory (Nielsen); he tells his blue-collar supporters, "A bunch of raggedly-rich over there [are] screaming 'Death to America,' and our president does nothing! The Ayrabs raised the price of oil four times in two years. And they'll raise it again. And what are we going to do about that?" The crowd cheers!

• At Hagreb's airport, Awad, the "religious fanatic," prays, saying he "must do God's will." Says Lockwood, King Awad "must respect Jews." Quips the CIA Chief, Jack Philindros (Spradlin), "Dead ones, yes!"

• An American spy satellite reveals an Arab "enemy training camp," complete with gunfire and explosions. Cut to in-training Palestinian "crackpots." One Palestinian trainee dies. Directing the Eye of Gaza radicals is Rafeeq. Boasts Rafeeq, "[I will commit any violent act, so long as] the cause [is advanced]. We plan to purify Islam."

- Washington, DC, agent Philindros explains that one month ago "two airliners exploded over Israel." Asked how people could go about planting bombs on secure planes, Philindros says, "Plastique, implanted by surgeons into the flesh of Rafeeq's agents." Explains the agent, Awad purchased two atomic bombs. Why? Because "the voices in the desert told him (King Awad) to." Warns the agent, Rafeeq will soon acquire the bombs, then detonate them. "[His primary] targets [are] Tel Aviv and Jerusalem."

- US General Wombat (Conrad), who heads the "task force fighting terrorism," tells the president, "Just press the button on that little black box. And in thirty minutes, WHAM! No more Arabs, no more oil crisis."

- At Rafeeq's camp, as Palestinians fire weapons into the air, Rafeeq demands from America, billions of dollars. He warns that unless Lockwood resigns, he will launch A-bombs, destroying "the people of New York City."

- Lockwood wants US troops to crush Hagreb's Arabs; to "blast 'em out of the ball park." Awad dies. Though the press claims Awad committed suicide, the CIA assassinated the ruler.

- In Hagreb, rampaging Arabs burn the American flag and toss grenades inside the Embassy.

- New York City. Angry pro-Arab radicals, wearing robes and kuffiyehs, scream, "No more lies; the Jews own television." As these troublemakers are wearing Arab garb the implication is they are either Arab students and/or Arab Americans. Policemen arrive and crush the protestors. One of Rafeeq's robed radicals blows himself up.

- Rafeeq becomes Hagreb's potentate. Immediately, the oil-rich ruler checks out a weapon that "makes killing a pleasure." Rafeeq tells reporters that oil prices are "going up to $22 a barrel." When asked about the fate of "the homeless Palestinians," he quips, "We'll sell them oil, of course." What about "the Israelis?" asks Unger. Chuckles Rafeeq, "They'll have to pay more, of course." And, when asked, "Why punish the people of Europe?" Rafeeq says, "You're all the same!" Cut to reporter Patrick Hale telling Americans, "The price of gas went up fifty cents a gallon, and [there's not] enough to go around." Cut to angry, panicked drivers lined up at US gas stations.

- At the Alamo, President Lockwood addresses a cheering crowd. Suddenly, an Arab wearing a checkered black-and-white headdress explodes himself, nearly killing Lockwood. The Arab's female cohort grabs an ice pick, fatally stabbing an FBI agent.

- General Wombat informs fellow Americans about Arab terror, "When the rats take over, call the exterminator, and blast off." Barks Wombat, "Turn us loose Mr. President and we'll blow 'em all to Hell."

- In Times Square, "Arab students" wearing robes and checkered kuffiyehs demonstrate, shouting, "Death to America"; "Death to the Jews"; "Kill the Jews." The police and angry Americans tussle with the Arab students; one student ignites herself.

- "The city of infidels," Washington, DC. Three Arab terrorists blow themselves up near the Capitol. "Insane" attacks also take place in "Chicago, Detroit."

- Rafeeq, or someone imitating his "suicidal" voice, warns that the Arab suicide bombings will not stop until Lockwood resigns. The voice threatens to release "two [pre-set] atom bombs [that] will destroy the city and people of New York." Cut to a scale model of New York, showing the bombs' impact on city residents and dwellings.

Finis: Viewers ascertain that the CIA, not Rafeeq, planted the two bogus A-bombs in New York. The camera shows CIA agents locating the bombs and disarming them—

"in the nick of time." Now, what happens? "War!" Believing Rafeeq's Arabs planted the A-bombs, Senator Mallory tells Lockwood, "You hit 'em. Hit 'em with everything you've got. But for God's sake, don't hit those oil wells." Barks General Wombat, "Attack! Pulverize 'em. We can wipe them off the map in five hours; let's kick ass." Cut to advancing US troops; our tanks and planes blast Hagreb, terminating Rafeeq.

Note: In exchange for prominent credit and "the assurance people would see the word Sony on every set," director Richard Brooks received $800,000 worth of [film] equipment on loan from Sony. Concerned viewers, mostly Arab Americans, criticized Sony executives for "endorsing a detrimental characterization of the Arab people." Reacting to complaints, William E. Baker, vice president of corporate affairs, said that Sony would be "more sensitive" in the future. VAR reports Baker said, in a letter to Middle East consultant Margaret Penner that this movie "caused us to review our approval procedure" (7 April 1982).

Wrongfully Accused (1998), WB. *Leslie Nielsen, Mina E. Mina.* W, P, D: Pat Proft. CAMEOS, SHEIKHS

This comedy focuses on an American who is framed for murder. Yet, an Arab Muslim is singled out for ridicule.

Scene: When screen credits cease rolling, the protagonist, Ryan (Nielsen), appears at a multi-millionaire's outdoor party, clasping a tennis racket. All the invited guests are Westerners, except for one—a white-burnoosed, mustachioed Arab (Mina). As the Arab walks past Ryan, he swings his racket, accidentally hitting the Arab below the belt. "Oh! Oh! My balls! Oh, Allah!" moans the Arab, falling to his knees. Quips Ryan, "Muslim prayers. That must be East." As Ryan starts to walk away, the frightened Arab again moans, "My hand!? Oh!"

A Yank in Libya (1942), Producers Releasing Corp. *H.B. Warner, Duncan Renaldo, Walter Woolf King, George Lewis, Amarilla Morris, Joan Woodbury.* S, SP: Arthur St. Claire, Sherman Lowe. See *Action in Arabia* (1944) and *I Cover the War* (1937). SHEIKHS, MAIDENS

This tiresome WWII set-in-Libya espionage drama reveals a heroic Yank reporter. Pro-Nazi Arab "tribes" fight pro-British Arabs.

Scene: The mythical kingdom of El-Muktar. Sheikh Ibrahim's (Lewis) pro-Nazi Arabs pursue an American reporter, Mike Malone (King). The Arab-clad Malone enters the British enclave, and rushes into Nancy Brooks' (Woodbury) room. Seeking a man clad in Arab garb, Nancy retreats, screaming, "What do you want?" Malone removes his Arab robe and headdress. Relieved, Nancy sighs, "Oh, I thought..." Nods Malone, "I know. You thought I was an Arab!" He shows Nancy a "Made In Germany" weapon, explaining, "The Germans... are supplying the Arabs with guns and ammunition."

• The Nazi agent, Herr Streyer (Vaughn), delivers some rifles to the Arab villain, Ibrahim. Intent on uniting and convincing the "tribes" to side with the Germans, Ibrahim tells potential allies, "We have powerful friends who will help us."

• The "faster than a racing camel" Ibrahim calls Malone an "unbeliever" and an "infidel pig." Barks Ibrahim, "Unbelieving dog, may your father cease to bark."

• At "the Foreign Club," Arab musicians perform. Ibrahim takes a knife, boasting,

"First in my heart is the crusade against the infidel." Suddenly, he and his cohorts attack Malone and his pal, Benny. Instantly, Benny grabs a large tray and bangs Arab heads.

• Benny also dupes the bellydancer Haditha (Morris) into helping Malone escape from jail. He hands her a string of pearls, purring, "[This] cost me fifteen cents at a five and dime store." Thinking the pearls are worth "the price of twenty camels," Haditha grunts, "Give to me."

• The movie's pro-British Arab, Sheikh David, (Renaldo), falls for Nancy, saying, "I am of my people." Sighs Nancy, "You are a fine person." Yet, they go their separate ways.

• Ibrahim's Arabs nab and bury Malone in the sand; only his head is visible. Malone's fate? "The Punishment of the Spears." Ibrahim's Arabs mount their horses and ride off, tossing spears and daggers at Malone. Fortunately, they miss their target. In time, Sheikh David appears, rescuing Malone.

• Herr Streyer deceives the Arab "tribes," telling them the British have killed their respected leader, Sheikh David. Abruptly, stock footage shows Arabs charging a British fort. As the attacking Arabs close in, the British sound an alarm, shouting, "Get the women and children into the fort." Stale Cowboy and Indians scenarios contained such scenes and dialogue. Often, as Indians closed in on outnumbered pioneers and US Cavalry members, they shouted similar lines.

• Sheikh David's Arabs arrive at the fort, repelling Ibrahim's men. Though wounded, Sheikh David helps rout the rogues, and he kills Ibrahim.

Dialogue: The clad-in-Arab-garb Benny mocks, thrice, Islam, saying: "By the beard of the prophet."

Yankee Pasha (1954), UNI. *Jeff Chandler, Rhonda Fleming, Mamie Van Doren, Bart Roberts, Hal March, Lee J. Cobb.* See *Pirates of Tripoli* (1955). VILLAINS, MAIDENS

American sailors bring down anti-Christian Moroccans. Arabs vs. Arabs. Islam is mocked; Arab women are slandered. Arab slavers appear. This sex-in-the-sand-saga also presents Miss Universe contestants as harem maidens.

Scene: Salem, Massachusetts, circa 1800. The delectable Roxana (Fleming) sets sail for France. Abruptly, pirates attack her ship, whisking "the tasty morsel" off to Morocco.

• Her beau, Jason (Chandler), the stalwart hero, learns of the assault. He asks whether Roxana "is still alive." Quips a Salem official, "If so, it would be kinder to accept her as dead than to think of her as a slave in Islam." He warns Jason not to go to Morocco, "you would be discovered and made a slave."

• In Morocco, the US Consul forewarns Jason, "The sultan considers all non-believers his subjects and his slaves. There are no free Christians in Morocco."

• The Moroccan sultan's (Cobb) desert palace boasts a prison, complete with torture gear. There's also a throne room, a grand hall, a bathing pool, and the ruler's harem quarters. Cut to the souk; prominently displayed is an Arab slaver's platform.

• Lilith (Van Doren), an Arab maiden tagged "the tattler" is delivered to Jason as a "present." When Jason balks, a Moroccan advises, "[Women] must be taught that the duty of a slave is prompt obedience to the will of the master." Such criteria do not apply to Roxana, the American heroine. She refuses to abide in Omar Id-Din's (Roberts) harem.

• American ships passing through the Mediterranean must pay the sultan monies. One sailor protests, "Someday we'll be able to sail without our government having to buy our safety."

• Though the Arabs jail Jason, he is freed by Hassan (March), the film's one and only "decent" Arab. Cut to Omar's sinister saber-swinging stooges attacking Jason and Hassan. American sailors to the rescue; they deliver solid uppercuts, flattening the Arabs.

• The US fighters render Morocco's "sultan a great service" by disposing "of the one man [Omar] whose ambition [to nab the throne] was a constant threat."

Finis: Finally, the sultan allows Jason to exchange Lilith for his true love, Roxana. She embraces Jason, saying, "[Morocco is] a strange and mysterious country where women are the slaves of men."

Young Sherlock Holmes (1985), PAR. *Nicholas Rowe, Sophie Ward, Anthony Higgins.* SP: Chris Colombo. P: Steven Spielberg. See *Back to the Future* (1985). CAMEOS, EGYPTIANS

Not only does Spielberg present Holmes' long-standing nemesis Dr. Moriarty as half-Egyptian, Spielberg shows young Holmes battling Moriarty and his Egyptian cult. These villains abduct and kill innocent girls. Would Sir Arthur Conan Doyle approve?

Scene: Mid-Victorian London's foggy streets. Amazingly, the camera reveals a run-down English pub run by, would you believe, an Arab speaking Arabic? Cut to a bellydancer. When young Holmes (Rowe) appears, the inn's scruffy Arabs draw guns.

• Introducing crazed Englishmen clad in Egyptian garb; they tag themselves, the Osiris group. Prowling the streets, Osiris' villains not only kidnap young English girls, they inject the women with hallucinogen-dipped darts, delivered by blowguns.

• The cult abducts five girls, whisking them off to their underground pyramid—a temple of doom. The extremists wrap the girls in white linen, douse them with oil, and burn them. Among those perishing is the film's heroine (Ward), Holmes' one and only love.

Note: Who is the villain responsible for mystifying and then directing fiendish idol-worshipers to burn these innocent young English girls? Professor Moriarty, an Egyptian-English villain. Had Spielberg stuck to the facts, he would have projected Moriarty not as a half-Egyptian heavy, but as a half-Jewish villain. Authorities on Sherlock Holmes point out that the inspiration for his arch-nemesis, Professor Moriarty, was Adam Worth, the son of German Jewish immigrants. Worth, a Civil War deserter, resided in New York City, where he rose from common pickpocket to criminal mastermind.[195]

Your Ticket Is No Longer Valid (1981), a.k.a. A Slow Descent Into Hell, a.k.a. Finishing Touch, Films RSL. *Richard Harris, George Peppard, Jennifer Dale, Jeanne Moreau.* SP: Leila Basen, Ian McLellan Hunter. P: Robert Lantos, Stephen J. Roth. Based on Romain Gary's novel. CAMEOS, SHEIKHS

Inflammatory dialogue. Arabs residing in Paris are "sons-of-bitches" out to "fuck a man's wife." And, those "goddamn [sheikhs] own half the world."

Scene: Jason (Harris), a financial mogul, tries to save the family business. Attending a lavish reception, he and his girlfriend, Laura (Dale), run into a fellow businessman, Jim (Peppard). Barks Jim, "Did you see those goddamn Arabs?... If you don't let 'em in the front door, they buy the place and change the locks. Sheikhs. You remember?" Cut to some bearded, robed Arabs wearing sunglasses and thobes. Continues Jim, "We used to buy them [Sheik condoms] in drugstores, four in a pack, one size fits all... but now sheikhs are giving us the shaft. The sons-of-bitches own half the world and got an option on the rest. Us white folks are outnumbered. The only thing holding those towelheads back is respect for our brainpower." Jim's slurs stand.

• A Parisian advises Jason, "If I were looking for a thief, I'd go to the foreign quarter, to the Café Tobruk." Inside the quarter, Arab music underscores scenes displaying seedy Arabs. One tells Jason, "I fuck your wife, you like? I fuck your wife, you watch, okay?" Instantly, the Arab starts pawing Laura. Jason tries to stop him; some Arabs pull knives. Jason yanks a pistol; he and Laura exit.

• At a live sex show, Jim and Jason watch a dark-complexioned man seducing a woman. Moans Jim, "God damn Arabs, they get the broads first and all we get is a dose of clap. I wonder if they really are better hung than we are." Quips Jason, "I doubt if he's an Arab. More like a gypsy. Probably from Spain." Retorts Jim, "They're all the same." Jason is silent.

INTRODUCTION

[1] Max Alvarez, "Heroes & Villains," *Extra!* September–October 1998: 27.

[2] Sydney Harris, "The World Shrinks and Stereotypes Fall," *Detroit Free Press* 11 April 1986: editorial page.

[3] John F. Kennedy, Commencement address, Yale University, 11 July 1962.

[4] The 22 Arab states are Algeria, Bahrain, Chad, Comoros, Djibouti, Egypt, Iraq, Jordan, Lebanon, Libya, Mauritania, Morocco, Oman, Palestine, Qatar, Saudi Arabia, Somalia, Sudan, Syria, Tunisia, United Arab Emirates, and Yemen.

[5] Jay Stone, *Ottawa Citizen* 16 March 1996.

[6] Richard Dreyfuss, quoted in "Hollywood, DC: A Tale of Two Cities," Bravo-TV, 6 November 2000.

[7] *CBS This Morning* 10 July 1999.

[8] William Greider, "Against the Grain," *Washington Post* 15 July 1979: 4E.

[9] Roger Ebert, *Chicago Sun Times* 6 November 1998.

[10] Sam Keen, Address to the Association of Editorial Cartoonists, San Diego, CA, 15 May 1986.

[11] Jerry Mander, *Four Arguments for the Elimination of Television* (New York: William Morrow, 1978).

[12] See ADC, "The Anti-Discrimination Hate Crimes," (Washington, DC, 1996).

[13] Henry Kissinger, "Stone's Nixon," *Washington Post* 24 January 1996.

[14] Magdoline Asfahani, "My Turn," *Newsweek* 2 December 1996.

[15] David Copelin, "The Television Image in American Film & TV," *Cineaste* XVII (1989):1.

[16] Jack G. Shaheen, "The Arab World as Place," *Beyond the Stars, Volume 4: Locales in American Popular Film*, ed. Paul Loukides and Linda K. Fuller (Bowling Green, OH: Bowling Green State University Press, 1993).

[17] Anthony Lane, *The New Yorker* 10 May 1999.

[18] Andrew Dowdy's *The Films of the Fifties: The American State of Mind* was originally published as *Movies are Better Than Ever: Wide-Screen Memories of the Fifties* (New York: William Morrow, 1973).

[19] Ken Weiss and Ed Goodgold, *To Be Continued...* (New York: Crown, 1972): vii–viii; 335–36.

[20] For movies featuring African-American actors destroying reel Arabs, see *Best Defense* (1984), *Iron Eagle* (1986), *The Delta Force* (1986), *Wanted: Dead or Alive* (1987), *Firewalker* (1986), *Kazaam* (1996), *The Siege* (1998), and *Rules of Engagement* (2000).

[21] Matthew Sweet, "Movie Targets: Arabs Are the Latest People to Suffer the Racial Stereotyping of Hollywood," *The Independent* 30 July 2000.

[22] Lawrence Suid, *Sailing on the Silver Screen: Hollywood and the U.S. Navy* (Annapolis, MD: Naval Institute Press, 1996): 151.

[23] Greider 1E.

[24] See *Chain of Command* (1993).

[25] Sweet.

[26] Edward W. Said, *Orientalism* (New York: Pantheon, 1978): 125.

[27] I.C.B. Dear and M.R.D. Foot, eds., *The Oxford Companion to World War II* (Oxford: Oxford University Press, 1995).

[28] William Zinsser, "In Search of Lawrence of Arabia," *Esquire* June 1961: 72.

[29] "Fencing By Ear," *Missou* Fall 1997: 11.

[30] Adolph Zukor, "Most Important Events of the Year," *Wid's Year Book* 1918. For more on Palestinian portraits, see my essay "Screen Images of Palestinians in the 1980s," *Beyond the Stars, Volume 1: Stock Characters in American Film*, ed. Paul Loukides and Linda K. Fuller (Bowling Green, OH: Bowling Green State University Press, 1990).

[31] Maureen Dowd, "Cuomos vs. Sopranos," *New York Times* 22 April 2001.

[32] Sidney Furie, speaking with Arthur Lord, *Today* on NBC-TV 12 January 1987.

[33] *Censored!*, documentary, American Movie Classics, 7 December 1999.

[34] Dowd.

[35] Gary Crowdus and Dan Georgakas, "Thinking about the Power of Images: An Interview with Spike Lee," *Cineaste* XXVI:2.

[36] *Moving Picture World* 18 May 1907: 167 and Charles Musser, "Role-playing and Film Comedy," *Unspeakable Images: Ethnicity and the American Cinema*, ed. Lester D. Friedman (Urbana, IL: University of Illinois Press): 52–53.

FILMS A–B

[37] Bob Furmanek and Ron Palumbo, *Abbott and Costello in Hollywood* (New York: Putnam, 1991): 200.

[38] Furmanek and Palumbo 201.

[39] Buster Crabbe's TV series *Captain Gallant of the Foreign Legion* is available from Video Resources: 1-800-442-7055.

[40] Jeff Rovin, *The Encyclopedia of Super Villains* (New York: Facts on File, 1987).

[41] Henry A. Giroux, *The Mouse That Roared: Disney and the End of Innocence* (New York, 1999): 104.

[42] "Romance is Inevitable," *Kuwait Times* 31 October 1995: 21.

[43] Daniel H. Cerone, "Robin Williams Back in," *TV Guide* 3 August 1996.

[44] Lynette Rice, "Aladdin Sequel Draws Complaints," *Los Angeles Times* 19 May 1994.

[45] "Toy Story," *Associated Press* 10 October 1999.

[46] See Jeff Rovin's comments on Aladdin in *The Encyclopedia of Super Villains*.

[47] Ann Lolordo, "Kuffiyeh is above Fashion, Faction," *The Baltimore Sun* 12 August 1998.

[48] Christopher Hitchens, "The Clinton–Douglas Debates," *The Nation* 16 November 1998.

[49] Liam O'Leary, *Rex Ingram: Master of the Silent Cinema* (London: British Film Institute, 1994).

[50] See Luther S. Luedtke's *Hawthorne and the Romance of the Orient* (Bloomington: Indiana University Press, 1989).

[51] Douglas Porch, *Conquest of Morocco* (Forward Movement, March 1986): 54, 531.

[52] Thanks to Linda Rafeedie for the *Good News* (1947) citation.

[53] Robert W. Lebling Jr., "Dos Passos in the Desert," *ARAMCO World* July/August 1997: 8–10.

FILMS C–F

[54] Ella Shohat, *Israeli Cinema: East/West and the Politics of Representation* (Austin: University of Texas Press, 1989).

[55] Donald Davidson, "Indy Yesterday," Indianapolis Motor Speedway Hall of Fame Museum.

[56] Janet Wallach, *Desert Queen* (New York: Doubleday, 1997).

[57] Thanks to Steve Ward of La Jolla, CA, for providing a copy of *The Attack of the Moors*.

[58] Marie Dennis et al., *St. Francis and the Foolishness of God* (New York: Orbis Books, 1993).

[59] Ann Zwicker Kerr, *Come with Me from Lebanon* (Syracuse: Syracuse University Press, 1994): 206–7.

[60] Amy Docker Marcus, "The Veil Is Old Hat, But Muslim Women Give It New Vogue," *Wall Street Journal* 1 May 1997.

[61] Kirk Honeycutt, "On the Screen, Lee Marvin Gets Even," *St. Louis Globe–Democrat* 15–16 February 1986.

[62] "Accents at the AFI," *Variety* 26 February 1986.

[63] Michael Elkin, "Terror on Film," *Jewish Exponent* 20 February 1987.

[64] Haya El Nasser, "More Arab-Bashing Feared in Hollywood Depictions," *USA Today* 3 January 1991.

[65] Bruce Fetter, ed., *Colonial Rule in Africa: Readings From Primary Sources* (Madison: University of Wisconsin Press, 1979): 46–49. See also Evelyn Baring's *Modern Egypt* (New York, 1908): Vol. 1: 4-6; Vol. 2: 146–248.

[66] "*Executive Decision*: Hollywood Actor Reveals the True Story," *The Minaret* April 1996.

[67] Art Stevens, *The Population Explosion* (Washington, DC: Acropolis Books, Ltd., 1985).

[68] Alan Gevinson, *Within Our Gates: Ethnicity in American Feature Films, 1911–1960* (Berkeley: University of California Press, 1997).

[69] For more on *Father of the Bride Part II*, see my essay, "Disney Has Done It Again," *Washington Report On Middle East Affairs* February/March 1996: 44.

[70] Charles Kennedy, "When the Streets of Cairo Met Main Street: Little Egypt and the Salome Dancers," Southeastern Middle East and Islamic Studies Seminar, Fall 1993. In his paper, Kennedy refers to Edo McCulloh's history of New York's Coney Island.

[71] David Nasaw, *Going Out* (New York: Basic Books, 1993): 77.

[72] Morey, *The Islamic Invasion* (Eugene, OR: Harvest House Publishers, 1992).

[73] John Buchan, *Greenmantle* (New York: Grosset & Dunlap, 1916): 58.

[74] Antoine de Saint Exupéry, *Wind, Sand, and Stars* (London: William Heinemann, 1939).

[75] Steve Shagan, *The Formula* (New York: William Morrow & Company, 1979): 162–64, 184–85, 195, 201, 265–66, 324–25.

[76] Porch 112.

[77] Sari Naisr, *The Arabs and the English* (London: Longman, 1978): 58.

[78] Joan DuPont, "Roman Polanski at 54 and *Frantic*," *New York Times* 27 March 1988: H29.

FILMS G–L

[79] Thanks to Michele & Robert Tasoff for the *Gladiator* (2000) citation.

[80] Kathleen Coleman, e-mail to Mehrunisa Quayyum, an American-Arab Anti-Discrimination (ADC) intern, 17 June 2000.

[81] See "De Imperatoribus Romanis: An Online Encyclopedia of Roman Emperors" at www.roman-emperors.org

[82] Thanks to Dr. Alfred Charles Richard Jr., author of *Censorship and Hollywood's Hispanic Image* (Westport, CT: Greenwood Press, 1993), for the *Guns and Guitars* (1936) citation.

[83] Julie Salamon, "Jill Clayburgh, in Undies Again, Tackles the Mideast," *Wall Street Journal* 29 September 1983.

[84] "Chicago Alert Costa-Gavras Film Yanked from Distribution," P.H.R.C. Newsletter January 1984.

[85] Aljean Harmetz, "Hollywood Tackles Hot Issues," *San Francisco Chronicle* 12 September 1983.

[86] Mark Langer, "Max and Dave Fleischer," *Film Comment* January/February 1975.

[87] For additional information on Hi Jolly, see Adele L. Younis and Philip M. Kayal, ed., *The Coming of the Arabic-Speaking People to the United States* (New York: Center for Migration Studies, 1995): 106–9.

[88] Thanks to David Wilt of College Park, MD, for the *Hey Rookie* (1944) citation.

[89] Miriam Rosen, "The Making of Omar Sharif: An Interview," *Cineaste* Vol 17 (1986): 20.

[90] John T. McManus and Louis Kronenberger, "Motion Pictures, the Theater, and Race Relations," *The Annals* March 1946: 153.

[91] Richard Harrington, Review of *Iron Eagle II*, *Washington Post* 15 November 1988.

[92] David Thompson, *Warren Beatty and Desert Eyes* (New York: Vintage, 1987): 442.

[93] "Arabs Kick Sand at Desert Comedy," *New York Post* 11 May 1987: 6.

[94] Peter Biskind, ed., "Inside Ishtar," *American Film* May 1987: 24, 26, 66.

[95] Thanks to Nancy and Salah Nasrallah for *Jerusalem* (1996) citation.

[96] Avner Eisenberg, "Avner the Eccentric," Self Family Arts Center, Hilton Head Island, SC, 24 February 1997.

[97] Erens, *The Jew in American Cinema* (Bloomington: Indiana University Press, 1984).

[98] Philip Sanford Marden, *Egyptian Days* (New York: Houghton Mifflin, 1912).

[99] Robert Birchard, letter to the author, 3 December 1994.

[100] James Swift of Kenrick-Glennon Seminary, letter to the author, 14 October 1989. See Bruce Metzger, ed. et al, *Great Events of Bible Times* (New York: Barnes & Noble Books, 1988): 131.

[101] Fouad Ajami, "History Reflected in a Cracked Mirror," *US News and World Report* 14 May 1996.

[102] Dennis et al.

[103] Joel Hudson, "Who Wrote *Lawrence of Arabia*?" *Cineaste* XX:4.

[104] Wallach.

[105] James Akins, letter to the author, 23 October 1989.

[106] David Fromkin, *Peace to End All Peace* (New York: Henry Holt, 1989).

[107] John Buchan, *Greenmantle* (New York: Grosset & Dunlap, 1916).

[108] Denis Mack Smith, *Mussolini's Roman Empire* (New York: Viking Press, 1976).

[109] "Israel Upset by Spy Novel," *New York Times* 6 July 1983.

[110] Nasaw 133.

[111] Thanks to Richard Hobson for *The Long Kiss Goodnight* (1996) citation.

[112] Roy Kinnard, *50 Years of Serial Thrills* (London: Scarecrow Press, Inc., 1983): 37.

[113] Weiss and Goodgold vii–viii.

[114] Thanks to Mon Ayash of Fall River, MA, for the *Lost in a Harem* (1944) citation.

[115] Furmanek and Palumbo.

[116] MAG 1444.

[117] O'Leary 194–97.

FILMS M–R

[118] See my "Hollywood's Distorted Picture of Arabs," *St. Louis Post–Dispatch* 1 August 1990.

[119] Suid.

[120] John Brady, *The Craft of the Screenwriter* (New York: Simon and Schuster, 1981).

[121] See John Law, "Arab Investors: Who They Are, What They Buy and Where" (New York: Chase World Information Corporation, 1980). See also the Winter 1980 issue of Laventhal and Horwath's *Perspective*, in which Benjamin Benson discusses US government reports on foreign investments in his essay "The Selling of America."

[122] Thanks to Michael Shaheen for the *Never Say Never Again* (1983) citation.

[123] Thanks to Robert Norberg for the *Office Space* (1999) citation.

[124] Thanks to David Wilt of College Park, MD, for the *Old Mother Riley* (1952) citation.

[125] Joy Al-Sofi, phone interview, 18 July 1997.

[126] "Gays, Baptists, and Disney," *USA Weekend* 18–20 July 1997: 20.

[127] Thanks to Gary Edgerton of the Communications Department, Goucher College, for this reference.

[128] "Solar Energy at Work for Future Generations," *Saudi Arabia* Winter 1987: 16.

[129] London's *Sunday Times* (4 October 1986) reports that, as early as 1986, Israel was ranked as the world's sixth largest producer of nuclear weapons. Since the mid-1960s, Israel's secret Negev Desert underground factory has produced between 100 and 200 nuclear warheads.

[130] Laurence Pope, Op-Ed essay: "Flickers of Our Anti-Islam Bigotry," *Los Angeles Times* 1 March 1985.

[131] Bob Cohn's comments were made at the Jewish Center, Clayton, MO, 8 January 1985.

[132] "Putting Saudi women to work," *The Economist* 26 September 1998.

[133] Nina Darnton, "Now It's Miss Hawn Goes to Washington," *New York Times* 23 December 1984.

[134] Joshua Hammer, "Outraged Arab-Americans Charge That Goldie Hawn's New Film Violates the Rules of *Protocol*," *People* 7 May 1984.

[135] Gregg Kilday, "Arabs Want Hollywood to Rewrite Their Fall-Guy Roles," *Los Angeles Herald Examiner* 28 July 1984.

[136] Bruce Handy, "The Force is Back," *Time* 10 February 1997.

[137] Gevinson 268.

[138] Philip and Joseph Kayal, *The Syrian-Lebanese in America* (Boston: Twayne Publishers, 1975): 74.

[139] Luedtke 194.

[140] Thanks to Professor Alfred Richard for the Popeye cartoon citation.

[141] Otto Friedrich, *City of Nets* (New York: Harper & Row, 1986).

[142] See Clyde Prestowitz Jr., *Trading Places* (New York: Basic Books, 1988) and Martin Tolchin, *Buying into America* (New York: Times Books, 1988).

[143] Nancy Anderson, "Believe That Fonda Believes," *Evening Outlook* 11 December 1981.

[144] "Quote of the Month," *New York Magazine* December 1982.

[145] Douglas Waller, "Hunt for a Mole," *Time* 19 May 1997.

[146] Chris Tricario and Marison Mull, "The Arab: No More Mr. Bad Guy?" *Los Angeles Times Calendar* 14 September 1986.

[147] Sana'a is the correct spelling.

[148] *ADC Action Alert* 12 April 2000.

[149] *CAIR Action Alert on* Rules of Engagement (11 April 2000).

[150] "*Rules of Engagement*: Former Navy Secretary Who Wrote Original Screenplay at First Objected to Film Version, Then Made Peace with It," *The Virginian-Pilot* 5 April 2000: E1.

FILMS S–Z

[151] See Clyde Jeavons, *A Pictorial History of War Films* (New Jersey: Citadel Press, 1974).

[152] Garth Jowett, *Film: The Democratic Art* (Boston: Little, Brown, 1976).

[153] Thanks to Will Brownell, a Valentino film buff, for *The Sheik* (1921) citation.

[154] Kenneth Anger, *Hollywood Babylon II* (New York: Dutton, 1984).

[155] Shohat 71.

[156] "Hollywood's 'The Siege' Besieged," *Washington Post* 6 November 1998: 1.

[157] Jack G. Shaheen, "We've Seen This Plot Too Many Times," *Washington Post* 15 November 1998: C3.

[158] This film's pre-release titles also included *Against All Enemies* and *Holy War.*

[159] Zwick, "Opinion: In the Hurt Game, Honesty Loses," *International Herald Tribune* 11 November 1998: 11.

[160] Matthew Miller, "Muslims: Enemy Depiction Is Unfair," *News Press* 27 November 1998.

[161] "Group Denounces Israeli Interrogations," *Associated Press* 10 May 1997.

[162] Andrew Dowdy, "Motion Pictures Classified by National Legion of Decency—February 1936–1955," *The Films of the Fifties* (New York: William Morrow & Company, 1973).

[163] Jim Harmon and Donald F. Glut, *The Great Movie Serials* (New York: Doubleday, 1972): 122.

[164] Thanks to David Wilt, College Park, MD, for the *Sorority House Massacre 2* (1992) citation.

[165] Tom Buckley, "At the Movies, Langella Tells of Egyptian Adventures," *New York Times* 1 February 1981.

[166] John M. McDougal, "When the Setting Calls for Pyramids, Filmmakers Avoid Egypt," *Christian Science Monitor* 31 July 1985.

[167] McDougal.

[168] Collier's Encyclopedia, 1960, s.v. "Suez Canal."

[169] Irwin Porges, *Edgar Rice Burroughs: The Man Who Created Tarzan* (Provo, UT: Brigham Young University Press, 1975).

[170] Porges 515.

[171] Edgar Maclean, "Reruns and Revivals: Profile of Ham Fisher," *The Comics Journal* 168 (May 1994).

[172] Cripps, "Making Movies Black," *Split Image: African-Americans in the Mass Media,* ed. Jannette L. Dates and William Barlow (Washington, DC: Howard University Press, 1990)

[173] Jack G. Shaheen, *The TV Arab* (Bowling Green, OH: Bowling Green State University Popular Press, 1984).

[174] David Finnigan, "Arab-Americans Cheer *3 Kings,*" *Hollywood Reporter* 1–3 October 1999: 1.

[175] Ray Hanania, "One of the Bad Guys," *Newsweek* 2 November 1998.

[176] "Neigh Sayers," *Newsweek* 1 November 1993.

[177] "No True Lies," *Topside Loaf* 6 August 1994.

[178] Russell Baker, "All in What Family?" 14 June 1994.

[179] "Hasta la Vista Fairness," *Los Angeles Times* August 1994.

[180] Pat Broeske and Nisid Hajari, "Burden of 'True'," *Entertainment Weekly* 5 August 1994.

[181] Carlo E. Cortés, "Knowledge, Construction, and Popular Culture: The Media As Multi-Cultural Educator," *Handbook for Research On Multi-Cultural Research Education,* ed. James A. Banks (Seattle: University of Washington, 1994).

[182] Broeske and Hajari.

[183] Thanks to ADC's Anne Marie Baylouny for the citation about *True Lies* (1994), a review of which appeared in *Entertainment Tonight* 18 July 1994.

[184] Nicci Gerrard, "Jamie Lee Curtis: Ready to Step into the Big Time," *Newswire* 21 September 1994.

[185] "Security Exercise Defames Arabs," *ADC Times* September 1993.

[186] John Ellis, *World War II: The Encyclopedia of Facts and Figures* (New York: Military Book Club, 1996).

[187] *World War Two Nation By Nation* (London: Arams and Armour, 1995): 205–209.

[188] Luedtke.

[189] Due to a newspaper strike in 1953, this quote from the *New York Times* never appeared in print.

[190] "Beware the Exploding Falafel," *Harper's* March 1989.

[191] Gary Crowdus, "Neil Jordan's Michael Collins," *Cineaste* Vol. XX11, No. 4.

[192] Fred Strickert, *The Holy Innocents,* unpublished text.

[193] Porch.

[194] Eugene Archer, "Wonders of Aladdin at Two Theaters," *New York Times* 23 December 1961.

[195] Ben Macintyre, *The Napoleon of Crime: The Life and Times of Adam Worth, Master Thief* (New York: Farrar, Straus & Giroux, 1997).

APPENDICES

A.K.A.—Alternate Titles

a.k.a.	*see:*
Abdullah's Harem	Abdulla the Great (1956)
Adventures of Sinbad the Sailor	The Adventures of Sinbad (1962)
The African Sorcerer	The Adventures of Prince Achmed (1925)
Aladdin and His Wonderful Lamp	Aladdin and the Magic Lamp (1982)
Aladdin and His Wonderful Lamp (1917)	Aladdin and the Wonderful Lamp (1917)
Amina and the Forty Thieves	The African Magician (unknown)
The Arab Conspiracy	The Next Man (1976)
Arabian naito: Shindobaddo no boken	The Adventures of Sinbad (1962)
Armor of God II: Operation Condor	Operation Condor (1997)
Ashanti: Land of No Mercy	Ashanti (1979)
L'Atlantide (1932)	Mistress of Atlantis (1932)
L'Atlantide (1961)	Journey beneath the Desert (1961)
Die Augen der Mummie Ma	Eyes of the Mummy (1918)
Bang, Bang You're Dead!	Our Man in Marrakesh (1966)
Baroud	Love in Morocco (1933)
Les belles de nuit	Beauties of the Night (1952)
Beyond the Door	Beyond Obsession (1982)
Bloodfist VI: Ground Zero	Ground Zero (1994)
Bomba and the Golden Idol	The Golden Idol (1954)
Bram Stoker's Legend of the Mummy	Legend of the Mummy (1997)
Brennender Sand	Blazing Sand (1960)
Burning Sands	Blazing Sand (1960)
Le cadeau	The Gift (1982)
Caesar's Wife	Another Dawn (1937)
Child Bride	Lola (1969)
The Chosen	Holocaust 2000 (1978)
Colt-Flight 802	Hostage (1986)
Conflict	Judith (1966)
The Courtesan of Babylon	The Queen of Babylon (1956)
Crazy House	Goodbye, New York (1985)
Dark Sands	Jericho (1937)
Daughter of Cleopatra	Cleopatra's Daughter (1961)
Delirium in a Studio	*Ali Barboyou et Ali Bouf a l'huile* (1907)
Desert Patrol	Sea of Sand (1958)
Due notte con Cleopatra	Two Nights with Cleopatra (1954)
The Evil Eye	Manhattan Baby (1986)
Eye of the Dead	Manhattan Baby (1986)

The Favorite	Intimate Power (1989)
Finishing Touch	Your Ticket is No Longer Valid (1981)
Il fiore delle mille e unanotte	Arabian Nights (1974)
Flying Aces	The Flying Deuces (1939)
The Four Feathers (1955)	Storm over the Nile (1955)
Giv'a 24 eina ona	Hill 24 Doesn't Answer (1955)
The Golden Mask	South of Algiers (1953)
Goliath, King of the Slaves	Beast of Babylon against the Son of Hercules (1963)
The Great American Bugs Bunny Road Runner Chase	The Bugs Bunny/Road Runner Movie (1979)
La haine	Hate (1995)
Hand of Night	Beast of Morocco (1966)
Hawk of Bagdad	Ali Baba and the Seven Saracens (1964)
Hello My Darlings	Sands of the Desert (1960)
Hero of Babylon	Beast of Babylon against the Son of Hercules (1963
His Majesty, Bunker Bean (1936)	Bunker Bean (1936)
Ice Cold in Alex	Desert Attack (1961)
John Carpenter's Escape from L.A.	Escape from L.A. (1996)
Jungle Trail of the Son of Tarzan	Son of Tarzan (1920)
King's Mate	The White Sheik (1928)
The Lamp	The Outing (1987)
The Lost World of Sinbad	The Adventures of Sinbad (1963)
Malaya	Fire over Africa (1954)
Man from Tangier	Thunder over Tangier (1957)
Maneater	Shark (1969)
Manhunt in the African Jungle	Secret Service in Darkest Africa (1943)
Mirakel der liebe	She (1925)
Mirror of Death	Dead of Night (1987)
Mohammed, Messenger of God	The Message (1976)
Nel segno di Roma	Sign of the Gladiator (1958)
Nerfertiti, regina del Nilo	Nefertiti, Queen of the Nile (1961)
A Night in Cairo	The Arab (1915)
No Time to Die	Tank Force (1958)
Not Quite Jerusalem	Not Quite Paradise (1986)
Nyoka and the Tigerman	Perils of Nyoka (1942)
Old Mother Riley's New Venture	Old Mother Riley (1952)
Once We Were Dreamers	Unsettled Land (1987)
The Peacemaker	The Ambassador (1984)
The Plot to Kill Roosevelt	Conspiracy in Teheran (1950)
Priority Red One	Delta Force Commando II (1990)
Ha pritza ha gdola	Eagles Attack at Dawn (1970)
Rebels against the Light	Sands of Beersheba (1966)
La Rosa di Bagdad	The Singing Princess (1967)
Semiramis	The Queen of Babylon (1956)
Il Sergente Klems	Man of Legend (1971)
Sherlock Holmes in Pursuit to Algiers	Pursuit to Algiers (1945)
Sinai Commandos	Sinai Commandos: The Story of the Six Day War (1968)
Sinai Guerillas	Blazing Sand (1960)

Sinbad the Sailor	Invitation to the Dance (1956)
A Slow Descent into Hell	Your Ticket Is No Longer Valid (1981)
Streets of Cairo	Dark Streets of Cairo (1940)
Sumurun	One Arabian Night (1920)
Target Embassy	Embassy (1972)
Teheran	Conspiracy in Teheran (1948)
The Thief and the Cobbler	Arabian Knight (1995)
Tom Mix in Arabia	Arabia (1922)
Twinky	Lola (1969)
The Unforgivable Sin	The White Man's Law (1918)
Warhead	Prisoner in the Middle (1974)
The Way Ahead	The Immortal Battalion (1944)
We're in the Legion Now	The Rest Cure (1936)

Best List

Ali: Fear Eats the Soul (1974)
Beyond the Walls (1984)
The Black Tent (1956)
Cup Final (1992)
Gambit (1966)
King Richard and the Crusaders (1954)
Lion of the Desert (1981)
Madame Rosa (1977)
Robin Hood: Prince of Thieves (1991)
The Thief of Bagdad (1924)
The 13th Warrior (1999)
Three Kings (1999)

Recommended Films

The Adventures of Prince Achmed (1925)
The Adventures of Sinbad (1962)
The Adventures of Sinbad (1979)
Aladdin and the Wonderful Lamp (1917)
Aladdin's Lamp (1907)
Ali Baba and the Forty Thieves (1944)
Ali and the Talking Camel (1960)
Antony and Cleopatra (1972)
Arabian Love (1922)
The Battle of Algiers (1965)
Ben Hur (1959)
Caesar and Cleopatra (1946)
The Camel Boy (1984)
Captain Sinbad (1963)
Cleopatra (1934)
Cleopatra (1963)
The Desert Hawk (1950)
The Desert Song (1929)
Escape from Zahrain (1962)
Fatima (1912)
Five Graves to Cairo (1943)
Flame of Araby (1951)
Flight from Ashiya (1964)
40,000 Horsemen (1942)
The Golden Voyage of Sinbad (1974)
Hamsin (1983)
Hanna K. (1983)
Hate (1995)
Jericho (1937)
Khartoum (1966)
King of the Wind (1989)
Kismet (1944)
Kismet (1955)

The Long Kiss Goodnight (1996)
Man of Legend (1971)
The Message (1976)
Overseas (1992)
Party Girl (1995)
A Perfect Murder (1998)
Princess Tam Tam (1935)
Private Worlds (1935)
Project Z (1987)
The Return of Chandu (1934)
Sahara (1943)
The Seventh Coin (1992)
The Sheik Steps Out (1937)
The Sheik's Wife (1922)
The Son of Cleopatra (1964)
Sudan (1945)
The Vigilante (1947)
What the Moon Saw (1990)

Worst List

Abdulla the Great (1956)
American Ninja 4: The Annihilation (1991)
Ashanti (1979)
Back to the Future (1985)
Beau Ideal (1931)
Best Defense (1984)
Beyond Justice (1992)
The Black Stallion (1979)
The Black Stallion Returns (1983)
Blink of an Eye (1991)
The Bonfire of the Vanities (1990)
Bulletproof (1988)
Cast a Giant Shadow (1966)
Chain of Command (1993)
Code Name Vengeance (1989)
Death before Dishonor (1987)
The Delta Force (1986)
Double Edge (1992)
Eagles Attack at Dawn (1970)
East of Sudan (1964)
Exodus (1960)
Follow That Camel (1967)
Freedom Strike (1998)
Ground Zero (1994)
Hell Squad (1985)
Hollywood Hot Tubs 2: Educating Crystal
   (1990)
Hostage (1986)
The Human Shield (1992)

Into the Sun (1991)
Iron Eagle (1986)
Ishtar (1987)
Jewel of the Nile (1985)
Killing Streets (1991)
Legion of the Doomed (1958)
Legion of Missing Men (1937)
Ministry of Vengeance (1989)
My Chauffeur (1986)
Navy SEALs (1990)
Network (1976)
Operation Condor (1997)
Paradise (1982)
Prisoner in the Middle (1974)
Protocol (1984)
Riding the Edge (1989)
Rollover (1982)
Rosebud (1975)
Rules of Engagement (2000)
The Sad Sack (1957)
Sahara (1983)
Sands of Beersheba (1966)
The Sheltering Sky (1990)
Son of the Pink Panther (1993)
Son of Tarzan (1920)
Sphinx (1981)
Tarzan the Tiger (1929)
Tarzan's Revenge (1938)
Terminal Entry (1986)
Terror in Beverly Hills (1988)
Things are Tough All Over (1982)
Tripoli (1950)
True Lies (1994)
Wanted: Dead or Alive (1987)
War Birds (1988)
Wrong Is Right (1982)

Cannon (Golan-Globus) Films

Aladdin (1986)
Allan Quatermain and the Lost City of Gold (1987)
The Ambassador (1984)
American Ninja 3: Blood Hunt (1989)
American Ninja 4: The Annihilation (1991)
American Samurai (1992)
Appointment with Death (1988)
Bloodsport (1988)
Bolero (1984)
Chain of Command (1993)
The Delta Force (1986)
The Delta Force 3: The Killing Game (1991)
Eagles Attack at Dawn (1970)
Firewalker (1986)
The Happy Hooker Goes to Washington (1977)
Hell Squad (1985)
The Hitman (1991)
The Human Shield (1992)
Invasion U.S.A. (1985)
King Solomon's Mines (1985)
A Man Called Sarge (1990)
Prison Heat (1993)
Sahara (1983)
Sinbad of the Seven Seas (1989)
Surrender (1987)
Trunk to Cairo (1967)

Epithets Directed at the Film Arab

Aliens
Animals
Ape
Arab wrangler
Arab ass
Arabian Gestapo
Assassins
Asshole
Atomic terrorist
Ayrab
Bad-ass terrorist
Bandit chief
Bandits
Barbarian
Bastard
Bastards
Bearded Arab
Boring oil billionaires
Brown devils
Buffoons
Butchers
Bunco artist
Buzzards of the jungle
Camel-dick
Camel-driver
Camel farts
Camel humper
Camel jockeys
Carpetbaggers
Cheap-suited camel jockey
Cheese-dick
Cockroach
Crackpots
Croaking bullfrog
Crocodile
Cutthroats
Damn camel jockey
Desert bandits
Desert outlaws
Desert rat
Devil
Devil of the desert
Devil worshipers
Dirty dog
Dirty, filthy swines
Dog
Dog monkey

Dune dumpers
Empty-headed old fool
Faggot
Fairies
Fakirs
Fanatic tribesmen
Fanatics
Fat ant-eater
Filth
Filthy animal
Filthy Arabs
Filthy Ayrabs
Filthy butcher
Filthy groveling pig
Filthy swine
Fink-face
Flea-bitten bunch of pirates
Fly-in-a-piece-of-shit
Foal of a camel
Fuckers
Fuckin' fag
Fuckin' pigs
Gangsters
Goat
Goddamn Arabs
Goons
Greedy dogs
Groveling pig
Gucci terrorist
Half-breed dog
Half-man, half-horse
Half-savage
Hashish-maddened horde
Heathen
Hippopotamus
Holy hyenas
Horrid brutal brute
Idiot
Injuns
Infidel pig
Infidels
Jackal
King of beggars
Lard bucket
Lean Arab
Little bastard
Little monster
Little pig with a moustache
Mad dog
Male chauvinist
Man-eating dark savages

Man-eating savages
Maniac
Medieval fanatics
Merciless desert cult
Mick-a-muck of Morocco
Mideast maggot
Mongol Oriental
Monkeys
Monster
Moorish whore
Motherfuckers
Musselmen
Nazis
Nitwits
Nuclear-terrorist
Old goat
Old horse-face
Old witch
Pack of dogs
Phonies
Piece of shit
Pig
Pinhead potentate
Poisonous snake
Possessed of devils
Prowling bedouins
Raghead
Raghead faggot
Rat
Rat-bastard
Riff-raff
Riffians
Roaches
Sand-diviner
Sand fleas
Sand-spider
Satan
Savages
Scavengers
Scum
Scum bucket
Scum bums
Scum of the earth
Scumbags
Serpent
Sharks in the sea
Sheiss (shit)
Shit
Slob
Snake
Sneaky Arabs

Son-of-a-bitch
Son-of-a-camel
Son-of-a-dog
Son-of-a-flea-bitten-camel
Son-of-a-flea-bitten-goat
Son-of-a-thief
Son-of-a-whore
Son-of-an-owl
Son-of-an-unnamed-goat
Sons-of-she-camels
Stateless savages (Palestinians)
Stinky fellow
Strange Arab
Stupid bastard
Stupid bitch
Swine
Swine of the alleys
Terrorists
Thoroughbred mongrel
Tiger claws
Toothless Arab
Total slime
Towel head
Towel-headed creep
Treacherous dog
Treacherous scamp
Treacherous toad
Turbaned gangster
Turbaned twit
Unbelievers
Unseeable ones
Vampire
Vulture
Walking bedsheets
Wicked wolf
Wild tribes
Witch of evil
Wog farmers
Wogs
Wolf of the desert
World's bloodiest terrorist
Yellow heathen
Yellow-livered ape
Your-disgrace-ful-ness
Your-worth-less-ness

Reel Arabia: Hollywood's Arab-Land

Abistan
Abu Karum
Agrabah
Ahad
Araba
Araban
Araby
Aramy
Arbi
Arizia
Ashanti
Barabeeha
Bari-Bari
Bashir
Benadeen
Bhustan
Bir Harari
Bondaria
Bukistan
Ceuta
Citra
El Arish
El-Akbar
El-Alahaim
El-Hamed
El-Jazir
El-Kubla
El-Marish
El-Muktar
El-Qutar
El-Sikkuri
Hagreeb
Hazak
Hidden City
Il Kharem
Ishram
Ishtar
Jadoor
Jemal
Jotse
Kafiristan
Karamesh
Karashar
Katar
Khalifa
Kuma
Lemuria

Libertahd
Lionia
Lugash
Madera
Magda
Makyad
Massura
Opar
Othar
Pomonia
Qumir
Ramalt
Republic of Hatay
Rungay
Samari
Soudan
Sumalia
Tamareed
Tarajan
Tarjan
Tongola
Trans-Berberite
United Hebrab Republic
Urah
Zaccahabar
Zambezi
Zanzibar

Silent Shorts, Travelogues, and Documentaries

Starred films are noted in Abdelmajid Hajji's dissertation, *"The Arab in American Silent Cinema: A Study of a Film Genre,"* University of Kansas, 1993.

*An African Village, North Africa. Pathe, US Rel. George Kleine. 1911.
*Aladdin-up-to-Date. Thomas Edison. 3 September 1912.
*Algeria, Old and New. Pathe. 15 April 1916.
Allahabad: The Arab Wizard. American Mutoscope & Biograph Co. 11 November 1902.
*Always the Woman. Betty Compson Prod., Dist. Goldwyn Distributing Corp. 11 July 1922.
*Ancient Port of Jaffa. Kalem. 11 September 1912.
Arab Act, Luna Park (Coney Island). American Mutoscope & Biograph Co. 1903.
*Arab Troops. Pathe. 31 August 1914.
The Arab Wizard. 1902.
*The Arab's Bride. Ambrosio. 28 September 1912.
*Arab's Vengeance. Mutual Film Corp. 16 December 1915.
*Arabia's Last Alarm. FOX. 2 November 1923.
*Arabian Cavalry. Independent Films. 29 May 1909.
*Arabian Customs. Éclair. 13 May 1912.
Arabian Gun Twirler. Thomas Edison. 20 March 1898.
*Arabian Infamy. Ambrosio. 25 September 1912.
*Arabian Pilgrimage. Pathe. 7 August 1909.
*Arabian Pottery. Éclair. 3 February 1912.
*Arabian Sports. Vitagraph. 9 November 1912.
*An Arabian Tragedy. Kalem. 19 June 1912.
*The Black Box (Installment #11: A Desert Vengeance). UNI. 10 May 1915.
*The Breath of Araby. 8 May 1915.
*Cairo, Egypt and its Environs. Pathe. 2 April 1913.
*Cheated Hearts. UNI. 12 December 1921.
*Christian and Moor. Thomas Edison. 1 August 1911.
*The City of Mosques. Éclair. 25 February 1912.
*The City of Tripoli. Cines. 19 March 1912.
*The Cobbler and the Caliph. Vitagraph. 10 July 1909.
*Conscience of Hassan Bey. Biograph. 18 December 1913.
Dance of the Seven Veils. Thomas Edison. 1893.
*Dark Secrets. Famous Players–Lasky, Dist. PAR. 21 January 1923.
*Date Culture in Iraq. Dept. of Agriculture. Circa 1928.
*Desert Bagdad. Source unknown. 1928.
*Desert Blues. Educational Films Corporation of America. 13 October 1924.
*Egypt. Kalem. 20 May 1912.
*Egypt, Land of the Pyramids. MGM. James A. Fitzpatrick's Traveltalks Series. 1930.
*Egypt, the Mysterious. Kalem. 15 May 1912.
*Egypt Sport. Kalem. 19 July 1912.
*An Egyptian Adventure. Four Stars Films. 1928.
Egyptian Boys in Swimming Race. Thomas Edison. 10 June 1903.
Egyptian Fakir with Dancing Monkey. Thomas Edison. 8 June 1903.
Egyptian Market Scene. Thomas Edison. June 1903.
Excavating Scene at the Pyramids of Sakkaroh. Thomas Edison. 1903.
*The Exiles. FOX. 14 October 1923.
*The Fall of Constantinople. Gaumont. 1 November 1913.
*Farming in Tunis. C.G.P.C. 30 January 1912.

*Fighting Dervishes of the Desert. Kalem. 27 May 1912.
*Fighting Love. DeMille Pictures, Dist. Producers Distributing Corp. 14 February 1927.
*Firemen of Cairo. Éclair. 20 August 1910.
*Flight from the Seraglio. Great Northern Film Co. 23 May 1908.
*The Forbidden Woman. DeMille Pictures, Dist. Pathe. 29 October 1927.
Fording the River Nile on Donkeys. Thomas Edison. June 1903.
*The Fortieth Door. New York. 1920.
*The 40th Door. Pathe. 17 August 1924.
*From Cairo to Khartoum. Eclipse. 10 August 1907.
*A Glimpse of Tripoli. Eclipse. 28 February 1912.
Going to Market, Luxor, Egypt. Thomas Edison. 17 June 1903.
*The Greed of Osman Bey. Thomas Edison. 28 July 1913.
*Grief in Bagdad. FOX. 4 January 1925.
*Grief in Bagdad. Hal Roach, Pathe. 10 April 1925.
*The Guerrillas of Algiers, a.k.a. The Mosque in the Desert. Éclair, Features Ideal Co.
    6 December1913.
*Hannigan's Dream. Pathe. 10 July 1913.
*The Harem Scarem Deacon. Joker, UNI. 15 July 1916.
*Her Purchase Price. Brunton B. Features, Inc., Dist. Robertson-Cole Corp. 1 September 1919.
Herd of Sheep on the Way to Jerusalem. Thomas Edison. 1903.
*Home of the Arabians. Independent Films. 29 May 1909.
*In the Shadow of the Mosque. Éclair. 22 April 1914.
*In the Sultan's Place. Selig Polyscope Co. 12 June 1909.
*Into the Desert. Thanhouser. 16 April 1912.
*Jaffa, the Seaport of Jerusalem. Thomas Edison. 22 October 1913.
*Jerusalem Delivered. 15 July 1911.
Jerusalem's Busiest Street, Showing Mt. Zion. Thomas Edison. 17 June 1903.
*Kairowan, Algiers. Source unknown. Circa 1905 (Library of Congress Paper Print Collection).
*The Lady Who Lied. First National Pictures. 12 July 1925.
*Little Journey in Tunis. C.G.P.C. 10 September 1912.
*The Lost Empire. Edward A. Salisbury, Dist Frederick J. Burgard. 15 March 1924.
*Lost in the Soudan. Selig Polyscope. 20 August 1910.
*Luxor, Egypt. Kalem. 25 May 1912.
*Making Arabian Pottery. Pathe. 3 October 1908.
*The Man from Egypt. Vitagraph. 14 July 1915.
Market Scene in Old Cairo, Egypt. Thomas Edison. 28 March 1903.
*The Mohammedan at Home. Producer unknown. 19 December 1908.
*Moon Madness. Haworth Studios, Dist. Robertson-Cole Distributing Corp. July 1920.
*The Moorish Bride. Cines. 9 May 1912.
*The Moslem Lady's Day. Éclair. 25 August 1912.
*Mosques and Towns of Caliphs and Mamelukes. Mutual. 8 May 1913.
*Mosques and Turkish Palaces. Cines. 29 October 1912.
*A Motor Trip to the Garden of Allah. Parker Read Productions. 8 June 1912.
*Native Industries in Sudan, Egypt. C.G.P.C. 28 February 1913.
*Native Life in Sudan. Pathe. 4 July 1908.
*The Next in Command. Pasquali American Co., Dist. Picture Playhouse Film Co.
    14 August 1914.
A Night in New Arabia. D: Thomas R. Mills. 1917.
*Nomadic Tribes in El-Kantara Gorges, Algeria. Pathe. Circa 1910.
*Oasis of Gabes. Pathe. 27 January 1914.
*Oasis in the Sahara Desert. Gaumont. 1 July 1911.

*Off to Morocco. Gaumont, Rel. Kleine Optical Co. 1908.

*Omar the Tentmaker. Richard Walton Tully Prod, Dist. Associated First National Pictures. December 1922.

*The Oriental Mystic. Vitagraph. 29 May 1909.

Outpost of the Foreign Legion. 1931.

Panoramic View of Beyrough; Syrian, Sharing Holiday Festivities. Thomas Edison. June 1903.

Panoramic View of an Egyptian Cattle Market. Thomas Edison. June 1903.

*Pasha's Daughter. Thanhouser Company. July 1911.

Passengers Embarking from SS *Augusta Victoria* at Beyrough. Thomas Edison. 1903.

*Plastered in Paris. FOX. 23 September 1928.

*Potters of the Nile. Kalem. 3 May 1912.

Primitive Irrigation in Egypt. Thomas Edison. June 1903.

*A Princess of the Desert. Thomas Edison. 18 April 1914.

*Prisoner of the Harem. Kalem. 19 July 1912.

*Pseudo-Sultan. Pathe. 27 January 1912.

*Quaint Spots in Cairo. Thomas Edison. 14 August 1913.

*Ramsese, King of Egypt. Cines. 12 August 1912.

*Roosevelt in Cairo. Urban-Eclipse, Rel. Kleine. 21 May 1910.

*The Rug Maker's Daughter. Bosworth Inc., with the Oliver Morosco Photoplay Inc. 5 July 1915.

*Rummy Act of Omar K.M. Mutual Film Co. 16 July 1916.

*Sahara Blues. Century. 15 October 1924.

*Saved from the Harem. Lubin Manufacturing Co., Dist. General Film Co. 27 December 1915.

*The Sea Hawk. Frank Lloyd Prod., Dist. First National Pictures. 2 June 1924.

*The Shadow of the East, a.k.a. Shadow of the Desert. Boston. 1921.

*Shadow of the East. FOX. 27 January 1924.

Shearing a Donkey in Egypt. Thomas Edison. June 1903.

*Sidi Hadji Moursouck. Pathe. 19 December 1912.

*The Silent Lover. First National Pictures. 21 November 1926.

*The Span of Life. Kinotophote Corp., Dist. State Rights. 7 December 1914.

A Street Arab. Thomas Edison. 21 April 1898.

Street Scene at Jaffa. Thomas Edison. June 1903.

Street's Zouaves and Wall Scaling. Thomas Edison. 1901.

*Sultana of the Desert. Selig Polyscope. 5 October 1915.

*The Syrian Immigrant. Eastern Star Film Co. September 1921.

*Tale of a Harem: The Caliph and the Pirate. Vitagraph. 12 September 1908.

Tourist on Donkeys for the Pyramids of Sakkarah. Thomas Edison. 1903

Tourist Embarking at Jaffa. Thomas Edison. 17 June 1903.

Tourist Returning on Donkeys from Mispah. Thomas Edison. 1903.

Tourist Taking Water from the River Jordan. Thomas Edison. 1903.

*The Towns of Tunis. Pathe. 29 April 1916.

*Tragedy of the Desert. Kalem. 1 July 1912.

*A Trip through Cairo. Circa 1920.

*A Trip through Syria. Faris and Debs. 12 February 1922.

*Tunis, Africa (The City of White). Gaumont. 6 May 1911.

*Under the Crescent (six part series), Gold Seal. UNI. May–June 1915.

1. The Purple Iris, 25 May
2. The Cage of the Golden Bars, 2 June
3. In the Shadow of the Pyramids, 8 June
4. For the Honor of a Woman, 16 June
5. In the Name of the King, 29 June
6. The Crown of Death, 29 June

*Under the Palm Trees of Tunis. Gaumont. 18 July 1911.
*The Unknown. Jesse Lasky Feature Play Co., Dist. PAR. 9 December 1915.
*The Virgin of Stamboul. UNI. 29 March 1920.
*A Visit to Biskra. Pathe. 11 September 1909.
*A Walk in Tunis. Lux. 13 May 1911.
*When the Desert Calls. Pyramid Pictures, Dist. American Releasing Corp. 8 October 1922.
*The White Black Sheep. Inspiration Pictures, Dist. First National Pictures. 12 December 1926.
*The Winding Stair. FOX. 25 October 1925.
With Allenby in Palestine and Lawrence of Arabia. Lowell Thomas. 1919.
*With Car and Camera around the World. Aloha Wanderwell. 11 November 1929.
*Won in the Desert. Selig Polyscope Co. 17 July 1909.
*Yussuf the Pirate. Raleigh & Robert, Rel. Kleine Optical Co. 1908.

Films for Future Review

Information on the following movies was gleaned from the following sources: AFIC, *Film Daily*, IMDb, *Monthly Film Bulletin, Motion Picture Guide*, MPH, *National Union Catalog*, NYT, VAR, and the *Washington Report on Middle East Affairs.*

Adventures in Cairo (1943).

The Adventures of Rabbi Jacob (1973), a.k.a. *Les adventures de Rabbi Jacob.* French. A Frenchman disguises himself as a rabbi, bringing in Arab complications.

Aida (1954), I.F.E. Italian. The Ethiopian princess Aida is loved by Radames, an Egyptian warrior.

El Alamein (1954), COL. The protagonists come across a bedouin tomb. Appearing are Selim, a slimy Arab, and Jara, his 17-year-old niece.

Alexandria...Why? (1978), a.k.a. *Iskanderija... lih?.* Egypt/Algeria. Two love affairs in wartime Alexandria. One, an aristocratic Arab woman and an English soldier; the other between a Muslim man and a Jewish girl.

Ali Baba (1954), a.k.a. *Ali Baba et les guarante.* French. This film stars the great French comic Fernandel. Surfacing are Ali Baba and Abdel, a bandit chief.

Arabian Duet (1922). Silent. A short "Music Film."

Brain of Blood (1971), a.k.a. *The Creature's Revenge.* Phil-Am Enterprises Ltd. Surfacing is "Mohammed."

Brothers in Arms (1989). French. An Arab and Jew contest Arab terrorists.

Candlelight in Algeria (1944). UK. International intrigue in Algiers.

Captive of the Desert (1990), a.k.a. *La captive du desert.* French. A young French woman is held captive by dark-complexioned bedouin.

The Cayman Triangle (1977), Hefalump. An Arab (Arek Jospeh) appears in this movie about lost vessels.

Circle of Deceit (1981), a.k.a. *Die falschung.* French/German. In Lebanon, a German journalist covers the civil war.

Clouds over Israel (1966). Israeli. An Israeli pilot crash lands in Egypt.

The Cohens and Kellys in Africa (1930), UNI. Actor Lloyd Whitlock portrays an Arab sheikh.

Crooks Tour (1940). UK. Tourists get mixed up with Arabs. Actor Charles Oliver portrays a sheikh; actor Abraham Sofaer plays Ali.

Daughter of the Sands (1952), a.k.a. *Les noces de sable.* French/Moroccan. After a young Arab prince dies, he is reunited with his sweetheart.

Desert Desperadoes (1959), a.k.a. *The Sinner,* RKO. An Arab merchant (Akim Tamiroff) flirts with the stranded-in-the-desert western heroine.

The Desert Sheik (1924), Truart Film. Silent.

Dinky Doodle in Egypt (1926), Bray. Silent.

Disraeli (1921). Silent. US. British Prime Minster Benjamin Disraeli moves to purchase the Suez Canal.

Disraeli (1929), a.k.a. *Disraeli the Noble Ladies of Scandal,* WB. Britian's Prime Minister plans to purchase the Suez Canal.

Every Bastard a King (1968). Israeli. The Israeli view of the "Six Day War."

The Fighting Wildcats (1957), REP. UK. An American gun-for-hire is directed to blow up an Arab dignitary. The mercenary's girlfriend sacrifices her life to save the Arab.

A Flame in My Heart (1990). French. A young Arab becomes obsessed with a Parisian actress.

Flesh and the Woman (1953), a.k.a. *Le grand jeu.* French/Italian. In Algiers, the foreign legion, and a prostitute.

La folle des grandeurs (1971). French. The protagonists are sold to Arab slave traders.

Forbidden Desert (1957), WB. In 1812, a Swiss explorer penetrates the dangerous Arab world disguised as a Damascene Arab.

The Foreign Legion (1928), UNI. Silent. The action takes place in the North African desert.

The Foreigner (1978), Rel. Amos Poe Visions. Appearing is "The Arab" played by Chirine Ed Khadem.

Fun Among the Pharoahs As Seen by Homer Grey (1920/1927).

The Golden Lady (1979). UK. Rivals bid for Arab oil. Female super-sleuths prevent an Arab country from falling into the KGB's grasp.

The Greek Tycoon (1978), UNI. A Greek shipping magnate wants to sell his fleet of ships to Arabs.

Green Pastures (1936), WB. In this Bible story, actor Ernest Whitman portrays a pharaoh.

Great Sadness (1983). Israeli. A young Jewish woman travels to Arab lands.

Guns (1980). French. Surfacing are gun-runners and oil-rich Arabs.

The Guns and the Fury (1983), A&Z/Bordeaux. Actors Peter Graves and Cameron Mitchell fight off Cossacks and Arabs.

His and Hers (1961). UK. The protagonist adopts bedouin dress and habits.

The House Opposite (1931). UK. Private eyes battle a mad Egyptian scientist and his fellow blackmailers.

Huge Scimitar (1927). Silent.

Island of Allah (1956), a.k.a. *Garden of Allah*, Studio Alliance Inc. Featured are four Arabs, and an "Arabian Dancing Girl."

Juggernaut (1937). UK. A noted doctor conducts research in Morocco.

Juggernaut (1974). UK. Roshan Seth portrays Azad, an Arab. Several bombs are planted on an ocean liner.

Labyrinth of Passion (1990). Spanish. A potentate's bisexual son picks up a friendly Arab terrorist.

Lady in a Harem (1916). Silent.

Last Man (1932), COL. Appearing in Port Said is an Egyptian spy (Johnny Eberts).

Little Egypt (1920). Silent.

The Little Soldier (1963), a.k.a. *Le petit soldat*. French. This Algerian War drama reveals an "Arab" (Laszlo Szabo).

The Lure of Egypt (1921), Federal Photoplays of California. Silent.

The Man from Morocco (1946). UK. The protagonist acquires names of Morocco's most trusted citizens.

Marco the Magnificent (1966), MGM. Omar Sharif portrays a friendly sheikh. Akim Tamiroff, portrays a villainous desert chieftain.

The Milky Way (1997), a.k.a. *Shvil Hahalav*, Sanabil Prod. Israel. The scenario focuses on Palestinian villagers in 1964, the final year of Israeli military occupation in the Galilee.

Miss Mona (1987). French. Miss Mona, a gay streetwalker befriends Samir, an Arab. Later, Samir commits murder to protect both himself and Miss Mona.

The Mole People (1956), UI. Actors Rodd Redwing, Joe Abdullah, and Billy Miller portray Arabs.

Mona Lisa (1986). UK. Appearing is an Arab servant (Raad Rawi).

Moses (1975). UK/Italy. Moses' conflict with Egypt's Pharaoh.

Mystic Circle Murder (1939), Fanchon Royer. Scenes reveal Egypt's sphinx and the pyramids.

Naked Earth (1958), TCF. Harold Kasket portrays an Arab captain.

Nervous Ticks (1992). US. An "Arab Woman" is played by Yomi Perry.

Oasis (1955), a.k.a. *Oase*, TCF. German. Moroccans appear in the background.

Oddball Hall (1990), Ravenhill. Appearing are two Arabs, "Meejaball" and "Salim."

Old Loves and New (1926), First National Pictures. Silent. The European protagonist, Lord Carew, resides in the desert, where he is regarded as a patriarch to the Arabs, who call him "El Hakim."

The Olive Trees of Justice (1967). French. This film presents balanced images of French and Algerians, dark and light. Muslim workers, labor problems, and Arab traditions.

Operation Camel (1960), a.k.a. *Soldaterkammerater pa vagt.* Denmark. An Egyptian appears.

Our Men in Bagdad (1967). Italian. This espionage thriller is set in the Arab world.

The Passenger (1975), MGM. Surfacing in Africa is an Arab and his camel; the Arab ignores the protagonist's plight.

The Passions of an Egyptian Princess (1911). Silent short. UK.

Peggy of the Secret Service (1925). Silent. Three Arabs are featured: Mahmoud el Akem, Abdullah, and Abdullah's Favorite Wife.

Peggy the Vamp (1925). Silent.

Petit con (1985). French. The French protagonist befriends a sexy Algerian girl.

Pharaoh (1966), a.k.a. *Faroan.* This historical epic focuses on the abuses of power in ancient Egypt.

Pretty Smart (1986), Balcor Film-Investors. The film focuses on happenings at a private school. A Lebanese man (Joseph Medawar) appears.

The Pure Hell of St. Trinian's (1961). UK. European maidens are delivered to the Emir's (Elwyn Brook-Jones) harem somewhere east of Suez.

The Question (1977), a.k.a. *La question.* French. French communists try to help the colonized Algerians achieve freedom. Scenes show French paratroopers torturing innocents.

Ramparts of Clay (1970). French. An Algerian woman copes with the modern world.

The Red Sheik (1961), a.k.a. *Lo sceisso rosso.* Italy/US. Set in nineteenth-century Morocco, this drama features an evil Arab potentate who enjoys making people suffer.

The Return of Mr. Moto (1965), TCF. In the Arab world, Mr. Moto foils Middle East curs who attempt to sabotage oil production.

Robinson Crusoe and Son (1932), UNI.

Salut Cousin! (1998). UK. An Algerian boy visits Paris and is taken in by his pathologically lying cousin.

The Scarab Murder Case (1936). UK. In London, an American detective uncovers a millionaire's murder.

Secret Agent Fireball (1966). A Lebanese man (Alcide Borik) appears in this movie about agents trying to secure an H-bomb formula.

The Serpent of Death (1989). Arabs appear.

Shadow of Egypt (1924). Silent. UK. Appearing is Sheik Hanan (Carlyle Blackwell, Sr.).

The Sheik (1922). Silent. UK. Appearing is the Sheik (Clive Brook).

The Sheik of Araby (1926), Artclass Pictures. Silent.

Ships of the Night (1928). Silent. US. Surfacing are Arab slavers.

Sob Sister (1931), FOX. Johnnie the Sheik is portrayed by George E. Stone.

Solomon Kinq (1974), WAL/WA. An ex-Green Beret hero leads a commando raid, crushing insurgents in an unnamed Arab country.

Song of the Sheik.

The Story of Joseph and His Brethern (1962). Italian. Robert Morley portrays a demented Egyptian slave-owner.

Sword of the Desert (1914). Silent.

Sword of the Desert (1960).

Table of the Sheik (1923). Silent.

Tangier Assignment (1955). UK. A European agent moves to bring down gun-runners.

Tangier Cop (1997).

Tale of Egypt (1998), UA.

Target for Killing (1966), a.k.a *Das geheimnis der gelben monche.* Austria/Italy/W. Germany. A secret agent protects a young woman from a Lebanese syndicate intent on harming her.

Tea in the Harem (1986). French. The protagonist lives in a housing project outside Paris with his Algerian-born parents.

That Lucky Touch (1975). UK. Arabs are cited in the credits.

That Man George (1966), a.k.a. *L' homme de Marrakesh*. Italian/Spanish. In the Moroccan desert, the protagonist (George Hamilton) nabs a shipment of gold.

That Man from Tangier (1950). Spain/US. Location footage reveals Arab-world-as-place.

They Were Ten (1961). Israeli. In the nineteenth century, ten Russian Jews establish a settlement.

The Unveiling Hand (1919), World Film Corp. Silent. Hassan, a guide, commits murder to protect the Western heroines.

Valentino (1977), UA. The movie is based on Brad Steiger's novel, "Valentino, An Intimate Exposé of the Sheik."

A Voice in Your Heart (1952). Italian. An Arab vs. Jew scenario.

Wedding in Galilee (1986). Israel/Belgium. The film focuses on a Palestinian village under Israeli occupation.

Weekend (1968), a.k.a. *Le weekend*. French. Appearing is an Algerian garbage collector advocating black power.

White Cargo (1973). UK. Innocent European maidens are kidnapped. The villain vows to sell the women to Arab sheikhs.

White Sister (1915). Silent. US. Based on play/novel by Francis Marion Crawford.

White Sister (1973). Italian/French/Spanish. The revolutionary government of Libya expels Sister Germana from her home.

White Sun of the Desert (1970), a.k.a. *Beloye solntse pustyni*. Soviet Union. Red Army soldier is chosen to guard a harem.

Why Sailors Leave Home (1930). UK. Two Arabs appear: Sheikh Sidi Ben and a "slave girl."

Wild Zone (1990).

The Wildcats of St. Trinian's (1980). UK. English schoolgirls hold an Arab's daughter hostage.

Wind (1992), TRI. Appearing is a sheikh (Bruce Epke).

Woman from Tangier (1948), COL. In Tangier, an American insurance agent investigates a theft.

You Pay Your Money (1957). UK. Arabs kidnap and hold hostage the protagonist.

Glossary

Abaya	Long toga-like robe, worn by a woman or man
Agal, Igal	Headband men wear over the headdress
Ageela	Water pipe; hubble-bubble; hookah
Ahlan wa Sahlan	Welcome
Al-Rawi	Storyteller
Allah	God
Allah Ma Cum	God be with you
Allahu Akbar	God is Great; Glory to God
Arak	An anise liquor
Assalamu Aleikum	Peace be upon you
Aswad	The color black
Babaganush	An eggplant dish
Baksheesh	Tip; money
Bedouin	Nomad
Bismallah	In the name of God
Burnoose	Headdress
Chador	(Persian) Muslim dress covering woman's head and body
Dabke	Arab folk dance
Derbuke	Drum
Falafeh	Bean dish
Feluca	A small, narrow sailboat
Hammam	Turkish bath
Hijab	Head scarf
Imam	Muslim religious leader
Imshe	Hurry; walk
Intifada	Uprising
Jihad	Struggle within oneself; Holy War
Kaaba	A holy shrine in Mecca
Khanjar	Curved dagger
Kuffiyeh	Checkered headdress
Ma'ssalameh	Goodbye; Go in peace
Mahdi	Expected prophet; enlightened man
Majnoon	A fool
Malik	Owner
Misbaha	Worry beads; prayer beads
Muezzin	Muslim announcing the call to prayer
Nargelih	Water pipe
Shams	Sun
Sharmoota	Whore
Shetan	Devil; Satan
Shookran	Thank you
Souk	Marketplace
Tarboosh	A red fez

Thobe	Robe; dress
Wog	Derogatory slang for a non-white person
Yahood, Yahoodi	Jew, Jews
Yallah	Hurry up; move
Yallah Habibi	Hurry, my love
Zaghareet	Trilling sound made by women

NDEX OF FILMS

B

C